国际海事条约汇编
（综合文本）
A COLLECTION OF INTERNATIONAL MARITIME TREATIES (CONSOLIDATED EDITION)

第一卷　国际海上人命安全公约
Volume I　International Convention for the Safety of Life at Sea

中华人民共和国交通运输部国际合作司
大连海事大学

大连海事大学出版社
DALIAN MARITIME UNIVERSITY PRESS

图书在版编目(CIP)数据

国际海事条约汇编：综合文本. 第一卷，国际海上人命安全公约：英汉对照 / 中华人民共和国交通运输部国际合作司，大连海事大学编译. — 大连：大连海事大学出版社，2023.9

书名原文：A COLLECTION OF INTERNATIONAL MARITIME TREATIES（CONSOLIDATED EDITION）Volume Ⅰ International Convention for the Safety of Life at Sea

ISBN 978-7-5632-4450-8

Ⅰ. ①国… Ⅱ. ①中… ②大… Ⅲ. ①海洋法-国际条约-汇编-英、汉 Ⅳ. ①D993.5

中国国家版本馆 CIP 数据核字(2023)第 158240 号

大连海事大学出版社出版

地址：大连市黄浦路523号 邮编：116026 电话：0411-84729665(营销部) 84729480(总编室)

http://press.dlmu.edu.cn E-mail:dmupress@dlmu.edu.cn

辽宁新华印务有限公司印装 大连海事大学出版社发行

2023 年 9 月第 1 版 2023 年 9 月第 1 次印刷

幅面尺寸：184 mm×260 mm 印张：64.5

字数：1503 千 印数：1~1000 册

出版人：刘明凯

责任编辑：李继凯 责任校对：王 琴

封面设计：解瑶瑶 版式设计：解瑶瑶

ISBN 978-7-5632-4450-8 定价：290.00 元

前　言

为满足广大航运、造船、船检、海事、外贸、保险、法律等部门的工作人员及相关的教学人员了解、掌握和执行国际海事条约的需要，1992年交通部外事司（现交通运输部国际合作司）曾在其译校和保存的有关条约的基础上，与大连海运学院（现大连海事大学）一起，以中英文对照的形式，编译出版了《国际海事条约汇编》（以下简称《汇编》）。在这30年间，《国际海上人命安全公约》《国际防止船舶造成污染公约》等重要的国际公约进行了多次的修改，《2006年海事劳工公约》《国际防止船舶造成污染公约1997年议定书》等多部新公约和议定书通过，《汇编》始终保持更新，保持本系列书籍内容的完整性。为了便利读者阅读和使用，编者认为有必要对重要的公约进行整理，以中英文对照综合文本的形式再次出版。

我国是名副其实的航运大国、造船大国、海员大国，在国际航运业中占有举足轻重的地位。我国是国际海事组织（IMO）A类理事国，在国际海事事务中扮演着越来越重要的角色。2021年12月15日，国际海事组织第32届大会通过了《国际海事组织公约》修正案，生效后中文文本将成为其正式文本之一。今年也是我国恢复国际海事组织合法席位50周年，在这一时刻，重新整理四个支柱性海事公约的中英文综合文本，既是《汇编》在新时代的传承，也是向我国恢复国际海事组织合法席位50周年献礼，具有重要的历史意义和现实意义。

本次出版的《国际海事条约汇编》（综合文本）共四卷，分别为《国际海上人命安全公约》《国际防止船舶造成污染公约》《1978年海员培训、发证和值班标准国际公约》《2006年海事劳工公约》，均收录了截至2023年12月31日前生效的公约修正案，整理成综合文本。编者后续将根据工作需要和公约修改的频率、程度出版其他公约的综合文本和更新现有版本，尽量与国际海事组织、国际劳工组织出版的公约综合文本保持同步。希望本系列书籍能够为相关行业从业人员在研究和实施公约的过程中提供参考。

本卷前言

1914 年 4 月 14 日，“泰坦尼克”号在北大西洋撞上冰山后沉没，这一举世震惊的海难催生了《1914 年国际海上人命安全公约》。这一公约在 1929 年、1948 年和 1960 年经历了三次修改。1974 年 10 月 21 日至 11 月 1 日，国际海上人命安全会议在英国伦敦召开。这是中国恢复在政府间海事协商组织（简称“海协”，国际海事组织前身）的合法席位后，首次参加该组织举办的外交大会。会议通过了《1974 年国际海上人命安全公约》（SOLAS 1974），中文被列为该公约的正式语言之一。中国于 1980 年 1 月 7 日加入该公约，同年 5 月 25 日即公约生效之日起对中国生效。

SOLAS 公约被公认为海上安全领域最重要的公约，也是国际海事法规体系中的支柱性公约之一，内容涉及船舶构造、救生、通信、航行安全、货物运输、安全管理、海上保安、极地航行等。

本卷所载 SOLAS 公约为 1974 年公约、1988 年议定书和生效日期在 2023 年 12 月 31 日及之前的两者修正案的综合文本。

在本卷编译过程中，交通运输部国际合作司王宏伟、李冠玉、陈星森、张琨琨，大连海事大学赵友涛，大连海事大学航海学院章文俊、韩佳霖、费珊珊、李桢、何庆华、王艳华、唐浩云，大连海事大学航海训练与工程实践中心刘锦程和大连海事大学出版社给予了大力支持，在此表示衷心感谢。由于编译工作时间仓促，书中难免有疏漏和错误，敬请读者批评指正。

Contents

目　录

国际海上人命安全公约

International Convention for the Safety of Life at Sea

Articles of the International Convention for the Safety of Life at Sea, 1974

1974 年国际海上人命安全公约

Articles of the International Convention for the Safety of Life at Sea, 1974

THE CONTRACTING GOVERNMENTS

BEING DESIROUS of promoting safety of life at sea by establishing in a common agreement uniform principles and rules directed thereto,

CONSIDERING that this end may best be achieved by the conclusion of a Convention to replace the International Convention for the Safety of Life at Sea, 1960, taking account of developments since that Convention was concluded,

HAVE AGREED as follows:

Article I
General obligations under the Convention

(a) The Contracting Governments undertake to give effect to the provisions of the present Convention and the annex thereto, which shall constitute an integral part of the present Convention. Every reference to the present Convention constitutes at the same time a reference to the annex.

(b) The Contracting Governments undertake to promulgate all laws, decrees, orders and regulations and to take all other steps which may be necessary to give the present Convention full and complete effect, so as to ensure that, from the point of view of safety of life, a ship is fit for the service for which it is intended.

Article II
Application[①]

The present Convention shall apply to ships entitled to fly the flag of States the Governments of which are Contracting Governments.

Article III
Laws, regulations[②]

The Contracting Governments undertake to communicate to and deposit with the Secretary-General of the Inter-Governmental Maritime Consultative Organization[③] (hereinafter referred to as "the Organization"):

---

① Refer to *Transfer of ships between States* (MSC/Circ.1140-MEPC/Circ.424).

② Refer to Article Ⅲ of the 1988 SOLAS Protocol; *Notification and circulation through the Global Integrated Shipping Information System (GISIS)* (resolution A.1074(28)).

③ The name of the Organization was changed to "International Maritime Organization" (IMO) by virtue of amendments to the Organization's Convention which entered into force on 22 May 1982.

1974 年国际海上人命安全公约

各缔约国政府

愿共同制定统一原则和有关规则，以增进海上人命安全；

考虑到 1960 年国际海上人命安全公约缔结以来的发展情况，重新缔结一个公约，以替代 1960 年公约，可以最好地达到这一目的；

特议定下列各条：

第 I 条
公约的一般义务

（a） 各缔约国政府承担义务实施本公约及其附则的各项规定，本公约附则与本公约构成一个整体。引用本公约即为同时引用其附则。

（b） 各缔约国政府承担义务颁布一切必要的法律、法令、命令和规则，并采取一切必要的其他措施，使本公约得以充分和完全实施，以从人命安全的角度确保船舶适合其预定的用途。

第 II 条
适用范围[①]

本公约适用于悬挂缔约国政府国旗的船舶。

第 III 条
法律、规则[②]

各缔约国政府承担义务向政府间海事协商组织[③]（以下称“本组织”）秘书长交存下列资料：

① 参见《船舶转换船旗国》（第 MSC/Circ.1140-MEPC/Circ.424 号通函）。
② 参见 SOLAS 1988 年议定书第三条；《在全球综合航运信息系统（GISIS）发布通知和通告》（第 A.1074(28) 号决议）。
③ 根据 1982 年 5 月 22 日生效的本组织公约修正案，本组织更名为“国际海事组织”（IMO）。

(**a**) a list of non-governmental agencies which are authorized to act in their behalf in the administration of measures for safety of life at sea for circulation to the Contracting Governments for the information of their officers;

(**b**) the text of laws, decrees, orders and regulations which shall have been promulgated on the various matters within the scope of the present Convention;

(**c**) a sufficient number of specimens of their certificates issued under the provisions of the present Convention for circulation to the Contracting Governments for the information of their officers.

Article IV
Cases of force majeure

(**a**) A ship, which is not subject to the provisions of the present Convention at the time of its departure on any voyage, shall not become subject to the provisions of the present Convention on account of any deviation from its intended voyage due to stress of weather or any other case of force majeure.

(**b**) Persons who are on board a ship by reason of force majeure or in consequence of the obligation laid upon the master to carry shipwrecked or other persons shall not be taken into account for the purpose of ascertaining the application to a ship of any provisions of the present Convention.

Article V
Carriage of persons in emergencies

(**a**) For the purpose of evacuating persons in order to avoid a threat to the security of their lives a Contracting Government may permit the carriage of a larger number of persons in its ships than is otherwise permissible under the present Convention.

(**b**) Such permission shall not deprive other Contracting Governments of any right of control under the present Convention over such ships which come within their ports.

(**c**) Notice of any such permission, together with a statement of the circumstances, shall be sent to the Secretary-General of the Organization by the Contracting Government granting such permission.

Article VI
Prior treaties and conventions

(**a**) As between the Contracting Governments, the present Convention replaces and abrogates the International Convention for the Safety of Life at Sea which was signed in London on 17 June 1960.

(a) 经授权代表其在管理海上人命安全措施方面行事的非政府机构的名单,以分发给各缔约国政府,供其官员参考;

(b) 就本公约范围内各种事项所颁布的法律、法令、命令和规则的文本;

(c) 根据本公约规定颁发的足够数量的证书样本,以分发给各缔约国政府,供其官员参考。

第 IV 条
不可抗力情况

(a) 在出航时不受本公约规定约束的船舶,并不因天气恶劣或任何其他不可抗力的原因偏离原定航线而受本公约规定的约束。

(b) 由于不可抗力或因船长负有搭载失事船舶人员或其他人员的义务而登上船的人员,在确定本公约的任何规定适用于该船时,都不应计算在内。

第 V 条
紧急情况下载运人员

(a) 为了避免对人命安全的威胁而撤离人员时,缔约国政府可准许其船舶载运多于本公约其他规定所允许的人数。

(b) 上述许可并不剥夺其他缔约国政府根据本公约享有的对到达其港口的这种船舶的任何监督权。

(c) 给予此项许可的缔约国政府应将任何这种许可的通知连同对当时情况的说明送交本组织秘书长。

第 VI 条
以前的条约和公约

(a) 在缔约国政府之间,本公约替代并废除 1960 年 6 月 17 日在伦敦签署的国际海上人命安全公约。

(**b**) All other treaties, conventions and arrangements relating to safety of life at sea, or matters appertaining thereto, at present in force between Governments parties to the present Convention shall continue to have full and complete effect during the terms thereof as regards:

(i) ships to which the present Convention does not apply;

(ii) ships to which the present Convention applies, in respect of matters for which it has not expressly provided.

(**c**) To the extent, however, that such treaties, conventions or arrangements conflict with the provisions of the present Convention, the provisions of the present Convention shall prevail.

(**d**) All matters which are not expressly provided for in the present Convention remain subject to the legislation of the Contracting Governments.

Article VII
Special rules drawn up by agreement

When in accordance with the present Convention special rules are drawn up by agreement between all or some of the Contracting Governments, such rules shall be communicated to the Secretary-General of the Organization for circulation to all Contracting Governments.

Article VIII
Amendments①

(**a**) The present Convention may be amended by either of the procedures specified in the following paragraphs.

(**b**) Amendments after consideration within the Organization:

(i) Any amendment proposed by a Contracting Government shall be submitted to the Secretary-General of the Organization, who shall then circulate it to all Members of the Organization and all Contracting Governments at least six months prior to its consideration.

(ii) Any amendment proposed and circulated as above shall be referred to the Maritime Safety Committee of the Organization for consideration.

(iii) Contracting Governments of States, whether or not Members of the Organization, shall be entitled to participate in the proceedings of the Maritime Safety Committee for the consideration and adoption of amendments.

---

① Refer to *Guidance on entry into force of amendments to the 1974 SOLAS Convention and related mandatory instruments* (MSC. 1/Circ. 1481) and *Guidance on drafting of amendments to the 1974 SOLAS Convention and related mandatory instruments* (MSC.1 /Circ.1500/Rev.1).

(b) 本公约缔约国政府之间目前继续有效的有关海上人命安全或其有关事项的所有其他条约、公约和协议,在其有效期间,对下列事项仍应继续充分和完全有效:

  (i) 不适用本公约的船舶;

  (ii) 适用本公约的船舶,但本公约未予明文规定的事项。

(c) 至于上述条约、公约或协议与本公约的规定有抵触时,应以本公约的规定为准。

(d) 本公约未予明文规定的一切事项,仍受缔约国政府的法律管辖。

第 VII 条
经协议订立的特殊规则

所有或某些缔约国政府之间,通过协议而按照本公约订立特殊规则时,应将这种规则送交本组织秘书长,由秘书长分发给所有缔约国政府。

第 VIII 条
修正[①]

(a) 本公约可按下列各款所规定的任一程序进行修正。

(b) 经本组织审议后的修正案:

  (i) 缔约国政府提出的任何修正案应提交给本组织秘书长,随后由秘书长在本组织审议前至少 6 个月将其分发给本组织所有成员和所有缔约国政府。

  (ii) 按上述所提议和分发的任何修正案应提交本组织海上安全委员会审议。

  (iii) 各缔约国政府,无论其是否为本组织成员,均有权参加海上安全委员会对修正案进行审议和通过的会议。

① 参见《1974 年 SOLAS 公约及其强制性文书修正案的生效指南》(第 MSC.1/Circ.1481 号通函)和《起草 1974 年 SOLAS 公约及其强制性文书修正案指南》(第 MSC.1 /Circ.1500/Rev.1 号通函)。

(iv) Amendments shall be adopted by a two-thirds majority of the Contracting Governments present and voting in the Maritime Safety Committee expanded as provided for in subparagraph (iii) of this paragraph (hereinafter referred to as "the expanded Maritime Safety Committee") on condition that at least one third of the Contracting Governments shall be present at the time of voting.

(v) Amendments adopted in accordance with subparagraph (iv) of this paragraph shall be communicated by the Secretary-General of the Organization to all Contracting Governments for acceptance.

(vi) (1) An amendment to an article of the Convention or to chapter I of the annex shall be deemed to have been accepted on the date on which it is accepted by two thirds of the Contracting Governments.

(2) An amendment to the annex other than chapter I shall be deemed to have been accepted

(aa) at the end of two years from the date on which it is communicated to Contracting Governments for acceptance; or

(bb) at the end of a different period, which shall not be less than one year, if so determined at the time of its adoption by a two-thirds majority of the Contracting Governments present and voting in the expanded Maritime Safety Committee.

However, if within the specified period either more than one third of Contracting Governments, or Contracting Governments the combined merchant fleets of which constitute not less than 50% of the gross tonnage of the world's merchant fleet, notify the Secretary-General of the Organization that they object to the amendment, it shall be deemed not to have been accepted.

(vii) (1) An amendment to an article of the Convention or to chapter I of the annex shall enter into force with respect to those Contracting Governments which have accepted it, six months after the date on which it is deemed to have been accepted, and with respect to each Contracting Government which accepts it after that date, six months after the date of that Contracting Government's acceptance.

(2) An amendment to the annex other than chapter I shall enter into force with respect to all Contracting Governments, except those which have objected to the amendment under subparagraph (vi)(2) of this paragraph and which have not withdrawn such objections, 6 months after the date on which it is deemed to have been accepted. However, before the date set for entry into force, any Contracting Government may give notice to the Secretary-General of the Organization that it exempts itself from giving effect to that amendment for a period not longer than one year from the date of its entry into force, or for such longer period as may be determined by a two-thirds majority of the Contracting Governments present and voting in the expanded Maritime Safety Committee at the time of the adoption of the amendment.

(iv) 修正案应在按本条(iii)所规定的扩大的海上安全委员会(以下称海上安全委员会扩大会议)上,经到会并投票的缔约国政府的三分之二多数通过,但在表决时应至少有三分之一的缔约国政府出席。

(v) 按本条(iv)通过的修正案应由本组织秘书长送交所有缔约国政府供其接受。

(vi) (1) 对本公约正文某一条款或附则第Ⅰ章的修正案,在三分之二的缔约国政府接受之日,应视为已被接受。

(2) 对除第Ⅰ章外的附则修正案,在下列情况下,应视为已被接受:

(aa) 从送交缔约国政府供其接受之日起的2年期限届满时;或

(bb) 在海上安全委员会扩大会议上,由到会并投票的缔约国政府的三分之二多数通过时所确定的不少于1年的不同期限届满时。

但在该规定期限内,有三分之一以上的缔约国政府,或拥有商船合计吨位数不少于世界商船总吨数50%的缔约国政府通知本组织秘书长其反对该修正案,则应视为该修正案未被接受。

(vii) (1) 对公约正文某一条款或附则第Ⅰ章的修正案,就那些业已接受该修正案的缔约国政府而言,应在其视为已接受之日起6个月后对其生效,而就该修正案在该接受日期之后接受的每一缔约国政府而言,应在其接受之日起6个月后对其生效。

(2) 对除第Ⅰ章外的附则修正案,就所有缔约国政府而言,应在其视为接受之日起6个月后对其生效,但按本条(vi)(2)规定反对该修正案且尚未撤销这种反对的缔约国政府除外。然而,在该修正案生效之日前,任何缔约国政府可通知本组织秘书长,在该修正案生效之日起不长于1年的期间内,或在海上安全委员会扩大会议通过修正案时,经到会并投票的缔约国政府的三分之二多数可能确定的更长的期间内,免于实行该修正案。

(c) Amendment by a Conference:

(i) Upon the request of a Contracting Government concurred in by at least one third of the Contracting Governments, the Organization shall convene a Conference of Contracting Governments to consider amendments to the present Convention.

(ii) Every amendment adopted by such a Conference by a two-thirds majority of the Contracting Governments present and voting shall be communicated by the Secretary-General of the Organization to all Contracting Governments for acceptance.

(iii) Unless the Conference decides otherwise, the amendment shall be deemed to have been accepted and shall enter into force in accordance with the procedures specified in subparagraphs (b)(vi) and (b)(vii) respectively of this article, provided that references in these paragraphs to the expanded Maritime Safety Committee shall be taken to mean references to the Conference.

(d) (i) A Contracting Government which has accepted an amendment to the annex which has entered into force shall not be obliged to extend the benefit of the present Convention in respect of the certificates issued to a ship entitled to fly the flag of a State the Government of which, pursuant to the provisions of subparagraph (b)(vi)(2) of this article, has objected to the amendment and has not withdrawn such an objection, but only to the extent that such certificates relate to matters covered by the amendment in question.

(ii) A Contracting Government which has accepted an amendment to the annex which has entered into force shall extend the benefit of the present Convention in respect of the certificates issued to a ship entitled to fly the flag of a State the Government of which, pursuant to the provisions of subparagraph (b)(vii)(2) of this article, has notified the Secretary-General of the Organization that it exempts itself from giving effect to the amendment.

(e) Unless expressly provided otherwise, any amendment to the present Convention made under this article, which relates to the structure of a ship, shall apply only to ships the keels of which are laid or which are at a similar stage of construction, on or after the date on which the amendment enters into force.

(f) Any declaration of acceptance of, or objection to, an amendment or any notice given under subparagraph (b)(vii)(2) of this article shall be submitted in writing to the Secretary-General of the Organization, who shall inform all Contracting Governments of any such submission and the date of its receipt.

(g) The Secretary-General of the Organization shall inform all Contracting Governments of any amendments which enter into force under this article, together with the date on which each such amendment enters into force.

(c) 会议修正：

(i) 经某一缔约国政府要请，并经至少三分之一缔约国政府的同意，本组织应召开一次缔约国政府会议，审议对本公约的修正案。

(ii) 经这一会议到会并投票的缔约国政府的三分之二多数通过的每一修正案，应由本组织秘书长送交所有缔约国政府供其接受。

(iii) 除会议另有决定外，该修正案应按本条(b)(vi)和(b)(vii)分别规定的程序视为已被接受和生效，但在这些条款中对海上安全委员会扩大会议的引述，应视为同时引述缔约国政府会议。

(d) (i) 已接受一项业已生效的附则修正案的某一缔约国政府，不得将本公约在签发证书方面的利益给予悬挂按本条(b)(vi)(2)规定反对该修正案且尚未撤销这种反对的某一国政府国旗的船舶，而应仅限于该修正案所涉及的与证书有关的事项范围。

(ii) 已接受一项业已生效的附则修正案的某一缔约国政府，应将本公约在签发证书方面的利益给予悬挂按本条(b)(vii)(2)规定已通知本组织秘书长免于实行该修正案的某一国政府国旗的船舶。

(e) 除另有明文规定外，按本条规定对本公约所做的任何修正案，凡涉及船舶结构者，应仅适用于在该修正案生效之日或以后安放龙骨或处于类似建造阶段的船舶。

(f) 按本条(b)(vii)(2)规定对某一修正案接受或反对的任何声明，或任何通知，应书面提交给本组织秘书长，并由秘书长将该提交的文件和收到的日期通知所有缔约国政府。

(g) 本组织秘书长应将按本条规定生效的任何修正案，连同每一项修正案的生效日期，通知所有缔约国政府。

Article IX
Signature, ratification, acceptance, approval and accession

(a) The present Convention shall remain open for signature at the Headquarters of the Organization from 1 November 1974 until 1 July 1975 and shall thereafter remain open for accession. States may become Parties to the present Convention by:

(i) signature without reservation as to ratification, acceptance or approval; or

(ii) signature subject to ratification, acceptance or approval, followed by ratification, acceptance or approval; or

(iii) accession.

(b) Ratification, acceptance, approval or accession shall be effected by the deposit of an instrument to that effect with the Secretary-General of the Organization.

(c) The Secretary-General of the Organization shall inform the Governments of all States which have signed the present Convention or acceded to it of any signature or of the deposit of any instrument of ratification, acceptance, approval or accession and the date of its deposit.

Article X
Entry into force

(a) The present Convention shall enter into force 12 months after the date on which not less than 25 States, the combined merchant fleets of which constitute not less than 50% of the gross tonnage of the world's merchant shipping, have become parties to it in accordance with article IX.

(b) Any instrument of ratification, acceptance, approval or accession deposited after the date on which the present Convention enters into force shall take effect three months after the date of deposit.

(c) After the date on which an amendment to the present Convention is deemed to have been accepted under article VIII, any instrument of ratification, acceptance, approval or accession deposited shall apply to the Convention as amended.

Article XI
Denunciation

(a) The present Convention may be denounced by any Contracting Government at any time after the expiry of five years from the date on which the Convention enters into force for that Government.

第 IX 条
签字、批准、接受、认可和加入

（a） 本公约自 1974 年 11 月 1 日起至 1975 年 7 月 1 日止在本组织总部开放供各国签字，以后继续开放供各国加入。各国可按下列方式成为本公约的缔约国：

（i） 签字并对批准、接受或认可无保留；或

（ii） 签字而有待批准、接受或认可，随后再予批准、接受或认可；或

（iii） 加入。

（b） 办理批准、接受、认可或加入，应向本组织秘书长交存一份相应的文件。

（c） 本组织秘书长应将任何签字，或批准、接受、认可，或加入的任何文件的交存及其交存日期，通知本公约所有签字国政府，或加入本公约的各国政府。

第 X 条
生效

（a） 本公约应在不少于 25 个国家，其拥有商船合计吨位数不少于世界商船总吨数的 50%，按第Ⅸ条规定成为本公约缔约国之日起 12 个月后生效。

（b） 在本公约生效日以后交存的批准、接受、认可或加入的任何文件，应在交存文件之日起 3 个月后对其生效。

（c） 在本公约的某一修正案在其按第Ⅷ条规定视为已被接受之日后交存的批准、接受、认可或加入的任何文件，应适用于经修正的公约。

第 XI 条
退出

（a） 任何缔约国政府在本公约对其生效满 5 年后，可随时退出本公约。

(b) Denunciation shall be effected by the deposit of an instrument of denunciation with the Secretary-General of the Organization who shall notify all the other Contracting Governments of any instrument of denunciation received and of the date of its receipt as well as the date on which such denunciation takes effect.

(c) A denunciation shall take effect one year, or such longer period as may be specified in the instrument of denunciation, after its receipt by the Secretary-General of the Organization.

Article XII
Deposit and registration

(a) The present Convention shall be deposited with the Secretary-General of the Organization who shall transmit certified true copies thereof to the Governments of all States which have signed the present Convention or acceded to it.

(b) As soon as the present Convention enters into force, the text shall be transmitted by the Secretary-General of the Organization to the Secretary-General of the United Nations for registration and publication, in accordance with Article 102 of the Charter of the United Nations.

Article XIII
Languages

The present Convention is established in a single copy in the Chinese, English, French, Russian and Spanish languages, each text being equally authentic. Official translations in the Arabic, German and Italian languages shall be prepared and deposited with the signed original.

IN WITNESS WHEREOF the undersigned,[①] being duly authorized by their respective Governments for that purpose, have signed the present Convention.

DONE AT LONDON this first day of November one thousand nine hundred and seventy-four.

① Signatures omitted.

(b) 退出本公约应向本组织秘书长交存一份退出文件,秘书长应将收到的退出本公约的任何文件和收到的日期以及退出生效的日期通知所有其他缔约国政府。

(c) 退出本公约应在本组织秘书长收到退出文件1年后,或在该文件中可能指明的较此为长的期限届满后生效。

第XII条
保存和登记

(a) 本公约应由本组织秘书长保存,本组织秘书长应将核准无误的本公约副本送交所有已签字或加入本公约的国家。

(b) 本公约一经生效,本组织秘书长应按《联合国宪章》第102条的规定,将其文本送交联合国秘书长登记并公布。

第XIII条
文字

本公约正本一份,用中文、英文、法文、俄文和西班牙文写成,每种文本具有同等效力。应备有阿拉伯文、德文和意大利文的官方译本,并与签署的正本一起保存。

下列具名的经各自政府为此目的正式授权的代表特签署本公约①,以昭信守。

1974年11月1日订于伦敦。

① 略去签字部分。

Protocol of 1988 relating to the International Convention for the Safety of Life at Sea, 1974

1974 年国际海上人命安全公约 1988 年议定书

Protocol of 1988 relating to the International Convention for the Safety of Life at Sea, 1974

THE PARTIES TO THE PRESENT PROTOCOL,

BEING PARTIES to the International Convention for the Safety of Life at Sea, done at London on 1 November 1974,

RECOGNIZING the need for the introduction into the above-mentioned Convention of provisions for survey and certification harmonized with corresponding provisions in other international instruments,

CONSIDERING that this need may best be met by the conclusion of a Protocol relating to the International Convention for the Safety of Life at Sea, 1974,

HAVE AGREED as follows:

Article I
General obligations

1 The Parties to the present Protocol undertake to give effect to the provisions of the present Protocol and the annex hereto, which shall constitute an integral part of the present Protocol. Every reference to the present Protocol constitutes at the same time a reference to the annex hereto.

2 As between the Parties to the present Protocol, the provisions of the International Convention for the Safety of Life at Sea, 1974, as amended, (hereinafter referred to as "the Convention") shall apply subject to the modifications and additions set out in the present Protocol.

3 With respect to ships entitled to fly the flag of a State which is not a Party to the Convention and the present Protocol, the Parties to the present Protocol shall apply the requirements of the Convention and the present Protocol as may be necessary to ensure that no more favourable treatment is given to such ships.

Article II
Prior treaties

1 As between the Parties to the present Protocol, the present Protocol replaces and abrogates the Protocol of 1978 relating to the Convention.

1974 年国际海上人命安全公约 1988 年议定书

本议定书各缔约国，

作为 1974 年 11 月 1 日在伦敦签署 1974 年国际海上人命安全公约的**缔约国**；

认识到需要在上述公约中引入检验和发证的规定，以与其他国际文件中相应的规定协调一致；

考虑到满足这一需要的最好办法是缔结一项关于 1974 年国际海上人命安全公约的议定书；

特议定下列各条：

第 I 条
一般义务

1 本议定书各缔约国承担义务实施本议定书及其附则的各项规定，本议定书附则与本议定书构成一个整体。引用本议定书即为同时引用其附则。

2 在本议定书各缔约国之间适用经修正的 1974 年国际海上人命安全公约（以下称“公约”）的规定时，亦应遵守本议定书列出的各项修订及补充规定。

3 对悬挂非公约和本议定书缔约国国旗的船舶，本议定书各缔约国应实施公约及本议定书的各项必要的规定，以确保不再给予此类船舶优惠的待遇。

第 II 条
以前的条约

1 在本议定书各缔约国之间，本议定书替代并废除公约 1978 年议定书。

2 Notwithstanding any other provisions of the present Protocol, any certificate issued under, and in accordance with, the provisions of the Convention and any supplement to such certificate issued under, and in accordance with, the provisions of the Protocol of 1978 relating to the Convention which is current when the present Protocol enters into force in respect of the Party by which the certificate or supplement was issued, shall remain valid until it expires under the terms of the Convention or the Protocol of 1978 relating to the Convention, as the case may be.

3 A Party to the present Protocol shall not issue certificates under, and in accordance with, the provisions of the International Convention for the Safety of Life at Sea, 1974, as adopted on 1 November 1974.

Article III
Communication of information①

The Parties to the present Protocol undertake to communicate to, and deposit with, the Secretary-General of the International Maritime Organization (hereinafter referred to as "the Organization"):

(**a**) the text of laws, decrees, orders and regulations and other instruments which have been promulgated on the various matters within the scope of the present Protocol;

(**b**) a list of nominated surveyors or recognized organizations which are authorized to act on their behalf in the administration of measures for safety of life at sea for circulation to the Parties for information of their officers, and a notification of the specific responsibilities and conditions of the authority delegated to those nominated surveyors or recognized organizations; and

(**c**) a sufficient number of specimens of their certificates issued under the provision of the present Protocol.

Article IV
Signature, ratification, acceptance, approval and accession

1 The present Protocol shall be open for signature at the Headquarters of the Organization from 1 March 1989 to 28 February 1990 and shall thereafter remain open for accession. Subject to the provisions of paragraph 3, States may express their consent to be bound by the present Protocol by:

(**a**) signature without reservation as to ratification, acceptance or approval; or

(**b**) signature subject to ratification, acceptance or approval, followed by ratification, acceptance or approval; or

(**c**) accession.

① Refer to *Notification and circulation through the Global Integrated Shipping Information System* (*CISIS*) (resolution A.1074(28)).

2 尽管有本议定书的其他规定,某一缔约国根据和按照公约规定所签发的任何证书以及根据和按照公约1978年议定书规定所签发的任何证书的附件,在本议定书对该缔约国生效时,应继续保持有效,直至视情况根据公约或公约1978年议定书规定期满时为止。

3 本议定书各缔约国应不再根据和按照1974年11月1日通过的1974年国际海上人命安全公约的规定签发证书。

第III条
资料的送交[①]

本议定书各缔约国承担义务,向国际海事组织(以下称"本组织")秘书长交存下列资料:

(a) 就本议定书范围内各种事项所颁布的法律、法令、命令、规则和其他文件的文本;

(b) 经授权代表其在管理海上人命安全措施方面行事的指定的验船师或认可的组织名单,以分发给各缔约国政府供其官员参考,以及这些指定的验船师或认可的组织具体职责和授权条件的通告;和

(c) 根据本议定书规定颁发的足够数量的证书样本。

第IV条
签字、批准、接受、认可和加入

1 本议定书自1989年3月1日起至1990年2月28日止在本组织总部开放供各国签字,此后继续开放供各国加入。除本条3规定外,各国可按下列方式同意承担本议定书的义务:

(a) 签字并对批准、接受或认可无保留;或

(b) 签字而有待批准、接受或认可,随后再予批准、接受或认可;或

(c) 加入。

---

① 参见《在全球综合航运信息系统(GISIS)发布通知和通告》(第A.1074(28)号决议)。

2 Ratification, acceptance, approval or accession shall be effected by the deposit of an instrument to that effect with the Secretary-General of the Organization.

3 The present Protocol may be signed without reservation, ratified, accepted, approved or acceded to only by States which have signed without reservation, ratified, accepted, approved or acceded to the Convention.

Article V
Entry into force

1 The present Protocol shall enter into force twelve months after the date on which both the following conditions have been met:

(a) not less than fifteen States, the combined merchant fleets of which constitute not less than 50% of the gross tonnage of the world's merchant shipping, have expressed their consent to be bound by it in accordance with article Ⅳ, and

(b) the conditions for the entry into force of the Protocol of 1988 relating to the International Convention on Load Lines, 1966, have been met,

provided that the present Protocol shall not enter into force before 1 February 1992.

2 For States which have deposited an instrument of ratification, acceptance, approval or accession in respect of the present Protocol after the conditions for entry into force thereof have been met but prior to the date of entry into force, the ratification, acceptance, approval or accession shall take effect on the date of entry into force of the present Protocol or three months after the date of deposit of the instrument, whichever is the later date.

3 Any instrument of ratification, acceptance, approval or accession deposited after the date on which the present Protocol enters into force shall take effect three months after the date of deposit.

4 After the date on which an amendment to the present Protocol is deemed to have been accepted under article Ⅵ, any instrument of ratification, acceptance, approval or accession deposited shall apply to the present Protocol as amended.

Article VI
Amendments①

The procedures set out in article Ⅷ of the Convention shall apply to amendments to the present Protocol, provided that:

(a) references in that article to the Convention and to Contracting Governments shall be taken to mean references to the present Protocol and to the Parties to the present Protocol respectively;

① Refer to *Guidance on entry into force of amendments to the 1974 SOLAS Convention and related mandatory instruments* (MSC.1/Circ.1481) and *Guidance on drafting of amendments to the 1974 SOLAS Convention and related mandatory instruments* (MSC.1/Circ.1500/Rev.1).

2 办理批准、接受、认可或加入,应向本组织秘书长交存一份相应的文件。

3 只有已对公约签字而无保留、批准、接受、认可或加入的国家,才可对本议定书签字而无保留、批准、接受、认可或加入。

第 V 条
生效

1 本议定书应在下列两个条件均满足之日起 12 个月后生效:

(a) 不少于 15 个国家,其拥有商船合计吨位数不少于世界商船总吨数的 50%,按第Ⅳ条规定已同意承担本议定书的义务,和

(b) 《1966 年国际载重线公约 1988 年议定书》的生效条件已经满足,

但本议定书不得早于 1992 年 2 月 1 日生效。

2 对于在本议定书生效条件予以满足之日后但在生效之日前已交存批准、接受、认可或加入本议定书文件的国家,其批准、接受、认可或加入应在本议定书生效之日时对其生效,或在交存该文件之日起 3 个月后对其生效,以日期较后者为准。

3 对于在本议定书生效之日后交存的任何批准、接受、认可或加入的文件,应在交存之日起 3 个月后对其生效。

4 对于在本议定书的修正案按第Ⅵ条规定视为已被接受之日后交存的任何批准、接受、认可或加入的文件,应适用于经修正的议定书。

第 VI 条
修正[①]

公约第Ⅷ条中规定的程序应适用于本议定书的修正,其条件是:

(a) 该条对公约和缔约国政府的引述,应视为同时分别引述本议定书和本议定书缔约国;

① 参见《1974 年 SOLAS 公约及其强制性文书修正案的生效指南》(第 MSC.1/Circ.1481 号通函)和《起草 1974 年 SOLAS 公约及其强制性文书修正案指南》(第 MSC.1/Circ.1500/Rev.1 号通函)。

(b) amendments to the articles of the present Protocol and to the annex thereto shall be adopted and brought into force in accordance with the procedure applicable to amendments to the articles of the Convention or to chapter I of the annex thereto; and

(c) amendments to the appendix to the annex to the present Protocol may be adopted and brought into force in accordance with the procedure applicable to amendments to the annex to the Convention other than chapter I.

Article VII
Denunciation

1 The present Protocol may be denounced by any Party at any time after the expiry of five years from the date on which the present Protocol enters into force for that Party.

2 Denunciation shall be effected by the deposit of an instrument of denunciation with the Secretary-General of the Organization.

3 A denunciation shall take effect one year, or such longer period as may be specified in the instrument of denunciation, after its receipt by the Secretary-General of the Organization.

4 A denunciation of the Convention by a Party shall be deemed to be a denunciation of the present Protocol by that Party. Such denunciation shall take effect on the same date as denunciation of the Convention takes effect according to paragraph (c) of article XI of the Convention.

Article VIII
Depositary

1 The present Protocol shall be deposited with the Secretary-General of the Organization (hereinafter referred to as "the depositary").

2 The depositary shall:

(a) inform the Governments of all States which have signed the present Protocol or acceded thereto of:

(i) each new signature or deposit of an instrument of ratification, acceptance, approval or accession, together with the date thereof;

(ii) the date of entry into force of the present Protocol;

(iii) the deposit of any instrument of denunciation of the present Protocol together with the date on which it was received and the date on which the denunciation takes effect;

(b) transmit certified true copies of the present Protocol to the Governments of all States which have signed the present Protocol or acceded thereto.

(b) 对本议定书条款及其附则的修正，应按对公约条款或其附则第Ⅰ章适用的修正程序予以通过和生效；和

(c) 对本议定书附则附录的修正可按对除第Ⅰ章以外适用的公约附则修正程序予以通过和生效。

第 VII 条
退出

1 任何缔约国政府在本议定书对其生效满5年后，可随时退出本议定书。

2 退出本议定书应向本组织秘书长交存一份退出文件。

3 退出本议定书应在本组织秘书长收到退出文件1年后，或在该文件中可能指明的较此为长的期限届满后生效。

4 一缔约国退出公约，即应视为该缔约国同时退出本议定书。在按公约第XI条(c)规定退出公约生效的同日，退出本议定书亦即生效。

第 VIII 条
保管人

1 本议定书应由本组织秘书长（以下称"保管人"）保存。

2 保管人应：

(a) 将下列情况通知所有已签字或加入本议定书的国家政府：

(i) 每一新的签字或批准、接受、认可或加入的文件交存及其日期；

(ii) 本议定书的生效日期；

(iii) 任何退出本议定书文件的交存，以及该文件的收到日期和退出生效日期；

(b) 将核准无误的本议定书副本送交所有已签字或加入本议定书的国家政府。

3 As soon as the present Protocol enters into force, a certified true copy thereof shall be transmitted by the depositary to the Secretariat of the United Nations for registration and publication in accordance with Article 102 of the Charter of the United Nations.

Article IX
Languages

The present Protocol is established in a single original in the Arabic, Chinese, English, French, Russian and Spanish languages, each text being equally authentic. An official translation into the Italian language shall be prepared and deposited with the signed original.

IN WITNESS WHEREOF the undersigned,[①] being duly authorized by their respective Governments for that purpose, have signed the present Protocol.

DONE AT LONDON this eleventh day of November one thousand nine hundred and eighty-eight.

① Signatures omitted.

3 本议定书一经生效，保管人应按《联合国宪章》第102条的规定，将一份核准无误的本议定书副本送交联合国秘书处登记并公布。

第IX条
文字

本议定书正本一份，用阿拉伯文、中文、英文、法文、俄文和西班牙文写成，每种文本具有同等效力。应备有意大利文的官方译本，并与签署的正本一起保存。

下列具名的经各自政府为此目的正式授权的代表特签署本议定书，[①]以昭信守。

1988年11月11日订于伦敦。

① 略去签字部分。

Consolidated text of the annex to the 1974 SOLAS Convention and the 1988 Protocol relating thereto

1974年国际海上人命安全公约及其1988年议定书附则的综合文本

Chapter Ⅰ General provisions

第 I 章　总则

Part A
Application, definitions, etc.

Regulation 1
Application①

(a) Unless expressly provided otherwise, the present regulations apply only to ships engaged on international voyages.

(b) The classes of ships to which each chapter applies are more precisely defined, and the extent of the application is shown, in each chapter.

P88 Regulation 2
Definitions

For the purpose of the present regulations, unless expressly provided otherwise:

(a) *Regulations* means the regulations contained in the annex to the present Convention.

(b) *Administration* means the Government of the State whose flag the ship is entitled to fly.

(c) *Approved* means approved by the Administration.

(d) *International voyage* means a voyage from a country to which the present Convention applies to a port outside such country, or conversely.

(e) A *passenger* is every person other than:

(i) the master and the members of the crew or other persons employed or engaged in any capacity on board a ship on the business of that ship; and

(ii) a child under one year of age.

(f) A *passenger ship* is a ship which carries more than twelve passengers.

(g) A *cargo ship* is any ship which is not a passenger ship.

(h) A *tanker* is a cargo ship constructed or adapted for the carriage in bulk of liquid cargoes of an inflammable② nature.

(i) A *fishing vessel* is a vessel used for catching fish, whales, seals, walrus or other living resources of the sea.

---

① For some specific type of ships, refer to other IMO instruments, such as the *Code of safety for special purpose ships, 2008* (resolution MSC.266(84)), as amended (2008 SPS Code); the *Code for the construction and equipment of mobile offshore drilling unit, 2009* (resolution A.1023(26)), as amended (2009 MODU Code); the *Code for the transport and handling of hazardous and noxious liquid substances in bulk on offshore support vessels* (resolution A.1122(30)) (OSV Chemical Code); the *Code of safety for diving systems, 1995* (resolution A.831(19)) (Diving Code, 1995) and so on.

② "Inflammable" has the same meaning as "flammable".

A 部分
适用范围、定义等

第 1 条
适用范围[①]

(a)　除另有明文规定外，本规则仅适用于从事国际航行的船舶。

(b)　本规则各章适用的船舶种类与适用的范围，在各章中予以明确规定。

P88 第 2 条
定义

除另有明文规定外，就本规则而言：

(a)　**规则**系指本公约附则内包含的规则条文。

(b)　**主管机关**系指船旗国政府。

(c)　**认可**系指经主管机关认可。

(d)　**国际航行**系指由适用本公约的一国驶往该国以外港口或与此相反的航行。

(e)　**乘客**系指除下列人员外的人员：

　(i)　船长和船员，或在船上以任何职位从事或参加该船业务的其他人员；和

　(ii)　一周岁以下儿童。

(f)　**客船**系指载客超过 12 人的船舶。

(g)　**货船**系指非客船的任何船舶。

(h)　**液货船**系指经建造或改建用于散装运输易燃[②]液体货品的货船。

(i)　**渔船**系指用于捕捞鱼类、鲸鱼、海豹、海象或其他海洋生物资源的船舶。

---

① 对于某些特殊类型船舶，参见其他 IMO 文书，例如《经修订的 2008 年特种用途船舶安全规则》(2008 SPS 规则)(第 MSC.266(84)号决议)；《经修订的 2009 年海上移动式钻井平台构造和设备规则》(2009 MODU 规则)(第 A.1023(26)号决议)；《近海供应船散装运输和装卸有毒有害液体物质规则》(OSV 化学品规则)(第 A.1122(30)号决议)；《1995 年潜水系统安全规则》(1995 潜水规则)(第 A.831(19)号决议)等。

② “Inflammable”与“flammable”意思相同。

(**j**) A *nuclear ship* is a ship provided with a nuclear power plant.

P88 (**k**) *New ship* means a ship the keel of which is laid or which is at a similar stage of construction on or after 25 May 1980.

(**l**) *Existing ship* means a ship which is not a new ship.

(**m**) A *mile* is 1,852 meters or 6,080 feet.

P88 (**n**) *Anniversary date* means the day and the month of each year which will correspond to the date of expiry of the relevant certificate.

Regulation 3
Exceptions

(**a**) The present regulations, unless expressly provided otherwise, do not apply to:

(i) Ships of war and troopships.

(ii) Cargo ships of less than 500 gross tonnage.

(iii) Ships not propelled by mechanical means.

(iv) Wooden ships of primitive build.

(v) Pleasure yachts not engaged in trade.

(vi) Fishing vessels.

(**b**) Except as expressly provided in chapter V, nothing herein shall apply to ships solely navigating the Great Lakes of North America and the River St Lawrence as far east as a straight line drawn from Cap des Rosiers to West Point, Anticosti Island and, on the north side of Anticosti Island, the 63rd meridian.

Regulation 4
Exemptions[①]

(**a**) A ship which is not normally engaged on international voyages but which, in exceptional circumstances, is required to undertake a single international voyage may be exempted by the Administration from any of the requirements of the present regulations provided that it complies with safety requirements which are adequate in the opinion of the Administration for the voyage which is to be undertaken by the ship.

① Refer to *Issue of Exemption Certificates under the 1974 SOLAS Convention and Amendments thereto*, as amended (SLS.14/Circ.115); *Port State concurrence with SOLAS exemptions* (MSC/Circ.606) and *Notification and circulation through the Global Integrated Shipping Information System (GISIS)* (resolution A.1074(28)).

(j)　**核能船舶**系指设有核动力装置的船舶。

P88 (k)　**新船**系指在 1980 年 5 月 25 日或以后安放龙骨或处于类似建造阶段的船舶。

(l)　**现有船舶**系指非新船。

(m)　**1 海里**(n mile)为 1 852 m 或 6 080 ft。

P88 (n)　**周年日期**系指与相关证书期满之日对应的每年的该月该日。

第 3 条
例外

(a)　除另有明文规定外,本规则不适用于下列船舶:

　(i)　军船和运兵船。

　(ii)　小于 500 总吨的货船。

　(iii)　非机动船。

　(iv)　制造简陋的木船。

　(v)　非营业性游艇。

　(vi)　渔船。

(b)　除第Ⅴ章另有明文规定外,本规则不适用于专门航行于北美洲五大湖和航行于圣劳伦斯河东至罗歇尔角与安提科斯提岛西点间所绘的直线以及在安提科斯提岛北面水域至西经 63°线的船舶。

第 4 条
免除[①]

(a)　对于通常不从事国际航行的船舶,在特殊情况下需要进行一次国际航行时,主管机关可予免除本规则中的任何要求,但该船应符合主管机关认为适合于其所担任航次的安全要求。

① 参见《经修订的按照 1974 年 SOLAS 公约及其修正案签发免除证书》(第 SLS.14/Circ.115 号通函);《港口国同意〈安全公约〉的免除》(第 MSC/Circ.606 号通函)和《通过全球航运综合信息系统(GISIS)发布通知和通告》(第 A.1074(28)号决议)。

(**b**) The Administration may exempt any ship which embodies features of a novel kind from any of the provisions of chapters Ⅱ-1, Ⅱ-2, Ⅲ and Ⅳ of these regulations the application of which might seriously impede research into the development of such features and their incorporation in ships engaged on international voyages. Any such ship shall, however, comply with safety requirements which, in the opinion of that Administration, are adequate for the service for which it is intended and are such as to ensure the overall safety of the ship and which are acceptable to the Governments of the States to be visited by the ship. The Administration which allows any such exemption shall communicate to the Organization particulars of same and the reasons therefor which the Organization shall circulate to the Contracting Governments for their information.

Regulation 5
Equivalents①

(**a**) Where the present regulations require that a particular fitting, material, appliance or apparatus, or type thereof, shall be fitted or carried in a ship, or that any particular provision shall be made, the Administration may allow any other fitting, material, appliance or apparatus, or type thereof, to be fitted or carried, or any other provision to be made in that ship, if it is satisfied by trial thereof or otherwise that such fitting, material, appliance or apparatus, or type thereof, or provision, is at least as effective as that required by the present regulations.

(**b**) Any Administration which so allows, in substitution, a fitting, material, appliance or apparatus, or type thereof, or provision, shall communicate to the Organization particulars thereof together with a report on any trials made and the Organization shall circulate such particulars to other Contracting Governments for the information of their officers.

① Refer to *Guidelines for the approval of alternatives and equivalents as provided for in various IMO instruments* (MSC.1/Circ.1455) and *Notification and circulation through the Global Integrated Shipping Information System* (*GISIS*) (resolution A.1074(28)).

（b）　对于具有新颖特性的任何船舶，如果应用本规则第Ⅱ-1章、第Ⅱ-2章、第Ⅲ章和第Ⅳ章的任何规定可能严重妨碍对发展这种特性的研究和在从事国际航行的船舶上对这些特性的采用时，主管机关可予免除这些要求。然而，任何此种船舶应符合该主管机关认为适于其预定的用途，并能保证船舶的全面安全，同时又为该船拟驶往的国家政府所接受的各项安全要求。允许任何这种免除的主管机关应把此次免除的详细资料和理由提交本组织，由本组织分发给各缔约国政府，供其参考。

第5条
等效[①]

（a）　对本规则要求船上所应装设或配备的专门装置、材料、设备或器具，或其型式，或本规则要求应设置的任何专门设施，主管机关可准许该船上装设或配备任何其他的装置、材料、设备或器具，或其型式，或设置任何其他的设施，但应通过试验或其他方法确信，这些装置、材料、设备或器具，或其型式，或其他设施，至少与本规则所要求者具有同等效能。

（b）　准许采用这种替代装置、材料、设备或器具，或其型式，或其他设施的任何主管机关，应将其详细资料连同所做的任何试验报告送交本组织，由本组织将该资料分发给其他缔约国政府，供其官员参考。

---

①　参见《多项IMO文书中的替代和等效措施批准导则》（第MSC.1/Circ.1455号通函）和《通过全球航运综合信息系统（GISIS）发布通知和通告》（第A.1074(28)号决议）。

Part B
Surveys and certificates[①]

P88 Regulation 6
Inspection and survey

(a) The inspection and survey of ships, so far as regards the enforcement of the provisions of the present regulations and the granting of exemptions therefrom, shall be carried out by officers of the Administration. The Administration may, however, entrust the inspections and surveys either to surveyors nominated for the purpose or to organizations recognized by it.

(b) An Administration nominating surveyors or recognizing organizations to conduct inspections and surveys as set forth in paragraph (a) shall as a minimum empower any nominated surveyor or recognized organization to:

(i) require repairs to a ship;

(ii) carry out inspections and surveys if requested by the appropriate authorities of a port State.

The Administration shall notify the Organization of the specific responsibilities and conditions of the authority delegated to nominated surveyors or recognized organizations.[②]

(c) When a nominated surveyor or recognized organization determines that the condition of the ship or its equipment does not correspond substantially with the particulars of the certificate or is such that the ship is not fit to proceed to sea without danger to the ship, or persons on board, such surveyor or organization shall immediately ensure that corrective action is taken and shall in due course notify the Administration. If such corrective action is not taken the relevant certificate should be withdrawn and the Administration shall be notified immediately; and, if the ship is in the port of another Party, the appropriate authorities of the port State shall also be notified immediately. When an officer of the Administration, a nominated surveyor or a recognized organization has notified the appropriate authorities of the port State, the Government of the port State concerned shall give such officer, surveyor or organization any necessary assistance to carry out their obligations under this regulation. When applicable, the Government of the port State concerned shall ensure that the ship shall not sail until it can proceed to sea, or leave port for the purpose of proceeding to the appropriate repair yard, without danger to the ship or persons on board.

---

① Refer to *Global and uniform implementation of the harmonized system of survey and certification* (*HSSC*) (resolution A.883(21)), *Survey Guidelines under the Harmonized System of Survey and Certification* (*HSSC*), 2019 (resolution A.1140(31), as may be amended), *Guidelines for pre-planning of surveys in dry dock of ships which are not subject to the enhanced programme of inspections* (MSC.1/Circ.1223), *Unified interpretation of the term "first survey" referred to in SOLAS regulations* (MSC.1/Circ.1290) and *Guidelines for Administrations to ensure the adequacy of transfer of class-related matters between recognized organizations* (*ROs*) (MSC-MEPC.5/Circ.2).

② Refer to the *Code for Recognized Organizations* (*RO Code*) (resolutions MSC.349(92) and MEPC.237(65)); *Communication of information on the authorization of recognized organizations* (*ROs*) (MSC/Circ.1010-MEPC/Circ.382) and *Notification and circulation through the Global Integrated Shipping Information System* (*GISIS*) (resolution A.1074(28)).

B 部分
检验与发证[①]

P88 第 6 条
检查与检验

（a） 为执行及为准予免除本规则的规定而对船舶进行的检查和检验，应由主管机关的官员进行。但主管机关可将这些检查和检验委托给为此目的而指定的验船师或由其认可的组织。

（b） 指定验船师或认可组织执行本条(a)所规定的检查和检验的主管机关，至少应就下列事项对其指定的验船师或认可的组织进行授权：

（i） 对船舶提出修理要求；

（ii） 在受到港口国有关当局请求时，进行检查和检验。

主管机关应将有关授权给指定的验船师或认可的组织的具体职责及条件通知本组织。[②]

（c） 当指定的验船师或认可的组织确定船舶或其设备的状况在实质上与证书所载内容不符，或会危及船舶或船上人员，因而船舶不适于出海航行时，该验船师或组织应确保立即采取纠正措施并及时通知主管机关。如果未能采取此种纠正措施，则应撤销有关证书并立即通知主管机关；如该船是在另一缔约国的港口内，则还应立即通知港口国的有关当局。当主管机关的官员、指定的验船师或认可的组织通知该港口国的有关当局后，有关的港口国政府应向该官员、验船师或组织提供履行本条规定的义务所必需的任何帮助。必要时，有关的港口国政府应确保该船在未具备不危及船舶或船上人员的条件前，不得开航或离港驶往合适的修船厂。

---

① 参见《全球统一实施检验和发证协调系统（HSSC）》（第 A.883(21) 号决议），《2019 年检验和发证协调系统（HSSC）检验导则》（第 A.1140(31) 号决议，可经修订），《不执行加强检验程序的船舶干坞检验预先计划导则》（第 MSC.1/Circ.1223 号通函），《〈安全公约〉条款中“初次检验”的统一解释》（第 MSC.1/Circ.1290 号通函），以及《主管机关确保船舶在被认可组织（ROs）间转级事宜的适合性指南》（第 MSC-MEPC.5/Circ.2 号通函）。

② 参见《认可组织规则》（RO 规则）（第 MSC.349(92) 号决议和第 MEPC.237(65) 号决议）；《关于被认可组织（RO）授权的资料送交》（第 MSC/Circ.1010-MEPC/Circ.382 号通函）和《通过全球航运综合信息系统（GISIS）发布通知和通告》（第 A.1074(28) 号决议）。

(**d**) In every case, the Administration shall fully guarantee the completeness and efficiency of the inspection and survey, and shall undertake to ensure the necessary arrangements to satisfy this obligation.

P88 Regulation 7
Surveys of passenger ships①

(**a**) A passenger ship shall be subject to the surveys specified below:

(i) an initial survey before the ship is put in service;

(ii) a renewal survey once every 12 months, except where regulation 14(b), (e), (f) and (g) is applicable;

(iii) additional surveys, as occasion arises.

(**b**) The surveys referred to above shall be carried out as follows:

(i) the initial survey shall include a complete inspection of the ship's structure, machinery and equipment, including the outside of the ship's bottom and the inside and outside of the boilers. This survey shall be such as to ensure that the arrangements, materials and scantlings of the structure, boilers and other pressure vessels and their appurtenances, main and auxiliary machinery, electrical installation, radio installations including those used in life-saving appliances, fire protection, fire safety systems and appliances, life-saving appliances and arrangements, shipborne navigational equipment, nautical publications, means of embarkation for pilots and other equipment fully comply with the requirements of the present regulations, and of the laws, decrees, orders and regulations promulgated as a result thereof by the Administration for ships of the service for which it is intended. The survey shall also be such as to ensure that the workmanship of all parts of the ship and its equipment is in all respects satisfactory, and that the ship is provided with the lights, shapes, means of making sound signals and distress signals as required by the provisions of the present regulations and the International Regulations for Preventing Collisions at Sea in force;

① Refer to *Surveys and inspections of ro-ro passenger ships* (resolution A.794(19)), *Guidelines for unscheduled inspections of ro-ro passenger ships by flag States* (MSC/Circ.956) and *Guidelines for the assessment of technical provisions for the performance of an in-water survey in lieu of bottom inspection in dry-dock to permit one dry-dock examination in any five-year period for passenger ships other than ro-ro passenger ships* (MSC.1/Circ.1348).

（d）　在所有情况下，主管机关均应充分保证检查和检验的完整性和有效性，确保为履行这一职责做出必要的安排。

P88 第 7 条
客船的检验[①]

（a）　客船应接受下列规定的检验：

（i）　初次检验，在船舶投入营运前进行；

（ii）　换证检验，每 12 个月进行一次，如适用第 14(b)、(e)、(f)和(g)条时除外；

（iii）　附加检验，在必要时进行。

（b）　应按下列规定进行上述检验：

（i）　初次检验应包括船舶结构、机器及设备，并包括船底外部，以及锅炉内、外部在内的全面检查。该检验应确保船舶的布置、材料、结构尺寸、锅炉和其他受压容器及其附件、主辅机、电气设备、无线电装置（包括救生设备中使用的无线电装置）、防火、消防安全系统和设备、救生设备和装置、船载导航设备、航海出版物、引航员登船设施和其他设备，完全符合本公约规则以及主管机关为此而颁布的对从事预定用途船舶的法律、法令、命令和规则的各项要求。该检验还应确保船舶所有部分及其设备的制造工艺在所有方面均属合格，并确保船舶已按本公约规则和现行国际海上避碰规则的规定备有号灯、号型，以及发出声响信号和遇险信号的设备；

---

① 参见《滚装客船的检查与检验》（第 A.749(19)号决议），《船旗国对滚装客船的不定期检查导则》（第 MSC./Circ.956 号通函）和《对滚装客船以外的客船，以水下检查代替坞内船底外部检验而通过五年期坞内检验的性能技术标准评估导则》（第 MSC.1/Circ.1348 号通函）。

(ii) the renewal survey shall include an inspection of the structure, boilers and other pressure vessels, machinery and equipment, including the outside of the ship's bottom. The survey shall be such as to ensure that the ship, as regards the structure, boilers and other pressure vessels and their appurtenances, main and auxiliary machinery, electrical installation, radio installations including those used in life-saving appliances, fire protection, fire safety systems and appliances, life-saving appliances and arrangements, shipborne navigational equipment, nautical publications, means of embarkation for pilots and other equipment is in satisfactory condition and is fit for the service for which it is intended, and that it complies with the requirements of the present regulations and of the laws, decrees, orders and regulations promulgated as a result thereof by the Administration. The lights, shapes, means of making sound signals and distress signals carried by the ship shall also be subject to the above-mentioned survey for the purpose of ensuring that they comply with the requirements of the present regulations and of the International Regulations for Preventing Collisions at Sea in force;

(**iii**) an additional survey either general or partial, according to the circumstances, shall be made after a repair resulting from investigations prescribed in regulation 11, or whenever any important repairs or renewals are made. The survey shall be such as to ensure that the necessary repairs or renewals have been effectively made, that the material and workmanship of such repairs or renewals are in all respects satisfactory, and that the ship complies in all respects with the provisions of the present regulations and of the International Regulations for Preventing Collisions at Sea in force, and of the laws, decrees, orders and regulations promulgated as a result thereof by the Administration.

(**c**) (i) the laws, decrees, orders and regulations referred to in paragraph (b) of this regulation shall be in all respects such as to ensure that, from the point of view of safety of life, the ship is fit for the service for which it is intended;

(ii) they shall among other things prescribe the requirements to be observed as to the initial and subsequent hydraulic or other acceptable alternative tests to which the main and auxiliary boilers, connections, steam pipes, high pressure receivers and fuel tanks for internal combustion engines are to be submitted including the test procedures to be followed and the intervals between two consecutive tests.

(ii) 换证检验应包括结构、锅炉及其他受压容器、机器及设备,并包括船底外部在内的检查。该检验应确保船舶结构、锅炉及其他受压容器及其附件、主辅机、电气设备、无线电装置(包括救生设备中使用的无线电装置)、防火、消防安全系统和设备、救生设备和装置、船载导航设备、航海出版物、引航员登船设施和其他设备,均处于合格状态,并适合其预定的用途,以及确保符合本公约规则和主管机关为此而颁布的法律、法令、命令和规则的各项要求。船舶所配备的号灯、号型,以及发出声响信号和遇险信号的设备也应接受上述检验,以确保其符合本公约规则和现行国际海上避碰规则的各项要求;

(iii) 附加检验,在第 11 条规定的检查结果进行修理后,或在任何重大修理或换新后,都应根据情况进行全面或部分检验。该检验应确保已有效进行了必要的修理或换新,确保此项修理或换新所用的材料和工艺在所有方面均属合格,并确保船舶在所有方面均符合本公约规则和现行国际海上避碰规则,以及主管机关为此而颁布的法律、法令、命令和规则的各项规定;

(c) (i) 本条(b)所指的法律、法令、命令和规则,应从人命安全的角度,在所有方面确保船舶适合其预定的用途;

(ii) 在上述法律、法令、命令和规则中,应规定对主辅锅炉、连接件、蒸汽管、高压容器以及内燃机用的燃油舱柜应进行的初次及其后的液压试验或其他可接受的替代试验所应遵循的各项要求,包括应遵循的试验程序和连续两次试验之间的间隔期。

P88 Regulation 8
Surveys of life-saving appliances and other equipment of cargo ships[①]

(a) The life-saving appliances and other equipment of cargo ships of 500 gross tonnage and upwards as referred to in paragraph (b)(i) shall be subject to the surveys specified below:

(i) an initial survey before the ship is put in service;

(ii) a renewal survey at intervals specified by the Administration but not exceeding 5 years, except where regulation 14(b), (e), (f) and (g) is applicable;

(iii) a periodical survey within three months before or after the second anniversary date or within three months before or after the third anniversary date of the Cargo Ship Safety Equipment Certificate which shall take the place of one of the annual surveys specified in paragraph (a)(iv);

(iv) an annual survey within 3 months before or after each anniversary date of the Cargo Ship Safety Equipment Certificate;

(v) an additional survey as prescribed for passenger ships in regulation 7(b)(iii).

(b) The surveys referred to in paragraph (a) shall be carried out as follows:

(i) the initial survey shall include a complete inspection of the fire safety systems and appliances, life-saving appliances and arrangements except radio installations, the shipborne navigational equipment, means of embarkation for pilots and other equipment to which chapters II-1, II-2, III and V apply to ensure that they comply with the requirements of the present regulations, are in satisfactory condition and are fit for the service for which the ship is intended. The fire control plans, nautical publications, lights, shapes, means of making sound signals and distress signals shall also be subject to the above-mentioned survey for the purpose of ensuring that they comply with the requirements of the present regulations and, where applicable, the International Regulations for Preventing Collisions at Sea in force;

(ii) the renewal and periodical surveys shall include an inspection of the equipment referred to in paragraph (b)(i) to ensure that it complies with the relevant requirements of the present regulations and the International Regulations for Preventing Collisions at Sea in force, is in satisfactory condition and is fit for the service for which the ship is intended;

---

① Refer to *Guidelines for construction, installation, maintenance and inspection/survey of means of embarkation and disembarkation* (MSC.1/Circ.1331); *Servicing of life-saving appliances and radiocommunication equipment under the Harmonized System of Survey and Certification* (HSSC) (MSC/Circ.955); *Guidelines for the performance and testing criteria and surveys of high-expansion foam concentrates for fixed-extinguishing systems* (MSC/Circ.670); *Guidelines for performance and testing criteria and surveys of medium expansion from concentrates for fixed fire-extinguishing systems* (MSC/Circ.798) *and Guidance on the survey and certification of compliance of ships with the requirement to transmit LRIT information* (MSC.1/Circ.1307).

P88 第 8 条
货船救生设备和其他设备的检验[①]

(a)　500 总吨及以上的货船救生设备和其他设备应按(b)(i)所述接受下列规定的检验:

　(i)　初次检验,在船舶投入营运前进行;

　(ii)　换证检验,按主管机关规定的间隔期进行,但不得超过 5 年,如适用第 14(b)、(e)、(f)和(g)条时除外;

　(iii)　定期检验,在货船设备安全证书的第二个周年日之前或之后 3 个月内或第三个周年日之前或之后 3 个月内进行,并应取代(a)(iv)规定的其中一次年度检验;

　(iv)　年度检验,在货船设备安全证书的每一周年日之前或之后 3 个月内进行;

　(v)　附加检验,按第 7(b)(iii)条对客船的规定进行。

(b)　本条(a)所述的检验应按下列规定进行:

　(i)　初次检验应包括消防安全系统和设备、救生设备和装置(无线电装置除外)、船载导航设备、引航员登船设施以及其他适用第Ⅱ-1、Ⅱ-2、Ⅲ和Ⅴ章的设备在内的全面检查,以确保其符合本公约规则的各项要求,均处于合格状态,并适合船舶预定的用途。防火控制图、航海出版物、号灯、号型,以及发出声响信号和遇险信号的设备也应接受上述检验,以确保其符合本公约规则的各项要求,以及如适用时,符合现行国际海上避碰规则的要求;

　(ii)　换证检验和定期检验应包括(b)(i)所述设备的检查,以确保设备符合本公约规则和现行国际海上避碰规则的各项要求,均处于合格状态,并适合船舶预定的用途;

---

① 参见《登离船设施的制造、安全、维护保养和检查/检验导则》(第 MSC.1/Circ.1331 号通函);《检验和发证协调系统(HSSC)下的救生设备和通信设备维护》(第 MSC/Circ.955 号通函);《固定式灭火系统中倍数泡沫浓度测试标准和检验导则》(第 MSC/Circ.670 号通函);《固定式灭火系统高倍数泡沫浓度测试标准和检验导则》(第 MSC/Circ.798 号通函)和《船舶 LRIT 信息传输设备符合性检验和发证指南》(第 MSC.1/Circ.1307 号通函)。

(iii) the annual survey shall include a general inspection of the equipment referred to in paragraph (b)(i) to ensure that it has been maintained in accordance with regulation 11(a) and that it remains satisfactory for the service for which the ship is intended.

(**c**) The periodical and annual surveys referred to in paragraphs (a)(iii) and (a)(iv) shall be endorsed on the Cargo Ship Safety Equipment Certificate.

P88 Regulation 9
Surveys of radio installations of cargo ships[①]

(**a**) The radio installations, including those used in life-saving appliances, of cargo ships to which chapters Ⅲ and Ⅳ apply shall be subject to the surveys specified below:

(i) an initial survey before the ship is put in service;

(ii) a renewal survey at intervals specified by the Administration but not exceeding five years, except where regulation 14(b), (e), (f) and (g) is applicable;

(iii) a periodical survey within three months before or after each anniversary date of the Cargo Ship Safety Radio Certificate;

(iv) an additional survey as prescribed for passenger ships in regulation 7(b)(iii).

(**b**) The surveys referred to in paragraph (a) shall be carried out as follows:

(i) the initial survey shall include a complete inspection of the radio installations of cargo ships, including those used in life-saving appliances, to ensure that they comply with the requirements of the present regulations;

(ii) the renewal and periodical surveys shall include an inspection of the radio installations of cargo ships, including those used in life-saving appliances, to ensure that they comply with the requirements of the present regulations.

(**c**) The periodical surveys referred to in paragraph (a)(iii) shall be endorsed on the Cargo Ship Safety Radio Certificate.

---

① Refer to *Servicing of life-saving appliances and radiocommunication equipment under the Harmonized System of Survey and Certification* (HSSC) (MSC/Circ.955).

（iii）　年度检验应包括(b)(i)所述设备的总体检查，以确保设备已按第11(a)条进行维护保养，并确保其继续满足船舶预定的用途。

（c）　本条(a)(iii)和(a)(iv)所述的定期检验和年度检验应在货船设备安全证书上予以签署。

P88 第9条
货船无线电装置的检验[①]

（a）　适用第Ⅲ章和第Ⅳ章的货船无线电装置(包括救生设备中使用的无线电装置)，应接受下列规定的检验：

（i）　初次检验，在船舶投入营运前进行；

（ii）　换证检验，按主管机关规定的间隔期进行，但不得超过5年，如果适用第14(b)、(e)、(f)和(g)条时除外；

（iii）　定期检验，在货船无线电安全证书的每一周年日之前或之后3个月内进行；

（iv）　附加检验，按第7(b)(iii)条对客船的规定进行。

（b）　本条(a)所述的检验应按下列规定进行：

（i）　初次检验应包括货船无线电装置，并包括救生设备中使用的无线电装置在内的全面检查，以确保设备符合本公约规则的各项要求；

（ii）　换证检验和定期检验应包括货船无线电装置，并包括救生设备中使用的无线电装置的检查，以确保设备符合本公约规则的各项要求。

（c）　本条(a)(iii)所述的定期检验应在货船无线电安全证书上予以签署。

---

① 参见《检验和发证协调系统(HSSC)下的救生设备和通信设备维护》(第MSC/Circ.955号通函)。

P88 Regulation 10
Surveys of structure, machinery and equipment of cargo ships①

(a) The structure, machinery and equipment (other than items in respect of which a Cargo Ship Safety Equipment Certificate and a Cargo Ship Safety Radio Certificate are issued) of a cargo ship as referred to in paragraph (b)(i) shall be subject to the surveys and inspections specified below:

(i) an initial survey including an inspection of the outside of the ship's bottom before the ship is put in service;

(ii) a renewal survey at intervals specified by the Administration but not exceeding 5 years, except where regulation 14(b), (e), (f) and (g) is applicable;

(iii) an intermediate survey within three months before or after the second anniversary date or within three months before or after the third anniversary date of the Cargo Ship Safety Construction Certificate, which shall take the place of one of the annual surveys specified in paragraph (a)(iv);

(iv) an annual survey within 3 months before or after each anniversary date of the Cargo Ship Safety Construction Certificate;

(v) a minimum of two inspections of the outside of the ship's bottom during any five-year period, except where regulation 14(e) or (f) is applicable. Where regulation 14(e) or (f) is applicable, this five-year period may be extended to coincide with the extended period of validity of the certificate. In all cases the interval between any two such inspections shall not exceed 36 months;

(vi) an additional survey as prescribed for passenger ships in regulation 7(b)(iii).

(b) The surveys and inspections referred to in paragraph (a) shall be carried out as follows:

(i) the initial survey shall include a complete inspection of the structure, machinery and equipment. This survey shall be such as to ensure that the arrangements, materials, scantlings and workmanship of the structure, boilers and other pressure vessels, their appurtenances, main and auxiliary machinery including steering gear and associated control systems, electrical installation and other equipment comply with the requirements of the present regulations, are in satisfactory condition and are fit for the service for which the ship is intended and that the required stability information is provided. In the case of tankers such a survey shall also include an inspection of the pump-rooms, cargo, bunker and ventilation piping systems and associated safety devices;

① Refer to *Guidance for planning the enhanced programme of inspections during surveys of bulk carriers and oil tankers* (MSC/Circ.655); *Guidelines for pre-planning of surveys in dry-dock of ships which are not subject to the Enhanced programme of inspections* (MSC./Circ.1223) and *Guidelines for bulk carrier hatch cover surveys and owner's inspections and maintenance* (MSC/Circ.1071).

P88 第 10 条
货船结构、机器和设备的检验[①]

(a) 货船结构、机器及设备(货船设备安全证书或货船无线电安全证书所含的项目除外),应按(b)(i)所述接受下列规定的检验和检查:

(i) 初次检验(包括船底外部的检查),在船舶投入营运前进行;

(ii) 换证检验,按主管机关规定的间隔期进行,但不得超过 5 年,如果适用第 14(b)、(e)、(f)和(g)条时除外;

(iii) 中间检验,在货船构造安全证书的第二个周年日之前或之后 3 个月内或第三个周年日之前或之后 3 个月内进行,并应取代(a)(iv)规定的其中一次年度检验;

(iv) 年度检验,在货船构造安全证书的每一周年日之前或之后 3 个月内进行;

(v) 在货船安全构造证书或货船安全证书的 5 年有效期内,船底外部应至少进行两次检查,但在第 14(e)或 14(f)条适用时除外。在第 14(e)或 14(f)条适用时,此 5 年期限可展期至与证书有效期的展期期限相一致。但在任何情况下,任何 2 次这种检查的间隔期不得超过 36 个月;

(vi) 附加检验,按第 7(b)(iii)条对客船的规定进行。

(b) 本条(a)所述的检验和检查应按下列规定进行:

(i) 初次检验应包括结构、机器和设备在内的全面检查。该检验应确保船舶的布置、材料、结构尺寸和工艺,锅炉和其他受压容器及其附件、主辅机(包括舵机及其相关的控制系统)、电气设备以及其他设备符合本公约规则的各项要求,均处于合格状态,适合船舶预定的用途,并确保备有要求的稳性资料。如果为液货船,则该检验还应包括泵舱,货油、燃油和透气管系及其相关的安全装置的检查;

① 参见《制定散货船和油船加强检验计划指南》(第 MSC/Circ.655 号通函);《为不适用加强检验计划的船舶提前计划干船坞检验的导则》(第 MSC.1/Circ.1223 号通函)和《散货船舱口盖检验及船东检查与维护指南》(第 MSC/Circ.1071 号通函)。

(ii) the renewal survey shall include an inspection of the structure, machinery and equipment as referred to in paragraph (b)(i) to ensure that they comply with the requirements of the present regulations, are in satisfactory condition and are fit for the service for which the ship is intended;

(iii) the intermediate survey shall include an inspection of the structure, boilers and other pressure vessels, machinery and equipment, the steering gear and the associated control systems and electrical installations to ensure that they remain satisfactory for the service for which the ship is intended. In the case of tankers, the survey shall also include an inspection of the pump-rooms, cargo, bunker and ventilation piping systems and associated safety devices and the testing of insulation resistance of electrical installations in dangerous zones;

(iv) the annual survey shall include a general inspection of the structure, machinery and equipment referred to in paragraph (b)(i), to ensure that they have been maintained in accordance with regulation 11(a) and that they remain satisfactory for the service for which the ship is intended;

(v) the inspection of the outside of the ship's bottom and the survey of related items inspected at the same time shall be such as to ensure that they remain satisfactory for the service for which the ship is intended.

(c) The intermediate and annual surveys and the inspections of the outside of the ship's bottom referred to in paragraphs (a)(iii), (a)(iv) and (a)(v) shall be endorsed on the Cargo Ship Safety Construction Certificate.

P88 Regulation 11

Maintenance of conditions after survey①

(a) The condition of the ship and its equipment shall be maintained to conform with the provisions of the present regulations to ensure that the ship in all respects will remain fit to proceed to sea without danger to the ship or persons on board.

(b) After any survey of the ship under regulations 7, 8, 9 or 10 has been completed, no change shall be made in the structural arrangements, machinery, equipment and other items covered by the survey, without the sanction of the Administration.

(c) Whenever an accident occurs to a ship or a defect is discovered, either of which affects the safety of the ship or the efficiency or completeness of its life-saving appliances or other equipment, the master or owner of the ship shall report at the earliest opportunity to the Administration, the nominated surveyor or recognized organization responsible for issuing the relevant certificate, who shall cause investigations to be initiated to determine whether a survey, as required by regulations 7, 8, 9 or 10, is necessary. If the ship is in a port of another Contracting Government, the master or owner shall also report immediately to the appropriate authorities of the port State and the nominated surveyor or recognized organization shall ascertain that such a report has been made.

① Refer to *Ship design, construction, repair and maintenance* (MSC/Circ.1070); *Shipboard technical operating and maintenance manuals* (MSC.1/Circ.1253) and the relevant instruments as referred to in the footnotes of other chapters.

(ii) 换证检验应包括(b)(i)所述结构、机器和设备的检查,以确保其符合本公约规则的各项要求,均处于合格状态,并适合船舶预定的用途;

(iii) 中间检验应包括结构、锅炉和其他受压容器、机器和设备、舵机及其相关的控制系统和电气设备的检查,以确保其继续满足船舶预定的用途。如果为液货船,则该检验还应包括泵舱,货油、燃油和透气管系及其相关的安全装置的检查和危险区域内电气设备绝缘电阻的测试;

(iv) 年度检验应包括(b)(i)所述结构、机器和设备的总体检查,以确保其已按第11(a)条进行维护保养,并确保其继续满足船舶预定的用途;

(v) 对船底外部的检查以及同时对相关项目的检验应确保其继续满足船舶预定的用途。

(c) 本条(a)(iii)、(a)(iv)和(a)(v)所述的中间检验、年度检验和船底外部的检查均应在货船构造安全证书上予以签署。

P88 第 11 条
检验后状况的维持[①]

(a) 应保持船舶及其设备状况符合本公约规则的各项规定,以确保船舶在所有方面保持适合于出海航行而不危及船舶及船上人员。

(b) 根据第 7、8、9 条或第 10 条的规定对船舶进行的任何检验完成后,未经主管机关许可,已经检验的结构布置、机器、设备及其他项目均不得做任何变动。

(c) 当船舶发生事故或发现缺陷,对该船的安全或其救生设备或其他设备的有效性或完整性产生影响时,该船船长或船东应尽早向负责签发有关证书的主管机关、指定的验船师或认可的组织报告。该主管机关、指定的验船师或认可的组织应立即着手调查以确定是否需要按第 7、8、9 条或第 10 条的要求进行检验。如果该船在另一缔约国的港口内,船长或船东还应立即向该港口国的有关当局报告,而指定的验船师或认可的组织应查明已进行了此项报告。

① 参见《船舶设计、建造、维修和维护保养》(第 MSC/Circ.1070 号通函);《船上技术操作和维护手册》(第 MSC.1/Circ.1253 号通函)以及其他章节脚注中提及的相关文书。

P88 Regulation 12
Issue or endorsement of certificates[①]

(a) (i) a certificate called a Passenger Ship Safety Certificate shall be issued after an initial or renewal survey to a passenger ship which complies with the relevant requirements of chapters II-1, II-2, III, IV and V and any other relevant requirements of the present regulations;

(ii) a certificate called a Cargo Ship Safety Construction Certificate shall be issued after an initial or renewal survey to a cargo ship which complies with the relevant requirements of chapters II-1 and II-2 (other than those relating to fire safety systems and appliances and fire control plans) and any other relevant requirements of the present regulations;

(iii) a certificate called a Cargo Ship Safety Equipment Certificate shall be issued after an initial or renewal survey to a cargo ship which complies with the relevant requirements of chapters II-1, II-2, III and V and any other relevant requirements of the present regulations;

(iv) a certificate called a Cargo Ship Safety Radio Certificate shall be issued after an initial or renewal survey to a cargo ship which complies with the relevant requirements of chapter IV and any other relevant requirements of the present regulations;

(v) (1) a certificate called a Cargo Ship Safety Certificate may be issued after an initial or renewal survey to a cargo ship which complies with the relevant requirements of chapters II-1, II-2, III, IV and V and any other relevant requirements of the present regulations, as an alternative to the certificates referred to in paragraph (a)(ii), (a)(iii) and (a)(iv);

(2) whenever in this chapter reference is made to a Cargo Ship Safety Construction Certificate, Cargo Ship Safety Equipment Certificate or Cargo Ship Safety Radio Certificate, it shall apply to a Cargo Ship Safety Certificate, if it is used as an alternative to these certificates;

(vi) the Passenger Ship Safety Certificate, the Cargo Ship Safety Equipment Certificate, the Cargo Ship Safety Radio Certificate and the Cargo Ship Safety Certificate, referred to in subparagraphs (i), (iii), (iv) and (v), shall be supplemented by a Record of Equipment;

(vii) when an exemption is granted to a ship under and in accordance with the provisions of the present regulations, a certificate called an Exemption Certificate shall be issued in addition to the certificates prescribed in this paragraph;

---

① Refer to *Recommendation on the use of national tonnage in applying international conventions* (resolution A.1073(28)); *Guidelines for the use of Electronic Certificates* (FAL.5/Circ.39/Rev.2 and Corr.1); *Guidance on the timing of replacement of existing certificates by the certificates issued after the entry into force of amendments to certificates in IMO instruments* (MSC-MEPC.5/Circ.6); *Unified interpretation on the expiration date of statutory certificates* (MSC-MEPC.5/Circ.13) and *Unified interpretation of the date of completion of the survey and verification on which the certificates are based* (MSC-MEPC.5/Circ.3).

P88 第12条
证书的签发或签注[①]

(a)　(i)客船经初次检验或换证检验,符合第Ⅱ-1、Ⅱ-2、Ⅲ、Ⅳ和Ⅴ章要求以及本公约规则其他有关要求,应予签发客船安全证书;

(ii)　货船经初次检验或换证检验,符合除有关消防安全系统和防火控制图要求以外的第Ⅱ-1章和第Ⅱ-2章要求以及本公约规则其他有关要求,应予签发货船构造安全证书;

(iii)　货船经初次检验或换证检验,符合第Ⅱ-1、Ⅱ-2、Ⅲ和Ⅴ章要求以及本公约规则其他有关要求,应予签发货船设备安全证书;

(iv)　货船经初次检验或换证检验,符合第Ⅳ章要求以及本公约规则其他有关要求,应予签发货船无线电安全证书;

(v)　(1)　货船经初次检验或换证检验,符合第Ⅱ-1、Ⅱ-2、Ⅲ、Ⅳ和Ⅴ章要求以及本公约规则其他有关要求,可予签发货船安全证书,以替代(a)(ii)、(a)(iii)和a(iv)所述的各证书;

(2)　如果货船安全证书用以替代货船构造安全证书、货船设备安全证书或货船无线电安全证书时,则任何在本章述及有关这些证书时,应适用于货船安全证书;

(vi)　上述(i)、(iii)、(iv)和(v)所述的客船安全证书、货船设备安全证书、货船无线电安全证书和货船安全证书均应附有一份设备记录;

(vii)　根据并按本公约规则的规定,对船舶准予免除某项规定后,除签发本条所述的证书以外,还应予签发免除证书;

---

① 参见《关于执行国际公约时采用国家吨位的建议案》(第A.1073(28)号决议);《电子证书使用导则》(第FAL.5/Circ.39/Rev.2及Corr.1号通函);《IMO文书修正案生效日后签发的证书替代原有证书的时间指南》(第MSC-MEPC.5/Circ.6号通函);《法定证书失效日期的统一解释》(第MSC-MEPC.5/Circ.13号通函)和《证书所依据的检验和验证完成日期的统一解释》(第MSC-MEPC.5/Circ.3号通函)。

(viii) the certificates referred to in this regulation shall be issued or endorsed either by the Administration or by any person or organization authorized by it. In every case, that Administration assumes full responsibility for the certificates.

(b) A Contracting Government shall not issue certificates under, and in accordance with, the provisions of the International Convention for the Safety of Life at Sea, 1960, 1948 or 1929, after the date on which acceptance of the present Convention by the Government takes effect.

P88 Regulation 13
Issue or endorsement of certificates by another Government

A Contracting Government may, at the request of the Administration, cause a ship to be surveyed and, if satisfied that the requirements of the present regulations are complied with, shall issue or authorize the issue of certificates to the ship and, where appropriate, endorse or authorize the endorsement of certificates on the ship in accordance with the present regulations. Any certificate so issued shall contain a statement to the effect that it has been issued at the request of the Government of the State the flag of which the ship is entitled to fly, and it shall have the same force and receive the same recognition as a certificate issued under regulation 12.

P88 Regulation 14
Duration and validity of certificates[①]

(a) A Passenger Ship Safety Certificate shall be issued for a period not exceeding 12 months. A Cargo Ship Safety Construction Certificate, Cargo Ship Safety Equipment Certificate and Cargo Ship Safety Radio Certificate shall be issued for a period specified by the Administration which shall not exceed five years. An Exemption Certificate shall not be valid for longer than the period of the certificate to which it refers.

(b) (i) notwithstanding the requirements of paragraph (a), when the renewal survey is completed within three months before the expiry date of the existing certificate, the new certificate shall be valid from the date of completion of the renewal survey to:

(1) for a passenger ship, a date not exceeding 12 months from the date of expiry of the existing certificate;

(2) for a cargo ship, a date not exceeding five years from the date of expiry of the existing certificate;

(ii) when the renewal survey is completed after the expiry date of the existing certificate, the new certificate shall be valid from the date of completion of the renewal survey to:

① Refer to *Recommended conditions for the period of a certificate* (MSC-MEPC.5/Circ.1); *Guidance on the timing of replacement of existing certificates by the certificates issued after the entry into force of amendments to certificates in IMO instruments* (MSC-MEPC.5/Circ.6); *Guidelines for the use of Electronic Certificate* (FAL.5/Circ.39/Rev.2 and Corr.1); *Unified interpretation on the expiration date of statutory certificates* (MSC-MEPC.5/Circ.13) and *Unified interpretation of the date of completion of the survey and verification are based*(MSC-MEPC.5/Circ.3).

(viii) 本条所述的各证书均应由主管机关或其授权的任何个人或组织签发或签署。在任何情况下,主管机关应对该证书负有全部责任。

(b) 在缔约国政府对本公约的接受生效之日后,不应再根据并按 1960 年、1948 年或 1929 年国际海上人命安全公约的规定签发证书。

P88 第 13 条
他国政府签发或签注的证书

缔约国政府应主管机关的申请,可对船舶进行检验,如果确信符合本公约规则的要求,应按本公约规则规定对该船签发或授权签发证书,并在适用时,为该船证书进行签署或授权签署。如此签发的任何证书均应载明系根据该船旗国政府的申请签发,并应与按第 12 条规定所签发的证书具有同等效力和得到同样的承认。

P88 第 14 条
证书的有效期限[①]

(a) 签发客船安全证书的有效期限不应超过 12 个月。签发货船构造安全证书、货船设备安全证书和货船无线电安全证书的有效期限应由主管机关规定,但不得超过 5 年。免除证书的有效期限不应长于其有关证书的有效期限。

(b) (i) 尽管有本条(a)的要求,如果换证检验在现有证书期满之日前 3 个月内完成,则新证书应从该换证检验完成之日起:

(1) 对客船,至现有证书期满之日起不超过 12 个月的日期内有效;

(2) 对货船,至现有证书期满之日起不超过 5 年的日期内有效;

(ii) 如果换证检验在现有证书期满之日后完成,则新证书应从该换证检验完成之日起:

① 参见《关于延长证书有效期限的建议条件》(第 MSC-MEPC.5/Circ.1 号通函);《IMO 文书修正案生效日后签发的证书替代原有证书的时间指南》(第 MSC-MEPC.5/Circ.6 号通函);《电子证书使用导则》(第 FAL.5/Circ.39/Rev.2 及 Corr.1 号通函);《法定证书失效日期的统一解释》(第 MSC-MEPC.5/Circ.13 号通函)和《证书所依据的检验和验证完成日期的统一解释》(第 MSC-MEPC.5/Circ.3 号通函)。

(1) for a passenger ship, a date not exceeding 12 months from the date of expiry of the existing certificate;

(2) for a cargo ship, a date not exceeding five years from the date of expiry of the existing certificate;

(iii) when the renewal survey is completed more than three months before the expiry date of the existing certificate, the new certificate shall be valid from the date of completion of the renewal survey to:

(1) for a passenger ship, a date not exceeding 12 months from the date of completion of the renewal survey;

(2) for a cargo ship, a date not exceeding five years from the date of completion of the renewal survey.

(c) If a certificate other than a Passenger Ship Safety Certificate is issued for a period of less than five years, the Administration may extend the validity of the certificate beyond the expiry date to the maximum period specified in paragraph (a), provided that the surveys referred to in regulations 8, 9 and 10 applicable when a certificate is issued for a period of 5 years are carried out as appropriate.

(d) If a renewal survey has been completed and a new certificate cannot be issued or placed on board the ship before the expiry date of the existing certificate, the person or organization authorized by the Administration may endorse the existing certificate and such a certificate shall be accepted as valid for a further period which shall not exceed 5 months from the expiry date.

(e) If a ship at the time when a certificate expires is not in a port in which it is to be surveyed, the Administration may extend the period of validity of the certificate but this extension shall be granted only for the purpose of allowing the ship to complete its voyage to the port in which it is to be surveyed, and then only in cases where it appears proper and reasonable to do so. No certificate shall be extended for a period longer than three months, and a ship to which an extension is granted shall not, on its arrival in the port in which it is to be surveyed, be entitled by virtue of such extension to leave that port without having a new certificate. When the renewal survey is completed, the new certificate shall be valid to:

(i) for a passenger ship, a date not exceeding 12 months from the date of expiry of the existing certificate before the extension was granted;

(ii) for a cargo ship, a date not exceeding 5 years from the date of expiry of the existing certificate before the extension was granted.

(f) A certificate issued to a ship engaged on short voyages which has not been extended under the foregoing provisions of this regulation may be extended by the Administration for a period of grace of up to one month from the date of expiry stated on it. When the renewal survey is completed, the new certificate shall be valid to:

(1) 对客船,至现有证书期满之日起不超过12个月的日期内有效;

(2) 对货船,至现有证书期满之日起不超过5年的日期内有效;

(iii) 如果换证检验在现有证书期满之日前3个月前完成,则新证书应从该换证检验完成之日起:

(1) 对客船,自换证检验完成之日起不超过12个月的日期内有效;

(2) 对货船,自换证检验完成之日起不超过5年的日期内有效。

(c) 除客船安全证书外,如果所发证书的有效期限少于5年,主管机关可将证书有效期自期满日延长至本条(a)规定的最长期限,条件是在签发5年期的证书时进行了第8、第9和第10条所述的相应的检验。

(d) 如果换证检验已完成,而新证书在现有证书期满之日前不能签发或不能存放船上,主管机关授权的人员或组织可在现有证书上签署,签署后的证书自期满之日起不超过5个月的期限内应视为继续有效。

(e) 如果证书期满时船舶不在应进行检验的港口,主管机关可延长该证书的有效期,但此项展期仅以能使船舶完成其驶抵应进行检验的港口的航次为限,并且仅在正当和合理的情况下才能如此办理。展期不得超过3个月。经展期的船舶在抵达应进行检验的港口后,不得因有此项展期而在未获得新证书前驶离该港口。换证检验完成后,新证书的有效期应:

(i) 对客船,自现有证书展期前的期满日起不超过12个月;

(ii) 对货船,自现有证书展期前的期满日起不超过5年。

(f) 发给短程航行船舶的证书未按本条前述之规定展期,主管机关可给予自该证书所示的期满之日起至多1个月的宽限期。换证检验完成后,新证书的有效期应:

(i) for a passenger ship, a date not exceeding 12 months from the date of expiry of the existing certificate before the extension was granted;

(ii) for a cargo ship, a date not exceeding 5 years from the date of expiry of the existing certificate before the extension was granted.

(g) In special circumstances, as determined by the Administration, a new certificate need not be dated from the date of expiry of the existing certificate as required by paragraphs (b)(ii), (e) or (f). In these special circumstances, the new certificate shall be valid to:

(i) for a passenger ship, a date not exceeding 12 months from the date of completion of the renewal survey;

(ii) for a cargo ship, a date not exceeding five years from the date of completion of the renewal survey.

(h) If an annual, intermediate or periodical survey is completed before the period specified in the relevant regulations then:

(i) the anniversary date shown on the relevant certificate shall be amended by endorsement to a date which shall not be more than three months later than the date on which the survey was completed;

(ii) the subsequent annual, intermediate or periodical survey required by the relevant regulations shall be completed at the intervals prescribed by these regulations using the new anniversary date;

(iii) the expiry date may remain unchanged provided one or more annual, intermediate or periodical surveys, as appropriate, are carried out so that the maximum intervals between the surveys prescribed by the relevant regulations are not exceeded.

(i) A certificate issued under regulation 12 or 13 shall cease to be valid in any of the following cases:

(i) if the relevant surveys and inspections are not completed within the periods specified under regulations 7(a), 8(a), 9(a) and 10(a);

(ii) if the certificate is not endorsed in accordance with the present regulations;

(iii) upon transfer of the ship to the flag of another State. A new certificate shall only be issued when the Government issuing the new certificate is fully satisfied that the ship is in compliance with the requirements of regulation 11(a) and (b). In the case of a transfer between Contracting Governments, if requested within three months after the transfer has taken place, the Government of the State whose flag the ship was formerly entitled to fly shall, as soon as possible, transmit to the Administration copies of the certificates carried by the ship before a transfer and, if available, copies of the relevant survey reports.

(i)　对客船，自现有证书展期前的期满日起不超过 12 个月；

(ii)　对货船，自现有证书展期前的期满日起不超过 5 年。

(g)　在特殊情况下（由主管机关确定），新证书无须按(b)(ii)、(e)或(f)的要求从现有证书的期满日起计算日期。在此特殊情况下，新证书的有效期应：

(i)　对客船，自换证检验完成之日起不超过 12 个月；

(ii)　对货船，自换证检验完成之日起不超过 5 年。

(h)　如果年度检验、中间检验或定期检验在相关规则规定的期限之前完成，则：

(i)　相关证书上所示的周年日应予签署修正，修正后的周年日应不多于检验完成之日起 3 个月；

(ii)　相关规则要求的其后的年度检验、中间检验或定期检验应使用新的周年日按这些规则规定的间隔期完成；

(iii)　如果进行一次或多次相应的年度检验、中间检验或定期检验，而使相关规则规定的检验最大间隔期不被超过，则该期满日可保持不变。

(i)　按第 12 或 13 条规定签发的证书，在下列任一情况下即应中止有效：

(i)　如果相关检验和检查未在第 7(a)、8(a)、9(a)和 10(a)条规定的期限内完成时；

(ii)　如果证书未按本公约规则规定予以签署时；

(iii)　船舶变更船旗国时。只有当换发新证书的政府确信该船符合第 11(a)和(b)条的要求时，才能签发新的证书。如果变更船旗系在缔约国之间进行，则在变更后的 3 个月内，前船旗国政府如收到申请，应尽快将变更船旗前该船所携证书的副本以及相关的检验报告（若备有）送交该船新的主管机关。

P88 Regulation 15
Forms of certificates and records of equipment[①]

The certificates and records of equipment shall be drawn up in the form corresponding to the models given in the appendix to the annex to the present Convention. If the language used is neither English nor French, the text shall include a translation into one of these languages.[②]

P88 Regulation 16
Availability of certificates[③]

The certificates issued under regulations 12 and 13 shall be readily available on board for examination at all times.

Regulation 17
Acceptance of certificates

Certificates issued under the authority of a Contracting Government shall be accepted by the other Contracting Governments for all purposes covered by the present Convention. They shall be regarded by the other Contracting Governments as having the same force as certificates issued by them.

Regulation 18
Qualification of certificates

(**a**) If in the course of a particular voyage a ship has on board a number of persons less than the total number stated in the Passenger Ship Safety Certificate and is in consequence, in accordance with the provisions of the present regulations, free to carry a smaller number of lifeboats and other life-saving appliances than that stated in the certificate, an annex may be issued by the Government, person or organization referred to in regulation 12 or 13 of this chapter.

(**b**) This annex shall state that in the circumstances there is no infringement of the provisions of the present regulations. It shall be annexed to the certificate and shall be substituted for it in so far as the life-saving appliances are concerned. It shall be valid only for the particular voyage for which it is issued.

---

① Refer to *Guidelines for the use of Electronic Certificate* (FAL.5/Circ.39/Rev.2 and Corr.1) and the information collected via the Global Integrated Shipping Information System (GISIS).

② Refer to *Translation of the text of certificates* (resolution A.561 (14)).

③ Refer to *Retention of original records/documents on board ships* (MSC-MEPC.4/Circ.1) and *Guidance on the timing of replacement of existing certificates by the certificates issued after the entry into force of amendments to certificates in IMO instruments* (MSC-MEPC.5/Circ.6).

P88 第 15 条
证书格式和设备记录[①]

各证书和设备记录应按本公约附则附录中所示样本相一致的格式写成。如果使用的文字既非英文又非法文,则文本应包含其中一种文字的译文。[②]

P88 第 16 条
证书的提供[③]

按第 12 和 13 条签发的船上证书应随时可提供,以供检查。

第 17 条
证书的承认

根据某一缔约国政府的授权所签发的证书,其他缔约国政府应在本公约涉及的全部范围内予以承认。其他缔约国政府应视这些证书与其所签发的证书具有同等的效力。

第 18 条
证书的资格证明

(a) 如果船舶在某一特定航次中船上人数少于客船安全证书中载明的总数,从而按本公约规则规定可配置少于证书中所载明的救生艇数量和其他救生设备,本章第 12 条或第 13 条所述的政府、个人或组织可签发一份证书附件。

(b) 该附件应说明在该情况下并无违反本公约规则规定之处。附件应附于证书之后,并仅在救生设备方面代替该证书。附件仅对该特定航次有效。

① 参见《电子证书使用导则》(第 FAL.5/Circ.39/Rev.2 及 Corr.1 号通函)和全球综合航运信息系统(GISIS)中收集的信息。

② 参见《证书文本的翻译》(第 A.561(14)号决议)。

③ 参见《船上原始记录/文件的留存》(第 MSC-MEPC.4/Circ.1 号通函)和《IMO 文书修正案生效日后签发的证书替代原有证书的时间指南》(第 MSC-MEPC.5/Circ.6 号通函)。

P88 Regulation 19
Control①

(a) Every ship when in a port of another Contracting Government is subject to control by officers duly authorized by such Government in so far as this control is directed towards verifying that the certificates issued under regulation 12 or regulation 13 are valid.

(b) Such certificates, if valid, shall be accepted unless there are clear grounds for believing that the condition of the ship or of its equipment does not correspond substantially with the particulars of any of the certificates or that the ship and its equipment are not in compliance with the provisions of regulation 11(a) and (b).

(c) In the circumstances given in paragraph (b) or where a certificate has expired or ceased to be valid, the officer carrying out the control shall take steps to ensure that the ship shall not sail until it can proceed to sea or leave the port for the purpose of proceeding to the appropriate repair yard without danger to the ship or persons on board.

(d) In the event of this control giving rise to an intervention of any kind, the officer carrying out the control shall forthwith inform, in writing, the Consul or, in his absence, the nearest diplomatic representative of the State whose flag the ship is entitled to fly of all the circumstances in which intervention was deemed necessary. In addition, nominated surveyors or recognized organizations responsible for the issue of the certificates shall also be notified. The facts concerning the intervention shall be reported to the Organization.

(e) The port State authority concerned shall notify all relevant information about the ship to the authorities of the next port of call, in addition to parties mentioned in paragraph (d), if it is unable to take action as specified in paragraphs (c) and (d) or if the ship has been allowed to proceed to the next port of call.

(f) When exercising control under this regulation all possible efforts shall be made to avoid a ship being unduly detained or delayed. If a ship is thereby unduly detained or delayed it shall be entitled to compensation for any loss or damage suffered.

Regulation 20
Privileges

The privileges of the present Convention may not be claimed in favour of any ship unless it holds appropriate valid certificates.

① Refer to *Procedures for port State control, 2019* (resolution A.1138(31)); *IMO Instruments Implementation Code* (III Code) (resolution A.1070(28)); *Guidance to port State control officers on the non-security related elements of the 2002 SOLAS amendments* (MSC/Circ.1113); *Measures to improve port State control procedures* (MSC/Circ.1011-MEPC/Circ.383); *Code of good practice for port State control officers* (MSC-MEPC.4/Circ.2); *National contact points for safety and pollution prevention and response* (MSC-MEPC.6/Circ.18, as may be amended), and the information collected via the Global Integrated Shipping Information System (GISIS).

P88 第 19 条
监督[①]

(a) 每艘船舶,当其在另一缔约国政府的港口时,应受该国政府正式授权的官员的监督。这种监督的目的在于查明按第 12 条或第 13 条所签发的证书是否有效。

(b) 除非有明显理由确信该船或其设备的状况在实质上与任何一份证书所载内容不符或该船及其设备不符合第 11(a)和(b)条的规定,这些证书如属有效,即应被承认。

(c) 在本条(b)所述情况下或当证书已期满或已中止有效时,执行监督的官员应采取措施,确保该船在未具备不危及船舶或船上人员的条件前,不得开航或离港驶往合适的修船厂。

(d) 因这种监督而产生任何干预时,执行监督的官员应将认为必须进行干预的一切情况,立即书面通知该船船旗国的领事,或当领事不在时,通知其最近的外交代表。此外,还应通知负责发证的指定的验船师或认可的组织。有关干预的事实应向本组织报告。

(e) 若未能按本条(c)和(d)的规定采取行动或如已允许该船驶往下一停靠港时,港口国有关当局除应将该船所有的相关信息通知本条(d)所述有关方外,还应通知下一停靠港当局。

(f) 按本条规定执行监督时,应尽力避免使船舶受到不当滞留或延误。如果船舶由此受到不当滞留或延误,应有权对其所受的任何损失或损坏要求赔偿。

第 20 条
特权

任何船舶,除持有相应的有效证书外,不可要求本公约所赋予的各项特权。

① 参见《2019 年港口国监督程序》(第 A.1138(31)号决议);《IMO 文书实施规则(III 规则)》(第 A.1070(28)号决议);《对港口国检查官在〈安全公约〉2002 年修正案中非保安相关要求的指南》(第 MSC/Circ.1113 号通函);《改进港口国监督程序的措施》(第 MSC/Circ.1011-MEPC/Circ.383 号通函);《港口国检查官良好行为准则》(第 MSC-MEPC.4/ Circ.2 号通函);《安全和污染应急与预防国家联络点》(第 MSC-MEPC.6/Circ.18 号通函,可经修订),以及全球综合航运信息系统(GISIS)中收集的信息。

Part C
Casualties

Regulation 21
Casualties[①]

(a) Each Administration undertakes to conduct an investigation of any casualty occurring to any of its ships subject to the provisions of the present Convention when it judges that such an investigation may assist in determining what changes in the present regulations might be desirable.

(b) Each Contracting Government undertakes to supply the Organization with pertinent information concerning the findings of such investigations. No reports or recommendations of the Organization based upon such information shall disclose the identity or nationality of the ships concerned or in any manner fix or imply responsibility upon any ship or person.

① See additional requirements for the investigation of marine casualties and incidents in regulation XI-1/6.

C 部分
事故

第 21 条
事故[①]

(a)　各主管机关承担义务对其受本公约规定约束的任何船舶所发生的任何事故，在其认为调查有助于确定本公约规则可能需要进行何种修改时，即应进行调查。

(b)　各缔约国政府承担义务将有关此项调查所获得的相关资料提供给本组织。本组织根据该资料所作的报告或建议，均不得泄露有关船舶的标识或国籍，或以任何方式确定或暗示任何船舶或个人承担的责任。

① 参见第Ⅺ-1/6 条关于海上事故和事件调查的附加要求。

Chapter Ⅱ-1 Construction – Structure, subdivision and stability, machinery and electrical installations

第Ⅱ-1章　构造——结构、分舱与稳性、机电设备

Part A
General

Regulation 1
Application①

1.1 Unless expressly provided otherwise, this chapter shall apply to ships the keels of which are laid or which are at a similar stage of construction on or after 1 January 2009.

1.1.1 Unless expressly provided otherwise, parts B, B-1, B-2 and B-4 of this chapter shall only apply to ships:

.1 for which the building contract is placed on or after 1 January 2020; or

.2 in the absence of a building contract, the keel of which is laid or which are at a similar stage of construction on or after 1 July 2020; or

.3 the delivery of which is on or after 1 January 2024.

1.1.2 Unless expressly provided otherwise, for ships not subject to the provisions of paragraph 1.1.1 but constructed on or after 1 January 2009, the Administration shall:

.1 ensure that the requirements for parts B, B-1, B-2 and B-4 which are applicable under chapter Ⅱ-1 of the International Convention for the Safety of Life at Sea, 1974, as amended by resolutions MSC.216(82), MSC.269(85) and MSC.325(90) are complied with; and

.2 ensure that the requirements of regulations 8-1.3 and 19-1 are complied with.

1.2 For the purpose of this chapter, the term *a similar stage of construction* means the stage at which:

.1 construction identifiable with a specific ship begins; and

.2 assembly of that ship has commenced comprising at least 50 tonnes 1% of the estimated mass of all structural material, whichever is less.

1.3 For the purpose of this chapter:

.1 the expression *ships constructed* means ships the keels of which are laid or which are at a similar stage of construction;

.2 the expression *all ships* means ships constructed before, on or after 1 January 2009;

.3 a cargo ship, whenever built, which is converted to a passenger ship shall be treated as a passenger ship constructed on the date on which such a conversion commences.

---

① Refer to *Unified interpretation of the application of regulations governed by the building contract date, the keel laying date and the delivery date for the requirements of the SOLAS and MARPOL Conventions* (MSC-MEPC.5/Circ.8).

A 部分
通则

第 1 条
适用范围[①]

1.1 除另有明文规定外，本章适用于 2009 年 1 月 1 日或以后安放龙骨或处于类似建造阶段的船舶。

1.1.1 除另有明文规定外，本章 B、B-1、B-2 和 B-4 部分应仅适用于下列船舶：

.1 2020 年 1 月 1 日及之后签订建造合同；或

.2 如无建造合同，2020 年 7 月 1 日及之后安放龙骨或处于类似建造阶段；或

.3 2024 年 1 月 1 日及之后交船。

1.1.2 除另有明文规定外，对于不受 1.1.1 规定约束但于 2009 年 1 月 1 日或以后建造的船舶，主管机关应：

.1 确保使其适用经第 MSC.216(82) 号、第 MSC.269(85) 号和第 MSC.325(90) 号决议修正的《安全公约》第Ⅱ-1 章第 B、B-1、B-2 和 B-4 部分的适用要求；和

.2 确保使其符合第 19-1 条的要求。

1.2 就本章而言，**类似建造阶段**系指在此阶段：

.1 可辨认出某一具体船舶建造开始；和

.2 该船业已开始的装配量至少为 50 t，或为全部结构材料估算重量的 1%，取较小者。

1.3 就本章而言：

.1 **建造的船舶**系指安放龙骨或处于类似建造阶段的船舶；

.2 **所有船舶**系指在 2009 年 1 月 1 日或以前或以后建造的船舶；

.3 无论何时建造的货船，一经改建成客船后，应视作在开始改建之日建造的客船；

① 参见《〈安全公约〉和〈防污公约〉中提及的建造合同日期、安放龙骨日期和交船日期的适用的统一解释》（第 MSC-MEPC.5/Circ.8 号通函）。

2 Unless expressly provided otherwise, for ships constructed before 1 January 2009, the Administration shall:

.1 ensure that the requirements which are applicable under chapter Ⅱ-1 of the International Convention for the Safety of Life at Sea, 1974, as amended by resolutions MSC.1(XLV), MSC.6(48), MSC.11(55), MSC.12(56), MSC.13(57), MSC.19(58), MSC.26(60), MSC.27(61), resolution 1 of the 1995 SOLAS Conference, MSC.47(66), MSC.57(67), MSC.65(68), MSC.69(69), MSC.99(73), MSC.134(76), MSC.151(78) and MSC.170(79) are complied with; and

.2 ensure that the requirements of regulations 8-1.3 and 19-1 are complied with.

3 All ships which undergo repairs, alterations, modifications and outfitting related thereto shall continue to comply with at least the requirements previously applicable to these ships. Such ships, if constructed before the date on which any relevant amendments enter into force, shall, as a rule, comply with the requirements for ships constructed on or after that date to at least the same extent as they did before undergoing such repairs, alterations, modifications or outfitting. Repairs, alterations and modifications of a major character and outfitting related thereto shall meet the requirements for ships constructed on or after the date on which any relevant amendments enter into force, insofar as the Administration deems reasonable and practicable.①

4 The Administration of a State may, if it considers that the sheltered nature and conditions of the voyage are such as to render the application of any specific requirements of this chapter unreasonable or unnecessary, exempt from those requirements individual ships or classes of ships entitled to fly the flag of that State which, in the course of their voyage, do not proceed more than 20 miles from the nearest land.

5 In the case of passenger ships which are employed in special trades for the carriage of large numbers of special trade passengers, such as the pilgrim trade, the Administration of the State whose flag such ships are entitled to fly, if satisfied that it is impracticable to enforce compliance with the requirements of this chapter, may exempt such ships from those requirements, provided that they comply fully with the provisions of:

.1 the rules annexed to the Special Trade Passenger Ships Agreement, 1971; and

.2 the rules annexed to the Protocol on Space Requirements for Special Trade Passenger Ships, 1973.

Regulation 2
Definitions

For the purpose of this chapter, unless expressly provided otherwise:

1 *Subdivision length* (L_s) of the ship is the greatest projected moulded length of that part of the ship at or below deck or decks limiting the vertical extent of flooding with the ship at the deepest subdivision draught.

① Refer to *Interpretation of alterations and modifications of a major character* (MSC.1/Circ.1246).

2 除另有明文规定外,对2009年1月1日以前建造的船舶,主管机关应:

.1 确保使其符合经第MSC.1(XLV)号决议、第MSC.6(48)号决议、第MSC.11(55)号决议、第MSC.12(56)号决议、第MSC.13(57)号决议、第MSC.19(58)号决议、第MSC.26(60)号决议、第MSC.27(61)号决议、1995年SOLAS缔约国会议决议第1号决议、第MSC.47(66)号决议、第MSC.57(67)号决议、第MSC.65(68)号决议、第MSC.69(69)号决议、第MSC.99(73)号决议、第MSC.134(76)号决议、第MSC.151(78)号决议和第MSC.170(79)号决议修正的《安全公约》第Ⅱ-1章的适用要求;和

.2 确保使其符合第8-1.3条和第19-1条的要求。

3 所有船舶在进行修理、改装以及与之有关的舾装时,应至少继续符合这些船舶原先适用的要求。上述船舶如果系在任何相关修正案生效之日以前建造,一般应至少按其修理、改装或舾装之前的同等程度,符合对该日或以后建造的船舶的要求。重大的修理、改装以及与之有关的舾装,在主管机关认为合理和可行的范围内,应满足对任何相关修正案生效之日或以后建造的船舶的要求。①

4 主管机关如果考虑到航程的遮蔽性及其条件而认为实施本章的任何具体要求不合理或不必要时,可对悬挂该国国旗,并在其距最近陆地不超过20 n mile的航线航行的个别船舶或某些类型船舶,免除这些要求。

5 对用于运输大量特别乘客(如朝圣的乘客)的客船,主管机关如果确信实施本章要求不切实际时,可对悬挂该国国旗的此类船舶免除这些要求,但应完全符合下列规定:

.1 《1971年特种业务客船协定》所附的规则;和

.2 《1973年特种业务客船舱室要求议定书》所附的规则。

第2条
定义

除另有明文规定外,就本章而言:

1 **船舶分舱长度**(L_s)系指船舶处于最深分舱吃水时,船舶在一层或数层限定垂向进水范围的甲板处或其以下部分的最大投影型长。

---

① 参见《主要部位的重大改装和改建统一解释》(第MSC.1/Circ.1246号通函)。

2 *Amidships* is at the middle of the length (L).

3 *Aft terminal* is the aft limit of the subdivision length.

4 *Forward terminal* is the forward limit of the subdivision length.

5 *Length* (L) is the length as defined in the International Convention on Load Lines in force.

6 *Freeboard deck* is the deck as defined in the International Convention on Load Lines in force.

7 *Forward perpendicular* is the forward perpendicular as defined in the International Convention on Load Lines in force.

8 *Breadth* (B) is the greatest moulded breadth of the ship at or below the deepest subdivision draught.

9 *Draught* (d) is the vertical distance from the keel line at:

.1 amidships, for ships subject to the provisions of regulation Ⅱ-1/1.1.1.1; and

.2 the mid-point of the subdivision length (L_s), for ships not subject to the provisions of regulation Ⅱ-1/1.1.1.1 but constructed on or after 1 January 2009, to the waterline in question.

10 *Deepest subdivision draught* (d_s) is the summer load line draught of the ship.

11 *Light service draught* (d_l) is the service draught corresponding to the lightest anticipated loading and associated tankage, including, however, such ballast as may be necessary for stability and/or immersion. Passenger ships should include the full complement of passengers and crew on board.

12 *Partial subdivision draught* (d_p) is the light service draught plus 60% of the difference between the light service draught and the deepest subdivision draught.

13 *Trim* is the difference between the draught forward and the draught aft, where the draughts are measured at the forward and aft:

.1 perpendiculars respectively, as defined in the International Convention on Load Lines in force, for ships subject to the provisions of regulation Ⅱ-1/1.1.1.1; and

.2 terminals respectively, for ships not subject to the provisions of regulation Ⅱ-1/1.1.1.1 but constructed on or after 1 January 2009,

disregarding any rake of keel.

14 *Permeability*(μ) of a space is the proportion of the immersed volume of that space which can be occupied by water.

15 *Machinery spaces* are spaces between the watertight boundaries of a space containing the main and auxiliary propulsion machinery, including boilers, generators and electric motors primarily intended for propulsion. In the case of unusual arrangements, the Administration may define the limits of the machinery spaces.

2　**船中**系指船长(L)的中点。

3　**后端点**系指分舱长度的后部界限。

4　**前端点**系指分舱长度的前部界限。

5　**船长**(L)系指现行《国际载重线公约》所定义的船长。

6　**干舷甲板**系指现行《国际载重线公约》所定义的甲板。

7　**首垂线**系指现行《国际载重线公约》所定义的首垂线。

8　**船宽**(B)系指船舶处于或低于最深分舱吃水时的最大型宽。

9　**吃水**(d):

.1　对于应符合第Ⅱ-1/1.1.1.1 条规定的船舶,系指从船中龙骨线至相关水线的垂直距离;和

.2　对于不受第Ⅱ-1/1.1.1.1 条约束但在 2009 年 1 月 1 日或以后建造的船舶,系指从分舱长度(L_s)中点处龙骨线至相关水线的垂直距离。

10　**最深分舱吃水**(d_s)系指船舶的夏季载重线吃水。

11　**轻载航行吃水**(d_l)系指相应于最轻预计装载量和相关液舱容量的航行吃水,但应计入稳性和/或浸水所可能需要的压载。客船应足额计入船上乘客和船员。

12　**部分分舱吃水**(d_p)系指轻载航行吃水加上轻载航行吃水与最深分舱吃水之差的 60%。

13　**纵倾**系指首吃水和尾吃水之差:

.1　对于应符合第Ⅱ-1/1.1.1.1 条的船舶,吃水分别在现行《国际载重线公约》中规定的首垂线和尾垂线处量取,不计龙骨斜度;

.2　对于不受第Ⅱ-1/1.1.1.1 条约束但在 2009 年 1 月 1 日或以后建造的船舶,吃水分别在前端点和后端点量取,

不计龙骨斜度。

14　**某一处所的渗透率**(μ)系指该处所能被水侵占的浸水容积比例。

15　**机器处所**系指介于一个处所的水密限界面之间,供安置主辅推进机械,包括主要供推进之用的锅炉、发电机和电动机的各个处所。对于特殊布置的船舶,主管机关可以规定机器处所的范围。

16 *Weathertight* means that in any sea conditions water will not penetrate into the ship.

17 *Watertight* means having scantlings and arrangements capable of preventing the passage of water in any direction under the head of water likely to occur in intact and damaged conditions. In the damaged condition, the head of water is to be considered in the worst situation at equilibrium, including intermediate stages of flooding.

18 *Design pressure* means the hydrostatic pressure for which each structure or appliance assumed watertight in the intact and damage stability calculations is designed to withstand.

19 *Bulkhead deck* in a passenger ship means the uppermost deck:

.1 to which the main bulkheads and the ship's shell are carried watertight, for ships subject to the provisions of regulation Ⅱ-1/1.1.1.1; and

.2 at any point in the subdivision length (L_s) to which the main bulkheads and the ship's shell are carried watertight and the lowermost deck from which passenger and crew evacuation will not be impeded by water in any stage of flooding for damage cases defined in regulation 8 and in part B-2 of this chapter, for ships not subject to the provisions of regulation Ⅱ-1/1.1.1.1 but constructed on or after 1 January 2009.

The bulkhead deck may be a stepped deck. In a cargo ship not subject to the provisions of regulation Ⅱ-1/1.1.1.1 but constructed on or after 1 January 2009, the freeboard deck may be taken as the bulkhead deck.

20 *Deadweight* is the difference in tonnes between the displacement of a ship in water of a specific gravity of 1.025 at the draught corresponding to the assigned summer freeboard and the lightweight of the ship.

21 *Lightweight* is the displacement of a ship in tonnes without cargo, fuel, lubricating oil, ballast water, fresh water and feedwater in tanks, consumable stores, and passengers and crew and their effects.

22 *Oil tanker* is the oil tanker defined in regulation 1 of Annex Ⅰ of the Protocol of 1978 relating to the International Convention for the Prevention of Pollution from Ships, 1973.

23 *Ro-ro* passenger ship means a passenger ship with ro-ro spaces or special category spaces as defined in regulation Ⅱ-2/3.42.

24 *Bulk carrier* means a bulk carrier as defined in regulation Ⅻ/1.1.

25 *Keel line* is a line parallel to the slope of the keel passing amidships through:

.1 the top of the keel at centreline or line of intersection of the inside of shell plating with the keel if a bar keel extends below that line, on a ship with a metal shell; or

.2 in wood and composite ships, the distance is measured from the lower edge of the keel rabbet. When the form at the lower part of the midship section is of a hollow character, or where thick garboards are fitted, the distance is measured from the point where the line of the flat of the bottom continued inward intersects the centreline amidships.

16　**风雨密**系指在任何海况下,水不会渗入船内。

17　**水密**系指构件尺寸和布置在完整和破损工况中可能产生的水头下,能防止水从任何方向进入。在破损工况中,水头应考虑在平衡时,包括进水的中间阶段中最差的状况。

18　**设计压力**系指完整和破损稳性计算所假定的各个水密结构或设备按设计所应承受的静水压力。

19　**客船舱壁甲板**:

.1　对于应符合第Ⅱ-1/1.1.1.1 条的船舶,系指主舱壁和船壳板保持水密的最高甲板;和

.2　对于不受第Ⅱ-1/1.1.1.1 条约束但在 2009 年 1 月 1 日或以后建造的船舶,系指在分舱长度(L_s)任何一点上,主舱壁和船壳板保持水密的最高甲板,以及在本章第 8 条和第 B-2 部分中定义的破损情况下,乘客和船员的撤离在任何浸水阶段亦不会受水阻碍的最低甲板。

舱壁甲板可为阶形甲板。对于不受第Ⅱ-1/1.1.1.1 条约束但在 2009 年 1 月 1 日或以后建造的货船,干舷甲板可视为舱壁甲板。

20　**载重量**系指船舶在比重为 1.025 的海水中,吃水相应于所勘绘的夏季干舷时,排水量与该船空船排水量之差,以吨计。

21　**空船排水量**系指船舶在没有货物,舱柜内无燃油、润滑油、压载水、淡水、锅炉给水,消耗物料,且无乘客、船员及其行李物品时的排水量,以吨计。

22　**油船**系指《1973 年国际防止船舶造成污染公约 1978 年议定书》附则Ⅰ第 1 条所定义的油船。

23　**滚装客船**系指具有第Ⅱ-2/3.42 条定义的滚装处所或特种处所的客船。

24　**散货船**系指第Ⅻ/1.1 条所定义的散货船。

25　**龙骨线**系指在船中穿过以下部位与龙骨斜面平行的线:

.1　金属船壳船舶中心线或船壳外板内侧与龙骨交线(如有方龙骨延伸至该线之下)处的龙骨顶端;或

.2　对木质和混合结构船舶,该距离自龙骨镶口下缘量起。当船中剖面下部为凹形时,或如果设有厚的龙骨翼板,则该距离自船底平面向内延伸线与船中心线的交点量起。

26 *2008 IS Code* means the International Code on Intact Stability, 2008, consisting of an introduction, part A (the provisions of which shall be treated as mandatory) and part B (the provisions of which shall be treated as recommendatory), as adopted by resolution MSC.267(85), provided that:

.1 amendments to the introduction and part A of the Code are adopted, brought into force and take effect in accordance with the provisions of article Ⅷ of the present Convention concerning the amendment procedures applicable to the annex other than chapter Ⅰ thereof; and

.2 amendments to part B of the Code are adopted by the Maritime Safety Committee in accordance with its Rules of Procedure.

27 *Goal-based Ship Construction Standards for Bulk Carriers and Oil Tankers* means the International Goal-Based Ship Construction Standards for Bulk Carriers and Oil Tankers, adopted by the Maritime Safety Committee by resolution MSC.287(87), as may be amended by the Organization, provided that such amendments are adopted, brought into force and take effect in accordance with the provisions of article Ⅷ of the present Convention concerning the amendment procedures applicable to the annex other than chapter Ⅰ thereof.

28 *ICF Code* means the International Code of Safety for Ships using Gases or other Low-Flashpoint Fuels as adopted by the Maritime Safety Committee of the Organization by resolution MSC.391(95), as may be amended by the Organization, provided that such amendments are adopted, brought into force and take effect in accordance with the provisions of article Ⅷ of the present Convention concerning the amendment procedures applicable to the annex other than chapter Ⅰ.

29 *Low-flashpoint fuel* means gaseous or liquid fuel having a flashpoint lower than otherwise permitted under regulation Ⅱ-2/4.2.1.1.

Regulation 3
Definitions relating to parts C, D and E

For the purpose of parts C, D and E, unless expressly provided otherwise:

1 *Steering gear control system* is the equipment by which orders are transmitted from the navigating bridge to the steering gear power units.

Steering gear control systems comprise transmitters, receivers, hydraulic control pumps and their associated motors, motor controllers, piping and cables.

2 *Main steering gear* is the machinery, rudder actuators, steering gear, power units, if any, and ancillary equipment and the means of applying torque to the rudder stock (e.g., tiller or quadrant) necessary for effecting movement of the rudder for the purpose of steering the ship under normal service conditions.

26 **《2008年国际完整稳性规则》(2008 IS规则)**系指以第MSC.267(85)号决议通过的《2008年国际完整稳性规则》,该规则包括引言,A部分(其规定须按照强制性对待)和B部分(其规定须按照建议性对待),条件是:

.1　对该规则引言和A部分的修正按照适用于公约附则(公约第Ⅰ章的规定除外)的修正程序的现公约第Ⅷ条予以通过和生效,并且

.2　对该规则B部分的修正由海上安全委员会按照其议事程序通过。

27 **《散货船和油船目标型新船建造标准》**系指海上安全委员会以第MSC.287(87)号决议通过的《国际散货船和油船目标型船舶建造标准》,该标准可由本组织修正,但修正案须按照本公约关于附则除第Ⅰ章外的适用修正程序的第Ⅷ(b)条规定予以通过、生效和实施。

28 **《气体或其他低闪点燃料动力船舶国际安全规则》(IGF规则)**系指本组织海上安全委员会以第MSC.391(95)号决议通过的《气体或其他低闪点燃料动力船舶国际安全规则》,该规则可由本组织修正,但其修正案应按照本公约第Ⅷ条有关其附则(除第Ⅰ章以外)的适用修正程序的规定通过、生效和实施。

29 **低闪点燃料**系指其闪点低于根据第Ⅱ-2/4.2.1.1条允许者的气体或液体燃料。

第3条
有关C、D和E部分的定义

除另有明文规定外,就C、D和E部分而言:

1 **操舵装置控制**系统系指将舵令由驾驶室传至操舵装置动力设备的设备。

操舵装置控制系统由发送器、接收器、液压控制泵及其电动机、电动机控制器、管系和电缆组成。

2 **主操舵装置**系指在正常情况下为操纵船舶而使舵产生动作所必需的机械、舵执行器、操舵动力设备(若设有)和附属设备以及对舵杆施加扭矩的装置(如舵柄或舵扇)。

3 *Steering gear power* unit is:

.1 in the case of electric steering gear, an electric motor and its associated electrical equipment;

.2 in the case of electrohydraulic steering gear, an electric motor and its associated electrical equipment and connected pump; or

.3 in the case of other hydraulic steering gear, a driving engine and connected pump.

4 *Auxiliary steering gear* is the equipment other than any part of the main steering gear necessary to steer the ship in the event of failure of the main steering gear but not including the tiller, quadrant or components serving the same purpose.

5 *Normal operational and habitable condition* is a condition under which the ship as a whole, the machinery, services, means and aids ensuring propulsion, ability to steer, safe navigation, fire and flooding safety, internal and external communications and signals, means of escape, and emergency boat winches, as well as the designed comfortable conditions of habitability, are in working order and functioning normally.

6 *Emergency condition* is a condition under which any services needed for normal operational and habitable conditions are not in working order due to failure of the main source of electrical power.

7 *Main source of electrical power* is a source intended to supply electrical power to the main switchboard for distribution to all services necessary for maintaining the ship in normal operational and habitable conditions.

8 *Dead ship condition* is the condition under which the main propulsion plant, boilers and auxiliaries are not in operation due to the absence of power.

9 *Main generating station* is the space in which the main source of electrical power is situated.

10 *Main switchboard* is a switchboard which is directly supplied by the main source of electrical power and is intended to distribute electrical energy to the ship's services.

11 *Emergency switchboard* is a switchboard which in the event of failure of the main electrical power supply system is directly supplied by the emergency source of electrical power or the transitional source of emergency power and is intended to distribute electrical energy to the emergency services.

12 *Emergency source of electrical power* is a source of electrical power, intended to supply the emergency switchboard in the event of a failure of the supply from the main source of electrical power.

13 *Power actuating system* is the hydraulic equipment provided for supplying power to turn the rudder stock, comprising a steering gear power unit or units, together with the associated pipes and fittings, and a rudder actuator. The power actuating systems may share common mechanical components (i.e., tiller, quadrant and rudder stock) or components serving the same purpose.

3　**操舵装置动力设备**系指：

.1　如果为电动操舵装置，系指电动机及有关的电气设备；

.2　如果为电动液压操舵装置，系指电动机及有关的电气设备和与之相连接的泵；或

.3　如果为其他液压操舵装置，系指驱动机及与之相连接的泵。

4　**辅助操舵装置**系指如主操舵装置失效时操纵船舶所必需的设备，其不属于主操舵装置的任何部分，但不包括舵柄、舵扇或作同样用途的部件。

5　**正常操作和居住条件**系指船舶作为一个整体，其机器、设施、确保推进的设备和辅助装置、操舵能力、安全航行、消防安全和防止进水、内外通信和信号、脱险通道，应急救生艇绞车以及设计要求的舒适居住条件，均处于工作状态并正常发挥效用。

6　**紧急状态**系指由于主电源发生故障以致正常操作和居住条件所需的设施，均处于工作失常的状态。

7　**主电源**系指向主配电板供电以给保持船舶正常操作和居住条件所必需的所有设施配电的电源。

8　**瘫船状态**系指由于缺少动力，致使主推进装置、锅炉和辅机不能运转的状态。

9　**主发电站**系指主电源所在的处所。

10　**主配电板**系指由主电源直接供电并将电能分配给船上各种设施的配电板。

11　**应急配电板**系指在主电源供电系统发生故障的情况下，由应急电源或临时应急电源直接供电，并将电能分配给应急用途的配电板。

12　**应急电源**系指在主电源供电发生故障的情况下，用于向应急配电板供电的电源。

13　**动力执行系统**系指提供动力以转动舵杆的液压设备，由一个或几个操舵装置动力设备，连同有关的管系和附件以及舵执行器组成。各个动力执行系统可共用某些机械部件（即舵柄、舵扇和舵杆）或共用有同样用途的部件。

14 *Maximum ahead service speed* is the greatest speed which the ship is designed to maintain in service at sea at the deepest seagoing draught.

15 *Maximum astern speed* is the speed which it is estimated the ship can attain at the designed maximum astern power at the deepest seagoing draught.

16 *Machinery spaces* are all machinery spaces of category A and all other spaces containing propelling machinery, boilers, oil fuel units, steam and internal-combustion engines, generators and major electrical machinery, oil filling stations, refrigerating, stabilizing, ventilation and air conditioning machinery, and similar spaces, and trunks to such spaces.

17 *Machinery spaces of category A* are those spaces and trunks to such spaces which contain:

.1 internal-combustion machinery used for main propulsion;

.2 internal-combustion machinery used for purposes other than main propulsion where such machinery has in the aggregate a total power output of not less than 375 kW; or

.3 any oil-fired boiler or oil fuel unit.

18 *Control stations* are those spaces in which the ship's radio or main navigating equipment or the emergency source of power is located or where the fire recording or fire control equipment is centralized.

19 *Chemical tanker* is a cargo ship constructed or adapted and used for the carriage in bulk of any liquid product listed in either:

.1 chapter 17 of the International Code for the Construction and Equipment of Ships Carrying Dangerous Chemicals in Bulk adopted by the Maritime Safety Committee by resolution MSC.4(48), hereinafter referred to as "the International Bulk Chemical Code", as may be amended by the Organization; or

.2 chapter Ⅵ of the Code for the Construction and Equipment of Ships Carrying Dangerous Chemicals in Bulk adopted by the Assembly of the Organization by resolution A.212(Ⅶ), hereinafter referred to as "the Bulk Chemical Code", as has been or may be amended by the Organization,

whichever is applicable.

20 *Gas carrier* is a cargo ship constructed or adapted and used for the carriage in bulk of any liquefied gas or other products listed in either:

.1 chapter 19 of the International Code for the Construction and Equipment of Ships Carrying Liquefied Gases in Bulk adopted by the Maritime Safety Committee by resolution MSC.5(48), hereinafter referred to as "the International Gas Carrier Code", as may be amended by the Organization; or

.2 chapter XIX of the Code for the Construction and Equipment of Ships Carrying Liquefied Gases in Bulk adopted by the Organization by resolution A.328(Ⅸ), hereinafter referred to as "the Gas Carrier Code", as has been or may be amended by the Organization,

whichever is applicable.

14　**最大营运前进航速**系指船舶在最大航海吃水情况下保持海上营运的最大设计航速。

15　**最大后退速度**系指船舶在最大航海吃水情况下用设计的最大倒退功率估计能够达到的速度。

16　**机器处所**系指所有A类机器处所和所有其他设有推进装置、锅炉、燃油装置、蒸汽机和内燃机、发电机和主要电动机、加油站、制冷机、防摇装置、通风机和空调机的处所，以及类似处所和通往这些处所的围壁通道。

17　**A类机器处所**系指设有下列设备的处所和通往这些处所的围壁通道：

.1　用作主推进的内燃机；

.2　用作非主推进合计总输出功率不小于375 kW的内燃机；或

.3　任何燃油锅炉或燃油装置。

18　**控制站**系指船舶无线电设备或主要航行设备或应急电源所在的处所，或火警指示器或消防控制设备集中的处所。

19　**化学品液货船**系指经建造或改建用于散装运输下述规则之一所列的任何液体货品的货船：

.1　经海上安全委员会第MSC.4(48)号决议通过的，并可能由本组织修正的《国际散装运输危险化学品船舶构造和设备规则》（以下简称《国际散化规则》）第17章；或

.2　经本组织第A.212(Ⅶ)号决议通过的，并已经或可能由本组织修正的《散装运输危险化学品船舶构造和设备规则》（以下简称《散化规则》）第Ⅵ章。

20　**气体运输船**系指经建造或改建用于散装运输下述规则之一所列的任何液化气体或其他货品的货船：

.1　经海上安全委员会第MSC.5(48)号决议通过的，并可能由本组织修正的《国际散装运输液化气体船舶构造和设备规则》（以下简称《国际气体运输船规则》）第19章；或

.2　经本组织第A.328(Ⅸ)号决议通过的，并已经或可能由本组织修正的《散装运输液化气体船舶构造和设备规则》（以下简称《气体运输船规则》）第ⅩⅨ章。

Part A-1
Structure of ships

Regulation 3-1
Structural, mechanical and electrical requirements for ships

In addition to the requirements contained elsewhere in the present regulations, ships shall be designed, constructed and maintained in compliance with the structural, mechanical and electrical requirements of a classification society which is recognized by the Administration in accordance with the provisions of regulation Ⅺ-1/1, or with applicable national standards of the Administration which provide an equivalent level of safety.

Regulation 3-2
Protective coatings of dedicated seawater ballast tanks in all types of ships and double-side skin spaces of bulk carriers①

1 Paragraphs 2 and 4 of this regulation shall apply to ships of not less than 500 gross tonnage:

.1 for which the building contract is placed on or after 1 July 2008; or

.2 in the absence of a building contract, the keels of which are laid or which are at a similar stage of construction on or after 1 January 2009; or

.3 the delivery of which is on or after 1 July 2012.②

2 All dedicated seawater ballast tanks arranged in ships and double-side skin spaces arranged in bulk carriers of 150 m in length and upwards shall be coated during construction in accordance with the *Performance standard for protective coatings for dedicated seawater ballast tanks in all types of ships and double-side skin spaces of bulk carriers*, adopted by the Maritime Safety Committee by resolution MSC.215(82), as may be amended by the Organization, provided that such amendments are adopted, brought into force and take effect in accordance with the provisions of article Ⅷ of the present Convention concerning the amendment procedures applicable to the annex other than chapter Ⅰ.

---

① Refer to *Guidelines for the selection, application and maintenance of corrosion prevention systems of dedicated seawater ballast tanks* (resolution A.798(19)).

② Refer to *Unified interpretation of "unforeseen delay in delivery of ships"* (MSC.1/Circ.1247).

A-1 部分
船舶结构

第 3-1 条
船舶的结构和机电设备要求

除符合本公约其他要求外，船舶的设计、建造和维护保养还应符合主管机关按第Ⅺ-1/1条的规定予以承认的船级社对结构和机电设备的要求，或应符合主管机关具有同等安全水平的适用的国家标准。

第 3-2 条
所有类型船舶的专用海水压载舱和散货船双舷侧处所的保护涂层①

1　本条 2 和 4 应适用于不小于 500 总吨的下列船舶：

.1　2008 年 7 月 1 日或以后签订建造合同；或

.2　如果无建造合同，2009 年 1 月 1 日或以后安放龙骨或处于类似建造阶段；或

.3　2012 年 7 月 1 日或以后交付。②

2　建造期间，船上配置的所有专用海水压载舱和船长 150 m 及以上的散货船双舷侧处所应按照所有类型船舶专用海水压载舱和散货船双舷侧处所保护涂层性能标准涂装涂层。该标准由海上安全委员会以第 MSC.215(82)号决议通过，并可能经本组织修正，但该修正案应按本公约第Ⅷ条有关适用于除第Ⅰ章外的附则修正程序的规定予以通过、生效和实施。

① 参见《专用海水压载舱防腐系统的选择、使用和维护导则》(第 A.798(19)号决议)。
② 参见《“不可预见的延迟交船”统一解释》(第 MSC.1/Circ.1247 号通函)。

3 All dedicated seawater ballast tanks arranged in oil tankers and bulk carriers constructed on or after 1 July 1998, for which paragraph 2 is not applicable, shall comply with the requirements of regulation Ⅱ-1/3-2 adopted by resolution MSC.47(66).

4 Maintenance of the protective coating system shall be included in the overall ship's maintenance scheme. The effectiveness of the protective coating system shall be verified during the life of a ship by the Administration or an organization recognized by the Administration, based on the guidelines developed by the Organization.①

Regulation 3-3
Safe access to tanker bows

1 For the purpose of this regulation and regulation 3-4, tankers include oil tankers as defined in regulation 2.22, chemical tankers as defined in regulation Ⅶ/8.2 and gas carriers as defined in regulation Ⅶ/11.2.

2 Every tanker shall be provided with the means to enable the crew to gain safe access to the bow even in severe weather conditions. Such means of access shall be approved by the Administration based on the guidelines developed by the Organization.②

Regulation 3-4
Emergency towing arrangements and procedures

1 Emergency towing arrangements on tankers

1.1 Emergency towing arrangements shall be fitted at both ends on board every tanker of not less than 20,000 tonnes deadweight.

1.2 For tankers constructed on or after 1 July 2002:

.1 the arrangements shall, at all times, be capable of rapid deployment in the absence of main power on the ship to be towed and easy connection to the towing ship. At least one of the emergency towing arrangements shall be pre-rigged ready for rapid deployment; and

.2 emergency towing arrangements at both ends shall be of adequate strength taking into account the size and deadweight of the ship, and the expected forces during bad weather conditions. The design and construction and prototype testing of emergency towing arrangements shall be approved by the Administration, based on the guidelines developed by the Organization.③

---

① Refer to *Guidelines for maintenance and repair of protective coatings* (MSC.1/Circ.1330).

② Refer to *Guidelines for safe access to tanker bows* (resolution MSC.62(67)).

③ Refer to *Guidelines on emergency towing arrangements for tankers* (resolution MSC.35(63), as amended) and LL.3/Circ.130, section 5.

3 1998年7月1日或以后建造的油船和散货船上配置的不适用2的所有专用海水压载舱应符合MSC.47(66)决议通过的第Ⅱ-1/3-2条的要求。

4 保护涂层系统的维护应包括在全船维护计划中。主管机关或主管机关认可的组织应根据本组织制定的导则①在船舶的使用寿命期间对保护涂层系统的有效性进行验证。

第3-3条
进入液货船船首的安全通道

1 就本条和第3-4条而言,液货船包括第2.22条所定义的油船、第Ⅶ/8.2条所定义的化学品液货船以及第Ⅶ/11.2条所定义的气体运输船。

2 每艘液货船应设置使船员即使在恶劣的气候条件下也能进入船首的安全通道。此类安全通道应由主管机关根据本组织制定的指南②予以认可。

第3-4条
应急拖带装置和程序

1 液货船应急拖带装置

1.1 应急拖带装置须安装于不小于20 000载重吨的每一液货船的两端。

1.2 对于2002年7月1日及以后建造的液货船:

.1 该装置应能始终在被拖船主动力失效时迅速展开并易于与拖船连接。至少1台应急拖带装置应预先设置为待命状态用于迅速展开;并且

.2 考虑到船舶大小和载重吨以及在恶劣气候条件下的预计受力,首尾两端的应急拖带装置应有足够的强度。应急拖带装置的设计、建造和原型实验须由主管机关根据本组织制定的导则③予以批准。

---

① 参见《防护涂层维护和保养导则》(第MSC.1/Circ.1330号通函)。
② 参见海上安全委员会第MSC.62(67)号决议通过的《进入液货船船首的安全通道指南》。
③ 参见《液货船应急拖带导则》(经修正的第MSC.35(63)号决议)和第LL.3/Circ.130号通函第5节。

1.3 For tankers constructed before 1 July 2002, the design and construction of emergency towing arrangements shall be approved by the Administration, based on the guidelines developed by the Organization.①

2 Emergency towing procedures on ships

2.1 This paragraph applies to:

.1 all passenger ships, not later than 1 January 2010;

.2 cargo ships constructed on or after 1 January 2010; and

.3 cargo ships constructed before 1 January 2010, not later than 1 January 2012.

2.2 Ships shall be provided with a ship-specific emergency towing procedure. Such a procedure shall be carried aboard the ship for use in emergency situations and shall be based on existing arrangements and equipment available on board the ship.

2.3 The procedure② shall include:

.1 drawings of fore and aft deck showing possible emergency towing arrangements;

.2 inventory of equipment on board that can be used for emergency towing;

.3 means and methods of communication; and

.4 sample procedures to facilitate the preparation for and conducting of emergency towing operations.

Regulation 3-5
New installation of materials containing asbestos③

1 This regulation shall apply to materials used for the structure, machinery, electrical installations and equipment covered by the present Convention.

2 From 1 January 2011, for all ships, new installation of materials which contain asbestos shall be prohibited.

Regulation 3-6
Access to and within spaces in, and forward of, the cargo area of oil tankers and bulk carriers

1 Application

---

① Refer to *Guidelines on emergency towing arrangements for tankers* (resolution MSC.35(63), as amended) and LL.3/Circ.130, section 5.

② Refer to *Guileless for owners/operators on preparing emergency towing procedures* (MSC.1/Circ.1255).

③ Refer to *Information on prohibiting the use of asbestos on board ships* (MSC.1/Circ.1374).

1.3　对于2002年7月1日之前建造的液货船，应急拖带装置的设计和建造应由主管机关根据本组织制定的导则①批准。

2　**船上应急拖带程序**

2.1　本段适用于：

.1　所有客船，不晚于2010年1月1日；

.2　2010年1月1日及以后建造的货船；和

.3　2010年1月1日以前建造的货船，但不晚于2012年1月1日。

2.2　船舶须配备船舶专用应急拖带程序。该程序须备于船上供应急情况下使用，并应根据船上现有装置和可用设备制定。

2.3　程序②应包括：

.1　标明可能的应急拖带装置的前甲板和后甲板示意图；

.2　船上可用于应急拖带的设备清单；

.3　通信手段和方法；和

.4　便于应急拖带作业的准备和操作的程序范例。

第3-5条
新装含有石棉的材料③

1　本条适用于本公约涉及的结构、机电装置和设备所使用的材料。

2　从2011年1月1日起，禁止所有船舶安装以含石棉的材料制成的新设备。

第3-6条
进入油船和散货船货物区域处所的通道和该区域处所内的通道以及该区域处所前部的通道

1　**适用范围**

---

① 参见《液货船应急拖带导则》（经修正的第MSC.35(63)号决议）和第LL.3/Circ.130号通函第5节。

② 参见《船东/船舶经营人制定应急拖带程序导则》（第MSC.1/Circ.1255号通函）。

③ 参见《禁止在船上使用石棉的相关信息》（第MSC.1/Circ.1374号通函）。

1.1 Except as provided for in paragraph 1.2, this regulation applies to oil tankers of 500 gross tonnage and over and bulk carriers, as defined in regulation Ⅸ/1, of 20,000 gross tonnage and over, constructed on or after 1 January 2006.

1.2 Oil tankers of 500 gross tonnage and over constructed on or after 1 October 1994 but before 1 January 2005 shall comply with the provisions of regulation Ⅱ-1/12-2 adopted by resolution MSC.27 (61).

2 Means of access to cargo and other spaces

2.1 Each space shall be provided with means of access to enable, throughout the life of a ship, overall and close-up inspections and thickness measurements of the ship's structures to be carried out by the Administration, the Company, as defined in regulation Ⅸ/1, and the ship's personnel and others as necessary. Such means of access shall comply with the requirements of paragraph 5 and with the *Technical provisions for means of access for inspections*, adopted by the Maritime Safety Committee by resolution MSC.133(76)①, as may be amended by the Organization, provided that such amendments are adopted, brought into force and take effect in accordance with the provisions of article Ⅷ of the present Convention concerning the amendment procedures applicable to the annex other than chapter Ⅰ.

2.2 Where a permanent means of access may be susceptible to damage during normal cargo loading and unloading operations or where it is impracticable to fit permanent means of access, the Administration may allow, in lieu thereof, the provision of movable or portable means of access, as specified in the Technical provisions, provided that the means of attaching, rigging, suspending or supporting the portable means of access forms a permanent part of the ship's structure. All portable equipment shall be capable of being readily erected or deployed by ship's personnel.

2.3 The construction and materials of all means of access and their attachment to the ship's structure shall be to the satisfaction of the Administration. The means of access shall be subject to survey prior to, or in conjunction with, its use in carrying out surveys in accordance with regulation Ⅰ/10.

3 Safe access to cargo holds, cargo tanks, ballast tanks and other spaces

3.1 Safe access② to cargo holds, cofferdams, ballast tanks, cargo tanks and other spaces in the cargo area shall be direct from the open deck and such as to ensure their complete inspection. Safe access to double bottom spaces or to forward ballast tanks may be from a pump-room, deep cofferdam, pipe tunnel, cargo hold, double-hull space or similar compartment not intended for the carriage of oil or hazardous cargoes.

---

① Amended by resolution MSC.158(78).

② Refer to *Revised recommendations for entering enclosed spaces aboard ships* (resolution A.1050(27)).

1.1　除1.2所述外，本条适用于2006年1月1日或以后建造的500总吨及以上的油船，和第Ⅸ/1条定义的20 000总吨及以上的散货船。

1.2　在1994年10月1日或以后，但在2005年1月1日以前建造的500总吨及以上的油船，应符合第MSC.27(61)号决议通过的第Ⅱ-1/12-2条的规定。

2　进入货舱和其他处所的通道

2.1　在船舶整个寿命期间内，每一处所均应设置通道，以供主管机关、第Ⅸ/1条所定义的船公司以及船上人员和其他人员必要时对船舶结构进行全面检查、近观检查和厚度测量。通道应符合本条5的要求和海上安全委员会第MSC.133(76)号[①]决议通过的《检查通道技术规定》，并可能经本组织修正，但该修正案应按本公约第Ⅷ条有关适用于除第Ⅰ章外的附则修正程序的规定予以通过、生效和实施。

2.2　如果永久通道在正常装卸货物作业时容易损坏，或如果设置永久通道不切实际时，主管机关可允许设置该技术规定中规定的移动式或便携式通道作为替代，但该连接、安装、悬吊或支撑便携式通道的装置应构成船舶结构的永久部分。所有便携式设备均应易于船上人员架设或布设。

2.3　所有通道的构造和材料及其与船舶结构连接的附件均应使主管机关满意。在按第Ⅰ/10条进行检验时，应在通道使用前或使用时对其进行检查。

3　进入货舱、液货舱、压载舱和其他处所的安全通道

3.1　货舱、隔离空舱、压载舱、液货舱和货物区域的其他处所的安全通道[②]应直接从开敞甲板进入并能确保对这些处所进行全面检查。双层底处所或前部各压载舱的安全通道可从泵舱、深隔离空舱、管隧、货舱、双壳处所或不拟载运油或危险货物的类似舱室进入。

① 经第MSC.158(78)号决议修订。
② 参见《关于进入船上围蔽处所的建议案》(第A.1050(27)号决议)。

3.2 Tanks, and subdivisions of tanks, having a length of 35 m or more, shall be fitted with at least two access hatchways and ladders, as far apart as practicable. Tanks less than 35 m in length shall be served by at least one access hatchway and ladder. When a tank is subdivided by one or more swash bulkheads or similar obstructions which do not allow ready means of access to the other parts of the tank, at least two hatchways and ladders shall be fitted.

3.3 Each cargo hold shall be provided with at least two means of access as far apart as practicable. In general, these accesses should be arranged diagonally, for example one access near the forward bulkhead on the port side, the other one near the aft bulkhead on the starboard side.

4 Ship Structure Access Manual

4.1 A ship's means of access to carry out overall and close-up inspections and thickness measurements shall be described in a Ship Structure Access Manual approved by the Administration, an updated copy of which shall be kept on board. The Ship Structure Access Manual shall include the following for each space:

.1 plans showing the means of access to the space, with appropriate technical specifications and dimensions;

.2 plans showing the means of access within each space to enable an overall inspection to be carried out, with appropriate technical specifications and dimensions. The plans shall indicate from where each area in the space can be inspected;

.3 plans showing the means of access within the space to enable close-up inspections to be carried out, with appropriate technical specifications and dimensions. The plans shall indicate the positions of critical structural areas, whether the means of access is permanent or portable and from where each area can be inspected;

.4 instructions for inspecting and maintaining the structural strength of all means of access and means of attachment, taking into account any corrosive atmosphere that may be within the space;

.5 instructions for safety guidance when rafting is used for close-up inspections and thickness measurements;

.6 instructions for the rigging and use of any portable means of access in a safe manner;

.7 an inventory of all portable means of access; and

.8 records of periodical inspections and maintenance of the ship's means of access.

4.2 For the purpose of this regulation "critical structural areas" are locations which have been identified from calculations to require monitoring or from the service history of similar or sister ships to be sensitive to cracking, buckling, deformation or corrosion which would impair the structural integrity of the ship.

3.2 长度为 35 m 或以上的液舱和液舱的分舱，应至少设置 2 个尽可能相互远离的出入舱口和梯子。长度小于 35 m 的液舱应至少有 1 个出入舱口和梯子。当 1 个液舱被 1 道或多道制荡舱壁或类似的隔堵所分开时，如果不易于布置从舱室的一端到另一端的通道，则至少应设置 2 个出入舱口和梯子。

3.3 每个货舱应至少设置 2 个尽可能相互远离的出入通道。通常，出入通道应按对角线布置，例如 1 个出入通道布置在左舷靠近货舱前端舱壁处，另 1 个出入通道布置在右舷靠近货舱后端舱壁处。

4　船舶结构通道手册

4.1 船上用于全面检查、近观检查和厚度测量的通道，应在经主管机关批准的船舶结构通道手册中予以说明，一份其最新版本的副本应保存在船上。船舶结构通道手册应包括每一处所的下述资料：

.1 该处所的出入通道图，并有相应的技术说明和尺寸；

.2 每一处所内能进行全面检查的通道图，并有相应的技术说明和尺寸。图中应标示该处所内的每一区域可从何处检查；

.3 该处所内能进行近观检查的通道图，并有相应的技术说明和尺寸。图中应标示临界结构区域的位置，是否为永久通道或是便携式通道，以及每一区域可从何处检查；

.4 检查和维护保养所有出入通道和附属设备结构强度的须知，其中应考虑处所内任何腐蚀气体的影响；

.5 当使用筏进行近观检查和厚度测量时，应有安全指导须知；

.6 任何便携式通道安全安装和使用须知；

.7 一份所有便携式通道的清单；和

.8 船上通道定期检查和维护保养的记录。

4.2 就本条而言，“临界结构区域”系指通过计算确定需要进行监控的局部区域，或类似船舶或姐妹船在营运史上易于发生会损害船舶结构完整性的裂缝、屈曲、变形或腐蚀的区域。

5 General technical specifications

5.1 For access through horizontal openings, hatches or manholes, the dimensions shall be sufficient to allow a person wearing a self-contained air-breathing apparatus and protective equipment to ascend or descend any ladder without obstruction and also provide a clear opening to facilitate the hoisting of an injured person from the bottom of the space. The minimum clear opening shall not be less than 600 mm × 600 mm. When access to a cargo hold is arranged through the cargo hatch, the top of the ladder shall be placed as close as possible to the hatch coaming. Access hatch coamings having a height greater than 900 mm shall also have steps on the outside in conjunction with the ladder.

5.2 For access through vertical openings, or manholes, in swash bulkheads, floors, girders and web frames providing passage through the length and breadth of the space, the minimum opening shall be not less than 600 mm × 800 mm at a height of not more than 600 mm from the bottom shell plating unless gratings or other footholds are provided.

5.3 For oil tankers of less than 5,000 tonnes deadweight, the Administration may approve, in special circumstances, smaller dimensions for the openings referred to in paragraphs 5.1 and 5.2, if the ability to traverse such openings or to remove an injured person can be proved to the satisfaction of the Administration.

Regulation 3-7
Construction drawings maintained on board and ashore

1 A set of as-built construction drawings① and other plans showing any subsequent structural alterations shall be kept on board a ship constructed on or after 1 January 2007.

2 An additional set of such drawings shall be kept ashore by the Company, as defined in regulation Ⅸ/1.2.

Regulation 3-8
Towing and mooring equipment

1 This regulation applies to ships constructed on or after 1 January 2007, but does not apply to emergency towing arrangements provided in accordance with regulation 3-4.

2 Ships shall be provided with arrangements, equipment and fittings of sufficient safe working load to enable the safe conduct of all towing and mooring operations associated with the normal operation of the ship.

3 Arrangements, equipment and fittings provided in accordance with paragraph 2 shall meet the appropriate requirements of the Administration or an organization recognized by the Administration under regulation Ⅰ/6.②

---

① Refer to *As-built construction drawings to be maintained on board the ship and ashore* (MSC/Circ.1135).

② Refer to *Guidance on shipboard towing and mooring equipment* (MSC/Circ.1175).

5 一般技术规定

5.1 通过水平开口、舱口或人孔的通道,其尺寸应足以使穿戴自储式呼吸装置和保护设备的人员上下梯子不受阻碍,而且净孔尺寸应便于将受伤人员从舱底提升上来。该最小净孔尺寸应不小于600 mm×600 mm。当货舱通道布置为通过货舱口进入时,梯子的顶部应尽可能靠近舱口围板;通道出入处舱口围板的高度如超过900 mm,则在舱口围板外侧还应有数级踏板与梯子相接。

5.2 通过制荡舱壁、肋板、纵桁和宽板肋骨上的垂向开口和人孔并可贯通处所的长度和宽度范围的通道,其最小开口尺寸应不小于600 mm×800 mm且应位于船底外板以上不超过600 mm处,除非设有格栅或其他立足处。

5.3 对载重量小于5 000 t的油船,如能证明这些开口的通行和转移伤员的能力并使主管机关满意,在特殊情况下,主管机关可允许设置尺寸小于上述5.1和5.2要求的开口。

第3-7条
船上和岸上保留的建造图纸

1 在2007年1月1日或以后建造的船上,应保存一套建造完工图纸[①]和表明任何后续结构改装的其他图纸。

2 这类图纸应由第Ⅸ/1.2条所定义的公司在岸上另存一套。

第3-8条
拖带和系泊设备

1 本条适用于2007年1月1日或以后建造的船舶,但不适用于按照第3-4条配备的应急拖带装置。

2 船舶所配备的装置、设备和附件的工作负荷应足以安全进行与船舶正常操作有关的所有拖带和系泊作业。

3 按照本条2配备的装置、设备和附件应满足主管机关或主管机关根据第Ⅰ/6条所认可组织的相应要求。[②]

① 参见《船上和岸上保留建造完工图纸》(第MSC/Circ.1135号通函)。
② 参见《船上拖带和系泊设备导则》(第MSC/Circ.1175号通函)。

4 Each fitting or item of equipment provided under this regulation shall be clearly marked with any restrictions associated with its safe operation, taking into account the strength of its attachment to the ship's structure.

Regulation 3-9
Means of embarkation on and disembarkation from ships

1 Ships constructed on or after 1 January 2010 shall be provided with means of embarkation on and disembarkation from ships for use in port and in port-related operations, such as gangways and accommodation ladders, in accordance with paragraph 2, unless the Administration deems that compliance with a particular provision is unreasonable or impractical.①

2 The means of embarkation and disembarkation required in paragraph 1 shall be constructed and installed based on the guidelines developed by the Organization.②

3 For all ships the means of embarkation and disembarkation shall be inspected and maintained① in suitable condition for their intended purpose, taking into account any restrictions related to safe loading. All wires used to support the means of embarkation and disembarkation shall be maintained as specified in regulation Ⅲ/20.4.

Regulation 3-10
Goal-based ship construction standards for bulk carriers and oil tankers

1 This regulation shall apply to oil tankers of 150 m in length and above and to bulk carriers of 150 m in length and above, constructed with single deck, top-side tanks and hopper side tanks in cargo spaces, excluding ore carriers and combination carriers:

.1 for which the building contract is placed on or after 1 July 2016; or

.2 in the absence of a building contract, the keels of which are laid or which are at a similar stage of construction on or after 1 July 2017; or

.3 the delivery of which is on or after 1 July 2020.

2 Ships shall be designed and constructed for a specified design life to be safe and environmentally friendly, when properly operated and maintained under the specified operating and environmental conditions, in intact and specified damage conditions, throughout their life.

---

① Circumstances where compliance may be deemed unreasonable or impractical may include where the ship:
.1 has small freeboards and is provided with boarding ramps; or
.2 is engaged in voyages between designated ports where appropriate shore accommodation/embarkation ladders (platforms) are provided.

② Refer to *Guidelines for construction, installation, maintenance and inspection/survey of means of embarkation and disembarkation* (MSC.1/Circ.1331).

4 根据本条配备的每一附件或每项设备均应清晰标有与其安全操作有关的任何限制，其中应计及这些附件和设备与船舶结构的连接强度。

第3-9条
登乘和离船设施

1 除非主管机关认为符合某一具体条款不合理或实践上不可行，2010年1月1日及以后建造的船舶，应根据本条第2款配备在港口和港口相关地点使用的登乘和离船设施，例如舷门和舷梯。①

2 本条第1款要求的登乘和离船设施应根据本组织制定的导则建造和安装。②

3 对于所有的船舶，登乘和离船设施须在适合其预期用途的条件下进行检查和维护①，并考虑到任何有关安全负载的限制。所有用于支持登乘和离船设施的线缆都须按照第Ⅲ/20.4条的要求进行维护。

第3-10条
散货船和油船目标型船舶建造标准

1 本条适用于长度为150 m及以上的油船和长度为150 m及以上、货物处所为单甲板、顶边舱和底边舱的散货船，但不包括矿砂船和兼用船：

.1 2016年7月1日或之后签订建造合同的；或

.2 如果没有建造合同，于2017年7月1日或以后铺放龙骨或处于类似建造阶段的；或

.3 于2020年7月1日或以后交船的。

2 船舶的设计和建造须使其具有明确的设计寿命，如果船舶在规定的营运和环境条件下操作和维护得当，在完整和规定的破损条件下，在其整个服务寿命期间安全和环境友好。

---

① 可认为不合理或不可行的船舶应满足以下情形：
　.1 干舷高度较小且设有登船踏板；或
　.2 在指定港口间航行，且港口配有登船舷梯/登乘梯（平台）。

② 参见《登离船装置制造、安装、维护和检查/检验导则》（第MSC.1/Circ.1311号通函）。

2.1 *Safe and environmentally friendly* means the ship shall have adequate strength, integrity and stability to minimize the risk of loss of the ship or pollution to the marine environment due to structural failure, including collapse, resulting in flooding or loss of watertight integrity.

2.2 *Environmentally friendly* also includes the ship being constructed of materials for environmentally acceptable recycling.

2.3 *Safety* also includes the ship's structure, fittings and arrangements providing for safe access, escape, inspection and proper maintenance and facilitating safe operation.

2.4 *Specified operating and environmental conditions* are defined by the intended operating area for the ship throughout its life and cover the conditions, including intermediate conditions, arising from cargo and ballast operations in port, waterways and at sea.

2.5 *Specified design life* is the nominal period that the ship is assumed to be exposed to operating and/or environmental conditions and/or the corrosive environment and is used for selecting appropriate ship design parameters. However, the ship's actual service life may be longer or shorter depending on the actual operating conditions and maintenance of the ship throughout its life cycle.

3 The requirements of paragraphs 2 to 2.5 shall be achieved through satisfying applicable structural requirements of an organization which is recognized by the Administration in accordance with the provisions of regulation Ⅺ-1/1, or national standards of the Administration, conforming to the functional requirements of the Goal-based Ship Construction Standards for Bulk Carriers and Oil Tankers.[①]

4 A Ship Construction File with specific information on how the functional requirements of the Goal-based Ship Construction Standards for Bulk Carriers and Oil Tankers have been applied in the ship design and construction shall be provided upon delivery of a new ship, and kept on board the ship and/or ashore and updated as appropriate throughout the ship's service. The contents of the Ship Construction File shall, at least, conform to the guidelines developed by the Organization.[②]

Regulation 3-11
Corrosion protection of cargo oil tanks of crude oil tankers

1 Paragraph 3 shall apply to crude oil tankers,[③] as defined in regulation 1 of Annex Ⅰ to the International Convention for the Prevention of Pollution from Ships, 1973, as modified by the Protocol of 1978 relating thereto, of 5,000 tonnes deadweight and above:

.1 for which the building contract is placed on or after 1 January 2013; or

---

① The *International goal-based ship construction standards for bulk carriers and oil tankers* were adopted by resolution MSC.287(87) and their verification should be carried out in accordance with the *Revised guidelines for verification of conformity with goal-based ship construction standards for bulk carriers and oil tankers* (resolution MSC.454(100)).

② Refer to *Guidelines for the information to be included in a Ship Construction File* (MSC.1/Circ.1343).

③ Refer to items 1.11.1 or 1.11.4 of the supplement to the International Oil Pollution Prevention Certificate (Form B).

2.1 **安全和环境友好**系指船舶须有足够的强度、完整性和稳性，以最大限度地减少船舶因结构失效（包括坍塌）导致浸水或丧失水密完整性而发生船舶灭失或海洋环境污染的风险。

2.2 **环境友好**还包括使用可环保回收的材料建造船舶。

2.3 **安全**还包括船舶的结构、装置和布置为安全进出、逃生、检查和妥善维护做出安排并便于安全操作。

2.4 **规定的操作和环境条件**被界定为船舶在其整个寿命中拟运营的航区，并包括在港口、航道和海上的货物和压载作业中出现的各种工况，包括过渡工况。

2.5 **规定的设计寿命**系指船舶设定的、承受运营和（或）环境条件和（或）腐蚀环境的标定期限，用于选择适当的船舶设计参数。但是，船舶的实际服役寿命取决于船舶在其整个寿命周期的实际运营条件和维护状况，可能更长或更短。

3 达到第 2 至第 2.5 款要求的方式，是满足符合《散货船和油船目标型船舶建造标准》①功能要求的、由主管机关按照第Ⅺ-1/1 条规定认可的组织的适用结构要求或主管机关的国家标准。

4 含有船舶设计和建造中如何适用《散货船和油船目标型船舶建造标准》功能要求的具体信息的船舶建造档案，须在新船交船时提供，在船舶的整个服役期间保存在船上和（或）岸上，并视情予以更新。船舶建造档案的内容须至少符合本组织制定的导则。②

第 3-11 条
原油油船货油舱防腐保护

1 第 3 款适用于《经 1978 年议定书修订的〈1973 年国际防止船舶造成污染公约〉》附则Ⅰ第 1 条界定的、5 000 载重吨及以上的下列原油油船③：

.1 在 2013 年 1 月 1 日或之后签订建造合同的；或

---

① 第 MSC.287（87）号决议通过的《散货船和油船目标型船舶建造标准》，其核验应根据《经修订的散货船和油船目标性船舶建造标准核验导则》（第 MSC.454（100）号决议）。

② 参见《船舶建造档案内容导则》（第 MSC.1/Circ.1343 号通函）。

③ 参见国际防止油污证书（格式 B）附件 1.11.1 或 1.11.4。

.2 in the absence of a building contract, the keels of which are laid or which are at a similar stage of construction on or after 1 July 2013; or

.3 the delivery of which is on or after 1 January 2016.

2 Paragraph 3 shall not apply to combination carriers or chemical tankers as defined in regulations 1 of Annexes Ⅰ and Ⅱ, respectively, to the International Convention for the Prevention of Pollution from Ships, 1973, as modified by the Protocol of 1978 relating thereto. For the purpose of this regulation, chemical tankers also include chemical tankers certified to carry oil.

3 All cargo oil tanks of crude oil tankers shall be:

.1 coated during the construction of the ship in accordance with the *Performance standard for protective coatings for cargo oil tanks of crude oil tankers*, adopted by the Maritime Safety Committee by resolution MSC. 288 (87), as may be amended by the Organization, provided that such amendments are adopted, brought into force and take effect in accordance with the provisions of article Ⅷ of the present Convention concerning the amendment procedures applicable to the annex other than chapter Ⅰ; or

.2 protected by alternative means of corrosion protection or utilization of corrosion resistance material to maintain required structural integrity for 25 years in accordance with the *Performance standard for alternative means of corrosion protection for cargo oil tanks of crude oil tankers*, adopted by the Maritime Safety Committee by resolution MSC. 289 (87), as may be amended by the Organization, provided that such amendments are adopted, brought into force and take effect in accordance with the provisions of article Ⅷ of the present Convention concerning the amendment procedures applicable to the annex other than chapter Ⅰ.

4 The Administration may exempt a crude oil tanker from the requirements of paragraph 3 to allow the use of novel prototype alternatives to the coating system specified in paragraph 3.1, for testing, provided they are subject to suitable controls, regular assessment and acknowledgement of the need for immediate remedial action if the system fails or is shown to be failing. Such exemption shall be recorded on an exemption certificate.

5 The Administration may exempt a crude oil tanker from the requirements of paragraph 3 if the ship is built to be engaged solely in the carriage of cargoes and cargo handling operations not causing corrosion.① Such exemption and conditions for which it is granted shall be recorded on an exemption certificate.

Regulation 3-12
Protection against noise

1 This regulation shall apply to ships of 1,600 gross tonnage and above:

① Refer to *Guidelines on procedures for in-service maintenance and repair of coating systems for cargo oil tankers of crude oil tankers* (MSC.1/Circ.1399) and *Guidelines on exemptions for crude oil tankers solely engaged in the carriage of cargoes and cargo-handling operations not causing corrosion* (MSC.1/Circ.1421).

.2　如果无建造合同,在2013年7月1日或之后安放龙骨或处于相似建造阶段的;或

.3　在2016年1月1日或之后交船的。

2　第3款不适用于分别在《经1978年议定书修订的〈1973年国际防止船舶造成污染公约〉》附则Ⅰ和附则Ⅱ第1条中界定的兼用船和化学品船。就本条规定而言,化学品船也包括其证书中规定可载运油类的化学品船。

3　原油油船的所有货油舱须:

.1　按照海上安全委员会以第MSC.288(87)号决议通过的《原油油船货油舱保护涂层性能标准》,在船舶建造时涂装涂层,该标准可由本组织修正,但修正案须按照本公约关于附则除第Ⅰ章外的适用修正程序的第Ⅷ条予以通过、生效和施行;或

.2　按照海上安全委员会以第MSC.289(87)号决议通过的《原油油船货油舱防腐保护替代方法性能标准》,以替代防腐方法或使用耐腐蚀材料获得保护,以保持所要求的结构完整性达25年,该标准可由本组织修正,但修正案须按照本公约关于附则除第Ⅰ章外的适用修正程序的第Ⅷ条予以通过、生效和施行。

4　主管机关可免除原油油船适用第3款的要求,以允许使用第3.1款规定的新颖原型替代涂层系统进行试验,但要对其进行适当监控、定期评估,并且在确认一旦该系统失灵或显示出会失灵时,立即采取纠正措施。此项免除须记录在免除证书中。

5　如果一艘原油油船仅为运输和装卸不会造成腐蚀①的货物而建造,主管机关可免除该船适用第3款的要求。此项免除及批准免除的条件须记录在免除证书中。

第3-12条
噪声的防护

1　本条须适用于1 600总吨及以上和:

① 参见《原油油船货油舱涂层在役期间维护和修理程序导则》(第MSC.1/Circ.1399号通函)和《仅用于运输和装卸不会造成腐蚀货物的原油油船免除导则》(第MSC.1/Circ.1421号通函)。

.1 for which the building contract is placed on or after 1 July 2014; or

.2 in the absence of a building contract, the keels of which are laid or which are at a similar stage of construction on or after 1 January 2015; or

.3 the delivery of which is on or after 1 July 2018,

unless the Administration deems that compliance with a particular provision is unreasonable or impractical.

2 On ships delivered before 1 July 2018 and:

.1 contracted for construction before 1 July 2014 and the keels of which are laid or which are at a similar stage of construction on or after 1 January 2009; or

.2 in the absence of a building contract, the keels of which are laid or which are at a similar stage of construction on or after 1 January 2009 but before 1 January 2015,

measures① shall be taken to reduce machinery noise in machinery spaces to acceptable levels as determined by the Administration②. If this noise cannot be sufficiently reduced the source of excessive noise shall be suitably insulated or isolated or a refuge from noise shall be provided if the space is required to be manned. Ear protectors shall be provided for personnel required to enter such spaces, if necessary.

3 Ships shall be constructed to reduce onboard noise and to protect personnel from the noise in accordance with the Code on Noise Levels on Board Ships, adopted by the Maritime Safety Committee by resolution MSC.337(91), as may be amended by the Organization, provided that such amendments are adopted, brought into force and take effect in accordance with the provisions of article Ⅷ of the present Convention concerning the amendment procedures applicable to the annex other than chapter Ⅰ. For the purpose of this regulation, although the Code on Noise Levels on Board Ships is treated as a mandatory instrument, recommendatory parts as specified in chapter Ⅰ of the Code shall be treated as non-mandatory, provided that amendments to such recommendatory parts are adopted by the Maritime Safety Committee in accordance with its Rules of Procedure.

4 Notwithstanding the requirements of paragraph 1, this regulation does not apply to types of ships listed in paragraph 1.3.4 of the Code on Noise Levels on Board Ships.

① Refer to the *Code on Noise Levels on Board Ships* (resolution A.468(Ⅻ)).

② Refer to *Guidelines for the reduction of underwater noise from commercial shipping to address adverse impacts on marine life* (MEPC.1/Circ.833).

.1　2014年7月1日或之后签订建造合同；或

.2　如无建造合同，2015年1月1日或之后安放龙骨或处于类似建造阶段；或

.3　2018年7月1日或之后交付的船舶，

但主管机关认为符合某一特定规定为不合理或不切实际者除外。

2　对于2018年7月1日之前交付和：

.1　2014年7月1日之前签订建造合同，并且在2009年1月1日或之后安放龙骨或处于类似建造阶段；或

.2　如无建造合同，2009年1月1日或之后，但在2015年1月1日之前安放龙骨或处于类似建造阶段的船舶，

应采取措施①将机器处所内的机器噪声降至主管机关确定的可接受等级②。如果不能充分降低该噪声，应对过度噪声源进行适当绝缘或隔离或，如果该处所要求有人值班，提供噪声庇护所。如必要，应对进入该类处所的人员提供听力保护用具。

3　船舶的构造须按照《船上噪声等级规则》降低船上噪声并保护人员免受噪声伤害。该规则由海上安全委员会以第MSC.337(91)号决议通过并可经本组织修正，但其修正案须按照本公约第Ⅷ条有关附则除第Ⅰ章外的适用修正程序的规定予以通过、生效和实施。就本条而言，虽然《船上噪声级规则》被视为强制性文件，但规则第Ⅰ章的建议性部分须被视为具有非强制性，条件是该建议性部分的修正案应由海上安全委员会按其议事规则予以通过。

4　尽管有本条第1款的要求，本条不适用于《船上噪声等级规则》第1.3.4款所列的船型。

---

①　参见《船舶噪声等级规则》(第A.468(Ⅻ)号决议)。
②　参见《为避免对海洋生物造成不良影响减小商船水下噪声导则》(第MSC.1/Circ.833号通函)。

Part B
Subdivision and stability

Regulation 4
General

1 Unless expressly provided otherwise, the requirements in parts B-1 to B-4 shall apply to passenger ships.

2 For cargo ships, the requirements in parts B-1 to B-4 shall apply as follows:

.1 In part B-1:

.1 unless expressly provided otherwise, regulation 5 shall apply to cargo ships and regulation 5-1 shall apply to cargo ships other than tankers, as defined in regulation Ⅰ/2(h);

.2 regulation 6 to regulation 7-3 shall apply to cargo ships having a length (L) of 80 m and upwards, but may exclude those ships subject to the following instruments and shown to comply with the subdivision and damage stability requirements of that instrument:

.1 Annex Ⅰ to MARPOL, except that combination carriers (as defined in SOLAS regulation Ⅱ-2/3.14) with type B freeboards shall be in compliance with regulation 6 to regulation 7-3;[①] or

.2 the International Code for the Construction and Equipment of Ships Carrying Dangerous Chemicals in Bulk (IBC Code);[①] or

.3 the International Code for the Construction and Equipment of Ships Carrying Liquefied Gases in Bulk (IGC Code);[①] or

.4 the damage stability requirements of regulation 27 of the 1966 Load Lines Convention as applied in compliance with resolutions A.320(Ⅸ) and A.514(13), provided that in the case of cargo ships to which regulation 27(9) applies, main transverse watertight bulkheads, to be considered effective, are spaced according to paragraph (12)(f) of resolution A.320(Ⅸ), except that ships intended for the carriage of deck cargo shall be in compliance with regulation 6 to regulation 7-3; or

.5 the damage stability requirements of regulation 27 of the 1988 Load Lines Protocol, except that ships intended for the carriage of deck cargo shall be in compliance with regulation 6 to regulation 7-3; or

① Refer to *Guidelines for verification of damage stability requirements for tankers* (MSC.1/Circ.1461).

B 部分
分舱与稳性

第 4 条
通则

1　除非另有明确规定，第 B-1 至 B-4 部分的要求须适用于客船。

2　对于货船，第 B-1 至 B-4 部分的要求须按如下适用：

.1　在第 B-1 部分中：

.1　除另有明文规定，第 5 条须适用于货船，第 5-1 条应适用于除第Ⅰ/2(h)条定义的液货船以外的货船；

.2　第 6 至 7-3 条须适用于船长(L)80 m 及以上的货船，但受下述文件约束并经证明符合该文件中分舱和破损稳性要求的船舶可除外：

.1　《防污公约》附则Ⅰ，但 B 型干舷兼装船(《安全公约》第Ⅱ-2/3.14 条定义的)须符合第 6 至 7-3 条[①]；或

.2　《国际散装运输危险化学品船舶构造和设备规则》(国际散化规则)[①]；或

.3　《国际散装运输液化气体船舶构造和设备规则》(国际气体船规则)[①]；或

.4　按第 A.320(Ⅸ)和 A.514(13)号决议执行的《1966 年载重线公约》第 27 条的破损稳性要求，但对适用第 27(9)条的货船，视为有效的主水密横舱壁应按第 A.320(Ⅸ)号决议第(12)(f)款予以间隔，但拟运输甲板货的船舶应符合第 6 至 7-3 条；或

.5　《1988 年载重线议定书》第 27 条对破损稳性的要求，但拟运输甲板货的船舶应符合第 6 至 7-3 条；或

---

①　参见《液货船破损稳性要求验证导则》(第 MSC.1/Circ.1461 号通函)。

.6 the subdivision and damage stability standards in other instruments① developed by the Organization.

.2 Unless expressly provided otherwise, the requirements in parts B-2 and B-4 shall apply to cargo ships.

3 The Administration may, for a particular ship or group of ships, accept alternative methodologies if it is satisfied that at least the same degree of safety as represented by these regulations is achieved. Any Administration which allows such alternative methodologies shall communicate to the Organization particulars thereof.

4 Ships shall be as efficiently subdivided as is possible having regard to the nature of the service for which they are intended. The degree of subdivision shall vary with the subdivision length (L_s) of the ship and with the service, in such manner that the highest degree of subdivision corresponds with the ships of greatest subdivision length (L_s), primarily engaged in the carriage of passengers.

5 Where it is proposed to fit decks, inner skins or longitudinal bulkheads of sufficient tightness to seriously restrict the flow of water, the Administration shall be satisfied that proper consideration is given to beneficial or adverse effects of such structures in the calculations.

① .1 For offshore supply vessels of not more than 100 m in length (L), the *Guidelines for the design and construction of offshore supply vessels*, *2006* (resolution MSC.235(82), as amended by resolution MSC.335(90)); or

.2 For special purpose ships, the *Code of Safety for Special Purpose Ships*, *2008* (resolution MSC.266(84), as amended).

.6　本组织制定的其他文书中的分舱和破损稳性标准①。

.2　除另有明文规定，第 B-2 和 B-4 部分的要求应适用于货船。

3　对特定船舶或特定类别船舶采用的替代方法，主管机关如确信至少可达到本部分规则所体现的同等安全程度，可予以接受。任何允许采用此类替代方法的主管机关，应将其详细资料送交本组织。

4　船舶应按其预定的用途尽可能做有效的分舱。分舱的程度应视船舶的分舱长度（L_s）与用途而变化，以载客为主的船舶，其分舱长度越大则分舱程度越高。

5　凡拟装设足够密性的甲板、内壳板或纵舱壁以严格限制水的流动者，在计算中对此类结构的有益或不利影响所做的适当考虑，应使主管机关满意。

① .1　对于船长（L）不超过 100 m 的近海供应船，参见《2006 年近海供应船设计和建造导则》（第 MSC.235（82）号决议，经第 MSC.335（90）号决议修正）；或

.2　对于特种用途船舶，参见《2008 年特种用途船舶安全规则》（经修正的第 MSC.266（84）号决议）。

Part B-1
Stability

Regulation 5
Intact stability

1 Every passenger ship, regardless of size, and every cargo ship having a length (L) of 24 m and upwards, shall be inclined upon its completion. The lightship displacement and the longitudinal, transverse and vertical position of its centre of gravity shall be determined. In addition to any other applicable requirements of the present regulations, ships having a length of 24 m and upwards shall as a minimum comply with the requirements of part A of the 2008 IS Code.

2 The Administration may allow the inclining test of an individual cargo ship to be dispensed with, provided basic stability data are available from the inclining test of a sister ship and it is shown to the satisfaction of the Administration that reliable stability information for the exempted ship can be obtained from such basic data, as required by regulation 5-1. A lightweight survey shall be carried out upon completion and the ship shall be inclined whenever, in comparison with the data derived from the sister ship, a deviation from the lightship displacement exceeding 1% for ships of 160 m or more in length and 2% for ships of 50 m or less in length and as determined by linear interpolation for intermediate lengths or a deviation from the lightship longitudinal centre of gravity exceeding 0.5% of L is found.

3 The Administration may also allow the inclining test of an individual ship or class of ships especially designed for the carriage of liquids or ore in bulk to be dispensed with when reference to existing data for similar ships clearly indicates that, due to the ship's proportions and arrangements, more than sufficient metacentric height will be available in all probable loading conditions.

4 Where any alterations are made to a ship so as to materially affect the stability information supplied to the master, amended stability information shall be provided. If necessary, the ship shall be re-inclined. The ship shall be re-inclined if anticipated deviations exceed one of the values specified in paragraph 5.

5 At periodical intervals not exceeding 5 years, a lightweight survey shall be carried out on all passenger ships to verify any changes in lightship displacement and longitudinal centre of gravity. The ship shall be re-inclined whenever, in comparison with the approved stability information, a deviation from the lightship displacement exceeding 2% or a deviation of the longitudinal centre of gravity exceeding 1% of L is found or anticipated.

6 Every ship shall have scales of draughts marked clearly at the bow and stern. In the case where the draught marks are not located where they are easily readable, or operational constraints for a particular trade make it difficult to read the draught marks, then the ship shall also be fitted with a reliable draught indicating system by which the bow and stern draughts can be determined.

B-1 部分
稳性

第 5 条
完整稳性资料

1 每艘客船不论其大小,以及船长(L)在 24 m 及以上的每艘货船,须在完工时进行倾斜试验。须确定空船排水量和其重心的纵向、横向和垂向位置。除现行规则的任何其他适用要求外,船长在 24 m 及以上的船舶还须至少符合《2008 IS 规则》A 部分的要求。

2 主管机关可允许对某一货船免除倾斜试验,但须具有其姊妹船所做倾斜试验的基本稳性数据,且令主管机关满意地认为可以从第 5-1 条要求的这些基本数据中获得被免除船舶的可靠稳性资料。在船舶完工时须进行空船重量测量,而且只要与从姊妹船获得的数据相比,空船排水量偏差就船长为 160 m 或以上船舶而言超过 1%,就船长为 50 m 或以下船舶而言超过 2%,就中间长度的船舶而言超过线性内插法确定的百分比,或发现空船纵向稳心高度偏差超过 L 的 0.5%,则须进行倾斜试验。

3 如果参考类似船舶的已有数据,清楚表示该船的尺度比例及布置,在所有可能的装载工况下具有足够有余的初稳性高度时,主管机关也可允许个别船舶或某一类船舶免做倾斜试验,特别是专门设计用于载运散装液体货物或矿砂的船舶。

4 如果船舶做某种改装而对向船长提供的稳性资料有实质性影响时,应提供经修正的稳性资料。必要时,船舶应重做倾斜试验。如果预计偏差超过本条 5 所规定的值之一,船舶应重做倾斜试验。

5 所有客船均应在不超过五年的间隔期内进行空船排水量检验,以验证空船排水量和纵向重心高度的任何变化。当与经核准的稳性资料相比,发现或预料到空船排水量偏差超过 2%,或纵向重心高度偏差超过 L 的 1%时,则须重新进行倾斜试验。

6 每艘船舶在船首和船尾应清楚标示吃水的水尺,如果水尺标志并非位于可见的位置,或因特定业务的操作限制而难以见到水尺标志时,船上应装设一套可靠的能确定首、尾吃水的吃水显示系统。

Regulation 5-1
Stability information to be supplied to the master[①]

1 The master shall be supplied with such information to the satisfaction of the Administration as is necessary to enable him by rapid and simple processes to obtain accurate guidance as to the stability of the ship under varying conditions of service. A copy of the stability information shall be furnished to the Administration.

2 The information should include:

.1 curves or tables of minimum operational metacentric height (*GM*) and maximum permissible trim versus draught which assures compliance with the intact and damage stability requirements where applicable, alternatively corresponding curves or tables of the maximum allowable vertical centre of gravity (*KG*) and maximum permissible trim versus draught, or with the equivalents of either of these curves or tables;

.2 instructions concerning the operation of cross-flooding arrangements; and

.3 all other data and aids which might be necessary to maintain the required intact stability and stability after damage.

3 The intact and damage stability information required by regulation 5-1.2 shall be presented as consolidated data and encompass the full operating range of draught and trim[②]. Applied trim values shall coincide in all stability information intended for use on board. Information not required for determination of stability and trim limits should be excluded from this information.

4 If the damage stability is calculated in accordance with regulation 6 to regulation 7-3 and, if applicable, with regulations 8 and 9.8, a stability limit curve is to be determined using linear interpolation between the minimum required *GM* assumed for each of the three draughts d_s, d_p, and d_l. When additional subdivision indices are calculated for different trims, a single envelope curve based on the minimum values from these calculations shall be presented. When it is intended to develop curves of maximum permissible *KG* it shall be ensured that the resulting maximum *KG* curves correspond with a linear variation of *GM*.

5 As an alternative to a single envelope curve, the calculations for additional trims may be carried out with one common *GM* for all of the trims assumed at each subdivision draught. The lowest values of each partial index A_s, A_p, and A_l across these trims shall then be used in the summation of the attained subdivision index *A* according to regulation 7.1. This will result in one *GM* limit curve based on the GM used at each draught. *A* trim limit diagram showing the assumed trim range shall be developed.

6 When curves or tables of minimum operational metacentric height (*GM*) or maximum allowable *KG* versus draught are not provided, the master shall ensure that the operating condition does not deviate from approved loading conditions, or verify by calculation that the stability requirements are satisfied for this loading condition.

---

① Refer also to the *Guidelines for the preparation of intact stability information* (MSC/Circ.456) and the *Revised guidance to the master for avoiding dangerous situations in adverse weather and sea conditions* (MSC.1/Circ.1228).

② Refer to *Guidelines for verification of damage stability requirements for tankers* (MSC.1/Circ.1461).

第5-1条
向船长提供的资料[①]

1 为使船长能在不同营运状态下迅速和简便地获得有关船舶稳性的准确指导，应向他提供令主管机关满意的所需资料。应将稳性资料的一份副本提供给主管机关。

2 这些资料应包括：

.1 确保符合有关完整和破损稳性要求的最小营运稳心高度（*GM*）与最大许用纵倾对吃水的关系曲线或表格（如适用），也可选择相应的最大许用重心高度（*KG*）与最大许用纵倾对吃水的关系曲线或表格，或与这些曲线图等效的其他资料；

.2 有关横贯进水装置的操作说明；和

.3 破损后维持要求的完整稳性和稳性所必需的所有其他数据和辅助措施。

3 第5-1.2条要求的完整和破损稳性资料须作为整体数据一并提供，并须包含所有营运吃水和纵倾范围[②]。船上拟使用的所有稳性资料中的适用纵倾值应一致。确定稳性和纵倾限值无须用到的信息不应包含在本资料中。

4 如果按第6至7-3条和第8至9.8条（如适用）计算破损稳性，应对 d_s、d_p 和 d_l 三种吃水中每种吃水所假定的最小要求 *GM*，采用线性内插法获得稳性限值曲线。当按不同纵倾计算附加分舱指数时，须能呈现基于这些计算取得的最小值基础上的单包络曲线。当拟绘制最大许用 *KG* 曲线时，应确保获得的最大 *KG* 曲线与 *GM* 的线性变化一致。

5 对于单包络曲线的替代，可对每一分舱吃水处假定的所有纵倾采用一个通用 *GM*，计算附加纵倾。然后按照第7.1条，采用按这些纵倾的每一部分指数 A_s、A_p 和 A_l 的最小值，求和得出达到的分舱指数 *A*。基于每一吃水处的 *GM*，将产生一条 *GM* 限值曲线。应绘制能显示假定纵倾范围的纵倾限值图。

6 如未提供最小营运稳心高度（*GM*）或最大许用 *KG* 对吃水的曲线图或表格，船长应确保营运工况不会偏离经批准的装载工况，或通过计算验证符合该装载工况的稳性要求。

① 参见《完整稳性资料编制指南》（第MSC/Circ.456号通函）；《现有液货船驳运作业时的完整稳性导则》（第MSC/Circ.706号通函）；以及《经修订的船长在恶劣气候条件和海况下避免险情导则》（第MSC.1/Circ.1228号通函）。

② 参见《液货船破损稳性要求核验导则》（第MSC.1/Circ.1461号通函）。

Regulation 6
Required subdivision index R[①]

1 The subdivision of a ship is considered sufficient if the attained subdivision index A, determined in accordance with regulation 7, is not less than the required subdivision index R calculated in accordance with this regulation and if, in addition, the partial indices A_s, A_p and A_l are not less than 0.9 R for passenger ships and 0.5 R for cargo ships.

2 For ships to which the damage stability requirements of this part apply, the degree of subdivision to be provided shall be determined by the required subdivision index R, as follows:

.1 In the case of cargo ships greater than 100 m in length (L_s):

$$R=1-\frac{128}{L_s+152}$$

.2 In the case of cargo ships not less than 80 m in length (L_s) and not greater than 100 m in length (L_s):

$$R=1-\frac{1}{1+\frac{L_s}{100}\times\frac{R_o}{1-R_o}}$$

where R_o is the value R as calculated in accordance with the formula in subparagraph.1.

.3 In the case of passenger ships:

Persons on board	R
$N<400$	$R=0.722$
$400\leqslant N\leqslant 1,350$	$R=\frac{N}{7,580}+0.66923$
$1,350<N\leqslant 6,000$	$R=0.0369\times\ln(N+89.048)+0.579$
$N>6,000$	$R=1-\frac{852.5+0.03875\times N}{N+5,000}$

where:
N= total number of persons on board.

① The Maritime Safety Committee, in adopting the regulations contained in parts B to B-4, invited Administrations to note that the regulations should be applied in conjunction with the explanatory notes developed by the Organization in order to ensure their uniform application.

第 6 条
要求的分舱指数 *R*[①]

1 如按第 7 条确定的达到的分舱指数 A 不小于按本条计算的要求的分舱指数 R，此外，如部分指数 A_s、A_p 和 A_l 对客船不小于 0.9 R 及对货船不小于 0.5 R，则船舶分舱可视为足够。

2 对适用本部分破损稳性要求的船舶，所具备的分舱程度须由以下所要求的分舱指数 R 来确定：

.1 对船长（L_s）大于 100 m 的船舶：

$$R = 1 - \frac{128}{L_s + 152}$$

.2 对船长（L_s）不小于 80 m，但不大于 100 m 的船舶：

$$R = 1 - \frac{1}{1 + \frac{L_s}{100} \times \frac{R_o}{1 - R_o}}$$

式中：R_o 为按本条 2.1 中公式计算的 R 值。

.3 对客船：

船上人数	R
$N<400$	$R=0.722$
$400 \leqslant N \leqslant 1\ 350$	$R=\frac{N}{7\ 580}+0.66923$
$1\ 350<N \leqslant 6\ 000$	$R=0.0369 \times \ln(N+89.048)+0.579$
$N>6\ 000$	$R=1-\frac{852.5+0.03875 \times N}{N+5\ 000}$

式中：

N = 船上总人数。

① 海上安全委员会在通过 B 至 B-4 部分的规则时，曾提请各国主管机关注意，这些规则应结合本组织为确保其统一执行规则而制定的解释性说明一起执行。

Regulation 7
Attained subdivision index *A*

1 An attained subdivision index A is obtained by the summation of the partial indices A_s, A_p, and A_l, (weighted as shown and calculated for the draughts d_s, d_p, and d_l defined in regulation 2 in accordance with the following formula:

$$A = 0.4A_s + 0.4A_p + 0.2A_l$$

Each partial index is a summation of contributions from all damage cases taken in consideration, using the following formula:

$$A = \sum p_i s_i$$

Where:

i represents each compartment or group of compartments under consideration,

p_i accounts for the probability that only the compartment or group of compartments under consideration may be flooded, disregarding any horizontal subdivision, as defined in regulation 7-1,

s_i accounts for the probability of survival after flooding the compartment or group of compartments under consideration, and includes the effect of any horizontal subdivision, as defined in regulation 7-2.

2 As a minimum, the calculation of A shall be carried out at the level trim for the deepest subdivision draught d_s and the partial subdivision draught d_p. The estimated service trim may be used for the light service draught d_l. If, in any anticipated service condition within the draught range from d_s to d_l, the trim variation in comparison with the calculated trims is greater than 0.5% of L, one or more additional calculations of A are to be performed for the same draughts but including sufficient trims to ensure that, for all intended service conditions, the difference in trim in comparison with the reference trim used for one calculation will be not more than 0.5% of L. Each additional calculation of A shall comply with regulation 6.1.

3 When determining the positive righting lever (GZ) of the residual stability curve in the intermediate and final equilibrium stages of flooding, the displacement used should be that of the intact loading condition. All calculations should be done with the ship freely trimming.

4 The summation indicated by the above formula shall be taken over the ship's subdivision length (L_s) for all cases of flooding in which a single compartment or two or more adjacent compartments are involved. In the case of unsymmetrical arrangements, the calculated A value should be the mean value obtained from calculations involving both sides. Alternatively, it should be taken as that corresponding to the side which evidently gives the least favourable result.

第7条
达到的分舱指数 A

1 达到的分舱指数 A 由按第2条定义的吃水 d_s、d_p 和 d_l 计算所得的如所示加权的局部指数 A_s、A_p 和 A_l 的总和求得，按下式计算：

$$A=0.4A_s+0.4A_p+0.2A_l$$

每个部分指数均为所考虑的全部破损情况所起作用的总和，所用公式如下：

$$A=\sum p_i s_i$$

式中：

i——表示所考虑的每一个舱或舱组；

p_i——如同第7-1条的定义，表示所考虑的舱或舱组可能进水的概率，不考虑任何水平分隔；

s_i——如同第7-2条的定义，表示所考虑的舱或舱组进水后生存概率，并包括任何水平分隔的影响。

2 应至少对最深分舱吃水 d_s 和局部分舱吃水 d_p 采用水平纵倾来计算 A。可将估算的营运纵倾用于轻载航行吃水 d_l。如果在 d_s 至 d_l 吃水范围内的任何预计营运工况下，与计算所得的纵倾相比较，纵倾变量大于 L 的0.5%，则需按相同吃水但包含足够纵倾进行一次或以上 A 的附加计算，使所有拟用营运工况下的纵倾与用于一次计算的参考纵倾相比较，纵倾的差异将小于 L 的0.5%。对于每一个 A 的附加计算须符合第6.1条。

3 在确定进水的中间和最终平衡阶段的剩余稳性曲线的正复原力臂（GZ）时，所用排水量应为完整装载工况的排水量。所有计算应在船舶自由纵倾下进行。

4 上述公式所表示的总和应计及整船分舱长度（L_s）范围内单个舱或两个或更多相邻舱进水的所有情况。对于非对称布置，A 的计算值应为按两舷所作计算求得的平均值。或者，该值相应于明显得出最不利结果的一舷计取。

5 Wherever wing compartments are fitted, contribution to the summation indicated by the formula shall be taken for all cases of flooding in which wing compartments are involved. Additionally, cases of simultaneous flooding of a wing compartment or group of compartments and the adjacent inboard compartment or group of compartments, but excluding damage of transverse extent greater than one half of the ship breadth B, may be added. For the purpose of this regulation, transverse extent is measured inboard from ship's side, at right angles to the centreline at the level of the deepest subdivision draught.

6 In the flooding calculations carried out according to the regulations, only one breach of the hull and only one free surface need to be assumed. The assumed vertical extent of damage is to extend from the baseline upwards to any watertight horizontal subdivision above the waterline or higher. However, if a lesser extent of damage will give a more severe result, such extent is to be assumed.

7 If pipes, ducts or tunnels are situated within the assumed extent of damage, arrangements are to be made to ensure that progressive flooding cannot thereby extend to compartments other than those assumed flooded. However, the Administration may permit minor progressive flooding if it is demonstrated that its effects can be easily controlled and the safety of the ship is not impaired.

Regulation 7-1
Calculation of the factor p_i

1 The factor p_i, for a compartment or group of compartments shall be calculated in accordance with paragraphs 1.1 and 1.2 using the following notations:

j = the aftmost damage zone number involved in the damage starting with No.1 at the stern;

n = the number of adjacent damage zones involved in the damage;

k = the number of a particular longitudinal bulkhead as barrier for transverse penetration in a damage zone counted from shell towards the centreline. The shell has $k = 0$;

$x1$ = the distance from the aft terminal of L_s to the aft end of the zone in question;

$x2$ = the distance from the aft terminal of L_s to the forward end of the zone in question;

b = the mean transverse distance in metres measured at right angles to the centreline at the deepest subdivision draught between the shell and an assumed vertical plane extended between the longitudinal limits used in calculating the factor p_i and which is a tangent to, or common with, all or part of the outermost portion of the longitudinal bulkhead under consideration. This vertical plane shall be so orientated that the mean transverse distance to the shell is a maximum, but not more than twice the least distance between the plane and the shell. If the upper part of a longitudinal bulkhead is below the deepest subdivision draught the vertical plane used for determination of b is assumed to extend upwards to the deepest subdivision waterline. In any case, b is not to be taken greater than $B/2$.

If the damage involves a single zone only:

5 如果设有边舱，边舱进水的所有情况应加入公式所表示的总和中。此外，边舱或舱组和其相邻的内侧舱或舱组同时进水的情况也可加入总和，但横向范围大于一半船宽 B 的破损除外。就本条而言，横向范围从舷侧向内垂直于最深分舱吃水线处的中线量取。

6 在根据规则进行进水计算时，只需假定船壳有一个破洞以及只有一个自由液面。破损的垂向范围假定为从基线向上扩展至水线以上或更高的任一水密水平分隔。然而，如果一个较小范围的破损会产生更为严重的后果，则须假定为该范围。

7 如果在假定破损范围内设有管子、管道或管隧，其布置应确保累进进水不会扩展到那些假定进水的舱室以外的其他舱室。然而，如果证实累进进水的影响能易于控制并且不损害船舶的安全，则主管机关可允许较小的累进进水。

第7-1条
因数 p_i 的计算

1 应按本条1.1和1.2并使用下列符号计算一个舱或舱组的因数 p_i：

j = 船尾以1起始的破损范围内最后部破损区编号；
n = 破损范围内相邻破损区编号；

k = 作为破损区横向穿透屏障的特定纵舱壁编号，从船壳向中心线计数。在船壳处的 $k = 0$；

$x1$ = 从 L_s 的后端点到所考虑的区后端的距离；

$x2$ = 从 L_s 的后端点到所考虑的区前端的距离；

b = 在最深分舱吃水处与中线成直角的、船壳板至假定垂直平面之间的平均横向距离（米），该垂直平面介于计算 p_i 因素所用的纵向极限之间，并与所考虑的纵舱壁离中心最远部分的全部或部分相切或相同。该垂直平面的定位方式须为：至船壳板的横向平均距离为最大值，但不超过平面至船壳板最小距离的两倍。如果纵舱壁的上部分在最深分舱吃水以下，则可假定用于确定 b 的垂直平面向上延伸至最深分舱水线。无论如何，所取的 b 不得大于 $B/2$。

如果破损仅涉及单个区：

$$p_i = p(x1_j, x2_j) \cdot [r(x1_j, x2_j, b_k) - r(x1_j, x2_j, b_{k-1})]$$

If the damage involves two adjacent zones:

$$p_i = p(x1_j, x2_{j+1}) \cdot [r(x1_j, x2_{j+1}, b_k) - r(x1_j, x2_{j+1}, b_{k-1})] - p(x1_j, x2_j) \cdot [r(x1_j, x2_j, b_k) - r(x1_j, x2_j, b_{k-1})] - p(x1_{j+1}, x2_{j+1}) \cdot [r(x1_{j+1}, x2_{j+1}, b_k) - r(x1_{j+1}, x2_{j+1}, b_{k-1})]$$

If the damage involves three or more adjacent zones:

$$p_i = p(x1_j, x2_{j+n-1}) \cdot [r(x1_j, x2_{j+n-1}, b_k) - r(x1_j, x2_{j+n-1}, b_{k-1})] - p(x1_j, x2_{j+n-2}) \cdot [r(x1_j, x2_{j+n-2}, b_k) - r(x1_j, x2_{j+n-2}, b_{k-1})] - p(x1_{j+1}, x2_{j+n-1}) \cdot [r(x1_{j+1}, x2_{j+n-1}, b_k) - r(x1_{j+1}, x2_{j+n-1}, b_{k-1})] + p(x1_{j+1}, x2_{j+n-2}) \cdot [r(x1_{j+1}, x2_{j+n-2}, b_k) - r(x1_{j+1}, x2_{j+n-2}, b_{k-1})]$$

and where $r(x1, x2, b_0) = 0$.

1.1 The factor $p(x1, x2)$ is to be calculated according to the following formulae:

Overall normalized max damage length: $J_{max} = 10/33$

Knuckle point in the distribution: $J_{kn} = 5/33$

Cumulative probability at J_{kn}: $P_k = 11/12$

Maximum absolute damage length: $l_{max} = 60$ m

Length where normalized distribution ends: $L^* = 260$ m

Probability density at $J = 0$:

$$b_0 = 2\left(\frac{p_k}{J_{kn}} - \frac{1-p_k}{J_{max} - J_{kn}}\right)$$

When $L_s \leqslant L^*$:

$$J_m = \min\left(J_{max}, \frac{l_{max}}{L_s}\right)$$

$$J_k = \frac{J_m}{2} + \frac{1 - \sqrt{1 + (1-2p_k) b_0 J_m + \frac{1}{4} b_0^2 J_m^2}}{b_0}$$

$$b_{12} = b_0$$

When $L_s > L^*$:

$$J_m^* = \min\left(J_{max}, \frac{l_{max}}{L^*}\right)$$

$$J_k = \frac{J_m^*}{2} + \frac{1 - \sqrt{1 + (1-2p_k) b_0 J_m^* + \frac{1}{4} b_0^2 J_m^{*2}}}{b_0}$$

$$p_i=p(x1_j,x2_j)\cdot[r(x1_j,x2_j,b_k)-r(x1_j,x2_j,b_{k-1})]$$

如果破损涉及两个相邻区：

$$p_i=p(x1_j,x2_{j+1})\cdot[r(x1_j,x2_{j+1},b_k)-r(x1_j,x2_{j+1},b_{k-1})]-p(x1_j,x2_j)\cdot[r(x1_j,x2_j,b_k)-r(x1_j,x2_j,b_{k-1})]-p(x1_{j+1},x2_{j+1})\cdot[r(x1_{j+1},x2_{j+1},b_k)-r(x1_{j+1},x2_{j+1},b_{k-1})]$$

如果破损涉及三个或更多相邻区：

$$p_i=p(x1_j,x2_{j+n-1})\cdot[r(x1_j,x2_{j+n-1},b_k)-r(x1_j,x2_{j+n-1},b_{k-1})]-p(x1_j,x2_{j+n-2})\cdot[r(x1_j,x2_{j+n-2},b_k)-r(x1_j,x2_{j+n-2},b_{k-1})]-p(x1_{j+1},x2_{j+n-1})\cdot[r(x1_{j+1},x2_{j+n-1},b_k)-r(x1_{j+1},x2_{j+n-1},b_{k-1})]+p(x1_{j+1},x2_{j+n-2})\cdot[r(x1_{j+1},x2_{j+n-2},b_k)-r(x1_{j+1},x2_{j+n-2},b_{k-1})]$$

式中：$r(x1,x2,b_0)=0$。

1.1 系数 $p(x1,x2)$ 按以下各式计算。

标准化最大破损总长： $J_{max}=10/33$

折角点分布： $J_{kn}=5/33$

在 J_{kn} 处累积概率： $p_k=11/12$

最大绝对破损长度： $l_{max}=60\ \text{m}$

标准化分布端点长度： $L^*=260\ \text{m}$

$J=0$ 时概率密度：

$$b_0=2\left(\frac{p_k}{J_{kn}}-\frac{1-p_k}{J_{max}-J_{kn}}\right)$$

当 $L_s\leqslant L^*$ 时：

$$J_m=\min\left(J_{max},\frac{l_{max}}{L_s}\right)$$

$$J_k=\frac{J_m}{2}+\frac{1-\sqrt{1+(1-2p_k)b_0J_m+\frac{1}{4}b_0^2J_m{}^2}}{b_0}$$

$$b_{12}=b_0$$

当 $L_s>L^*$ 时：

$$J_m^*=\min\left(J_{max},\frac{l_{max}}{L^*}\right)$$

$$J_k=\frac{J_m^*}{2}+\frac{1-\sqrt{1+(1-2p_k)b_0J_m^*+\frac{1}{4}b_0^2J_m^{*2}}}{b_0}$$

$$J_m = \frac{J_m^* \cdot I^*}{L_s}$$

$$J_k = \frac{J_k^* \cdot L^*}{L_s}$$

$$b_{12} = 2\left(\frac{p_k}{J_k} - \frac{1-p_k}{J_m - J_k}\right)$$

$$b_{11} = 4\frac{1-p_k}{(J_m - J_k)J_k} - 2\frac{p_k}{J_k^2}$$

$$b_{21} = -2\frac{1-p_k}{(J_m - J_k)^2}$$

$$b_{22} = -b_{21}J_m$$

The non-dimensional damage length:

$$J = \frac{(x2 - x1)}{L_s}$$

The normalized length of a compartment or group of compartments:

J_n is to be taken as the lesser of J and J_m

1.1.1 Where neither limit of the compartment or group of compartments under consideration coincides with the aft or forward terminals:

$J \leq J_k$:

$$p(x1, x2) = p_1 = \frac{1}{6}J^2(b_{11}J + 3b_{12})$$

$J > J_k$:

$$p(x1, x2) = p_2 = -\frac{1}{3}b_{11}J_k^3 + \frac{1}{2}(b_{11}J - b_{12})J_k^2 + b_{12}JJ_k - \frac{1}{3}b_{21}(J_n^3 - J_k^3) + \frac{1}{2}(b_{21}J - b_{22})(J_n^2 - J_k^2) + b_{22}J(J_n - J_k)$$

1.1.2 Where the aft limit of the compartment or group of compartments under consideration coincides with the aft terminal or the forward limit of the compartment or group of compartments under consideration coincides with the forward terminal:

$J \leq J_k$:

$$p(x1, x2) = \frac{1}{2}(p_1 + J)$$

$J \leq J_k$:

$$p(x1, x2) = \frac{1}{2}(p_2 + J)$$

$$J_m = \frac{J_m^* \cdot L^*}{L_s}$$

$$J_k = \frac{J_k^* \cdot L^*}{L_s}$$

$$b_{12} = 2\left(\frac{p_k}{J_k} - \frac{1-p_k}{J_m - J_k}\right)$$

$$b_{11} = 4\frac{1-p_k}{(J_m - J_k)J_k} - 2\frac{p_k}{J_k^2}$$

$$b_{21} = -2\frac{1-p_k}{(J_m - J_k)^2}$$

$$b_{22} = -b_{21}J_m$$

无因次破损长度：

$$J = \frac{(x2 - x1)}{L_s}$$

舱室或舱组标准化长度：

J_n 取为 J 和 J_m 的小者

1.1.1 如果所计及的舱或舱组的界限不与后端点或前端点重合：

$J \leqslant J_k$：

$$p(x1,\ x2) = p_1 = \frac{1}{6}J^2(b_{11}J + 3b_{12})$$

$J > J_k$：

$$p(x1,\ x2) = p_2 = -\frac{1}{3}b_{11}J_k^3 + \frac{1}{2}(b_{11}J - b_{12})J_k^2 + b_{12}JJ_k - \frac{1}{3}b_{21}(J_n^3 - J_k^3) + \frac{1}{2}(b_{21}J - b_{22})(J_n^2 - J_k^2) + b_{22}J(J_n - J_k)$$

1.1.2 如果所计及的舱或舱组的后部界限与后端点重合或所计及的舱或舱组的前部界限与前端点重合：

$J \leqslant J_k$：

$$p(x1,\ x2) = \frac{1}{2}(p_1 + J)$$

$J \leqslant J_k$：

$$p(x1,\ x2) = \frac{1}{2}(p_2 + J)$$

1.1.3 Where the compartment or groups of compartments considered extends over the entire subdivision length (L_s):

$$p(x1,x2) = 1$$

1.2 The factor $r(x1,x2,b)$ shall be determined by the following formuiae:

$$r(x1,x2,b) = 1-(1-C)\cdot\left(1-\frac{G}{p(x1,x2)}\right)$$

where:

$$C = 12\,J_b\cdot(-45\cdot J_b+4)\text{, where}$$

$$J_b = \frac{b}{15\cdot B}$$

1.2.1 Where the compartment or groups of compartments considered extends over the entire subdivision length (L_s):

$$G = G_1 = \frac{1}{2}b_{11}J_b^{\,2} + b_{12}J_b$$

1.2.2 Where neither limit of the compartment or group of compartments under consideration coincides with the aft or forward terminals:

$$G = G_2 = -\frac{1}{3}b_{11}J_0^{\,3} + \frac{1}{2}(b_{11}J-b_{12})J_0^{\,2} + b_{12}JJ_0\text{, where}$$

$$J_0 = \min(J,J_b)$$

1.2.3 Where the aft limit of the compartment or group of compartments under consideration coincides with the aft terminal or the forward limit of the compartment or group of compartments under consideration coincides with the forward terminal:

$$G = \frac{1}{2}(G_2 + G_1\cdot J)$$

Regulation 7-2
Calculation of the factor s_i

1 The factor s_i shall be determined for each case of assumed flooding, involving a compartment or group of compartments, in accordance with the following notations and the provisions in this regulation.

θ_e is the equilibrium heel angle in any stage of flooding, in degrees;

θ_v is the angle, in any stage of flooding, where the righting lever becomes negative, or the angle at which an opening incapable of being closed weathertight becomes submerged;

1.1.3　如果所计及的舱或舱组延伸至整个分舱长度（L_s）：

$$p(x1,x2)=1$$

1.2　系数 $r(x1,x2,b)$ 按以下各式计算：

$$r(x1,x2,b)=1-(1-C)\left(1-\frac{G}{p(x1,x2)}\right)$$

式中：

$$C=12\cdot J_b\cdot(-45\cdot J_b+4)\text{，其中}$$

$$J_b=\frac{b}{15\cdot B}$$

1.2.1　如果所计及的舱或舱组延伸至整个分舱长度（L_s）：

$$G=G_1=\frac{1}{2}b_{11}J_b^{\ 2}+b_{12}J_b$$

1.2.2　如果所计及的舱或舱组的界限不与后端点或前端点重合：

$$G=G_2=-\frac{1}{3}b_{11}J_0^{\ 3}+\frac{1}{2}(b_{11}J-b_{12})J_0^{\ 2}+b_{12}JJ_0\text{，其中}$$

$$J_0=\min(J,J_b)$$

1.2.3　如果所计及的舱或舱组的后部界限与后端点重合或所计及的舱或舱组的前部界限与前端点重合：

$$G=\frac{1}{2}(G_2+G_1\cdot J)$$

第 7-2 条
因数 s_i 的计算

1　应按照本条的以下注释和规定，确定每种假定进水情况下舱或舱组的因数 s_i。

θ_e 是任何进水阶段的平衡横倾角（°）；

θ_v 是任何进水阶段复原力臂变负的角度，或不能水密关闭的开口被水浸没的角度；

GZ_{max} is the maximum positive righting lever, in metres, up to the angle θ_v;

Range is the range of positive righting levers, in degrees, measured from the angle θ_e. The positive range is to be taken up to the angle θ_v;

Flooding stage is any discrete step during the flooding process, including the stage before equalization (if any), until final equilibrium has been reached.

1.1 The factor s_i, for any damage case at any initial loading condition, d_i, shall be obtained from the formula:

$$s_i = \text{minimum}\ (s_{intermediate,\ i}\ \text{or}\ s_{final,\ i} \cdot s_{mom,\ i})$$

Where:

$s_{intermediate,\ i}$ is the probability to survive all intermediate flooding stages until the final equilibrium stage, and is calculated in accordance with paragraph 2;

$s_{final,i}$ is the probability to survive in the final equilibrium stage of flooding. It is calculated in accordance with paragraph 3;

$s_{mom,i}$ is the probability to survive heeling moments, and is calculated in accordance with paragraph 4.

2 For passenger ships, and cargo ships fitted with cross-flooding devices, the factor $s_{intermediate,i}$ is taken as the least of the s-factors obtained from all flooding stages including the stage before equalization, if any, and is to be calculated as follows:

$$s_{intermediate,i} = \left(\frac{GZ_{max}}{0.05} \cdot \frac{Range}{7}\right)^{\frac{1}{4}}$$

where GZ_{max} is not to be taken as more than 0.05 m and *Range* as not more than 7°. $s_{intermediate,i} = 0$, if the intermediate heel angle exceeds 15° for passenger ships and 30° for cargo ships.

For cargo ships not fitted with cross-flooding devices the factor $s_{intermediate,i}$ is taken as unity, except if the Administration considers that the stability in intermediate stages of flooding may be insufficient, it should require further investigation thereof.

For passenger and cargo ships, where cross-flooding devices are fitted, the time for equalization shall not exceed 10 min.

3 The factor $s_{final,i}$, shall be obtained from the formula:

$$s_{final,i} = K \cdot \left(\frac{GZ_{max}}{TGZ_{max}} \cdot \frac{Range}{TRange}\right)^{\frac{1}{4}}$$

where:

GZ_{max} is not to be taken as more than TGZ_{max};

Range is not to be taken as more than *TRange*;

GZ_{max}是 θ_v 角范围内最大正复原力臂(m)；

范围是从 θ_e 角量取的正复原力臂范围(°)。正值范围取为达到 θ_v 角度；

进水阶段是进水过程中任何的一步，包括达到最终平衡之前的采取平衡措施前阶段(如果有)。

1.1　任何初始装载工况 d_i 下的任何破损情况的因数 s_i 应按下式计算：

$$s_i = \min(s_{intermediate,i} \text{或} s_{final,i} \cdot s_{mom,i})$$

式中：

$s_{intermediate,i}$是在最终平衡阶段之前所有进水中间阶段的残存概率，按本条2计算；

$s_{final,i}$是进水最终平衡阶段的残存概率，按本条3计算；

$s_{mom,i}$是经受住横倾力矩的残存概率，按本条4计算。

2　对于客船和设有横贯进水装置的货船，因数 $s_{intermediate,i}$取为所有进水阶段，包括采取平衡作业前阶段(如有)的最小 s-因数，按以下公式计算：

$$s_{intermediate,\ i} = \left(\frac{GZ_{max}}{0.05} \cdot \frac{Range}{7}\right)^{\frac{1}{4}}$$

式中所取 GZ_{max}不大于0.05 m且Range不大于7°。如果对于客船，中间横倾角大于15°，或对于货船，中间横倾角大于30°，则 $s_{intermediate,\ i} = 0$。

对于未设横贯进水装置的货船，因数 $s_{intermediate,\ i}$取值取1，除非如果主管机关认为在进水的中间阶段的稳性可能不足，则其应要求进行进一步调查。

对于设有横贯进水装置的客船和货船，平衡时间不得超过10 min。

3　因数 $s_{final,i}$应按以下公式计算：

$$s_{final,\ i} = K \cdot \left(\frac{GZ_{max}}{TGZ_{max}} \cdot \frac{Range}{TRange}\right)^{\frac{1}{4}}$$

式中：

GZ_{max}不大于 TGZ_{max}；

$Range$ 不大于 $TRange$；

TGZ_{max} = 0.20 m, for ro-ro passenger ships each damage case that involves a ro-ro space,

TGZ_{max} = 0.12 m, otherwise;

$TRange$ = 20°, for ro-ro passenger ships each damage case that involves a ro-ro space,

$TRange$ = 16°, otherwise;

$K = 1$ if $\theta_e \leqslant \theta_{min}$,

$K = 0$ if $\theta_e \geqslant \theta_{max}$,

$$K = \sqrt{\frac{\theta_{max} - \theta_e}{\theta_{max} - \theta_{min}}} \text{ otherwise},$$

where:

θ_{min} is 7° for passenger ships and 25° for cargo ships; and

θ_{max} is 15° for passenger ships and 30° for cargo ships.

4 The factor $s_{mom,i}$ is applicable only to passenger ships (for cargo ships $s_{mom,i}$ shall be taken as unity) and shall be calculated at the final equilibrium from the formula:

$$s_{mom,i} = \frac{(GZ_{max} - 0.04) \cdot Displacement}{M_{heel}}$$

where:

Displacement is the intact displacement at the subdivision draught (d_s, d_p or d_l);

M_{heel} is the maximum assumed heeling moment as calculated in accordance with paragraph 4.1; and

$s_{mom,i} \leqslant 1$

4.1 The heeling moment M_{heel} is to be calculated as follows:

$$M_{heel} = \text{maximum } (M_{passenger} \text{ or } M_{wind} \text{ or } M_{Survivalcraft})$$

4.1.1 $M_{passenger}$ is the maximum assumed heeling moment resulting from movement of passengers, and is to be obtained as follows:

$$M_{passenger} = (0.075 \cdot N_p) \cdot (0.45 \cdot B) \quad (t \cdot m)$$

where:

N_p is the maximum number of passengers permitted to be on board in the service condition corresponding to the deepest subdivision draught under consideration; and

B is the breadth of the ship as defined in regulation 2.8.

对于滚装客船涉及滚装处所的每一破损情况：$TGZ_{max}=0.20$ m，

对于其他情况：$TGZ_{max}=0.12$ m；

对于滚装客船涉及滚装处所的每一破损情况：$TRange=20°$，

对于其他情况：$TRange=16°$；

如果 $\theta_e \leqslant \theta_{min}$，$K=1$，

如果 $\theta_e \geqslant \theta_{max}$，$K=0$，

其他情况下，$K=\sqrt{\dfrac{\theta_{max}-\theta_e}{\theta_{max}-\theta_{min}}}$，

式中：

θ_{min}对于客船为7°，对于货船为25°；且

θ_{max}对于客船为15°，对于货船为30°。

4　因数$s_{mom,i}$仅适用于客船（对货船而言，$s_{mom,i}$应取一）且须在最终平衡状态下按以下公式计算：

$$s_{mom,i}=\frac{(GZ_{max}-0.04)\cdot Displacement}{M_{heel}}$$

式中：

排水量（Displacement）系指处于各相应吃水（d_s、d_p 或 d_l）时的完整排水量；

M_{heel}系指按照第4.1项计算所得的最大假定横倾力矩；和

$s_{mom,i} \leqslant 1$

4.1　横倾力矩 M_{heel}按以下公式计算：

$$M_{heel}=\text{maximum}(M_{passenger}\text{或}M_{wind}\text{或}M_{survivalcraft})$$

4.1.1　$M_{passenger}$系指乘客移动所导致的最大假定横倾力矩，并按以下公式计算：

$$M_{passenger}=(0.075\cdot N_p)\cdot(0.45\cdot B)\qquad(\text{t}\cdot\text{m})$$

式中：

N_p 系指对应所考虑的最深分舱吃水的营运条件下船上所允许运载的最大乘客数；和

B 系指按照第2.8条定义的船宽。

Alternatively, the heeling moment may be calculated assuming the passengers are distributed with 4 persons per square metre on available deck areas towards one side of the ship on the decks where muster stations are located and in such a way that they produce the most adverse heeling moment. In doing so, a weight of 75 kg per passenger is to be assumed.

4.1.2 M_{wind} is the maximum assumed wind moment acting in a damage situation:

$$M_{wind} = \frac{(P \cdot A \cdot Z)}{9{,}806} \qquad (t \cdot m)$$

where:

P = 120 N/m^2;

A = projected lateral area above waterline;

Z= distance from centre of lateral projected area above waterline to $T/2$; and

T = respective draught (d_s, d_p or d_l).

4.1.3 $M_{survivalcraft}$ is the maximum assumed heeling moment due to the launching of all fully loaded davit-launched survival craft on one side of the ship. It shall be calculated using the following assumptions:

.1 all lifeboats and rescue boats fitted on the side to which the ship has heeled after having sustained damage shall be assumed to be swung out fully loaded and ready for lowering;

.2 for lifeboats which are arranged to be launched fully loaded from the stowed position, the maximum heeling moment during launching shall be taken;

.3 a fully loaded davit-launched liferaft attached to each davit on the side to which the ship has heeled after having sustained damage shall be assumed to be swung out ready for lowering;

.4 persons not in the life-saving appliances which are swung out shall not provide either additional heeling or righting moment; and

.5 life-saving appliances on the side of the ship opposite to the side to which the ship has heeled shall be assumed to be in a stowed position.

5 Unsymmetrical flooding is to be kept to a minimum consistent with the efficient arrangements. Where it is necessary to correct large angles of heel, the means adopted shall, where practicable, be self-acting, but in any case where controls to equalization devices are provided they shall be operable from above the bulkhead deck of passenger ships and the freeboard deck of cargo ships. These fittings together with their controls shall be acceptable to the Administration.① Suitable information concerning the use of equalization devices shall be supplied to the master of the ship.

① Reference is made to the *Revised recommendation on a standard method for evaluating cross-flooding arrangements*, adopted by the Organization by resolution MSC.362(92), as may be amended.

或者,为计算横倾力矩,假定乘客按照每平方米4人分布在集合站所在的各层甲板的一舷可供站立的甲板区域,且其产生最不利的横倾力矩。这样的话,则可以假定每名乘客的重量为75 kg。

4.1.2 M_{wind}系指在破损情况下产生作用的最大假定风力:

$$M_{wind}=\frac{(P\cdot A\cdot Z)}{9\,806}\qquad (t\cdot m)$$

式中:

$P=120\ N/m^2$;

A=水线以上突出的侧面面积;

Z=水线以上突出侧面面积中间至$T/2$的距离;和

T=相应吃水(d_s、d_p或d_l)。

4.1.3 $M_{survivalcraft}$是因在船舶一舷满载降放所有的吊架降落式救生艇筏而造成的最大假定横倾力矩,应采用以下假定进行计算:

.1　假定船舶破损后位于倾斜一舷的所有救生艇和救助艇,均满载悬挂于舷外并准备降放;

.2　对从存放位置满载降落布置的救生艇,应考虑在降落过程中的最大横倾力矩;

.3　假定船舶破损后位于倾斜一舷的每个吊架上,均吊有满载的吊架降落式救生筏,救生筏已悬挂于舷外并准备降放;

.4　不在悬挂于舷外的救生设备内的人员不增加倾侧力矩或复原力矩;和

.5　位于船舶倾斜相反一舷的救生设备假定为处于存放位置。

5　应使不对称进水降至与有效布置相称的最低程度。在需要校正大横倾角时,所采用的方法应尽可能是自动的,但在任何情况下,当设有控制平衡装置的设备时,此项设备应能在客船舱壁甲板和货船干舷甲板以上操作。这些装置连同其控制设备应被主管机关接受①。关于使用平衡装置的相关资料应提供给船长。

① 参见《经修订的评估横贯进水装置标准方法建议》(第MSC.362(92)号决议,可经修正)。

5.1 Tanks and compartments taking part in such equalization shall be fitted with air pipes or equivalent means of sufficient cross-section to ensure that the flow of water into the equalization compartments is not delayed.

5.2 The factor s_i is to be taken as zero in those cases where the final waterline, taking into account sinkage, heel and trim, immerses:

.1 the lower edge of openings through which progressive flooding may take place and such flooding is not accounted for in the calculation of factor s_i. Such openings shall include air pipes, ventilators and openings which are closed by means of weathertight doors or hatch covers; and

.2 any part of the bulkhead deck in passenger ships considered a horizontal evacuation route for compliance with chapter Ⅱ-2.

5.3 The factor s_i is to be taken as zero if, taking into account sinkage, heel and trim, any of the following occur in any intermediate stage or in the final stage of flooding:

.1 immersion of any vertical escape hatch in the bulkhead deck of passenger ships and the freeboard deck of cargo ships intended for compliance with chapter Ⅱ-2;

.2 any controls intended for the operation of watertight doors, equalization devices, valves on piping or on ventilation ducts intended to maintain the integrity of watertight bulkheads from above the bulkhead deck of passenger ships and the freeboard deck of cargo ships become inaccessible or inoperable; and

.3 immersion of any part of piping or ventilation ducts located within the assumed extent of damage and carried through a watertight boundary if this can lead to the progressive flooding of compartments not assumed as flooded.

5.4 However, where compartments assumed flooded due to progressive flooding are taken into account in the damage stability calculations, multiple values of $s_{\text{intermediate},i}$ may be calculated, assuming equalization in additional flooding phases.

5.5 Except as provided in paragraph 5.3.1, openings closed by means of watertight manhole covers and flush scuttles, remotely operated sliding watertight doors, sidescuttles of the non-opening type as well as watertight access doors and watertight hatch covers required to be kept closed at sea need not be considered.

6 Where horizontal watertight boundaries are fitted above the waterline under consideration, the s-value calculated for the lower compartment or group of compartments shall be obtained by multiplying the value as determined in paragraph 1.1 by the reduction factor v_m according to paragraph 6.1, which represents the probability that the spaces above the horizontal subdivision will not be flooded.

6.1 The factor v_m shall be obtained from the formula:

$$v_m = v(H_{j,n,m}, d) - v(H_{j,n,m-1}, d)$$

where:

5.1 参与这种平衡的液舱和舱室应设有横截面足够的空气管或等效装置，以确保进入平衡舱室的水流不受阻碍。

5.2 若虑及下沉、横倾和纵倾后的最终水线浸没以下部位，则因数 s_i 取为零：

.1 某些开口的下缘，通过这些开口可能发生累进进水，而这种进水在计算因数 s_i 时不予考虑。这些开口应包括空气管、通风筒和用风雨密门或舱口盖关闭的开口；和

.2 客船中为符合Ⅱ-2章要求而视为水平撤离通道的舱壁甲板任何部分。

5.3 若虑及下沉、横倾和纵倾后，在进水的任何中间阶段或最终阶段发生任一以下情况，则因数 s_i 取为零：

.1 浸没旨在符合第Ⅱ-2章的、客船舱壁甲板和货船干舷甲板任何垂直逃生舱口；

.2 用于在客船舱壁甲板和货船干舷甲板上方操作水密门、平衡装置、用于保持水密舱壁完整性的管路阀或通风管道阀变得无法通达或无法操作；和

.3 位于假定破损范围内且通过水密界限面的管路或通风管道的任何部分被水浸没，如可能导致未被假定为进水舱室的累进进水。

5.4 但是，如在破损稳性计算中计入假定因累进进水而进水的舱室，则可计算多个 $s_{\text{intermediate},i}$ 值并假定附加进水时处于平衡状态。

5.5 除第5.3.1款另有规定外，不必虑及依靠水密人孔盖和平面舱盖关闭的开口、遥控操作的滑动水密门、永闭型舷窗以及需要在海上航行中保持关闭的水密出入门和舱口盖。

6 如果水平水密限界面设在所计及水线以上，则对下面的舱室或舱组，s 计算值应按本条6.1以本条1.1所得的值乘以表示该水平分隔以上处所不进水概率的缩减因数 v_m 求得。

6.1 因数 v_m 应按下式计算：

$$v_m = v(H_{j,n,m}, d) - v(H_{j,n,m-1}, d)$$

式中：

$H_{j,n,m}$ is the least height above the baseline, in metres, within the longitudinal range of $x_{1(j)}...x_{2(j+n-1)}$ of the mth horizontal boundary which is assumed to limit the vertical extent of flooding for the damaged compartments under consideration;

$H_{j,n,m-1}$ is the least height above the baseline, in metres, within the longitudinal range of $x_{1(j)}...x(_{2j+n-1})$ of the $(m-1)^{th}$ horizontal boundary which is assumed to limit the vertical extent of flooding for the damaged compartments under consideration;

j signifies the aft terminal of the damaged compartments under consideration;

m represents each horizontal boundary counted upwards from the waterline under consideration;

d is the draught in question as defined in regulation 2; and

x_1 and x_2 represent the terminals of the compartment or group of compartments considered in regulation 7-1.

6.1.1 The factors $v(H_{j,n,m}, d)$ and $v(H_{j,n,m-1}, d)$ shall be obtained from the formulae:

$$v(H, d) = 0.8\frac{(H-d)}{7.8}, \text{ if } (H_m-d) \text{ is less than, or equal to, 7.8 m;}$$

$$v(H, d) = 0.8 + 0.2\left[\frac{(H-d)-7.8}{4.7}\right] \text{in all other cases,}$$

where

$v(H_{j,n,m}, d)$ is to be taken as 1, if H_m coincides with the uppermost watertight boundary of the ship within the range $(x_{1(j)} \cdots x_{2(j+n-1)})$, and

$v(H_{j,n,0}, d)$ is to be taken as 0.

In no case is v_m to be taken as less than zero or more than 1.

6.2 In general, each contribution dA to the index A in the case of horizontal subdivisions is obtained from the formula:

$$dA = p_i \cdot [v_1 \cdot s_{min1} + (v_2-v_1) \cdot s_{min2} + \cdots + (1-v_{m-1}) \cdot s_{minm}]$$

where:

v_m = the v-value calculated in accordance with paragraph 6.1;

s_{min} = the least s-factor for all combinations of damages obtained when the assumed damage extends from the assumed damage height H_m downwards.

$H_{j,n,m}$是假定限制所计及破损舱室垂向浸水范围的 m^{th} 水平限界面在 $x_{1(j)}\cdots x_{2(j+n-1)}$ 纵向范围内基线以上的最小高度，m；

$H_{j,n,m-1}$是假定限制所计及破损舱室垂向浸水范围的 $(m-1)^{th}$ 水平限界面在 $x_{1(j)}\cdots x_{2(j+n-1)}$ 纵向范围内基线以上的最小高度，m；

j 表示所计及破损舱室的后端点；

m 代表从所计及水线向上计数的每一水平限界面；

d 是所考虑的吃水，定义见第 2 条；以及

x_1 和 x_2 代表第 7-1 条所计及的舱室或舱组的端点。

6.1.1　因数 $v(H_{j,n,m},d)$ 和 $v(H_{j,n,m-1},d)$ 应按下式计算：

$v(H,d) = 0.8\dfrac{(H-d)}{7.8}$，如果 (H_m-d) 小于或等于 7.8 m，则

在所有其他情况下，$v(H,d) = 0.8 + 0.2\left[\dfrac{(H-d)-7.8}{4.7}\right]$

式中：

如果 H_m 与船舶最上部水密限界面在 $x_{1(j)}\ldots x_{2(j+n-1)}$ 范围内重合，则 $v(H_{j,n,m},d)$ 取为 1，

$v(H_{j,n,0},d)$ 取为 0。

v_m 在任何情况下均不得取为小于零或大于 1。

6.2　一般就水平分舱而言，作用于指数 A 的每个 dA 由下式求得：

$$dA = p_i\cdot[v_1\cdot s_{min1} + (v_2 - v_1)\cdot s_{min2} + \cdots + (1-v_{m-1})\cdot s_{minm}]$$

式中：

v_m = 按本条 6.1 计算的 v 值；

s_{min} = 当假定破损从假定破损高度 H_m 向下延伸时，所有破损组合的最小 s-因数。

Regulation 7-3
Permeability

1 For the purpose of the subdivision and damage stability calculations of the regulations, the permeability of each general compartment or part of a compartment shall be as follows:

Spaces	Permeability
Appropriated to stores	0.60
Occupied by accommodation	0.95
Occupied by machinery	0.85
Void spaces	0.95
Intended for liquids	0 or 0.95[a]

a: Whichever results in the more severe requirement.

2 For the purpose of the subdivision and damage stability calculations of the regulations, the permeability of each cargo compartment or part of a compartment shall be as follows:

Spaces	Permeability at draught d_s	Permeability at draught d_p	Permeability at draught d_l
Dry cargo spaces	0.70	0.80	0.95
Container spaces	0.70	0.80	0.95
Ro-ro spaces	0.90	0.90	0.95
Cargo liquids	0.70	0.80	0.95

3 Other figures for permeability may be used if substantiated by calculations.

Regulation 8
Special requirements concerning passenger ship stability

1 A passenger ship intended to carry 400 or more persons shall have watertight subdivision abaft the collision bulkhead so that $s_i = 1$ for a damage involving all the compartments within $0.08L$ measured from the forward perpendicular for the three loading conditions used to calculate the attained subdivision index A. If the attained subdivision index A is calculated for different trims, this requirement shall also be satisfied for those loading conditions.

2 A passenger ship intended to carry 36 or more persons is to be capable of withstanding damage along the side shell to an extent specified in paragraph 3. Compliance with this regulation is to be achieved by demonstrating that s_i, as defined in regulation 7-2, is not less than 0.9 for the three loading conditions used to calculate the attained subdivision index A. If the attained subdivision index A is calculated for different trims, this requirement shall also be satisfied for those loading conditions.

第 7-3 条
渗透率

1　本规则的分舱和破损稳性计算中，每一普通舱室或某舱室的一部分的渗透率应按以下规定取值：

处所	渗透率
贮物处所	0.60
起居处所	0.95
机器处所	0.85
空舱处所	0.95
液体处所	0 或 0.95[a]

a：取会得出更严格标准的值。

2　就本规则的分舱和破损稳性计算而言，每个货舱或某舱室的一部分的渗透率应按以下规定取值：

处所	吃水时渗透率 d_s	吃水时渗透率 d_p	吃水时渗透率 d_l
干货处所	0.70	0.80	0.95
集装箱处所	0.70	0.80	0.95
滚装处所	0.90	0.90	0.95
液货	0.70	0.80	0.95

3　如果经计算证实，渗透率可用其他数字。

第 8 条
关于客船稳性的特殊要求

1　拟载运 400 名或更多乘客的客船须具备防撞舱壁往后的水密分舱，以在计算达到的分舱指数 A 所依据的三种装载工况下及发生从首垂线量起 $0.08L$ 以内的所有舱室的破损时，$s_i = 1$。如果为不同纵倾计算达到的分舱指数 A，那些装载工况同样须满足这一要求。

2　拟载运 36 名或更多乘客的客船须能够承受沿着舷侧外板至第 3 款所述范围内的破损。通过证明在作为计算达到的分舱指数 A 所依据的三种装载工况下，第 7-2 条界定的 s_i 不小于 0.9，即认为符合本条规定。如果为不同纵倾计算达到的分舱指数 A，那些装载工况同样须满足这一要求。

3 The damage extent① to be assumed when demonstrating compliance with paragraph 2 is to be dependent on the total number of persons carried, and L, such that:

.1 the vertical extent of damage is to extend from the ship's moulded baseline to a position up to 12.5 m above the position of the deepest subdivision draught as defined in regulation 2, unless a lesser vertical extent of damage were to give a lower value of s_i, in which case this reduced extent is to be used;

.2 where 400 or more persons are to be carried, a damage length of $0.03L$, but not less than 3 m is to be assumed at any position along the side shell, in conjunction with a penetration inboard of $0.1B$ but not less than 0.75 m measured inboard from the ship side, at right angles to the centreline at the level of the deepest subdivision draught;

.3 where fewer than 400 persons are carried, damage length is to be assumed at any position along the shell side between transverse watertight bulkheads provided that the distance between two adjacent transverse watertight bulkheads is not less than the assumed damage length. If the distance between adjacent transverse watertight bulkheads is less than the assumed damage length, only one of these bulkheads shall be considered effective for the purpose of demonstrating compliance with paragraph 2;

.4 where 36 persons are carried, a damage length of $0.015L$ but not less than 3 m is to be assumed, in conjunction with a penetration inboard of $0.05B$ but not less than 0.75 m; and

.5 where more than 36, but fewer than 400, persons are carried, the values of damage length and penetration inboard, used in the determination of the assumed extent of damage, are to be obtained by linear interpolation between the values of damage length and penetration which apply for ships carrying 36 persons and 400 persons as specified in subparagraphs .4 and .2.

Regulation 8-1

System capabilities and operational information after a flooding casualty on passenger ships

1 Application

Passenger ships having length, as defined in regulation Ⅱ-1/2.5, of 120 m or more or having three or more main vertical zones shall comply with the provisions of this regulation.

2 Availability of essential systems in case of flooding damage②

A passenger ship shall be designed so that the systems specified in regulation Ⅱ-2/21.4 remain operational when the ship is subject to flooding of any single watertight compartment.

---

① Refer to the appendix of the *Revised guidance for watertight doors on passenger ships which may be opened during navigation* (MSC.1/Circ.1564).

② Refer to the *Interim Explanatory Notes for the assessment of passenger ship systems' capabilities after a fire or flooding casualty* (MSC.1/Circ.1369 and MSC.1/Circ.1369/Add.1).

3　若证明符合第 2 款，假定的破损范围①将取决于载运的总人数和 L：

.1　垂向破损范围从船舶型基线延伸至第 2 条所定义的最深分舱吃水位置以上 12.5 m 处，除非垂向破损范围较小而使 s_i 值较低，在此情况下应使用此减小的范围；

.2　如果载运 400 名或更多乘客，则可在沿着舷侧外板任何位置假设破损长度为 0.03L，但不小于 3 m，连同船内渗水 0.1B，但从船内侧量起至最深分舱吃水水平面中心线的直角距离不应小于 0.75 m；

.3　如果载客人数少于 400 人，则应在水密横舱壁之间的舷侧外板任何一处假定破损长度，但相邻两水密横舱壁的间距应不小于假定的破损长度。如果相邻两水密横舱壁的间距小于假定的破损长度，就证实符合本条 2 的要求而言，应仅将这两个舱壁中的一个视为有效；

.4　如载运 36 名乘客，则可假设破损长度为 0.015L 但不小于 3 m，连同 0.05B 但不小于 0.75 m 的船内渗水；和

.5　如果载客人数多于 36 人但少于 400 人，则用以确定假定破损范围的破损长度值和舷内穿透值，应在适用于上述.4 和.2 规定的载客人数为 36 人和载客人数为 400 人的船舶破损长度值和穿透值间用线性内插法求得。

第 8-1 条
客船进水事故后的系统性能

1　适用范围

船长（按第Ⅱ-1/2.5 条定义）为 120 m 或以上或有 3 个或以上主竖区的客船应符合本条规定。

2　发生进水破损时重要系统的有效性②

客船的设计应使船舶在任何单个水密舱室进水时，第Ⅱ-2/21.4 条规定的系统保持运行。

---

① 参见《经修订的客船在航行期间可开启的水密门指南》（第 MSC.1/Circ.1564 号通函）附录。
② 参见《火灾或进水事故后客船系统能力巩固临时解释》（第 MSC.1/Circ.1369 和 MSC.1/Circ.1369/Add.1 号通函）。

3 Operational information after a flooding casualty

3.1 For the purpose of providing operational information to the master for safe return to port after a flooding casualty, passenger ships, as specified in paragraph 1, shall have:

.1 an onboard stability computer; or

.2 shore-based support,

based on the guidelines developed by the Organization.①

3.2 Passenger ships constructed before 1 January 2014 shall comply with the provisions in paragraph 3.1 not later than the first renewal survey after 1 January 2025.

① Refer to the *Guidelines on operational information for masters of passenger ships for safe return to port by own power or under tow* (MSC.1/Circ.1400) for ships constructed on or after 1 January 2014 but before 13 May 2016, or the *Revised guidelines on operational information for masters of passenger ships for safe return to port* (MSC.1/Circ.1532/Rev.1) for ships constructed on or after 13 May 2016, or the *Guidelines on operational information for masters in case of flooding* for passenger ships constructed before 1 January 2014 (MSC./Circ.1589).

3 进水事故后的操作资料

3.1 根据本组织制定的导则①,为向船长提供进水事故后安全返港的操作资料,.1 款所述客船应配备:

.1 船上稳性计算机;或

.2 岸基支持。

3.2 2014 年 1 月 1 日前建造的客船须不迟于 2025 年 1 月 1 日或之后的第一个换证检验日符合第 3.1 款的规定。

① 2014 年 1 月 1 日及以后、2016 年 5 月 13 日以前建造的船舶,参见《为用船舶自身动力或被拖带安全返港向客船船长提供的操作信息导则》(第 MSC.1/Circ.1400 号通函);2016 年 5 月 13 日或以后建造的船舶,参见《经修订的为船舶安全返港向客船船长提供的操作信息导则》(第 MSC.1/Circ.1532/Rev.1 号通函);2014 年 1 月 1 日以前建造的客船,参见《向船长提供的船舶进水情况下的操作信息》(第 MSC.1/Circ.1589 号通函)。

Part B-2
Subdivision, watertight and weathertight integrity

Regulation 9
Double bottoms in passenger ships and cargo ships other than tankers

1 A double bottom shall be fitted extending from the collision bulkhead to the afterpeak bulkhead, as far as this is practicable and compatible with the design and proper working of the ship.

2 Where a double bottom is required to be fitted, the inner bottom shall be continued out to the ship's sides in such a manner as to protect the bottom to the turn of the bilge. Such protection will be deemed satisfactory if the inner bottom is not lower at any part than a plane parallel with the keel line and which is located not less than a vertical distance h measured from the keel line, as calculated by the formula:

$$h = B/20$$

However, in no case is the value of h to be less than 760 mm, and need not be taken as more than 2,000 mm.

3.1 Small wells constructed in the double bottom in connection with drainage arrangements shall not extend downward more than necessary. The vertical distance from the bottom of such a well to a plane coinciding with the keel line shall not be less than $h/2$ or 500 mm, whichever is greater, or compliance with paragraph 8 of this regulation shall be shown for that part of the ship.

3.2 Other wells (e. g. for lubricating oil under main engines) may be permitted by the Administration if satisfied that the arrangements give protection equivalent to that afforded by a double bottom complying with this regulation.

3.2.1 For a cargo ship of 80 m in length and upwards or for a passenger ship, proof of equivalent protection is to be shown by demonstrating that the ship is capable of withstanding bottom damages as specified in paragraph 8. Alternatively, wells for lubricating oil below main engines may protrude into the double bottom below the boundary line defined by the distance h provided that the vertical distance between the well bottom and a plane coinciding with the keel line is not less than $h/2$ or 500 mm, whichever is greater.

3.2.2 For cargo ships of less than 80 m in length the arrangements shall provide a level of safety to the satisfaction of the Administration.

4 A double bottom need not be fitted in way of watertight tanks, including dry tanks of moderate size, provided the safety of the ship is not impaired in the event of bottom or side damage.

B-2部分
分舱、水密和风雨密完整性

第9条
客船和货船(除液货船外)双层底

1 双层底设置应在适应船舶设计及船舶正常作业的情况下,尽实际可能自防撞舱壁延伸至尾尖舱舱壁。

2 如果需设置双层底时,其内底应延伸至船舷两侧,以保护船底至舭部弯曲部位。此项保护如果能使内底板在任何部分都不低于与龙骨线平行且自龙骨线量起垂直高度不低于 h 的水平面,即认为满意。h 按下式计算:

$$h = B/20$$

但在任何情况下,h 值不得小于760 mm,也不必取为大于2 000 mm。

3.1 设于双层底内且与排水装置相连的小井,不得向下延伸至超过所需的深度。从这种井的底部至与龙骨线重合的水平面的垂直距离不得小于 $h/2$ 或500 mm,取大者,或者证明船舶的该部分符合本条第8款的要求。

3.2 其他井(如主机下的润滑油井)的布置与符合本条的双层底具有等效的保护作用,则主管机关可允许设置。

3.2.1 对于船长80 m及以上的货船或对于客船,可通过证明船舶能够经受本条第8款规定的船底破损以证实提供等效的保护。或者,主机下的润滑油井可延伸至按距离 h 所定义的边界线下的双层底,只要井的底部至与龙骨线重合的水平面的垂直距离不小于 $h/2$ 或500 mm,取大者。

3.2.2 对于船长小于80 m的货船,其他井的布置须能提供令主管机关满意的安全水平。

4 在大小适度的水密液舱(包括干的液舱)处,如果舱的底部或侧面破损时不致有损于船舶的安全,则不必设双层底。

5 In the case of passenger ships to which the provisions of regulation 1.5 apply and which are engaged on regular service within the limits of a short international voyage as defined in regulation Ⅲ/3.22, the Administration may permit a double bottom to be dispensed with if satisfied that the fitting of a double bottom in that part would not be compatible with the design and proper working of the ship.

6 Any part of a cargo ship of 80 m in length and upwards or of a passenger ship that is not fitted with a double bottom in accordance with paragraphs 1, 4 or 5, as specified in paragraph 2, shall be capable of withstanding bottom damages, as specified in paragraph 8, in that part of the ship. For cargo ships of less than 80 m in length the alternative arrangements shall provide a level of safety to the satisfaction of the Administration.

7 In the case of unusual bottom arrangements in a cargo ship of 80 m in length and upwards or a passenger ship, it shall be demonstrated that the ship is capable of withstanding bottom damages as specified in paragraph 8. For cargo ships of less than 80 m in length the alternative arrangements shall provide a level of safety to the satisfaction of the Administration.

8 Compliance with paragraphs 3.1,3.2.1, 6 or 7 is to be achieved by demonstrating that s_i, when calculated in accordance with regulation 7-2, is not less than 1 for all service conditions when subject to bottom damage with an extent specified in sub-paragraph .2 below for any position in the affected part of the ship:

.1 Flooding of such spaces shall not render emergency power and lighting, internal communication, signals or other emergency devices inoperable in other parts of the ship.

.2 Assumed extent of damage shall be as follows:

	For 0.3L from the forward perpendicular of the ship	Any other part of the ship
Longitudinal extent	$1/3L^{2/3}$ or 14.5 m, whichever is less	$1/3L^{2/3}$ or 14.5 m, whichever is less
Transverse extent	$B/6$ or 10 m, whichever is less	$B/6$ or 5 m, whichever is less
Vertical extent, measured from the keel line	$B/20$, to be taken not less than 0.76 m and not more than 2 m	$B/20$, to be taken not less than 0.76 m and not more than 2 m

.3 If any damage of a lesser extent than the maximum damage specified in .2 would result in a more severe condition, such damage should be considered.

9 In case of large lower holds in passenger ships, the Administration may require an increased double-bottom height of not more than $B/10$ or 3 m, whichever is less, measured from the keel line. Alternatively, bottom damages may be calculated for these areas, in accordance with paragraph 8, but assuming an increased vertical extent.

5 适用第1.5条规定并在第Ⅲ/3.22条定义的短程国际航行范围内营运的客船，主管机关如果确信设置双层底与该船的设计及船舶正常作业不相适应，可允许在该部分免设双底层。

6 按第2款规定，船长80 m及以上的货船或客船按照第1、4或5款未设双层底的任何部分，须能承受在船舶该部分发生如第8款所述的船底破损。对于船长小于80 m的货船，替代布置须能提供令主管机关满意的安全水平。

7 对于船长80 m及以上的货船或客船的非常规船底布置，须证明该船能承受第8款所述的船底破损。对于船长小于80 m的货船，替代布置须能提供令主管机关满意的安全水平。

8 通过证明在船舶受影响部分的任何一处经受以下.2款所述的破损范围的船底破损时，若按照第7-2条计算，s_i 在所有营运情况下不小于1，则可符合第3.1、3.2.1项、第6或7款的要求：

.1 这类处所进水不得导致船舶其他部分的应急电源和照明系统、内部通信、信号或其他应急装置无法操作。

.2 假设破损范围须如下所示：

	自船首垂线起0.3L	船舶任何其他部分
纵向范围	1/3$L^{2/3}$或14.5 m，取较小者	1/3$L^{2/3}$或14.5 m，取较小者
横向范围	B/6或10 m，取较小者	B/6或5 m，取较小者
垂向范围，从龙骨线量起	B/20，取不小于0.76 m且不大于2 m	B/20，取不小于0.76 m且不大于2 m

.3 如果任何破损小于第.2项所述的最大破损范围但会导致更加严重的状况时，则应虑及此种破损。

9 客船如有大的底舱，主管机关可要求将双层底高度增至从龙骨线量起不大于B/10或3 m，取小者。或者，可按照本条8计算这些区域的船底破损，但应假定垂直范围增大。

Regulation 10
Construction of watertight bulkheads

1 Each watertight subdivision bulkhead, whether transverse or longitudinal, shall be constructed having scantlings as specified in regulation 2. 17. In all cases, watertight subdivision bulkheads shall be capable of supporting at least the pressure due to a head of water up to the bulkhead deck of passenger ships and the freeboard deck of cargo ships.

2 Steps and recesses in watertight bulkheads shall be as strong as the bulkhead at the place where each occurs.

Regulation 11
Initial testing of watertight bulkheads, etc.

1 Testing watertight spaces not intended to hold liquids and cargo holds intended to hold ballast by filling them with water is not compulsory. When testing by filling with water is not carried out, a hose test shall be carried out where practicable. This test shall be carried out in the most advanced stage of the fitting out of the ship. Where a hose test is not practicable because of possible damage to machinery, electrical equipment insulation or outfitting items, it may be replaced by a careful visual examination of welded connections, supported where deemed necessary by means such as a dye penetrant test or an ultrasonic leak test or an equivalent test. In any case a thorough inspection of the watertight bulkheads shall be carried out.

2 The forepeak, double bottom (including duct keels) and inner skins shall be tested with water to a head corresponding to the requirements of regulation 10.1.

3 Tanks which are intended to hold liquids, and which form part of the watertight subdivision of the ship, shall be tested for tightness and structural strength with water to a head corresponding to its design pressure. The water head is in no case to be less than the top of the air pipes or to a level of 2.4 m above the top of the tank, whichever is the greater.

4 The tests referred to in paragraphs 2 and 3 are for the purpose of ensuring that the subdivision structural arrangements are watertight and are not to be regarded as a test of the fitness of any compartment for the storage of oil fuel or for other special purposes for which a test of a superior character may be required, depending on the height to which the liquid has access in the tank or its connections.

第 10 条
水密舱壁的构造

1　每一水密分隔舱壁，无论横向或纵向，其构造须具有第 2.17 条所述的船材。在任何情况下，水密分隔舱壁须至少能够支持高达客船舱壁甲板和货船干舷甲板的水头压力。

2　水密舱壁上的阶层和凹入应与阶层或凹入处的舱壁具有同样强度。

第 11 条
水密舱壁等的初次试验

1　对拟不装载液体的水密处所和拟压载的货舱的灌水试验不是强制性的。如果不进行灌水试验，则在实际可行情况下应做冲水试验。此试验应在船舶的舾装工作进行到最后阶段时进行。如果由于冲水试验可能造成机械、电气设备绝缘或舾装件的损坏而不可行，则可用对焊接缝的细致目视检查予以替代，且在认为必要时，还应由类似于着色渗透试验或超声波测漏试验或等效试验加以支持。在任何情况下，都应对水密舱壁进行彻底检查。

2　首尖舱、双层底（包括箱形龙骨）及内壳板均应以相应于第 10.1 条要求的水头做试验。

3　供装载液体并形成船舶分舱部分的舱柜，应以相当于其设计压力的水头试验其密性和结构强度。该水头无论如何不得低于空气管顶或该舱舱顶以上 2.4 m，取大者。

4　本条 2 和 3 所述试验的目的在于确保分舱结构布置是水密的，而不应视为对任何用于储存燃油或其他特殊用途舱室的适应性试验，而此类试验按液体进入舱内或其连接部分的高度，可能要求更为严格。

Regulation 12
Peak and machinery space bulkheads, shaft tunnels, etc.

1 A collision bulkhead shall be fitted which shall be watertight up to the bulkhead deck of passenger ships and the freeboard deck of cargo ships. This bulkhead shall be located at a distance from the forward perpendicular of not less than $0.05L$ or 10 m, whichever is less, and, except as may be permitted by the Administration, not more than $0.08L$ or $0.05L$ + 3 m, whichever is the greater.

2 The ship shall be so designed that s_i calculated in accordance with regulation 7-2 will not be less than 1 at the deepest subdivision draught loading condition, level trim or any forward trim loading conditions, if any part of the ship forward of the collision bulkhead is flooded without vertical limits.

3 Where any part of the ship below the waterline extends forward of the forward perpendicular, e.g. a bulbous bow, the distances stipulated in paragraph 1 shall be measured from a point either:

.1 at the mid-length of such extension;

.2 at a distance $0.015L$ forward of the forward perpendicular; or

.3 at a distance 3 m forward of the forward perpendicular,

whichever gives the smallest measurement.

4 The bulkhead may have steps or recesses provided they are within the limits prescribed in paragraph 1 or 3.

5 No doors, manholes, access openings, ventilation ducts or any other openings shall be fitted in the collision bulkhead below the bulkhead deck of passenger ships and the freeboard deck of cargo ships.

6.1 Except as provided in paragraph 6.2, the collision bulkhead may be pierced below the bulkhead deck of passenger ships and the freeboard deck of cargo ships by not more than one pipe for dealing with fluid in the forepeak tank, provided that the pipe is fitted with a screw-down valve capable of being operated from above the bulkhead deck of passenger ships and the freeboard deck of cargo ships, the valve being located inside the forepeak at the collision bulkhead. The Administration may, however, authorize the fitting of this valve on the after side of the collision bulkhead provided that the valve is readily accessible under all service conditions and the space in which it is located is not a cargo space. Alternatively, for cargo ships, the pipe may be fitted with a butterfly valve suitably supported by a seat or flanges and capable of being operated from above the freeboard deck. All valves shall be of steel, bronze or other approved ductile material. Valves of ordinary cast iron or similar material are not acceptable.

第12条
尖舱及机器处所的舱壁、轴隧等

1 应设置防撞舱壁，其舱壁水密应至客船舱壁甲板和货船干舷甲板。此舱壁应位于距首垂线不小于0.05L或10 m处（取较小者），且除非经主管机关许可，不大于0.08L或0.05L+3 m（取较大者）处。

2 船舶的设计应能使得在船舶防撞舱壁以前的任一部分进水，且进水在垂直方向无限制值时，按第7-2条计算的s_i在最深分舱吃水装载工况、水平纵倾或任何首纵倾装载工况下不小于1。

3 如果船舶水线以下的任何部分自首垂线向前延伸，例如球鼻首，则应从下列任一点来测量第1款规定的距离：

.1　此类延伸部分的长度中点；

.2　首垂线前端的0.015L处；或

.3　首垂线前方3 m处，

取最小测量值。

4 舱壁可以有阶层或凹入，但其应在第1或3款规定的限度内。

5 在客船舱壁甲板和货船干舷甲板以下的防撞舱壁内不得设置门、人孔、通道开口、通风管道或任何其他开口。

6.1 除第6.2款规定者外，在客船舱壁甲板和货船干舷甲板以下的防撞舱壁上可穿过1根管子用以处理首尖舱内的液体，但是该管子应设有能在客船舱壁甲板和货船干舷甲板以上操作的螺旋阀，其阀体应位于首尖舱内的防撞舱壁上。如果阀位于在所有营运工况下均可到达之处，且其所在处所不是货物处所，则主管机关可允许该阀设于防撞舱壁的后侧。或者，对于货船，管子可以设在一个能在干舷甲板以上操作的由阀座或法兰适当支撑的蝶形阀上。所有阀应以钢、铜或其他经认可的韧性材料制成。不得采用普通铸铁或类似材料制成的阀。

6.2 If the forepeak is divided to hold two different kinds of liquids, the Administration may allow the collision bulkhead to be pierced below the bulkhead deck of passenger ships and the freeboard deck of cargo ships by two pipes, each of which is fitted as required by paragraph 6.1, provided the Administration is satisfied that there is no practical alternative to the fitting of such a second pipe and that, having regard to the additional subdivision provided in the forepeak, the safety of the ship is maintained.

7 Where a long forward superstructure is fitted, the collision bulkhead shall be extended weathertight to the deck next above the bulkhead deck of passenger ships and the freeboard deck of cargo ships. The extension need not be fitted directly above the bulkhead below provided that all parts of the extension, including any part of the ramp attached to it, are located within the limits prescribed in paragraph 1 or 3, with the exception permitted by paragraph 8, and that the part of the deck which forms the step is made effectively weathertight. The extension shall be so arranged as to preclude the possibility of the bow door or ramp, where fitted, causing damage to it in the case of damage to, or detachment of, a bow door or any part of the ramp.

8 Where bow doors are fitted and a sloping loading ramp forms part of the extension of the collision bulkhead above the bulkhead deck of passenger ships and the freeboard deck of cargo ships, the ramp shall be weathertight over its complete length. In cargo ships, the part of the ramp which is more than 2.3 m above the freeboard deck may extend forward of the limit specified in paragraph 1 or 3. Ramps not meeting the above requirements shall be disregarded as an extension of the collision bulkhead.

9 The number of openings in the extension of the collision bulkhead above the freeboard deck shall be restricted to the minimum compatible with the design and normal operation of the ship. All such openings shall be capable of being closed weathertight.

10 Bulkheads shall be fitted separating the machinery space from cargo and accommodation spaces forward and aft and made watertight up to the bulkhead deck of passenger ships and the freeboard deck of cargo ships. An afterpeak bulkhead shall also be fitted and made watertight up to the bulkhead deck or the freeboard deck. The afterpeak bulkhead may, however, be stepped below the bulkhead deck or the freeboard deck, provided the degree of safety of the ship as regards subdivision is not thereby diminished.

11 In all cases stern tubes shall be enclosed in watertight spaces of moderate volume. In passenger ships the stern gland shall be situated in a watertight shaft tunnel or other watertight space separate from the stern tube compartment and of such volume that, if flooded by leakage through the stern gland, the bulkhead deck will not be immersed. In cargo ships other measures to minimize the danger of water penetrating into the ship in case of damage to stern tube arrangements may be taken at the discretion of the Administration.

6.2　如果首尖舱被分隔成用来装载两种不同的液体，主管机关可允许在客船舱壁甲板和货船干舷甲板以下的防撞舱壁上穿过 2 根管子，每根管子均按照第 6.1 款要求进行设置，但应使主管机关确信除装设第二根管子外无其他切实可行的办法，并考虑了首尖舱内增设分舱仍能维持船舶安全。

7　如船舶设有长的前部上层建筑，则防撞舱壁须风雨密延伸至客船舱壁甲板和货船干舷甲板上一层的甲板。此延伸部分不必直接设于下面舱壁之上，但延伸的所有部分，包括其连接的坡道的任何部分应位于第 1 或 3 款规定的限度内（第 8 款允许的情况除外），且形成阶层的甲板部分应有效地风雨密。此延伸部分的布置须避免在首门或者坡道的任何部分发生破损或脱落时对其造成损坏的可能性。

8　如设有首门且装货斜坡道形成客船舱壁甲板和货船干舷甲板以上的防撞舱壁的延伸部分，坡道全长范围内均须风雨密。就货船而言，高出干舷甲板 2.3 m 的坡道部分可从第 1 或 3 款规定的限度向前延伸。不符合上述要求的坡道不得视为防撞舱壁的延伸。

9　干舷甲板以上防撞舱壁延伸处的开口数量，须在适应船舶设计和正常作业的情况下减至最少。所有这类开口须能关闭成风雨密。

10　应设置舱壁将机器处所与前后货物和起居处所隔开，该舱壁须水密延伸到客船舱壁甲板和货船干舷甲板。还须设置尾尖舱舱壁，该舱壁须水密延伸到舱壁甲板或干舷甲板。但是，只要不降低船舶分舱的安全程度，尾尖舱舱壁可在舱壁甲板或干舷甲板下方做成阶层。

11　在所有情况下，尾管须封闭于适当容积的水密处所内。就客船而言，尾填料函压盖须装设于水密轴隧内或与尾管舱室分开的其他水密处所内，且该处所的容积足以在尾填料函压盖渗漏而进水时不至于浸没舱壁甲板。就货船而言，经主管机关酌定可采取其他措施，以在尾管布置受损的情况下向船内渗水的危险降至最低。

Regulation 13

Openings in watertight bulkheads below the bulkhead deck in passenger ships[①]

1 The number of openings in watertight bulkheads shall be reduced to the minimum compatible with the design and proper working of the ship; satisfactory means shall be provided for closing these openings.

2.1 Where pipes, scuppers, electric cables, etc., are carried through watertight bulkheads, arrangements shall be made to ensure the watertight integrity of the bulkheads.

2.2 Valves not forming part of a piping system shall not be permitted in watertight bulkheads.

2.3 Lead or other heat-sensitive materials shall not be used in systems which penetrate watertight bulkheads, where deterioration of such systems in the event of fire would impair the watertight integrity of the bulkheads.

3 No doors, manholes, or access openings are permitted in watertight transverse bulkheads dividing a cargo space from an adjoining cargo space, except as provided in paragraph 9.1 and in regulation 14.

4 Subject to paragraph 10, not more than one door, apart from the doors to shaft tunnels, may be fitted in each watertight bulkhead within spaces containing the main and auxiliary propulsion machinery, including boilers serving the needs of propulsion. Where two or more shafts are fitted, the tunnels shall be connected by an intercommunicating passage. There shall be only one door between the machinery space and the tunnel spaces where two shafts are fitted and only two doors where there are more than two shafts. All these doors shall be of the sliding type and shall be so located as to have their sills as high as practicable. The hand gear for operating these doors from above the bulkhead deck shall be situated outside the spaces containing the machinery.

5.1 Watertight doors, except as provided in paragraph 9.1 or regulation 14, shall be power-operated sliding doors complying with the requirements of paragraph 7 capable of being closed simultaneously from the central operating console at the navigation bridge in not more than 60 s with the ship in the upright position.

5.2 The means of operation, whether by power or by hand, of any power-operated sliding watertight door shall be capable of closing the door with the ship listed to 15° either way. Consideration shall also be given to the forces which may act on either side of the door as may be experienced when water is flowing through the opening, applying a static head equivalent to a water height of at least 1 m above the sill on the centreline of the door.

---

① Refer to *Revised guidance for watertight doors on passenger ships which may be opened during navigation* (MSC.1/Circ.1564).

第13条
客船舱壁甲板以下水密舱壁上的开口[①]

1　水密舱壁上开口的数量应在适应船舶设计及船舶正常作业的情况下减至最少,这些开口均应设有可靠的关闭设备。

2.1　如果管子、排水管和电缆等通过水密舱壁时,应设有保证该舱壁水密完整性的设施。

2.2　不得在水密舱壁上装设与构成管系无关的阀。

2.3　铅或其他易熔材料不应用于穿过水密舱壁的管系上,因为发生火灾时这种管系的损坏将会损害舱壁的水密完整性。

3　分隔相邻货物处所的水密横舱壁不准设门、人孔或通道开口,但本条9.1和第14条规定者除外。

4　除符合本条10的规定外,在主、辅推进机械包括推进所需的锅炉的处所内,其每一水密舱壁上,除通往轴隧的门外,只可设置1扇门。如果装有2根或更多的轴,其轴隧之间应设有一个互通的连接通道。如果装设2根轴者,在机器处所与轴隧间仅准设1扇门;如果装设2根轴以上者,则只准设2扇门。所有这些门均应为滑动式,且应设置于使其门槛尽可能高之处。在机器处所以外,应装设从舱壁甲板上操纵这些门的手动装置。

5.1　除本条9.1或第14条规定外,水密门应为符合本条7要求的动力滑动门,当船舶在正浮位置时,应能从驾驶室的总控制台于不超过60 s内同时关闭这些门。

5.2　任何动力滑动水密门的操纵装置,无论是动力式还是手动式,均应能在船舶向任一舷横倾至15°的情况下将门关闭。还应考虑当水从开口处涌入时,在门的任一侧受到一个相当于在门的中心线处门槛以上至少1 m高度的静水压头的作用力。

① 参见《经修订的客船在航行期间可开启的水密门指南》(第MSC.1/Circ.1564号通函)。

5.3 Watertight door controls, including hydraulic piping and electric cables, shall be kept as close as practicable to the bulkhead in which the doors are fitted, in order to minimize the likelihood of them being involved in any damage which the ship may sustain. The positioning of watertight doors and their controls shall be such that if the ship sustains damage within one fifth of the breadth of the ship, as defined in regulation 2, such distance being measured at right angles to the centreline at the level of the deepest subdivision draught, the operation of the watertight doors clear of the damaged portion of the ship is not impaired.

6 All power-operated sliding watertight doors shall be provided with means of indication which will show at all remote operating positions whether the doors are open or closed. Remote operating positions shall only be at the navigation bridge as required by paragraph 7.1.5 and at the location where hand operation above the bulkhead deck is required by paragraph 7.1.4.

7.1 Each power-operated sliding watertight door:

.1 shall have a vertical or horizontal motion;

.2 shall, subject to paragraph 10, be normally limited to a maximum clear opening width of 1.2 m. The Administration may permit larger doors only to the extent considered necessary for the effective operation of the ship provided that other safety measures, including the following, are taken into consideration:

.1 special consideration shall be given to the strength of the door and its closing appliances in order to prevent leakages; and

.2 the door shall be located inboard the damage zone $B/5$;

.3 shall be fitted with the necessary equipment to open and close the door using electric power, hydraulic power, or any other form of power that is acceptable to the Administration;

.4 shall be provided with an individual hand-operated mechanism. It shall be possible to open and close the door by hand at the door itself from either side, and in addition, close the door from an accessible position above the bulkhead deck with an all round crank motion or some other movement providing the same degree of safety acceptable to the Administration. Direction of rotation or other movement is to be clearly indicated at all operating positions. The time necessary for the complete closure of the door, when operating by hand gear, shall not exceed 90 s with the ship in the upright position;

.5 shall be provided with controls for opening and closing the door by power from both sides of the door and also for closing the door by power from the central operating console at the navigation bridge;

5.3 水密门的操纵装置，包括液压管路和电缆，应尽可能靠近装设该门的舱壁，以减少当船舶遭受破损时这些装置也被损坏的可能性。水密门及其操纵装置的位置应满足当船舶在如第 2 条定义的 1/5 船宽（在最深分舱吃水线上向中心线垂直量计）范围内遭受破损时，位于船舶破损部位以外的水密门的操纵不受妨碍。

6 所有动力滑动水密门在其遥控操纵位置均应设有显示这些门是否开启的指示设施，遥控操纵位置只能设在本条 7.1.5 要求的驾驶室内和本条 7.1.4 要求的舱壁甲板以上的手动操纵处。

7.1 每一动力滑动水密门：

.1 应为竖动式或横动式；

.2 除按本条 10 规定外，最大净开口宽度一般还应限制为 1.2 m。只有在考虑到船舶实际操作需要时，主管机关可允许设更宽的门，但应考虑包括以下要求的其他安全措施：

.1 对该门的强度和关闭设备应特殊考虑，以防止渗漏；和

.2 该门应位于 *B*/5 的破损区域之外；

.3 应设有使用电力、液压或主管机关接受的其他动力开启和关闭门的必要设备；

.4 应设置一套独立的手动机械装置。该装置能从门的任何一侧用手开启和关闭；此外，还能在舱壁甲板上可到达之处用全周旋摇柄转动或主管机关接受的具有同样安全程度的其他动作关闭该门。在所有操纵位置处须清楚地标明旋转方向或其他动作的方向。在船舶正浮时，手动操纵装置将门完全关闭的时间应不超过 90 s；

.5 应设置从门的两侧用动力开启和关闭该门的控制装置。还应在驾驶室设置从总控制台用动力关闭该门的控制装置；

.6 shall be provided with an audible alarm, distinct from any other alarm in the area, which will sound whenever the door is closed remotely by power and which shall sound for at least 5 s but no more than 10 s before the door begins to move and shall continue sounding until the door is completely closed. In the case of remote hand operation it is sufficient for the audible alarm to sound only when the door is moving. Additionally, in passenger areas and areas of high ambient noise the Administration may require the audible alarm to be supplemented by an intermittent visual signal at the door; and

.7 shall have an approximately uniform rate of closure under power. The closure time, from the time the door begins to move to the time it reaches the completely closed position, shall in no case be less than 20 s or more than 40 s with the ship in the upright position.

7.2 The electrical power required for power-operated sliding watertight doors shall be supplied from the emergency switchboard either directly or by a dedicated distribution board situated above the bulkhead deck. The associated control, indication and alarm circuits shall be supplied from the emergency switchboard either directly or by a dedicated distribution board situated above the bulkhead deck and be capable of being automatically supplied by the transitional source of emergency electrical power required by regulation 42.3.1.3 in the event of failure of either the main or emergency source of electrical power.

7.3 Power-operated sliding watertight doors shall have either:

.1 a centralized hydraulic system with two independent power sources each consisting of a motor and pump capable of simultaneously closing all doors. In addition, there shall be for the whole installation hydraulic accumulators of sufficient capacity to operate all the doors at least three times, i.e., closed-open-closed, against an adverse list of 15°. This operating cycle shall be capable of being carried out when the accumulator is at the pump cut-in pressure. The fluid used shall be chosen considering the temperatures liable to be encountered by the installation during its service. The power operating system shall be designed to minimize the possibility of having a single failure in the hydraulic piping adversely affect the operation of more than one door. The hydraulic system shall be provided with a low-level alarm for hydraulic fluid reservoirs serving the power-operated system and a low gas pressure alarm or other effective means of monitoring loss of stored energy in hydraulic accumulators. These alarms are to be audible and visual and shall be situated on the central operating console at the navigation bridge; or

.6 应设置一个与该区域内其他报警器不同的听觉报警器。当该门用动力遥控关闭时,这种报警器应在门开始移动前至少5 s但不超过10 s发出声响,且连续发出声响直至该门完全关闭。在手动遥控操纵的情况下,只要当门移动时听觉报警器能发出声响即可。此外,在乘客区域和高环境噪声区域,主管机关可以要求在门上的听觉报警器增配一个间歇发光信号器;和

.7 用动力关闭门时关闭速率应大致均匀。在船舶正浮时,从门开始移动至门完全关闭的时间,在任何情况下应不少于20 s或不大于40 s。

7.2 动力滑动水密门需要的电源应由应急配电板直接供电,或由位于舱壁甲板上方的专用配电板直接供电。与其关联的控制装置、指示器和报警电路也应由应急配电板直接供电或由位于舱壁甲板上方的专用配电板供电,并且当主电源或应急电源发生故障时,能自动转换为由第42.3.1.3条要求的临时应急电源供电。

7.3 动力滑动水密门应设有下列任一系统:

.1 设有一套具有两个独立动力源的集中液压系统,每一动力源由一台能同时关闭所有门的电动机和泵组成。此外,应设有用于整个装置的具有足够能量的液压蓄能器,能在不利的15°横倾时至少操纵所有的门3次,即关闭—开启—关闭。这个操作循环应能在泵为蓄能器加入压力的状态下进行。所选用的液体应考虑该装置工作时可能达到的温度。该动力操作系统的设计应使当液压管路中发生某一故障时多于1扇门的操纵受到不利影响的可能性降至最小,该液压系统应设有用于动力操纵系统储液箱的低液位报警器和低压报警器,或其他能监控液压蓄能器内能量损耗的有效装置。这些报警器应为听觉和视觉型,并应装设在驾驶室内的集中控制台上;或

.2 an independent hydraulic system for each door with each power source consisting of a motor and pump capable of opening and closing the door. In addition, there shall be a hydraulic accumulator of sufficient capacity to operate the door at least three times, i.e., closed-open-closed, against an adverse list of 15°. This operating cycle shall be capable of being carried out when the accumulator is at the pump cut-in pressure. The fluid used shall be chosen considering the temperatures liable to be encountered by the installation during its service. A low gas pressure group alarm or other effective means of monitoring loss of stored energy in hydraulic accumulators shall be provided at the central operating console on the navigation bridge. Loss of stored energy indication at each local operating position shall also be provided; or

.3 an independent electrical system and motor for each door with each power source consisting of a motor capable of opening and closing the door. The power source shall be capable of being automatically supplied by the transitional source of emergency electrical power as required by regulation 42.4.2 — in the event of failure of either the main or emergency source of electrical power and with sufficient capacity to operate the door at least three times, i.e. closed-open-closed, against an adverse list of 15°.

For the systems specified in paragraphs 7.3.1, 7.3.2 and 7.3.3, provision should be made as follows: Power systems for power-operated watertight sliding doors shall be separate from any other power system. A single failure in the electric or hydraulic power-operated systems excluding the hydraulic actuator shall not prevent the hand operation of any door.

7.4 Control handles shall be provided at each side of the bulkhead at a minimum height of 1.6 m above the floor and shall be so arranged as to enable persons passing through the doorway to hold both handles in the open position without being able to set the power closing mechanism in operation accidentally. The direction of movement of the handles in opening and closing the door shall be in the direction of door movement and shall be clearly indicated.

7.5 As far as practicable, electrical equipment and components for watertight doors shall be situated above the bulkhead deck and outside hazardous areas and spaces.

7.6 The enclosures of electrical components necessarily situated below the bulkhead deck shall provide suitable protection against the ingress of water.[①]

7.7 Electric power, control, indication and alarm circuits shall be protected against fault in such a way that a failure in one door circuit will not cause a failure in any other door circuit. Short circuits or other faults in the alarm or indicator circuits of a door shall not result in a loss of power operation of that door. Arrangements shall be such that leakage of water into the electrical equipment located below the bulkhead deck will not cause the door to open.

---

① Refer to the following publication IEC 60529:1989:

.1 electrical motors, associated circuits and control components; protected to IPX 7 standard;

.2 door position indicators and associated circuit components; protected to IPX 8 standard; and

.3 door movement warning signals; protected to IPX 6 standard.

Other arrangements for the enclosures of electrical components may be fitted provided the Administration is satisfied that an equivalent protection is achieved. The water pressure IPX 8 shall be based on the pressure that may occur at the location of the component during flooding for a period of 36 h.

.2　为每扇门装设一套具有各自动力源的独立液压系统，由一台能启闭该门的电动机和泵组成。此外，还应装有一个具有足够能量的液压蓄能器，能在不利的15°横倾时至少操作该门3次，即关闭—开启—关闭。这个操作循环应能在泵为蓄能器加入压力的状态下进行。所用液体的选择应考虑该装置工作时可能达到的温度。在驾驶台的集中控制台上应设一组低压报警器或其他能监控液压蓄能器内能量损耗的有效装置。在每个就地操作位置还应设置储蓄能量损耗的指示器；或

.3　为每扇门装设一套具有各自动力源的独立电力系统和电动机，其由一台能启闭该门的电动机组成。该动力源在主电源或应急电源发生故障时应能自动地转换为由第42.4.2条所要求的临时应急电源供电，且应具有足够的能量，以能在不利的15°横倾时至少操纵该门3次，即关闭—开启—关闭。

上述7.3.1、7.3.2和7.3.3所规定的各系统应符合以下要求：动力滑动水密门的动力系统应和任何其他动力系统分开。电力或液压动力操作系统（不包含液压执行器）中的某一故障应不妨碍任何门的手工操作。

7.4　控制手柄应装设在舱壁两侧地板以上至少1.6 m的高处，并且其布置应使通过该门的人员能保持两侧手柄均处于开启位置，防止意外操作而启动动力关闭装置。开启和关闭门时手柄的运动方向应与门移动的方向一致，并应清楚地标明。

7.5　水密门的电气设备和部件应尽可能设于舱壁甲板以上及危险区域和危险处所之外。

7.6　必须装设在舱壁甲板以下的电气部件的外壳应设有防止进水的适当保护措施。①

7.7　电源、控制装置、指示器和报警电路应设置下述方式的防止故障保护，即某一扇门的电路中的故障不应引起任何其他门的电路故障。一扇门的报警器或指示器的电路中的短路或其他故障不应导致丧失该门的动力操纵。其布置应保证水渗漏进位于舱壁甲板以下的电气设备时不致使门开启。

---

①　参见下列IEC 60519：1989出版物：
.1　达到IPX7保护标准的电机、相关电路及控制部件；
.2　达到IPX8保护标准的门位置指示器及相关电路部件；和
.3　达到IPX6保护标准的门移动报警信号器。
如果主管机关确信能达到同等保护程度，可对电气部件的外壳做其他布置。IPX8水压应基于该部件位置处浸水36 h过程中可能出现的压力。

7.8 A single electrical failure in the power operating or control system of a power-operated sliding watertight door shall not result in a closed door opening. Availability of the power supply should be continuously monitored at a point in the electrical circuit as near as practicable to each of the motors required by paragraph 7.3. Loss of any such power supply should activate an audible and visual alarm at the central operating console at the navigation bridge.

8.1 The central operating console at the navigation bridge shall have a "master mode" switch with two modes of control: a "local control" mode which shall allow any door to be locally opened and locally closed after use without automatic closure, and a "doors closed" mode which shall automatically close any door that is open. The "doors closed" mode shall automatically close any door that is open. The "doors closed" mode shall permit doors to be opened locally and shall automatically re-close the doors upon release of the local control mechanism. The "master mode" switch shall normally be in the "local control" mode. The "doors closed" mode shall only be used in an emergency or for testing purposes. Special consideration shall be given to the reliability of the "master mode" switch.

8.2 The central operating console at the navigation bridge shall be provided with a diagram showing the location of each door, with visual indicators to show whether each door is open or closed. A red light shall indicate a door is fully open and a green light shall indicate a door is fully closed. When the door is closed remotely the red light shall indicate the intermediate position by flashing. The indicating circuit shall be independent of the control circuit for each door.

8.3 It shall not be possible to remotely open any door from the central operating console.

9.1 If the Administration is satisfied that such doors are essential, watertight doors of satisfactory construction may be fitted in watertight bulkheads dividing cargo between deck spaces. Such doors may be hinged, rolling or sliding doors but shall not be remotely controlled. They shall be fitted at the highest level and as far from the shell plating as practicable, but in no case shall the outboard vertical edges be situated at a distance from the shell plating which is less than one fifth of the breadth of the ship, as defined in regulation 2, such distance being measured at right angles to the centreline at the level of the deepest subdivision draught.

9.2 Should any such doors be accessible during the voyage, they shall be fitted with a device which prevents unauthorized opening. When it is proposed to fit such doors, the number and arrangements shall receive the special consideration of the Administration.

10 Portable plates on bulkheads shall not be permitted except in machinery spaces. The Administration may permit not more than one power-operated sliding watertight door in each watertight bulkhead larger than those specified in paragraph 7.1.2 to be substituted for these portable plates, provided these doors are intended to remain closed during navigation except in case of urgent necessity at the discretion of the master. These doors need not meet the requirements of paragraph 7.1.4 regarding complete closure by hand-operated gear in 90 s.

7.8 动力滑动水密门的动力操纵系统或控制系统中的单一电气故障，不应导致一扇关闭的门被开启。在尽可能靠近本条 7.3 所要求的每台电动机的供电线路上的某一点，应连续监控电源供电的有效性。任何这种供电失效，应在驾驶室集控台上发出听觉和视觉报警。

8.1 驾驶台内的集控台应有一个“控制模式”开关，其应具有两套控制模式：一套是“就地控制”模式，其不使用自动关闭装置即能使任何门就地开启和就地关闭，另一套是“关闭门”模式，其应能自动关闭任何开启着的门。该“关闭门”模式应准许门被就地开启，而当脱开就地控制机构时应能自动重新关闭该门。“控制模式”开关一般处于“就地控制”模式挡内。“关闭门”模式仅在紧急情况下或为试验的目的才使用。应特别重视“控制模式”开关的可靠性。

8.2 驾驶台内的集控台应设有标明每扇门位置的图，并附有发光指示器，以显示出每扇门的开启或关闭状态。应使用红灯表示一扇门完全开启，而绿灯表示一扇门完全关闭。当遥控关闭门时，红灯应以闪烁表示门处于关闭过程中。指示器电路应与每扇门的控制电路分开。

8.3 应不能从集控台遥控开启任何一扇门。

9.1 如果主管机关确信必需设有此类门，可在甲板处所之间分隔货物的水密舱壁上装设适当构造的水密门。此类门可为铰链式、滚动式或滑动式，但不应是遥控的。门应装在最高处并尽可能远离外板，但其靠近舷侧的垂直边缘概不得位于如第 2 条所规定的距外板少于船宽的 1/5 处，此距离在最深分舱吃水线水平面上向船中心线垂直量计。

9.2 如果有在航行中可以通过的门，则任何此类门应设有适当装置，以防未经授权的开启。在提出设置此类门时，主管机关应对其数量及布置予以特殊考虑。

10 活动门板不允许用于舱壁上，但在机器处所内除外。主管机关可允许在每一水密舱壁上设一扇宽度超过本条 7.1.2 规定的动力滑动水密门取代此类活动门板，但这些门在航行中除在紧急情况下船长认为必需外应保持关闭。这些门不必满足本条7.1.4关于在 90 s 内用手动操作装置完全关闭的要求。

11.1 Where trunkways or tunnels for access from crew accommodation to the machinery spaces, for piping or for any other purpose, are carried through watertight bulkheads, they shall be watertight and in accordance with the requirements of regulation 16-1. The access to at least one end of each such tunnel or trunkway, if used as a passage at sea, shall be through a trunk extending watertight to a height sufficient to permit access above the bulkhead deck. The access to the other end of the trunkway or tunnel may be through a watertight door of the type required by its location in the ship. Such trunkways or tunnels shall not extend through the first subdivision bulkhead abaft the collision bulkhead.

11.2 Where it is proposed to fit tunnels piercing watertight bulkheads, these shall receive the special consideration of the Administration.

11.3 Where trunkways in connection with refrigerated cargo and ventilation or forced draught trunks are carried through more than one watertight bulkhead, the means of closure at such openings shall be operated by power and be capable of being closed from a central position situated above the bulkhead deck.

Regulation 13-1
Openings in watertight bulkheads and internal decks in cargo ships

1 The number of openings in watertight subdivisions is to be kept to a minimum compatible with the design and proper working of the ship. Where penetrations of watertight bulkheads and internal decks are necessary for access, piping, ventilation, electrical cables, etc., arrangements are to be made to maintain the watertight integrity. The Administration may permit relaxation in the watertightness of openings above the freeboard deck, provided that it is demonstrated that any progressive flooding can be easily controlled and that the safety of the ship is not impaired.

2 Doors provided to ensure the watertight integrity of internal openings which are used while at sea are to be sliding watertight doors capable of being remotely closed from the bridge and are also to be operable locally from each side of the bulkhead. Indicators are to be provided at the control position showing whether the doors are open or closed, and an audible alarm is to be provided at the door closure. The power, control and indicators are to be operable in the event of main power failure. Particular attention is to be paid to minimizing the effect of control system failure. Each power-operated sliding watertight door shall be provided with an individual hand-operated mechanism. It shall be possible to open and close the door by hand at the door itself from both sides.

3 Access doors and access hatch covers normally closed at sea, intended to ensure the watertight integrity of internal openings, shall be provided with means of indication locally and on the bridge showing whether these doors or hatch covers are open or closed. A notice is to be affixed to each such door or hatch cover to the effect that it is not to be left open.

11.1 凡从船员舱室进入机器处所的围壁通道或隧道，或用于管路或任何其他用途的围壁通道或隧道，如穿过水密舱壁，须为水密并符合第16-1条的要求。在航行中用作通路的每一围壁通道或隧道，至少其一端的出口须通过保持水密到足够高度的围壁并能从舱壁甲板以上出入。围壁通道或隧道的另一端出通道，可经过一水密门，其型号按其所在位置决定，此类围壁通道或隧道不得通过防撞舱壁之后的第一个分舱舱壁。

11.2 如果需装设穿过水密舱壁的隧道，主管机关应予以特别考虑。

11.3 如果连接冷藏货物处所和通风设备的围壁通道或强力通风隧道穿过一个以上水密舱壁，此类开口的关闭装置应由动力操纵，并应能从位于舱壁甲板上方的集控位置处将其关闭。

第13-1条
货船水密舱壁和内部甲板上的开口

1 水密分隔上的开口应在适合船舶设计和船舶正常作业的情况下保持最少数量。如果因出入、管路、通风、电缆等而必须贯穿水密舱壁和内部甲板，则应设有保持水密完整性的装置。如果证实任何累计进水能易于控制并且不损害船舶安全，则主管机关可允许放宽对干舷甲板以上的开口的水密性要求。

2 为确保在海上使用的内部开口的水密完整性而设置的门应是滑动水密门，能从驾驶台遥控关闭，也可从舱壁每侧就地操纵。在控制位置应装设显示门是开启或关闭的指示器，并且在门关闭时发出听觉报警。在主动力失灵时，动力、控制和指示器应能工作。特别应注意减少控制系统失灵的影响。每一个动力操纵的滑动水密门应有一个独立的手动机械操纵装置。该装置应能从门的两侧用手开启和关闭该门。

3 用以保证内部开口的水密完整性且通常在航行时关闭的出入门和舱盖，应在该处和驾驶台装设显示这些门或舱盖是开启还是关闭的设施。每一个此类门或舱盖应附贴一个通告牌，其大意是不应让其处于开启状态。

4 Watertight doors or ramps of satisfactory construction may be fitted to internally subdivide large cargo spaces, provided that the Administration is satisfied that such doors or ramps are essential. These doors or ramps may be hinged, rolling or sliding doors or ramps, but shall not be remotely controlled. Should any of the doors or ramps be accessible during the voyage, they shall be fitted with a device which prevents unauthorized opening.

5 Other closing appliances which are kept permanently closed at sea to ensure the watertight integrity of internal openings shall be provided with a notice which is to be affixed to each such closing appliance to the effect that it is to be kept closed. Manholes fitted with closely bolted covers need not be so marked.

Regulation 14
Passenger ships carrying goods vehicles and accompanying personnel

1 This regulation applies to passenger ships designed or adapted for the carriage of goods vehicles and accompanying personnel.

2 If in such a ship the total number of passengers, which includes personnel accompanying vehicles, does not exceed $12 + A_d/25$, where A_d = total deck area (square metres) of spaces available for the stowage of goods vehicles and where the clear height at the stowage position and at the entrance to such spaces is not less than 4 m, the provisions of regulations 13.9.1 and 13.9.2 in respect of watertight doors apply except that the doors may be fitted at any level in watertight bulkheads dividing cargo spaces. Additionally, indicators are required on the navigation bridge to show automatically when each door is closed and all door fastenings are secured.

3 The ship may not be certified for a higher number of passengers than assumed in paragraph 2, if a watertight door has been fitted in accordance with this regulation.

Regulation 15
Openings in the shell plating below the bulkhead deck of passenger ships and the freeboard deck of cargo ships

1 The number of openings in the shell plating shall be reduced to the minimum compatible with the design and proper working of the ship.

2 The arrangement and efficiency of the means for closing any opening in the shell plating shall be consistent with its intended purpose and the position in which it is fitted and generally to the satisfaction of the Administration.

3.1 Subject to the requirements of the International Convention on Load Lines in force, no sidescuttle shall be fitted in such a position that its sill is below a line drawn parallel to the bulkhead deck at side and having its lowest point 2.5% of the breadth of the ship above the deepest subdivision draught, or 500 mm, whichever is the greater.

4　可以装设结构良好的水密门或坡道用作大型货物处所的内部分隔,条件是主管机关确信此种门或坡道是必要的。这些门或坡道可以是铰链的、滚动的或滑动的门或坡道,但不应是遥控操纵的。如果在航程中需要通过任何此类门或坡道,则应设有适当装置以防未经授权的开启。

5　为保证内部开口的水密完整性,在海上保持永久关闭的其他关闭装置,应有一个通告牌贴于其上,其大意是应保持关闭状态。用螺栓紧固盖子的人孔不必设此通告牌。

第14条
载运货车和随车人员的客船

1　本条适用于为载运货车和随车人员而设计或改做此用的客船。

2　如果这类船上的乘客总数(包括随车人员在内)不超过 $12+A_d/25$,其中 A_d 为能用于装载货车处所的甲板总面积(m^2),以及装货车辆处所及其出入口的净高度不小于 4 m,则关于水门密门可应用第13.9.1和13.9.2条的规定,但这些门可设置在分隔装货处所水密舱壁的任何高度上。此外,要求在驾驶室设置指示器,以自动指示何时每扇门关闭和何时所有门闩已扣紧。

3　如果已按本条装设一扇水密门,船舶核准搭载的最大乘客数不可超过本条2所假定的乘客数。

第15条
客船舱壁甲板和货船干舷甲板以下外板上的开口

1　外板上的开口数量应在适应船舶设计及船舶正常作业情况下减至最少。

2　关闭任何外板开口设备的布置及效用,应与其预定的用途及装设位置相适应,一般应使主管机关满意。

3.1　根据现行《国际载重线公约》的要求,舷窗的位置应不至于使其窗槛低于平行于舱壁甲板边线所绘的线,此线的最低点在最深分舱载重线以上为船宽的2.5%,或500 mm,取较大者。

3.2 All sidescuttles the sills of which are below the bulkhead deck of passenger ships and the freeboard deck of cargo ships, as permitted by paragraph 3.1, shall be of such construction as will effectively prevent any person opening them without the consent of the master of the ship.

4 Efficient hinged inside deadlights, so arranged that they can be easily and effectively closed and secured watertight, shall be fitted to all sidescuttles except that, abaft one eighth of the ship's length from the forward perpendicular and above a line drawn parallel to the bulkhead deck at side and having its lowest point at a height of 3.7 m plus 2.5% of the breadth of the ship above the deepest subdivision draught, the deadlights may be portable in passenger accommodation, unless the deadlights are required by the International Convention on Load Lines in force to be permanently attached in their proper positions. Such portable deadlights shall be stowed adjacent to the sidescuttles they serve.

5.1 No sidescuttles shall be fitted in any spaces which are appropriated exclusively to the carriage of cargo.

5.2 Sidescuttles may, however, be fitted in spaces appropriated alternatively to the carriage of cargo or passengers, but they shall be of such construction as will effectively prevent any person opening them or their deadlights without the consent of the master.

6 Automatic ventilating sidescuttles shall not be fitted in the shell plating below the bulkhead deck of passenger ships and the freeboard deck of cargo ships without the special sanction of the Administration.

7 The number of scuppers, sanitary discharges and other similar openings in the shell plating shall be reduced to the minimum either by making each discharge serve for as many as possible of the sanitary and other pipes or in any other satisfactory manner.

8.1 All inlets and discharges in the shell plating shall be fitted with efficient and accessible arrangements for preventing the accidental admission of water into the ship.

8.2.1 Subject to the requirements of the International Convention on Load Lines in force, and except as provided in paragraph 8.3, each separate discharge led through the shell plating from spaces below the bulkhead deck of passenger ships and the freeboard deck of cargo ships shall be provided with either one automatic non-return valve fitted with a positive means of closing it from above the bulkhead deck of passenger ships and the freeboard deck of cargo ships or with two automatic non-return valves without positive means of closing, provided that the inboard valve is situated above the deepest subdivision draught and is always accessible for examination under service conditions. Where a valve with positive means of closing is fitted, the operating position above the bulkhead deck of passenger ships and the freeboard deck of cargo ships shall always be readily accessible and means shall be provided for indicating whether the valve is open or closed.

8.2.2 The requirements of the International Convention on Load Lines in force shall apply to discharges led through the shell plating from spaces above the bulkhead deck of passenger ships and the freeboard deck of cargo ships.

3.2 本条3.1准许的所有舷窗，凡窗槛低于客船舱壁甲板和货船干舷甲板者，其构造应能有效地防止任何人未经船长许可而开启。

4 所有舷窗均须装设有效的内部铰链舷窗盖，其布置须能便利和有效地关闭及紧固成水密，但在距首垂线1/8船长以后，且在平行于舱壁甲板边线及最低点在最深分舱吃水以上3.7 m加船宽的2.5%所绘的线以上者，则乘客舱室的舷窗盖可为可移式的，但按现行《国际载重线公约》要求需永久附着于其相应位置者除外。这些可移式舷窗盖应存放于其所属的舷窗附近。

5.1 凡专供载货用的处所，不得装设舷窗。

5.2 供交替载货或载客的处所，可装设舷窗，但其构造应能有效地防止任何人未经船长许可而开启舷窗或舷窗盖。

6 未经主管机关特准，不应在客船舱壁甲板和货船干舷甲板以下的外板上装设自动通风舷窗。

7 外板上的泄水孔、卫生水排泄孔及其他类似开口，应减至最低数量。可采取每个排水孔供尽可能多的卫生水管及其他管道共用，或采用其他适当的办法。

8.1 外板上的所有进水孔及排水孔，均应装设防止海水意外进入船内的有效并可到达的装置。

8.2.1 取决于现行《国际载重线公约》的要求，且除第8.3款规定者外，凡从客船舱壁甲板和货船干舷甲板以下处所引出穿过船壳板的每一独立排水孔，须设有一个自动止回阀，此阀须具有从客船舱壁甲板和货船干舷甲板以上将其关闭的可靠装置，或者须设有两个无此类关闭装置的自动止回阀，但内侧一阀须设置在最深分舱吃水以上，且能在营运工况下随时接近以做检查。如设置有可靠关闭装置的阀，则在客船舱壁甲板和货船干舷甲板以上的操作位置须随时易于到达，并须设有指示阀门开启或关闭的装置。

8.2.2 现行《国际载重线公约》的要求适用于从客船舱壁甲板和货船干舷甲板以上处所引出穿过外板的排水孔。

8.3 Machinery space, main and auxiliary sea inlets and discharges in connection with the operation of machinery shall be fitted with readily accessible valves between the pipes and the shell plating or between the pipes and fabricated boxes attached to the shell plating. In manned machinery spaces the valves may be controlled locally and shall be provided with indicators showing whether they are open or closed.

8.4 Moving parts penetrating the shell plating below the deepest subdivision draught shall be fitted with a watertight sealing arrangement acceptable to the Administration. The inboard gland shall be located within a watertight space of such volume that, if flooded, the bulkhead deck of passenger ships and the freeboard deck of cargo ships will not be submerged. The Administration may require that if such compartment is flooded, essential or emergency power and lighting, internal communication, signals or other emergency devices must remain available in other parts of the ship.

8.5 All shell fittings and valves required by this regulation shall be of steel, bronze or other approved ductile material. Valves of ordinary cast iron or similar material are not acceptable. All pipes to which this regulation refers shall be of steel or other equivalent material to the satisfaction of the Administration.

9 Gangway, cargo and fuelling ports fitted below the bulkhead deck of passenger ships and the freeboard deck of cargo ships shall be watertight and in no case be so fitted as to have their lowest point below the deepest subdivision draught.

10.1 The inboard opening of each ash-chute, rubbish-chute, etc., shall be fitted with an efficient cover.

10.2 If the inboard opening is situated below the bulkhead deck of passenger ships and the freeboard deck of cargo ships, the cover shall be watertight and, in addition, an automatic non-return valve shall be fitted in the chute in an easily accessible position above the deepest subdivision draught.

Regulation 15-1
External openings in cargo ships

1 All external openings leading to compartments assumed intact in the damage analysis, which are below the final damage waterline, are required to be watertight.

2 External openings required to be watertight in accordance with paragraph 1 shall, except for cargo hatch covers, be fitted with indicators on the bridge.

3 Openings in the shell plating below the deck limiting the vertical extent of damage shall be fitted with a device that prevents unauthorized opening if they are accessible during the voyage.

4 Other closing appliances which are kept permanently closed at sea to ensure the watertight integrity of external openings shall be provided with a notice affixed to each appliance to the effect that it is to be kept closed. Manholes fitted with closely bolted covers need not be so marked.

8.3 与机器运转有关的机器处所的主、辅海水进水孔和排水孔，应在管子与外板之间或管子与装配在外板上的阀箱之间装设易于到达的阀。在有人值守的机器处所内，这些阀可就地控制，并应设有表明阀开启或关闭的指示器。

8.4 穿过最深分舱吃水以下船壳板的活动部分须装设主管机关认可的水密封闭装置。舷内填料函压盖须位于水密处所内，且其容积能使它进水后不会导致客船舱壁甲板和货船干舷甲板被淹没。主管机关可以要求船舶其他部分的基本或应急电源和照明、内部通信、信号或其他应急装置须在此类舱室浸水后仍可使用。

8.5 所有本条要求的外板配件和阀应为钢质、青铜或其他认可的延性材料。普通铸铁或类似材料的阀不能采用。本条所指的所有管子应为钢质或主管机关满意的其他等效材料。

9 设于客船舱壁甲板和货船干舷甲板以下的舷门、装货门及装燃料门均应水密，并且其最低点无论如何不得低于最深分舱吃水。

10.1 每个出灰管、垃圾管等的舷内开口均应设有有效盖子。

10.2 如果舷内开口位于客船舱壁甲板和货船干舷甲板以下，则盖子应为水密，并且在最深分舱吃水以上易于到达处的排出管上还应设有一个自动止回阀。

第15-1条
货船外部开口

1 所有通向在破损分析中假定为完整的且位于最终水线以下的舱室的外部开口，应要求水密。

2 根据本条1要求水密的外部开口除货舱盖外，应在驾驶室设有指示器。

3 在限制垂向破损范围的甲板以下的船壳外板上的开口如果在航程中可以通过，则应设有适当装置以防未经授权的开启。

4 为保证外部开口的水密完整性，在海上保持永久关闭的其他关闭装置，应有一个通告牌贴于其上，其大意是应保持关闭状态。用螺栓紧固盖子的人孔不必设此通告牌。

Regulation 16
Construction and initial tests of watertight closures

1.1 The design, materials and construction of all watertight closures such as doors, hatches, sidescuttles, gangway and cargo ports, valves, pipes, ash-chutes and rubbish chutes referred to in these regulations shall be to the satisfaction of the Administration.

1.2 Such valves, doors, hatches and mechanisms shall be suitably marked to ensure that they may be properly used to provide maximum safety.

1.3 The frames of vertical watertight doors shall have no groove at the bottom in which dirt might lodge and prevent the door closing properly.

2 Watertight doors and hatches shall be tested by water pressure to the maximum head of water they might sustain in a final or intermediate stage of flooding. For cargo ships not covered by damage stability requirements, watertight doors and hatches shall be tested by water pressure to a head of water measured from the lower edge of the opening to 1 m above the freeboard deck. Where testing of individual doors and hatches is not carried out because of possible damage to insulation or outfitting items, testing of individual doors and hatches may be replaced by a prototype pressure test of each type and size of door or hatch with a test pressure corresponding at least to the head required for the individual location. The prototype test shall be carried out before the door or hatch is fitted. The installation method and procedure for fitting the door or hatch on board shall correspond to that of the prototype test. When fitted on board, each door or hatch shall be checked for proper seating between the bulkhead, the frame and the door or between deck, the coaming and the hatch.

Regulation 16-1
Construction and initial tests of watertight decks, trunks, etc.

1 Watertight decks, trunks, tunnels, duct keels and ventilators shall be of the same strength as watertight bulkheads at corresponding levels. The means used for making them watertight, and the arrangements adopted for closing openings in them, shall be to the satisfaction of the Administration. Watertight ventilators and trunks shall be carried at least up to the bulkhead deck in passenger ships and up to the freeboard deck in cargo ships.

2 In passenger ships, where a ventilation trunk passing through a structure penetrates a watertight area of the bulkhead deck, the trunk shall be capable of withstanding the water pressure that may be present within the trunk, after having taken into account the maximum heel angle during flooding, in accordance with regulation 7-2.

3 In ro-ro passenger ships, where all or part of the penetration of the bulkhead deck is on the main ro-ro deck, the trunk shall be capable of withstanding impact pressure due to internal water motions (sloshing) of water trapped on the ro-ro deck.

4 After completion, a hose or flooding test shall be applied to watertight decks and a hose test to watertight trunks, tunnels and ventilators.

第16条
水密关闭装置的构造和初次试验

1.1　本条所述的所有水密关闭装置，例如门、舱口、舷窗、舷门和装货门、阀门、管道、出灰管及垃圾管的设计、材料和构造，均须令主管机关满意；

1.2　此类阀门、门、舱口及装置须做适当标志，以确保可以适当地使用它们从而最大限度地保证安全；和

1.3　直立式水密门的门框，其底部不得有可能积聚污秽的槽，以免妨碍门的正常关闭。

2　水密门和舱口须以其在进水最终或中间阶段可能承受的最大水头做水压试验。对于不受破损稳性要求约束的货船，水密门和舱口须以从开口下缘量至干舷甲板以上1 m的水头做水压试验。如因可能损坏绝缘件或舾装件而未对个别门和舱口做试验，可用最起码相应于预定位置所要求的试验压力对每种类型和尺寸的门进行原型试验取代对每一扇门的试验。该原型试验须在门或舱口安装之前进行。门或舱口在船上安装的方法和程序应与原型试验所用安装方法和程序相一致。当在船上装妥后，须检查每扇门或舱口，以核查舱壁、门框和门之间，或甲板、围板和舱口之间是否正确就位。

第16-1条
水密甲板、围壁通道等的构造和初次试验

1　水密甲板、围壁通道、隧道、箱形龙骨及通风管道，均应与相应高度的水密舱壁具有同等强度。其水密及关闭其开口的装置，均应使主管机关满意。水密通风管道及围壁通道在客船上应至少向上延伸到舱壁甲板，在货船上应至少向上延伸到干舷甲板。

2　在客船上，如穿过某一结构的通风管道贯穿舱壁甲板的水密区域，在按照第7-2条计及进水时的最大横倾角后，该通风管道须能承受可能出现于其中的水压。

3　在滚装客船上，如果舱壁甲板的穿透结构全部或部分位于滚装主甲板上，该通风管道须能够承受滚装甲板积水的内部水运动（晃动）引起的冲击压力。

4　完工后，水密甲板应做冲水或灌水试验，而水密围壁通道、隧道和通风管道则应做冲水试验。

Regulation 17
Internal watertight integrity of passenger ships above the bulkhead deck

1 The Administration may require that all reasonable and practicable measures shall be taken to limit the entry and spread of water above the bulkhead deck. Such measures may include partial bulkheads or webs. When partial watertight bulkheads and webs are fitted on the bulkhead deck, above or in the immediate vicinity of watertight bulkheads, they shall have watertight shell and bulkhead deck connections so as to restrict the flow of water along the deck when the ship is in a heeled damaged condition. Where the partial watertight bulkhead does not line up with the bulkhead below, the bulkhead deck between shall be made effectively watertight. Where openings, pipes, scuppers, electric cables, etc., are carried through the partial watertight bulkheads or decks within the immersed part of the bulkhead deck, arrangements shall be made to ensure the watertight integrity of the structure above the bulkhead deck.①

2 All openings in the exposed weather deck shall have coamings of ample height and strength and shall be provided with efficient means for expeditiously closing them weathertight. Freeing ports, open rails and scuppers shall be fitted as necessary for rapidly clearing the weather deck of water under all weather conditions.

3 Air pipes terminating within a superstructure which are not fitted with watertight means of closure shall be considered as unprotected openings when applying regulation 7-2.6.1.1.

4 Sidescuttles, gangway, cargo and fuelling ports and other means for closing openings in the shell plating above the bulkhead deck shall be of efficient design and construction and of sufficient strength having regard to the spaces in which they are fitted and their positions relative to the deepest subdivision draught.②

5 Efficient inside deadlights, so arranged that they can be easily and effectively closed and secured watertight, shall be provided for all sidescuttles to spaces below the first deck above the bulkhead deck.

Regulation 17-1
Integrity of the hull and superstructure, damage prevention and control on ro-ro passenger ships

1.1 Subject to the provisions of paragraphs 1.2 and 1.3, all accesses that lead to spaces below the bulkhead deck shall have a lowest point which is not less than 2.5 m above the bulkhead deck.

---

① Refer to *Guidance notes on the integrity of flooding boundaries above the bulkhead deck of passenger ships for proper application of regulations Ⅱ-1/8 and 20, paragraph 1, of SOLAS 1974, as amended* (MSC/Circ.541, as may be amended).

② Refer to *Recommendation on strength and security and locking arrangements of shell doors on ro-ro passenger ships* (resolution A.793(19)).

第17条
客船舱壁甲板以上的内部水密完整性

1　主管机关可要求采取一切合理和可行的措施，以限制海水在舱壁甲板以上进入及漫流。此类措施可包括装设局部舱壁或桁材。当局部水密舱壁和桁材装于水密舱壁上方或附近的舱壁甲板上时，应与外板及舱壁甲板水密连接，以使在船舶破损横倾的情况下限制海水沿甲板漫流。如果局部水密舱壁与其下方的舱壁错开，则两者间的舱壁甲板应做有效的水密。如果开口、管子、排水管和电缆等通过舱壁甲板浸没范围内的局部水密舱壁，应设有保证舱壁甲板以上结构水密完整性的设施。①

2　露天甲板上的所有开口，应设有足够高度和强度的围板，并应设有能迅速关闭成风雨密的有效装置。应按需要装设排水舷口、栏杆及流水孔，以便在任何天气情况下均能迅速排除露天甲板上的积水。

3　在适用第7-2.6.1.1条时，终止于上层建筑内的未设水密关闭装置的空气管应被视作未受保护的开口。

4　在舱壁甲板以上外板上的舷窗、舷门、装货门和装燃料门以及关闭开口的其他装置，应考虑到所装设的处所及其相对于最深分舱吃水的位置，做有效的设计与构造，并应具有足够的强度。②

5　在舱壁甲板以上第一层甲板以下处所内的所有舷窗，应设有有效的内侧舷窗盖，其布置应能易于有效地水密关闭并紧固。

第17-1条
滚装客船船体和上层建筑的完整性、破损的预防和控制

1.1　除满足本条1.2和1.3的要求外，所有通向舱壁甲板以下处所的通道口的最低点至少应高出舱壁甲板2.5 m。

---

①　参见《正确应用经修正的1974年SOLAS公约第Ⅱ-1/8条和第20.1条关于客船舱壁甲板以上进水边界完整性的导则》（第MSC/Circ.541号通函，可能经修正）。

②　参见《关于滚装客船舷门强度、紧固和锁闭装置的建议案》（第A.793(19)号决议）。

1.2 Where vehicle ramps are installed to give access to spaces below the bulkhead deck, their openings shall be able to be closed weathertight to prevent ingress of water below, alarmed and indicated to the navigation bridge.

1.3 The Administration may permit the fitting of particular accesses to spaces below the bulkhead deck provided they are necessary for the essential working of the ship, e.g. the movement of machinery and stores, subject to such accesses being made watertight, alarmed and indicated on the navigation bridge.

2 Indicators shall be provided on the navigation bridge for all shell doors, loading doors and other closing appliances which, if left open or not properly secured, could, in the opinion of the Administration, lead to flooding of a special category space or ro-ro space. The indicator system shall be designed on the fail-safe principle and shall show by visual alarms if the door is not fully closed or if any of the securing arrangements are not in place and fully locked and by audible alarms if such door or closing appliances become open or the securing arrangements become unsecured. The indicator panel on the navigation bridge shall be equipped with a mode selection function "harbour/sea voyage" so arranged that an audible alarm is given on the navigation bridge if the ship leaves harbour with the bow doors, inner doors, stern ramp or any other side shell doors not closed or any closing device not in the correct position. The power supply for the indicator system shall be independent of the power supply for operating and securing the doors.

3 Television surveillance and a water leakage detection system shall be arranged to provide an indication to the navigation bridge and to the engine control station of any leakage through inner and outer bow doors, stern doors or any other shell doors which could lead to flooding of special category spaces or ro-ro spaces.

1.2 在设有通向舱壁甲板以下处所的车辆坡道的情况下,坡道开口关闭时应能保持风雨密,以防止下层处所进水,并在驾驶室设有报警与指示装置。

1.3 主管机关可以允许为船上的某些必需的工作(如机器与物料的移动)设置通向舱壁甲板以下处所的特别通道。但该通道应为水密,并在驾驶台设有报警与指示装置。

2 主管机关认为任其开启或未适当紧固会导致特种处所或滚装处所进水的所有舷门、装货门和其他关闭设备应在驾驶室配备指示器。指示器系统应按故障安全原则设计,如果门未完全关闭,或任一紧固装置未到位或未完全锁好,该指示器应以视觉报警显示;如果这类门或关闭装置开启或紧固装置松开,指示器应以听觉报警显示。在驾驶台的指示器面板上配备的“在港/航行中”模式选择功能应使船舶离港时,如果首门、内门、尾坡道或任何其他舷门未关闭或任何关闭装置未处于正确位置,在驾驶台发出听觉报警。用于指示器系统的动力源应独立于用于操作和紧固这些门的动力源。

3 应设置电视监视和水渗漏探测系统,将可能通过内、外首门、尾门或任何其他舷门导致特种处所或滚装处所进水的任何渗漏情况提供给驾驶室及发动机控制站。

Part B-3
Subdivision load line assignment for passenger ships

Regulation 18
Assigning, marking and recording of subdivision load lines for passenger ships

1 In order that the required degree of subdivision shall be maintained, a load line corresponding to the approved subdivision draught shall be assigned and marked on the ship's sides. A ship intended for alternating modes of operation may, if the owners desire, have one or more additional load lines assigned and marked to correspond with the subdivision draughts which the Administration may approve for the alternative service configurations. Each service configuration so approved shall comply with part B-1 of this chapter independently of the results obtained for other modes of operation.

2 The subdivision load lines assigned and marked shall be recorded in the Passenger Ship Safety Certificate, and shall be distinguished by the notation P1 for the principal passenger service configuration, and P2, P3, etc., for the alternative configurations. The principal passenger configuration shall be taken as the mode of operation in which the required subdivision index *R* will have the highest value.

3 The freeboard corresponding to each of these load lines shall be measured at the same position and from the same deck line as the freeboards determined in accordance with the International Convention on Load Lines in force.

4 The freeboard corresponding to each approved subdivision load line and the service configuration for which it is approved shall be clearly indicated on the Passenger Ship Safety Certificate.

5 In no case shall any subdivision load line mark be placed above the deepest load line in salt water as determined by the strength of the ship or the International Convention on Load Lines in force.

6 Whatever may be the position of the subdivision load line marks, a ship shall in no case be loaded so as to submerge the load line mark appropriate to the season and locality as determined in accordance with the International Convention on Load Lines in force.

7 A ship shall in no case be so loaded that when it is in salt water the subdivision load line mark appropriate to the particular voyage and service configuration is submerged.

B-3 部分
客船分舱载重线的核定

第 18 条
客船分舱载重线的核定、勘绘与记载

1 为了保持所要求的分舱程度，应在船舶两舷核定并勘绘相应于所核准分舱吃水的载重线。对拟交替营运模式的船舶，如果船东要求，可核定和勘绘一个或数个相应于主管机关核准的交替营运配置的分舱吃水的附加载重线。按此批准的每一营运配置均应符合本章 B-1 部分的要求，不受其他营运模式所得结果的影响。

2 所核定和勘绘的分舱载重线应载入客船安全证书，并以符号 P1 表示主要载客营运配置；P2、P3 等分别表示其他交替配置。主要载客配置应视为要求的分舱指数 R 值最高的营运模式。

3 相应于每一载重线的干舷，应按现行《国际载重线公约》确定的干舷在同一位置从同一甲板线进行测量。

4 相应于每一经核准的分舱载重线的干舷以及对其所核准的营运配置，均应清楚地记载在客船安全证书内。

5 任何分舱载重线标志均不得勘绘于按船舶强度或现行《国际载重线公约》所确定的海水中最深载重线以上。

6 不论分舱载重线标志的位置如何，船舶装载均不得使按现行《国际载重线公约》所确定的适合于所在季节和区域的载重线标志浸没于水中。

7 当船舶在海水中时，其装载在任何情况下均不得使适合于该航次及营运配置的分舱载重线标志浸没于水中。

Part B-4
Stability management

Regulation 19
Damage control information[①]

1 There shall be permanently exhibited, or readily available on the navigation bridge, for the guidance of the officer in charge of the ship, plans showing clearly for each deck and hold the boundaries of the watertight compartments, the openings therein with the means of closure and position of any controls thereof, and the arrangements for the correction of any list due to flooding. In addition, booklets containing the aforementioned information shall be made available to the officers of the ship.

2 General precautions to be included shall consist of a listing of equipment, conditions, and operational procedures considered by the Administration to be necessary to maintain watertight integrity under normal ship operations.

3 Specific precautions to be included shall consist of a listing of elements (i.e. closures, security of cargo, sounding of alarms, etc.) considered by the Administration to be vital to the survival of the ship, passengers and crew.

4 In case of ships to which damage stability requirements of part B-1 apply, damage stability information shall provide the master with a simple and easily understandable way of assessing the ship's survivability in all damage cases involving a compartment or group of compartments.

Regulation 19-1
Damage control drills for passenger ships

1 This regulation applies to passenger ships constructed before, on or after 1 January 2020.

2 A damage control drill shall take place at least every three months. The entire crew need not participate in every drill, but only those crew members with damage control responsibilities.

3 The damage control drill scenarios shall vary each drill so that emergency conditions are simulated for different damage conditions and shall, as far as practicable, be conducted as if there were an actual emergency.

4 Each damage control drill shall include:

.1 for crew members with damage control responsibilities, reporting to stations and preparing for the duties described in the muster list required by regulation Ⅲ/8;

① Refer to the *Guidelines for damage control plans and information to the master* (MSC.1/Circ.1245, as amended by MSC.1/Circ.1570) and to the *Guidelines for verification of damage stability requirements for tankers* (MSC.1/Circ.1461).

B-4 部分
稳性管理

第 19 条
破损控制资料[①]

1　驾驶台应设有永久展示或随时可用的控制图,用于指导船上负责的高级船员,图上应清晰显示每层甲板及货舱的水密舱室限界面,上面的开口及其关闭装置和任何控制位置,以及扶正由于进水产生的横倾的装置。此外,还应给船上高级船员提供包含上述资料的小册子。

2　应收入资料的一般预防措施应包括主管机关认为在船舶正常营运时为保持水密完整性所需的设备、条件和操作程序清单。

3　应收入资料的特殊预防措施应包括主管机关认为对船舶、乘客和船员的生存至关重要的各种事项(即关闭装置、货物系固和听觉报警等)。

4　对适用 B-1 部分破损稳性要求的船舶,破损稳性资料应为船长提供一种简单易懂的方式评估船舶在涉及一个或一组舱室的所有破损情况下的残存能力。

第 19-1 条
客船破损控制演习

1　本条适用于在 2020 年 1 月 1 日或之前或之后建造的客船。

2　应至少每三个月进行一次客船破损控制演习。每一次演习无须所有船员参加,仅需承担破损控制责任的船员参加。

3　每一次破损控制演习的场景须各有不同,以模拟不同破损状况下的紧急情况。演习须尽实际可能做到像真正发生了紧急情况。

4　每一次破损控制演习须包括:

　.1　对于承担破损控制责任的船员,向集合站报到,并准备执行第Ⅲ/8 条规定的应急部署表所述的任务;

① 参见《向船长提供破损控制图和资料导则》(第 MSC.1/Circ.1245 号通函,经 MSC.1/Circ.1570 号通函修订)和《液货船破损稳性要求核验导则》(第 MSC.1/Circ.1461 号通函)。

.2 use of the damage control information and the onboard damage stability computer, if fitted, to conduct stability assessments for the simulated damage conditions;

.3 establishment of the communications link between the ship and shore-based support, if provided;

.4 operation of watertight doors and other watertight closures;

.5 demonstrating proficiency in the use of the flooding detection system, if fitted, in accordance with muster list duties;

.6 demonstrating proficiency in the use of cross-flooding and equalization systems, if fitted, in accordance with muster list duties;

.7 operation of bilge pumps and checking of bilge alarms and automatic bilge pump starting systems; and

.8 instruction in damage survey and use of the ship's damage control systems.

5 At least one damage control drill each year shall include activation of the shore-based support, if provided in compliance with regulation Ⅱ-1/8-1.3, to conduct stability assessments for the simulated damage conditions.

6 Every crew member with assigned damage control responsibilities shall be familiarized with their duties and about the damage control information before the voyage begins.

7 A record of each damage control drill shall be maintained in the same manner as prescribed for the other drills in regulation Ⅲ/19.5.

Regulation 20
Loading of ships

1 On completion of loading of the ship and prior to its departure, the master shall determine the ship's trim and stability and also ascertain and record that the ship is upright and in compliance with stability criteria in relevant regulations. The determination of the ship's stability shall always be made by calculation or by ensuring that the ship is loaded according to one of the precalculated loading conditions within the approved stability information. The Administration may accept the use of an electronic loading and stability computer or equivalent means for this purpose.

2 Water ballast should not in general be carried in tanks intended for oil fuel. In ships in which it is not practicable to avoid putting water in oil fuel tanks, oily-water separating equipment to the satisfaction of the Administration shall be fitted, or other alternative means, such as discharge to shore facilities, acceptable to the Administration shall be provided for disposing of the oily-water ballast.

3 The provisions of this regulation are without prejudice to the provisions of the International Convention for the Prevention of Pollution from Ships in force.

.2 使用破损控制资料和船上破损稳性计算机(如设有)进行模拟破损工况的稳性评估;

.3 建立船舶和岸基支持的通信连接,如设有;

.4 操作水密门和其他水密关闭装置;

.5 按照应急部署表上的职责,演示对进水探测系统(如设有)的熟练使用;

.6 按照应变部署表上的职责,演示对横贯进水和平衡系统(如设有)的熟练使用;

.7 操作舱底泵和检查舱底报警和舱底泵自动启动系统;和

.8 破损检验和船舶破损控制系统的使用说明。

5 每年至少有一次破损控制演习须涵盖启动岸基支持,如按照第Ⅱ-1/8-1.3条要求设有以进行对模拟破损工况的稳性评估。

6 每位被指定承担破损控制责任的船员,应在开航前熟悉其职责和破损控制资料。

7 每次破损控制演习的记录须按照第Ⅲ/19.5条对其他演习规定的保存方式进行保存。

第20条
船舶装载

1 在船舶完成装载并在其启航之前,船长须确定船舶的纵倾和稳性,并查明和记录该船是否正浮和符合有关规则的稳性衡准。须始终通过计算来确定船舶的稳性或通过确保船舶按预先计算的装载工况之一装载并具有经批准的稳性资料来确定稳性。主管机关可接受采用电子装载仪和稳性计算机或等效装置。

2 压载水一般不应装于拟装载燃油的舱内。对实际上不能避免将水装入燃油舱的船舶,应设置使主管机关满意的油水分离设备,或为主管机关接受的处理含油压载水的其他设施,如排至岸上的接收设施。

3 本条规定与现行《国际防止船舶造成污染公约》的规定并不矛盾。

Regulation 21
Periodical operation and inspection of watertight doors, etc., in passenger ships

1 Operational tests of watertight doors, sidescuttles, valves and closing mechanisms of scuppers, ash-chutes and rubbish-chutes shall take place weekly. In ships in which the voyage exceeds one week in duration a complete set of operational tests shall be held before the voyage commences, and others thereafter at least once a week during the voyage.

2 All watertight doors, both hinged and power-operated, in watertight bulkheads, in use at sea, shall be operated daily.

3 The watertight doors and all mechanisms and indicators connected therewith, all valves the closing of which is necessary to make a compartment watertight, and all valves the operation of which is necessary for damage control cross-connections shall be periodically inspected at sea at least once a week.

4 A record of all operational tests and inspections required by this regulation shall be recorded in the logbook with an explicit record of any defects which may be disclosed.

Regulation 22
Prevention and control of water ingress, etc.

1 All watertight doors shall be kept closed during navigation except that they may be opened during navigation as specified in paragraphs 3. Watertight doors of a width of more than 1.2 m in machinery spaces as permitted by regulation 13.10 may only be opened in the circumstances detailed in that regulation. Any door which is opened in accordance with this paragraph shall be ready to be immediately closed.

2 Watertight doors located below the bulkhead deck of passenger ships and the freeboard deck of cargo ships having a maximum clear opening width of more than 1.2 m shall be kept closed during navigation, except for limited periods when absolutely necessary as determined by the Administration.

3 A watertight door may be opened during navigation to permit the passage of passengers or crew, or when work in the immediate vicinity of the door necessitates it being opened. The door must be immediately closed when transit through the door is complete or when the task which necessitated it being open is finished. The Administration shall authorize that such a watertight door may be opened during navigation only after careful consideration of the impact on ship operations and survivability taking into account guidance issued by the Organization.① A watertight door permitted to be opened during navigation shall be clearly indicated in the ship's stability information and shall always be ready to be immediately closed.

---

① Refer to the *Revised guidance for watertight doors on passenger ships which may be opened during navigation* (MSC.1/Circ. 1564).

第21条
客船水密门等的定期操作和检查

1 水密门、舷窗、阀门以及流水口、出灰管与垃圾管的关闭机械装置的操作试验，应每周进行一次。对航程超过一周的船舶，在离港前须进行一次全面的操作试验，此后在航行中每周至少进行一次。

2 水密舱壁上的所有铰链操作和动力操作的水密门，凡需在航行中使用的，应每天进行操作。

3 水密门及与其连接的所有装置和指示器，所有为使舱室水密而需关闭的阀及所有为破损控制横贯连通而需操作的阀，均应在航行中进行定期检查，每周至少一次。

4 本条要求的所有操作试验和检查记录均须记入航海日志，并明确记载可能发现的任何缺陷。

第22条
进水的预防和控制等

1 除本条3规定的航行中可以开启的门外，所有水密门在航行中应保持关闭。第13.10条准许的机器处所内宽度大于1.2 m的水密门仅在该条所述的环境下可以开启。任何按本规定开启的门均应处于可随时立即关闭的状态。

2 在航行时，客船舱壁甲板和货船干舷甲板以下最大净开口宽度大于1.2 m的水密门须保持关闭，但经主管机关确定的绝对必要的有限时段除外。

3 在航行途中，为准许乘客或船员通行，或因在紧靠门的附近作业而必需时，可以开启水密门。当通过该门的通行已结束或需开启门的作业已完成时，须立即关闭该门。主管机关须在仔细考虑了对船舶操作和残存能力的影响后，才能授权在航行途中开启此种水密门，同时考虑到本组织散发的指南①。准许在航行途中开启的水密门须明确标示在船舶的稳性资料内，并须可随时立即关闭。

---

① 参见《经修订的客船在航行期间可开启的水密门指南》（第MSC.1/Circ.1564号通函）。

4 Portable plates on bulkheads shall always be in place before the voyage commences and shall not be removed during navigation except in case of urgent necessity at the discretion of the master. The necessary precautions shall be taken in replacing them to ensure that the joints are watertight. Power-operated sliding watertight doors permitted in machinery spaces in accordance with regulation 13.10 shall be closed before the voyage commences and shall remain closed during navigation except in case of urgent necessity at the discretion of the master.

5 Watertight doors fitted in watertight bulkheads dividing cargo between deck spaces in accordance with regulation 13.9.1 shall be closed before the voyage commences and shall be kept closed during navigation. The time at which such doors are opened or closed shall be recorded in such logbook as may be prescribed by the Administration.

6 Gangway, cargo and fuelling ports fitted below the bulkhead deck of passenger ships and the freeboard deck of cargo ships shall be effectively closed and secured watertight before voyage commences, and shall be kept closed during navigation.

7 The following doors, located above the bulkhead deck of passenger ships and the freeboard deck of cargo ships, shall be closed and locked before the voyage commences and shall remain closed and locked until the ship is at its next berth:

.1 cargo loading doors in the shell or the boundaries of enclosed superstructures;

.2 bow visors fitted in positions as indicated in paragraph 7.1;

.3 cargo loading doors in the collision bulkhead; and

.4 ramps forming an alternative closure to those defined in paragraphs 7.1 to 7.3 inclusive.

8 Where a door cannot be opened or closed while the ship is at the berth, such a door may be opened or left open while the ship approaches or draws away from the berth, but only so far as may be necessary to enable the door to be immediately operated. In any case, the inner bow door must be kept closed.

9 Notwithstanding the requirements of paragraphs 7.1 and 7.4, the Administration may authorize that particular doors can be opened at the discretion of the master, if necessary for the operation of the ship or the embarking and disembarking of passengers when the ship is at safe anchorage and provided that the safety of the ship is not impaired.

10 The master shall ensure that an effective system of supervision and reporting of the closing and opening of the doors referred to in paragraph 7 is implemented.

11 The master shall ensure, before any voyage commences, that an entry in such logbook as may be prescribed by the Administration is made of the time the doors specified in paragraph 12 are closed and the time at which particular doors are opened in accordance with paragraph 13.

12 Hinged doors, portable plates, sidescuttles, gangway, cargo and bunkering ports and other openings, which are required by these regulations to be kept closed during navigation, shall be closed before the voyage commences. The time at which such doors are opened and closed (if permissible under these regulations) shall be recorded in such logbook as may be prescribed by the Administration.

4　在开航前,舱壁上可移动平板门须就位并不得被移走,在紧急情况下船长认为必需者除外。须采取必要的预防措施把它们放回原处以保证接缝水密。根据第 13.10 条准许设在机舱处所内的动力式滑动水密门须在启航前关闭,并须在航行中保持关闭,但在船长认为具有紧迫必要性时除外。

5　按照第 13.9.1 条在分隔甲板处所之间的货物的水密舱壁上设置的水密门应在启航前关闭,并在航行中保持关闭;此类门开启或关闭的时间应记入主管机关所规定的航海日志。

6　设置在客船舱壁甲板和货船干舷甲板以下的舷门、装货门及装燃料门在开航前应有效关闭和紧固成水密,并在航行中保持关闭。

7　位于客船舱壁甲板和货船干舷甲板以上的下列门,须在启航前关闭并紧锁,且在船舶到达下一个泊位之前保持关闭并紧锁:

.1　船壳或封闭上层建筑围壁上的装货门;

.2　装载第 7.1 项所述位置上的罩式首门;

.3　防撞舱壁中的装货门;和

.4　作为替代包括第 7.1 至 7.3 项所述的门的替代围闭装置的坡道。

8　如果船舶在泊位停泊时,门不能开启或关闭,则在船舶靠、离泊位时此门可开启或保持开启状态,但仅就必要时能对此门进行即时操作而言。在任何情况下,内首门必须保持关闭。

9　尽管有本条第 7.1 和 7.4 款的要求,当船舶位于安全锚地时,若其安全不受妨碍,出于船舶作业或乘客上下船特殊情况的需要,主管机关可以授权船长酌定开启特定的门。

10　船长须保证对第 7 款所述门的关闭和开启实施有效的监督和报告制度。

11　在开始任何航行之前,船长须确保将第 12 款所述门的关闭时间,和按第 13 款所述的特定门的开启时间记录在主管机关所规定的航海日志中。

12　本章条款要求在航行途中保持关闭的铰链门、平移门、舷窗、舷门、装货门、装燃料门和其他开口,须在开航前关闭。关闭和开启这些开口(如果本规则允许)的时间须记载于主管机关所规定的航海日志中。

13 Where in a between-deck, the sills of any of the sidescuttles referred to in regulation 15.3.2 are below a line drawn parallel to the bulkhead deck at side of passenger ships and the freeboard deck at side of cargo ships, and having its lowest point 1.4 m plus 2.5% of the breadth of the ship above the water when the voyage commences, all the sidescuttles in that between-deck shall be closed watertight and locked before the voyage commences, and they shall not be opened before the ship arrives at the next port. In the application of this paragraph the appropriate allowance for fresh water may be made when applicable.

.1 The time at which such sidescuttles are opened in port and closed and locked before the voyage commences shall be recorded in such logbook as may be prescribed by the Administration.

.2 For any ship that has one or more sidescuttles so placed that the requirements of paragraph 13 would apply when it was floating at its deepest subdivision draught, the Administration may indicate the limiting mean draught at which these sidescuttles will have their sills above the line drawn parallel to the bulkhead deck at side of passenger ships and the freeboard deck at side of cargo ships, and having its lowest point 1.4 m plus 2.5% of the breadth of the ship above the waterline corresponding to the limiting mean draught, and at which it will therefore be permissible for the voyage to commence without them being closed and locked and to be opened during navigation on the responsibility of the master during navigation. In tropical zones as defined in the International Convention on Load Lines in force, this limiting draught may be increased by 0.3 m.

14 Sidescuttles and their deadlights which will not be accessible during navigation shall be closed and secured before the voyage commences.

15 If cargo is carried in spaces referred to in regulation 15.5.2, the sidescuttles and their deadlights shall be closed watertight and locked before the cargo is shipped and the time at which such scuttles and deadlights are closed and locked shall be recorded in such logbook as may be prescribed by the Administration.

16 When a rubbish-chute, etc. is not in use, both the cover and the valve required by regulation 15.10.2 shall be kept closed and secured.

Regulation 22-1

Flooding detection systems for passenger ships carrying 36 or more persons

A flooding detection system for watertight spaces below the bulkhead deck shall be provided based on the guidelines developed by the Organization. ①

① Refer to *Guidelines for flooding detection systems on passenger ships* (MSC.1/Circ.1291).

13 在甲板夹层中，如第15.3.2条所述的任何舷窗的窗槛低于平行于客船舱壁甲板和货船干舷甲板边线所绘的线且其最低点在船舶离港前水面以上1.4 m加2.5%船宽，则在甲板夹层的所有舷窗须在开航之前关闭成水密并锁紧，且在船舶到达下一港口之前不得开启。在适用本款规定时，可视情对淡水留出适当的余量。

.1 在港口开启这些舷窗的时间和在启航之前关闭并锁紧它们的时间应记载于主管机关规定的航海日志中。

.2 如某船在浮于其最深分舱吃水时有一个或数个舷窗位置适用第13款的要求，主管机关可指明其限制平均吃水；在此吃水时这些舷窗窗槛将高于平行于客船舱壁甲板和货船干舷甲板边线所绘的、其最低点在对应于限制平均吃水的水线以上1.4 m加2.5%船宽的一条线；在该限制吃水时，准许启航而不必事先将这类舷窗关闭和锁紧，在航行中开启这些舷窗由船长负责。在现行《国际载重线公约》所定义的热带区域内，该限制吃水可增加0.3 m。

14 在航行时够不着的舷窗及其舷窗盖须在启航之前关闭并紧固。

15 如在第15.5.2条所述的处所装载货物，舷窗及其舷窗盖应在装货前关闭成水密并锁紧，这类舷窗和舷窗盖的闭锁时间应载入主管机关所规定的航海日志中。

16 垃圾管等不在使用时，第15.10.2条要求的管盖和管阀应保持关闭和紧固。

第22-1条
载客36人或以上的客船浸水探测系统

舱壁甲板以下水密处所的浸水探测系统应基于本组织制定的导则①配备。

① 参见《客船浸水探测系统指南》（第MSC.1/Circ.1291号通函）。

Regulation 23
Special requirements for ro-ro passenger ships

1 Special category spaces and ro-ro spaces shall be continuously patrolled or monitored by effective means, such as television surveillance, so that any movement of vehicles in adverse weather conditions and unauthorized access by passengers thereto can be detected during navigation.

2 Documented operating procedures for closing and securing all shell doors, loading doors and other closing appliances which, if left open or not properly secured, could, in the opinion of the Administration, lead to flooding of a special category space or ro-ro space, shall be kept on board and posted at an appropriate place.

3 All accesses from the ro-ro deck and vehicle ramps that lead to spaces below the bulkhead deck shall be closed before the voyage commences and shall remain closed until the ship is at its next berth.

4 The master shall ensure that an effective system of supervision and reporting of the closing and opening of such accesses referred to in paragraph 3 is implemented.

5 The master shall ensure, before the voyage commences, that an entry in the logbook, as required by regulation 22.12, is made of the time of the last closing of the accesses referred to in paragraph 3.

6 Notwithstanding the requirements of paragraph 3, the Administration may permit some accesses to be opened during the voyage, but only for a period sufficient to permit through passage and, if required, for the essential working of the ship.

7 All transverse or longitudinal bulkheads which are taken into account as effective to confine the seawater accumulated on the ro-ro deck shall be in place and secured before the voyage commences and remain in place and secured until the ship is at its next berth.

8 Notwithstanding the requirements of paragraph 7, the Administration may permit some accesses within such bulkheads to be opened during the voyage but only for sufficient time to permit through passage and, if required, for the essential working of the ship.

9 In all ro-ro passenger ships, the master or the designated officer shall ensure that, without the express consent of the master or the designated officer, no passengers are allowed access to an enclosed ro-ro deck during navigation.

Regulation 24
Additional requirements for prevention and control of water ingress, etc. in cargo ships

1 Openings in the shell plating below the deck limiting the vertical extent of damage shall be kept permanently closed during navigation.

第23条
对滚装客船的特殊要求

1　特种处所和滚装处所应不断巡查或以有效手段(如电视监视)不断监控,以便在航行期间能够发现车辆在恶劣气候条件下的任何移动和乘客的擅自进入。

2　关闭和系固所有舷门、装货门和主管机关认为在未关闭或未做适当系固的情况下可能导致特种处所或滚装货物处所浸水的其他关闭装置的书面操作程序,应随船携带并张贴在适当的地方。

3　从滚装甲板和车辆坡道通向舱壁甲板以下处所的所有通道,在启航之前均应关闭,并在船舶抵达下一泊位之前保持关闭。

4　船长须确保对第3款所述通道的关闭和开启实施有效的监督和报告制度。

5　在开航之前,船长应确保把最后关闭第3款所述通道的时间,按照第22.12条的要求记载于航海日志中。

6　尽管有第3款的要求,主管机关可允许在航行期间开启某些通道,但开启时间仅限于通行和船舶必要工作所需要的时间。

7　所有能有效控制滚装甲板上积聚的海水的横舱壁或纵舱壁须在启航之前就位并固定,并保持到船舶抵达下一个泊位。

8　尽管有第7款的要求,主管机关仍可允许在航行期间开启此种舱壁的一些通道,但开启时间仅限于通行和船舶必不可少的工作所需要的时间。

9　在所有滚装客船上,船长或指定的高级船员应确保,当船舶在航行时,任何乘客未经其明确同意,不得进入封闭的滚装甲板。

第24条
防止和控制货船进水

1　在航行中,应一直关闭位于限制垂直破损范围的甲板以下的船壳板上的开口。

2 Notwithstanding the requirements of paragraph 3, the Administration may authorize that particular doors may be opened at the discretion of the master, if necessary for the operation of the ship and provided that the safety of the ship is not impaired.

3 Watertight doors or ramps fitted to internally subdivide large cargo spaces shall be closed before the voyage commences and shall be kept closed during navigation. The time at which such doors are opened or closed shall be recorded in such logbook as may be prescribed by the Administration.

4 The use of access doors and hatch covers intended to ensure the watertight integrity of internal openings shall be authorized by the officer of the watch.

Regulation 25
Water level detectors on single hold cargo ships other than bulk carriers

1 Single hold cargo ships other than bulk carriers constructed before 1 January 2007 shall comply with the requirements of this regulation not later than 31 December 2009.

2 Ships having a length (*L*) of less than 80 m, or 100 m if constructed before 1 July 1998, and a single cargo hold below the freeboard deck or cargo holds below the freeboard deck which are not separated by at least one bulkhead made watertight up to that deck shall be fitted in such space or spaces with water level detectors. ①

3 The water level detectors required by paragraph 2 shall:

.1 give an audible and visual alarm at the navigation bridge when the water level above the inner bottom in the cargo hold reaches a height of not less than 0.3 m, and another when such level reaches not more than 15% of the mean depth of the cargo hold; and

.2 be fitted at the aft end of the hold, or above its lowest part where the inner bottom is not parallel to the designed waterline. Where webs or partial watertight bulkheads are fitted above the inner bottom, Administrations may require the fitting of additional detectors.

4 The water level detectors required by paragraph 2 need not be fitted in ships complying with regulation Ⅻ/12, or in ships having watertight side compartments each side of the cargo hold length extending vertically at least from inner bottom to freeboard deck.

---

① Refer to *Performance standards for water level detectors on bulk carriers and single hold cargo ships other than bulk carriers* (resolution MSC.188(79)).

2 尽管有本条3的要求,如果为了船舶的操纵需要并且不损害船舶的安全,主管机关仍可授权船长根据需要打开某些特殊的门。

3 为内部分隔宽大货物处所而设置的水密门或车辆坡道应在开航之前关闭,并在航行中保持关闭;开启或关闭此类门的时间应记录在主管机关所规定的航海日志中。

4 用以确保内部开口水密完整性的出入门和舱盖的使用应经值班驾驶员批准。

第25条
散货船以外的单舱货船水位探测器

1 2007年1月1日以前建造的散货船以外的单舱货船应不迟于2009年12月31日符合本条要求。

2 对船长(L)小于80 m或1998年7月1日以前建造的、船长小于100 m的船舶,如果干舷甲板以下设置单一货舱或干舷甲板以下设置数个货舱未由至少一道达到该层甲板的水密舱壁所分隔,则应在该单一处所或数个处所内装设水位探测器①。

3 本条2要求的水位探测器应:

.1 当货舱水位达到内底以上不少于0.3 m时发出一次听觉和视觉报警,当水位达到不超过货舱平均深度15%时再发出一次听觉和视觉报警;和

.2 设在货舱后端,或货舱最低部分以上(如内底不与设计水线相平行时)。如果桁材或局部水密舱壁设在内底以上,主管机关可要求增设探测器。

4 符合第Ⅻ/12条的船舶,或在货舱长度范围内每舷侧设有至少从内底垂向延伸至干舷甲板的水密边舱的船舶,不必装设本条2要求的水位探测器。

① 参见《散货船和除散货船以外的单舱货船水位探测器性能标准》(第MSC.188(79)号决议)。

Part C
Machinery installations

(Except where expressly provided otherwise part C applies to passenger ships and cargo ships)

Regulation 26
General

1 The machinery, boilers and other pressure vessels, associated piping systems and fittings shall be of a design and construction adequate for the service for which they are intended and shall be so installed and protected as to reduce to a minimum any danger to persons on board, due regard being paid to moving parts, hot surfaces and other hazards. The design shall have regard to materials used in construction, the purpose for which the equipment is intended, the working conditions to which it will be subjected and the environmental conditions on board.①

2 The Administration shall give special consideration to the reliability of single essential propulsion components and may require a separate source of propulsion power sufficient to give the ship a navigable speed, especially in the case of unconventional arrangements.

3 Means shall be provided whereby normal operation of propulsion machinery can be sustained or restored even though one of the essential auxiliaries becomes inoperative. Special consideration shall be given to the malfunctioning of:

.1 a generating set which serves as a main source of electrical power;

.2 the sources of steam supply;

.3 the boiler feedwater systems;

.4 the fuel oil supply systems for boilers or engines;②

.5 the sources of lubricating oil pressure;

.6 the sources of water pressure;

.7 a condensate pump and the arrangements to maintain vacuum in condensers;

.8 the mechanical air supply for boilers;

.9 an air compressor and receiver for starting or control purposes; and

.10 the hydraulic, pneumatic or electrical means for control in main propulsion machinery including controllable pitch propellers.

---

① Refer to *Guidelines for engine-room layout, design and arrangement* (MSC/Circ.834).

② Refer to *Guidelines to minimize leakages from flammable liquid systems* (MCS/Circ.647), and *Guidelines on engine-room oil fuel systems* (MSC/Circ.851).

C 部分
机器设备

（除另有明文规定者外，C 部分适用于客船和货船）

第 26 条
通则

1　机器、锅炉和其他受压容器、相关管系和附件的设计和建造应适合于其预定用途，其安装和防护应使其对船上人员的危险性降至最低程度，并应充分考虑到运动部件、热表面和其他危险。设计应考虑到建造中使用的材料、设备的预定用途以及将要遇到的工作条件和船上环境条件。[①]

2　主管机关应特别注意单个重要推进部件的可靠性；而且可以要求设有一个独立推进动力源，足以使船舶保持一个可航行速度，特别是在非常规布置的情况下。

3　应设有措施，在任一重要辅机失效时，使推进机械的正常运转能够维持或恢复。应特别注意下列设备的故障：

.1　作为主电源的发电机组；

.2　蒸汽供应源；

.3　锅炉给水系统；

.4　锅炉或发动机的燃油供给系统；[②]

.5　润滑油压力源；

.6　水压源；

.7　凝水泵和保持冷凝器真空的装置；

.8　锅炉的机械送风；

.9　空气压缩机和启动或控制用空气瓶；和

.10　主推进装置（包括可调螺距螺旋桨）的液压、气动或电气控制装置。

---

① 参见《机舱的设置、设计和布置指南》（第 MSC/Circ.834 号通函）。

② 参见《关于最大限度减少可燃液体系统泄漏指南》（第 MSC/Circ.647 号通函）和《关于机舱燃油系统指南》（第 MSC/Circ.851 号通函）。

However, the Administration, having regard to overall safety considerations, may accept a partial reduction in propulsion capability from normal operation.

4 Means shall be provided to ensure that the machinery can be brought into operation from the dead ship condition without external aid.

5 All boilers, all parts of machinery, all steam, hydraulic, pneumatic and other systems and their associated fittings which are under internal pressure shall be subjected to appropriate tests including a pressure test before being put into service for the first time.

6 Main propulsion machinery and all auxiliary machinery essential to the propulsion and the safety of the ship shall, as fitted in the ship, be designed to operate when the ship is upright and when inclined at any angle of list up to and including 15° either way under static conditions and 22.5° under dynamic conditions (rolling) either way and simultaneously inclined dynamically (pitching) 7.5° by bow or stern. The Administration may permit deviation from these angles, taking into consideration the type, size and service conditions of the ship.

7 Provision shall be made to facilitate cleaning, inspection and maintenance of main propulsion and auxiliary machinery including boilers and pressure vessels.

8 Special consideration shall be given to the design, construction and installation of propulsion machinery systems so that any mode of their vibrations shall not cause undue stresses in this machinery in the normal operating ranges.

9 Non-metallic expansion joints in piping systems, if located in a system which penetrates the ship's side and both the penetration and the non-metallic expansion joint are located below the deepest load waterline, shall be inspected as part of the surveys prescribed in regulation Ⅰ/10(a) and replaced as necessary, or at an interval recommended by the manufacturer.

10 Operating and maintenance instructions and engineering drawings for ship machinery and equipment essential to the safe operation of the ship shall be written in a language understandable by those officers and crew members who are required to understand such information in the performance of their duties.

11 Location and arrangement of vent pipes for fuel oil service, settling and lubrication oil tanks shall be such that in the event of a broken vent pipe this shall not directly lead to the risk of ingress of seawater splashes or rainwater. Two fuel oil service tanks for each type of fuel used on board necessary for propulsion and vital systems or equivalent arrangements shall be provided on each new ship, with a capacity of at least 8 h at maximum continuous rating of the propulsion plant and normal operating load at sea of the generator plant.① This paragraph applies only to ships constructed on or after 1 July 1998.

① Refer to regulation Ⅱ-2/4.2, Arrangements for oil fuel, lubrication oil and other flammable oils.

但是,当主管机关对整体安全性做考虑后,可以接受将正常运行的推进能力做部分降低。

4 应设有措施确保在没有外来帮助的情况下能使机器从瘫船状态运转起来。

5 所有锅炉、机器的所有部件,所有蒸汽、液压、气动和其他系统,以及有关的承受内部压力的附件,在首次投入使用前均应经受包括压力试验在内的相应试验。

6 主推进装置以及船舶推进和安全必需的所有辅机均应设计成安装于船上后,能在船舶正浮时以及静态工况下向任一舷横倾至15°和动态工况下向任一舷横摇至22.5°,并同时在首或尾纵摇7.5°时工作。主管机关可允许偏离这些角度,并考虑到船舶的类型、尺度和营运条件。

7 应有便于对主推进装置和辅机,包括锅炉和受压容器,进行清洁、检查和维护保养的措施。

8 对推进装置系统的设计、制造和安装应予以特殊考虑,使其任何振动模式均不致在正常运转范围内对机器内部引起过大的应力。

9 管系中的非金属膨胀接头,如果位于贯穿船侧的管系中且贯穿位置和非金属膨胀接头均位于最深载重线以下,则应作为第Ⅰ/10(a)条所规定检验的一部分进行检查,并在必要时或按制造商建议的间隔期予以更换。

10 操作和维护保养须知以及船舶安全运行所必需的机器和设备的工程图纸,应以在履行职责时须看懂这些资料的高级船员和普通船员所能理解的语言编制。

11 燃油日用柜、沉淀柜和润滑油舱柜透气管的位置和布置应使透气管在破裂时不会直接导致海水溅入或雨水淋入的危险。每艘新建船舶应对推进系统及重要系统或等效装置所必需的每一种燃油配备两个燃油日用柜,其容量应至少能供船舶推进装置在最大持续功率下,以及发电机装置在海上正常负荷下工作8 h。① 本规定仅适用于1998年7月1日或以后建造的船舶。

① 参见SOLAS公约第Ⅱ-2/4.2条,燃油、润滑油和其他易燃油类的布置。

Regulation 27
Machinery

1 Where risk from overspeeding of machinery exists, means shall be provided to ensure that the safe speed is not exceeded.

2 Where main or auxiliary machinery including pressure vessels or any parts of such machinery are subject to internal pressure and may be subject to dangerous overpressure, means shall be provided where practicable to protect against such excessive pressure.

3 All gearing and every shaft and coupling used for transmission of power to machinery essential for the propulsion and safety of the ship or for the safety of persons on board shall be so designed and constructed that they will withstand the maximum working stresses to which they may be subjected in all service conditions, and due consideration shall be given to the type of engines by which they are driven or of which they form part.

4 Internal combustion engines of a cylinder diameter of 200 mm or a crankcase volume of 0.6 m^3 and above shall be provided with crankcase explosion relief valves of a suitable type with sufficient relief area. The relief valves shall be arranged or provided with means to ensure that discharge from them is so directed as to minimize the possibility of injury to personnel.

5 Main turbine propulsion machinery and, where applicable, main internal combustion propulsion machinery and auxiliary machinery shall be provided with automatic shutoff arrangements in the case of failures such as lubricating oil supply failure which could lead rapidly to complete breakdown, serious damage or explosion. The Administration may permit provisions for overriding automatic shutoff devices.

Regulation 28
Means of going astern[①]

1 Sufficient power for going astern shall be provided to secure proper control of the ship in all normal circumstances.

2 The ability of the machinery to reverse the direction of thrust of the propeller in sufficient time, and so to bring the ship to rest within a reasonable distance from maximum ahead service speed, shall be demonstrated and recorded.

3 The stopping times, ship headings and distances recorded on trials, together with the results of trials to determine the ability of ships having multiple propellers to navigate and manoeuvre with one or more propellers inoperative, shall be available on board for the use of the master or designated personnel.

① Refer to *Provision and the display of manoeuvring information on board ships* (resolution A.601(15)), *Standards for ship manoeuvrability* (resolution MSC.137(76)), and *Explanatory Notes to the Standards for ship manoeuvrability* (MSC/Circ.1053).

第27条
机器

1　如果存在机器超速的危险，则应设有确保不超过安全速度的装置。

2　如果主机或辅机（包括受压容器）或这类机器的任何部件承受内部压力并可能受到危险的超压，则应设有防止这种过大压力的装置（若可行）。

3　对船舶推进、船舶安全或船上人员安全必要的机器，其动力传递用的所有齿轮装置和每根轴与每个联轴器的设计和构造应使其能承受所有运行工况下可能产生的最大工作应力，并应充分考虑到被驱动的或作为组成部分的发动机的类型。

4　缸径为200 mm或曲轴箱容积为0.6 m^3及以上的内燃机，应设有适当型式并具备足够释压面积的曲轴箱防爆安全阀。安全阀的布置或所设装置应确保将阀排出的气体造成人身伤害的可能性降至最低程度。

5　主涡轮推进机械和（若适用）主内燃推进机械及副机，应设有在发生诸如滑油供给故障等可能迅速导致其完全破坏、严重损坏或爆炸的故障时能自动停车的装置。主管机关可允许采用自动停车的越控装置。

第28条
倒车装置[①]

1　船舶应具有足够的后退动力，以保证在所有正常情况下均能正确控制船舶。

2　应证实并记录机器在足够的时间内调换螺旋桨的推力方向，从而在一段合理的距离内使船舶从最大营运前进航速停止的能力。

3　船上应备有航行中试验停车滑行时间、船舶首向和航行距离的记录，以及为确定多螺旋桨船舶在一个或几个螺旋桨失效时的航行和操纵能力所做试验的结果，以供船长或指定人员使用。

---

①　参见《关于船上配备和显示操纵资料的建议》（第A.601（15）号决议）、《船舶操纵性标准》（第MSC.137（76）号决议）和《船舶操纵性标准的解释性说明》（第MSC/Circ.1053号通函）。

4 Where the ship is provided with supplementary means for manoeuvring or stopping, the effectiveness of such means shall be demonstrated and recorded as referred to in paragraphs 2 and 3.

Regulation 29
Steering gear①

1 Unless expressly provided otherwise, every ship shall be provided with a main steering gear and an auxiliary steering gear to the satisfaction of the Administration. The main steering gear and the auxiliary steering gear shall be so arranged that the failure of one of them will not render the other one inoperative.

2.1 All the steering gear components and the rudder stock shall be of sound and reliable construction to the satisfaction of the Administration. Special consideration shall be given to the suitability of any essential component which is not duplicated. Any such essential component shall, where appropriate, utilize antifriction bearings such as ball-bearings, roller-bearings or sleeve-bearings which shall be permanently lubricated or provided with lubrication fittings.

2.2 The design pressure for calculations to determine the scantlings of piping and other steering gear components subjected to internal hydraulic pressure shall be at least 1.25 times the maximum working pressure to be expected under the operational conditions specified in paragraph 3.2, taking into account any pressure which may exist in the low-pressure side of the system. At the discretion of the Administration, fatigue criteria shall be applied for the design of piping and components, taking into account pulsating pressures due to dynamic loads.

2.3 Relief valves shall be fitted to any part of the hydraulic system which can be isolated and in which pressure can be generated from the power source or from external forces. The setting of the relief valves shall not exceed the design pressure. The valves shall be of adequate size and so arranged as to avoid an undue rise in pressure above the design pressure.

3 The main steering gear and rudder stock shall be:

.1 of adequate strength and capable of steering the ship at maximum ahead service speed which shall be demonstrated;

.2 capable of putting the rudder over from 35° on one side to 35° on the other side with the ship at its deepest seagoing draught and running ahead at maximum ahead service speed and, under the same conditions, from 35° on either side to 30° on the other side in not more than 28 s; where it is impractical to demonstrate compliance with this requirement during sea trials with the ship at its deepest seagoing draught and running ahead at the speed corresponding to the number of maximum continuous revolutions of the main engine and maximum design pitch, ships regardless of date of construction may demonstrate compliance with this requirement by one of the following methods:

① Refer to *Improved steering gear standards for passenger and cargo ships* (resolution A.415 (XI)) and *Examination of steering gears on existing tankers* (resolution A.416(XI)).

4 如果船舶设有操纵或停车的补充装置,则应按本条2和3所述证实这些装置的有效性并予记录。

第29条
操舵装置[①]

1 除另有明文规定外,每艘船舶应设有一台主操舵装置和一台辅助操舵装置并使主管机关满意。该主操舵装置和辅助操舵装置的布置应使其中一台发生的故障不会导致另一台失效。

2.1 所有操舵装置的部件和舵杆应为主管机关满意的坚固和可靠的构造。对于非双套的必要部件的适用性应特别注意。任何这类必要部件,在合适时,应采用耐磨轴承,如球轴承、滚子轴承或者能持久润滑或设有润滑装置的套筒轴承。

2.2 对于承受内部液压的管系和其他操舵装置的部件,确定其尺寸计算所用的设计压力应至少为本条3.2所指运行状况下可能出现的最大工作压力的1.25倍,同时应考虑在该系统低压一侧可能存在的压力。根据主管机关的意见,管系和部件的设计应采用疲劳衡准,同时考虑动力负荷所产生的脉动压力。

2.3 凡在液压系统中能被隔断的和由于动力源或外力作用能产生压力的任何部件,应设置安全阀。安全阀的调定应不超过设计压力。安全阀应有足够尺寸并布置成能够避免过度升高的压力超过设计压力。

3 主操舵装置和舵杆应:

.1 具有足够强度,并能在最大营运前进航速下操纵船舶,此应予以证实;

.2 能在船舶处于最深航海吃水并以最大营运航速前进时将舵自一舷35°转至另一舷35°以及于相同条件下在不超过28 s内将舵自任一舷35°转至另一舷30°;如船舶在海试期间,以最深航行吃水并以主机最大持续转速及最大设计螺距相应的航速前进时,证明符合该要求不切实际,则该船舶无论何时建造均可通过下列方法之一证明符合该要求:

① 参见《关于改进的客货船操舵装置标准》(第A.415(Ⅺ)号决议)和《关于现有液货船操舵装置的检查》(第A.416(Ⅺ)号决议)。

.1 during sea trials the ship is at even keel and the rudder fully submerged whilst running ahead at the speed corresponding to the number of maximum continuous revolutions of the main engine and maximum design pitch; or

.2 where full rudder immersion during sea trials cannot be achieved, an appropriate ahead speed shall be calculated using the submerged rudder blade area in the proposed sea trial loading condition. The calculated ahead speed shall result in a force and torque applied to the main steering gear which is at least as great as if it was being tested with the ship at its deepest seagoing draught and running ahead at the speed corresponding to the number of maximum continuous revolutions of the main engine and maximum design pitch; or

.3 the rudder force and torque at the sea trial loading condition have been reliably predicted and extrapolated to the full load condition. The speed of the ship shall correspond to the number of maximum continuous revolutions of the main engine and maximum design pitch of the propeller;

.3 operated by power where necessary to meet the requirements of paragraph 3.2 and in any case when the Administration requires a rudder stock of over 120 mm diameter in way of the tiller, excluding strengthening for navigation in ice; and

.4 so designed that they will not be damaged at maximum astern speed; however, this design requirement need not be proved by trials at maximum astern speed and maximum rudder angle.

4 The auxiliary steering gear shall be:

.1 of adequate strength and capable of steering the ship at navigable speed and of being brought speedily into action in an emergency;

.2 capable of putting the rudder over from 15° on one side to 15° on the other side in not more than 60 s with the ship at its deepest seagoing draught and running ahead at one half of the maximum ahead service speed or 7 knots, whichever is the greater; where it is impractical to demonstrate compliance with this requirement during sea trials with the ship at its deepest seagoing draught and running ahead at one half of the speed corresponding to the number of maximum continuous revolutions of the main engine and maximum design pitch or 7 knots, whichever is greater, ships regardless of date of construction, including those constructed before 1 January 2009, may demonstrate compliance with this requirement by one of the following methods:

.1 during sea trials the ship is at even keel and the rudder fully submerged whilst running ahead at one half of the speed corresponding to the number of maximum continuous revolutions of the main engine and maximum design pitch or 7 knots, whichever is greater; or

.1　船舶在海试期间，以主机最大持续转速及最大设计螺距相应的航速前进时呈平浮状态，且舵完全浸没；或

.2　如海试期间无法实现舵完全浸没，则须采取在所建议的海试载荷条件下的舵叶浸没面积计算出适当的前进速度。所计算出的前进速度，其结果须使作用于主操舵装置的力及力矩至少与测试中的船舶在以最深航行吃水并以主机最大持续转速及最大设计螺距相应的航速前进时同样大；或

.3　在海试载荷条件下的舵力和力矩业经可靠预测并推算至满载荷条件。船速应与主机的最大持续转速和螺旋桨的最大设计螺距相对应；

.3　动力操纵，以必要时满足本条 3.2 的要求，以及满足任何情况下主管机关对舵柄处的舵杆直径大于 120 mm（不包括冰区加强）的要求；和

.4　设计成在最大后退航速下不致损坏；但这一设计要求不必用最大后退航速和最大舵角下的试航证明。

4　辅助操舵装置应：

.1　具有足够强度和足以在可航行的航速下操纵船舶，并能在紧急情况下迅速投入工作；

.2　能在船舶处于最深航海吃水并以最大营运前进航速的一半或 7 kn（取大者）前进时，在不超过 60 s 内将舵自一舷 15°转至另一舷 15°；如船舶在海试期间，以最深航行吃水并以主机最大持续转速及最大设计螺距相应航速的一半或 7 kn（取大者）前进时，证明符合该要求不切实际，则该船舶无论何时建造（包括 2009 年 1 月 1 日之前建造的船舶）均可通过下列方法之一证明符合该要求：

.1　船舶在海试期间，以主机最大持续转速及最大设计螺距相应航速的一半或7 kn（取大者）前进时处于正浮状态，且舵完全浸没；或

.2 where full rudder immersion during sea trials cannot be achieved, an appropriate ahead speed shall be calculated using the submerged rudder blade area in the proposed sea trial loading condition. The calculated ahead speed shall result in a force and torque applied to the auxiliary steering gear which is at least as great as if it was being tested with the ship at its deepest seagoing draught and running ahead at one half of the speed corresponding to the number of maximum continuous revolutions of the main engine and maximum design pitch or 7 knots, whichever is greater; or

.3 the rudder force and torque at the sea trial loading condition have been reliably predicted and extrapolated to the full load condition; and

.3 operated by power where necessary to meet the requirements of paragraph 4.2 and in any case when the Administration requires a rudder stock of over 230 mm diameter in way of the tiller, excluding strengthening for navigation in ice.

5 Main and auxiliary steering gear power units shall be:

.1 arranged to restart automatically when power is restored after a power failure; and

.2 capable of being brought into operation from a position on the navigation bridge. In the event of a power failure to any one of the steering gear power units, an audible and visual alarm shall be given on the navigation bridge.

6.1 Where the main steering gear comprises two or more identical power units, an auxiliary steering gear need not be fitted, provided that:

.1 in a passenger ship, the main steering gear is capable of operating the rudder as required by paragraph 3.2 while any one of the power units is out of operation;

.2 in a cargo ship, the main steering gear is capable of operating the rudder as required by paragraph 3.2 while operating with all power units;

.3 the main steering gear is so arranged that after a single failure in its piping system or in one of the power units the defect can be isolated so that steering capability can be maintained or speedily regained.

6.2 The Administration may, until 1 September 1986, accept the fitting of a steering gear which has a proven record of reliability but does not comply with the requirements of paragraph 6.1.3 for a hydraulic system.

6.3 Steering gears, other than of the hydraulic type, shall achieve standards equivalent to the requirements of this paragraph to the satisfaction of the Administration.

7 Steering gear control shall be provided:

.1 for the main steering gear, both on the navigation bridge and in the steering gear compartment;

.2　如海试期间无法实现舵完全浸没，则须采取在所建议的海试载荷条件下的舵叶浸没面积计算出适当的前进速度。所计算出的前进速度，其结果须使作用于主操舵装置的力及力矩至少与测试中的船舶在以最深航行吃水并以主机最大持续转速及最大设计螺距相应航速的一半或 7 kn（取大者）前进时同样大；或

.3　在海试载荷条件下的舵力和力矩业经可靠预测并推算至满载荷条件；和

.3　动力操纵，以必要时满足本条 4.2 的要求，以及满足任何情况下主管机关对舵柄处的舵杆直径大于 230 mm（不包括冰区加强）的要求。

5　主操舵装置和辅助操舵装置的动力设备应：

.1　布置成电源发生故障后恢复供电时能自动再启动；和

.2　能从驾驶台某一位置投入工作。操舵装置的任何 1 台动力设备失电时，应在驾驶台里发出听觉和视觉报警。

6.1　如果操舵装置包括有 2 台或更多相同的动力设备，则不必装设辅助操舵装置，但：

.1　在客船上，当任何 1 台动力设备不能运转时，主操舵装置应能按本条 3.2 的要求操舵；

.2　在货船上，当所有动力设备都运转时，主操舵装置应能按本条 3.2 的要求操舵；

.3　主操舵装置应布置成当其管系或 1 台动力设备发生单项故障后，此故障能被隔离，使操舵能力能够保持或迅速恢复。

6.2　直至 1986 年 9 月 1 日止，主管机关可以接受设置经证实具有可靠性记录但不符合本条 6.1.3 对液压系统要求的操舵装置。

6.3　非液压型式的操舵装置应达到等效的标准，并使主管机关满意。

7　应按下列要求设有操舵装置的控制装置：

.1　对于主操舵装置，在驾驶台和舵机舱；

.2 where the main steering gear is arranged in accordance with paragraph 6, by two independent control systems, both operable from the navigation bridge. This does not require duplication of the steering wheel or steering lever. Where the control system consists of a hydraulic telemotor, a second independent system need not be fitted, except in a tanker, chemical tanker or gas carrier of 10,000 gross tonnage and upwards;

.3 for the auxiliary steering gear, in the steering gear compartment and, if power-operated, it shall also be operable from the navigation bridge and shall be independent of the control system for the main steering gear.

8 Any main and auxiliary steering gear control system operable from the navigation bridge shall comply with the following:

.1 if electric, it shall be served by its own separate circuit supplied from a steering gear power circuit from a point within the steering gear compartment, or directly from switchboard busbars supplying that steering gear power circuit at a point on the switchboard adjacent to the supply to the steering gear power circuit;

.2 means shall be provided in the steering gear compartment for disconnecting any control system operable from the navigation bridge from the steering gear it serves;

.3 the system shall be capable of being brought into operation from a position on the navigation bridge;

.4 in the event of a failure of electrical power supply to the control system, an audible and visual alarm shall be given on the navigation bridge; and

.5 short circuit protection only shall be provided for steering gear control supply circuits.

9 The electrical power circuits and the steering gear control systems with their associated components, cables and pipes required by this regulation and by regulation 30 shall be separated as far as is practicable throughout their length.

10 A means of communication shall be provided between the navigation bridge and the steering gear compartment.

11 The angular position of the rudder shall:

.1 if the main steering gear is power-operated, be indicated on the navigation bridge. The rudder angle indication shall be independent of the steering gear control system;

.2 be recognizable in the steering gear compartment.

12 Hydraulic power-operated steering gear shall be provided with the following:

.1 arrangements to maintain the cleanliness of the hydraulic fluid taking into consideration the type and design of the hydraulic system;

.2 a low-level alarm for each hydraulic fluid reservoir to give the earliest practicable indication of hydraulic fluid leakage. Audible and visual alarms shall be given on the navigation bridge and in the machinery space where they can be readily observed; and

.2　如果主操舵装置按照本条6布置并由两个独立的控制系统控制，该两个控制系统均能从驾驶台操作，但不必设置两套操舵手轮或操舵手柄。如果控制系统是由液压遥控传动装置组成，则除10 000总吨及以上的油船、化学品船或气体运输船外，不必设置第二套独立控制系统；

.3　对于位于舵机舱的辅助操舵装置，如系动力操纵，也应能在驾驶台进行操作，并应独立于主操舵装置的控制系统。

8　能从驾驶台操作的任何主操舵装置和辅助操舵装置的控制系统应符合下列要求：

.1　如果系电动者，应由在舵机舱内操舵装置电源电路上的一点所设独立电路供电，或由向操舵装置电力线路供电的配电板上邻近该电力线路处的一点直接供电；

.2　应在舵机室内设有将驾驶台操作的控制系统与其所控制的操舵装置断开的装置；

.3　系统能从驾驶台某一位置投入工作；

.4　当控制系统的电源供应发生故障时，应在驾驶室发出听觉和视觉报警；和

.5　应仅对操舵装置控制供电线路设有短路保护。

9　本条和第30条要求的电力线路和操舵装置系统以及相关的部件、电缆和管子应在其整个长度范围内尽可能地分离。

10　驾驶台与舵机舱之间应设有通信设施。

11　舵角位置应：

.1　当主操舵装置系动力操纵时，在驾驶台显示。舵角指示器应独立于操舵装置控制系统；

.2　能在舵机舱内辨认出。

12　液压操纵的操舵装置应设有下列设施：

.1　能针对该液压系统的型式和设计保持液体清洁的装置；

.2　每个液体贮存器设低位警报器，以便确切和尽早地指示液体泄漏。应在驾驶台和机器处所内易于观察的地方发出听觉和视觉报警；和

.3 a fixed storage tank having sufficient capacity to recharge at least one power actuating system including the reservoir, where the main steering gear is required to be power-operated. The storage tank shall be permanently connected by piping in such a manner that the hydraulic systems can be readily recharged from a position within the steering gear compartment and shall be provided with a contents gauge.

13 The steering gear compartments shall be:

.1 readily accessible and, as far as practicable, separated from machinery spaces; and

.2 provided with suitable arrangements to ensure working access to steering gear machinery and controls. These arrangements shall include handrails and gratings or other nonslip surfaces to ensure suitable working conditions in the event of hydraulic fluid leakage.

14 Where the rudder stock is required to be over 230 mm diameter in way of the tiller, excluding strengthening for navigation in ice, an alternative power supply, sufficient at least to supply the steering gear power unit which complies with the requirements of paragraph 4.2 and also its associated control system and the rudder angle indicator, shall be provided automatically, within 45 s, either from the emergency source of electrical power or from an independent source of power located in the steering gear compartment. This independent source of power shall be used only for this purpose. In every ship of 10,000 gross tonnage and upwards, the alternative power supply shall have a capacity for at least 30 min of continuous operation and in any other ship for at least 10 min.

15 In every tanker, chemical tanker or gas carrier of 10,000 gross tonnage and upwards and in every other ship of 70,000 gross tonnage and upwards, the main steering gear shall comprise two or more identical power units complying with the provisions of paragraph 6.

16 Every tanker, chemical tanker or gas carrier of 10,000 gross tonnage and upwards shall, subject to paragraph 17, comply with the following:

.1 the main steering gear shall be so arranged that in the event of loss of steering capability due to a single failure in any part of one of the power actuating systems of the main steering gear, excluding the tiller, quadrant or components serving the same purpose, or seizure of the rudder actuators, steering capability shall be regained in not more than 45 s after the loss of one power actuating system;

.2 the main steering gear shall comprise either:

.1 two independent and separate power actuating systems, each capable of meeting the requirements of paragraph 3.2; or

.2 at least two identical power actuating systems which, acting simultaneously in normal operation, shall be capable of meeting the requirements of paragraph 3.2. Where necessary to comply with this requirement, interconnection of hydraulic power actuating systems shall be provided. Loss of hydraulic fluid from one system shall be capable of being detected and the defective system automatically isolated so that the other actuating system or systems shall remain fully operational;

.3 steering gears other than of the hydraulic type shall achieve equivalent standards.

.3　如果主操舵装置要求动力操纵，设置一个固定储存柜，其容量足以至少为一个动力执行系统（包括贮存器）进行再充液。储存柜应用管系固定联结以使能从舵机舱内容易地再次为液压系统充液，并应设有液位指示器。

13　舵机舱应：

.1　易于到达，并尽可能与机器处所分开；和

.2　有适当的布置以保证有到达操舵装置和控制器的工作通道。这些布置应包括扶手栏杆和格子板或其他防滑地板以确保液体泄漏时有适宜的工作条件。

14　如果要求舵柄处舵杆直径超过230 mm（不包括冰区加强），应设有一个由应急电源或舵机舱内的一个独立动力源在45 s内自动供电的替代动力源，其容量至少足以向符合本条4.2要求的操舵装置动力设备及其相关控制系统和舵角指示器供电。此独立动力源应只用于上述目的。在每艘10 000总吨及以上的船舶上，该替代动力源应具有至少连续运转30 min的能力，在任何其他船舶上则至少为10 min。

15　每艘10 000总吨及以上的油船、化学品船或气体运输船和每艘70 000总吨及以上的其他船舶，主操舵装置应由符合本条6规定的两台或两台以上相同的动力设备组成。

16　每艘10 000总吨及以上的油船、化学品船或气体运输船，除满足本条17的规定外，应符合如下要求：

.1　主操舵装置应布置成当由于主操舵装置的一个动力执行系统的任何部件（舵柄、舵扇或为同样目的服务的部件除外）发生单项故障，或由于舵执行器卡住以致操舵能力丧失时，操舵能力应在一个动力执行系统失效后不大于45 s内重新获得；

.2　主操舵装置应包括：

.1　两个独立和分开的动力执行系统，每个系统均满足本条3.2的要求；或

.2　至少两个相同的动力执行系统，在正常运转中同时工作时，应能满足本条3.2的要求。如果需要符合此要求，液压动力执行系统应设有交叉联结。一个系统中液体的流失应能发现，有缺陷的系统应能自动隔离，以使另一个或几个执行系统能保持全面运转；

.3　非液压型式的操舵装置应能达到等效标准。

17 For tankers, chemical tankers or gas carriers of 10,000 gross tonnage and upwards, but of less than 100,000 tonnes deadweight, solutions other than those set out in paragraph 16, which need not apply the single failure criterion to the rudder actuator or actuators, may be permitted provided that an equivalent safety standard is achieved and that:

.1 following loss of steering capability due to a single failure of any part of the piping system or in one of the power units, steering capability shall be regained within 45 s; and

.2 where the steering gear includes only a single rudder actuator, special consideration is given to stress analysis for the design including fatigue analysis and fracture mechanics analysis, as appropriate, to the material used, to the installation of sealing arrangements and to testing and inspection and to the provision of effective maintenance. In consideration of the foregoing, the Administration shall adopt regulations which include the provisions of the Guidelines for acceptance of non-duplicated rudder actuators for tankers, chemical tankers and gas carriers of 10,000 gross tonnage and above but less than 100,000 tonnes deadweight, adopted by the Organization. ①

18 For a tanker, chemical tanker or gas carrier of 10,000 gross tonnage and upwards, but less than 70,000 tonnes deadweight, the Administration may, until 1 September 1986, accept a steering gear system with a proven record of reliability which does not comply with the single failure criterion required for a hydraulic system in paragraph 16.

19 Every tanker, chemical tanker or gas carrier of 10,000 gross tonnage and upwards, constructed before 1 September 1984, shall comply, not later than 1 September 1986, with the following:

.1 the requirements of paragraphs 7.1, 8.2, 8.4, 10, 11, 12.2, 12.3 and 13.2;

.2 two independent steering gear control systems shall be provided each of which can be operated from the navigation bridge. This does not require duplication of the steering wheel or steering lever;

.3 if the steering gear control system in operation fails, the second system shall be capable of being brought into immediate operation from the navigation bridge; and

.4 each steering gear control system, if electric, shall be served by its own separate circuit supplied from the steering gear power circuit or directly from switchboard busbars supplying that steering gear power circuit at a point on the switchboard adjacent to the supply to the steering gear power circuit.

20 In addition to the requirements of paragraph 19, in every tanker, chemical tanker or gas carrier of 40,000 gross tonnage and upwards, constructed before 1 September 1984, the steering gear shall, not later than 1 September 1988, be so arranged that, in the event of a single failure of the piping or of one of the power units, steering capability can be maintained or the rudder movement can be limited so that steering capability can be speedily regained. This shall be achieved by:

---

① Refer to *Guidelines for acceptance of non-duplicated rudder actuators for tankers, chemical tankers and gas carriers of 10,000 tons gross tonnage and above but less than 100,000 tons deadweight* (resolution A.467(XII)).

17 对于10 000总吨及以上但小于100 000载重吨的油船、化学品船或气体运输船，如果能达到等效安全标准，则可允许采用不同于本条16所述的解决办法，即对舵的一个或几个执行器不必应用单项故障衡准，而且：

.1 由于管系或一台动力设备的任何部件发生单项故障而丧失了操舵能力，应在45 s内重新获得操舵能力；和

.2 如果操舵装置只包括单个舵执行器，则应特别注意在设计中对所使用的材料、密封装置的安装、试验检查和有效维护的要求进行包括疲劳分析和断裂力学分析（若适用）在内的应力分析。在考虑上述情况时，主管机关应采用包括本组织通过的《10 000总吨及以上但小于100 000载重吨的油船、化学品船和气体运输船非双套舵执行器验收指南》的各项规定。①

18 对于10 000总吨及以上但小于70 000载重吨的油船、化学品船或气体运输船，至1986年9月1日止，主管机关可接受具有可靠性记录但不符合本条16中对液压系统要求的单项故障衡准的操舵装置系统。

19 1984年9月1日以前建造的每艘10 000总吨及以上的油船、化学品船或气体运输船应不迟于1986年9月1日符合下列要求：

.1 本条7.1、8.2、8.4、10、11、12.2、12.3和13.2的要求；

.2 应设有两个独立操舵装置控制系统，每个系统均能从驾驶台操作。但并不要求双套舵轮或操舵柄；

.3 如果在操作中操舵装置控制系统发生损坏，第二套系统应能从驾驶台立即投入操作；和

.4 每个操舵装置控制系统，如果系电动者，应由操舵装置电力线路设独立电路供电，或从向操舵装置电力线路供电的电路板上邻近该电力线路处的一点直接供电。

20 除本条19的要求外，1984年9月1日以前建造的每艘40 000总吨及以上的油船、化学品船或气体运输船，其操舵装置应不迟于1988年9月1日布置成当管系或其中1台动力设备发生单项故障时，能够保持操舵能力，或舵的运动能加以限制，以使操舵能力迅速重新获得。这应由下列措施实现：

---

① 参见《10 000总吨及以上但小于100 000载重吨的油船、化学品船和气体运输船非双套舵执行器验收指南》（第A.467（Ⅻ）号决议）。

.1 an independent means of restraining the rudder; or

.2 fast-acting valves which may be manually operated to isolate the actuator or actuators from the external hydraulic piping together with a means of directly refilling the actuators by a fixed independent power-operated pump and piping system; or

.3 an arrangement such that, where hydraulic power systems are interconnected, loss of hydraulic fluid from one system shall be detected and the defective system isolated either automatically or from the navigation bridge so that the other system remains fully operational.

Regulation 30
Additional requirements for electric and electrohydraulic steering gear

1 Means for indicating that the motors of electric and electrohydraulic steering gear are running shall be installed on the navigation bridge and at a suitable main machinery control position.

2 Each electric or electrohydraulic steering gear comprising one or more power units shall be served by at least two exclusive circuits fed directly from the main switchboard; however, one of the circuits may be supplied through the emergency switchboard. An auxiliary electric or electrohydraulic steering gear associated with a main electric or electrohydraulic steering gear may be connected to one of the circuits supplying this main steering gear. The circuits supplying an electric or electrohydraulic steering gear shall have adequate rating for supplying all motors which can be simultaneously connected to them and may be required to operate simultaneously.

3 Short circuit protection and an overload alarm shall be provided for such circuits and motors. Protection against excess current, including starting current, if provided, shall be for not less than twice the full load current of the motor or circuit so protected, and shall be arranged to permit the passage of the appropriate starting currents. Where a three-phase supply is used an alarm shall be provided that will indicate failure of any one of the supply phases. The alarms required in this paragraph shall be both audible and visual and shall be situated in a conspicuous position in the main machinery space or control room from which the main machinery is normally controlled and as may be required by regulation 51.

4 When in a ship of less than 1,600 gross tonnage an auxiliary steering gear which is required by regulation 29.4.3 to be operated by power is not electrically powered or is powered by an electric motor primarily intended for other services, the main steering gear may be fed by one circuit from the main switchboard. Where such an electric motor primarily intended for other services is arranged to power such an auxiliary steering gear, the requirement of paragraph 3 may be waived by the Administration if satisfied with the protection arrangement together with the requirements of regulation 29.5.1 and .2 and 29.7.3 applicable to auxiliary steering gear.

.1　独立的限舵设施;或

.2　可人工操作速动阀将一个或几个执行器与外部液压管系隔离开,以及用固定的独立动力泵和管系直接补充执行器的设施;或

.3　如果各液压动力系统是交叉联结的,则应做适当布置以保证一个系统中液体的流失能被发现,有缺陷的系统能自动地或从驾驶台加以隔离,以使其他系统能保持全面运转。

第30条
电动和电动液压操舵装置的附加要求

1　对于电动和电动液压操舵装置,应在驾驶台和适当的主机控制位置装设指示其电动机正在运转的设备。

2　由1台或几台动力设备组成的每一电动或电动液压操舵装置至少应由两个自主配电板直接供电的专用电路供电;但是,其中之一可以由应急配电板供电。一个与电动或电动液压主操舵装置相连的电动或电动液压辅助操舵装置可与向此主操舵装置供电的电路之一连接。向电动或电动液压操舵装置供电的电路应有足够额定容量,向能同时与其连接且可能需要同时工作的所有电动机供电。

3　这类电路和电动机应设有短路保护和过载报警装置。如果设有过载电流保护装置(包括启动电流),其允许使用的电流应不小于所保护电动机或电路满载电流的两倍,且其布置应能允许适当的启动电流通过。如果采用三相供电,应设有能指示任何一相所发生故障的报警装置。所要求的报警应为听觉和视觉报警,并应设于正常控制主机的主机处所或控制室内的明显位置,符合第51条适用的要求。

4　在小于1 600总吨的船上,按第29.4.3条要求为动力操作的辅助操舵装置,如果非电力驱动或由原来用作其他用途的电动机驱动,则主操舵装置可由来自主配电板的一个电路供电。当这类原来用作其他用途的电动机作为这种辅助操舵装置的动力时,如果主管机关对其保护装置表示满意,并认为其满足适用于辅助操舵装置的第29.5.1条和29.5.2条和第29.7.3条的要求时,可免除本条3的要求。

Regulation 31
Machinery controls

1 Main and auxiliary machinery essential for the propulsion and safety of the ship shall be provided with effective means for its operation and control.

2 Where remote control of propulsion machinery from the navigation bridge is provided and the machinery spaces are intended to be manned, the following shall apply:

.1 the speed, direction of thrust and, if applicable, the pitch of the propeller shall be fully controllable from the navigation bridge under all sailing conditions, including manoeuvring;

.2 the remote control shall be performed, for each independent propeller, by a control device so designed and constructed that its operation does not require particular attention to the operational details of the machinery. Where multiple propellers are designed to operate simultaneously, they may be controlled by one control device;

.3 the main propulsion machinery shall be provided with an emergency stopping device on the navigation bridge which shall be independent of the navigation bridge control system;

.4 propulsion machinery orders from the navigation bridge shall be indicated in the main machinery control room or at the manoeuvring platform as appropriate;

.5 remote control of the propulsion machinery shall be possible only from one location at a time; at such locations interconnected control positions are permitted. At each location there shall be an indicator showing which location is in control of the propulsion machinery. The transfer of control between the navigation bridge and machinery spaces shall be possible only in the main machinery space or the main machinery control room. This system shall include means to prevent the propelling thrust from altering significantly when transferring control from one location to another;

.6 it shall be possible to control the propulsion machinery locally, even in the case of failure in any part of the remote control system;

.7 the design of the remote control system shall be such that in case of its failure an alarm will be given. Unless the Administration considers it impracticable the preset speed and direction of thrust of the propellers shall be maintained until local control is in operation;

.8 indicators shall be fitted on the navigation bridge for:

.1 propeller speed and direction of rotation in the case of fixed pitch propellers;

.2 propeller speed and pitch position in the case of controllable pitch propellers;

第31条
机器的控制

1　船舶推进和安全所必需的主机和辅机应设有有效的操作和控制装置。

2　如果推进机械由驾驶台遥控而机器处所有人值班,则应适用下列要求:

.1　航速、推进方向以及(若适用)螺旋桨螺距应在所有航行(包括操纵)工况下,均可从驾驶台完全控制;

.2　每一独立的螺旋桨应由一个控制装置进行遥控,该控制装置的设计和制造应使其操作不需对机器的操作细节予以特别注意。如果多螺旋桨设计为同时运行,则可由一个控制装置进行控制;

.3　主推进机械应在驾驶台设有一个独立于驾驶台控制系统的紧急停机装置;

.4　驾驶台发出的推进机械指令应视具体情况在主机控制室或操纵台显示;

.5　推进机械在同一时间内应只能从一处进行遥控;在这种处所允许有互相连接的控制位置。每一处所均应有指示器显示何处在控制推进机械的。驾驶台和机器处所之间的控制转换应只能在主机处所或主机控制室内进行。此系统应包括将控制由一处转换到另一处时防止推力发生较大变化的装置;

.6　即使在遥控系统的任一部分发生故障时,推进机械应仍能就地控制;

.7　遥控系统应设计成在其发生故障时给出报警。除主管机关认为不可行外,应在实行就地控制动前保持预设的螺旋桨转速和推力方向;

.8　驾驶台应装有指示器,用以指示:

.1　固定螺距螺旋桨的转速和转动方向;

.2　可调螺距螺旋桨的转速和螺距位置;

.9 an alarm shall be provided on the navigation bridge and in the machinery space to indicate low starting air pressure which shall be set at a level to permit further main engine starting operations. If the remote control system of the propulsion machinery is designed for automatic starting, the number of automatic consecutive attempts which fail to produce a start shall be limited in order to safeguard sufficient starting air pressure for starting locally.

3 Where the main propulsion and associated machinery, including sources of main electrical supply, are provided with various degrees of automatic or remote control and are under continuous manual supervision from a control room the arrangements and controls shall be so designed, equipped and installed that the machinery operation will be as safe and effective as if it were under direct supervision; for this purpose regulations 46 to 50 shall apply as appropriate. Particular consideration shall be given to protect such spaces against fire and flooding.

4 In general, automatic starting, operational and control systems shall include provisions for manually overriding the automatic controls. Failure of any part of such systems shall not prevent the use of the manual override.

5 Ships constructed on or after 1 July 1998 shall comply with the requirements of paragraphs 1 to 4, as amended, as follows:

.1 paragraph 1 is replaced by the following:

"**1** Main and auxiliary machinery essential for the propulsion, control and safety of the ship shall be provided with effective means for its operation and control. All control systems essential for the propulsion, control and safety of the ship shall be independent or designed such that failure of one system does not degrade the performance of another system.";

.2 in the second and third lines of paragraph 2, the words "and the machinery spaces are intended to be manned" are deleted;

.3 the first sentence of paragraph 2.2 is replaced by the following:

"**.2** the control shall be performed by a single control device for each independent propeller, with automatic performance of all associated services, including, where necessary, means of preventing overload of the propulsion machinery.";

.4 paragraph 2.4 is replaced by the following:

"**.4** propulsion machinery orders from the navigation bridge shall be indicated in the main machinery control room and at the manoeuvring platform;";

.5 a new sentence is added at the end of paragraph 2.6 to read as follows:

"It shall also be possible to control the auxiliary machinery, essential for the propulsion and safety of the ship, at or near the machinery concerned;"; and

.6 paragraphs 2.8, 2.8.1 and 2.8.2 are replaced by the following:

.9 应在驾驶台和机器处所各设一个报警器，用以指示仍能多次启动主机的启动空气的规定低压。如果推进机械的遥控系统设计成自动启动，对于启动失败的自动连续启动次数应予限制，以保证有足够的启动空气压力进行就地启动。

3 如果主推进机械和相关机械（包括主电源）设有不同程度的自动控制或遥控，并在控制室有值班人员连续监管，则其布置和控制装置的设计、配备和安装应使机器的运转与处于直接监管下同样安全和有效；为此，应视具体情况适用第46条至第50条的要求。对于这类处所的防火和防止进水应予特别考虑。

4 一般情况下，自动启动、操作和控制系统应包括人工越控自动控制的装置。这些系统的任何部分发生故障应不致妨碍使用人工越控功能。

5 1998年7月1日或以后建造的船舶应符合如下经修正的本条1至4的要求：

.1 本条1由如下文字替代：

"1 对船舶推进、控制和安全所必需的主机和辅机应设有有效的操作和控制装置。船舶推进、控制和安全所必需的所有控制系统应是独立的，或设计成在某一系统失效时不会降低其他系统的功能。"；

.2 删除本条2中"而机器处所有人值班"的文字；

.3 本条2.2第一句由如下文字替代：

".2 每一独立的螺旋桨应使用单一控制装置进行控制，所有有关的设备具有自动性能，如果必要，具有防止推进机械超负荷运转的装置。"；

.4 本条2.4由如下文字替代：

".4 驾驶台发出的推进机械指令应在主机控制室和操纵台上显示；"；

.5 本条2.6后新增如下文字：

"对船舶推进和安全所必需的辅机也能就地或在其附近进行控制；"和

.6 本条2.8、2.8.1和2.8.2由如下文字替代：

“**.8** indicators shall be fitted on the navigation bridge, the main machinery control room and at the manoeuvring platform, for:

.1 propeller speed and direction of rotation in the case of fixed pitch propellers; and

.2 propeller speed and pitch position in the case of controllable pitch propellers;”

6 Ships constructed on or after 1 July 2004 shall comply with the requirements of paragraphs 1 to 5, as amended, as follows:

.1 a new subparagraph .10 is added to paragraph 2 to read as follows:

“**.10** automation systems shall be designed in a manner which ensures that threshold warning of impending or imminent slowdown or shutdown of the propulsion system is given to the officer in charge of the navigational watch in time to assess navigational circumstances in an emergency. In particular, the systems shall control, monitor, report, alert and take safety action to slow down or stop propulsion while providing the officer in charge of the navigational watch an opportunity to manually intervene, except for those cases where manual intervention will result in total failure of the engine and/or propulsion equipment within a short time, for example in the case of overspeed.”

Regulation 32
Steam boilers and boiler feed systems

1 Every steam boiler and every unfired steam generator shall be provided with not less than two safety valves of adequate capacity. However, having regard to the output or any other features of any boiler or unfired steam generator, the Administration may permit only one safety valve to be fitted if it is satisfied that adequate protection against overpressure is thereby provided.

2 Each oil-fired boiler which is intended to operate without manual supervision shall have safety arrangements which shut off the fuel supply and give an alarm in the case of low water level, air supply failure or flame failure.

3 Water tube boilers serving turbine propulsion machinery shall be fitted with a high water level alarm.

4 Every steam generating system which provides services essential for the safety of the ship, or which could be rendered dangerous by the failure of its feedwater supply, shall be provided with not less than two separate feedwater systems from and including the feed pumps, noting that a single penetration of the steam drum is acceptable. Unless overpressure is prevented by the pump characteristics, means shall be provided which will prevent overpressure in any part of the systems.

5 Boilers shall be provided with means to supervise and control the quality of the feedwater. Suitable arrangements shall be provided to preclude, as far as practicable, the entry of oil or other contaminants which may adversely affect the boiler.

“.8　在驾驶台、主机控制室和操纵台应设置指示器，以显示：

.1　固定螺距螺旋桨的转速和转动方向；和

.2　可调螺距螺旋桨的转速和螺距位置；”

6　2004年7月1日或以后建造的船舶应符合如下经修正的本条1至5的要求：

.1　在2之后新增.10如下：

“.10　自动控制系统的设计应确保向负责航行值班的驾驶员及时发出推进系统即将或快要减速或停车的临界报警，以评估紧急情况下的航行条件。尤其是该系统在为负责航行值班的驾驶员提供手动干预机会的同时，应控制、监视、报告、发出报警并采取减速或停车的安全措施，但短时间内由于手动干预而导致发动机和/或推进设备完全失效（例如过速）的情况除外。”

第32条
蒸汽锅炉和锅炉给水系统

1　每台蒸汽锅炉和每台非燃烧的蒸汽发生器，均应至少设有两个排量足够的安全阀。但是，在主管机关对任何锅炉或非燃烧蒸汽发生器考虑到其蒸汽产量或任何其他特性后，如果确信对超压已有充分防护，可允许只设一个安全阀。

2　每台无人监控的燃油锅炉均应设有在出现低水位、空气供给故障或火焰熄灭时能关闭燃油供应和发出警报的安全装置。

3　用于涡轮推进机械的水管式锅炉应装有高水位报警装置。

4　船舶安全所必需的或由于给水故障可能导致危险的每一蒸汽发生系统，应设有不少于两套从给水泵开始并包括给水泵在内的独立给水系统，并应注意到可以接受在汽鼓上有一处贯穿。除非泵的特性能防止超压，否则应设有防止此系统任何部分超压的装置。

5　锅炉应设有监视和控制给水质量的设施。应有适当布置尽可能地阻止对锅炉产生不利影响的油或其他污物进入锅炉。

6 Every boiler essential for the safety of the ship and designed to contain water at a specified level shall be provided with at least two means for indicating its water level, at least one of which shall be a direct reading gauge glass.

Regulation 33
Steam pipe systems

1 Every steam pipe and every fitting connected thereto through which steam may pass shall be so designed, constructed and installed as to withstand the maximum working stresses to which it may be subjected.

2 Means shall be provided for draining every steam pipe in which dangerous water hammer action might otherwise occur.

3 If a steam pipe or fitting may receive steam from any source at a higher pressure than that for which it is designed a suitable reducing valve, relief valve and pressure gauge shall be fitted.

Regulation 34
Air pressure systems

1 In every ship means shall be provided to prevent overpressure in any part of compressed air systems and wherever water jackets or casings of air compressors and coolers might be subjected to dangerous overpressure due to leakage into them from air pressure parts. Suitable pressure relief arrangements shall be provided for all systems.

2 The main starting air arrangements for main propulsion internal combustion engines shall be adequately protected against the effects of backfiring and internal explosion in the starting air pipes.

3 All discharge pipes from starting air compressors shall lead directly to the starting air receivers, and all starting pipes from the air receivers to main or auxiliary engines shall be entirely separate from the compressor discharge pipe system.

4 Provision shall be made to reduce to a minimum the entry of oil into the air pressure systems and to drain these systems.

Regulation 35
Ventilating systems in machinery spaces

Machinery spaces of category A shall be adequately ventilated so as to ensure that when machinery or boilers therein are operating at full power in all weather conditions including heavy-weather, an adequate supply of air is maintained to the spaces for the safety and comfort of personnel and the operation of the machinery. Any other machinery space shall be adequately ventilated appropriate for the purpose of that machinery space.

6　船舶安全所必需并设计有规定水位的每台锅炉，应至少设有两个水位指示装置，其中至少有一个应是直接读数的玻璃水位表。

第33条
蒸汽管系

1　每一蒸汽管和蒸汽可能通过的每一附件，其设计、制造和安装应使其能承受可能遇到的最大工作应力。

2　可能发生危险的水锤作用的每一蒸汽管均应设有泄水装置。

3　如果蒸汽管或管件可能从任何来源接受压力高于其设计压力的蒸汽，则应装设适当的减压阀、释放阀和压力表。

第34条
空气压力系统

1　在每艘船上，压缩空气系统的任何部分以及可能由于空气压力部件漏气而受到危险超压的空气压缩机的水套或外壳以及冷却器，均应设有防止超压的装置。所有系统均应设有适当的压力释放装置。

2　主推进内燃机的主启动空气装置，应对其启动空气管内的回火和爆炸的影响有充分防护。

3　启动空气压缩机的所有排出管应直接通至启动空气瓶，由空气瓶通至主机或辅机的所有启动空气管应与压缩机的排出管系完全分开。

4　应采取措施尽量减少进入空气压力系统的油和排空这些系统。

第35条
机器处所的通风系统

A类机器处所应有足够的通风，以确保其中的机器或锅炉在包括恶劣气候在内的所有气候条件下全功率运转时，该处所能有充足的空气供应，以保证人员的安全和舒适，以及机器的运转。任何其他机器处所应有适合于该机器处所的适当通风。

Regulation 35-1
Bilge pumping arrangements

1 This regulation applies to ships constructed on or after 1 January 2009.

2 Passenger ships and cargo ships

2.1 An efficient bilge pumping system shall be provided, capable of pumping from and draining any watertight compartment other than a space permanently appropriated for the carriage of fresh water, water ballast, oil fuel or liquid cargo and for which other efficient means of pumping are provided, under all practical conditions. Efficient means shall be provided for draining water from insulated holds.

2.2 Sanitary, ballast and general service pumps may be accepted as independent power bilge pumps if fitted with the necessary connections to the bilge pumping system.

2.3 All bilge pipes used in or under coal bunkers or fuel storage tanks or in boiler or machinery spaces, including spaces in which oil-settling tanks or oil fuel pumping units are situated, shall be of steel or other suitable material.

2.4 The arrangement of the bilge and ballast pumping system shall be such as to prevent the possibility of water passing from the sea and from water ballast spaces into the cargo and machinery spaces, or from one compartment to another. Provision shall be made to prevent any deep tank having bilge and ballast connections being inadvertently flooded from the sea when containing cargo, or being discharged through a bilge pump when containing water ballast.

2.5 All distribution boxes and manually operated valves in connection with the bilge pumping arrangements shall be in positions which are accessible under ordinary circumstances.

2.6 Provision shall be made for the drainage of enclosed cargo spaces situated on the bulkhead deck of a passenger ship and on the freeboard deck of a cargo ship, provided that the Administration may permit the means of drainage to be dispensed with in any particular compartment of any ship or class of ship if it is satisfied that by reason of size or internal subdivision of those spaces the safety of the ship is not thereby impaired. For ships subject to the provisions of regulation Ⅱ-1/1.1.1.1, for the special hazards associated with loss of stability when fitted with fixed pressure water-spraying fire-extinguishing systems refer to regulation Ⅱ-2/20.6.1.4.

2.6.1 Where the freeboard to the bulkhead deck or the freeboard deck, respectively, is such that the deck edge is immersed when the ship heels more than 5°, the drainage shall be by means of a sufficient number of scuppers of suitable size discharging directly overboard, fitted in accordance with the requirements of regulation 15 in the case of a passenger ship and the requirements for scuppers, inlets and discharges of the International Convention on Load Lines in force in the case of a cargo ship.

第35-1条
舱底水泵送装置

1　本条适用于2009年1月1日或以后建造的船舶。

2　客船与货船

2.1　应设有有效的舱底水泵送系统，在所有实际工况下均能抽除及排干任何水密舱室的水，但固定用于装载淡水、压载水、燃油或液货并设有其他有效排水设备的处所除外。冷藏舱应设置有效的排水装置。

2.2　卫生泵、压载泵及通用泵如与舱底水泵送系统有必要的连接，均可接受为独立的动力舱底泵。

2.3　用于煤舱或燃油贮存舱柜内及其下方处所，或用于锅炉舱或机器处所内，包括设置沉淀油柜或燃油泵组所在处所内的所有舱底水管，应为钢质或采用其他合适的材料。

2.4　舱底排水管及压载管系，应布置成能防止由海上或来自压载舱的水进入货舱及机器处所，或自一舱进入另一舱的可能性。对于与舱底排水管系及压载管有连接的任何深舱，应采取措施以防在深舱装有货物时不慎灌入海水，或在深舱装有压载水时通过舱底排水管抽出压载水。

2.5　所有与舱底水泵送装置相连接的分配箱和手动阀，应设在通常情况下可以到达的位置。

2.6　位于客船舱壁甲板上和货船干舷甲板上封闭的货物处所应设有排水装置，对于任何船舶或任何级别船舶的任何特殊舱室，如果主管机关确信这些处所的尺度或内部分舱不会因免除其内部的排水装置而损害船舶的安全，可准许此类处所免设排水装置。对于须符合第Ⅱ-1/1.1.1.1条规定的船舶，对于安装固定压力喷水消防系统后与稳性丧失相关的特殊风险，见第Ⅱ-2/20.6.1.4条。

2.6.1　当船舶横倾超过5°时，至舱壁甲板或至干舷甲板的干舷分别使甲板边缘浸水，则应设有足够数量适当尺度的泄水孔直接将水排向舷外。此类泄水孔的设置，对客船应符合第15条的要求，对货船应符合现行《国际载重线公约》中关于泄水孔、进水孔和排水孔的要求。

2.6.2 Where the freeboard is such that the edge of the bulkhead deck or the edge of the freeboard deck, respectively, is immersed when the ship heels 5° or less, the drainage of the enclosed cargo spaces on the bulkhead deck or on the freeboard deck, respectively, shall be led to a suitable space, or spaces, of adequate capacity, having a high water level alarm and provided with suitable arrangements for discharge overboard. In addition it shall be ensured that:

.1 the number, size and disposition of the scuppers are such as to prevent unreasonable accumulation of free water;

.2 the pumping arrangements required by this regulation for passenger ships or cargo ships, as applicable, take account of the requirements for any fixed pressure water-spraying fire-extinguishing system;

.3 water contaminated with petrol or other dangerous substances is not drained to machinery spaces or other spaces where sources of ignition may be present; and

.4 where the enclosed cargo space is protected by a carbon dioxide fire-extinguishing system the deck scuppers are fitted with means to prevent the escape of the smothering gas.

2.6.3 Provisions for the drainage of closed vehicle and ro-ro spaces and special category spaces shall also comply with regulations Ⅱ-2/20.6.1.4 and Ⅱ-2/20.6.1.5.

3 Passenger ships

3.1 The bilge pumping system required by paragraph 2.1 shall be capable of operation under all practicable conditions after a casualty whether the ship is upright or listed. For this purpose wing suctions shall generally be fitted except in narrow compartments at the end of the ship where one suction may be sufficient. In compartments of unusual form, additional suctions may be required. Arrangements shall be made whereby water in the compartment may find its way to the suction pipes. Where, for particular compartments, the Administration is satisfied that the provision of drainage may be undesirable, it may allow such provision to be dispensed with if calculations made in accordance with the conditions laid down in regulations 7 and 8 show that the survival capability of the ship will not be impaired.

3.2 At least three power pumps shall be fitted connected to the bilge main, one of which may be driven by the propulsion machinery. Where the bilge pump numeral is 30 or more, one additional independent power pump shall be provided.
The bilge pump numeral shall be calculated as follows:

when P_1 is greater than P: bilge pump numeral $= 72 \cdot \left(\frac{M+2P_1}{V+P_1-P}\right)$

in other cases: bilge pump numeral $= 72 \cdot \left(\frac{M+2P}{V}\right)$

where:

L = the length of the ship (metres), as defined in regulation 2;

2.6.2 当船舶横倾为5°或小于5°时，其干舷分别使舱壁甲板边缘或干舷甲板边缘浸水，则舱壁甲板或干舷甲板上的封闭货物处所内排出的水应导向一个或多个容量足够的处所，这类处所应设有高水位报警器和向舷外排放的合适装置。此外，还应确保：

.1 泄水孔的数量、尺度与布置应能防止自由水的不合理积聚；

.2 本条对客船或货船要求的排水装置（若适用），应考虑任何一种固定压力水雾灭火系统的要求；

.3 受汽油或其他危险物质污染的水，不应排向机器处所或其他可能存在火源的处所；和

.4 如果封闭的货物处所由二氧化碳灭火系统保护，则甲板泄水孔应设有防止此类窒息性气体逸漏的装置。

2.6.3 封闭式车辆和滚装处所和特种处所的排水设备亦须符合第Ⅱ-2/20.6.1.4和Ⅱ-2/20.6.1.5条。

3　客船

3.1 本条2.1要求的舱底水泵送系统，在海损后所有实际情况下，无论船舶是正浮或横倾，均应能操作。为此，通常应设几根侧吸水管，但在船舶端部的狭窄舱室内，设1根吸水管可能已够用。对形状特殊的舱可要求增设吸水管。舱内的布置应使水能流至吸水管。对于某些特殊舱室，如果主管机关确信设置排水设备可能不需要，并按第7条和第8条规定的条件计算证明无损于船舶的残存能力时，可准予免除设置。

3.2 至少应有3台动力泵与舱底总管连接，其中1台可由推进机械驱动。如果其舱底泵数为30或大于30，则应增设1台独立动力泵。

舱底泵数应按下式计算：

当P_1大于P时：舱底泵数$=72\cdot\left(\frac{M+2P_1}{V+P_1-P}\right)$

在其他情况下：舱底泵数$=72\cdot\left(\frac{M+2P}{V}\right)$

式中：

L——第2条定义的船长，m；

M = the volume of the machinery space (cubic metres), as defined in regulation 2, that is below the bulkhead deck; with the addition thereto of the volume of any permanent oil fuel bunkers which may be situated above the inner bottom and forward of, or abaft, the machinery space;

P = the whole volume of the passenger and crew spaces below the bulkhead deck (cubic metres) which are provided for the accommodation and use of passengers and crew, excluding baggage, store and provision rooms;

V = the whole volume of the ship below the bulkhead deck (cubic metres);

$P_1 = KN$,

where:

N = the number of passengers for which the ship is to be certified; and

$K = 0.056L$

However, where the value of KN is greater than the sum of P and the whole volume of the actual passenger spaces above the bulkhead deck, the figure to be taken as P_1 is that sum or two-thirds KN, whichever is the greater.

3.3 Where practicable, the power bilge pumps shall be placed in separate watertight compartments and so arranged or situated that these compartments will not be flooded by the same damage. If the main propulsion machinery, auxiliary machinery and boilers are in two or more watertight compartments, the pumps available for bilge service shall be distributed as far as is possible throughout these compartments.

3.4 On a ship of 91.5 m in length L and upwards or having a bilge pump numeral, calculated in accordance with paragraph 3.2, of 30 or more, the arrangements shall be such that at least one power bilge pump shall be available for use in all flooding conditions which the ship is required to withstand, and, for ships subject to the provisions of regulation Ⅱ-1/1.1.1.1, in all flooding conditions derived from consideration of minor damages as specified in regulation 8 as follows:

.1 one of the required bilge pumps shall be an emergency pump of a reliable submersible type having a source of power situated above the bulkhead deck; or

.2 the bilge pumps and their sources of power shall be so distributed throughout the length of the ship that at least one pump in an undamaged compartment will be available.

3.5 With the exception of additional pumps which may be provided for peak compartments only, each required bilge pump shall be so arranged as to draw water from any space required to be drained by paragraph 2.1.

3.6 Each power bilge pump shall be capable of pumping water through the required main bilge pipe at a speed of not less than 2 m/s. Independent power bilge pumps situated in machinery spaces shall have direct suctions from these spaces, except that not more than two such suctions shall be required in any one space. Where two or more such suctions are provided, there shall be at least one on each side of the ship. The Administration may require independent power bilge pumps situated in other spaces to have separate direct suctions. Direct suctions shall be suitably arranged and those in a machinery space shall be of a diameter not less than that required for the bilge main.

M——第2条定义的机器处所的容积，m^3，其位于舱壁甲板以下；加上机器处所前方或后方位于内底以上的任何固定燃油舱的容积；

P——舱壁甲板以下乘客和船员处所的全部容积（m^3），这是提供给乘客和船员居住和使用的处所，不包括行李间、储藏间和物料间；

V——舱壁甲板以下的船舶总容积，m^3；

P_1——KN，

其中：

N——核准该船搭载的乘客数；和

K——$0.056L$

但是，如果 KN 的数值大于 P 与舱壁甲板以上的实际乘客处所总容积之和，则 P_1 应取上述之和或 KN 值的 2/3，取较大者。

3.3 如果实际可行，动力舱底泵应置于分开的水密舱内，其布置或位置应使这些舱室不致因同一破损而进水。如果主推进装置、辅机和锅炉置于2个或2个以上的水密舱内，则可用于舱底排水的各泵应尽可能遍布于这些舱内。

3.4 在船长（L）为91.5 m及以上的船上或按照第3.2款计算的舱底泵数量为30或更多者，其布置须使至少一台动力舱底泵可在要求船舶经受的各种浸水状态中使用，以及，对于须符合第Ⅱ-1/1.1.1.1条的船舶，其泵的布置应能在考虑第8条所述的较小破损时出现的所有进水情况下，至少有一台动力舱底泵可供使用如下：

.1 所需各泵中的1台应是可靠的可潜式应急泵，其动力源位于舱壁甲板以上；或

.2 舱底泵及其动力源应在整个船长范围内分布，使未破损的一舱内至少有1台泵可供使用。

3.5 除仅供尖舱专用的附加泵外，所需的每一台舱底泵的布置应能从本条2.1所要求排水的任何处所抽水。

3.6 每台动力舱底泵应能通过所需的排水总管用不小于2 m/s的速度抽水。位于机器处所内的独立动力舱底泵应有引自这些处所的直接吸水管，但此种吸水管在任一处所内应不多于2根。如果设有2根或以上的此种吸水管，则至少每舷应有1根。主管机关可要求在其他处所内的各独立动力舱底泵配有单独的直接吸水管。各直接吸水管应适当地布置，而在机器处所内直接吸水管的直径，应不小于舱底排水总管所要求的直径。

3.7.1 In addition to the direct bilge suction or suctions required by paragraph 3.6, a direct suction from the main circulating pump leading to the drainage level of the machinery space and fitted with a non-return valve shall be provided in the machinery space. The diameter of this direct suction pipe shall be at least two thirds of the diameter of the pump inlet in the case of steamships, and of the same diameter as the pump inlet in the case of motorships.

3.7.2 Where, in the opinion of the Administration, the main circulating pump is not suitable for this purpose, a direct emergency bilge suction shall be led from the largest available independent power-driven pump to the drainage level of the machinery space; the suction shall be of the same diameter as the main inlet of the pump used. The capacity of the pump so connected shall exceed that of a required bilge pump by an amount deemed satisfactory by the Administration.

3.7.3 The spindles of the sea inlet and direct suction valves shall extend well above the engine-room platform.

3.8 All bilge suction piping up to the connection to the pumps shall be independent of other piping.

3.9 The diameter d of the bilge main shall be calculated according to the following formula. However, the actual internal diameter of the bilge main may be rounded off to the nearest standard size acceptable to the Administration:

$$d = 25 + 1.68\sqrt{L(B+D)}$$

where:

d is the internal diameter of the bilge main (millimetres);

L and B are the length and the breadth of the ship (metres) as defined in regulation 2; and

D is the moulded depth of the ship to the bulkhead deck (metres) provided that, in a ship having an enclosed cargo space on the bulkhead deck which is internally drained in accordance with the requirements of paragraph 2.6.2 and which extends for the full length of the ship, D shall be measured to the next deck above the bulkhead deck. Where the enclosed cargo spaces cover a lesser length, D shall be taken as the moulded depth to the bulkhead deck plus lh/L where l and h are the aggregate length and height, respectively, of the enclosed cargo spaces (metres). The diameter of the bilge branch pipes shall meet the requirements of the Administration.

3.10 Provision shall be made to prevent the compartment served by any bilge suction pipe being flooded in the event of the pipe being severed or otherwise damaged by collision or grounding in any other compartment. For this purpose, where the pipe is at any part situated nearer the side of the ship than one fifth of the breadth of the ship (as defined in regulation 2 and measured at right angles to the centreline at the level of the deepest subdivision load line), or is in a duct keel, a non-return valve shall be fitted to the pipe in the compartment containing the open end. For ships subject to the provisions of regulation Ⅱ-1/1.1.1.1, the deepest subdivision load line shall be taken as the deepest subdivision draught.

3.7.1 除直接舱底吸水管或本条 3.6 要求的吸水管外，在机器处所内应增设 1 根自主循环水泵引至机器处所排水液面的直接吸水管，此管应装有止回阀。此直接吸水管的直径，对蒸汽机船至少应为循环水泵进口直径 2/3，对柴油机船应与循环水泵进口的直径相等。

3.7.2 如果主管机关认为主循环水泵不适宜作此用途，则应自可用的最大独立动力泵引 1 根应急的直接舱底吸水管至机器处所排水液面；此管的直径应与所用泵的主进水管口直径相同。这样连接的泵，其排量应超过所需舱底泵的排量，超过量应使主管机关满意。

3.7.3 海水进水阀及直接吸水管阀的阀杆，应延伸至远高于机舱平台处。

3.8 所有舱底吸水管系，直至与泵连接为止，应独立于其他管系。

3.9 舱底总管的直径 d 应按下列公式计算，但是舱底总管的实际内径可按主管机关所接受的最接近标准尺度取整：

$$d = 25 + 1.68\sqrt{L(B+D)}$$

式中：

d——舱底总管的内径，mm；

L、B——第 2 条定义所指的船长和船宽，m；和

D——至舱壁甲板的船舶型深，m。但如果舱壁甲板上有一延伸至船舶全长且按本条 2.6.2 要求在内部排水的封闭货物处所，则 D 应量至舱壁甲板以上的第一层甲板。如果封闭货物处所的长度较短，D 应取为至舱壁甲板的型深加上 lh/L，此处 l 和 h 分别为此类封闭货物处所的累计长度和高度，以 m 计。舱底支管的直径应符合主管机关的要求。

3.10 应采取措施防止装有舱底吸水管的舱室因其他舱室由于碰撞或搁浅而使管子断裂或其他损坏所引起进水。为此，凡此水管的任何部分位于距舷侧不到 1/5 船宽（按第 2 条定义，且在最深分舱载重线水平面上向纵中剖面方向垂直量计）处或在箱形龙骨内，应在其开口端所在舱室内的管子上装有止回阀。对于应符合第Ⅱ-1/1.1.1.1 条的船舶，最深分舱载重线须取作最深分舱吃水。

3.11 Distribution boxes, cocks and valves in connection with the bilge pumping system shall be so arranged that, in the event of flooding, one of the bilge pumps may be operative on any compartment; in addition, damage to a pump or its pipe connecting to the bilge main outboard of a line drawn at one fifth of the breadth of the ship shall not put the bilge system out of action. If there is only one system of pipes common to all the pumps, the necessary valves for controlling the bilge suctions must be capable of being operated from above the bulkhead deck. Where, in addition to the main bilge pumping system, an emergency bilge pumping system is provided, it shall be independent of the main system and so arranged that a pump is capable of operating on any compartment under flooding condition as specified in paragraph 3.1; in that case only the valves necessary for the operation of the emergency system need be capable of being operated from above the bulkhead deck.

3.12 All cocks and valves referred to in paragraph 3.11 which can be operated from above the bulkhead deck shall have their controls at their place of operation clearly marked and shall be provided with means to indicate whether they are open or closed.

4 Cargo ships

At least two power pumps connected to the main bilge system shall be provided, one of which may be driven by the propulsion machinery. If the Administration is satisfied that the safety of the ship is not impaired, bilge pumping arrangements may be dispensed with in particular compartments.

Regulation 36[①]

Regulation 37
Communication between navigation bridge and machinery space

1 At least two independent means shall be provided for communicating orders from the navigation bridge to the position in the machinery space or in the control room from which the engines are normally controlled: one of these shall be an engine-room telegraph which provides visual indication of the orders and responses both in the machinery space and on the navigation bridge. Appropriate means of communication shall be provided to any other positions from which the engines may be controlled.

2 For ships constructed on or after 1 October 1994 the following requirements apply in lieu of the provisions of paragraph 1:

① This regulation is deliberately left blank.

3.11 与舱底水泵送系统相连的分配箱、旋塞及阀，应布置成万一进水时，舱底泵之一能用于任何舱室；此外，在距舷侧 1/5 船宽处所绘一线以外的舱底泵或其与舱底总管连接的管子有损坏时，不应使整个舱底排水系统丧失作用。如果仅有一路管系为所有的泵共用，则控制舱底吸水管所需的阀必须能从舱壁甲板以上操作。如果除主舱底水泵送系统外还设有应急舱底水泵送系统，则此应急系统应独立于主系统，并应布置成在本条 3.1 规定的进水情况下，有一泵能用于任一舱室；在此情况下，只有应急系统操作所需的阀才要求能在舱壁甲板以上操作。

3.12 本条 3.11 所述的能自舱壁甲板以上操作的所有旋塞和阀，在其操作处所应有明显标志的控制器，并应设有指示其开启或关闭的设施。

4　货船

至少应设有与主舱底排水系统相连接的 2 台动力泵，其中 1 台可由推进机械驱动。如果主管机关确信船舶的安全不会受到损害，则个别舱室可免设舱底水泵送装置。

第 36 条[①]

第 37 条
驾驶台与机器处所之间的通信

1 应至少设有两套独立的设备，将驾驶台的指令传至机器处所或控制室中通常控制发动机的位置：其中一套应为在机器处所和驾驶台均能以视觉方式显示指令和响应的车钟。其他能控制发动机的任何处所也应配备适当的通信设备。

2 对于 1994 年 10 月 1 日或以后建造的船舶，适用下列要求以替代本条 1 的规定：

① 本条目前留空。

At least two independent means shall be provided for communicating orders from the navigation bridge to the position in the machinery space or in the control room from which the speed and direction of thrust of the propellers are normally controlled; one of these shall be an engine-room telegraph which provides visual indication of the orders and responses both in the machinery spaces and on the navigation bridge. Appropriate means of communication shall be provided from the navigation bridge and the engine-room to any other position from which the speed or direction of thrust of the propellers may be controlled.

Regulation 38
Engineers' alarm

An engineers' alarm shall be provided to be operated from the engine control room or at the manoeuvring platform as appropriate, and shall be clearly audible in the engineers' accommodation.

Regulation 39
Location of emergency installations in passenger ships

Emergency sources of electrical power, fire pumps, bilge pumps except those specifically serving the spaces forward of the collision bulkhead, any fixed fire-extinguishing system required by chapter Ⅱ-2 and other emergency installations which are essential for the safety of the ship, except anchor windlasses, shall not be installed forward of the collision bulkhead.

从驾驶台到机器处所或控制室中通常控制推进器速度和方向的位置上至少应设置2套独立的通信设施，其中1套应为在机器处所和驾驶台均能直接显示指令和回令的车钟。其他任何可以控制推进器速度和方向的位置也应配备适当的通信设施，以便接收来自驾驶台和机舱的指令。

第38条
轮机员的报警装置

应设有一个从发动机控制室或操纵平台（视具体情况而定）进行操作的轮机员报警装置，且报警信号应能在轮机员居住舱室清晰地听到。

第39条
客船应急装置的位置

应急电源、消防泵、舱底泵（防撞舱壁前方的处所专用舱底泵除外）、第Ⅱ-2章要求的任何固定式灭火系统，以及为船舶安全所必需的其他应急装置（除锚机外）不应安装在防撞舱壁前方。

Part D
Electrical installations

(Except where expressly provided otherwise part D applies to passenger ships and cargo ships)

Regulation 40
General

1 Electrical installations shall be such that:

.1 all electrical auxiliary services necessary for maintaining the ship in normal operational and habitable conditions will be ensured without recourse to the emergency source of electrical power;

.2 electrical services essential for safety will be ensured under various emergency conditions; and

.3 the safety of passengers, crew and ship from electrical hazards will be ensured.

2 The Administration shall take appropriate steps to ensure uniformity in the implementation and application of the provisions of this part in respect of electrical installations. ①

Regulation 41
Main source of electrical power and lighting systems

1.1 A main source of electrical power of sufficient capacity to supply all those services mentioned in regulation 40.1.1 shall be provided. This main source of electrical power shall consist of at least two generating sets.

1.2 The capacity of these generating sets shall be such that in the event of any one generating set being stopped it will still be possible to supply those services necessary to provide normal operational conditions of propulsion and safety. Minimum comfortable conditions of habitability shall also be ensured which include at least adequate services for cooking, heating, domestic refrigeration, mechanical ventilation, sanitary and fresh water.

1.3 The arrangements of the ship's main source of electrical power shall be such that the services referred to in regulation 40.1.1 can be maintained regardless of the speed and direction of rotation of the propulsion machinery or shafting.

① Refer to the recommendations published by the International Electrotechnical Commission and, in particular, publication IEC 60092, *Electrical installations in ships*.

D 部分
电气装置

(除另有明文规定外,D 部分适用于客船和货船)

第 40 条
通则

1　电气装置应能

.1　在不借助应急电源的情况下,确保对所有为船舶正常操作和居住条件所必需的电气辅助设备供电;

.2　在各种应急情况下,确保对安全所必需的电气设备供电;和

.3　确保乘客、船员和船舶的安全,免受各种电气灾害。

2　主管机关应采取相应措施,以确保本部分关于电气装置的各项规定能得到统一的执行和应用。①

第 41 条
主电源和照明系统

1.1　应配备向第 40.1.1 条所述的所有设备供电的足够容量的主电源。主电源至少应由2 台发电机组组成。

1.2　这些发电机组的容量,应是当任一发电机组停止供电时,仍能对正常推进操作和安全所必需的设备供电。还应确保最低舒适居住条件,包括至少为烹调、取暖、食品冷冻、机械通风、卫生和淡水等设备充分供电。

1.3　船舶的主电源应布置成不论推进机械和轴系的速度和转动方向如何,第 40.1.1 条所述设备均能保持工作状态。

---

①　参见国际电工委员会出版的建议性标准,特别是 IEC60092 出版物《船舶电气装置》。

1.4 In addition, the generating sets shall be such as to ensure that with any one generator or its primary source of power out of operation, the remaining generating sets shall be capable of providing the electrical services necessary to start the main propulsion plant from a dead ship condition. The emergency source of electrical power may be used for the purpose of starting from a dead ship condition if its capability either alone or combined with that of any other source of electrical power is sufficient to provide at the same time those services required to be supplied by regulations 42.2.1 to 42.2.3 or 43.2.1 to 43.2.4.

1.5 Where transformers constitute an essential part of the electrical supply system required by this paragraph, the system shall be so arranged as to ensure the same continuity of the supply as is stated in this paragraph.

2.1 A main electric lighting system which shall provide illumination throughout those parts of the ship normally accessible to and used by passengers or crew shall be supplied from the main source of electrical power.

2.2 The arrangement of the main electric lighting system shall be such that a fire or other casualty in spaces containing the main source of electrical power, associated transforming equipment, if any, the main switchboard and the main lighting switchboard, will not render the emergency electric lighting system required by regulations 42.2.1 and 42.2.2 or 43.2.1, 43.2.2 and 43.2.3 inoperative.

2.3 The arrangement of the emergency electric lighting system shall be such that a fire or other casualty in spaces containing the emergency source of electrical power, associated transforming equipment, if any, the emergency switchboard and the emergency lighting switchboard will not render the main electric lighting system required by this regulation inoperative.

3 The main switchboard shall be so placed relative to one main generating station that, as far as is practicable, the integrity of the normal electrical supply may be affected only by a fire or other casualty in one space. An environmental enclosure for the main switchboard, such as may be provided by a machinery control room situated within the main boundaries of the space, is not to be considered as separating the switchboards from the generators.

4 Where the total installed electrical power of the main generating sets is in excess of 3 MW, the main busbars shall be subdivided into at least two parts which shall normally be connected by removable links or other approved means; so far as is practicable, the connection of generating sets and any other duplicated equipment shall be equally divided between the parts. Equivalent arrangements may be permitted to the satisfaction of the Administration.

5 Ships constructed on or after 1 July 1998:

.1 in addition to paragraphs 1 to 3, shall comply with the following:

.1 where the main source of electrical power is necessary for propulsion and steering of the ship, the system shall be so arranged that the electrical supply to equipment necessary for propulsion and steering and to ensure safety of the ship will be maintained or immediately restored in the case of loss of any one of the generators in service;

1.4 此外,发电机组应在任一发电机组或其原动力源失效时,确保其余发电机组仍能对主推进装置从瘫船状态启动所必需的设备供电。如果应急电源单凭自身功率或与任何其他电源的组合功率足以同时对第 42.2.1 至 42.2.3 条或第 43.2.1 至 43.2.4 条所述设备供电,则应急电源可用于从瘫船状态启动的目的。

1.5 如果变压器构成本条所要求供电系统的一个重要部分,则变压器系统的布置应能确保如本条所述同样的供电连续性。

2.1 为船上通常可供船员或乘客进入并使用的部位提供全部照明的主电气照明系统,应由主电源供电。

2.2 主电气照明系统的布置应能在主电源、相关的变换设备(若设有)、主配电板和主照明配电板所在处所发生火灾或其他事故时,不会导致第 42.2.1 和 42.2.2 条或第 43.2.1、43.2.2和 43.2.3 条所要求的应急电气照明系统失效。

2.3 应急电气照明系统的布置应在应急电源、相关的变换设备(若设有)、应急配电板和应急照明配电板所在处所发生火灾或其他事故时,不会导致本条所要求的主电气照明系统失效。

3 主配电板应相对于一个主发电站设置,以尽实际可能使正常供电的完整性只有在一个处所发生火灾或其他事故时才可能受到影响。主配电板的环境围蔽,例如位于该处所主限界面以内的机器控制室提供的围蔽,不应视为将配电板与发电机隔开。

4 如果主发电机组的总装机功率超过 3 MW,则主汇流排应至少分成两段,通常应由可拆装的连接件或其他认可的装置加以连接,并应尽实际可能将各发电机组和其他双套设备均等地连接在各分段上。可允许采用等效的布置并使主管机关满意。

5 1998 年 7 月 1 日或以后建造的船舶:

.1 除本条 1 至 3 外,还应符合如下要求:

.1 如果主电源对船舶推进和操舵是必需的,则该系统的布置应在运行中的任何一台发电机发生故障时,对推进和操舵以及确保船舶安全必需的设备的供电能维持或立即恢复供电;

.2 load shedding or other equivalent arrangements shall be provided to protect the generators required by this regulation against sustained overload;

.3 where the main source of electrical power is necessary for propulsion of the ship, the main busbar shall be subdivided into at least two parts which shall normally be connected by circuit breakers or other approved means; so far as is practicable, the connection of generating sets and other duplicated equipment shall be equally divided between the parts; and

.2 need not comply with paragraph 4.

6 In passenger ships constructed on or after 1 July 2010, supplementary lighting shall be provided in all cabins to clearly indicate the exit so that occupants will be able to find their way to the door. Such lighting, which may be connected to an emergency source of power or have a self-contained source of electrical power in each cabin, shall automatically illuminate when power to the normal cabin lighting is lost and remain on for a minimum of 30 min.

Regulation 42
Emergency source of electrical power in passenger ships

(Paragraphs 2.6.1 and 4.2 of this regulation apply to ships constructed on or after 1 February 1992)

1.1 A self-contained emergency source of electrical power shall be provided.

1.2 The emergency source of electrical power, associated transforming equipment, if any, transitional source of emergency power, emergency switchboard and emergency lighting switchboard shall be located above the uppermost continuous deck and shall be readily accessible from the open deck. They shall not be located forward of the collision bulkhead.

1.3 The location of the emergency source of electrical power and associated transforming equipment, if any, the transitional source of emergency power, the emergency switchboard and the emergency electric lighting switchboards in relation to the main source of electrical power, associated transforming equipment, if any, and the main switchboard shall be such as to ensure to the satisfaction of the Administration that a fire or other casualty in spaces containing the main source of electrical power, associated transforming equipment, if any, and the main switchboard or in any machinery space of category A will not interfere with the supply, control and distribution of emergency electrical power. As far as practicable, the space containing the emergency source of electrical power, associated transforming equipment, if any, the transitional source of emergency electrical power and the emergency switchboard shall not be contiguous to the boundaries of machinery spaces of category A or those spaces containing the main source of electrical power, associated transforming equipment, if any, or the main switchboard.

1.4 Provided that suitable measures are taken for safeguarding independent emergency operation under all circumstances, the emergency generator may be used exceptionally, and for short periods, to supply non-emergency circuits.

.2 应设有卸载或其他等效装置以保护本条所要求的发电机避免发生超载；

.3 如果主电源对船舶的推进必不可少，则主汇流排应至少分成两段，通常应由断路器或其他经认可的装置加以连接；并应尽实际可能将各发电机组和其他双套设备均等地连接在各分段上；和

.2 不必符合本条4的要求。

6 在2010年7月1日或以后建造的客船上，所有舱室均须设有辅助照明，以清楚地示明出口，使旅客能够找到通向门的通道。辅助照明可与应急电源相连，或在每一舱室中配有自备电源，在舱室正常照明失去电源时自动点亮，并延续至少30 min。

第42条
客船应急电源

（本条2.6.1和4.2适用于1992年2月1日或以后建造的船舶）

1.1 应设有一独立的应急电源。

1.2 应急电源、相关的变换设备（若设有）、临时应急电源、应急配电板和应急照明配电板应位于最高连续甲板之上，并应从露天甲板易于到达。它们不应位于防撞舱壁的前方。

1.3 应急电源、相关的变换设备（若设有）、临时应急电源、应急配电板和应急照明配电板与主电源、相关变换设备（若设有）与主配电板的相对位置应确保使主管机关确信，主电源、相关的变换设备（若设有）和主配电板所在处所或任何A类机器处所发生火灾或其他事故时，不会妨碍应急电源的供电、控制和配电。应急电源、相关的变换设备（若设有）、临时应急电源和应急配电板所在处所应尽可能不与A类机器处所或主电源、相关的变换设备（若设有）或主配电板所在处所的限界面相邻接。

1.4 如果采取适当措施以在各种情况下确保独立的应急操作，则应急发电机可例外用于短时间内向非应急电路供电。

2 The electrical power available shall be sufficient to supply all those services that are essential for safety in an emergency, due regard being paid to such services as may have to be operated simultaneously. The emergency source of electrical power shall be capable, having regard to starting currents and the transitory nature of certain loads, of supplying simultaneously at least the following services for the periods specified hereinafter, if they depend upon an electrical source for their operation:

2.1 For a period of 36 h, emergency lighting:

.1 at every muster and embarkation station and over the sides as required by regulations Ⅲ/11.4 and Ⅲ/16.7;

.2 in alleyways, stairways and exits giving access to the muster and embarkation stations, as required by regulation Ⅲ/11.5;

.3 in all service and accommodation alleyways, stairways and exits, personnel lift cars;

.4 in the machinery spaces and main generating stations including their control positions;

.5 in all control stations, machinery control rooms, and at each main and emergency switchboard;

.6 at all stowage positions for firemen's outfits;

.7 at the steering gear; and

.8 at the fire pump, the sprinkler pump and the emergency bilge pump referred to in paragraph 2.4 and at the starting position of their motors.

2.2 For a period of 36 h:

.1 the navigation lights and other lights required by the International Regulations for Preventing Collisions at Sea in force; and

.2 on ships constructed on or after 1 February 1995, the VHF radio installation required by regulation Ⅳ/7.1.1 and Ⅳ/7.1.2; and, if applicable:

.1 the MF radio installation required by regulations Ⅳ/9.1.1, Ⅳ/9.1.2, Ⅳ/10.1.2 and Ⅳ/10.1.3;

.2 the ship earth station required by regulation Ⅳ/10.1.1; and

.3 the MF/HF radio installation required by regulations Ⅳ/10.2.1, Ⅳ/10.2.2 and Ⅳ/11.1.

2.3 For a period of 36 h:

.1 all internal communication equipment required in an emergency;

.2 the shipborne navigational equipment as required by regulation Ⅴ/19; where such provision is unreasonable or impracticable the Administration may waive this requirement for ships of less than 5,000 gross tonnage;

2 可用的电源功率应足够向应急情况下安全所必需的所有设备供电，并充分考虑到这些设备可能要同时使用。应急电源应能在下述时间内足以同时至少对下列设备供电（如果这些设备由电力驱动），同时应考虑到某些负载的启动电流和瞬变特性：

2.1 对下列处所供电 36 h，应急照明：

.1 第Ⅲ/11.4 条和第Ⅲ/16.7 条所要求的每一集合地点、登乘地点和舷侧；

.2 第Ⅲ/11.5 条所要求的通达集合地点与登乘地点的走廊、梯道和出口；

.3 所有服务和居住处所的走廊、梯道、出口和载人电梯；

.4 机器处所和主发电站，包括其控制位置；

.5 所有控制站、机器控制室和每一主配电板和应急配电板处；

.6 消防员装备的所有存放处所；

.7 操舵装置处；和

.8 消防泵、喷水泵和本条 2.4 所指的应急舱底泵以及其电动机启动位置。

2.2 对下列设备供电 36 h：

.1 现行《国际海上避碰规则》所要求的航行灯和其他信号灯；和

.2 对 1995 年 2 月 1 日或以后建造的船舶，第Ⅳ/7.1.1 条和第Ⅳ/7.1.2 条所要求的甚高频无线电装置；和如果适用时：

.1 第Ⅳ/9.1.1、Ⅳ/9.1.2、Ⅳ/10.1.2 和Ⅳ/10.1.3 条所要求的中频无线电装置；

.2 第Ⅳ/10.1.1 条所要求的船舶地面站；和

.3 第Ⅳ/10.2.1、Ⅳ/10.2.2 和Ⅳ/11.1 条所要求的中频/高频无线电装置。

2.3 对下列设备供电 36 h：

.1 紧急情况下所需要的所有内部通信设备；

.2 第Ⅴ/12 条所要求的船上航行设备；当此项规定为不合理或不可行时，主管机关可对小于 5 000 总吨的船舶免除此项要求；

.3 the fire detection and fire alarm system, and the fire door holding and release system; and

.4 for intermittent operation of the daylight signalling lamp, the ship's whistle, the manually operated call points, and all internal signals that are required in an emergency;

unless such services have an independent supply for the period of 36 h from an accumulator battery suitably located for use in an emergency.

2.4 For a period of 36 h:

.1 one of the fire pumps required by regulation II-2/10.2.2.2 and II-2/10.2.2.3;

.2 the automatic sprinkler pump, if any; and

.3 the emergency bilge pump and all the equipment essential for the operation of electrically powered remote controlled bilge valves.

2.5 For the period of time required by regulation 29.14 the steering gear if required to be so supplied by that regulation.

2.6 For a period of half an hour:

.1 any watertight doors required by regulation 15 to be power-operated together with their indicators and warning signals;

.2 the emergency arrangements to bring the lift cars to deck level for the escape of persons. The passenger lift cars may be brought to deck level sequentially in an emergency.

2.7 In a ship engaged regularly on voyages of short duration, the Administration if satisfied that an adequate standard of safety would be attained may accept a lesser period than the 36 h period specified in paragraphs 2.1 to 2.5 but not less than 12 h.

3 The emergency source of electrical power may be either a generator or an accumulator battery, which shall comply with the following:

3.1 Where the emergency source of electrical power is a generator, it shall be:

.1 driven by a suitable prime mover with an independent supply of fuel having a flashpoint (closed cup test) of not less than 43 ℃;

.2 started automatically upon failure of the electrical supply from the main source of electrical power and shall be automatically connected to the emergency switchboard; those services referred to in paragraph 4 shall then be transferred automatically to the emergency generating set. The automatic starting system and the characteristic of the prime mover shall be such as to permit the emergency generator to carry its full rated load as quickly as is safe and practicable, subject to a maximum of 45 s; unless a second independent means of starting the emergency generating set is provided, the single source of stored energy shall be protected to preclude its complete depletion by the automatic starting system; and

.3　探火和失火报警系统，以及防火门的吸持和释放系统；和

.4　白昼信号灯、船舶号笛、手动报警按钮和紧急情况下需要的所有内部信号的断续操作；

除非这些装置在紧急情况下，置于适当位置的蓄电池可以提供 36 h 的独立供电。

2.4　对下列设备供电 36 h：

.1　第Ⅱ-2/10.2.2.2 和Ⅱ-2/10.2.2.3 条要求的消防泵之一；

.2　自动喷水泵（若设有）；和

.3　应急舱底泵和操作电动遥控舱底阀所必需的所有设备。

2.5　按第 29.14 条要求的时间对操舵装置供电，如果该条要求如此供电时。

2.6　对下列设备供电 0.5 h：

.1　第 15 条要求的动力操作水密门，以及其指示器和报警信号；

.2　将电梯提升至甲板高度以便人员脱逃的应急装置，在紧急情况下乘客电梯可按序提升至甲板高度。

2.7　定期从事短途航行的船舶，主管机关如果确信能达到适当的安全标准，则可接受比本条 2.1 至 2.5 所规定的 36 h 更短的时间，但应不少于 12 h。

3　应急电源可以是一台发电机或一蓄电池组，其应满足下列要求：

3.1　应急电源如为一台发电机，其应：

.1　由一台独立供给燃油的适当原动机驱动，燃油闪点（闭杯试验）不低于 43 ℃；

.2　在主电源供电发生故障时自动启动，并应自动与应急配电板接通，本条 4 所指的设备也应自动转由应急发电机组供电。原动机的自动启动系统及其特性，应能尽快地在最多 45 s 内使应急发电机安全和实际可行地承载其额定负载；除设有应急发电机组的第二套独立启动装置外，应对单一的储存能源加以保护，以防止其被自动启动系统全部耗尽；和

.3 provided with a transitional source of emergency electrical power according to paragraph 4.

3.2 Where the emergency source of electrical power is an accumulator battery, it shall be capable of:

.1 carrying the emergency electrical load without recharging while maintaining the voltage of the battery throughout the discharge period within 12% above or below its nominal voltage;

.2 automatically connecting to the emergency switchboard in the event of failure of the main source of electrical power; and

.3 immediately supplying at least those services specified in paragraph 4.

3.3 The following provisions in paragraph 3.1.2 shall not apply to ships constructed on or after 1 October 1994:

Unless a second independent means of starting the emergency generating set is provided, the single source of stored energy shall be protected to preclude its complete depletion by the automatic starting system.

3.4 For ships constructed on or after 1 July 1998, where electrical power is necessary to restore propulsion, the capacity shall be sufficient to restore propulsion to the ship in conjunction with other machinery, as appropriate, from a dead ship condition within 30 min after blackout.

4 The transitional source of emergency electrical power required by paragraph 3.1.3 shall consist of an accumulator battery suitably located for use in an emergency which shall operate without recharging while maintaining the voltage of the battery throughout the discharge period within 12% above or below its nominal voltage and be of sufficient capacity and so arranged as to supply automatically in the event of failure of either the main or emergency source of electrical power at least the following services, if they depend upon an electrical source for their operation:

4.1 For half an hour:

.1 the lighting required by paragraphs 2.1 and 2.2;

.2 all services required by paragraphs 2.3.1, 2.3.3 and 2.3.4 unless such services have an independent supply for the period specified from an accumulator battery suitably located for use in an emergency.

4.2 Power to operate the watertight doors, as required by regulation 13.7.3.3, but not necessarily all of them simultaneously, unless an independent temporary source of stored energy is provided. Power to the control, indication and alarm circuits as required by regulation 13.7.2 for half an hour.

5.1 The emergency switchboard shall be installed as near as is practicable to the emergency source of electrical power.

.3　设有本条4规定的临时应急电源。

3.2　如果应急电源为蓄电池组,其应能:

.1　承载应急负载而不必再充电。在整个供电时间保持其电压变化在额定电压的±12%以内;

.2　在主电源供电发生故障时,自动与应急配电板接通;和

.3　立即至少对本条4所指的那些设备供电。

3.3　本条3.1.2中的下列规定不适用于1994年10月1日或以后建造的船舶:

除非设有应急发电机组的第二套独立启动装置,否则单一储备的能源应加以保护,以免被自动启动系统全部耗尽。

3.4　1998年7月1日或以后建造的船舶,如果必须使用电源恢复推进,其功率应足以在全船失电后30 min内,使之连同其他机器(视具体情况而定)从瘫船状态恢复至推进状态。

4　本条3.1.3要求的临时应急电源,应由一个设置于适当处所供紧急情况下使用的蓄电池组组成。该蓄电池组应在整个供电期间将蓄电池的电压保持在其额定电压的±12%以内而不需重新充电,并具有足够的容量,且布置成能在主电源或应急电源发生故障时自动至少对下列设备供电(如果这些设备由电力驱动):

4.1　对下列设备供电0.5 h:

.1　本条2.1和2.2要求的照明;

.2　本条2.3.1、2.3.3和2.3.4要求的所有设备,除非这些设备是由设置于应急时便于使用处所的蓄电池组在指定时间独立供电。

4.2　第13.7.3.3条要求动力操作的水密门,但不要求同时操作所有的水密门,除非设有一独立的过渡性储备能源。并应对第13.7.2条要求的动力控制、指示和报警电路供电0.5 h。

5.1　应急配电板应尽实际可能设置在靠近应急电源处。

5.2 Where the emergency source of electrical power is a generator, the emergency switchboard shall be located in the same space unless the operation of the emergency switchboard would thereby be impaired.

5.3 No accumulator battery fitted in accordance with this regulation shall be installed in the same space as the emergency switchboard. An indicator shall be mounted in a suitable place on the main switchboard or in the machinery control room to indicate when the batteries constituting either the emergency source of electrical power or the transitional source of emergency electrical power referred to in paragraph 3.1.3 or 4 are being discharged.

5.4 The emergency switchboard shall be supplied during normal operation from the main switchboard by an interconnector feeder which is to be adequately protected at the main switchboard against overload and short circuit and which is to be disconnected automatically at the emergency switchboard upon failure of the main source of electrical power. Where the system is arranged for feedback operation, the interconnector feeder is also to be protected at the emergency switchboard at least against short circuit.

5.5 In order to ensure ready availability of the emergency source of electrical power, arrangements shall be made where necessary to disconnect automatically non-emergency circuits from the emergency switchboard to ensure that power shall be available to the emergency circuits.

6 The emergency generator and its prime mover and any emergency accumulator battery shall be so designed and arranged as to ensure that they will function at full rated power when the ship is upright and when inclined at any angle of list up to 22.5° or when inclined up to 10° either in the fore or aft direction, or is in any combination of angles within those limits.

7 Provision shall be made for the periodic testing of the complete emergency system and shall include the testing of automatic starting arrangements.

Regulation 42-1
Supplementary emergency lighting for ro-ro passenger ships

(*This regulation applies to all passenger ships with ro-ro cargo spaces or special category spaces as defined in regulation Ⅱ-2/3, except that for ships constructed before 22 October 1989, this regulation shall apply not later than 22 October 1990*)

1 In addition to the emergency lighting required by regulation 42.2, on every passenger ship with ro-ro cargo spaces or special category spaces as defined in regulation Ⅱ-2/3:

5.2 如果应急电源是一台发电机，则除会妨碍应急配电板的操作外，应急配电板应与应急电源位于同一处所。

5.3 按本条规定装设的蓄电池组不得与应急配电板安装在同一处所。应在主配电板上或机器控制室内的适当位置安装一个指示器，用以显示作为本条3.1.3或4所述的应急电源或临时应急电源的蓄电池组正在放电。

5.4 应急配电板在正常工作时应用互连馈线由主配电板供电，此互连馈线在主配电板上应设有适当的过载和短路保护，并应在主电源发生故障时在应急配电板处自动断开。如果该系统布置成反向供电，则该互连馈线还应在应急配电板上至少设有短路保护。

5.5 为确保应急电源随时可用，其布置应在必要时可将非应急电路从应急配电板自动断开，以确保向应急电路有效供电。

6 应急发电机及其原动机和任何应急蓄电池组应设计和布置成在船舶处于正浮状态和横倾达22.5°，或首、尾纵倾达10°，或在这些范围内出现的任何组合的倾斜角度时，确保其仍能以全额定功率发挥效用。

7 应做出规定对整个应急系统进行定期测试，并应包括自动启动装置的测试。

第42-1条
滚装客船的附加应急照明

（本条适用于设有第Ⅱ-2/3条定义的滚装装货处所或特种处所的所有客船，但对1989年10月22日以前建造的船舶，本条应不迟于1990年10月22日起适用）

1 除第42.2条要求的应急照明外，在每艘设有第Ⅱ-2/3条定义的滚装装货处所或特种处所的客船上：

.1 all passenger public spaces and alleyways shall be provided with supplementary electric lighting that can operate for at least 3 h when all other sources of electrical power have failed and under any condition of heel. The illumination provided shall be such that the approach to the means of escape can be readily seen. The source of power for the supplementary lighting shall consist of accumulator batteries located within the lighting units that are continuously charged, where practicable, from the emergency switchboard. Alternatively, any other means of lighting which is at least as effective may be accepted by the Administration. The supplementary lighting shall be such that any failure of the lamp will be immediately apparent. Any accumulator battery provided shall be replaced at intervals having regard to the specified service life in the ambient conditions that they are subject to in service; and

.2 a portable rechargeable battery operated lamp shall be provided in every crew space alleyway, recreational space and every working space which is normally occupied unless supplementary emergency lighting, as required by subparagraph .1, is provided.

Regulation 43
Emergency source of electrical power in cargo ships

1.1 A self-contained emergency source of electrical power shall be provided.

1.2 The emergency source of electrical power, associated transforming equipment, if any, transitional source of emergency power, emergency switchboard and emergency lighting switchboard shall be located above the uppermost continuous deck and shall be readily accessible from the open deck. They shall not be located forward of the collision bulkhead, except where permitted by the Administration in exceptional circumstances.

1.3 The location of the emergency source of electrical power, associated transforming equipment, if any, the transitional source of emergency power, the emergency switchboard and the emergency lighting switchboard in relation to the main source of electrical power, associated transforming equipment, if any, and the main switchboard shall be such as to ensure to the satisfaction of the Administration that a fire or other casualty in the space containing the main source of electrical power, associated transforming equipment, if any, and the main switchboard, or in any machinery space of category A will not interfere with the supply, control and distribution of emergency electrical power. As far as practicable the space containing the emergency source of electrical power, associated transforming equipment, if any, the transitional source of emergency electrical power and the emergency switchboard shall not be contiguous to the boundaries of machinery spaces of category A or those spaces containing the main source of electrical power, associated transforming equipment, if any, and the main switchboard.

1.4 Provided that suitable measures are taken for safeguarding independent emergency operation under all circumstances, the emergency generator may be used, exceptionally, and for short periods, to supply non-emergency circuits.

.1 所有乘客公共处所和走廊都应设有附加照明设备，在所有其他电源发生故障时和任何横倾条件下，至少能维持照明 3 h。所提供的照明应能易于看见脱险通道。附加照明的电源应位于照明设备内部并由能连续充电的蓄电池组组成，该蓄电池组在实际可行时能从应急配电板充电。作为替代，主管机关可以接受至少如上述一样有效的其他照明设备。该附加照明设备应使灯的故障能立即被发现。所设的蓄电池应定期更换，间隔期应考虑到根据蓄电池使用中所处的环境条件而定的使用寿命；和

.2 在每一船员处所的走廊、娱乐处所和通常有人的每一工作处所，除非设有本条.1 所要求的附加应急照明，否则均应配备可携式充电电池灯。

第 43 条
货船应急电源

1.1 应设有一独立的应急电源。

1.2 应急电源、相关的变换设备（若设有）、临时应急电源、应急配电板和应急照明配电板应位于最高连续甲板之上，并应从露天甲板易于到达。除在例外情况下经主管机关允许外，它们不应位于防撞舱壁的前方。

1.3 应急电源、相关的变换设备（若设有）、临时应急电源、应急配电板和应急照明配电板与主电源、相关的变换设备（若设有）和主配电板的相对位置应使主管机关满意，以确保在主电源、相关的变换设备（若设有）和主配电板所在处所或任何 A 类机器处所发生火灾或其他事故时，不会妨碍应急电源的供电、控制和配电。应急电源、相关的变换设备（若设有）、临时应急电源和应急配电板所在处所应尽可能不与 A 类机器处所或主电源、相关的变换设备（若设有）和主配电板所在处所的限界面相邻接。

1.4 如采取适当措施以在各种情况下确保独立的应急操作，则应急发电机可例外用于短时间内向非应急电路供电。

2 The electrical power available shall be sufficient to supply all those services that are essential for safety in an emergency, due regard being paid to such services as may have to be operated simultaneously. The emergency source of electrical power shall be capable, having regard to starting currents and the transitory nature of certain loads, of supplying simultaneously at least the following services for the periods specified hereinafter, if they depend upon an electrical source for their operation:

2.1 For a period of 3 h, emergency lighting at every muster and embarkation station and over the sides as required by regulations Ⅲ/11.4 and Ⅲ/16.7.

2.2 For a period of 18 h, emergency lighting:

.1 in all service and accommodation alleyways, stairways and exits, personnel lift cars and personnel lift trunks;

.2 in the machinery spaces and main generating stations including their control positions;

.3 in all control stations, machinery control rooms, and at each main and emergency switchboard;

.4 at all stowage positions for firemen's outfits;

.5 at the steering gear;

.6 at the fire pump referred to in paragraph 2.5, at the sprinkler pump, if any, and at the emergency bilge pump, if any, and at the starting positions of their motors; and

.7 in all cargo pump-rooms of tankers constructed on or after 1 July 2002.

2.3 For a period of 18 h:

.1 the navigation lights and other lights required by the International Regulations for Preventing Collisions at Sea in force;

.2 on ships constructed on or after 1 February 1995 the VHF radio installation required by regulation Ⅳ/7.1.1 and Ⅳ/7.1.2; and, if applicable:

.1 the MF radio installation required by regulations Ⅳ/9.1.1, Ⅳ/9.1.2, Ⅳ/10.1.2 and Ⅳ/10.1.3;

.2 the ship earth station required by regulation Ⅳ/10.1.1; and

.3 the MF/HF radio installation required by regulations Ⅳ/10.2.1, Ⅳ/10.2.2 and Ⅳ/11.1.

2.4 For a period of 18 h:

.1 all internal communication equipment as required in an emergency;

.2 the shipborne navigational equipment as required by regulation Ⅴ/19; where such provision is unreasonable or impracticable the Administration may waive this requirement for ships of less than 5,000 gross tonnage;

2 可用的电源功率应足够向应急情况下安全所必需的所有设备供电，并充分考虑到这些设备可能要同时使用。应急电源应能在下述时间内足以同时至少对下列设备供电（若这些设备由电力驱动），同时应考虑到某些负载的启动电流和瞬变特性：

2.1 对第Ⅲ/11.4 条和第Ⅲ/16.7 条所要求的每一集合和登乘地点和舷侧供电 3 h，应急照明。

2.2 对下列处所供电 18 h，应急照明：

.1 所有服务和居住处所的走廊、梯道和出口、载人电梯及其围井；

.2 机器处所和主发电站，包括其控制位置；

.3 所有控制站、机器控制室和每一主配电板及应急配电板处；

.4 消防员装备的所有存放位置；

.5 操舵装置处；

.6 本条 2.5 所指的消防泵，喷水泵（若设有）和应急舱底泵（若设有）和其电动机启动位置；和

.7 在 2002 年 7 月 1 日或以后建造的液货船的所有货泵舱内。

2.3 对下列设备供电 18 h：

.1 现行《国际海上避碰规则》所要求的航行灯和其他信号灯；

.2 对 1995 年 2 月 1 日或以后建造的船舶，第Ⅳ/7.1.1 和第Ⅳ/7.1.2 条所要求的甚高频无线电装置；及如适用时：

.1 第Ⅳ/9.1.1、Ⅳ/9.1.2、Ⅳ/10.1.2 和Ⅳ/10.1.3 条所要求的中频无线电装置；

.2 第Ⅳ/10.1.1 条所要求的船舶地面站；和

.3 第Ⅳ/10.2.1、Ⅳ/10.2.2 和Ⅳ/11.1 条所要求的中频/高频无线电装置。

2.4 对下列设备供电 18 h：

.1 紧急情况下所需要的所有内部通信设备；

.2 第Ⅴ/19 条所要求的船上航行设备，如果此项规定不合理或不可行，主管机关可对小于 5 000 总吨的船舶免除此项要求；

.3 the fire detection and fire alarm system; and

.4 intermittent operation of the daylight signalling lamp, the ship's whistle, the manually operated call points and all internal signals that are required in an emergency;

unless such services have an independent supply for the period of 18 h from an accumulator battery suitably located for use in an emergency.

2.5 For a period of 18 h one of the fire pumps required by regulation Ⅱ-10.2.2.2 and Ⅱ-2/10.2.2.3; if dependent upon the emergency generator for its source of power.

2.6.1 For the period of time required by regulation 29.14 the steering gear where it is required to be so supplied by that regulation.

2.6.2 In a ship engaged regularly in voyages of short duration, the Administration if satisfied that an adequate standard of safety would be attained may accept a lesser period than the 18 h period specified in paragraphs 2.2 to 2.5 but not less than 12 h.

3 The emergency source of electrical power may be either a generator or an accumulator battery, which shall comply with the following:

3.1 Where the emergency source of electrical power is a generator, it shall be:

.1 driven by a suitable prime mover with an independent supply of fuel, having a flashpoint (closed-cup test) of not less than 43 ℃;

.2 started automatically upon failure of the main source of electrical power supply unless a transitional source of emergency electrical power in accordance with paragraph 3.1.3 is provided; where the emergency generator is automatically started, it shall be automatically connected to the emergency switchboard; those services referred to in paragraph 4 shall then be connected automatically to the emergency generator; and unless a second independent means of starting the emergency generator is provided the single source of stored energy shall be protected to preclude its complete depletion by the automatic starting system; and

.3 provided with a transitional source of emergency electrical power as specified in paragraph 4 unless an emergency generator is provided capable both of supplying the services mentioned in that paragraph and of being automatically started and supplying the required load as quickly as is safe and practicable subject to a maximum of 45 s.

3.2 Where the emergency source of electrical power is an accumulator battery it shall be capable of:

.1 carrying the emergency electrical load without recharging while maintaining the voltage of the battery throughout the discharge period within 12% above or below its nominal voltage;

.2 automatically connecting to the emergency switchboard in the event of failure of the main source of electrical power; and

.3 immediately supplying at least those services specified in paragraph 4.

.3 探火和失火报警系统；和

.4 用于断续操作的白昼信号灯、船舶号笛、手动报警按钮和紧急时需要使用的所有船内信号；

除非这些装置在紧急情况下，置于适当位置的蓄电池可以提供 18 h 的独立供电。

2.5 如果以应急发电机作为动力源，则应对第Ⅱ-2/10.2.2.2 和Ⅱ-2/10.2.2.3 条所要求的消防泵之一供电 18 h。

2.6.1 按第 29.14 条要求的时间对操舵装置供电，如果该条要求如此供电时。

2.6.2 定期从事短途航行的船舶，主管机关如果确信能达到适当的安全标准，则可接受比本条 2.2 至 2.5 规定的 18 h 更短的时间，但应不少于 12 h。

3 应急电源可以是 1 台发电机，或者是 1 组蓄电池，其应符合下列要求：

3.1 应急电源如为一台发电机，其应：

.1 由一台独立供给燃油的适当原动机驱动，燃油闪点（闭杯试验）不低于 43 ℃；

.2 在主电源发生故障时自动启动，除非按本条 3.1.3 设有临时应急电源；应急发电机如系自动启动，则应自动与应急配电板接通；本条 4 所述各项设备应随后自动接通应急发电机；除设有应急发电机的第二套独立启动装置外，单一的储存能源加以保护，以防止其被自动启动系统全部耗尽；和

.3 按本条 4 的规定设有一个临时应急电源，除非设有应急发电机，能对本条 4 所述各项设备供电且能在安全和实际可行限度内尽快（但不超过 45 s）自动启动并对规定的负载供电。

3.2 应急电源如果为蓄电池组，其应能：

.1 承载应急电力负载而不需重新充电，并在整个供电期间将蓄电池的电压保持在其额定电压的±12%以内；

.2 在主电源发生故障时，自动与应急配电板接通；和

.3 立即至少对本条 4 规定的各项设备供电。

3.3 The following provision in paragraph 3.1.2 shall not apply to ships constructed on or after 1 October 1994:

Unless a second independent means of starting the emergency generating set is provided, the single source of stored energy shall be protected to preclude its complete depletion by the automatic starting system.

3.4 For ships constructed on or after 1 July 1998, where electrical power is necessary to restore propulsion, the capacity shall be sufficient to restore propulsion to the ship in conjunction with other machinery, as appropriate, from a dead ship condition within 30 min after blackout.

4 The transitional source of emergency electrical power where required by paragraph 3.1.3 shall consist of an accumulator battery suitably located for use in an emergency which shall operate without recharging while maintaining the voltage of the battery throughout the discharge period within 12% above or below its nominal voltage and be of sufficient capacity and shall be so arranged as to supply automatically in the event of failure of either the main or the emergency source of electrical power for half an hour at least the following services if they depend upon an electrical source for their operation:

.1 the lighting required by paragraphs 2.1, 2.2 and 2.3.1. For this transitional phase, the required emergency electric lighting, in respect of the machinery space and accommodation and service spaces may be provided by permanently fixed, individual, automatically charged, relay operated accumulator lamps; and

.2 all services required by paragraphs 2.4.1, 2.4.3 and 2.4.4 unless such services have an independent supply for the period specified from an accumulator battery suitably located for use in an emergency.

5.1 The emergency switchboard shall be installed as near as is practicable to the emergency source of electrical power.

5.2 Where the emergency source of electrical power is a generator, the emergency switchboard shall be located in the same space unless the operation of the emergency switchboard would thereby be impaired.

5.3 No accumulator battery fitted in accordance with this regulation shall be installed in the same space as the emergency switchboard. An indicator shall be mounted in a suitable place on the main switchboard or in the machinery control room to indicate when the batteries constituting either the emergency source of electrical power or the transitional source of electrical power referred to in paragraph 3.2 or 4 are being discharged.

5.4 The emergency switchboard shall be supplied during normal operation from the main switchboard by an interconnector feeder which is to be adequately protected at the main switchboard against overload and short circuit and which is to be disconnected automatically at the emergency switchboard upon failure of the main source of electrical power. Where the system is arranged for feedback operation, the interconnector feeder is also to be protected at the emergency switchboard at least against short circuit.

3.3　本条3.1.2中的下列规定不适用于1994年10月1日或以后建造的船舶：

除非设有应急发电机组的第二套独立启动装置，否则单一储备的能源应加以保护，以免被自动启动系统全部耗尽。

3.4　1998年7月1日或以后建造的船舶，如果电源对恢复推进是必需的，其功率应能在全船失电后30 min内，使之连同其他机器（如适合）一起从瘫船状态恢复至船舶的推进。

4　本条3.1.3要求的临时应急电源，应由一个位于适合应急使用处所的蓄电池组组成。该蓄电池组应在整个供电期间将蓄电池的电压保持在其额定电压的±12%以内而不需重新充电，并具有足够的容量，且布置成能在主电源或应急电源发生故障时自动对下列设备（如这些设备由电力驱动）至少供电0.5 h：

.1　本条2.1、2.2和2.3.1要求的照明。在此过渡阶段，机器处所和居住及服务区域所要求的应急照明可由固定安装、自动充电并用继电器控制的专用蓄电池灯提供；和

.2　本条2.4.1、2.4.3和2.4.4要求的所有设备，除非这些设备是由位于适合应急使用处所的蓄电池组按规定的时间独立供电。

5.1　应急配电板应尽实际可能设置在靠近应急电源处。

5.2　如果应急电源是一台发电机，则除会妨碍应急配电板的操作外，应急配电板应与应急电源位于同一处所。

5.3　按本条规定装设的蓄电池组不得与应急配电板安装在同一处所。应在主配电板上或机器控制室内的适当位置安装一个指示器，用以显示作为本条3.2或4所述的应急电源或临时应急电源的蓄电池组正在放电。

5.4　应急配电板在正常工作时应用互连馈线由主配电板供电，此互连馈线在主配电板上应设有适当的过载和短路保护，并应在主电源发生故障时在应急配电板处自动断开。如果该系统布置成反向供电，则该互连馈线还应在应急配电板上至少设有短路保护。

5.5 In order to ensure ready availability of the emergency source of electrical power, arrangements shall be made where necessary to disconnect automatically non-emergency circuits from the emergency switchboard to ensure that electrical power shall be available automatically to the emergency circuits.

6 The emergency generator and its prime mover and any emergency accumulator battery shall be so designed and arranged as to ensure that they will function at full rated power when the ship is upright and when inclined at any angle of list up to 22.5° or when inclined up to 10° either in the fore or aft direction, or is in any combination of angles within those limits.

7 Provision shall be made for the periodic testing of the complete emergency system and shall include the testing of automatic starting arrangements.

Regulation 44
Starting arrangements for emergency generating sets

1 Emergency generating sets shall be capable of being readily started in their cold condition at a temperature of 0 ℃. If this is impracticable, or if lower temperatures are likely to be encountered, provision acceptable to the Administration shall be made for the maintenance of heating arrangements, to ensure ready starting of the generating sets.

2 Each emergency generating set arranged to be automatically started shall be equipped with starting devices approved by the Administration with a stored energy capability of at least three consecutive starts. A second source of energy shall be provided for an additional three starts within 30 min unless manual starting can be demonstrated to be effective.

2.1 Ships constructed on or after 1 October 1994, in lieu of the provision of the second sentence of paragraph 2, shall comply with the following requirements:

The source of stored energy shall be protected to preclude critical depletion by the automatic starting system, unless a second independent means of starting is provided. In addition, a second source of energy shall be provided for an additional three starts within 30 min unless manual starting can be demonstrated to be effective.

3 The stored energy shall be maintained at all times, as follows:

.1 electrical and hydraulic starting systems shall be maintained from the emergency switchboard;

.2 compressed air starting systems may be maintained by the main or auxiliary compressed air receivers through a suitable non-return valve or by an emergency air compressor which, if electrically driven, is supplied from the emergency switchboard;

.3 all of these starting, charging and energy storing devices shall be located in the emergency generator space; these devices are not to be used for any purpose other than the operation of the emergency generating set. This does not preclude the supply to the air receiver of the emergency generating set from the main or auxiliary compressed air system through the non-return valve fitted in the emergency generator space.

5.5　为确保应急电源随时可用，其布置应在必要时可将非应急电路从应急配电板自动断开，以确保向应急电路有效供电。

6　应急发电机及其原动机和任何应急蓄电池组应设计和布置成在船舶处于正浮状态和横倾达22.5°，或首、尾纵倾达10°，或在这些范围内出现的任何组合的倾斜角度时，确保其仍能以全额定功率发挥效用。

7　应做出规定对整个应急系统进行定期测试，并应包括自动启动装置的测试。

第44条
应急发电机组的启动装置

1　应急发电机组应在温度为0 ℃的冷机状态下，仍能立即启动。如果这无法做到，或如果可能遇到更低的温度，则应采取主管机关可接受的措施保有加热装置，以确保发电机组能立即启动。

2　凡属自动启动的应急发电机组，均应设有主管机关认可的启动装置，其储能容量至少能供连续三次启动。除能证明人工启动有效外，还应设有在30 min内再启动3次的第二能源。

2.1　对1994年10月1日或以后建造的船舶，应符合下述要求，以替代本条2中第二句的规定：

储备的能源应受到保护，以免被自动启动系统耗尽，除非设有第二套独立的启动装置。此外，还应设有能在30 min内启动三次的第二能源，除非人工启动能被证明是有效的。

3　储备的能源应一直保持如下：

.1　电力和液压启动系统应由应急配电板保持能量；

.2　压缩空气启动系统可由主或辅压缩空气瓶通过一个合适的止回阀保持供气，或由一个应急空气压缩机保持供气，该空气压缩机如果系电力驱动，则应由应急配电板供电；

.3　所有这些启动、充电和储能装置均应设置在应急发电机处所内；这些装置除操纵应急发电机组外，不得有任何其他用途。但这并不排除通过设在应急发电机处所内的一个止回阀，由主或辅压缩空气系统向应急发电机组的空气瓶供气。

4.1 Where automatic starting is not required, manual starting is permissible, such as manual cranking, inertia starters, manually charged hydraulic accumulators, or powder charge cartridges, where they can be demonstrated as being effective.

4.2 When manual starting is not practicable, the requirements of paragraphs 2 and 3 shall be complied with except that starting may be manually initiated.

Regulation 45
Precautions against shock, fire and other hazards of electrical origin

(Paragraphs 10 and 11 of this regulation apply to ships constructed on or after 1 January 2007)

1.1 Exposed metal parts of electrical machines or equipment which are not intended to be live but which are liable under fault conditions to become live shall be earthed unless the machines or equipment are:

.1 supplied at a voltage not exceeding 50 V direct current or 50 V root mean square between conductors; auto-transformers shall not be used for the purpose of achieving this voltage; or

.2 supplied at a voltage not exceeding 250 V by safety isolating transformers supplying only one consuming device; or

.3 constructed in accordance with the principle of double insulation.

1.2 The Administration may require additional precautions for portable electrical equipment for use in confined or exceptionally damp spaces where particular risks due to conductivity may exist.

1.3 All electrical apparatus shall be so constructed and so installed as not to cause injury when handled or touched in the normal manner.

2 Main and emergency switchboards shall be so arranged as to give easy access as may be needed to apparatus and equipment, without danger to personnel. The sides and the rear and, where necessary, the front of switchboards shall be suitably guarded. Exposed live parts having voltages to earth exceeding a voltage to be specified by the Administration shall not be installed on the front of such switchboards. Where necessary, non-conducting mats or gratings shall be provided at the front and rear of the switchboard.

3.1 The hull return system of distribution shall not be used for any purpose in a tanker, or for power, heating, or lighting in any other ship of 1,600 gross tonnage and upwards.

3.2 The requirement of paragraph 3.1 does not preclude under conditions approved by the Administration the use of:

.1 impressed current cathodic protective systems;

.2 limited and locally earthed systems; or

4.1 如果不要求自动启动,则可允许人工启动,例如手摇曲柄、惯性启动器、人工充液液压蓄能器或火药填充筒(如能证明其有效)。

4.2 当人工启动不可行时,应符合本条2和3的要求,但可用人工启动者除外。

第45条
触电、电气火灾及其他电气灾害的预防措施

(本条10和11适用于2007年1月1日或以后建造的船舶)

1.1 电机或电气设备的裸露金属部件,原系不带电但在各种故障情况下易于变为带电者,应予以接地,但下列电机或电气设备除外:

.1 供电电压直流不超过50 V,或导体间电压(均方根值)不超过50 V;且不应使用自耦变压器获得该电压者;或

.2 由安全隔离变压器供电,电压不超过250 V,且该变压器只对一个用电设备供电者;或

.3 根据双重绝缘原理制造者。

1.2 对用于狭窄或特别潮湿处所的便携式电气设备,如果这些处所由于导电而可能特别危险,则主管机关可要求增加预防措施。

1.3 所有电器的制造和安装应使其在正常操作或接触时不致造成伤害。

2 主配电板和应急配电板应布置成需要时易于接近电器和设备,且对人员无危险。配电板的侧面和背面,必要时包括正面,均应有适当的防护。对地电压超过主管机关规定电压的裸露带电部件,不应安装在这种配电板的正面。若有必要,应在配电板的正面和背面铺设不导电的垫或格栅。

3.1 液货船上任何配电系统或1 600总吨及以上任何其他船舶上的动力、电热或照明用的配电系统,都不得采用以船体作回路的配电系统。

3.2 本条3.1的要求并不排除在主管机关批准的条件下使用:

.1 外加电流阴极保护系统;

.2 有限的局部接地系统;或

.3 insulation level monitoring devices provided the circulation current does not exceed 30 mA under the most unfavourable conditions.

3.2-1 For ships constructed on or after 1 October 1994, the requirement of paragraph 3.1 does not preclude the use of limited and locally earthed systems, provided that any possible resulting current does not flow directly through any dangerous spaces.

3.3 Where the hull return system is used, all final subcircuits, i.e. all circuits fitted after the last protective device, shall be two-wire and special precautions shall be taken to the satisfaction of the Administration.

4.1 Earthed distribution systems shall not be used in a tanker. The Administration may exceptionally permit in a tanker the earthing of the neutral for alternating current power networks of 3,000 V (line to line) and over, provided that any possible resulting current does not flow directly through any of the dangerous spaces.

4.2 When a distribution system, whether primary or secondary, for power, heating or lighting, with no connection to earth is used, a device capable of continuously monitoring the insulation level to earth and of giving an audible or visual indication of abnormally low insulation values shall be provided.

4.3 Ships constructed on or after 1 October 1994, in lieu of the provisions of paragraph 4.1, shall comply with the following requirements:

.1 Except as permitted by paragraph 4.3.2, earthed distribution systems shall not be used in a tanker.

.2 The requirement of paragraph 4.3.1 does not preclude the use of earthed intrinsically safe circuits and in addition, under conditions approved by the Administration, the use of the following earthed systems:

.1 power-supplied control circuits and instrumentation circuits where technical or safety reasons preclude the use of a system with no connection to earth, provided the current in the hull is limited to not more than 5 A in both normal and fault conditions; or

.2 limited and locally earthed systems, provided that any possible resulting current does not flow directly through any of the dangerous spaces; or

.3 alternating current power networks of 1,000 V root mean square (line to line) and over, provided that any possible resulting current does not flow directly through any of the dangerous spaces.

5.1 Except as permitted by the Administration in exceptional circumstances, all metal sheaths and armour of cables shall be electrically continuous and shall be earthed.

5.2 All electric cables and wiring external to equipment shall be at least of a flame-retardant type and shall be so installed as not to impair their original flame-retarding properties. Where necessary for particular applications the Administration may permit the use of special types of cables such as radio frequency cables, which do not comply with the foregoing.

.3　绝缘电阻监测装置，但循环电流在最不利工况下应不超过 30 mA。

3.2-1　对于 1994 年 10 月 1 日或以后建造的船舶，本条 3.1 的要求不妨碍使用有限的局部接地系统，只要任何可能产生的电流不会直接流经任何危险处所。

3.3　如果使用以船体作回路的配电系统，其所有最后分路，即最末保护设备以后装设的所有电路均应为双导线的，并应采取使主管机关满意的特殊预防措施。

4.1　液货船上不应采用接地配电系统。主管机关可以例外地允许在液货船上使用的 3 000 V（线电压）及以上的交流电力系统采用中性点接地的配电系统，但由此可能产生的任何电流不应直接流经任何危险处所。

4.2　当动力、加热或照明使用不接地的配电系统时，不论一级系统还是二级系统，均应设有一个能连续监测对地绝缘电阻并对异常低的电阻值做出听觉或视觉显示的装置。

4.3　对 1994 年 10 月 1 日或以后建造的船舶，应符合下述要求，以替代本条 4.1 中的规定：

.1　除本条 4.3.2 允许者外，液货船上不得使用接地配电系统。

.2　本条 4.3.1 的要求不排除使用接地的本质安全型线路；此外，在主管机关认可的情况下，可以使用下列接地系统：

.1　对于电源供给控制电路和仪器仪表电路，由于技术或安全的原因不得不使系统接地的只要能确保在正常工况及故障情况下流经船体的电流被限制在5 A以内；或

.2　有限的和局部的接地系统，只要能确保任何可能产生的电流不会直接流经任何危险处所；或

.3　均方根电压（线电压）为 1 000 V 及以上的交流电网，只要能确保任何可能产生的电流不会直接流经任何危险处所。

5.1　除在例外情况下经主管机关许可外，电缆的所有金属护套和铠装均应连续导电并应接地。

5.2　设备外面的所有电缆和电线至少应为滞燃型，敷设方式应不损及其原有的滞燃性能。如果因特殊用途而有必要，主管机关可允许使用不符合此项要求的特种电缆，如射频电缆。

5.3 Cables and wiring serving essential or emergency power, lighting, internal communications or signals shall so far as practicable be routed clear of galleys, laundries, machinery spaces of category A and their casings and other high fire risk areas. In ro-ro passenger ships, cabling for emergency alarms and public address systems installed on or after 1 July 1998 shall be approved by the Administration having regard to the recommendations developed by the Organization.① Cables connecting fire pumps to the emergency switchboard shall be of a fire-resistant type where they pass through high fire risk areas. Where practicable all such cables should be run in such a manner as to preclude their being rendered unserviceable by heating of the bulkheads that may be caused by a fire in an adjacent space.

5.4 Where cables which are installed in hazardous areas introduce the risk of fire or explosion in the event of an electrical fault in such areas, special precautions against such risks shall be taken to the satisfaction of the Administration.

5.5 Cables and wiring shall be installed and supported in such a manner as to avoid chafing or other damage.

5.6 Terminations and joints in all conductors shall be so made as to retain the original electrical, mechanical, flame-retarding and, where necessary, fire-resisting properties of the cable.

6.1 Each separate circuit shall be protected against short circuit and against overload, except as permitted in regulations 29 and 30 or where the Administration may exceptionally otherwise permit.

6.2 The rating or appropriate setting of the overload protective device for each circuit shall be permanently indicated at the location of the protective device.

7 Lighting fittings shall be so arranged as to prevent temperature rises which could damage the cables and wiring, and to prevent surrounding material from becoming excessively hot.

8 All lighting and power circuits terminating in a bunker or cargo space shall be provided with a multiple-pole switch outside the space for disconnecting such circuits.

9.1 Accumulator batteries shall be suitably housed, and compartments used primarily for their accommodation shall be properly constructed and efficiently ventilated.

9.2 Electrical or other equipment which may constitute a source of ignition of flammable vapours shall not be permitted in these compartments except as permitted in paragraph 10.

9.3 Accumulator batteries shall not be located in sleeping quarters except where hermetically sealed to the satisfaction of the Administration.

10 No electrical equipment shall be installed in any space where flammable mixtures are liable to collect, e.g. in compartments assigned principally to accumulator batteries, in paint lockers, acetylene stores or similar spaces, unless the Administration is satisfied that such equipment is:

---

① Refer to *Recommendation on performance standards for public address systems on passenger ships, including cabling* (MSC/Circ. 808).

5.3 重要或应急动力、照明、内部通信或信号所用的电缆和电线应尽可能避开厨房、洗衣间、A 类机器处所及其机舱篷和其他有高度失火危险的区域。在滚装客船上，于1998 年7 月 1 日或以后安装的用于应急报警和公共广播系统的电缆系统需经主管机关在根据本组织制定的有关建议案①做考虑后认可。连接消防泵与应急配电板的电缆如通过有高度失火危险的区域，则应为耐火型。如果实际可行，所有这些电缆的敷设方式应使其不会因相邻处所失火引起的舱壁发热而失效。

5.4 如果敷设在危险区域的电缆存在因这类危险区内的电气故障而引起火灾或爆炸的危险，则应采取使主管机关满意的防止这类危险的特殊预防措施。

5.5 电缆和电线的敷设和支承应能避免其被磨损或受到其他损坏。

5.6 所有导体的端子和接头均应能保持电缆原有的电气、机械、阻燃和必要的耐火性能。

6.1 除第 29 条和第 30 条所许可者或经主管机关特许者外，每个独立电路均应设短路保护和过载保护。

6.2 每个电路的过载保护装置的额定值或相应的整定值，应在该保护装置所在位置有永久性标示。

7 照明附具的布置应能防止其温度升高而损坏电缆和电线，并能防止其周围的材料发生过热现象。

8 在燃料舱或货舱内终止的所有照明和动力电路，均应在该处所外设有用以断开这些馈电线的多极开关。

9.1 蓄电池组应放置在适当的处所，主要用于放置蓄电池组的舱室应有适当的构造和有效的通风。

9.2 除本条 10 所许可者外，凡可能构成易燃蒸气引燃源的电气设备或其他设备，不准设在有易燃蒸气的舱室内。

9.3 蓄电池组不应放置在卧室区域内，但主管机关满意的密封式蓄电池组除外。

10 电气设备不应安装在易燃混合气体易于积聚的任何处所（包括液货船上的这类处所）内，或主要用于存放蓄电池的舱室、油漆间、乙炔贮存室或类似处所内，除非主管机关确信该设备：

---

① 参见《关于客船公共广播系统，包括电缆系统的性能标准建议案》（第 MSC/Circ.808 号通函）。

.1 essential for operational purposes;

.2 of a type which will not ignite the mixture concerned;

.3 appropriate to the space concerned; and

.4 appropriately certified for safe usage in the dusts, vapours or gases likely to be encountered.

11 In tankers, electrical equipment, cables and wiring shall not be installed in hazardous locations unless it conforms with standards not inferior to those acceptable to the Organization.① However, for locations not covered by such standards, electrical equipment, cables and wiring which do not conform to the standards may be installed in hazardous locations based on a risk assessment to the satisfaction of the Administration, to ensure that an equivalent level of safety is assured.

12 In a passenger ship, distribution systems shall be so arranged that fire in any main vertical zone as is defined in regulation Ⅱ-2/3.32 will not interfere with services essential for safety in any other such zone. This requirement will be met if main and emergency feeders passing through any such zone are separated both vertically and horizontally as widely as is practicable.

① Refer to the standards published by the International Electrotechnical Commission, and in particular IEC 60092-502:1999, *Electrical installations in ships–Tankers*.

.1　为操作所必需；

.2　不会引燃有关混合气体的型式；

.3　适合于有关处所；和

.4　持有相应证书可在可能遇到的灰尘、蒸气或气体中安全使用。

11　在液货船中，电气设备、电缆和接线不应安装在危险场所，除非其所符合的标准不低于本组织接受的标准①。然而，对于这类标准不适用的场所，不符合标准的电气设备、电缆和接线可根据风险评估安装在危险场所并使主管机关满意，确保达到同等的安全等级。

12　在客船上，配电系统的布置应使第Ⅱ-2/3.32条所定义的任何主竖区内发生的火灾，不致妨碍任何其他主竖区内安全所必需的设备的使用。如果通过任何主竖区的主馈电线路和应急馈电线路在垂直和水平方向均尽可能相互远离，即满足了此项要求。

① 参见国际电工委员会出版的标准，特别是IEC60092-502：1999《船舶电气装置——液货船》。

Part E
Additional requirements for periodically unattended machinery spaces

(*Part E applies to cargo ships except that regulation 54 refers to passenger ships*)

Regulation 46
General

1 The arrangements provided shall be such as to ensure that the safety of the ship in all sailing conditions, including manoeuvring, is equivalent to that of a ship having the machinery spaces manned.

2 Measures shall be taken to the satisfaction of the Administration to ensure that the equipment is functioning in a reliable manner and that satisfactory arrangements are made for regular inspections and routine tests to ensure continuous reliable operation.

3 Every ship shall be provided with documentary evidence, to the satisfaction of the Administration, of its fitness to operate with periodically unattended machinery spaces.

Regulation 47
Fire precautions

1 Means shall be provided to detect and give alarms at an early stage in case of fires:

.1 in boiler air supply casings and exhausts (uptakes); and

.2 in scavenging air belts of propulsion machinery,

unless the Administration considers this to be unnecessary in a particular case.

2 Internal combustion engines of 2,250 kW and above or having cylinders of more than 300 mm bore shall be provided with crankcase oil mist detectors or engine bearing temperature monitors or equivalent devices.

Regulation 48
Protection against flooding

1 Bilge wells in periodically unattended machinery spaces shall be located and monitored in such a way that the accumulation of liquids is detected at normal angles of trim and heel, and shall be large enough to accommodate easily the normal drainage during the unattended period.

2 Where the bilge pumps are capable of being started automatically, means shall be provided to indicate when the influx of liquid is greater than the pump capacity or when the pump is operating more frequently than would normally be expected. In these cases, smaller bilge wells to cover a reasonable period of time may be permitted. Where automatically controlled bilge pumps are provided, special attention shall be given to oil pollution prevention requirements.

E 部分
周期性无人值班机器处所的附加要求

(除第 54 条涉及客船外,E 部分适用于货船)

第 46 条
通则

1　各项布置应可确保在包括操纵的所有航海工况下,船舶与机器处所有人值班的船舶具有同等安全。

2　应采取使主管机关满意的措施确保设备的功能可靠并对定期检查和例行试验做出妥善的安排,以确保持续可靠运行。

3　每艘船舶均应备有使主管机关满意的证明文件,用以证明其适合于在机器处所周期性无人值班的情况下运行。

第 47 条
防火措施

1　除主管机关在特殊情况下认为不必要外,应在下列位置设有探火及火灾早期阶段的报警装置:

.1　锅炉供气箱及排气管(烟道);和

.2　推进装置的扫气总管,

除非主管机关认为其在特殊情况下不必要。

2　2 250 kW 及以上或气缸内径大于 300 mm 的内燃机,应设有曲轴箱油雾探测器或发动机轴承温度监测器或等效装置。

第 48 条
防止进水

1　周期性无人值班机器处所的舱底污水井的位置和监测,应使液体的积聚能在正常纵倾和横倾角度下探知,且其大小应足以易于容纳无人值班期间的正常泄水量。

2　如果舱底泵能自动启动,应设有装置在流入液量大于泵的排量时或泵的工作次数比通常所预期的更为频繁时予以显示。在这种情况下,可以允许设置能维持一段合理时间的较小舱底污水井。如果设有自动控制的舱底泵,则应特别注意防止油类污染的要求。

3 The location of the controls of any valve serving a sea inlet, a discharge below the waterline or a bilge injection system shall be so sited as to allow adequate time for operation in case of influx of water to the space, having regard to the time likely to be required in order to reach and operate such controls. If the level to which the space could become flooded with the ship in the fully loaded condition so requires, arrangements shall be made to operate the controls from a position above such level.

Regulation 49
Control of propulsion machinery from the navigation bridge

1 Under all sailing conditions, including manoeuvring, the speed, direction of thrust and, if applicable, the pitch of the propeller shall be fully controllable from the navigation bridge.

1.1 Such remote control shall be performed by a single control device for each independent propeller, with automatic performance of all associated services, including, where necessary, means of preventing overload of the propulsion machinery.

1.2 The main propulsion machinery shall be provided with an emergency stopping device on the navigation bridge which shall be independent of the navigation bridge control system.

2 Propulsion machinery orders from the navigation bridge shall be indicated in the main machinery control room or at the propulsion machinery control position as appropriate.

3 Remote control of the propulsion machinery shall be possible only from one location at a time; at such locations interconnected control positions are permitted. At each location there shall be an indicator showing which location is in control of the propulsion machinery. The transfer of control between the navigation bridge and machinery spaces shall be possible only in the main machinery space or in the main machinery control room. The system shall include means to prevent the propelling thrust from altering significantly when transferring control from one location to another.

4 It shall be possible for all machinery essential for the safe operation of the ship to be controlled from a local position, even in the case of failure in any part of the automatic or remote control systems.

5 The design of the remote automatic control system shall be such that in case of its failure an alarm will be given. Unless the Administration considers it impracticable, the preset speed and direction of thrust of the propeller shall be maintained until local control is in operation.

6 Indicators shall be fitted on the navigation bridge for:

.1 propeller speed and direction of rotation in the case of fixed pitch propellers; or

.2 propeller speed and pitch position in the case of controllable pitch propellers.

3 用于海水进口、水线下排水或舱底喷射系统任何阀的操纵装置，其位置应是当水注入该处所时能有足够时间操作，并应顾及到达和操作这些操纵装置所需的时间。如果所要求的位置可能于船舶满载情况下被水所浸，则应做出布置，以便能在该位置以上地点操作这些操纵装置。

第49条
驾驶室对推进装置的控制

1 在包括操纵的所有航海工况下，螺旋桨的转速、推力方向和（如适用）螺距应完全可从驾驶台控制。

1.1 这种遥控对于每一独立的螺旋桨均应由单一控制装置执行，所有相关设备，如果有必要还包括防止推进装置超载的装置，均应自动进行操作。

1.2 主推进装置应备有能在驾驶室紧急停机的装置，该装置应独立于驾驶室控制系统。

2 来自驾驶台的推进装置指令，应在主机控制室或适当的推进装置控制位置显示。

3 推进装置的遥控在同一时间只能在一处进行；在这些地点允许互连控制位置。在每一控制地点应有一个指示器以指明哪个控制地点正在控制推进装置。驾驶台和机器处所之间的控制转换，应只能在主要机器处所或主机控制室进行。此系统应包含由一个到另一个控制地点转换时防止推力发生显著变更的装置。

4 对于安全操作船舶所必需的所有机器，即使自动或遥控系统的任何部分发生故障，也应能就地进行控制。

5 自动遥控系统的设计应使其发生故障时能发出报警。除主管机关认为不可行外，螺旋桨的预设转速和推力方向应保持到进行就地控制为止。

6 驾驶台应安装指示器，以指示：

.1 固定螺距螺旋桨转速和转动方向；或

.2 可调螺距螺旋桨转速和螺距位置。

7 The number of consecutive automatic attempts which fail to produce a start shall be limited to safeguard sufficient starting air pressure. An alarm shall be provided to indicate low starting air pressure set at a level which still permits starting operations of the propulsion machinery.

Regulation 50
Communication

A reliable means of vocal communication shall be provided between the main machinery control room or the propulsion machinery control position as appropriate, the navigation bridge and the engineer officers' accommodation.

Regulation 51
Alarm system

1 An alarm system shall be provided indicating any fault requiring attention and shall:

.1 be capable of sounding an audible alarm in the main machinery control room or at the propulsion machinery control position, and indicate visually each separate alarm function at a suitable position;

.2 have a connection to the engineers' public rooms and to each of the engineers' cabins through a selector switch, to ensure connection to at least one of those cabins. Administrations may permit equivalent arrangements;

.3 activate an audible and visual alarm on the navigation bridge for any situation which requires action by or attention of the officer on watch;

.4 as far as is practicable be designed on the fail-to-safety principle; and

.5 activate the engineers' alarm required by regulation 38 if an alarm function has not received attention locally within a limited time.

2.1 The alarm system shall be continuously powered and shall have an automatic change-over to a stand-by power supply in case of loss of normal power supply.

2.2 Failure of the normal power supply of the alarm system shall be indicated by an alarm.

3.1 The alarm system shall be able to indicate at the same time more than one fault and the acceptance of any alarm shall not inhibit another alarm.

3.2 Acceptance at the position referred to in paragraph 1 of any alarm condition shall be indicated at the positions where it was shown. Alarms shall be maintained until they are accepted and the visual indications of individual alarms shall remain until the fault has been corrected, when the alarm system shall automatically reset to the normal operating condition.

7 启动失败的连续自动启动次数应加以限制，以确保足够的启动空气压力。应设有报警装置，以指示仍然能进行推进装置启动操作的最低启动空气压力。

第50条
通信

在主机控制室或推进装置控制位置（视具体情况而定）、驾驶台和轮机员居住舱室之间应设有可靠的语音通信设备。

第51条
报警系统

1 应设有报警系统以指示任何需要注意的故障，此报警系统应：

.1 能在主机控制室或推进装置控制位置发出听觉报警，并能在适当位置以视觉方式显示出每一独立的报警功能；

.2 通过选择开关与轮机员公用舱室和每一个轮机员居住舱室相连，以确保至少与这些舱室的其中一个相连。主管机关可允许采用等效布置；

.3 对要求值班驾驶员采取行动或加以注意的任何情况，在驾驶台启动听觉和视觉报警；

.4 尽实际可能按故障安全原理设计；和

.5 如果报警在一个限定时间内未能就地引起注意，启动第38条要求的轮机员报警装置。

2.1 报警系统应持续得到供电，并应在失去正常供电的情况下自动转换成备用电源供电。

2.2 报警系统的正常供电失效时应报警指示。

3.1 报警系统应能同时提示一个以上故障，且任一报警的接受不应妨碍其他报警。

3.2 在本条1所述位置对任何报警的接受，应在表明存在该报警状态的各个位置显示。报警应保持到其被接受，各个报警的视觉显示应保持到故障被排除，此时报警系统应自动复位到正常运行状态。

Regulation 52
Safety systems

A safety system shall be provided to ensure that serious malfunction in machinery or boiler operations, which presents an immediate danger, shall initiate the automatic shutdown of that part of the plant and that an alarm shall be given. Shutdown of the propulsion system shall not be automatically activated except in cases which could lead to serious damage, complete breakdown, or explosion. Where arrangements for overriding the shutdown of the main propelling machinery are fitted, these shall be such as to preclude inadvertent operation. Visual means shall be provided to indicate when the override has been activated.

Regulation 53
Special requirements for machinery, boiler and electrical installations

1 The special requirements for the machinery, boiler and electrical installations shall be to the satisfaction of the Administration and shall include at least the requirements of this regulation.

2 The main source of electrical power shall comply with the following:

2.1 Where the electrical power can normally be supplied by one generator, suitable load-shedding arrangements shall be provided to ensure the integrity of supplies to services required for propulsion and steering as well as the safety of the ship. In the case of loss of the generator in operation, adequate provision shall be made for automatic starting and connecting to the main switchboard of a stand-by generator of sufficient capacity to permit propulsion and steering and to ensure the safety of the ship with automatic restarting of the essential auxiliaries including, where necessary, sequential operations. The Administration may dispense with this requirement for a ship of less than 1,600 gross tonnage, if it is considered impracticable.

2.2 If the electrical power is normally supplied by more than one generator simultaneously in parallel operation, provision shall be made, for instance by load shedding, to ensure that, in case of loss of one of these generating sets, the remaining ones are kept in operation without overload to permit propulsion and steering, and to ensure the safety of the ship.

3 Where stand-by machines are required for other auxiliary machinery essential to propulsion, automatic change-over devices shall be provided.

4 Automatic control and alarm system

4.1 The control system shall be such that the services needed for the operation of the main propulsion machinery and its auxiliaries are ensured through the necessary automatic arrangements.

4.2 An alarm shall be given on the automatic change-over.

4.3 An alarm system complying with regulation 51 shall be provided for all important pressures, temperatures and fluid levels and other essential parameters.

第52条
安全系统

应设有一套安全系统,以确保机器或锅炉在工作中发生会立即造成危险的严重故障时自动关闭该部分设备并发出警报。除会导致严重损坏、完全破坏或爆炸的情况外,推进系统的关停不应自动启动。如果对主推进装置的关停设有越控装置,该装置应能防止误操作。对已启动的越控应有视觉显示。

第53条
机器、锅炉和电气装置的特殊要求

1 机器、锅炉和电气装置的特殊要求应使主管机关满意,并应至少包括本条的要求。

2 主电源应符合下列规定:

2.1 如果电力通常能由1台发电机供应,应设有适当的卸载装置以确保推进、操舵和船舶安全所需各种设备的供电完整性。在处于运转中的发电机损坏时,应有充分的措施自动启动一台具有足够功率的备用发电机并与其主配电板接通以供推进和操舵,并自动重新启动重要的辅机(如有必要则包括顺序运转)以确保船舶的安全。如果主管机关认为本要求对小于1 600总吨的船舶不切实际时,可予以免除。

2.2 如果电力通常由1台以上同时并联运转的发电机供应,应有措施(例如卸载)确保在其中1台发电机组发生故障时,其余各台能保持运转以供推进和操舵而不发生过载,并确保船舶安全。

3 如果推进所必需的其他辅机要求有备用机器,则应设有自动转换装置。

4 **自动控制和报警系统**

4.1 控制系统应通过必要的自动装置确保主推进装置及其辅机运转所需的各项服务。

4.2 在自动转换时应发出报警。

4.3 对于所有重要的压力、温度、液位和其他必需的参数,应设有符合第51条的报警系统。

4.4 A centralized control position shall be arranged with the necessary alarm panels and instrumentation indicating any alarm.

5 Means shall be provided to keep the starting air pressure at the required level where internal combustion engines are used for main propulsion.

Regulation 54
Special consideration in respect of passenger ships

Passenger ships shall be specially considered by the Administration as to whether or not their machinery spaces may be periodically unattended and if so whether additional requirements to those stipulated in these regulations are necessary to achieve equivalent safety to that of normally attended machinery spaces.

4.4　集中控制位置应设置必要的报警控制板和指示任何报警的测试仪表。

5　如果内燃机用于主推进，则应设有使启动空气压力保持在所要求压力水平的装置。

第54条
关于客船的特殊考虑

客船的机器处所是否可以为周期性无人值班，应经主管机关特别考虑；如果可以，则应考虑除这些规则规定以外是否还需附加要求，以达到与通常有人值班的机器处所具有同等安全。

Part F
Alternative design and arrangements

Regulation 55
Alternative design and arrangements

1 Purpose

The purpose of this regulation is to provide a methodology for alternative design and arrangements for machinery, electrical installations and low-flashpoint fuel storage and distribution systems.

2 General

2.1 Machinery, electrical installation and low-flashpoint fuel storage and distribution systems design and arrangements may deviate from the requirements set out in parts C, D, E or G, provided that the alternative design and arrangements meet the intent of the requirements concerned and provide an equivalent level of safety to this chapter.

2.2 When alternative design or arrangements deviate from the prescriptive requirements of parts C, D, E or G, an engineering analysis, evaluation and approval of the design and arrangements shall be carried out in accordance with this regulation.

3 Engineering analysis

The engineering analysis shall be prepared and submitted to the Administration, based on the guidelines developed by the Organization① and shall include, as a minimum, the following elements:

.1 determination of the ship type, machinery, electrical installations, low-flashpoint fuel storage and distribution systems and space(s) concerned;

.2 identification of the prescriptive requirement(s) with which the machinery, electrical installations and low-flashpoint fuel storage and distribution systems will not comply;

.3 identification of the reason the proposed design will not meet the prescriptive requirements supported by compliance with other recognized engineering or industry standards;

.4 determination of the performance criteria for the ship, machinery, electrical installation, low-flashpoint fuel storage and distribution system or the space(s) concerned addressed by the relevant prescriptive requirement(s):

.1 performance criteria shall provide a level of safety not inferior to the relevant prescriptive requirements contained in parts C, D, E or G; and

① Refer to the *Revised guidelines on alternative design and arrangements for SOLAS chapters Ⅱ-1 and Ⅲ* (MSC.1/Circ.1212/Rev.1) and the *Guidelines for the approval of alternatives and equivalents as provided for in various IMO instruments* (MSC.1/Circ.1455).

F 部分
替代设计与布置

第 55 条
替代设计与布置

1　目的

本条的目的是为机电设备和低闪点燃料储存及分配系统的提供替代设计和布置的方法。

2　通则

2.1　机电设备和低闪点燃料储存及分配系统的设计和布置可偏离 C、D、E 或 G 部分所列的要求，但这些替代设计和布置应满足有关要求的意图并提供与本章等效的安全水准。

2.2　如果替代设计和布置偏离 C、D、E 或 G 部分规定的要求，须按照本条规定对设计和布置进行工程技术分析、评估与认可。

3　工程技术分析

工程技术分析须按照本组织制定的导则①编写并提交给主管机关，并须至少包含下列内容：

.1　确定船舶类型、机电设备、低闪点燃料储存及分配系统以及有关处所；

.2　认定机电设备和低闪点燃料储存及分配系统不符合的规定性要求；

.3　认定建议的设计不满足规定性要求的理由，并通过符合其他公认的工程或行业标准予以支持；

.4　确定相关规定性要求提及的船舶、机电设备、低闪点燃料储存及分配系统或相关处所的性能标准：

　.1　性能标准须提供不低于 C、D、E 或 G 部分中相关规定性要求的安全水平；和

---

①　参见《〈安全公约〉第Ⅱ-1章和第Ⅲ章关于替代设计和布置的导则》（第 MSC.1/Circ.1212/Rev.1 号通函）和《各类 IMO 文书规定的替代和等效批准指南》（第 MSC.1/Circ.1455 号通函）。

.2 performance criteria shall be quantifiable and measurable;

.5 detailed description of the alternative design and arrangements, including a list of the assumptions used in the design and any proposed operational restrictions or conditions;

.6 technical justification demonstrating that the alternative design and arrangements meet the safety performance criteria; and

.7 risk assessment based on identification of the potential faults and hazards associated with the proposal.

4 Evaluation of the alternative design and arrangements

4.1 The engineering analysis required in paragraph 3 shall be evaluated and approved by the Administration, taking into account the guidelines developed by the Organization①.

4.2 A copy of the documentation, as approved by the Administration, indicating that the alternative design and arrangements comply with this regulation shall be carried on board the ship.

5 Exchange of information

The Administration shall communicate to the Organization pertinent information concerning alternative design and arrangements approved by them for circulation to all Contracting Governments.

6 Re-evaluation due to change of conditions

If the assumptions and operational restrictions that were stipulated in the alternative design and arrangements are changed, the engineering analysis shall be carried out under the changed condition and shall be approved by the Administration.

① Refer to *Revised guidelines on alternative design and arrangements for SOLAS chapters Ⅱ-1 and Ⅲ* (MSC.1/Circ.1212/Rev.1).

.2　性能标准须可量化并可衡量；

.5　替代设计和布置的详细描述，包括列出设计中所用假设及任何建议的操作限制或条件；

.6　证明替代设计和布置满足安全性能标准的技术证据；和

.7　基于对潜在的与建议相关的缺陷和危险进行识别的风险评估。

4　替代设计与布置的评估

4.1　主管机关应参照本组织制定的导则[①]对第3款所要求的工程分析进行评估及认可。

4.2　船上须带有经主管机关认可的证明替代设计与布置符合本条规定的文件的副本。

5　交换资料

主管机关须向本组织通报其所认可的有关替代设计与布置的相关资料，以向所有缔约政府转发。

6　条件变化后的重新评估

如果替代设计与布置中规定的假设和操作限制出现变化，须按照变化后的条件进行工程评估，并获得主管机关的认可。

① 参见《〈安全公约〉第Ⅱ-1章和第Ⅲ章关于替代设计和布置的导则》（第MSC.1/Circ.1212/Rev.1号通函）。

Part G
Ships using low-flashpoint fuels

Regulation 56
Application

1 Except as provided for in paragraphs 4 and 5, this part shall apply to ships using low-flashpoint fuels:

.1 for which the building contract is placed on or after 1 January 2017;

.2 in the absence of a building contract, the keels of which are laid or which are at a similar stage of construction on or after 1 July 2017; or

.3 the delivery of which is on or after 1 January 2021.

Such ships using low-flashpoint fuels shall comply with the requirements of this part in addition to any other applicable requirements of the present regulations.

2 Except as provided for in paragraphs 4 and 5, a ship, irrespective of the date of construction, including one constructed before 1 January 2009, which converts to using low-flashpoint fuels on or after 1 January 2017 shall be treated as a ship using low-flashpoint fuels on the date on which such conversion commenced.

3 Except as provided for in paragraphs 4 and 5, a ship using low-flashpoint fuels, irrespective of the date of construction, including one constructed before 1 January 2009, which, on or after 1 January 2017, undertakes to use low-flashpoint fuels different from those which it was originally approved to use before 1 January 2017 shall be treated as a ship using low-flashpoint fuels on the date on which such undertaking commenced.

4 This part shall not apply to gas carriers, as defined in regulation Ⅶ/11.2:

.1 using their cargoes as fuel and complying with the requirements of the IGC Code, as defined in regulation Ⅶ/11.1; or

.2 using other low-flashpoint gaseous fuels provided that the fuel storage and distribution systems design and arrangements for such gaseous fuels comply with the requirements of the IGC Code for gas as a cargo.

5 This part shall not apply to ships owned or operated by a Contracting Government and used, for the time being, only in government non-commercial service. However, ships owned or operated by a Contracting Government and used, for the time being, only in Government non-commercial service are encouraged to act in a manner consistent, so far as reasonable and practicable, with this part.

G 部分
使用低闪点燃料的船舶

第 56 条
适用范围

1　除第 4 和 5 款规定外,本部分适用于使用低闪点燃料的下列船舶:

.1　2017 年 1 月 1 日或以后签订建造合同者;

.2　如无建造合同,2017 年 7 月 1 日或以后安放龙骨或处于类似建造阶段者;或

.3　2021 年 1 月 1 日或以后交付者。

除各条款的任何其他适用要求以外,使用低闪点燃料的此类船舶还须符合本部分的要求。

2　除第 4 和 5 款规定外,无论何时建造的船舶(包括 2009 年 1 月 1 日前建造),在 2017 年 1 月 1 日或以后改建成使用低闪点燃料,应被视作在开始改建之日使用低闪点燃料的船舶。

3　除第 4 和 5 款规定外,无论何时建造的使用低闪点燃料的船舶(包括 2009 年 1 月 1 日前建造),在 2017 年 1 月 1 日或以后承诺使用有别于 2017 年 1 月 1 日前被批准使用的低闪点燃料,须被视作在开始承诺之日使用低闪点燃料的船舶。

4　本部分不适用于第Ⅶ/11.2 条定义的下列气体运输船:

.1　经第Ⅶ/11.1 条定义,用货物作为燃料并且符合《IGC 规则》的要求;或

.2　使用其他低闪点气体燃料,只要该气体燃料的储存及分配系统设计和布置符合《IGC 规则》对该气体货物的要求。

5　本部分不适用于由缔约国政府拥有或经营的、目前仅用于政府非商业性服务的船舶。但是仍鼓励由缔约国政府拥有或经营的、目前仅用于政府非商业性服务的船舶在合理和可行的范围内符合本部分的要求。

Regulation 57
Requirements for ships using low-flashpoint fuels

Except as provided in regulations 56.4 and 56.5, ships using low-flashpoint fuels shall comply with the requirements of the IGF Code.

第 57 条
对使用低闪点燃料船舶的要求

除第 56.4 和 56.5 条规定外，使用低闪点燃料的船舶应符合《IGF 规则》的要求。

Chapter Ⅱ-2 Construction – Fire protection, fire detection and fire extinction

第Ⅱ-2章　构造——防火、探火和灭火

Part A
General

Regulation 1[①]
Application

1 Application

1.1 Unless expressly provided otherwise, this chapter shall apply to ships constructed on or after 1 July 2012.

1.2 For the purpose of this chapter:

.1 the expression *ships constructed* means ships the keels of which are laid or which are at a similar stage of construction;

.2 the expression *all ships* means ships, irrespective of type, constructed before, on or after 1 July 2012; and

.3 a cargo ship, whenever built, which is converted to a passenger ship shall be treated as a passenger ship constructed on the date on which such a conversion commences.

1.3 For the purpose of this chapter, the expression *a similar stage of construction* means the stage at which:

.1 construction identifiable with a specific ship begins; and

.2 assembly of that ship has commenced comprising at least 50 tonnes or 1% of the estimated mass of all structural material, whichever is less.

2 Applicable requirements to existing ships

2.1 Unless expressly provided otherwise, for ships constructed before 1 July 2012, the Administration shall ensure that the requirements which are applicable under chapter Ⅱ-2 of the International Convention for the Safety of Life at Sea, 1974, as amended by resolutions MSC.1(XLV), MSC.6(48), MSC.13(57), MSC.22(59), MSC.24(60), MSC.27(61), MSC.31(63), MSC.57(67), MSC.99(73), MSC.134(76), MSC.194(80), MSC.201(81), MSC.216(82), MSC.256(84), MSC.269(85) and MSC.291(87) are complied with.

2.2 Ships constructed before 1 July 2002 shall also comply with:

.1 paragraphs 3, 6.5 and 6.7 as appropriate;

① The application date of 1 July 2012 was introduced by resolution MSC.308(88). However, this resolution amended, under chapter Ⅱ-2, regulations Ⅱ-2/3.23 (definition of "Fire Test Procedures Code") and Ⅱ-2/7.4.1 (new subparagraph .3) only, and all other regulations with the original application date of 1 July 2002 were not amended.

A 部分
通则

第 1 条[①]
适用范围

1　适用范围

1.1　除另有明文规定外，本章适用于 2012 年 7 月 1 日或以后安放龙骨或处于类似建造阶段的船舶。

1.2　就本章而言：

.1　**建造的船舶**系指安放龙骨或处于类似建造阶段的船舶；

.2　**所有船舶**系指在 2012 年 7 月 1 日或以前或以后建造的船舶，不论其类型；和

.3　无论何时建造的货船，一经改建成客船后，应视作在开始改建之日建造的客船。

1.3　就本章而言，**类似建造阶段**系指在此阶段：

.1　可辨认出某一具体船舶建造开始；和

.2　该船业已开始的装配量至少为 50 t，或为全部结构材料估算重量的 1%，取较小者。

2　适用于现有船舶的要求

2.1　除另有明文规定外，对 2012 年 7 月 1 日以前建造的船舶，主管机关须确保使之符合经第 MSC.1(XLV)、MSC.6(48)、MSC.13(57)、MSC.22(59)、MSC.24(60)、MSC.27(61)、MSC.31(63)、MSC.57(67)、MSC.99(73)、MSC.134(76)、MSC.194(80)、MSC.201(81)、MSC.216(82)、MSC.256(84)、MSC.269(85)和 MSC.291(87)号决议经修正的《1974 年国际海上人命安全公约》第Ⅱ-2 章的适用要求。

2.2　2002 年 7 月 1 日以前建造的船舶还应：

.1　符合本条 3、6.5 和 6.7 的相应要求；

---

① 2012 年 7 月 1 日的适用日期由第 MSC.308(88)款决议修正。然而，该决议仅对第Ⅱ-2 章中的第Ⅱ-2/3.23 条(《耐火试验程序规则》的定义)和第Ⅱ-2/7.4.1 条(新增的.3 款)进行修正，而对原适用日期为 2002 年 7 月 1 日的所有其他条文，并未进行修正。

.2 regulations 13.3.4.2 to 13.3.4.5, 13.4.3 and part E, except regulations 16.3.2.2 and 16.3.2.3 thereof, as appropriate, not later than the date of the first survey① after 1 July 2002;

.3 regulations 10.4.1.3 and 10.6.4 for new installations only;

.4 regulation 10.5.6 not later than 1 October 2005 for passenger ships of 2,000 gross tonnage and above;

.5 regulations 5.3.1.3.2 and 5.3.4 to passenger ships not later than the date of the first survey after 1 July 2008; and

.6 regulation 4.5.7.1

2.3 Ships constructed on or after 1 July 2002 and before 1 July 2010 shall comply with paragraphs 7.1.1, 7.4.4.2, 7.4.4.3 and 7.5.2.1.2 of regulation 9, as adopted by resolution MSC.99(73).

2.4 The following ships, with cargo spaces intended for the carriage of packaged dangerous goods, shall comply with regulation 19.3, except when carrying dangerous goods specified as classes 6.2 and 7 and dangerous goods in limited quantities② and excepted quantities③ in accordance with tables 19.1 and 19.3, not later than the date of the first renewal survey on or after 1 January 2011:

.1 cargo ships of 500 gross tonnage and upwards and passenger ships constructed on or after 1 September 1984 but before 1 January 2011; and

.2 cargo ships of less than 500 gross tonnage constructed on or after 1 February 1992 but before 1 January 2011,

and notwithstanding these provisions:

.3 cargo ships of 500 gross tonnage and upwards and passenger ships constructed on or after 1 September 1984 but before 1 July 1986 need not comply with regulation 19.3.3 provided that they comply with regulation 54.2.3 as adopted by resolution MSC. 1 (XLV);

.4 cargo ships of 500 gross tonnage and upwards and passenger ships constructed on or after 1 July 1986 but before 1 February 1992 need not comply with regulation 19.3.3 provided that they comply with regulation 54.2.3 as adopted by resolution MSC.6(48);

.5 cargo ships of 500 gross tonnage and upwards and passenger ships constructed on or after 1 September 1984 but before 1 July 1998 need not comply with regulations 19.3.10.1 and 19.3.10.2;

.6 cargo ships of less than 500 gross tonnage constructed on or after 1 February 1992 but before 1 July 1998 need not comply with regulations 19.3.10.1 and 19.3.10.2.

---

① Refer to the *Unified interpretation of the term "first survey" referred to in SOLAS regulations* (MSC.1/Circ.1290).

② Refer to chapter 3.4 of the IMDG Code.

③ Refer to chapter 3.5 of the IMDG Code.

.2　不迟于2002年7月1日以后的第一次检验[①]日期符合第13.3.4.2至13.3.4.5条、13.4.3条以及除第16.3.2.2和16.3.2.3条以外的E部分的相应要求；

.3　符合第10.4.1.3和10.6.4条仅适用于新装置的要求；

.4　对于2 000总吨及以上客船，不迟于2005年10月1日符合第10.5.6条的要求；

.5　不迟于2008年7月1日以后的第一次检验日期符合第5.3.1.3.2和5.3.4条对客船的要求；和

.6　第4.5.7.1条。

2.3　2002年7月1日及之后并2010年7月1日之前建造的船舶须符合第MSC.99(73)号决议所通过的第9条规定的第7.1.1，7.4.4.2，7.4.4.3和7.5.2.1.2款的要求。

2.4　具有拟装运包装危险货物处所的下列船舶，除按照表19.1和表19.3装运定为6.2类和7类危险货物及限量内[②]和免除数量[③]危险货物外，须在不迟于2011年1月1日或之后的第一次更新检验之日符合规则第19.3条的要求：

.1　1984年9月1日及之后，但在2011年1月1日之前建造的客船和500总吨及以上的货船；和

.2　1992年2月1日及之后，但在2011年1月1日之前建造的500总吨以下的货船，

尽管有此规定：

.3　1984年9月1日及之后，但在1986年7月1日之前建造的客船和500总吨及以上的货船，如果符合经第MSC.1(XLV)号决议所通过的规定第54.2.3条要求，则无须符合规则第19.3.3条的要求；

.4　1986年7月1日及之后，但在1992年2月1日之前建造的客船和500总吨及以上的货船，如果符合经第MAC.6(48)号决议所通过的规定第54.2.3条要求，则无须符合规则19.3.3条的要求；

.5　1984年9月1日及之后，但在1998年7月1日之前建造的客船和500总吨及以上的货船，无须符合规则19.3.10.1条和19.3.10.2条的要求；和

.6　1992年2月1日之后，但在1998年7月1日之前建造的500总吨以下的货船，无须符合规则9.3.10.1条和19.3.10.2条的要求。

---

① 参见《SOLAS规则所述的术语“第一次检验”的统一解释》(第MSC.1/Circ.1290号通函)。
② 参见IMDG规则第3.4章。
③ 参见IMDG规则第3.5章。

.7 cargo ships of 500 gross tonnage and upwards and passenger ships constructed on or after 1 February 1992 but before 1 july 2002 need not comply with regulation 19.3.3 provided that they comply with regulation 54.2.3 as adopted by resolution MSC.13(57); and

.8 cargo ships of 500 gross tonnage and upwards and passenger ships constructed on or after 1 September 1984 but before 1 July 2002 need not comply with regulations 19.3.1, 19.3.5, 19.3.6, 19.3.9, provided that they comply with regulations 54.2.1, 54.2.5, 54.2.6, 54.2.9 as adopted by resolution MSC.1(XLV).

2.5 Ships constructed before 1 July 2012 shall also comply with regulation 10.10.1.2, as adopted by resolution MSC.338(91).

2.6 Vehicle carriers constructed before 1 January 2016, including those constructed before 1 July 2012, shall comply with paragraph 2.2 of regulation 20-1, as adopted by resolution MSC.365(93).

2.7 Tankers constructed before 1 January 2016, including those constructed before 1 July 2012, shall comply with regulation 16.3.3 except 16.3.3.3.

2.8 Regulations 4.5.5.1.1 and 4.5.5.1.3 apply to ships constructed on or after 1 July 2002 but before 1 January 2016, and regulation 4.5.5.2.1 applies to all ships constructed before 1 January 2016.

2.9 Regulation 10.5.1.2.2, as amended by resolution MSC.409(97), applies to ships constructed before 1 January 2020, including those constructed before 1 July 2012.

3 Repairs, alterations, modifications and outfitting

3.1 All ships which undergo repairs, alterations, modifications and outfitting related thereto shall continue to comply with at least the requirements previously applicable to these ships. Such ships, if constructed before 1 July 2012, shall, as a rule, comply with the requirements for ships constructed on or after that date to at least the same extent as they did before undergoing such repairs, alterations, modifications or outfitting.

3.2 Repairs, alterations and modifications which substantially alter the dimensions of a ship or the passenger accommodation spaces, or substantially increase a ship's service life and outfitting related thereto, shall meet the requirements for ships constructed on or after 1 July 2012 in so far as the Administration deems reasonable and practicable.

4 Exemptions

4.1 The Administration may, if it considers that the sheltered nature and conditions of the voyage are such as to render the application of any specific requirements of this chapter unreasonable or unnecessary, exempt[①] from those requirements individual ships or classes of ships entitled to fly the flag of its State, provided that such ships, in the course of their voyage, do not sail at distances of more than 20 miles from the nearest land.

① Refer to *Port State concurrence with SOLAS exemptions* (MSC/Circ.606).

.7　1992年2月1日或以后，但在2002年7月1日以前建造的货船（500总吨及以上）和客船，若符合第MSC.13(57)号决议所通过的第54.2.3条，则不必符合第19.3.3条；和

.8　1984年9月1日或以后，但在2002年7月1日以前建造的货船（500总吨及以上）和客船，若符合第MSC.1(XLV)号决议所通过的第54.2.1、54.2.5、54.2.6和54.2.9条，则不必符合第19.3.1、19.3.5、19.3.6和19.3.9条。

2.5　2012年7月1日以前建造的船舶还须符合第MSC.338(91)号决议所通过的第10.10.1.2条。

2.6　在2016年1月1日之前建造的、包括2012年7月1日之前建造的那些车辆运输船须符合经第MSC.365(93)号决议通过的第20-1条第2.2款的要求。

2.7　在2016年1月1日之前建造的、包括2012年7月1日之前建造的那些液货船须符合第16.3.3(第16.3.3.3条除外)的要求。

2.8　第4.5.5.1.1和4.5.5.1.3条适用于在2002年1月1日或之后但在2016年1月1日之前建造的船舶，而第4.5.5.2.1条适用于在2016年1月1日之前建造的所有船舶。

2.9　经第MSC.409(97)号决议修正的第10.5.1.2.2条适用于在2020年1月1日之前建造的船舶，包括在2012年7月1日之前建造的船舶。

3　修理、改装和舾装

3.1　所有船舶在进行修理、改装以及与之有关的舾装时，应至少继续符合这些船舶原先适用的要求。上述船舶如系在2012年7月1日以前建造，一般应至少按其修理、改装或舾装之前的同等程度，符合对该日或以后建造的船舶的要求。

3.2　对船舶尺度或乘客起居处所做出实质性改变，或大幅度增加船舶营运期限的修理、改装以及与之有关的舾装，在主管机关认为合理和可行的范围内，应满足对在2012年7月1日或以后建造的船舶的要求。

4　免除

4.1　主管机关如考虑到航程的遮蔽性及其条件而认为实施本章的任何具体要求不合理或不必要时，可对悬挂其国旗的个别船舶或某些类型船舶免除①这些要求，但此类船舶须在其距最近陆地不超过20海里的航线航行。

① 参见《港口国同意SOLAS的免除》(第MSC/Circ.606号通函)。

4.2 In the case of passenger ships which are employed in special trades for the carriage of large numbers of special trade passengers, such as the pilgrim trade, the Administration, if satisfied that it is impracticable to enforce compliance with the requirements of this chapter, may exempt such ships from those requirements, provided that they comply fully with the provisions of:

.1 the rules annexed to the Special Trade Passenger Ships Agreement, 1971; and

.2 the rules annexed to the Protocol on Space Requirements for Special Trade Passenger Ships, 1973.

5 Applicable requirements depending on ship type

Unless expressly provided otherwise:

.1 requirements not referring to a specific ship type shall apply to ships of all types; and

.2 requirements referring to "tankers" shall apply to tankers subject to the requirements specified in paragraph 6 below.

6 Application of requirements for tankers

6.1 Requirements for tankers in this chapter shall apply to tankers carrying crude oil or petroleum products having a flashpoint not exceeding 60℃ (closed-cup test), as determined by an approved flashpoint apparatus, and a Reid vapour pressure which is below the atmospheric pressure or other liquid products having a similar fire hazard.

6.2 Where liquid cargoes other than those referred to in paragraph 6.1 or liquefied gases which introduce additional fire hazards are intended to be carried, additional safety measures shall be required, having due regard to the provisions of the International Bulk Chemical Code, as defined in regulation Ⅶ/8.1, the Bulk Chemical Code, the International Gas Carrier Code, as defined in regulation Ⅶ/11.1, and the Gas Carrier Code, as appropriate.

6.2.1 A liquid cargo with a flashpoint of less than 60 ℃ for which a regular foam fire-fighting system complying with the Fire Safety Systems Code is not effective, is considered to be a cargo introducing additional fire hazards in this context. The following additional measures are required:

.1 the foam shall be of alcohol-resistant type;

.2 the type of foam concentrates for use in chemical tankers shall be to the satisfaction of the Administration, taking into account the guidelines developed by the Organization;[①] and

① Refer to *Revised guidelines for the performance and testing criteria, and surveys of foam concentrates for fixed fire-extinguishing systems* (MSC.1/Circ.1312 and Corr.1).

4.2 对用于载运大量特别乘客(如朝圣者)的客船,主管机关如确信实施本章要求不切实际时,可对悬挂该国国旗的此类船舶免除这些要求,但应完全符合下列规定:

.1 《1971年特种业务客船协定》所附的规则;和

.2 《1973年特种业务客船舱室要求议定书》所附的规则。

5　视船型而定的适用要求

除另有明文规定外:

.1 凡不涉及具体船舶类型的要求应适用于所有类型的船舶;和

.2 凡涉及"液货船"的要求应适用于受本条6规定之要求约束的液货船。

6　对液货船要求的应用

6.1 本章对液货船的要求应适用于载运闪点不超过60 ℃(闭杯试验,由认可的闪点仪测定),且雷德蒸气压力低于大气压力的原油或成品油或具有类似失火危险的其他液体货品的液货船。

6.2 如果拟载运本条6.1所述液货以外的能引起额外失火危险的液体货物或液化气体,则应要求采取附加的安全措施,并应根据情况,充分注意到第Ⅶ/8.1条定义的《国际散化规则》、《散化规则》、第Ⅶ/11.1条定义的《国际气体运输船规则》和《气体运输船规则》的规定。

6.2.1 在这方面,闪点低于60 ℃且符合《消防安全系统规则》规定的常规泡沫灭火系统对之不起作用的液体货物,应视为能引起额外失火危险的货物。为此应采取下列附加措施:

.1 泡沫液应为抗醇型;

.2 用于化学品液货船的泡沫浓缩液类型应参照本组织制定的指南,并使主管机关满意;[①]和

① 参见经修订的《固定式灭火系统用泡沫浓缩液性能、试验衡准和检验指南》(第MSC.1/Circ.1312号通函和Corr.1)。

.3 the capacity and application rates of the foam extinguishing system shall comply, with chapter 11 of the International Bulk Chemical Code, except that lower application rates may be accepted based on performance tests. For tankers fitted with inert gas systems, a quantity of foam concentrate sufficient for 20 min of foam generation may be accepted.①

6.2.2 For the purpose of this regulation, a liquid cargo with a vapour pressure greater than 1.013 bar absolute at 37.8 ℃ is considered to be a cargo introducing additional fire hazards. Ships carrying such substances shall comply with paragraph 15.14 of the International Bulk Chemical Code. When ships operate in restricted areas and at restricted times, the Administration concerned may agree to waive the requirements for refrigeration systems in accordance with paragraph 15.14.3 of the International Bulk Chemical Code.

6.3 Liquid cargoes with a flashpoint exceeding 60 ℃ other than oil products or liquid cargoes subject to the requirements of the International Bulk Chemical Code are considered to constitute a low fire risk, not requiring the protection of a fixed foam extinguishing system.

6.4 Tankers carrying petroleum products with a flashpoint exceeding 60 ℃ (closed cup test), as determined by an approved flashpoint apparatus, shall comply with the requirements provided in regulations 10.2.1.4.4 and 10.10.2.3 and the requirements for cargo ships other than tankers, except that, in lieu of the fixed fire-extinguishing system required in regulation 10.7, they shall be fitted with a fixed deck foam system which shall comply with the provisions of the Fire Safety Systems Code.

6.5 Combination carriers constructed before, on or after 1 July 2002 shall not carry cargoes other than oil unless all cargo spaces are empty of oil and gas-freed or unless the arrangements provided in each case have been approved by the Administration taking into account the guidelines developed by the Organization.②

6.6 Chemical tankers and gas carriers shall comply with the requirements for tankers, except where alternative and supplementary arrangements are provided to the satisfaction of the Administration, having due regard to the provisions of the International Bulk Chemical Code and the International Gas Carrier Code, as appropriate.

6.7 The requirements of regulations 4.5.10.1.1 and 4.5.10.1.4 and a system for continuous monitoring of the concentration of hydrocarbon gases shall be fitted on all tankers constructed before 1 July 2002 by the date of the first scheduled dry-docking after 1 July 2002, but not later than 1 July 2005. Sampling points or detector heads shall be located in suitable positions in order that potentially dangerous leakages are readily detected. When the hydrocarbon gas concentration reaches a pre-set level which shall not be higher than 10% of the lower flammable limit, a continuous audible and visual alarm signal shall be automatically effected in the pump-room and cargo control room to alert personnel to the potential hazard. However, existing monitoring systems already fitted having a pre-set level not greater than 30% of the lower flammable limit may be accepted.

---

① Refer to *Information on flashpoint and recommended fire-fighting media for chemicals to which neither the IBC nor BCH Codes apply* (MSC/Circ.553)

② Refer to *Guidelines for inert gas systems* (MSC/Circ.353, as amended by MSC/Circ.387).

.3 泡沫灭火系统的容量和施放率应符合《国际散化规则》第 11 章的规定，但可在性能试验基础上接受较低的施放率。对设有惰性气体系统的液货船，可接受足以产生 20 min 泡沫的泡沫浓缩液量①。

6.2.2 就本条而言，在 37.8 ℃时蒸气绝对压力大于 1.013 bar 的液体货物视为能引起额外失火危险的货物。载运此类物质的船舶应符合《国际散化规则》第 15.14 条的要求。如果船舶在限制时间内航行于限制区域，有关主管机关可根据《国际散化规则》第 15.14.3条免除对制冷系统的要求。

6.3 除成品油外，闪点超过 60 ℃的液体货物或应符合《国际散化规则》要求的液体货物视为具有较小火灾风险，不要求用固定式泡沫灭火系统保护。

6.4 载运闪点超过 60 ℃（闭杯试验，由认可的闪点仪测定）成品油的液货船应符合第 10.2.1.4.4和 10.10.2.3 条的要求以及对液货船以外的货船的要求，但应安装符合《消防安全系统规则》规定的固定式甲板泡沫系统替代第 10.7 条所要求的固定式灭火系统。

6.5 2002 年 7 月 1 日或以前或以后建造的兼装船，除非所有货物处所的油已卸空且经除气，或除非对每种情况所做的布置经主管机关参照本组织制定的指南②予以批准，不得载运油类以外的货物。

6.6 除非提供了使主管机关满意的替代和补充布置并充分考虑到《国际散化规则》和《国际气体运输船规则》的相应规定，化学品液货船和气体运输船应符合对液货船的要求。

6.7 2002 年 7 月 1 日以前建造的所有液货船，应于 2002 年 7 月 1 日以后的第一次计划坞修之日，但不迟于 2005 年 7 月 1 日安装第 4.5.10.1.1 和 4.5.10.1.4 条要求的装置和一个碳氢气体浓度连续监测系统。采样点或探测头应设置在适当位置，以随时探测到有潜在危险的渗漏。当碳氢气体浓度达到预先设定的水平（应不高于可燃气体爆炸下限的 10%）时，应在货泵舱和货物控制室内自动激发连续视听报警信号，以引起有关人员对潜在危险的警觉。但是，可以接受已经安装好且预先设定水平不高于可燃气体爆炸下限 30%的现有监测系统。

① 参见《既不适用 IBC 规则也不适用 BCH 规则的化学品闪点及建议的灭火介质资料》（第 MSC/Circ.553 号通函）。
② 参见《惰性气体系统指南》（经第 MSC/Circ.387 号通函修正的第 MSC/Circ.353 号通函）。

Regulation 2
Fire safety objectives and functional requirements

1 Fire safety objectives

1.1 The fire safety objectives of this chapter are to:

.1 prevent the occurrence of fire and explosion;

.2 reduce the risk to life caused by fire;

.3 reduce the risk of damage caused by fire to the ship, its cargo and the environment;

.4 contain, control and suppress fire and explosion in the compartment of origin; and

.5 provide adequate and readily accessible means of escape for passengers and crew.

2 Functional requirements

2.1 In order to achieve the fire safety objectives set out in paragraph 1, the following functional requirements are embodied in the regulations of this chapter as appropriate:

.1 division of the ship into main vertical and horizontal zones by thermal and structural boundaries;

.2 separation of accommodation spaces from the remainder of the ship by thermal and structural boundaries;

.3 restricted use of combustible materials;

.4 detection of any fire in the zone of origin;

.5 containment and extinction of any fire in the space of origin;

.6 protection of means of escape and access for fire fighting;

.7 ready availability of fire-extinguishing appliances; and

.8 minimization of possibility of ignition of flammable cargo vapour.

3 Achievement of the fire safety objectives

The fire safety objectives set out in paragraph 1 shall be achieved by ensuring compliance with the prescriptive requirements specified in parts B, C, D, E or G, or by alternative design and arrangements which comply with part F. A ship shall be considered to meet the functional requirements set out in paragraph 2 and to achieve the fire safety objectives set out in paragraph 1 when either:

.1 the ship's design and arrangements, as a whole, comply with the relevant prescriptive requirements in parts B, C, D, E or G;

.2 the ship's design and arrangements, as a whole, have been reviewed and approved in accordance with part F; or

第2条
消防安全目标和功能要求

1　消防安全目标

1.1　本章消防安全目标为：

.1　防止火灾和爆炸的发生；

.2　减少火灾造成的生命危险；

.3　减少火灾对船舶、船上货物和环境的破坏危险；

.4　将火灾和爆炸抑制、控制和扑灭在火源舱室内；和

.5　为乘客和船员提供充分和随时可用的脱险通道。

2　功能要求

2.1　为了达到本条1所述的消防安全目标，下列功能要求体现在本章相应的条文中：

.1　用耐热与结构性限界面，将船舶划分为若干主竖区和水平区；

.2　用耐热与结构性限界面，将起居处所与船舶其他处所隔开；

.3　限制可燃材料的使用；

.4　探知火源区域内的任何火灾；

.5　遏制和扑灭火源处所内的任何火灾；

.6　保护脱险通道和消防通道；

.7　灭火设备的随时可用性；和

.8　将易燃货物蒸气着火的可能性减至最低。

3　消防安全目标的实现

本条1所述消防安全目标应通过确保符合B、C、D、E或G部分的规定性要求实现，或通过符合F部分的替代设计和布置实现。船舶满足以下条件之一，即应视为已满足本条2所述功能要求，并达到了本条1所述消防安全目标：

.1　船舶的整体设计和布置符合B、C、D、E或G部分的相关规定性要求；

.2　船舶的整体设计和布置已按F部分的要求审核并认可；或

.3 part(s) of the ship's design and arrangements have been reviewed and approved in accordance with part F and the remaining parts of the ship comply with the relevant prescriptive requirements in parts B, C, D, E or G.

Regulation 3
Definitions

For the purpose of this chapter, unless expressly provided otherwise, the following definitions shall apply:

1 *Accommodation spaces* are those spaces used for public spaces, corridors, lavatories, cabins, offices, hospitals, cinemas, game and hobby rooms, barber shops, pantries containing no cooking appliances and similar spaces.

2 "A" *class divisions* are those divisions formed by bulkheads and decks which comply with the following criteria:

.1 they are constructed of steel or other equivalent material;

.2 they are suitably stiffened;

.3 they are insulated with approved non-combustible materials such that the average temperature of the unexposed side will not rise more than 140 ℃ above the original temperature, nor will the temperature, at any one point, including any joint, rise more than 180 ℃ above the original temperature, within the time listed below:

class "A-60"	60 min
class "A-30"	30 min
class "A-15"	15 min
class "A-0"	0 min

.4 they are so constructed as to be capable of preventing the passage of smoke and flame to the end of the one-hour standard fire test; and

.5 the Administration required a test of a prototype bulkhead or deck in accordance with the Fire Test Procedures Code to ensure that it meets the above requirements for integrity and temperature rise.

3 *Atriums* are public spaces within a single main vertical zone spanning three or more open decks.

4 "B" *class divisions* are those divisions formed by bulkheads, decks, ceilings or linings which comply with the following criteria:

.1 they are constructed of approved non-combustible materials and all materials used in the construction and erection of "B" class divisions are non-combustible, with the exception that combustible veneers may be permitted provided they meet other appropriate requirements of this chapter;

.3 船舶的部分设计和布置已按F部分的要求审核并认可,船舶的其他部分符合B、C、D、E或G部分的相关规定性要求。

第3条
定义

除另有明文规定外,就本章而言:

1 **起居处所**系指用作公共处所、走廊、盥洗室、居住舱室、办公室、医务室、电影院、游戏娱乐室、理发室、无烹调设备的配膳室的处所以及类似的处所。

2 **"A"级分隔**系指由符合下列衡准的舱壁与甲板所组成的分隔:

.1 用钢或其他等效的材料制成;

.2 有适当的防挠加强;

.3 用认可的不燃材料隔热,使之在下列时间内,其背火一面的平均温度较初始温度升高不超过140 ℃,且在包括任何接头在内的任何一点的温度较初始温度升高不超过180 ℃:

"A-60"级	60 min
"A-30"级	30 min
"A-15"级	15 min
"A-0"级	0 min

.4 其构造应在1 h的标准耐火试验至结束时能防止烟及火焰通过;和

.5 主管机关已要求按《耐火试验程序规则》对原型舱壁或甲板进行一次试验,以确保满足上述完整性和温升的要求。

3 **天井**系指在单一主竖区内跨越三层或以上开敞甲板的公共处所。

4 **"B"级分隔**系指由符合下列衡准的舱壁、甲板、天花板或衬板所组成的分隔:

.1 用认可的不燃材料制成,且"B"级分隔建造和装配中所用的一切材料均为不燃材料,但并不排除可燃装饰板的使用,只要这些材料符合本章的其他相应要求;

.2 they have an insulation value such that the average temperature of the unexposed side will not rise more than 140 ℃ above the original temperature, nor will the temperature at any one point, including any joint, rise more than 225 ℃ above the original temperature, within the time listed below:
class "B-15" 15 min
class "B-0" 0 min

.3 they are so constructed as to be capable of preventing the passage of flame to the end of the first half hour of the standard fire test; and

.4 the Administration required a test of a prototype division in accordance with the Fire Test Procedures Code to ensure that it meets the above requirements for integrity and temperature rise.

5 *Bulkhead deck* is the uppermost deck up to which the transverse watertight bulkheads are carried.

6 *Cargo area* is that part of the ship that contains cargo holds, cargo tanks, slop tanks and cargo pump-rooms including pump-rooms, cofferdams, ballast and void spaces adjacent to cargo tanks and also deck areas throughout the entire length and breadth of the part of the ship over the aforementioned spaces.

7 *Cargo ship* is a ship as defined in regulation Ⅰ/2(g).

8 *Cargo spaces* are spaces used for cargo, cargo oil tanks, tanks for other liquid cargo and trunks to such spaces.

9 *Central control station* is a control station in which the following control and indicator functions are centralized:

.1 fixed fire detection and fire alarm systems;

.2 automatic sprinkler, fire detection and fire alarm systems;

.3 fire door indicator panels;

.4 fire door closure;

.5 watertight door indicator panels;

.6 watertight door closures;

.7 ventilation fans;

.8 general/fire alarms;

.9 communication systems including telephones; and

.10 microphones to public address systems.

10 "C" *class divisions* are divisions constructed of approved non-combustible materials. They need meet neither requirements relative to the passage of smoke and flame nor limitations relative to the temperature rise. Combustible veneers are permitted provided they meet the requirements of this chapter.

.2 具有的隔热值使之在下列时间内，其背火一面的平均温度较初始温度升高不超过140 ℃，且在包括任何接头在内的任何一点的温度较初始温度升高不超过225 ℃：

“B-15”级　　15 min

“B-0”级　　0 min

.3 其构造应在标准耐火试验最初的0.5 h结束时能防止火焰通过；和

.4 主管机关已要求按《耐火试验程序规则》对原型分隔进行一次试验，以确保满足上述完整性和温升的要求。

5 **舱壁甲板**系指横向水密舱壁所到达的最高一层甲板。

6 **货物区域**系指船上包含货舱、液货舱、污油舱和货泵舱的部分，包括相邻液货舱的泵舱、隔离空舱、压载舱和空舱处所，以及前述处所上方的船舶这一部分的整个长度和宽度范围内的甲板区域。

7 **货船**系指第Ⅰ/2(g)条所定义的船舶。

8 **货物处所**系指用作装载货物的处所、货油舱、装载其他液体货物的液货舱和通往此种处所的围壁通道。

9 **集中控制站**系指具有下列集中控制和显示功能的控制站：

.1 固定式探火和失火报警系统；

.2 自动喷水器、探火和失火报警系统；

.3 防火门位置指示；

.4 防火门锁闭；

.5 水密门位置指示；

.6 水密门锁闭；

.7 风机；

.8 通用/失火报警；

.9 包括电话在内的通信系统；和

.10 公共广播系统的扩音器。

10 **“C”级分隔**系指用认可的不燃材料制成的分隔，不必满足防止烟和火焰通过以及限制温升的要求。允许使用可燃装饰板，只要这些材料满足本章的要求。

11 *Chemical tanker* is a cargo ship constructed or adapted and used for the carriage in bulk of any liquid product of a flammable nature listed in chapter 17 of the International Bulk Chemical Code, as defined in regulation Ⅶ/8.1.

12 *Closed ro-ro spaces* are ro-ro spaces which are neither open ro-ro spaces nor weather decks.

13 *Closed vehicle spaces* are vehicle spaces which are neither open vehicle spaces nor weather decks.

14 *Combination carrier* is a cargo ship designed to carry both oil and solid cargoes in bulk.

15 *Combustible material* is any material other than a non-combustible material.

16 *Continuous "B" class ceilings or linings* are those "B" class ceilings or linings which terminate at an "A" or "B" class division.

17 *Continuously manned central control station* is a central control station which is continuously manned by a responsible member of the crew.

18 *Control stations* are those spaces in which the ship's radio or main navigating equipment or the emergency source of power is located or where the fire recording or fire control equipment is centralized. Spaces where the fire recording or fire control equipment is centralized are also considered to be a fire control station.

19 *Crude oil* is any oil occurring naturally in the earth, whether or not treated to render it suitable for transportation, and includes crude oil where certain distillate fractions may have been removed from or added to.

20 *Dangerous goods* are those goods referred to in the IMDG Code, as defined in regulation Ⅶ/1.1.

21 *Deadweight* is the difference in tonnes between the displacement of a ship in water of a specific gravity of 1.025 at the load waterline corresponding to the assigned summer freeboard and the lightweight of the ship.

22 *Fire Safety Systems Code* means the International Code for Fire Safety Systems as adopted by the Maritime Safety Committee of the Organization by resolution MSC.98(73), as may be amended by the Organization, provided that such amendments are adopted, brought into force and take effect in accordance with the provisions of article Ⅷ of the present Convention concerning the amendment procedures applicable to the annex other than chapter Ⅰ thereof.

11　**化学品液货船**系指经建造或改建用于散装运输第Ⅶ/8.1 条定义的《国际散化规则》第 17 章所列的任何易燃性液体货品的货船。

12　**闭式滚装处所**系指既不是开式滚装处所,也不是露天甲板的滚装处所。

13　**闭式车辆处所**系指既不是开式车辆处所,也不是露天甲板的车辆处所。

14　**兼装船**系指设计为散装运输油类和固体货物的货船。

15　**可燃材料**系指除不燃材料以外的任何材料。

16　**连续"B"级天花板或衬板**系指终止于"A"级或"B"级分隔处的"B"级天花板或衬板。

17　**连续有人值班的集中控制站**系指有一名负责的船员连续值班的集中控制站。

18　**控制站**系指船舶无线电设备或主要航行设备或应急电源所在的处所,或火警指示器或消防控制设备集中的处所。火警指示器或消防控制设备集中的处所亦视为消防控制站。

19　**原油**系指自然呈现于地下的油,不论是否为适合运输而做过处理,并包括可能已去除或添加了某些馏分的原油。

20　**危险货物**系指第Ⅶ/1.1 条定义的 IMDG 规则所列的货物。

21　**载重量**系指船舶在相对密度为 1.025 的海水中,相应于所勘绘的夏季干舷载重水线排水量与该船空船排水量之差,以吨计。

22　**《消防安全系统规则》**系指本组织海上安全委员会 MSC.98(73)决议通过的《国际消防安全系统规则》,该规则可能经本组织修正,但该修正案应按本公约第Ⅷ条有关适用于除第Ⅰ章外的附则修正程序的规定予以通过、生效和实施。

23 *Fire Test Procedures Code* means the International Code for Application of Fire Test Procedures, 2010(2010 FTP Code) as adopted by the Maritime Safety Committee of the Organization by resolution MSC.307(88), as may be amended by the Organization, provided that such amendments are adopted, brought into force and take effect in accordance with the provisions of article Ⅷ of the present Convention concerning the amendment procedures applicable to the annex other than chapter Ⅰ.①

24 *Flashpoint* is the temperature in degrees Celsius (closed cup test) at which a product will give off enough flammable vapour to be ignited, as determined by an approved flashpoint apparatus.

25 *Gas carrier* is a cargo ship constructed or adapted and used for the carriage in bulk of any liquefied gas or other products of a flammable nature listed in chapter 19 of the International Gas Carrier Code, as defined in regulation Ⅶ/11.1.

26 *Helideck* is a purpose-built helicopter landing area located on a ship including all structure, fire-fighting appliances and other equipment necessary for the safe operation of helicopters.

27 *Helicopter facility* is a helideck including any refuelling and hangar facilities.

28 *Lightweight* is the displacement of a ship in tonnes without cargo, fuel, lubricating oil, ballast water, fresh water and feedwater in tanks, consumable stores, and passengers and crew and their effects.

29 *Low flame-spread* means that the surface thus described will adequately restrict the spread of flame, this being determined in accordance with the Fire Test Procedures Code.

30 *Machinery spaces* are machinery spaces of category A and other spaces containing propulsion machinery, boilers, oil fuel units, steam and internal combustion engines, generators and major electrical machinery, oil filling stations, refrigerating, stabilizing, ventilation and air conditioning machinery, and similar spaces, and trunks to such spaces.

31 *Machinery spaces of category A* are those spaces and trunks to such spaces which contain either:

.1 internal combustion machinery used for main propulsion;

.2 internal combustion machinery used for purposes other than main propulsion where such machinery has in the aggregate a total power output of not less than 375 kW; or

.3 any oil-fired boiler or oil fuel unit, or any oil-fired equipment other than boilers, such as inert gas generators, incinerators, etc.

32 *Main vertical zones* are those sections into which the hull, superstructure and deckhouses are divided by "A" class divisions, the mean length and width of which on any deck does not in general exceed 40 m.

① The list of laboratories recognized by Administrations which are able to conduct fire tests in accordance with the provisions of the 2010 FTP Code are circulated through the Global Integrated Shipping information System (GISIS) (resolution A.1074(28)) under the module called "Test Laboratories and Halon Facilities".

23 **《耐火试验程序规则》**系指本组织海上安全委员会以第 MSC.307(88)号决议通过的《2010 年国际耐火试验程序应用规则》(2010 年 FTP 规则),该规则可能经本组织修正,但该修正案应按本公约第Ⅷ条有关适用于除第Ⅰ章外的附则修正程序的规定予以通过、生效和实施。[①]

24 **闪点**系指某货品发出足以被引燃的可燃蒸气时的温度(闭杯试验),以摄氏度计,由认可的闪点仪测得。

25 **气体运输船**系指经建造或改建用于散装运输第Ⅶ/11.1 条定义的《国际气体运输船规则》第 19 章所列的任何液化气体或其他易燃性货品的货船。

26 **直升机甲板**系指船上专门建造的直升机降落区域,包括所有结构物、消防设备和其他为直升机的安全操作所必需的设备。

27 **直升机设施**系指包含任何加油和机库设施的直升机甲板。

28 **空船排水量**系指船舶在无货物,舱柜内无燃油、润滑油、压载水、淡水、锅炉给水,无消耗物料,且无乘客、船员及其行李物品时的排水量,以吨计。

29 **低播焰**系指所述表面能有效地限制火焰的蔓延,这根据《耐火试验程序规则》确定。

30 **机器处所**系指 A 类机器处所和其他装有推进装置、锅炉、燃油装置、蒸汽机和内燃机、发电机和主要电动机械、加油站、冷藏机、防摇装置、通风机和空调机的处所,以及类似的处所和通往这些处所的围壁通道。

31 **A 类机器处**所系指装有下列设备的处所和通往这些处所的围壁通道:

.1 用作主推进的内燃机;

.2 用作非主推进,合计总输出功率不小于 375 kW 的内燃机;或

.3 任何燃油锅炉或燃油装置,或锅炉以外的任何燃油设备,如惰性气体发生器、焚烧炉等。

32 **主竖区**系指由“A”级分隔分成的船体、上层建筑和甲板室区段,其在任何一层甲板上的平均长度和宽度一般不超过 40 m。

---

① 根据 2021 年 FTP 规则的规定,经主管机关认可能够进行耐火试验的实验室名单通过全球综合航运信息系统(GISIS)(第 A.1074(28)号决议)下名为“测试试验室和哈龙接收设施”的模块公布。

33 *Non-combustible material* is a material which neither burns nor gives off flammable vapours in sufficient quantity for self-ignition when heated to approximately 750 ℃, this being determined in accordance with the Fire Test Procedures Code.

34 *Oil fuel unit* is the equipment used for the preparation of oil fuel for delivery to an oil-fired boiler, or equipment used for the preparation for delivery of heated oil to an internal combustion engine, and includes any oil pressure pumps, filters and heaters dealing with oil at a pressure of more than 0.18 N/mm^2.

35 *Open ro-ro spaces* are those ro-ro spaces which are either open at both ends or have an opening at one end, and are provided with adequate natural ventilation effective over their entire length through permanent openings distributed in the side plating or deckhead or from above, having a total area of at least 10% of the total area of the space sides.

36 *Open vehicle spaces* are those vehicle spaces which are either open at both ends or have an opening at one end and are provided with adequate natural ventilation effective over their entire length through permanent openings distributed in the side plating or deckhead or from above, having a total area of at least 10% of the total area of the space sides.

37 *Passenger ship* is a ship as defined in regulation Ⅰ/2(f).

38 *Prescriptive requirements* means the construction characteristics, limiting dimensions, or fire safety systems specified in parts B, C, D, E or G.

39 *Public spaces* are those portions of the accommodation which are used for halls, dining rooms, lounges and similar permanently enclosed spaces.

40 *Rooms containing furniture and furnishings of restricted fire risk*, for the purpose of regulation 9, are those rooms containing furniture and furnishings of restricted fire risk (whether cabins, public spaces, offices or other types of accommodation) in which:

.1 case furniture such as desks, wardrobes, dressing tables, bureaux, or dressers are constructed entirely of approved non-combustible materials, except that a combustible veneer not exceeding 2 mm may be used on the working surface of such articles;

.2 free-standing furniture such as chairs, sofas, or tables are constructed with frames of non-combustible materials;

.3 draperies, curtains and other suspended textile materials have qualities of resistance to the propagation of flame not inferior to those of wool having a mass of 0.8 kg/m^2, this being determined in accordance with the Fire Test Procedures Code;

.4 floor coverings have low flame-spread characteristics;

.5 exposed surfaces of bulkheads, linings and ceilings have low flame-spread characteristics;

.6 upholstered furniture has qualities of resistance to the ignition and propagation of flame, this being determined in accordance with the Fire Test Procedures Code; and

.7 bedding components have qualities of resistance to the ignition and propagation of flame, this being determined in accordance with the Fire Test Procedures Code.

33 **不燃材料**系指某种材料加热至约750 ℃时，既不燃烧，也不发出足以造成自燃的易燃蒸气，根据《耐火程序试验规则》确定。

34 **燃油装置**系指准备为燃油锅炉输送燃油或准备为内燃机输送加热燃油的设备，并包括用于处理油类而压力超过0.18 N/mm^{2}的任何压力油泵、过滤器和加热器。

35 **开式滚装处所**系指两端开口或一端开口的滚装处所，该处所通过分布在侧壁或天花板上的固定开口或从上部，提供遍及整个长度的充分有效的自然通风。固定开口的总面积至少为处所侧面总面积的10%。

36 **开式车辆处所**系指两端开口或一端开口的车辆处所，该处所通过分布在侧壁或天花板上的固定开口或从上部，提供遍及整个长度的充分有效的自然通风。固定开口的总面积至少为处所侧面总面积的10%。

37 **客船**系指第Ⅰ/2(f)条定义的船舶。

38 **规定性要求**系指B、C、D、E或G部分规定的构造特性、限定的尺寸或消防安全系统。

39 **公共处所**系指起居处所中用作大厅、餐室、休息室的部分以及类似的固定围蔽处所。

40 **设有限制失火危险的家具和陈设的房间**，就第9条而言，系指设有限制失火危险的家具和陈设的那些房间（无论居住舱室、公共处所、办公室或其他类型的起居处所）：

.1 框架式家具，如书桌、衣橱、梳妆台、书柜或餐具柜，除其使用面可采用不超过2 mm的可燃装饰板外，应完全用认可的不燃材料制成；

.2 独立式家具，如椅子、沙发或桌子，其骨架应用不燃材料制成；

.3 帷幔、窗帘以及其他悬挂的纺织品材料，其阻止火焰蔓延的性能不次于质量为0.8 kg/m^{2}的毛织品，根据《耐火试验程序规则》确定；

.4 地板覆盖物具有低播焰性；

.5 舱壁、衬板及天花板的外露表面具有低播焰性；

.6 装有垫套的家具具有阻止着火和火焰蔓延的性能，根据《耐火试验程序规则》确定；和

.7 床上用品具有阻止着火和火焰蔓延的性能，根据《耐火试验程序规则》确定。

41 *Ro-ro spaces* are spaces not normally subdivided in any way and normally extending to either a substantial length or the entire length of the ship in which motor vehicles with fuel in their tanks for their own propulsion and/or goods (packaged or in bulk, in or on rail or road cars, vehicles (including road or rail tankers), trailers, containers, pallets, demountable tanks or in or on similar stowage units or other receptacles) can be loaded and unloaded normally in a horizontal direction.

42 *Ro-ro passenger ship* means a passenger ship with ro-ro spaces or special category spaces.

43 *Steel or other equivalent material* means any non-combustible material which, by itself or due to insulation provided, has structural and integrity properties equivalent to steel at the end of the applicable exposure to the standard fire test (e. g. aluminium alloy with appropriate insulation).

44 *Sauna* is a hot room with temperatures normally varying between 80 ℃ and 120℃ where the heat is provided by a hot surface (e.g. by an electrically heated oven). The hot room may also include the space where the oven is located and adjacent bathrooms.

45 *Service spaces* are those spaces used for galleys, pantries containing cooking appliances, lockers, mail and specie rooms, store-rooms, workshops other than those forming part of the machinery spaces, and similar spaces and trunks to such spaces.

46 *Special category spaces* are those enclosed vehicle spaces above and below the bulkhead deck, into and from which vehicles can be driven and to which passengers have access. Special category spaces may be accommodated on more than one deck provided that the total overall clear height for vehicles does not exceed 10 m.

47 *A standard fire test* is a test in which specimens of the relevant bulkheads or decks are exposed in a test furnace to temperatures corresponding approximately to the standard time–temperature curve in accordance with the test method specified in the Fire Test Procedures Code.

48 *Tanker* is a ship as defined in regulation Ⅰ/2(h).

49 *Vehicle spaces* are cargo spaces intended for carriage of motor vehicles with fuel in their tanks for their own propulsion.

50 *Weather deck* is a deck which is completely exposed to the weather from above and from at least two sides.

51 *Safe area* in the context of a casualty is, from the perspective of habitability, any area(s) which is not flooded or which is outside the main vertical zone(s) in which a fire has occurred such that it can safely accommodate all persons on board to protect them from hazards to life or health and provide them with basic services.

52 *Safety centre* is a control station dedicated to the management of emergency situations. Safety systems' operation, control and/or monitoring are an integral part of the safety centre.

53 *Cabin balcony* is an open deck space which is provided for the exclusive use of the occupants of a single cabin and has direct access from such a cabin.

41　**滚装处所**系指通常不予分隔并通常延伸至船舶的大部分长度或整个长度的处所，能以水平方向正常装卸油箱内备有自用燃料的机动车辆和/或货物（在铁路或公路车辆、运载车辆（包括公路或铁路槽罐车）、拖车、集装箱、货盘、可拆槽罐之内或之上，或在类似装载单元或其他容器之内或之上的包装或散装货物）。

42　**滚装客船**系指设有滚装处所或特种处所的客船。

43　**钢或其他等效材料**系指本身或由于所设置隔热物，经过标准耐火试验规定的适用曝火时间后，在结构性和完整性上与钢具有等效性能的任何不燃材料（例如设有适当隔热材料的铝合金）。

44　**桑拿房**系指一种温度通常在80~120 ℃的加温室，其热量由一种热表面提供（如电加热炉）。此加温室还可包括加热炉所在的处所和邻近的浴房。

45　**服务处所**系指用作厨房、设有烹调设备的配膳室、储物间、邮件及贵重物品室、储藏室、不属于机器处所组成部分的工作间，以及类似处所和通往这些处所的围壁通道。

46　**特种处所**系指在舱壁甲板以上或以下围蔽的车辆处所，车辆能够驶进驶出，并有乘客进出通道。若用于停放车辆的全部总净高度不超过10 m，特种处所占用的甲板可多于一层。

47　**标准耐火试验**系指将相关舱壁或甲板的试样置于试验炉内，根据《耐火试验程序规则》规定的试验方法加温到大致相当于标准时间-温度曲线的一种试验。

48　**液货船**系指第Ⅰ/2(h)条定义的船舶。

49　**车辆处所**系指拟用于装载油箱内备有自用燃料的机动车辆的货物处所。

50　**露天甲板**系指在上方且至少有两侧完全暴露于露天的甲板。

51　**事故中的安全区**系指从可居住性的角度而言，任何未进水的或发生火灾的主竖区之外的区域，其中可安全地容纳船上所有人员，使其不受生命或健康威胁，并向其提供基本服务。

52　**安全中心**系指专用于管理紧急情况的控制站。对安全系统的运作，控制和（或）监测是该安全中心的组成部分。

53　**客舱阳台**系指单个客舱的居住者专用的且从该客舱可直接进入的开敞甲板处所。

54 *Fire damper* is, for the purpose of implementing regulation 9.7 adopted by resolution MSC. 365(93), as may be amended, a device installed in a ventilation duct, which under normal conditions remains open allowing flow in the duct, and is closed during a fire, preventing the flow in the duct to restrict the passage of fire. In using the above definition the following terms may be associated:

.1 *automatic fire damper* is a fire damper that closes independently in response to exposure to fire products;

.2 *manual fire damper* is a fire damper that is intended to be opened or closed by the crew by hand at the damper itself; and

.3 *remotely operated fire damper* is a fire damper that is closed by the crew through a control located at a distance away from the controlled damper.

55 *Smoke damper* is, for the purpose of implementing regulation 9.7 adopted by resolution MSC.365(93), as may be amended, a device installed in a ventilation duct, which under normal conditions remains open allowing flow in the duct, and is closed during a fire, preventing the flow in the duct to restrict the passage of smoke and hot gases. A smoke damper is not expected to contribute to the integrity of a fire rated division penetrated by a ventilation duct. In using the above definition the following terms may be associated:

.1 *automatic smoke damper* is a smoke damper that closes independently in response to exposure to moke or hot gases;

.2 *manual smoke damper* is a smoke damper intended to be opened or closed by the crew by hand at the damper itself; and

.3 *remotely operated smoke damper* is a smoke damper that is closed by the crew through a control located at a distance away from the controlled damper.

56 *Vehicle carrier* means a cargo ship which only carries cargo in ro-ro spaces or vehicle spaces, and which is designed for the carriage of unoccupied motor vehicles without cargo, as cargo.

57 *Helicopter landing area* is an area on a ship designated for occasional or emergency landing of helicopters but not designed for routine helicopter operations.

58 *Winching area* is a pick-up area provided for the transfer by helicopter of personnel or stores to or from the ship, while the helicopter hovers above the deck.

54 **挡火闸**系指，为实施经第 MSC.365(93) 号决议通过的、可能经修正的第 9.7 条，在通风导管上安装的一种装置，其在正常情况下保持开启使气流进入导管，而在火灾时关闭，以阻隔导管流通而抑制火焰通行。在使用上述定义时，可结合下列术语：

.1　自动挡火闸系指因遭受火灾而能自行关闭的挡火闸；

.2　手动挡火闸系指拟由船员在挡火闸处手动开启或关闭的挡火闸；和

.3　遥控操作挡火闸系指由船员通过离受控闸一定距离处的操纵装置关闭的挡火闸。

55 **挡烟闸**系指，为实施经第 MSC.365(93) 号决议通过的、可能经修正的第 9.7 条，在通风导管上安装的一种装置，其在正常情况下保持开启使气流进入导管，而在失火时关闭，以阻隔导管流通而抑制烟和热气的通行。不能期望挡烟闸有助于被通风导管穿透的防火分隔的完整性。在使用上述定义时，可结合下列术语：

.1　自动挡烟闸系指暴露于烟或热气而自行关闭的挡烟闸；

.2　手动挡烟闸系指拟由船员在挡烟闸处手动开启或关闭的挡烟闸；和

.3　遥控操作挡烟闸系指由船员通过离受控闸一定距离处的操纵装置关闭挡烟闸。

56 **车辆运输船**系指仅在滚装处所或车辆处所载运货物、且设计成载运空载无人无货的机动车辆作为货物的货船。

57 **直升机降落区域**系指船上用于直升机偶尔或应急降落但不用于直升机例行作业的区域。

58 **悬停操作区域**系指用于直升机悬停在甲板上方时运送人员或物料往来船舶的搭乘区域。

Part B
Prevention of fire and explosion[①]

Regulation 4
Probability of ignition

1 Purpose

The purpose of this regulation is to prevent the ignition of combustible materials or flammable liquids. For this purpose, the following functional requirements shall be met:

.1 means shall be provided to control leaks of flammable liquids;

.2 means shall be provided to limit the accumulation of flammable vapours;

.3 the ignitability of combustible materials shall be restricted;

.4 ignition sources shall be restricted;

.5 ignition sources shall be separated from combustible materials and flammable liquids; and

.6 the atmosphere in cargo tanks shall be maintained out of the explosive range.

2 Arrangements for oil fuel, lubrication oil and other flammable oils

2.1 Limitations in the use of oils as fuel

The following limitations shall apply to the use of oil as fuel:

.1 except as otherwise permitted by this paragraph, no oil fuel with a flashpoint of less than 60 ℃ shall be used;[②]

.2 in emergency generators, oil fuel with a flashpoint of not less than 43 ℃ may be used;

.3 the use of oil fuel having a flashpoint of less than 60 ℃ but not less than 43 ℃ may be permitted (e. g. for feeding the emergency fire pump's engines and the auxiliary machines which are not located in the machinery spaces of category A) subject to the following:

  .1 fuel oil tanks except those arranged in double-bottom compartments shall be located outside of machinery spaces of category A;

  .2 provisions for the measurement of oil temperature are provided on the suction pipe of the oil fuel pump;

---

① Refer to *Guidelines for measures to prevent fires in engine-rooms and cargo pump-rooms* (MSC.1/Circ.1321).

② Refer to *Recommended procedures to prevent the illegal or accidental use of low flashpoint cargo oil as fuel* (resolution A.565(14)).

B 部分
火灾和爆炸的预防[①]

第 4 条
引燃的可能性

1　目的

本条的目的是防止可燃材料或易燃液体被引燃。为达到这一目的,应满足下列功能要求:

.1　应采取控制易燃液体渗漏的措施;

.2　应采取限制易燃蒸气聚集的措施;

.3　应限制可燃材料的可燃性;

.4　应限制着火源;

.5　应将着火源与可燃材料和易燃液体隔离开;和

.6　应将液货舱内的空气保持在不会发生爆炸的范围内。

2　燃油、润滑油和其他易燃油类的布置

2.1　燃油的使用限制

燃油的使用应受到下列限制:

.1　除本要求另有许可外,不得使用闪点低于 60 ℃的燃油;[②]

.2　应急发电机可使用闪点不低于 43 ℃的燃油;

.3　如果符合下述条件,可以使用闪点低于 60 ℃但不低于 43 ℃的燃油(例如为应急消防泵发动机和位于 A 类机器处所以外的辅机供油):

.1　除布置在双层底舱内的燃油舱柜外,其他燃油舱柜应位于 A 类机器处所外;

.2　在燃油泵的吸油管上设有油温测量装置;

① 参见《机舱和货泵舱防火措施指南》(第 MSC.1/Circ.1321 号通函)。
② 参见本组织第 A.565(14)号决议通过的《关于防止非法或意外使用低闪点货油作为燃料的建议程序》。

.3 stop valves and/or cocks are provided on the inlet side and outlet side of the oil fuel strainers; and

.4 pipe joints of welded construction or of circular cone type or spherical type union joint are applied as much as possible;

.4 in cargo ships, to which part G of chapter Ⅱ-1 is not applicable, the use of oil fuel having a lower flashpoint than otherwise specified in paragraph 2.1.1, for example crude oil, may be permitted provided that such fuel is not stored in any machinery space and subject to the approval by the Administration of the complete installation; and

.5 in ships, to which part G of chapter Ⅱ-1 is applicable, the use of oil fuel having a lower flashpoint than otherwise specified in paragraph 2.1.1 is permitted.

2.2 Arrangements for oil fuel

In a ship in which oil fuel is used, the arrangements for the storage, distribution and utilization of the oil fuel shall be such as to ensure the safety of the ship and persons on board and shall at least comply with the following provisions.

2.2.1 Location of oil fuel systems

As far as practicable, parts of the oil fuel system containing heated oil under pressure exceeding 0.18 N/mm^2 shall not be placed in a concealed position such that defects and leakage cannot readily be observed. The machinery spaces in way of such parts of the oil fuel system shall be adequately illuminated.

2.2.2 Ventilation of machinery spaces

The ventilation of machinery spaces shall be sufficient under normal conditions to prevent accumulation of oil vapour.

2.2.3 Oil fuel tanks

2.2.3.1 Fuel oil, lubrication oil and other flammable oils shall not be carried in forepeak tanks.

2.2.3.2 As far as practicable, oil fuel tanks shall be part of the ship's structure and shall be located outside machinery spaces of category A. Where oil fuel tanks, other than double-bottom tanks, are necessarily located adjacent to or within machinery spaces of category A, at least one of their vertical sides shall be contiguous to the machinery space boundaries, and shall preferably have a common boundary with the double-bottom tanks, and the area of the tank boundary common with the machinery spaces shall be kept to a minimum.① Where such tanks are situated within the boundaries of machinery spaces of category A they shall not contain oil fuel having a flashpoint of less than 60 ℃. In general, the use of free-standing oil fuel tanks shall be avoided. When such tanks are employed their use shall be prohibited in category A machinery spaces on passenger ships. Where permitted, they shall be placed in an oil-tight spill tray of ample size having a suitable drain pipe leading to a suitably sized spill oil tank.

① Refer to *Unified interpretations of SOLAS chapter Ⅱ-2* (MSC.1/Circ.1322).

.3 燃油滤净器的进口侧和出口侧均设有截止阀和/或旋塞；和

.4 尽可能使用焊接结构的或圆锥形的或球形的管接头；

.4 对于不适用第Ⅱ-1章G部分的货船，可准许使用闪点低于本条第2.1.1款规定的燃油，例如原油，但此种燃油不得储存在任何机器处所内，且整套装置应经主管机关认可；以及

.5 对于适用第Ⅱ-1章G部分的船舶，可准许使用闪点低于本条第2.1.1款规定的燃油。

2.2 燃油的布置

使用燃油的船舶，其燃油储存、输送和使用的布置应能确保船舶和船上人员的安全，并应至少符合下述规定。

2.2.1 燃油系统的位置

在燃油系统中凡含有压力超过0.18 N/mm^2的加热燃油的任何部件，应尽实际可能不布置在隐闭处所，以免不易察觉其缺陷和渗漏。在机器处所内包括燃油系统此类部件的位置应有足够的照明。

2.2.2 机器处所的通风

机器处所的通风在正常情况下，机器处所应有充分的通风，以防止油气聚集。

2.2.3 燃油舱柜

2.2.3.1 不得在首尖舱内装载燃油、润滑油和其他易燃油类。

2.2.3.2 燃油舱柜应尽实际可能作为船体结构的一部分，并位于A类机器处所之外。除双层底舱外，如果其他燃油舱柜必需邻近A类机器处所或位于其内，其垂直面中至少有一面应与该机器处所的限界面相邻接，并最好与双层底舱具有共同的限界面，且燃油舱柜与机器处所的共同限界面的面积应减至最小。① 若此种燃油舱柜位于A类机器处所的限界面之内，则其中不得储存闪点低于60 ℃的燃油。一般应避免使用独立式燃油柜。在使用此种油柜时，应禁止在客船的A类机器处所内使用。若准许使用，该油柜应置于尺寸足够大的油密溢油盘内，溢油盘应设有合适的排泄管通向尺寸合适的溢油柜。

---

① 参见《SOLAS公约第Ⅱ-2章的统一解释》（第MSC.1/Circ.1322号通函）。

2.2.3.3 No oil fuel tank shall be situated where spillage or leakage therefrom can constitute a fire or explosion hazard by falling on heated surfaces.

2.2.3.4 Oil fuel pipes, which, if damaged, would allow oil to escape from a storage, settling or daily service tank having a capacity of 500 L and above situated above the double bottom, shall be fitted with a cock or valve directly on the tank capable of being closed from a safe position outside the space concerned in the event of a fire occurring in the space in which such tanks are situated. In the special case of deep tanks situated in any shaft or pipe tunnel or similar space, valves on the tank shall be fitted, but control in the event of fire may be effected by means of an additional valve on the pipe or pipes outside the tunnel or similar space. If such an additional valve is fitted in the machinery space, it shall be operated from a position outside this space. The controls for remote operation of the valve for the emergency generator fuel tank shall be in a separate location from the controls for remote operation of other valves for tanks located in machinery spaces.

2.2.3.5 Safe and efficient means of ascertaining the amount of oil fuel contained in any oil fuel tank shall be provided.

2.2.3.5.1 Where sounding pipes are used, they shall not terminate in any space where the risk of ignition of spillage from the sounding pipe might arise. In particular, they shall not terminate in passenger or crew spaces. As a general rule, they shall not terminate in machinery spaces. However, where the Administration considers that these latter requirements are impracticable, it may permit termination of sounding pipes in machinery spaces on condition that all of the following requirements are met:

.1 an oil-level gauge is provided meeting the requirements of paragraph 2.2.3.5.2;

.2 the sounding pipes terminate in locations remote from ignition hazards unless precautions are taken, such as the fitting of effective screens, to prevent the oil fuel in the case of spillage through the terminations of the sounding pipes from coming into contact with a source of ignition; and

.3 the terminations of sounding pipes are fitted with self-closing blanking devices and with a small-diameter self-closing control cock located below the blanking device for the purpose of ascertaining before the blanking device is opened that oil fuel is not present. Provisions shall be made so as to ensure that any spillage of oil fuel through the control cock involves no ignition hazard.

2.2.3.5.2 Other oil-level gauges may be used in place of sounding pipes subject to the following conditions:

.1 in passenger ships, such gauges shall not require penetration below the top of the tank and their failure or overfilling of the tanks shall not permit release of fuel; and

.2 in cargo ships, the failure of such gauges or overfilling of the tank shall not permit release of fuel into the space. The use of cylindrical gauge glasses is prohibited. The Administration may permit the use of oil-level gauges with flat glasses and self-closing valves between the gauges and fuel tanks.

2.2.3.3 燃油舱柜不得设在从燃油舱柜溢出或渗漏的燃油可能落于热表面而构成火灾或爆炸危险的地方。

2.2.3.4 对于如有损坏会使燃油从设在双层底以上的容积 500 L 及以上的储存柜、沉淀柜或日用柜溢出的燃油管，应为其在油柜上直接装设一个旋塞或阀门，该旋塞或阀门应能在此种油柜所在处所失火时从有关处所外的安全位置予以关闭。在深舱位于轴隧或管隧或类似处所内的特殊情况下，深舱应装设阀门，但在失火时，可由隧道或类似处所外的管路上加装的一个阀进行控制。如果该加装的阀位于机器处所内，应在机器处所外的位置对其进行操纵。应急发电机燃油柜阀门的遥控操作控制应位于一单独的位置，与位于机器处所内的油柜的其他阀门的遥控操作控制的位置相分开。

2.2.3.5 应设有确定任何燃油舱柜内存油量的安全有效装置。

2.2.3.5.1 如果使用测深管，则其不得终止于测深管溢油有被引燃危险的任何处所。特别是测深管不得终止于乘客或船员处所。一般而言，测深管不得终止于机器处所。但是，主管机关如认为后者的要求不可行，则以满足下列所有要求为条件，可准许测深管终止于机器处所：

.1 设有满足本条 2.2.3.5.2 要求的油位计；

.2 测深管终止于远离着火危险的位置，否则应采取预防措施，例如装设有效的防火网，以防止从测深管终端溢出的燃油与着火源相接触；和

.3 测量管终端装有自闭式关断装置并在该装置下面设有一个小直径的自闭式控制旋塞，用于确定该关断装置打开前无燃油存在。应采取措施确保从控制旋塞溢出的燃油无着火危险。

2.2.3.5.2 如果满足下述条件，可使用其他油位计代替测深管：

.1 在客船上，此种油位计不得在舱柜顶部以下贯穿，且在其失效或舱柜注油过量时不可有燃油溢出；和

.2 在货船上，此种油位计失效或舱柜注油过量时不可有燃油溢到舱内。禁止使用圆柱形玻璃管油位计。主管机关可允许使用装有平板玻璃且在油位计和油柜之间设有自闭阀的油位计。

2.2.3.5.3 The means prescribed in paragraph 2.2.3.5.2 which are acceptable to the Administration shall be maintained in the proper condition to ensure their continued accurate functioning in service.

2.2.4 Prevention of overpressure

Provisions shall be made to prevent overpressure in any oil tank or in any part of the oil fuel system, including the filling pipes served by pumps on board. Air and overflow pipes and relief valves shall discharge to a position where there is no risk of fire or explosion from the emergence of oils and vapour and shall not lead into crew spaces, passenger spaces nor into special category spaces, closed ro-ro spaces, machinery spaces or similar spaces.

2.2.5 Oil fuel piping

2.2.5.1 Oil fuel pipes and their valves and fittings shall be of steel or other approved material, except that restricted use of flexible pipes shall be permissible in positions where the Administration is satisfied that they are necessary.① Such flexible pipes and end attachments shall be of approved fire-resisting materials of adequate strength and shall be constructed to the satisfaction of the Administration. For valves fitted to oil fuel tanks and under static pressure, steel or spheroidal-graphite cast iron may be accepted. However, ordinary cast iron valves may be used in piping systems where the design pressure is lower than 7 bar and the design temperature is below 60 ℃.

2.2.5.2 External high-pressure fuel delivery lines between the high-pressure fuel pumps and fuel injectors shall be protected with a jacketed piping system capable of containing fuel from a high-pressure line failure. A jacketed pipe incorporates an outer pipe into which the high-pressure fuel pipe is placed, forming a permanent assembly. The jacketed piping system shall include a means for collection of leakages and arrangements shall be provided with an alarm in case of a fuel line failure.

2.2.5.3 Oil fuel lines shall not be located immediately above or near units of high temperature, including boilers, steam pipelines, exhaust manifolds, silencers or other equipment required to be insulated by paragraph 2.2.6. As far as practicable, oil fuel lines shall be arranged far apart from hot surfaces, electrical installations or other sources of ignition and shall be screened or otherwise suitably protected to avoid oil spray or oil leakage onto the sources of ignition. The number of joints in such piping systems shall be kept to a minimum.

2.2.5.4 Components of a diesel engine fuel system shall be designed considering the maximum peak pressure which will be experienced in service, including any high-pressure pulses which are generated and transmitted back into the fuel supply and spill lines by the action of fuel injection pumps. Connections within the fuel supply and spill lines shall be constructed having regard to their ability to prevent pressurized oil fuel leaks while in service and after maintenance.

---

① Refer to recommendations published by the International Organization for Standardization, in particular publications ISO 15540:1999, *Ships and marine technology—Fire resistance of hose assemblies—Test methods* and ISO 15541:1999, *Ships and marine technology—Fire resistance of hose assemblies—Requirements for the test bench.*

2.2.3.5.3 主管机关可以接受的本条 2.2.3.5.2 所述的装置应保持处于正常状态，以确保其在使用中持续精确运转。

2.2.4 防止超压

任一油舱柜或燃油系统的任何部分，包括由船上油泵供油的注入管在内，应设有防止超压的装置。空气管和溢流管以及安全阀应排向不会由于油和蒸气的存在而导致失火或爆炸危险的位置，且不得排向船员处所和乘客处所，也不得排向特种处所、闭式滚装处所、机器处所或类似处所。

2.2.5 燃油管路

2.2.5.1 燃油管及其阀件和附件应用钢材或其他认可的材料制成，但在主管机关认为必要的地方，可允许有限制地使用挠性管[①]。这种挠性管及其端部附件应用具有足够强度的认可的耐火材料制成，且其构造应使主管机关满意。对于安装在燃油舱柜上和承受静压力的阀件，可以接受用钢材或球墨铸铁制成。但是如果设计压力低于 7 bar 且设计温度低于 60 ℃，在管系中也可使用普通铸铁阀件。

2.2.5.2 高压燃油泵与燃油喷油器之间的外部高压燃油输送管线应使用能在高压管线发生故障时容纳泄漏燃油的套管系统加以保护。这种套管包括内装高压燃油管的外管，构成一个固定组装件。套管系统应包括收集漏油的装置，并应设有在燃油管线发生故障时报警的装置。

2.2.5.3 燃油管线不应紧靠高温装置，包括锅炉、蒸汽管线、排气总管、消音器或本条2.2.6要求加以隔热的其他设备的上方和附近。应尽实际可能使燃油管线布置在远离热表面、电气装置或其他着火源之处，并应予以围罩或其他适当保护，以避免燃油喷到或渗漏到着火源上。此类管系的接头数量应尽量减少。

2.2.5.4 柴油机燃油系统组件的设计应考虑到工作时将出现的最高峰值压力，包括由燃油喷射泵的动作所产生并传递回供油和溢油管线的任何高压脉冲。对供油和溢油管线上的接头的结构，应考虑到其在工作时和维修后具有防止受压燃油渗漏的性能。

---

① 参见国际标准化组织出版的建议案，特别是出版物 ISO15540：1999《软管组件耐火性——试验方法》和出版物 ISO 15541：1999《软管组件耐火性——试验台要求》。

2.2.5.5 In multi-engine installations which are supplied from the same fuel source, means of isolating the fuel supply and spill piping to individual engines shall be provided. The means of isolation shall not affect the operation of the other engines and shall be operable from a position not rendered inaccessible by a fire on any of the engines.

2.2.5.6 Where the Administration may permit the conveying of oil and combustible liquids through accommodation and service spaces, the pipes conveying oil or combustible liquids shall be of a material approved by the Administration having regard to the fire risk.

2.2.6 Protection of high-temperature surfaces

2.2.6.1 Surfaces with temperatures above 220 ℃ which may be impinged as a result of a fuel system failure shall be properly insulated.

2.2.6.2 Precautions shall be taken to prevent any oil that may escape under pressure from any pump, filter or heater from coming into contact with heated surfaces.

2.3 Arrangements for lubricating oil

2.3.1 The arrangements for the storage, distribution and utilization of oil used in pressure lubrication systems shall be such as to ensure the safety of the ship and persons on board. The arrangements made in machinery spaces of category A, and whenever practicable in other machinery spaces, shall at least comply with the provisions of paragraphs 2.2.1, 2.2.3.3, 2.2.3.4, 2.2.3.5, 2.2.4, 2.2.5.1, 2.2.5.3 and 2.2.6, except that:

.1 this does not preclude the use of sight-flow glasses in lubricating systems provided that they are shown by testing to have a suitable degree of fire resistance; and

.2 sounding pipes may be authorized in machinery spaces; however, the requirements of paragraphs 2.2.3.5.1.1 and 2.2.3.5.1.3 need not be applied on condition that the sounding pipes are fitted with appropriate means of closure.

2.3.2 The provisions of paragraph 2.2.3.4 shall also apply to lubricating oil tanks except those having a capacity less than 500 L, storage tanks on which valves are closed during the normal operation mode of the ship, or where it is determined that an unintended operation of a quick-closing valve on the oil lubricating tank would endanger the safe operation of the main propulsion and essential auxiliary machinery.

2.4 Arrangements for other flammable oils

The arrangements for the storage, distribution and utilization of other flammable oils employed under pressure in power transmission systems, control and activating systems and heating systems shall be such as to ensure the safety of the ship and persons on board. Suitable oil collecting arrangements for leaks shall be fitted below hydraulic valves and cylinders. In locations where means of ignition are present, such arrangements shall at least comply with the provisions of paragraphs 2.2.3.3, 2.2.3.5, 2.2.5.3 and 2.2.6 and with the provisions of paragraphs 2.2.4 and 2.2.5.1 in respect of strength and construction.

2.2.5.5 在使用同一供油来源的多台发动机装置中，应设有隔离各台发动机供油和溢油管线的装置。隔离装置不得影响其他发动机的工作，并应能从不会因任何发动机失火而无法靠近的位置操作。

2.2.5.6 如果主管机关可允许穿过起居处所和服务处所输送油或可燃液体，输送油或可燃液体的管路应用主管机关在考虑了失火危险后认可的材料制成。

2.2.6 高温表面的保护

2.2.6.1 所有温度超过 220 ℃且可能因燃油系统故障而受到影响的表面均应妥善隔热。

2.2.6.2 应采取预防措施防止在压力作用下可能从任何油泵、过滤器或加热器逸出的任何油类接触热表面。

2.3 润滑油的布置

2.3.1 压力润滑系统的滑油的储藏、输送和使用的布置，应保证船舶和船上人员的安全。在 A 类机器处所以及（只要切实可行）在其他机器处所内所做的布置，应至少符合本条 2.2.1、2.2.3.3、2.2.3.4、2.2.3.5、2.2.4、2.2.5.1、2.2.5.3 和 2.2.6 的规定，但下列情况除外：

.1 如果经试验表明具有适当的耐火等级，不排除在润滑系统中使用窥流镜；和

.2 机器处所内可准许使用测深管；然而，如果测深管装有适当的关闭装置，可不必适用本条 2.2.3.5.1.1 和 2.2.3.5.1.3 的要求。

2.3.2 本条 2.2.3.4 的规定还应适用于润滑油舱柜，但容积小于 500 L 的润滑油舱柜、在船舶正常操作模式下阀门关闭的储油舱柜，或如果确定润滑油舱柜上的速闭阀的意外操作会危及主推进装置和重要辅机的安全运转者除外。

2.4 其他易燃油类的布置

在压力下用于动力传递系统、控制和启动系统以及加热系统的其他易燃油类，其储存、分配和使用的布置应确保船舶和船上人员的安全。在液压阀和油缸下应布置适当的收集渗漏油的装置。在含有点火装置的位置，这类布置应至少符合本条 2.2.3.3、2.2.3.5、2.2.5.3 和 2.2.6 的规定，并符合本条 2.2.4 和 2.2.5.1 有关强度和构造的规定。

2.5 Arrangements for oil fuel in periodically unattended machinery spaces

In addition to the requirements of paragraphs 2.1 to 2.4, the oil fuel and lubricating oil systems in a periodically unattended machinery space shall comply with the following:

.1 where daily service oil fuel tanks are filled automatically, or by remote control, means shall be provided to prevent overflow spillages. Other equipment which treats flammable liquids automatically (e.g. oil fuel purifiers) which, whenever practicable, shall be installed in a special space reserved for purifiers and their heaters, shall have arrangements to prevent overflow spillages; and

.2 where daily service oil fuel tanks or settling tanks are fitted with heating arrangements, a high temperature alarm shall be provided if the flashpoint of the oil fuel can be exceeded.

3 Arrangements for gaseous fuel for domestic purposes

Gaseous fuel systems used for domestic purposes shall be approved by the Administration. Storage of gas bottles shall be located on the open deck or in a well-ventilated space which opens only to the open deck.

4 Miscellaneous items of ignition sources and ignitability

4.1 Electric radiators

Electric radiators, if used, shall be fixed in position and so constructed as to reduce fire risks to a minimum. No such radiators shall be fitted with an element so exposed that clothing, curtains, or other similar materials can be scorched or set on fire by heat from the element.

4.2 Waste receptacles

Waste receptacles shall be constructed of non-combustible materials with no openings in the sides or bottom.

4.3 Insulation surfaces protected against oil penetration

In spaces where penetration of oil products is possible, the surface of insulation shall be impervious to oil or oil vapours.

4.4 Primary deck coverings

Primary deck coverings, if applied within accommodation and service spaces and control stations, or if applied on cabin balconies of passenger ships constructed on or after 1 July 2008, shall be of approved material which will not readily ignite, this being determined in accordance with the Fire Test Procedures Code.

2.5　周期性无人值班机器处所的燃油布置

周期性无人值班机器处所的燃油和润滑油系统除应符合本条2.1至2.4的要求外，还应符合以下规定：

.1　燃油日用柜如系自动或遥控注油，则应设有防止溢油的装置。其他自动处理易燃液体的设备(例如燃油净化器)，在可行情况下应安装在专供净化器及其加热器使用的处所内并应有防止溢油的装置；和

.2　燃油日用柜或沉淀柜若设有加热装置且若有可能超过燃油的闪点，则应装设高温报警器。

3　生活用气体燃料的布置

生活用气体燃料系统应经主管机关认可。气瓶应存放于开敞甲板或开口仅朝向开敞甲板的通风良好的处所。

4　有关着火源和引燃性的其他事项

4.1　电取暖器

如果使用电取暖器，应予固定装设，其构造应能使失火危险减至最低。不得装设因某一暴露元件的热度而可能使衣服、窗帘或其他类似物料被烤焦或起火的电取暖器。

4.2　废物箱

废物箱应用不燃材料制成，四周和底部应无开口。

4.3　保护隔热表面防止油类渗透

在成品油可能渗透的处所，隔热层表面应能防止油或油气的渗透。

4.4　甲板基层敷料

如果在起居处所、服务处所和控制站内使用甲板基层敷料，或如果用于2008年7月1日或以后建造的客船的客舱阳台上，则该敷料应为不易引燃的认可材料，根据《耐火试验程序规则》确定。

5 Cargo areas of tankers

5.1 Separation of cargo oil tanks

5.1.1 Cargo pump-rooms, cargo tanks, slop tanks and cofferdams shall be positioned forward of machinery spaces. However, oil fuel bunker tanks need not be forward of machinery spaces. Cargo tanks and slop tanks shall be isolated from machinery spaces by cofferdams, cargo pump-rooms, oil bunker tanks or ballast tanks. Pump-rooms containing pumps and their accessories for ballasting those spaces situated adjacent to cargo tanks and slop tanks and pumps for oil fuel transfer shall be considered as equivalent to a cargo pump-room within the context of this regulation provided that such pump-rooms have the same safety standard as that required for cargo pump-rooms. Pump-rooms intended solely for ballast or oil fuel transfer, however, need not comply with the requirements of regulation 10.9. The lower portion of the pump-room may be recessed into machinery spaces of category A to accommodate pumps, provided that the deck head of the recess is in general not more than one third of the moulded depth above the keel, except that in the case of ships of not more than 25,000 tonnes deadweight, where it can be demonstrated that for reasons of access and satisfactory piping arrangements this is impracticable, the Administration may permit a recess in excess of such height, but not exceeding one half of the moulded depth above the keel.

5.1.2 Main cargo control stations, control stations, accommodation and service spaces (excluding isolated cargo handling gear lockers) shall be positioned aft of cargo tanks, slop tanks, and spaces which isolate cargo or slop tanks from machinery spaces, but not necessarily aft of the oil fuel bunker tanks and ballast tanks, and shall be arranged in such a way that a single failure of a deck or bulkhead shall not permit the entry of gas or fumes from the cargo tanks into main cargo control stations, control stations, or accommodation and service spaces. A recess provided in accordance with paragraph 5.1.1 need not be taken into account when the position of these spaces is being determined.

5.1.3 However, where deemed necessary, the Administration may permit main cargo control stations, control stations, accommodation and service spaces forward of the cargo tanks, slop tanks and spaces which isolate cargo and slop tanks from machinery spaces, but not necessarily forward of oil fuel bunker tanks or ballast tanks. Machinery spaces, other than those of category A, may be permitted forward of the cargo tanks and slop tanks provided they are isolated from the cargo tanks and slop tanks by cofferdams, cargo pump-rooms, oil fuel bunker tanks or ballast tanks, and have at least one portable fire extinguisher. In cases where they contain internal combustion machinery, one approved foam-type extinguisher of at least 45 L capacity or equivalent shall be arranged in addition to portable fire extinguishers. If operation of a semi-portable fire extinguisher is impracticable, this fire extinguisher may be replaced by two additional portable fire extinguishers. Main cargo control stations, control stations and accommodation and service spaces shall be arranged in such a way that a single failure of a deck or bulkhead shall not permit the entry of gas or fumes from the cargo tanks into such spaces. In addition, where deemed necessary for the safety or navigation of the ship, the Administration may permit machinery spaces containing internal combustion machinery not being main propulsion machinery having an output greater than 375 kW to be located forward of the cargo area provided the arrangements are in accordance with the provisions of this paragraph.

5　液货船的货物区域

5.1　货油舱的隔离

5.1.1　货油泵舱、货油舱、污油舱和隔离空舱应位于机器处所的前方。但是,燃油舱不必位于机器处所的前方。货油舱和污油舱应通过隔离空舱、货油泵舱、燃油舱和压载舱与机器处所隔开。凡设有供相邻于货油舱和污油舱的处所进行压载的泵及其附件的泵舱和设有燃油驳运泵的泵舱,如果这类泵舱所具有的安全标准与货油泵舱要求的安全标准相同,均应视为等效于本条内的货油泵舱。但是,只用于压载或燃油驳运的泵舱不必满足第10.9条的要求。泵舱的下部可以凹入A类机器处所,以便安置泵,但凹入部分的顶板高度自龙骨以上一般不得超过型深的1/3,但对于载重量不超过25 000 t的船舶,如果能证明这一高度由于通道和妥善布置管系的原因而不切实际,则主管机关可准许凹入部分高度超过此限,但其高度自龙骨以上不得超过型深的一半。

5.1.2　货油主控制站、控制站、起居处所和服务处所(不包括独立的起货设备小间)应位于货油舱、污油舱以及将货油舱或污油舱与机器处所隔开的处所的后方,但不必位于燃油舱或压载舱的后方,且其布置应使任何甲板或舱壁的单个破损不会导致货油舱的气体或油雾进入货油主控制站、控制站,或起居处所和服务处所。在确定这些处所的位置时,不必考虑根据本条5.1.1所设的凹入部分。

5.1.3　但是,主管机关如果认为有必要,可准许货油主控制站、控制站、起居处所和服务处所位于货油舱、污油舱以及将货油舱或污油舱与机器处所隔开的处所的前方,但不必位于燃油舱或压载舱的前方。除A类机器处所以外的其他机器处所可准予位于货油舱的前方,但须将其与货油舱和污油舱用隔离空舱、货油泵舱、燃油舱或压载舱隔开,且至少配备1个手提式灭火器。在设有内燃机的处所,除手提式灭火器外,还应布置容量至少为45 L的经认可的泡沫灭火器或等效灭火设备。如果使用半手提式灭火器不切实际,可添加2个手提式灭火器替代。货油主控制站、控制站和起居处所以及服务处所的布置应使任何甲板或舱壁的单个破损不会导致货油舱气体或油雾进入这类处所。此外,主管机关如果认为对船舶的安全或航行有必要,则可允许设有功率大于375 kW,但不用作主推进装置的内燃机的机器处所位于货物区域的前方,但其布置应符合本条的规定。

5.1.4 In combination carriers only:

.1 The slop tanks shall be surrounded by cofferdams except where the boundaries of the slop tanks are part of the hull, main cargo deck, cargo pump-room bulkhead or oil fuel bunker tank. These cofferdams shall not be open to a double bottom, pipe tunnel, pump-room or other enclosed space, nor shall they be used for cargo or ballast and shall not be connected to piping systems serving oil cargo or ballast. Means shall be provided for filling the cofferdams with water and for draining them. Where the boundary of a slop tank is part of the cargo pump-room bulkhead, the pump-room shall not be open to the double bottom, pipe tunnel or other enclosed space; however, openings provided with gastight bolted covers may be permitted;

.2 Means shall be provided for isolating the piping connecting the pump-room with the slop tanks referred to in paragraph 5.1.4.1. The means of isolation shall consist of a valve followed by a spectacle flange or a spool piece with appropriate blank flanges. This arrangement shall be located adjacent to the slop tanks, but where this is unreasonable or impracticable, it may be located within the pump-room directly after the piping penetrates the bulkhead. A separate permanently installed pumping and piping arrangement incorporating a manifold, provided with a shut-off valve and a blank flange, shall be provided for discharging the contents of the slop tanks directly to the open deck for disposal to shore reception facilities when the ship is in the dry cargo mode. When the transfer system is used for slop transfer in the dry cargo mode, it shall have no connection to other systems. Separation from other systems by means of removal of spool pieces may be accepted;

.3 Hatches and tank cleaning openings to slop tanks shall only be permitted on the open deck and shall be fitted with closing arrangements. Except where they consist of bolted plates with bolts at watertight spacing, these closing arrangements shall be provided with locking arrangements under the control of the responsible ship's officer; and

.4 Where cargo wing tanks are provided, cargo oil lines below deck shall be installed inside these tanks. However, the Administration may permit cargo oil lines to be placed in special ducts provided these are capable of being adequately cleaned and ventilated to the satisfaction of the Administration. Where cargo wing tanks are not provided, cargo oil lines below deck shall be placed in special ducts.

5.1.5 Where the fitting of a navigation position above the cargo area is shown to be necessary, it shall be for navigation purposes only and it shall be separated from the cargo tank deck by means of an open space with a height of at least 2 m. The fire protection requirements for such a navigation position shall be those required for control stations, as specified in regulation 9.2.4.2 and other provisions for tankers, as applicable.

5.1.6 Means shall be provided to keep deck spills away from the accommodation and service areas. This may be accomplished by provision of a permanent continuous coaming of a height of at least 300 mm, extending from side to side. Special consideration shall be given to the arrangements associated with stern loading.

5.1.4 仅对于兼装船：

.1 污油舱应以隔离空舱围隔，但限界面为船体、主货物甲板、货油泵舱舱壁或燃油舱之一部分的污油舱除外。这些隔离空舱不得设有通向双层底、管隧、泵舱或其他封闭处所的开口，不得用于装载货物或压载，也不得与货物或压载水的管系相连接。应设有向隔离空舱灌水或排水的装置。如果污油舱的限界面为货油泵舱舱壁的一部分，该泵舱不得设有通向双层底、管隧或其他封闭处所的开口；但可允许设有装设气密螺栓盖的开口；

.2 应设有切断连接泵舱和本条 5.1.4.1 所述污油舱的管系的装置。该切断装置应包括 1 个阀门，阀门后装有 1 个双环法兰或 1 个具有适当盲板法兰的短管。此布置应邻接污油舱，但如果此管系不合理或不可行，也可设置在泵舱内直接位于穿过舱壁的管路之后。应设有一个独立的固定式泵和管系装置，包括一个歧管并带有一个关闭阀和一个盲板法兰，以便在船舶从事干货运输时，将污油舱内的污油水直接通过开敞甲板排放到岸上的接收设施中去。如果驳运系统在运载干货时被用于输送污油水，该系统不得与其他系统相连接。可以接受通过拆除短管的方式与其他系统相分离；

.3 污舱的舱口和洗舱开口只允许设在开敞甲板上，并应设有关闭装置。这些关闭装置应有锁紧装置并由负责的高级船员控制，但采用螺栓固定的盖板且螺栓的间距能保证水密者除外；和

.4 如果设有边货油舱，甲板下的货油管系应设在这些边舱内。但是，主管机关可允许货油管系设在专门导管内，但这些导管须能充分清洗和通风并使主管机关满意。如果未设边货油舱，则甲板下的货油管系应设在专门导管内。

5.1.5 如果证实有必要把驾驶位置设在货物区域的上方，则此处所应仅用于驾驶的目的，并且应用高度至少 2 m 的开敞空间使之与货油舱甲板隔开。这种驾驶位置的防火要求应是第 9.2.4.2 条对控制站规定的要求和其他适用于液货船的规定。

5.1.6 应设有使甲板上的溢油远离起居和服务区域的设备。可以通过安装高度至少为 300 mm 并延伸至两舷的连续固定挡板达到这一目的。对布置在船尾的注装油装置，应给予特别考虑。

5.2 Restriction on boundary openings

5.2.1 Except as permitted in paragraph 5.2.2, access doors, air inlets and openings to accommodation spaces, service spaces, control stations and machinery spaces shall not face the cargo area. They shall be located on the transverse bulkhead not facing the cargo area or on the outboard side of the superstructure or deckhouse at a distance of at least 4% of the length of the ship, but not less than 3 m from the end of the superstructure or deckhouse facing the cargo area. This distance need not exceed 5 m.

5.2.2 The Administration may permit access doors in boundary bulkheads facing the cargo area or within the 5 m limits specified in paragraph 5.2.1, to main cargo control stations and to such service spaces used as provision rooms, store-rooms and lockers, provided they do not give access directly or indirectly to any other space containing or providing for accommodation, control stations or service spaces such as galleys, pantries or workshops, or similar spaces containing sources of vapour ignition. The boundary of such a space shall be insulated to "A-60" class standard, with the exception of the boundary facing the cargo area. Bolted plates for the removal of machinery may be fitted within the limits specified in paragraph 5.2.1. Wheelhouse doors and windows may be located within the limits specified in paragraph 5.2.1 so long as they are designed to ensure that the wheelhouse can be made rapidly and efficiently gastight and vapourtight.

5.2.3 Windows and sidescuttles facing the cargo area and on the sides of the superstructures and deckhouses within the limits specified in paragraph 5.2.1 shall be of the fixed (non-opening) type. Such windows and sidescuttles, except wheelhouse windows, shall be constructed to "A-60" class standard except that "A-0" class standard is acceptable for windows and sidescuttles outside the limit specified in regulation 9.2.4.2.5.

5.2.4 Where there is permanent access from a pipe tunnel to the main pump-room, a watertight door shall be fitted complying with the requirements of regulation Ⅱ-1/13-1.2 and, in addition, with the following:

.1 in addition to the bridge operation, the watertight door shall be capable of being manually closed from outside the main pump-room entrance; and

.2 the watertight door shall be kept closed during normal operations of the ship except when access to the pipe tunnel is required.

5.2.5 Permanent approved gastight lighting enclosures for illuminating cargo pump-rooms may be permitted in bulkheads and decks separating cargo pump-rooms and other spaces provided they are of adequate strength and the integrity and gastightness of the bulkhead or deck is maintained.

5.2.6 The arrangement of ventilation inlets and outlets and other deckhouse and superstructure boundary space openings shall be such as to complement the provisions of paragraph 5.3 and regulation 11.6. Such vents, especially for machinery spaces, shall be situated as far aft as practicable. Due consideration in this regard shall be given when the ship is equipped to load or discharge at the stern. Sources of ignition such as electrical equipment shall be so arranged as to avoid an explosion hazard.

5.2　限界面开口的限制

5.2.1　除本条 5.2.2 准许的情况以外，通往起居处所、服务处所、控制站和机器处所的出入门、空气进口和开口，均不应面向货物区域，而应位于不面向货物区域的横舱壁上，或位于上层建筑或甲板室外侧距离上层建筑或甲板室面向货物区域的端壁至少为船舶长度的 4%，但不少于 3 m 处。此距离不必超过 5 m。

5.2.2　主管机关可准许在面向货物区域的限界面舱壁，或在本条 5.2.1 规定的 5 m 限制范围内设置通向货物主控制站和诸如食品间、储藏室及物料间这类服务处所的出入门，但是这些出入门不得直接或间接通往包括有或用作起居处所、控制站的任何其他处所，或诸如厨房、配膳室或工作间的服务处所，或含有油气着火源的类似处所。这种处所的限界面应隔热至“A-60”级标准，但面向货物区域的限界面除外。在本条 5.2.1 规定的限制范围内可设置拆移机器时用的由螺栓紧固的门板。驾驶室的门窗可以位于本条 5.2.1 规定的限制范围内，只要其设计能确保驾驶室迅速而有效地达到气密和油气密。

5.2.3　面向货物区域和在本条 5.2.1 规定的限制范围内的上层建筑及甲板室侧壁上的窗和舷窗应为永闭(不能开启)型。这种窗和舷窗应按“A-60”级标准建造，但驾驶室的窗除外，除非对第 9.2.4.2.5 条规定的限制范围外的窗和舷窗可接受“A-0”级标准。

5.2.4　如果从管隧到主泵舱有永久性通道，应安装除符合第Ⅱ-1/13-1.2 条要求外，还应符合下述要求的水密门：

.1　除能从驾驶室操作外，该水密门还应能从主泵舱入口外侧手动关闭；和

.2　在船舶正常作业期间，水密门应保持关闭，但在需要进入管隧时除外。

5.2.5　可以准许在分隔货油泵舱和其他处所的舱壁和甲板上，安装用于货油泵舱照明的认可型永固式气密围罩照明灯，但这种照明灯应具有足够强度并应保持舱壁或甲板的完整性和气密性。

5.2.6　通风出口和入口以及甲板室和上层建筑边界处所的其他开口，其布置应与本条 5.3 和第 11.6 条的规定相符。这种通风口，特别是机器处所的通风口，应尽实际可能位于后部。当船舶设有尾部装卸设备时，对这一点应给以充分考虑。诸如电气设备之类着火源，其布置应避免造成爆炸危险。

5.3 Cargo tank venting

5.3.1 General requirements

The venting systems of cargo tanks shall be entirely distinct from the air pipes of the other compartments of the ship. The arrangements and position of openings in the cargo tank deck from which emission of flammable vapours can occur shall be such as to minimize the possibility of flammable vapours being admitted to enclosed spaces containing a source of ignition, or collecting in the vicinity of deck machinery and equipment which may constitute an ignition hazard. In accordance with this general principle, the criteria in paragraphs 5.3.2 to 5.3.5 and regulation 11.6 will apply.

5.3.2 Venting arrangements

5.3.2.1 The venting arrangements in each cargo tank may be independent or combined with other cargo tanks and may be incorporated into the inert gas piping.

5.3.2.2 Where the arrangements are combined with other cargo tanks, either stop valves or other acceptable means shall be provided to isolate each cargo tank. Where stop valves are fitted, they shall be provided with locking arrangements which shall be under the control of the responsible ship's officer. There shall be a clear visual indication of the operational status of the valves or other acceptable means. Where tanks have been isolated, it shall be ensured that relevant isolating valves are opened before cargo loading or ballasting or discharging of those tanks is commenced. Any isolation must continue to permit the flow caused by thermal variations in a cargo tank in accordance with regulation 11.6.1.1. For tankers constructed on or after 1 January 2017, any isolation shall also continue to permit the passage of large volumes of vapour, air or inert gas mixtures during cargo loading and ballasting, or during discharging in accordance with regulation 11.6.1.2.

5.3.2.3 If cargo loading and ballasting or discharging of a cargo tank or cargo tank group which is isolated from a common venting system is intended, that cargo tank or cargo tank group shall be fitted with a means for over-pressure or under-pressure protection as required in regulation 11.6.3.2.

5.3.2.4 The venting arrangements shall be connected to the top of each cargo tank and shall be self-draining to the cargo tanks under all normal conditions of trim and list of the ship. Where it may not be possible to provide self-draining lines, permanent arrangements shall be provided to drain the vent lines to a cargo tank.

5.3.3 Safety devices in venting systems

The venting system shall be provided with devices to prevent the passage of flame into the cargo tanks. The design, testing and locating of these devices shall comply with the requirements established by the Administration based on the guidelines developed by the Organization.[①] Ullage openings shall not be used for pressure equalization. They shall be provided with self-closing and tightly sealing covers. Flame arresters and screens are not permitted in these openings.

---

① Refer to *Revised standards for the design, testing and locating of devices to prevent the passage of flame into cargo tanks in tankers* (MSC/Circ.677, as amended) and *Revised factors to be taken into consideration when designing cargo tank venting and gas-freeing arrangements* (MSC/Circ.731).

5.3 液货舱透气

5.3.1 一般要求

液货舱的透气系统应完全区别于船舶其他舱室的空气管。凡液货舱甲板上能散发出可燃蒸气的开口,其布置和部位应使可燃蒸气进入含有着火源的围蔽处所或聚集在可能构成着火危险的甲板机械和设备附近的可能性减至最低。按照这一总的原则,本条 5.3.2 至5.3.5 及第 11.6 条的衡准适用。

5.3.2 透气装置

5.3.2.1 每一液货舱的透气装置可以是独立的,亦可以同其他液货舱连在一起,还可以与惰性气体管系并为一体。

5.3.2.2 如果该装置与其他液货舱连在一起,则应装有截止阀和其他可接受的装置,以隔绝每一液货舱。如安装截止阀,应为其配备锁闭装置并由负责的高级船员控制。截止阀或其他可接受的装置的工作状态应有清楚的视觉指示。如果液货舱已被隔离,应确保在这些液货舱开始装卸货或压载之前开启有关隔离阀。任何隔离措施都必须按照第 11.6.1.1 条的规定使由于液货舱内温度变化所产生的气体能继续流通无阻。对于 2017 年 1 月 1 日或以后建造的液货船,任何隔离措施还须按照第 11.6.1.2 条,在装载和压载或卸载过程中,使大量蒸气、空气或惰性气体混合物能够继续通过。

5.3.2.3 如要对与公共透气系统隔离的某一或某组液货舱进行装卸货或压载,则该液货舱或该组液货舱应按第 11.6.3.2 条的要求装有超压或负压保护装置。

5.3.2.4 透气装置应接至每一液货舱的顶部,并在船舶所有正常的纵倾和横倾工况下,能自行把液体排泄到液货舱。如果不能装设自行排泄管路,则应装设永久性装置,以将透气管路中的液体排泄至液货舱中。

5.3.3 透气系统

透气系统的安全装置透气系统应设有防止火焰进入液货舱的装置。这些装置的设计、试验和安装位置应符合主管机关依据本组织制定的指南①而规定的要求。液位测量孔不得用于平衡压力。液位测量孔应装有能自行关闭并密封的盖。在这些开口上不允许设置阻焰器和防火网。

---

① 参见《经修订的液货船防止火焰进入液货舱装置的设计、试验和安装位置标准》(经修正的第 MSC/Circ.677 号通函)以及《经修订的液货舱透气和除气布置设计时应考虑的因素》(第 MSC/Circ.731 号通函)。

5.3.4 Vent outlets for cargo handling and ballasting

5.3.4.1 Vent outlets for cargo loading, discharging and ballasting required by regulation 11.6.1.2 shall:

.1.1 permit the free flow of vapour mixtures; or

.1.2 permit the throttling of the discharge of the vapour mixtures to achieve a velocity of not less than 30 m/s;

.2 be so arranged that the vapour mixture is discharged vertically upwards;

.3 where the method is by free flow of vapour mixtures, be such that the outlet shall be not less than 6 m above the cargo tank deck or fore and aft gangway if situated within 4 m of the gangway and located not less than 10 m measured horizontally from the nearest air intakes and openings to enclosed spaces containing a source of ignition and from deck machinery, which may include anchor windlass and chain locker openings, and equipment which may constitute an ignition hazard; and

.4 where the method is by high-velocity discharge, be located at a height not less than 2 m above the cargo tank deck and not less than 10 m measured horizontally from the nearest air intakes and openings to enclosed spaces containing a source of ignition and from deck machinery, which may include anchor windlass and chain locker openings, and equipment which may constitute an ignition hazard. These outlets shall be provided with high-velocity devices of an approved type.

5.3.4.2 The arrangements for the venting of vapours displaced from the cargo tanks during loading and ballasting shall comply with paragraph 5.3 and regulation 11.6 and shall consist of either one or more mast risers, or a number of high-velocity vents. The inert gas supply main may be used for such venting.

5.3.5 Isolation of slop tanks in combination carriers

In combination carriers, the arrangements for isolating slop tanks containing oil or oil residues from other cargo tanks shall consist of blank flanges which will remain in position at all times when cargoes other than liquid cargoes referred to in regulation 1.6.1 are carried.

5.4 Ventilation

5.4.1 Ventilation systems in cargo pump-rooms

Cargo pump-rooms shall be mechanically ventilated and discharges from the exhaust fans shall be led to a safe place on the open deck. The ventilation of these rooms shall have sufficient capacity to minimize the possibility of accumulation of flammable vapours. The number of air changes shall be at least 20 per hour, based upon the gross volume of the space. The air ducts shall be arranged so that all of the space is effectively ventilated. The ventilation shall be of the suction type using fans of the non-sparking type.

5.3.4　用于液货装卸和压载的透气出口

5.3.4.1　第11.6.1.2条所要求的用于液货装卸和压载的透气出口应：

.1.1　使蒸气混合物能自由流通；或

.1.2　使蒸气混合物的排泄节流速度达到不小于30 m/s；

.2　布置为使蒸气混合物垂直向上排出；

.3　如果采用蒸气混合物自由排出的方式，布置成该出口在液货舱甲板以上高度不少于6 m，或者如果该出口位于距步桥4 m以内，则布置成在前后步桥以上高度不少于6 m，且与含有着火源的围蔽处所的最近进气口和开口以及可能构成着火危险的甲板机械（可包括起锚机和锚链舱开口）和设备的水平距离不少于10 m；和

.4　如果采用高速排气的方式，布置成在液货舱甲板以上高度不少于2 m，且与含有着火源的围蔽处所的最近进气口和开口以及可能构成着火危险的甲板机械（可包括起锚机和锚链舱开口）和设备的水平距离不少于10 m。这些出口应设有认可型的高速装置。

5.3.4.2　在装载和压载期间从液货舱排出蒸气的透气装置应符合本条5.3和第11.6条的规定，并应由一个或多个桅杆透气管或多个高速排气口组成。惰性气体总管可以用于这种透气。

5.3.5　兼装船污油舱的隔离

对于兼装船，用于将含有油或残油的污油舱与其他货油舱隔离的装置应由盲板法兰组成，当载运第1.6.1条所述液体货物以外的货物时，这些法兰应始终保持在原位。

5.4　通风

5.4.1　液货泵舱内的通风系统

液货泵舱应采用机械通风，从通风机排出的气体应引至开敞甲板上的安全地点。这些舱室的通风能力应足以最大限度降低可燃蒸气聚集的可能性。换气次数应至少为每小时20次，根据该处所的总容积确定。通风管道的布置应使该处所的所有空间均能得到有效通风。应采用抽吸式通风并使用无火星型风机。

5.4.2 Ventilation systems in combination carriers

In combination carriers, cargo spaces and any enclosed spaces adjacent to cargo spaces shall be capable of being mechanically ventilated. The mechanical ventilation may be provided by portable fans. An approved fixed gas warning system capable of monitoring flammable vapours shall be provided in cargo pump-rooms, pipe ducts and cofferdams, as referred to in paragraph 5.1.4, adjacent to slop tanks. Suitable arrangements shall be made to facilitate measurement of flammable vapours in all other spaces within the cargo area. Such measurements shall be made possible from the open deck or easily accessible positions.

5.5 Inert gas systems

5.5.1 Application

5.5.1.1 For tankers of 20,000 tonnes deadweight and upwards constructed on or after 1 July 2002 but before 1 January 2016, the protection of the cargo tanks shall be achieved by a fixed inert gas system in accordance with the requirements of the Fire Safety Systems Code, as adopted by resolution MSC.98(73), except that the Administration may accept other equivalent systems or arrangements, as described in paragraph 5.5.4.

5.5.1.2 For tankers of 8,000 tonnes deadweight and upwards constructed on or after 1 January 2016 when carrying cargoes described in regulation 1.6.1 or 1.6.2, the protection of the cargo tanks shall be achieved by a fixed inert gas system in accordance with the requirements of the Fire Safety Systems Code, except that the Administration may accept other equivalent systems or arrangements, as described in paragraph 5.5.4.

5.5.1.3 Tankers operating with a cargo tank cleaning procedure using crude oil washing shall be fitted with an inert gas system complying with the Fire Safety Systems Code and with fixed tank washing machines. However, inert gas systems fitted on tankers constructed on or after 1 July 2002 but before 1 January 2016 shall comply with the Fire Safety Systems Code, as adopted by resolution MSC.98(73).

5.5.1.4 Tankers required to be fitted with inert gas systems shall comply with the following provisions:

.1 double-hull spaces shall be fitted with suitable connections for the supply of inert gas;

.2 where hull spaces are connected to a permanently fitted inert gas distribution system, means shall be provided to prevent hydrocarbon gases from the cargo tanks entering the double-hull spaces through the system; and

.3 where such spaces are not permanently connected to an inert gas distribution system, appropriate means shall be provided to allow connection to the inert gas main.

5.5.2 Inert gas systems of chemical tankers and gas carriers

5.5.2.1 The requirements for inert gas systems contained in the Fire Safety Systems Code need not be applied to chemical tankers constructed before 1 January 2016, including those constructed before 1 July 2012, and all gas carriers:

5.4.2　兼装船的通风系统

对于兼装船,载货处所及与其相邻的围蔽处所应能进行机械通风。机械通风可用移动式风机进行。在货油泵舱、管道以及本条5.1.4所述的邻接于污油舱的隔离空舱内,应设有认可的能监测可燃蒸气的固定式气体报警系统。应有适当的布置,为测量货物区域内所有其他处所的可燃蒸气提供方便。这种测量应能在开敞甲板上或易于到达的位置上进行。

5.5　惰性气体系统

5.5.1　适用范围

5.5.1.1　对于在2002年7月1日或之后但在2016年1月1日之前建造的20 000载重吨及以上的液货船,其液货舱须通过一个符合经第MSC.98(73)号决议通过的《消防安全系统规则》要求的固定式惰性气体系统获得保护,但主管机关可接受第5.5.4款中所述的其他等效系统或安排。

5.5.1.2　对于在2016年1月1日或之后建造的8 000载重吨及以上的液货船,在载运第1.6.1或1.6.2条中所述的货物时,其液货舱须通过一个符合《消防安全系统规则》要求的固定惰性气体系统获得保护,但主管机关可接受第5.5.4款中所述的其他等效系统或安排。

5.5.1.3　在货舱清洗工序中使用原油来清洗的液货船须装有符合《消防安全系统规则》的惰性气体系统和固定式洗舱机。但安装在2002年7月1日或之后但在2016年1月1日之前建造的液货船上的惰性气体系统须符合经第MSC.98(73)号决议通过的《消防安全系统规则》。

5.5.1.4　要求安装惰性气体系统的液货船须符合以下规定:

.1　双层壳处所须装有供应惰性气体的适当连接管;

.2　如这些处所被接至一个固定安装的惰性气体分配系统上,须采取措施防止碳氢化合物气体从货油舱通过该系统进入双层壳处所;及

.3　如此类处所未被接至固定安装的惰性气体分配系统上,须采取适当措施允许其与惰性气体主管相连接。

5.5.2　化学品液货船和气体运输船的惰性气体系统

5.5.2.1　《消防安全系统规则》中关于惰性气体系统的要求不必适用于在2016年1月1日之前建造的化学品液货船(包括2012年7月1日之前建造的那些船)及所有气体运输船:

.1 when carrying cargoes described in regulation 1.6.1, provided that they comply with the requirements for inert gas systems on chemical tankers established by the Administration, based on the guidelines developed by the Organization;[①] or

.2 when carrying flammable cargoes other than crude oil or petroleum products such as cargoes listed in chapters 17 and 18 of the International Bulk Chemical Code, provided that the capacity of tanks used for their carriage does not exceed 3,000 m^3 and the individual nozzle capacities of tank washing machines do not exceed 17.5 m^3/h and the total combined throughput from the number of machines in use in a cargo tank at any one time does not exceed 110 m^3/h.

5.5.3 General requirements for inert gas systems

5.5.3.1 The inert gas system shall be capable of inerting, purging and gas-freeing empty tanks and maintaining the atmosphere in cargo tanks with the required oxygen content.

5.5.3.2 Tankers fitted with a fixed inert gas system shall be provided with a closed ullage system.

5.5.4 Requirements for equivalent systems

5.5.4.1 The Administration may, after having given consideration to the ship's arrangement and equipment, accept other fixed installations, in accordance with regulation Ⅰ/5 and paragraph 5.5.4.3.

5.5.4.2 For tankers of 8,000 tonnes deadweight and upwards but less than 20,000 tonnes deadweight constructed on or after 1 January 2016, in lieu of fixed installations as required by paragraph 5.5.4.1, the Administration may accept other equivalent arrangements or means of protection in accordance with regulation Ⅰ/5 and paragraph 5.5.4.3.

5.5.4.3 Equivalent systems or arrangements shall:

.1 be capable of preventing dangerous accumulations of explosive mixtures in intact cargo tanks during normal service throughout the ballast voyage and necessary in-tank operations; and

.2 be so designed as to minimize the risk of ignition from the generation of static electricity by the system itself.

5.6 Inerting, purging and gas-freeing

5.6.1 Arrangements for purging and/or gas-freeing shall be such as to minimize the hazards due to dispersal of flammable vapours in the atmosphere and to flammable mixtures in a cargo tank.

5.6.2 The procedure for cargo tank purging and/or gas-freeing shall be carried out in accordance with regulation 16.3.2.

---

① Refer to *Regulation for inert gas systems on chemical tankers* (resolution A.567(14) and Corr.1).

.1　载运第 1.6.1 条所述货物，只要其符合主管机关根据本组织制定的导则[①]规定的对化学品液货船惰性气体系统的要求；或

.2　载运原油或石油产品以外的易燃货物，例如《国际散化规则》第 17 和 18 章中所列货物，只要用于装载这些货物的液货舱容积不超过 3 000 m^3，洗舱机单支水枪的能力不超过 17.5 m^3/h，且任一时刻在一个货舱内所用的几个洗舱机的总喷出量不超过 110 m^3/h。

5.5.3　惰性气体系统的一般要求

5.5.3.1　惰性气体系统须能对空舱进行惰化、驱气和除气，并使货舱内的空气维持所要求的含氧量。

5.5.3.2　安装有固定式惰性气体系统的液货船须配备封闭式液位测量系统。

5.5.4　对等效系统的要求

5.5.4.1　主管机关考虑到船舶的布置和设备，可根据第Ⅰ/5 条和第 5.5.4.3 款接受其他固定式装置。

5.5.4.2　对于在 2016 年 1 月 1 日或之后建造的 8 000 载重吨及以上但小于 20 000 载重吨的液货船，主管机关可根据第Ⅰ/5 条和第 5.5.4.3 款同意用其他等效保护的布置或措施来代替第 5.5.4.1 款中所要求的固定式装置。

5.5.4.3　等效系统或布置须：

.1　在正常压载航行的整个航程中以及必要的舱内作业期间，能防止爆炸性混合物在完整的液货舱内产生危险的积聚；以及

.2　如此设计以致该系统本身产生静电而着火的危险性降至最低程度。

5.6　惰化、驱气和除气

5.6.1　驱气和/或除气的布置应能使由于空气中可燃气体的散布和液货舱内可燃混合气体的存在而造成的危险减至最低。

5.6.2　液货舱的驱气和/或除气程序应按第 16.3.2 条的规定执行。

---

① 参见《化学品液货船惰性气体系统规则》（第 A.567(14)号决议和 Corr.1）。

5.6.3 The arrangements for inerting, purging or gas-freeing of empty tanks as required in paragraph 5.5.3.1 shall be to the satisfaction of the Administration and shall be such that the accumulation of hydrocarbon vapours in pockets formed by the internal structural members in a tank is minimized and that:

.1 on individual cargo tanks, the gas outlet pipe, if fitted, shall be positioned as far as practicable from the inert gas/air inlet and in accordance with paragraph 5.3 and regulation 11.6. The inlet of such outlet pipes may be located either at deck level or at not more than 1 m above the bottom of the tank;

.2 the cross-sectional area of such gas outlet pipe referred to in paragraph 5.6.3.1 shall be such that an exit velocity of at least 20 m/s can be maintained when any three tanks are being simultaneously supplied with inert gas. Their outlets shall extend not less than 2 m above deck level; and

.3 each gas outlet referred to in paragraph 5.6.3.2 shall be fitted with suitable blanking arrangements.

5.7 Gas measurement and detection

5.7.1 Portable instrument

Tankers shall be equipped with at least one portable instrument for measuring oxygen and one for measuring flammable vapour concentrations, together with a sufficient set of spares. Suitable means shall be provided for the calibration of such instruments.

5.7.2 Arrangements for gas measurement in double-hull spaces and double-bottom spaces

5.7.2.1 Suitable portable instruments for measuring oxygen and flammable vapour concentrations in double-hull spaces and double-bottom spaces shall be provided. In selecting these instruments, due attention shall be given to their use in combination with the fixed gas sampling line systems referred to in paragraph 5.7.2.2.

5.7.2.2 Where the atmosphere in double-hull spaces cannot be reliably measured using flexible gas sampling hoses, such spaces shall be fitted with permanent gas sampling lines. The configuration of gas sampling lines shall be adapted to the design of such spaces.

5.7.2.3 The materials of construction and dimensions of gas sampling lines shall be such as to prevent restriction. Where plastic materials are used, they shall be electrically conductive.

5.7.3 Arrangements for fixed hydrocarbon gas detection systems in double-hull and double-bottom spaces of oil tankers

5.7.3.1 In addition to the requirements in paragraphs 5.7.1 and 5.7.2, oil tankers of 20,000 tonnes deadweight and above, constructed on or after 1 January 2012, shall be provided with a fixed hydrocarbon gas detection system complying with the Fire Safety Systems Code for measuring hydrocarbon gas concentrations in all ballast tanks and void spaces of double-hull and double-bottom spaces adjacent to the cargo tanks, including the forepeak tank and any other tanks and spaces under the bulkhead deck adjacent to cargo tanks.

5.6.3 本条5.5.3.1所要求的空液货舱的惰化、驱气或除气的布置应使主管机关满意，并应使碳氢化合物蒸气在液货舱内部构件形成的空穴内的积聚减至最低，并且：

.1 对单个液货舱，如果安装了排气管，该排气管的位置应尽实际可能远离惰性气体/空气的进口，并符合本条5.3和第11.6条的规定。这种排气管的进口可以位于与甲板相平的高度或位于液货舱舱底以上不超过1 m处；

.2 本条5.6.3.1所述排气管之横截面面积应为：当同时向任何三个货油舱供给惰性气体时，排气速度至少为20 m/s。其出口应伸出甲板之上至少2 m；和

.3 本条5.6.3.2所述的每一排气口应装有适当的盲断装置。

5.7　气体测量和探测

5.7.1　便携式仪器

液货船须至少配备一台用于测量易燃气体浓度的便携式仪器及充足备件。须为这种仪器提供适当的校准方法。

5.7.2　测量双层壳和双层底处所内气体的布置

5.7.2.1 须配备在双层壳和双层底处所内测量氧气和易燃气体浓度的适当便携式仪器。在选择这些仪器时，须充分注意其与本条第5.7.2.2款中提到的固定式气体取样管路系统的组合使用。

5.7.2.2 如果使用挠性的气体取样软管无法可靠地测量双层壳处所的气体，此类处所须安装固定式气体取样管路。取样管路的走向须与此类处所的设计相适应。

5.7.2.3 气体取样管路的制造材料和尺寸须防止在管内发生限流。如果使用塑料材料，须具有导电性。

5.7.3　油船双层壳和双层底处所内的固定式碳氢化合物气体探测系统的布置

5.7.3.1 除第5.7.1和5.7.2款的要求以外，2012年1月1日或之后建造的20 000载重吨及以上的油船须安装一个符合《国际消防安全系统规则》的固定式碳氢化合物气体探测系统，用于测量所有压载舱和与货舱相邻的双层壳和双层底空舱处所（包括首尖舱和舱壁甲板下与货舱相邻的任何其他舱室和处所）内的碳氢化合物气体浓度。

5.7.3.2 Oil tankers provided with constant operative inerting systems for such spaces need not be equipped with fixed hydrocarbon gas detection equipment.

5.7.3.3 Notwithstanding the above, cargo pump-rooms subject to the provisions of paragraph 5.10 need not comply with the requirements of this paragraph.

5.8 Air supply to double-hull spaces and double-bottom spaces

Double-hull spaces and double–bottom spaces shall be fitted with suitable connections for the supply of air.

5.9 Protection of cargo area

Drip pans for collecting cargo residues in cargo lines and hoses shall be provided in the area of pipe and hose connections under the manifold area. Cargo hoses and tank washing hoses shall have electrical continuity over their entire lengths, including couplings and flanges (except shore connections), and shall be earthed for removal of electrostatic charges.

5.10 Protection of cargo pump-rooms

5.10.1 In tankers:

.1 cargo pumps, ballast pumps and stripping pumps, installed in cargo pump–rooms and driven by shafts passing through pump–room bulkheads shall be fitted with temperature sensing devices for bulkhead shaft glands, bearings and pump casings. A continuous audible and visual alarm signal shall be automatically effected in the cargo control room or the pump control station;

.2 lighting in cargo pump–rooms, except emergency lighting, shall be interlocked with ventilation such that the ventilation shall be in operation when switching on the lighting. Failure of the ventilation system shall not cause the lighting to go out;

.3 a system for continuous monitoring of the concentration of hydrocarbon gases shall be fitted. Sampling points or detector heads shall be located in suitable positions in order that potentially dangerous leakages are readily detected. When the hydrocarbon gas concentration reaches a pre-set level, which shall not be higher than 10% of the lower flammable limit, a continuous audible and visual alarm signal shall be automatically effected in the pump–room, engine control room, cargo control room and navigation bridge to alert personnel to the potential hazard; and

.4 all pump-rooms shall be provided with bilge level monitoring devices together with appropriately located alarms.

5.7.3.2 在这种处所装有恒定运作惰性气体系统的油船无须安装固定式碳氢化合物气体探测系统。

5.7.3.3 尽管有以上要求,受本条第5.10款规定约束的货泵舱无须符合本款的要求。

5.8 双壳体处所和双层底处所的空气供给

双壳体处所和双层底处所应装有用于供给空气的适当接管。

5.9 货物区域的保护

在总管区域的管子和软管的接头部位应设有收集液货管路和软管中液货残余物的滴盘。液货软管和洗舱软管应在其整个长度上具有导电连续性,包括管箍和法兰(通岸接头除外),并应接地以消除静电。

5.10 液货泵舱的保护

5.10.1 对于液货船:

.1 装在液货泵舱内并由穿过泵舱舱壁的轴驱动的液货泵、压载泵和扫舱泵,其舱壁轴填料函、轴承和泵壳应装设温度传感装置。在货物控制室或泵控制站内应能自动激发连续听觉和视觉报警信号;

.2 除应急照明外,液货泵舱的照明应与通风联锁,在开启照明时即开始通风。通风系统失灵不应使照明熄灭;

.3 应安装一个持续监测碳氢化合物气体浓度的系统。采样点或探测头应设置在适当位置,以随时探测到潜在的危险泄漏。如果碳氢化合物气体浓度达到预先设定的水平(应不高于可燃气体爆炸下限的10%),应在泵舱、轮机控制室、货物控制室和驾驶室内自动激发连续听觉和视觉报警信号,以引起有关人员对潜在危险的警觉;和

.4 所有泵舱应安装舱底水位监测装置及布设在适当位置的报警装置。

Regulation 5
Fire growth potential

1 Purpose

The purpose of this regulation is to limit the fire growth potential in every space of the ship. For this purpose, the following functional requirements shall be met:

.1 means of control for the air supply to the space shall be provided;

.2 means of control for flammable liquids in the space shall be provided; and

.3 the use of combustible materials shall be restricted.

2 Control of air supply and flammable liquid to the space

2.1 Closing appliances and stopping devices of ventilation

2.1.1 The main inlets and outlets of all ventilation systems shall be capable of being closed from outside the spaces being ventilated. The means of closing shall be easily accessible as well as prominently and permanently marked and shall indicate whether the shut-off is open or closed.

2.1.2 Power ventilation of accommodation spaces, service spaces, cargo spaces, control stations and machinery spaces shall be capable of being stopped from an easily accessible position outside the space being served. This position shall not be readily cut off in the event of a fire in the spaces served.

2.1.3 In passenger ships carrying more than 36 passengers, power ventilation, except machinery space and cargo space ventilation and any alternative system which may be required under regulation 8.2, shall be fitted with controls so grouped that all fans may be stopped from either of two separate positions which shall be situated as far apart as practicable. Fans serving power ventilation systems to cargo spaces shall be capable of being stopped from a safe position outside such spaces.

2.2 Means of control in machinery spaces

2.2.1 Means of control shall be provided for opening and closure of skylights, closure of openings in funnels which normally allow exhaust ventilation and closure of ventilator dampers.

2.2.2 Means of control shall be provided for stopping ventilating fans. Controls provided for the power ventilation serving machinery spaces shall be grouped so as to be operable from two positions, one of which shall be outside such spaces. The means provided for stopping the power ventilation of the machinery spaces shall be entirely separate from the means provided for stopping ventilation of other spaces.

第5条
潜在的火势增大

1　目的

本条的目的是限制船舶各种处所内潜在的火势增大。为此,应满足下列功能要求:

.1　应设有控制处所空气供给的装置;

.2　应设有控制处所内易燃液体的装置;和

.3　应限制可燃材料的使用。

2　处所内空气供给和易燃液体的控制

2.1　通风的关闭和停止装置

2.1.1　所有通风系统的主要进气口和出气口都应能从通风处所的外部关闭。关闭装置操作位置应易于到达,有显著的永久性标志,且应指示出关闭装置是处在开启位置还是处在关闭位置。

2.1.2　起居处所、服务处所、货物处所、控制站和机器处所的动力通风,应能从其所通风的处所外部易于到达的位置将其停止。此位置在其服务的处所失火时应不易被切断。

2.1.3　对于载客超过36人的客船,除机器处所和货物处所的通风以及可根据第8.2条要求的任何替代系统外,动力通风应有集中控制装置,以便在两个尽可能彼此远离的位置均可停止所有通风机。服务于货物处所动力通风系统的风机应能从该处所外的安全位置予以关闭。

2.2　机器处所的控制装置

2.2.1　应设有供天窗开启和关闭、在烟囱上正常排气通风开口关闭和通风挡火闸关闭用的控制装置。

2.2.2　应设有停止通风机的控制装置。对服务于机器处所的动力通风应设有能从两个位置集中控制的装置,其中之一应位于这种处所的外面。机器处所内的动力通风停止装置应与其他处所内的通风停止装置完全分开。

2.2.3 Means of control shall be provided for stopping forced and induced draught fans, oil fuel transfer pumps, oil fuel unit pumps, lubricating oil service pumps, thermal oil circulating pumps and oil separators (purifiers). However, paragraphs 2.2.4 and 2.2.5 need not apply to oily water separators.

2.2.4 The controls required in paragraphs 2.2.1 to 2.2.3 and in regulation 4.2.2.3.4 shall be located outside the space concerned so they will not be cut off in the event of fire in the space they serve.

2.2.5 In passenger ships, the controls required in paragraphs 2.2.1 to 2.2.4 and in regulations 8.3.3 and 9.5.2.3 and the controls for any required fire-extinguishing system shall be situated at one control position or grouped in as few positions as possible to the satisfaction of the Administration. Such positions shall have a safe access from the open deck.

2.3 Additional requirements for means of control in periodically unattended machinery spaces

2.3.1 For periodically unattended machinery spaces, the Administration shall give special consideration to maintaining the fire integrity of the machinery spaces, the location and centralization of the fire-extinguishing system controls, the required shutdown arrangements (e.g. ventilation, fuel pumps, etc.) and that additional fire-extinguishing appliances and other fire-fighting equipment and breathing apparatus may be required.

2.3.2 In passenger ships, these requirements shall be at least equivalent to those of machinery spaces normally attended.

3 Fire protection materials

3.1 Use of non-combustible materials

3.1.1 Insulating materials

Insulating materials shall be non-combustible, except in cargo spaces, mail rooms, baggage rooms and refrigerated compartments of service spaces. Vapour barriers and adhesives used in conjunction with insulation, as well as the insulation of pipe fittings for cold service systems, need not be of non-combustible materials, but they shall be kept to the minimum quantity practicable and their exposed surfaces shall have low flame-spread characteristics.

3.1.2 Ceilings and linings

3.1.2.1 In passenger ships, except in cargo spaces, all linings, grounds, draught stops and ceilings shall be of non-combustible material except in mail rooms, baggage rooms, saunas or refrigerated compartments of service spaces.

3.1.2.2 In cargo ships, all linings, ceilings, draught stops and their associated grounds shall be of non-combustible materials in the following spaces:

.1 in accommodation and service spaces and control stations for ships where method Ⅰ C is specified as referred to in regulation 9.2.3.1; and

2.2.3 应设有停止强力鼓风机和抽风机、燃油驳运泵、燃油装置所用的泵、润滑油供应泵、热油循环泵和油分离器(净油器)的控制装置。但是,本条2.2.4和2.2.5的规定不必适用于油水分离器。

2.2.4 本条2.2.1至2.2.3和第4.2.2.3.4条要求的控制装置应位于各有关处所的外部,从而不会在其所服务的处所失火时被切断。

2.2.5 对于客船,本条2.2.1至2.2.4和第8.3.3和9.5.2.3条所要求的控制装置以及任何所要求的灭火系统的控制装置应位于一个控制位置或集中在主管机关满意的尽可能少的地点。这些地点应能从开敞甲板安全进出。

2.3 对周期性无人值班机器处所控制装置的附加要求

2.3.1 对于周期性无人值班的机器处所,主管机关应对保持机器处所的耐火完整性、灭火系统控制装置的位置和集中性以及所要求的切断布置(例如通风、燃油泵等)予以特别考虑,为此可以要求配备额外的灭火设施和其他消防设备以及呼吸器。

2.3.2 在客船上,这些要求应至少等效于对通常有人值班机器处所的要求。

3 防火材料

3.1 不燃材料的使用

3.1.1 隔热材料

除在货物处所、邮件舱、行李室和服务处所的冷藏室外,隔热材料应为不燃材料。与隔热物一起使用的防潮层和黏合剂,以及制冷机系统管件的隔热物,不必为不燃材料,但应保持在实际可行的最低数量,且其外露表面应具有低播焰性。

3.1.2 天花板和衬板

3.1.2.1 在客船上,除了货物处所、邮件舱、行李室、桑拿房或服务处所的冷藏室外,所有衬板、衬挡、风挡和天花板应为不燃材料。

3.1.2.2 在货船上,以下处所内的所有衬板、天花板、风挡和其附属衬挡应为不燃材料:

.1 在第9.2.3.1条中被指定采用ⅠC法的船舶起居处所、服务处所和控制站内;和

.2 in corridors and stairway enclosures serving accommodation and service spaces and control stations for ships where methods ⅡC or ⅢC are specified as referred to in regulation 9.2.3.1.

3.1.3 Partial bulkheads and decks on passenger ships

3.1.3.1 Partial bulkheads or decks used to subdivide a space for utility or artistic treatment shall be of non-combustible materials.

3.1.3.2 Linings, ceilings and partial bulkheads or decks used to screen or to separate adjacent cabin balconies shall be of non-combustible materials. Cabin balconies on passenger ships constructed before 1 July 2008 shall comply with the requirements of this paragraph by the first survey after 1 July 2008.

3.2 Use of combustible materials

3.2.1 General

3.2.1.1 In passenger ships, "A", "B" or "C" class divisions in accommodation and service spaces and cabin balconies which are faced with combustible materials, facings, mouldings, decorations and veneers shall comply with the provisions of paragraphs 3.2.2 to 3.2.4 and regulation 6. However, traditional wooden benches and wooden linings on bulkheads and ceilings are permitted in saunas and such materials need not be subject to the calculations prescribed in paragraphs 3.2.2 and 3.2.3. However, the provisions of paragraph 3.2.3 need not be applied to cabin balconies.

3.2.1.2 In cargo ships, non-combustible bulkheads, ceilings and linings fitted in accommodation and service spaces may be faced with combustible materials, facings, mouldings, decorations and veneers provided such spaces are bounded by non-combustible bulkheads, ceilings and linings in accordance with the provisions of paragraphs 3.2.2 to 3.2.4 and regulation 6.

3.2.2 Maximum calorific value of combustible materials

Combustible materials used on the surfaces and linings specified in paragraph 3.2.1 shall have a calorific value[①] not exceeding 45 MJ/m^2 of the area for the thickness used. The requirements of this paragraph are not applicable to the surfaces of furniture fixed to linings or bulkheads.

3.2.3 Total volume of combustible materials

Where combustible materials are used in accordance with paragraph 3.2.1, they shall comply with the following requirements:

.1 The total volume of combustible facings, mouldings, decorations and veneers in accommodation and service spaces shall not exceed a volume equivalent to 2.5 mm veneer on the combined area of the walls and ceiling linings. Furniture fixed to linings, bulkheads or decks need not be included in the calculation of the total volume of combustible materials; and

① Refer to the recommendations published by the International Organization for Standardization, in particular ISO/DIS 1716, *Reaction to fire tests for products—Determination of the gross heat of combustion (calorific value)*.

.2　在第 9.2.3.1 条中被指定采用ⅡC 法或ⅢC 法的供船舶起居处所、服务处所和控制站使用的走廊和梯道环围内。

3.1.3　客船上的局部舱壁和甲板

3.1.3.1　为了实用或艺术处理而用作某一处所内部分隔的局部舱壁或甲板应为不燃材料。

3.1.3.2　衬板、天花板和用作遮蔽或分隔相邻客舱阳台的局部舱壁或甲板应为不燃材料。2008 年 7 月 1 日以前建造的客船上的客舱阳台应在 2008 年 7 月 1 日以后的第一次检验之前符合本要求。

3.2　可燃材料的使用

3.2.1　通则

3.2.1.1　在客船上,起居处所和服务处所及客舱阳台内表面加装可燃材料的“A”、“B”或“C”级分隔,其贴面、嵌条、装饰物及装饰板应符合本条 3.2.2 至 3.2.4 和第 6 条的规定。但是,在桑拿房内允许采用传统的木制长凳以及在舱壁和天花板上铺木衬板,且对这种材料不必进行本条 3.2.2 和 3.2.3 所规定的计算。然而,3.2.3 的规定不必适用于客舱阳台。

3.2.1.2　在货船上,起居处所和服务处所内安装的不燃性舱壁、天花板和衬板的表面可加装易燃材料贴面、嵌条、装饰物及装饰板,但这种处所应按本条 3.2.2 至 3.2.4 和第 6 条的规定由不燃舱壁、天花板和衬板所围闭。

3.2.2　可燃材料的最大发热值

本条 3.2.1 所规定的用于表面和衬板的可燃材料,按所用厚度的面积所具有的发热值①不得超过 45 MJ/m^2。本要求不适用于固定在衬板或舱壁上的家具表面。

3.2.3　可燃材料的总体积

如果按本条 3.2.1 的要求使用了可燃材料,所用可燃材料应符合以下要求:

.1　起居处所和服务处所内的可燃贴面、嵌条、装饰物及装饰板的总体积,不得超过相当于各围壁和天花板衬板合计面积上厚 2.5 mm 装饰板的体积。固定在衬板、舱壁或甲板上的家具不必包括在可燃材料总体积的计算之中;和

① 参见国际标准化组织出版的建议案,特别是 ISO/DIS 1716《产品耐火试验反应——总发热量(热值)测定》。

.2 in the case of ships fitted with an automatic sprinkler system complying with the provisions of the Fire Safety Systems Code, the above volume may include some combustible material used for erection of "C" class divisions.

3.2.4 Low flame-spread characteristics of exposed surfaces

The following surfaces shall have low flame-spread characteristics in accordance with the Fire Test Procedures Code:

3.2.4.1 In passenger ships:

.1 exposed surfaces in corridors and stairway enclosures and of bulkhead and ceiling linings in accommodation and service spaces (except saunas) and control stations;

.2 surfaces and grounds in concealed or inaccessible spaces in accommodation and service spaces and control stations; and

.3 exposed surfaces of cabin balconies, except for natural hard wood decking systems.

3.2.4.2 In cargo ships:

.1 exposed surfaces in corridors and stairway enclosures and of ceilings in accommodation and service spaces (except saunas) and control stations; and

.2 surfaces and grounds in concealed or inaccessible spaces in accommodation and service spaces and control stations.

3.3 Furniture in stairway enclosures of passenger ships

Furniture in stairway enclosures shall be limited to seating. It shall be fixed, limited to six seats on each deck in each stairway enclosure, be of restricted fire risk determined in accordance with the Fire Test Procedures Code, and shall not restrict the passenger escape route. The Administration may permit additional seating in the main reception area within a stairway enclosure if it is fixed, non-combustible and does not restrict the passenger escape route. Furniture shall not be permitted in passenger and crew corridors forming escape routes in cabin areas. In addition to the above, lockers of non-combustible material, providing storage for non-hazardous safety equipment required by these regulations, may be permitted. Drinking water dispensers and ice cube machines may be permitted in corridors provided they are fixed and do not restrict the width of the escape routes. This applies as well to decorative flower or plant arrangements, statues or other objects of art such as paintings and tapestries in corridors and stairways.

3.4 Furniture and furnishings on cabin balconies of passenger ships

On passenger ships, furniture and furnishings on cabin balconies shall comply with regulations 3.40.1, 3.40.2, 3.40.3, 3.40.6 and 3.40.7 unless such balconies are protected by a fixed pressure water-spraying and fixed fire detection and fire alarm systems complying with regulations 7.10 and 10.6.1.3. Passenger ships constructed before 1 July 2008 shall comply with the requirements of this paragraph by the first survey after 1 July 2008.

.2　如果船舶装有符合《消防安全系统规则》规定的自动喷水器系统，则上述体积可包含某种用于建立"C"级分隔的可燃材料。

3.2.4　外露表面的低播焰性

下述表面应按《耐火试验程序规则》的规定具有低播焰性：

3.2.4.1　对于客船：

.1　走廊和梯道的环围以及起居处所、服务处所（桑拿房除外）和控制站的舱壁和天花板衬板的外露表面；

.2　起居处所、服务处所和控制站内隐蔽或不能到达之处的表面和衬挡；和

.3　客舱阳台的外露表面，但天然硬木甲板铺板除外。

3.2.4.2　对于货船：

.1　走廊和梯道的环围以及起居处所、服务处所（桑拿房除外）和控制站的天花板的外露表面；和

.2　起居处所、服务处所和控制站内隐蔽或不能到达之处的表面和衬挡。

3.3　客船梯道环围内的家具

设在梯道环围内的家具应仅限于座位。这些座位应予固定，在每一梯道环围内的每一层甲板的座位数量不得超过6个，按《耐火试验程序规则》确定为限制失火危险，且不得阻塞乘客脱险通道。如果座位是固定式的，由不燃材料制成且不阻塞乘客脱险通道，主管机关可允许在梯道环围内的主接待区增加座位数。在居住舱室区域构成脱险通道的乘客和船员用走廊内不允许设置家具。此外，还可允许在梯道环围内布置这些规则要求的由不燃材料制成的存放无危害的安全设备的储物柜。可允许在走廊设置饮水器和制冰机，但其应为固定式且不限制脱险通道的宽度。此要求还适用于走廊和梯道内的装饰花木布置、塑像或其他艺术品，如画和挂毯等。

3.4　客船客舱阳台上的家具和陈设

在客船上，客舱阳台的家具和陈设应符合第3.40.1、3.40.2、3.40.3、3.40.6和3.40.7条，除非阳台在符合第7.10和10.6.1.3条的固定式压力水雾和固定式探火和失火报警系统的保护之下。2008年7月1日以前建造的客船应在2008年7月1日以后的第一次检验之前符合本要求。

Regulation 6
Smoke generation potential and toxicity

1 Purpose

The purpose of this regulation is to reduce the hazard to life from smoke and toxic products generated during a fire in spaces where persons normally work or live. For this purpose, the quantity of smoke and toxic products released from combustible materials, including surface finishes, during fire shall be limited.

2.1 Paints, varnishes and other finishes

Paints, varnishes and other finishes used on exposed interior surfaces shall not be capable of producing excessive quantities of smoke and toxic products, this being determined in accordance with the Fire Test Procedures Code.

2.2 On passenger ships constructed on or after 1 July 2008, paints, varnishes and other finishes used on exposed surfaces of cabin balconies, excluding natural hard wood decking systems, shall not be capable of producing excessive quantities of smoke and toxic products, this being determined in accordance with the Fire Test Procedures Code.

3.1 Primary deck coverings

Primary deck coverings, if applied within accommodation and service spaces and control stations, shall be of approved material which will not give rise to smoke or toxic or explosive hazards at elevated temperatures, this being determined in accordance with the Fire Test Procedures Code.

3.2 On passenger ships constructed on or after 1 July 2008, primary deck coverings on cabin balconies shall not give rise to smoke, toxic or explosive hazards at elevated temperatures, this being determined in accordance with the Fire Test Procedures Code.

第6条
潜在的烟气产生和毒性

1　目的

本条的目的是减少在通常有人工作或生活的处所发生火灾时产生的烟气和生成的毒性物质所造成的生命危险。为此，应限制可燃材料，包括表面涂料在火灾中释放出的烟气和毒性物质的数量。

2.1　油漆、清漆和其他饰面涂料

用于外露表面的油漆、清漆和其他饰面涂料应不能产生过量的烟气及毒性产物，根据《耐火试验程序规则》确定。

2.2　在2008年7月1日或以后建造的客船上，客舱阳台的外露表面（天然硬木甲板铺板除外）使用的油漆、清漆和其他饰面涂料应不致产生过量的烟气及毒性物质，根据《耐火试验程序规则》确定。

3.1　甲板基层敷料

如果在起居处所、服务处所和控制站使用甲板基层敷料，应采用在高温下不致产生烟气、毒性物质或爆炸危险的认可材料，根据《耐火试验程序规则》确定。

3.2　在2008年7月1日或以后建造的客船上，客舱阳台的甲板基层敷料应在高温下不致产生烟气、毒性物质或爆炸危险，根据《耐火试验程序规则》确定。

Part C
Suppression of fire

Regulation 7
Detection and alarm

1 Purpose

The purpose of this regulation is to detect a fire in the space of origin and to provide for alarm for safe escape and fire-fighting activity. For this purpose, the following functional requirements shall be met:

.1 fixed fire detection and fire alarm system installations shall be suitable for the nature of the space, fire growth potential and potential generation of smoke and gases;

.2 manually operated call points shall be placed effectively to ensure a readily accessible means of notification; and

.3 fire patrols shall provide an effective means of detecting and locating fires and alerting the navigation bridge and fire teams.

2 General requirements

2.1 A fixed fire detection and fire alarm system shall be provided in accordance with the provisions of this regulation.

2.2 A fixed fire detection and fire alarm system and a sample extraction smoke detection system required in this regulation and other regulations in this part shall be of an approved type and comply with the Fire Safety Systems Code.

2.3 Where a fixed fire detection and fire alarm system is required for the protection of spaces other than those specified in paragraph 5.1, at least one detector complying with the Fire Safety Systems Code shall be installed in each such space.

2.4 A fixed fire detection and fire alarm system for passenger ships shall be capable of remotely and individually identifying each detector and manually operated call point.

3 Initial and periodical tests

3.1 The function of fixed fire detection and fire alarm systems required by the relevant regulations of this chapter shall be tested under varying conditions of ventilation after installation.

3.2 The function of fixed fire detection and fire alarm systems shall be periodically tested to the satisfaction of the Administration by means of equipment producing hot air at the appropriate temperature, or smoke or aerosol particles having the appropriate range of density or particle size, or other phenomena associated with incipient fires to which the detector is designed to respond.

C 部分
火灾的抑制

第 7 条
探测和报警

1　目的

本条的目的是探测火源处的火灾，并规定发出安全撤离和采取灭火行动的警报。为此，应满足下列功能性要求：

.1　固定式探火和失火报警系统装置应适合于处所的性质、潜在的火势增大和潜在的烟气产生；

.2　应有效设置手动报警按钮，以确保有随时可使用的报警通知方式；和

.3　消防巡逻应能作为一种有效方式探测和确定火灾位置以及向驾驶台和船上消防队发出警报。

2　一般要求

2.1　应按照本条的规定设有固定式探火和失火报警系统。

2.2　本条和本部分其他规则所要求的固定式探火和失火报警系统以及抽烟探火系统应为认可型并符合《消防安全系统规则》。

2.3　如果要求用固定式探火和失火报警系统对本条 5.1 所规定处所以外的处所提供保护，在每一这种处所至少应安装一个符合《消防安全系统规则》的探火装置。

2.4　客船固定式探火和失火报警系统须能够远距离单独识别每一个探测器及手动报点。

3　初始试验和定期试验

3.1　本章有关规则所要求的固定式探火和失火报警系统的功能应在安装后经过各种通风条件下的试验。

3.2　固定式探火和失火报警系统的功能应定期进行试验，并使主管机关满意。试验所用设备应按探测器的设计反应，产生相应温度下的热空气，或具有相应浓度或颗粒尺寸范围的烟雾或悬浮微粒，或与早期火灾相关的其他现象。

4 Protection of machinery spaces

4.1 Installation

A fixed fire detection and fire alarm system shall be installed in:

.1 periodically unattended machinery spaces;

.2 machinery spaces where:

  .1 the installation of automatic and remote control systems and equipment has been approved in lieu of continuous manning of the space; and

  .2 the main propulsion and associated machinery, including the main sources of electrical power, are provided with various degrees of automatic or remote control and are under continuous manned supervision from a control room; and

.3 enclosed spaces containing incinerators.

4.2 Design

The fixed fire detection and fire alarm system required in paragraph 4.1.1 shall be so designed and the detectors so positioned as to detect rapidly the onset of fire in any part of those spaces and under any normal conditions of operation of the machinery and variations of ventilation as required by the possible range of ambient temperatures. Except in spaces of restricted height and where their use is specially appropriate, detection systems using only thermal detectors shall not be permitted. The detection system shall initiate audible and visual alarms distinct in both respects from the alarms of any other system not indicating fire, in sufficient places to ensure that the alarms are heard and observed on the navigation bridge and by a responsible engineer officer. When the navigation bridge is unmanned, the alarm shall sound in a place where a responsible member of the crew is on duty.

5 Protection of accommodation and service spaces and control stations

5.1 Smoke detectors in accommodation spaces

Smoke detectors shall be installed in all stairways, corridors and escape routes within accommodation spaces as provided in paragraphs 5.2, 5.3 and 5.4. Consideration shall be given to the installation of special purpose smoke detectors within ventilation ducting.

5.2 Requirements for passenger ships carrying more than 36 passengers

A fixed fire detection and fire alarm system shall be so installed and arranged as to provide smoke detection in service spaces, control stations and accommodation spaces, including corridors, stairways and escape routes within accommodation spaces. Smoke detectors need not be fitted in private bathrooms and galleys. Spaces having little or no fire risk such as voids, public toilets, carbon dioxide rooms and similar spaces need not be fitted with a fixed fire detection and alarm system. Detectors fitted in cabins, when activated, shall also be capable of emitting, or cause to be emitted, an audible alarm within the space where they are located.

4　机器处所的保护

4.1　安装

应在下列处所安装一套固定式探火和失火报警系统：

.1　周期性无人值班的机器处所；

.2　下述机器处所：

　.1　自动和遥控系统以及设备的安装业经认可，用以代替处所的连续有人值班；和

　.2　主推进装置及其相关装置，包括主电源，采用不同程度的自动控制或遥控，并在控制室连续有人监视；和

.3　设有焚烧炉的封闭处所。

4.2　设计

本条4.1.1所要求的固定式探火和失火报警系统的设计和探测器的布置应能在上述处所的任何部位，在机器的任何正常工作状况和可能的环境温度范围内所要求的通风变化下，迅速探出火灾征兆。除处所的高度受到限制和特别适合使用的情况之外，不允许安装仅使用感温探测器的探火系统。探火系统应能在足够地点启动听觉和视觉报警，且这两种信号应不同于任何其他非火灾报警系统的信号，以确保驾驶台和负责的轮机员听到和看到该报警信号。当驾驶台无人值班时，应能在负责船员的值班处发出听觉报警。

5　起居处所和服务处所及控制站的保护

5.1　起居处所的感烟探测器

在起居处所内的所有梯道、走廊和脱险通道内应安装本条5.2、5.3和5.4规定的感烟探测器。还应考虑在通风管道内安装专用的感烟探测器。

5.2　对载客超过36人客船的要求

在服务处所、控制站和起居处所，包括起居处所内的走廊、梯道和脱险通道，应安装和布置固定式探火和失火报警系统，以探测这些处所的烟雾。客房内的盥洗室和厨房不必安装感烟探测器。极少有失火危险或无失火危险的处所，如空舱、公共盥洗室、二氧化碳室以及类似处所，不必安装固定式探火和报警系统。安装在舱室中的探测器在被触发时，须能够在其所在处所中发出或引发声响警报。

5.3 Requirements for passenger ships carrying not more than 36 passengers

There shall be installed throughout each separate zone, whether vertical or horizontal, in all accommodation and service spaces and, where it is considered necessary by the Administration, in control stations, except spaces which afford no substantial fire risk such as void spaces, sanitary spaces, etc., either:

.1 a fixed fire detection and fire alarm system so installed and arranged as to detect the presence of fire in such spaces and providing smoke detection in corridors, stairways and escape routes within accommodation spaces. Detectors fitted in cabins, when activated, shall also be capable of emitting, or cause to be emitted, an audible alarm within the space where they are located; or

.2 an automatic sprinkler, fire detection and fire alarm system of an approved type complying with the relevant requirements of the Fire Safety Systems Code and so installed and arranged as to protect such spaces and, in addition, a fixed fire detection and fire alarm system and so installed and arranged as to provide smoke detection in corridors, stairways and escape routes within accommodation spaces.

5.4 Protection of atriums in passenger ships

The entire main vertical zone containing the atrium shall be protected throughout with a smoke detection system.

5.5 Cargo ships

Accommodation and service spaces and control stations of cargo ships shall be protected by a fixed fire detection and fire alarm system and/or an automatic sprinkler, fire detection and fire alarm system as follows, depending on a protection method adopted in accordance with regulation 9.2.3.1.

5.5.1 *Method IC*—A fixed fire detection and fire alarm system shall be so installed and arranged as to provide smoke detection in all corridors, stairways and escape routes within accommodation spaces.

5.5.2 *Method IIC*—An automatic sprinkler, fire detection and fire alarm system of an approved type complying with the relevant requirements of the Fire Safety Systems Code shall be so installed and arranged as to protect accommodation spaces, galleys and other service spaces, except spaces which afford no substantial fire risk such as void spaces, sanitary spaces, etc. In addition, a fixed fire detection and fire alarm system shall be so installed and arranged as to provide smoke detection in all corridors, stairways and escape routes within accommodation spaces.

5.5.3 *Method IIIC*—A fixed fire detection and fire alarm system shall be so installed and arranged as to detect the presence of fire in all accommodation spaces and service spaces, providing smoke detection in corridors, stairways and escape routes within accommodation spaces, except spaces which afford no substantial fire risk such as void spaces, sanitary spaces, etc. In addition, a fixed fire detection and fire alarm system shall be so installed and arranged as to provide smoke detection in all corridors, stairways and escape routes within accommodation spaces.

5.3　对载客不超过36人客船的要求

除基本上无失火危险的处所,如空舱和卫生处所等以外,在所有起居处所和服务处所内的每一独立分隔区内(无论其为垂直还是水平)以及主管机关认为必要的位置以及控制站,均应按其整体范围安装下列两者之一:

.1　一个固定式探火和失火报警系统,其安装和布置能够探知上述处所的火灾并探测起居处所的走廊、梯道和脱险通道内的烟雾;安装在舱室中的探测器在被触发时,须能够在其所在处所中发出或引发声响警报;或

.2　一个符合《消防安全系统规则》相关要求的认可型自动喷水器、探火和失火报警系统,其安装和布置能够保护上述处所,此外还有一个固定式探火和失火报警系统,其安装和布置能够探测起居处所的走廊、梯道和脱险通道内的烟雾。

5.4　客船天井的保护

内含天井的整个主竖区应按其整体范围由感烟探测系统保护。

5.5　货船

货船的起居处所和服务处所及控制站应依据第9.2.3.1条所采用的保护方法,由以下固定式探火和失火报警系统和/或自动喷水器、探火和失火报警系统保护。

5.5.1　**ⅠC法**——应安装和布置一个固定式探火和失火报警系统,以探测起居处所的所有走廊、梯道和脱险通道内的烟雾。

5.5.2　**ⅡC法**——应安装和布置一个符合《消防安全系统规则》相关要求的认可型自动喷水器、探火和失火报警系统,以保护起居处所、厨房和其他服务处所,但空舱、卫生处所等基本上无失火危险的处所除外。此外,还应安装和布置一个固定式失火和探火报警系统,以探测起居处所的所有走廊、梯道和脱险通道内的烟雾。

5.5.3　**ⅢC法**——应安装和布置一个固定式探火和失火报警系统,以探测所有起居处所和服务处所内的火灾,以及各起居处所内所有的走廊、梯道和脱险通道内的烟雾,但空舱、卫生处所等基本上无失火危险的处所除外。

6 Protection of cargo spaces in passenger ships

A fixed fire detection and fire alarm system or a sample extraction smoke detection system shall be provided in any cargo space which, in the opinion of the Administration, is not accessible, except where it is shown to the satisfaction of the Administration that the ship is engaged on voyages of such short duration that it would be unreasonable to apply this requirement.

7 Manually operated call points

Manually operated call points complying with the Fire Safety Systems Code shall be installed throughout the accommodation spaces, service spaces and control stations. One manually operated call point shall be located at each exit. Manually operated call points shall be readily accessible in the corridors of each deck such that no part of the corridor is more than 20 m from a manually operated call point.

8 Fire patrols in passenger ships

8.1 Fire patrols

For ships carrying more than 36 passengers, an efficient patrol system shall be maintained so that an outbreak of fire may be promptly detected. Each member of the fire patrol shall be trained to be familiar with the arrangements of the ship as well as the location and operation of any equipment he may be called upon to use.

8.2 Inspection hatches

The construction of ceilings and bulkheads shall be such that it will be possible, without impairing the efficiency of the fire protection, for the fire patrols to detect any smoke originating in concealed and inaccessible places, except where in the opinion of the Administration there is no risk of fire originating in such places.

8.3 Two-way portable radiotelephone apparatus

Each member of the fire patrol shall be provided with a two-way portable radiotelephone apparatus.

9 Fire alarm signalling systems in passenger ships[①]

9.1 Passenger ships shall at all times when at sea, or in port (except when out of service), be so manned or equipped as to ensure that any initial fire alarm is immediately received by a responsible member of the crew.

9.2 The control panel of fixed fire detection and fire alarm systems shall be designed on the fail-safe principle (e.g. an open detector circuit shall cause an alarm condition).

---

① Refer to the *Code on alerts and indicators, 2009* (resolution A.1021(26), as may be amended).

6　客船上货物处所的保护

在主管机关认为不易到达的任何货物处所应装设固定式探火和失火报警系统或抽烟探火系统，但主管机关确信船舶所从事的短程航行证明应用本要求为不合理时除外。

7　手动报警按钮

符合《消防安全系统规则》的手动报警按钮应遍布起居处所、服务处所和控制站。每一出口都应装有手动报警按钮点。在每一层甲板的走廊内，手动报警按钮的位置应便于到达，且走廊的任何部位距手动报警按钮的距离都不得超过 20 m。

8　客船上的消防巡逻

8.1　消防巡逻

在载客超过 36 人的客船上应保持有效的巡逻制度，以便迅速探知火灾的发生。应对每名消防巡逻员进行培训，使其熟悉船舶的布置以及可能需要由他使用的任何设备的位置和操作方法。

8.2　检查孔

天花板及舱壁的构造应在不降低其防火效能的情况下，能使消防巡逻人员探知隐蔽和不易到达之处的烟源，但主管机关认为不致产生失火危险的地方除外。

8.3　双向便携式无线电话机

应为每名消防巡逻员配备双向便携式无线电话机。

9　客船的失火报警信号系统①

9.1　客船在海上或在港口的所有时间内（非营运时除外）的船员配置或设备配备应确保负责船员能立即接到任何初始失火报警。

9.2　固定式探火和失火报警系统的控制屏应根据自动防止故障原理（例如探测器开式回路应造成报警的条件）设计。

① 参见《2009 年报警器和指示器规则》（可能经修正的 A.1021(26)决议）。

9.3 Passenger ships carrying more than 36 passengers shall have the fire detection alarms for the systems required by paragraph 5.2 centralized in a continuously manned central control station. In addition, controls for remote closing of the fire doors and shutting down the ventilation fans shall be centralized in the same location. The ventilation fans shall be capable of reactivation by the crew at the continuously manned control station. The control panels in the central control station shall be capable of indicating open or closed positions of fire doors and closed or off status of the detectors, alarms and fans. The control panel shall be continuously powered and shall have an automatic change-over to standby power supply in case of loss of normal power supply. The control panel shall be powered from the main source of electrical power and the emergency source of electrical power defined by regulation Ⅱ-1/42 unless other arrangements are permitted by the regulations, as applicable.

9.4 A special alarm, operated from the navigation bridge or fire control station, shall be fitted to summon the crew. This alarm may be part of the ship's general alarm system and shall be capable of being sounded independently of the alarm to the passenger spaces.

10 Protection of cabin balconies on passenger ships

A fixed fire detection and fire alarm system complying with the provisions of the Fire Safety Systems Code shall be installed on cabin balconies of ships to which regulation 5.3.4 applies, when furniture and furnishings on such balconies are not as defined in regulations 3.40.1, 3.40.2, 3.40.3, 3.40.6 and 3.40.7.

Regulation 8
Control of smoke spread

1 Purpose

The purpose of this regulation is to control the spread of smoke in order to minimize the hazards from smoke. For this purpose, means for controlling smoke in atriums, control stations, machinery spaces and concealed spaces shall be provided.

2 Protection of control stations outside machinery spaces

Practicable measures shall be taken for control stations outside machinery spaces in order to ensure that ventilation, visibility and freedom from smoke are maintained so that, in the event of fire, the machinery and equipment contained therein may be supervised and continue to function effectively. Alternative and separate means of air supply shall be provided and air inlets of the two sources of supply shall be so disposed that the risk of both inlets drawing in smoke simultaneously is minimized. At the discretion of the Administration, such requirements need not apply to control stations situated on, and opening onto, an open deck or where local closing arrangements would be equally effective. The ventilation system serving safety centres may be derived from the ventilation system serving the navigation bridge, unless located in an adjacent main vertical zone.

9.3 载客超过36人的客船应将本条5.2要求的系统所使用的探火报警装置集中于一个连续有人值班的集中控制站。此外，遥控关闭防火门和遥控停止风机的控制装置也应集中于同一处所。风机应能在连续有人值班的控制站由船员重新启动。集中控制站的控制屏应能显示防火门开启或关闭的状态和探测器、报警器和风机的接通或断开状态。控制屏应能够得到连续供电，并在万一正常供电电路失电时自动切换到备用供电电路。除非有相应的适用规定允许其他布置，控制屏应由第Ⅱ-1/42条规定的主电源和应急电源供电。

9.4 应设置一个由驾驶室或消防控制站操纵的召集船员的专用报警器。该报警器可以是船上通用报警系统的一部分，并应能与乘客处所的报警分开而单独发出报警。

10　客船客舱阳台的保护

在第5.3.4条适用的船舶的客舱阳台上，当其家具与陈设不是第3.40.1、3.40.2、3.40.3、3.40.6和3.40.7条所定义者时，应安装符合《消防安全系统规则》规定的固定式探火和失火报警系统。

第8条
控制烟气蔓延

1　目的

本条的目的是控制烟气的蔓延，以最大限度减少烟气的危害。为此，应有控制天井、控制站、机器处所和隐蔽处所内烟气的装置。

2　机器处所外面的控制站的保护

应采取实际可行的措施确保机器处所外面的控制站保持通风和能见度，且不受烟气妨碍，以便在失火时，位于其中的机械和设备可以受到监管并继续有效地运转。应设有交替和分开的供气装置，这两个供气源的进气口布置应使两个进气口同时吸进烟气的危险性减至最小。经主管机关同意，上述要求不必适用于位于开敞甲板上和开口通向开敞甲板的控制站，或具有同等效用就地关闭装置的控制站。安全中心的通风系统可为驾驶室通风系统的分支，但位于相邻主竖区者除外。

3 Release of smoke from machinery spaces

3.1 The provisions of this paragraph shall apply to machinery spaces of category A and, where the Administration considers it desirable, to other machinery spaces.

3.2 Suitable arrangements shall be made to permit the release of smoke, in the event of fire, from the space to be protected, subject to the provisions of regulation 9.5.2.1 The normal ventilation systems may be acceptable for this purpose.

3.3 Means of control shall be provided for permitting the release of smoke and such controls shall be located outside the space concerned so that they will not be cut off in the event of fire in the space they serve.

3.4 In passenger ships, the controls required by paragraph 3.3 shall be situated at one control position or grouped in as few positions as possible to the satisfaction of the Administration. Such positions shall have a safe access from the open deck.

4 Draught stops

Air spaces enclosed behind ceilings, panelling or linings shall be divided by close-fitting draught stops spaced not more than 14 m apart. In the vertical direction, such enclosed air spaces, including those behind linings of stairways, trunks, etc., shall be closed at each deck.

5 Smoke extraction systems in atriums of passenger ships

Atriums shall be equipped with a smoke extraction system. The smoke extraction system shall be activated by the required smoke detection system and be capable of manual control. The fans shall be sized such that the entire volume within the space can be exhausted in 10 min or less.

Regulation 9
Containment of fire

1 Purpose

The purpose of this regulation is to contain a fire in the space of origin. For this purpose, the following functional requirements shall be met:

- .1 the ship shall be subdivided by thermal and structural boundaries;
- .2 thermal insulation of boundaries shall have due regard to the fire risk of the space and adjacent spaces; and
- .3 the fire integrity of the divisions shall be maintained at openings and penetrations.

2 Thermal and structural boundaries

2.1 Thermal and structural subdivision

Ships of all types shall be subdivided into spaces by thermal and structural divisions having regard to the fire risks of the spaces.

3 机器处所烟气的排出

3.1 本节规定应适用于 A 类机器处所,如果主管机关认为合适,并适用于其他机器处所。

3.2 在满足第 9.5.2.1 条的前提下,应通过适当布置,允许在失火时烟气从被保护的处所排出。通常的通风系统可接受用于此目的。

3.3 应设有允许烟气排出的控制装置,这种控制装置应位于有关处所的外面,从而在其所服务的处所发生火灾时不致被隔断。

3.4 在客船上,3.3 所要求的控制装置应位于一个控制位置或集中于尽可能少的位置,并使主管机关满意。这些位置应能从开敞甲板安全到达。

4 挡风条

封闭在天花板、镶板或衬板后面的空隙应以紧密安装且间距不超过 14 m 的挡风条做分隔。在垂直方向上,此类封闭空隙,包括梯道、围壁通道等衬板后的空隙在内,应在每层甲板处加以封堵。

5 客船天井内的抽烟系统

天井应装设抽烟系统。该抽烟系统应由所要求的感烟探测系统启动,并能够手动控制。风机的容量应能在 10 min 或更短的时间内将该处所容纳的全部烟气排出。

第 9 条
火灾的限制

1 目的

本条的目的是将火灾遏制在火源处所内。为此,应满足下列功能要求:

.1 应通过耐热和结构性限界面将船舶分隔成若干区;

.2 限界面的隔热应充分考虑到处所及其相邻处所的火灾危险;和

.3 在开口和贯穿件处应保持分隔的耐火完整性。

2 耐热和结构性限界面

2.1 耐热和结构性分隔

对于各类船舶,都应在考虑了各处所的失火危险的基础上,通过耐热和结构性分隔划分为若干处所。

2.2 Passenger ships

2.2.1 Main vertical zones and horizontal zones

2.2.1.1.1 In ships carrying more than 36 passengers, the hull, superstructure and deckhouses shall be subdivided into main vertical zones by "A-60" class divisions. Steps and recesses shall be kept to a minimum, but where they are necessary they shall also be "A-60" class divisions. Where a category (5), (9) or (10) space defined in paragraph 2.2.3.2.2 is on one side or where fuel oil tanks are on both sides of the division the standard may be reduced to "A-0".

2.2.1.1.2 In ships carrying not more than 36 passengers, the hull, superstructure and deckhouses in way of accommodation and service spaces shall be subdivided into main vertical zones by "A" class divisions. These divisions shall have insulation values in accordance with tables in paragraph 2.2.4.

2.2.1.2 As far as practicable, the bulkheads forming the boundaries of the main vertical zones above the bulkhead deck shall be in line with watertight subdivision bulkheads situated immediately below the bulkhead deck. The length and width of main vertical zones may be extended to a maximum of 48 m in order to bring the ends of main vertical zones to coincide with watertight subdivision bulkheads or in order to accommodate a large public space extending for the whole length of the main vertical zone provided that the total area of the main vertical zone is not greater than 1,600 m^2 on any deck. The length or width of a main vertical zone is the maximum distance between the furthermost points of the bulkheads bounding it.

2.2.1.3 Such bulkheads shall extend from deck to deck and to the shell or other boundaries.

2.2.1.4 Where a main vertical zone is subdivided by horizontal "A" class divisions into horizontal zones for the purpose of providing an appropriate barrier between a zone with sprinklers and a zone without sprinklers, the divisions shall extend between adjacent main vertical zone bulkheads and to the shell or exterior boundaries of the ship and shall be insulated in accordance with the fire insulation and integrity values given in table 9.4.

2.2.1.5.1 On ships designed for special purposes, such as automobile or railroad car ferries, where the provision of main vertical zone bulkheads would defeat the purpose for which the ship is intended, equivalent means for controlling and limiting a fire shall be substituted and specifically approved by the Administration. Service spaces and ship stores shall not be located on ro-ro decks unless protected in accordance with the applicable regulations.

2.2.1.5.2 However, in a ship with special category spaces, such spaces shall comply with the applicable provisions of regulation 20 and, where such compliance would be inconsistent with other requirements for passenger ships specified in this chapter, the requirements of regulation 20 shall prevail.

2.2 客船

2.2.1 主竖区和水平区

2.2.1.1.1 载客超过36人的客船，其船体、上层建筑和甲板室应以"A-60"级分隔分为若干主竖区。阶层和壁龛应保持在最低限度，但若有必要，其也应为"A-60"级分隔。如果在主竖区分隔一侧的处所为本条2.2.3.2.2所定义的(5)、(9)或(10)类处所，或在分隔的两侧均为燃油舱，则该主竖区分隔标准可降为"A-0"级。

2.2.1.1.2 载客不超过36人的客船，在其起居处所和服务处所的船体、上层建筑及甲板室应以"A"级分隔分为若干主竖区。此分隔的隔热值，应符合本条2.2.4中相应的表列规定。

2.2.1.2 只要实际可行，舱壁甲板以上形成主竖区限界面的舱壁，应与直接在舱壁甲板以下的水密分舱舱壁位于同一直线上。为使主竖区的端部与水密分舱舱壁相一致，或为提供一个长度伸及主竖区全长的大型公共处所，主竖区的长度和宽度最大可延伸至48 m，但在任一层甲板上主竖区的总面积不得大于1 600 m^2。主竖区的长度或宽度范围为主竖区限界面舱壁的最远点之间的最大距离。

2.2.1.3 这种舱壁应由甲板延伸至甲板，并延伸至船壳或其他限界面。

2.2.1.4 如果某一主竖区以水平"A"级分隔再分为若干水平区，用以在船上设有喷水器系统区域与未设有喷水器系统区域之间提供一适当的屏障，此项水平分隔应在相邻两个主竖区舱壁之间延伸且延伸至船舶的壳板或外部限界面，并应按表9.4所列的耐火隔热性和完整性的等级予以隔热。

2.2.1.5.1 为特殊用途而设计的船舶，例如汽车或铁路车辆渡船，如果设置主竖区舱壁将影响船舶预期的用途，应以能控制和限制火灾的等效装置代替，并应经主管机关专门认可。除非根据适用的规则予以保护，否则服务处所和船舶储物舱不得位于滚装甲板。

2.2.1.5.2 但是，在设有特种处所的船上，此种处所应符合第20条的适用规定，并且如果符合该条规定与本章关于客船的其他要求有矛盾，应以第20条的规定为准。

2.2.2 Bulkheads within a main vertical zone

2.2.2.1 For ships carrying more than 36 passengers, bulkheads which are not required to be "A" class divisions shall be at least "B" class or "C" class divisions as prescribed in the tables in paragraph 2.2.3.

2.2.2.2 For ships carrying not more than 36 passengers, bulkheads within accommodation and service spaces which are not required to be "A" class divisions shall be at least "B" class or "C" class divisions as prescribed in the tables in paragraph 2.2.4. In addition, corridor bulkheads, where not required to be "A" class, shall be "B" class divisions which shall extend from deck to deck except:

.1 when continuous "B" class ceilings or linings are fitted on both sides of the bulkhead, the portion of the bulkhead behind the continuous ceiling or lining shall be of material which, in thickness and composition, is acceptable in the construction of "B" class divisions, but which shall be required to meet "B" class integrity standards only in so far as is reasonable and practicable in the opinion of the Administration; and

.2 in the case of a ship protected by an automatic sprinkler system complying with the provisions of the Fire Safety Systems Code, the corridor bulkheads may terminate at a ceiling in the corridor provided such bulkheads and ceilings are of "B" class standard in compliance with paragraph 2.2.4. All doors and frames in such bulkheads shall be of non-combustible materials and shall have the same fire integrity as the bulkhead in which they are fitted.

2.2.2.3 Bulkheads required to be "B" class divisions, except corridor bulkheads as prescribed in paragraph 2.2.2.2, shall extend from deck to deck and to the shell or other boundaries. However, where a continuous "B" class ceiling or lining is fitted on both sides of a bulkhead which is at least of the same fire resistance as the adjoining bulkhead, the bulkhead may terminate at the continuous ceiling or lining.

2.2.3 Fire integrity of bulkheads and decks in ships carrying more than 36 passengers

2.2.3.1 In addition to complying with the specific provisions for fire integrity of bulkheads and decks of passenger ships, the minimum fire integrity of all bulkheads and decks shall be as prescribed in tables 9.1 and 9.2. Where, due to any particular structural arrangements in the ship, difficulty is experienced in determining from the tables the minimum fire integrity value of any divisions, such values shall be determined to the satisfaction of the Administration.

2.2.3.2 The following requirements shall govern application of the tables:

.1 Table 9.1 shall apply to bulkheads not bounding either main vertical zones or horizontal zones. Table 9.2 shall apply to decks not forming steps in main vertical zones nor bounding horizontal zones.

2.2.2　主竖区内的舱壁

2.2.2.1　对载客超过36人的客船，不要求为“A”级分隔的舱壁应至少为本条2.2.3的表列“B”级或“C”级分隔。

2.2.2.2　对载客不超过36人的客船，其起居处所和服务处所内不要求为“A”级分隔的舱壁应至少为本条2.2.4的表列“B”级或“C”级分隔。此外，不要求为“A”级分隔的走廊舱壁应为从甲板延伸至甲板的“B”级分隔，但下列情况除外：

.1　当在舱壁的两侧设置连续“B”级天花板或衬板时，连续天花板或衬板后面的舱壁部分所用材料的厚度和构成应适合于“B”级分隔结构，但只有在主管机关认为合理和可行的范围内，才应要求该材料达到“B”级完整性标准；和

.2　对由符合《消防安全系统规则》规定的自动喷水器系统所保护的船舶，只要走廊舱壁和天花板符合本条2.2.4的“B”级标准，走廊舱壁可在走廊内天花板处终止。这些舱壁上的所有门和门框应为不燃材料，并与其所安装处的舱壁具有同样的耐火完整性。

2.2.2.3　除了本条2.2.2.2规定的走廊舱壁外，要求为“B”级分隔的舱壁应由甲板延伸至甲板，并延伸至船壳或其他限界面。但若在舱壁两侧均设有至少与邻接舱壁具有同样耐火性能的连续“B”级天花板或衬板，该舱壁可终止于连续的天花板或衬板。

2.2.3　载客超过36人的船舶舱壁和甲板的耐火完整性

2.2.3.1　除符合客船舱壁和甲板耐火完整性的具体规定外，所有舱壁和甲板的最低耐火完整性还应符合表9.1和9.2的规定。如果因船舶的特殊结构布置而使任何分隔的最低耐火完整性等级难于根据这些表予以确定时，此种等级的确定应使主管机关满意。

2.2.3.2　各表的适用范围应以下列要求为准：

.1　表9.1应适用于不作为主竖区或水平区限界面的舱壁。表9.2应适用于不在主竖区内形成阶层也不构成水平区限界面的甲板。

.2 For determining the appropriate fire integrity standards to be applied to boundaries between adjacent spaces, such spaces are classified according to their fire risk as shown in categories (1) to (14) below. Where the contents and use of a space are such that there is a doubt as to its classification for the purpose of this regulation, or where it is possible to assign two or more classifications to a space, it shall be treated as a space within the relevant category having the most stringent boundary requirements. Smaller, enclosed rooms within a space that have less than 30% communicating openings to that space are considered separate spaces. The fire integrity of the boundary bulkheads and decks of such smaller rooms shall be as prescribed in tables 9.1 and 9.2. The title of each category is intended to be typical rather than restrictive. The number in parentheses preceding each category refers to the applicable column or row in the tables.

(**1**) Control stations

Spaces containing emergency sources of power and lighting.

Wheelhouse and chartroom.

Spaces containing the ship's radio equipment.

Fire control stations.

Control room for propulsion machinery when located outside the propulsion machinery space.

Spaces containing centralized fire alarm equipment.

Spaces containing centralized emergency public address system stations and equipment.

(**2**) Stairways

Interior stairways, lifts, totally enclosed emergency escape trunks, and escalators (other than those wholly contained within the machinery spaces) for passengers and crew and enclosures thereto.

In this connection, a stairway which is enclosed at only one level shall be regarded as part of the space from which it is not separated by a fire door.

(**3**) Corridors

Passenger and crew corridors and lobbies.

(**4**) Evacuation stations and external escape routes

Survival craft stowage area.

Open deck spaces and enclosed promenades forming lifeboat and liferaft embarkation and lowering stations.

Assembly stations, internal and external.

.2　为了确定相邻处所限界面所适用的相应耐火完整性标准,这类处所按其失火危险程度分为下列(1)至(14)类。如果某一处所内的东西和用途致使按本条规定进行分类存在疑问,或有可能为某一处所指定两个或以上类别,则该处所应视作具有最严格限界面要求的相关类别的处所。一个处所内各个较小的围蔽舱室,如果其与该处所相通的开口小于30%,则视为单独处所。这种较小舱室的限界面舱壁和甲板的耐火完整性应符合表9.1和9.2的规定。每一类别的名称系典型举例,而非限制性规定。每类前面括号内的数字是指表内相应的列或行。

(1)　控制站

设有应急电源和应急照明电源的处所。

驾驶室和海图室。

设有船舶无线电设备的处所。

消防控制站。

位于推进装置处所外面的推进装置控制室。

设有集中失火报警设备的处所。

设有集中应急公共广播系统站和设备的处所。

(2)　梯道

乘客和船员用的内部梯道、升降机、完全封闭的紧急脱险围井、自动扶梯(完全设在机器处所内者除外),以及通往上述梯道的环围。

对此,仅在一层甲板设有环围的梯道应视为未用防火门与其隔开的处所的一部分。

(3)　走廊

乘客及船员用的走廊和门厅。

(4)　撤离站和外部脱险通道

救生艇筏存放区。

作为救生艇和救生筏登乘与降落站的开敞甲板处所和围蔽游步甲板处所。

内部和外部集合站。

External stairs and open decks used for escape routes.

The ship's side to the waterline in the lightest seagoing condition, superstructure and deckhouse sides situated below and adjacent to the liferaft and evacuation slide embarkation areas.

(**5**) Open deck spaces

Open deck spaces and enclosed promenades clear of lifeboat and liferaft embarkation and lowering stations. To be considered in this category, enclosed promenades shall have no significant fire risk, meaning that furnishings shall be restricted to deck furniture. In addition, such spaces shall be naturally ventilated by permanent openings.

Air spaces (the space outside superstructures and deckhouses).

(**6**) Accommodation spaces of minor fire risk

Cabins containing furniture and furnishings of restricted fire risk.

Offices and dispensaries containing furniture and furnishings of restricted fire risk.

Public spaces containing furniture and furnishings of restricted fire risk and having a deck area of less than 50 m^2.

(**7**) Accommodation spaces of moderate fire risk

Spaces as in category (6) above but containing furniture and furnishings of other than restricted fire risk.

Public spaces containing furniture and furnishings of restricted fire risk and having a deck area of 50 m^2 or more.

Isolated lockers and small store-rooms in accommodation spaces having areas less than 4 m^2(in which flammable liquids are not stowed).

Motion picture projection and film stowage rooms. Diet kitchens (containing no open flame).

Cleaning gear lockers (in which flammable liquids are not stowed).

Laboratories (in which flammable liquids are not stowed).

Pharmacies.

Small drying rooms (having a deck area of 4 m^2 or less).

Specie rooms.

Operating rooms.

用作脱险通道的外部梯道和开敞甲板。

最轻载航行水线之上的舷侧,位于救生艇筏和撤离滑道的登乘区域下方且相邻的上层建筑和甲板室舷侧。

（5） 开敞甲板处所

救生艇和救生筏登乘与降落站以外的开敞甲板处所和围蔽游步甲板处所。如果考虑将围蔽游步甲板处所归为此类,其应无大的失火危险,即其内应只设有甲板家具。此外,此类处所还应通过固定开口进行自然通风。露天处所(上层建筑和甲板室外面的处所)。

（6） 具有较小失火危险的起居处所

设有限制失火危险的家具和陈设的居住舱室。

设有限制失火危险的家具和陈设的办公室和诊疗室。设有限制失火危险的家具和陈设的公共处所,且其甲板面积小于 50 m^2。

（7） 具有中等失火危险的起居处所

如同上述第(6)类的处所,但其内设有未限制失火危险的家具和陈设。

设有限制失火危险的家具和陈设的公共处所,其甲板面积等于或大于 50 m^2。

起居处所内面积小于 4 m^2 的独立小间及小储物间(不储存易燃液体)。

电影放映室和影片储藏室。厨房(无明火者)。

清洁用具储藏室(不存放易燃液体)。

实验室(不存放易燃液体)。

药房。

小干燥间(面积等于或小于 4 m^2)。

贵重物品保管室。

手术室。

(**8**) Accommodation spaces of greater fire risk

Public spaces containing furniture and furnishings of other than restricted fire risk and having a deck area of 50 m^2 or more.

Barber shops and beauty parlours.

Saunas.

Sale shops.

(**9**) Sanitary and similar spaces

Communal sanitary facilities, showers, baths, water closets, etc.

Small laundry rooms.

Indoor swimming pool area.

Isolated pantries containing no cooking appliances in accommodation spaces.

Private sanitary facilities shall be considered a portion of the space in which they are located.

(**10**) Tanks, voids and auxiliary machinery spaces having little or no fire risk

Water tanks forming part of the ship's structure.

Voids and cofferdams.

Auxiliary machinery spaces which do not contain machinery having a pressure lubrication system and where storage of combustibles is prohibited, such as:

> ventilation and air-conditioning rooms; windlass room; steering gear room; stabilizer equipment room; electrical propulsion motor room; rooms containing section switchboards and purely electrical equipment other than oil-filled electrical transformers (above 10 kVA); shaft alleys and pipe tunnels; and spaces for pumps and refrigeration machinery (not handling or using flammable liquids).

Closed trunks serving the spaces listed above.

Other closed trunks such as pipe and cable trunks.

(**11**) Auxiliary machinery spaces, cargo spaces, cargo and other oil tanks and other similar spaces of moderate fire risk

Cargo oil tanks.

Cargo holds, trunkways and hatchways.

Refrigerated chambers.

Oil fuel tanks (where installed in a separate space with no machinery).

（**8**）　具有较大失火危险的起居处所

设有未限制失火危险的家具和陈设的公共处所，且其甲板面积等于或大于 50 m^2。

理发室和美容室。

桑拿房。

小卖部。

（**9**）　卫生间及类似处所

公共卫生设施、淋浴室、盆浴室、厕所等。

小洗衣间。

室内游泳场所。

起居处所内无烹调设备的单独配膳室。

个人卫生设施应视为所在处所的一部分。

（**10**）　极少或无失火危险的液舱、空舱及辅机处所构成船体结构部分的水舱

作为船舶结构的水箱。

空舱及隔离空舱。

不设置具有压力润滑系统的机器的辅机处所，且在该处所内禁止储存可燃物品，例如：

通风机和空调机室；锚机室；舵机室；减摇设备室；电力推进电动机室；设有分区配电板和除浸油式电力变压器（10 kVA 以上）以外的纯电气设备舱室；轴隧及管隧；泵及制冷机处所（不输送或使用易燃液体）。

为上述处所服务的封闭围井。

其他封闭围井，如管道和电缆围井。

（**11**）　具有中等失火危险的辅机处所、货物处所、货油舱和其他油舱以及其他类似处所

货油舱。

货舱、货舱围壁通道及舱口。

冷藏室。

燃油舱（设在无机器的单独处所内）。

Shaft alleys and pipe tunnels allowing storage of combustibles.

Auxiliary machinery spaces as in category (10) which contain machinery having a pressure lubrication system or where storage of combustibles is permitted.

Oil fuel filling stations.

Spaces containing oil-filled electrical transformers (above 10 kVA).

Spaces containing turbine and reciprocating steam engine driven auxiliary generators and small internal combustion engines of power output up to 110 kW driving generators, sprinkler, drencher or fire pumps, bilge pumps, etc.

Closed trunks serving the spaces listed above.

(**12**) Machinery spaces and main galleys

Main propulsion machinery rooms (other than electric propulsion motor rooms) and boiler rooms.

Auxiliary machinery spaces other than those in categories (10) and (11) which contain internal combustion machinery or other oil-burning, heating or pumping units.

Main galleys and annexes.

Trunks and casings to the spaces listed above.

(**13**) Store-rooms, workshops, pantries, etc.

Main pantries not annexed to galleys.

Main laundry.

Large drying rooms (having a deck area of more than 4 m^2).

Miscellaneous stores.

Mail and baggage rooms.

Garbage rooms.

Workshops (not part of machinery spaces, galleys, etc.).

Lockers and store-rooms having areas greater than 4 m^2, other than those spaces that have provisions for the storage of flammable liquids.

(**14**) Other spaces in which flammable liquids are stowed

Paint lockers.

Store-rooms containing flammable liquids (including dyes, medicines, etc.).

Laboratories (in which flammable liquids are stowed).

允许储存可燃物的轴隧和管隧。

第(10)类中所述的辅机处所,其内设置具有压力润滑系统的机器或允许储藏可燃物。

燃油加油站。

设有浸油式电力变压器(10 kVA 以上)的处所。

设有由涡轮机及往复式蒸汽机驱动的辅助发电机、由输出功率为110 kW及以下的小内燃机驱动的发电机、喷水器泵、水幕喷头泵或消防泵、舱底泵等的处所。

用于上述处所的封闭围井。

(12) 机器处所和主厨房

主推进机舱(电力推进电动机舱除外)及锅炉舱。

第(10)和(11)类以外的设有内燃机或其他燃油、加热或泵送装置的辅机处所。

主厨房及其附属间。

上述处所的围井及舱篷。

(13) 储藏室、工作间、配膳室等

不属于厨房的主配膳室。

主洗衣间。

大干燥间(甲板面积大于4 m^2)。

杂物间。

邮件和行李室。

垃圾间。

工作间(不是机器处所、厨房等的一部分)。

面积大于4 m^2 的储藏间和储物间,存放易燃液体的处所除外。

(14) 储藏易燃液体的其他处所

油漆间。

存放易燃液体的储物间(包括染料、药品等)。

实验室(室内存放易燃液体)。

.3 Where a single value is shown for the fire integrity of a boundary between two spaces, that value shall apply in all cases.

.4 Notwithstanding the provisions of paragraph 2. 2. 2, there are no special requirements for material or integrity of boundaries where only a dash appears in the tables.

.5 The Administration shall determine in respect of category (5) spaces whether the insulation values in table 9. 1 shall apply to ends of deckhouses and superstructures, and whether the insulation values in table 9.2 shall apply to weather decks. In no case shall the requirements of category (5) of tables 9.1 or 9.2 necessitate enclosure of spaces which in the opinion of the Administration need not be enclosed.

Table 9.1 Bulkheads not bounding either main vertical zones or horizontal zones

Spaces		(1)	(2)	(3)	(4)	(5)	(6)	(7)	(8)	(9)	(10)	(11)	(12)	(13)	(14)
Control stations	(1)	B-0[a]	A-0	A-0	A-0	A-0	A-60	A-60	A-60	A-0	A-0	A-60	A-60	A-60	A-60
Stairways	(2)		A-0[a]	A-0	A-0	A-0	A-0	A-15	A-15	A-0[c]	A-0	A-15	A-30	A-15	A-30
Corridors	(3)			B-15	A-60	A-0	B-15	B-15	B-15	B-15	A-0	A-15	A-30	A-0	A-30
Evacuation stations and external escape routes	(4)					A-0	A-60[b,d]	A-60[b,d]	A-60[b,d]	A-0[d]	A-0	A-60[b]	A-60[b]	A-60[b]	A-60[b]
Open deck spaces	(5)						A-0	A-0	A-0	A-0	A-0	A-0	A-0	A-0	A-0
Accommodation spaces of minor fire risk	(6)						B-0	B-0	B-0	C	A-0	A-0	A-30	A-0	A-30
Accommodation spaces of moderate fire risk	(7)							B-0	B-0	C	A-0	A-15	A-60	A-15	A-60
Accommodation spaces of greater fire risk	(8)								B-0	C	A-0	A-30	A-60	A-15	A-60
Sanitary and similar spaces	(9)									C	A-0	A-0	A-0	A-0	A-0
Tanks, voids and auxiliary machinery spaces having little or no fire risk	(10)										A-0[a]	A-0	A-0	A-0	A-0
Auxiliary machinery spaces, cargo spaces, cargo and other oil tanks and other similar spaces of moderate fire risk	(11)											A-0[a]	A-0	A-0	A-15
Machinery spaces and main galleys	(12)												A-0[a]	A-0	A-60
Store-rooms, workshops, pantries, etc.	(13)													A-0[a]	A-0
Other spaces in which flammable liquids are stowed	(14)														A-30

See notes following table 9.2.

.3　如果两个处所之间的限界面的耐火完整性在表中仅有一个等级，则该等级适用于各种情况。

.4　尽管有本条2.2.2的规定，但如在表中只标有“—”，则对限界面的材料或完整性无具体要求。

.5　对于第(5)类处所，主管机关应确定表9.1的隔热值是否适用于甲板室及上层建筑的末端，以及表9.2的隔热值是否适用于露天甲板。如果主管机关认为不必围蔽，则应无须按表9.1或9.2中的第(5)类要求围蔽处所。

表9.1　不作为主竖区或水平区限界面的舱壁

处所		(1)	(2)	(3)	(4)	(5)	(6)	(7)	(8)	(9)	(10)	(11)	(12)	(13)	(14)
控制站	(1)	B-0[a]	A-0	A-0	A-0	A-0	A-60	A-60	A-60	A-0	A-0	A-60	A-60	A-60	A-60
梯道	(2)		A-0[a]	A-0	A-0	A-0	A-0	A-15	A-15	A-0[c]	A-0	A-15	A-30	A-15	A-30
走廊	(3)			B-15	A-60	A-0	B-15	B-15	B-15	B-15	A-0	A-15	A-30	A-0	A-30
撤离站和外部脱险通道	(4)					A-0	A-60[b,d]	A-60[b,d]	A-60[b,d]	A-0[d]	A-0	A-60[b]	A-60[b]	A-60[b]	A-60[b]
开敞甲板处所	(5)						A-0	A-0	A-0	A-0	A-0	A-0	A-0	A-0	A-0
具有较小失火危险的起居处所	(6)						B-0	B-0	B-0	C	A-0	A-0	A-30	A-0	A-30
具有中等失火危险的起居处所	(7)							B-0	B-0	C	A-0	A-15	A-60	A-15	A-60
具有较大失火危险的起居处所	(8)								B-0	C	A-0	A-30	A-60	A-15	A-60
卫生间及类似处所	(9)									C	A-0	A-0	A-0	A-0	A-0
极少或无失火危险的液舱、空舱及辅机处所	(10)										A-0[a]	A-0	A-0	A-0	A-0
具有中等失火危险的辅机处所、货物处所、货油舱和其他油舱以及其他类似处所	(11)											A-0[a]	A-0	A-0	A-15
机器处所和主厨房	(12)												A-0[a]	A-0	A-60
储藏室、工作间、配膳室等	(13)													A-0[a]	A-0
储藏易燃液体的其他处所	(14)														A-30

见表9.2的注释。

Table 9.2 Decks not forming steps in main vertical zones nor bounding horizontal zones

Space below ↓ Space above →		(1)	(2)	(3)	(4)	(5)	(6)	(7)	(8)	(9)	(10)	(11)	(12)	(13)	(14)
Control stations	(1)	A-30	A-30	A-15	A-0	A-0	A-0	A-15	A-30	A-0	A-0	A-0	A-60	A-0	A-60
Stairways	(2)	A-0	A-0	A-0	A-0	A-0	A-0	A-0	A-0	A-0	A-0	A-0	A-30	A-0	A-30
Corridors	(3)	A-15	A-0	A-0[a]	A-60	A-0	A-0	A-15	A-15	A-0	A-0	A-0	A-30	A-0	A-30
Evacuation stations and external escape routes	(4)	A-0	A-0	A-0	A-0	–	A-0	A-0	A-0	A-0	A-0	A-0	A-0	A-0	A-0
Open deck spaces	(5)	A-0	A-0	A-0	A-0	–	A-0	A-0	A-0	A-0	A-0	A-0	A-0	A-0	A-0
Accommodation spaces of minor fire risk	(6)	A-60	A-15	A-0	A-60	A-0	A-0	A-0	A-0	A-0	A-0	A-0	A-0	A-0	A-0
Accommodation spaces of moderate fire risk	(7)	A-60	A-15	A-15	A-60	A-0	A-0	A-15	A-15	A-0	A-0	A-0	A-0	A-0	A-0
Accommodation spaces of greater fire risk	(8)	A-60	A-15	A-15	A-60	A-0	A-15	A-15	A-30	A-0	A-0	A-0	A-0	A-0	A-0
Sanitary and similar spaces	(9)	A-0	A-0	A-0	A-0	A-0	A-0	A-0	A-0	A-0	A-0	A-0	A-0	A-0	A-0
Tanks, voids and auxiliary machinery spaces having little or no fire risk	(10)	A-0	A-0	A-0	A-0	A-0	A-0	A-0	A-0	A-0	A-0[a]	A-0	A-0	A-0	A-0
Auxiliary machinery spaces, cargo spaces, cargo and other oil tanks and other similar spaces of moderate fire risk	(11)	A-60	A-60	A-60	A-60	A-0	A-0	A-15	A-30	A-0	A-0	A-0[a]	A-0	A-0	A-30
Machinery spaces and main galleys	(12)	A-60	A-60	A-60	A-60	A-0	A-60	A-60	A-60	A-0	A-0	A-30	A-30[a]	A-0	A-60
Store-rooms, workshops, pantries, etc.	(13)	A-60	A-30	A-15	A-60	A-0	A-15	A-30	A-30	A-0	A-0	A-0	A-0	A-0	A-0
Other spaces in which flammable liquids are stowed	(14)	A-60	A-60	A-60	A-60	A-0	A-30	A-60	A-60	A-0	A-0	A-0	A-0	A-0	A-0

Notes: To be applied to tables 9.1 and 9.2, as appropriate.

a Where adjacent spaces are in the same numerical category and superscript "a" appears, a bulkhead or deck between such spaces need not be fitted if deemed unnecessary by the Administration. For example, in category (12) a bulkhead need not be required between a galley and its annexed pantries provided the pantry bulkhead and decks maintain the integrity of the galley boundaries. A bulkhead is, however, required between a galley and machinery space even though both spaces are in category (12).

b The ship's side, to the waterline in the lightest seagoing condition, superstructure and deckhouse sides situated below and adjacent to liferafts and evacuation slides may be reduced to "A-30".

c Where public toilets are installed completely within the stairway enclosure, the public toilet bulkhead within the stairway enclosure can be of "B" class integrity.

d Where spaces of categories (6), (7), (8) and (9) are located completely within the outer perimeter of the assembly station, the bulkheads of these spaces are allowed to be of "B-0" class integrity. Control positions for audio, video and light installations may be considered as part of the assembly station.

2.2.3.3 Continuous "B" class ceilings or linings, in association with the relevant decks or bulkheads, may be accepted as contributing, wholly or in part, to the required insulation and integrity of a division.

表 9.2　在主竖区内既不形成阶层也不作为水平区限界面的甲板

甲板下处所↓　　甲板上处所→	(1)	(2)	(3)	(4)	(5)	(6)	(7)	(8)	(9)	(10)	(11)	(12)	(13)	(14)
控制站　(1)	A-30	A-30	A-15	A-0	A-0	A-0	A-15	A-30	A-0	A-0	A-0	A-60	A-0	A-60
梯道　(2)	A-0	A-0	A-0	A-0	A-0	A-0	A-0	A-0	A-0	A-0	A-0	A-30	A-0	A-30
走廊　(3)	A-15	A-0	A-0[a]	A-60	A-0	A-0	A-15	A-15	A-0	A-0	A-0	A-30	A-0	A-30
撤离站和外部脱险通道　(4)	A-0	A-0	A-0	A-0	—	A-0	A-0	A-0	A-0	A-0	A-0	A-0	A-0	A-0
开敞甲板处所　(5)	A-0	A-0	A-0	A-0	—	A-0	A-0	A-0	A-0	A-0	A-0	A-0	A-0	A-0
具有较小失火危险的起居处所　(6)	A-60	A-15	A-0	A-60	A-0	A-0	A-0	A-0	A-0	A-0	A-0	A-0	A-0	A-0
具有中等失火危险的起居处所　(7)	A-60	A-15	A-15	A-60	A-0	A-0	A-15	A-15	A-0	A-0	A-0	A-0	A-0	A-0
具有较大失火危险的起居处所　(8)	A-60	A-15	A-15	A-60	A-0	A-15	A-15	A-30	A-0	A-0	A-0	A-0	A-0	A-0
卫生间及类似处所　(9)	A-0	A-0	A-0	A-0	A-0	A-0	A-0	A-0	A-0	A-0	A-0	A-0	A-0	A-0
极少或无失火危险的液舱、空舱及辅机处所　(10)	A-0	A-0	A-0	A-0	A-0	A-0	A-0	A-0	A-0	A-0[a]	A-0	A-0	A-0	A-0
具有中等失火危险的辅机处所、货物处所、货油舱和其他油舱以及其他类似处所　(11)	A-60	A-60	A-60	A-60	A-0	A-0	A-15	A-30	A-0	A-0	A-0[a]	A-0	A-0	A-30
机器处所和主厨房　(12)	A-60	A-60	A-60	A-60	A-0	A-60	A-60	A-60	A-0	A-0	A-30	A-30[a]	A-0	A-60
储藏室、工作间、配膳室等　(13)	A-60	A-30	A-15	A-60	A-0	A-15	A-30	A-30	A-0	A-0	A-0	A-0	A-0	A-0
储藏易燃液体的其他处所　(14)	A-60	A-60	A-60	A-60	A-0	A-30	A-60	A-60	A-0	A-0	A-0	A-0	A-0	A-0

注：视情况适用于表 9.1 和 9.2。

a　属于同一数字类别且标有上标“a”的相邻处所，如果主管机关认为不必要时，在此类处所之间不必设置舱壁和甲板。例如，在第(12)类内的厨房及其所属配膳室之间，只要配膳室的舱壁和甲板能保持厨房限界面的完整性，则不必要求设置舱壁。但是，厨房和机器处所之间要求设置舱壁，即使这两个处所都属于第(12)类。

b　最轻载航行水线之上的船侧、位于救生艇筏和撤离滑道的登乘区域下方且相邻的上层建筑和甲板室舷侧可降低为“A-30”级。

c　如果公共盥洗室完全设在梯道环围内，在梯道环围内的公共盥洗室的舱壁可具有“B”级耐火完整性。

d　如果第(6)、(7)、(8)和(9)类处所完全位于集合站的外边界之内，这些处所的舱壁允许具有“B-0”级耐火完整性。听觉、视觉和灯光装置的控制位置可视为集合站的一部分。

2.2.3.3　连续“B”级天花板或衬板连同有关的甲板和舱壁，可视为全部或部分地起到分隔所要求的隔热性和完整性的作用。

2.2.3.4 Construction and arrangement of saunas

2.2.3.4.1 The perimeter of the sauna shall be of "A" class boundaries and may include changing rooms, showers and toilets. The sauna shall be insulated to "A-60" standard against other spaces except those inside of the perimeter and spaces of categories (5), (9) and (10).

2.2.3.4.2 Bathrooms with direct access to saunas may be considered as part of them. In such cases, the door between sauna and the bathroom need not comply with fire safety requirements.

2.2.3.4.3 The traditional wooden lining on the bulkheads and ceiling are permitted in the sauna. The ceiling above the oven shall be lined with a non-combustible plate with an air gap of at least 30 mm. The distance from the hot surfaces to combustible materials shall be at least 500 mm or the combustible materials shall be protected (e.g. non-combustible plate with an air gap of at least 30 mm).

2.2.3.4.4 The traditional wooden benches are permitted to be used in the sauna.

2.2.3.4.5 The sauna door shall open outwards by pushing.

2.2.3.4.6 Electrically heated ovens shall be provided with a timer.

2.2.4 Fire integrity of bulkheads and decks in ships carrying not more than 36 passengers

2.2.4.1 In addition to complying with the specific provisions for fire integrity of bulkheads and decks of passenger ships, the minimum fire integrity of bulkheads and decks shall be as prescribed in tables 9.3 and 9.4.

2.2.4.2 The following requirements shall govern application of the tables:

.1 Tables 9.3 and 9.4 shall apply respectively to the bulkheads and decks separating adjacent spaces.

.2 For determining the appropriate fire integrity standards to be applied to divisions between adjacent spaces, such spaces are classified according to their fire risk as shown in categories (1) to (11) below. Where the contents and use of a space are such that there is a doubt as to its classification for the purpose of this regulation, or where it is possible to assign two or more classifications to a space, it shall be treated as a space within the relevant category having the most stringent boundary requirements. Smaller, enclosed rooms within a space that have less than 30% communicating openings to that space are considered separate spaces. The fire integrity of the boundary bulkheads and decks of such smaller rooms shall be as prescribed in tables 9.3 and 9.4. The title of each category is intended to be typical rather than restrictive. The number in parentheses preceding each category refers to the applicable column or row in the tables.

(**1**) Control stations

Spaces containing emergency sources of power and lighting.

Wheelhouse and chartroom.

2.2.3.4　桑拿房的构造和布置

2.2.3.4.1　桑拿房的周界应为“A”级限界面，可将更衣室、淋浴室和洗手间包括在内。桑拿房应同其他处所隔热至“A-60”级标准，但桑拿房周界内的处所和第（5）、（9）和（10）类处所除外。

2.2.3.4.2　直接通向桑拿房的浴室可视为桑拿房的一部分。在这种情况下，桑拿房和浴室之间的门不必符合消防安全要求。

2.2.3.4.3　在桑拿房内允许舱壁和天花板上采用传统的木衬板。蒸汽炉上方的天花板应衬有不燃衬板，并至少留有30 mm厚的空隙。从热表面到可燃材料之间的距离至少应为500 mm，或将不燃材料保护起来（例如采用不燃材料板且至少留有30 mm的空隙）。

2.2.3.4.4　在桑拿房内允许使用传统的木制长凳。

2.2.3.4.5　桑拿房的开门方式应为向外推开。

2.2.3.4.6　电加热蒸汽炉应设有定时器。

2.2.4　载客不超过36人的客船舱壁及甲板的耐火完整性

2.2.4.1　除符合客船舱壁和甲板耐火完整性的具体规定外，所有舱壁和甲板的最低耐火完整性还应符合表9.3和9.4的规定。

2.2.4.2　各表的适用范围应以下列要求为准：

.1　表9.3和9.4应分别适用于分隔相邻处所的舱壁和甲板。

.2　为确定相邻处所之间分隔所适用的相应耐火完整性标准，这类处所按其失火危险程度分为下列（1）至（11）类。如果某一处所内的东西和用途致使按本条规定进行分类存在疑问，或有可能为某一处所指定两个或以上类别，则该处所应视作具有最严格限界面要求的相关类别的处所。一个处所内各个较小的围蔽舱室，如果其与该处所相通的开口小于30%，则视为单独处所。这种较小舱室的限界面舱壁和甲板的耐火完整性应符合表9.3和9.4的规定。每一类别的名称系典型举例，而非限制性规定。每类前面括号内的数字是指表内相应的列或行。

（1）　控制站

设有应急电源和应急照明电源的处所。

驾驶室和海图室。

Spaces containing the ship's radio equipment.

Fire control stations.

Control room for propulsion machinery when located outside the machinery space.

Spaces containing centralized fire alarm equipment.

(2) Corridors

Passenger and crew corridors and lobbies.

(3) Accommodation spaces

Spaces as defined in regulation 3.1 excluding corridors.

(4) Stairways

Interior stairways, lifts, totally enclosed emergency escape trunks, and escalators (other than those wholly contained within the machinery spaces) and enclosures thereto.

In this connection, a stairway which is enclosed only at one level shall be regarded as part of the space from which it is not separated by a fire door.

(5) Service spaces (low risk)

Lockers and store-rooms not having provisions for the storage of flammable liquids and having areas less than 4 m^2 and drying rooms and laundries.

(6) Machinery spaces of category A

Spaces as defined in regulation 3.31.

(7) Other machinery spaces

Electrical equipment rooms (auto-telephone exchange, air-conditioning duct spaces). Spaces as defined in regulation 3.30 excluding machinery spaces of category A.

(8) Cargo spaces

All spaces used for cargo (including cargo oil tanks) and trunkways and hatchways to such spaces, other than special category spaces.

(9) Service spaces (high risk)

Galleys, pantries containing cooking appliances, paint lockers, lockers and store-rooms having areas of 4 m^2 or more, spaces for the storage of flammable liquids, saunas and workshops other than those forming part of the machinery spaces.

设有船舶无线电设备的处所。

消防控制站。

位于推进装置处所外面的推进装置控制室。

设有集中失火报警设备的处所。

（2）　走廊

乘客及船员用的走廊和门厅。

（3）　起居处所

第3.1条所定义的处所，不包括走廊。

（4）　梯道内部

梯道、升降机、完全封闭的紧急脱险围井、自动扶梯（完全设在机器处所内者除外），以及通往上述梯道的环围。

对此，仅在一层甲板设有环围的梯道应视为未用防火门与其隔开的处所的一部分。

（5）　具有较小失火危险的服务处所

不存放易燃液体且面积小于4 m^2 的小间和储物间、干燥间和洗衣间。

（6）　A类机器处所

第3.31条所定义的处所。

（7）　其他机器处所

电气设备间（自动电话交换机室、空调管道处所）。除A类机器处所外，第3.30条所定义的各处所。

（8）　货物处所

所有用于装运货物的处所（包括货油舱）以及通往这些处所的围井通道和舱口，特种处所除外。

（9）　具有较大失火危险的服务处所

厨房、设有烹调设备的配膳室、油漆间、面积为4 m^2 及以上的小间和储物间、存放易燃液体的处所、桑拿房和不构成机器处所一部分的工作间。

(**10**) Open decks

Open deck spaces and enclosed promenades having little or no fire risk. To be considered in this category, enclosed promenades shall have no significant fire risk, meaning that furnishing shall be restricted to deck furniture. In addition, such spaces shall be naturally ventilated by permanent openings.

Air spaces (the space outside superstructures and deckhouses).

(**11**) Special category and ro-ro spaces

Spaces as defined in regulations 3.41 and 3.46.

.3 In determining the applicable fire integrity standard of a boundary between two spaces within a main vertical zone or horizontal zone which is not protected by an automatic sprinkler system complying with the provisions of the Fire Safety Systems Code or between such zones neither of which is so protected, the higher of the two values given in the tables shall apply.

.4 In determining the applicable fire integrity standard of a boundary between two spaces within a main vertical zone or horizontal zone which is protected by an automatic sprinkler system complying with the provisions of the Fire Safety Systems Code or between such zones both of which are so protected, the lesser of the two values given in the tables shall apply. Where a zone with sprinklers and a zone without sprinklers meet within accommodation and service spaces, the higher of the two values given in the tables shall apply to the division between the zones.

Table 9.3 Fire integrity of bulkheads separating adjacent spaces

Spaces		(1)	(2)	(3)	(4)	(5)	(6)	(7)	(8)	(9)	(10)	(11)
Control stations	(1)	A-0[c]	A-0	A-60	A-0	A-15	A-60	A-15	A-60	A-60	*	A-60
Corridors	(2)		C[e]	B-0[e]	A-0[a] B-0[e]	B-0[e]	A-60	A-0	A-0	A-15 A-0[d]	*	A-30[g]
Accommodation spaces	(3)			C[e]	A-0[a] B-0[e]	B-0[e]	A-60	A-0	A-0	A-15 A-0[d]	*	A-30 A-0[d]
Stairways	(4)				A-0[a] B-0[e]	A-0[a] B-0[e]	A-60	A-0	A-0	A-15 A-0[d]	*	A-30[g]
Service spaces (low risk)	(5)					C[e]	A-60	A-0	A-0	A-0	*	A-0
Machinery spaces of category A	(6)						*	A-0	A-0	A-60	*	A-60
Other machinery spaces	(7)							A-0[b]	A-0	A-0	*	A-0
Cargo spaces	(8)								*	A-0	*	A-0
Service spaces (high risk)	(9)									A-0[b]	*	A-30
Open decks	(10)											A-0
Special category and ro-ro spaces	(11)											A-30[g]

See notes following table 9.4.

（10）开敞甲板

开敞甲板处所和极少或无失火危险的围蔽游步甲板处所。如果考虑将围蔽游步甲板处所归为此类，其应无大的失火危险，即其内应只设有甲板用具。此外，此类处所还应通过固定开口进行自然通风。露天处所（上层建筑和甲板室外的处所）。

（11）特种和滚装处所

第3.41和3.46条所定义的处所。

.3 对位于未受到符合《消防安全系统规则》规定的自动喷水器系统保护的主竖区或水平区内的两个处所之间的限界面，或位于均无此种保护的主竖区和水平区之间的限界面，在确定其所适用的耐火完整性标准时，应采用表列两个等级中的较高等级。

.4 对位于受到符合《消防安全系统规则》规定的自动喷水器系统保护的主竖区或水平区内的两个处所之间的限界面，或位于均受到此种保护的主竖区和水平区之间的限界面，在确定其所适用的耐火完整性标准时，应采用表列两个等级中的较低等级。如果在起居处所和服务处所内，一个装有喷水器的区域邻接一个未装有喷水器的区域，这两个区域之间的分隔应采用表列两个等级中的较高等级。

表9.3 分隔相邻处所舱壁的耐火完整性

处所		(1)	(2)	(3)	(4)	(5)	(6)	(7)	(8)	(9)	(10)	(11)
控制站	(1)	A-0[c]	A-0	A-60	A-0	A-15	A-60	A-15	A-60	A-60	*	A-60
走廊	(2)		C[e]	B-0[e]	A-0[a] B-0[e]	B-0[e]	A-60	A-0	A-0	A-15 A-0[d]	*	A-30[g]
起居处所	(3)			C[e]	A-0[a] B-0[e]	B-0[e]	A-60	A-0	A-0	A-15 A-0[d]	*	A-30 A-0[d]
梯道	(4)				A-0[a] B-0[e]	A-0[a] B-0[e]	A-60	A-0	A-0	A-30[g] A-0[d]	*	A-30[g]
具有较小失火危险的服务处所	(5)					C[e]	A-60	A-0	A-0	A-0	*	A-0
A类机器处所	(6)						*	A-0	A-0	A-60	*	A-60
其他机器处所	(7)							A-0[b]	A-0	A-0	*	A-0
货物处所	(8)								*	A-0	*	A-0
具有较大失火危险的服务处所	(9)									A-0[b]	*	A-30
开敞甲板	(10)											A-0
特种和滚装处所	(11)											A-30[g]

见表9.4的注释。

Table 9.4 Fire integrity of decks separating adjacent spaces

Space below ↓ Space above →		(1)	(2)	(3)	(4)	(5)	(6)	(7)	(8)	(9)	(10)	(11)
Control stations	(1)	A-0	A-0	A-0	A-0	A-0	A-60	A-0	A-0	A-0	*	A-60[g]
Corridors	(2)	A-0	*	*	A-0	*	A-60	A-0	A-0	A-0	*	A-30[g]
Accommodation spaces	(3)	A-60	A-0	*	A-0	*	A-60	A-0	A-0	A-0	*	A-30 A-0[d]
Stairways	(4)	A-0	A-0	A-0	*	A-0	A-60	A-0	A-0	A-0	*	A-30[g]
Service spaces(low risk)	(5)	A-15	A-0	A-0	A-0	*	A-60	A-0	A-0	A-0	*	A-0
Machinery spaces of category A	(6)	A-60	A-60	A-60	A-60	A-60	*	A-60[f]	A-30	A-60	*	A-60
Other machinery spaces	(7)	A-15	A-0	A-0	A-0	A-0	A-0	*	A-0	A-0	*	A-0
Cargo spaces	(8)	A-60	A-0	A-0	A-0	A-0	A-0	A-0	*	A-0	*	A-0
Service spaces(high risk)	(9)	A-60	A-30 A-0[d]	A-30 A-0[d]	A-30 A-0[d]	A-0	A-60	A-0	A-0	A-0	*	A-30
Open decks	(10)	*	*	*	*	*	*	*	*	*	–	A-0
Special category and ro-ro spaces	(11)	A-60	A-30[g]	A-30 A-0[d]	A-30[g]	A-0	A-60[g]	A-0	A-0	A-30	A-0	A-30[g]

Notes: To be applied to both tables 9.3 and 9.4 as appropriate.

a For clarification as to which applies, see paragraphs 2.2.2 and 2.2.5.

b Where spaces are of the same numerical category and superscript "b" appears, a bulkhead or deck of the rating shown in the tables is only required when the adjacent spaces are for a different purpose (e.g. in category(9)). A galley next to a galley does not require a bulkhead, but a galley next to a paint room requires an "A-0" bulkhead.

c Bulkheads separating the wheelhouse and chartroom from each other may have a "B-0" rating. No fire rating is required for those partitions separating the navigation bridge and the safety centre when the latter is within the navigation bridge.

d See paragraphs 2.2.4.2.3 and 2.2.4.2.4.

e For the application of paragraph 2.2.1.1.2, "B-0" and "C", where appearing in table 9.3, shall be read as "A-0".

f Fire insulation need not be fitted if the machinery space in category(7), in the opinion of the Administration, has little or no fire risk.

g Ships constructed before 1 July 2014 shall comply, as a minimum, with the previous requirements applicable at the time the ship was constructed, as specified in regulation 1.2.

* Where an asterisk appears in the tables, the division is required to be of steel or other equivalent material, but is not required to be of "A" class standard. However, where a deck, except in a category (10) space, is penetrated for the passage of electric cables, pipes and vent ducts, such penetrations shall be made tight to prevent the passage of flame and smoke. Divisions between control stations (emergency generators) and open decks may have air intake openings without means for closure, unless a fixed gas fire-extinguishing system is fitted.

For the application of paragraph 2.2.1.1.2, an asterisk, where appearing in table 9.4, except for categories(8) and(10), shall be read as "A-0".

2.2.4.3 Continuous "B" class ceilings or linings, in association with the relevant decks or bulkheads, may be accepted as contributing, wholly or in part, to the required insulation and integrity of a division.

2.2.4.4 External boundaries which are required in regulation 11.2 to be of steel or other equivalent material may be pierced for the fitting of windows and sidescuttles provided that there is no requirement for such boundaries of passenger ships to have "A" class integrity. Similarly, in such boundaries which are not required to have "A" class integrity, doors may be constructed of materials which are to the satisfaction of the Administration.

表 9.4 分隔相邻处所甲板的耐火完整性

甲板下处所↓ 甲板上处所→		(1)	(2)	(3)	(4)	(5)	(6)	(7)	(8)	(9)	(10)	(11)
控制站	(1)	A-0	A-0	A-0	A-0	A-0	A-60	A-0	A-0	A-0	*	A-60[g]
走廊	(2)	A-0	*	*	A-0	*	A-60	A-0	A-0	A-0	*	A-30[g]
起居处所	(3)	A-60	A-0	*	A-0	*	A-60	A-0	A-0	A-0	*	A-30 A-0[d]
梯道	(4)	A-0	A-0	A-0	*	A-0	A-60	A-0	A-0	A-0	*	A-30[g]
具有较小失火危险的服务处所	(5)	A-15	A-0	A-0	A-0	*	A-60	A-0	A-0	A-0	*	A-0
A类机器处所	(6)	A-60	A-60	A-60	A-60	A-60	*	A-60[f]	A-30	A-60	*	A-60
其他机器处所	(7)	A-15	A-0	A-0	A-0	A-0	A-0	*	A-0	A-0	*	A-0
货物处所	(8)	A-60	A-0	A-0	A-0	A-0	A-0	A-0	*	A-0	*	A-0
具有较大失火危险的服务处所	(9)	A-60	A-30 A-0[d]	A-30 A-0[d]	A-30 A-0[d]	A-0	A-60	A-0	A-0	A-0	*	A-30
开敞甲板	(10)	*	*	*	*	*	*	*	*	*	-	A-0
特种和滚装处所	(11)	A-60	A-30[g]	A-30 A-0[d]	A-30[g]	A-0	A-60[g]	A-0	A-0	A-30	A-0	A-30[g]

注:根据情况适用于表 9.3 和 9.4。

a 为分清适用哪一等级,见本条 2.2.2 和 2.2.5。

b 属于同一数字类别且有上标“b”的相邻处所,只有当相邻处所用途不同时,才要求表中所示等级的舱壁或甲板(例如第(9)类)。相邻的厨房之间不要求用舱壁分隔,但厨房与油漆间相邻则要求用“A-0”级舱壁分隔。

c 分隔驾驶室和海图室的舱壁可以为“B-0”级。当安全中心位于驾驶室之中时,驾驶室和安全中心之间的隔断不需要耐火等级。

d 见本条 2.2.4.2.3 和 2.2.4.2.4。

e 在应用本条 2.2.1.1.2 时,表 9.3 中的“B-0”级和“C”级应为“A-0”级。

f 如果主管机关认为第(7)类中的机器处所极少或无失火危险,可不必设置防火隔热。

g 2014 年 7 月 1 日以前建造的船舶须至少符合第 1.2 条所述的船舶建造时适用的原有要求。

* 表中出现星号 * 处,表示指分隔要求为钢质或等效材料,但不要求为“A”级标准。但是,除第(10)类处所以外,如果甲板被贯穿以供电缆、管线和通风管道通过,应对此类贯穿处进行密封以防止火焰和烟气通过。除非安装了固定式气体灭火系统,控制站(应急发电机室)和开敞甲板之间的分隔可以设有不带关闭装置的空气进入开口。

在应用本条 2.2.1.1.2 时,表 9.4 中的 * 号应视为“A-0”级,但第(8)和(10)类除外。

2.2.4.3 可以接受连续“B”级天花板或衬板连同有关甲板或舱壁对分隔所要求的隔热性和完整性起到全部或部分作用。

2.2.4.4 第 11.2 条所要求的钢质或其他等效材料外部限界面,可为安装窗或舷窗的目的而开孔,只要未要求客船的这类限界面具有“A”级完整性。同样,在不要求具有“A”级完整性的限界面上,门可以使用主管机关满意的材料制成。

2.2.4.5 Saunas shall comply with paragraph 2.2.3.4.

2.2.5 Protection of stairways and lifts in accommodation area

2.2.5.1 Stairways shall be within enclosures formed of "A" class divisions, with positive means of closure at all openings, except that:

.1 a stairway connecting only two decks need not be enclosed, provided the integrity of the deck is maintained by proper bulkheads or self-closing doors in one 'tween-deck space. When a stairway is closed in one 'tween-deck space, the stairway enclosure shall be protected in accordance with the tables for decks in paragraphs 2.2.3 or 2.2.4; and

.2 stairways may be fitted in the open in a public space, provided they lie wholly within the public space.

2.2.5.2 Lift trunks shall be so fitted as to prevent the passage of smoke and flame from one 'tween-deck to another and shall be provided with means of closing so as to permit the control of draught and smoke. Machinery for lifts located within stairway enclosures shall be arranged in a separate room, surrounded by steel boundaries, except that small passages for lift cables are permitted. Lifts which open into spaces other than corridors, public spaces, special category spaces, stairways and external areas shall not open into stairways included in the means of escape.

2.2.6 Arrangement of cabin balconies

On passenger ships constructed on or after 1 July 2008, non-load-bearing partial bulkheads which separate adjacent cabin balconies shall be capable of being opened by the crew from each side for the purpose of fighting fires.

2.2.7 Protection of atriums

2.2.7.1 Atriums shall be within enclosures formed of "A" class divisions having a fire rating determined in accordance with tables 9.2 and 9.4, as applicable.

2.2.7.2 Decks separating spaces within atriums shall have a fire rating determined in accordance with tables 9.2 and 9.4, as applicable.

2.3 Cargo ships except tankers

2.3.1 Methods of protection in accommodation area

2.3.1.1 One of the following methods of protection shall be adopted in accommodation and service spaces and control stations:

.1 *Method IC*—The construction of internal divisional bulkheads of non-combustible "B" or "C" class divisions generally without the installation of an automatic sprinkler, fire detection and fire alarm system in the accommodation and service spaces, except as required by regulation 7.5.5.1; or

2.2.4.5 桑拿房应符合本条2.2.3.4。

2.2.5 起居处所内的梯道和升降机的保护

2.2.5.1 梯道应位于"A"级分隔形成的环围之内,并在一切开口处设有可靠的关闭装置,但下列情况除外:

.1 仅连接两层甲板的梯道,如果在一甲板间具有适当的舱壁或自闭门使甲板的完整性得以保持,则不必环围。如果梯道在一个甲板间被环围,其梯道环围应按本条2.2.3或2.2.4的表中所列对甲板的要求加以保护;和

.2 梯道可设于公共处所的开敞部位,但应完全位于公共处所内。

2.2.5.2 升降机围井的设置,应能防止烟和火焰从一个甲板间通至另一个甲板间,并应设置关闭装置,以能控制气流和烟气的流通。位于梯道环围内的升降机械应布置在一个独立的舱室内,由钢质限界面环围,但允许设有升降机电缆使用的小通道。通往除走廊、公共处所、特种处所、梯道和外部区域之外的处所的升降机,不得通往脱险通道内的梯道。

2.2.6 客舱阳台的布置

在2008年7月1日或以后建造的客船上,分隔相邻客舱阳台的非承重局部舱壁应能够由船员从每一侧打开以便灭火。

2.2.7 中庭的保护

2.2.7.1 中庭须位于"A"级分隔结构的围壁之中。其围壁的耐火等级按照所适用的列表9.2和9.4确定。

2.2.7.2 分隔中庭内处所的甲板,其耐火等级须按照所适用的列表9.2和9.4确定。

2.3 液货船以外的货船

2.3.1 起居处所的保护方法

2.3.1.1 在起居处所、服务处所和控制站内应采取下列保护方法之一:

.1 **ⅠC法**——除第7.5.5.1条的要求外,在起居处所和服务处所内以不燃的"B"级或"C"级分隔作内部分隔舱壁,一般不设有自动喷水器、探火和失火报警系统;或

.2 *Method ⅡC*—The fitting of an automatic sprinkler, fire detection and fire alarm system as required by regulation 7.5.5.2 for the detection and extinction of fire in all spaces in which fire might be expected to originate, generally with no restriction on the type of internal divisional bulkheads; or

.3 *Method ⅢC*—The fitting of a fixed fire detection and fire alarm system as required by regulation 7.5.5.3 in spaces in which a fire might be expected to originate, generally with no restriction on the type of internal divisional bulkheads, except that in no case shall the area of any accommodation space or spaces bounded by an "A" or "B" class division exceed 50 m^2. However, consideration may be given by the Administration to increasing this area for public spaces.

2.3.1.2 The requirements for the use of non-combustible materials in the construction and insulation of boundary bulkheads of machinery spaces, control stations, service spaces, etc., and the protection of the above stairway enclosures and corridors will be common to all three methods outlined in paragraph 2.3.1.1.

2.3.2 Bulkheads within accommodation area

2.3.2.1 Bulkheads required to be "B" class divisions shall extend from deck to deck and to the shell or other boundaries. However, where a continuous "B" class ceiling or lining is fitted on both sides of the bulkhead, the bulkhead may terminate at the continuous ceiling or lining.

2.3.2.2 *Method ⅠC*—Bulkheads not required by this or other regulations for cargo ships to be "A" or "B" class divisions shall be of at least "C" class construction.

2.3.2.3 *Method ⅡC*—There shall be no restriction on the construction of bulkheads not required by this or other regulations for cargo ships to be "A" or "B" class divisions except in individual cases where "C" class bulkheads are required in accordance with table 9.5.

2.3.2.4 *Method ⅢC*—There shall be no restriction on the construction of bulkheads not required for cargo ships to be "A" or "B" class divisions except that the area of any accommodation space or spaces bounded by a continuous "A" or "B" class division shall in no case exceed 50 m^2, except in individual cases where "C" class bulkheads are required in accordance with table 9.5. However, consideration may be given by the Administration to increasing this area for public spaces.

2.3.3 Fire integrity of bulkheads and decks

2.3.3.1 In addition to complying with the specific provisions for fire integrity of bulkheads and decks of cargo ships, the minimum fire integrity of bulkheads and decks shall be as prescribed in tables 9.5 and 9.6.

2.3.3.2 The following requirements shall govern application of the tables:

.1 Tables 9.5 and 9.6 shall apply respectively to the bulkheads and decks separating adjacent spaces.

.2　ⅡC法——在可能成为失火源的所有处所，按第7.5.5.2条的要求装设用于探火及灭火的自动喷水器、探火和失火报警系统，一般对内部分隔舱壁的型式不予限制；或

.3　ⅢC法——在可能成为失火源的处所，按第7.5.5.3条的要求装设固定式探火和失火报警系统，一般对内部分隔舱壁的型式不予限制，但无论在何种情况下任一起居处所，或用“A”级或“B”级分隔作为限界面的各个处所的面积不得超过50 m^2。但对于公共处所，主管机关可考虑增加这一面积。

2.3.1.2　对机器处所、控制站、服务处所等限界面舱壁的构造和隔热使用不燃材料的要求以及对上述梯道环围和走廊的保护要求，是对本条2.3.1.1所概述的三种方法的共同要求。

2.3.2　起居处所内的舱壁

2.3.2.1　要求为“B”级分隔的舱壁，应由甲板延伸至甲板，并延伸至船壳和其他限界面。但是，如果在舱壁的两侧均设有连续“B”级天花板或衬板，这种舱壁可终止于连续天花板或衬板。

2.3.2.2　ⅠC法——本条或其他关于货船的条文未规定为“A”级或“B”级分隔的舱壁，至少应为“C”级结构。

2.3.2.3　ⅡC法——除在个别情况下根据表9.5要求为“C”级舱壁外，本条或其他关于货船的条文未规定为“A”级或“B”级分隔的舱壁，其构造应不受限制。

2.3.2.4　ⅢC法——除在个别情况下根据表9.5要求为“C”级舱壁外，凡对货船不要求为“A”级或“B”级分隔的舱壁，其构造应不受限制，但无论在何种情况下，任一起居处所，或用连续“A”级或“B”级分隔作为限界面的各个处所的面积不得超过50 m^2。但对于公共处所，主管机关可考虑增加这一面积。

2.3.3　舱壁和甲板的耐火完整性

2.3.3.1　除符合货船舱壁和甲板耐火完整性的具体规定外，所有舱壁和甲板的最低耐火完整性还应符合表9.5和9.6的规定。

2.3.3.2　各表的适用范围应以下列要求为准：

.1　表9.5和9.6分别适用于分隔相邻处所的舱壁和甲板。

.2 For determining the appropriate fire integrity standards to be applied to divisions between adjacent spaces, such spaces are classified according to their fire risk as shown in categories (1) to (11) below. Where the contents and use of a space are such that there is a doubt as to its classification for the purpose of this regulation, or where it is possible to assign two or more classifications to a space, it shall be treated as a space within the relevant category having the most stringent boundary requirements. Smaller, enclosed rooms within a space that have less than 30% communicating openings to that space are considered separate spaces. The fire integrity of the boundary bulkheads and decks of such smaller rooms shall be as prescribed in tables 9.5 and 9.6. The title of each category is intended to be typical rather than restrictive. The number in parentheses preceding each category refers to the applicable column or row in the tables.

(**1**) Control stations

Spaces containing emergency sources of power and lighting.

Wheelhouse and chartroom.

Spaces containing the ship's radio equipment.

Fire control stations.

Control room for propulsion machinery when located outside the machinery space.

Spaces containing centralized fire alarm equipment.

(**2**) Corridors

Corridors and lobbies.

(**3**) Accommodation spaces

Spaces as defined in regulation 3.1, excluding corridors.

(**4**) Stairways

Interior stairway, lifts, totally enclosed emergency escape trunks, and escalators (other than those wholly contained within the machinery spaces) and enclosures thereto.

In this connection, a stairway which is enclosed only at one level shall be regarded as part of the space from which it is not separated by a fire door.

(**5**) Service spaces (low risk)

Lockers and store-rooms not having provisions for the storage of flammable liquids and having areas less than 4 m^2 and drying rooms and laundries.

(**6**) Machinery spaces of category A

Spaces as defined in regulation 3.31.

.2 为确定相邻处所之间分隔所适用的相应耐火完整性标准,这种处所按其失火危险程度分为下列(1)至(11)类。如果某一处所内的东西和用途致使按本条规定进行分类存在疑问,或有可能为某一处所指定两个或以上类别,则该处所应按具有最严格限界面要求的相关类别的处所对待。一个处所内各个较小的围蔽舱室,如果其与该处所相通的开口小于30%,则视为单独处所。这种较小舱室的限界面舱壁和甲板的耐火完整性应符合表9.5和9.6的规定。每一类别的名称系典型举例,而不是限制性规定。每类前面括号内的数字系指表内相应的列或行。

(1) 控制站

设有应急电源和应急照明电源的处所。

驾驶室和海图室。

设有船舶无线电设备的处所。

消防控制站。

位于推进装置处所外面的推进装置控制室。

设有集中失火报警设备的处所。

(2) 走廊

走廊和门厅。

(3) 起居处所

第3.1条所定义的处所,不包括走廊。

(4) 梯道内部

梯道、升降机、完全封闭的紧急脱险围井、自动扶梯(完全设在机器处所内者除外),以及通往上述梯道的环围。

对此,仅在一层甲板设有环围的梯道应视为未用防火门与其隔开的处所的一部分。

(5) 具有较小失火危险的服务处所

不存放易燃液体且面积小于4 m^2 的小间和储物间、干燥室和洗衣间。

(6) A类机器处所

第3.31条所定义的处所。

(**7**) Other machinery spaces

Electrical equipment rooms (auto-telephone exchange, air-conditioning duct spaces). Spaces as defined in regulation 3.30, excluding machinery spaces of category A.

(**8**) Cargo spaces

All spaces used for cargo (including cargo oil tanks) and trunkways and hatchways to such spaces.

(**9**) Service spaces (high risk)

Galleys, pantries containing cooking appliances, saunas, paint lockers and store-rooms having areas of 4 m^2 or more, spaces for the storage of flammable liquids, and workshops other than those forming part of the machinery spaces.

(**10**) Open decks

Open deck spaces and enclosed promenades having little or no fire risk. To be considered in this category, enclosed promenades shall have no significant fire risk, meaning that furnishings shall be restricted to deck furniture. In addition, such spaces shall be naturally ventilated by permanent openings.

Air spaces (the space outside superstructures and deckhouses).

(**11**) Ro-ro and vehicle spaces

Ro-ro spaces as defined in regulation 3.41.

Vehicle spaces as defined in regulation 3.49.

Table 9.5 Fire integrity of bulkheads separating adjacent spaces

Spaces		(1)	(2)	(3)	(4)	(5)	(6)	(7)	(8)	(9)	(10)	(11)
Control stations	(1)	A-0[e]	A-0	A-60	A-0	A-15	A-60	A-15	A-60	A-60	*	A-60
Corridors	(2)		C	B-0	B-0 A-0[c]	B-0	A-60	A-0	A-0	A-0	*	A-30
Accommodation spaces	(3)			C[a,b]	B-0 A-0[c]	B-0	A-60	A-0	A-0	A-0	*	A-30
Stairways	(4)				B-0 A-0[c]	B-0 A-0[c]	A-60	A-0	A-0	A-0	*	A-30
Service spaces (low risk)	(5)					C	A-60	A-0	A-0	A-0	*	A-0
Machinery spaces of category A	(6)						*	A-0	A-0[g]	A-60	*	A-60[f]
Other machinery spaces	(7)							A-0[d]	A-0	A-0	*	A-0
Cargo spaces	(8)								*	A-0	*	A-0
Service spaces (high risk)	(9)									A-0[d]	*	A-30
Open decks	(10)										–	A-0
Ro-ro and vehicle spaces	(11)											A-30[j]

See notes following table 9.6.

(**7**)　其他机器处所

电气设备间(自动电话交换机室、空调管道处所)。除 A 类机器处所外，第 3.30 条所定义的各处所。

(**8**)　货物处所

所有用于装运货物的处所(包括货油舱)以及通往这些处所的围井通道和舱口。

(**9**)　具有较大失火危险的服务处所

厨房、设有烹调设备的配膳室、桑拿房、面积为 4 m^2 及以上的油漆间和储物间、存放易燃液体的处所和不构成机器处所一部分的工作间。

(**10**)　开敞甲板

开敞甲板处所和极少或无失火危险的围蔽游步甲板处所。如果考虑将围蔽游步甲板处所归为此类，其应无大的失火危险，即其内应只设有甲板用具。此外，此类处所还应通过固定开口自然通风。

露天处所(上层建筑和甲板室外的处所)。

(**11**)　滚装和车辆处所

第 3.41 条所定义的滚装处所。

第 3.49 条所定义的车辆处所。

表 9.5　分隔相邻处所舱壁的耐火完整性

处所		(1)	(2)	(3)	(4)	(5)	(6)	(7)	(8)	(9)	(10)	(11)
控制站	(1)	A-0[e]	A-0	A-60	A-0	A-15	A-60	A-15	A-60	A-60	*	A-60
走廊	(2)		C	B-0	B-0 A-0[c]	B-0	A-60	A-0	A-0	A-0	*	A-30
起居处所	(3)			C[a,b]	B-0 A-0[c]	B-0	A-60	A-0	A-0	A-0	*	A-30
梯道	(4)				B-0 A-0[c]	B-0 A-0[c]	A-60	A-0	A-0	A-0	*	A-30
具有较小失火危险的服务处所	(5)					C	A-60	A-0	A-0	A-0	*	A-0
A 类机器处所	(6)						*	A-0	A-0[g]	A-60	*	A-60[f]
其他机器处所	(7)							A-0[d]	A-0	A-0	*	A-0
货物处所	(8)								*	A-0	*	A-0
具有较大失火危险的服务处所	(9)									A-0[d]	*	A-30
开敞甲板	(10)										—	A-0
滚装和车辆处所	(11)											A-30[j]

见表 9.6 的注释。

Table 9.6 Fire integrity of decks separating adjacent spaces

Space below ↓ Space above→		(1)	(2)	(3)	(4)	(5)	(6)	(7)	(8)	(9)	(10)	(11)
Control stations	(1)	A-0	A-0	A-0	A-0	A-0	A-60	A-0	A-0	A-0	*	A-60
Corridors	(2)	A-0	*	*	A-0	*	A-60	A-0	A-0	A-0	*	A-30
Accommodation spaces	(3)	A-60	A-0	*	A-0	*	A-60	A-0	A-0	A-0	*	A-30
Stairways	(4)	A-0	A-0	A-0	*	A-0	A-60	A-0	A-0	A-0	*	A-30
Service spaces(low risk)	(5)	A-15	A-0	A-0	A-0	*	A-60	A-0	A-0	A-0	*	A-0
Machinery spaces of category A	(6)	A-60	A-60	A-60	A-60	A-60	*	A-60[i]	A-30	A-60	*	A-60
Other machinery spaces	(7)	A-15	A-0	A-0	A-0	A-0	A-0	*	A-0	A-0	*	A-0
Cargo spaces	(8)	A-60	A-0	A-0	A-0	A-0	A-0	A-0	*	A-0	*	A-0
Service spaces(high risk)	(9)	A-60	A-0	A-0	A-0	A-0	A-60	A-0	A-0	A-0[d]	*	A-30
Open decks	(10)	*	*	*	*	*	*	*	*	*	–	A-0[j]
Ro-ro and vehicle spaces	(11)	A-60	A-30	A-30	A-30	A-0	A-60	A-0	A-0	A-30	A-0[j]	A-30[j]

Notes: To be applied to tables 9.5 and 9.6, as appropriate.

a No special requirements are imposed upon bulkheads in methods ⅡC and ⅢC fire protection.

b In case of method ⅢC, "B" class bulkheads of "B-0" rating shall be provided between spaces or groups of spaces of 50 m^2 and over in area.

c For clarification as to which applies, see paragraphs 2.3.2 and 2.3.4.

d Where spaces are of the same numerical category and superscript "d" appears, a bulkhead or deck of the rating shown in the tables is only required when the adjacent spaces are for a different purpose (e.g. in category (9)). A galley next to a galley does not require a bulkhead, but a galley next to a paint room requires an "A-0" bulkhead.

e Bulkheads separating the wheelhouse, chartroom and radio room from each other may have a "B-0" rating.

f An "A-0" rating may be used if no dangerous goods are intended to be carried or if such goods are stowed not less than 3 m horizontally from such a bulkhead.

g For cargo spaces in which dangerous goods are intended to be carried, regulation 19.3.8 applies.

h Deleted.

i Fire insulation need not be fitted in the machinery space in category (7) if, in the opinion of the Administration, it has little or no fire risk.

j Ships constructed before 1 July 2014 shall comply, as a minimum, with the previous requirements applicable at the time the ship was constructed, as specified in regulation 1.2.

* Where an asterisk appears in the tables, the division is required to be of steel or other equivalent material but is not required to be of "A" class standard. However, where a deck, except an open deck, is penetrated for the passage of electric cables, pipes and vent ducts, such penetrations shall be made tight to prevent the passage of flame and smoke. Divisions between control stations (emergency generators) and open decks may have air intake openings without means for closure, unless a fixed gas fire-extinguishing system is fitted.

2.3.3.3 Continuous "B" class ceilings or linings, in association with the relevant decks or bulkheads, may be accepted as contributing, wholly or in part, to the required insulation and integrity of a division.

2.3.3.4 External boundaries which are required in regulation 11.2 to be of steel or other equivalent material may be pierced for the fitting of windows and sidescuttles provided that there is no requirement for such boundaries of cargo ships to have "A" class integrity. Similarly, in such boundaries which are not required to have "A" class integrity, doors may be constructed of materials which are to the satisfaction of the Administration.

表 9.6　相邻处所分隔甲板的耐火完整性

甲板下处所↓　　甲板上处所→		(1)	(2)	(3)	(4)	(5)	(6)	(7)	(8)	(9)	(10)	(11)
控制站	(1)	A-0	A-0	A-0	A-0	A-0	A-60	A-0	A-0	A-0	*	A-60
走廊	(2)	A-0	*	*	A-0	*	A-60	A-0	A-0	A-0	*	A-30
起居处所	(3)	A-60	A-0	*	A-0	*	A-60	A-0	A-0	A-0	*	A-30
梯道	(4)	A-0	A-0	A-0	*	A-0	A-60	A-0	A-0	A-0	*	A-30
具有较小失火危险的服务处所	(5)	A-15	A-0	A-0	A-0	*	A-60	A-0	A-0	A-0	*	A-0
A类机器处所	(6)	A-60	A-60	A-60	A-60	A-60	*	A-60[i]	A-30	A-60	*	A-60
其他机器处所	(7)	A-15	A-0	A-0	A-0	A-0	A-0	*	A-0	A-0	*	A-0
货物处所	(8)	A-60	A-0	A-0	A-0	A-0	A-0	A-0	*	A-0	*	A-0
具有较大失火危险的服务处所	(9)	A-60	A-0	A-0	A-0	A-0	A-60	A-0	A-0	A-0[d]	*	A-30
开敞甲板	(10)	*	*	*	*	*	*	*	*	*	—	A-0[j]
滚装和车辆处所	(11)	A-60	A-30	A-30	A-30	A-0	A-60	A-0	A-0	A-30	A-0[j]	A-30[j]

注:根据情况适用于表 9.5 和 9.6。

a　在ⅡC 及ⅢC 法中对舱壁无特殊要求。

b　在ⅢC 法中,面积为 50 m^2 及以上的各处所或各组处所之间应装设"B-0 级"舱壁。

c　为分清适用哪一等级,见本条 2.3.2 和 2.3.4。

d　属于同一数字类别且有上标"d"的处所,只有当相邻处所用途不同时,才要求表中所示等级的舱壁或甲板(例如第(9)类)。相邻的厨房之间不要求用舱壁分隔,但厨房与油漆间相邻则要求用"A-0"级舱壁分隔。

e　分隔驾驶室、海图室和无线电室的舱壁可以为"B-0"级。

f　如果不拟载运危险货物,或危险货物的堆存处与舱壁的水平距离不少于 3 m,该舱壁可为 A-0 级。

g　拟用于载运危险货物的货物处所适用第 19.3.8 条。

h　删除。

i　如果主管机关认为第(7)类中的机器处所极少或无失火危险,可不必设置防火隔热。

j　2014 年 7 月 1 日以前建造的船舶须至少符合第 1.2 条所述的船舶建造时适用的原有要求。

*　表中出现星号" * "处,表示分隔要求为钢质或等效材料,但不要求为"A"级标准。但是,除开敞甲板以外,如果甲板被贯穿以供电缆、管线和通风管道通过,应对此类贯穿处进行密封以防止火焰和烟气通过。除非安装了固定式气体灭火系统,控制站(应急发电机)和开敞甲板之间的分隔可以设有不带关闭装置的空气进入开口。

2.3.3.3　连续"B"级天花板或衬板连同有关的甲板和舱壁,可以认为全部或部分地起到分隔所要求的隔热性和完整性的作用。

2.3.3.4　第 11.2 条所要求的钢质或其他等效材料外部限界面,可为安装窗或舷窗的目的而开孔,只要未要求货船的这类限界面具有"A"级完整性。同样,在不要求具有"A"级完整性的限界面上,门可以使用主管机关满意的材料制成。

2.3.3.5 Saunas shall comply with paragraph 2.2.3.4.

2.3.4 Protection of stairways and lift trunks in accommodation spaces, service spaces and control stations

2.3.4.1 Stairways which penetrate only a single deck shall be protected, at a minimum, at one level by at least "B-0" class divisions and self-closing doors. Lifts which penetrate only a single deck shall be surrounded by "A-0" class divisions with steel doors at both levels. Stairways and lift trunks which penetrate more than a single deck shall be surrounded by at least "A-0" class divisions and be protected by self-closing doors at all levels.

2.3.4.2 On ships having accommodation for 12 persons or less, where stairways penetrate more than a single deck and where there are at least two escape routes direct to the open deck at every accommodation level, the "A-0" requirements of paragraph 2.3.4.1 may be reduced to "B-0".

2.4 Tankers

2.4.1 Application

For tankers, only method ⅠC as defined in paragraph 2.3.1.1 shall be used.

2.4.2 Fire integrity of bulkheads and decks

2.4.2.1 In lieu of paragraph 2.3 and in addition to complying with the specific provisions for fire integrity of bulkheads and decks of tankers, the minimum fire integrity of bulkheads and decks shall be as prescribed in tables 9.7 and 9.8.

2.4.2.2 The following requirements shall govern application of the tables:

.1 Tables 9.7 and 9.8 shall apply respectively to the bulkhead and decks separating adjacent spaces.

.2 For determining the appropriate fire integrity standards to be applied to divisions between adjacent spaces, such spaces are classified according to their fire risk as shown in categories (1) to (10) below. Where the contents and use of a space are such that there is a doubt as to its classification for the purpose of this regulation, or where it is possible to assign two or more classifications to a space, it shall be treated as a space within the relevant category having the most stringent boundary requirements. Smaller, enclosed areas within a space that have less than 30% communicating openings to that space are considered separate areas. The fire integrity of the boundary bulkheads and decks of such smaller spaces shall be as prescribed in tables 9.7 and 9.8. The title of each category is intended to be typical rather than restrictive. The number in parentheses preceding each category refers to the applicable column or row in the tables.

(**1**) Control stations

Spaces containing emergency sources of power and lighting.

Wheelhouse and chartroom.

2.3.3.5 桑拿房应符合本条2.2.3.4。

2.3.4 起居处所、服务处所和控制站内的梯道和升降机围井的保护

2.3.4.1 仅穿过一层甲板的梯道，最低限度应在一层甲板上至少用“B-0”级分隔及自闭式门保护。仅穿过一层甲板的升降机，应在两层甲板上用装有钢质门的“A-0”级分隔环围。穿过一层以上甲板的梯道及升降机围井应在各层甲板上至少用“A-0”级分隔环围，并用自闭式门保护。

2.3.4.2 在设有容纳12人或少于12人的起居处所的船上，如果梯道穿过多于一层甲板，且如果每层起居处所甲板上至少有2条直接通往开敞甲板的脱险通道，则本条2.3.4.1所要求的“A-0”级可降为“B-0”级。

2.4 液货船

2.4.1 适用范围

对于液货船，应仅采用本条2.3.1.1所定义的ⅠC法。

2.4.2 舱壁和甲板的耐火完整性

2.4.2.1 取代本条2.3。除应符合关于液货船舱壁和甲板耐火完整性的具体规定外，所有舱壁和甲板的最低耐火完整性还应符合表9.7和9.8的规定。

2.4.2.2 各表的适用范围应以下列要求为准：

.1 表9.7和9.8分别适用于分隔相邻处所的舱壁和甲板。

.2 为了确定相邻处所限界面所适用的相应耐火完整性标准，这种处所按其失火危险程度分为下列(1)至(10)类。如果某一处所内的东西和用途致使按本条规定进行分类存在疑问，或有可能为某一处所指定两个或以上类别，则该处所应按具有最严格限界面要求的相关类别的处所对待。一个处所内各个较小的围蔽区域，如果其与该处所相通的开口小于30%，则视为单独区域。这种较小舱室的限界面舱壁和甲板的耐火完整性应符合表9.7和9.8的规定。每一类别的名称系典型举例，而不是限制性规定。每类前面括号内的数字是指表内相应的列或行。

(1) 控制站

设有应急电源和应急照明电源的处所。

驾驶室和海图室。

Spaces containing the ship's radio equipment.

Fire control stations.

Control room for propulsion machinery when located outside the machinery space.

Spaces containing centralized fire alarm equipment.

(2) Corridors

Corridors and lobbies.

(3) Accommodation spaces

Spaces as defined in regulation 3.1, excluding corridors.

(4) Stairways

Interior stairways, lifts, totally enclosed emergency escape trunks, and escalators (other than those wholly contained within the machinery spaces) and enclosures thereto.

In this connection, a stairway which is enclosed only at one level shall be regarded as part of the space from which it is not separated by a fire door.

(5) Service spaces (low risk)

Lockers and store-rooms not having provisions for the storage of flammable liquids and having areas less than 4 m^2 and drying rooms and laundries.

(6) Machinery spaces of category A

Spaces as defined in regulation 3.31.

(7) Other machinery spaces

Electrical equipment rooms (auto-telephone exchange and air-conditioning duct spaces). Spaces as defined in regulation 3.30, excluding machinery spaces of category A.

(8) Cargo pump-rooms

Spaces containing cargo pumps and entrances and trunks to such spaces.

(9) Service spaces (high risk)

Galleys, pantries containing cooking appliances, saunas, paint lockers and store-rooms having areas of 4 m^2 or more, spaces for the storage of flammable liquids and workshops other than those forming part of the machinery spaces.

设有船舶无线电设备的处所。

消防控制站。

位于推进装置处所外面的推进装置控制室。

设有集中失火报警设备的处所。

（2）　走廊

走廊和门厅。

（3）　起居处所

第3.1条所定义的处所，不包括走廊。

（4）　梯道

内部梯道、升降机、完全封闭的紧急脱险围井、自动扶梯（完全设在机器处所内者除外），以及通往上述梯道的环围。

对此，仅在一层甲板设有环围的梯道应视为未用防火门与其隔开的处所的一部分。

（5）　具有较小失火危险的服务处所

不存放易燃液体且面积小于4 m^2 的小间和储物间、干燥室和洗衣间。

（6）　A类机器处所

第3.31条所定义的处所。

（7）　其他机器处所

电气设备间（自动电话交换机室、空调管道处所）。除A类机器处所外，第3.30条所定义的各处所。

（8）　液货泵舱

设有液货泵的处所以及通往这些处所的入口和围壁通道。

（9）　具有较大失火危险的服务处所

厨房、设有烹调设备的配膳室、桑拿房、面积为4 m^2 及以上的油漆间和储物间、存放易燃液体的处所和不构成机器处所一部分的工作间。

(**10**) Open decks

Open deck spaces and enclosed promenades having little or no fire risk. To be considered in this category, enclosed promenades shall have no significant fire risk, meaning that furnishings shall be restricted to deck furniture. In addition, such spaces shall be naturally ventilated by permanent openings.

Air spaces (the space outside superstructures and deckhouses).

Table 9.7 Fire integrity of bulkheads separating adjacent spaces

Spaces		(1)	(2)	(3)	(4)	(5)	(6)	(7)	(8)	(9)	(10)
Control stations	(1)	A-0[c]	A-0	A-60	A-0	A-15	A-60	A-15	A-60	A-60	*
Corridors	(2)		C	B-0	B-0 A-0[a]	B-0	A-60	A-0	A-60	A-0	*
Accommodation spaces	(3)			C	B-0 A-0[a]	B-0	A-60	A-0	A-60	A-0	*
Stairways	(4)				B-0 A-0[a]	B-0 A-0[a]	A-60	A-0	A-60	A-0	*
Service spaces (low risk)	(5)					C	A-60	A-0	A-60	A-0	*
Machinery spaces of category A	(6)						*	A-0	A-0[d]	A-60	*
Other machinery spaces	(7)							A-0[b]	A-0	A-0	*
Cargo pump-rooms	(8)								*	A-60	*
Service spaces (high risk)	(9)									A-0[b]	*
Open decks	(10)										–

See notes following table 9.8.

Table 9.8 Fire integrity of decks separating adjacent spaces

Space below ↓ Space above →		(1)	(2)	(3)	(4)	(5)	(6)	(7)	(8)	(9)	(10)
Control stations	(1)	A-0	A-0	A-0	A-0	A-0	A-60	A-0	–	A-0	*
Corridors	(2)	A-0	*	*	A-0	*	A-60	A-0	–	A-0	*
Accommodation spaces	(3)	A-60	A-0	*	A-0	*	A-60	A-0	–	A-0	*
Stairways	(4)	A-0	A-0	A-0	*	A-0	A-60	A-0	–	A-0	*
Service spaces (low risk)	(5)	A-15	A-0	A-0	A-0	*	A-60	A-0	–	A-0	*
Machinery spaces of category A	(6)	A-60	A-60	A-60	A-60	A-60	*	A-60[e]	A-0	A-60	*
Other machinery spaces	(7)	A-15	A-0	A-0	A-0	A-0	A-0	*	A-0	A-0	*
Cargo pump rooms	(8)	–	–	–	–	–	A-0[d]	A-0	*	–	*
Service spaces (high risk)	(9)	A-60	A-0	A-0	A-0	A-0	A-60	A-0	–	A-0[b]	*
Open decks	(10)	*	*	*	*	*	*	*	*	*	–

Notes: To be applied to tables 9.7 and 9.8 as appropriate.

a For clarification as to which applies, see paragraphs 2.3.2 and 2.3.4.

b Where spaces are of the same numerical category and superscript "b" appears, a bulkhead or deck of the rating shown in the tables is only required when the adjacent spaces are for a different purpose (e.g. in category (9)). A galley next to a galley does not require a bulkhead but a galley next to a paint room requires an "A-0" bulkhead.

（10）　开敞甲板

开敞甲板处所和极少或无失火危险的围蔽游步甲板处所。如果考虑将围蔽游步甲板处所归为此类,其应无大的失火危险,即其内应只设有甲板用具。此外,此类处所还应通过固定开口自然通风。

露天处所(上层建筑和甲板室外的处所)。

表 9.7　分隔相邻处所舱壁的耐火完整性

处所		(1)	(2)	(3)	(4)	(5)	(6)	(7)	(8)	(9)	(10)
控制站	(1)	A-0[c]	A-0	A-60	A-0	A-15	A-60	A-15	A-60	A-60	*
走廊	(2)		C	B-0	B-0 A-0[a]	B-0	A-60	A-0	A-60	A-0	*
起居处所	(3)			C	B-0 A-0[a]	B-0	A-60	A-0	A-60	A-0	*
梯道	(4)				B-0 A-0[a]	B-0 A-0[a]	A-60	A-0	A-60	A-0	*
具有较小失火危险的服务处所	(5)					C	A-60	A-0	A-60	A-0	*
A类机器处所	(6)						*	A-0	A-0d	A-60	*
其他机器处所	(7)							A-0[b]	A-0	A-0	*
液货泵舱	(8)								*	A-60	*
具有较大失火危险的服务处所	(9)									A-0[b]	*
开敞甲板	(10)										—

见表 9.8 的注释。

表 9.8　分隔相邻处所甲板的耐火完整性

甲板下处所↓　　甲板上处所→		(1)	(2)	(3)	(4)	(5)	(6)	(7)	(8)	(9)	(10)
控制站	(1)	A-0	A-0	A-0	A-0	A-0	A-60	A-0	—	A-0	*
走廊	(2)	A-0	*	*	A-0	*	A-60	A-0	—	A-0	*
起居处所	(3)	A-60	A-0	*	A-0	*	A-60	A-0	—	A-0	*
梯道	(4)	A-0	A-0	A-0	*	A-0	A-60	A-0	—	A-0	*
具有较小失火危险的服务处所	(5)	A-15	A-0	A-0	A-0	*	A-60	A-0	—	A-0	*
A类机器处所	(6)	A-60	A-60	A-60	A-60	A-60	*	A-60[e]	A-0	A-60	*
其他机器处所	(7)	A-15	A-0	A-0	A-0	A-0	A-0	*	A-0	A-0	*
液货泵舱	(8)	—	—	—	—	—	A-0[d]	A-0	*	—	*
具有较大失火危险的服务处所	(9)	A-60	A-0	A-0	A-0	A-0	A-60	A-0	—	A-0[b]	*
开敞甲板	(10)	*	*	*	*	*	*	*	*	*	—

注:根据情况适用于表 9.7 和 9.8。

a　为分清适用哪一等级,见本条 2.3.2 和 2.3.4。

b　属于同一数字类别且有上标“b”的处所,只有当相邻处所用途不同时,才要求表中所示等级的舱壁或甲板(例如第(9)类)。相邻的厨房之间不要求用舱壁分隔,但厨房与油漆间相邻则要求用“A-0”级舱壁分隔。

c Bulkheads separating the wheelhouse, chartroom and radio room from each other may have a "B-0" rating.

d Bulkheads and decks between cargo pump-rooms and machinery spaces of category A may be penetrated by cargo pump shaft glands and similar gland penetrations, provided that gastight seals with efficient lubrication or other means of ensuring the permanence of the gas seal are fitted in way of the bulkheads or deck.

e Fire insulation need not be fitted in the machinery space in category (7) if, in the opinion of the Administration, it has little or no fire risk.

* Where an asterisk appears in the table, the division is required to be of steel or other equivalent material, but is not required to be of "A" class standard. However, where a deck, except an open deck, is penetrated for the passage of electric cables, pipes and vent ducts, such penetrations shall be made tight to prevent the passage of flame and smoke. Divisions between control stations (emergency generators) and open decks may have air intake openings without means for closure, unless a fixed gas fire-extinguishing system is fitted.

2.4.2.3 Continuous "B" class ceilings or linings, in association with the relevant decks or bulkheads, may be accepted as contributing, wholly or in part, to the required insulation and integrity of a division.

2.4.2.4 External boundaries which are required in regulation 11.2 to be of steel or other equivalent material may be pierced for the fitting of windows and sidescuttles provided that there is no requirement for such boundaries of tankers to have "A" class integrity. Similarly, in such boundaries which are not required to have "A" class integrity, doors may be constructed of materials which are to the satisfaction of the Administration.

2.4.2.5 Exterior boundaries of superstructures and deckhouses enclosing accommodation and including any overhanging decks which support such accommodation shall be constructed of steel and insulated to "A-60" standard for the whole of the portions which face the cargo area and on the outward sides for a distance of 3 m from the end boundary facing the cargo area. The distance of 3 m shall be measured horizontally and parallel to the middle line of the ship from the boundary which faces the cargo area at each deck level. In the case of the sides of those superstructures and deckhouses, such insulation shall be carried up to the underside of the deck of the navigation bridge.

2.4.2.6 Skylights to cargo pump-rooms shall be of steel, shall not contain any glass and shall be capable of being closed from outside the pump-room.

2.4.2.7 Construction and arrangement of saunas shall comply with paragraph 2.2.3.4.

3 Penetrations in fire-resisting divisions and prevention of heat transmission

3.1 Where "A" class divisions are penetrated, such penetrations shall be tested in accordance with the Fire Test Procedures Code, subject to the provisions of paragraph 4.1.1.6. In the case of ventilation ducts, paragraphs 7.1.2 and 7.3.1 apply. However, where a pipe penetration is made of steel or equivalent material having a thickness of 3 mm or greater and a length of not less than 900 mm (preferably 450 mm on each side of the division), and there are no openings, testing is not required. Such penetrations shall be suitably insulated by extension of the insulation at the same level of the division.

c　分隔驾驶室、海图室和无线电室的舱壁可以为“B-0”级。

d　在液货泵舱和A类机器处所之间的舱壁和甲板可以让货油泵轴的填料函盖以及类似的填料函盖贯穿件穿过，但应在舱壁或甲板的贯穿处采用有效润滑达到气密或采用其他能保证永久性气密的装置。

e　如果主管机关认为第(7)类中的机器处所极少或无失火危险，可不必设置防火隔热。

*　表中出现星号*处，表示分隔要求为钢质或等效材料，但不要求为“A”级标准。但是，除开敞甲板以外，如果甲板被贯穿以供电缆、管线和通风管道通过，应对此类贯穿件进行密封以防止火焰和烟气通过。除非安装了固定式气体灭火系统，控制站(应急发电机室)和开敞甲板之间的分隔可以设有不带关闭装置的空气进入开口。

2.4.2.3　连续“B”级天花板或衬板连同有关的甲板和舱壁，可以认为全部或部分地起到分隔所要求的隔热性和完整性的作用。

2.4.2.4　第11.2条所要求的钢质或其他等效材料外部限界面，可为安装窗或舷窗的目的而开孔，只要未要求液货船的这类限界面具有“A”级完整性。同样，在不要求具有“A”级完整性的限界面上，门可以使用主管机关满意的材料制成。

2.4.2.5　环围起居处所的上层建筑和甲板室的外部限界面并包括支承该起居处所的悬伸甲板，其面向货物区域的所有部分以及从面向货物区域的限界面端部起3 m之内的外表面，应用钢材制成并隔热至“A-60”级标准。该3 m距离应在每层甲板上从面向货物区域的限界面起平行于船舶中线按水平面量取。对于这种上层建筑和甲板室的各个侧面，此种隔热应延伸到驾驶台甲板的底面。

2.4.2.6　液货泵舱的天窗应为钢质，不得镶有玻璃，并应能在泵舱外部予以关闭。

2.4.2.7　桑拿房的构造和布置应符合本条2.2.3.4。

3　耐火分隔上的贯穿及防止热传递

3.1　如贯穿“A”级分隔，该贯穿件应在符合本条4.1.1.6规定的前提下，根据《耐火试验程序规则》进行试验。对于通风管道，应适用本条7.1.2和7.3.1。但是，如果贯穿套管系由厚度3 mm及以上，长度不小于900 mm(以该分隔两侧各450 mm为宜)的钢或等效材料制成，且无开口，则不要求进行试验。该贯穿件应通过延伸与该分隔同样级别的隔热材料适当隔热。

3.2 Where "B" class divisions are penetrated for the passage of electric cables, pipes, trunks, ducts, etc., or for the fitting of ventilation terminals, lighting fixtures and similar devices, arrangements shall be made to ensure that the fire resistance is not impaired, subject to the provisions of paragraph 7.3.2. Pipes other than steel or copper that penetrate "B" class divisions shall be protected by either:

.1 a fire-tested penetration device suitable for the fire resistance of the division pierced and the type of pipe used; or

.2 a steel sleeve, having a thickness of not less than 1.8 mm and a length of not less than 900 mm for pipe diameters of 150 mm or more and not less than 600 mm for pipe diameters of less than 150 mm (preferably equally divided to each side of the division). The pipe shall be connected to the ends of the sleeve by flanges or couplings; or the clearance between the sleeve and the pipe shall not exceed 2.5 mm; or any clearance between pipe and sleeve shall be made tight by means of non-combustible or other suitable material.

3.3 Uninsulated metallic pipes penetrating "A" or "B" class divisions shall be of materials having a melting temperature which exceeds 950 ℃ for "A-0" and 850 ℃ for "B-0" class divisions.

3.4 In approving structural fire protection details, the Administration shall have regard to the risk of heat transmission at intersections and terminal points of required thermal barriers. The insulation of a deck or bulkhead shall be carried past the penetration, intersection or terminal point for a distance of at least 450 mm in the case of steel and aluminium structures. If a space is divided with a deck or a bulkhead of "A" class standard having insulation of different values, the insulation with the higher value shall continue on the deck or bulkhead with the insulation of the lesser value for a distance of at least 450 mm.

4 Protection of openings in fire-resisting divisions

4.1 Openings in bulkheads and decks in passenger ships

4.1.1 Openings in "A" class divisions

4.1.1.1 Except for hatches between cargo, special category, store, and baggage spaces, and between such spaces and the weather decks, openings shall be provided with permanently attached means of closing which shall be at least as effective for resisting fires as the divisions in which they are fitted.

4.1.1.2 The construction of doors and door frames in "A" class divisions, with the means of securing them when closed, shall provide resistance to fire as well as to the passage of smoke and flame equivalent to that of the bulkheads in which the doors are situated, this being determined in accordance with the Fire Test Procedures Code. Such doors and door frames shall be constructed of steel or other equivalent material. Doors approved without the sill being part of the frame, which are installed on or after 1 July 2010, shall be installed such that the gap under the door does not exceed 12 mm. A non-combustible sill shall be installed under the door such that floor coverings do not extend beneath the closed door.

3.2 如果贯穿"B"级分隔,用于电缆、管道、围壁通道、导管等的通过,或安装通风端口、照明灯具和类似装置,应在符合本条7.3.2的规定的前提下做出适当布置,以确保其耐火性不被削弱。应通过以下二者之一对贯穿"B"级分隔的钢管或铜管以外的管道加以保护:

.1 一个经过耐火试验的贯穿装置,具有适合于被穿透的分隔和所用管道类型的耐火性能;或

.2 厚度不小于1.8 mm的钢质套管,对直径为150 mm及以上的管道,长度不小于900 mm,对直径小于150 mm的管道,长度不小于600 mm(以该分隔两侧的长度相等为宜)。管道应通过法兰或管箍与套管的两端连接;或套管与管道之间的空隙不得超过2.5 mm;或管道和套管之间的任何空隙应用不燃材料或其他合适的材料填实。

3.3 穿"A"级或"B"级分隔的未经隔热的金属管,其材料的熔点对"A-0"级分隔应超过950 ℃,对"B-0"级分隔应超过850 ℃。

3.4 主管机关在对结构防火的细节进行认可时,应考虑到所要求隔热物的接头处和终止点的热传递危险。对于钢或铝结构的甲板或舱壁,其隔热应至少延伸至超过贯穿处、接头处或终止点450 m。如果由"A"级标准的甲板或舱壁分隔的处所有不同的隔热等级,等级高的隔热应在隔热等级低的甲板或舱壁上至少延伸450 m。

4 耐火分隔上开口的保护

4.1 客船舱壁和甲板上的开口

4.1.1 "A"级分隔上的开口

4.1.1.1 除货物处所、特种处所、储藏间和行李室之间的舱口以及这些处所与露天甲板之间的舱口外,开口应设有永久附连于其上的关闭装置,其耐火性能应至少与其所在的分隔相等。

4.1.1.2 "A"级分隔上所有门和门框的结构及其在关闭时的锁紧装置,其耐火和阻止烟气及火焰通过的性能应与其所在舱壁的此种性能等效,根据《耐火试验程序规则》确定。这些门及门框应由钢或其他等效材料建造。在2010年7月1日或之后安装的,已获核准的门槛并非门框一部分的门,其门下间隙须不超过12 mm。门下须装设不燃门槛,地板敷料不得延续至关闭的门之下。

4.1.1.3 Watertight doors need not be insulated.

4.1.1.4 It shall be possible for each door to be opened and closed from each side of the bulkhead by one person only.

4.1.1.5 Fire doors in main vertical zone bulkheads, galley boundaries and stairway enclosures other than power-operated watertight doors and those which are normally locked shall satisfy the following requirements:

.1 the doors shall be self-closing and be capable of closing with an angle of inclination of up to 3.5° opposing closure;

.2 the approximate time of closure for hinged fire doors shall be no more than 40 s and no less than 10 s from the beginning of their movement with the ship in upright position. The approximate uniform rate of closure for sliding doors shall be of no more than 0.2 m/s and no less than 0.1 m/s with the ship in upright position;

.3 the doors, except those for emergency escape trunks, shall be capable of remote release from the continuously manned central control station, either simultaneously or in groups, and shall be capable of release also individually from a position at both sides of the door. Release switches shall have an on-off function to prevent automatic resetting of the system;

.4 hold-back hooks not subject to central control station release are prohibited;

.5 a door closed remotely from the central control station shall be capable of being re-opened from both sides of the door by local control. After such local opening, the door shall automatically close again;

.6 indication shall be provided at the fire door indicator panel in the continuously manned central control station whether each door is closed;

.7 the release mechanism shall be so designed that the door will automatically close in the event of disruption of the control system or central power supply;

.8 local power accumulators for power-operated doors shall be provided in the immediate vicinity of the doors to enable the doors to be operated at least 10 times (fully opened and closed) after disruption of the control system or central power supply using the local controls;

.9 disruption of the control system or central power supply at one door shall not impair the safe functioning of the other doors;

.10 remote-released sliding or power-operated doors shall be equipped with an alarm that sounds at least 5 s but no more than 10 s, after the door is released from the central control station and before the door begins to move and continues sounding until the door is completely closed;

.11 a door designed to re-open upon contacting an object in its path shall re-open not more than 1 m from the point of contact;

4.1.1.3 水密门不必隔热。

4.1.1.4 应只需1人就能开启和关闭舱壁每一面的每扇门。

4.1.1.5 除动力操纵的水密门和通常锁闭的门外，主竖区舱壁、厨房限界面及梯道环围上的防火门应满足以下要求：

.1 门应为自闭型，并应在门朝关闭的反方向倾斜至3.5°时仍能自动关闭；

.2 在船舶处于正浮状态时，铰链式防火门的大致关闭时间从动作开始至关闭，应不超过40 s，但不少于10 s。在船舶处于正浮状态时，滑动式防火门的大致平均关闭速率应不超过0.2 m/s，但不少于0.1 m/s；

.3 除紧急脱险通道的门以外，所有防火门应能从连续有人值班的集中控制站同时或成组遥控释放关闭，并应能从门两侧的位置单独释放关闭。释放开关应具有通—断功能，以防止系统自动复位；

.4 禁止使用不能由集中控制站脱开的门背钩；

.5 从集中控制站遥控关闭的门应能从门的两则通过就地控制重新开启。就地开启以后，应能再次自动关闭；

.6 连续有人值班的集中控制站内的防火门显示屏上应显示出每扇门是否都已关闭；

.7 释放装置应设计成在控制系统或主电源出现故障时，门将自动关闭；

.8 对于动力操纵的防火门，应在紧靠门的位置设有局部蓄能器，以使该门能在控制系统或主电源出现故障后，通过就地控制至少可操作（全开和关闭）10次；

.9 某一个门处的控制系统或主电源故障不得妨害其他门的安全工作；

.10 遥控释放关闭的滑动门或动力操纵的门应装有听觉报警装置，在门由集中控制站释放后和门开始动作前至少5 s，但不超过10 s，发出听觉报警并持续至门完全关闭；

.11 被设计成在关闭过程中遇到障碍物时重新开启的门，其重新开启度从接触点开始不得超过1 m；

.12 double-leaf doors equipped with a latch necessary for their fire integrity shall have a latch that is automatically activated by the operation of the doors when released by the system;

.13 doors giving direct access to special category spaces which are power-operated and automatically closed need not be equipped with the alarms and remote-release mechanisms required in paragraphs 4.1.1.5.3 and 4.1.1.5.10;

.14 the components of the local control system shall be accessible for maintenance and adjusting;

.15 power-operated doors shall be provided with a control system of an approved type which shall be able to operate in case of fire and be in accordance with the Fire Test Procedures Code. This system shall satisfy the following requirements:

.1 the control system shall be able to operate the door at the temperature of at least 200 ℃ for at least 60 min, served by the power supply;

.2 the power supply for all other doors not subject to fire shall not be impaired; and

.3 at temperatures exceeding 200 ℃, the control system shall be automatically isolated from the power supply and shall be capable of keeping the door closed up to at least 945 ℃.

4.1.1.6 In ships carrying not more than 36 passengers, where a space is protected by an automatic sprinkler fire detection and fire alarm system complying with the provisions of the Fire Safety Systems Code or fitted with a continuous "B" class ceiling, openings in decks not forming steps in main vertical zones nor bounding horizontal zones shall be closed reasonably tight and such decks shall meet the "A" class integrity requirements in so far as is reasonable and practicable in the opinion of the Administration.

4.1.1.7 The requirements for "A" class integrity of the outer boundaries of a ship shall not apply to glass partitions, windows and sidescuttles, provided that there is no requirement for such boundaries to have "A" class integrity in paragraph 4.1.3.3. The requirements for "A" class integrity of the outer boundaries of the ship shall not apply to exterior doors, except for those in superstructures and deckhouses facing life-saving appliances, embarkation and external assembly station areas, external stairs and open decks used for escape routes. Stairway enclosure doors need not meet this requirement.

4.1.1.8 Except for watertight doors, weathertight doors (semi-watertight doors), doors leading to the open deck and doors which need to be reasonably gastight, all "A" class doors located in stairways, public spaces and main vertical zone bulkheads in escape routes shall be equipped with a self-closing hose port. The material, construction and fire resistance of the hose port shall be equivalent to the door into which it is fitted, and shall be a 150 mm square clear opening with the door closed and shall be inset into the lower edge of the door, opposite the door hinges or, in the case of sliding doors, nearest the opening.

.12 装有耐火完整性所必需的压紧装置的双叶门,在被控制系统释放时,其压紧装置应随门的动作而自动工作;

.13 直接通向特种处所的动力操纵和自动关闭门,不必装设本条4.1.1.5.3和4.1.1.5.10要求的报警装置和遥控释放装置;

.14 就地控制系统的组件应易于进行维护和调整;

.15 动力操纵的门应设有符合《耐火试验程序规则》且能在发生火灾时操作的认可型的控制装置。该装置应满足以下要求:

.1 在有电力供应时,控制装置应能在不低于 200 ℃的温度下操作门至少达到 60 min;

.2 所有未受火灾影响的其他门的供电不得受到妨害;和

.3 在温度超过 200 ℃时,控制装置应自动与供电电源断开,并能在不低于945 ℃温度下使门保持关闭。

4.1.1.6 对载客不超过 36 人的客船,如果某一处所由符合《消防安全系统规则》规定的自动喷水器、探火和失火报警系统保护,或设有连续"B"级天花板,则在主竖区内未形成阶层亦不作为水平区限界面的甲板上的开口,应能适度紧密关闭,并且在主管机关认为合理和实际可行的范围内,这类甲板应满足"A"级完整性的要求。

4.1.1.7 对船舶外部限界面的"A"级完整性的要求不适用于玻璃隔板、窗及舷窗,只要本条4.1.3.3 对这类限界面不要求有"A"级耐火完整性。对船舶外部限界面的"A"级完整性的要求不适用于外门,但上层建筑和甲板室面对救生设备、登乘站和外部集合站区域、外部梯道和用作脱险通道的开敞甲板的外门除外。梯道环围的门不必满足这一要求。

4.1.1.8 除水密门、风雨密门(半风雨密门)、通往开敞甲板的门和需要适度气密的门以外,所有位于脱险通道内的梯道、公共处所和主竖区舱壁上的"A"级门,应装有一个自闭式消防水管通道。该消防水管通道的材料、结构和耐火性能应与其所在的门相当,其开口净尺寸在门处于关闭状态下应为 150 mm×150 mm,并应嵌入门的下边缘与铰链相对之处,或对于滑动门,则该开口应位于与门开口最接近之处。

4.1.1.9 Where it is necessary that a ventilation duct passes through a main vertical zone division, a fail-safe automatic closing fire damper shall be fitted adjacent to the division. The damper shall also be capable of being manually closed from each side of the division. The operating position shall be readily accessible and be marked in red light-reflecting colour. The duct between the division and the damper shall be of steel or other equivalent material and, if necessary, insulated to comply with the requirements of paragraph 3.1. The damper shall be fitted on at least one side of the division with a visible indicator showing whether the damper is in the open position.

4.1.2 Openings in "B" class divisions

4.1.2.1 Doors and door frames in "B" class divisions and means of securing them shall provide a method of closure which shall have resistance to fire equivalent to that of the divisions, this being determined in accordance with the Fire Test Procedures Code except that ventilation openings may be permitted in the lower portion of such doors. Where such opening is in or under a door, the total net area of any such opening or openings shall not exceed 0.05 m^2. Alternatively, a non-combustible air balance duct routed between the cabin and the corridor, and located below the sanitary unit, is permitted where the cross-sectional area of the duct does not exceed 0.05 m^2. All ventilation openings shall be fitted with a grill made of non-combustible material. Doors shall be non-combustible. Doors approved without the sill being part of the frame, which are installed on or after 1 July 2010, shall be installed such that the gap under the door does not exceed 25 mm.

4.1.2.2 Cabin doors in "B" class divisions shall be of a self-closing type. Hold-back hooks are not permitted.

4.1.2.3 The requirements for "B" class integrity of the outer boundaries of a ship shall not apply to glass partitions, windows and sidescuttles. Similarly, the requirements for "B" class integrity shall not apply to exterior doors in superstructures and deckhouses. For ships carrying not more than 36 passengers, the Administration may permit the use of combustible materials in doors separating cabins from the individual interior sanitary spaces such as showers.

4.1.2.4 In ships carrying not more than 36 passengers, where an automatic sprinkler system complying with the provisions of the Fire Safety Systems Code is fitted:

.1 openings in decks not forming steps in main vertical zones nor bounding horizontal zones shall be closed reasonably tight and such decks shall meet the "B" class integrity requirements in so far as is reasonable and practicable in the opinion of the Administration; and

.2 openings in corridor bulkheads of "B" class materials shall be protected in accordance with the provisions of paragraph 2.2.2.

4.1.1.9 如果通风导管必须通过主竖区分隔,应在分隔邻近处装设故障安全型自动关闭挡火闸。该挡火闸还应能从分隔的每一侧都可手动关闭。其操作位置应易于到达,并用红的反光颜色标出。分隔与挡火闸之间的导管应为钢质或其他等效材料,并在必要时其隔热应符合本条 3.1 的要求。挡火闸应至少在分隔的一侧装设显示器,指明挡火闸是否处于开启的位置。

4.1.2 "B"级分隔上的开口

4.1.2.1 "B"级分隔的门和门框及其锁紧装置的关闭方式所达到的耐火性能应等效于该级分隔的耐火性能,根据《耐火试验程序规则》确定,但允许在门的下部设置通风开口。如果这种通风开口是开在门上或门以下,则任一或所有这种开口的总净面积应不超过 0.05 m^2。作为该布置的替代,允许使用在居住舱室和走廊之间及卫生设施之下布设的不燃空气平衡导管,但这种导管的横截面积不得超过0.05 m^2。所有通风开口应设有不燃材料制成的格栅。门应具有不燃性。经批准,在 2010 年 7 月 1 日及之后安装的门框上不含门槛的门,安装时,门下的间隙不得超过 25 mm。

4.1.2.2 在"B"级分隔上的居住舱室的门应为自闭型,不允许使用门背钩。

4.1.2.3 对船舶外部限界面的"B"级完整性要求,不适用于玻璃隔板、窗及舷窗。同样,"B"级完整性要求也不适用于上层建筑及甲板室的外门。对载客不超过 36 人的客船,主管机关可允许分隔居住舱室与单独的内部卫生处所(如淋浴间)的门使用可燃材料。

4.1.2.4 载客不超过 36 人的客船,如设有符合《消防安全系统规则》规定的自动喷水器系统,则:

.1 在主竖区内未形成阶层亦不作为水平区限界面的甲板上的开口,应能适度紧密关闭,并且在主管机关认为合理和实际可行的范围内,这类甲板应满足"B"级完整性的要求;和

.2 "B"级材料走廊舱壁上的开口,应按本条 2.2.2 的规定加以保护。

4.1.3 Windows and sidescuttles

4.1.3.1 Windows and sidescuttles in bulkheads within accommodation and service spaces and control stations other than those to which the provisions of paragraphs 4.1.1.7 and 4.1.2.3 apply shall be so constructed as to preserve the integrity requirements of the type of bulkheads in which they are fitted, this being determined in accordance with the Fire Test Procedures Code.

4.1.3.2 Notwithstanding the requirements of tables 9.1 to 9.4, windows and sidescuttles in bulkheads separating accommodation and service spaces and control stations from weather shall be constructed with frames of steel or other suitable material. The glass shall be retained by a metal glazing bead or angle.

4.1.3.3 Windows facing life-saving appliances, embarkation and assembly stations, external stairs and open decks used for escape routes, and windows situated below liferaft and escape slide embarkation areas shall have fire integrity as required in table 9.1. Where automatic dedicated sprinkler heads are provided for windows, "A-0" windows may be accepted as equivalent. To be considered under this paragraph, the sprinkler heads shall either be:

.1 dedicated heads located above the windows, and installed in addition to the conventional ceiling sprinklers; or

.2 conventional ceiling sprinkler heads arranged such that the window is protected by an average application rate of at least 5 L/min/m^2 and the additional window area is included in the calculation of the area of coverage; or

.3 water-mist nozzles that have been tested and approved in accordance with the guidelines approved by the Organization. ①

Windows located in the ship's side below the lifeboat embarkation area shall have fire integrity at least equal to "A-0" class.

4.1.3.4 Notwithstanding the requirement in paragraph 4.1.3.3, the requirements in paragraphs 4.1.3.5 and 4.1.3.6 shall apply to ships constructed on or after 1 January 2020.

4.1.3.5 For ships carrying more than 36 passengers, windows facing survival craft, embarkation and assembly stations, external stairs and open decks used for escape routes, and windows situated below liferaft and escape slide embarkation areas shall have fire integrity as required in table 9.1. Where automatic dedicated sprinkler heads are provided for windows, "A-0" windows may be accepted as equivalent. To be considered under this paragraph, the sprinkler heads must either be:

.1 dedicated heads located above the windows, and installed in addition to the conventional ceiling sprinklers; or

.2 conventional ceiling sprinkler heads arranged such that the window is protected by an average application rate of at least 5 L/min/m^2 and the additional window area is included in the calculation of the area of coverage; or

---

① Refer to *Revised guidelines for approval of sprinkler systems equivalent to that referred to in SOLAS regulation Ⅱ-2/12* (resolution A.800(19), as amended).

4.1.3　窗和舷窗

4.1.3.1　起居处所、服务处所和控制站舱壁上的窗和舷窗，除那些应符合本条4.1.1.7和4.1.2.3规定者外，其构造应能保持对其所在舱壁类型的完整性要求，根据《耐火试验程序规则》确定。

4.1.3.2　尽管有表9.1至9.4的要求，分隔起居处所、服务处所和控制站与露天处所的舱壁上的窗和舷窗，应配有用钢材或其他适合材料建造的框架。窗的玻璃应用金属镶边或镶角加以固定。

4.1.3.3　面向救生设备、登乘和集合点、外部梯道和用作脱险通道的开敞甲板的窗以及位于救生筏和撤离滑道登乘区以下的窗，应具有表9.1所要求的耐火完整性。如果这些窗配有专用的自动喷水器喷头，则可以接受"A-0"级窗作为等效窗。根据本节考虑，喷水器喷头应为下述二者之一：

.1　除安装常规的天花板喷水器外，在窗的上方安装专用喷头；或

.2　常规天花板喷水器喷头的布置，使窗受到平均喷水率至少5 L/min/m^2的保护，在计算喷水覆盖面积时计入窗的附加面积；或

.3　按照本组织批准的导则①经过试验并得到批准的水雾喷嘴。

4.1.3.4　尽管有第4.1.3.3款的要求，第4.1.3.5和4.1.3.6款的要求须适用于2020年1月1日或以后建造的船舶。

4.1.3.5　对于载运超过36名乘客的船舶，面向救生艇筏、登乘和集合站、外部梯道和用作脱险通道的开敞甲板的窗，以及位于救生筏和撤离滑道登乘区以下的窗，须具有表9.1所要求的耐火完整性。如果这些窗配有专用的自动喷水器喷头，则可以接受"A-0"级窗作为等效替代。出于本款的考虑，喷水器喷头须为下述之一：

.1　除安装常规的天花板喷水器之外，在窗的上方安装专用喷头；或

.2　常规天花板喷水器喷头，其布置须使窗受到平均喷水率至少为5 L/min/m^2的保护，在计算喷水覆盖面积时计入窗的附加面积；或

① 参见《经修订的与SOLAS公约第Ⅱ-2/12条规定等效的喷水器系统认可导则》(经修正的第A.800(19)号决议)。

.3 water-mist nozzles that have been tested and approved in accordance with the guidelines approved by the Organization①; and

windows located in the ship's side below the lifeboat embarkation area shall have fire integrity at least equal to "A-0" class.

4.1.3.6 For ships carrying not more than 36 passengers, windows facing survival craft and escape slide, embarkation areas and windows situated below such areas shall have fire integrity at least equal to "A-0" class.

4.2 Doors in fire-resisting divisions in cargo ships

4.2.1 The fire resistance of doors shall be equivalent to that of the division in which they are fitted, this being determined in accordance with the Fire Test Procedures Code. Doors approved as "A" class without the sill being part of the frame, which are installed on or after 1 July 2010, shall be installed such that the gap under the door does not exceed 12 mm and a non-combustible sill shall be installed under the door such that floor coverings do not extend beneath the closed door. Doors approved as "B" class without the sill being part of the frame, which are installed on or after 1 July 2010, shall be installed such that the gap under the door does not exceed 25 mm. Doors and door frames in "A" class divisions shall be constructed of steel. Doors in "B" class divisions shall be non-combustible. Doors fitted in boundary bulkheads of machinery spaces of category A shall be reasonably gastight and self-closing. In ships constructed according to method ⅠC, the Administration may permit the use of combustible materials in doors separating cabins from individual interior sanitary accommodation such as showers.

4.2.2 Doors required to be self-closing shall not be fitted with hold-back hooks. However, hold-back arrangements fitted with remote release devices of the fail-safe type may be utilized.

4.2.3 In corridor bulkheads, ventilation openings may be permitted in and under the doors of cabins and public spaces. Ventilation openings are also permitted in "B" class doors leading to lavatories, offices, pantries, lockers and store-rooms. Except as permitted below, the openings shall be provided only in the lower half of a door. Where such an opening is in or under a door, the total net area of any such opening or openings shall not exceed 0.05 m^2. Alternatively, a non-combustible air balance duct routed between the cabin and the corridor, and located below the sanitary unit, is permitted where the cross-sectional area of the duct does not exceed 0.05 m^2. Ventilation openings, except those under the door, shall be fitted with a grill made of non-combustible material.

4.2.4 Watertight doors need not be insulated.

5 Protection of openings in machinery space boundaries

5.1 Application

5.1.1 The provision of this paragraph shall apply to machinery spaces of category A and, where the Administration considers it desirable, to other machinery spaces.

① Refer to the *Revised guidelines for approval of sprinkler systems equivalent to that referred to in SOLAS regulation Ⅱ-2/12* (*resdution A.800(19), as amended*).

.3 已按本组织批准的导则[①]试验和认可的水雾喷嘴。

位于救生艇登乘区以下的舷侧窗须至少具有相当于“A-0”级的耐火完整性。

4.1.3.6 对于载运不超过 36 名乘客的船舶，面向救生艇筏和撤离滑道、登乘区的窗以及位于此类区域以下的窗，须至少具有相当于“A-0”级的耐火完整性。

4.2 货船耐火分隔上的门

4.2.1 门的耐火性能应与其所在分隔的耐火性能相同，根据《耐火试验程序规则》确定。在 2010 年 7 月 1 日或之后安装的，已获核准的门槛并非门框一部分的“A”类门，其门下间隙须不超过 12 mm，并且门下须装设不燃门槛，地板敷料不得延续至关闭的门之下。在 2010 年 7 月 1 日或之后安装的，已获核准的门槛并非门框一部分的“B”类门，其门下间隙不得超过 25 mm。在“A”级分隔上的门及门框应为钢质结构。在“B”级分隔上的门应为不燃材料。装设在 A 类机器处所限界面舱壁上的门，应适度气密和能够自闭。按ⅠC 法建造的船舶，主管机关可允许在分隔居住舱室与单独的内部卫生间(如淋浴室)的门上使用可燃材料。

4.2.2 要求自闭的门不得装设门背钩。但是，可以使用装有故障安全型遥控释放设备的门背钩装置。

4.2.3 在走廊舱壁上，可允许在居住舱室和公共处所的门上及门以下开设通风开口。还允许在通往盥洗室、办公室、厨房、储物柜和储藏室的“B”级门上开设通风开口。除下列允许者外，开口应仅设在门的下半部。如果这种开口是开在门上或门以下，则任一或所有这种开口的总净面积不得超过 0.05 m^2。作为这种布置的替代，允许使用在居住舱室和走廊之间及卫生设施之下布设的不燃空气平衡导管，但这种导管的横截面积不得超过 0.05 m^2。通风开口除设在门以下者外，应设有不燃材料制成的格栅。

4.2.4 水密门不必隔热。

5 机器处所限界面上开口的保护

5.1 适用范围

5.1.1 本规定适用于 A 类机器处所以及主管机关认为需要的其他机器处所。

① 参见《经修订的与 SOLAS 公约第Ⅱ-2/12 条规定等效的喷水器系统认可导则》(经修正的第 A.800(19)号决议)。

5.2 Protection of openings in machinery space boundaries

5.2.1 The number of skylights, doors, ventilators, openings in funnels to permit exhaust ventilation and other openings to machinery spaces shall be reduced to a minimum consistent with the needs of ventilation and the proper and safe working of the ship.

5.2.2 Skylights shall be of steel and shall not contain glass panels.

5.2.3 Means of control shall be provided for closing power-operated doors or actuating release mechanisms on doors other than power-operated watertight doors. The controls shall be located outside the space concerned, where they will not be cut off in the event of fire in the space it serves.

5.2.4 In passenger ships, the means of control required in paragraph 5.2.3 shall be situated at one control position or grouped in as few positions as possible, to the satisfaction of the Administration. Such positions shall have safe access from the open deck.

5.2.5 In passenger ships, doors, other than power-operated watertight doors, shall be so arranged that positive closure is assured in case of fire in the space by power-operated closing arrangements or by the provision of self-closing doors capable of closing against an inclination of 3.5° opposing closure, and having a fail-safe hold-back arrangement, provided with a remotely operated release device. Doors for emergency escape trunks need not be fitted with a fail-safe hold-back facility and a remotely operated release device.

5.2.6 Windows shall not be fitted in machinery space boundaries. However, this does not preclude the use of glass in control rooms within the machinery spaces.

6 Protection of cargo space boundaries

6.1 In passenger ships carrying more than 36 passengers, the boundary bulkheads and decks of special category and ro-ro spaces shall be insulated to "A-60" class standard. However, where a category (5), (9) or (10) space, as defined in paragraph 2.2.3, is on one side of the division, the standard may be reduced to "A-0". Where fuel oil tanks are below a special category space, the integrity of the deck between such spaces may be reduced to "A-0" standard.

6.2 In passenger ships, indicators shall be provided on the navigation bridge which shall indicate when any fire door leading to or from the special category spaces is closed.

6.3 In tankers, for the protection of cargo tanks carrying crude oil and petroleum products having a flashpoint not exceeding 60 ℃, materials readily rendered ineffective by heat shall not be used for valves, fittings, tank opening covers, cargo vent piping and cargo piping so as to prevent the spread of fire to the cargo.

7 Ventilation systems

(*This paragraph applies to ships constructed on or after 1 January 2016*)

5.2 机器处所限界面上开口的保护

5.2.1 天窗、门、通风筒、烟囱上供排气通风用的开口以及机器处所的其他开口的数量应减少到符合通风和船舶正常安全工作所需的最低数量。

5.2.2 天窗应为钢质,且不应含有玻璃板。

5.2.3 应设有控制装置关闭动力操纵门或启动除动力操纵水密门以外的门的释放装置。控制装置应位于有关处所的外部,且在其所服务的处所失火时不致被切断的位置。

5.2.4 在客船上,本条5.2.3所要求的控制装置应位于一个控制位置或集中于尽可能少的位置内,并使主管机关满意。此种位置应具有通往开敞甲板的安全通道。

5.2.5 在客船上,除动力操纵的水密门外,门的布置应能够在所在处所失火时,由动力操纵的关闭装置,或通过能够在门朝关闭的反方向倾斜3.5°时关闭并设有故障安全型门背钩及遥控释放装置的自闭门保证其确实关闭。紧急脱险通道的门不必安装故障安全型门背钩装置和遥控释放装置。

5.2.6 在机器处所的限界面上不应设窗。但这并不排除在机器处所内的控制室使用玻璃。

6 货物处所限界面的保护

6.1 载客超过36人的客船,特种处所和滚装处所的限界面舱壁和甲板应隔热至“A-60”级标准,但如果分隔的一侧为本条2.2.3所定义的第(5)、(9)和(10)类处所,该标准可降至“A-0”级。如果燃油舱位于特种处所的下面,则两处所间甲板的完整性可降至“A-0”级标准。

6.2 在客船上,应在驾驶室内设有指示器,该指示器应能指示出任何出入特种处所的门是否已关闭。

6.3 在液货船上,为了保护装载闪点不超过60 ℃的原油和成品油的液货舱,阀门、附件、液舱开口封盖、货物透气管道和液货管道不得使用遇热易于失效的材料,以防止火灾蔓延到货物。

7 通风系统

(本款适用于2016年1月1日或之后建造的船舶。)

7.1 General

7.1.1 Ventilation ducts, including single and double wall ducts, shall be of steel or equivalent material except flexible bellows of short length not exceeding 600 mm used for connecting fans to the ducting in air-conditioning rooms. Unless expressly provided otherwise in paragraph 7.1.6, any other material used in the construction of ducts, including insulation, shall also be non-combustible. However, short ducts, not generally exceeding 2 m in length and with a free cross-sectional area① not exceeding 0.02 m^2, need not be of steel or equivalent material, subject to the following conditions:

.1 the ducts shall be made of non-combustible material, which may be faced internally and externally with membranes having low flame-spread characteristics and, in each case, a calorific value② not exceeding 45 MJ/m^2 of their surface area for the thickness used;

.2 the ducts are only used at the end of the ventilation device; and

.3 the ducts are not situated less than 600 mm, measured along the duct, from an opening in an "A" or "B" class division, including continuous "B" class ceiling.

7.1.2 The following arrangements shall be tested in accordance with the Fire Test Procedures Code:

.1 fire dampers, including their relevant means of operation, however, the testing is not required for dampers located at the lower end of the duct in exhaust ducts for galley ranges, which must be of steel and capable of stopping the draught in the duct; and

.2 duct penetrations through "A" class divisions. However, the test is not required where steel sleeves are directly joined to ventilation ducts by means of riveted or screwed Connections or by welding.

7.1.3 Fire dampers shall be easily accessible. Where they are placed behind ceilings or linings, these ceilings or linings shall be provided with an inspection hatch on which the identification number of the fire damper is marked. The fire damper identification number shall also be marked on any remote controls provided.

7.1.4 Ventilation ducts shall be provided with hatches for inspection and cleaning. The hatches shall be located near the fire dampers.

7.1.5 The main inlets and outlets of ventilation systems shall be capable of being closed from outside the spaces being ventilated. The means of closing shall be easily accessible as well as prominently and permanently marked and shall indicate the operating position of the closing device.

7.1.6 Combustible gaskets in flanged ventilation duct connections are not permitted within 600 mm of openings in "A" or "B" class divisions and in ducts required to be of "A" class construction.

---

① The term *free cross-sectional area* means, even in the case of a pre-insulated duct, the area calculated on the basis of the inner dimensions of the duct itself and not the insulation.

② Refer to the recommendations published by the International Organization for Standardization, in particular publication ISO 1716:2002, *Reaction to fire tests for building products—Determination of the heat of combustion.*

7.1 总则

7.1.1 通风导管(包括单层及双层壁导管)须由钢或等效材料制成,但用于连接风扇至空调室内导管的、不超过 600 mm 的短节柔性波纹管除外。除第 7.1.6 款中明文规定者外,用于导管的构造包括绝缘体的任何其他材料亦须是不可燃材料。但一般长度不超过 2 m 且有效横截面积①不超过 0.02 m^2 的短节导管,如满足下列条件,则不必用钢或等效材料制成:

.1 导管须用不可燃材料制成,其内外表面可加装低播焰性的膜,且在每种情况下,其所用厚度的表面面积的热值②不超过 45 MJ/m^2;

.2 导管只用在通风装置的末端;且

.3 导管不要敷设在沿导管的方向距"A"或"B"级分隔(包括连续"B"级天花板)上的开口小于 600 mm 之处。

7.1.2 以下布置须根据《耐火试验程序规则》进行试验:

.1 挡火闸,包括其相关操作装置;但对厨房炉灶排气导管中位于导管下端的挡火闸不要求进行试验,该挡火闸必须是钢质的并能阻止导管中的气流;和

.2 贯穿"A"级分隔的导管。但是,如钢套管通过铆接或螺纹接头或焊接直接与通风导管连接,则不要求进行试验。

7.1.3 挡火闸须易于接近。如挡火闸位于天花板或衬板的后面,这些天花板或衬板须设有一个检查口,在检查口上须标明挡火闸的识别号。挡火闸识别号还须标示在所设的任何遥控装置上。

7.1.4 通风导管须设有检查和清洁口。检查和清洁口的位置须靠近挡火闸。

7.1.5 通风系统的主要进气口和出气口须能从通风处所的外部关闭。关闭装置须易于到达,以及有显著和永久性标志,并须指明关闭装置的操作位置。

7.1.6 法兰式通风导管接头中的易燃垫片不准用于"A"或"B"级分隔上开口的 600 mm 范围内和要求为"A"级结构的导管上。

① 术语有效横截面积,系指根据导管内径而非绝缘层计算的面积,即使是预装隔热的导管。
② 参见国际标准化组织出版的建议案,特别是 ISO 1716:2002《建筑产品耐火试验反应——燃烧热值测定》。

7.1.7 Ventilation openings or air balance ducts between two enclosed spaces shall not be provided except as permitted by paragraphs 4.1.2.1 and 4.2.3.

7.2 Arrangement of ducts

7.2.1 The ventilation systems for machinery spaces of category A, vehicle spaces, ro-ro spaces, galleys, special category spaces and cargo spaces shall, in general, be separated from each other and from the ventilation systems serving other spaces. However, the galley ventilation systems on cargo ships of less than 4,000 gross tonnage and in passenger ships carrying not more than 36 passengers need not be completely separated from other ventilation systems, but may be served by separate ducts from a ventilation unit serving other spaces. In such a case, an automatic fire damper shall be fitted in the galley ventilation duct near the ventilation unit.

7.2.2 Ducts provided for the ventilation of machinery spaces of category A, galleys, vehicle spaces, ro-ro spaces or special category spaces shall not pass through accommodation spaces, service spaces, or control stations unless they comply with paragraph 7.2.4.

7.2.3 Ducts provided for the ventilation of accommodation spaces, service spaces or control stations shall not pass through machinery spaces of category A, galleys, vehicle spaces, ro-ro spaces or special category spaces unless they comply with paragraph 7.2.4.

7.2.4 As permitted by paragraphs 7.2.2 and 7.2.3 ducts shall be either:

.1.1 constructed of steel having a thickness of at least 3 mm for ducts with a free cross-sectional area of less than 0.075 m^2, at least 4 mm for ducts with a free cross-sectional area of between 0.075 m^2 and 0.45 m^2, and at least 5 mm for ducts with a free cross-sectional area of over 0.45 m^2;

.1.2 suitably supported and stiffened;

.1.3 fitted with automatic fire dampers close to the boundaries penetrated; and

.1.4 insulated to "A-60" class standard from the boundaries of the spaces they serve to a point at least 5 m beyond each fire damper;

or

.2.1 constructed of steel in accordance with paragraphs 7.2.4.1.1 and 7.2.4.1.2; and

.2.2 insulated to "A-60" class standard throughout the spaces they pass through, except for ducts that pass through spaces of category (9) or (10) as defined in paragraph 2.2.3.2.2.

7.2.5 For the purposes of paragraphs 7.2.4.1.4 and 7.2.4.2.2, ducts shall be insulated over their entire cross sectional external surface. Ducts that are outside but adjacent to the specified space, and share one or more surfaces with it, shall be considered to pass through the specified space, and shall be insulated over the surface they share with the space for a distance of 450 mm past the duct.[①]

① Sketches of such arrangements are contained in the *Unified interpretations of SOLAS chapter Ⅱ-2* (MSC.1/Circ.1276).

7.1.7 除第 4.1.2.1 和 4.2.3 款准许者外,在两个围蔽处所之间不得设通风开口或空气平衡导管。

7.2 导管的布置

7.2.1 A 类机器处所、车辆处所、滚装处所、厨房、特种处所和货物处所的通风系统一般须相互分开并与用于其他处所的通风系统分开。但小于 4 000 总吨的货船和载客不超过 36 人的客船的厨房通风系统不必与其他通风系统完全分开,而是可以利用服务于其他处所的通风装置通过其分开的通风导管通风。在此情况下,在厨房通风导管靠近通风装置处须装设自动挡火闸。

7.2.2 A 类机器处所、厨房、车辆处所、滚装处所或特种处所的通风导管不得穿过起居处所、服务处所或控制站,但其符合第 7.2.4 款者除外。

7.2.3 起居处所、服务处所或控制站的通风导管不得穿过 A 类机器处所、厨房、车辆处所、滚装处所或特种处所,除非其符合第 7.2.4 款。

7.2.4 第 7.2.2 和 7.2.3 款准许的导管须为:

.1.1 钢制成,对导管有效横截面积小于 0.075 m^2 者,管壁厚度至少为 3 mm;对导管有效横截面积在 0.075 m^2 和 0.45 m^2 之间者,管壁厚度至少为 4 mm;以及对导管有效横截面积大于 0.45 m^2 者,管壁厚度至少为 5 mm;

.1.2 有适当的支撑和加强;

.1.3 在靠近导管贯穿界面处设有自动挡火闸;及

.1.4 从其服务处所的边界到每个挡火闸以外至少 5 m 处按“A-60”级标准隔热;

或

.2.1 按第 7.2.4.1.1 和 7.2.4.1.2 款为钢制成;及

.2.2 在其穿过的所有处所均按“A-60”级标准隔热,但贯穿第 2.2.3.2.2 款中所界定的第(9)或(10)类处所的导管除外。

7.2.5 就第 7.2.4.1.4 和 7.2.4.2.2 款而言,导管的整个横截外表面均须隔热。对于指定处所之外部但邻近该处所、并与其共用一个或多个表面的导管,须视为贯穿该指定处所,并须对其共用表面进行隔热,其隔热范围应延伸至超过导管 450 mm 处①。

① 此类装置的示意图见《SOLAS 公约第Ⅱ-2 章的统一解释》(第 MSC.1/Circ.1276 号通函)。

7.2.6 Where it is necessary that a ventilation duct passes through a main vertical zone division, an automatic fire damper shall be fitted adjacent to the division. The damper shall also be capable of being manually closed from each side of the division. The control location shall be readily accessible and be clearly and prominently marked. The duct between the division and the damper shall be constructed of steel in accordance with paragraphs 7.2.4.1.1 and 7.2.4.1.2 and insulated to at least the same fire integrity as the division penetrated. The damper shall be fitted on at least one side of the division with a visible indicator showing the operating position of the damper.

7.3 Details of fire dampers and duct penetrations

7.3.1 Ducts passing through "A" class divisions shall meet the following requirements:

.1 where a thin plated duct with a free cross-sectional area equal to, or less than, 0.02 m^2 passes through "A" class divisions, the opening shall be fitted with a steel sheet sleeve having a thickness of at least 3 mm and a length of at least 200 mm, divided preferably into 100 mm on each side of a bulkhead or, in the case of a deck, wholly laid on the lower side of the decks penetrated;

.2 where ventilation ducts with a free cross-sectional area exceeding 0.02 m^2, but not more than 0.075 m^2, pass through "A" class divisions, the openings shall be lined with steel sheet sleeves. The ducts and sleeves shall have a thickness of at least 3 mm and a length of at least 900 mm. When passing through bulkheads, this length shall be divided preferably into 450 mm on each side of the bulkhead. These ducts, or sleeves lining such ducts, shall be provided with fire insulation. The insulation shall have at least the same fire integrity as the division through which the duct passes; and

.3 automatic fire dampers shall be fitted in all ducts with a free cross-sectional area exceeding 0.075 m^2 that pass through "A" class divisions. Each damper shall be fitted close to the division penetrated and the duct between the damper and the division penetrated shall be constructed of steel in accordance with paragraphs 7.2.4.1.1 and 7.2.4.1.2. The fire damper shall operate automatically, but shall also be capable of being closed manually from both sides of the division. The damper shall be fitted with a visible indicator which shows the operating position of the damper. Fire dampers are not required, however, where ducts pass through spaces surrounded by "A" class divisions, without serving those spaces, provided those ducts have the same fire integrity as the divisions which they penetrate. A duct of cross-sectional area exceeding 0.075 m^2 shall not be divided into smaller ducts at the penetration of an "A" class division and then recombined into the original duct once through the division to avoid installing the damper required by this provision.

7.3.2 Ventilation ducts with a free cross-sectional area exceeding 0.02 m^2 passing through "B" class bulkheads shall be lined with steel sheet sleeves of 900 mm in length, divided preferably into 450 mm on each side of the bulkheads unless the duct is of steel for this length.

7.2.6 如通风导管必须通过主竖区分隔,应在分隔邻近处装设自动挡火闸。该挡火闸还须能从分隔的每一侧均可手动关闭。其控制位置应易于到达,并清晰、显著地标出。分隔与挡火闸之间的导管须按第 7.2.4.1.1 和 7.2.4.1.2 款由钢制成,并至少按与其贯穿的分隔同等的耐火完整性进行隔热。挡火闸须至少在分隔的一侧装设可视指示牌,指明挡火闸的操作位置。

7.3 挡火闸和导管贯穿的细节

7.3.1 穿过“A”级分隔的导管须满足下列要求:

.1 如有效横截面积等于或小于 0.02 m^2 的薄壁导管穿过“A”级分隔,开口须装设厚度至少为 3 mm 和长度至少为 200 mm 的钢套管,该套管分布舱壁两侧长度各 100 mm 为宜,或者如穿过甲板,则全部敷设在所穿过甲板的底侧;

.2 如有效横截面积大于 0.02 m^2 但不超过 0.075 m^2 的通风导管穿过“A”级分隔,开口应衬有钢套管。导管和套管的厚度应至少为 3 mm,长度至少为 900 mm。在穿过舱壁时,此长度须分布舱壁两侧各 450 mm 为宜。这些导管或其所衬套管须设有耐火隔热材料。该隔热材料至少须具有与导管穿过的分隔同等的耐火完整性;和

.3 穿过“A”级分隔的有效横截面积超过 0.075 m^2的所有导管均须装设自动挡火闸。每个挡火闸均须靠近所贯穿的分隔,挡火闸和所贯穿分隔之间的导管须按第 7.2.4.1.1 和 7.2.4.1.2 款由钢制成。挡火闸须自动工作,但也能从分隔的两侧手动关闭。挡火闸须装有可视指示牌,指明挡火闸的操作位置。但是,如导管穿过被“A”级分隔包围的处所而又不用于这些处所,只要这些导管具有与其所穿过的分隔同等的耐火完整性,则不要求设置挡火闸。有效横截面积超过 0.075 m^2 的导管须不得为避免安装本规定所要求的挡火闸而在“A”级分隔的贯穿处分成较小的导管穿过分隔后再重组为原有的导管。

7.3.2 穿过“B”级舱壁且有效横截面积超过 0.02 m^2 的通风导管须衬有长度为 900 mm 的钢板套管,该套管分布舱壁两侧各 450 mm 为宜,但在此长度范围内为钢质导管者除外。

7.3.3 All fire dampers shall be capable of manual operation. The dampers shall have a direct mechanical means of release or, alternatively, be closed by electrical, hydraulic, or pneumatic operation. All dampers shall be manually operable from both sides of the division. Automatic fire dampers, including those capable of remote operation, shall have a failsafe mechanism that will close the damper in a fire even upon loss of electrical power or hydraulic or pneumatic pressure loss. Remotely operated fire dampers shall be capable of being reopened manually at the damper.

7.4 Ventilation systems for passenger ships carrying more than 36 passengers

7.4.1 In addition to the requirements in sections 7.1, 7.2 and 7.3, the ventilation system of a passenger ship carrying more than 36 passengers shall also meet the following requirements.

7.4.2 In general, the ventilation fans shall be so arranged that the ducts reaching the various spaces remain within a main vertical zone.

7.4.3 Stairway enclosures shall be served by an independent ventilation fan and duct system (exhaust and supply) which shall not serve any other spaces in the ventilation systems.

7.4.4 A duct, irrespective of its cross-section, serving more than one 'tween-deck accommodation space, service space or control station, shall be fitted, near the penetration of each deck of such spaces, with an automatic smoke damper that shall also be capable of being closed manually from the protected deck above the damper. Where a fan serves more than one 'tween-deck space through separate ducts within a main vertical zone, each dedicated to a single 'tween-deck space, each duct shall be provided with a manually operated smoke damper fitted close to the fan.

7.4.5 Vertical ducts shall, if necessary, be insulated as required by tables 9.1 and 9.2. Ducts shall be insulated as required for decks between the space they serve and the space being considered, as applicable.

7.5 Exhaust ducts from galley ranges

7.5.1 Requirements for passenger ships carrying more than 36 passengers

7.5.1.1 In addition to the requirements in sections 7.1, 7.2 and 7.3, exhaust ducts from galley ranges shall be constructed in accordance with paragraphs 7.2.4.2.1 and 7.2.4.2.2 and insulated to "A-60" class standard throughout accommodation spaces, service spaces, or control stations they pass through. They shall also be fitted with:

.1 a grease trap readily removable for cleaning unless an alternative approved grease removal system is fitted;

.2 a fire damper located in the lower end of the duct at the junction between the duct and the galley range hood which is automatically and remotely operated and, in addition, a remotely operated fire damper located in the upper end of the duct close to the outlet of the duct;

7.3.3 所有挡火闸均须能手动操作。挡火闸须通过直接的机械方式开启，或者，作为替代方式，通过电力、液压或气压操作进行关闭。所有挡火闸均须从分隔的两侧手动操作。自动挡火闸（包括能遥控操作的挡火闸）须设有故障保护装置，即便在火灾中失去电力、液压或气压动力，仍可关闭挡火闸。遥控操作的挡火闸须能于挡火闸处被手动重新开启。

7.4 载客超过 36 人的客船的通风系统

7.4.1 除第 7.1、7.2 和 7.3 节的要求外，载客超过 36 人的客船的通风系统还须满足下列要求。

7.4.2 通风机的分布，一般须使通往各处所的导管保持在同一主竖区内。

7.4.3 梯道围蔽须由独立的风机和不服务于通风系统中任何其他处所的导管系统（排气和供气）来通风。

7.4.4 服务于 1 个以上甲板间起居处所、服务处所或者控制站的导管，无论其横截面大小，须在靠近此类处所的每一甲板的贯穿处装设自动挡烟闸，且亦须从其上方的受保护甲板处能将其手动关闭。如在一个主竖区内通风机通过分开的导管服务于 1 个以上的甲板间处所，而每个导管专门服务于单个甲板间处所，则须在每个导管靠近通风机处装设手动操作的挡烟闸。

7.4.5 对垂直导管须在必要时按表 9.1 和 9.2 的要求进行隔热。对导管在其所服务处所和所计及的处所之间的甲板处须适当地按要求进行隔热。

7.5 厨房炉灶的排气导管

7.5.1 对载客超过 36 人的客船的要求

7.5.1.1 除满足第 7.1、7.2 和 7.3 节的要求外，厨房炉灶的排气导管还须按第 7.2.4.2.1 和 7.2.4.2.2 款建造并在其穿过的起居处所、服务处所或控制站处按“A-60”级标准进行隔热。这些导管还须装设：

.1 一个易于拆下清洗的集油器，但另装有经认可的油垢清除装置者除外；

.2 一个位于导管和厨房炉灶罩接头处导管下端的自动和遥控操作的挡火闸，此外，还须在导管上端靠近其出口处装设 1 个遥控操作的挡火闸；

.3 a fixed means for extinguishing a fire within the duct;①

.4 remote-control arrangements for shutting off the exhaust fans and supply fans, for operating the fire dampers mentioned in paragraph 7.5.1.1.2 and for operating the fire-extinguishing system, which shall be placed in a position outside the galley close to the entrance to the galley. Where a multibranch system is installed, a remote means located with the above controls shall be provided to close all branches exhausting through the same main duct before an extinguishing medium is released into the system; and

.5 suitably located hatches for inspection and cleaning, including one provided close to the exhaust fan and one fitted in the lower end where grease accumulates.

7.5.1.2 Exhaust ducts from ranges for cooking equipment installed on open decks shall conform to paragraph 7.5.1.1, as applicable, when passing through accommodation spaces or spaces containing combustible materials.

7.5.2 Requirements for cargo ships and passenger ships carrying not more than 36 passengers

When passing through accommodation spaces or spaces containing combustible materials, the exhaust ducts from galley ranges shall be constructed in accordance with paragraphs 7.2.4.1.1 and 7.2.4.1.2. Each exhaust duct shall be fitted with:

.1 a grease trap readily removable for cleaning;

.2 an automatically and remotely operated fire damper located in the lower end of the duct at the junction between the duct and the galley range hood and, in addition, a remotely operated fire damper in the upper end of the duct close to the outlet of the duct;

.3 arrangements, operable from within the galley, for shutting off the exhaust and supply fans; and

.4 fixed means for extinguishing a fire within the duct.①

7.6 Ventilation rooms serving machinery spaces of category A containing internal combustion machinery

7.6.1 Where a ventilation room serves only such an adjacent machinery space and there is no fire division between the ventilation room and the machinery space, the means for closing the ventilation duct or ducts serving the machinery space shall be located outside of the ventilation room and machinery space.

7.6.2 Where a ventilation room serves such a machinery space as well as other spaces and is separated from the machinery space by an "A-0" class division, including penetrations, the means for closing the ventilation duct or ducts for the machinery space can be located in the ventilation room.

---

① Refer to the recommendations published by the International Organization for Standardization, in particular, publication ISO 15371:2009, *Ships and marine technology—Fire-extinguishing systems for protection of galley cooking equipment.*

.3　用于导管内部灭火的固定式灭火装置；[①]

.4　用于关闭排气风机和送风机、用于操作第 7.5.1.1.2 款所述的挡火闸和用于操作灭火系统的遥控装置，这些遥控装置须装设在厨房外接近厨房入口的位置。如所安装的排气系统具有若干分支，则须在上述控制处装设一个遥控装置，以在灭火剂释放进入该系统前关闭通向同一主排气导管的所有支管；和

.5　适当分布的检查和清洁口，其中一个设在靠近排气风机及另一个装在油垢堆积处的下端。

7.5.1.2　安装在开敞甲板上的烹饪设备的炉灶排气导管，如其穿过起居处所或含有可燃材料的处所，须酌情遵守第 7.5.1.1 款的规定。

7.5.2　对载客不超过 36 人的货船和客船的要求

如厨房炉灶的排气导管穿过起居处所或含有可燃材料的处所，该排气导管须按第 7.2.4.1.1 和 7.2.4.1.2 款建造。每一排气导管均须装设：

.1　一个易于拆下清洗的集油器；

.2　一个位于导管和厨房炉灶罩接头处导管下端的自动和遥控操作的挡火闸，此外，还须在导管上端靠近其出口处装设 1 个遥控操作的挡火闸；

.3　可在厨房内操作的排气风机和送风机关闭装置；和

.4　用于导管内部灭火的固定式灭火装置。[①]

7.6　服务于设有内燃机的 A 类机器处所的排风机房

7.6.1　如排风机房仅服务于 1 个邻近的机器处所，且在排风机房和机器处所之间无防火分隔，服务于机器处所的一个或多个通风导管的关闭装置须设在排风机房和机器处所外。

7.6.2　如排风机房服务于机器处所以及其他处所，且通过“A-0”级分隔与机器处所隔开（包括贯穿处），用于机器处所的 1 个或多个通风导管的关闭装置可设在排风机房内。

---

① 参见国际标准化组织出版的建议案，特别是 ISO 15371:2009《船舶和海洋技术——保护厨房烹饪设备的灭火系统》。

7.7 Ventilation systems for laundries in passenger ships carrying more than 36 passengers

Exhaust ducts from laundries and drying rooms of category (13) spaces as defined in paragraph 2.2.3.2.2 shall be fitted with:

.1 filters readily removable for cleaning purposes;

.2 a fire damper located in the lower end of the duct which is automatically and remotely operated;

.3 remote-control arrangements for shutting off the exhaust fans and supply fans from within the space and for operating the fire damper mentioned in paragraph 7.7.2; and

.4 suitably located hatches for inspection and cleaning.

Regulation 10
Fire fighting

1 Purpose

1.1 The purpose of this regulation is to suppress and swiftly extinguish a fire in the space of origin, except for paragraph 1.2. For this purpose, the following functional requirements shall be met:

.1 fixed fire-extinguishing systems shall be installed having due regard to the fire growth potential of the protected spaces; and

.2 fire-extinguishing appliances shall be readily available.

1.2 For open-top container holds① and on deck container stowage areas on ships designed to carry containers on or above the weather deck, constructed on or after 1 January 2016, fire protection arrangements shall be provided for the purpose of containing a fire in the space or area of origin and cooling adjacent areas to prevent fire spread and structural damage.

2 Water supply systems

Ships shall be provided with fire pumps, fire mains, hydrants and hoses complying with the applicable requirements of this regulation.

2.1 Fire mains and hydrants

2.1.1 General

① For a definition of this term, refer to Interim guidelines for open-top containerships (MSC/Circ.608/Rev.1).

7.7　载客超过36人客船的洗衣房的通风系统

第**2.2.3.2.2**款中所界定的(**13**)类处所的洗衣房和烘干间的排气导管须装设:

.1　易于拆下用于清洗的过滤器;

.2　一个位于导管下端的自动和遥控操作的挡火闸;

.3　用于关闭处所内的排气风机和送风机和用于操作第7.7.2款所述的挡火闸的遥控装置;和

.4　在适当位置的检查和清洁口。

第10条
灭火

1　目的

1.1　本条旨在抑制火灾并迅速将其扑灭在火源处,但第1.2款除外。为此,须满足下列功能要求:

.1　须安装固定式灭火系统,并充分考虑到受保护处所火势扩大的可能;以及

.2　灭火器材须随时可用。

1.2　对于2016年1月1日或以后建造的敞口集装箱船货舱[①]和设计用于在露天甲板或其上方装载集装箱的船舶甲板集装箱堆装区域,应提供防火布置,以将火灾抑制在火源处所或区域,并冷却邻近区域以防止火灾蔓延和结构损坏。

2　供水系统

船舶应设有符合本条适用要求的消防泵、消防总管、消火栓和消防水带。

2.1　消防总管和消火栓

2.1.1　通则

① 该条术语的定义参见《敞口集装箱船暂行指南》(第MSC/Circ.608/Rev.1号通函)。

Materials readily rendered ineffective by heat shall not be used for fire mains and hydrants unless adequately protected. The pipes and hydrants shall be so placed that the fire hoses may be easily coupled to them. The arrangement of pipes and hydrants shall be such as to avoid the possibility of freezing. Suitable drainage provisions shall be provided for fire main piping. Isolation valves shall be installed for all open deck fire main branches used for purposes other than fire fighting. In ships where deck cargo may be carried, the positions of the hydrants shall be such that they are always readily accessible and the pipes shall be arranged as far as practicable to avoid risk of damage by such cargo.

2.1.2 Ready availability of water supply

The arrangements for the ready availability of water supply shall be:

.1 in passenger ships:

.1 of 1,000 gross tonnage and upwards such that at least one effective jet of water is immediately available from any hydrant in an interior location and so as to ensure the continuation of the output of water by the automatic starting of one required fire pump;

.2 of less than 1,000 gross tonnage by automatic start of at least one fire pump or by remote starting from the navigation bridge of at least one fire pump. If the pump starts automatically or if the bottom valve cannot be opened from where the pump is remotely started, the bottom valve shall always be kept open; and

.3 if fitted with periodically unattended machinery spaces in accordance with regulation Ⅱ-1/54, the Administration shall determine provisions for fixed water fire-extinguishing arrangements for such spaces equivalent to those required for normally attended machinery spaces;

.2 in cargo ships:

.1 to the satisfaction of the Administration; and

.2 with a periodically unattended machinery space or when only one person is required on watch, there shall be immediate water delivery from the fire main system at a suitable pressure, either by remote starting of one of the main fire pumps with remote starting from the navigation bridge and fire control station, if any, or permanent pressurization of the fire main system by one of the main fire pumps, except that the Administration may waive this requirement for cargo ships of less than 1,600 gross tonnage if the fire pump starting arrangement in the machinery space is in an easily accessible position.

2.1.3 Diameter of fire mains

The diameter of the fire main and water service pipes shall be sufficient for the effective distribution of the maximum required discharge from two fire pumps operating simultaneously, except that in the case of cargo ships, other than those included in paragraph 7.3.2, the diameter need only be sufficient for the discharge of 140 m^3/h.

遇热易于失效的材料，除非其有充分的保护，不得用于消防总管和消火栓。管子和消火栓的位置应便于连接消防水带。管子和消火栓的布置应防止冻结的可能性。消防总管应设有适当的排水设施。用于消防以外目的的所有开敞甲板上消防总管的支管应装有隔离阀。在可载运甲板货物的船上，消火栓应位于随时易于到达的位置，消防管的布置应尽实际可能避免被甲板货物损坏的危险。

2.1.2　随时可以供水

随时可以供水的布置应：

.1　对于客船：

.1　1 000 总吨及以上的客船，至少从内部位置的任何消火栓上可立即喷出一股有效的水柱，并确保由 1 台所要求的自动启动的消防泵持续出水；

.2　1 000 总吨以下的客船，有至少 1 台自动启动的消防泵或至少 1 台由驾驶室遥控启动的消防泵。如果消防泵为自动启动，或如果消防泵的底阀不能在遥控启动的位置打开，则底阀应始终保持开启状态；和

.3　如果根据第Ⅱ-1/54 条设有周期无人值班机器处所，主管机关应对这种处所的固定式喷水灭火装置做出规定，这些规定应与通常有人值班机器处所的要求相当。

.2　对于货船：

.1　使主管机关满意；和

.2　在设有周期无人值班机器处所或仅有 1 人值班的货船上，应通过遥控启动能由驾驶室或消防控制站（若设有）遥控启动的主消防泵中的 1 台，或通过由主消防泵中的 1 台使消防总管系统保持恒定的压力的方法，以适当的压力从消防总管系统立即供水，但对 1 600 总吨以下的货船，如果布置在机器处所的消防泵启动装置的位置易于到达，主管机关可免除此要求。

2.1.3　消防总管的直径

消防总管和消防水管的直径应足以有效分配 2 台消防泵同时工作所需的最大排水量，但对于除第 7.3.2 款规定以外的货船，上述管子直径仅需足以排送 140 m^3/h 水量。

2.1.4 Isolating valves and relief valves

2.1.4.1 Isolating valves to separate the section of the fire main within the machinery space containing the main fire pump or pumps from the rest of the fire main shall be fitted in an easily accessible and tenable position outside the machinery spaces. The fire main shall be so arranged that when the isolating valves are shut all the hydrants on the ship, except those in the machinery space referred to above, can be supplied with water by another fire pump or an emergency fire pump. The emergency fire pump, its seawater inlet, and suction and delivery pipes and isolating valves shall be located outside the machinery space. If this arrangement cannot be made, the sea-chest may be fitted in the machinery space if the valve is remotely controlled from a position in the same compartment as the emergency fire pump and the suction pipe is as short as practicable. Short lengths of suction or discharge piping may penetrate the machinery space, provided they are enclosed in a substantial steel casing or are insulated to "A-60" class standards. The pipes shall have substantial wall thickness, but in no case less than 11 mm, and shall be welded except for the flanged connection to the sea inlet valve.

2.1.4.2 A valve shall be fitted to serve each fire hydrant so that any fire hose may be removed while the fire pumps are in operation.

2.1.4.3 Relief valves shall be provided in conjunction with fire pumps if the pumps are capable of developing a pressure exceeding the design pressure of the water service pipes, hydrants and hoses. These valves shall be so placed and adjusted as to prevent excessive pressure in any part of the fire main system.

2.1.4.4 In tankers, isolation valves shall be fitted in the fire main at the poop front in a protected position and on the tank deck at intervals of not more than 40 m to preserve the integrity of the fire main system in case of fire or explosion.

2.1.5 Number and position of hydrants

2.1.5.1 The number and position of hydrants shall be such that at least two jets of water not emanating from the same hydrant, one of which shall be from a single length of hose, may reach any part of the ship normally accessible to the passengers or crew while the ship is being navigated and any part of any cargo space when empty, any ro-ro space or any vehicle space, in which latter case the two jets shall reach any part of the space, each from a single length of hose. Furthermore, such hydrants shall be positioned near the accesses to the protected spaces.

2.1.5.2 In addition to the requirements in paragraph 2.1.5.1, passenger ships shall comply with the following:

.1 in the accommodation, service and machinery spaces, the number and position of hydrants shall be such that the requirements of paragraph 2.1.5.1 may be complied with when all watertight doors and all doors in main vertical zone bulkheads are closed; and

2.1.4　隔离阀和释放阀

2.1.4.1　用于将布置在设有主消防泵或泵组的机器处所内的消防总管部分与消防总管其他部分分开的隔离阀，应设在机器处所之外易于到达并站得住的位置。消防总管应布置成当隔离阀关闭时，船上除上述机器处所内的消火栓外，其他所有消火栓能由另1台消防泵或1台应急消防泵供水。应急消防泵及其海水入口、吸水以及送水管和隔离阀应位于机器处所的外部。无法做到这种布置时，如果对该阀门进行遥控的位置与应急消防泵在同一舱室，可在机器处所安装通海阀箱，吸水管要尽可能短。吸水管和排水管的一小部分可以贯穿机器处所，但应由坚固的钢质外套包裹，或隔热至“A-60”级标准。管子应有足实的壁厚，无论如何不得小于11 mm，并且除与海水进口阀门的连接采用法兰外，所有接头均应采用焊接连接。

2.1.4.2　应为每一消火栓装设一个阀门，以在消防泵工作时可以卸下任何消防水带。

2.1.4.3　如果消防泵能够产生超出消防水管、消火栓和水带设计压力的压力，应在消防泵上附设释放阀。这些阀的布置和调整应能避免在消防总管系统的任何部分出现超压。

2.1.4.4　在液货船上，隔离阀应装设在尾楼前端消防总管受保护的位置，其在液货舱甲板上的间距不得超过40 m，以在发生火灾或爆炸时维持消防总管系统的完整性。

2.1.5　消火栓的数量和位置

2.1.5.1　消火栓的数量和位置，应至少能使两股不是由同一消火栓喷出的水柱（其中一股水柱应仅用1节消防水带）可射至船舶在航行时乘客或船员通常可以到达的任何部分、任何货物处所空舱时的任何部分、任何滚装处所或任何车辆处所，在任一后者情况下，两股水柱中每股均应仅用1节消防水带射至该处所的任何部分。此外，上述消火栓应位于靠近被保护处所的出入口处。

2.1.5.2　除应符合本条2.1.5.1的要求外，客船还应符合下列要求：

.1　在起居处所、服务处所和机器处所，当所有水密门和所有主竖区舱壁上的门均关闭时，消火栓的数量和位置应使本条2.1.5.1的要求可以满足；和

.2 where access is provided to a machinery space of category A at a low level from an adjacent shaft tunnel, two hydrants shall be provided external to, but near the entrance to, that machinery space. Where such access is provided from other spaces, in one of those spaces two hydrants shall be provided near the entrance to the machinery space of category A. Such provision need not be made where the tunnel or adjacent spaces are not part of the escape route.

2.1.6 Pressure at hydrants

With the two pumps simultaneously delivering water through the nozzles specified in paragraph 2.3.3, with the quantity of water as specified in paragraph 2.1.3, through any adjacent hydrants, the following minimum pressures shall be maintained at all hydrants:

.1 for passenger ships:

4,000 gross tonnage and upwards

0.40 N/mm^2

less than 4,000 gross tonnage

0.30 N/mm^2

.2 for cargo ships:

6,000 gross tonnage and upwards

0.27 N/mm^2

less than 6,000 gross tonnage

0.25 N/mm^2

and

.3 the maximum pressure at any hydrant shall not exceed that at which the effective control of a fire hose can be demonstrated.

2.1.7 International shore connection

2.1.7.1 Ships of 500 gross tonnage and upwards shall be provided with at least one international shore connection complying with the Fire Safety Systems Code.

2.1.7.2 Facilities shall be available enabling such a connection to be used on either side of the ship.

2.2 Fire pumps

2.2.1 Pumps accepted as fire pumps

Sanitary, ballast, bilge or general service pumps may be accepted as fire pumps, provided that they are not normally used for pumping oil and that if they are subject to occasional duty for the transfer or pumping of oil fuel, suitable change-over arrangements are fitted.

2.2.2 Number of fire pumps

Ships shall be provided with independently driven fire pumps as follows:

.1 in passenger ships of:

.2　如果从与A类机器处所相邻的轴隧至A类机器处所在下层位置设有通道，则应在该机器处所入口之外，但在其附近设置2个消火栓。如果从其他处所至A类机器处所设有此类通道，则应在那些处所中的一个处所靠近A类机器处所入口之处设置2个消火栓。如果轴隧或相邻处所不属于脱险通道部分，则不必采取上述措施。

2.1.6　消火栓的压力

在2台泵同时通过本条2.3.3所规定的水枪从任何相邻的消火栓输送本条2.1.3所规定的水量时，所有消火栓应维持下述最低压力：

.1　对于客船：

4 000总吨及以上　　0.40 N/mm^2

4 000总吨以下　　0.30 N/mm^2

.2　对于货船：

6 000总吨及以上　　0.27 N/mm^2

6 000总吨以下　　0.25 N/mm^2

和

.3　任何消火栓的最大压力不得超过经证实可有效控制消防水带的压力。

2.1.7　国际通岸接头

2.1.7.1　500总吨及以上的船舶应设有至少一个符合《消防安全系统规则》的国际通岸接头。

2.1.7.2　应有使这种接头在船舶任何一舷都能使用的设施。

2.2　消防泵

2.2.1　接受作为消防泵的泵

卫生泵、压载泵、舱底泵或通用泵均可接受作为消防泵，但其通常不得用于抽送油类，且如其偶尔用于驳运或泵送燃油，应装设合适的转换装置。

2.2.2　消防泵的数量

船舶应按下述要求配备独立驱动的消防泵：

.1　对于客船：

4,000 gross tonnage and upwards	at least three
less than 4,000 gross tonnage	at least two

.2 in cargo ships of:

1,000 gross tonnage and upwards	at least two
less than 1,000 gross tonnage	at least two power-driven pumps, one of which shall be independently driven

2.2.3 Arrangement of fire pumps and fire mains

2.2.3.1 Fire pumps

The arrangement of sea connections, fire pumps and their sources of power shall be as to ensure that:

.1 in passenger ships of 1,000 gross tonnage and upwards, in the event of a fire in any one compartment, all the fire pumps will not be put out of action; and

.2 in passenger ships of less than 1,000 gross tonnage and in cargo ships, if a fire in any one compartment could put all the pumps out of action, there shall be an alternative means consisting of an emergency fire pump complying with the provisions of the Fire Safety Systems Code with its source of power and sea connection located outside the space where the main fire pumps or their sources of power are located.

2.2.3.2 Requirements for the space containing the emergency fire pump

2.2.3.2.1 Location of the space

The space containing the fire pump shall not be contiguous to the boundaries of machinery spaces of category A or those spaces containing main fire pumps. Where this is not practicable, the common bulkhead between the two spaces shall be insulated to a standard of structural fire protection equivalent to that required for a control station.

2.2.3.2.2 Access to the emergency fire pump

No direct access shall be permitted between the machinery space and the space containing the emergency fire pump and its source of power. When this is impracticable, the Administration may accept an arrangement where the access is by means of an airlock with the door of the machinery space being of "A-60" class standard and the other door being at least steel, both reasonably gastight, self-closing and without any hold-back arrangements. Alternatively, the access may be through a watertight door capable of being operated from a space remote from the machinery space and the space containing the emergency fire pump and unlikely to be cut off in the event of fire in those spaces. In such cases, a second means of access to the space containing the emergency fire pump and its source of power shall be provided.

2.2.3.2.3 Ventilation of the emergency fire pump space

Ventilation arrangements to the space containing the independent source of power for the emergency fire pump shall be such as to preclude, as far as practicable, the possibility of smoke from a machinery space fire entering or being drawn into that space.

4 000 总吨及以上	至少 3 台
4 000 总吨以下	至少 2 台

.2　对于货船：

1 000 总吨及以上	至少 2 台
1 000 总吨以下	至少 2 台动力泵，其中之一应为独立驱动

2.2.3　消防泵和消防总管的布置

2.2.3.1　消防泵

通海连接件、消防泵及其动力源的布置应确保：

.1　1 000 总吨及以上的客船，在任何一个舱室失火时，不会使所有消防泵失去作用；和

.2　1 000 总吨以下的客船和货船，如果任何一个舱室失火时可能使所有消防泵失去作用，应配备 1 台符合《消防安全系统规则》的应急消防泵作为替代设备，该泵的动力源和通海连接件位于主消防泵或其电源所在处所之外。

2.2.3.2　对应急消防泵所在处所的要求

2.2.3.2.1　处所的位置

应急消防泵所在处所不得与 A 类机器处所或内设主消防泵处所的限界面相邻接。如果此种布置不可行，两个处所间共用的舱壁应隔热至相当于对控制站所要求的结构防火标准。

2.2.3.2.2　通往应急消防泵的通道

机器处所与应急消防泵及其动力源所在处所之间，不允许有直接通道。当此种布置不可行时，主管机关可以接受这样一种布置，即通道有一个气锁设施，其内机器处所的门达到"A-60"级标准，另一门至少为钢质，2 个门均适度气密、自闭且不设门背钩。作为替代，可利用能从远离机器处所和应急消防泵所在处所的位置操作并在这些处所失火时不会被阻断的水密门作为通道。在此种情况下，应急消防泵及其动力源所在处所应设有第 2 个通道。

2.2.3.2.3　应急消防泵处所的通风

应急消防泵独立动力源所在处所通风的布置，应尽可能杜绝机器处所失火时产生的烟气进入或被吸入该处所的可能。

2.2.3.3 Additional pumps for cargo ships

In addition, in cargo ships where other pumps, such as general service, bilge and ballast, etc., are fitted in a machinery space, arrangements shall be made to ensure that at least one of these pumps, having the capacity and pressure required by paragraphs 2.1.6.2 and 2.2.4.2, is capable of providing water to the fire main.

2.2.4 Capacity of fire pumps

2.2.4.1 Total capacity of required fire pumps

The required fire pumps shall be capable of delivering for fire-fighting purposes a quantity of water, at the pressure specified in paragraph 2.1.6, as follows:

.1 pumps in passenger ships: the quantity of water is not less than two thirds of the quantity required to be dealt with by the bilge pumps when employed for bilge pumping; and

.2 pumps in cargo ships, other than any emergency pump: the quantity of water is not less than four thirds of the quantity required under regulation Ⅱ-1/35-1 to be dealt with by each of the independent bilge pumps in a passenger ship of the same dimension when employed in bilge pumping, provided that in no cargo ship, other than those included in paragraph 7.3.2, need the total required capacity of the fire pumps exceed 180 m^3/h.

2.2.4.2 Capacity of each fire pump

Each of the required fire pumps (other than any emergency pump required in paragraph 2.2.3.1.2 for cargo ships) shall have a capacity not less than 80% of the total required capacity divided by the minimum number of required fire pumps, but in any case not less than 25 m^3/h, and each such pump shall in any event be capable of delivering at least the two required jets of water. These fire pumps shall be capable of supplying the fire main system under the required conditions. Where more pumps than the minimum of required pumps are installed, such additional pumps shall have a capacity of at least 25 m^3/h and shall be capable of delivering at least the two jets of water required in paragraph 2.1.5.1.

2.3 Fire hoses and nozzles

2.3.1 General specifications

2.3.1.1 Fire hoses shall be of non-perishable material approved by the Administration and shall be sufficient in length to project a jet of water to any of the spaces in which they may be required to be used. Each hose shall be provided with a nozzle and the necessary couplings. Hoses specified in this chapter as "fire hoses" shall, together with any necessary fittings and tools, be kept ready for use in conspicuous positions near the water service hydrants or connections. Additionally, in interior locations in passenger ships carrying more than 36 passengers, fire hoses shall be connected to the hydrants at all times. Fire hoses shall have a length of at least 10 m, but not more than:

.1 15 m in machinery spaces;

2.2.3.3　货船的附加泵

此外，在货船机器处所设置的其他泵，如通用泵、舱底泵和压载泵等，其布置应确保这些泵中至少有1台具有本条2.1.6.2和2.2.4.2所要求的排量和压力，能向消防总管供水。

2.2.4　消防泵的排量

2.2.4.1　所要求的消防泵总排量

所要求的消防泵应能按本条2.1.6所规定的压力输送以下排量的消防用水：

.1　客船上的消防泵：该排量不少于各舱底泵用于舱底水泵送时所要求排量的三分之二；和

.2　货船上除任何应急泵以外的消防泵：该排量不少于第Ⅱ-1/35-1条对同样尺度客船的每一独立舱底泵用于舱底水泵送时所要求排量的三分之四，但除第7.3.2款所列船舶以外的货船的消防泵的要求总排量不必超过180 m^3/h。

2.2.4.2　每台消防泵的排量

所要求的每台消防泵（本条2.2.3.1.2对货船要求的应急消防泵除外），其排量应不少于所要求总排量的80%除以所要求的最少消防泵数，但在任何情况下不得少于25 m^3/h，并且每台这样的消防泵应至少能在任何情况下提供所要求的两股水柱。这些消防泵应能按所要求的条件向消防总管系统供水。如果所设泵数多于所要求的最低泵数，则这些额外泵的排量应至少为25 m^3/h，并且应至少能够提供本条2.1.5.1所要求的两股水柱。

2.3　消防水带和水枪

2.3.1　一般规格

2.3.1.1　消防水带应由经主管机关认可的不腐蚀材料制成，其长度应足以将水柱喷射到可能需要使用消防水带的任一处所。每条消防水带应配有一支水枪和必要的接头。在本章中规定为"消防水带"的水带，连同必要的配件和工具，应存放在供水消火栓或接头附近的明显位置，以备随时取用。此外，在载客超过36人的客船的各内部处所，消防水带应一直保持与消火栓相连接。消防水带的长度应至少为10 m，但不应超过下列规定的最大长度：

.1　在机器处所内为15 m；

.2 20 m in other spaces and open decks; and

.3 25 m for open decks on ships with a maximum breadth in excess of 30 m.

2.3.1.2 Unless one hose and nozzle is provided for each hydrant in the ship, there shall be complete interchangeability of hose couplings and nozzles.

2.3.2 Number and diameter of fire hoses

2.3.2.1 Ships shall be provided with fire hoses, the number and diameter of which shall be to the satisfaction of the Administration.

2.3.2.2 In passenger ships, there shall be at least one fire hose for each of the hydrants required by paragraph 2.1.5 and these hoses shall be used only for the purposes of extinguishing fires or testing the fire-extinguishing apparatus at fire drills and surveys.

2.3.2.3 In cargo ships:

.1 of 1,000 gross tonnage and upwards, the number of fire hoses to be provided shall be one for each 30 m length of the ship and one spare, but in no case less than five in all. This number does not include any hoses required in any engine-room or boiler room. The Administration may increase the number of hoses required so as to ensure that hoses in sufficient number are available and accessible at all times, having regard to the type of ship and the nature of trade in which the ship is employed. Ships carrying dangerous goods in accordance with regulation 19 shall be provided with three hoses and nozzles, in addition to those required above; and

.2 of less than 1,000 gross tonnage, the number of fire hoses to be provided shall be calculated in accordance with the provisions of paragraph 2.3.2.3.1. However, the number of hoses shall in no case be less than three.

2.3.3 Size and types of nozzles

2.3.3.1 For the purposes of this chapter, standard nozzle sizes shall be 12 mm, 16 mm and 19 mm or as near thereto as possible. Larger diameter nozzles may be permitted at the discretion of the Administration.

2.3.3.2 For accommodation and service spaces, a nozzle size greater than 12 mm need not be used.

2.3.3.3 For machinery spaces and exterior locations, the nozzle size shall be such as to obtain the maximum discharge possible from two jets at the pressure mentioned in paragraph 2.1.6 from the smallest pump, provided that a nozzle size greater than 19 mm need not be used.

2.3.3.4 Nozzles shall be of an approved dual-purpose type (i.e.spray/jet type) incorporating a shutoff.

.2　在其他处所内和开敞甲板上为 20 m；和

.3　在最大型宽大于 30 m 船舶的开敞甲板上为 25 m。

2.3.1.2　除非船上每一消火栓均配备 1 条消防水带和 1 支水枪，否则各消防水带接头与各水枪应能完全互换使用。

2.3.2　消防水带的数量和直径

2.3.2.1　船舶配备的消防水带的数量和直径应使主管机关满意。

2.3.2.2　对于客船，本条 2.1.5 所要求的每个消火栓应至少配有 1 条消防水带，并且这些水带应仅用于灭火或在消防演习和检验时试验灭火设备。

2.3.2.3　对于货船：

.1　1 000 总吨及以上的货船，应配备的消防水带数量为每 30 m 船长配备 1 条并有 1 条备用，但无论如何总数不得少于 5 条。这一数字不包括机舱或锅炉舱所要求的水带。考虑到船舶类型和船舶所从事贸易的性质，主管机关可增加所要求消防水带的数量，以确保随时有数量足够的消防水带可供使用。符合第 19 条要求载运危险货物的船舶除应满足上述要求外，还应备有 3 组水带和水枪；和

.2　1 000 总吨以下的货船，应配备的消防水带的数量应根据本条 2.3.2.3.1 的规定进行计算。但在任何情况下，水带的数量不得少于 3 根。

2.3.3　水枪的尺寸和类型

2.3.3.1　就本章而言，标准水枪的尺寸应为 12 mm、16 mm 和 19 mm，或尽可能与之相近。经主管机关同意，可允许使用直径更大的水枪。

2.3.3.2　在起居处所和服务处所，不必使用尺寸大于 12 mm 的水枪。

2.3.3.3　在机器处所和外部场所，水枪尺寸应能从最小的泵在本条 2.1.6 所述压力下，从两股水柱获得最大限度水量，但不必使用尺寸大于 19 mm 的水枪。

2.3.3.4　水枪应为经认可的设有关闭装置的两用型（水雾/水柱型）。

3 Portable fire extinguishers[①]

3.1 Type and design

Portable fire extinguishers shall comply with the requirements of the Fire Safety Systems Code.

3.2 Arrangement of fire extinguishers

3.2.1 Accommodation spaces, service spaces and control stations shall be provided with portable fire extinguishers of appropriate types and in sufficient number to the satisfaction of the Administration. Ships of 1,000 gross tonnage and upwards shall carry at least five portable fire extinguishers.

3.2.2 One of the portable fire extinguishers intended for use in any space shall be stowed near the entrance to that space.

3.2.3 Carbon dioxide fire extinguishers shall not be placed in accommodation spaces. In control stations and other spaces containing electrical or electronic equipment or appliances necessary for the safety of the ship, fire extinguishers shall be provided whose extinguishing media are neither electrically conductive nor harmful to the equipment and appliances.

3.2.4 Fire extinguishers shall be situated ready for use at easily visible places, which can be reached quickly and easily at any time in the event of a fire, and in such a way that their serviceability is not impaired by the weather, vibration or other external factors. Portable fire extinguishers shall be provided with devices which indicate whether they have been used.

3.3 Spare charges

3.3.1 Spare charges shall be provided for 100% of the first ten extinguishers and 50% of the remaining fire extinguishers capable of being recharged on board. Not more than 60 total spare charges are required. Instructions for recharging shall be carried on board.

3.3.2 For fire extinguishers which cannot be recharged on board, additional portable fire extinguishers of the same quantity, type, capacity and number as determined in paragraph 3.3.1 above shall be provided in lieu of spare charges.

4 Fixed fire-extinguishing systems

4.1 Types of fixed fire-extinguishing systems

4.1.1 A fixed fire-extinguishing system required by paragraph 5 below may be any of the following systems:

.1 a fixed gas fire-extinguishing system complying with the provisions of the Fire Safety Systems Code;

---

① Refer to *Improved guidelines for marine portable fire extinguishers* (resolution A.951(23)) and *Unified interpretation of SOLAS chapter Ⅱ-2 on the number and arrangement of portable fire extinguishers on board ships* (MSC.1/ Circ.1275 and Corr.1).

3　手提式灭火器①

3.1　型式和设计

手提式灭火器应符合《消防安全系统规则》的要求。

3.2　灭火器的布置

3.2.1　起居处所、服务处所和控制站内应配备使主管机关满意的型式适用和数量足够的手提式灭火器。1 000 总吨及以上的船舶应至少备有 5 具手提式灭火器。

3.2.2　用于任何处所的手提式灭火器,其中应有 1 具存放在该处所的入口附近。

3.2.3　在起居处所内不得布置二氧化碳灭火器。在控制站和其他设有船舶安全所必需的电气或电子设备或装置的其他处所,所配备灭火器的灭火剂应既不导电也不会对设备和装置产生危害。

3.2.4　灭火器应位于易于看到的位置并随时可用。该位置应在失火时能迅速和便于到达,且灭火器所处位置应不会使其可用性受到天气、振动或其他外部因素的影响。手提式灭火器应配有表明其是否已被用过的标志。

3.3　备用灭火剂

3.3.1　能在船上重新充装的灭火器,其备用灭火剂的数量应按前 10 个灭火器的 100% 和其余灭火器的 50% 进行配备。备用灭火剂的总数不必超过 60 份。船上应备有充装说明。

3.3.2　对于不能在船上重新充装的灭火器,应额外配备本条 3.3.1 所确定的相同灭火剂量、型式、容量和数量的手提式灭火器以代替备用灭火剂。

4　固定式灭火系统

4.1　固定式灭火系统的类型

4.1.1　本条 5 所要求的固定式灭火系统可以为以下任何系统:

.1　符合《消防安全系统规则》规定的固定式气体灭火系统;

---

①　参见《船用手提式灭火器改进导则》(第 A.951(23)号决议)和《SOLAS 公约第Ⅱ-2 章船上手提式灭火器数量和布置的统一解释》(第 MSC.1/Circ.1275 号通函和 Corr.1)。

.2 a fixed high-expansion foam fire-extinguishing system complying with the provisions of the Fire Safety Systems Code; and

.3 a fixed pressure water-spraying fire-extinguishing system complying with the provisions of the Fire Safety Systems Code.

4.1.2 Where a fixed fire-extinguishing system not required by this chapter is installed, it shall meet the requirements of the relevant regulations of this chapter and the Fire Safety Systems Code.

4.1.3 Fire-extinguishing systems using Halon 1211, 1301, and 2402 and perfluorocarbons shall be prohibited.①

4.1.4 In general, the Administration shall not permit the use of steam as a fire-extinguishing medium in fixed fire-extinguishing systems. Where the use of steam is permitted by the Administration, it shall be used only in restricted areas as an addition to the required fire-extinguishing system and shall comply with the requirements of the Fire Safety System Code.

4.1.5 By the first scheduled dry-docking after 1 January 2010, fixed carbon dioxide fire-extinguishing systems for the protection of machinery spaces and cargo pump-rooms on ships constructed before 1 July 2002 shall comply with the provisions of paragraph 2.2.2 of chapter 5 of the Fire Safety Systems Code.

4.2 Closing appliances for fixed gas fire-extinguishing systems

Where a fixed gas fire-extinguishing system is used, openings which may admit air to, or allow gas to escape from, a protected space shall be capable of being closed from outside the protected space.

4.3 Storage rooms of fire-extinguishing medium

When the fire-extinguishing medium is stored outside a protected space, it shall be stored in a room which is located behind the forward collision bulkhead, and is used for no other purposes. Any entrance to such a storage room shall preferably be from the open deck and shall be independent of the protected space. If the storage space is located below deck, it shall be located no more than one deck below the open deck and shall be directly accessible by a stairway or ladder from the open deck. Spaces which are located below deck or spaces where access from the open deck is not provided shall be fitted with a mechanical ventilation system designed to take exhaust air from the bottom of the space and shall be sized to provide at least six air changes per hour. Access doors shall open outwards, and bulkheads and decks, including doors and other means of closing any opening therein, which form the boundaries between such rooms and adjacent enclosed spaces shall be gastight. For the purpose of the application of tables 9.1 to 9.8, such storage rooms shall be treated as fire control stations.

① The list of halon banking and reception facilities to recharge or decommission existing fire-extinguishing systems are circulated through the Global Integrated Shipping Information System (GISIS) (resolution A.1074(28)), under the module "Test Laboratories and Halon Facilities".

.2　符合《消防安全系统规则》规定的固定式高倍泡沫灭火系统；和

.3　符合《消防安全系统规则》规定的固定式压力水雾灭火系统。

4.1.2　如果安装了非本章要求的固定式灭火系统，则该灭火系统应满足本章有关规则和《消防安全系统规则》的要求。

4.1.3　禁止使用以卤代烷 1211、1301 和 2402 以及全氟化碳作为灭火剂的灭火系统。①

4.1.4　一般而言，主管机关应不允许在固定式灭火系统中使用蒸汽作为灭火剂。如果主管机关允许使用蒸汽，应仅用于限定区域内作为所要求灭火系统的附加灭火措施，并应符合《消防安全系统规则》的要求。

4.1.5　到 2010 年 1 月 1 日后的第一次计划的干坞检验时，2002 年 7 月 1 日之前建造的船舶上用于保护机器处所和液货泵舱的固定二氧化碳灭火系统须符合《消防安全系统规则》第 5 章第 2.2.2 款的要求。

4.2　固定式气体灭火系统的关闭装置

如果使用固定式气体灭火系统，可以让空气进入或允许气体排出的被保护处所的开口应能从该处所外部予以关闭。

4.3　灭火剂储存室

当灭火剂储存在被保护处所的外面时，应储存在前防撞舱壁之后的舱室内，且该舱室不作他用。这种储存室的任何入口应最好从开敞甲板进入，并应独立于被保护处所。如果储存处所位于甲板以下，则该处所的位置不得低于开敞甲板下一层，并应能由梯道或梯子从开敞甲板直接进出。位于甲板下或未设从开敞甲板进出布置的处所，应设有机械通风装置，用于排出处所底部的废气。通风装置应具有至少每小时换气 6 次的能力。入口的门应向外开启，并且在这种储存室和毗连围蔽处所之间构成限界面的舱壁和甲板，包括门和关闭其任何开口的其他装置，均应气密。就表 9.1 至 9.8 的适用范围而言，上述储存室应视作消防控制站。

① 用于重装或正式停用现有灭火系统的哈龙加注和接收设施名单通过全球综合航运信息系统（GISIS）（第 A.1074（28）号决议）下名为“测试试验室和哈龙接收设施”的模块公布。

4.4 Water pumps for other fire-extinguishing systems

Pumps, other than those serving the fire main, required for the provision of water for fire-extinguishing systems required by this chapter, their sources of power and their controls shall be installed outside the space or spaces protected by such systems and shall be so arranged that a fire in the space or spaces protected will not put any such system out of action.

5 Fire-extinguishing arrangements in machinery spaces

5.1 Machinery spaces of category A containing oil-fired boilers or oil fuel units

5.1.1 Fixed fire-extinguishing systems

Machinery spaces of category A containing oil-fired boilers or oil fuel units shall be provided with any one of the fixed fire-extinguishing systems in paragraph 4.1. In each case, if the engine-room and boiler room are not entirely separate, or if fuel oil can drain from the boiler room into the engine-room, the combined engine and boiler rooms shall be considered as one compartment.

5.1.2 Additional fire-extinguishing arrangements①

5.1.2.1 There shall be in each boiler room or at an entrance outside of the boiler room at least one portable foam applicator unit complying with the provisions of the Fire Safety Systems Code.

5.1.2.2 There shall be at least two portable foam extinguishers or equivalent in each firing space in each boiler room and in each space in which a part of the oil fuel installation is situated. There shall be not less than one approved foam-type extinguisher of at least 135 L capacity or equivalent in each boiler room. These extinguishers shall be provided with hoses on reels suitable for reaching any part of the boiler room. In the case of domestic boilers of less than 175 kW, or boilers protected by fixed water-based local application fire-extinguishing systems as required by paragraph 5.6, an approved foam-type extinguisher of at least 135 L capacity is not required.

5.1.2.3 In each firing space there shall be a receptacle containing at least 0.1 m^3 sand, sawdust impregnated with soda, or other approved dry material, along with a suitable shovel for spreading the material. An approved portable extinguisher may be substituted as an alternative.

5.2 Machinery spaces of category A containing internal combustion machinery

5.2.1 Fixed fire-extinguishing systems

Machinery spaces of category A containing internal combustion machinery shall be provided with one of the fixed fire-extinguishing systems in paragraph 4.1.

---

① Refer to *Unified interpretation of SOLAS chapter Ⅱ-2 on the number and arrangement of portable fire extinguishers on board ships* (MSC.1/Circ.1275 and Corr.1).

4.4　其他灭火系统的水泵

除用于消防总管的泵以外，需为本章所要求的各灭火系统供水的泵及其电源和控制装置应安装在该系统所保护的处所外部，且其布置应在被保护处所失火时，不会造成任何此种系统停止工作。

5　机器处所的灭火设备

5.1　设有燃油锅炉或燃油装置的机器处所

5.1.1　固定式灭火系统

内设燃油锅炉或燃油装置的A类机器处所，应设有本条4.1中规定的任何一种固定式灭火系统。在各种情况下，如机舱和锅炉舱未完全隔开，或如燃油能从锅炉舱流入机舱，则机舱和锅炉舱两者应视为一个舱室。

5.1.2　附加灭火设备①

5.1.2.1　每一锅炉舱内或锅炉舱入口外侧应至少设有1套符合《消防安全系统规则》规定的手提式泡沫枪装置。

5.1.2.2　每一锅炉舱内的每一生火处所和部分燃油装置所在的每一处所，至少应设置2具手提式泡沫灭火器或等效灭火器。在每一锅炉舱内应至少设有容量至少135 L的认可的泡沫型灭火器或与之等效的灭火器1具。这些灭火器应备有绕在卷筒上足以达到锅炉舱任何部位的软管。对小于175 kW的生活锅炉，或按第5.6款要求由固定水基局部使用灭火系统保护的锅炉，可不要求设有容量至少为135 L的经认可的泡沫灭火器。

5.1.2.3　每一生火处所应设有容器1具，内装至少0.1 m^3的沙、浸透苏打的锯屑或其他认可的干燥物，并配有1把合适的铲子用于扬撒这些干燥物。也可用1具认可的手提式灭火器作为替代。

5.2　装有内燃机的A类机器处所

5.2.1　固定式灭火系统

设有内燃机的A类机器处所应设有本条4.1中规定的一种固定式灭火系统。

① 参见SOLAS公约第Ⅱ-2章船上手提式灭火器数量和布置的统一解释（第MSC.1/CIrc.1275号通函和Corr.1）。

5.2.2 Additional fire-extinguishing arrangements①

5.2.2.1 There shall be at least one portable foam applicator unit complying with the provisions of the Fire Safety Systems Code.

5.2.2.2 There shall be in each such space approved foam-type fire extinguishers, each of at least 45 L capacity or equivalent, sufficient in number to enable foam or its equivalent to be directed onto any part of the fuel and lubricating oil pressure systems, gearing and other fire hazards. In addition, there shall be provided a sufficient number of portable foam extinguishers or equivalent which shall be so located that no point in the space is more than 10 m walking distance from an extinguisher and that there are at least two such extinguishers in each such space. For smaller spaces of cargo ships the Administration may consider relaxing this requirement.

5.3 Machinery spaces containing steam turbines or enclosed steam engines

5.3.1 Fixed fire-extinguishing systems

In spaces containing steam turbines or enclosed steam engines used for main propulsion or other purposes having in the aggregate a total output of not less than 375 kW, one of the fire-extinguishing systems specified in paragraph 4.1 shall be provided if such spaces are periodically unattended.

5.3.2 Additional fire-extinguishing arrangements

5.3.2.1 There shall be approved foam fire extinguishers, each of at least 45 L capacity or equivalent, sufficient in number to enable foam or its equivalent to be directed on to any part of the pressure lubrication system, on to any part of the casings enclosing pressure-lubricated parts of the turbines, engines or associated gearing, and any other fire hazards. However, such extinguishers shall not be required if protection, at least equivalent to that required by this subparagraph, is provided in such spaces by a fixed fire-extinguishing system fitted in compliance with paragraph 4.1.

5.3.2.2 There shall be a sufficient number of portable foam extinguishers② or equivalent which shall be so located that no point in the space is more than 10 m walking distance from an extinguisher and that there are at least two such extinguishers in each such space, except that such extinguishers shall not be required in addition to any provided in compliance with paragraph 5.1.2.2.

5.4 Other machinery spaces

Where, in the opinion of the Administration, a fire hazard exists in any machinery space for which no specific provisions for fire-extinguishing appliances are prescribed in paragraphs 5.1, 5.2 and 5.3, there shall be provided in, or adjacent to, that space such a number of approved portable fire extinguishers or other means of fire extinction as the Administration may deem sufficient.

---

① Refer to *Unified interpretation of SOLAS chapter Ⅱ-2 on the number and arrangement of portable fire extinguishers on board ships* (MSC.1/Circ.1275 and Corr.1).

② Refer to *Unified interpretation of SOLAS chapter Ⅱ-2 on the number and arrangement of portable fire extinguishers on board ships* (MSC.1/Circ.1275).

5.2.2　附加灭火设备[①]

5.2.2.1　应至少设有1套符合《消防安全系统规则》规定的手提式泡沫枪装置。

5.2.2.2　在该每一处所内，应设有每具容量至少45 L的经认可的泡沫灭火器或等效灭火器，其数量足以使泡沫或等效物能射到燃油和润滑油压力系统、传动装置和其他有失火危险的任何部分。此外，还应设有足够数量的手提式泡沫灭火器或等效灭火器，其布置应使该处所内任何一点到达1具灭火器的步行距离不大于10 m，且该每处所至少设有2具这样的灭火器。对于货船上设有内燃机的较小处所，主管机关可以考虑放宽此项要求。

5.3　设有汽轮机或闭式蒸汽机的处所

5.3.1　固定式灭火系统

设有总输出功率不少于375 kW的汽轮机或闭式蒸汽机的处所，无论其用于主推进或用于其他目的，如果该处所为周期性无人值班，应设有本条4.1规定的一种固定式灭火系统。

5.3.2　附加灭火设备

5.3.2.1　应设有每具容量至少为45 L的经认可的泡沫灭火器或等效灭火器，其数量足以使泡沫或其等效物能射到压力润滑油系统的任何部分，汽轮机闭式压力润滑部件的罩壳、发动机或其传动装置的任何部分以及其他有失火危险之处。但是，如果按本条4.1安装的固定式灭火系统对上述处所提供的保护至少等效于本规定所要求的保护，不应要求设有上述灭火器。

5.3.2.2　应设有足够数量的手提式泡沫灭火器[②]或等效灭火器，其布置应使该处所的任何一点到达1具灭火器的步行距离不大于10 m，且每一这种处所至少设有2具这种灭火器。但如果设有的灭火器符合本条5.1.2.2的要求，则不应要求增设上述灭火器。

5.4　其他机器处所

在本条5.1、5.2和5.3对灭火设备未做具体规定的任何机器处所，如果主管机关认为存在失火危险，应在该处所内或与其相邻处按主管机关认为足够的数量设置认可的手提式灭火器或其他灭火装置。

---

① 参见SOLAS公约第Ⅱ-2章船上手提式灭火器数量和布置的统一解释（第MSC.1/CIrc.1275号通函和Corr.1）。

② 参见《1974年国际海上人命安全公约》第Ⅱ-2章船上手提式灭火器数量和布置的统一解释（第MSC.1/Circ.1275号通函）。

5.5 Additional requirements for passenger ships

In passenger ships carrying more than 36 passengers, each machinery space of category A shall be provided with at least two suitable water fog applicators.①

5.6 Fixed local application fire-extinguishing systems

5.6.1 Paragraph 5.6 shall apply to passenger ships of 500 gross tonnage and above and cargo ships of 2,000 gross tonnage and above.

5.6.2 Machinery spaces of category A above 500 m^3 in volume shall, in addition to the fixed fire-extinguishing system required in paragraph 5.1.1, be protected by an approved type of fixed water-based or equivalent local application fire-extinguishing system, based on the guidelines developed by the Organization.② In the case of periodically unattended machinery spaces, the fire-extinguishing system shall have both automatic and manual release capabilities. In the case of continuously manned machinery spaces, the fire-extinguishing system is only required to have a manual release capability.

5.6.3 Fixed local application fire-extinguishing systems are to protect areas such as the following without the necessity of engine shutdown, personnel evacuation, or sealing of the spaces:

.1 the fire hazard portions of internal combustion machinery or, for ships constructed before 1 July 2014, the fire hazard portions of internal combustion machinery used for the ship's main propulsion and power generation;

.2 boiler fronts;

.3 the fire hazard portions of incinerators; and

.4 purifiers for heated fuel oil.

5.6.4 Activation of any local application system shall give a visual and distinct audible alarm in the protected space and at continuously manned stations. The alarm shall indicate the specific system activated. The system alarm requirements described within this paragraph are in addition to, and not a substitute for, the detection and fire alarm system required elsewhere in this chapter.

6 Fire-extinguishing arrangements in control stations, accommodation and service spaces

6.1 Sprinkler and water-spraying systems in passenger ships

---

① A water fog applicator might consist of a metal L-shaped pipe, the long limb being about 2 m in length, capable of being fitted to a fire hose, and the short limb being about 250 mm in length, fitted with a fixed water fog nozzle or capable of being fitted with a water spray nozzle.

② Refer to *Revised guidelines for the approval of fixed water-based local application fire-fighting systems for use in category A machinery spaces* (MSC/Circ.913) (MSC.1/Circ.1387), *Unified interpretations of the Guidelines for the approval of fixed water-based local application fire-fighting systems* (MSC/Circ.913) (MSC/Circ.1082) and *Unified interpretations of SOLAS chapter Ⅱ-2* (MSC.1/Circ.1276).

5.5 对客船的附加要求

载客超过36人的客船,其每一A类机器处所应至少设有2具适合的水雾枪[①]。

5.6 固定式局部使用灭火系统

5.6.1 本条5.6应适用于500总吨及以上的客船和2 000总吨及以上的货船。

5.6.2 容积超过500 m^3 的A类机器处所,除应装设本条5.1.1要求的固定式灭火系统外,还应根据本组织制定的指南[②],由一个经认可的固定式水基或等效的局部灭火系统保护。对于周期性无人值班机器处所,该灭火系统应能自动和手动释放。对于连续有人值班的机器处所,仅要求该灭火系统能手动释放。

5.6.3 固定式局部使用灭火系统用于保护下列区域,而无须关闭发动机、撤离人员或封闭这些处所:

.1 内燃机上有失火危险的部分,或对于2014年7月1日以前建造的船舶,为船舶主推进和发电所用的内燃机上有失火危险的部分;

.2 锅炉正面;

.3 焚烧炉有失火危险的部分;和

.4 加热燃油的净化器。

5.6.4 任何局部使用灭火系统启动时,应在被保护的处所和连续有人值班的处所发出视觉报警和清晰的听觉报警。该报警应指明所启动的具体系统。本规定所述的系统报警要求是对本章其他部分要求的探火和失火报警系统的补充,而不是替代。

6 控制站、起居处所和服务处所的灭火设备

6.1 客船上的喷水器和水雾系统

---

① 水雾枪可由L形金属管组成,其长肢长约2 m,能与消防水带相连接,其短肢长约250 mm,装有一个固定水雾枪或能够接上一个喷水枪。

② 参见《用于A类机器处所的固定式水基局部使用灭火系统认可指南》(第MSC/Circ.913号通函)(第MSC.1/Circ.1387号通函)、《〈固定式水基局部使用灭火系统认可指南〉(第MSC/Circ.913号通函)的统一解释》(第MSC/Circ.1082号通函)和《SOLAS第Ⅱ-2章的统一解释》(第MSC.1/Circ.1276号通函)。

6.1.1 Passenger ships carrying more than 36 passengers shall be equipped with an automatic sprinkler, fire detection and fire alarm system of an approved type complying with the requirements of the Fire Safety Systems Code in all control stations, accommodation and service spaces, including corridors and stairways. Alternatively, control stations, where water may cause damage to essential equipment, may be fitted with an approved fixed fire-extinguishing system of another type. Spaces having little or no fire risk such as voids, public toilets, carbon dioxide rooms and similar spaces need not be fitted with an automatic sprinkler system.

6.1.2 In passenger ships carrying not more than 36 passengers, when a fixed smoke detection and fire alarm system complying with the provisions of the Fire Safety Systems Code is provided only in corridors, stairways and escape routes within accommodation spaces, an automatic sprinkler system shall be installed in accordance with regulation 7.5.3.2.

6.1.3 A fixed pressure water-spraying fire-extinguishing system complying with the provisions of the Fire Safety Systems Code shall be installed on cabin balconies of ships to which regulation 5.3.4 applies, where furniture and furnishings on such balconies are not as defined in regulations 3.40.1, 3.40.2, 3.40.3, 3.40.6 and 3.40.7.

6.2 Sprinkler systems for cargo ships

In cargo ships in which method ⅡC specified in regulation 9.2.3.1.1.2 is adopted, an automatic sprinkler, fire detection and fire alarm system shall be fitted in accordance with the requirements in regulation 7.5.5.2.

6.3 Spaces containing flammable liquid

6.3.1 Paint lockers shall be protected by:

.1 a carbon dioxide system, designed to give a minimum volume of free gas equal to 40% of the gross volume of the protected space;

.2 a dry powder system, designed for at least 0.5 kg powder/m^3;

.3 a water-spraying or sprinkler system, designed for 5 L/m^2 min. Water-spraying systems may be connected to the fire main of the ship; or

.4 a system providing equivalent protection, as determined by the Administration.

In all cases, the system shall be operable from outside the protected space.

6.3.2 Flammable liquid lockers shall be protected by an appropriate fire-extinguishing arrangement approved by the Administration.

6.3.3 For lockers of a deck area of less than 4 m^2, which do not give access to accommodation spaces, a portable carbon dioxide fire extinguisher sized to provide a minimum volume of free gas equal to 40% of the gross volume of the space may be accepted in lieu of a fixed system. A discharge port shall be arranged in the locker to allow the discharge of the extinguisher without having to enter into the protected space. The required portable fire extinguisher shall be stowed adjacent to the port. Alternatively, a port or hose connection may be provided to facilitate the use of fire main water.

6.1.1　载客超过 36 人的客船，应在所有控制站、起居处所和服务处所，包括走廊和梯道装设符合《消防安全系统规则》要求的认可型式的自动喷水器、探火和失火报警系统。作为替代，在水可能造成关键设备损坏的控制站，可以安装其他类型的认可型式的灭火系统。在极少有失火危险或无失火危险的处所，如空舱、公共卫生间、二氧化碳间和类似处所，不必安装自动喷水器系统。

6.1.2　载客不超过 36 人的客船，如果仅在起居处所的走廊、梯道和脱险通道设有符合《消防安全系统规则》规定的固定式探火和失火报警系统，应根据第 7.5.3.2 条安装自动喷水器系统。

6.1.3　在第 5.3.4 条适用的船舶的客舱阳台上，如果其家具与陈设不是第 3.40.1、3.40.2、3.40.3、3.40.6 和 3.40.7 条所定义的，应安装符合《消防安全系统规则》规定的固定式压力水雾灭火系统。

6.2　货船的喷水器系统

对于采用第 9.2.3.1.1.2 条规定的ⅡC 法的货船，应根据第 7.5.5.2 条的要求安装自动喷水器、探火和失火报警系统。

6.3　存有易燃液体的处所

6.3.1　油漆间应由下列系统保护：

.1　二氧化碳系统，设计成能至少放出相当于所保护处所总容积 40%的自由气体；

.2　干粉系统，设计能力至少为 0.5 kg 干粉/m^3；

.3　水雾或喷水器系统，设计供水能力为 5 L/m^2/min。水雾系统可连接在船舶消防总管上；或

.4　主管机关认为能提供等效保护的系统。

在任何情况下，该系统均应能从所保护处所的外部进行操作。

6.3.2　易燃液体储藏室应由经主管机关认可的相应的灭火设备予以保护。

6.3.3　对于不通往起居处所甲板的面积小于 4 m^2 的易燃液体储藏室，可以接受用手提式二氧化碳灭火器代替固定式灭火系统，该灭火器应能至少放出相当于所保护处所总容积 40%的自由气体。在储藏室上应设有喷放孔，无须进入该受保护处所就可以用灭火器向内喷放。所要求的手提式灭火器应存放在喷放孔附近。作为替代，可以布置注水口或水带接头以便于使用消防总管的水。

6.4 Deep-fat cooking equipment

Deep-fat cooking equipment installed in enclosed spaces or on open decks shall be fitted with the following:

.1 an automatic or manual fire-extinguishing system tested to an international standard acceptable to the Organization;①

.2 a primary and backup thermostat with an alarm to alert the operator in the event of failure of either thermostat;

.3 arrangements for automatically shutting off the electrical power upon activation of the fire-extinguishing system;

.4 an alarm for indicating operation of the fire-extinguishing system in the galley where the equipment is installed; and

.5 controls for manual operation of the fire-extinguishing system which are clearly labelled for ready use by the crew.

7 Fire-extinguishing arrangements in cargo spaces

7.1 Fixed gas fire-extinguishing systems for general cargo

7.1.1 Except as provided for in paragraph 7.2, the cargo spaces of passenger ships of 1,000 gross tonnage and upwards shall be protected by a fixed carbon dioxide or inert gas fire-extinguishing system complying with the provisions of the Fire Safety Systems Code or by a fixed high-expansion foam fire-extinguishing system which gives equivalent protection.

7.1.2 Where it is shown to the satisfaction of the Administration that a passenger ship is engaged on voyages of such short duration that it would be unreasonable to apply the requirements of paragraph 7.1.1 and also in ships of less than 1,000 gross tonnage, the arrangements in cargo spaces shall be to the satisfaction of the Administration, provided that the ship is fitted with steel hatch covers and effective means of closing all ventilators and other openings leading to the cargo spaces.

7.1.3 Except for ro-ro and vehicle spaces, cargo spaces on cargo ships of 2,000 gross tonnage and upwards shall be protected by a fixed carbon dioxide or inert gas fire-extinguishing system complying with the provisions of the Fire Safety Systems Code, or by a fire-extinguishing system which gives equivalent protection.

---

① Refer to the recommendations by the International Organization for Standardization, in particular publication ISO 15371:2009, *Ships and marine technology—Fire-extinguishing systems for protection of galley cooking equipment.*

6.4　深油烹饪设备

安装在围蔽处所中或开敞甲板上的深油烹饪设备应装有下列装置：

.1　按本组织所接受的国际标准①试验过的自动或手动灭火系统；

.2　1个主恒温器和1个后备恒温器，以及1个在任一恒温器出现故障时引起操作人员警觉的报警装置；

.3　在灭火系统启动后自动关闭电源的装置；

.4　1个表明厨房内安装的灭火系统操作的报警装置；和

.5　灭火系统的手动操作控制器，为便于船员使用，其上应有清晰的标志。

7　货物处所的灭火设备

7.1　用于普通货物的固定式气体灭火系统

7.1.1　除本条7.2的规定外，1 000总吨及以上的客船的货物处所应由符合《消防安全系统规则》规定的固定式二氧化碳灭火系统或固定式惰性气体灭火系统加以保护，或由能提供等效保护的固定式高倍泡沫灭火系统给予保护。

7.1.2　如果能证明并使主管机关确信对航程短的客船以及对1 000总吨以下的船舶应用本条7.1.1的要求为不合理，则货物处所灭火系统的布置应使主管机关满意，但该船须安装有钢质舱口盖和关闭所有通风口及其他通往货物处所开口的有效装置。

7.1.3　除滚装处所和车辆处所外，2 000总吨及以上货船上的货物处所应由符合《消防安全系统规则》规定的固定式二氧化碳灭火系统或固定式惰性气体灭火系统加以保护，或由能提供等效保护的灭火系统给予保护。

---

①　参见国际标准化组织的建议案，特别是出版物ISO 15371：2009《船舶和船用技术——保护厨房烹饪设备的灭火系统》。

7.1.4 The Administration may exempt from the requirements of paragraphs 7.1.3 and 7.2 cargo spaces of any cargo ship if constructed, and solely intended, for the carriage of ore, coal, grain, unseasoned timber, non-combustible cargoes or cargoes which, in the opinion of the Administration, constitute a low fire risk.① Such exemptions may be granted only if the ship is fitted with steel hatch covers and effective means of closing all ventilators and other openings leading to the cargo spaces. When such exemptions are granted, the Administration shall issue an Exemption Certificate, irrespective of the date of construction of the ship concerned, in accordance with regulation Ⅰ/12(a)(vi), and shall ensure that the list of cargoes the ship is permitted to carry is attached to the Exemption Certificate.

7.2 Fixed gas fire-extinguishing systems for dangerous goods

A ship engaged in the carriage of dangerous goods in any cargo spaces shall be provided with a fixed carbon dioxide or inert gas fire-extinguishing system complying with the provisions of the Fire Safety Systems Code or with a fire-extinguishing system which, in the opinion of the Administration, gives equivalent protection for the cargoes carried.

7.3 Firefighting for ships constructed on or after 1 January 2016 designed to carry containers on or above the weather deck

7.3.1 Ships shall carry, in addition to the equipment and arrangements required by paragraphs 1 and 2, at least one water mist lance.

7.3.1.1 The water mist lance shall consist of a tube with a piercing nozzle which is capable of penetrating a container wall and producing water mist inside a confined space (container, etc.) when connected to the fire main.

7.3.2 Ships designed to carry five or more tiers of containers on or above the weather deck shall carry, in addition to the requirements of paragraph 7.3.1, mobile water monitors② as follows:

(1) ships with breadth less than 30 m: at least two mobile water monitors; or

(2) ships with breadth of 30 m or more: at least four mobile water monitors.

7.3.2.1 The mobile water monitors, all necessary hoses, fittings and required fixing hardware shall be kept ready for use in a location outside the cargo space area not likely to be cut off in the event of a fire in the cargo spaces.

7.3.2.2 A sufficient number of fire hydrants shall be provided such that:

.1 all provided mobile water monitors can be operated simultaneously for creating effective water barriers forward and aft of each container bay;

---

① Refer to the IMSBC Code (resolution MSC.268(85), as amended), appendix 1, entry for coal, and to the *Lists of solid bulk cargoes for which a fixed gas fire-extinguishing system may be exempted or for which a fixed gas fire-extinguishing system is ineffective* (MSC./Circ.1395/Rev.4).

② Refer to *Guidelines for the design, performance, testing and approval of mobile water monitors used for the protection of on-deck cargo areas of ships designed and constructed to carry five or more tiers of containers on or above the weather deck* (MSC. 1/Circ. 1472).

7.1.4 对于专门为载运矿砂、煤、粮食、未干透的木材、不燃货物或主管机关认为具有较小失火危险的货物而建造的货船，主管机关可免除本条 7.1.3 和 7.2 对其货物处所的要求。[①] 只有在船舶安装有钢质舱口盖和关闭所有通风口及其他通往货物处所开口的有效装置时才准予上述免除。在准予此种免除时，无论该船舶何时建造，主管机关均应按第Ⅰ/12(a)(vi)条签发免除证书，并应确保免除证书附有船舶准许载运货物种类的清单。

7.2　用于危险货物的固定式气体灭火系统

使用任何货物处所载运危险货物的船舶应设有符合《消防安全系统规则》规定的固定式二氧化碳或惰性气体灭火系统，或设有主管机关认为能为所载运货物提供等效保护的灭火系统。

7.3　2016 年 1 月 1 日或以后建造的、设计在露天甲板或其上方载运集装箱的船舶消防

7.3.1 除第 1 和第 2 款所要求的设备和装置外，船舶还应至少配备一具水雾枪。

7.3.1.1 水雾枪应包括一个带有穿刺喷嘴的管子，当连接至消防总管时能刺穿集装箱壁并将水雾喷入密闭空间(集装箱等)。

7.3.2 设计在露天甲板或其上方载运五层或五层以上集装箱的船舶，除满足第 7.3.1 款的要求外，还应配备如下移动式消防水炮[②]：

(1)　船宽不超过 30 m 的船舶：至少 2 具移动式消防水炮；或

(2)　船宽为 30 m 或以上的船舶：至少 4 具移动式消防水炮。

7.3.2.1 移动式消防水炮、所有必要的软管、配件和要求的固定装置应存放在货物处所区域之外且在货物处所内发生火灾时不会被阻隔的位置以供随时使用。

7.3.2.2 应配备足够数量的消火栓以使：

.1　所有配备的移动式消防水炮可以同时在每一集装箱箱跨的首尾处产生有效的水障；

① 参见《国际海运固体散货规则》(第 MSC.268(85)号决议通过，经修正的)附录 1 关于煤的细目以及《固定式气体灭火系统可予免除或固定式气体灭火系统不起作用的固体散货清单》(第 MSC.1/ Circ.1395/Rev.4 号通函)。

② 参见《用于保护拟设计和建造为在露天甲板或其上方装载五层或五层以上集装箱的船舶的甲板上货物区域的移动式消防水炮的设计、性能、试验和认可指南》(第 MSC.1/Circ.1472 号通函)。

.2 the two jets of water required by paragraph 2.1.5.1 can be supplied at the pressure required by paragraph 2.1.6; and

.3 each of the required mobile water monitors can be supplied by separate hydrants at the pressure necessary to reach the top tier of containers on deck.

7.3.2.3 The mobile water monitors may be supplied by the fire main, provided the capacity of fire pumps and fire main diameter are adequate to simultaneously operate the mobile water monitors and two jets of water from fire hoses at the required pressure values. If carrying dangerous goods, the capacity of fire pumps and fire main diameter shall also comply with regulation 19.3.1.5, as far as applicable to on-deck cargo areas.

7.3.2.4 The operational performance of each mobile water monitor shall be tested during initial survey on board the ship to the satisfaction of the Administration. The test shall verify that:

.1 the mobile water monitor can be securely fixed to the ship structure ensuring safe and effective operation; and

.2 the mobile water monitor jet reaches the top tier of containers with all required monitors and water jets from fire hoses operated simultaneously.

8 Cargo tank protection

8.1 Fixed deck foam fire-extinguishing systems

8.1.1 For tankers of 20,000 tonnes deadweight and upwards, a fixed deck foam fire-extinguishing system shall be provided complying with the provisions of the Fire Safety Systems Code, except that, in lieu of the above, the Administration, after having given consideration to the ship's arrangement and equipment, may accept other fixed installations if they afford protection equivalent to the above, in accordance with regulation Ⅰ/5. The requirements for alternative fixed installations shall comply with the requirements in paragraph 8.1.2.

8.1.2 In accordance with paragraph 8.1.1, where the Administration accepts an equivalent fixed installation in lieu of the fixed deck foam fire-extinguishing system, the installation shall:

.1 be capable of extinguishing spill fires and also preclude ignition of spilled oil not yet ignited; and

.2 be capable of combating fires in ruptured tanks.

8.1.3 Tankers of less than 20,000 tonnes deadweight shall be provided with a deck foam fire-extinguishing system complying with the requirements of the Fire Safety Systems Code.

9 Protection of cargo pump-rooms in tankers

9.1 Fixed fire-extinguishing systems

Each cargo pump-room shall be provided with one of the following fixed fire-extinguishing systems operated from a readily accessible position outside the pump-room. Cargo pump-rooms shall be provided with a system suitable for machinery spaces of category A.

.2　可以第 2.1.6 款所要求的压力提供第 2.1.5.1 款所要求的两股水柱；和

.3　每具所要求的移动消防水炮可由不同的消火栓供水，其压力足以达到甲板上最高一层集装箱。

7.3.2.3　如果消防泵的排量和消防总管的直径足以同时供应移动式消防水炮并从消防水带产生两股达到所要求压力值的水柱，则移动式消防水炮可由消防总管供水。如果载运危险货物，则对甲板上的货物区域而言，消防泵的排量和消防总管的直径还应符合第 19.3.1.5 条的要求。

7.3.2.4　在船上进行初次检验时，须对每具移动式消防水炮的运行性能进行试验，并使主管机关满意。试验须验证：

.1　移动式消防水炮能安全地固定在船体结构上，并保证安全有效地运行；和

.2　所有要求的移动式消防水炮和消防水带的喷水器同时运行时，移动式消防水炮的水柱可以达到最高一层集装箱。

8　液货舱保护

8.1　固定式甲板泡沫灭火系统

8.1.1　20 000 载重吨及以上的液货船应安装符合《消防安全系统规则》规定的固定式甲板泡沫灭火系统，但主管机关考虑到船舶的布置和设备情况，可以根据第Ⅰ/5 条接受其他固定式装置代替上述系统，只要这些装置能提供与上述系统等效的保护。对替代的固定式装置的要求应与本条 8.1.2 的要求相符。

8.1.2　如果主管机关根据本条 8.1.1 接受用等效固定式装置代替固定式甲板泡沫灭火系统，该装置应：

.1　能够扑灭溢油失火，并能防止尚未着火的溢油着火；和

.2　能够扑灭破裂液货舱内的火灾。

8.1.3　20 000 以下载重吨的液货船应设有符合《消防安全系统规则》要求的甲板泡沫灭火系统。

9　液货船液货泵舱的保护

9.1　固定式灭火系统

每一液货泵舱应安装下述固定式灭火系统之一，且可以在液货泵舱外部的一个易于到达的位置进行操作。液货泵舱应安装一个适合于 A 类机器处所的灭火系统。

9.1.1 A carbon dioxide fire-extinguishing system complying with the provisions of the Fire Safety Systems Code and with the following:

.1 the alarms giving audible warning of the release of fire-extinguishing medium shall be safe for use in a flammable cargo vapour/air mixture; and

.2 a notice shall be exhibited at the controls stating that, due to the electrostatic ignition hazard, the system is to be used only for fire extinguishing and not for inerting purposes.

9.1.2 A high-expansion foam fire-extinguishing system complying with the provisions of the Fire Safety Systems Code, provided that the foam concentrate supply is suitable for extinguishing fires involving the cargoes carried.

9.1.3 A fixed pressure water-spraying fire-extinguishing system complying with the provisions of the Fire Safety Systems Code.

9.2 Quantity of fire-extinguishing medium

Where the fire-extinguishing medium used in the cargo pump-room system is also used in systems serving other spaces, the quantity of medium provided or its delivery rate need not be more than the maximum required for the largest compartment.

10 Fire-fighter's outfits

10.1 Types of fire-fighter's outfits

10.1.1 Fire-fighter's outfits shall comply with the Fire Safety Systems Code.

10.1.2 Self-contained compressed air breathing apparatus of fire-fighter's outfits shall comply with paragraph 2.1.2.2 of chapter 3 of the Fire Safety Systems Code by 1 July 2019.

10.2 Number of fire-fighter's outfits

10.2.1 Ships shall carry at least two fire-fighter's outfits.

10.2.2 In addition, in passenger ships there shall be provided:

.1 for every 80 m, or part thereof, of the aggregate of the lengths of all passenger spaces and service spaces on the deck which carries such spaces or, if there is more than one such deck, on the deck which has the largest aggregate of such lengths, two fire-fighter's outfits and, in addition, two sets of personal equipment, each set comprising the items stipulated in the Fire Safety Systems Code. In passenger ships carrying more than 36 passengers, two additional fire-fighter's outfits shall be provided for each main vertical zone. However, for stairway enclosures which constitute individual main vertical zones and for the main vertical zones in the fore or aft end of a ship which do not contain spaces of categories (6), (7), (8) or (12) defined in regulation 9.2.2.3, no additional fire-fighter's outfits are required; and

.2 on ships carrying more than 36 passengers, for each pair of breathing apparatus, one water fog applicator which shall be stored adjacent to such apparatus.

9.1.1 一个符合《消防安全系统规则》规定的二氧化碳系统，该系统并符合下列要求：

.1 释放灭火剂时发出声响警告的报警装置应能安全用于易燃货物蒸气/空气混合物中；和

.2 在控制部位应展示一个提示，说明由于静电着火危险，本系统应仅用于灭火而不能用于惰化的目的。

9.1.2 一个符合《消防安全系统规则》规定的高倍泡沫灭火系统，但泡沫浓缩剂的供给应适合扑灭涉及所载货物的火灾。

9.1.3 一个符合《消防安全系统规则》规定的固定式压力水雾灭火系统。

9.2 灭火剂的数量

如果用于液货泵舱系统的灭火剂也用于为其他处所服务的系统，则所配备的灭火剂数量或其施放率不必超过最大舱室所需的最大量。

10 消防员装备

10.1 消防员装备的类型

10.1.1 消防员装备应符合《消防安全系统规则》；和

10.1.2 消防员装备的自给式压缩空气呼吸器须自 2019 年 7 月 1 日起符合《消防安全系统规则》第 3 章第 2.1.2.2 款。

10.2 消防员装备的数量

10.2.1 船舶应携带至少 2 套消防员装备。

10.2.2 此外，对于客船：

.1 对设有乘客处所和服务处所的甲板，按其乘客处所和服务处所的合计长度，或如这种甲板多于一层，按其一层甲板乘客处所和服务处所的最大长度，每80 m（不足 80 m 以 80 m 计）应备有 2 套消防员装备以及 2 套个人配备，每套配备包括《消防安全系统规则》中所规定的项目。对载客超过 36 人的客船，每一主竖区内应增配 2 套消防员装备。但对于构成独立主竖区的梯道环围和分布在船舶首端或尾端且未设有第 9.2.2.3 条所定义的(6)、(7)、(8)或(12)类处所的主竖区，则无须增配消防员装备；和

.2 对载客超过 36 人的船舶，应为每副呼吸器配备 1 具水雾枪，水雾枪应邻近于该呼吸器存放。

10.2.3 In addition, in tankers, two fire-fighter's outfits shall be provided.

10.2.4 The Administration may require additional sets of personal equipment and breathing apparatus, having due regard to the size and type of the ship.

10.2.5 Two spare charges shall be provided for each required breathing apparatus. Passenger ships carrying not more than 36 passengers and cargo ships that are equipped with suitably located means for fully recharging the air cylinders free from contamination need carry only one spare charge for each required apparatus. In passenger ships carrying more than 36 passengers, at least two spare charges for each breathing apparatus shall be provided.

10.2.6 Passenger ships carrying more than 36 passengers constructed on or after 1 July 2010 shall be fitted with a suitably located means for fully recharging breathing air cylinders, free from contamination. The means for recharging shall be either:

.1 breathing air compressors supplied from the main and emergency switchboard, or independently driven, with a minimum capacity of 60 L/min per required breathing apparatus, not to exceed 420 L/min; or

.2 self-contained high-pressure storage systems of suitable pressure to recharge the breathing apparatus used on board, with a capacity of at least 1,200 L per required breathing apparatus, not to exceed 50,000 L of free air.

10.3 Storage of fire-fighter's outfits

10.3.1 The fire-fighter's outfits or sets of personal equipment shall be kept ready for use in an easily accessible location that is permanently and clearly marked and, where more than one fire-fighter's outfit or more than one set of personal equipment is carried, they shall be stored in widely separated positions.

10.3.2 In passenger ships, at least two fire-fighter's outfits and, in addition, one set of personal equipment shall be available at any one position. At least two fire-fighter's outfits shall be stored in each main vertical zone.

10.4 Fire-fighter's communication

For ships constructed on or after 1 July 2014, a minimum of two two-way portable radiotelephone apparatus for each fire party for fire-fighter's communication shall be carried on board. Those two-way portable radiotelephone apparatus shall be of an explosion-proof type or intrinsically safe. Ships constructed before 1 July 2014 shall comply with the requirements of this paragraph not later than the first survey after 1 July 2018.

10.2.3　此外,液货船上应配备2套消防员装备。

10.2.4　主管机关在充分考虑到船舶大小和类型的情况下,可以要求增加个人配备和呼吸器的数量。

10.2.5　每副所要求的呼吸器均应配备2个备用充气瓶。对载客不超过36人的客船以及货船,其在适当的位置配有无污染重新充装全部气瓶的设备时,只需为每副所要求的呼吸器配备1个备用充气瓶。对载客超过36人的客船,则应为每副呼吸器至少配备2个备用充气瓶。

10.2.6　在2010年7月1日及之后建造的载客超过36人以上的客船须在适当位置设有无沾染完全再充装呼吸气瓶的装置。再充装装置须是:

.1　由主配电盘和应急配电盘供电的,或独立驱动的呼吸气体压缩机,其最小容量为每具所要求的呼吸器60 L/min,但不超过420 L/min;或

.2　压力适于再充装船用呼吸器的独立式高压存储系统,其容量为每具所要求的呼吸器至少1 200 L,但不超过50 000 L的自由空气。

10.3　消防员装备的存放

10.3.1　消防员装备和个人配备应存放在有永久性清晰标记且易于到达的位置,以备随时取用。如果所配备的消防员装备或个人配备不止1套,其存放位置应彼此远离。

10.3.2　在客船上,应在任一位置可获得至少2套消防员装备外加1套个人配备。在每一主竖区内应至少存放2套消防员装备。

10.4　消防员通信

对于2014年7月1日或以后建造的船舶,船上每一消防队须携带至少两部双向便携式无线电话机用于消防员的通信。这些双向便携式无线电话机须为防爆型或本质安全型。2014年7月1日以前建造的船舶须不迟于2018年7月1日以后的第一次检验符合本要求。

Regulation 11
Structural integrity

1 Purpose

The purpose of this regulation is to maintain structural integrity of the ship, preventing partial or whole collapse of the ship structures due to strength deterioration by heat. For this purpose, materials used in the ships' structure shall ensure that the structural integrity is not degraded due to fire.

2 Material of hull, superstructures, structural bulkheads, decks and deckhouses

The hull, superstructures, structural bulkheads, decks and deckhouses shall be constructed of steel or other equivalent material. For the purpose of applying the definition of steel or other equivalent material as given in regulation 3.43, the "applicable fire exposure" shall be according to the integrity and insulation standards given in tables 9.1 to 9.4. For example, where divisions such as decks or sides and ends of deckhouses are permitted to have "B-0" fire integrity, the "applicable fire exposure" shall be half an hour.

3 Structure of aluminium alloy

Unless otherwise specified in paragraph 2, in cases where any part of the structure is of aluminium alloy, the following shall apply:

.1 the insulation of aluminium alloy components of "A" or "B" class divisions, except structure which, in the opinion of the Administration, is non-load-bearing, shall be such that the temperature of the structural core does not rise more than 200 ℃ above the ambient temperature at any time during the applicable fire exposure to the standard fire test; and

.2 special attention shall be given to the insulation of aluminium alloy components of columns, stanchions and other structural members required to support lifeboat and liferaft stowage, launching and embarkation areas, and "A" and "B" class divisions to ensure:

.1 that for such members supporting lifeboat and liferaft areas and "A" class divisions, the temperature rise limitation specified in paragraph 3.1 shall apply at the end of one hour; and

.2 that for such members required to support "B" class divisions, the temperature rise limitation specified in paragraph 3.1 shall apply at the end of half an hour.

4 Machinery spaces of category A

4.1 Crowns and casings

Crowns and casings of machinery spaces of category A shall be of steel construction and shall be insulated as required by tables 9.5 and 9.7, as appropriate.

第11条
结构完整性

1　目的

本条的目的是保持船舶的结构完整性,防止由于热量造成强度降低而使船舶结构部分或全部破坏。为此,船舶结构中使用的材料应确保结构完整性不会由于失火而削弱。

2　船体、上层建筑、结构舱壁、甲板以及甲板室的材料

船体、上层建筑、结构舱壁、甲板以及甲板室应用钢或其他等效材料建造。就应用第3.43条对钢或其他等效材料的定义而言,“适用曝火时间”应根据表9.1至9.4规定的完整性和隔热标准确定。例如,如果甲板或甲板室侧壁和端壁之类的分隔允许具有“B-0”级耐火完整性,则“适用曝火时间”应为30 min。

3　铝合金结构

除本条2中另有规定外,如结构的任一部分为铝合金结构,则应适用下列要求:

.1　“A”级或“B”级分隔的铝合金部件的隔热,在标准耐火试验适用曝火时间内的任何时候,应能使结构芯材的温升不超过环境温度以上200 ℃,主管机关认为属于非承载的结构除外;和

.2　应特别注意用于支承救生艇筏的存放、降落和登乘区域以及“A”级和“B”级分隔的立柱、支柱和其他结构部件中的铝合金件的隔热要求,以确保:

　.1　对用于支承救生艇筏区域以及“A”级分隔的构件,本条3.1规定的温升限制应在标准耐火试验1 h结束时适用;和

　.2　对要求用于支承“B”级分隔的构件,本条3.1规定的温升限制应在标准耐火试验30 min结束时适用。

4　A类机器处所

4.1　顶盖和舱篷

A类机器处所的顶盖和舱篷应为钢结构,并应按表9.5和9.7的相应要求予以隔热。

4.2 Floor plating

The floor plating of normal passageways in machinery spaces of category A shall be made of steel.

5 Materials of overboard fittings

Materials readily rendered ineffective by heat shall not be used for overboard scuppers, sanitary discharges, and other outlets which are close to the waterline and where the failure of the material in the event of fire would give rise to danger of flooding.

6 Protection of cargo tank structure against pressure or vacuum in tankers

6.1 General

The venting arrangements shall be so designed and operated as to ensure that neither pressure nor vacuum in cargo tanks shall exceed design parameters and be such as to provide for:

.1 the flow of the small volumes of vapour, air or inert gas mixtures caused by thermal variations in a cargo tank in all cases through pressure/vacuum valves; and

.2 the passage of large volumes of vapour, air or inert gas mixtures during cargo loading and ballasting, or during discharging.

6.2 Openings for small flow by thermal variations

Openings for pressure release required by paragraph 6.1.1 shall:

.1 have as great a height as is practicable above the cargo tank deck to obtain maximum dispersal of flammable vapours, but in no case less than 2 m above the cargo tank deck; and

.2 be arranged at the furthest distance practicable, but not less than 5 m , from the nearest air intakes and openings to enclosed spaces containing a source of ignition and from deck machinery and equipment which may constitute an ignition hazard. Anchor windlass and chain locker openings constitute an ignition hazard.

For tankers constructed on or after 1 January 2017, the openings shall be arranged in accordance with regulation 4.5.3.4.1.

6.3 Safety measures in cargo tanks

6.3.1 Preventive measures against liquid rising in the venting system

Provisions shall be made to guard against liquid rising in the venting system to a height which would exceed the design head of cargo tanks. This shall be accomplished by high-level alarms or overflow control systems or other equivalent means, together with independent gauging devices and cargo tank filling procedures. For the purposes of this regulation, spill valves are not considered equivalent to an overflow system.

4.2 地板

A 类机器处所内正常通道的地板应为钢质。

5 舷外装置的材料

遇热易失效的材料不得用于舷外排水口、卫生间排泄口和在火灾时由于材料失效可能造成进水危险的其他接近水线的出口。

6 液货船上针对压力或真空的液货舱结构保护

6.1 通则

透气装置的设计和操作应能确保液货舱内压力和真空均不得超过设计参数，并确保：

.1 在任何情况下，由于液货舱内温度变化所产生的少量蒸气、空气或惰性气体混合物能流经压力/真空阀；和

.2 在液货装载和压载或卸载过程中，大量蒸气、空气或惰性气体混合物能够通过。

6.2 温度变化所产生的少量气流的开口

本条 6.1.1 所要求的压力释放口应：

.1 在液货舱甲板以上尽可能高的位置，以达到最大程度扩散易燃气体。但无论如何，该位置在液货舱甲板以上的高度不得小于 2 m；和

.2 布置在距含有着火源的围蔽处所的最近进气口和开口以及可能构成失火危险的甲板机械和设备尽可能远的地方，但不得小于 5 m。锚机和锚链舱的开口为构成失火危险处。

对于 2017 年 1 月 1 日或以后建造的液货船，须按照第 4.5.3.4.1 条布置开口。

6.3 液货舱内的安全措施

6.3.1 预防透气系统液体上升的措施

应采取预防措施，以防止透气系统内液体上升至可能超过液货舱设计压头的高度。应通过采用高位报警器或溢流控制系统或其他等效措施，连同独立测量装置和液货舱充装程序实现。就本条而言，溢流阀不能视为等效于溢流系统。

6.3.2 Secondary means for pressure/vacuum relief

A secondary means of allowing full flow relief of vapour, air or inert gas mixtures shall be provided to prevent over-pressure or under-pressure in the event of failure of the arrangements in paragraph 6.1.2. In addition, for tankers constructed on or after 1 January 2017, the secondary means shall be capable of preventing over-perssure or under-pressure in the event of damage to, or inadvertent closing of, the means of isolation required in regulation 4.5.3.2.2. Alternatively, pressure sensors may be fitted in each tank protected by the arrangement required in paragraph 6.1.2, with a monitoring system in the ship's cargo control room or the position from which cargo operations are normally carried out. Such monitoring equipment shall also provide an alarm facility which is activated by detection of over-pressure or under-pressure conditions within a tank.

6.3.3 Bypasses in vent mains

Pressure/vacuum valves required by paragraph 6.1.1 may be provided with a bypass arrangement when they are located in a vent main or masthead riser. Where such an arrangement is provided there shall be suitable indicators to show whether the bypass is open or closed.

6.3.4 Pressure/vacuum-breaking devices

One or more pressure/vacuum-breaking devices shall be provided to prevent the cargo tanks from being subject to:

.1 a positive pressure, in excess of the test pressure of the cargo tank, if the cargo were to be loaded at the maximum rated capacity and all other outlets are left shut; and

.2 a negative pressure in excess of 700 mm water gauge if the cargo were to be discharged at the maximum rated capacity of the cargo pumps and the inert gas blowers were to fail.

Such devices shall be installed on the inert gas main unless they are installed in the venting system required by regulation 4.5.3.1 or on individual cargo tanks. The location and design of the devices shall be in accordance with regulation 4.5.3 and paragraph 6.

6.4 Size of vent outlets

Vent outlets for cargo loading, discharging and ballasting required by paragraph 6.1.2 shall be designed on the basis of the maximum designed loading rate multiplied by a factor of at least 1.25 to take account of gas evolution, in order to prevent the pressure in any cargo tank from exceeding the design pressure. The master shall be provided with information regarding the maximum permissible loading rate for each cargo tank and, in the case of combined venting systems, for each group of cargo tanks.

6.3.2 辅助压力/真空释放装置

应装设允许蒸气、空气或惰性气体混合物充分释放的辅助装置,防止本条 6.1.2 所述的布置发生故障时出现超压或欠压。此外,对于 2017 年 1 月 1 日或以后建造的液货船,如果第 4.5.3.2.2 条要求的隔离装置发生损坏或误关闭时,辅助装置须能防止超压或欠压。作为替代,可以在由本条 6.1.2 所要求措施保护的每一液货舱内安装压力传感器,传感器的监测系统应设于船舶货物控制室或通常进行货物操作的位置。监测设备上还应设有报警装置,在探测到液货舱内出现超压或欠压时启动。

6.3.3 透气总管的旁通装置

如果本条 6.1.1 所要求的压力/真空阀位于透气总管或桅顶通气管上,可以装设旁通装置。如果装有这种旁通装置,应有适当的指示器以显示旁通装置是否打开或关闭。

6.3.4 压力/真空断开装置

应设有一个或多个压力/真空断开装置,以防止液货舱受到:

.1 在以最大额定容量装货而所有其他排气口未打开时所产生的超过液货舱试验压力的正压;和

.2 在以液货泵的最大额定流量卸载而惰性气体鼓风机失灵时所产生的超过700 mm水位压力的负压。

除非在第 4.5.3.1 条所要求的透气系统或各个液货舱上安装了该装置,否则应在惰性气体总管上安装该装置。该装置的位置和设计应符合第 4.5.3 条和本条 6 的要求。

6.4 透气出口的尺寸

考虑到放出的气体,为防止任何液货舱的压力超过设计压力,本条 6.1.2 所要求的用于液货装卸和压载的透气出口,其设计应根据最大设计装载速率乘以至少 1.25 的系数。应向船长提供有关每一液货舱最大允许装载速率的资料,对于组合透气系统,则应提供每一组液货舱的资料。

Part D
Escape

Regulation 12
Notification of crew and passengers

1 Purpose

The purpose of this regulation is to notify crew and passengers of a fire for safe evacuation. For this purpose, a general emergency alarm system and a public address system shall be provided.

2 General emergency alarm system

A general emergency alarm system required by regulation Ⅲ/6.4.2 shall be used for notifying crew and passengers of a fire.

3 Public address systems in passenger ships

A public address system or other effective means of communication complying with the requirements of regulation Ⅲ/6.5 shall be available throughout the accommodation and service spaces and control stations and open decks.

Regulation 13
Means of escape

1 Purpose

The purpose of this regulation is to provide means of escape so that persons on board can safely and swiftly escape to the lifeboat and liferaft embarkation deck. For this purpose, the following functional requirements shall be met:

.1 safe escape routes shall be provided;

.2 escape routes shall be maintained in a safe condition, clear of obstacles; and

.3 additional aids for escape shall be provided as necessary to ensure accessibility, clear marking, and adequate design for emergency situations.

2 General requirements

2.1 Unless expressly provided otherwise in this regulation, at least two widely separated and ready means of escape shall be provided from all spaces or groups of spaces.

2.2 Lifts shall not be considered as forming one of the means of escape as required by this regulation.

D 部分
脱险

第 12 条
通知船员和乘客

1　目的

本条的目的是将失火情况通知船员和乘客，以便安全撤离。为此，应装设 1 套通用应急报警系统和 1 套公共广播系统。

2　通用应急报警系统

应使用第Ⅲ/6.4.2 条所要求的通用应急报警系统将失火情况通知船员和乘客。

3　客船上的公共广播系统

符合第Ⅲ/6.5 条要求的公共广播系统或其他有效通信设施应在遍及所有起居处所、服务处所、控制站和开敞甲板的范围均可通用。

第 13 条
脱险通道

1　目的

本条的目的是提供脱险通道，从而使船上人员能够安全迅速撤向救生艇和救生筏登乘甲板。为此，应满足下列功能要求：

.1　应提供安全的脱险通道；

.2　脱险通道应保持安全状况，无障碍物；和

.3　应提供其他必要的辅助逃生设施，确保其易于到达、标志清晰、设计能满足紧急情况需要。

2　一般要求

2.1　除本条另有明文规定外，应为所有处所或处所群至少提供 2 条彼此远离并随时可用的脱险通道。

2.2　不得将升降机视为构成本条所要求的脱险通道之一。

3 Means of escape from control stations, accommodation spaces and service spaces

3.1 General requirements

3.1.1 Stairways and ladders shall be so arranged as to provide ready means of escape to the lifeboat and liferaft embarkation deck from passenger and crew accommodation spaces and from spaces in which the crew is normally employed, other than machinery spaces.

3.1.2 Unless expressly provided otherwise in this regulation, a corridor, lobby, or part of a corridor from which there is only one route of escape shall be prohibited. Dead-end corridors used in service areas which are necessary for the practical utility of the ship, such as fuel oil stations and athwartship supply corridors, shall be permitted, provided such dead-end corridors are separated from crew accommodation areas and are inaccessible from passenger accommodation areas. Also, a part of a corridor that has a depth not exceeding its width is considered a recess or local extension and is permitted.

3.1.3 All stairways in accommodation and service spaces and control stations shall be of steel frame construction except where the Administration sanctions the use of other equivalent material.

3.1.4 If a radiotelegraph station has no direct access to the open deck, two means of escape from, or access to, the station shall be provided, one of which may be a porthole or window of sufficient size or other means to the satisfaction of the Administration.

3.1.5 Doors in escape routes shall, in general, open in way of the direction of escape, except that:

.1 individual cabin doors may open into the cabins in order to avoid injury to persons in the corridor when the door is opened; and

.2 doors in vertical emergency escape trunks may open out of the trunk in order to permit the trunk to be used both for escape and for access.

3.2 Means of escape in passenger ships

3.2.1 Escape from spaces below the bulkhead deck

3.2.1.1 Below the bulkhead deck, two means of escape, at least one of which shall be independent of watertight doors, shall be provided from each watertight compartment or similarly restricted space or group of spaces. Exceptionally, the Administration may dispense with one of the means of escape for crew spaces that are entered only occasionally, if the required escape route is independent of watertight doors.

3.2.1.2 Where the Administration has granted dispensation under the provisions of paragraph 3.2.1.1, this sole means of escape shall provide safe escape. However, stairways shall not be less than 800 mm in clear width with handrails on both sides.

3.2.2 Escape from spaces above the bulkhead deck

Above the bulkhead deck there shall be at least two means of escape from each main vertical zone or similarly restricted space or group of spaces, at least one of which shall give access to a stairway forming a vertical escape.

3 控制站、起居处所和服务处所的脱险通道

3.1 一般要求

3.1.1 乘客及船员起居处所和除机器处所外通常有船员的处所，其梯道和梯子的布置应提供到达救生艇和救生筏登乘甲板的随时可用的脱险通道。

3.1.2 除本条另有明文规定外，应禁止仅设1条脱险通道的走廊、门厅或局部走廊。准许船舶实际效用所必需的用于服务区域的端部封闭走廊，如燃油站和横向供应走廊，但这种端部封闭的走廊应与船员起居处所分开，且不能从乘客起居处所进入。此外，准许设置深度不超过宽度的一段局部走廊，其可视为凹入或局部延伸。

3.1.3 起居处所、服务处所和控制站内的所有梯道应为钢质框架结构，但主管机关批准使用其他等效材料者除外。

3.1.4 如果无线电报站无直接通往开敞甲板的出口，则该站应设有2条脱险或出入通道，其中之一个可为尺寸足够的舷窗或窗，或主管机关满意的其他设施。

3.1.5 脱险通道上的门一般应向逃生的方向开启，但下述情况除外：

.1 个别客舱的门可开向客舱内侧，以防在门打开时对走廊内的人员造成伤害；和

.2 垂直紧急脱险围井上的门可开向围井外侧，以使围井既能用于逃生也能用于出入。

3.2 客船的脱险通道

3.2.1 舱壁甲板以下处所的脱险通道

3.2.1.1 在舱壁甲板以下，每一水密舱或类似的限界处所或处所群，应设有2条脱险通道，其中至少1条应独立于水密门。在特殊情况下，如果所要求的脱险通道独立于水密门，主管机关可对只是偶尔进入的船员处所免除其中1条脱险通道。

3.2.1.2 如果主管机关根据本条3.2.1.1的规定免除了1条脱险通道，则剩下的唯一脱险通道应能提供安全逃生。但是，梯道的净宽不得小于800 mm，且梯道两侧须设有扶手。

3.2.2 舱壁甲板以上处所的脱险通道

在舱壁甲板以上，每一主竖区或类似的限界处所或处所群，应至少设有2条脱险通道，其中应至少有1条通往形成垂直脱险通道的梯道。

3.2.3 Direct access to stairway enclosures

Stairway enclosures in accommodation and service spaces shall have direct access from the corridors and be of a sufficient area to prevent congestion, having in view the number of persons likely to use them in an emergency. Within the perimeter of such stairway enclosures, only public toilets, lockers of non-combustible material providing storage for non-hazardous safety equipment and open information counters are permitted. Only corridors, lifts, public toilets, special category spaces and open ro-ro spaces to which any passengers carried can have access, other escape stairways required by paragraph 3.2.4.1 and external areas are permitted to have direct access to these stairway enclosures. Public spaces may also have direct access to stairway enclosures except for the backstage of a theatre. Small corridors or "lobbies" used to separate an enclosed stairway from galleys or main laundries may have direct access to the stairway provided they have a minimum deck area of 4.5 m^2, a width of no less than 900 mm and contain a fire hose station.

3.2.4 Details of means of escape

3.2.4.1 At least one of the means of escape required by paragraphs 3.2.1.1 and 3.2.2 shall consist of a readily accessible enclosed stairway, which shall provide continuous fire shelter from the level of its origin to the appropriate lifeboat and liferaft embarkation decks, or to the uppermost weather deck if the embarkation deck does not extend to the main vertical zone being considered. In the latter case, direct access to the embarkation deck by way of external open stairways and passageways shall be provided and shall have emergency lighting in accordance with regulation Ⅲ/11.5 and slip-free surfaces underfoot. Boundaries facing external open stairways and passageways forming part of an escape route and boundaries in such a position that their failure during a fire would impede escape to the embarkation deck shall have fire integrity, including insulation values, in accordance with tables 9.1 to 9.4, as appropriate.

3.2.4.2 Protection of access from the stairway enclosures to the lifeboat and liferaft embarkation areas shall be provided either directly or through protected internal routes which have fire integrity and insulation values for stairway enclosures as determined by tables 9.1 to 9.4, as appropriate.

3.2.4.3 Stairways serving only a space and a balcony in that space shall not be considered as forming one of the required means of escape.

3.2.4.4 Each level within an atrium shall have two means of escape, one of which shall give direct access to an enclosed vertical means of escape meeting the requirements of paragraph 3.2.4.1.

3.2.4.5 The widths, number and continuity of escapes shall be in accordance with the requirements in the Fire Safety Systems Code.

3.2.5 Marking of escape routes

3.2.3　梯道环围的直接出入口

起居处所和服务处所的梯道环围应设有直接通向走廊的出入口,且应考虑到紧急情况下可能使用梯道环围的人数而有足够的面积,以避免出现拥挤。在这种梯道环围的周界内,只允许布置公共盥洗室、由不燃材料建成的用于存放无危害的安全设备的储藏柜和开式服务台。只有走廊、升降机、公共盥洗室、特种处所和所载的任何乘客均能进入的开式滚装处所、本条3.2.4.1所要求的其他脱险梯道以及船舶外部区域才允许设有直接通向这些梯道环围的出入口。公共处所亦可具有直通楼梯间的通道,但剧场后台除外。用于将围蔽梯道与厨房或主洗衣房隔开的小的走廊或"门厅"可直接通向梯道,但其最小甲板面积应为4.5 m^2,宽度不小于900 mm,并设有消防水带箱。

3.2.4　脱险通道的细节

3.2.4.1　本条3.2.1.1和3.2.2所要求的脱险通道中至少应有1条是可随时出入的围蔽梯道,此梯道应设有连续的防火遮蔽,该防火遮蔽自其起点的一层一直到达适当的救生艇和救生筏登乘甲板,或在登乘甲板未延伸至所计及的主竖区情况下,到达最上层露天甲板。在后者情况下,应设有利用外部露天梯道和过道通向登乘甲板的直接通路,沿该通路应设置符合第Ⅲ/11.5条要求的应急照明,其地面应为防滑地面。面向作为脱险通道一部分的外部露天梯道和过道的限界面以及位于在失火时遭受破坏后会阻碍撤向登乘甲板处的限界面,应具有符合表9.1至9.4的相应耐火完整性和隔热等级。

3.2.4.2　自梯道环围至救生艇和救生筏登乘区域的通道的保护,应通过直接保护或通过按表9.1至9.4确定的相应梯道环围耐火完整性和隔热等级的受保护内部通道实现。

3.2.4.3　仅服务于1个处所和该处所的阳台的梯道不得视为构成所要求的脱险通道之一。

3.2.4.4　天井的每一层应有2条脱险通道,其中之一应直接通向符合本条3.2.4.1要求的围蔽垂直脱险通道。

3.2.4.5　脱险通道的宽度、数量和连续性应满足《消防安全系统规则》的要求。

3.2.5　脱险通道的标志

3.2.5.1 In addition to the emergency lighting required by regulations Ⅱ-1/42 and Ⅲ/11.5, the means of escape, including stairways and exits, shall be marked by lighting or photoluminescent strip indicators placed not more than 300 mm above the deck at all points of the escape route, including angles and intersections. The marking must enable passengers to identify the routes of escape and readily identify the escape exits. If electric illumination is used, it shall be supplied by the emergency source of power and it shall be so arranged that the failure of any single light or cut in a lighting strip will not result in the marking being ineffective. Additionally, escape route signs and fire equipment location markings shall be of photoluminescent material or marked by lighting. The Administration shall ensure that such lighting or photoluminescent equipment has been evaluated, tested and applied in accordance with the Fire Safety Systems Code.

3.2.5.2 In passenger ships carrying more than 36 passengers, the requirements of the paragraph 3.2.5.1 shall also apply to the crew accommodation areas.

3.2.5.3 In lieu of the escape route lighting system required by paragraph 3.2.5.1, alternative evacuation guidance systems may be accepted if approved by the Administration based on the guidelines developed by the Organization. ①

3.2.6 Normally locked doors that form part of an escape route

3.2.6.1 Cabin and stateroom doors shall not require keys to unlock them from inside the room. Neither shall there be any doors along any designated escape route which require keys to unlock them when moving in the direction of escape.

3.2.6.2 Escape doors from public spaces that are normally latched shall be fitted with a means of quick release. Such means shall consist of a door-latching mechanism incorporating a device that releases the latch upon the application of a force in the direction of escape flow. Quick release mechanisms shall be designed and installed to the satisfaction of the Administration and, in particular:

.1 consist of bars or panels, the actuating portion of which extends across at least one half of the width of the door leaf, at least 760 mm and not more than 1,120 mm above the deck;

.2 cause the latch to release when a force not exceeding 67 N is applied; and

.3 not be equipped with any locking device, set screw or other arrangement that prevents the release of the latch when pressure is applied to the releasing device.

3.2.7 Evacuation analysis for passenger ships②

3.2.7.1 Escape routes shall be evaluated by an evacuation analysis early in the design process. This analysis shall apply to:

---

① Refer to *Functional requirements and performance standards for the assessment of evacuation guidance systems* (MSC/Circ. 1167) and *Interim guidelines for the testing, approval and maintenance of evacuation guidance systems used as an alternative to low-location lighting systems* (MSC/Circ.1168).

② Refer to the *Revised guidelines on evacuation analysis for new and existing passenger ships* (MSC.1/Circ.1533), as may be amended.

3.2.5.1 除了应符合第Ⅱ-1/42和Ⅲ/11.5条关于应急照明的要求外,包括梯道和出口在内的脱险通道应在脱险通道所有各点(包括拐弯和交叉处),用位于甲板以上不超过300 mm的照明或荧光条指示装置予以标示。此标示必须使乘客能够辨认脱险通道并易于识别脱险出口。如果使用电力照明,应由应急电源供电,并应布置为任何单个灯的故障或一个照明条的切除不会导致标示失效。此外,脱险路线的标志和消防设备位置的标志应采用荧光材料或用照明标示。主管机关应确保该照明或荧光设备的鉴定、测试和使用符合《消防安全系统规则》。

3.2.5.2 对于载客超过36人的客船,本条3.2.5.1的要求还应适用于船员起居区域。

3.2.5.3 如果获主管机关根据本组织制定的导则①所给予的认可,亦可接受替代撤离导向系统以取代第3.2.5.1款所要求的脱险通道照明系统。

3.2.6　构成脱险通道部分的通常闭锁的门

3.2.6.1 居住舱室和特等客舱的门应不用钥匙即可从舱室内打开。沿着任何指定的逃生路线朝逃生方向运动时,途中的任何门也都应不用钥匙即可打开。

3.2.6.2 通常闩扣着的公共处所通往脱险通道的门应装有快速松开装置。这种装置应由一个门闩机构组成并带有朝逃生方向一推即松开栓销的装置。快速松开机构的设计和安装应使主管机关满意,并且特别要符合下列要求:

.1 由扳动杆或扳动条构成,其扳动部分至少横向延伸到门扇宽度一半,并位于甲板以上至少760 mm,但不超过1 120 mm;

.2 在施力不超过67 N时使门闩松开;和

.3 不设任何在对松开装置施压后阻止栓销打开的锁死装置、止动螺丝或其他装置。

3.2.7　客船撤离分析②

3.2.7.1 须在设计过程的早期,通过撤离分析对脱险通道进行评估。这种分析须适用于:

① 参见《用于评估撤离引导系统的功能要求和性能标准》(第MSC/Circ.1167号通函)以及《用作替代低位照明系统的撤离引导系统试验、认可和维护暂行指南》(第MSC/Circ.1168号通函)

② 参见可能经修正的《经修订的新客船和现有客船撤离分析指南》(第MSC.1/Circ.1533号通函)。

.1 ro-ro passenger ships constructed on or after 1 July 1999; and

.2 other passenger ships constructed on or after 1 January 2020 carrying more than 36 passengers.

3.2.7.2 The analysis shall be used to identify and eliminate, as far as practicable, congestion which may develop during an abandonment, due to normal movement of passengers and crew along escape routes, including the possibility that crew may need to move along these routes in a direction opposite to the movement of passengers. In addition, the analysis shall be used to demonstrate that escape arrangements are sufficiently flexible to provide for the possibility that certain escape routes, assembly stations, embarkation stations or survival craft may not be available as a result of a casualty.

3.3 Means of escape in cargo ships

3.3.1 General

At all levels of accommodation there shall be provided at least two widely separated means of escape from each restricted space or group of spaces.

3.3.2 Escape from spaces below the lowest open deck

Below the lowest open deck the main means of escape shall be a stairway and the second escape may be a trunk or a stairway.

3.3.3 Escape from spaces above the lowest open deck

Above the lowest open deck the means of escape shall be stairways or doors to an open deck or a combination thereof.

3.3.4 Dead-end corridors

No dead-end corridors having a length of more than 7 m shall be accepted.

3.3.5 Width and continuity of escape routes

The width, number and continuity of escape routes shall be in accordance with the requirements in the Fire Safety Systems Code.

3.3.6 Dispensation from two means of escape

Exceptionally, the Administration may dispense with one of the means of escape, for crew spaces that are entered only occasionally, if the required escape route is independent of watertight doors.

3.4 Emergency escape breathing devices[①]

3.4.1 Emergency escape breathing devices shall comply with the Fire Safety Systems Code. Spare emergency escape breathing devices shall be kept on board.

① Refer to *Guidelines for the performance, location use and care of emergency escape breathing devices* (EEBDs) (MSC/Circ. 849).

.1 1999年7月1日或以后建造的滚装客船;和

.2 2020年1月1日或以后建造的载客超过36名的其他客船。

3.2.7.2 此种分析须用于确定并尽可能消除在弃船中由于乘客和船员沿脱险通道正常移动时可能造成的拥挤,包括可能有船员需要沿这些通道与乘客逆向移动时造成的拥挤。此外,此种分析还须用于证实逃生布置具有充足的灵活性以适应可能由于事故而导致某些脱险通道、集合站、登乘站或救生筏不能使用的情况。

3.3 货船的脱险通道

3.3.1 通则

在起居处所的各层,从每一限界处所或处所群应至少有2条彼此远离的脱险通道。

3.3.2 最低开敞甲板以下处所的脱险通道

在最低开敞甲板以下,主要的脱险通道应为梯道,次要的脱险通道可为围井或梯道。

3.3.3 最低开敞甲板以上处所的脱险通道

在最低开敞甲板以上,脱险通道应为梯道或通往开敞甲板的门或两者的组合。

3.3.4 端部封闭的走廊

不允许设有长度超过7 m的端部封闭的走廊。

3.3.5 脱险通道的宽度和连续性

脱险通道的宽度、数量和连续性应符合《消防安全系统规则》的要求。

3.3.6 对2条脱险通道要求的免除

在特殊情况下,如果所要求的脱险通道独立于水密门,主管机关可对只是偶尔进入的船员处所免除其中1条脱险通道。

3.4 紧急逃生呼吸装置①

3.4.1 紧急逃生呼吸装置应符合《消防安全系统规则》。船上应存有备用紧急逃生呼吸装置。

① 参见《紧急逃生呼吸装置性能、位置、使用和保养指南》(EEBDs)(第MSC/Circ.849号通函)。

3.4.2 All ships shall carry at least two emergency escape breathing devices within accommodation spaces.

3.4.3 In all passenger ships, at least two emergency escape breathing devices shall be carried in each main vertical zone.

3.4.4 In all passenger ships carrying more than 36 passengers, two emergency escape breathing devices, in addition to those required in paragraph 3.4.3 above, shall be carried in each main vertical zone.

3.4.5 However, paragraphs 3.4.3 and 3.4.4 do not apply to stairway enclosures which constitute individual main vertical zones and to the main vertical zones in the fore or aft end of a ship which do not contain spaces of categories (6), (7), (8) or (12) as defined in regulation 9.2.2.3.

4 Means of escape from machinery spaces

4.1 Means of escape on passenger ships

Means of escape from each machinery space in passenger ships shall comply with the following provisions.

4.1.1 Escape from spaces below the bulkhead deck

Where the space is below the bulkhead deck, the two means of escape shall consist of either:

.1 two sets of steel ladders, as widely separated as possible, leading to doors in the upper part of the space, similarly separated and from which access is provided to the appropriate lifeboat and liferaft embarkation decks. One of these ladders shall be located within a protected enclosure that satisfies regulation 9.2.2.3, category (2), or regulation 9.2.2.4, category (4), as appropriate, from the lower part of the space it serves to a safe position outside the space. Self-closing fire doors of the same fire integrity standards shall be fitted in the enclosure. The ladder shall be fixed in such a way that heat is not transferred into the enclosure through non-insulated fixing points. The protected enclosure shall have minimum internal dimensions of at least 800 mm × 800 mm, and shall have emergency lighting provisions; or

.2 one steel ladder leading to a door in the upper part of the space from which access is provided to the embarkation deck and additionally, in the lower part of the space and in a position well separated from the ladder referred to, a steel door capable of being operated from each side and which provides access to a safe escape route from the lower part of the space to the embarkation deck.

4.1.2 Escape from spaces above the bulkhead deck

Where the space is above the bulkhead deck, the two means of escape shall be as widely separated as possible and the doors leading from such means of escape shall be in a position from which access is provided to the appropriate lifeboat and liferaft embarkation decks. Where such means of escape require the use of ladders, these shall be of steel.

3.4.2 所有船舶应在起居处所内配备至少2套紧急逃生呼吸装置。

3.4.3 在所有客船上的每一主竖区,应配备至少2套紧急逃生呼吸装置。

3.4.4 载客超过36人的所有客船,除应配备本条3.4.3要求的紧急逃生呼吸装置外,还应在每一主竖区配备2套紧急逃生呼吸装置。

3.4.5 但是,本条3.4.3和3.4.4不适用于形成各个主竖区的梯道环围和不含第9.2.2.3条所定义的第(6)、(7)、(8)或(12)类处所的船舶首端或尾端的主竖区。

4 机器处所的脱险通道

4.1 客船的脱险通道

客船上每一机器处所的脱险通道应符合下列规定。

4.1.1 舱壁甲板以下处所的脱险通道

如果处所位于舱壁甲板以下,2条脱险通道应为下述二者之一:

.1 两部彼此尽可能远离的钢梯,通往该处所上部彼此类似远离的门,从门至相应的救生艇和救生筏登乘甲板设有通道。其中1部钢梯应位于一个受保护环围内,该环围满足第9.2.2.3条第(2)类或第9.2.2.4条第(4)类的相应要求,从其所服务的处所的下部通到该处所以外的安全位置。在该环围内应设有达到相同耐火完整性标准的自闭式防火门。钢梯的安装方式应使热量不致通过未隔热固定点传入环围内。受保护环围的内部尺寸应至少为800 mm×800 mm,并应设有应急照明;或

.2 通往该处所上部1扇门的1部钢梯,从该门至登乘甲板设有通道,此外,在该处所下部和远离上述钢梯的位置,设有1扇能从两面操纵的钢门,从该处所下部经该门可进入通往登乘甲板的安全脱险通道。

4.1.2 舱壁甲板以上处所的脱险通道

如果处所位于舱壁甲板以上,2条脱险通道应尽可能彼此远离,且在该脱险通道的门处应设有通往相应救生艇和救生筏登乘甲板的通道。如果该脱险通道需设梯子,这些梯子应为钢质。

4.1.3 Dispensation from two means of escape

In a ship of less than 1,000 gross tonnage, the Administration may dispense with one of the means of escape, due regard being paid to the width and disposition of the upper part of the space. In a ship of 1,000 gross tonnage and above, the Administration may dispense with one means of escape from any such space, including a normally unattended auxiliary machinery space, so long as either a door or a steel ladder provides a safe escape route to the embarkation deck, due regard being paid to the nature and location of the space and whether persons are normally employed in that space. In the steering gear space, a second means of escape shall be provided when the emergency steering position is located in that space unless there is direct access to the open deck.

4.1.4 Escape from machinery control rooms

Two means of escape shall be provided from a machinery control room located within a machinery space, at least one of which will provide continuous fire shelter to a safe position outside the machinery space.

4.1.5 Inclined ladders and stairways

For ships constructed on or after 1 January 2016, all inclined ladders/stairways fitted to comply with paragraph 4.1.1 with open treads in machinery spaces being part of or providing access to escape routes but not located within a protected enclosure shall be made of steel. Such ladders/stairways shall be fitted with steel shields attached to their undersides, such as to provide escaping personnel protection against heat and flame from beneath.

4.1.6 Escape from main workshops within machinery spaces

For ships constructed on or after 1 January 2016, two means of escape shall be provided from the main workshop within a machinery space. At least one of these escape routes shall provide a continuous fire shelter to a safe position outside the machinery space.

4.2 Means of escape on cargo ships

Means of escape from each machinery space in cargo ships shall comply with the following provisions.

4.2.1 Escape from machinery spaces of category A

Except as provided in paragraph 4.2.2, two means of escape shall be provided from each machinery space of category A. In particular, one of the following provisions shall be complied with:

.1 two sets of steel ladders, as widely separated as possible, leading to doors in the upper part of the space, similarly separated and from which access is provided to the open deck. One of these ladders shall be located within a protected enclosure that satisfies regulation 9.2.3.3, category (4), from the lower part of the space it serves to a safe position outside the space. Self-closing fire doors of the same fire integrity standards shall be fitted in the enclosure. The ladder shall be fixed in such a way that heat is not transferred into the enclosure through non-insulated fixing points. The enclosure shall have minimum internal dimensions of at least 800 mm × 800 mm, and shall have emergency lighting provisions; or

4.1.3　对2条脱险通道要求的免除

小于1 000总吨的船舶，主管机关在充分考虑到该处所上部的宽度及布置后，可免除其中1条脱险通道。1 000总吨及以上的船舶，只要任何此种处所（包括通常无人值班的辅机处所）中有1扇门或1部钢梯可提供抵达登乘甲板的安全脱险通道，则主管机关在充分考虑到该处所的性质和位置以及是否经常有人在内工作后，可免除其中1条脱险通道。在舵机处所，如果应急操舵装置位于该处所，应提供第2条脱险通道，但该处所设有直接通向开敞甲板通道者除外。

4.1.4　机器控制室的脱险通道

位于机器处所的机器控制室应设有2条脱险通道，其中至少1条能提供通往机器处所外部安全位置的连续防火遮蔽。

4.1.5　斜梯与梯道

对于2016年1月1日或之后建造的船舶，在机器处所内为符合第4.1.1款要求而装设的、有开放踏板的、作为脱险通道的一部分或者通向脱险通道但并不位于受保护围蔽内的所有斜梯/梯道均应由钢制成。此类梯子/梯道的底面须装设钢质护板供逃生人员用于防护来自下方的高温和火焰。

4.1.6　器处所内的主工作间脱险通道

对于2016年1月1日或之后建造的船舶，在机器处所内的主工作间须设有2条脱险通道，其中至少1条脱险路线须提供通往机器处所外部安全位置的连续防火遮蔽。

4.2　货船的脱险通道

货船上每一机器处所的脱险通道应符合下列规定。

4.2.1　A类机器处所的脱险通道

除本条4.2.2规定者外，每一A类机器处所均应设有2条脱险通道。特别是应符合下列规定之一：

.1　2部彼此尽可能远离的钢梯通往该处所上部彼此类似远离的门，从门至开敞甲板设有通道。其中1部钢梯应位于一个满足第9.2.3.3条第（4）类要求的受到保护的环围内，并从其所在处所的下部通到该处所以外的安全位置。在该环围内应设有达到相同耐火完整性标准的自闭式防火门。钢梯的安装方式应使热量不能通过未隔热的固定点传入该环围内。该环围的最小内部尺寸应至少为800 mm×800 mm，并应设有应急照明；或

.2 one steel ladder leading to a door in the upper part of the space from which access is provided to the open deck and, additionally, in the lower part of the space and in a position well separated from the ladder referred to, a steel door capable of being operated from each side and which provides access to a safe escape route from the lower part of the space to the open deck.

4.2.2 Dispensation from two means of escape

In a ship of less than 1,000 gross tonnage, the Administration may dispense with one of the means of escape required under paragraph 4.2.1, due regard being paid to the dimension and disposition of the upper part of the space. In addition, the means of escape from machinery spaces of category A need not comply with the requirement for an enclosed fire shelter listed in paragraph 4.2.1.1. In the steering gear space, a second means of escape shall be provided when the emergency steering position is located in that space unless there is direct access to the open deck.

4.2.3 Escape from machinery spaces other than those of category A

From machinery spaces other than those of category A, two escape routes shall be provided except that a single escape route may be accepted for spaces that are entered only occasionally and for spaces where the maximum travel distance to the door is 5 m or less.

4.2.4 Inclined ladders and stairways

For ships constructed on or after 1 January 2016, all inclined ladders/stairways fitted to comply with paragraph 4.2.1 with open treads in machinery spaces being part of or providing access to escape routes but not located within a protected enclosure shall be made of steel. Such ladders/stairways shall be fitted with steel shields attached to their undersides, such as to provide escaping personnel protection against heat and flame from beneath.

4.2.5 Escape from machinery control rooms in machinery spaces of category A

For ships constructed on or after 1 January 2016, two means of escape shall be provided from the machinery control room located within a machinery space. At least one of these escape routes shall provide a continuous fire shelter to a safe position outside the machinery space.

4.2.6 Escape from main workshops in machinery spaces of category A

For ships constructed on or after 1 January 2016, two means of escape shall be provided from the main workshop within a machinery space. At least one of these escape routes shall provide a continuous fire shelter to a safe position outside the machinery space.

4.3 Emergency escape breathing devices

4.3.1 On all ships, within the machinery spaces, emergency escape breathing devices shall be situated ready for use at easily visible places, which can be reached quickly and easily at any time in the event of fire. The location of emergency escape breathing devices shall take into account the layout of the machinery space and the number of persons normally working in the spaces.①

---

① Refer to *Guidelines for the performance, location, use and care of emergency escape breathing devices* (EEBDs) (MSC/Circ. 849).

.2 1部钢梯通往该处所上部的1扇门,从该门至开敞甲板设有通道,此外,在该处所下部远离上述钢梯的位置应设有1扇能从每侧操作的钢门,由此门可进入从该处所下部通往开敞甲板的安全脱险通道。

4.2.2 对2条脱险通道要求的免除

小于1 000总吨的船舶,主管机关在充分考虑到该处所上部的尺寸及布置后,可免除本条4.2.1中所要求的2条脱险通道之一。此外,A类机器处所的脱险通道不必符合本条4.2.1.1所列的防火遮蔽的要求。在舵机处所,如果应急操舵装置位于该处所,应提供第2条脱险通道,但该处所设有直接通向开敞甲板通道者除外。

4.2.3 A类以外机器处所的脱险通道

A类以外机器处所应设有2条脱险通道,但对于只是偶尔进入的处所和到门的最大步行距离为5 m或以下的处所,可以接受单条脱险通道。

4.2.4 斜梯与梯道

对于2016年1月1日或之后建造的船舶,机器处所内为符合第4.2.1款要求而装设的、有开放踏板的、作为脱险通道的一部分或者通向脱险通道但并不位于受保护围蔽内的所有斜梯/梯道均须由钢制成。此类梯子/梯道的底面须装设钢质护板,如此供逃生人员用于防护来自下方的高温和火焰。

4.2.5 A类机器处所内机器控制室的脱险通道

对于2016年1月1日或之后建造的船舶,在机器处所内的机器控制室须设有2条脱险通道,其中至少1条脱险路线须提供通往机器处所外部安全位置的连续防火遮蔽。

4.2.6 A类机器处所内主工作间的脱险通道

对于2016年1月1日或之后建造的船舶,在机器处所内的主工作间须设有2条脱险通道,其中至少1条脱险路线须提供通往机器处所外部安全位置的连续防火遮蔽。

4.3 紧急逃生呼吸装置

4.3.1 在所有船上的机器处所内,紧急逃生呼吸装置应位于易于看到的位置,随时可用。在发生火灾时,这些位置应能随时迅速和容易地到达。紧急逃生呼吸装置位置的确定应考虑到机器处所的布置和通常在该处所工作的人员数量。①

① 参见《紧急逃生呼吸装置性能、位置、使用和保养指南》(EEBDs)(第MSC/Circ.849号通函)。

4.3.2 The number and location of these devices shall be indicated in the fire control plan required in regulation 15.2.4.

4.3.3 Emergency escape breathing devices shall comply with the Fire Safety Systems Code.

5 Means of escape on passenger ships from special category and open ro-ro spaces to which any passengers carried can have access

5.1 In special category and open ro-ro spaces to which any passengers carried can have access, the number and locations of the means of escape both below and above the bulkhead deck shall be to the satisfaction of the Administration and, in general, the safety of access to the embarkation deck shall be at least equivalent to that provided for under paragraphs 3.2.1.1, 3.2.2, 3.2.4.1 and 3.2.4.2. Such spaces shall be provided with designated walkways to the means of escape with a breadth of at least 600 mm. The parking arrangements for the vehicles shall maintain the walkways clear at all times.

5.2 One of the escape routes from the machinery spaces where the crew is normally employed shall avoid direct access to any special category space.

6 Means of escape from ro-ro spaces

At least two means of escape shall be provided in ro-ro spaces where the crew are normally employed. The escape routes shall provide a safe escape to the lifeboat and liferaft embarkation decks and shall be located at the fore and aft ends of the space.

7 Additional requirements for ro-ro passenger ships

7.1 General

7.1.1 Escape routes shall be provided from every normally occupied space on the ship to an assembly station. These escape routes shall be arranged so as to provide the most direct route possible to the assembly station,① and shall be marked with symbols based on the guidelines developed by the Organization.②

7.1.2 The escape route from cabins to stairway enclosures shall be as direct as possible, with a minimum number of changes in direction. It shall not be necessary to cross from one side of the ship to the other to reach an escape route. It shall not be necessary to climb more than two decks up or down in order to reach an assembly station or open deck from any passenger space.

7.1.3 External routes shall be provided from open decks, as referred to in paragraph 7.1.2, to the survival craft embarkation stations.

7.1.4 Where enclosed spaces adjoin an open deck, openings from the enclosed space to the open deck shall, where practicable, be capable of being used as an emergency exit.

---

① Refer to *Indication of the assembly station in passenger ships* (MSC/Circ.777).

② Refer to *Symbols related to life-saving appliances and arrangements* (resolution A.760(18), as amended) and/or tables 1 and 2 of *Escape route signs and equipment location makings* (resolution A.1116(30)), as appropriate. Refer to the new symbols in tables 1 and 2 of resolution A.1116(30) where the symbols for a specific item are differently expressed in resolutions A.760(18), as amended and A.1116(30).

4.3.2 这些装置的数量和位置应在第15.2.4条所要求的防火控制图中标出。

4.3.3 紧急逃生呼吸装置应符合《消防安全系统规则》。

5 客船特种处所和所载任何乘客均能进入的开式滚装处所的脱险通道

5.1 在特种处所和所载任何乘客均能进入的开式滚装处所，舱壁甲板以下和以上处所的脱险通道数量和位置应使主管机关满意，并且，通向登乘甲板的通道安全性一般应至少等效于本条3.2.1.1、3.2.2、3.2.4.1和3.2.4.2规定的通道安全性。此类处所应设有通往脱险通道的专用过道，宽度至少为600 mm。车辆的停车布置应使该过道在任何时候畅通无阻。

5.2 通常有船员工作的机器处所的脱险通道，其中之一应避免直接通向任何特种处所。

6 滚装处所的脱险通道

通常有船员在内工作的滚装处所应设有至少2条脱险通道。脱险通道应能安全通向救生艇和救生筏登乘甲板，并位于该处所的前后两端。

7 对滚装客船的附加要求

7.1 通则

7.1.1 从船上每一通常有人的处所至集合站均应设有脱险通道。脱险通道的布置应尽可能提供通往集合站①的最直接通道，并应根据本组织制定的指南②用符号标出。

7.1.2 从居住舱室到梯道环围的脱险通道应尽可能笔直，并尽可能少改变方向。应不必从船舶的一舷走到另一舷才能到达脱险通道。为从任何乘客处所到达集合站或开敞甲板而向上或向下所通过的甲板应不必超过两层。

7.1.3 本条7.1.2所述之开敞甲板应设有通往救生艇筏登乘站的外部脱险通道。

7.1.4 如果围蔽处所邻接开敞甲板，该围蔽处所开向开敞甲板的开口在实际可行情况下应能用作应急出口。

---

① 参见《客船集合站的指示》（第MSC/Circ.777号通函）。

② 参见《与救生设备和装置有关的符号》（第A.760(18)号决议，经修正的）和/或相应的《脱险通道标志和设备位置标识》（第A.1116(30)号决议）中的表1和2。参见第A.1116(30)号决议中的表1和2，其中某一特定项目的符号与经修正的第A.760(18)号决议有不同的表达方式。

7.1.5 Escape routes shall not be obstructed by furniture and other obstructions. With the exception of tables and chairs which may be cleared to provide open space, cabinets and other heavy furnishings in public spaces and along escape routes shall be secured in place to prevent shifting if the ship rolls or lists. Floor coverings shall also be secured in place. When the ship is under way, escape routes shall be kept clear of obstructions such as cleaning carts, bedding, luggage and boxes of goods.

7.2 Instruction for safe escape

7.2.1 Decks shall be sequentially numbered, starting with "1" at the tank top or lowest deck. The numbers shall be prominently displayed at stair landings and lift lobbies. Decks may also be named, but the deck number shall always be displayed with the name.

7.2.2 Simple "mimic" plans showing the "you are here" position and escape routes marked by arrows shall be prominently displayed on the inside of each cabin door and in public spaces. The plan shall show the directions of escape and shall be properly oriented in relation to its position on the ship.

7.3 Strength of handrails and corridors

7.3.1 Handrails or other handholds shall be provided in corridors along the entire escape route so that a firm handhold is available at every step of the way, where possible, to the assembly stations and embarkation stations. Such handrails shall be provided on both sides of longitudinal corridors more than 1.8 m in width and transverse corridors more than 1 m in width. Particular attention shall be paid to the need to be able to cross lobbies, atriums and other large open spaces along escape routes. Handrails and other handholds shall be of such strength as to withstand a distributed horizontal load of 750 N/m applied in the direction of the centre of the corridor or space, and a distributed vertical load of 750 N/m applied in the downward direction. The two loads need not be applied simultaneously.

7.3.2 The lowest 0.5 m of bulkheads and other partitions forming vertical divisions along escape routes shall be able to sustain a load of 750 N/m to allow them to be used as walking surfaces from the side of the escape route with the ship at large angles of heel.

7.1.5 脱险通道不得被家具或其他障碍物阻塞。除可被搬走以腾出开敞处所的桌子和椅子以外,公共处所内以及脱险通道沿线的橱柜和其他重家具应固定在原地,以防止在船舶横摇或倾侧时发生移动。地板覆盖物亦应原地固定。在船舶航行中,脱险通道内不得有清洁车、寝具、行李和什物箱等障碍物。

7.2 安全逃生指示

7.2.1 对各层甲板应编有序号,由内底板或最下层甲板起为"1"。序号应显著地显示在楼梯平台和升降机门廊处。也可给甲板命名,但甲板序号应始终与甲板名称一起显示。

7.2.2 用"你在这"标出当前位置并用箭头标出脱险通道的简明"模拟"平面图应明显地张贴在每一居住舱室门的内侧和公共处所内。该图应显示脱险通道的方向并正确地指明其在船上的方位。

7.3 扶手和走廊的强度

7.3.1 在脱险通道沿线的所有走廊内应设置扶手或其他手扶物,以便在通向集合站和登乘站的通道内可能有的每一台阶处,都有坚固的手扶物。此种扶手应设在宽度超过 1.8 m 的纵向走廊和宽度超过 1 m 的横向走廊的两侧。应特别注意需能穿过脱险通道沿线的大厅、天井和其他较大开敞处所。扶手和其他手扶物的强度应能承受走廊或处所中心线方向 750 N/m 的水平分布荷载以及 750 N/m 的垂直向下分布荷载。这两种荷载不必同时施加。

7.3.2 脱险通道沿线的舱壁和其他构成垂直分隔的隔板最下部 0.5 m 部分应能承受 750 N/m的荷载,从而在船舶处于大角度倾斜状态时,允许在脱险通道的侧表面上通行。

Part E
Operational requirements

Regulation 14
Operational readiness and maintenance

1 Purpose

The purpose of this regulation is to maintain and monitor the effectiveness of the fire safety measures the ship is provided with. For this purpose, the following functional requirements shall be met:

.1 fire protection systems and fire-fighting systems and appliances shall be maintained ready for use; and

.2 fire protection systems and fire-fighting systems and appliances shall be properly tested and inspected.

2 General requirements

At all times while the ship is in service, the requirements of paragraph 1.1 shall be complied with. A ship is not in service when:

.1 it is in for repairs or lay-up (either at anchor or in port) or in dry-dock;

.2 it is declared not in service by the owner or the owner's representative; and

.3 in the case of passenger ships, there are no passengers on board.

2.1 Operational readiness

2.1.1 The following fire protection systems shall be kept in good order so as to ensure their required performance if a fire occurs:

.1 structural fire protection, including fire-resisting divisions, and protection of openings and penetrations in these divisions;

.2 fire detection and fire alarm systems; and

.3 means of escape systems and appliances.

2.1.2 Fire-fighting systems and appliances shall be kept in good working order and readily available for immediate use. Portable extinguishers which have been discharged shall be immediately recharged or replaced with an equivalent unit.

2.2 Maintenance, testing and inspections

2.2.1 Maintenance, testing and inspections shall be carried out based on the guidelines developed by the Organization① and in a manner having due regard to ensuring the reliability of fire-fighting systems and appliances.

① Refer to *Revised guidelines for the maintenance and inspection of fire protection systems and appliances* (MSC.1/Circ.1432, as amended by MSC.1/Circ.1516).

E 部分
操作性要求

第14条
操作准备状态和维护保养

1　目的

本条的目的是保持和监控船舶所具备的消防安全措施的有效性。为此,应满足下列功能要求:

.1　应对防火系统和灭火系统及设备进行维护保养,以备随时使用;和

.2　应对防火系统和灭火系统及设备进行适当试验和检查。

2　一般要求

船舶在营运期间的任何时候,都应符合本条1.1的要求。船舶不在营运期间系指:

.1　船舶修理或搁置(在锚地或在港内)或在干坞时;

.2　船东或船东代表宣布船舶停止营运时;和

.3　对于客船,船上无乘客时。

2.1　操作准备状态

2.1.1　下列防火系统应保持完好状态,以确保其在发生火灾时能发挥所要求的效能:

.1　结构防火,包括耐火分隔,以及在这些分隔上的开口和贯穿处的保护;

.2　探火和失火报警系统;和

.3　脱险通道系统和设备。

2.1.2　灭火系统和设备应保持良好的工作状态并随时可立即使用。已用过的手提式灭火器应立即予以重新充装或用等效装置替换。

2.2　维护保养、试验和检查

2.2.1　维护保养、试验和检查应根据本组织制定的指南①进行,所采用的方式应充分考虑到确保灭火系统及设备的可靠性。

① 参见《经修订的防火系统和设备维护保养和检查指南》(第MSC.1/Circ.1432号通函,经第MSC.1/Circ.1516号通函修订)。

2.2.2 The maintenance plan shall be kept on board the ship and shall be available for inspection whenever required by the Administration.

2.2.3 The maintenance plan shall include at least the following fire protection systems and fire-fighting systems and appliances, where installed:

.1 fire mains, fire pumps and hydrants, including hoses, nozzles and international shore connections;

.2 fixed fire detection and fire alarm systems;

.3 fixed fire-extinguishing systems and other fire-extinguishing appliances;

.4 automatic sprinkler, fire detection and fire alarm systems;

.5 ventilation systems, including fire and smoke dampers, fans and their controls;

.6 emergency shutdown of fuel supply;

.7 fire doors, including their controls;

.8 general emergency alarm systems;

.9 emergency escape breathing devices;

.10 portable fire extinguishers, including spare charges; and

.11 fire-fighter's outfits.

2.2.4 The maintenance programme may be computer-based.

3 Additional requirements for passenger ships

In addition to the fire protection systems and appliances listed in paragraph 2.2.3, ships carrying more than 36 passengers shall develop a maintenance plan for low-location lighting and public address systems.

4 Additional requirements for tankers

In addition to the fire protection systems and appliances listed in paragraph 2.2.3, tankers shall have a maintenance plan for:

.1 inert gas systems;

.2 deck foam systems;

.3 fire safety arrangements in cargo pump-rooms; and

.4 flammable gas detectors.

2.2.2 维护保养计划应保存在船上,并在主管机关要求时供其检查。

2.2.3 维护保养计划应至少包括下列防火系统和灭火系统及设备(若已安装):

.1 消防总管、消防泵和消火栓,包括水带、水枪和国际通岸接头;

.2 固定式探火和失火报警系统;

.3 固定式灭火系统和其他灭火设备;

.4 自动喷水器、探火和失火报警系统;

.5 通风系统,包括挡火闸、挡烟闸、风机及其控制装置;

.6 燃油供给紧急切断装置;

.7 防火门,包括其控制装置;

.8 通用应急报警系统;

.9 紧急逃生呼吸装置;

.10 手提式灭火器,包括备用气瓶;和

.11 消防员装备。

2.2.4 维护保养程序可用计算机编制。

3　对客船的附加要求

除本条 2.2.3 所列的防火系统和设备维护保养计划外,载客超过 36 人的客船还应编制低位照明和公共广播系统的维护保养计划。

4　对液货船的附加要求

除本条 2.2.3 所列的防火系统和设备维护保养计划外,液货船还应为下列系统和装置编制维护保养计划:

.1 惰性气体系统;

.2 甲板泡沫系统;

.3 液货泵舱的消防安全装置;和

.4 易燃气体探测器。

Regulation 15
Instructions, on-board training and drills

1 Purpose

The purpose of this regulation is to mitigate the consequences of fire by means of proper instructions for training and drills of persons on board in correct procedures under emergency conditions. For this purpose, the crew shall have the necessary knowledge and skills to handle fire emergency cases, including passenger care.

2 General requirements

2.1 Instructions, duties and organization

2.1.1 Crew members shall receive instruction on fire safety on board the ship.

2.1.2 Crew members shall receive instructions on their assigned duties.

2.1.3 Parties responsible for fire extinguishing shall be organized. These parties shall have the capability to complete their duties at all times while the ship is in service.

2.2 On-board training and drills

2.2.1 Crew members shall be trained to be familiar with the arrangements of the ship as well as the location and operation of any fire-fighting systems and appliances that they may be called upon to use.

2.2.2 Training in the use of the emergency escape breathing devices shall be considered as part of on-board training.

2.2.3 Performance of crew members assigned fire-fighting duties shall be periodically evaluated by conducting on-board training and drills to identify areas in need of improvement, to ensure competency in fire-fighting skills is maintained, and to ensure the operational readiness of the fire-fighting organization.

2.2.4 On-board training in the use of the ship's fire-extinguishing systems and appliances shall be planned and conducted in accordance with the provisions of regulation Ⅲ/19.4.1.

2.2.5 Fire drills shall be conducted and recorded in accordance with the provisions of regulations Ⅲ/19.3 and Ⅲ/19.5.

2.2.6 An onboard means of recharging breathing apparatus cylinders used during drills shall be provided or a suitable number of spare cylinders shall be carried on board to replace those used.

2.3 Training manuals

2.3.1 A training manual shall be provided in each crew mess room and recreation room or in each crew cabin.

2.3.2 The training manual shall be written in the working language of the ship.

第15条
指导、船上培训和演习

1　目的

本条的目的是通过对船上人员的培训和演习的实际指导，使其能在紧急情况下执行正确的程序减轻火灾的影响。为此，船员应具备处理火灾紧急情况，包括照顾乘客的必要知识和技能。

2　一般要求

2.1　指导、职责和组织

2.1.1　船员应得到船上消防安全的有关指导。

2.1.2　船员应得到其所承担职责的有关指导。

2.1.3　应组织负责灭火的小组。在船舶营运期间时，这些小组应具备在任何时候都能完成其职责的能力。

2.2　船上培训和演习

2.2.1　应培训船员熟悉船舶的布置和可能需要其使用的任何灭火系统和设备的位置及操作。

2.2.2　紧急逃生呼吸装置的使用训练应视为船上培训的一部分。

2.2.3　对承担灭火职责的船员，应通过开展船上培训和演习对其履行职责的能力进行定期评估，以发现需要提高的方面，从而确保其灭火技能方面的适任性得以保持，并确保灭火组织处于操作就绪状态。

2.2.4　船上使用船舶灭火系统和设备的训练应按第Ⅲ/19.4.1条的规定予以规划和实施。

2.2.5　应按第Ⅲ/19.3和Ⅲ/19.5条的规定进行消防演习并做记录。

2.2.6　须为演习期间所使用的呼吸器气瓶配备船上充气装置或船上须配备适当数量的备用气瓶以替换已使用的气瓶。

2.3　培训手册

2.3.1　应在每一船员餐厅和娱乐室或在每一船员居住舱室内配备1本培训手册。

2.3.2　培训手册应用船舶的工作语言写成。

2.3.3 The training manual, which may comprise several volumes, shall contain the instructions and information required in paragraph 2.3.4 in easily understood terms and illustrated wherever possible. Any part of such information may be provided in the form of audio-visual aids in lieu of the manual.

2.3.4 The training manual shall explain the following in detail:

.1 general fire safety practice and precautions related to the dangers of smoking, electrical hazards, flammable liquids and similar common shipboard hazards;

.2 general instructions on fire-fighting activities and fire-fighting procedures, including procedures for notification of a fire and use of manually operated call points;

.3 meanings of the ship's alarms;

.4 operation and use of fire-fighting systems and appliances;

.5 operation and use of fire doors;

.6 operation and use of fire and smoke dampers; and

.7 escape systems and appliances.

2.4 Fire control plans[①]

2.4.1 General arrangement plans shall be permanently exhibited for the guidance of the ship's officers, showing clearly for each deck the control stations, the various fire sections enclosed by "A" class divisions, the sections enclosed by "B" class divisions together with particulars of the fire detection and fire alarm systems, the sprinkler installation, the fire-extinguishing appliances, means of access to different compartments, decks, etc., and the ventilating system, including particulars of the fan control positions, the position of dampers and identification numbers of the ventilating fans serving each section. Alternatively, at the discretion of the Administration, the aforementioned details may be set out in a booklet, a copy of which shall be supplied to each officer, and one copy shall at all times be available on board in an accessible position. Plans and booklets shall be kept up to date; any alterations thereto shall be recorded as soon as practicable. Description in such plans and booklets shall be in the language or languages required by the Administration. If the language is neither English nor French, a translation into one of those languages shall be included.

2.4.2 A duplicate set of fire control plans or a booklet containing such plans shall be permanently stored in a prominently marked weathertight enclosure outside the deckhouse for the assistance of shore-side fire-fighting personnel.[②]

3 Additional requirements for passenger ships

① Refer to *Graphical symbols for shipboard fire control plans* (resolution A.952(23)) and/or table 3 of *Escape route signs and equipment location markings* (resolution A.1116(30)), as appropriate. Refer to the symbols in table 3 of resolution A.1116(30) where the symbols for a specific item are differently expressed in resolutions A.952(23) and A.1116(30).

② Refer to *Guidance concerning the location of fire control plans for the assistance of shoreside fire-fighting personnel* (MSC/Circ. 451).

2.3.3 培训手册可分成若干分册,应包含本条2.3.4所要求的须知和资料并应用易懂的措辞写成,如有可能应配以图解说明。这些资料的任何部分都可以用视听辅助教材形式提供,用以替代手册。

2.3.4 培训手册应详细解释以下内容:

.1 有关烟气危害、电气危险、易燃液体和船上类似常见危险的一般消防安全操作和预防措施;

.2 关于灭火行动和灭火程序的一般须知,包括报告火灾及使用手动报警按钮的程序;

.3 船舶各种报警的含义;

.4 灭火系统和设备的操作和使用;

.5 防火门的操作和使用;

.6 挡火闸和挡烟闸的操作和使用;和

.7 脱险通道系统和设备。

2.4 防火控制图①

2.4.1 应有永久展示的总布置图向高级船员提供指导,该图应清晰标明每层甲板的控制站、"A"级分隔围蔽的各防火区域、"B"级分隔围蔽的各防火区域,连同探火和失火报警系统、喷水器装置、灭火设备和各舱室、甲板等的出入通道以及通风系统的细节,包括风机控制位置、挡火闸位置和服务于每一区域的通风机识别号码的细节。作为替代,经主管机关同意,上述细节可合并成册,每位高级船员人手一份,而在船上易于到达的位置应有一份副本可供随时取用。控制图和小册子应保持更新;任何改动应尽快予以记录。该防火控制图和小册子的说明文字应以主管机关要求的一种或几种语言写成。如果该语言既不是英文也不是法文,则应包括其中一种语言的译文。

2.4.2 一套防火控制图或含有防火控制图小册子的副本应永久存放于甲板室外标有明显标志的风雨密盒中,供岸上消防人员使用。②

3 对客船的附加要求

① 参见《船舶防火控制图识别符号》(第A.952(23)号决议)和/或相应的《脱险通道标志和设备位置标识》(第A.1116(30)号决议)中的表3。参见第A.1116(30)号决议中的表3,其中某一特定项目的符号与第A.952(23)号决议有不同的表达方式。

② 参见《关于为岸上消防人员提供帮助的防火控制图位置导则》(第MSC/Circ.451号通函)。

3.1 Fire drills

In addition to the requirement of paragraph 2.2.3, fire drills shall be conducted in accordance with the provisions of regulation Ⅲ/30, having due regard to notification of passengers and movement of passengers to assembly stations and embarkation decks.

3.2 Fire control plans

In ships carrying more than 36 passengers, plans and booklets required by this regulation shall provide information regarding fire protection, fire detection and fire extinction based on the guidelines developed by the Organization.①

Regulation 16
Operations

1 Purpose

The purpose of this regulation is to provide information and instructions for proper ship and cargo handling operations in relation to fire safety. For this purpose, the following functional requirements shall be met:

.1 fire safety operational booklets shall be provided on board; and

.2 flammable vapour releases from cargo tank venting shall be controlled.

2 Fire safety operational booklets

2.1 The required fire safety operational booklet shall contain the necessary information and instructions for the safe operation of the ship and cargo handling operations in relation to fire safety. The booklet shall include information concerning the crew's responsibilities for the general fire safety of the ship while loading and discharging cargo and while under way. Necessary fire safety precautions for handling general cargoes shall be explained. For ships carrying dangerous goods and flammable bulk cargoes, the fire safety operational booklet shall also provide reference to the pertinent fire-fighting and emergency cargo handling instructions contained in the International Maritime Solid Bulk Cargoes (IMSBC) Code, the International Bulk Chemical Code, the International Gas Carrier Code and the International Maritime Dangerous Goods Code, as appropriate.

2.2 The fire safety operational booklet shall be provided in each crew mess room and recreation room or in each crew cabin.

2.3 The fire safety operational booklet shall be written in the working language of the ship.

2.4 The fire safety operational booklet may be combined with the training manuals required in regulation 15.2.3.

① Refer to *Guidelines on the information to be provided with fire control plans and booklets required by SOLAS regulations Ⅱ-2/20 and 41-2* (resolution A.756(18)).

3.1　消防演习

除本条2.2.3的要求外，消防演习还应按第Ⅲ/30条的规定进行，并充分考虑到通知乘客及乘客向集合站和登乘甲板的移动。

3.2　防火控制图

在载客超过36人的客船上，本条所要求的防火控制图和小册子应按本组织制定的指南提供有关防火、探火和灭火的资料。①

第16条
操作

1　目的

本条的目的是为与消防安全有关的正确的船舶操作和货物装卸操作提供资料和须知。为此，应满足下列功能要求：

.1　船上应备有消防安全操作手册；和

.2　应控制从液货舱透气系统释放出的易燃蒸气。

2　消防安全操作手册

2.1　所要求的消防安全操作手册应包含与消防安全有关的船舶安全操作和货物装卸安全操作所必需的信息和须知。该手册应包括关于船员在船舶装卸货物时和航行时对船舶总体消防安全所负责任方面的信息。还应对装卸一般货物时需采取的消防安全预防措施进行解释。对于载运危险货物和易燃散货的船舶，消防安全操作手册还应相应提及《国际海运固体散装货物安全操作规则》、《国际散化规则》、《国际气体运输船规则》和《国际海运危险货物规则》中有关消防和紧急货物装卸的须知。

2.2　应在每一船员餐厅和娱乐室或在每一船员居住舱室内配备一份消防安全操作手册。

2.3　消防安全操作手册应以船上的工作语言写成。

2.4　消防安全操作手册可与第15.2.3条要求的培训手册合并。

① 参见本组织第A.756(18)号决议通过的《关于SOLAS公约第Ⅱ-2/20和41-2条要求的防火控制图和小册子提供资料指南》。

3 Additional requirements for tankers

3.1 General

The fire safety operational booklet referred to in paragraph 2 shall include provisions for preventing fire spread to the cargo area due to ignition of flammable vapours and include procedures of cargo tank gas-purging and/or gas-freeing, taking into account the provisions in paragraph 3.2.

3.2 Procedures for cargo tank purging and/or gas-freeing

3.2.1 When the ship is provided with an inert gas system, the cargo tanks shall first be purged in accordance with the provisions of regulation 4.5.6 until the concentration of hydrocarbon vapours in the cargo tanks has been reduced to less than 2% by volume. Thereafter, gas-freeing may take place at the cargo tank deck level.

3.2.2 When the ship is not provided with an inert gas system, the operation shall be such that the flammable vapour is discharged initially through:

.1 the vent outlets as specified in regulation 4.5.3.4;

.2 outlets at least 2 m above the cargo tank deck level with a vertical efflux velocity of at least 30 m/s maintained during the gas-freeing operation; or

.3 outlets at least 2 m above the cargo tank deck level with a vertical efflux velocity of at least 20 m/s and which are protected by suitable devices to prevent the passage of flame.

3.2.3 The above outlets shall be located not less than 10 m, measured horizontally, from the nearest air intakes and openings to enclosed spaces containing a source of ignition and from deck machinery, which may include anchor windlass and chain locker openings, and equipment which may constitute an ignition hazard.

3.2.4 When the flammable vapour concentration at the outlet has been reduced to 30% of the lower flammable limit, gas-freeing may be continued at cargo tank deck level.

3.3 Operation of inert gas system

3.3.1 The inert gas system for tankers required in accordance with regulation 4.5.5.1 shall be so operated as to render and maintain the atmosphere of the cargo tanks non-flammable, except when such tanks are required to be gas-free.

3.3.2 Notwithstanding the above, for chemical tankers, the application of inert gas may take place after the cargo tank has been loaded, but before commencement of unloading and shall continue to be applied until that cargo tank has been purged of all flammable vapours before gas-freeing. Only nitrogen is acceptable as inert gas under this provision.

3　对液货船的附加要求

3.1　总则

本条2所述的消防安全操作手册应包括防止火灾由于易燃蒸气着火而蔓延至货物区域的规定，并包括液货舱驱气和/或除气的程序，该程序应考虑到本条3.2的规定。

3.2　液货舱驱气和/或除气程序

3.2.1　如果船舶设有惰性气体系统，应首先按照第4.5.6条的规定进行液货舱驱气，直到液货舱内碳氢化合物蒸气的浓度（按体积计算）降至2%以下。在此之后，可在液货舱甲板面上进行除气。

3.2.2　如果船舶未设有惰性气体系统，其操作应首先排除易燃气体：

.1　通过第4.5.3.4条规定的透气出口；

.2　通过液货舱甲板面以上至少2 m的出口，并且在除气作业期间至少维持30 m/s的垂直出气速度；或

.3　通过液货舱甲板面以上至少2 m的出口，并且至少有20 m/s的垂直出气速度，出口有适当的保护装置以防火焰通过。

3.2.3　以上出口距含有着火源的封闭处所的最近空气进口和开口以及甲板机械，包括锚机间和锚链舱上的开口，和可能构成失火危险的设备的水平距离应不少于10 m。

3.2.4　如果出口处的易燃蒸气浓度已减至可燃下限的30%，可在液货舱甲板面上继续除气。

3.3　惰性气体系统操作

3.3.1　按照第4.5.5.1条所要求的液货船惰性气体系统须如此操作以使液货舱内的空气不可燃并保持不可燃，但要求除气的此类液货舱除外。

3.3.2　尽管有上述规定，对于化学品液货船，可在液货舱装载之后、但在卸载开始之前施用惰性气体，且须继续施用，直至该液货舱内所有易燃蒸气在除气作业前均已驱除。就本条而言，只有氮气可作为惰性气体。

3.3.3 Notwithstanding regulation 1.2.2.2, the provisions of this paragraph shall only apply to tankers constructed on or after 1 January 2016. If the oxygen content of the inert gas exceeds 5% by volume, immediate action shall be taken to improve the gas quality. Unless the quality of the gas improves, all operations in those cargo tanks to which inert gas is being supplied shall be suspended so as to avoid air being drawn into the cargo tanks, the gas regulating valve, if fitted, shall be closed and the off specification gas shall be vented to atmosphere.

3.3.4 In the event that the inert gas system is unable to meet the requirement in paragraph 16.3.3.1 and it has been assessed that it is impractical to effect a repair, then cargo discharge and cleaning of those cargo tanks requiring inerting shall only be resumed when suitable emergency procedures have been followed, taking into account guidelines developed by the Organization.①

① Refer to *Clarification of inert gas system requirements under SOLAS 1974 as amended* (MSC/Circ.485) and *Revised guidelines for inert gas systems* (MSC/Circ.353, as amended by MSC/Circ.387).

3.3.3　尽管有第1.2.2.2条规定，本款的规定仅适用于2016年1月1日或之后建造的液货船。如惰性气体中氧气含量按体积计超过5%，须立即采取行动提高气体质量。如气体质量没有提高，须暂停液货舱中正在输送惰性气体的所有操作，以避免将空气引入液货舱中。如装设气体调节阀，须将其关闭，且将不合格的气体排到空气中。

3.3.4　如惰性气体系统不能达到第16.3.3.1款的要求且经评估认为进行修理不切实际，则需惰化的液货舱的货物卸载和清洁应只有在采用合适应急程序后才能继续进行，并考虑到本组织制定的导则。[①]

① 参见经修正的《对SOLAS 1974公约中惰性气体系统要求的澄清》(第MSC/Circ.485号通函)和《经修订的惰性气体系统指南》(经第MSC/Circ.387号通函修正的第MSC/Circ.353号通函)。

Part F
Alternative design and arrangements

Regulation 17
Alternative design and arrangements

1 Purpose

The purpose of this regulation is to provide a methodology for alternative design and arrangements for fire safety.

2 General

2.1 Fire safety design and arrangements may deviate from the prescriptive requirements set out in parts B, C, D, E or G, provided that the design and arrangements meet the fire safety objectives and the functional requirements.

2.2 When fire safety design or arrangements deviate from the prescriptive requirements of this chapter, engineering analysis, evaluation and approval of the alternative design and arrangements shall be carried out in accordance with this regulation.

3 Engineering analysis

The engineering analysis shall be prepared and submitted to the Administration, based on the guidelines developed by the Organization,[①] and shall include, as a minimum, the following elements:

.1 determination of the ship type and space(s) concerned;

.2 identification of prescriptive requirement(s) with which the ship or the space(s) will not comply;

.3 identification of the fire and explosion hazards of the ship or the space(s) concerned, including:

  .1 identification of the possible ignition sources;

  .2 identification of the fire growth potential of each space concerned;

  .3 identification of the smoke and toxic effluent generation potential for each space concerned;

  .4 identification of the potential for the spread of fire, smoke or of toxic effluents from the space (s) concerned to other spaces;

① Refer to *Guidelines on alternative design and arrangements for fire safety* (MSC/Circ.1002 and its Corr.1, Corr.2 and Corr.3, as amended by MSC.1/Circ.1552).

F部分
替代设计和布置

第17条
替代设计和布置

1　目的

本条的目的是提供消防安全替代设计和布置的方法。

2　总则

2.1　消防安全设计和布置可以偏离本章B、C、D、E或G部分的规定要求，但这些设计和布置须符合本章的消防安全目标和功能要求。

2.2　如果消防安全设计或布置偏离了本章的规定性要求，该替代设计和布置应按本条进行工程分析、评估和认可。

3　工程分析

工程分析应根据本组织制定的指南[①]编写并提交主管机关，并应至少包括下列要素：

.1　确定有关船型和处所；

.2　判定船舶或处所不符合的规定要求；

.3　判定有关船舶或处所的失火和爆炸危险，包括：

　　.1　判定可能的着火源；

　　.2　判定各有关处所火势增大的可能性；

　　.3　判定各有关处所产生烟气和有毒物的可能性；

　　.4　判定火灾、烟气和有毒物从有关处所向其他处所蔓延的可能性；

① 参见《消防安全替代设计和布置指南》(经第MSC.1/Circ.1552号通函修正的第MSC/Circ.1002号通函及其Corr.1、Corr.2和Corr.3)。

.4 determination of the required fire safety performance criteria for the ships or the space(s) concerned addressed by the prescriptive requirement(s), in particular:

.1 performance criteria shall be based on the fire safety objectives and on the functional requirements of this chapter;

.2 performance criteria shall provide a degree of safety not less than that achieved by using the prescriptive requirements;

.3 performance criteria shall be quantifiable and measurable;

.5 detailed description of the alternative design and arrangements, including a list of the assumptions used in the design and any proposed operational restrictions or conditions; and

.6 technical justification demonstrating that the alternative design and arrangements meet the required fire safety performance criteria.

4 Evaluation of the alternative design and arrangements

4.1 The engineering analysis required in paragraph 3 shall be evaluated and approved by the Administration, taking into account the guidelines developed by the Organization.[①]

4.2 A copy of the documentation, as approved by the Administration, indicating that the alternative design and arrangements comply with this regulation shall be carried on board the ship.

5 Exchange of information

The Administration shall communicate to the Organization pertinent information concerning alternative design and arrangements approved by them for circulation to all Contracting Governments.

6 Re-evaluation due to change of conditions

If the assumptions and operational restrictions that were stipulated in the alternative design and arrangements are changed, the engineering analysis shall be carried out under the changed condition and shall be approved by the Administration.

---

① Refer to *Guidelines on alternative design and arrangements for fire safety* (MSC/Circ.1002 and its Corr.1, Corr.2 and Corr.3, as amended by MSC.1/Circ.1552).

.4 确定规定性要求对有关船舶或处所提出的消防安全性能衡准：

.1 性能衡准应基于本章的消防安全目标和功能要求；

.2 性能衡准所规定的安全度应不低于应用规定性要求所达到的安全度；

.3 性能衡准应可量化并具备可测量性；

.5 替代设计和布置的细节描述，包括列出设计时采用的假设，以及所建议的任何操作限制或条件；和

.6 表明替代设计和布置符合所要求的安全性能衡准的技术论据。

4 替代设计和布置的评估

4.1 本条3所要求的工程分析应由主管机关予以评估和批准，并考虑到本组织制定的指南①。

4.2 经主管机关批准的指明替代设计和布置符合本条要求的文件副本应随船携带。

5 信息交流

主管机关应将其所批准的替代设计和布置的有关信息送交本组织，以分发给所有缔约国政府。

6 条件改变后的再评估

如果替代设计和布置所规定的假设和操作限制发生了改变，应根据改变后的条件进行工程分析并应经主管机关批准。

① 参见《消防安全替代设计和布置指南》（经第MSC.1/Circ.1552号通函修正的第MSC/Circ.1002号通函及其Corr.1、Corr.2和Corr.3）。

Part G
Special Requirements

Regulation 18
Helicopter facilities

1 Purpose

The purpose of this regulation is to provide additional measures in order to address the fire safety objectives of this chapter for ships fitted with special facilities for helicopters. For this purpose, the following functional requirements shall be met:

.1 helideck structure shall be adequate to protect the ship from the fire hazards associated with helicopter operations;

.2 fire-fighting appliances shall be provided to adequately protect the ship from the fire hazards associated with helicopter operations;

.3 refuelling and hangar facilities and operations shall provide the necessary measures to protect the ship from the fire hazards associated with helicopter operations; and

.4 operation manuals and training shall be provided.

2 Application

2.1 In addition to complying with the requirements of regulations in parts B, C, D and E, as appropriate, ships equipped with helidecks shall comply with the requirements of this regulation.

2.2 Where helicopters land or conduct winching operations on an occasional or emergency basis on ships without helidecks, fire-fighting equipment fitted in accordance with the requirements in part C may be used. This equipment shall be made readily available in close proximity to the landing or winching areas during helicopter operations.

2.3 Notwithstanding the requirements of paragraph 2.2 above, ships constructed on or after 1 January 2020, having a helicopter landing area, shall be provided with foam firefighting appliances which comply with the relevant provisions of chapter 17 of the Fire Safety Systems Code.

2.4 Notwithstanding the requirements of paragraph 2.2 or 2.3 above, ro-ro passenger ships without helidecks shall comply with regulation Ⅲ/28.

3 Structure

3.1 Construction of steel or other equivalent material

G 部分
特殊要求

第 18 条
直升机设施

1　目的

本条的目的是为设有直升机专用设施的船舶达到本章的消防安全目标而规定附加措施。为此,应满足下列功能要求:

.1　直升机甲板结构应足以保护船舶免受与直升机作业有关的火灾危险;

.2　应配备足以保护船舶免受与直升机作业有关的火灾危险的消防设备;

.3　对加油和机库设施及操作采取必要措施以保护船舶免受与直升机作业有关的火灾危险;和

.4　应备有操作手册并提供培训。

2　适用范围

2.1　除符合本章 B、C、D 和 E 部分各条的相应要求外,设有直升机甲板的船舶还应符合本条的要求。

2.2　对于只是在偶尔或紧急情况下才有直升机降落或进行绞车作业的未设直升机甲板的船舶,可以使用按 C 部分的要求安装的灭火设备。在直升机作业期间,这些设备应在紧靠降落或绞车作业区域处随时可用。

2.3　尽管有上述第 2.2 款的要求,2020 年 1 月 1 日或以后建造的设有直升机降落区域的船舶须备有符合《消防安全系统规则》第 17 章相关规定的泡沫消防设备。

2.4　尽管有上述第 2.2 或 2.3 款的要求,未设直升机甲板的滚装客船仍须符合第Ⅲ/28 条。

3　结构

3.1　钢或其他等效材料结构

In general, the construction of the helidecks shall be of steel or other equivalent materials. If the helideck forms the deckhead of a deckhouse or superstructure, it shall be insulated to "A-60" class standard.

3.2 Construction of aluminium or other low melting point metals

If the Administration permits aluminium or other low melting point metal construction that is not made equivalent to steel, the following provisions shall be satisfied:

.1 if the platform is cantilevered over the side of the ship, after each fire on the ship or on the platform, the platform shall undergo a structural analysis to determine its suitability for further use; and

.2 if the platform is located above the ship's deckhouse or similar structure, the following conditions shall be satisfied:

.1 the deckhouse top and bulkheads under the platform shall have no openings;

.2 windows under the platform shall be provided with steel shutters; and

.3 after each fire on the platform or in close proximity, the platform shall undergo a structural analysis to determine its suitability for further use.

4 Means of escape

A helideck shall be provided with both a main and an emergency means of escape and access for fire fighting and rescue personnel. These shall be located as far apart from each other as is practicable and preferably on opposite sides of the helideck.

5 Fire-fighting appliances

5.1 In close proximity to the helideck, the following fire-fighting appliances shall be provided and stored near the means of access to that helideck:

.1 at least two dry powder extinguishers having a total capacity of not less than 45 kg;①

.2 carbon dioxide extinguishers of a total capacity of not less than 18 kg or equivalent;①

.3 a suitable foam application system consisting of monitors or foam-making branch pipes capable of delivering foam to all parts of the helideck in all weather conditions in which helicopters can operate. The system shall be capable of delivering a discharge rate as required in table 18.1 for at least 5 min;

Table 18.1 Foam discharge rates

Category	Helicopter overall length	Discharge rate foam solution (L/min)
H1	up to but not including 15 m	250
H2	from 15 m up to but not including 24 m	500
H3	from 24 m up to but not including 35 m	800

① Refer to *Unified interpretation of SOLAS chapter Ⅱ-2 on the number and arrangement of portable fire extinguishers on board ships* (MSC.1/Circ.1275 and its Corr.1).

直升机甲板一般应为钢或其他等效材料结构。如果直升机甲板构成甲板室或上层建筑的顶甲板，则应将其按“A-60”级标准隔热。

3.2　铝或其他低熔点金属结构

如果主管机关允许使用铝或其他不与钢等效的低熔点金属结构，则应符合下列规定：

.1　如果平台是位于船舷的悬臂结构，在船舶或平台每次失火后，应对平台进行一次结构分析以确定其是否适于继续使用；和

.2　如果平台位于船舶甲板室或类似结构以上，则应满足下列条件：

.1　平台以下的甲板室的顶部和舱壁应无开口；

.2　平台以下的窗应设有钢质窗盖；和

.3　在平台或紧靠平台处每次失火后，都应对平台进行一次结构分析以确定其是否适于继续使用。

4　脱险通道

直升机甲板应设有1条主脱险通道和1条应急脱险通道，以及供消防和救助人员用的通道。这些通道应尽可能相互远离，最好位于直升机甲板上相对的两侧。

5　消防设备

5.1　在紧靠直升机甲板处，应在通往该直升机甲板的通道附近配备和存放下列消防设备：

.1　至少2具干粉灭火器，总容量不小于45 kg；①

.2　总容量不小于18 kg的二氧化碳灭火器或等效设备；①

.3　一个由泡沫炮或泡沫发生支管组成的合适的泡沫灭火系统，能在直升机能作业的所有气候条件下将泡沫喷射至直升机甲板的所有部分。该系统应能按表18.1所要求的喷射率工作至少5 min；

表18.1　泡沫喷射率

类别	直升机总长	泡沫液喷射率(L/min)
H1	15 m以下(不含15 m)	250
H2	15 m至24 m以下(不含24 m)	500
H3	24 m至35 m以下(不含35 m)	800

① 参见《SOLAS第Ⅱ-2章船上手提式灭火器数量和布置的统一解释》(第MSC.1/Circ.1275号通函及其Corr.1)。

.4 the principal agent shall be suitable for use with salt water and conform to performance standards not inferior to those acceptable to the Organization;①

.5 at least two nozzles of an approved dual-purpose type (jet/spray) and hoses sufficient to reach any part of the helideck;

.6 in lieu of the requirements of paragraphs 5.1.3 through 5.1.5, on ships constructed on or after 1 January 2020 having a helideck, foam firefighting appliances which comply with the provisions of the Fire Safety Systems Code;

.7 in addition to the requirements of regulation 10.10, two sets of fire-fighter's outfits; and

.8 at least the following equipment shall be stored in a manner that provides for immediate use and protection from the elements:

.1 adjustable wrench;

.2 blanket, fire-resistant;

.3 cutters, bolt, 60 cm;

.4 hook, grab or salving;

.5 hacksaw, heavy duty complete with 6 spare blades;

.6 ladder;

.7 lift line 5 mm diameter and 15 m in length;

.8 pliers, side-cutting;

.9 set of assorted screwdrivers; and

.10 harness knife complete with sheath.

6 Drainage facilities

Drainage facilities in way of helidecks shall be constructed of steel and shall lead directly overboard independent of any other system and shall be designed so that drainage does not fall onto any part of the ship.

7 Helicopter refuelling and hangar facilities

Where the ship has helicopter refuelling and hangar facilities, the following requirements shall be complied with:

.1 a designated area shall be provided for the storage of fuel tanks which shall be:

.1 as remote as is practicable from accommodation spaces, escape routes and embarkation stations; and

.2 isolated from areas containing a source of vapour ignition;

① Refer to the *International Civil Aviation Organization Airport Services Manual*, part 1, Rescue and Fire Fighting, chapter 8, Extinguishing Agent Characteristics, paragraph 8.1.5, Foam Specifications table 8-1, level "B".

.4 主要灭火剂应适于与盐水一起使用，其所符合的性能标准应不低于本组织接受的性能标准①；

.5 至少2具经认可的两用型（水柱/水雾）水枪和足以达到直升机甲板任何部分的水带；

.6 取代第5.1.3至5.1.5款的要求，在2020年1月1日或以后建造的设有直升机甲板的船上，备有符合《消防安全系统规则》规定的泡沫消防设备。

.7 除第10.10条的要求外，另备2套消防员装备；和

.8 应至少存有下列设备，存放方式应使其可立即使用且有风雨防护：

.1 活络扳手；
.2 耐火毯；
.3 60 cm螺栓刀具；
.4 抓钩或捞钩；
.5 高负荷钢锯，配有6根备用锯条；
.6 梯子；
.7 5 mm直径起重绳，长15 m；
.8 侧剪钳子；
.9 全套分类螺丝刀；和
.10 带有可配挂刀鞘的工具刀。

6 排水设施

直升机甲板上的排水设施应为钢质构造，独立于任何其他系统，直接将水排向舷外，且其设计应使排出的水不会落到船上任何部分。

7 直升机加油和机库设施

如果船上有直升机加油和机库设施，则应符合以下要求：

.1 应设有用于储存燃料罐的专门区域，该区域应：

.1 尽可能远离起居处所、脱险通道和登乘站；和

.2 与含有蒸气引燃源的区域隔离；

① 参见《国际民航组织机场服务手册》第1部分“救助和灭火”第8章“灭火剂特性”8.1.5“泡沫规格，表8-1，‘B’级”。

.2 the fuel storage area shall be provided with arrangements whereby fuel spillage may be collected and drained to a safe location;

.3 tanks and associated equipment shall be protected against physical damage and from a fire in an adjacent space or area;

.4 where portable fuel storage tanks are used, special attention shall be given to:

.1 design of the tank for its intended purpose;

.2 mounting and securing arrangements;

.3 electric bonding; and

.4 inspection procedures;

.5 storage tank fuel pumps shall be provided with means which permit shutdown from a safe remote location in the event of a fire. Where a gravity fuelling system is installed, equivalent closing arrangements shall be provided to isolate the fuel source;

.6 the fuel pumping unit shall be connected to one tank at a time. The piping between the tank and the pumping unit shall be of steel or equivalent material, as short as possible, and protected against damage;

.7 electrical fuel pumping units and associated control equipment shall be of a type suitable for the location and potential hazards;

.8 fuel pumping units shall incorporate a device which will prevent over-pressurization of the delivery or filling hose;

.9 equipment used in refuelling operations shall be electrically bonded;

.10 "NO SMOKING" signs shall be displayed at appropriate locations;

.11 hangar, refuelling and maintenance facilities shall be treated as category A machinery spaces with regard to structural fire protection, fixed fire-extinguishing and detection system requirements;

.12 enclosed hangar facilities or enclosed spaces containing refuelling installations shall be provided with mechanical ventilation, as required by regulation 20.3 for closed ro-ro spaces of cargo ships. Ventilation fans shall be of non-sparking type; and

.13 electric equipment and wiring in enclosed hangars or enclosed spaces containing refuelling installations shall comply with regulations 20.3.2, 20.3.3 and 20.3.4.

8 Operations manual and fire-fighting arrangements

8.1 Each helicopter facility shall have an operations manual, including a description and a checklist of safety precautions, procedures and equipment requirements. This manual may be part of the ship's emergency response procedures.

.2　燃料储存区域应设有将溢漏燃料收集起来并排往安全位置的装置；

.3　对油罐及所属设备应加以保护,防止受到机械损坏以及邻近处所或区域火灾造成的危害；

.4　如果采用移动式燃料储存罐,应特别注意：

.1　罐的设计符合其预期用途；

.2　安放和紧固布置；

.3　电气屏蔽接地；和

.4　检查程序；

.5　储存罐的燃料泵应设有在失火时能从远处安全位置关闭的装置。如果安装了重力式加油系统,应设有隔离燃料源的等效关闭装置；

.6　燃料泵送装置应一次与 1 个燃料罐连接。燃料罐与泵送装置之间的管路应用钢或等效材料制成,尽可能短,并加以保护,防止受到损坏；

.7　电动燃料泵送装置及相关控制设备的类型应适合其位置及潜在的危险；

.8　燃料泵送装置中应附有 1 个防止输油或注油软管超压的装置；

.9　加油作业使用的设备应予以电气屏蔽接地；

.10　应在各相应位置设有“禁止吸烟”标志；

.11　机库、加油和维护保养设施的结构防火、固定式灭火和探火系统要求应按 A 类机器处所考虑；

.12　围蔽的机库设施或内设加油设备的围蔽处所应设有本章第 20.3 条对货船闭式滚装处所要求的机械通风。风机应为无火花型；和

.13　围蔽的机库或内设加油设备的围蔽处所中的电气设备和线路应符合第 20.3.2、20.3.3 和 20.3.4 条的要求。

8　操作手册和灭火布置

8.1　每一直升机设施应备有一份操作手册,包括一份对安全预防措施、程序和设备要求的说明和一份检查清单。此手册可为船舶应急响应程序的一部分。

8.2 The procedures and precautions to be followed during refuelling operations shall be in accordance with recognized safe practices and contained in the operations manual.

8.3 Fire-fighting personnel, consisting of at least two persons trained for rescue and fire-fighting duties, and fire-fighting equipment shall be immediately available at all times when helicopter operations are expected.

8.4 Fire-fighting personnel shall be present during refuelling operations. However, the fire-fighting personnel shall not be involved with refuelling activities.

8.5 On-board refresher training shall be carried out and additional supplies of fire-fighting media shall be provided for training and testing of the equipment.

Regulation 19
Carriage of dangerous goods①

1 Purpose

The purpose of this regulation is to provide additional safety measures in order to address the fire safety objectives of this chapter for ships carrying dangerous goods. For this purpose, the following functional requirements shall be met:

.1 fire protection systems shall be provided to protect the ship from the added fire hazards associated with carriage of dangerous goods;

.2 dangerous goods shall be adequately separated from ignition sources; and

.3 appropriate personnel protective equipment shall be provided for the hazards associated with the carriage of dangerous goods.

2 General requirements

2.1 In addition to complying with the requirements of regulations in parts B, C, D, E and regulations 18 and 20,② as appropriate, ship types and cargo spaces, referred to in paragraph 2.2, intended for the carriage of dangerous goods shall comply with the requirements of this regulation, as appropriate, except when carrying dangerous goods in limited quantities③ and excepted quantities④ unless such requirements have already been met by compliance with the requirements elsewhere in this chapter. The types of ships and modes of carriage of dangerous goods are referred to in paragraph 2.2 and in table 19.1. Cargo ships of less than 500 gross tonnage shall comply with this regulation, but Administrations may reduce the requirements and such reduced requirements shall be recorded in the document of compliance referred to in paragraph 4.

2.2 The following ship types and cargo spaces shall govern the application of tables 19.1 and 19.2:

---

① Refer to *Interim guidelines for open-top containerships* (MSC/Circ.608/Rev.1).

② Refer to part 7 of the IMDG Code.

③ Refer to chapter 3.4 of the IMDG Code.

④ Refer to chapter 3.5 of the IMDG Code.

8.2 在加油作业时应遵守的程序和预防措施应符合公认的安全操作方式并包括在操作手册内。

8.3 在预计将进行直升机作业时,消防人员(至少为2名受过救助和消防职责及消防设备培训的人)应能随时立即到场工作。

8.4 在加油作业时应有消防人员在场。但是,消防人员不应参与加油工作。

8.5 应在船上开展复习培训并应为培训和设备试验提供额外的灭火剂。

第19条
危险货物运输[①]

1　目的

本条的目的是为载运危险货物的船舶规定附加安全措施,以达到本章的消防安全目标。为此,应满足下列功能要求:

.1　应配备防火系统以保护船舶免受因载运危险货物而带来的额外火灾危险;

.2　应将危险货物与着火源充分隔开;和

.3　应针对因载运危险货物而带来的危险配备适当的人员保护设备。

2　一般要求

2.1 除符合本章B、C、D、E部分各条和第18条以及20条[②]的相应要求外,本条2.2所述的拟用于载运危险货物的船舶类型和货物处所还应符合本条的相应要求,但在载运有限数量和免除数量的危险货物[③]时,且此种要求[④]已通过符合本章的其他要求而得到满足时除外。船舶类型和载运危险货物的方式见本条2.2和表19.1。小于500总吨的货船应符合本条,但主管机关可以降低要求,且该降低的要求应记录在本条4中所述的符合证明中。

2.2 表19.1和表19.2的适用范围应以下列船舶类型和货物处所为准:

---

① 参见《敞口集装箱船暂行指南》(第MSC/Circ.608/Rev.1号通函)。
② 参见《国际海运危险货物规则》第7部分。
③ 参见《国际海运危险货物规则》第3.4章。
④ 参见《国际海运危险货物规划》第3.5章。

.1 ships and cargo spaces not specifically designed for the carriage of freight containers, but intended for the carriage of dangerous goods in packaged form, including goods in freight containers and portable tanks;

.2 purpose-built containerships and cargo spaces intended for the carriage of dangerous goods in freight containers and portable tanks;

.3 ro-ro ships and ro-ro spaces intended for the carriage of dangerous goods;

.4 ships and cargo spaces intended for the carriage of solid dangerous goods in bulk; and

.5 ships and cargo spaces intended for carriage of dangerous goods other than liquids and gases in bulk in shipborne barges.

3 Special requirements

Unless otherwise specified, the following requirements shall govern the application of tables 19.1, 19.2 and 19.3 to both "on-deck" and "under-deck" stowage of dangerous goods where the numbers of the following paragraphs are indicated in the first column of the tables.

3.1 Water supplies

3.1.1 Arrangements shall be made to ensure immediate availability of a supply of water from the fire main at the required pressure either by permanent pressurization or by suitably placed remote arrangements for the fire pumps.

3.1.2 The quantity of water delivered shall be capable of supplying four nozzles of a size and at pressures as specified in regulation 10.2, capable of being trained on any part of the cargo space when empty. This amount of water may be applied by equivalent means to the satisfaction of the Administration.

3.1.3 Means shall be provided for effectively cooling the designated under-deck cargo space by at least 5 L/min per square metre of the horizontal area of cargo spaces, either by a fixed arrangement of spraying nozzles or by flooding the cargo space with water. Hoses may be used for this purpose in small cargo spaces and in small areas of larger cargo spaces at the discretion of the Administration. However, the drainage and pumping arrangements shall be such as to prevent the build-up of free surfaces. The drainage system shall be sized to remove no less than 125% of the combined capacity of both the water-spraying system pumps and the required number of fire hose nozzles. The drainage system valves shall be operable from outside the protected space at a position in the vicinity of the extinguishing system controls. Bilge wells shall be of sufficient holding capacity and shall be arranged at the side shell of the ship at a distance from each other of not more than 40 m in each watertight compartment. If this is not possible, the adverse effect upon stability of the added weight and free surface of water shall be taken into account to the extent deemed necessary by the Administration in its approval of the stability information.①

① Refer to *Recommendation on fixed fire-extinguishing systems for special category spaces* (resolution A.123(V)).

.1　船舶和货物处所并非专门设计用于载运货物集装箱，而是拟用于载运包装危险货物，包括装在集装箱和可移动罐柜内的危险货物；

.2　为拟载运装在集装箱和可移动罐柜内的危险货物而建造的专用集装箱船和货物处所；

.3　拟用于载运危险货物的滚装船和滚装处所；

.4　拟用于载运固体散装危险货物的船舶和货物处所；和

.5　拟用于载运除船载驳船内散装液体和气体以外的其他危险货物的船舶和货物处所。

3　特殊要求

除另有规定外，表19.1、19.2和19.3对"甲板上"和"甲板下"的危险货物积载的适用范围应以下列要求为准，其下列各节的编号在这些表的第一栏中显示。

3.1　供水

3.1.1　供水布置应通过固定加压或通过位于适当位置的遥控装置启动消防泵，确保能够立即从消防总管按所要求的压力供水。

3.1.2　输送的水量应能向本章第10.2条所规定尺寸的4具水枪以该条规定的压力供水，当空舱时能射到货物处所的任何部分。此水量可以采用主管机关满意的等效方式获得。

3.1.3　应设有固定式喷雾器设备或用水浸入货物处所的设备，以使指定甲板下的货物处所通过按货物处所水平区域面积计每平方米至少5 L/min的水量得到有效冷却。经主管机关决定，对小型货物处所和较大货物处所内的小区域可使用消防水带达到这一目的。但是，排水和抽水装置应能防止形成自由液面。排水系统的尺度所达到的排量应不低于水雾系统泵和所要求数量的消防水枪的组合容量的125%。排水系统的阀门应能从所保护处所的外部靠近灭火系统控制装置的位置进行操作。舱底污水井应具有足够的容量，应布置在船侧，且在每一水密舱内相互间距不得超过40 m。如果不可能这样，主管机关在批准稳性资料时应按其认为必要的程度，考虑增加的水重量和自由液面对船舶稳性的不利影响。[①]

① 参见《关于特种处所固定式灭火系统的建议》(第A.123(Ⅴ)号决议)。

3.1.4 Provision to flood a designated under-deck cargo space with suitable specified media may be substituted for the requirements in paragraph 3.1.3.

3.1.5 The total required capacity of the water supply shall satisfy paragraphs 3.1.2 and 3.1.3, if applicable, simultaneously calculated for the largest designated cargo space. The capacity requirements of paragraph 3.1.2 shall be met by the total capacity of the main fire pump(s), not including the capacity of the emergency fire pump, if fitted. If a drencher system is used to satisfy paragraph 3.1.3, the drencher pump shall also be taken into account in this total capacity calculation.

3.2 Sources of ignition

Electrical equipment and wiring shall not be fitted in enclosed cargo spaces or vehicle spaces unless it is essential for operational purposes in the opinion of the Administration. However, if electrical equipment is fitted in such spaces, it shall be of a certified safe type① for use in the dangerous environments to which it may be exposed unless it is possible to completely isolate the electrical system (e.g. by removal of links in the system, other than fuses). Cable penetrations of the decks and bulkheads shall be sealed against the passage of gas or vapour. Through runs of cables and cables within the cargo spaces shall be protected against damage from impact. Any other equipment which may constitute a source of ignition of flammable vapour shall not be permitted.

3.3 Detection system

Ro-ro spaces shall be fitted with a fixed fire detection and fire alarm system complying with the requirements of the Fire Safety Systems Code. All other types of cargo spaces shall be fitted with either a fixed fire detection and fire alarm system or a sample extraction smoke detection system complying with the requirements of the Fire Safety Systems Code. If a sample extraction smoke detection system is fitted, particular attention shall be given to paragraph 2.1.3 in chapter 10 of the Fire Safety Systems Code in order to prevent the leakage of toxic fumes into occupied areas.

3.4 Ventilation arrangement

3.4.1 Adequate power ventilation shall be provided in enclosed cargo spaces. The arrangement shall be such as to provide for at least six air changes per hour in the cargo space, based on an empty cargo space, and for removal of vapours from the upper or lower parts of the cargo space, as appropriate.

3.4.2 The fans shall be such as to avoid the possibility of ignition of flammable gas/air mixtures. Suitable wire mesh guards shall be fitted over inlet and outlet ventilation openings.

3.4.3 Natural ventilation shall be provided in enclosed cargo spaces intended for the carriage of solid dangerous goods in bulk, where there is no provision for mechanical ventilation.

3.5 Bilge pumping

---

① Refer to the recommendations of the International Electrotechnical Commission, in particular publication IEC 60092, *Electrical installations in ships*.

3.1.4 由适当的专门介质淹没指定的甲板下货物处所的措施，可替代本条3.1.3中的要求。

3.1.5 所要求的总供水流量按最大的指定货物处所同时计算，应满足本条3.1.2和3.1.3的适用要求。应通过主消防泵的总流量满足本条3.1.2所要求的流量，其中不包括应急消防泵（若设有）的流量。如果安装了喷射泵系统以满足本条3.1.3的要求，则在计算总流量时还应计及喷射泵。

3.2 着火源

除非主管机关认为在操作上极为必要，否则电气设备和电线不应安装在围蔽的货物处所或车辆处所内。然而，如果电气设备安装在这种处所内，其应为可以暴露在危险环境中使用的合格防爆型设备①，但能完全隔离电气系统（例如通过拆除系统内除保险丝外的连接线）者除外。电缆穿过的甲板和舱壁应予以密封，以防止气体或蒸气通过。贯穿电缆和货物处所内部的电缆应予以保护，以防止被碰损。禁止使用任何其他可能构成易燃蒸气着火源的设备。

3.3 探测系统

滚装处所应装设1个符合《消防安全系统规则》的固定式探火和失火报警系统。所有其他类型的货物处所应装有符合《消防安全系统规则》要求的1个固定式探火和失火报警系统或1个烟雾探火系统。如果安装了1个烟雾探火系统，应特别注意《消防安全系统规则》第10章2.1.3节，以防止有毒烟气泄漏到有人区域。

3.4 通风布置

3.4.1 应向围蔽货物处所提供足够的动力通风。货物处所的通风布置应以空货物处所为基础每小时至少换气6次，并从货物处所的上部或下部相应位置排除蒸气。

3.4.2 风机应能避免易燃气体和空气混合物着火的可能性。通风系统的入口和出口处应设有适合的金属丝网保护。

3.4.3 用于载运固体散装危险货物的围蔽货物处所如果未提供机械通风，应设有自然通风。

3.5 舱底水泵送

① 参见国际电工委员会的建议，特别是IEC 60092出版物《船舶电气装置》。

3.5.1 Where it is intended to carry flammable or toxic liquids in enclosed cargo spaces, the bilge pumping system shall be designed to protect against inadvertent pumping of such liquids through machinery space piping or pumps. Where large quantities of such liquids are carried, consideration shall be given to the provision of additional means of draining those cargo spaces.

3.5.2 If the bilge drainage system is additional to the system served by pumps in the machinery space, the capacity of the system shall be not less than 10 m^3/h per cargo space served. If the additional system is common, the capacity need not exceed 25 m^3/h. The additional bilge system need not be arranged with redundancy.

3.5.3 Whenever flammable or toxic liquids are carried, the bilge line into the machinery space shall be isolated either by fitting a blank flange or by a closed lockable valve.

3.5.4 Enclosed spaces outside machinery spaces containing bilge pumps serving cargo spaces intended for carriage of flammable or toxic liquids shall be fitted with separate mechanical ventilation giving at least six air changes per hour. If the space has access from another enclosed space, the door shall be self-closing.

3.5.5 If bilge drainage of cargo spaces is arranged by gravity drainage, the drainage shall be either led directly overboard or to a closed drain tank located outside the machinery spaces. The tank shall be provided with a vent pipe to a safe location on the open deck. Drainage from a cargo space into bilge wells in a lower space is only permitted if that space satisfies the same requirements as the cargo space above.

3.6 Personnel protection

3.6.1 Four sets of full protective clothing, resistant to chemical attack, shall be provided in addition to the firefighter's outfits required by regulation 10.10 and shall be selected taking into account the hazards associated with the chemicals being transported and the standards developed by the Organization according to the class and physical state.① The protective clothing shall cover all skin, so that no part of the body is unprotected.

3.6.2 At least two self-contained breathing apparatuses additional to those required by regulation 10.10 shall be provided. Two spare charges suitable for use with the breathing apparatus shall be provided for each required apparatus. Passenger ships carrying not more than 36 passengers and cargo ships that are equipped with suitably located means for fully recharging the air cylinders free from contamination need carry only one spare charge for each required apparatus.

---

① For solid bulk cargoes, the protective clothing should satisfy the equipment provisions specified in the respective schedules of the IMSBC Code for the individual substances. For packaged goods, the protective clothing should satisfy the equipment provisions specified in the *Revised Emergency Response Procedures for Ships Carrying Dangerous Goods* (*EmS Guide*) (MSC.1/Circ.1588, as may be amended) of the Supplement to the IMDG Code for the individual substances.

3.5.1 如果拟在围蔽货物处所内载运易燃或有毒液体,舱底水泵送系统的设计应能防止由于疏忽而将这种液体输往机器处所的管路或泵。如果大量载运这种液体,应考虑为这些处所配备附加的排放装置。

3.5.2 如果舱底排放系统是机器处所内舱底泵系统的附加系统,则对于所服务的每个货物处所,该系统的排量不得小于 10 m^3/h。如果附加系统是公用的,则其排量不必超过 25 m^3/h。附加舱底系统的布置不需要有冗余。

3.5.3 只要载运易燃或有毒液体,通往机器处所的舱底泵管路就应安装盲板法兰或可锁的封闭阀门予以隔离。

3.5.4 在设有服务于装载易燃或有毒液体货物处所的舱底泵的机器处所外面的围蔽处所,应设有独立的机械通风,并能每小时至少换气 6 次。如果该处所设有通往其他围蔽处所的通道,其门应为自闭型。

3.5.5 如果货物处所的舱底排放系统是通过重力排放,该排放应直接通往舷外或通往位于机器处所外面的封闭泄放舱。泄放舱应设有透气管,通向开敞甲板上的一个安全位置。允许将舱底水从货物处所排往一个较低处所的舱底污水井中,但该较低处所必须满足与上述货物处所相同的要求。

3.6 人员保护

3.6.1 除按第 10.10 条要求配备消防员装备外,还应配备 4 套抗化学侵蚀的全面防护服,并须在考虑到与所运化学品相关的危害及本组织所制定的标准①,根据货物类别和物理状态加以选择。防护服应罩没全部皮肤,使身体的所有部分都得到保护。

3.6.2 除按第 10.10 条要求配备呼吸器外,还应配备至少 2 套自给式呼吸器。对所要求的每个呼吸器应配备 2 个适合于其使用的备用充气瓶。载客不超过 36 人的客船和货船,如在适当位置装有为所有气瓶重新充满洁净空气的设备,则所要求的每套呼吸器只需配备 1 个备用气瓶。

---

① 对固体散货,防护服应满足 IMSBC 规则在各种物质的相应细则中所做的设备规定。对包装货物,防护服应满足 IMDG 规则附件在各种物质的经修订的运输危险货物船舶应急响应程序(EmS 指引)(第 MSC.1/Circ.1588 号通函,可能经修正)中所做的设备规定。

3.7 Portable fire extinguishers[①]

Portable fire extinguishers with a total capacity of at least 12 kg of dry powder or equivalent shall be provided for the cargo spaces. These extinguishers shall be in addition to any portable fire extinguishers required elsewhere in this chapter.

3.8 Insulation of machinery space boundaries

Bulkheads forming boundaries between cargo spaces and machinery spaces of category A shall be insulated to "A-60" class standard, unless the dangerous goods are stowed at least 3 m horizontally away from such bulkheads. Other boundaries between such spaces shall be insulated to "A-60" class standard.

3.9 Water-spray system

Each open ro-ro space having a deck above it and each space deemed to be a closed ro-ro space not capable of being sealed shall be fitted with an approved fixed pressure water-spraying system for manual operation which shall protect all parts of any deck and vehicle platform in the space, except that the Administration may permit the use of any other fixed fire-extinguishing system that has been shown by full-scale test to be no less effective. However, the drainage and pumping arrangements shall be such as to prevent the build-up of free surfaces. The drainage system shall be sized to remove no less than 125% of the combined capacity of both the water-spraying system pumps and the required number of fire hose nozzles. The drainage system valves shall be operable from outside the protected space at a position in the vicinity of the extinguishing system controls. Bilge wells shall be of sufficient holding capacity and shall be arranged at the side shell of the ship at a distance from each other of not more than 40 m in each watertight compartment. If this is not possible, the adverse effect upon stability of the added weight and free surface of water shall be taken into account to the extent deemed necessary by the Administration in its approval of the stability information.[②]

3.10 Separation of ro-ro spaces

3.10.1 In ships having ro-ro spaces, a separation shall be provided between a closed ro-ro space and an adjacent open ro-ro space. The separation shall be such as to minimize the passage of dangerous vapours and liquids between such spaces. Alternatively, such separation need not be provided if the ro-ro space is considered to be a closed cargo space over its entire length and fully complies with the relevant special requirements of this regulation.

3.10.2 In ships having ro-ro spaces, a separation shall be provided between a closed ro-ro space and the adjacent weather deck. The separation shall be such as to minimize the passage of dangerous vapours and liquids between such spaces. Alternatively, a separation need not be provided if the arrangements of the closed ro-ro spaces are in accordance with those required for the dangerous goods carried on adjacent weather decks.

---

① Refer to *Unified interpretation of SOLAS chapter Ⅱ-2 on the number and arrangement of portable fire extinguishers on board ships* (MSC.1/Circ.1275 and its Corr.1).

② Refer to *Recommendation on fixed fire-extinguishing systems for special category spaces* (resolution A.123(V)).

3.7　手提式灭火器①

货物处所应配备总容量至少为 12 kg 干粉或与其等效的手提式灭火器。这些灭火器应附加于本章其他部分所要求的手提式灭火器。

3.8　机器处所限界面的隔热

构成货物处所和 A 类机器处所限界面的舱壁应隔热至“A-60”级标准,但危险货物的堆放处与这些舱壁的水平距离至少为 3 m 者除外。此类处所之间的其他限界面应隔热至“A-60”级标准。

3.9　水雾系统

每一个在上方有甲板的开式滚装处所和每一个被视作闭式滚装处所但不能密封的处所,应装设经认可的手动操作的固定式压力水雾系统。该水雾系统应保护该处所内的任何甲板和车辆平台的所有部位,但主管机关可以允许在该处所使用已经过实尺度试验证明其效能不低于固定式压力水雾系统的任何其他固定式灭火系统。但是,排水和抽水装置应能防止形成自由液面。排水系统的尺度所达到的排量应不低于水雾系统泵和所要求数量的消防水枪的组合容量的 125%。排水系统的阀门应能从所保护位置的外部靠近灭火系统控制装置的位置进行操作。舱底污水井应具有足够的容量,并应布置在船侧,其在每一水密舱内相互间的距离不得超过 40 m。如果不可能做到,则主管机关在批准稳性资料时,应在其认为必要的范围内考虑到增加的水重量和自由液面对船舶稳性的不利影响。②

3.10　滚装处所的分隔

3.10.1　在设有滚装处所的船上,应在闭式滚装处所和相邻的开式滚装处所之间加以分隔。该分隔应使这些处所之间危险蒸气和液体的通路减至最小。如果滚装处所在其整个长度上视为一个封闭的货物处所并完全符合本条的有关特殊要求,则不必进行此种分隔。

3.10.2　在设有滚装处所的船上,应在闭式滚装处所和相邻的露天甲板之间加以分隔。该分隔应使这些处所之间危险蒸气和液体的通路减至最小。如果闭式滚装处所的布置与对邻近的露天甲板载运危险货物所要求的布置相符,则不必进行分隔。

---

① 参见《SOLAS 第Ⅱ-2 章船上手提式灭火器数量和布置的统一解释》(第 MSC.1/Circ.1275 号通函及其 Corr.1)。

② 参见《关于特种处所固定式灭火系统的建议》(第 A.123(Ⅴ)号决议)。

Table 19.1 Application of the requirements to different modes of carriage of dangerous goods in ships and cargo spaces

Where × appears in table 19.1, it means this requirement is applicable to all classes of dangerous goods as given in the appropriate line of table 19.3, except as indicated by the notes.

Regulation 19.2.2 / Regulation 19	Weather decks (.1 to .5 inclusive)	.1 Not specifically designed	.2 Closed ro-ro spaces	.3		.4 Solid dangerous goods in bulk	.5 Shipborne barges
				Closed ro-ro spaces[5]	Open ro-ro spaces		
.3.1.1	×	×	×	×	×	For application of requirements of regulation 19 to different classes of dangerous goods, see table 19.2	×
.3.1.2	×	×	×	×	×		–
.3.1.3	–	×	×	×	×		×
.3.1.4	–	×	×	×	×		×
.3.2	–	×	×	×	×		×[4]
.3.3	–	×	×	×	–		×[4]
.3.4.1	–	×	×[1]	×	–		×[4]
.3.4.2	–	×	×[1]	×	–		×[4]
.3.5	–	×	×	×	–		–
.3.6.1	×	×	×	×	×		–
.3.6.2	×	×	×	×	×		–
.3.7	×	×	–	–	×		–
.3.8	×	×	×[2]	×	×		–
.3.9	–	–	–	×[3]	×		–
.3.10.1	–	–	–	×	–		–
.3.10.2	–	–	–	×	–		–

Notes:

1 For classes 4 and 5.1 solids not applicable to closed freight containers. For classes 2, 3, 6.1 and 8 when carried in closed freight containers, the ventilation rate may be reduced to not less than two air changes per hour. For classes 4 and 5.1 liquids when carried in closed freight containers, the ventilation rate may be reduced to not less than two air changes per hour. For the purpose of this requirement, a portable tank is a closed freight container.

2 Applicable to decks only.

3 Applies only to closed ro-ro spaces, not capable of being sealed.

4 In the special case where the barges are capable of containing flammable vapours or alternatively if they are capable of discharging flammable vapours to a safe space outside the barge carrier compartment by means of ventilation ducts connected to the barges, these requirements may be reduced or waived to the satisfaction of the Administration.

5 Special category spaces shall be treated as closed ro-ro spaces when dangerous goods are carried.

表 19.1　以不同方式载运危险货物的船舶和货物处所的适用要求

表 19.1 中的×表示该要求适用于表 19.3 相应行中所列的所有类别的危险货物，有注释者除外。

第 19.2.2 条 / 第 19 条	露天甲板 .1 至.5（含.5）	.1 非特别设计	.2 集装箱货物处所	.3		.4 圆体散装危险货物	.5 船载驳船
				闭式滚装处所[5]	开式滚装处所		
.3.1.1	×	×	×	×	×	对不同类别的危险货物应用第 19 条的要求，见表 19.2	×
.3.1.2	×	×	×	×	×		—
.3.1.3	—	×	×	×	×		×
.3.1.4	—	×	×	×	×		×
.3.2	—	×	×	×	×		×[4]
.3.3	—	×	×	×	—		×[4]
.3.4.1	—	×	×[1]	×	—		×[4]
.3.4.2	—	×	×[1]	×	—		×[4]
.3.5	—	×	×	×	—		—
.3.6.1	×	×	×	×	×		—
.3.6.2	×	×	×	×	×		—
.3.7	×	×	—	—	×		—
.3.8	×	×	×[2]	×	×		—
.3.9	—	—	—	×[3]	×		—
.3.10.1	—	—	—	×	—		—
.3.10.2	—	—	—	×	—		—

注：

1　对于不适用于封闭货运集装箱的第 4 类和第 5.1 类的固体。对于第 2,3,6.1 和 8 类，当装于封闭货运集装箱内时，通风率可减至不少于每小时换气两次。对于第 4 类和第 5.1 类的液体，当装于封闭货运集装箱内时，通风率可减至不少于每小时换气两次。就本要求而言，封闭式可移动罐即为封闭的集装箱。

2　只适用于甲板。

3　只适用于不能密封的闭式滚装处所。

4　在驳船能够容纳易燃蒸气或能够通过与其连接的通风管道将易燃蒸气排向驳船载运舱室之外的安全处所的特殊情况下，可以按主管机关满意的方式降低或放弃这些要求。

5　特种处所在装载危险货物时应视为闭式滚装处所。

Table 19.2 Application of the requirements to different classes of dangerous goods for ships and cargo spaces carrying solid dangerous goods in bulk

Regulation 19 \ Class	4.1	4.2	4.3[6]	5.1	6.1	8	9
.3.1.1	×	×	–	×	–	–	×
.3.1.2	×	×	–	×	–	–	×
.3.2	×	×[7]	×	×[8]	–	–	×[8]
.3.4.1	–	×[7]	×	–	–	–	–
.3.4.2	×[9]	×[7]	×	×[7, 9]	–	–	×[7, 9]
.3.4.3	×	×	×	×	×	×	×
.3.6	×	×	×	×	×	×	×
.3.8	×	×	×	×[7]	–	–	×[10]

Notes:

6 The hazards of substances in this class which may be carried in bulk are such that special consideration shall be given by the Administration to the construction and equipment of the ship involved in addition to meeting the requirements enumerated in this table.

7 Only applicable to Seedcake containing solvent extractions, to Ammonium nitrate and to Ammonium nitrate fertilizers.

8 Only applicable to Ammonium nitrate and to Ammonium nitrate fertilizers. However, a degree of protection in accordance with standards contained in the International Electrotechnical Commission publication IEC 60079, *Electrical apparatus for explosive gas atmospheres*, is sufficient.

9 Only suitable wire mesh guards are required.

10 The requirements of the IMSBC Code, as amended, are sufficient.

表 19.2 载运不同类别危险货物的散装运输固体危险货物船舶和货物处所的适用要求

第19条 / 类别	4.1	4.2	4.3[6]	5.1	6.1	8	9
.3.1.1	×	×	—	×	—	—	×
.3.1.2	×	×	—	×	—	—	×
.3.2	×	×[7]	×	×[8]	—	—	×[8]
.3.4.1	—	×[7]	×	—	—	—	—
.3.4.2	×[9]	×[7]	×	×[7，9]	—	—	×[7，9]
.3.4.3	×	×	×	×	×	×	×
.3.6	×	×	×	×	×	×	×
.3.8	×	×	×	×[7]	—	—	×[10]

注：

6 鉴于此类可散装运输物质的危害性，有关船舶除应满足本表所列要求外，主管机关还应对其构造和设备给予特殊考虑。

7 只适用于含有溶剂萃取物的种子饼、硝酸铵和硝酸铵化肥。

8 只适用于硝酸铵和硝酸铵化肥。但是，保护程度符合国际电工委员会 IEC 60079 出版物《爆炸性气体环境内的电气设备》所含标准即可。

9 只要求有适合的防火网保护。

10 满足经修正的《国际海运固体散装货物安全操作规则》的要求即可。

Table 19.3 Application of the requirements to different classes of dangerous goods except solid dangerous goods in bulk

Regulation 19 \ Class	1.1 to 1.6	1.4S	2.1	2.2	2.3 flamm-able[20]	2.3 non-flammable	3 FP15 <23 ℃	3 FP[15] ≥23 ℃ to ≤60 ℃	4.1	4.2	4.3 liquids[21]	4.3 solids	5.1	5.2[16]	6.1 liquids FP[15] <23 ℃	6.1 liquids FP[15] ≥23 ℃ to ≤60 ℃	6.1 liquids	6.1 solids	8 liquids FP[15] <23 ℃	8 liquids FP[15] ≥23 ℃ to ≤60 ℃	8 liquids	8 solids	9
.3.1.1	×	×	×	×	×	×	×	×	×	×	×	×	×	×	×	×	×	×	×	×	×	×	×
.3.1.2	×	×	×	×	×	×	×	×	×	×	×	×	×	×	×	×	×	×	×	×	×	×	–
.3.1.3	×	–	–	–	–	–	–	–	–	–	–	–	–	–	–	–	–	–	–	–	–	–	–
.3.1.4	×	–	–	–	–	–	–	–	–	–	–	–	–	–	–	–	–	–	–	–	–	–	–
.3.2	×	–	×	–	×	–	×	–	–	×[18]	×[18]	–	–	–	×	–	–	–	×	–	–	–	×[17]
.3.3	×	×	×	×	–	×	×	×	×	×	×	×	×	–	×	×	×	×	×	×	×	×	–
.3.4.1	–	–	×	–	–	×	×	–	×[11]	×	×	×	×[11]	–	×	×	–	×[11]	×	×	–	–	×[11]
.3.4.2	–	–	×	–	–	–	×	–	–	–	–	–	–	–	×	–	–	–	×	–	–	–	×[17]
.3.5	–	–	–	–	–	–	×	–	–	–	–	–	–	–	×	×	×	–	×	×[19]	×[19]	–	–
.3.6	–	–	×	×	×	×	×	×	×	×	×	×	×	×	×	×	×	×	×	×	×	×	×[14]
.3.7	–	–	–	–	–	–	×	×	×	×	×	×	×	–	×	×	–	–	×	×	–	–	–
.3.8	×[12]	–	×	×	×	×	×	×	×	×	×	×	×[13]	×	×	×	–	–	×	×	–	–	–
.3.9	×	×	×	×	×	×	×	×	×	×	×	×	×	×	×	×	×	×	×	×	×	×	×
.3.10.1	×	×	×	×	×	×	×	×	×	×	×	×	×	×	×	×	×	×	×	×	×	×	×
.3.10.2	×	×	×	×	×	×	×	×	×	×	×	×	×	×	×	×	×	×	×	×	×	×	×

Notes:

11 When "mechanically-ventilated spaces" are required by the IMDG Code, as amended.
12 Stow 3 m horizontally away from the machinery space boundaries in all cases.
13 Refer to the IMDG Code.
14 As appropriate to the goods to be carried.
15 FP means flashpoint.
16 Under the provisions of the IMDG Code, stowage of class 5.2 dangerous goods under deck or in enclosed ro-ro spaces is prohibited.
17 Only applicable to dangerous goods evolving flammable vapour listed in the IMDG Code.
18 Only applicable to dangerous goods having a flashpoint less than 23 ℃ listed in the IMDG Code.
19 Only applicable to dangerous goods having a subsidiary risk class 6.1.
20 Under the provisions of the IMDG Code, stowage of class 2.3 having subsidiary risk class 2.1 under deck or in enclosed ro-ro spaces is prohibited.
21 Under the provisions of the IMDG Code, stowage of class 4.3 liquids having a flashpoint less than 23 ℃ under deck or in enclosed ro-ro spaces is prohibited.

表 19.3　除固体散装危险货物外其他不同类别危险货物的适用要求

第19条 \ 类别	1.1至1.6	1.4S	2.1	2.2	2.3 易燃[20]	2.3 不可燃	3 闪点[15] <23 ℃	3 闪点[15] ≥23 ℃ 至≤60 ℃	4.1	4.2	4.3 液体[21]	4.3 固体	5.1	5.2[16]	6.1 liquids FP[15] <23 ℃	6.1 液体闪点[15] ≥23 ℃ 至 ≤60 ℃	6.1 液体	6.1 固体	8 液体 闪点[15] <23 ℃	8 液体闪点[15] ≥23 ℃ 至 ≤60 ℃	8 液体	8 固体	9
.3.1.1	×	×	×	×	×	×	×	×	×	×	×	×	×	×	×	×	×	×	×	×	×	×	×
.3.1.2	×	×	×	×	×	×	×	×	×	×	×	×	×	×	×	×	×	×	×	×	×	×	—
.3.1.3	×	—	—	—	—	—	—	—	—	—	—	—	—	—	—	—	—	—	—	—	—	—	—
.3.1.4	×	—	—	—	—	—	—	—	—	—	—	—	—	—	—	—	—	—	—	—	—	—	—
.3.2	×	—	×	—	×	—	×	—	—	×[18]	×[18]	—	—	—	×	—	—	—	×	—	—	—	×[17]
.3.3	×	×	×	×	—	×	×	×	×	×	×	×	×	—	×	×	×	×	×	×	×	×	—
.3.4.1	—	—	×	—	—	×	×	—	×[11]	×	×	×	×[11]	—	×	×	—	×[11]	×	×	—	—	×[11]
.3.4.2	—	—	×	—	—	—	×	—	—	—	—	—	—	—	×	—	—	—	×	—	—	—	×[17]
.3.5	—	—	—	—	—	—	×	—	—	—	—	—	—	—	×	×	×	—	×	×[19]	×[19]	—	—
.3.6	—	—	×	×	×	×	×	×	×	×	×	×	×	×	×	×	×	×	×	×	×	×	×[14]
.3.7	—	—	—	—	—	—	×	×	×	×	×	×	×	—	×	×	—	—	×	×	—	—	—
.3.8	×[12]	—	×	×	×	×	×	×	×	×	×	×	×[13]	×	×	×	—	—	×	×	—	—	—
.3.9	×	×	×	×	×	×	×	×	×	×	×	×	×	×	×	×	×	×	×	×	×	×	×
.3.10.1	×	×	×	×	×	×	×	×	×	×	×	×	×	×	×	×	×	×	×	×	×	×	×
.3.10.2	×	×	×	×	×	×	×	×	×	×	×	×	×	×	×	×	×	×	×	×	×	×	×

注：

11　当经修正的《国际海运危险货物规则》要求"机械通风处所"时。

12　在所有情况下，货物堆装处与机器处所限界面的水平距离应至少为 3 m。

13　参见经修正的《国际海运危险货物规则》。

14　视所载运的货物而定。

15　指闪点。

16　根据经修正的《国际海运危险货物规则》的规定，禁止在甲板下或在闭式滚装处所内堆装 5.2 类危险货物。

17　仅适用于 IMDG 规则列出的释放易燃蒸气的危险货物。

18　仅适用于 IMDG 规则列出的闪点低于 23 ℃的危险货物。

19　仅适用于具有 6.1 类次风险的危险货物。

20　根据 IMDG 规则的规定，禁止在甲板下或在闭式滚装处所内堆装具有 2.1 类次风险的 2.3 类危险货物。

21　根据 IMDG 规则的规定，禁止在甲板下或在闭式滚装处所内堆装闪点低于 23 ℃的 4.3 类液体。

4 Document of compliance[①]

The Administration shall provide the ship with an appropriate document as evidence of compliance of construction and equipment with the requirements of this regulation. Certification for dangerous goods, except solid dangerous goods in bulk, is not required for those cargoes specified as class 6.2 and 7 and dangerous goods in limited quantities and excepted quantities.

Regulation 20
Protection of vehicle, special category and ro-ro spaces

1 Purpose

The purpose of this regulation is to provide additional safety measures in order to address the fire safety objectives of this chapter for ships fitted with vehicle, special category and ro-ro spaces. For this purpose, the following functional requirements shall be met:

.1 fire protection systems shall be provided to adequately protect the ship from the fire hazards associated with vehicle, special category and ro-ro spaces;

.2 ignition sources shall be separated from vehicle, special category and ro-ro spaces; and

.3 vehicle, special category and ro-ro spaces shall be adequately ventilated.

2 General requirements

2.1 Application

2.1.1 In addition to complying with the requirements of regulations in parts B, C, D and E, as appropriate, vehicle, special category and ro-ro spaces shall comply with the requirements of this regulation.

2.1.2 On all ships, vehicles with fuel in their tanks for their own propulsion may be carried in cargo spaces other than vehicle, special category or ro-ro spaces, provided that all the following conditions are met:

.1 the vehicles do not use their own propulsion within the cargo spaces;

.2 the cargo spaces are in compliance with the appropriate requirements of regulation 19; and

.3 the vehicles are carried in accordance with the IMDG Code, as defined in regulation Ⅶ/1.1.

---

① Refer to *Document of compliance with the special requirements for ships carrying dangerous goods under the provisions of regulation Ⅱ-2/19 of the 1974 SOLAS Convention, as amended, and paragraph 7.17 of the 2000 HSC Code, as amended* (MSC.1/Circ.1266).

4　符合证明[①]

主管机关应向船舶提供一份适当的证明,作为其构造和设备符合本条要求的证据。除固体散装危险货物外,对于被确定为第 6.2 和 7 类的货物和数量有限及免除数量的危险货物,不要求危险货物证书。

第 20 条
车辆处所、特种处所和滚装处所的保护

1　目的

本条的目的是为设有车辆处所、特种处所和滚装处所的船舶规定附加的安全措施,以达到本章的消防安全目标。为此,应满足下列功能要求:

.1　应配备能充分保护船舶免受与车辆处所、特种处所和滚装处所有关的火灾危险的防火系统;

.2　着火源应与车辆处所、特种处所和滚装处所隔开;和

.3　车辆处所、特种处所和滚装处所应充分通风。

2　一般要求

2.1　适用范围

2.1.1　除符合本章 B、C、D 和 E 部分各条的相应要求外,车辆处所、特种处所和滚装处所还应符合本条的要求。

2.1.2　只要满足以下全部条件,在所有船舶上,除车辆处所、特种处所或滚装处所以外的货物处所可载运油箱内备有自用燃料的机动车辆:

.1　车辆在货物处所内不使用其自身驱动;

.2　货物处所符合第 19 条的相应要求;和

.3　车辆按照第 Ⅶ/1.1 条定义的《国际危规》载运。

---

① 参见《按经修正的 1974 年 SOLAS 公约第Ⅱ-2/19 条和经修正的 2000 年 HSC 规则 7.17 款的规定对载运危险货物船舶特殊要求的符合证明》(第 MSC.1/Circ.1266 号通函)。

2.2 Basic principles for passenger ships

2.2.1 The basic principle underlying the provisions of this regulation is that the main vertical zoning required by regulation 9.2 may not be practicable in vehicle spaces of passenger ships and, therefore, equivalent protection must be obtained in such spaces on the basis of a horizontal zone concept and by the provision of an efficient fixed fire-extinguishing system. Based on this concept, a horizontal zone for the purpose of this regulation may include special category spaces on more than one deck provided that the total overall clear height for vehicles does not exceed 10 m.

2.2.2 The basic principle underlying the provisions of paragraph 2.2.1 is also applicable to ro-ro spaces.

2.2.3 The requirements of ventilation systems, openings in "A" class divisions and penetrations in "A" class divisions for maintaining the integrity of vertical zones in this chapter shall be applied equally to decks and bulkheads forming the boundaries separating horizontal zones from each other and from the remainder of the ship.

3 Precaution against ignition of flammable vapours in closed vehicle spaces, closed ro-ro spaces and special category spaces

3.1 Ventilation systems[①]

3.1.1 Capacity of ventilation systems

There shall be provided an effective power ventilation system sufficient to give at least the following air changes:

.1 Passenger ships:

Special category spaces	10 air changes per hour
Closed ro-ro and vehicle spaces other than special category spaces for ships carrying more than 36 passengers	10 air changes per hour
Closed ro-ro and vehicle spaces other than special category spaces for ships carrying not more than 36 passengers	6 air changes per hour

.2 Cargo ships: 6 air changes per hour

The Administration may require an increased number of air changes when vehicles are being loaded and unloaded.

3.1.2 Performance of ventilation systems

3.1.2.1 In passenger ships, the power ventilation system shall be separate from other ventilation systems. The power ventilation system shall be operated to give at least the number of air changes required in paragraph 3.1.1 at all times when vehicles are in such spaces, except where an air quality control system in accordance with paragraph 3.1.2.4 is provided. Ventilation ducts serving such cargo spaces capable of being effectively sealed shall be separated for each such space. The system shall be capable of being controlled from a position outside such spaces.

---

① Refer to *Design guidelines and operational recommendations for ventilation systems in ro-ro cargo spaces* (MSC/Circ.729).

2.2 对客船的基本原则

2.2.1 本条各项规定的基本原则是，在客船的车辆处所内，第9.2条所要求的主竖区划分可能不切实际，因而在此类处所必须基于水平区的概念通过配备有效的固定式灭火系统获得等效的保护。根据这一概念，就本条而言，只要用于停放车辆的总净高不超过10 m，则一个水平区可以包括多于一层甲板的若干特种处所。

2.2.2 本条2.2.1中各项规定的基本原则也适用于滚装处所。

2.2.3 本章中为保持主竖区完整性而对通风系统、“A”级分隔上的开口和“A”级分隔上的贯穿件提出的要求，应同样适用于构成分隔水平区之间及水平区与船舶其他部分限界面的甲板和舱壁。

3 闭式车辆处所、闭式滚装处所和特种处所内易燃蒸气引燃的预防措施

3.1 通风系统[①]

3.1.1 通风系统的能力

应设有效的动力通风系统，其足以提供至少以下换气次数：

.1 客船：

特种处所	每小时换气10次
载客超过36人的客船上除特种处所以外的闭式滚装处所和车辆处所	每小时换气10次
载客不超过36人的客船上除特种处所以外的闭式滚装处所和车辆处所	每小时换气6次

.2 货船：　每小时换气6次

主管机关可要求在装载或卸载车辆时增加换气次数。

3.1.2 通风系统的性能

3.1.2.1 对于客船，动力通风系统须与其他通风系统分开，并且当车辆处于这类处所时，通风系统须一直工作以提供至少本条第3.1.1款要求的换气次数，但按照本条第3.1.2.4款设有空气质量控制系统者除外。服务于此类货物处所的能有效封闭的通风导管须与每一此类处所分开。该系统须能从此类处所以外的位置进行控制。

① 参见《滚装货物处所通风系统设计指南和操作建议》（第MSC/Circ.729号通函）。

3.1.2.2 In cargo ships, the ventilation fans shall normally be run continuously and give at least the number of air changes required in paragraph 3.1.1 whenever vehicles are on board, except where an air quality control system in accordance with paragraph 3.1.2.4 is provided. Where this is impracticable, they shall be operated for a limited period daily as weather permits and in any case for a reasonable period prior to discharge, after which period the ro-ro or vehicle space shall be proved gas free. One or more portable combustible gas detecting instruments shall be carried for this purpose. The system shall be entirely separate from other ventilation systems. Ventilation ducts serving ro-ro or vehicle spaces shall be capable of being effectively sealed for each cargo space. The system shall be capable of being controlled from a position outside such spaces.

3.1.2.3 The ventilation system shall be such as to prevent air stratification and the formation of air pockets.

3.1.2.4 For all ships, where an air quality control system is provided based on the guidelines developed by the Organization,① the ventilation system may be operated at a decreased number of air changes and/or a decreased amount of ventilation. This relaxation does not apply to spaces to which at least 10 air changes per hour is required by paragraph 3.2.2 of this regulation and spaces subject to regulations 19.3.4.1 and 20-1.

3.1.3 Indication of ventilation systems

Means shall be provided on the navigation bridge to indicate any loss of the required ventilating capacity.

3.1.4 Closing appliances and ducts

3.1.4.1 Arrangements shall be provided to permit a rapid shutdown and effective closure of the ventilation system from outside of the space in case of fire, taking into account the weather and sea conditions.

3.1.4.2 Ventilation ducts, including dampers, within a common horizontal zone shall be made of steel. In passenger ships, ventilation ducts that pass through other horizontal zones or machinery spaces shall be "A-60" class steel ducts constructed in accordance with regulations 9.7.2.4.1.1 and 9.7.2.4.1.2.

3.1.5 Permanent openings

Permanent openings in the side plating, the ends or deckhead of the space shall be so situated that a fire in the cargo space does not endanger stowage areas and embarkation stations for survival craft and accommodation spaces, service spaces and control stations in superstructures and deckhouses above the cargo spaces.

3.2 Electrical equipment and wiring

3.2.1 Except as provided in paragraph 3.2.2, electrical equipment and wiring shall be of a type suitable for use in an explosive petrol and air mixture.②

---

① Refer to the *Revised design guidelines and operational recommendations for ventilation systems in ro-ro cargo spaces* (MSC/Circ. 1515).

② Refer to the recommendations of the International Electrotechnical Commission, in particular publication IEC 60079, *Electrical apparatus for explosive gas atmospheres*.

3.1.2.2 对于货船,当船上有车辆时,风机通常须连续运转并提供至少本条第 3.1.1 款所要求的换气次数,但按照本条第 3.1.2.4 款设有空气质量控制系统者除外。如这样做不可行,在天气允许的情况下,风机须每天在限定的时间内运转且无论如何应在卸货前一段合理的时间内开始运转,经过这段时间的运转后,须证明滚装处所或车辆处所已经除气。为此,须配备 1 套或 1 套以上便携式可燃气体探测仪。该系统须与其他通风系统完全分开。对每一货物处所,服务于滚装或车辆处所的通风导管须可以有效封闭。该系统须能从此类处所以外的位置进行控制。

3.1.2.3 通风系统须能防止空气分层及形成气囊。

3.1.2.4 对于所有船舶,如根据本组织制定的导则①设有空气质量控制系统,通风系统工作时可减少换气次数和/或通风量。此种放宽要求不适用于本条第 3.2.2 款要求每小时至少换气 10 次的处所以及第 19.3.4.1 条和第 20-1 条所述处所。

3.1.3 通风系统的显示

驾驶台应设有显示所要求的通风能力任何损失的装置。

3.1.4 关闭装置和导管

3.1.4.1 应结合气候情况和海况,设有在发生火灾时可从处所外部快速关闭和有效封闭通风系统的装置。

3.1.4.2 包括挡火闸在内的、设在共同水平区内的通风导管应为钢质。在客船上,通过其他水平区或机器处所的通风导管应为根据第 9.7.2.4.1.1 条和 9.7.2.4.1.2 条建造的“A-60”级钢质导管。

3.1.5 永久性开口

处所侧板、端部和天花板上的永久性开口的位置应使货物处所内的火灾不会威胁到救生艇筏的存放区和登乘站以及货物处所上部的上层建筑和甲板室中的起居处所、服务处所和控制站。

3.2 电气设备和电线

3.2.1 除本条 3.2.2 中规定者外,电气设备和电线应为适于在易爆炸性汽油和空气混合物中使用的型式。②

---

① 参见《经修订的滚装货物处所通风系统设计指南和操作建议》(第 MSC/Circ.1515 号通函)。
② 参见国际电工委员会的建议,特别是 IEC 60079 出版物《爆炸性气体环境内的电气设备》。

3.2.2 In case of other than special category spaces below the bulkhead deck, notwithstanding the provisions in paragraph 3.2.1, above a height of 450 mm from the deck and from each platform for vehicles, if fitted, except platforms with openings of sufficient size permitting penetration of petrol gases downwards, electrical equipment of a type so enclosed and protected as to prevent the escape of sparks shall be permitted as an alternative, on condition that the ventilation system is so designed and operated as to provide continuous ventilation of the cargo spaces at the rate of at least ten air changes per hour whenever vehicles are on board.

3.3 Electrical equipment and wiring in exhaust ventilation ducts

Electrical equipment and wiring, if installed in an exhaust ventilation duct, shall be of a type approved for use in explosive petrol and air mixtures and the outlet from any exhaust duct shall be sited in a safe position, having regard to other possible sources of ignition.

3.4 Other ignition sources

Other equipment which may constitute a source of ignition of flammable vapours shall not be permitted.

3.5 Scuppers and discharges

Scuppers shall not be led to machinery or other spaces where sources of ignition may be present.

4 Detection and alarm

4.1 Fixed fire detection and fire alarm systems

Except as provided in paragraph 4.3.1, there shall be provided a fixed fire detection and fire alarm system complying with the requirements of the Fire Safety Systems Code. The fixed fire detection system shall be capable of rapidly detecting the onset of fire. The type of detectors and their spacing and location shall be to the satisfaction of the Administration, taking into account the effects of ventilation and other relevant factors. After being installed, the system shall be tested under normal ventilation conditions and shall give an overall response time to the satisfaction of the Administration.

4.2 Sample extraction smoke detection systems

Except open ro-ro spaces, open vehicle spaces and special category spaces, a sample extraction smoke detection system complying with the requirements of the Fire Safety Systems Code may be used as an alternative for the fixed fire detection and fire alarm system required in paragraph 4.1.

4.3 Special category spaces

4.3.1 An efficient fire patrol system shall be maintained in special category spaces. If an efficient fire patrol system is maintained by a continuous fire watch at all times during the voyage, a fixed fire detection and fire alarm system is not required.

4.3.2 Manually operated call points shall be spaced so that no part of the space is more than 20 m from a manually operated call point, and one shall be placed close to each exit from such spaces.

3.2.2 对于除舱壁甲板以下特种处所以外的处所，尽管有本条3.2.1的规定，在甲板和每层车辆平台（若设有）以上高于450 mm处，应允许装设加以封闭并受到保护以防止火星外漏的电气设备作为一种替代方式，但开口尺寸足以使汽油气体向下渗透的平台除外。采取上述替代方式的条件是在船上有车辆时，通风系统的设计和运转能够以每小时至少换气10次的速率对货物处所提供持续通风。

3.3 排气通风导管内的电气设备和电线

如果在排气通风导管内装有电气设备和电线，这些电气设备和电线应为经认可能在易爆炸性汽油和空气混合物中使用的型式，并且任何排气导管的出口，考虑到其他可能的着火源，应位于一个安全的位置。

3.4 其他着火源

不允许使用可能构成易燃气体着火源的其他设备。

3.5 泄水孔和排水孔

泄水孔不得通向机器处所或其他可能存在着火源的处所。

4 探测和报警

4.1 固定式探火和失火报警系统

除本条4.3.1规定者外，应设有符合《消防安全系统规则》要求的一个有效的固定式探火和失火报警系统。该固定式探火系统应能迅速探知火灾的出现。探测器的型式及其间距和位置应使主管机关在考虑到通风和其他相关因素影响后满意。该系统在安装后，应在正常的通风条件下进行测试，且其总体响应时间应使主管机关满意。

4.2 烟雾探火系统

除开式滚装处所、开式车辆处所和特种处所外，作为本条4.1所要求的固定式探火和失火报警系统的一种替代，可使用符合《消防安全系统规则》要求的烟雾探火系统。

4.3 特种处所

4.3.1 在特种处所内应保持有效的消防巡逻制度。如果在整个航行期间能够保证通过连续的消防值班保持有效的消防巡逻，则不要求配备固定式探火和失火报警系统。

4.3.2 手动报警按钮的间距应使处所内的任一部分到手动报警按钮的距离都不超过20 m，且在靠近此类处所的每个出口处应布置1个手动报警按钮。

5 Structural fire protection

Notwithstanding the provisions of regulation 9.2.2, in passenger ships carrying more than 36 passengers, the boundary bulkheads and decks of special category spaces and ro-ro spaces shall be insulated to "A-60" class standard. However, where a category (5), (9) or (10) space, as defined in regulation 9.2.2.3, is on one side of the division, the standard may be reduced to "A-0". Where fuel oil tanks are below a special category space or a ro-ro space, the integrity of the deck between such spaces may be reduced to "A-0" standard.

6 Fire extinction

6.1 Fixed fire、lextinguishing systems

(The requirements of paragraphs 6.1.1 and 6.1.2 shall apply to ships constructed on or after 1 July 2014. Ships constructed before 1 July 2014 shall comply with the previously applicable requirements of paragraphs 6.1.1 and 6.1.2)

6.1.1 Vehicle spaces and ro-ro spaces, which are not special category spaces and are capable of being sealed from a location outside of the cargo spaces, shall be fitted with one of the following fixed fire-extinguishing systems:

.1 a fixed gas fire-extinguishing system complying with the provisions of the Fire Safety Systems Code;

.2 a fixed high-expansion foam fire-extinguishing system complying with the provisions of the Fire Safety Systems Code; or

.3 a fixed water-based fire-fighting system for ro-ro spaces and special category spaces complying with the provisions of the Fire Safety Systems Code and paragraphs 6.1.2.1 to 6.1.2.4.

6.1.2 Vehicle spaces and ro-ro spaces not capable of being sealed and special category spaces shall be fitted with a fixed water-based fire-fighting system for ro-ro spaces and special category spaces complying with the provisions of the Fire Safety Systems Code which shall protect all parts of any deck and vehicle platform in such spaces. Such a water-based fire-fighting system shall have:

.1 a pressure gauge on the valve manifold;

.2 clear marking on each manifold valve indicating the spaces served;

.3 instructions for maintenance and operation located in the valve room; and

.4 a sufficient number of drainage valves to ensure complete drainage of the system.

6.1.3 The Administration may permit the use of any other fixed fire-extinguishing system① that has been shown, by a full-scale test in conditions simulating a flowing petrol fire in a vehicle space or a ro-ro space, to be not less effective in controlling fires likely to occur in such a space.

---

① Refer to *Guidelines for the approval of fixed water-based fire-fighting systems for ro-ro spaces and special category spaces equivalent to that referred to in resolution* A.123(Ⅴ) (MSC.1/Circ.1272) and *Revised Guidelines for the design and approval of fixed water-based fire-fighting systems for ro-ro spaces and special category spaces* (MSC.1/Circ.1430).

5　结构防火

尽管有本章第 9.2.2 条的规定，对于载客超过 36 人的客船，特种处所和滚装处所的限界面舱壁和甲板应隔热至“A-60”级标准。但是，如果本章第 9.2.2.3 条所定义的第(5)类、第(9)类或第(10)类处所位于分隔的一侧，该标准可降为“A-0”级。如果燃油舱位于特种处所或滚装处所以下，此类处所之间的甲板完整性可降为“A-0”级标准。

6　灭火

6.1　固定式灭火系统

(第 6.1.1 和 6.1.2 款的要求须适用于 2014 年 7 月 1 日或以后建造的船舶。2014 年 7 月 1 日以前建造的船舶须符合第 6.1.1 和 6.1.2 款的原有适用要求。)

6.1.1　不是特种处所且能从货物处所外部某一位置加以密封的车辆处所和滚装处所，须装设下列之一的固定式灭火系统：

.1　符合《消防安全系统规则》规定的固定式气体灭火系统；

.2　符合《消防安全系统规则》规定的固定式高倍泡沫灭火系统；或

.3　符合《消防安全系统规则》和第 6.1.2.1 至 6.1.2.4 款规定的滚装处所和特种处所固定式水基灭火系统。

6.1.2　不能加以密封的车辆处所和滚装处所以及特种处所须装有符合《消防安全系统规则》规定的滚装处所和特种处所固定式水基灭火系统，该系统须保护此类处所的任何甲板和车辆平台的所有部分。该水基灭火系统须：

.1　在阀门总管上有 1 个压力表；

.2　在每一总管阀门上清楚标出其所服务的处所；

.3　在阀门间内有维护保养和操作说明；和

.4　有足够数量的排水阀以确保系统完全排空。

6.1.3　主管机关可允许使用经过实尺度试验已表明对控制车辆处所或滚装处所可能发生的火灾同样有效的任何其他固定式灭火系统①，该试验应在模拟此类处所内流动的汽油火灾条件下进行。

① 参见《等效于 A.123(V)决议要求的用于滚装处所和特种处所的固定式水基灭火系统认可指南》(第 MSC.1/Circ.1272 号通函)和《经修订的滚装处所和特种处所固定式水基灭火系统设计和认可指南》(第 MSC.1/Circ.1430 号通函)。

6.1.4 The requirement of this paragraph shall apply to ships constructed on or after 1 January 2010. Ships constructed on or after 1 July 2002 and before 1 January 2010 shall comply with the previously applicable requirements of paragraph 6.1.4, as amended by resolution MSC.99(73). When fixed pressure water-spraying systems are fitted, in view of the serious loss of stability which could arise due to large quantities of water accumulating on the deck or decks during the operation of the fixed pressure water-spraying system, the following arrangements shall be provided:

.1 in passenger ships:

.1.1 in the spaces above the bulkhead deck, scuppers shall be fitted so as to ensure that such water is rapidly discharged directly overboard, taking into account the guidelines developed by the Organization;[①]

.1.2.1 in ro-ro passenger ships, discharge valves for scuppers, fitted with positive means of closing operable from a position above the bulkhead deck in accordance with the requirements of the International Convention on Load Lines in force, shall be kept open while the ships are at sea;

.1.2.2 any operation of valves referred to in paragraph 6.1.4.1.2.1 shall be recorded in the log-book;

.1.3 in the spaces below the bulkhead deck, the Administration may require pumping and drainage facilities to be provided additional to the requirements of regulation Ⅱ-1/35-1. In such case, the drainage system shall be sized to remove no less than 125% of the combined capacity of both the water-spraying system pumps and the required number of fire hose nozzles, taking into account the guidelines developed by the Organization[①]. The drainage system valves shall be operable from outside the protected space at a position in the vicinity of the extinguishing system controls. Bilge wells shall be of sufficient holding capacity and shall be arranged at the side shell of the ship at a distance from each other of not more than 40 m in each watertight compartment;

.2 in cargo ships, the drainage and pumping arrangements shall be such as to prevent the build-up of free surfaces. In such case, the drainage system shall be sized to remove no less than 125% of the combined capacity of both the water-spraying system pumps and the required number of fire hose nozzles, taking into account the guidelines developed by the Organization[①]. The drainage system valves shall be operable from outside the protected space at a position in the vicinity of the extinguishing system controls. Bilge wells shall be of sufficient holding capacity and shall be arranged at the side shell of the ship at a distance from each other of not more than 40 m in each watertight compartment. If this is not possible, the adverse effect upon stability of the added weight and free surface of water shall be taken into account to the extent deemed necessary by the Administration in its approval of the stability information.[②] Such information shall be included in the stability information supplied to the master as required by regulation Ⅱ-1/5-1.

---

① Refer to *Guidelines for the drainage of fire-fighting water from enclosed vehicle and ro-ro spaces and special category spaces of passenger and cargo ships* (MSC.1/Circ.1320).

② Refer to *Recommendation on fixed fire-extinguishing systems for special category spaces* (resolution A.123(Ⅴ)).

6.1.4 本款要求须适用于2010年1月1日及之后建造的船舶。2002年7月1日及之后，2010年1月1日之前建造的船舶须符合以前适用的经第MSC.99(73)号决议修正的第6.1.4款的要求。如果安装了固定式压力水雾灭火系统，鉴于在固定式压力水雾灭火系统工作期间有大量的水积聚在一层或几层甲板上会导致稳性的严重削弱，须做出下列安排：

.1 对于客船：

.1.1 在舱壁甲板以上处所，须设有泄水孔以保证这些水能被迅速地直接排往舷外，同时考虑到本组织制定的导则；①

.1.2.1 在滚装客船上，当船舶在海上航行时泄水孔的阀门须保持在打开状态，该阀门须装有符合现行有效的《国际载重线公约》的能从舱壁甲板以上的位置操作的可靠关闭装置；

.1.2.2 第6.1.4.1.2.1款所述阀门的任何操作均须记录在航海日志中；

.1.3 在舱壁甲板以下处所，主管机关可要求在第Ⅱ-1/35-1条的要求以外另装抽水和排水设施。在这种情况下，排水系统的能力须能够排掉不低于水雾系统泵和所要求数目的消防水枪的组合能力的125%，并考虑到本组织制定的导则①。排水系统的阀门须能够从所保护位置的外部靠近灭火系统控制的位置进行操作。污水井须具有足够的容量，并须布置在船侧，在每一水密舱内彼此间距不得超过40 m；

.2 对于货船，排水和抽水装置须能够防止形成自由液面。在这种情况下，排水系统的能力须能够排掉不低于水雾系统泵和所要求数目的消防水枪的组合能力的125%，并考虑到本组织制定的导则①。排水系统的阀门须能够从所保护位置的外部靠近灭火系统控制的位置进行操作。污水井须具有足够的容量，并须布置在船侧，在每一水密舱内彼此间距不得超过40 m。如果不可能做到，主管机关在认可稳性资料②时须按其认为必要的程度，考虑到水所增加的重量和自由液面对船舶稳性的不利影响。这些信息须包括在第Ⅱ-1/5-1条所要求的向船长提供的稳性资料中。

---

① 参见《客船和货船封闭式车辆和滚装处所以及特种处所的消防水排水系统导则》(第MSC.1/Circ.1320号通函)。

② 参见《关于特种处所固定式灭火系统的建议》(第A.123(Ⅴ)号决议)。

6.1.5 On all ships, for closed vehicles and ro-ro spaces and special category spaces, where fixed pressure water-spraying systems are fitted, means shall be provided to prevent the blockage of drainage arrangements, taking into account the guidelines developed by the Organization.① Ships constructed before 1 January 2010 shall comply with the requirements of this paragraph by the first survey after 1 January 2010.

6.2 Portable fire extinguishers

6.2.1 Portable fire extinguishers shall be provided at each deck level in each hold or compartment where vehicles are carried, spaced not more than 20 m apart on both sides of the space. At least one portable fire extinguisher shall be located at each access to such a cargo space.①

6.2.2 In addition to the provision of paragraph 6.2.1, the following fire-extinguishing appliances shall be provided in vehicle, ro-ro and special category spaces intended for the carriage of motor vehicles with fuel in their tanks for their own propulsion:

.1 at least three water-fog applicators; and

.2 one portable foam applicator unit complying with the provisions of the Fire Safety Systems Code, provided that at least two such units are available in the ship for use in such spaces.

Regulation 20-1
Requirements for vehicle carriers carrying motor vehicles with compressed hydrogen or natural gas in their tanks for their own propulsion as cargo

1 Purpose

The purpose of this regulation is to provide additional safety measures in order to address the fire safety objectives of this chapter for vehicle carriers with vehicle and ro-ro spaces intended for carriage of motor vehicles with compressed hydrogen or compressed natural gas in their tanks for their own propulsion as cargo.

2 Application

2.1 In addition to complying with the requirements of regulation 20, as appropriate, vehicle carriers constructed on or after 1 January 2016 intended for the carriage of motor vehicles with compressed hydrogen or compressed natural gas in their tanks for their own propulsion as cargo shall comply with the requirements in paragraphs 3 to 5 of this regulation.

---

① Refer to *Unified interpretation of SOLAS chapter Ⅱ-2 on the number and arrangement of portable fire extinguishers on board ships* (MSC.1/Circ.1275 and its Corr.1).

6.1.5 在所有船舶上，装备有固定式压力水雾灭火系统的封闭式车辆和滚装处所须提供防止排水设备堵塞的装置，并考虑到本组织制定的导则①。2010 年 1 月 1 日之前建造的船舶须在 2010 年 1 月 1 日之后的第 1 次检验时符合本段的要求。

6.2 手提式灭火器

6.2.1 在装载车辆的每个货舱或舱室的每层甲板应备有手提式灭火器，灭火器应布置在处所的两侧，间距不超过 20 m。此类货物处所的每一出入口处应至少有 1 具手提式灭火器。①

6.2.2 除符合本条 6.2.1 的规定外，用于装载油箱内备有自用燃料的机动车辆的车辆处所、滚装处所和特种处所内还应配备以下灭火设备：

.1 至少 3 具水雾枪；和

.2 1 套符合《消防安全系统规则》规定的手提式泡沫枪装置，但船上应至少备有 2 套用于这些处所的该装置。

第 20-1 条
对载运作为货物的其储罐内有压缩氢气或天然气作为自身动力燃料的机动车辆的车辆运输船的要求

1 目的

本条的目的是为拟用于载运储罐内有压缩氢气或天然气作为自身动力燃料的机动车辆的车辆运输船和滚装处所达到本章消防安全目标而规定附加安全措施。

2 适用范围

2.1 除符合第 20 条的相应要求外，对于在 2016 年 1 月 1 日或以后建造的、拟载运作为货物的储罐内有自用压缩氢气或天然气作为自身动力燃料的机动车辆的车辆运输船还须符合本条第 3 至 5 款的要求。

---

① 参见《SOLAS 公约第Ⅱ-2 章船上手提式灭火器数量和布置的统一解释》（第 MSC.1/Circ.1275 号通函及其 Corr.1）。

2.2 In addition to complying with the requirements of regulation 20, as appropriate, vehicle carriers constructed before 1 January 2016, including those constructed before 1 July 2012,[①] shall comply with the requirements in paragraph 5 of this regulation.

3 Requirements for spaces intended for carriage of motor vehicles with compressed natural gas in their tanks for their own propulsion as cargo

3.1 Electrical equipment and wiring

All electrical equipment and wiring shall be of a certified safe type for use in an explosive methane and air mixture.[②]

3.2 Ventilation arrangement

3.2.1 Electrical equipment and wiring, if installed in any ventilation duct, shall be of a certified safe type for use in explosive methane and air mixtures.

3.2.2 The fans shall be such as to avoid the possibility of ignition of methane and air mixtures. Suitable wire mesh guards shall be fitted over inlet and outlet ventilation openings.

3.3 Other ignition sources

Other equipment which may constitute a source of ignition of methane and air mixtures shall not be permitted.

4 Requirements for spaces intended for carriage of motor vehicles with compressed hydrogen in their tanks for their own propulsion as cargo

4.1 Electrical equipment and wiring

All electrical equipment and wiring shall be of a certified safe type for use in an explosive hydrogen and air mixture.[①]

4.2 Ventilation arrangement

4.2.1 Electrical equipment and wiring, if installed in any ventilation duct, shall be of a certified safe type for use in explosive hydrogen and air mixtures and the outlet from any exhaust duct shall be sited in a safe position, having regard to other possible sources of ignition.

4.2.2 The fans shall be designed such as to avoid the possibility of ignition of hydrogen and air mixtures. Suitable wire mesh guards shall be fitted over inlet and outlet ventilation openings.

4.3 Other ignition sources

Other equipment which may constitute a source of ignition of hydrogen and air mixtures shall not be permitted.

---

① Refer to *Recommendation on safety measures for existing vehicle carriers carrying motor vehicles with compressed hydrogen or natural gas in their tanks for their own propulsion as cargo* (MSC.1/Circ.1471).

② Refer to the recommendations of the International Electrotechnical Commission, in particular, publication IEC 60079.

2.2　除符合第20条的相应要求外，对于在2016年1月1日之前建造的车辆运输船，包括2012年7月1日之前建造的车辆运输船①，还须符合本条第5款的要求。

3　对拟载运作为货物的储罐内有压缩天然气作为自身动力燃料的机动车辆的处所的要求

3.1　电气设备和电线

所有的电气设备和电线均须为可在易爆的甲烷和空气混合物的环境中使用的合格防爆型。①

3.2　通风布置

3.2.1　安装在任何通风导管上的电气设备和电线须为可在易爆的甲烷和空气混合物的环境中使用的合格防爆型。

3.2.2　风机须能避免甲烷和空气混合物着火的可能性。通风口的进出口处须设有合适的金属丝网护罩。

3.3　其他着火源

不准使用可能构成甲烷和空气混合物着火源的其他设备。

4　对拟载运作为货物的储罐内有压缩氢气作为自身动力燃料的机动车辆的处所的要求

4.1　电气设备和电线

所有的电气设备和电线均须为可在易爆的氢气和空气混合物的环境中使用的合格防爆型。②

4.2　通风布置

4.2.1　安装在任何通风导管上的电气设备和电线须为可在易爆的氢气和空气混合物的环境中使用的合格防爆型。并考虑到其他可能的着火源，任何排气导管的出口须设在一个安全的位置。

4.2.2　风机须设计成能避免氢气和空气混合物着火的可能性。通风口的进出口处须设有适当的金属丝网护罩。

4.3　其他着火源

不准使用可能构成氢气和空气混合物着火源的其他设备。

---

①　参见《载运作为货物的储罐内有压缩氢气或天然气作为自身动力燃料的机动车辆的现有车辆运输船安全措施建议案》(第MSC.1/Circ.1471号通函)。
②　参见国际电工委员会的建议案，特别是IEC 60079出版物。

5 Detection

When a vehicle carrier carries as cargo one or more motor vehicles with either compressed hydrogen or compressed natural gas in their tanks for their own propulsion, at least two portable gas detectors shall be provided. Such detectors shall be suitable for the detection of the gas fuel and be of a certified safe type for use in the explosive gas and air mixture.

Regulation 21
Casualty threshold, safe return to port and safe areas

1 Application

Passenger ships constructed on or after 1 July 2010 having a length, as defined in regulation Ⅱ-1/2.5, of 120 m or more or having three or more main vertical zones shall comply with the provisions of this regulation.

2 Purpose

The purpose of this regulation is to establish design criteria for a ship's safe return to port under its own propulsion after a casualty that does not exceed the casualty threshold stipulated in paragraph 3 and also provides functional requirements and performance standards for safe areas.

3 Casualty threshold

The casualty threshold, in the context of a fire, includes:

.1 loss of space of origin up to the nearest "A" class boundaries, which may be a part of the space of origin, if the space of origin is protected by a fixed fire-extinguishing system; or

.2 loss of the space of origin and adjacent spaces up to the nearest "A" class boundaries which are not part of the space of origin.

4 Safe return to port[①]

When fire damage does not exceed the casualty threshold indicated in paragraph 3, the ship shall be capable of returning to port while providing a safe area as defined in regulation 3.51. To be deemed capable of returning to port, the following systems shall remain operational in the remaining part of the ship not affected by fire:

.1 propulsion;

.2 steering systems and steering-control systems;

.3 navigational systems;

.4 systems for fill, transfer and service of fuel oil;

---

① Refer to *Interim Explanatory Notes for the assessment of passenger ship systems' capabilities after a fire or flooding casualty* (MSC.1/Circ.1369/Add.1).

5　探测

如果车辆运输船载运作为货物的其储罐内有压缩氢气或压缩天然气作为自身动力燃料的1辆或多辆机动车辆，须至少配备2个便携式气体探测器。此种探测器须适合于探测气体燃料，且须为可在易爆气体和空气混合物的环境中使用的合格防爆型。

第21条
事故界限、安全返港和安全区

1　适用范围

2010年7月1日及以后建造、按照第Ⅱ-1/2.5条的定义长度为120 m及以上，或具有3个及以上主竖区的客船须符合本条的规定。

2　目的

本条款的目的是确定设计标准，使船舶在发生未超出第3款所界定的事故界限的事故后，依靠自身动力安全返港；本条款还提出了安全区的功能要求和性能标准。

3　事故界限

就失火而言，事故界限包括：

.1　原发处所受损直至最近的"A"级边界，如该原发处所受固定式灭火系统保护，该边界可以是原发处所的一部分；或

.2　原发处所以及相邻处所受损直至最近的"A"级边界，该边界并非原发处所的一部分。

4　安全返港①

如果火损未超出第3款所界定的事故界限，当提供第3.51条所界定的安全区时，船舶应能够返港。为被视为有能力返港，在船上未受失火影响部分的下列系统须维持运转：

.1　推进系统；

.2　操舵系统和操舵-控制系统；

.3　导航系统；

.4　燃油注入、转输和服务系统；

① 参见《客船发生火灾或进水事故后系统能力评估的暂行解释性说明》（第MSC.1/Circ.1369/Add.1号通函）。

.5 internal communication between the bridge, engineering spaces, safety centre, fire-fighting and damage-control teams, and as required for passenger and crew notification and mustering;

.6 external communication;

.7 fire main system;

.8 fixed fire-extinguishing systems;

.9 fire and smoke detection system;

.10 bilge and ballast system;

.11 power-operated watertight and semi-watertight doors;

.12 systems intended to support "safe areas" as indicated in paragraph 5.1.2;

.13 flooding detection systems; and

.14 other systems determined by the Administration to be vital to damage control efforts.

5 Safe area(s)

5.1 Functional requirements

.1 the safe area(s) shall generally be an internal space(s); however, the use of an external space as a safe area may be allowed by the Administration taking into account any restriction due to the area of operation and relevant expected environmental conditions;

.2 the safe area(s) shall provide all occupants with the following basic services[①] to ensure that the health of passengers and crew is maintained:

.1 sanitation;

.2 water;

.3 food;

.4 alternate space for medical care;

.5 shelter from the weather;

.6 means of preventing heat stress and hypothermia;

.7 light; and

.8 ventilation;

.3 ventilation design shall reduce the risk of smoke and hot gases that could affect the use of the safe area(s); and

① Refer to *Interim Explanatory Notes for the assessment of passenger ship systems' capabilities after a fire or flooding casualty* (MSC.1/Circ.1369/Add.1).

.5 驾驶台、轮机处所、安全中心、灭火队及控损队之间的内部通信系统，以及通知和集合旅客和船员所需的内部通信系统；

.6 对外通信系统；

.7 消防总管系统；

.8 固定式灭火系统；

.9 火、烟探测系统；

.10 舱底水及压载系统；

.11 动力操作的水密和半水密门；

.12 预计支持第5.1.2款所述“安全区”的系统；

.13 进水探测系统；和

.14 主管机关认定的对控损努力至关重要的其他系统。

5 安全区

5.1 功能要求

.1 安全区一般须为内部处所，但主管机关在考虑到运营区域的任何限制和有关预期环境状况后，亦可允许将某外部处所用作安全区；

.2 安全区须向所有居住者提供下列基本服务[①]，以确保旅客和船员的健康得以维持：

.1 卫生设施；

.2 水；

.3 食物；

.4 后备医疗处所；

.5 风雨遮蔽；

.6 防暑防寒设施；

.7 照明；和

.8 通风；

.3 通风设计须减少可能影响安全区使用的烟和热气风险；和

① 参见《客船发生火灾或进水事故后系统能力评估的暂行解释性说明》（第MSC.1/Circ.1369/Add.1号通函）。

.4 means of access to life-saving appliances shall be provided from each area identified or used as a safe area, taking into account that a main vertical zone may not be available for internal transit.

5.2 Alternate space for medical care

Alternate space for medical care shall conform to a standard acceptable to the Administration.①

Regulation 22
Design criteria for systems to remain operational after a fire casualty

1 Application

Passenger ships constructed on or after 1 July 2010 having a length, as defined in regulation Ⅱ-1/2.5, of 120 m or more or having three or more main vertical zones shall comply with the provisions of this regulation.

2 Purpose

The purpose of this regulation is to provide design criteria for systems required to remain operational for supporting the orderly evacuation and abandonment of a ship, if the casualty threshold, as defined in regulation 21.3, is exceeded.

3 Systems②

3.1 In case any one main vertical zone is unserviceable due to fire, the following systems shall be so arranged and segregated as to remain operational:

.1 fire main;

.2 internal communications (in support of fire fighting as required for passenger and crew notification and evacuation);

.3 means of external communications;

.4 bilge systems for removal of fire-fighting water;

.5 lighting along escape routes, at assembly stations and at embarkation stations of life-saving appliances; and

.6 guidance systems for evacuation shall be available.

3.2 The above systems shall be capable of operation for at least 3 h based on the assumption of no damage outside the unserviceable main vertical zone. These systems are not required to remain operational within the unserviceable main vertical zones.

---

① Refer to *Guidance on the establishment of medical and sanitation related programmes for passenger ships* (MSC/Circ.1129).
② Refer to *Interim Explanatory Notes for the assessment of passenger ship systems' capabilities after a fire or flooding casualty* (MSC.1/Circ.1369).

.4 考虑到某一主竖区可能无法从内部通过,应为每个被标识或用作安全区的区域提供通往救生设备的通道。

5.2 替代医疗处所

替代医疗处所应符合主管机关认可的标准。①

第22条
在失火事故后维持运行的系统的设计标准

1 适用范围

2010年7月1日及之后建造,按照Ⅱ-1/2.5条的定义长度为120 m及以上,或具有3个及以上主竖区的客船须符合本条的规定。

2 目的

本规定的目的是为在超出第21.3款界定的事故界限后,为支持有序撤离及弃船而需要维持运行的系统定出设计标准。

3 系统②

3.1 一旦任何一个主竖区因失火而无法使用,下列系统的布置与分隔须能确保维持运行:

.1 消防总管;

.2 内部通信(支持通知和集合旅客和船员所需要的灭火工作);

.3 对外通信手段;

.4 排除灭火用水的舱底水系统;

.5 逃生通道沿线、集中站和救生设备登乘站的照明;和

.6 须设有撤离导向系统。

3.2 上述系统,在假设无法使用的主竖区之外无损坏的情况下,须能运行至少3 h。这些系统无须在无法使用的主竖区内维持运行。

---

① 参见《客船建立医疗和卫生设施相关计划指南》(第MSC/Circ.1129号通函)。

② 参见《客船发生火灾或进水事故后系统能力评估的暂行解释性说明》(第MSC.1/Circ.1369号通函)。

3.3 Cabling and piping within a trunk constructed to an "A-60" standard shall be deemed to remain intact and serviceable while passing through the unserviceable main vertical zone for the purposes of paragraph 3.1. An equivalent degree of protection for cabling and piping may be approved by the Administration.

Regulation 23
Safety centre on passenger ships

1 Application

Passenger ships constructed on or after 1 July 2010 shall have on board a safety centre complying with the requirements of this regulation.

2 Purpose

The purpose of this regulation is to provide a space to assist with the management of emergency situations.

3 Location and arrangement

The safety centre shall either be a part of the navigation bridge or be located in a separate space adjacent, but having direct access, to the navigation bridge, so that the management of emergencies can be performed without distracting watch officers from their navigational duties.

4 Layout and ergonomic design

The layout and ergonomic design of the safety centre shall take into account the guidelines developed by the Organization,① as appropriate.

5 Communications

Means of communication between the safety centre, the central control station, the navigation bridge, the engine control room, the storage room(s) for fire-extinguishing system(s) and fire equipment lockers shall be provided.

6 Control and monitoring of safety systems

Notwithstanding the requirements set out elsewhere in the Convention, the full functionality (operation, control, monitoring or any combination thereof, as required) of the safety systems listed below shall be available from the safety centre:

.1 all powered ventilation systems;

.2 fire doors;

.3 general emergency alarm system;

.4 public address system;

① Refer to the guidelines to be developed by the Organization. Refer also to *Interim Clarifications of SOLAS chapter Ⅱ-2 requirements regarding interrelation between the central control station, navigation bridge and safety centre* (MSC.1/Circ.1368).

3.3 就3.1款而言，在按照“A-60”标准建造的围井之内穿过无法使用的主竖区的电缆和管线须被视为完好及可用。主管机关可认可同等程度的电缆及管线保护。

第23条
客船上的安全中心

1 适用范围

2010年7月1日及之后建造的客船须在船上设有符合本条要求的安全中心。

2 目的

本条旨在为协助管理紧急情况的处所做出规定。

3 位置与布置

安全中心必须为驾驶台的一部分或者位于与驾驶台相邻的处所但有直通驾驶台的入口，以使对紧急情况的管理不致影响到当班驾驶员的驾驶职责。

4 布局和人机工程设计

安全中心的布局和人机工程设计须酌情考虑到本组织制定的指南。①

5 通信

安全中心、中央控制站、驾驶台、机舱控制室、消防系统储藏室和消防设备储藏间之间须设有通信手段。

6 安全系统的控制与监测

尽管公约中有其他要求，安全中心必须具有下列安全系统的全部功能（操作、控制、监测或所需要的任何组合）：

.1 所有动力通风系统；

.2 防火门；

.3 通用应急报警系统；

.4 公共广播系统；

---

① 参见将由本组织制定的导则，还参见《SOLAS公约第Ⅱ-2章关于中心控制站、船舶驾驶台和安全中心之间关联性的暂行澄清》（第MSC.1/Circ.1368号通函）。

.5 electrically powered evacuation guidance systems;

.6 watertight and semi-watertight doors;

.7 indicators for shell doors, loading doors and other closing appliances;

.8 water leakage of inner/outer bow doors, stern doors and any other shell door;

.9 television surveillance system;

.10 fire detection and alarm system;

.11 fixed fire-fighting local application system(s);

.12 sprinkler and equivalent systems;

.13 water-based fire-extinguishing systems for machinery spaces;

.14 alarm to summon the crew;

.15 atrium smoke extraction system;

.16 flooding detection systems; and

.17 fire pumps and emergency fire pumps.

.5　电动撤离导向系统；

.6　水密和半水密门；

.7　船壳门、装货门和其他关闭装置的显示器；

.8　内(外)首门、尾门及任何其他船壳门的漏水；

.9　电视监视系统；

.10　探火及报警系统；

.11　固定式局部灭火系统；

.12　洒水和同类系统；

.13　机器处所的水基灭火系统；

.14　召集船员用的警报系统；

.15　中庭排烟系统；

.16　进水探测系统；和

.17　消防泵及应急消防泵。

Chapter Ⅲ Life-saving appliances and arrangements

第Ⅲ章　救生设备和装置

Part A
General

Regulation 1
Application

1 Unless expressly provided otherwise, this chapter shall apply to ships the keels of which are laid or which are at a similar stage of construction on or after 1 July 1998.

2 For the purpose of this chapter the term *a similar stage of construction* means the stage at which:

.1 construction identifiable with a specific ship begins; and

.2 assembly of that ship has commenced comprising at least 50 tonnes or 1% of the estimated mass of all structural material, whichever is less.

3 For the purpose of this chapter:

.1 the expression *ships constructed* means "ships the keels of which are laid or which are at a similar stage of construction";

.2 the expression *all ships* means ships constructed before, on or after 1 July 1998; the expressions *all passenger ships* and *all cargo ships* shall be construed accordingly;

.3 a cargo ship, whenever built, which is converted to a passenger ship shall be treated as a passenger ship constructed on the date on which such a conversion commences.

4 For ships constructed before 1 July 1998, the Administration shall:

.1 ensure that, subject to the provisions of paragraph 4.2, the requirements which are applicable under chapter III of the International Convention for the Safety of Life at Sea, 1974, in force prior to 1 July 1998 to new or existing ships as prescribed by that chapter are complied with;

.2 ensure that when life-saving appliances or arrangements on such ships are replaced or such ships undergo repairs, alterations or modifications of a major character which involve replacement of, or any addition to, their existing life-saving appliances or arrangements, such life-saving appliances or arrangements, in so far as is reasonable and practicable, comply with the requirements of this chapter. However, if a survival craft other than an inflatable liferaft is replaced without replacing its launching appliance, or vice versa, the survival craft or launching appliance may be of the same type as that replaced; and

.3 ensure that the requirements of regulations 30.3 and 37.3.9 are complied with.

A 部分
通则

第 1 条
适用范围

1　除另有明文规定者外,本章应适用于 1998 年 7 月 1 日或以后安放龙骨或处于类似建造阶段的船舶。

2　就本章而言,类似建造阶段系指在此阶段:

.1　可辨认出某一具体船舶建造开始;和

.2　该船业已开始的装配量至少为 50 t,或为全部结构材料估算重量的 1%,取较小者。

3　就本章而言:

.1　建造的船舶系指"安放龙骨或处于类似建造阶段的船舶";

.2　所有船舶系指在 1998 年 7 月 1 日或以前或以后建造的船舶;所有客船和所有货船均应照此解释;

.3　无论何时建造的货船,一经改建成客船后,应视作在开始改建之日建造的客船。

4　对于 1998 年 7 月 1 日以前建造的船舶,主管机关须:

.1　确保在满足第 4.2 款规定的前提下,使其符合 1998 年 7 月 1 日以前有效的《1974 年国际海上人命安全公约》第Ⅲ章中对新船或现有船舶所规定的各项适用要求;

.2　保证当此类船舶更换救生设备或装置时,或当此类船舶进行涉及更换或增加其现有救生设备或装置的重大修理、改装或改建时,这些救生设备和装置在合理可行的情况下符合本章要求。但是,如果更换的只是除气胀式救生筏以外的救生艇筏而不更换其降落设备,或是与之相反,则救生艇筏或降落设备与被更换者可以为相同类型;和

.3　确保符合第 30.3 和 37.3.9 条的要求。

5 Notwithstanding paragraph 4.2, for all ships, not later than the first scheduled dry-docking after 1 July 2014, but not later than 1 July 2019, lifeboat on-load release mechanisms not complying with paragraphs 4.4.7.6.4 to 4.4.7.6.6 of the Code shall be replaced with equipment that complies with the International Life-Saving Appliance (LSA) Code.①

Regulation 2
Exemptions

1 The Administration may, if it considers that the sheltered nature and conditions of the voyage are such as to render the application of any specific requirements of this chapter unreasonable or unnecessary, exempt from those requirements individual ships or classes of ships which, in the course of their voyage, do not proceed more than 20 miles from the nearest land.

2 In the case of passenger ships which are employed in special trades for the carriage of large numbers of special trade passengers, such as the pilgrim trade, the Administration, if satisfied that it is impracticable to enforce compliance with the requirements of this chapter, may exempt such ships from those requirements, provided that such ships comply fully with the provisions of:

.1 the rules annexed to the Special Trade Passenger Ships Agreement, 1971; and

.2 the rules annexed to the Protocol on Space Requirements for Special Trade Passenger Ships, 1973.

Regulation 3
Definitions

For the purpose of this chapter, unless expressly provided otherwise:

1 *Anti-exposure suit* is a protective suit designed for use by rescue boat crews and marine evacuation system parties.

2 *Certificated person* is a person who holds a certificate of proficiency in survival craft issued under the authority of, or recognized as valid by, the Administration in accordance with the requirements of the International Convention on Standards of Training, Certification and Watchkeeping for Seafarers, in force; or a person who holds a certificate issued or recognized by the Administration of a State not a Party to that Convention for the same purpose as the convention certificate.

3 *Detection* is the determination of the location of survivors or survival craft.

4 *Embarkation ladder* is the ladder provided at survival craft embarkation stations to permit safe access to survival craft after launching.

---

① Refer to *Guidelines for evaluation and replacement of lifeboat release and retrieval systems* (MSC.1/Circ.1392 and its Corr.1, as amended by MSC.1/Circ.1584).

5　尽管有第4.2款的要求，对所有船舶，在不迟于2014年7月1日以后第一个计划的干坞期，但不迟于2019年7月1日，其不符合《国际救生设备规则》第4.4.7.6.4至4.4.7.6.6款要求的救生艇负载释放装置须更换为符合该《规则》的设备①。

第2条
免除

1　主管机关如考虑到航程的遮蔽性及其条件而认为实施本章的任何具体要求不合理或不必要时，可对在其距最近陆地不超过20海里的航线航行的个别船舶或某些类型船舶，免除这些要求。

2　对用于运输大量特别乘客（如朝觐的乘客）的客船，主管机关如确信实施本章要求不切实际时，可对此类船舶免除这些要求，但应完全符合下列规定：

.1　《1971年特种业务客船协定》所附的规则；和

.2　《1973年特种业务客船舱室要求议定书》所附的规则。

第3条
定义

除另有明文规定外，就本章而言：

1　**抗暴露服**系指设计成供救助艇艇员和海上撤离系统人员使用的防护服。

2　**持证人员**系指持有主管机关按照现行的《海员培训、发证和值班标准国际公约》要求，授权签发的或承认有效的精通救生艇筏业务证书的人员；或持有非该公约缔约国的主管机关为公约证书同一目的而签发或承认的证书的人员。

3　**探测**系指幸存者或救生艇筏位置的测定。

4　**登乘梯**系指设置在救生艇筏登乘站以供安全登入降落下水后的救生艇筏的梯子。

① 参加《救生艇释放和回收系统评估和更换导则》（第MSC.1/Circ.1392号通函及经MSC.1/Circ.1584修订的Corr.1）。

5 *Float-free launching* is that method of launching a survival craft whereby the craft is automatically released from a sinking ship and is ready for use.

6 *Free-fall launching* is that method of launching a survival craft whereby the craft with its complement of persons and equipment on board is released and allowed to fall into the sea without any restraining apparatus.

7 *Immersion suit* is a protective suit which reduces the body heat loss of a person wearing it in cold water.

8 *Inflatable appliance* is an appliance which depends upon non-rigid, gas-filled chambers for buoyancy and which is normally kept uninflated until ready for use.

9 *Inflated appliance* is an appliance which depends upon non-rigid, gas-filled chambers for buoyancy and which is kept inflated and ready for use at all times.

10 *International Life-Saving Appliance* (LSA) Code (referred to as "the Code" in this chapter) means the International Life-Saving Appliance (LSA) Code adopted by the Maritime Safety Committee of the Organization by resolution MSC.48(66), as it may be amended by the Organization, provided that such amendments are adopted, brought into force and take effect in accordance with the provisions of article Ⅷ of the present Convention concerning the amendment procedures applicable to the annex other than chapter Ⅰ.

11 *Launching appliance or arrangement* is a means of transferring a survival craft or rescue boat from its stowed position safely to the water.

12 *Length* is 96% of the total length on a waterline at 85% of the least moulded depth measured from the top of the keel, or the length from the fore-side of the stem to the axis of the rudder stock on that waterline, if that be greater. In ships designed with a rake of keel the waterline on which this is measured shall be parallel to the designed waterline.

13 *Lightest seagoing condition* is the loading condition with the ship on even keel, without cargo, with 10% stores and fuel remaining and in the case of a passenger ship with the full number of passengers and crew and their luggage.

14 *Marine evacuation system* is an appliance for the rapid transfer of persons from the embarkation deck of a ship to a floating survival craft.

15 *Moulded depth*

.1 *The moulded depth* is the vertical distance measured from the top of the keel to the top of the freeboard deck beam at side. In wood and composite ships the distance is measured from the lower edge of the keel rabbet. Where the form at the lower part of the midship section is of a hollow character, or where thick garboards are fitted, the distance is measured from the point where the line of the flat of the bottom continued inwards cuts the side of the keel.

.2 In ships having rounded gunwales, the moulded depth shall be measured to the point of intersection of the moulded lines of the deck and side shell plating, the lines extending as though the gunwale were of angular design.

5　**自由漂浮下水**系指救生艇筏从下沉中的船舶自动脱开并立即可用的降落方法。

6　**自由降落下水**系指释放(或脱开)载足全部乘员和属具的救生艇筏,并在没有任何约束装置的情况下,任其下降到海面的降落方法。

7　**救生服**系指减少在冷水中穿着该服人员体热损失的防护服。

8　**气胀式设备**系指依靠非刚性的充气室作浮力,而且在准备使用前通常保持不充气状态的设备。

9　**充气式设备**系指依靠非刚性的充气室作浮力,而且一直保持充气备用状态的设备。

10　**国际救生设备(LSA)规则(本章内称"《规则》")**系指本组织海上安全委员会MSC.48(66)决议通过的《国际救生设备(LSA)规则》,该规则可能经本组织修正,但该修正案应按本公约第Ⅷ条有关适用于除第Ⅰ章外的附则修正程序的规定予以通过、生效和实施。

11　**降落设备或装置**系指将救生艇筏或救助艇从其存放位置安全地转移到水上的设施。

12　**长度**系指量自龙骨上面的最小型深85%处水线总长的96%,或沿该水线从首柱前缘量至舵杆中心线的长度,取较大者。对设计为具有倾斜龙骨的船舶,其计量长度的水线应与设计水线平行。

13　**最轻载航行状态**系指船舶处于平浮,无货物,剩有10%的备品和燃料的装载状态;对客船而言,船舶处于载足全额乘客和船员及其行李的装载状态。

14　**海上撤离系统**系指将人员从船舶的登乘甲板迅速转移到漂浮的救生艇筏上的设备。

15　**型深**

.1　**型深**系指从龙骨上面量至船舷处的干舷甲板横梁上面的垂直距离。对木质船舶和混合结构船舶,此垂直距离从龙骨槽口的下缘量起。如船舶中横剖面的下部具有凹形,或如装有厚龙骨翼板,此垂直距离从船底平坦部分向内延伸线与龙骨侧面相交之点量起。

.2　具有圆弧形舷边的船舶,型深应量至甲板型线和船舶外板型线相交之点,这些线的延伸是把该舷边看作设计为角形。

.3 Where the freeboard deck is stepped and the raised part of the deck extends over the point at which the moulded depth is to be determined, the moulded depth shall be measured to a line of reference extending from the lower part of the deck along a line parallel with the raised part.

16 *Novel life-saving appliance or arrangement* is a life-saving appliance or arrangement which embodies new features not fully covered by the provisions of this chapter or the Code but which provides an equal or higher standard of safety.

17 *Positive stability* is the ability of a craft to return to its original position after the removal of a heeling moment.

18 *Recovery time* for a rescue boat is the time required to raise the boat to a position where persons on board can disembark to the deck of the ship. Recovery time includes the time required to make preparations for recovery on board the rescue boat such as passing and securing a painter, connecting the rescue boat to the launching appliance, and the time to raise the rescue boat. Recovery time does not include the time needed to lower the launching appliance into position to recover the rescue boat.

19 *Rescue boat* is a boat designed to rescue persons in distress and to marshal survival craft.

20 *Retrieval* is the safe recovery of survivors.

21 *Ro-ro passenger ship* means a passenger ship with ro-ro cargo spaces or special category spaces as defined in regulation Ⅱ-2/3.

22 *Short international voyage* is an international voyage in the course of which a ship is not more than 200 miles from a port or place in which the passengers and crew could be placed in safety. Neither the distance between the last port of call in the country in which the voyage begins and the final port of destination nor the return voyage shall exceed 600 miles. The final port of destination is the last port of call in the scheduled voyage at which the ship commences its return voyage to the country in which the voyage began.

23 *Survival craft* is a craft capable of sustaining the lives of persons in distress from the time of abandoning the ship.

24 *Thermal protective aid* is a bag or suit made of waterproof material with low thermal conductance.

25 *Requirements for maintenance, thorough examination, operational testing, overhaul and repair* means the Requirements for maintenance, thorough examination, operational testing, overhaul and repair of lifeboats and rescue boats, launching appliances and release gear, adopted by the Maritime Safety Committee of the Organization by resolution MSC. 402(96), as may be amended by the Organization, provided that such amendments are adopted, brought into force and take effect in accordance with the provisions of article Ⅷ of the present Convention concerning the amendment procedures applicable to the annex other than chapter Ⅰ.

.3 如干舷甲板为阶梯形并且其升高部分延伸到超过决定型深的点，则型深应量至甲板较低部分与升高部分平行的延伸线。

16 **新颖救生设备或装置**系指具有本章或《规则》之规定未全部包括的新型特征，但达到等效的或更高的安全标准的救生设备或装置。

17 **正稳性**系指艇筏在移去一横倾力矩后回复到其初始位置的能力。

18 **救助艇的回收时间**系指该艇被提升至某一位置，而使艇上人员可从该处登上大船甲板所需的时间。回收时间包括在救助艇上做的回收准备工作所需的时间，诸如抛投和系住首缆，连接救助艇与降落设备，以及提升救助艇的时间。回收时间不包括把降落设备降低至回收救助艇的位置所需要的时间。

19 **救助艇**系指为救助遇险人员及集结救生艇筏而设计的艇。

20 **拯救**系指安全寻回幸存者。

21 **滚装客船**系指具有第Ⅱ-2/3 条定义的滚装装货处所或特种处所的客船。

22 **短程国际航行**系指在航行中，船舶距离能够安全安置乘客和船员的港口或地点不超过200 海里的国际航行。启航国最后停靠港至最终目的港之间距离与返航航程均应不超过 600 海里。最终目的港系指船舶开始返航回到启航国前的计划航次中的最后停靠港。

23 **救生艇筏**系指从弃船时起能维持遇险人员生命的艇筏。

24 **保温用具**系指采用低导热率的防水材料制成的袋子或衣服。

25 **维护保养、彻底检查、操作测试、大修和修理要求**系指本组织海上安全委员会以第MSC.402(96)号决议通过并可能经本组织修改的，救生艇和救助艇、降落设备装置和释放装置的维护保养、彻底检查、操作测试、大修和修理要求，只要此类修正案是按本公约第Ⅷ条关于除第Ⅰ章外适用的附则修正程序的规定予以通过、生效和实施。

Regulation 4
Evaluation, testing and approval of life-saving appliances and arrangements

1 Except as provided in paragraphs 5 and 6, life-saving appliances and arrangements required by this chapter shall be approved by the Administration.

2 Before giving approval to life-saving appliances and arrangements, the Administration shall ensure that such life-saving appliances and arrangements:

.1 are tested, to confirm that they comply with the requirements of this chapter and the Code, in accordance with the recommendations of the Organization; ①or

.2 have successfully undergone, to the satisfaction of the Administration, tests which are substantially equivalent to those specified in those recommendations.

3 Before giving approval to novel life-saving appliances or arrangements, the Administration shall ensure that such:

.1 appliances provide safety standards at least equivalent to the requirements of this chapter and the Code and have been evaluated and tested based on the guidelines developed by the Organization; ②or

.2 arrangements have successfully undergone an engineering analysis, evaluation and approval in accordance with regulation 38.

4 Procedures adopted by the Administration for approval shall also include the conditions whereby approval would continue or would be withdrawn.

5 Before accepting life-saving appliances and arrangements that have not been previously approved by the Administration, the Administration shall be satisfied that life-saving appliances and arrangements comply with the requirements of this chapter and the Code.

6 Life-saving appliances required by this chapter for which detailed specifications are not included in the Code shall be to the satisfaction of the Administration.

Regulation 5
Production tests

The Administration shall require life-saving appliances to be subjected to such production tests as are necessary to ensure that the life-saving appliances are manufactured to the same standard as the approved prototype.

---

① Refer to *Recommendation on testing of life-saving appliances* (resolution A.689(17)). For life-saving appliances installed on board on or after 1 July 1999, refer to *Revised Recommendations on testing of life-saving appliances* (resolution MSC.81(70)).

② Refer to the guidelines to be developed by the Organization.

第4条
救生设备和装置的鉴定、试验及认可

1　除按照本条第5和6款的规定外,本章规定的救生设备和装置应经主管机关认可。

2　在对救生设备和装置予以认可之前,主管机关应确保该救生设备和装置:

.1　按本组织的建议案进行试验,确认其符合本章和规则的要求①;或

.2　业已成功进行了实质上等效于该建议案规定的试验,并使主管机关满意。

3　在认可新颖救生设备或布置之前,主管机关须确保:

.1　此设备所达到的安全标准至少与本章和《规则》的要求相等,并已根据本组织制定的指南加以评估及测试②;或

.2　此布置已按照第38条成功地进行了工程分析、评估与认可。

4　主管机关所采用的认可程序还应包括继续认可或撤销认可的条件。

5　在接受主管机关原先未予认可的救生设备和装置之前,主管机管应确信该救生设备和装置符合本章和《规则》的要求。

6　本章所要求的救生设备,如其详细的技术规定未列入《规则》,应使主管机关满意。

第5条
生产试验

主管机关应要求救生设备经受必要的生产试验,以确保救生设备是按已认可的原型设备的同一标准进行制造。

① 参见本组织以第A.689(17)号决议通过的《关于救生设备试验的建议案》。对1999年7月1日或以后安装在船上的救生设备,参见本组织海上安全委员会第MSC.80(71)号决议通过的《经修订的关于救生设备试验的建议案》。

② 参见本组织将制定的导则。

Part B
Requirements for ships and life-saving appliances

Section Ⅰ
Passenger ships and cargo ships

Regulation 6
Communications

1 Paragraph 2 applies to all passenger ships and to all cargo ships of 300 gross tonnage and upwards.

2 Radio life-saving appliances

2.1 Two-way VHF radiotelephone apparatus

2.1.1 At least three two-way VHF radiotelephone apparatus shall be provided on every passenger ship and on every cargo ship of 500 gross tonnage and upwards. At least two two-way VHF radiotelephone apparatus shall be provided on every cargo ship of 300 gross tonnage and upwards but less than 500 gross tonnage. Such apparatus shall conform to performance standards not inferior to those adopted by the Organization.[①] If a fixed two-way VHF radiotelephone apparatus is fitted in a survival craft it shall conform to performance standards not inferior to those adopted by the Organization.[①]

2.1.2 Two-way VHF radiotelephone apparatus provided on board ships prior to 1 February 1992 and not complying fully with the performance standards adopted by the Organization may be accepted by the Administration until 1 February 1999 provided the Administration is satisfied that they are compatible with approved two-way VHF radiotelephone apparatus.

① Refer to the Performance standards for survival craft two-way VHF radiotelephone apparatus (resolution A.809(19), as it may be amended, annex 1 or annex 2, as applicable), and resolution MSC.149(77).

B 部分
船舶和救生设备的要求

第 1 节
客船与货船

第 6 条
通信

1　本条第 2 款适用于所有客船和 300 总吨及以上的所有货船。

2　无线电救生设备

2.1　双向甚高频(VHF)无线电话设备

2.1.1　每艘客船和每艘 500 总吨及以上的货船,应至少配备 3 台双向甚高频(VHF)无线电话设备。每艘 300 总吨及以上,但小于 500 总吨的货船,应至少配备 2 台双向 VHF 无线电话设备。该设备所符合的性能标准应不低于本组织通过的性能标准①。如果在救生艇筏上装有固定式双向 VHF 无线电话设备,其所符合的性能标准也应不低于本组织通过的性能标准4。

2.1.2　1992 年 2 月 1 日以前在船上配备的,且不完全符合本组织通过的性能标准的双向 VHF 无线电话设备,只要主管机关确信它们同经认可的双向 VHF 无线电话设备相容,在 1999 年 2 月 1 日前仍可被主管机关接受。

① 参见《救生艇筏双向甚高频(VHF)无线电话设备性能标准》(可能经修正的第 A.809(19)号决议的附件 1 或附件 2,如适用)和第 MSC.149(77)号决议。

2.2 Search and rescue locating devices

At least one search and rescue locating device shall be carried on each side of every passenger ship and of every cargo ship of 500 gross tonnage and upwards. At least one search and rescue locating device shall be carried on every cargo ship of 300 gross tonnage and upwards but less than 500 gross tonnage. Such search and rescue locating devices shall conform to the applicable performance standards not inferior to those adopted by the Organization①. The search and rescue locating devices② shall be stowed in such location that they can be rapidly placed in any survival craft other than the liferaft or liferafts required by regulation 31.1.4. Alternatively one search and rescue locating device shall be stowed in each survival craft other than those required by regulation 31.1.4. On ships carrying at least two search and rescue locating devices and equipped with free-fall lifeboats one of the search and rescue locating devices shall be stowed in a free-fall lifeboat and the other located in the immediate vicinity of the navigation bridge so that it can be utilized on board and ready for transfer to any of the other survival craft.

3 Distress flares

Not less than 12 rocket parachute flares, complying with the requirements of section 3.1 of the Code, shall be carried and be stowed on or near the navigation bridge.

4 On-board communications and alarm systems

4.1 An emergency means comprised of either fixed or portable equipment or both shall be provided for two-way communications between emergency control stations, muster and embarkation stations and strategic positions on board.

4.2 A general emergency alarm system complying with the requirements of paragraph 7.2.1 of the Code shall be provided and shall be used for summoning passengers and crew to muster stations and to initiate the actions included in the muster list. The system shall be supplemented by either a public address system complying with the requirements of paragraph 7.2.2 of the Code or other suitable means of communication. Entertainment sound systems shall automatically be turned off when the general emergency alarm system is activated.

4.3 The general emergency alarm system shall be audible throughout all the accommodation and normal crew working spaces. On passenger ships, the system shall also be audible on all open decks.

4.4 On ships fitted with a marine evacuation system communication between the embarkation station and the platform or the survival craft shall be ensured.

5 Public address systems on passenger ships

① Refer to *Recommendation on performance standards for survival craft radar transponders for use in search and rescue operations* (resolution A.802(19), as amended by resolution MSC.247(83)), and *Recommendation on performance standards for survival craft AIS Search and Rescue Transmitters (AIS-SART) for use in search and rescue operations* (resolution MSC.246(83)).

② One of these search and rescue locating devices may be the search and rescue locating device required by regulation Ⅳ/7.1.3.

2.2　搜救定位装置

所有客船和所有500总吨及以上的货船每舷须配备至少一个搜救定位装置。所有300总吨及以上但低于500总吨的货船须配备至少一个搜救定位装置。该搜救定位装置须符合适用的性能标准,该性能标准不低于本组织通过的性能标准[①]。该搜救定位装置[②]的存放位置须使其能够被迅速地放置到除第31.1.4条要求的救生筏以外的所有救生艇筏上。也可以在每艘救生艇筏(第31.1.4条要求的救生艇筏除外)安置一个搜救定位装置。至少配备两个搜救定位装置,配备有自落式救生艇的船舶须在自落式救生艇中安置一个搜救定位装置并将另一个搜救定位装置安置于最靠近驾驶台的地方以便于在船上使用并转移到另一艘救生艇筏上。

3　遇险火焰信号

应配备不少于12支符合《规则》3.1要求的火箭降落伞火焰信号,并应存放在驾驶室或其附近。

4　船上通信与报警系统

4.1　应配备1套固定式或手提式设备构成的或由这两种型式构成的应急设施,供船上应急控制站、集合站和登乘站及要害位置之间的双向通信联系使用。

4.2　应配备符合《规则》7.2.1要求的通用应急报警系统,以供召集乘客与船员至集合站和采取应变部署表所列行动之用。该系统应以符合《规则》7.2.2要求的公共广播系统或其他适宜的通信设施作为补充。当通用应急报警系统启动时,娱乐声响系统应自动关闭。

4.3　通用应急报警系统应在所有起居处所和船员通常工作处所都能听到其报警。在客船上,该系统也应在所有开敞甲板上都能听到其报警。

4.4　配备海上撤离系统的船舶应确保登乘站和平台或救生艇筏之间的通信联络。

5　客船公共广播系统

---

① 参见《供搜救作业适用的救生艇筏雷达应答器性能标准的建议案》(第MSC.247(83)号决议修正的第A.802(19)号决议),和《供搜救作业适用的救生艇筏搜救AIS应答器(AIS-SART)性能标准的建议案》(第MSC.246(83)号决议)。

② 这些搜救定位装置其中之一可以是第Ⅳ/7.1.3条要求的搜救定位装置。

5.1 In addition to the requirements of regulation Ⅱ-2/12.3 and of paragraph 4.2, all passenger ships shall be fitted with a public address system. With respect to passenger ships constructed before 1 July 1997 the requirements of paragraphs 5.2 and 5.4, subject to the provisions of paragraph 5.5, shall apply not later than the date of the first periodical survey after 1 July 1997.

5.2 The public address system shall be clearly audible above the ambient noise in all spaces, prescribed by paragraph 7.2.2.1 of the Code, and shall be provided with an override function controlled from one location on the navigation bridge and such other places on board as the Administration deems necessary, so that all emergency messages will be broadcast if any loudspeaker in the spaces concerned has been switched off, its volume has been turned down or the public address system is used for other purposes.

5.3 On passenger ships constructed on or after 1 July 1997:

.1 the public address system shall have at least two loops which shall be sufficiently separated throughout their length and have two separate and independent amplifiers; and

.2 the public address system and its performance standards shall be approved by the Administration having regard to the recommendations adopted by the Organization①.

5.4 The public address system shall be connected to the emergency source of electrical power required by regulation Ⅱ-1/42.2.2.

5.5 Ships constructed before 1 July 1997 which are already fitted with the public address system approved by the Administration which complies substantially with those required by sections 5.2 and 5.4 and paragraph 7.2.2.1 of the Code are not required to change their system.

Regulation 7
Personal life-saving appliances

1 Lifebuoys

1.1 Lifebuoys complying with the requirements of paragraph 2.1.1 of the Code shall be:

.1 so distributed as to be readily available on both sides of the ship and as far as practicable on all open decks extending to the ship's side; at least one shall be placed in the vicinity of the stern; and

.2 so stowed as to be capable of being rapidly cast loose, and not permanently secured in any way.

① Refer to *Recommendation on performance standards for public address systems on passenger ships, including cabling* (MSC/Circ. 808).

5.1 除第Ⅱ-2/12.3 及本条 4.2 的要求外,所有客船还应设置一套公共广播系统。对于 1997 年 7 月 1 日以前建造的客船,除 5.5 的规定外,5.2 和 5.4 的要求应不迟于 1997 年 7 月 1 日以后第一次定期检验的日期适用。

5.2 公共广播系统应按《规则》7.2.2.1 所述,在所有处所内其播音都高于环境噪声,并能被清晰地听到。该系统还应配备一个可从驾驶室的某一位置以及主管机关认为必需的船上的其他位置进行控制的越控功能,以便当有关处所内的任一扩音器已被关闭,其音量已被关小或公共广播系统供作他用时,也能广播所有的紧急信息。

5.3 对 1997 年 7 月 1 日或以后建造的客船:

.1 公共广播系统至少应有两个在整个线路上完全独立的回路,并应有两个分开和独立的扩音器;和

.2 公共广播系统及其性能标准应经主管机关考虑本组织所通过的建议案后予以认可①。

5.4 公共广播系统应与第Ⅱ-1/42.2.2 条要求的应急电源相连接。

5.5 对 1997 年 7 月 1 日以前建造的船舶,如已设有经主管机关认可且实质上与 5.2、5.4 和《规则》7.2.2.1 所要求相符的公共广播系统,则不要求改变该系统。

第 7 条
个人救生设备

1　救生圈

1.1 符合《规则》2.1.1 要求的救生圈:

.1 应分布在船舶两舷易于拿到之处,并在可行范围内,分放在所有延伸到船舷的露天甲板上;至少有 1 个应放在船尾附近;和

.2 其存放应能随时迅速取下,且不应以任何方式永久系牢。

---

① 参加《关于客船公共广播系统,包括其布线的性能标准建议案》(第 MSC/Circ.808 号通函)。

1.2 At least one lifebuoy on each side of the ship shall be fitted with a buoyant lifeline complying with the requirements of paragraph 2.1.4 of the Code equal in length to not less than twice the height at which it is stowed above the waterline in the lightest seagoing condition, or 30 m, whichever is the greater.

1.3 Not less than one half of the total number of lifebuoys shall be provided with lifebuoy self-igniting lights complying with the requirements of paragraph 2.1.2 of the Code; not less than two of these shall also be provided with lifebuoy self-activating smoke signals complying with the requirements of paragraph 2.1.3 of the Code and be capable of quick release from the navigation bridge; lifebuoys with lights and those with lights and smoke signals shall be equally distributed on both sides of the ship and shall not be the lifebuoys provided with lifelines in compliance with the requirements of paragraph 1.2.

1.4 Each lifebuoy shall be marked in block capitals of the Roman alphabet with the name and port of registry of the ship on which it is carried.

2 Lifejackets

2.1 A lifejacket complying with the requirements of paragraph 2.2.1 or 2.2.2 of the Code shall be provided for every person on board the ship and, in addition:

.1 for passenger ships on voyages of less than 24 hours, a number of infant lifejackets equal to at least 2.5% of the number of passengers on board shall be provided;

.2 for passenger ships on voyages of 24 hours or greater, infant lifejackets shall be provided for each infant on board;

.3 a number of lifejackets suitable for children equal to at least 10% of the number of passengers on board shall be provided or such greater number as may be required to provide a lifejacket for each child;

.4 a sufficient number of lifejackets shall be carried for persons on watch and for use at remotely located survival craft stations. The lifejackets carried for persons on watch should be stowed on the bridge, in the engine control room and at any other manned watch station; and

.5 if the adult lifejackets provided are not designed to fit persons weighing up to 140 kg and with a chest girth of up to 1,750 mm, a sufficient number of suitable accessories shall be available on board to allow them to be secured to such persons.

2.2 Lifejackets shall be so placed as to be readily accessible and their position shall be plainly indicated. Where, due to the particular arrangements of the ship, the lifejackets provided in compliance with the requirements of paragraph 2.1 may become inaccessible, alternative provisions shall be made to the satisfaction of the Administration which may include an increase in the number of lifejackets to be carried.

2.3 The lifejackets used in totally enclosed lifeboats, except free-fall lifeboats, shall not impede entry into the lifeboat or seating, including operation of the seat belts in the lifeboat.

1.2　船舶每舷至少有 1 个救生圈应设有符合《规则》2.1.4 要求的可浮救生索，其长度不少于其存放处在最轻载航行水线以上高度的 2 倍，或 30 m，取大者。

1.3　不少于总数一半的救生圈应设有符合《规则》2.1.2 要求的自亮灯；这些救生圈中不少于 2 个还应设有符合《规则》2.1.3 要求的自发烟雾信号，并能从驾驶室迅速抛投；设有自亮灯的救 生圈和设有自亮灯及自发烟雾信号的救生圈，应均等分布在船舶两舷，这类救生圈不应是按本条 1.2 要求装有救生索的救生圈。

1.4　每个救生圈应以粗体罗马大写字母标明其所属船舶的船名和船籍港。

2　救生衣

2.1　应为船上每个人配备 1 件符合《规则》2.2.1 或 2.2.2 要求的救生衣，此外还应：

.1　对于航行时间在 24 小时以下的客船，应配备若干婴儿救生衣，其数量至少等于船上乘客总数的 2.5%；

.2　对于航行时间在 24 小时及其以上的客船，应为在船上的每个婴儿配备婴儿救生衣；

.3　配备若干适合儿童穿着的救生衣，其数量至少相等于船上乘客总数的 10%，或为每个儿童配备 1 件救生衣而可能需要的更多数量；和

.4　配备足够数量的救生衣，以供值班人员使用，并供设置在远处的救生艇筏站使用。供值班人员使用的救生衣应存放在驾驶室、机舱控制室和任何其他有人值班的地方。

.5　如果设计配备的成人救生衣不适合最大胸围为 1 750 mm 的人员，则船上应提供足够数量适合的附属件使救生衣可以系于此类人员身上。

2.2　救生衣应置放于易于到达之处，且其位置应予明显标示。如由于船舶的特殊布置而使按本条 2.1 要求配备的救生衣可能无法拿到时，可制定使主管机关满意的变通措施，其中可包括增加救生衣的配备数量。

2.3　除自由降落救生艇外，用于全封闭救生艇上的救生衣应不妨碍人员进入救生艇或在艇内就座，包括系好安全带。

2.4 Lifejackets selected for free-fall lifeboats, and the manner in which they are carried or worn, shall not interfere with entry into the lifeboat, occupant safety or operation of the lifeboat.

3 Immersion suits and anti-exposure suits

An immersion suit, complying with the requirements of section 2.3 of the Code or an anti-exposure suit complying with section 2.4 of the Code, of an appropriate size, shall be provided for every person assigned to crew the rescue boat or assigned to the marine evacuation system party. If the ship is constantly engaged in warm climates① where, in the opinion of the Administration thermal protection is unnecessary, this protective clothing need not be carried.

Regulation 8
Muster list and emergency instructions

1 This regulation applies to all ships.

2 Clear instructions to be followed in the event of an emergency shall be provided for every person on board. In the case of passenger ships these instructions shall be drawn up in the language or languages required by the ship's flag State and in the English language.

3 Muster lists and emergency instructions complying with the requirements of regulation 37 shall be exhibited in conspicuous places throughout the ship including the navigation bridge, engine-room and crew accommodation spaces.

4 Illustrations and instructions in appropriate languages shall be posted in passenger cabins and be conspicuously displayed at muster stations and other passenger spaces to inform passengers of:

.1 their muster station;

.2 the essential actions they must take in an emergency; and

.3 the method of donning lifejackets.

Regulation 9
Operating instructions

1 This regulation applies to all ships.

2 Posters or signs shall be provided on or in the vicinity of survival craft and their launching controls and shall:

.1 illustrate the purpose of controls and the procedures for operating the appliance and give relevant instructions or warnings;

.2 be easily seen under emergency lighting conditions; and

---

① Refer to *Guidelines for the assessment of thermal protection* (MSC/Circ.1046).

2.4　为自由降落救生艇选用的救生衣及其存放和穿着方式应不妨碍人员进入救生艇、乘员安全或该艇的操作。

3　**救生服和抗暴露服**

应为每位被指派为救助艇员或海上撤离系统工作人员的人配备1件尺寸适宜且符合《规则》第2.3节要求的救生服或符合《规则》第2.4节要求的抗暴露服。如果船舶一直在主管机关认为不需温度保护的温暖气候区域①航行,则不必配备该防护服。

第8条
应变部署表与应变须知

1　本条适用于所有船舶。

2　应为船上每个人员配备1份在紧急情况下必须遵循的明确的须知。如为客船,这些须知应使用船旗国要求的一种或数种语言以及英语写成。

3　符合第37条要求的应变部署表和应变须知应在全船各显著部位展示,包括驾驶台、机舱和船员起居处所。

4　应在乘客舱室内张贴配有适当文字的示意图和应变须知,并在集合站及其他乘客处所的显著位置予以展示,以告知乘客:

.1　他们的集合站;

.2　他们在紧急情况下必须采取的重要行动;和

.3　救生衣的穿着方法。

第9条
操作须知

1　本条适用于所有船舶。

2　应在救生艇筏及其降落操纵器上或附近设置告示或标志,其应:

.1　有示意图说明操纵器的用途及此项设备的操作程序,并告知有关须知或注意事项;

.2　在应急照明条件下容易看清;和

① 参见《温度保护评估导则》(第MSC/Circ.1046号通函)。

.3 use symbols in accordance with the recommendations of the Organization①.

Regulation 10
Manning of survival craft and supervision

1 This regulation applies to all ships.

2 There shall be a sufficient number of trained persons on board for mustering and assisting untrained persons.

3 There shall be a sufficient number of crew members, who may be deck officers or certificated persons, on board for operating the survival craft and launching arrangements required for abandonment by the total number of persons on board.

4 A deck officer or certificated person shall be placed in charge of each survival craft to be used. However, the Administration, having due regard to the nature of the voyage, the number of persons on board and the characteristics of the ship, may permit persons practised in the handling and operation of liferafts to be placed in charge of liferafts in lieu of persons qualified as above. A second-in-command shall also be nominated in the case of lifeboats.

5 The person in charge of the survival craft shall have a list of the survival craft crew and shall see that the crew under his command are acquainted with their duties. In lifeboats the second-in-command shall also have a list of the lifeboat crew.

6 Every motorized survival craft shall have a person assigned who is capable of operating the engine and carrying out minor adjustments.

7 The master shall ensure the equitable distribution of persons referred to in paragraphs 2, 3 and 4 among the ship's survival craft.

Regulation 11
Survival craft muster and embarkation arrangements

1 Lifeboats and liferafts for which approved launching appliances are required shall be stowed as close to accommodation and service spaces as possible.

2 Muster stations shall be provided close to the embarkation stations. Each muster station shall have sufficient clear deck space to accommodate all persons assigned to muster at that station, but at least 0.35 m^2 per person.

3 Muster and embarkation stations shall be readily accessible from accommodation and work areas.

---

① Refer to *Symbols related to life-saving appliances and arrangements* (resolution A.760(18), as amended) and/or tables 1 and 2 of *Escape route signs and equipment location markings* (resolution A.1116(30)), as appropriate. Refer to the new symbols in tables 1 and 2 of resolution A.1116(30) where the symbols for a specific item are differently expressed in resolutions A.760(18), as amended and A.1116(30).

.3　使用符合本组织建议案的符号①。

第 10 条
救生艇筏的配员与监督

1　本条适用于所有船舶。

2　船上应有足够数量受过培训的人员进行召集和协助未受培训的人员。

3　船上应有足够数量的船员(他们可以是甲板部高级船员或持证人员)对船上全体人员弃船所需要的救生艇筏及其降落装置进行操作。

4　每艘要使用的救生艇筏,均应指定 1 名甲板部高级船员或持证人员负责指挥。但主管机关经适当考虑到航程的性质、船上人数和船舶的特点后,可以准许精通救生筏操纵和操作的人员代替具有上述资格的人员负责指挥救生筏。如为救生艇,还应指派 1 名副指挥。

5　救生艇筏负责人应有一份该救生艇筏船员名单,并应确保在其指挥下的船员是熟悉其任务的。救生艇的副指挥亦应有一份该救生艇船员名单。

6　应为每艘机动救生艇筏指派 1 名能操作发动机并能进行微调的人员。

7　船长应确保在船舶的救生艇筏之间合理分配本条 2、3 和 4 中所述的人员。

第 11 条
救生艇筏的集合与登乘布置

1　须有认可的降落设备的救生艇和救生筏,应存放在尽可能靠近起居处所和服务处所的地方。

2　集合站应设在紧靠登乘站的地方。每个集合站应在甲板上有足够的无障碍场地,以容纳指定在该站集合的所有人员,但人均面积至少为 0.35 m^2。

3　集合站与登乘站均应设在容易从起居和工作区域到达的地方。

①　参见《与救生设备和装置有关的符号》(经修订的第 760(18)号决议)以及《逃生路线标志及设备位置标识》(经修订的第 A.1116(30)号决议)中的表 1 和表 2。参见经修订的第 A.1116(30)号决议的表 1、表 2 中的新标志,其中具体项目的标志与经修订的第 A.760(18)号决议表述不同。

4 Muster and embarkation stations shall be adequately illuminated by lighting supplied from the emergency source of electrical power required by regulation Ⅱ-1/42 or Ⅱ-1/43, as appropriate.

5 Alleyways, stairways and exits giving access to the muster and embarkation stations shall be lighted. Such lighting shall be capable of being supplied by the emergency source of electrical power required by regulation Ⅱ-1/42 or Ⅱ-1/43, as appropriate. In addition to and as part of the markings required under regulation Ⅱ-2/13.3.2.5.1, routes to muster stations shall be indicated with the muster station symbol, intended for that purpose, in accordance with the recommendations of the Organization.①

6 Davit-launched and free-fall launched survival craft muster and embarkation stations shall be so arranged as to enable stretcher cases to be placed in survival craft.

7 An embarkation ladder complying with the requirements of paragraph 6.1.6 of the Code extending, in a single length, from the deck to the waterline in the lightest seagoing condition under all conditions of trim of up to 10° and a list of up to 20° either way shall be provided at each embarkation station or at every two adjacent embarkation stations for survival craft launched down the side of the ship. However, the Administration may permit such ladders to be replaced by approved devices to afford access to the survival craft when waterborne, provided that there shall be at least one embarkation ladder on each side of the ship. Other means of embarkation enabling descent to the water in a controlled manner may be permitted for the liferafts required by regulation 31.1.4.

8 Where necessary, means shall be provided for bringing the davit-launched survival craft against the ship's side and holding them alongside so that persons can be safely embarked.

Regulation 12
Launching stations

Launching stations shall be in such positions as to ensure safe launching having particular regard to clearance from the propeller and steeply overhanging portions of the hull and so that, as far as possible, survival craft, except survival craft specially designed for free-fall launching, can be launched down the straight side of the ship. If positioned forward, they shall be located abaft the collision bulkhead in a sheltered position and, in this respect, the Administration shall give special consideration to the strength of the launching appliance.

Regulation 13
Stowage of survival craft

1 Each survival craft shall be stowed:

---

① Refer to *Symbols related to life-saving appliances and arrangements* (resolution A.760(18), as amended) and/or tables 1 and of *Escape route signs and equipment location markings* (resolution A.1116(30)), as appropriate. Refer to the new symbols in tables 1 and 2 of resolution A.1116(30) where the symbols for a specific item are differently expressed in resolutions A.760(18), as amended and A.1116(30). Refer also to *Guidelines for the evaluation, testing and application of low-location lighting on passenger ships* (resolution A.752(18)).

4　集合站与登乘站应根据情况，由第Ⅱ-1/42 或Ⅱ-1/43 条所要求的应急电源照明系统提供足够的照明。

5　通往集合站与登乘站的通道、梯道和出口应予照明。该照明系统应能根据情况由第Ⅱ-1/42或Ⅱ-1/43 条所要求的应急电源供电。此外，作为第Ⅱ-2/13.3.2.5.1 条要求的标志的一部分，通往集合站的路线应按本组织为此用途而提出的建议案用集合站的符号标明①。

6　吊艇架降落和自由降落的救生艇筏集合站与登乘站的布置，应能用担架把病人抬进救生艇筏。

7　在船舷降落的救生艇筏的每处登乘站或每二处相邻的登乘站均应设置一个符合《规则》6.1.6 要求的登乘梯，其单根长度在船舶纵倾至 10°和任何一舷横倾至 20°的所有情况下可从甲板延伸至最轻载航行水线。然而，主管机关可准许用经认可的能进入已在水中的救生艇筏的装置代替这些梯子，但船舶的两舷均应设有至少一个登乘梯。对于第 31.1.4 条要求的救生筏，可准许使用以受控方式下降至水面的其他登乘设施。

8　如有必要，应设有将吊艇架降落的救生艇筏贴靠并系留在船舷的装置，以使人员能安全登乘。

第 12 条
降落站

降落站的位置应确保救生艇筏安全降落，并特别注意避开螺旋桨及船体陡斜悬空部分，除专门设计为自由降落的救生艇筏外，应尽可能使救生艇筏能从船舷平直部分降落下水。如降落站设置在船的前部，则应位于防撞舱壁后方有遮蔽的位置，对此，主管机关应对降落设备的强度予以特别考虑。

第 13 条
救生艇筏的存放

1　每艘救生艇筏的存放应：

---

①　参见《与救生设备和装置有关的符号》（第 760（18）号决议）以及《逃生路线标志及设备位置标识》（第 A.1116（30）号决议）中的表 1 和表 2。参见第 A.1116（30）号决议的表 1、表 2 中的新标志，其中具体项目的标志与经修订的第 A.760（18）号决议表述不同。参见《客船低位照明的评估、测试和应用导则》（第 A.752（18）号决议）。

.1 so that neither the survival craft nor its stowage arrangements will interfere with the operation of any other survival craft or rescue boat at any other launching station;

.2 as near the water surface as is safe and practicable and, in the case of a survival craft other than a liferaft intended for throw-overboard launching, in such a position that the survival craft in the embarkation position is not less than 2 m above the waterline with the ship in the fully loaded condition under unfavourable conditions of trim of up to 10° and listed up to 20° either way, or to the angle at which the ship's weather deck edge becomes submerged, whichever is less;

.3 in a state of continuous readiness so that two crew members can carry out preparations for embarkation and launching in less than 5 min;

.4 fully equipped as required by this chapter and the Code; and

.5 as far as practicable, in a secure and sheltered position and protected from damage by fire and explosion. In particular, survival craft on tankers, other than the liferafts required by regulation 31.1.4, shall not be stowed on or above a cargo tank, slop tank, or other tank containing explosive or hazardous cargoes.

2 Lifeboats for lowering down the ship's side shall be stowed as far forward of the propeller as practicable. On cargo ships of 80 m in length and upwards but less than 120 m in length, each lifeboat shall be so stowed that the after end of the lifeboat is not less than the length of the lifeboat forward of the propeller. On cargo ships of 120 m in length and upwards and passenger ships of 80 m in length and upwards, each lifeboat shall be so stowed that the after end of the lifeboat is not less than 1.5 times the length of the lifeboat forward of the propeller. Where appropriate, the ship shall be so arranged that lifeboats, in their stowed positions, are protected from damage by heavy seas.

3 Lifeboats shall be stowed attached to launching appliances.

4.1 Every liferaft shall be stowed with its painter permanently attached to the ship.

4.2 Each liferaft or group of liferafts shall be stowed with a float-free arrangement complying with the requirements of paragraph 4.1.6 of the Code so that each floats free and, if inflatable, inflates automatically when the ship sinks.

4.3 Liferafts shall be so stowed as to permit manual release of one raft or container at a time from their securing arrangements.

4.4 Paragraphs 4.1 and 4.2 do not apply to liferafts required by regulation 31.1.4.

5 Davit-launched liferafts shall be stowed within reach of the lifting hooks, unless some means of transfer is provided which is not rendered inoperable within the limits of trim and list prescribed in paragraph 1.2 or by ship motion or power failure.

6 Liferafts intended for throw-overboard launching shall be so stowed as to be readily transferable for launching on either side of the ship unless liferafts, of the aggregate capacity required by regulation 31.1 to be capable of being launched on either side, are stowed on each side of the ship.

.1　使该救生艇筏或其存放装置不会妨碍存放在任何其他降落站的任何其他救生艇筏或救助艇的操作；

.2　在安全和可行的情况下尽可能靠近水面，除需抛出船外降落的救生筏外，在船舶满载时纵倾至 10°和任何一舷横倾至 20°或横倾至船舶露天甲板的边缘浸入水中的角度（取较小者）的不利情况下，其存放处应使其登乘位置在水线以上不少于 2 m；

.3　持续处于备用状态，使 2 名船员能在不到 5 min 内完成登乘和降落准备工作；

.4　配齐本章和《规则》所要求的属具；和

.5　尽可能位于安全并有遮蔽的地方，并加以保护以免火灾和爆炸造成损坏。特别是，油船上的救生艇筏，除第 31.1.4 条要求的救生筏外，不应存放在货油舱、污油舱或其他含有爆炸性或危险性货物的液舱上或其上方。

2　顺船舷降落的救生艇应存放在推进器前方尽量远的地方。对船长大于 80 m 但小于 120 m 的货船，救生艇应存放在使该救生艇尾端在螺旋桨前方不少于该救生艇长度的地方。对船长为 120 m 及以上的货船和船长为 80 m 及以上的客船，救生艇应存放在使该救生艇尾端在螺旋桨前方不小于该救生艇一倍半长度的地方。船舶的布置应视情对在存放位置的救生艇加以保护，以免受大风浪损坏。

3　存放的救生艇应附连于其降落设备。

4.1　每只救生筏的存放应将其首缆牢固地系在船上。

4.2　每只救生筏或每组救生筏的存放应设有一个符合《规则》4.1.6 要求的自由漂浮装置，以使每只救生筏能自由漂浮，如为气胀式，在船舶下沉时能自动充气。

4.3　救生筏的存放应能用手动方式，一次将 1 只筏或容器从其系固装置上释放。

4.4　上述 4.1 和 4.2 不适用于第 31.1.4 条要求的救生筏。

5　吊放式救生筏应存放在吊筏钩可到达的范围内，除非设有某种搬移设备，该设备在本条 1.2 所规定的纵倾和横倾范围内不致无法操作，也不致因船舶运动或动力故障而无法操作。

6　抛出舷外降落的救生筏的存放，应可易于转移到船舶的任一舷降落，除非救生筏已按第 31.1 条要求的总容量存放于船舶两舷，并能在任一舷降落。

Regulation 14
Stowage of rescue boats

Rescue boats shall be stowed:

.1 in a state of continuous readiness for launching in not more than 5 min, and, if the inflated type, in a fully inflated condition at all times;

.2 in a position suitable for launching and recovery;

.3 so that neither the rescue boat nor its stowage arrangements will interfere with the operation of any survival craft at any other launching station; and

.4 if it is also a lifeboat, in compliance with the requirements of regulation 13.

Regulation 15
Stowage of marine evacuation systems

1 The ship's side shall not have any openings between the embarkation station of the marine evacuation system and the waterline in the lightest seagoing condition and means shall be provided to protect the system from any projections.

2 Marine evacuation systems shall be in such positions as to ensure safe launching having particular regard to clearance from the propeller and steeply overhanging positions of the hull and so that, as far as practicable, the system can be launched down the straight side of the ship.

3 Each marine evacuation system shall be stowed so that neither the passage nor platform nor its stowage or operational arrangements will interfere with the operation of any other life-saving appliance at any other launching station.

4 Where appropriate, the ship shall be so arranged that the marine evacuation systems in their stowed positions are protected from damage by heavy seas.

Regulation 16
Survival craft launching and recovery arrangements

1 Unless expressly provided otherwise, launching and embarkation appliances complying with the requirements of section 6.1 of the Code shall be provided for all survival craft except those which are:

.1 boarded from a position on deck less than 4.5 m above the waterline in the lightest seagoing condition and which have a mass of not more than 185 kg; or

第 14 条
救助艇的存放

救助艇的存放应：

.1 持续处于备用状态，不超过 5 min 即可降落，如果为充气式，随时处于充足气状态；

.2 在适宜于降落和回收的位置；

.3 使该救助艇及其存放装置，均不会妨碍存放在任何其他降落站的任何救生艇筏的操作；和

.4 在其兼作救生艇时，符合第 13 条的要求。

第 15 条
海上撤离系统的存放

1 在海上撤离系统的登乘站和最轻载航行水线之间的船侧不应有任何开口，并应设有保护该系统免受任何突出物影响的设施。

2 海上撤离系统应布置在能安全降落的位置，并特别注意避开螺旋桨及船体陡斜悬空部分，以尽可能使海上撤离系统能从船舷平直部分降落下水。

3 每一海上撤离系统的存放应使通道或平台，或其存放或操作装置均不会妨碍任何其他救生设备在任何其他降落站的操作。

4 船舶的布置应视情对在存放位置的海上撤离系统加以保护，以免受大风浪损坏。

第 16 条
救生艇筏的降落与回收装置

1 除另有明文规定外，所有救生艇筏应配备符合《规则》第 6.1 节要求的降落和登乘设备，但下列艇筏除外：

.1 距最轻载航行水线以上高度小于 4.5 m 高度的甲板上登乘的救生艇筏，且其质量不大于 185 kg；或

.2 boarded from a position on deck less than 4.5 m above the waterline in the lightest seagoing condition and which are stowed for launching directly from the stowed position under unfavourable conditions of trim of up to 10° and list of up to 20° either way; or

.3 carried in excess of the survival craft for 200% of the total number of persons on board the ship and which have a mass of not more than 185 kg; or

.4 carried in excess of the survival craft for 200% of the total number of persons on board the ship, are stowed for launching directly from the stowed position under unfavourable conditions of trim of up to 10° and list of up to 20° either way; or

.5 provided for use in conjunction with a marine evacuation system, complying with the requirements of section 6.2 of the Code and stowed for launching directly from the stowed position under unfavourable conditions of trim of up to 10° and list of up to 20° either way.

2 Each lifeboat shall be provided with an appliance which is capable of launching and recovering the lifeboat. In addition there shall be provision for hanging-off the lifeboat to free the release gear for maintenance.

3 Launching and recovery arrangements shall be such that the appliance operator on the ship is able to observe the survival craft at all times during launching and for lifeboats during recovery.

4 Only one type of release mechanism shall be used for similar survival craft carried on board the ship.

5 Preparation and handling of survival craft at any one launching station shall not interfere with the prompt preparation and handling of any other survival craft or rescue boat at any other station.

6 Falls, where used, shall be long enough for the survival craft to reach the water with the ship in its lightest seagoing condition, under unfavourable conditions of trim of up to 10° and list of up to 20° either way.

7 During preparation and launching, the survival craft, its launching appliance, and the area of water into which it is to be launched shall be adequately illuminated by lighting supplied from the emergency source of electrical power required by regulation Ⅱ-1/42 or Ⅱ-1/43, as appropriate.

8 Means shall be available to prevent any discharge of water onto survival craft during abandonment.

9 If there is a danger of the survival craft being damaged by the ship's stabilizer wings, means shall be available, powered by an emergency source of energy, to bring the stabilizer wings inboard; indicators operated by an emergency source of energy shall be available on the navigating bridge to show the position of the stabilizer wings.

.2 距最轻载航行水线以上高度小于 4.5 m 的甲板上登乘的救生艇筏，且存放方式为可在纵倾至 10°和任何一舷横倾至 20°的不利情况下直接从存放地点降落下水；或

.3 超过按船上总人数 200%所配备的救生艇筏，且其质量不大于 185 kg；或

.4 超过按船上总人数 200%所配备的救生艇筏，且存放方式为可在纵倾至 10°和任何一舷横倾至 20°的不利情况下直接从存放地点降落下水；或

.5 供连同海上撤离系统一起使用并符合《规则》第 6.2 节要求的救生艇筏，且存放方式为可在纵倾至 10°和任何一舷横倾至 20°的不利情况下直接从存放地点降落下水。

2 每艘救生艇应设有 1 台能降落和回收该救生艇的设备。此外，还应配备放开救生艇的装置，以便释放装置在不受载的情况下进行维护保养。

3 降落与回收装置应使该设备的操作人员在救生艇筏降落期间以及救生艇回收期间，能随时在船上观察到救生艇筏。

4 船上所配备的类似救生艇筏应仅使用同一种型式的释放机械装置。

5 在任一降落站，救生艇筏的准备和操作不应妨碍任何其他降落站的任何其他救生艇筏或救助艇的迅速准备和操作。

6 吊艇索（如使用）应有足够的长度，在船舶最轻载航行时纵倾至 10°和任何一舷横倾至 20°的不利情况下，可使救生艇筏到达水面。

7 在准备和降落过程中，救生艇筏和其降落设备以及降落的水域，应根据情况使用第Ⅱ-1/42 或Ⅱ-1/43 条所要求的应急电源供电的照明系统提供足够的照明。

8 在弃船过程中，应有能防止船舶的任何排水排放到救生艇筏内的设施。

9 如救生艇筏有被船舶减摇翼损坏的危险，则应有由应急电源驱动的、能将减摇翼收回船内的设施；驾驶台应设有应急电源操纵的指示减摇翼位置的指示器。

10 If partially enclosed lifeboats complying with the requirements of section 4.5 of the Code are carried, a davit span shall be provided, fitted with not less than two lifelines of sufficient length to reach the water with the ship in its lightest seagoing condition, under unfavourable conditions of trim of up to 10° and list of up to 20° either way.

Regulation 17
Rescue boat embarkation, launching and recovery arrangements

1 The rescue boat embarkation and launching arrangements shall be such that the rescue boat can be boarded and launched in the shortest possible time.

2 If the rescue boat is one of the ship's survival craft, the embarkation arrangements and launching station shall comply with the requirements of regulations 11 and 12.

3 Launching arrangements shall comply with the requirements of regulation 16. However, all rescue boats shall be capable of being launched, where necessary utilizing painters, with the ship making headway at speeds up to 5 knots in calm water.

4 Recovery time of the rescue boat shall be not more than 5 min in moderate sea conditions when loaded with its full complement of persons and equipment. If the rescue boat is also a lifeboat, this recovery time shall be possible when loaded with its lifeboat equipment and the approved rescue boat complement of at least six persons.

5 Rescue boat embarkation and recovery arrangements shall allow for safe and efficient handling of a stretcher case. Foul weather recovery strops shall be provided for safety if heavy fall blocks constitute a danger.

Regulation 17-1
Recovery of persons from the water

1 All ships shall have ship-specific plans and procedures for recovery of persons from the water, taking into account the guidelines developed by the Organization①. The plans and procedures shall identify the equipment intended to be used for recovery purposes and measures to be taken to minimize the risk to shipboard personnel involved in recovery operations. Ships constructed before 1 July 2014 shall comply with this requirement by the first periodical or renewal safety equipment survey of the ship to be carried out after 1 July 2014, whichever comes first.

2 Ro-ro passenger ships which comply with regulation 26.4 shall be deemed to comply with this regulation.

① Refer to *Guidelines for the development of plans and procedures for recovery of persons from the water* (MSC.1/Circ.1447).

10 如配备符合《规则》第 4.5 节要求的部分封闭救生艇,应装设吊艇架横张索,在其上设置不少于 2 根足够长度的救生索,以便船舶在最轻载航行时在纵倾至 10°和任何一舷横倾至 20°的不利情况下,可使救生索到达水面。

第 17 条
救助艇的登乘、降落与回收装置

1 救助艇的登乘与降落装置,应使救助艇能在尽可能短的时间内登乘和降落。

2 如救助艇是船舶救生艇筏中的一艘,其登乘装置与降落站应符合第 11 条和第 12 条的要求。

3 降落装置应符合第 16 条的要求。但是,所有救助艇均应能在船舶于平静水面上前进航速达到 5 kn 时降落,如必要可用艇首缆。

4 救助艇在载足额定乘员及属具时的中等海况下的回收时间应不超过 5 min。如救助艇兼作救生艇,应能在此时间内回收载有救生艇属具及认可额定乘员(至少为 6 人)的救助艇。

5 救助艇登乘和回收装置应能做到安全而有效地搬运担架病人。如果重型吊艇滑车构成危险,为安全起见应设有供恶劣天气下使用的回收环索。

第 17-1 条
营救落水人员

1 所有船舶须参照本组织制定的导则①备有针对本船的落水人员营救计划和程序。计划和程序须列明拟用于营救的设备和为最大程度减少对船上从事营救人员的风险而拟采取的措施。2014 年 7 月 1 日以前建造的船舶须在 2014 年 7 月 1 日以后的第一次定期检验或设备安全更新检验(以较早者为准)时符合本要求。

2 符合第 26.4 条要求的滚装客船应视为符合本条要求。

---

① 参见《落水人员营救的计划与程序编制导则》(第 MSC.1/Circ.1447 号通函)。

Regulation 18
Line-throwing appliances

A line-throwing appliance complying with the requirements of section 7.1 of the Code shall be provided.

Regulation 19
Emergency training and drills

1 This regulation applies to all ships.

2 Familiarity with safety installations and practice musters

2.1 Every crew member with assigned emergency duties shall be familiar with these duties before the voyage begins.

2.2 On a ship engaged on a voyage where passengers are scheduled to be on board for more than 24 h, musters of newly-embarked passengers shall take place prior to or immediately upon departure. Passengers shall be instructed in the use of the lifejackets and the action to take in an emergency.

2.3 Whenever new passengers embark, a passenger safety briefing shall be given immediately before departure, or immediately after departure. The briefing shall include the instructions required by regulations 8.2 and 8.4, and shall be made by means of an announcement, in one or more languages likely to be understood by the passengers. The announcement shall be made on the ship's public address system, or by other equivalent means likely to be heard at least by the passengers who have not yet heard it during the voyage. The briefing may be included in the muster required by paragraph 2.2. Information cards or posters or video programmes displayed on ships video displays may be used to supplement the briefing, but may not be used to replace the announcement.

3 Drills

3.1 Drills shall, as far as practicable, be conducted as if there were an actual emergency.

3.2 Every crew member shall participate in at least one abandon ship drill and one fire drill every month. The drills of the crew shall take place within 24 h of the ship leaving a port if more than 25% of the crew have not participated in abandon ship and fire drills on board that particular ship in the previous month. When a ship enters service for the first time, after modification of a major character or when a new crew is engaged, these drills shall be held before sailing. The Administration may accept other arrangements that are at least equivalent for those classes of ships for which this is impracticable.

3.3 Crew members with enclosed space entry or rescue responsibilities shall participate in an enclosed space entry and rescue drill to be held on board the ship at least once every two months.

第 18 条
抛绳器

应配备一具符合《规则》第 7.1 节要求的抛绳器。

第 19 条
应急培训与演习

1 本条适用于所有船舶。

2 熟悉安全装置与集合演习

2.1 每位被指派为具有应急职责的船员,应在开航前熟悉这些职责。

2.2 若乘客按行程将在船上停留 24 小时以上,从事此种航行的船舶须在开航前或开航后立即集合新上船的乘客,并向乘客介绍救生衣的使用方法以及在紧急情况下应采取的行动。

2.3 每当新乘客上船时,应在即将启航前,或在启航后立即向乘客做安全介绍。该介绍应包括第 8.2 和 8.4 条所要求的须知,并应以一种或多种易被乘客听懂的语言进行宣讲。宣讲须使用船上的公共广播系统进行,或者使用至少让在航行中尚未听到该宣讲的乘客能够听到的其他等效方式进行。该介绍可包括在上述第 2.2 款要求的集合之内。可以使用信息卡片或宣传画,或者在船上的视频显示屏幕上播出的视频节目来辅助介绍,但不可用其代替宣讲。

3 演习

3.1 演习应尽实际可能做到像真正发生了紧急情况。

3.2 每名船员每月应至少参加一次弃船演习和一次消防演习。如有 25%以上的船员未参加船上上个月的弃船和消防演习,应在该船离港后 24 h 内举行该两项船员演习。当船舶在经重大改装后首次投入营运时,或有新船员时,应在开航前举行这些演习。主管机关对无法这样做的各类船舶,可以接受至少是等效的其他安排。

3.3 具有进入封闭处所或救助职责的船员须参加船上至少每两个月举行一次的进入封闭处所和救助的演练。

3.4 Abandon ship drill

3.4.1 Each abandon ship drill shall include:

.1 summoning of passengers and crew to muster stations with the alarm required by regulation 6.4.2 followed by drill announcement on the public address or other communication system and ensuring that they are made aware of the order to abandon ship;

.2 reporting to stations and preparing for the duties described in the muster list;

.3 checking that passengers and crew are suitably dressed;

.4 checking that lifejackets are correctly donned;

.5 lowering of at least one lifeboat after any necessary preparation for launching;

.6 starting and operating the lifeboat engine;

.7 operation of davits used for launching liferafts;

.8 a mock search and rescue of passengers trapped in their staterooms; and

.9 instruction in the use of radio life-saving appliances.

3.4.2 Different lifeboats shall, as far as practicable, be lowered in compliance with the requirements of paragraph 3.4.1.5 at successive drills.

3.4.3 Except as provided in paragraphs 3.4.4 and 3.4.5, each lifeboat shall be launched, and manoeuvred in the water by its assigned operating crew, at least once every three months during an abandon ship drill.

3.4.4 In the case of a lifeboat arranged for free-fall launching, at least once every three months during an abandon ship drill the crew shall board the lifeboat, properly secure themselves in their seats and commence launch procedures up to, but not including, the actual release of the lifeboat (i.e., the release hook shall not be released). The lifeboat shall then either be free-fall launched with only the required operating crew on board, or lowered into the water by means of the secondary means of launching with or without the operating crew on board. In both cases, the lifeboat shall thereafter be manoeuvred in the water by the operating crew. At intervals of not more than six months, the lifeboat shall either be launched by free fall with only the operating crew on board, or simulated launching shall be carried out in accordance with the guidelines developed by the Organization①.

3.4.5 The Administration may allow ships operating on short international voyages not to launch the lifeboats on one side if their berthing arrangements in port and their trading patterns do not permit launching of lifeboats on that side. However, all such lifeboats shall be lowered at least once every three months and launched at least annually.

① Refer to *Measures to prevent accidents with lifeboats* (MSC.1/Circ.1206/Rev.1).

3.4　弃船演习

3.4.1　每次弃船演习应包括：

.1　先使用第6.4.2条所要求的报警系统，然后通过公共广播或其他通信系统宣布进行演习，将乘客和船员召集至集合站，并确保他们知道弃船命令；

.2　向集合站报到，并准备执行应变部署表所述的任务；

.3　查看乘客和船员穿着是否合适；

.4　查看是否正确地穿好救生衣；

.5　在完成任何必要的降落准备工作后，至少降下一艘救生艇；

.6　启动并操作救生艇发动机；

.7　操作降落救生筏所用的吊艇架；

.8　模拟搜救几位被困于客舱中的乘客；和

.9　介绍无线电救生设备的使用。

3.4.2　不同的救生艇应尽可能按本条3.4.1.5要求，在相继的演习中轮流降放。

3.4.3　除本条3.4.4和3.4.5规定外，每艘救生艇应在弃船演习中每3个月至少有一次乘载被指派的操艇船员降落下水，并在水上进行操纵。

3.4.4　如果救生艇作自由降落下水，在弃船演习中每3个月至少有一次船员应登上救生艇，在其座位中正确系固并开始降落下水程序直至但不包括实际释放救生艇(即释放钩不应松开)。随后，救生艇应仅搭载必需的操艇船员自由降落下水，或用辅助降落下水装置搭载或不搭载操艇船员降放至水面。在这两种情况下，救生艇均应由操艇船员在水中操纵。救生艇应按不超过六个月的间隔期，仅搭载操艇船员自由降落下水，或按本组织制定的指南进行模拟降落下水。①

3.4.5　对于从事短程国际航行的船舶，如果由于港口泊位的安排及其运输方式不允许救生艇在某一舷降落下水，主管机关可准许救生艇不在该舷降落下水。但是，所有这些救生艇应至少每3个月下降一次并每年至少降落下水一次。

① 参见《防止救生艇事故措施》(第MSC.1/Circ.1206/Rev.1号通函)。

3.4.6 As far as is reasonable and practicable, rescue boats other than lifeboats which are also rescue boats, shall be launched each month with their assigned crew aboard and manoeuvred in the water. In all cases this requirement shall be complied with at least once every three months.

3.4.7 If lifeboat and rescue boat launching drills are carried out with the ship making headway, such drills shall, because of the dangers involved, be practised in sheltered waters only and under the supervision of an officer experienced in such drills.

3.4.8 If a ship is fitted with marine evacuation systems, drills shall include exercising of the procedures required for the deployment of such a system up to the point immediately preceding actual deployment of the system. This aspect of drills should be augmented by regular instruction using the on-board training aids required by regulation 35.4. Additionally every system party member shall, as far as practicable, be further trained by participation in a full deployment of a similar system into water, either on board a ship or ashore, at intervals of not longer than two years, but in no case longer than three years. This training can be associated with the deployments required by regulation 20.8.2.

3.4.9 Emergency lighting for mustering and abandonment shall be tested at each abandon ship drill.

3.5 Fire drills

3.5.1 Fire drills should be planned in such a way that due consideration is given to regular practice in the various emergencies that may occur depending on the type of ships and the cargo.

3.5.2 Each fire drill shall include:

.1 reporting to stations and preparing for the duties described in the muster list required by regulation 8;

.2 starting of a fire pump, using at least the two required jets of water to show that the system is in proper working order;

.3 checking of fireman's outfit and other personal rescue equipment;

.4 checking of relevant communication equipment;

.5 checking the operation of watertight doors, fire doors, fire dampers and main inlets and outlets of ventilation systems in the drill area; and

.6 checking the necessary arrangements for subsequent abandoning of the ship.

3.5.3 The equipment used during drills shall immediately be brought back to its fully operational condition and any faults and defects discovered during the drills shall be remedied as soon as possible.

3.6 Enclosed space entry and rescue drills

3.4.6 除兼作救生艇的救助艇外，其他救助艇均应在合理和可行的范围内，每个月搭载指定的船员降落下水并在水上进行操纵。在任何情况下，应至少每 3 个月按此要求进行一次。

3.4.7 如救生艇与救助艇的降落下水演习是在船舶前进航行中进行，由于涉及危险，该项演习应仅在有遮蔽的水域，并在有此项演习经验的高级船员监督下进行。

3.4.8 如船上配备海上撤离系统，演习应包括按对该系统布放所要求的程序，演练至即将实际布放这一系统的程度。这方面的演习应按常规程序强化并使用第 35.4 条要求的船上培训教具进行。此外，该系统的每一成员还应尽可能，通过在船上或岸上参加类似系统在水中的全面布放而进行进一步的培训，参加的间隔期应不超过 2 年，但无论如何不得超过 3 年。此种培训可同第 20.8.2 条要求的布放结合起来进行。

3.4.9 在每次弃船演习时，应测试用于集合与弃船的应急照明系统。

3.5 消防演习

3.5.1 在制定消防演习计划时，对根据船型和货物类型下而可能发生的各种紧急情况下的常规操作，应给予充分考虑。

3.5.2 每次消防演习应包括：

.1 向集合站报到，并准备执行第 8 条要求的应变部署表所述的任务；

.2 启动一个消防泵，要求至少有 2 根消防水喉正常出水，以表明该系统是处于正常的工作状态；

.3 检查消防员装备和其他个人救援设备；

.4 检查有关的通信设备；

.5 检查演习区域内的水密门、防火门和挡火闸以及通风系统主要进出口的工作情况；和

.6 检查供随后弃船用的必要装置。

3.5.3 演习中使用过的设备应立即恢复到完好的操作状况；演习中发现的任何故障和缺陷，应尽快予以消除。

3.6 进入封闭处所和救助的演练

3.6.1 Enclosed space entry and rescue drills should be planned and conducted in a safe manner, taking into account, as appropriate, the guidance provided in the recommendations developed by the Organization.①

3.6.2 Each enclosed space entry and rescue drill shall include:

.1 checking and use of personal protective equipment required for entry;

.2 checking and use of communication equipment and procedures;

.3 checking and use of instruments for measuring the atmosphere in enclosed spaces;

.4 checking and use of rescue equipment and procedures; and

.5 instructions in first aid and resuscitation techniques.

4 On-board training and instructions

4.1 On-board training in the use of the ship's life-saving appliances, including survival craft equipment, and in the use of the ship's fire-extinguishing appliances shall be given as soon as possible but not later than two weeks after a crew member joins the ship. However, if the crew member is on a regularly scheduled rotating assignment to the ship, such training shall be given not later than two weeks after the time of first joining the ship. Instructions in the use of the ship's fire-extinguishing appliances, life-saving appliances, and in survival at sea shall be given at the same interval as the drills. Individual instruction may cover different parts of the ship's life-saving and fire-extinguishing appliances, but all the ship's life-saving and fire-extinguishing appliances shall be covered within any period of two months.

4.2 Every crew member shall be given instructions which shall include but not necessarily be limited to:

.1 operation and use of the ship's inflatable liferafts;

.2 problems of hypothermia, first-aid treatment for hypothermia and other appropriate first-aid procedures;

.3 special instructions necessary for use of the ship's life-saving appliances in severe weather and severe sea conditions;

.4 operation and use of fire-extinguishing appliances; and

.5 risks associated with enclosed spaces and onboard procedures for safe entry into such spaces which should take into account, as appropriate, the guidance provided in recommendations developed by the Organization.①

---

① Refer to the *Revised Recommendation for entering enclosed spaces aboard ships* (resolution A.1050(27)).

3.6.1 进入封闭处所和救助的演练须以安全的方式计划和执行,并视具体情况考虑到本组织制定的建议案中提供的指导。①

3.6.2 每次进入封闭处所和救助的演练均须包括:

.1 检查并使用进入所需的个人保护设备;

.2 检查并使用通信设备和程序;

.3 检查并使用测量封闭处所内空气的仪器;

.4 检查并使用救助设备和程序;和

.5 急救和复苏技术的指导。

4 船上培训与授课

4.1 船员上船后,应尽快在不迟于 2 个星期内,对其进行有关使用包括救生艇筏属具在内的船上救生设备和使用船上消防设备的船上培训。但是,如果船员是定期安排轮派上船,则这种培训应在不迟于船员第一次上船后 2 个星期内进行。应讲授船舶消防设备和救生设备的用法以及海上救生的课程,授课间隔期与演习间隔期相同。每次授课可以包括船舶救生设备和消防设备的各个不同部分,但在任何 2 个月的授课期内应包括该船的全部救生和消防设备。

4.2 每位船员均应听课, 课程应包括但不限于:

.1 船舶气胀式救生筏的操作与使用;

.2 低温保护问题,体温过低的急救护理和其他合适的急救程序;

.3 在恶劣气候和恶劣海况中使用船舶救生设备所必需的专门课程;

.4 消防设备的操作与使用;和

.5 封闭处所的相关风险和安全进入此类处所的船上程序,应视具体情况考虑到本组织制定的建议案中提供的指导。①

---

① 参见本组织以第 A.1050(27)号决议通过的《经修订的进入船上封闭处所的建议案》。

4.3 On-board training in the use of davit-launched liferafts shall take place at intervals of not more than four months on every ship fitted with such appliances. Whenever practicable this shall include the inflation and lowering of a liferaft. This liferaft may be a special liferaft intended for training purposes only, which is not part of the ship's life-saving equipment; such a special liferaft shall be conspicuously marked.

5 Records

The date when musters are held, details of abandon ship drills and fire drills, enclosed space entry and rescue drills, drills of other life-saving appliances and on-board training shall be recorded in such logbook as may be prescribed by the Administration. If a full muster, drill or training session is not held at the appointed time, an entry shall be made in the logbook stating the circumstances and the extent of the muster, drill or training session held.

Regulation 20
Operational readiness, maintenance and inspections

1 This regulation applies to all ships. The requirements of paragraphs 3.2, 3.3 and 6.2 shall be complied with, as far as is practicable, on ships constructed before 1 July 1986.

2 Operational readiness

Before the ship leaves port and at all times during the voyage, all life-saving appliances shall be in working order and ready for immediate use.

3 Maintenance

3.1 Maintenance, testing and inspections of life-saving appliances shall be carried out in a manner having due regard to ensuring reliability of such appliances.

3.2 Instructions for on-board maintenance of life-saving appliances complying with regulation 36 shall be provided and maintenance shall be carried out accordingly.

3.3 The Administration may accept, in compliance with the requirements of paragraph 3.2, a shipboard planned maintenance programme, which includes the requirements of regulation 36.

4 Maintenance of falls

Falls used in launching shall be inspected periodically① with special regard for areas passing through sheaves, and renewed when necessary due to deterioration of the falls or at intervals of not more than five years, whichever is the earlier.

5 Spares and repair equipment

Spares and repair equipment shall be provided for life-saving appliances and their components which are subject to excessive wear or consumption and need to be replaced regularly.

---

① Refer to *Measures to prevent accidents with lifeboats* (MSC.1/Circ.1206/Rev.1).

4.3　在每艘装有吊放式救生筏的船上，应按不超过 4 个月的间隔期举行一次此项设备用法的船上培训。凡可行时，此项培训应包括一个救生筏的充气与下降。这个救生筏可以是培训专用救生筏，而不是船舶救生设备的组成部分，并应明显地标出专用救生筏标志。

5　记录

举行集合的日期、弃船演习和消防演习、进入封闭处所和救助的演习的详细情况、其他救生设备演习以及船上培训均应记载于可由主管机关规定的航海日志内。如果在指定时间内未举行全部集合、演习或培训项目，则应在航海日志内记述其原因和已举行的集合、演习或培训项目的范围。

第 20 条
使用准备状态、维护保养与检查

1　本条适用于所有船舶。1986 年 7 月 1 日以前建造的船舶，应尽可能符合本条 3.2、3.3 和 6.2 的要求。

2　使用准备状态

在船舶离港前以及在航行期间的任何时候，所有救生设备均应处于工作状态，并立即可用。

3　维护保养

3.1　救生设备的维护保养、测试和检查的进行须充分考虑到确保此类设备的可靠性。

3.2　应备有符合第 36 条要求的救生设备船上维护保养须知，并应按须知进行维护保养。

3.3　主管机关可按 3.2 的要求，接受包括第 36 条的要求在内的船上计划维护保养程序。

4　吊艇索的保养

降落所用的吊艇索应定期检查[①]，要特别注意穿过滑轮的位置，并在由于吊艇索磨损而需要换新时或按不超过 5 年的间隔期（取早者）予以换新。

5　备件与修理设备

救生设备及其易损或易耗而需要定期更换的部件，应配有备件与修理设备。

---

① 参见《防止救生艇事故措施》（第 MSC.1/Circ.1206/Rev.1 号通函）。

6 Weekly inspection

The following tests and inspections shall be carried out weekly and a report of the inspection shall be entered in the logbook:

.1 all survival craft, rescue boats and launching appliances shall be visually inspected to ensure that they are ready for use. The inspection shall include, but is not limited to, the condition of hooks, their attachment to the lifeboat and the on-load release gear being properly and completely reset;

.2 all engines in lifeboats and rescue boats shall be run for a total period of not less than 3 min, provided the ambient temperature is above the minimum temperature required for starting and running the engine. During this period of time, it should be demonstrated that the gearbox and gearbox train are engaging satisfactorily. If the special characteristics of an outboard motor fitted to a rescue boat would not allow it to be run other than with its propeller submerged for a period of 3 min, a suitable water supply may be provided. In special cases, the Administration may waive this requirement for ships constructed before 1 July 1986;

.3 lifeboats, except free-fall lifeboats, on cargo ships shall be moved from their stowed position, without any persons on board, to the extent necessary to demonstrate satisfactory operation of launching appliances, if weather and sea conditions so allow; and

.4 the general emergency alarm shall be tested.

7 Monthly inspections

7.1 All lifeboats, except free-fall lifeboats, shall be turned out from their stowed position, without any persons on board if weather and sea conditions so allow.

7.2 Inspection of the life-saving appliances, including lifeboat equipment, shall be carried out monthly using the checklist required by regulation 36.1 to ensure that they are complete and in good order. A report of the inspection shall be entered in the logbook.

8 Servicing of inflatable liferafts, inflatable lifejackets, marine evacuation systems, and maintenance and repair of inflated rescue boats

8.1 Every inflatable liferaft, inflatable lifejacket, and marine evacuation system shall be serviced:

.1 at intervals not exceeding 12 months, provided where in any case this is impracticable, the Administration may extend this period to 17 months; and

.2 at an approved servicing station which is competent to service them, maintains proper servicing facilities and uses only properly trained personnel.①

8.2 Rotational deployment of marine evacuation systems

① Refer to *Recommendation on conditions for the approval of servicing stations for inflatable liferafts* (resolution A.761(18), as amended).

6　每周检查

每周应进行下列试验和检查,并把检查报告写进航海日志:

.1　所有救生艇筏、救助艇及降落设备应进行目视检查,以确保其立即可用。检查应包括,但不限于吊钩、吊钩及其与救生艇的连接以及上载装置均状态良好且完全复位;

.2　只要环境温度在启动和运转发动机所要求的最低温度以上,所有救生艇和救助艇的发动机应进行运转试验,总时间不少于 3 min。在这段时间内, 应证实齿轮箱和齿轮箱传动系统运行正常。安装在救助艇上的舷外发动机如果由于其特殊性而不能在螺旋桨没有浸没的情况下运转 3 min,可适当供水。在特殊情况下,主管机关对于 1986 年 7 月 1 日以前建造的船舶,可不坚持此项要求;

.3　如果天气和海况允许,货船上除自由降落式救生艇外,应将救生艇在不载人的情况下从其存放位置做必要的移动,以证实降落设备可正常操作;和

.4　通用应急报警系统应进行试验。

7　月度检查

7.1　如果天气和海况允许,除自由降落式救生艇外的所有救生艇应在不载人的情况下移离其存放位置。

7.2　每月应使用第 36.1 条所要求的检查清单对救生设备(包括救生艇属具)检查,以确保其完整无缺并处于良好状态。检查报告应载入航海日志。

8　气胀式救生筏、气胀式救生衣、海上撤离系统的检修及充气式救助艇的维修保养

8.1　每一气胀式救生筏、每件气胀式救生衣和每一海上撤离系统均应按下列规定检修:

.1　间隔期不超过 12 个月,但在任何情况下都不可行时,主管机关可将此期限展至 17 个月;和

.2　在经认可的检修站进行检修,该检修站应胜任检修工作,备有适当的检修设施并仅使用受过适当培训的人员①。

8.2　海上撤离系统的轮换布放

① 参见《关于气胀式救生筏检修站认可条件的建议案》(经修正的第 A.761(18)号决议)。

In addition to or in conjunction with the servicing intervals of marine evacuation systems required by paragraph 8.1, each marine evacuation system should be deployed from the ship on a rotational basis at intervals to be agreed by the Administration provided that each system is to be deployed at least once every six years.

8.3 An Administration which approves new and novel inflatable liferaft arrangements pursuant to regulation 4 may allow for extended service intervals on the following conditions:

8.3.1 The new and novel liferaft arrangement has proved to maintain the same standard, as required by testing procedure, during extended service intervals.

8.3.2 The liferaft system shall be checked on board by certified personnel according to paragraph 8.1.1.

8.3.3 Service at intervals not exceeding five years shall be carried out in accordance with the recommendations of the Organization.①

8.4 All repairs and maintenance of inflated rescue boats shall be carried out in accordance with the manufacturer's instructions. Emergency repairs may be carried out on board the ship; however, permanent repairs shall be effected at an approved servicing station.

8.5 An Administration which permits extension of liferaft service intervals in accordance with paragraph 8.3 shall notify the Organization of such action in accordance with regulation Ⅰ/5(b).

9 Periodic servicing of hydrostatic release units

Hydrostatic release units, other than disposable hydrostatic release units, shall be serviced:

.1 at intervals not exceeding 12 months, provided where in any case this is impracticable, the Administration may extend this period to 17 months;②and

.2 at a servicing station which is competent to service them, maintains proper servicing facilities and uses only properly trained personnel.

10 Marking of stowage locations

Containers, brackets, racks, and other similar stowage locations for life-saving equipment shall be marked with symbols in accordance with the recommendations of the Organization,③ indicating the devices stowed in that location for that purpose. If more than one device is stowed in that location, the number of devices shall also be indicated.

11 Maintenance, thorough examination, operational testing, overhaul and repair of lifeboats, rescue boats and fast rescue boats, launching appliances and release gear

① Refer to *Recommendation of conditions for the approval of servicing stations for inflatable liferafts* (resolution A.761(18), as amended).

② Refer to *Servicing of life-saving appliances and radiocommunication equipment under the harmonized system of survey and Certification* (*HSSC*) (MSC/Circ.955).

③ Refer to *Symbols related to life-saving appliances and arrangements* (resolution A.760(18), as amended) and/or tables 1 and 2 of *Escape route signs and equipment location markings* (resolution A.1116(30)), as appropriate. Refer to the new symbols in tables 1 and 2 of resolution A.1116(30) where the symbols for a specific item are differently expressed in resolutions A.760(18), as amended and A.1116(30).

除上述 8.1 所要求的海上撤离系统检修间隔期外,或与该检修间隔期相结合,每一海上撤离系统还应以主管机关同意的间隔期从船上轮流布放,但每个系统每 6 年应至少布放 1 次。

8.3　主管机关对按第 4 条认可的新颖气胀式救生筏装置,可根据以下条件允许检修期限展期:

8.3.1　在检修间隔期展期内,按试验程序的要求,已证实新颖气胀式救生筏装置保持同一标准。

8.3.2　救生筏系统应由持证人员按 8.1.1 的要求在船上进行检查。

8.3.3　检修间隔期不应超过 5 年并应按本组织的建议案①进行。

8.4　充气式救助艇的所有修理和维护保养应按制造商的说明书要求进行。应急修理可在船上进行;但是彻底检修应在经认可的检修站进行。

8.5　主管机关如按 8.3 要求允许救生筏检修间隔期展期,则应根据第Ⅰ/5(b)条将此情况通知本组织。

9　静水压力释放器的定期检修

静水压力释放器,除一次性静水压力释放器外,应按下列规定检修:

.1　间隔期不超过 12 个月,但在任何情况下都不可行时,主管机关可将此期限展至17 个月;②和

.2　在检修站进行检修,该检修站应胜任检修工作,备有适当的检修设施并仅使用受过适当培训的人员。

10　存放位置的标记

救生设备的容器、支架、搁架及其他类似存放装置的位置,应按本组织的建议案③用符号加以标记,表明该位置存放的设备及用途。如这个位置存放有一个以上的设备,则应表明其数量。

11　救生艇、救助艇和快速救助艇,降落设备和释放装置的维护保养、彻底检查、操作测试、大修和修理

① 参见《关于气胀式救生筏检修站认可条件的建议案》(经修正的第 A.761(18)号决议)。

② 参见《检验和发证协调系统(HSSC)救生设备和无线电设备的检修》(第 MSC/Circ.955 号通函)。

③ 参见《与救生设备和装置有关的符号》(第 760(18)号决议)以及《逃生路线标志及设备位置标识》(第 A.1116(30)号决议)中的表 1 和表 2。参见第 A.1116(30)号决议的表 1、表 2 中的新标志,其中具体项目的标志与经修订的第 A.760(18)号决议表述不同。

11.1 Launching appliances shall be:

.1 subject to a thorough examination at the annual surveys required by regulations Ⅰ/7 or Ⅰ/8, as applicable; and

.2 upon completion of the examination referred to in paragraph 11.1.1, subjected to a dynamic test of the winch brake at maximum lowering speed. The load to be applied shall be the mass of the survival craft or rescue boat without persons on board, except that, at intervals of at least once every five years, the test shall be carried out with a proof load equal to 1.1 times the weight of the survival craft or rescue boat and its full complement of persons and equipment.

11.2 Lifeboat and rescue boat release gear, including fast rescue boat release gear and free-fall lifeboat release systems, shall be:

.1 subject to a thorough examination and operational test during the annual surveys required by regulations Ⅰ/7 and Ⅰ/8;

.2 in case of on-load release gear, operationally tested under a load of 1.1 times the total mass of the boat when loaded with its full complement of persons and equipment whenever the release gear is overhauled. Such overhauling and operational test shall be carried out at least once every five years;① and

.3 notwithstanding paragraph 11.2.2, the operational testing of free-fall lifeboat release systems shall be performed either by free-fall launch with only the operating crew on board or by a test without launching the lifeboat carried out based on the Requirements for maintenance, thorough examination, operational testing, overhaul and repair.

11.3 Davit-launched liferaft automatic release hooks shall be:

.1 subject to a thorough examination and operational test during the annual surveys required by regulations Ⅰ/7 and Ⅰ/8; and

.2 operationally tested under a load of 1.1 times the total mass of the liferaft when loaded with its full complement of persons and equipment whenever the automatic release hook is overhauled. Such overhauling and operational test shall be carried out at least once every five years.

11.4 Lifeboats and rescue boats, including fast rescue boats, shall be subject to a thorough examination and operational test during the annual surveys required by regulations Ⅰ/7 and Ⅰ/8.

11.5 The thorough examination, operational testing and overhaul required by paragraphs 11.1 to 11.4 and the maintenance and repair of equipment specified in paragraphs 11.1 to 11.4 shall be carried out in accordance with the Requirements for maintenance, thorough examination, operational testing, overhaul and repair, and the instructions for onboard maintenance as required by regulation 36.

---

① Refer to *Recommendation on testing of life-saving appliance* (resolution A.689(17), as amended). For life-saving appliances installed on board on or after 1 July 1999, refer to *Revised Recommendations on testing of life-saving appliances* (resolution MSC.81(70), as amended).

11.1　降落设备须：

.1　在第Ⅰ/7 或Ⅰ/8 条(如适用)要求的年度检验时进行彻底检查;和

.2　在完成第 11.1.1 款所述的检查后,以最大降落速度对绞车制动器进行动力测试。所加负荷须为救生筏或救助艇无乘员时的质量,但至少在每 5 年的间隔里,须用相等于救生筏或救助艇载足额定乘员和设备时重量 1.1 倍的验证负荷进行测试。

11.2　救生艇和救助艇的释放装置,包括快速救助艇释放装置和自由降落救生艇释放系统须：

.1　在第Ⅰ/7 和Ⅰ/8 条要求的年度检验时进行彻底检查和操作测试;

.2　凡当承载释放装置大修时,用艇载足额定乘员和设备时总质量 1.1 倍的负荷进行操作测试。此种大修和操作测试须至少每 5 年进行一次;①和

.3　尽管有第 11.2.2 款的规定,自由降落救生艇释放系统的操作测试须仅搭载操艇船员自由降落下水或按照维护保养、彻底检查、操作测试、大修和修理要求进行试验而无须降落救生艇下水。

11.3　吊放式救生筏的自动释放钩须：

.1　在第Ⅰ/7 和Ⅰ/8 条要求的年度检验时进行彻底检查和操作测试;和

.2　凡当自动释放钩大修时,用救生筏载足额定乘员和设备时总质量 1.1 倍的负荷进行操作测试。此种大修和操作测试须至少每 5 年进行一次。

11.4　救生艇和救助艇,包括快速救助艇,须在第Ⅰ/7 和Ⅰ/8 条要求的年度检验时进行彻底检查和操作测试。

11.5　须按照维护保养、彻底检查、操作测试、大修和修理要求和第 36 条要求的船上维护保养须知进行第 11.1 至 11.4 款要求的全面检查、操作测试和检修以及第 11.1 至 11.4 款规定的设备维护保养和修理。

---

①　参见本组织第 A.689(17)号决议通过的《经修正的关于救生设备试验的建议案》。对 1999 年 7 月 1 日或以后安装在船上的救生设备,参见本组织海上安全委员会第 MSC.80(71)号决议通过的《经修订的关于救生设备试验的建议案》。

Section Ⅱ
Passenger ships (additional requirements)

Regulation 21
Survival craft and rescue boats

1 Survival craft

1.1 Passenger ships engaged on international voyages which are not short international voyages shall carry:

.1 partially or totally enclosed lifeboats complying with the requirements of section 4.5 or 4.6 of the Code on each side of such aggregate capacity as will accommodate not less than 50% of the total number of persons on board. The Administration may permit the substitution of lifeboats by liferafts of equivalent total capacity provided that there shall never be less than sufficient lifeboats on each side of the ship to accommodate 37.5% of the total number of persons on board. The inflatable or rigid liferafts shall comply with the requirements of section 4.2 or 4.3 of the Code and shall be served by launching appliances equally distributed on each side of the ship; and

.2 in addition, inflatable or rigid liferafts complying with the requirements of section 4.2 or 4.3 of the Code of such aggregate capacity as will accommodate at least 25% of the total number of persons on board. These liferafts shall be served by at least one launching appliance on each side which may be those provided in compliance with the requirements of paragraph 1.1.1 or equivalent approved appliances capable of being used on both sides. However, stowage of these liferafts need not comply with the requirements of regulation 13.5.

1.2 Passenger ships engaged on short international voyages shall carry:

.1 partially or totally enclosed lifeboats complying with the requirements of section 4.5 or 4.6 of the Code of such aggregate capacity as will accommodate at least 30% of the total number of persons on board. The lifeboats shall, as far as practicable, be equally distributed on each side of the ship. In addition inflatable or rigid liferafts complying with the requirements of section 4.2 or 4.3 of the Code shall be carried of such aggregate capacity that, together with the lifeboat capacity, the survival craft will accommodate the total number of persons on board. The liferafts shall be served by launching appliances equally distributed on each side of the ship; and

第 2 节
客船(附加要求)

第 21 条
救生艇筏与救助艇

1　救生艇筏

1.1　从事非短程国际航行的客船应配备:

.1　符合《规则》第 4.5 或 4.6 节要求的部分封闭或全封闭救生艇,其在每舷的总容量应能容纳不少于船上人员总数的 50%。主管机关可准许以相等总容量的救生筏代替救生艇,但船舶每舷必须配备足够容纳不少于船上人员总数 37.5% 的救生艇。气胀式或刚性救生筏应符合《规则》第 4.2 或 4.3 节的要求,而且应使用均等分布在船舶每舷的降落设备;和

.2　此外,符合《规则》第 4.2 或 4.3 节要求的气胀式或刚性救生筏的总容量应至少能容纳船上人员总数的 25%。这些救生筏应使用每舷至少 1 台降落设备,该设备可以是按本条 1.1.1 要求装设的设备,或是能在两舷均可使用的等效认可设备。但是,这些救生筏的存放不必符合第 13.5 条的要求。

1.2　从事短程国际航行的客船应配备:

.1　符合《规则》第 4.5 或 4.6 节要求的部分封闭或全封闭救生艇,其总容量应至少能容纳船上人员总数的 30%。救生艇应尽可能均等分布在船舶各舷。此外,符合《规则》第 4.2 或 4.3 节要求的气胀式或刚性救生筏的总容量,连同救生艇的总容量,应能容纳船上人员总数。这些救生筏应使用均等分布在船舶每舷的降落设备;和

.2 in addition, inflatable or rigid liferafts complying with the requirements of section 4.2 or 4.3 of the Code of such aggregate capacity as will accommodate at least 25% of the total number of persons on board. These liferafts shall be served by at least one launching appliance on each side which may be those provided in compliance with the requirements of paragraph 1.2.1 or equivalent approved appliances capable of being used on both sides. However, stowage of these liferafts need not comply with the requirements of regulation 13.5.

1.3 All survival craft required to provide for abandonment by the total number of persons on board shall be capable of being launched with their full complement of persons and equipment within a period of 30 min from the time the abandon ship signal is given after all persons have been assembled, with lifejackets donned.

1.4 In lieu of meeting the requirements of paragraph 1.1 or 1.2, passenger ships of less than 500 gross tonnage where the total number of persons on board is less than 200, may comply with the following:

.1 they shall carry on each side of the ship, inflatable or rigid liferafts complying with the requirements of section 4.2 or 4.3 of the Code and of such aggregate capacity as will accommodate the total number of persons on board;

.2 unless the liferafts required by paragraph 1.4.1 are stowed in a position providing for easy side-to-side transfer at a single open deck level, additional liferafts shall be provided so that the total capacity available on each side will accommodate 150% of the total number of persons on board;

.3 if the rescue boat required by paragraph 2.2 is also a partially or totally enclosed lifeboat complying with the requirements of section 4.5 or 4.6 of the Code, it may be included in the aggregate capacity required by paragraph 1.4.1, provided that the total capacity available on either side of the ship is at least 150% of the total number of persons on board; and

.4 in the event of any one survival craft being lost or rendered unserviceable, there shall be sufficient survival craft available for use on each side, including those which are stowed in a position providing for easy side-to-side transfer at a single open deck level, to accommodate the total number of persons on board.

1.5 A marine evacuation system or systems complying with section 6.2 of the Code may be substituted for the equivalent capacity of liferafts and launching appliances required by paragraph 1.1.1 or 1.2.1.

2 Rescue boats

2.1 Passenger ships of 500 gross tonnage and over shall carry at least one rescue boat complying with the requirements of section 5.1 of the Code on each side of the ship.

2.2 Passenger ships of less than 500 gross tonnage shall carry at least one rescue boat complying with the requirements of section 5.1 of the Code.

.2 此外,符合《规则》第 4.2 或 4.3 节要求的气胀式或刚性救生筏的总容量应至少能容纳船上人员总数的 25%。这些救生筏应使用每舷至少 1 台降落设备,该设备可以是按本条 1.2.1 要求装设的设备,或是能在两舷均可使用的等效认可设备。但是,这些救生筏的存放不必符合第 13.5 条的要求。

1.3 为船上全体人员弃船所需配备的所有救生艇筏在所有人员集合并穿妥救生衣后,应能在发出弃船信号后 30 min 内载足额定乘员及属具降落水面。

1.4 为代替满足本条 1.1 或 1.2 的要求,500 总吨以下的客船,凡船上人员总数少于 200 人者,可符合下列要求:

.1 船舶每舷配备符合《规则》第 4.2 或 4.3 节要求的气胀式或刚性救生筏,其总容量应能容纳船上全体人员;

.2 除非本条 1.4.1 所要求的救生筏是存放在一个能在单层开敞甲板上易于做舷对舷转移的位置,否则应配备附加救生筏,使每舷可用的总容量能容纳船上人员总数的 150%;

.3 如本条 2.2 所要求的救助艇也是符合《规则》第 4.5 或 4.6 节要求的部分封闭或全封闭救生艇,则可计入本条 1.4.1 所要求的总容量,但是船舶任何一舷的总容量应至少是船上人员总数的 150%;和

.4 在任何一艘救生艇筏掉失或不能使用时,每舷可供使用的救生艇筏,包括存放在一个能在单层开敞甲板上易于做舷对舷转移的位置的救生艇筏,应能足够容纳船上的全体人员。

1.5 符合《规则》第 6.2 节要求的一个或几个海上撤离系统可用以替代本条 1.1.1 或 1.2.1 要求的救生筏和降落设备的等效容量。

2　救助艇

2.1 500 总吨及以上的客船应在船舶每舷至少配备一艘符合《规则》第 5.1 节要求的救助艇。

2.2 500 总吨以下的客船应至少配备一艘符合《规则》第 5.1 节要求的救助艇。

2.3 A lifeboat may be accepted as a rescue boat provided that it and its launching and recovery arrangements also comply with the requirements for a rescue boat.

3 Marshalling of liferafts

3.1 The number of lifeboats and rescue boats that are carried on passenger ships shall be sufficient to ensure that in providing for abandonment by the total number of persons on board not more than six liferafts need be marshalled by each lifeboat or rescue boat.

3.2 The number of lifeboats and rescue boats that are carried on passenger ships engaged on short international voyages shall be sufficient to ensure that in providing for abandonment by the total number of persons on board not more than nine liferafts need be marshalled by each lifeboat or rescue boat.

Regulation 22
Personal life-saving appliances

1 Lifebuoys

1.1 A passenger ship shall carry not less than the number of lifebuoys complying with the requirements of regulation 7.1 and section 2.1 of the Code prescribed in the following table:

Length of ship in metres	Minimum number of lifebuoys
Under 60	8
60 and under 120	12
120 and under 180	18
180 and under 240	24
240 and over	30

1.2 Notwithstanding regulation 7.1.3, passenger ships of under 60 m in length shall carry not less than six lifebuoys provided with self-igniting lights.

2 Lifejackets

2.1 In addition to the lifejackets required by regulation 7.2, every passenger ship shall carry lifejackets for not less than 5% of the total number of persons on board. These lifejackets shall be stowed in conspicuous places on deck or at muster stations.

2.2 Where lifejackets for passengers are stowed in staterooms which are located remotely from direct routes between public spaces and muster stations, the additional lifejackets for these passengers required under regulation 7.2.2, shall be stowed either in the public spaces, the muster stations, or on direct routes between them. The lifejackets shall be stowed so that their distribution and donning does not impede orderly movement to muster stations and survival craft embarkation stations.

2.3 如果救生艇及其降落和回收装置也符合对救助艇的要求，则可以接受此救生艇作为救助艇。

3　救生筏的集结

3.1 配备于客船上的救生艇和救助艇的数量应能足以确保在供船上全体人员弃船使用时，每艘救生艇或救助艇需要集结的救生筏不多于 6 只。

3.2 配备于从事短程国际航行的客船上的救生艇和救助艇的数量应能足以确保在供船上全体人员弃船使用时，每艘救生艇或救助艇需要集结的救生筏不多于 9 只。

第 22 条
个人救生设备

1　救生圈

1.1 客船应配备符合第 7.1 条和《规则》第 2.1 节要求的救生圈，其数量应不少于下表规定：

船长（m）	救生圈最少数量
60 以下	8
60 至 120 以下	12
120 至 180 以下	18
180 至 240 以下	24
240 及以上	30

1.2 尽管有第 7.1.3 条的要求，长度为 60 m 以下的客船仍应配备不少于 6 只带有自亮灯的救生圈。

2　救生衣

2.1 除第 7.2 条要求的救生衣外，每艘客船还应配备不少于船上人员总数 5% 的救生衣。这些救生衣应存放在甲板上或集合站明显易见的地方。

2.2 如果乘客的救生衣存放在远离公共处所与集合站之间直接脱险通道的客舱内，则按第 7.2.2 条要求的这些乘客的附加救生衣应存放在公共处所、集合站或这二者之间的直接脱险通道上。这些救生衣的存放应使其分布和乘客穿着不妨碍有秩序地向集合站和救生艇筏登乘站移动。

3 Lifejacket lights

3.1 On all passenger ships each lifejacket shall be fitted with a light complying with the requirements of paragraph 2.2.3 of the Code.

3.2 Lights fitted on lifejackets on board passenger ships prior to 1 July 1998 and not complying fully with paragraph 2.2.3 of the Code may be accepted by the Administration until the lifejacket light would normally be replaced or until the first periodical survey after 1 July 2002, whichever is the earliest.

4 Immersion suits and thermal protective aids

4.1 All passenger ships shall carry for each lifeboat on the ship at least three immersion suits complying with the requirements of section 2.3 of the Code and, in addition, a thermal protective aid complying with the requirements of section 2.5 of the Code for every person to be accommodated in the lifeboat and not provided with an immersion suit. These immersion suits and thermal protective aids need not be carried:

.1 for persons to be accommodated in totally or partially enclosed lifeboats; or

.2 if the ship is constantly engaged on voyages in warm climates① where, in the opinion of the Administration, they are unnecessary.

4.2 The provisions of paragraph 4.1.1 also apply to partially or totally enclosed lifeboats not complying with the requirements of section 4.5 or 4.6 of the Code, provided they are carried on ships constructed before 1 July 1986.

Regulation 23
Survival craft and rescue boat embarkation arrangements

1 On passenger ships, survival craft embarkation arrangements shall be designed for:

.1 all lifeboats to be boarded and launched either directly from the stowed position or from an embarkation deck but not both; and

.2 davit-launched liferafts to be boarded and launched from a position immediately adjacent to the stowed position or from a position to which, in compliance with the requirements of regulation 13.5, the liferaft is transferred prior to launching.

2 Rescue boat arrangements shall be such that the rescue boat can be boarded and launched directly from the stowed position with the number of persons assigned to crew the rescue boat on board. Notwithstanding the requirements of paragraph 1.1, if the rescue boat is also a lifeboat and the other lifeboats are boarded and launched from an embarkation deck, the arrangements shall be such that the rescue boat can also be boarded and launched from the embarkation deck.

---

① Refer to *Guidelines for the assessment of thermal protection* (MSC/Circ.1046).

3　救生衣灯

3.1　在所有客船上,每件救生衣应设有 1 盏符合《规则》2.2.3 要求的灯。

3.2　1998 年 7 月 1 日以前在客船上的救生衣,其救生衣灯如不完全符合《规则》2.2.3 要求,主管机关可允许其使用至正常替换时或至 2002 年 7 月 1 日以后的第一次定期检验时,取较早者。

4　救生服和保温用具

4.1　所有客船上每艘救生艇应配备至少 3 件符合《规则》第 2.3 节要求的救生服,此外,还应为救生艇中没有配备救生服的每个人配备符合《规则》第 2.5 节要求的保温用具。在下列情况下,不必配备这些救生服和保温用具:

.1　全封闭或部分封闭救生艇中的人员;或

.2　如果船舶一直在主管机关认为不需救生服和保温用具的温暖气候区域[①]航行。

4.2　本条 4.1.1 的规定还适用于 1986 年 7 月 1 日以前建造的船舶所配备的不符合《规则》第 4.5 或 4.6 节要求的部分封闭或全封闭救生艇。

第 23 条
救生艇筏与救助艇的登乘布置

1　在客船上,救生艇筏登乘布置应设计为:

.1　所有救生艇从存放处或者从登乘甲板直接登乘并降落,但不是从两处登乘并降落;和

.2　吊艇架降落的救生筏从紧邻存放处的位置登乘并降落,或从在降落前按第 13.5 条要求所转移到的位置登乘并降落。

2　救助艇的布置应使救助艇在载足其指定船员的情况下,能够从存放处直接登乘并降落。不论本条 1.1 如何要求,如救助艇兼作救生艇,并且其他救生艇均为从登乘甲板登乘及降落,则其布置应使救助艇也能从登乘甲板登乘并降落。

---

① 参见《热保护评定指南》(第 MSC/Circ.1046 号通函)。

Regulation 24
Stowage of survival craft

The stowage height of a survival craft on a passenger ship shall take into account the requirements of regulation 13.1.2, the escape provisions of regulation Ⅱ-2/13, the size of the ship, and the weather conditions likely to be encountered in its intended area of operation. For a davit-launched survival craft, the height of the davit head with the survival craft in embarkation position, shall, as far as practicable, not exceed 15 m to the waterline when the ship is in its lightest seagoing condition.

Regulation 25
Muster stations

Every passenger ship shall, in addition to complying with the requirements of regulation 11, have passenger muster stations which shall:

.1 be in the vicinity of, and permit ready access for the passengers to, the embarkation stations unless in the same location; and

.2 have ample room for marshalling and instruction of the passengers, but at least 0.35 m^2 per passenger.

Regulation 26
Additional requirements for ro-ro passenger ships

1 This regulation applies to all ro-ro passenger ships. Ro-ro passenger ships constructed:

.1 on or after 1 July 1998 shall comply with the requirements of paragraphs 2.3, 2.4, 3.1, 3.2, 3.3, 4 and 5;

.2 on or after 1 July 1986 and before 1 July 1998 shall comply with the requirements of paragraph 5 not later than the first periodical survey after 1 July 1998 and with the requirements of paragraphs 2.3, 2.4, 3 and 4 not later than the first periodical survey after 1 July 2000;

.3 before 1 July 1986 shall comply with the requirements of paragraph 5 not later than the first periodical survey after 1 July 1998 and with the requirements of paragraphs 2.1, 2.2, 2.3, 2.4, 3 and 4 not later than the first periodical survey after 1 July 2000; and

.4 before 1 July 2004 shall comply with the requirements of paragraph 2.5 not later than the first survey on or after that date.

第 24 条
救生艇筏的存放

客船上救生艇筏的存放高度应考虑到第 13.1.2 条要求、第Ⅱ-2/13 条的脱险通道规定、船舶的尺度以及在拟定营运的海区可能遇到的气象状况。对吊艇架降落的救生艇筏，其在登乘位置的吊艇架顶部至最轻载航行水线之间的高度应尽可能不超过 15 m。

第 25 条
集合站

除符合第 11 条要求外，每艘客船应设有乘客集合站，其应：

.1　设在登乘站附近，并可使乘客易于到达登乘站，除非其与登乘站设在同一处；和

.2　有集结和指挥乘客用的宽敞场地，每位乘客所占面积至少为 0.35 m^2。

第 26 条
滚装客船的附加要求

1　本条适用于所有滚装客船：

.1　1998 年 7 月 1 日或以后建造的滚装客船应符合本条 2.3、2.4、3.1、3.2、3.3、4 和 5 款的要求；

.2　1986 年 7 月 1 日或以后，但在 1998 年 7 月 1 日以前建造的滚装客船，应在不迟于 1998 年 7 月 1 日后的第一次定期检验时符合本条 5 款的要求，并在不迟于 2000 年 7 月 1 日后的第一次定期检验时符合本条 2.3、2.4、3 和 4 款的要求；

.3　1986 年 7 月 1 日以前建造的滚装客船，应在不迟于 1998 年 7 月 1 日后的第一次定期检验时符合本条 5 款的要求，并在不迟于 2000 年 7 月 1 日后的第一次定期检验时符合本条 2.1、2.2、2.3、2.4、3 和 4 款的要求；和

.4　2004 年 7 月 1 日以前建造的滚装客船，应在不迟于该日期或该日期后的第一次检验时符合本条 2.5 款的要求。

2 Liferafts

2.1 The ro-ro passenger ship's liferafts shall be served by marine evacuation systems complying with the requirements of section 6.2 of the Code or launching appliances complying with the requirements of paragraph 6.1.5 of the Code, equally distributed on each side of the ship.

2.2 Every liferaft on ro-ro passenger ships shall be provided with float-free stowage arrangements complying with the requirements of regulation 13.4.

2.3 Every liferaft on ro-ro passenger ships shall be of a type fitted with a boarding ramp complying with the requirements of paragraph 4.2.4.1 or 4.3.4.1 of the Code, as appropriate.

2.4 Every liferaft on ro-ro passenger ships shall either be automatically self-righting or be a canopied reversible liferaft which is stable in a seaway and is capable of operating safely whichever way up it is floating. Alternatively, the ship shall carry automatically self-righting liferafts or canopied reversible liferafts, in addition to its normal complement of liferafts, of such aggregate capacity as will accommodate at least 50% of the persons not accommodated in lifeboats. This additional liferaft capacity shall be determined on the basis of the difference between the total number of persons on board and the number of persons accommodated in lifeboats. Every such liferaft shall be approved by the Administration having regard to the recommendations adopted by the Organization.①

2.5 Liferafts carried on ro-ro passenger ships shall be fitted with a search and rescue locating device in the ratio of one search and rescue locating device for every four liferafts. The search and rescue locating device shall be mounted inside the liferaft so its antenna is more than 1 m above the sea level when the liferaft is deployed, except that for canopied reversible liferafts the search and rescue locating device shall be so arranged as to be readily accessed and erected by survivors. Each search and rescue locating device shall be arranged to be manually erected when the liferaft is deployed. Containers of liferafts fitted with search and rescue locating devices shall be clearly marked.

3 Fast rescue boats

3.1 At least one of the rescue boats on a ro-ro passenger ship shall be a fast rescue boat complying with section 5.1.4 of the Code.①

3.2 Each fast rescue boat shall be served by a suitable launching appliance complying with section 6.1.7 of the Code.①

3.3 At least two crews of each fast rescue boat shall be trained and drilled regularly having regard to the Seafarers' Training, Certification and Watchkeeping (STCW) Code and recommendations adopted by the Organization②, including all aspects of rescue, handling, manoeuvring, operating these craft in various conditions, and righting them after capsize.

---

① Refer to *Recommendation for canopied reversible liferafts, automatically self-righting liferafts and fast rescue boats, including testing, on ro-ro passenger ships* (MSC/Circ.809).

② Refer to *Recommendation on training requirements for crews of fast rescue boats* (resolution A.771(18) and to section A-Ⅵ/2, table A-Ⅵ/2-2, specification of the minimum standard of competence in fast rescue boats, of the STCW Code.

2　救生筏

2.1　滚装客船的救生筏应使用符合《规则》第 6.2 节要求的海上撤离系统或符合《规则》6.1.5 要求的降落设备，并应均等地分布在船舶两侧。

2.2　滚装客船的每只救生筏应配备符合第 13.4 条要求的自由漂浮式存放装置。

2.3　滚装客船的每只救生筏应设置符合《规则》4.2.4.1 或 4.3.4.1 要求（视何者适用）的登筏踏板。

2.4　滚装客船的每只救生筏应为自行扶正的或为带顶篷两面可用的救生筏，其在海上应是稳定的，不论哪一面朝上，都能安全操作。或者，船上除了配备正常额定救生筏之外，还应配备自行扶正救生筏或带顶篷两面可用的救生筏，其总容量至少为救生艇所未容纳者的 50%。该附加的救生筏容量应根据船上总人数与救生艇乘员数之间的差值决定。每只这样的救生筏应经主管机关在考虑了本组织通过的建议案后予以认可。①

2.5　滚装客船上配备的救生筏应每四艘救生筏配备一个搜救定位装置。该搜救定位装置须安装在救生筏内使其天线在救生筏布放时高于海平面一米以上，但对于带有顶棚的可反转救生筏，搜救定位装置的装配须使幸存者能容易地拿到并安装。每个搜救定位装置均的装配应使其在救生筏布放时能够手动安装。存放配备有搜救定位装置的救生筏的容器须具有清楚的标记。

3　快速救助艇

3.1　滚装客船上的救助艇中应至少有一艘为符合《规则》第 5.1.4 节的快速救助艇。①

3.2　每艘快速救助艇应使用符合《规则》第 6.1.7 节的适当的降落设备。①

3.3　每艘快速救助艇应至少有 2 名船员参照《海员培训、发证和值班（STCW）规则》和本组织通过的建议案②接受培训并定期演习，包括救助的各个方面，艇在各种条件下的降放、操纵、操作以及倾覆后的扶正。

---

① 参见《关于滚装客船上带顶棚两面可用救生筏、自动扶正救生筏和快速救助艇（包括试验）的建议案》（第 MSC/Circ. 809 号通函）。

② 参见《快速救助艇船员培训要求建议案》（第 A.771（18）号决议）和 STCW 规则第 A-Ⅵ/2 节，表 A-Ⅵ/2-2《快速救助艇最低适任标准规定》。

3.4 In the case where the arrangement or size of a ro-ro passenger ship, constructed before 1 July 1997, is such as to prevent the installation of the fast rescue boat required by paragraph 3.1, the fast rescue boat may be installed in place of an existing lifeboat which is accepted as a rescue boat or, in the case of ships constructed prior to 1 July 1986, boats for use in an emergency, provided that all of the following conditions are met:

.1 the fast rescue boat installed is served by a launching appliance complying with the provisions of paragraph 3.2;

.2 the capacity of the survival craft lost by the above substitution is compensated by the installation of liferafts capable of carrying at least an equal number of persons served by the lifeboat replaced; and

.3 such liferafts are served by the existing launching appliances or marine evacuation systems.

4 Means of rescue①

4.1 Each ro-ro passenger ship shall be equipped with efficient means for rapidly recovering survivors from the water and transferring survivors from rescue units or survival craft to the ship.

4.2 The means of transfer of survivors to the ship may be part of a marine evacuation system, or may be part of a system designed for rescue purposes.

4.3 If the slide of a marine evacuation system is intended to provide the means of transfer of survivors to the deck of the ship, the slide shall be equipped with handlines or ladders to aid in climbing up the slide.

5 Lifejackets

5.1 Notwithstanding the requirements of regulations 7.2 and 22.2, a sufficient number of lifejackets shall be stowed in the vicinity of the muster stations so that passengers do not have to return to their cabins to collect their lifejackets.

5.2 In ro-ro passenger ships, each lifejacket shall be fitted with a light complying with the requirements of paragraph 2.2.3 of the Code.

Regulation 27
Information on passengers

1 All persons on board all passenger ships shall be counted prior to departure.

2 Details of persons who have declared a need for special care or assistance in emergency situations shall be recorded and communicated to the master prior to departure.

---

① Refer to *Recommendation on means of rescue on ro-ro passenger ships* (MSC/Circ.810).

3.4 对1997年7月1日以前建造的滚装客船，如按其布置或尺度不能安装按本条3.1要求的快速救助艇，则可以安装快速救助艇以替代现有作为救助艇的救生艇，或替代1986年7月1日以前建造的船舶在紧急情况下使用的艇，但应满足下列所有条件：

.1 安装的快速救助艇使用符合本条3.2规定的降落设备；

.2 因上述替代而损失的救生艇筏容量由安装救生筏予以补偿，这些救生筏能至少容纳被替代的救生艇所能容纳的等量的人数；和

.3 这些救生筏使用现有的降落设备或海上撤离系统。

4　救助设备①

4.1 每艘滚装客船应配置有效的设备以从水中迅速救回幸存者并把他们从救助装置或救生艇筏转移到船上。

4.2 转移幸存者到船上的设备可以是海上撤离系统的一部分，或是为救助目的而设计的系统的一部分。

4.3 如海上撤离系统的滑板是用以将幸存者转移到船上甲板的设备，则该滑道配备扶手或梯子，以便于沿滑道向上爬。

5　救生衣

5.1 尽管有第7.2和22.2条的要求，仍应有足够数量的救生衣存放在集合站附近，这样乘客不必回到自己的舱室去取救生衣。

5.2 在滚装客船上，每件救生衣应设有1盏符合《规则》2.2.3要求的灯。

第27条
乘客资料

1 所有客船上的所有人员，在开航前应予点数。

2 已申报在紧急状态下需要特殊照顾或需要帮助的人员的详细信息，在开航之前，应进行记录并通知船长。

① 参见《关于滚装客船救助设备的建议案》（第MSC/Circ.810号通函）。

3 In addition, not later than 1 January 1999, the names and gender of all persons on board, distinguishing between adults, children and infants shall be recorded for search and rescue purposes.

4 The information required by paragraphs 1, 2 and 3 shall be kept ashore and made readily available to search and rescue services when needed.

5 Administrations may exempt passenger ships from the requirements of paragraph 3, if the scheduled voyages of such ships render it impracticable for them to prepare such records.

Regulation 28
Helicopter landing and pick-up areas

1 All ro-ro passenger ships shall be provided with a helicopter pick-up area approved by the Administration having regard to the recommendations adopted by the Organization.①

2 Ro-ro② passenger ships of 130 m in length and upwards, constructed on or after 1 July 1999, shall be fitted with a helicopter landing area approved by the Administration having regard to the recommendations adopted by the Organization.③

Regulation 29
Decision support system for masters of passenger ships

1 This regulation applies to all passenger ships. Passenger ships constructed before 1 July 1997 shall comply with the requirements of this regulation not later than the date of the first periodical survey after 1 July 1999.

2 In all passenger ships, a decision support system for emergency management shall be provided on the navigation bridge.

3 The system shall, as a minimum, consist of a printed emergency plan or plans.④ All foreseeable emergency situations shall be identified in the emergency plan or plans, including, but not limited to, the following main groups of emergencies:

.1 fire;

.2 damage to ship;

.3 pollution;

---

① Refer to the *International Aeronautical and Maritime Search and Rescue Manual* (IAMSAR Manual).

② Refer to *Application of SOLAS regulation III/28.2 concerning helicopter landing areas on non-ro-ro passenger ship* (MSC/Circ. 907).

③ Refer to *Recommendation on helicopter landing areas on ro-ro passenger ships* (MSC/Circ.895, as amended by MSC.1/Circ. 1524) and *Guidelines for approval of helicopter foam fire-fighting appliances* (MSC.1/Circ.1431).

④ Refer to *Revised guidelines for a structure of an integrated system of contingency planning for shipboard emergencies* (resolution A.1072(28) and Corr.1).

3　此外，为了搜索和救助目的，不迟于1999年1月1日，应对船上所有人员的姓名和性别，分为成人、儿童和婴儿记录在册。

4　上述1、2和3所要求的资料应保留在岸上，需要时应随即提供搜救机构使用。

5　如果客船预定的航线按上述3款的要求进行这类记录不可行时，主管机关可对这些客船免除此项要求。

第28条
直升机降落和搭乘区域

1　所有滚装客船应设有一个直升机搭乘区域，并应经主管机关在考虑了本组织通过的建议案[①]后予以认可。

2　1999年7月1日或以后建造，船长为130 m及以上的滚装客船[②]，应设有一个直升机降落区域，并应经主管机关在考虑了本组织通过的建议案后予以认可。[③]

第29条
客船船长决策支持系统

1　本条适用于所有客船。1997年7月1日以前建造的客船应在不迟于1999年7月1日以后的第一次定期检验时符合本条要求。

2　所有客船，应在驾驶室设有一个处理紧急情况的决策支持系统。

3　该支持系统应至少由1个或几个纸质应急计划构成[④]。所有可预计的紧急状况均应在应急计划中标明，包括但不限于下列各类主要的紧急情况：

.1　火灾；

.2　船舶破损；

.3　污染；

---

① 参见《国际航空和航海搜救手册》(IAMSAR手册)。
② 参见《有关SOLAS公约第Ⅲ/28.2条对非滚装客船直升机降落区域的适用》(第MSC/Circ.907号通函)。
③ 参见《关于滚装客船直升机降落区域的建议案》(经第MSC.1/Circ.1524号修订的第MSC/Circ.895号通函)和《直升机泡沫灭火设备认可指南》(第MSC.1/Circ.1431号通函)。
④ 参见《经修订的船上紧急情况应急计划整体系统构成指南》(第A.107(28)号决议和Corr.1)。

.4 unlawful acts threatening the safety of the ship and the security of its passengers and crew;

.5 personnel accidents;

.6 cargo-related accidents; and

.7 emergency assistance to other ships.

4 The emergency procedures established in the emergency plan or plans shall provide decision support to masters for handling any combination of emergency situations.

5 The emergency plan or plans shall have a uniform structure and be easy to use. Where applicable, the actual loading condition as calculated for the passenger ship's voyage stability shall be used for damage control purposes.

6 In addition to the printed emergency plan or plans, the Administration may also accept the use of a computer-based decision support system on the navigation bridge which provides all the information contained in the emergency plan or plans, procedures, checklists, etc., which is able to present a list of recommended actions to be carried out in foreseeable emergencies.

Regulation 30
Drills

1 This regulation applies to all passenger ships.

2 On passenger ships, an abandon ship drill and fire drill shall take place weekly. The entire crew need not be involved in every drill, but each crew member must participate in an abandon ship drill and a fire drill each month as required in regulation 19.3.2. Passengers shall be strongly encouraged to attend these drills.

3 Damage control drills shall be conducted as required in regulation Ⅱ-1/19-1.

Section Ⅲ
Cargo ships (additional requirements)

Regulation 31
Survival craft and rescue boats

1 Survival craft

1.1 Cargo ships shall carry:

.1 one or more totally enclosed lifeboats complying with the requirements of section 4.6 of the Code of such aggregate capacity on each side of the ship as will accommodate the total number of persons on board; and

.4　威胁到船舶安全及乘客和船员保安的非法行为；

.5　人身意外伤害；

.6　与货物相关的事故；和

.7　对其他船舶的应急援助。

4　应急计划中所建立的应急程序，应向船长提供用以处理各种紧急状况同时发生的决策支持方案。

5　应急计划应有统一的格式并易于操作。如适用，为客船航行稳性而计算的实际装载工况应用于破损控制。

6　除纸质应急计划外，主管机关也可接受在驾驶台使用电脑决策支持系统，该系统能提供应急计划中包括的所有信息、程序、检查清单等，能针对可预计的紧急情况提出拟采取的建议措施的清单。

第 30 条
演习

1　本条适用于所有客船。

2　客船每周应举行一次弃船演习和消防演习。全体船员不必都参与每次演习，但每个船员均必须按第 19.3.2 条要求每月参加一次弃船和消防演习。应尽力鼓励乘客参与这些演习。

3　须按第Ⅱ-1/19-1 条的要求进行破损控制演习。

第 3 节
货船（附加要求）

第 31 条
救生艇筏与救助艇

1　救生艇筏

1.1　货船应配备：

.1　每舷一艘或多艘符合《规则》第 4.6 节要求的全封闭救生艇，其总容量应能容纳船上人员总数；和

.2 in addition, one or more inflatable or rigid liferafts, complying with the requirements of section 4.2 or 4.3 of the Code, of a mass of less than 185 kg and stowed in a position providing for easy side-to-side transfer at a single open deck level, and of such aggregate capacity as will accommodate the total number of persons on board. If the liferaft or liferafts are not of a mass of less than 185 kg and stowed in a position providing for easy side-to-side transfer at a single open deck level, the total capacity available on each side shall be sufficient to accommodate the total number of persons on board.

1.2 In lieu of meeting the requirements of paragraph 1.1, cargo ships may carry:

.1 one or more free-fall lifeboats, complying with the requirements of section 4.7 of the Code, capable of being free-fall launched over the stern of the ship of such aggregate capacity as will accommodate the total number of persons on board; and

.2 in addition, one or more inflatable or rigid liferafts complying with the requirements of section 4.2 or 4.3 of the Code, on each side of the ship, of such aggregate capacity as will accommodate the total number of persons on board. The liferafts on at least one side of the ship shall be served by launching appliances.

1.3 In lieu of meeting the requirements of paragraph 1.1 or 1.2, cargo ships of less than 85 m in length other than oil tankers, chemical tankers and gas carriers, may comply with the following:

.1 they shall carry on each side of the ship, one or more inflatable or rigid liferafts complying with the requirements of section 4.2 or 4.3 of the Code and of such aggregate capacity as will accommodate the total number of persons on board;

.2 unless the liferafts required by paragraph 1.3.1 are of a mass of less than 185 kg and stowed in a position providing for easy side-to-side transfer at a single open deck level, additional liferafts shall be provided so that the total capacity available on each side will accommodate 150% of the total number of persons on board;

.3 if the rescue boat required by paragraph 2 is also a totally enclosed lifeboat complying with the requirements of section 4.6 of the Code, it may be included in the aggregate capacity required by paragraph 1.3.1, provided that the total capacity available on either side of the ship is at least 150% of the total number of persons on board; and

.4 in the event of any one survival craft being lost or rendered unserviceable, there shall be sufficient survival craft available for use on each side, including any which are of a mass of less than 185 kg and stowed in a position providing for easy side-to-side transfer at a single open deck level, to accommodate the total number of persons on board.

1.4 Cargo ships where the horizontal distance from the extreme end of the stem or stern of the ship to the nearest end of the closest survival craft is more than 100 m shall carry, in addition to the liferafts required by paragraphs 1.1.2 and 1.2.2, a liferaft stowed as far forward or aft, or one as far forward and another as far aft, as is reasonable and practicable. Such liferaft or liferafts may be securely fastened so as to permit manual release and need not be of the type which can be launched from an approved launching device.

.2　另有符合《规则》第 4.2 或 4.3 节要求的 1 只或多只气胀式或刚性救生筏，其质量小于 185 kg，存放在一个能在单层开敞甲板上易于做舷对舷转移的位置，且其总容量能容纳船上人员总数。如果该救生筏或这些救生筏的质量大于 185 kg，且不是存放在一个能在单层开敞甲板上易于做舷对舷转移的位置，则每舷可用的总容量应能足以容纳船上人员总数。

1.2　为代替满足本条 1.1 的要求，货船可配备：

.1　一艘或多艘符合《规则》第 4.7 节要求的能在船尾自由降落下水的救生艇，其总容量应能容纳船上人员总数；和

.2　另有船舶每舷 1 只或多只符合《规则》第 4.2 或 4.3 节要求的气胀式或刚性救生筏，其总容量应能容纳船上人员总数。至少在船舶一舷的救生筏应使用降落设备。

1.3　为代替满足本条 1.1 或 1.2 的要求，除油船、化学品液货船和气体运输船外的长度为 85 m 以下的货船可符合下列要求：

.1　船舶每舷配备 1 只或多只符合《规则》第 4.2 或 4.3 节要求的气胀式或刚性救生筏，其总容量应能容纳船上人员总数；

.2　除非本条 1.3.1 要求的救生筏质量小于 185 kg，并存放在一个能在单层开敞甲板上易于做舷对舷转移的位置，否则应配备附加救生筏，使每舷可用的总容量能容纳船上人员总数的 150%；

.3　如本条 2 所要求的救助艇也是符合《规则》第 4.6 节要求的全封闭救生艇，则可计入本条 1.3.1 所要求的总容量，但船舶任何一舷可用的总容量应至少是船上人员总数的 150%；和

.4　在任何一艘救生艇筏掉失或不能使用的情况下，每舷可供使用的救生艇筏，包括任何质量小于 185 kg 并存放在一个能在单层开敞甲板上易于做舷对舷转移的位置的救生艇筏，应能足够容纳船上人员总数。

1.4　对于从船首最前端或船尾最末端至最近的救生艇筏最近一端的水平距离超过 100 m 的货船，除配备本条 1.1.2 和 1.2.2 要求的救生筏外，还应在合理可行的范围内配备 1 只救生筏，尽量靠前或靠后存放，或 2 只救生筏，1 只尽量靠前，另 1 只尽量靠后存放。所述救生筏可用能手动脱开的方式系牢，而不必为能用认可的降落设备降落的类型。

1.5 With the exception of the survival craft referred to in regulation 16.1.1, all survival craft required to provide for abandonment by the total number of persons on board shall be capable of being launched with their full complement of persons and equipment within a period of 10 min from the time the abandon ship signal is given.

1.6 Chemical tankers and gas carriers carrying cargoes emitting toxic vapours or gases① shall carry, in lieu of totally enclosed lifeboats complying with the requirements of section 4.6 of the Code, lifeboats with a self-contained air support system complying with the requirements of section 4.8 of the Code.

1.7 Oil tankers, chemical tankers and gas carriers carrying cargoes having a flashpoint not exceeding 60 ℃ (closed-cup test) shall carry, in lieu of totally enclosed lifeboats complying with the requirements of section 4.6 of the Code, fire-protected lifeboats complying with the requirements of section 4.9 of the Code.

1.8 Notwithstanding the requirements of paragraph 1.1, bulk carriers as defined in regulation Ⅸ/1.6 constructed on or after 1 July 2006 shall comply with the requirements of paragraph 1.2.

2 Rescue boats

Cargo ships shall carry at least one rescue boat complying with the requirements of section 5.1 of the Code. A lifeboat may be accepted as a rescue boat, provided that it and its launching and recovery arrangements also comply with the requirements for a rescue boat.

3 In addition to their lifeboats, all cargo ships constructed before 1 July 1986 shall carry:

.1 one or more liferafts capable of being launched on either side of the ship and of such aggregate capacity as will accommodate the total number of persons on board. The liferaft or liferafts shall be equipped with a lashing or an equivalent means of securing the liferaft which will automatically release it from a sinking ship; and

.2 where the horizontal distance from the extreme end of the stem or stern of the ship to the nearest end of the closest survival craft is more than 100 m, in addition to the liferafts required by paragraph 3.1, a liferaft stowed as far forward or aft, or one as far forward and another as far aft, as is reasonable and practicable. Notwithstanding the requirements of paragraph 3.1, such liferaft or liferafts may be securely fastened so as to permit manual release.

Regulation 32
Personal life-saving appliances

1 Lifebuoys

1.1 Cargo ships shall carry not less than the number of lifebuoys complying with the requirements of regulation 7.1 and section 2.1 of the Code prescribed in the following table:

① Refer to the products for which emergency escape respiratory protection is required in chapter 17 of the IBC Code (resolution MSC.4(48), as amended), and in chapter 19 of the IGC Code (resolution MSC.5(48), as amended).

1.5 除第16.1.1条所述的救生艇筏外，船上全部人员弃船所需配备的所有救生艇筏，应能在发出弃船信号后10 min内，载足额定乘员及属具降落水面。

1.6 载运散发有毒蒸气或毒气①的货物的化学品液货船和气体运输船，应配备符合《规则》第4.8节要求的有自备空气补给系统的救生艇，以替代符合《规则》第4.6节要求的全封闭救生艇。

1.7 载运闪点不超过60 ℃（闭杯试验）货物的油船、化学品液货船和气体运输船应配备符合《规则》第4.9节要求的耐火救生艇，以替代符合《规则》第4.6节要求的全封闭救生艇。

1.8 尽管有1.1的要求，第Ⅸ/1.6条定义的在2006年7月1日或以后建造的散货船应符合1.2的要求。

2　救助艇

货船应至少配备一艘符合《规则》第5.1节要求的救助艇。如果救生艇及其降落和回收装置也符合对救助艇的要求，则可以接受此救生艇作为救助艇。

3 所有1986年7月1日以前建造的货船，除其救生艇外，还应配备：

.1 1只或多只能在船舶任一舷降落的救生筏，其总容量应能容纳船上人员总数。该救生筏或这些救生筏应设有能与下沉中船舶自动脱开的系牢救生筏的绑扎装置或等效装置；和

.2 如从船首最前端或船尾最末端至最近的救生艇筏最近一端的水平距离超过100 m，除配备本条3.1要求的救生筏外，还应在合理可行的范围内配备1只救生筏，尽量靠前或靠后存放，或2只救生筏，1只尽量靠前，另1只尽量靠后存放。尽管有3.1的要求，所述救生筏可用能手动脱开的方式系牢。

第32条
个人救生设备

1　救生圈

1.1 货船应配备符合第7.1条和《规则》第2.1节要求的救生圈，其数量应不少于下表规定：

① 参见IBC规则（经修正的第MSC.4(48)号决议）第17章和IGC规则（经修正的第MSC.5(48)号决议）第19章中紧急脱险需加呼吸保护的货品。

Length of ship in metres	Minimum number of lifebuoys
Under 100	8
100 and under 150	10
150 and under 200	12
200 and over	14

1.2 Self-igniting lights for lifebuoys on tankers required by regulation 7.1.3 shall be of an electric battery type.

2 Lifejacket lights

2.1 This paragraph applies to all cargo ships.

2.2 On cargo ships, each lifejacket shall be fitted with a lifejacket light complying with the requirements of paragraph 2.2.3 of the Code.

2.3 Lights fitted on lifejackets on board cargo ships prior to 1 July 1998 and not complying fully with paragraph 2.2.3 of the Code may be accepted by the Administration until the lifejacket light would normally be replaced or until the first periodical survey after 1 July 2001, whichever is the earliest.

3 Immersion suits

3.1 This paragraph applies to all cargo ships. However, with respect to cargo ships constructed before 1 July 2006, paragraphs 3.2 to 3.5 shall be complied with not later than the first safety equipment survey on or after 1 July 2006.

3.2 An immersion suit of an appropriate size complying with the requirements of section 2.3 of the Code shall be provided for every person on board the ship. However, for ships other than bulk carriers, as defined in regulation Ⅺ/1, these immersion suits need not be required if the ship is constantly engaged on voyages in warm climates[①] where, in the opinion of the Administration, immersion suits are unnecessary.

3.3 If a ship has any watch or work stations which are located remotely from the place or places where immersion suits are normally stowed, including remotely located survival craft carried in accordance with regulation 31.1.4, additional immersion suits of an appropriate size shall be provided at these locations for the number of persons normally on watch or working at those locations at any time.

3.4 Immersion suits shall be so placed as to be readily accessible and their position shall be plainly indicated.

3.5 The immersion suits required by this regulation may be used to comply with the requirements of regulation 7.3.

---

① Refer to *Guidelines for the assessment of thermal protection* (MSC/Circ.1046).

船长(m)	救生圈最少数量
100 以下	8
100 至 150 以下	10
150 至 200 以下	12
200 及以上	14

1.2 第 7.1.3 条要求的配在液货船上的救生圈用自亮灯,应为电池型。

2 救生衣灯

2.1 本要求适用于所有货船。

2.2 在货船上,每件救生衣都应设有 1 盏符合《规则》2.2.3 要求的灯。

2.3 1998 年 7 月 1 日以前在客船上的救生衣,其救生衣灯如不完全符合《规则》2.2.3 要求,主管机关可允许其使用至正常替换时或至 2002 年 7 月 1 日以后的第一次定期检验时,取较早者。

3 救生服

3.1 本节适用于所有货船。但 2006 年 7 月 1 日以前建造的货船应在不迟于 2006 年 7 月 1 日或以后的第一次安全设备检验时符合 3.2 至 3.5 的规定。

3.2 应为船上每个人配备一件合身的且符合《规则》第 2.3 节要求的救生服。但对除了第Ⅸ/1 条所定义的散货船外的船,如果该船一直在主管机关认为不需救生服的温暖气候区域①航行,则不必要求配备这些救生服。

3.3 如果船舶有任何值班站或工作站远离通常存放救生服的地方(包括按第 31.1.4 条配备且位于远处的救生艇筏),则任何时候均应另外为通常在这些场所值班或工作的人员按其人数配备合身的救生服。

3.4 救生服应放在容易拿到的地方,其位置应予明显标示。

3.5 本条要求的救生服可用于符合第 7.3 条的要求。

① 参见《热保护评定指南》(第 MSC/Circ.1046 号通函)。

Regulation 33
Survival craft embarkation and launching arrangements

1 Cargo ship survival craft embarkation arrangements shall be so designed that lifeboats can be boarded and launched directly from the stowed position and davit-launched liferafts can be boarded and launched from a position immediately adjacent to the stowed position or from a position to which the liferaft is transferred prior to launching in compliance with the requirements of regulation 13.5.

2 On cargo ships of 20,000 gross tonnage and upwards, lifeboats shall be capable of being launched, where necessary utilizing painters, with the ship making headway at speeds up to 5 knots in calm water.

Section Ⅳ
Life-saving appliances and arrangements requirements

Regulation 34

All life-saving appliances and arrangements shall comply with the applicable requirements of the Code.

Section Ⅴ
Miscellaneous

Regulation 35
Training manual and on-board training aids

1 This regulation applies to all ships.

2 A training manual complying with the requirements of paragraph 3 shall be provided in each crew mess room and recreation room or in each crew cabin.

3 The training manual, which may comprise several volumes, shall contain instructions and information, in easily understood terms illustrated wherever possible, on the life-saving appliances provided in the ship and on the best methods of survival. Any part of such information may be provided in the form of audio-visual aids in lieu of the manual. The following shall be explained in detail:

.1 donning of lifejackets, immersion suits and anti-exposure suits, as appropriate;

.2 muster at the assigned stations;

第 33 条
救生艇筏的登乘与降落装置

1　货船救生艇筏的登乘布置的设计应使救生艇能从其存放位置直接登乘和降落，以及吊放式救生筏能从紧邻其存放处的位置或降落前按第 13.5 条将救生筏移至的位置登乘和降落。

2　20 000 总吨及以上的货船，其救生艇应能在该船于平静水域前进速度达 5 kn 时降落，必要时可利用艇首缆。

第 4 节
救生设备和装置的要求

第 34 条

所有救生设备和装置均应符合《规则》的适用要求。

第 5 节
其他

第 35 条
培训手册和船上培训教具

1　本条适用于所有船舶。

2　每一船员餐厅和娱乐室，或每一船员舱室内均应配备 1 本符合本条 3 要求的培训手册。

3　培训手册可分成若干分册，应包含关于船上所配备的救生设备和最佳救生方法的须知和资料并应用易懂的措辞写成，如有可能应配以图解说明。这些资料的任何部分都可以用视听辅助教材形式提供。下列各项应予详细解释：

.1　救生衣、救生服和抗暴露服的穿着法（酌情而定）；

.2　在指定地点集合；

.3 boarding, launching, and clearing the survival craft and rescue boats, including, where applicable, use of marine evacuation systems;

.4 method of launching from within the survival craft;

.5 release from launching appliances;

.6 methods and use of devices for protection in launching areas, where appropriate;

.7 illumination in launching areas;

.8 use of all survival equipment;

.9 use of all detection equipment;

.10 with the assistance of illustrations, the use of radio life-saving appliances;

.11 use of drogues;

.12 use of engine and accessories;

.13 recovery of survival craft and rescue boats including stowage and securing;

.14 hazards of exposure and the need for warm clothing;

.15 best use of the survival craft facilities in order to survive;

.16 methods of retrieval, including the use of helicopter rescue gear (slings, baskets, stretchers), breeches buoy and shore life-saving apparatus and ship's line-throwing apparatus;

.17 all other functions contained in the muster list and emergency instructions; and

.18 instructions for emergency repair of the life-saving appliances.

4 Every ship fitted with a marine evacuation system shall be provided with on-board training aids in the use of the system.

5 The training manual shall be written in the working language of the ship.

Regulation 36
Instructions for on-board maintenance

Instructions for on-board maintenance of life-saving appliances shall be easily understood, illustrated wherever possible, and, as appropriate, shall include the following for each appliance:

.1 a checklist for use when carrying out the inspections required by regulation 20.7;

.2 maintenance and repair instructions;

.3 schedule of periodic maintenance;

.3 救生艇筏和救助艇的登乘、降落和离开,包括(如适用)海上撤离系统的使用;

.4 在救生艇筏内降落的方法;

.5 从降落设备上脱开;

.6 降落区域内防护方法与防护设备的用法(如适用);

.7 降落区域的照明;

.8 所有救生设备的用法;

.9 所有探测装备的用法;

.10 用图解说明无线电救生设备的用法;

.11 海锚的用法;

.12 发动机及其附件的用法;

.13 救生艇筏和救助艇的回收,包括存放和系固;

.14 暴露的危害性和穿用保暖衣服的必要性;

.15 为求生而使用救生艇筏设备的最佳方法;

.16 拯救的方法,包括直升机救助装置(吊索、吊篮、担架)、连裤救生圈、沿岸救生工具和船舶抛绳设备的用法;

.17 应变部署表与应变须知所列出的所有其他措施;和

.18 救生设备应急修理须知。

4 配有海上撤离系统的每艘船舶应设有用于该系统的船上培训教具。

5 培训手册应以船上的工作语言撰写。

第36条
船上维护保养须知

救生设备的船上维护保养须知应易于理解,如有可能应配以图解说明,并且按适用情况,每一设备应包括下列各项:

.1 进行第20.7条要求的检查时所用的检查清单;

.2 维护保养与修理须知;

.3 定期维护保养计划;

.4 diagram of lubrication points with the recommended lubricants;

.5 list of replaceable parts;

.6 list of sources of spare parts; and

.7 log for records of inspections and maintenance.

Regulation 37
Muster list and emergency instructions

1 The muster list shall specify details of the general emergency alarm and public address system prescribed by section 7.2 of the Code and also action to be taken by crew and passengers when this alarm is sounded. The muster list shall also specify how the order to abandon ship will be given.

2 Each passenger ship shall have procedures in place for locating and rescuing passengers trapped in their staterooms.

3 The muster list shall show the duties assigned to the different members of the crew including:

.1 closing of the watertight doors, fire doors, valves, scuppers, sidescuttles, skylights, portholes and other similar openings in the ship;

.2 equipping of the survival craft and other life-saving appliances;

.3 preparation and launching of survival craft;

.4 general preparations of other life-saving appliances;

.5 muster of passengers;

.6 use of communication equipment;

.7 manning of fire parties assigned to deal with fires;

.8 special duties assigned in respect to the use of fire-fighting equipment and installations; and

.9 for passenger ships only, damage control for flooding emergencies.

4 The muster list shall specify which officers are assigned to ensure that life-saving and fire appliances are maintained in good condition and are ready for immediate use.

5 The muster list shall specify substitutes for key persons who may become disabled, taking into account that different emergencies may call for different actions.

6 The muster list shall show the duties assigned to members of the crew in relation to passengers in case of emergency. These duties shall include:

.1 warning the passengers;

.4　润滑点示意图，并注明建议用的润滑剂；

.5　可替换部件一览表；

.6　备件来源一览表；和

.7　检查和维护保养记录簿。

第 37 条
应变部署表与应变须知

1　应变部署表应详细说明《规则》第 7.2 节规定的通用紧急报警信号和公共广播系统，以及该警报发出时船员和乘客应采取的行动。应变部署表还应写明弃船命令将如何发出。

2　每艘客船应具有寻找并救出困在客舱内乘客的适当的程序。

3　应变部署表应写明分派给不同船员的任务，包括：

.1　船上水密门、防火门、阀、泄水孔、舷窗、天窗、装货舷门和其他类似开口的关闭；

.2　救生艇筏和其他救生设备的属具配备；

.3　救生艇筏的准备工作和降落；

.4　其他救生设备的一般准备工作；

.5　集合乘客；

.6　通信设备的使用；

.7　安排指定的处理火灾的消防组人员；

.8　就使用消防设备及装置而指派的专门任务；和

.9　进水紧急情况下的破损控制，仅针对客船。

4　应变部署表应规定指定的高级船员负责确保维护保养救生和消防设备，使其处于完好状态，并立即可用。

5　应变部署表应规定关键人员失去能力后的替代人员，要考虑到不同的紧急情况可能要求采取不同的行动。

6　应变部署表应说明在紧急情况下，指派给船员的与乘客有关的各项任务。这些任务应包括：

.1　向乘客发出警告；

.2 seeing that they are suitably clad and have donned their lifejackets correctly;

.3 assembling passengers at muster stations;

.4 keeping order in the passageways and on the stairways and generally controlling the movements of the passengers; and

.5 ensuring that a supply of blankets is taken to the survival craft.

7 The muster list shall be prepared before the ship proceeds to sea. After the muster list has been prepared, if any change takes place in the crew which necessitates an alteration in the muster list, the master shall either revise the list or prepare a new list.

8 The format of the muster list used on passenger ships shall be approved.

.2　查看乘客是否穿妥衣服，以及是否正确地穿好救生衣；

.3　召集乘客于各集合站；

.4　维持通道及梯道上的秩序，并大体上控制乘客的动向；和

.5　确保把毛毯送到救生艇筏上。

7　应变部署表应在船舶出航前制定。在应变部署表制定后，如果船员有所变动而必需更改应变部署表，船长应修订该表，或制定新表。

8　客船上使用的应变部署表的格式应经认可。

Part C
Alternative design and arrangements

Regulation 38
Alternative design and arrangements

1 Purpose

The purpose of this regulation is to provide a methodology for alternative design and arrangements for life-saving appliances and arrangements.

2 General

2.1 Life-saving appliances and arrangements may deviate from the requirements set out in part B, provided that the alternative design and arrangements meet the intent of the requirements concerned and provide an equivalent level of safety to this chapter.

2.2 When alternative design or arrangements deviate from the prescriptive requirements of part B, an engineering analysis, evaluation and approval of the design and arrangements shall be carried out in accordance with this regulation.

3 Engineering analysis

The engineering analysis shall be prepared and submitted to the Administration, based on the guidelines developed by the Organization① and shall include, as a minimum, the following elements:

.1 determination of the ship type and the life-saving appliance and arrangements concerned;

.2 identification of the prescriptive requirement(s) with which the life-saving appliance and arrangements will not comply;

.3 identification of the reason the proposed design will not meet the prescriptive requirements supported by compliance with other recognized engineering or industry standards;

.4 determination of the performance criteria for the ship and the life-saving appliance and arrangements concerned addressed by the relevant prescriptive requirement(s):

  .1 performance criteria shall provide a level of safety not inferior to the relevant prescriptive requirements contained in part B; and

  .2 performance criteria shall be quantifiable and measurable;

① Refer to *Revised guidelines on alternative design and arrangements for SOLAS Chapter Ⅱ-1 and Ⅲ* (MSC.1/Circ.1212/Rev.1).

C 部分
替代设计与布置

第 38 条
替代设计与布置

1　目的

本条旨在为救生设备与布置提供替代设计与布置的方法。

2　通则

2.1　如其替代设计与布置能满足有关要求的意图并能提供和本章同等的安全水平，救生设备与布置可以偏离 B 部分中的要求。

2.2　当替代设计与布置偏离于 B 部分中的条文要求时，须按照本条规定对该设计与布置进行工程分析、评估与认可。

3　工程分析

工程分析须按本组织制定的指南[①]编写并向主管机关提交，并须至少包含下列内容：

.1　确定船舶类型和有关救生设备与布置；

.2　给出该救生设备与布置不满足的条文要求；

.3　给出拟议设计不满足该条文要求的理由并以符合其他公认的工程或工业标准为证据；

.4　确定有关条文要求所阐明的关于该船舶和救生设备与布置的性能标准：

　　.1　性能标准所达到的安全水平须不低于 B 部分中相关条文要求；及

　　.2　性能标准须能量化并能衡量；

① 参见经修订的《SOLAS 第Ⅱ-1 章和第Ⅲ章的替代设计和布置指南》（第 MSC.1/Circ.1212/Rev.1 号通函）。

.5 detailed description of the alternative design and arrangements, including a list of the assumptions used in the design and any proposed operational restrictions or conditions;

.6 technical justification demonstrating that the alternative design and arrangements meet the safety performance criteria; and

.7 risk assessment based on identification of the potential faults and hazards associated with the proposal.

4 Evaluation of the alternative design and arrangements

4.1 The engineering analysis required in paragraph 3 shall be evaluated and approved by the Administration, taking into account the guidelines developed by the Organization. ①

4.2 A copy of the documentation, as approved by the Administration, indicating that the alternative design and arrangements comply with this regulation, shall be carried on board the ship.

5 Exchange of information

The Administration shall communicate to the Organization pertinent information concerning alternative design and arrangements approved by them for circulation to all Contracting Governments.

6 Re-evaluation due to change of conditions

If the assumptions and operational restrictions that were stipulated in the alternative design and arrangements are changed, the engineering analysis shall be carried out under the changed condition and shall be approved by the Administration.

① Refer to *Revised guidelines on alternative design and arrangements for SOLAS chapters Ⅱ-1 and Ⅲ* (MSC.1/Circ.1212/Rev.1).

.5　替代设计和布置的详细描述,包括列明设计中所使用的假设及任何建议的操作限制或条件

.6　证明替代设计和布置达到安全性能标准的技术证据;及

.7　识别该建议的有关潜在缺陷和危险后所做的风险评估。

4　替代设计与布置的评估

4.1　主管机关须参照本组织①制定的指南对第 3 款所要求的工程分析加以评估及认可。

4.2　船上须带有经主管机关认可的证明替代设计与布置符合本条规定的文件的副本。

5　交换资料

主管机关须向本组织通报其认可的有关替代设计与布置的相关资料,以向所有缔约政府转发。

6　条件变化后的重新评估

如替代设计与布置中规定的假设和操作限制出现变化,须按照变化后的条件进行工程评估,并获得主管机关的认可。

① 参见经修订的《SOLAS 第Ⅲ章的替代设计和布置指南》(第 MSC.1/Circ.1212/Rev.1 号通函)。

Chapter Ⅳ Radiocommunications

第Ⅳ章　无线电通信

Part A
General

Regulation 1
Application

1 Unless expressly provided otherwise, this chapter applies to all ships to which the present regulations apply and to cargo ships of 300 gross tonnage and upwards.

2 This chapter does not apply to ships to which the present regulations would otherwise apply while such ships are being navigated within the Great Lakes of North America and their connecting and tributary waters as far east as the lower exit of the St Lambert Lock at Montreal in the Province of Quebec, Canada.①

3 No provision in this chapter shall prevent the use by any ship, survival craft or person in distress, of any means at their disposal to attract attention, make known their position and obtain help.

Regulation 2
Terms and definitions

1 For the purpose of this chapter, the following terms shall have the meanings defined below:

.1 *Bridge-to-bridge communications* means safety communications between ships from the position from which the ships are normally navigated.

.2 *Continuous watch* means that the radio watch concerned shall not be interrupted other than for brief intervals when the ship's receiving capability is impaired or blocked by its own communications or when the facilities are under periodical maintenance or checks.

.3 *Digital selective calling* (DSC) means a technique using digital codes which enables a radio station to establish contact with, and transfer information to, another station or group of stations, and complying with the relevant recommendations of the International Radio Consultative Committee (CCIR).②

.4 *Direct-printing telegraphy* means automated telegraphy techniques which comply with the relevant recommendations of the International Radio Consultative Committee (CCIR).②

.5 *General radiocommunications* means operational and public correspondence traffic, other than distress, urgency and safety messages, conducted by radio.

---

① Such ships are subject to special requirements relative to radio for safety purposes, as contained in the relevant agreement between Canada and the United States of America.

② The name of the Committee was changed to "ITU Radiocommunication Sector" (ITU-R) due to Article 1 of the International Telecommunication Constitution, Geneva, 1992.

A 部分
通则

第 1 条
适用范围

1　除另有明文规定外，本章适用于本规则所适用的所有船舶和 300 总吨及以上的货船。

2　本章不适用于在北美洲五大湖及其东至加拿大魁北克省蒙特利尔的圣拉姆伯特船闸下游出口处为止的相连水域和支流航行的船舶，而这些船舶在其他情况下应适用本规则①。

3　本章的规定不应妨碍遇险的任何船舶、救生艇筏或人员使用任何方法以引起注意、表明其位置并获得援助。

第 2 条
术语和定义

1　就本章而言：

.1　**驾驶台对驾驶台的通信**系指在船舶通常驾驶位置进行的船舶之间的安全通信。

.2　**连续值班**系指有关的无线电值班不应中断，除非当船舶接收能力由于自身通信被削弱或阻塞时，或当设备处于定期维护或检查时，而引起短暂间隔。

.3　**数字选择呼叫**(DSC)系指使用数码，使一个无线电台与另一个电台或一组电台建立联系和传递信息，并符合国际无线电咨询委员会(CCIR)②有关建议案的一种技术。

.4　**直接印字电报**系指符合国际无线电咨询委员会(CCIR)②有关建议案的自动电报技术。

.5　**一般无线电通信**系指通过无线电进行的除遇险、紧急和安全信息通信以外的业务和公共通信。

---

①　此类船舶为安全目的而受有关无线电的特殊要求约束，这些要求载于加拿大与美利坚合众国的有关协议内。
②　因 1992 年日内瓦《国际电信联盟组织法》第 1 条规定，该委员会名称改为“ITU 无线电通信部”(ITU-R)。

.6 *Inmarsat*[①] means the Organization established by the Convention on the International Maritime Satellite Organization adopted on 3 September 1976.

.7 *International NAVTEX Service* means the coordinated broadcast and automatic reception on 518 kHz of maritime safety information by means of narrow-band direct-printing telegraphy using the English language.[②]

.8 *Locating* means the finding of ships, aircraft, units or persons in distress.

.9 *Maritime safety information* means navigational and meteorological warnings, meteorological forecasts and other urgent safety-related messages broadcast to ships.

.10 *Polar orbiting satellite service* means a service which is based on polar orbiting satellites which receive and relay distress alerts from satellite EPIRBs and which provides their position.

.11 *Radio Regulations* means the Radio Regulations annexed to, or regarded as being annexed to, the most recent International Telecommunication Convention which is in force at any time.

.12 *Sea area A1* means an area within the radiotelephone coverage of at least one VHF coast station in which continuous DSC alerting is available, as may be defined by a Contracting Government.[③]

.13 *Sea area A2* means an area, excluding sea area A1, within the radiotelephone coverage of at least one MF coast station in which continuous DSC alerting is available, as may be defined by a Contracting Government.[③]

.14 *Sea area A3* means an area, excluding sea areas A1 and A2, within the coverage of an Inmarsat geostationary satellite in which continuous alerting is available.

.15 *Sea area A4* means an area outside sea areas A1, A2 and A3.

.16 *Global Maritime Distress and Safety System (GMDSS)* identities means maritime mobile services identity, the ship's call sign, recognized mobile satellite service identities and serial number identity which may be transmitted by the ship's equipment and used to identify the ship.

.17 Recognized mobile satellite service means any service which operates through a satellite system and is recognized by the Organization, for use in the Global Maritime Distress and Safety System(GMDSS).

2 All other terms and abbreviations which are used in this chapter and which are defined in the Radio Regulations and in the International Convention on Maritime Search and Rescue (SAR), 1979, as may be amended, shall have the meanings as defined in those Regulations and the SAR Convention.

---

① The name of the Organization was changed to "International Mobile Satellite Organization" (Inmarsat) by virtue of amendments to its Convention and Operating Agreement adopted by the 10th(extraordinary) Assembly(5 to 9 December 1994).

② Refer to the NAVTEX Manual.

③ Refer to *Provision of radio services for the Global Maritime Distress and Safety System (GMDSS)* (resolution A.801(19), as amended).

.6　**国际海事卫星组织**[①]系指按 1976 年 9 月 3 日通过的国际海事卫星组织公约成立的组织。

.7　**国际奈伏泰斯**业务系指在 518 kHz 上,使用窄带直接印字电报手段,用英语协调广播和自动接收海上安全信息。[②]

.8　**定位**系指发现遇险的船舶、航空器、海上设施或人员。

.9　**海上安全信息**系指向船舶播发的航行和气象警报、气象预报和与安全有关的其他紧急信息。

.10　**极轨道卫星业务**系指利用极轨道卫星接收和转发来自卫星紧急无线电示位标的遇险报警,并提供其位置的业务。

.11　**《无线电规则》**系指任何时候实施的最新《国际电信公约》所附或视为其附件的《无线电规则》。

.12　**A1 海区**系指至少由一个具有连续 DSC 报警能力的甚高频海岸电台的无线电话所覆盖的区域,该区域可由各缔约国政府规定。[③]

.13　**A2 海区**系指除 A1 海区以外,至少由一个具有连续 DSC 报警能力的中频海岸电台的无线电话所覆盖的区域,该区域可由各缔约国政府规定。[③]

.14　**A3 海区**系指除 A1 和 A2 海区以外,由具有连续报警能力的 Inmarsat 对地静止卫星所覆盖的区域。

.15　**A4 海区**系指 A1、A2 和 A3 海区以外的区域。

.16　**全球海上遇险和安全系统**(GMDSS)标识系指可由船舶设备发送并用于识别船舶的海上移动业务识别码、船舶呼号、Inmarsat 识别码和系列号识别码。

.17　**经认可的移动卫星业务**系指任何通过卫星系统运作并经本组织认可用于全球海上遇险和安全系统(GMDSS)的业务。

2　本章所使用的并在《无线电规则》和可能经修正的《1979 年国际海上搜索与救助(SAR)公约》中已定义的所有其他术语和缩略语,具有与该规则和 SAR 公约所定义的相同含义。

---

① 按国际海事卫星组织第 10 次(特别)大会(1994 年 12 月 5 日至 9 日)通过的对其公约和操作协议的修正案,该组织名称改为“国际移动卫星组织”(Inmarsat)。

② 参见 NAVTEX 手册。

③ 参见经修订的第 A.801(19)号决议《关于全球海上遇险和安全系统(GMDSS)无线电业务的规定》。

Regulation 3
Exemptions

1 The Contracting Governments consider it highly desirable not to deviate from the requirements of this chapter; nevertheless the Administration may grant partial or conditional exemptions to individual ships from the requirements of regulations 7 to 11 provided:

.1 such ships comply with the functional requirements of regulation 4; and

.2 the Administration has taken into account the effect such exemptions may have upon the general efficiency of the service for the safety of all ships.

2 An exemption may be granted under paragraph 1 only:

.1 if the conditions affecting safety are such as to render the full application of regulations 7 to 11 unreasonable or unnecessary;

.2 in exceptional circumstances, for a single voyage outside the sea area or sea areas for which the ship is equipped.

3 Each Administration shall submit to the Organization, as soon as possible after the first of January in each year, a report showing all exemptions granted under paragraphs 1 and 2 during the previous calendar year and giving the reasons for granting such exemptions.

Regulation 4
Functional requirements①

1 Every ship, while at sea, shall be capable:

.1 except as provided in regulations 8.1.1 and 10.1.4.3, of transmitting ship-to-shore distress alerts by at least two separate and independent means, each using a different radiocommunication service;

.2 of receiving shore-to-ship distress alerts;

.3 of transmitting and receiving ship-to-ship distress alerts;

.4 of transmitting and receiving search and rescue coordinating communications;

.5 of transmitting and receiving on-scene communications;

.6 of transmitting and, as required by regulation Ⅴ/19.2.3.2, receiving signals for locating;②

.7 of transmitting and receiving③ maritime safety information;

① It should be noted that ships performing GMDSS functions should use *Guidance for avoidance of false distress alerts* (resolution A.814(19)).

② Refer to *Carriage of radar operating in the frequency band 9,300–9,500 MHz* (resolution A.614(15)).

③ It should be noted that ships may have a need for reception of certain maritime safety information while in port.

第3条
免除

1　虽然缔约国政府认为不背离本章的要求是极其必要的，但主管机关可准许个别船舶部分地或有条件地免除第7条至第11条的要求，只要：

.1　此类船舶符合第4条的功能要求；和

.2　主管机关已考虑到这些免除对所有船舶安全业务总的有效性的影响。

2　按本条1所给予的免除，仅适用于下列情况：

.1　如果影响安全的条件致使完全执行第7条至第11条为不合理或不必要时；

.2　在例外情况下，船舶在其配备所依据的海区或多个海区外进行单次航行。

3　各主管机关应在每年的1月1日后尽快向本组织提交1份报告，列出上一日历年度内按本条1和2准予的所有免除并阐明准予免除的理由。

第4条
功能要求[①]

1　每艘船舶在海上时均应能：

.1　除第8.1.1条和第10.1.4.3条的规定外，由至少两台分开的和独立的装置发送船对岸遇险报警，且每台装置应使用不同的无线电通信业务；

.2　接收岸对船遇险报警；

.3　发送和接收船对船遇险报警；

.4　发送和接收搜救协调通信；

.5　发送和接收现场通信；

.6　发送和按第Ⅴ/19.2.3.2条要求接收定位信号[②]；

.7　发送和接收海上安全信息[③]；

---

① 应注意船舶执行GMDSS功能应使用本组织第A.814(19)号决议通过的《避免错误的遇险报警指南》。
② 参见第A.614(15)号决议《关于在9 300~9 500 MHz频带上工作的雷达配备》。
③ 应注意船舶在港口时可能有必要接收某些海上安全信息。

.8 of transmitting and receiving general radiocommunications to and from shore-based radio systems or networks subject to regulation 15.8; and

.9 of transmitting and receiving bridge-to-bridge communications.

Regulation 4-1
GMDSS satellite providers

The Maritime Safety Committee shall determine the criteria, procedures and arrangements for the evaluation, recognition, review and oversight of the provision of mobile satellite communication services in the Global Maritime Distress and Safety System (GMDSS) pursuant to the provisions of this chapter.①

① Refer to *Criteria for the provision of mobile satellite communication systems in the Global Maritime Distress and Safety System (GMDSS)* (resolution A.1001(25)) and *Guidance to prospective GMDSS satellite service providers* (MSC.1/Circ.1414).

.8　向海岸无线电系统或网络发送和接收第 15.8 条所述的一般无线电通信；和

.9　发送和接收驾驶室对驾驶室的通信。

第 4-1 条
GMDSS 卫星服务提供商

海上安全委员会应对全球海上遇险和安全系统（GMDSS）的移动卫星通信服务，按本章规定确定评估、认可、评审和监管的衡准、程序和布置。[①]

① 参见《用于全球海上遇险和安全系统（GMDSS）的移动卫星通信系统配备衡准》（第 A.1001（25）号决议）和《未来 GMDSS 卫星服务提供商导则》（第 MSC.1/Circ.1414 号通函）。

Part B
Undertakings by Contracting Governments[①]

Regulation 5
Provision of radiocommunication services

1 Each Contracting Government undertakes to make available, as it deems practical and necessary either individually or in cooperation with other Contracting Governments, appropriate shore-based facilities for space and terrestrial radiocommunication services having due regard to the recommendations of the Organization.[②] These services are:

.1 a radiocommunication service utilizing geostationary satellites in the maritime mobile-satellite service;

.2 a radiocommunication service utilizing polar orbiting satellites in the mobile-satellite service;

.3 the maritime mobile service in the bands between 156 MHz and 174 MHz;

.4 the maritime mobile service in the bands between 4,000 kHz and 27,500 kHz; and

.5 the maritime mobile service in the bands between 415 kHz and 535 kHz[③] and between 1,605 kHz and 4,000 kHz.

2 Each Contracting Government undertakes to provide the Organization with pertinent information concerning the shore-based facilities in the maritime mobile service, mobile-satellite service and maritime mobile-satellite service, established for sea areas which it has designated off its coasts.[④]

Regulation 5-1
Global Maritime Distress and Safety System identities

1 This regulation applies to all ships on all voyages.

2 Each Contracting Government undertakes to ensure that suitable arrangements are made for registering Global Maritime Distress and Safety System (GMDSS) identities and for making information on these identities available to rescue co-ordination centres on a 24-hour basis. Where appropriate, international organizations maintaining a registry of these identities shall be notified by the Contracting Government of these assignments.

---

① 1 Each Contracting Government is not required to provide all radiocommunication services.
2 The requirements should be specified for shore-based facilities to cover the various sea areas.

② Refer to *Provision of radio services for the Global Maritime Distress and Safety System (GMDSS)* (resolution A.801(19), as amended).

③ Refer to *Implementation of the NAVTEX system as a component of the World-Wide Navigational Warning Service* (resolution A.617(15)).

④ The Master Plan of shore-based facilities for the GMDSS based on information provided by Contracting Governments is included in the Organization's Global Integrated Shipping Information System (GISIS).

B 部分
缔约国政府的承诺①

第 5 条
无线电通信业务的规定

1　各缔约国政府承担义务在其认为可行和必要时,充分考虑本组织的建议案②单独或与其他缔约国政府合作,为空间和地面无线电通信业务提供适当的岸基设施。这些业务是:

.1　在海上移动卫星业务中利用对地静止卫星的无线电通信业务;

.2　在移动卫星业务中利用极轨道卫星的无线电通信业务;

.3　在 156~174 MHz 频带内的海上移动业务;

.4　在 4 000~27 500 kHz 频带内的海上移动业务;和

.5　在 415~535 kHz③ 及 1 605~4 000 kHz 频带内的海上移动业务。

2　各缔约国政府承担义务向本组织提供关于在其沿海指定海区建立的海上移动业务、移动卫星业务和海上移动卫星业务的岸基设施的有关资料④。

第 5-1 条
全球海上遇险和安全系统标识

1　本条适用于在所有航线上航行的所有船舶。

2　各缔约国政府承担义务确保做出适当安排以登记全球海上遇险和安全系统(GMDSS)识别码,并使救助协调中心全天 24 h 能获得这些识别码。如果适合,缔约国政府应向保存这些识别码登记的国际组织通报所授予的识别码。

---

①　1　并不要求每一缔约国政府提供所有无线电通信业务。
　　2　对覆盖不同海区的岸基设施的要求应具体规定。

②　参见《关于全球海上遇险和安全系统(GMDSS)无线电业务的规定》(经修正的第 A.801(19)号决议)。

③　参见《关于作为世界范围航行警告业务一部分的 NAVTEX 系统的实施》(第 A.617(15)号决议)。

④　根据缔约国政府提供的信息,GMDSS 岸基设施的总布置图被纳入本组织的全球综合航运信息系统(GISIS)。

Part C
Ship requirements

Regulation 6
Radio installations

1 Every ship shall be provided with radio installations capable of complying with the functional requirements prescribed by regulation 4 throughout its intended voyage and, unless exempted under regulation 3, complying with the requirements of regulation 7 and, as appropriate for the sea area or areas through which it will pass during its intended voyage, the requirements of either regulation 8, 9, 10 or 11.

2 Every radio installation shall:

.1 be so located that no harmful interference of mechanical, electrical or other origin affects its proper use, and so as to ensure electromagnetic compatibility and avoidance of harmful interaction with other equipment and systems;

.2 be so located as to ensure the greatest possible degree of safety and operational availability;

.3 be protected against harmful effects of water, extremes of temperature and other adverse environmental conditions;

.4 be provided with reliable, permanently arranged electrical lighting, independent of the main and emergency sources of electrical power, for the adequate illumination of the radio controls for operating the radio installation; and

.5 be clearly marked with the call sign, the ship station identity and other codes as applicable for the use of the radio installation.

3 Control of the VHF radiotelephone channels, required for navigational safety, shall be immediately available on the navigation bridge convenient to the conning position and, where necessary, facilities should be available to permit radiocommunications from the wings of the navigation bridge. Portable VHF equipment may be used to meet the latter provision.

4 In passenger ships, a distress panel shall be installed at the conning position. This panel shall contain either one single button which, when pressed, initiates a distress alert using all radiocommunication installations required on board for that purpose or one button for each individual installation. The panel shall clearly and visually indicate whenever any button or buttons have been pressed. Means shall be provided to prevent inadvertent activation of the button or buttons. If the satellite EPIRB is used as the secondary means of distress alerting and is not remotely activated, it shall be acceptable to have an additional EPIRB installed in the wheelhouse near the conning position.

C 部分
船舶要求

第 6 条
无线电装置

1 每艘船舶应设有在其整个预定航程中均能符合第 4 条所述功能要求的无线电装置;除非按第 3 条已免除外,所有无线电装置应能符合第 7 条的要求以及第 8、9、10 或 11 条的要求(视预定航程所通过的海区或多个海区而定)。

2 每台无线电装置应:

.1 安装在机械、电气或其他干扰源的有害干扰不会影响其正常使用的地方,从而确保电磁兼容性,避免与其他设备和系统产生有害的相互干扰;

.2 安装在最安全和易操作的地方;

.3 防止受水、极端温度和其他不利环境条件的有害影响;

.4 配备独立于主电源和应急电源的可靠的、永久布置的电气照明,为操纵无线电装置的无线电控制台提供足够照明;和

.5 清楚地标明船舶呼号,船舶电台识别码及适于无线电装置使用的其他代码。

3 航行安全所需的 VHF 无线电话频道控制器,应设在驾驶台指挥位置附近,可供立即使用,必要时,应具有能从驾驶台两翼进行无线电通信的设施,此要求可由手提式 VHF 设备予以满足。

4 在客船上,遇险控制板应安装在指挥位置。该控制板可以设有一个单独按钮,当按下这个按钮时,船上所有具有遇险报警功能的无线电通信装置发出遇险警报,或者为各个装置各设有一个按钮。无论单按钮或多个按钮被按下时,控制板上均应有清晰的视觉显示。应设有防止单按钮或多个按钮误操作的设施。如果卫星紧急无线电示位标用作发送遇险警报的第二种措施,且不能被遥控,则应可在驾驶室指挥位置附近安装一个附加的卫星紧急无线电示位标。

5 In passenger ships, information on the ship's position shall be continuously and automatically provided to all relevant radiocommunication equipment to be included in the initial distress alert when the button or buttons on the distress panel is pressed.

6 In passenger ships, a distress alarm panel shall be installed at the conning position. The distress alarm panel shall provide visual and aural indication of any distress alert or alerts received on board and shall also indicate through which radiocommunication service the distress alerts have been received.

Regulation 7
Radio equipment: General

1 Every ship shall be provided with:

.1 a VHF radio installation capable of transmitting and receiving:

.1 DSC on the frequency 156.525 MHz (channel 70). It shall be possible to initiate the transmission of distress alerts on channel 70 from the position from which the ship is normally navigated;① and

.2 radiotelephony on the frequencies 156.300 MHz (channel 6), 156.650 MHz (channel 13) and 156.800 MHz (channel 16);

.2 a radio installation capable of maintaining a continuous DSC watch on VHF channel 70 which may be separate from, or combined with, that required by subparagraph 1.1;①

.3 a search and rescue locating device capable of operating either in the 9 GHz band or on frequencies dedicated for AIS, which:

.1 shall be so stowed that it can be easily utilized; and

.2 may be one of those required by regulation Ⅲ/6.2.2 for a survival craft;

.4 a receiver capable of receiving international NAVTEX service broadcasts if the ship is engaged on voyages in any area in which an international NAVTEX service is provided;

.5 a radio facility for reception of maritime safety information by a recognized mobile satellite service enhanced group calling system if the ship is engaged on voyages in sea area A1, or A2 or A3 but in which an international NAVTEX service is not provided. However, ships engaged exclusively on voyages in areas where an HF direct-printing telegraphy maritime safety information service is provided and fitted with equipment capable of receiving such service, may be exempt from this requirement.②

---

① Certain ships may be exempted from this requirement (see regulation Ⅳ/9.4).

② Refer to the *Recommendation on promulgation of maritime safety information* adopted by the Organization by resolution A.705(17), as amended.

5 客船按下遇险控制板上的按钮时,应能连续和自动地将船舶位置资料传送至初始遇险警报动用的所有相关无线电通信设备。

6 对于客船,遇险报警板应安装在指挥位置。遇险报警板应能对任何遇险报警或船上收到的警告发出视觉和听觉指示,并且还应指示出通过何种无线电通信业务接收到该遇险警报。

第7条
无线电设备:通则

1 每艘船舶应设有:

.1 1台能发送和接收的VHF无线电装置:

.1 在156.525 MHz(70频道)频率上的DSC。其应能从船舶通常驾驶的位置,在70频道上启动遇险报警的发送;[①]和

.2 在156.300 MHz(6频道)、156.650 MHz(13频道)和156.800 MHz(16频道)频率上的无线电话;

.2 1台能在VHF-70频道上保持连续DSC值班的无线电装置,该装置可以与第7.1.1.1条所要求的功能分开或相结合;[①]

.3 1只能够以9 GHz波段或自动识别系统指定频率操作的搜救定位装置,该装置:

.1 应安装在可方便使用的地方;和

.2 可以是第Ⅲ/6.2.2条对救生艇筏要求的搜救定位装置之一;

.4 1台能接收国际NAVTEX业务广播的接收机(如果船舶航行在具有国际NAVTEX业务的任何区域);

.5 1台接收来自经认可的移动卫星业务增强群呼系统的海上安全信息的无线电设备(如果船舶航行在A1或A2或A3,但不具有国际NAVTEX业务的海区)。但是,如果船舶仅航行在具有高频(HF)直接印字电报海上安全信息业务的区域,而且该船已装设了能接收这种业务的设备,则可免除本要求。[②]

---

① 某些船舶可免除该要求(见第Ⅳ/9.4条)。
② 参见《关于发布海上安全信息的建议案》(经修订的第A.705(17)号决议)。

.6 subject to the provisions of regulation 8.3, a satellite emergency position-indicating radio beacon (satellite EPIRB)① which shall be:

.1 capable of transmitting a distress alert through the polar orbiting satellite service operating in the 406 MHz band;

.2 installed in an easily accessible position;

.3 ready to be manually released and capable of being carried by one person into a survival craft;

.4 capable of floating free if the ship sinks and of being automatically activated when afloat; and

.5 capable of being activated manually.

2 Every passenger ship shall be provided with means for two-way on-scene radiocommunications for search and rescue purposes using the aeronautical frequencies 121.5 MHz and 123.1 MHz from the position from which the ship is normally navigated.

Regulation 8
Radio equipment: Sea area A1

1 In addition to meeting the requirements of regulation 7, every ship engaged on voyages exclusively in sea area A1 shall be provided with a radio installation capable of initiating the transmission of ship-to-shore distress alerts from the position from which the ship is normally navigated, operating either:

.1 on VHF using DSC; this requirement may be fulfilled by the EPIRB prescribed by paragraph 3, either by installing the EPIRB close to, or by remote activation from, the position from which the ship is normally navigated; or

.2 through the polar orbiting satellite service on 406 MHz; this requirement may be fulfilled by the satellite EPIRB, required by regulation 7.1.6, either by installing the satellite EPIRB close to, or by remote activation from, the position from which the ship is normally navigated; or

.3 if the ship is engaged on voyages within coverage of MF coast stations equipped with DSC, on MF using DSC; or

.4 on HF using DSC; or

.5 through a recognized mobile satellite service; this requirement may be fulfilled by:

.1 a ship earth station;② or

---

① Refer to Search and rescue homing capability (resolution A.616(15)).

② This requirement can be met by recognized mobile satellite service ship earth stations capable of two-way communications, such as Fleet-77 (resolutions A.808(19) and MSC.130(75)) or Inmarsat-C (resolution A.807(19), as amended) ship earth stations. Unless otherwise specified, this footnote applies to all requirements for a recognized mobile satellite service ship earth station prescribed by this chapter.

.6　1 台卫星紧急无线电示位标（卫星 EPIRB）[1]，且应考虑到第 8.3 条的规定，该示位标应：

.1　能够通过 406 MHz 频带上工作的极轨道卫星业务发送遇险报警；

.2　安装在易于接近的位置；

.3　可随时由人工释放并能由一人携入救生艇筏；

.4　当船舶沉没时，能自由漂浮，并当浮起时，能自动启动发送遇险报警；和

.5　能人工启动发送遇险报警。

2　每艘客船都应设有从船舶通常驾驶的位置与现场用航空频率 121.5 MHz 和 123.1 MHz 进行以搜救为目的的双向无线电通信的设备。

第 8 条
无线电设备：A1 海区

1　除满足第 7 条的要求外，仅航行于 A1 海区的每艘船舶还应装设 1 台无线电装置，该装置能从船舶通常驾驶的位置启动发送船对岸遇险报警，且能：

.1　在 VHF 频带上使用 DSC 工作。此要求可由本条 3 所规定的 EPIRB 予以满足，该 EPIRB 应位于靠近船舶通常驾驶的位置，或能从船舶通常驾驶的位置遥控启动；或

.2　通过在 406 MHz 频率上工作的极轨道卫星业务工作。此要求可由第 7.1.6 条所要求的卫星 EPIRB 予以满足，该卫星 EPIRB 应位于靠近船舶通常驾驶的位置或能从船舶通常驾驶的位置遥控启动；或

.3　在 MF 频带上使用 DSC 工作（如果船舶航行在具有 DSC 的 MF 海岸电台所覆盖的区域内）；或

.4　在 HF 频带上使用 DSC 工作；或

.5　通过经认可的移动卫星业务工作；该要求可由以下设备予以满足：

.1　1 台船舶地面站[2]；或

① 参见《搜救寻位能力》（第 A.616（15）号决议）。
② 此要求可由能进行双向通信的公认移动卫星服务船用地面站予以满足，如 Fleet-77（第 A.808（19）号决议和第 MSC.130（75）号决议）或 Inmarsat-C（经修正的第 A.807（19）号决议）。除另有说明外，本脚注适用于对本章规定的公认移动卫星服务船舶地面站的所有要求。

.2 the satellite EPIRB, required by regulation 7.1.6, either by installing the satellite EPIRB close to, or by remote activation from, the position from which the ship is normally navigated.

2 The VHF radio installation, required by regulation 7.1.1, shall also be capable of transmitting and receiving general radiocommunications using radiotelephony.

3 Ships engaged on voyages exclusively in sea area A1 may carry, in lieu of the satellite EPIRB required by regulation 7.1.6, an EPIRB which shall be:

.1 capable of transmitting a distress alert using DSC on VHF channel 70 and providing for locating by means of a radar transponder operating in the 9 GHz band;

.2 installed in an easily accessible position;

.3 ready to be manually released and capable of being carried by one person into a survival craft;

.4 capable of floating free if the ship sinks and being automatically activated when afloat; and

.5 capable of being activated manually.

Regulation 9
Radio equipment: Sea areas A1 and A2

1 In addition to meeting the requirements of regulation 7, every ship engaged on voyages beyond sea area A1, but remaining within sea area A2, shall be provided with:

.1 an MF radio installation capable of transmitting and receiving, for distress and safety purposes, on the frequencies:

.1 2,187.5 kHz using DSC; and

.2 2,182 kHz using radiotelephony;

.2 a radio installation capable of maintaining a continuous DSC watch on the frequency 2,187.5 kHz which may be separate from, or combined with, that required by subparagraph .1.1; and

.3 means of initiating the transmission of ship-to-shore distress alerts by a radio service other than MF operating either:

.1 through the polar orbiting satellite service on 406 MHz; this requirement may be fulfilled by the satellite EPIRB, required by regulation 7.1.6, either by installing the satellite EPIRB close to, or by remote activation from, the position from which the ship is normally navigated; or

.2 on HF using DSC; or

.3 through a recognized mobile satellite service by a ship earth station.

.2　第 7.1.6 条所要求的卫星 EPIRB，该卫星 EPIRB 应位于靠近船舶通常驾驶的位置或能从船舶通常驾驶的位置遥控启动。

2　第 7.1.1 条所要求的 VHF 无线电装置还应能用无线电话发送和接收一般无线电通信。

3　仅航行于 A1 海区的船舶可以装有 1 台 EPIRB 以代替第 7.1.6 条所要求的卫星 EPIRB。该 EPIRB 应：

.1　能在 VHF 的 70 频道上使用 DSC 发送遇险报警，并通过在 9 GHz 频带上工作的雷达应答器提供定位；

.2　经认可的移动卫星业务船舶地面站。

.3　可随时由人工释放并能由一人携入救生艇筏；

.4　当船舶沉没时，能自由漂浮，并在浮起时，能自动启动发送遇险报警；和

.5　能人工启动发送遇险报警。

第 9 条
无线电设备：A1 和 A2 海区

1　超过 A1 海区，但仍在 A2 海区范围内航行的每艘船舶，除满足第 7 条的要求外，还应设有：

.1　1 台能在下述频率上为遇险和安全目的进行发送和接收的 MF 无线电装置：

.1　在 2 187.5 kHz 率上使用 DSC 工作；和

.2　在 2 182 kHz 频率上使用无线电话工作；

.2　1 台能在 2 187.5 kHz 频率上保持连续 DSC 值班的无线电装置。该装置可与.1.1 所要求的功能分开或相结合；和

.3　通过除 MF 以外的无线电业务启动发送船对岸遇险报警的装置，该遇险报警的发送可：

.1　通过在 406 MHz 频率上工作的极轨道卫星业务进行；此要求可由第 7.1.6 条所要求的卫星 EPIRB 予以满足，该卫星 EPIRB 应位于靠近船舶通常驾驶的位置，或能从船舶通常驾驶的位置遥控启动；或

.2　在 HF 频带上使用 DSC 进行；或

.3　由一船舶地面站通过经认可的移动卫星业务进行。

2 It shall be possible to initiate transmission of distress alerts by the radio installations specified in paragraphs 1.1 and 1.3 from the position from which the ship is normally navigated.

3 The ship shall, in addition, be capable of transmitting and receiving general radiocommunications using radiotelephony or direct-printing telegraphy by either:

.1 a radio installation operating on working frequencies in the bands between 1,605 kHz and 4,000 kHz or between 4,000 kHz and 27,500 kHz. This requirement may be fulfilled by the addition of this capability in the equipment required by paragraph 1.1; or

.2 a recognized mobile satellite service ship earth station.

4 The Administration may exempt ships constructed before 1 February 1997, which are engaged exclusively on voyages within sea area A2, from the requirements of regulations 7.1.1.1 and 7.1.2 provided such ships maintain, when practicable, a continuous listening watch on VHF channel 16. This watch shall be kept at the position from which the ship is normally navigated.

Regulation 10
Radio equipment: Sea areas A1, A2 and A3

1 In addition to meeting the requirements of regulation 7, every ship engaged on voyages beyond sea areas A1 and A2, but remaining within sea area A3, shall, if it does not comply with the requirements of paragraph 2, be provided with:

.1 a recognized mobile satellite service ship earth station capable of:

.1 transmitting and receiving distress and safety communications using direct-printing telegraphy;

.2 initiating and receiving distress priority calls;

.3 maintaining watch for shore-to-ship distress alerts, including those directed to specifically defined geographical areas;

.4 transmitting and receiving general radiocommunications, using either radiotelephony or direct-printing telegraphy; and

.2 an MF radio installation capable of transmitting and receiving, for distress and safety purposes, on the frequencies:

.1 2,187.5 kHz using DSC; and

.2 2,182 kHz using radiotelephony; and

.3 a radio installation capable of maintaining a continuous DSC watch on the frequency 2, 187.5 kHz which may be separate from or combined with that required by subparagraph .2.1; and

.4 means of initiating the transmission of ship-to-shore distress alerts by a radio service operating either:

2 本条 1.1 和 1.3 所要求的无线电装置应能从船舶通常驾驶的位置启动发送遇险报警。

3 此外,船舶应能使用下列设备用无线电话或直接印字电报发送和接收一般无线电通信:

.1 1 台在 1 605~4 000 kHz 或 4 000~27 500 kHz 频率工作的无线电装置。此要求可由本条 1.1 所要求的设备增加该性能予以满足;或

.2 1 台经认可的移动卫星业务船舶地面站。

4 对 1997 年 2 月 1 日以前建造的且仅航行于 A2 海区的船舶,在实际可行时,只要这些船舶在其通常驾驶的位置在 VHF16 频道上保持连续守听值班,主管机关可免除第 7.1.1.1 条和第7.1.2 条的要求。

第 10 条
无线电设备:A1、A2 和 A3 海区

1 超出 A1 和 A2 海区,但仍在 A3 海区范围内航行的每艘船舶,除满足第 7 条的要求外,如果不符合本条 2 的要求,则还应设有:

.1 1 台经认可的移动卫星业务船舶地面站,它能:

.1 使用直接印字电报发送和接收遇险和安全通信;

.2 启动发送并接收遇险优先呼叫;

.3 保持岸对船遇险报警的值班,包括对特别定义的地理区域的遇险报警的值班;

.4 使用无线电话或直接印字电报发送和接收一般无线电通信;和

.2 1 台能在下述频率上为遇险和安全目的进行发送和接收的 MF 无线电装置:

.1 在 2 187.5 kHz 频率上使用 DSC 工作;和

.2 在 2 182 kHz 频率上使用无线电话工作;和

.3 1 台能在 2 187.5 kHz 频率上保持连续 DSC 值班的无线电装置。该装置可与.2.1 所要求的功能分开或相结合;和

.4 通过下述无线电业务启动发送船对岸遇险报警的无线电装置,该遇险报警的发送可:

.1 through the polar orbiting satellite service on 406 MHz; this requirement may be fulfilled by the satellite EPIRB, required by regulation 7.1.6, either by installing the satellite EPIRB close to, or by remote activation from, the position from which the ship is normally navigated; or

.2 on HF using DSC; or

.3 through a recognized mobile satellite service by an additional ship earth station.

2 In addition to meeting the requirements of regulation 7, every ship engaged on voyages beyond sea areas A1 and A2, but remaining within sea area A3, shall, if it does not comply with the requirements of paragraph 1, be provided with:

.1 an MF/HF radio installation capable of transmitting and receiving, for distress and safety purposes, on all distress and safety frequencies in the bands between 1,605 kHz and 4,000 kHz and between 4,000 kHz and 27,500 kHz:

.1 using DSC;

.2 using radiotelephony; and

.3 using direct-printing telegraphy; and

.2 equipment capable of maintaining DSC watch on 2,187.5 kHz, 8,414.5 kHz and on at least one of the distress and safety DSC frequencies 4,207.5 kHz, 6,312 kHz, 12,577 kHz or 16,804.5 kHz; at any time, it shall be possible to select any of these DSC distress and safety frequencies. This equipment may be separate from, or combined with, the equipment required by subparagraph. 1; and

.3 means of initiating the transmission of ship-to-shore distress alerts by a radiocommunication service other than HF operating either:

.1 through the polar orbiting satellite service on 406 MHz; this requirement may be fulfilled by the satellite EPIRB, required by regulation 7.1.6, either by installing the satellite EPIRB close to, or by remote activation from, the position from which the ship is normally navigated; or

.2 through a recognized mobile satellite service by a ship earth station; and

.4 in addition, ships shall be capable of transmitting and receiving general radiocommunications using radiotelephony or direct-printing telegraphy by an MF/HF radio installation operating on working frequencies in the bands between 1,605 kHz and 4,000 kHz and between 4,000 kHz and 27,500 kHz. This requirement may be fulfilled by the addition of this capability in the equipment required by subparagraph .1.

3 It shall be possible to initiate transmission of distress alerts by the radio installations specified in paragraphs 1.1, 1.2, 1.4, 2.1 and 2.3 from the position from which the ship is normally navigated.

.1 通过在 406 MHz 频率上工作的极轨道卫星业务进行；此要求可由第 7.1.6 条所要求的卫星 EPIRB 予以满足，该卫星 EPIRB 应位于靠近船舶通常驾驶的位置，或能从船舶通常驾驶的位置遥控启动；或

.2 在 HF 频带上使用 DSC 进行；或

.3 由另一船舶地面站通过经认可的移动卫星业务进行。

2 超出 A1 和 A2 海区，但仍在 A3 海区范围内航行的每艘船舶，除满足第 7 条的要求外，如果不符合本条 1 的要求，则还应设有：

.1 1 台在 1 605~4 000 kHz 和 4 000~27 500 kHz 频带内的所有遇险和安全频率上，为遇险和安全目的进行发送和接收的中/高频(MF/HF)无线电装置：

.1 使用 DSC；

.2 使用无线电话；和

.3 使用直接印字电报；和

.2 能在 2 187.5 kHz、8 414.5 kHz 频率上以及至少在遇险和安全 DSC 频率 4 207.5 kHz、6 312 kHz、12 577 kHz 或 16 804.5 kHz 中的一个频率上保持 DSC 值班的设备；在任何时候，应能选择这些 DSC 遇险和安全频率中的任一频率。该设备可以与上述.1 所要求的装置分开或与其合为一体；和

.3 通过除 HF 以外的无线电通信业务启动发送船对岸遇险报警的装置，该遇险报警的发送可以：

.1 通过在 406 MHz 频率上工作的极轨道卫星业务进行；此要求可由第 7.1.6 条所要求的卫星 EPIRB 予以满足，该卫星 EPIRB 应位于靠近船舶通常驾驶的位置，或能从船舶通常驾驶的位置遥控启动；或

.2 由一船舶地面站通过经认可的移动卫星业务进行；

.4 此外，船舶应能通过在 1 605~4 000 kHz 和 4 000~27 500 kHz 频带内的工作频率上工作的 MF/HF 无线电装置，使用无线电话或直接印字电报进行发送和接收一般无线电通信。此要求可由上述.1 所要求的设备增加该性能予以满足。

3 在本条 1.1、1.2、1.4、2.1 和 2.3 中所规定的无线电装置应能从船舶通常驾驶的位置启动发送遇险报警。

4 The Administration may exempt ships constructed before 1 February 1997, and engaged exclusively on voyages within sea areas A2 and A3, from the requirements of regulations 7.1.1.1 and 7.1.2 provided such ships maintain, when practicable, a continuous listening watch on VHF channel 16. This watch shall be kept at the position from which the ship is normally navigated.

Regulation 11
Radio equipment: Sea areas A1, A2, A3 and A4

1 In addition to meeting the requirements of regulation 7, ships engaged on voyages in all sea areas shall be provided with the radio installations and equipment required by regulation 10.2, except that the equipment required by regulation 10.2.3.2 shall not be accepted as an alternative to that required by regulation 10.2.3.1, which shall always be provided. In addition, ships engaged on voyages in all sea areas shall comply with the requirements of regulation 10.3.

2 The Administration may exempt ships constructed before 1 February 1997, and engaged exclusively on voyages within sea areas A2, A3 and A4, from the requirements of regulations 7.1.1.1 and 7.1.2 provided such ships maintain, when practicable, a continuous listening watch on VHF channel 16. This watch shall be kept at the position from which the ship is normally navigated.

Regulation 12
Watches

1 Every ship, while at sea, shall maintain a continuous watch:

.1 on VHF DSC channel 70, if the ship, in accordance with the requirements of regulation 7.1.2, is fitted with a VHF radio installation;

.2 on the distress and safety DSC frequency 2,187.5 kHz, if the ship, in accordance with the requirements of regulation 9.1.2 or 10.1.3, is fitted with an MF radio installation;

.3 on the distress and safety DSC frequencies 2,187.5 kHz and 8,414.5 kHz and also on at least one of the distress and safety DSC frequencies 4,207.5 kHz, 6,312 kHz, 12,577 kHz or 16,804.5 kHz, appropriate to the time of day and the geographical position of the ship, if the ship, in accordance with the requirements of regulation 10.2.2 or 11.1, is fitted with an MF/HF radio installation. This watch may be kept by means of a scanning receiver;

.4 for satellite shore-to-ship distress alerts, if the ship, in accordance with the requirements of regulation 10.1.1, is fitted with a recognized mobile satellite service ship earth station.

2 Every ship, while at sea, shall maintain a radio watch for broadcasts of maritime safety information on the appropriate frequency or frequencies on which such information is broadcast for the area in which the ship is navigating.

4 对 1997 年 2 月 1 日以前建造的且仅航行于 A2 和 A3 海区的船舶，在实际可行时，只要这些船舶在其通常驾驶的位置在 VHF16 频道上保持连续守听值班，主管机关可免除第 7.1.1.1条和 7.1.2 条的要求。

第 11 条
无线电设备：A1、A2、A3 和 A4 海区

1 航行于所有海区的船舶，除满足第 7 条的要求外，还应设有第 10.2 条所要求的无线电装置和设备，但不应接受用第 10.2.3.2 条所要求的设备替代第 10.2.3.1 条所要求的设备，且应始终设有第 10.2.3.1 条所要求的设备。此外，航行于所有海区的船舶还应满足第 10.3 条的要求。

2 1997 年 2 月 1 日以前建造的且仅航行于 A2、A3 和 A4 海区的船舶，在实际可行时，只要这些船舶在其通常驾驶的位置在 VHF16 频道上保持连续守听值班，主管机关可免除第 7.1.1.1条和 7.1.2 条的要求。

第 12 条
值班

1 每艘船舶在海上时：

.1 根据第 7.1.2 条的要求，如该船安装有 VHF 无线电装置，应在 VHF 的 DSC70 频道保持连续值班；

.2 根据第 9.1.2 条或 10.1.3 条的要求，如果该船安装有 MF 无线电装置，应在 DSC 遇险和安全频率 2 187.5 kHz 上保持连续值班；

.3 根据第 10.2.2 条或 11.1 条的要求，如果该船安装有 MF/HF 无线电装置，在 DSC 遇险和安全频率 2 187.5 kHz 和 8,414.5 kHz 频率上以及至少在 DSC 遇险和安全频率 4 07.5 kHz、6 312 kHz、12 77 kHz 或 16 04.5 kHz 中的一个频率上保持连续值班，视一天中的时间和船舶所在的地理位置而定。可用扫描接收机保持该值班；

.4 根据第 10.1.1 条的要求，如果该船安装有经认可的移动卫星业务船舶地面站，应对卫星岸对船的遇险报警保持连续值班。

2 艘船舶在海上时，应在向该船航行区域发布海上安全信息的相应频率上，对海上安全信息的播发保持无线电值班。

3 Until 1 February 1999 or until such other date as may be determined by the Maritime Safety Committee,① every ship while at sea shall maintain, when practicable, a continuous listening watch on VHF channel 16. This watch shall be kept at the position from which the ship is normally navigated.

Regulation 13
Sources of energy

1 There shall be available at all times, while the ship is at sea, a supply of electrical energy sufficient to operate the radio installations and to charge any batteries used as part of a reserve source or sources of energy for the radio installations.

2 A reserve source or sources of energy shall be provided on every ship, to supply radio installations, for the purpose of conducting distress and safety radiocommunications, in the event of failure of the ship's main and emergency sources of electrical power. The reserve source or sources of energy shall be capable of simultaneously operating the VHF radio installation required by regulation 7.1.1 and, as appropriate for the sea area or sea areas for which the ship is equipped, either the MF radio installation required by regulation 9.1.1, the MF/HF radio installation required by regulation 10.2.1 or 11.1, or the Inmarsat ship earth station required by regulation 10.1.1 and any of the additional loads mentioned in paragraphs 4, 5 and 8 for a period of at least:

.1 1 h on ships provided with an emergency source of electrical power, if such source of power complies fully with all relevant provisions of regulation Ⅱ-1/42 or 43, including the supply of such power to the radio installations; and

.2 6 h on ships not provided with an emergency source of electrical power complying fully with all relevant provisions of regulation Ⅱ-1/42 or 43, including the supply of such power to the radio installations.②

The reserve source or sources of energy need not supply independent HF and MF radio installations at the same time.

3 The reserve source or sources of energy shall be independent of the propelling power of the ship and the ship's electrical system.

4 Where, in addition to the VHF radio installation, two or more of the other radio installations, referred to in paragraph 2, can be connected to the reserve source or sources of energy, they shall be capable of simultaneously supplying, for the period specified, as appropriate, in paragraph 2.1 or 2.2, the VHF radio installation and:

.1 all other radio installations which can be connected to the reserve source or sources of energy at the same time; or

① Refer to *Maintenance of a continuous listening watch on VHF channel* 16 *by SOLAS ships whilst at sea after* 1 *February* 1999 *and installation of VHF DSC facilities on non-SOLAS ships* (resolution MSC.131(75)).

② For guidance, the following formula is recommended for determining the electrical load to be supplied by the reserve source of energy for each radio installation required for distress conditions: 1/2 of the current consumption necessary for transmission + the current consumption necessary for reception + the current consumption of any additional loads.

3 至 1999 年 2 月 1 日或截至海上安全委员会可能确定的其他日期①,每艘船舶在海上时,如果实际可行,应在船舶通常驾驶的位置在 VHF16 频道上保持连续守听值班。

第 13 条
电源

1 舶在海上时,应始终可获得足够的电源供无线电装置工作,并对作为无线电装置的 1 个或多个备用电源组成部分的蓄电池进行充电。

2 艘船舶应设有 1 个或多个备用电源,当船舶主电源和应急电源发生故障时,向无线电装置供电,以便进行遇险和安全通信。该 1 个或多个备用电源应能同时供电给第 7.1.1 条所要求的 VHF 无线电装置,和第 9.1.1 条所要求的 MF 无线电装置、第 10.2.1 或 11.1 条所要求的 MF/HF 无线电装置,或第 10.1.1 条所要求的 Inmarsat 船舶地面站(视船舶配备所依据的海区或多个海区而定),以及供电给本条 4、5 和 8 所提及的任何附加负载,其供电时间至少为:

.1 对于船舶配有的应急电源,如果其完全符合第Ⅱ-1/42 条或 43 条所有相关要求(包括向无线电装置供电),1 h;和

.2 对于船舶配有的应急电源,如果其不完全符合第Ⅱ-1/42 条或 43 条所有相关要求(包括向无线电装置供电),6 h②。

1 个或多个备用电源不必同时向各自独立的 HF 和 MF 无线电装置供电。

3 1 个或多个备用电源应独立于船舶推进动力及船舶电力系统。

4 VHF 无线电装置以外,当本条 2 所提及的 2 个或 2 个以上其他无线电装置能同 1 个或多个备用电源相连时,应能在本条 2.1 或 2.2(视何者适用)所规定的时间内,同时向 VHF 无线电装置和下述装置供电:

.1 能同时与 1 个或多个备用电源相连的所有其他无线电装置;或

---

① 海上安全委员会决定(第 MSC.131(75)号决议),所有 GMDSS 船舶在海上时,如果切实可行,仍应继续在 VHF16 频道上保持连续守听值班。

② 作为指导,建议用以下公式确定在遇险情况下对于每台无线电装置备用电源所能供给的电负荷:1/2 发射所消耗的电流+接收所消耗的电流+任何附加负载消耗的电流。

.2 whichever of the other radio installations will consume the most power, if only one of the other radio installations can be connected to the reserve source or sources of energy at the same time as the VHF radio installation.

5 The reserve source or sources of energy may be used to supply the electrical lighting required by regulation 6.2.4.

6 Where a reserve source of energy consists of a rechargeable accumulator battery or batteries:

.1 a means of automatically charging such batteries shall be provided which shall be capable of recharging them to minimum capacity requirements within 10 h; and

.2 the capacity of the battery or batteries shall be checked, using an appropriate method,① at intervals not exceeding 12 months, when the ship is not at sea.

7 The siting and installation of accumulator batteries which provide a reserve source of energy shall be such as to ensure:

.1 the highest degree of service;

.2 a reasonable lifetime;

.3 reasonable safety;

.4 that battery temperatures remain within the manufacturer's specifications whether under charge or idle; and

.5 that when fully charged, the batteries will provide at least the minimum required hours of operation under all weather conditions.

8 If an uninterrupted input of information from the ship's navigational or other equipment to a radio installation required by this chapter, including the navigation receiver referred to in regulation 18, is needed to ensure its proper performance, means shall be provided to ensure the continuous supply of such information in the event of failure of the ship's main or emergency source of electrical power.

① One method of checking the capacity of an accumulator battery is to fully discharge and recharge the battery, using normal operating current and period (e.g. 10 h). Assessment of the charge condition can be made at any time, but it should be done without significant discharge of the battery when the ship is at sea.

.2　如果其他无线电装置中仅1台能同时和VHF无线电装置一起与1个或多个备用电源相连,则应取其他无线电装置中耗电最大的1台。

5　1个或多个备用电源可用于向第6.2.4条所要求的电气照明供电。

6　如果一备用电源是由1个或多个可充电的蓄电池组成,则:

.1　应设有对这些蓄电池自动充电的装置,该装置应能在10 h内通过充电使蓄电池达到最小容量要求;和

.2　应按不超过12个月的间隔期,使用适当的方法①对不在海上的船舶检查蓄电池或蓄电池组的容量。

7　作为备用电源的蓄电池的位置和安装应确保:

.1　最有效的使用;

.2　合理的寿命;

.3　合理的安全;

.4　不论充电与否,蓄电池的温度保持在出厂说明书规定的温度范围内;和

.5　在任何气候条件下,充足电的蓄电池至少达到所要求的最少工作小时数。

8　如果需要将船舶的导航或其他设备的信息连续输入本章要求的无线电装置(包括第18条中所述的导航接收装置)中以确保其适当的性能,应具有能确保在船舶主电源或应急电源发生故障时继续提供此类信息的措施。

① 检查蓄电池容量的一种方法是,用正常工作电流和时间(例如10 h)对蓄电池彻底放电和充电。在任何时候都可对充电情况进行评定,但当船舶在海上时,该评定应在不大量放电的情况下进行。

Regulation 14
Performance standards

1 All equipment to which this chapter applies shall be of a type approved by the Administration. Such equipment shall conform to appropriate performance standards not inferior to those adopted by the Organization. ①

Regulation 15
Maintenance requirements

1 Equipment shall be so designed that the main units can be replaced readily, without elaborate recalibration or readjustment.

2 Where applicable, equipment shall be so constructed and installed that it is readily accessible for inspection and on-board maintenance purposes.

---

① Refer to:

.1 *Revised Performance standards for narrow-band direct-printing telegraph equipment for the reception of navigational and meteorological warnings and urgent information to ships (NAVTEX)* (resolution MSC.148(77), as amended).

.2 *General requirements for shipborne radio equipment forming part of the global maritime distress and safety system (GMDSS) and for electronic navigational aids* (resolution A.694(17)).

.3 *Performance standards for ship earth stations capable of two-way communications* (resolution A.808(19)); *Type approval of ship earth stations* (resolution A.570(14)); *Performance standards for Inmarsat ship earth stations capable of two-way communications* (resolution MSC.130(75)); and *Performance standards for a ship earth station for use in the GMDSS* (resolution MSC.434(98)).

.4 *Performance standards for shipborne VHF radio installations capable of voice communication and digital selective calling* (resolution A.803(19), as amended).

.5 *Performance standards for shipborne MF radio installations capable of voice communication and digital selective calling* (resolution A.804(19), as amended).

.6 *Performance standards for shipborne MF/HF radio installations capable of voice communication, narrow-band directprinting and digital selective calling* (resolution A.806(19), as amended).

.7 *Performance standards for float-free satellite emergency position-indicating radio beacons (EPIRBs) operating on* 406 *MHz* (resolution A.810(19), as amended); *Type approval of satellite emergency position-indicating radio beacons (EPIRBs) operating in the Cospas-Sarsat system* (resolution A.696(17)); and *Performance standards for float-free emergency position-indicating radio beacons (EPIRBs) operating on 406 MHz* (resolution MSC.471(101)).

.8 *Performance standards for survival craft radar transponders for use in search and rescue operations* (resolution A.802(19), as amended).

.9 *Performance standards for float-free VHF emergency position-indicating radio beacons* (resolution A.805(19)).

.10 *Performance standards for Inmarsat-C ship earth stations capable of transmitting and receiving direct-printing communications* (resolution A.807(19), as amended).

.11 *Revised Performance standards for enhanced group call (EGC) equipment* (resolution MSC.306(87), as amended).

.12 *Performance standards for float-free release and activation arrangements for emergency radio equipment* (resolution A.662(16)).

.13 *System performance standard for the promulgation and co-ordination of maritime safety information using high-frequency narrow-band direct printing* (resolution A.699(17)).

.14 *Performance standards for a shipborne integrated radio-communication system (IRCS) when used in the GMDSS* (resolution A.811 (19)).

.15 *Performance standards for on-scene (aeronautical) two-way portable VHF radiotelephone apparatus* (resolution MSC.80(70), annex 1).

第 14 条
性能标准

1 本章适用的所有设备应为主管机关认可的型式。这些设备所符合的相应性能标准应不低于本组织通过的性能标准①。

第 15 条
维护要求

1 设备的设计应使主要部件能易于更换而无须仔细地重新校准或调整。

2 如果适合,设备的构造和安装应易于进行检查和船上维护。

① 参见:

.1 《船舶接收航行和气象警报以及紧急信息用窄带直接印字电报设备性能标准(NAVTEX)》(第 MSC.148(77)号决议)。

.2 《作为全球海上遇险和安全系统(GMDSS)组成部分的船载无线电设备和电子导航设备一般要求》(第 A.694(17)号决议)。

.3 《能进行双向通信的船舶地面站性能标准》(第 A.808(19)号决议),《船舶地面站型式认可》(第 A.570(14)号决议),《能进行双向通信的 Inmarsat 船舶地面站性能标准》(第 MSC.130(75)号决议),以及《GMDSS 中使用的船舶地面站性能标准》(第 MSC.434(98)号决议)。

.4 《能进行通话和数字选择呼叫的船载 VHF 无线电装置性能标准》(第 A.803(19)号决议,经修订的)。

.5 《能进行通话和数字选择呼叫的船载 MF 无线电装置性能标准》(第 A.804(19)号决议,经修订的)。

.6 《能进行通话、窄带直接印字和数字选择呼叫的船载 MF/ HF 无线电装置性能标准》(第 A.806(19)号决议,经修订的)。

.7 《在 406 MHz 频率上工作的自浮式卫星紧急无线电示位标(EPIRBs)性能标准》(第 A.810(19)号决议,经修订的),《在 COSPAS-SARSAT 系统工作的卫星紧急无线电示位标(EPIRBs)型式认可》(第 A.696(17)号决议),以及《在 406 MHz 频率上工作的自浮式紧急无线电示位标(EPIRB)性能标准》(第 MSC.471(101)号决议)。

.8 《用于搜救作业的救生艇筏雷达应答器性能标准》(第 A.802(19)号决议,经修订的)。

.9 《自浮式 VHF 紧急无线电示位标性能标准》(第 A.805(19)号决议)。

.10 《能发射和接收直接印字通信的 Inmarsat-C 船舶地面站性能标准》(第 A.807(19)号决议,经修订的)。

.11 《增强群呼(EGC)设备性能标准》(第 MSC.306(87)号决议,经修订的)。

.12 《应急无线电设备自浮释放和启动装置性能标准》(第 A.662(16)号决议)。

.13 《使用高频窄带直接印字技术进行海上安全信息播发和协调的系统性能标准》(第 A.699(17)号决议)。

.14 《在 GMDSS 中使用的船载综合无线电通信系统(IRCS)性能标准》(第 A.811(19)号决议)。

.15 《现场(航空)双向便携式 VHF 无线电话设备性能标准》(第 MSC.80(70)号决议,附件 1)。

3 Adequate information shall be provided to enable the equipment to be properly operated and maintained, taking into account the recommendations of the Organization.①

4 Adequate tools and spares shall be provided to enable the equipment to be maintained.

5 The Administration shall ensure that radio equipment required by this chapter is maintained to provide the availability of the functional requirements specified in regulation 4 and to meet the recommended performance standards of such equipment.

6 On ships engaged on voyages in sea areas A1 and A2, the availability shall be ensured by using such methods as duplication of equipment, shore-based maintenance or at-sea electronic maintenance capability, or a combination of these, as may be approved by the Administration.

7 On ships engaged on voyages in sea areas A3 and A4, the availability shall be ensured by using a combination of at least two methods such as duplication of equipment, shore-based maintenance or at-sea electronic maintenance capability, as may be approved by the Administration, taking into account the recommendations of the Organization.②

8 While all reasonable steps shall be taken to maintain the equipment in efficient working order to ensure compliance with all the functional requirements specified in regulation 4, malfunction of the equipment for providing the general radiocommunications required by regulation 4.8 shall not be considered as making a ship unseaworthy or as a reason for delaying the ship in ports where repair facilities are not readily available, provided the ship is capable of performing all distress and safety functions.

9 Satellite EPIRBs shall be:

.1 annually tested for all aspects of operational efficiency, with special emphasis on checking the emission on operational frequencies, coding and registration, at intervals as specified below:

.1 on passenger ships, within 3 months before the expiry date of the Passenger Ship Safety Certificate; and

.2 on cargo ships, within 3 months before the expiry date, or 3 months before or after the anniversary date, of the Cargo Ship Safety Radio Certificate.

The test may be conducted on board the ship or at an approved testing station; and

.2 subject to maintenance at intervals not exceeding five years, to be performed at an approved shore-based maintenance facility.

---

① Refer to *Recommendation on general requirements for shipborne radio equipment forming part of the global maritime distress and safety system and for electronic navigational aids* (resolution A.694(17)), *General requirements for electromagnetic compatibility (EMC) for all electrical and electronic ship's equipment* (resolution A.813(19)), and *Clarifications of certain requirements in IMO performance standards for GMDSS equipment* (MSC/Circ.862).

② Refer to *Radio maintenance guidelines for the global maritime distress and safety system related to sea areas A3 and A4* (resolution A.702(17)).

3　应备有足够的资料以能对设备进行正确的操作和维护，并考虑到本组织的建议案①。

4　应备有足够的工具和备件以能对设备进行维护。

5　主管机关应确保本章要求的无线电设备可予以维护，以确保第 4 条规定的功能要求的有效性，并达到对这些设备所建议的性能标准。

6　航行在 A1 和 A2 海区的船舶，应使用可能经主管机关认可的方法，如双套设备、岸基维护或海上电子维护能力，或其组合，以确保功能要求的有效性。

7　航行在 A3 和 A4 海区的船舶，应使用可能经主管机关认可的至少两种组合方法，如双套设备、岸基维护或海上电子维护能力，以确保功能要求的有效性，并考虑到本组织的建议案②。

8　在应采取一切合理的步骤使设备保持有效的工作状态，以确保符合第 4 条规定的所有功能要求的情况下，只要船舶能实施所有的遇险安全功能，则第 4.8 条所要求的用于提供一般无线电通信的设备发生故障时不应视为该船舶不适航，或作为使船舶滞留在不易提供维修设施的港口的理由。

9　卫星紧急无线电示位标（EPIRB）应：

.1　每年按以下规定的间隔期进行全方位操作效用试验，着重检查操作频率发射、编码和登记：

.1　客船在客船安全证书期满日之前 3 个月内；和

.2　货船在货船无线电安全证书期满日之前 3 个月内或周年日前后 3 个月内。

试验可以在船上进行，也可以在一个经认可的试验站进行；和

.2　按不超过 5 年的间隔期在经认可的岸基维护站进行维护。

---

①　参见本组织第 A.694（17）号决议通过的《关于作为全球海上遇险和安全系统组成部分的船载无线电设备和电子导航设备一般要求的建议案》，以及第 A.813（19）号决议《所有船舶电气和电子设备电磁兼容性（EMC）的一般要求》和第 MSC/Circ.862 号通函《IMO 对 GMDSS 设备性能标准有关要求的澄清》。

②　参见第 A.702（17）号决议《全球海上遇险和安全系统 A3 和 A4 海区无线电维修指南》。

Regulation 16
Radio personnel

1 Every ship shall carry personnel qualified for distress and safety radiocommunication purposes to the satisfaction of the Administration.① The personnel shall be holders of certificates specified in the Radio Regulations as appropriate, any one of whom shall be designated to have primary responsibility for radiocommunications during distress incidents.

2 In passenger ships, at least one person qualified in accordance with paragraph 1 shall be assigned to perform only radiocommunication duties during distress incidents.

Regulation 17
Radio records

A record shall be kept, to the satisfaction of the Administration and as required by the Radio Regulations, of all incidents connected with the radiocommunication service which appear to be of importance to safety of life at sea.

Regulation 18
Position-updating

All two-way communication equipment carried on board a ship to which this chapter applies which is capable of automatically including the ship's position in the distress alert shall be automatically provided with this information from an internal or external navigation receiver, if either is installed. If such a receiver is not installed, the ship's position and the time at which the position was determined shall be manually updated at intervals not exceeding 4 h, while the ship is under way, so that it is always ready for transmission by the equipment.

---

① Refer to the STCW Code, chapter Ⅳ, section B-Ⅳ/2.

第 16 条
无线电人员

1　每艘船舶应配有主管机关满意的、能胜任遇险和安全无线电通信的人员。① 这些人员应持有《无线电规则》中规定的相应证书。在遇险时，应指定其中任何人员担负起无线电通信的主要职责。

2　客船上，至少应指派一名按本条 1 要求的有资格的人员，在遇险时只执行无线电通信责任。

第 17 条
无线电记录

应备有使主管机关满意并符合《无线电规则》要求的无线电记录，该记录应记载对于海上人命安全显然具有重要性的与无线电通信业务有关的所有遇险事故。

第 18 条
船位更新

适用本章的船舶，其船上备有的能在遇险报警时自动报告船位的所有双向通信设备，均应自动从内部或外部导航接收装置（若设有）获得该信息。如果未安装这种接收装置，则船舶在航行中的位置以及船位确定的时间应按不超过 4 h 的间隔期手动更新，以便随时可由该设备发送。

① 参见 STCW 规则第Ⅳ章第 B-Ⅳ/2 节。

Chapter V Safety of navigation

第Ⅴ章　航行安全

Regulation 1
Application

1 Unless expressly provided otherwise, this chapter shall apply to all ships on all voyages, except:

.1 warships, naval auxiliaries and other ships owned or operated by a Contracting Government and used only on government non-commercial service; and

.2 ships solely navigating the Great Lakes of North America and their connecting and tributary waters as far east as the lower exit of the St Lambert Lock at Montreal in the Province of Quebec, Canada.

However, warships, naval auxiliaries or other ships owned or operated by a Contracting Government and used only on Government non-commercial service are encouraged to act in a manner consistent, so far as reasonable and practicable, with this chapter.

2 The Administration may decide to what extent this chapter shall apply to ships operating solely in waters landward of the baselines which are established in accordance with international law.

3 A rigidly connected composite unit of a pushing vessel and associated pushed vessel, when designed as a dedicated and integrated tug and barge combination, shall be regarded as a single ship for the purpose of this chapter.

4 The Administration shall determine to what extent the provisions of regulations 15, 16, 17, 18, 19, 20, 21, 22, 23, 24, 25, 26, 27 and 28 do not apply to the following categories of ships:

.1 ships below 150 gross tonnage engaged on any voyage;

.2 ships below 500 gross tonnage not engaged on international voyages; and

.3 fishing vessels.

Regulation 2
Definitions

For the purpose of this chapter:

1 *Constructed* in respect of a ship means a stage of construction where:

.1 the keel is laid; or

.2 construction identifiable with a specific ship begins; or

.3 assembly of the ship has commenced comprising at least 50 tonnes or 1% of the estimated mass of all structural material, whichever is less.

第1条
适用范围

1　除另有明文规定外,本章应适用于在所有航线上航行的所有船舶,但下列情况除外:

.1　军舰、海军辅助船和由缔约国政府拥有或经营的仅用于政府非商业性服务的其他船舶;和

.2　专门航行于北美洲五大湖及其东至加拿大魁北克省蒙特利尔的圣拉姆伯特船闸下游出口处为止的相连水域和支流的船舶。

但是,仍鼓励军舰、海军辅助船或由缔约国政府拥有或经营的仅用于政府非商业性服务的其他船舶在合理和可行的范围内遵守本章的要求。

2　主管机关可决定本章对仅在按国际法规定的基线以内(向陆地一侧)水域营运的船舶的适用范围。

3　就本章而言,顶推船舶和被顶推船舶的刚性连接组合单元,当其设计成专用的整体拖船和驳船组合体时,应视为单一船舶。

4　主管机关应确定第15、16、17、18、19、20、21、22、23、24、25、26、27和28条对下列各类船舶的不适用范围:

.1　从事任何航行的150总吨以下的船舶;

.2　从事非国际航行的500总吨以下的船舶;和

.3　渔船。

第2条
定义

就本章而言:

1　**船舶的建造**系指下述建造阶段:

.1　安放龙骨;或

.2　可辨认出某一具体船舶建造开始;或

.3　该船业已开始的装配量至少为50 t,或为全部结构材料估算重量的1%,取较小者。

2 *Nautical chart or nautical publication* is a special-purpose map or book, or a specially compiled database from which such a map or book is derived, that is issued officially by or on the authority of a Government, authorized Hydrographic Office or other relevant government institution and is designed to meet the requirements of marine navigation.①

3 *All ships* means any ship, vessel or craft irrespective of type and purpose.

4 *Length* of a ship means its length overall.

5 *Search and rescue service*. The performance of distress monitoring, communication, co-ordination and search and rescue functions, including provision of medical advice, initial medical assistance, or medical evacuation, through the use of public and private resources including cooperating aircraft, ships, vessels and other craft and installations.

6 *High-speed craft* means a craft as defined in regulation X/1.3.

7 *Mobile offshore drilling unit* means a mobile offshore drilling unit as defined in regulation XI-2/1.1.5.

Regulation 3
Exemptions and equivalents

1 The Administration may grant general exemptions from the requirements of regulations 15, 17, 18, 19 (except 19.2.1.7), 20, 22, 24, 25, 26, 27 and 28 to ships without mechanical means of propulsion.

2 The Administration may grant to individual ships exemptions or equivalents of a partial or conditional nature, when any such ship is engaged on a voyage where the maximum distance of the ship from the shore, the length and nature of the voyage, the absence of general navigational hazards, and other conditions affecting safety are such as to render the full application of this chapter unreasonable or unnecessary, provided that the Administration has taken into account the effect such exemptions and equivalents may have upon the safety of all other ships.

3 Each Administration shall submit to the Organization, as soon as possible after 1 January in each year, a report summarizing all new exemptions and equivalents granted under paragraph 2 of this regulation during the previous calendar year and giving the reasons for granting such exemptions and equivalents. The Organization shall circulate such particulars to other Contracting Governments for information.

Regulation 4
Navigational warnings

Each Contracting Government shall take all steps necessary to ensure that, when intelligence of any dangers is received from whatever reliable source, it shall be promptly brought to the knowledge of those concerned and communicated to other interested Governments.②

① Refer to appropriate resolutions and recommendations of the International Hydrographic Organization concerning the authority and responsibilities of coastal States in the provision of charting in accordance with regulation 9.

② Refer to Guidance on the IMO/IHO World-Wide Navigational Warning Service (resolution A.706(17), as amended).

2 **海图或航海出版物**系指专用的图或书,或支持这种图或书的经特殊编辑的数据库,由政府主管机关,经授权的水文局或其他相关的政府机构正式颁布,用于满足航海要求。①

3 **所有船舶**系指所有船或艇,而不论其类型和用途。

4 **船舶长度**系指其总长度。

5 **搜救服务**。通过利用公共和私人资源,包括协作的飞机、船舶、船只和其他艇筏及设备,执行遇险监控、通信、协调和搜救职能,包括提供医疗建议、初步医疗援助或医疗撤离。

6 **高速船**系指第Ⅹ/1.3 条所定义的船艇。

7 **海上移动式钻井平台**系指第Ⅺ-2/1.1.5 条定义的海上移动式钻井平台。

第 3 条
免除和等效

1 主管机关对无机械推进装置的船舶可准予免除第 15、17、18、19(除 19.2.1.7 外)、20、22、24、25、26、27 和 28 条的要求。

2 当个别船舶所从事的航行,其距岸的最大距离、航程的长短和性质、大体上无航行危险以及影响安全的其他情况使得完全实施本章的规定不合理或不必要时,主管机关可对任何这种船舶准予部分或有条件的免除或等效,但主管机关必须事先考虑到这种免除和等效对所有其他船舶的安全可能产生的影响。

3 各主管机关应在每年的 1 月 1 日后尽快向本组织提交一份报告,汇总上一日历年度内按本条第 2 款准予的所有新的免除和等效并阐明准予免除和等效的理由。本组织应将这些内容分发给其他缔约国政府。

第 4 条
航行警报

各缔约国政府应采取所有必要的措施,确保其从任何可靠的来源获悉危险的情报时,迅速通知有关各方并发送至其他相关的国家政府。②

① 参见国际水道测量组织关于沿岸国根据第 9 条提供海图的权利和责任的相关决议和建议。
② 参见《IMO/IHO 全球航行警报服务指南》(第 A.706(17)号决议,经修订的)。

Regulation 5
Meteorological services and warnings

1 Contracting Governments undertake to encourage the collection of meteorological data by ships at sea and to arrange for their examination, dissemination and exchange in the manner most suitable for the purpose of aiding navigation.① Administrations shall encourage the use of meteorological instruments of a high degree of accuracy and shall facilitate the checking of such instruments upon request. Arrangements may be made by appropriate national meteorological services for this checking to be undertaken, free of charge to the ship.

2 In particular, Contracting Governments undertake to carry out, in cooperation, the following meteorological arrangements:

.1 To warn ships of gales, storms and tropical cyclones by the issue of information in text and, as far as practicable, graphic form, using the appropriate shore-based facilities for terrestrial and space radiocommunications services.

.2 To issue, at least twice daily, by terrestrial and space radiocommunication services,② as appropriate, weather information suitable for shipping containing data, analyses, warnings and forecasts of weather, waves and ice. Such information shall be transmitted in text and, as far as practicable, graphic form, including meteorological analysis and prognosis charts transmitted by facsimile or in digital form for reconstitution on board the ship's data processing system.

.3 To prepare and issue such publications as may be necessary for the efficient conduct of meteorological work at sea and to arrange, if practicable, for the publication and making available of daily weather charts for the information of departing ships.

.4 To arrange for a selection of ships to be equipped with tested marine meteorological instruments (such as a barometer, a barograph, a psychrometer and suitable apparatus for measuring sea temperature) for use in this service, and to take, record and transmit meteorological observations at the main standard times for surface synoptic observations (i.e. at least four times daily, whenever circumstances permit) and to encourage other ships to take, record and transmit observations in a modified form, particularly when in areas where shipping is sparse.

.5 To encourage companies to involve as many of their ships as practicable in the making and recording of weather observations; these observations to be transmitted using the ship's terrestrial or space radiocommunications facilities for the benefit of the various national meteorological services.

.6 The transmission of these weather observations is free of charge to the ships concerned.

---

① Refer to *Recommendation on weather routeing* (resolution A.528(13)).

② Refer to regulations IV/7.1.4 and IV/7.1.5.

第5条
气象服务和警报

1　各缔约国政府承担义务,鼓励海上船舶收集气象资料,并用最适宜于助航目的的方式安排这些资料的审查、传送和交换①。主管机关应鼓励使用高精度的气象仪器,并应于接到校核此种仪器的请求时给予便利。国家相应的气象服务机构可做出安排,免费向船舶提供这种校核。

2　特别是,各缔约国政府承担义务在执行下列气象安排方面进行合作:

.1　使用地面和空间无线电通信服务机构的岸基设备以文字,并尽可能以图像形式发出信息,警告船舶注意强风、风暴和热带气旋。

.2　每日至少2次通过相应的地面和空间无线电通信服务发出适用于航运的气象信息②,其中包括天气、波浪和冰的数据、分析、警报和预报。这些信息应以文字,并尽可能以图像形式发送,其中包括通过传真或以数字形式发送的气象分析和预测图像,供船上数据处理系统重新编排。

.3　编制并发行供海上顺利开展气象工作可能需要的出版物(如可行),并安排发布及提供每日天气图供出航船舶参考。

.4　安排选定的船舶配备经过校验的船用气象仪器(例如气压计、气压记录仪、湿度计及适当的测量海水温度的仪器),用于气象服务,并使其在基本天气观测时间进行气象观测且记录和发送观测结果,用于海面天气观测(如环境允许,每日至少4次),并鼓励其他船舶用变通方式进行观测且记录和发送观测结果,特别是在航船稀少的区域。

.5　鼓励船公司尽可能让更多船舶参与天气观测和记录工作中;观测结果使用船舶地面或空间无线电通信设备发送,以使各国气象服务机构受益。

.6　这些天气观测结果免费向有关船舶发送。

---

①　参见《关于气象航线划定的建议》(第A.528(13)号决议)。

②　参见第Ⅳ/7.1.4条和第Ⅳ/7.1.5条。

.7 When in the vicinity of a tropical cyclone, or of a suspected tropical cyclone, ships should be encouraged to take and transmit their observations at more frequent intervals whenever practicable, bearing in mind navigational preoccupations of ships' officers during storm conditions.

.8 To arrange for the reception and transmission of weather messages from and to ships, using the appropriate shore-based facilities for terrestrial and space radiocommunications services.

.9 To encourage masters to inform ships in the vicinity and also shore stations whenever they experience a wind speed of 50 knots or more (force 10 on the Beaufort scale).

.10 To endeavour to obtain a uniform procedure in regard to the international meteorological services already specified, and as far as practicable, to conform to the technical regulations and recommendations made by the World Meteorological Organization, to which Contracting Governments may refer, for study and advice, any meteorological question which may arise in carrying out the present Convention.

3 The information provided for in this regulation shall be furnished in a form for transmission and be transmitted in the order of priority prescribed by the Radio Regulations. During transmission "to all stations" of meteorological information, forecasts and warnings, all ship stations must conform to the provisions of the Radio Regulations.

4 Forecasts, warnings, synoptic and other meteorological data intended for ships shall be issued and disseminated by the national meteorological service in the best position to serve various coastal and high seas areas, in accordance with mutual arrangements made by Contracting Governments, in particular as defined by the World Meteorological Organization's system for the preparation and dissemination of meteorological forecasts and warnings for the high seas under the Global Maritime Distress and Safety System (GMDSS).

Regulation 6
Ice Patrol Service

1 The Ice Patrol contributes to safety of life at sea, safety and efficiency of navigation and protection of the marine environment in the North Atlantic. Ships transiting the region of icebergs guarded by the Ice Patrol during the ice season are required to make use of the services provided by the Ice Patrol.

2 The Contracting Governments undertake to continue an ice patrol and a service for study and observation of ice conditions in the North Atlantic. During the whole of the ice season, i.e., for the period from 15 February through 1 July of each year, the south-eastern, southern and south-western limits of the region of icebergs in the vicinity of the Grand Banks of Newfoundland shall be guarded for the purpose of informing passing ships of the extent of this dangerous region; for the study of ice conditions in general; and for the purpose of affording assistance to ships and crews requiring aid within the limits of operation of the patrol ships and aircraft. During the rest of the year the study and observation of ice conditions shall be maintained as advisable.

.7　当船舶在热带气旋或疑似热带气旋附近时，应鼓励其尽可能增加观测和发送观测结果的次数，但应使船上驾驶员牢记在风暴条件下航行的注意事项。

.8　使用地面和空间无线电通信服务机构的相应岸基设备，安排接收来自船舶和向船舶发送天气信息。

.9　鼓励船长在遇到风速 50 kn 或以上（蒲福风级 10 级）时，通知附近船舶及海岸电台。

.10　努力使上述国际气象服务获得统一程序，并尽可能符合世界气象组织提出的技术规则和建议。各缔约国政府可以将执行本公约过程中可能产生的任何气象问题提交世界气象组织研究和征求意见。

3　应以发送格式提交本条所规定的信息，并按《无线电规则》规定的优先顺序发送，在“向所有电台”发送气象信息、预报和警报时，所有船舶电台都必须遵守《无线电规则》的规定。

4　供船舶使用的预报、警报、天气形势和其他气象数据，应按缔约国政府间的共同协定，特别是按世界气象组织根据全球海上遇险和安全系统（GMDSS）要求建立的在公海编制和发布气象预报和警报系统的要求，由具备最佳位置为多海区和公海区域服务的国家气象服务机构进行发布和传播。

第 6 条
冰区巡逻服务

1　冰区巡逻有助于在北大西洋内的海上人命安全、航行安全和航行效率以及海洋环境保护。在冰季期间，穿越由冰区巡逻警戒的冰山区的船舶，应要求使用冰区巡逻所提供的服务。

2　各缔约国政府承担义务，继续担任北大西洋冰区巡逻和冰情的研究与观测服务。在整个冰季期间，即每年的 2 月 15 日至 7 月 1 日，在纽芬兰大浅滩附近冰山区的东南、南及西南界限应予警戒，以便将该危险区的范围通知过往船舶，观测冰情以及在巡逻船舶和飞机操作限度内为船舶和船员提供所需的帮助。在一年其余时间内也应适当保持对冰情的研究与观测。

3 Ships and aircraft used for the Ice Patrol Service and the study and observation of ice conditions may be assigned other duties provided that such other duties do not interfere with the primary purpose or increase the cost of this service.

4 The Government of the United States of America agrees to continue the overall management of the Ice Patrol Service and the study and observation of ice conditions, including the dissemination of information therefrom.

5 The terms and conditions governing the management, operation and financing of the Ice Patrol are set forth in the Rules for the management, operation and financing of the North Atlantic Ice Patrol appended to this chapter, which shall form an integral part of this chapter.

6 If, at any time, the United States and/or Canadian Governments should desire to discontinue providing these services, it may do so and the Contracting Governments shall settle the question of continuing these services in accordance with their mutual interests. The United States and/or Canadian Governments shall provide 18 months' written notice to all Contracting Governments whose ships entitled to fly their flag and whose ships are registered in territories to which those Contracting Governments have extended this regulation benefit from these services before discontinuing providing these services.

Regulation 7
Search and rescue services

1 Each Contracting Government undertakes to ensure that necessary arrangements are made for distress communication and coordination in their area of responsibility and for the rescue of persons in distress at sea around its coasts. These arrangements shall include the establishment, operation and maintenance of such search and rescue facilities as are deemed practicable and necessary, having regard to the density of the seagoing traffic and the navigational dangers, and shall, so far as possible, provide adequate means of locating and rescuing such persons.①

2 Each Contracting Government undertakes to make available information to the Organization concerning its existing search and rescue facilities and the plans for changes therein, if any.

3 Passenger ships to which chapter I applies shall have on board a plan for cooperation with appropriate search and rescue services in the event of an emergency. The plan shall be developed in cooperation between the ship, the company, as defined in regulation IX/1, and the search and rescue services. The plan shall include provisions for periodic exercises to be undertaken to test its effectiveness. The plan shall be developed based on the guidelines developed by the Organization.

---

① Refer to the International Convention on Maritime Research and Rescue (SAR), 1979, and to the following resolutions adopted by the Organization: *Homing capability of search and rescue (SAR) aircraft* (resolution A.225(VII)), *Use of radar transponders for search and rescue purposes* (resolution A.530(13)), *Search and rescue homing capability* (resolution A.616(15)) and *International Aeronautical and Maritime Search and Rescue (IAMSAR) Manual* (resolution A.894(21), as amended).

3　用于冰区巡逻服务及研究与观测冰情的船舶和飞机，也可承担其他任务，但这些其他任务不得妨碍本服务工作的原有目的或增加其费用。

4　美利坚合众国政府同意继续全面管理冰区巡逻服务及冰情的研究与观测，包括传播由此得到的信息。

5　在本章的附录《北大西洋冰区巡逻的管理、运作和费用规则》中列明了冰区巡逻的管理、运作和费用的各项条件，该附录是本章一个组成部分。

6　无论何时，美利坚合众国政府和/或加拿大政府如欲中止提供这些服务，即可以这样做，并且各缔约国政府应根据其共同利益解决继续这些服务的问题。美利坚合众国和/或加拿大政府对于在中止提供这些服务之前受益于这些服务且获准悬挂缔约国国旗的船舶和在缔约国政府已沿用本条要求的领土内注册的船舶，应提前 18 个月向所有有关缔约国政府发出中止服务的书面通知。

第 7 条
搜寻与救助服务

1　各缔约国政府承诺，确保为其责任区内的遇险通信和相互协调并为营救其沿岸附近的海上遇险者做出必要的安排。这些安排，应包括实际可行和必要的搜救设施的建立、运转和维护，虑及海上交通的密度和航行障碍物的密度，并应尽可能提供足够的定位和营救遇险人员的设备。①

2　各缔约国政府承诺，向本组织提供其现有搜救设施的资料以及对其中内容所做的更改方案（如有）。

3　适用第Ⅰ章的客船，应备有在紧急情况下与相应的搜寻和救助机构合作的计划。该计划应由船舶、第Ⅸ/1 条所定义的公司以及搜救机构共同制定。该计划应包括要进行定期演习以证明该计划有效性的规定。该计划应根据本组织制定的导则编制。

---

①　参见《1979 年国际海上搜寻和救助公约（SAR）》，以及本组织通过的下列决议：《搜救航空器的归航能力》（第 A.225（Ⅶ）号决议）、《雷达应答器在搜寻和救助中的使用》（第 A.530（13）号决议）、《搜寻和救助归航能力》（第 A.616（15）号决议）和《国际航空和海上搜寻救助（IAMSAR）手册》（第 A.894（21）号决议）。

Regulation 8
Life-saving signals

Contracting Governments undertake to arrange that life-saving signals are used by search and rescue facilities engaged in search and rescue operations when communicating with ships or persons in distress.

Regulation 9
Hydrographic services

1 Contracting Governments undertake to arrange for the collection and compilation of hydrographic data and the publication, dissemination and keeping up to date of all nautical information necessary for safe navigation.

2 In particular, Contracting Governments undertake to cooperate in carrying out, as far as possible, the following nautical and hydrographic services, in the manner most suitable for the purpose of aiding navigation:

.1 to ensure that hydrographic surveying is carried out, as far as possible, adequate to the requirements of safe navigation;

.2 to prepare and issue nautical charts, sailing directions, lists of lights, tide tables and other nautical publications, where applicable, satisfying the needs of safe navigation;

.3 to promulgate notices to mariners in order that nautical charts and publications are kept, as far as possible, up to date; and

.4 to provide data management arrangements to support these services.

3 Contracting Governments undertake to ensure the greatest possible uniformity in charts and nautical publications and to take into account, whenever possible, relevant international resolutions and recommendations.①

4 Contracting Governments undertake to coordinate their activities to the greatest possible degree in order to ensure that hydrographic and nautical information is made available on a world-wide scale as timely, reliably, and unambiguously as possible.

Regulation 10
Ships' routeing

1 Ships' routeing systems contribute to safety of life at sea, safety and efficiency of navigation and/or protection of the marine environment. Ships' routeing systems are recommended for use by, and may be made mandatory for, all ships, certain categories of ships or ships carrying certain cargoes, when adopted and implemented in accordance with the guidelines and criteria developed by the Organization.

① Refer to the appropriate resolutions and recommendations adopted by the International Hydrographic Organization.

第8条
救生信号

各缔约国政府承诺，使从事搜救工作的搜救设施在与遇险船舶或遇险人员通信时使用救生信号。

第9条
水文服务

1 各缔约国政府承诺，安排水文资料的收集和编制，并且出版、传播以及不断更新安全航行所需的所有航海信息。

2 特别是，各缔约国政府承诺尽可能进行合作，以最适合于助航目的的方式进行下列助航和水文服务：

.1 确保尽可能按安全航行的要求进行水文勘测；

.2 编制和发布海图、航路指南、灯标表、潮汐表和其他航海出版物（如适用）以满足安全航行的需要；

.3 向海员颁布通告使其海图和航海出版物尽可能及时更新；和

.4 提供数据管理安排以支持这些服务。

3 各缔约国政府承诺，确保尽最大可能统一海图和航海出版物，并且考虑到有关的国际决议和建议。①

4 各缔约国政府承诺尽最大可能协调其活动，确保在全球范围内尽可能及时、可靠并明确地提供水文和航海信息。

第10条
船舶定线制

1 船舶定线制有利于海上人命安全、航行安全及效率和/或海洋环境保护。建议使用船舶定线制，也可强制用于所有船舶、某些类型船舶或载运某些货物的船舶。定线制的通过和实施应根据本组织制定的导则和标准。

---

① 参见国际水道测量组织通过的有关决议和建议。

2 The Organization is recognized as the only international body for developing guidelines, criteria and regulations on an international level for ships' routeing systems. Contracting Governments shall refer proposals for the adoption of ships' routeing systems to the Organization. The Organization will collate and disseminate to Contracting Governments all relevant information with regard to any adopted ships' routeing systems.

3 The initiation of action for establishing a ships' routeing system is the responsibility of the Government or Governments concerned. In developing such systems for adoption by the Organization, the guidelines and criteria developed by the Organization shall be taken into account.

4 Ships' routeing systems should be submitted to the Organization for adoption. However, a Government or Governments implementing ships' routeing systems not intended to be submitted to the Organization for adoption or which have not been adopted by the Organization are encouraged to take into account, wherever possible, the guidelines and criteria developed by the Organization.①

5 Where two or more Governments have a common interest in a particular area, they should formulate joint proposals for the delineation and use of a routeing system therein on the basis of an agreement between them. Upon receipt of such proposal and before proceeding with consideration of it for adoption, the Organization shall ensure that details of the proposal are disseminated to the Governments which have a common interest in the area, including countries in the vicinity of the proposed ships' routeing system.

6 Contracting Governments shall adhere to the measures adopted by the Organization concerning ships' routeing. They shall promulgate all information necessary for the safe and effective use of adopted ships' routeing systems. A Government or Governments concerned may monitor traffic in those systems. Contracting Governments shall do everything in their power to secure the appropriate use of ships' routeing systems adopted by the Organization.

7 A ship shall use a mandatory ships' routeing system adopted by the Organization as required for its category or cargo carried and in accordance with the relevant provisions in force unless there are compelling reasons not to use a particular ships' routeing system. Any such reason shall be recorded in the ships' log.

8 Mandatory ships' routeing systems shall be reviewed by the Contracting Government or Governments concerned in accordance with the guidelines and criteria developed by the Organization.

9 All adopted ships' routeing systems and actions taken to enforce compliance with those systems shall be consistent with international law, including the relevant provisions of the 1982 United Nations Convention on the Law of the Sea.

10 Nothing in this regulation nor its associated guidelines and criteria shall prejudice the rights and duties of Governments under international law or the legal regimes of straits used for international navigation and archipelagic sea lanes.

① Refer to General provisions on ships' routeing (resolution A.572(14), as amended).

2　本组织是公认的为船舶定线制制定国际性导则、标准和规则的唯一国际机构。各缔约国政府应将通过船舶定线制的提案提交本组织。本组织将整理和向缔约国政府发布所有已通过的船舶定线制的全部相关信息。

3　发起建立船舶定线制是各有关国家政府的责任。在制定需本组织通过的定线制时，应考虑到本组织制定的导则及标准。

4　船舶定线制应提交本组织通过。但是，对于一国或几国政府实施的船舶定线制如不准备提交本组织通过或未经本组织通过，则鼓励其尽可能考虑本组织制定的导则及标准。①

5　如果两国或两国以上政府在某一特定区域具有共同利益，应在他们之间达成协议的基础上制定联合提案明确说明他们对该区域船舶定线制的划界和使用。收到此提案并开始考虑其是否通过之前，本组织应确保把该提案的详细内容分发给在此地区具有共同利益的政府，包括在此船舶定线制附近的国家。

6　缔约国政府应遵循本组织通过的关于船舶定线制的措施。他们应公布安全有效地使用已通过的船舶定线制所必需的资料。有关的一国或多国政府可监督定线制的运行。各缔约国政府应在其权力范围内全力确保本组织通过的船舶定线制的正常使用。

7　船舶应按其船型或载运货物的要求，使用本组织通过的强制性船舶定线制，并遵守现行的有关规定，除非有令人信服的理由。所有这些理由应记录于航海日志内。

8　强制性的船舶定线制应由各有关缔约国政府按本组织制定的导则和标准予以审核。

9　所有已通过的船舶定线制和为实施定线制所采取的行动应符合国际法，包括《1982 年联合国海洋法公约》的有关规定。

10　本条及其相关导则和标准的任何内容均不得损害各国政府根据国际法或国际航行海峡及群岛海道的法律制度所具有的权利和义务。

① 参见《船舶定线制的一般规定》（第 A.572（14）号决议，经修订的）。

Regulation 11
Ship reporting systems[①]

1 Ship reporting systems contribute to safety of life at sea, safety and efficiency of navigation and/or protection of the marine environment. A ship reporting system, when adopted and implemented in accordance with the guidelines and criteria developed by the Organization[②] pursuant to this regulation, shall be used by all ships or certain categories of ships or ships carrying certain cargoes in accordance with the provisions of each system so adopted.

2 The Organization is recognized as the only international body for developing guidelines, criteria and regulations on an international level for ship reporting systems. Contracting Governments shall refer proposals for the adoption of ship reporting systems to the Organization. The Organization will collate and disseminate to Contracting Governments all relevant information with regard to any adopted ship reporting system.

3 The initiation of action for establishing a ship reporting system is the responsibility of the Government or Governments concerned. In developing such systems, provision of the guidelines and criteria developed by the Organization[②] shall be taken into account.

4 Ship reporting systems not submitted to the Organization for adoption do not necessarily need to comply with this regulation. However, Governments implementing such systems are encouraged to follow, wherever possible, the guidelines and criteria developed by the Organization. Contracting Governments may submit such systems to the Organization for recognition.

5 Where two or more Governments have a common interest in a particular area, they should formulate proposals for a coordinated ship reporting system on the basis of agreement between them. Before proceeding with a proposal for adoption of a ship reporting system, the Organization shall disseminate details of the proposal to those Governments which have a common interest in the area covered by the proposed system. Where a coordinated ship reporting system is adopted and established, it shall have uniform procedures and operations.

6 After adoption of a ship reporting system in accordance with this regulation, the Government or Governments concerned shall take all measures necessary for the promulgation of any information needed for the efficient and effective use of the system. Any adopted ship reporting system shall have the capability of interaction and the ability to assist ships with information when necessary. Such systems shall be operated in accordance with the guidelines and criteria developed by the Organization[②] pursuant to this regulation.

7 The master of a ship shall comply with the requirements of adopted ship reporting systems and report to the appropriate authority all information required in accordance with the provisions of each such system.

---

① This regulation does not address ship reporting systems established by Governments for search and rescue purposes, which are covered by chapter 5 of the 1979 SAR Convention, as amended.

② Refer to revised *Guidelines and criteria for ship reporting systems* (MSC.433(98)) and *General principles for ship reporting requirements, including guidelines for reporting incidents involving dangerous goods, harmful substances and/or marine pollutants* (resolution A.851(20), as amended).

第 11 条
船舶报告制[①]

1 船舶报告制有利于海上人命安全、航行安全及效率和/或海洋环境保护。船舶报告制在按本组织根据本条的要求制定的导则和标准[②]予以通过并实施后,应按每个所通过的系统的规定适用于所有船舶或某些类型船舶或载运某些货物的船舶。

2 本组织是公认的为船舶报告制制定国际性导则、标准和规则的唯一国际机构。各缔约国政府应将采用船舶报告制的提案送交本组织。本组织将整理和向缔约国政府发布所有已通过的船舶报告制的全部相关信息。

3 发起建立船舶报告制是各有关国家政府的责任。在建立报告制时,应考虑到本组织制定的导则和标准[②]中的规定。

4 未提交本组织通过的船舶报告制不需遵守本条要求。但是,鼓励缔约国在实施报告制时尽可能遵循本组织制定的导则和标准。各缔约国政府可向本组织提交报告制由本组织认可。

5 如果两国或两国以上政府在某一特定区域具有共同利益,应在他们之间达成协议的基础上制定一个经协调的船舶报告制的提案。在开始考虑通过船舶报告制的提案之前,本组织应向在该报告制覆盖的区域内具有共同利益的缔约国政府通报该提案的详细内容。如果通过并建立了一个经协调的船舶报告系统,则该报告制应具有一致的程序和操作。

6 在按本条的要求通过船舶报告制后,各有关国家政府应采取所有必要的措施公布有效使用该系统所需的所有信息。任何已通过的船舶报告制应具有交互功能以及在必要时为船舶提供信息的能力。这种报告制应按本组织根据本条的要求制定的导则和标准[②]进行操作。

7 船长应遵守已通过的各个船舶报告制的要求,并按其中每一系统的规定向相应主管机关报告所要求的所有资料。

---

① 本条不涉及各国政府为搜救目的建立的船舶报告系统,适用经修订的 SAR 1979 公约第五章。

② 参见《船舶报告系统导则和标准》(第 MSC.433(98)号决议)、《船舶报告要求的一般原则,包括涉及危险货物、有害物质和/或海洋污染物的事故报告导则》(第 A.851(20)号决议,经修订的)。

8 All adopted ship reporting systems and actions taken to enforce compliance with those systems shall be consistent with international law, including the relevant provisions of the United Nations Convention on the Law of the Sea.

9 Nothing in this regulation or its associated guidelines and criteria shall prejudice the rights and duties of Governments under international law or the legal regimes of straits used for international navigation and archipelagic sea lanes.

10 The participation of ships in accordance with the provisions of adopted ship reporting systems shall be free of charge to the ships concerned.

11 The Organization shall ensure that adopted ship reporting systems are reviewed under the guidelines and criteria developed by the Organization.

Regulation 12
Vessel traffic services

1 Vessel traffic services (VTS) contribute to safety of life at sea, safety and efficiency of navigation and protection of the marine environment, adjacent shore areas, work sites and offshore installations from possible adverse effects of maritime traffic.

2 Contracting Governments undertake to arrange for the establishment of VTS where, in their opinion, the volume of traffic or the degree of risk justifies such services.

3 Contracting Governments planning and implementing VTS shall, wherever possible, follow the guidelines developed by the Organization.① The use of VTS may only be made mandatory in sea areas within the territorial seas of a coastal State.

4 Contracting Governments shall endeavour to secure the participation in, and compliance with, the provisions of vessel traffic services by ships entitled to fly their flag.

5 Nothing in this regulation or the guidelines adopted by the Organization shall prejudice the rights and duties of Governments under international law or the legal regimes of straits used for international navigation and archipelagic sea lanes.

Regulation 13
Establishment and operation of aids to navigation

1 Each Contracting Government undertakes to provide, as it deems practical and necessary, either individually or in cooperation with other Contracting Governments, such aids to navigation as the volume of traffic justifies and the degree of risk requires.

2 In order to obtain the greatest possible uniformity in aids to navigation, Contracting Governments undertake to take into account the international recommendations and guidelines② when establishing such aids.

---

① Refer to *Guidelines on vessel traffic services* (resolution A.857(20)).

② Refer to the appropriate recommendations and guidelines of IALA and to Maritime buoyage system (SN.1/Circ.297).

8　所有已通过的船舶报告制和为实施报告制所采取的行动应符合国际法,包括《联合国海洋法公约》的有关规定。

9　本条及其相关导则和标准的任何内容均不得损害各国政府根据国际法或国际航行海峡及群岛海道的法律制度所具有的权利和义务。

10　船舶按已通过的船舶报告制的规定进入,应对有关船舶免收费用。

11　本组织应确保根据本组织制定的导则和标准,对已通过的船舶报告制进行审核。

第12条
船舶交通服务

1　船舶交通服务(VTS)有利于海上人命安全、航行安全及效率和/或保护海洋环境、近岸区域、作业区和海上设施免受海洋运输可能带来的不利影响。

2　各缔约国政府承诺,在其认为因交通量和危险程度而需要船舶交通服务的情况下做出建立这种服务的安排。

3　规划和实施船舶交通服务的缔约国政府,应尽可能遵循本组织制定的指南[①]。船舶交通服务的使用,仅在沿海国领海所属的海域内才可作为强制性要求。

4　缔约国政府应确保悬挂其国旗的船舶参与船舶交通服务并遵守该服务的规定。

5　本条或本组织通过的指南的任何内容均不得损害各国政府根据国际法或国际航行海峡及群岛海道的法律制度所具有的权利和义务。

第13条
助航标志的设置和运行

1　各缔约国政府承诺,在其认为可行和必要时,根据交通量和危险程度的需要,单独或与其他缔约国政府合作提供助航标志。

2　为尽最大可能达到助航标志的一致性,各缔约国政府承诺在设置这些助航标志时,注意到国际上的建议和指南[②]。

① 参见《船舶交通服务指南》(第A.857(20)号决议)。
② 参见IALA相关导则和建议,以及《海上浮标系统》(SN/Circ.297)。

3 Contracting Governments undertake to arrange for information relating to aids to navigation to be made available to all concerned. Changes in the transmissions of position-fixing systems which could adversely affect the performance of receivers fitted in ships shall be avoided as far as possible and only be effected after timely and adequate notice has been promulgated.

Regulation 14
Ships' manning

1 Contracting Governments undertake, each for its national ships, to maintain, or, if it is necessary, to adopt, measures for the purpose of ensuring that, from the point of view of safety of life at sea, all ships shall be sufficiently and efficiently manned.①

2 For every ship to which chapter I applies, the Administration shall:

.1 establish appropriate minimum safe manning following a transparent procedure, taking into account the relevant guidance adopted by the Organization;① and

.2 issue an appropriate minimum safe manning document or equivalent as evidence of the minimum safe manning considered necessary to comply with the provisions of paragraph 1.

3 On all ships, to ensure effective crew performance in safety matters, a working language shall be established and recorded in the ship's logbook. The company, as defined in regulation IX/1, or the master, as appropriate, shall determine the appropriate working language. Each seafarer shall be required to understand and, where appropriate, give orders and instructions and to report back in that language. If the working language is not an official language of the State whose flag the ship is entitled to fly, all plans and lists required to be posted shall include a translation into the working language.

4 On ships to which chapter I applies, English shall be used on the bridge as the working language for bridge-to-bridge and bridge-to-shore safety communications as well as for communications on board between the pilot and bridge watchkeeping personnel,② unless those directly involved in the communication speak a common language other than English.

Regulation 15
Principles relating to bridge design, design and arrangement of navigational systems and equipment and bridge procedures

All decisions which are made for the purpose of applying the requirements of regulations 19, 22, 24, 25, 27 and 28 and which affect bridge design, the design and arrangement of navigational systems and equipment on the bridge and bridge procedures③ shall be taken with the aim of:

---

① Refer to *Principles of minimum safe manning* (resolution A.1047(27)).

② Refer to the *IMO Standard Marine Communication Phrases* (resolution A.918(22), as amended).

③ Refer to *Guidelines on ergonomic criteria for bridge equipment and layout* (MSC/Circ.982) and *Guidelines for bridge equipment and systems, their arrangement and integration* (BES) (SN.1/Circ.288) and, for INS, to revised *Recommendation on performance standards for an integrated navigational system* (resolution MSC.252(83), as amended).

3　各缔约国政府承诺，向所有有关方面提供与助航标志有关的信息。尽可能避免对船上接收设备的性能产生不利影响的定位系统信息传输的变化，仅在及时和广泛发布通告之后才可实行。

第14条
船舶配员

1　各缔约国政府承诺，各自对本国船舶保持或在必要时采取措施，以确保从海上人命安全的观点出发，所有船舶配备足够数量和适任的船员。①

2　对适用第Ⅰ章的每艘船舶，主管机关应：

.1　根据一个透明程序确定适当的最低安全配员，并考虑到本组织通过的相关指南；①和

.2　签发一份适当的最低安全配员证明或等效证明，作为符合本条第1款规定所需的最低安全配员的凭证。

3　在所有船舶上，为确保船员在安全事务上起到有效作用，应规定一种工作语言并将其记录在船舶航海日志上。第Ⅸ/1条所定义的公司或船长（合适者）应确定适当的工作语言。应要求每个船员能懂得这种语言，并在合适情况下使用这种语言下达指令和指示以及应答。如果该工作语言不是船旗国的官方语言，则所有需张贴的计划和表格内应有该工作语言的译文。

4　在适用第Ⅰ章的船舶上，应使用英语作为驾驶台的工作语言，用以进行驾驶台对驾驶台、驾驶台对岸的安全通信以及用于引航员和驾驶台值班人员之间在船上的交流②，除非直接参与通信的人员都讲英语以外的一种共同语言。

第15条
关于驾驶台设计、航行系统和设备的设计和布置以及驾驶台程序的原则

所有为应用本章第19、22、24、25、27和28条要求而做出并影响驾驶台设计、驾驶台航行系统和设备的设计和布置以及驾驶台程序③的决定，都应旨在：

---

① 参见《最低安全配员原则》（第A.1047(27)号决议）。

② 参见《IMO标准海上通信用语》（第A.918(22)号决议，经修订的）。

③ 参见《驾驶台设备和布置的人体工程学标准导则》（第MSC/Circ.982号通函）和《驾驶台设备和系统的安排和整合（BES）》（SN.1/Circ.288），对于INS，参见经修订的《组合导航系统性能标准建议》（第MSC.252(83)号决议，经修订的）。

.1 facilitating the tasks to be performed by the bridge team and the pilot in making full appraisal of the situation and in navigating the ship safely under all operational conditions;

.2 promoting effective and safe bridge resource management;

.3 enabling the bridge team and the pilot to have convenient and continuous access to essential information which is presented in a clear and unambiguous manner, using standardized symbols and coding systems for controls and displays;

.4 indicating the operational status of automated functions and integrated components, systems and/or sub-systems;

.5 allowing for expeditious, continuous and effective information processing and decision-making by the bridge team and the pilot;

.6 preventing or minimizing excessive or unnecessary work and any conditions or distractions on the bridge which may cause fatigue or interfere with the vigilance of the bridge team and the pilot; and

.7 minimizing the risk of human error and detecting such error, if it occurs, through monitoring and alarm systems, in time for the bridge team and the pilot to take appropriate action.

Regulation 16
Maintenance of equipment

1 The Administration shall be satisfied that adequate arrangements are in place to ensure that the performance of the equipment required by this chapter is maintained.

2 Except as provided in regulations I/7(b)(ii), I/8 and I/9, while all reasonable steps shall be taken to maintain the equipment required by this chapter in efficient working order, malfunctions of that equipment shall not be considered as making the ship unseaworthy or as a reason for delaying the ship in ports where repair facilities are not readily available, provided suitable arrangements are made by the master to take the inoperative equipment or unavailable information into account in planning and executing a safe voyage to a port where repairs can take place.

Regulation 17
Electromagnetic compatibility

1 Administrations shall ensure that all electrical and electronic equipment on the bridge or in the vicinity of the bridge, on ships constructed on or after 1 July 2002, is tested for electromagnetic compatibility, taking into account the recommendations developed by the Organization.①

① Refer to *General requirements for electromagnetic compatibility (EMC) for all electrical and electronic ship's equipment* (resolution A.813(19)).

.1 通过对情况进行全面评估和在所有操作条件下安全操纵船舶,帮助驾驶台团队和引航员执行任务;

.2 促进有效和安全的管理驾驶台资源;

.3 使驾驶台团队和引航员能够方便和连续地获取重要信息。这些重要信息以清晰和明确的方式表达,并使用用于控制和显示的标准化符号和编码系统;

.4 指示自动功能和集成部件、系统和/或分系统的操作状态;

.5 使驾驶台团队和引航员能迅速、连续和有效地处理信息和做出决策;

.6 防止或最大限度减少驾驶台内可能导致驾驶台团队和引航员疲劳或干扰其警惕性的过多或不必要的工作及任何情况或分散注意力的事物;和

.7 通过监视和报警系统最大限度降低人为失误的风险并在发生人为失误时可探测到,以使驾驶台团队和引航员及时采取相应行动。

第 16 条
设备的维护保养

1 应具有使主管机关满意的适当安排,以确保本章所要求设备的性能得到维护。

2 除第Ⅰ/7(b)(ii)、Ⅰ/8 和Ⅰ/9 条规定者外,在应采取一切合理的措施使本章所要求的设备保持有效的工作状态下,船长在考虑到设备故障或无法获得信息后做出适当安排仍能安全抵达修理港,则设备故障不应视为船舶不适航或将船舶滞留在无法修理设备的港口的理由。

第 17 条
电磁兼容性

1 各国主管机关应确保安装在 2002 年 7 月 1 日或以后建造的船舶上,对位于驾驶台或邻近驾驶台的所有电气和电子设备进行电磁兼容性试验,并考虑到本组织制定的建议案。[①]

① 参见《所有船舶电子电气设备电磁兼容性(EMC)的通用要求》(第 A.813(19)号决议)。

2 Electrical and electronic equipment shall be so installed that electromagnetic interference does not affect the proper function of navigational systems and equipment.

3 Portable electrical and electronic equipment shall not be operated on the bridge if it may affect the proper function of navigational systems and equipment.

Regulation 18

Approval, surveys and performance standards of navigational systems and equipment and voyage data recorder

1 Systems and equipment required to meet the requirements of regulations 19 and 20 shall be of a type approved by the Administration.

2 Systems and equipment, including associated back-up arrangements, where applicable, installed on or after 1 July 2002 to perform the functional requirements of regulations 19 and 20 shall conform to appropriate performance standards not inferior to those adopted by the Organization.①

---

① Refer to:
Recommendations on general requirements for shipborne radio equipment forming part of the global maritime distress and safety system (GMDSS) and for electronic navigational aids (resolution A.694(17));
Recommendation on performance standards for gyro-compasses (resolution A.424(XI));
Recommendation on performance standards for radar equipment (resolution MSC.64(67), annex 4);
Revised Recommendation on performance standards for radar equipment (resolution MSC.192(79));
Performance standards for automatic radar plotting aids (ARPAs) (resolution A.823(19));
Recommendation on performance standards for electronic chart display and information systems (ECDIS) (resolution A.817(19), as amended);
Recommendation on performance standards for shipborne Loran-C and Chayka receivers (resolution A.818(19));
Recommendation on performance standards for shipborne global positioning system (GPS) receiver equipment (resolution A.819(19), as amended);
Recommendation on performance standards for shipborne GLONASS receiver equipment (resolution MSC.53(66), as amended);
Recommendation on performance standards for shipborne DGPS and DGLONASS maritime radio beacon receiver equipment (resolution MSC.64(67), annex 2, as amended);
Recommendation on performance standards for shipborne combined GPS/GLONASS receiver equipment (resolution MSC.74(69), annex 1, as amended);
Performance standards for shipborne Galileo receiver equipment (resolution MSC. 233(82));
Performance standards for shipborne Beidou Satellite Navigation System (BDS) receiver equipment (resolution MSC. 379(93));
Performance standards for multi-system shipborne radionavigation receiver (resolution MSC. 401(95), as amended);
Performance standards for shipborne Indian Regional Navigation Satellite System (IRNSS) receiver equipment (resolution MSC. 449(99));
Recommendation on performance standards for heading control systems (resolution MSC.64(67), annex 3);
Recommendation on performance standards for track control systems (resolution MSC.74(69), annex 2);
Recommendation on performance standards for a universal shipborne automatic identification system (AIS) (resolution MSC.74(69), annex 3);
Recommendation on performance standards for echo-sounding equipment (resolution A.224(VII), as amended);
Recommendation on performance standards for devices to indicate speed and distance (resolution A.824(19), as amended);
Performance standards for rate-of-turn indicators (resolution A.526(13));
Recommendation on performance standards for radar reflectors (resolution A.384(X), as amended);
Recommendation on performance standards for daylight signaling lamps (resolution MSC.95(72));
Recommendation on performance standards for sound reception systems (resolution MSC.86(70), annex 1);
Recommendation on performance standards for shipborne voyage data recorders (VDRs) (resolution MSC.333(90));
Recommendation on performance standards for shipborne simplified voyage data recorders (S-VDRs) (resolution MSC.163(78), as amended);
Recommendation on performance standards for marine transmitting heading devices (THDs) (resolution MSC.116(73));
Performance standards for a bridge navigational watch alarm system (BNWAS) (resolution MSC.128(75)).

2　电气和电子设备的安装应使电磁干扰不会影响航行系统和设备的正常功能。

3　如果便携式电气和电子设备可能影响航行系统和设备的正常功能,则其不应在驾驶台进行操作。

第18条
航行系统和设备以及航行数据记录仪的认可、检验和性能标准

1　满足本章第19条和20条要求的系统和设备应经过主管机关的型式认可。

2　在2002年7月1日或以后安装,用于执行第19条和20条功能要求的系统和设备,包括相关的后备装置(如适用),其所达到的相应性能标准应不低于本组织通过的性能标准。①

① 参见:
《关于作为全球海上遇险和安全系统(GMDSS)组成部分的船载无线电设备和电子导航设备的通用要求的建议》(第A.694(17)号决议);
《关于陀螺经性能标准的建议》(第A.424(Ⅺ)号决议);
《关于雷达设备性能标准的建议》(第MSC.64(67)号决议,附件4);
《经修订的〈关于雷达设备性能标准的建议〉》(第MSC.192(79)号决议);
《自动雷达标绘仪(ARPAs)性能标准》(第A.823(19)号决议);
《关于电子海图显示与信息系统(ECDIS)性能标准的建议》(第A.817(19)号决议,经修订的);
《关于船载Loran-C和Chayka接收机性能标准的建议》(第A.818(19)号决议);
《关于船载全球定位系统(GPS)接收设备性能标准的建议》(第A.819(19)号决议,经修订的);
《关于船载GLONASS接收设备性能标准的建议》(第MSC.53(66)号决议,经修订的);
《关于船载DGPS和DGLONASS海上无线电信号接收设备性能标准的建议》(第MSC.64(67)号决议,附件2,经修订的);
《关于船载组合GPS/GLONASS接收设备性能标准的建议》(第MSC.74(69)号决议,附件1,经修订的);
《船载伽利略(Galileo)接收设备性能标准》(第MSC.233(82)号决议);
《船载北斗卫星导航系统(BDS)接收设备性能标准》(第MSC.379(93)号决议);
《多系统船载无线电导航接收机性能标准》(第MSC.401(95)号决议,经修订的);
《印度区域导航卫星系统(IRNSS)接收设备性能标准》(第MSC.449(99)号决议);
《关于航向控制系统性能标准的建议》(第MSC.64(67)号决议,附件3);
《关于航迹控制系统性能标准的建议》(第MSC.74(69)号决议,附件2);
《关于全球船载自动识别系统(AIS)性能标准的建议》(第MSC.74(69)号决议,附件3);
《关于回声测深设备性能标准的建议》(第A.224(Ⅶ)号决议,经修订的);
《关于航速和航程指示装置性能标准的建议》(第A.824(19)号决议,经修订的);
《船用航向变化率指示器性能标准》(第A.526(13)号决议);
《关于雷达反射器性能标准的建议》(第A.384(Ⅹ)号决议,经修订的);
《关于白昼信号灯性能标准的建议》(第MSC.95(72)号决议);
《关于声响接收系统性能标准的建议》(第MSC.86(70)号决议,附件1);
《关于船载航行数据记录仪(VDRs)性能标准的建议》(第MSC.333(90)号决议);
《关于船载简易型航行数据记录仪(S-VDRs)性能标准的建议》(第MSC.163(78)号决议,经修订的);
《关于首向发送设备(THDs)性能标准的建议》(第MSC.116(73)号决议);
《驾驶台航行值班报警系统(BNWAS)性能标准》(第MSC.128(75)号决议)。

3 When systems and equipment are replaced or added to on ships constructed before 1 July 2002, such systems and equipment shall, in so far as is reasonable and practicable, comply with the requirements of paragraph 2.

4 Systems and equipment installed prior to the adoption of performance standards by the Organization may subsequently be exempted from full compliance with such standards at the discretion of the Administration, having due regard to the recommended criteria adopted by the Organization. However, for an electronic chart display and information system (ECDIS) to be accepted as satisfying the chart carriage requirement of regulation 19.2.1.4, that system shall conform to the relevant performance standards not inferior to those adopted by the Organization in effect on the date of installation, or, for systems installed before 1 January 1999, not inferior to the performance standards adopted by the Organization on 23 November 1995.①

5 The Administration shall require that the manufacturers have a quality control system audited by a competent authority to ensure continuous compliance with the type approval conditions. Alternatively, the Administration may use final product verification procedures where the compliance with the type approval certificate is verified by a competent authority before the product is installed on board ships.

6 Before giving approval to systems or equipment embodying new features not covered by this chapter, the Administration shall ensure that such features support functions at least as effective as those required by this chapter.

7 When equipment, for which performance standards have been developed by the Organization, is carried on ships in addition to those items of equipment required by regulations 19 and 20, such equipment shall be subject to approval and shall, as far as practicable, comply with performance standards not inferior to those adopted by the Organization.

8 The voyage data recorder system, including all sensors, shall be subjected to an annual performance test. The test shall be conducted by an approved testing or servicing facility to verify the accuracy, duration and recoverability of the recorded data. In addition, tests and inspections shall be conducted to determine the serviceability of all protective enclosures and devices fitted to aid location. A copy of the certificate of compliance issued by the testing facility, stating the date of compliance and the applicable performance standards, shall be retained on board the ship.

---

① Refer to *Recommendation on performance standards for shipborne simplified voyage data recorders (S-VDRs)* (resolution MSC.163(78), as amended), *Revised performance standards for electronic chart display and information systems (ECDIS)* (resolution MSC. 232(82)), *Recommendation on performance standards for electronic chart display and information systems (ECDIS)* (resolution A.817(19), as amended), and *Revised performance standards and functional requirements for the long-range identification and tracking of ships* (resolution MSC.263(84), as amended).

3 在2002年7月1日以前建造的船舶上替换或加装系统和设备时，这些系统和设备应在合理和可行的范围内符合本条第2款的要求。

4 在本组织通过相关的性能标准之前安装的系统和设备，主管机关在充分考虑了本组织通过的建议标准后，可以对其免除完全符合该标准的要求。但是，用于满足第19.2.1.4条海图配备要求的电子海图显示与信息系统（ECDIS），系统所达到的相关性能标准应不低于本组织通过的且在其安装之日有效的性能标准，或者，对于在1999年1月1日以前安装的系统，应不低于本组织在1995年11月23日通过的性能标准。①

5 主管机关应要求制造商具有一个由主管机关审核的质量控制系统，以确保持续符合型式认可条件。作为替代，主管机关可以在该产品安装上船之前使用最终产品验证程序，由主管机关验证其是否符合型式认可证书。

6 在对具有本章未涉及的新特征的航行系统或设备认可之前，主管机关应确保这种特征支持的功能与本章的要求至少同样有效。

7 如果除第19条和20条要求的各项设备以外，船上还配有本组织已制定性能标准的设备，则这种设备应经过认可且所达到的性能标准应尽可能不低于本组织通过的性能标准。

8 航行数据记录仪系统，包括所有传感器，应进行年度性能试验。试验应由认可的试验或检修机构进行，以验证所记录数据的精度、持续时间和再现性。此外还应进行试验和检查，以确定所有保护容器和辅助定位装置的性能。船上应保留一份由试验机构颁发的载明符合日期和适用性能标准的符合证书的副本。

① 参见《关于船载简易型航行数据记录仪（S-VDRs）性能标准的建议》（第MSC.163(78)号决议，经修订的），《经修订的电子海图显示与信息系统（ECDIS）性能标准》（第MSC.232(82)号决议），《关于电子海图显示与信息系统（ECDIS）性能标准的建议》（第A.817(19)号决议，经修订的），以及《经修订的船舶远距离识别和跟踪系统性能标准和功能要求》（第MSC.263(84)号决议，经修订的）。

9 The automatic identification system (AIS) shall be subjected to an annual test. The test shall be conducted by an approved surveyor or an approved testing or servicing facility. The test shall verify the correct programming of the ship static information, correct data exchange with connected sensors as well as verifying the radio performance by radio frequency measurement and on-air test using, e.g., a Vessel Traffic Service (VTS). A copy of the test report shall be retained on board the ship.

Regulation 19

Carriage requirements for shipborne navigational systems and equipment

1 Application and requirements

Subject to the provisions of regulation 1.4:

1.1 Ships constructed on or after 1 July 2002 shall be fitted with navigational systems and equipment which will fulfil the requirements prescribed in paragraphs 2.1 to 2.9.

1.2 Ships constructed before 1 July 2002 shall:

.1 subject to the provisions of paragraphs 1.2.2, 1.2.3, and 1.2.4 unless they comply fully with this regulation, continue to be fitted with equipment which fulfils the requirements prescribed in regulations V/11, V/12 and V/20 of the International Convention for the Safety of Life at Sea, 1974 in force prior to 1 July 2002;

.2 be fitted with the equipment or systems required in paragraph 2.1.6 not later than the first survey① after 1 July 2002, at which time the radio direction-finding apparatus referred to in V/12(p) of the International Convention for the Safety of Life at Sea, 1974 in force prior to 1 July 2002 shall no longer be required;

.3 be fitted with the system required in paragraph 2.4 not later than the dates specified in paragraphs 2.4.2 and 2.4.3; and

.4 be fitted with the system required in paragraph 2.2.3, as follows:

.1 passenger ships irrespective of size, not later than the first survey② after 1 January 2016;

.2 cargo ships of 3,000 gross tonnage and upwards, not later than the first survey② after 1 January 2016;

.3 cargo ships of 500 gross tonnage and upwards but less than 3,000 gross tonnage, not later than the first survey② after 1 January 2017; and

---

① Refer to *Unified interpretation of the term "first survey" referred to in SOLAS regulations* (MSC.1/Circ.1290).

② Refer to appendix 6, Back-up requirements, of *Performance standards for electronic chart display and information systems (ECDIS)* (resolution A.817(19), as amended). An appropriate folio of paper nautical charts may be used as a back-up arrangement for ECDIS. Other back-up arrangements for ECDIS are acceptable.

9　船舶自动识别系统(AIS)须进行年度检测。检测须由经认可的验船师或经认可的检测或检修机构进行。检测须验证船舶静态信息的录入是否正常,与连接传感器的数据交换是否正确,并且通过无线电频率测量和使用船舶交通服务(VTS)等进行广播检测验证无线电性能。船上须保留一份检测报告的副本。

第19条
船载航行系统和设备的配备要求

1　适用范围和要求

在符合第1.4条规定的条件下:

1.1　在2002年7月1日或以后建造的船舶,应配备满足本条2.1至2.9款规定要求的航行系统和设备。

1.2　在2002年7月1日以前建造的船舶应:

.1　根据本条1.2.2、1.2.3和1.2.4的规定,除非这些船舶全部满足本条的要求,继续配备满足2002年7月1日以前生效的《1974年国际海上人命安全公约》第V/11、V/12和V/20条规定要求的设备;

.2　不迟于2002年7月1日以后的第一次检验[①],配备本条2.1.6要求的设备或系统,此时应不再要求设有2002年7月1日以前实施的《1974年国际海上人命安全公约》第V/12(p)条所述的无线电测向设备;

.3　不迟于本条2.4.2和2.4.3规定的日期,配备本条2.4款要求的系统;和

.4　按如下日期配备本条第2.2.3款要求的系统:

.1　对客船,不论其尺度大小,不迟于2016年1月1日以后的第一次检验[②];

.2　对3 000总吨及以上的货船,不迟于2016年1月1日以后的第一次检验;[②]

.3　对500总吨及以上但小于3 000总吨的货船,不迟于2017年1月1日以后的第一次检验[②];和

---

① 参见SOLAS条文所述的术语“第一次检验”的统一解释(海安会第MSC.1/Circ.1290号通函)。

② 参见《电子海图显示与信息系统(ECDIS)性能标准》(第A.817(19)号决议,经修订的),附件6后备要求。合适的纸质海图可以作为ECDIS的备用。其他ECDIS的备用安排也是可以接受的。

.4 cargo ships of 150 gross tonnage and upwards but less than 500 gross tonnage, not later than the first survey[①] after 1 January 2018.

The bridge navigational watch alarm system shall be in operation whenever the ship is underway at sea.

The provisions of paragraph 2.2.4 shall also apply to ships constructed before 1 July 2002.

1.3 Administrations may exempt ships from the application of the requirement of paragraph 1.2.4 when such ships will be taken permanently out of service within two years after the implementation date specified in subparagraphs 1.2.4.1 to 1.2.4.4.

2 Shipborne navigational equipment and systems

2.1 All ships, irrespective of size, shall have:

.1 a properly adjusted standard magnetic compass, or other means, independent of any power supply, to determine the ship's heading and display the reading at the main steering position;

.2 a pelorus or compass bearing device, or other means, independent of any power supply, to take bearings over an arc of the horizon of 360°;

.3 means of correcting heading and bearings to true at all times;

.4 nautical charts and nautical publications to plan and display the ship's route for the intended voyage and to plot and monitor positions throughout the voyage. An electronic chart display and information system (ECDIS) is also accepted as meeting the chart carriage requirements of this subparagraph. Ships to which paragraph 2.10 applies shall comply with the carriage requirements for ECDIS detailed therein;

.5 back-up arrangements to meet the functional requirements of subparagraph .4, if this function is partly or fully fulfilled by electronic means;[①]

.6 a receiver for a global navigation satellite system or a terrestrial radionavigation system, or other means, suitable for use at all times throughout the intended voyage to establish and update the ship's position by automatic means;

.7 if less than 150 gross tonnage and if practicable, a radar reflector, or other means, to enable detection by ships navigating by radar at both 9 and 3 GHz;

.8 when the ship's bridge is totally enclosed and unless the Administration determines otherwise, a sound reception system, or other means, to enable the officer in charge of the navigational watch to hear sound signals and determine their direction;

.9 a telephone, or other means, to communicate heading information to the emergency steering position, if provided.

---

① Refer to appendix 6, Back-up requirements, of *Performance standards for electronic chart display and information systems (ECDIS)* (resolution A.817(19), as amended). An appropriate folio of paper nautical charts may be used as a back-up arrangement for ECDIS. Other back-up arrangements for ECDIS are acceptable.

.4　对150总吨及以上但小于500总吨的货船，不迟于2018年1月1日以后的第一次检验①。

船舶在海上航行时，驾驶台航行值班报警系统须始终处于工作状态。

2.2.4的规定还适用于2002年7月1日以前建造的船舶。

1.3　如果船舶在1.2.4.1至1.2.4.4中规定的实施日期以后两年内永久退役，主管机关可对这些船舶免除适用第1.2.4款的要求。

2　船载航行设备和系统

2.1　所有船舶，不论其尺度大小，均应设有：

.1　1台经过校准的标准磁罗经或其他装置，不依靠任何电源，用于确定船舶首向并在主操舵位置显示其读数；

.2　1台罗经刻度盘或罗经方位装置或其他装置，不依靠任何电源，用于在水平360°弧度范围内量取方位；

.3　用于随时校正首向和方位的装置；

.4　配备海图和航海出版物以计划和显示船舶预定航程的航线，并且全程标绘和监测船位。电子海图显示与信息系统（ECDIS）也可作为满足本款海图配备要求的设备。第2.10款所适用的船舶应符合该款详述的关于电子海图显示与信息系统的配备要求；

.5　若该功能全部或部分由电子装置完成，应有满足上述.4功能要求的备用装置；①

.6　1台全球导航卫星系统或陆地无线电导航系统的接收机，或其他装置，适合于在船舶整个预定航程内随时自动确定和更新船位；

.7　如果船舶小于150总吨且可行，1台雷达反射器，或其他装置，使船舶能被其他航行船舶通过9 GHz和3 GHz雷达探测到；

.8　若船舶驾驶室是完全封闭的和除非主管机关另有规定，1套声响接收系统，或其他装置，使值班驾驶员能够听到声响信号并确定其方向；

.9　1部电话，或其他装置，用于向应急操舵位置（如有）传递首向信息。

① 参见《电子海图显示与信息系统（ECDIS）性能标准》（第A.817（19）号决议，经修订的），附件6后备要求。合适的纸质海图可以作为ECDIS的备用。其他ECDIS的备用安排也是可以接受的。

2.2 All ships of 150 gross tonnage and upwards and passenger ships irrespective of size shall, in addition to the requirements of paragraph 2.1, be fitted with:

.1 a spare magnetic compass, interchangeable with the magnetic compass as referred to in paragraph 2.1.1, or other means to perform the function referred to in paragraph 2.1.1 by means of replacement or duplicate equipment;

.2 a daylight signalling lamp, or other means, to communicate by light during day and night using an energy source of electrical power not solely dependent upon the ship's power supply.

.3 a bridge navigational watch alarm system (BNWAS), as follows:

.1 cargo ships of 150 gross tonnage and upwards and passenger ships irrespective of size constructed on or after 1 July 2011;

.2 passenger ships irrespective of size constructed before 1 July 2011, not later than the first survey① after 1 July 2012;

.3 cargo ships of 3,000 gross tonnage and upwards constructed before 1 July 2011, not later than the first survey① after 1 July 2012;

.4 cargo ships of 500 gross tonnage and upwards but less than 3,000 gross tonnage constructed before 1 July 2011, not later than the first survey① after 1 July 2013; and

.5 cargo ships of 150 gross tonnage and upwards but less than 500 gross tonnage constructed before 1 July 2011, not later than the first survey① after 1 July 2014.

The bridge navigational watch alarm system shall be in operation whenever the ship is underway at sea;

.4 a bridge navigational watch alarm system (BNWAS) installed prior to 1 July 2011 may subsequently be exempted from full compliance with the standards adopted by the Organization, at the discretion of the Administration.

2.3 All ships of 300 gross tonnage and upwards and passenger ships irrespective of size shall, in addition to meeting the requirements of paragraph 2.2, be fitted with:

.1 an echo-sounding device, or other electronic means, to measure and display the available depth of water;

.2 a 9 GHz radar, or other means, to determine and display the range and bearing of radar transponders and of other surface craft, obstructions, buoys, shorelines and navigational marks to assist in navigation and in collision avoidance;

.3 an electronic plotting aid, or other means, to plot electronically the range and bearing of targets to determine collision risk;

① Refer to *Unified interpretation of the term "first survey" referred to in SOLAS regulations* (MSC.1/Circ.1290).

2.2 所有150总吨及以上的船舶和不论尺度大小的客船,除满足本条2.1的要求外,还应设有:

.1 1台备用磁罗经,可与本条2.1.1中所述的磁罗经进行互换,或其他装置,以替代或备用设备实现2.1.1所述的功能;

.2 1套白昼信号灯,或其他装置,用于在白天和夜晚通过灯光进行联络,使用电源,但非仅依靠船上电源供电。

.3 按以下要求配备驾驶台航行值班报警系统(BNWAS):

.1 2011年7月1日或以后建造的150总吨及以上的货船和无论大小的客船;

.2 2011年7月1日以前建造的无论大小的客船,不迟于2012年7月1日以后的第一次检验①;

.3 2011年7月1日以前建造的3 000总吨及以上的货船,不迟于2012年7月1日以后的第一次检验①;

.4 2011年7月1日以前建造的500总吨及以上但小于3 000总吨的货船,不迟于2013年7月1日以后的第一次检验①;和

.5 2011年7月1日以前建造的150总吨及以上但小于500总吨的货船,不迟于2014年7月1日以后的第一次检验①。

每当船舶在海上航行时,驾驶台航行值班报警系统须处于运转状态;

.4 对于在2011年7月1日以前安装的驾驶台航行值班报警系统(BNWAS),主管机关可免除其完全符合本组织通过的标准。

2.3 所有300总吨及以上的船舶和不论大小的客船,除满足本条2.2款的要求外,还应设有:

.1 1台回声测深仪,或其他电子装置,用于测量和显示可用水深;

.2 1台9 GHz雷达,或其他装置,用于确定和显示雷达应答器、其他水上船艇、障碍物、浮标、海岸线和航标的距离和方位,借以助航和避碰;

.3 1套电子标绘装置,或其他装置,用电子方式标绘目标的距离和方位,以便确定碰撞危险;

① 参见SOLAS公约中对"第一次检验"的统一解释(第MSC.1/Circ.1290号通函)。

.4 speed and distance measuring device, or other means, to indicate speed and distance through the water;

.5 a properly adjusted transmitting heading device, or other means, to transmit heading information for input to the equipment referred to in paragraphs 2.3.2, 2.3.3 and 2.4.

2.4 All ships of 300 gross tonnage and upwards engaged on international voyages and cargo ships of 500 gross tonnage and upwards not engaged on international voyages and passenger ships irrespective of size shall be fitted with an automatic identification system (AIS), as follows:

.1 ships constructed on or after 1 July 2002;

.2 ships engaged on international voyages constructed before 1 July 2002:

.1 in the case of passenger ships, not later than 1 July 2003;

.2 in the case of tankers, not later than the first survey① for safety equipment② on or after 1 July 2003;

.3 in the case of ships, other than passenger ships and tankers, of 50,000 gross tonnage and upwards, not later than 1 July 2004;

.4 in the case of ships, other than passenger ships and tankers, of 300 gross tonnage and upwards but less than 50,000 gross tonnage, not later than the first safety equipment survey③ after 1 July 2004 or by 31 December 2004, whichever occurs earlier; and

.3 ships not engaged on international voyages constructed before 1 July 2002, not later than 1 July 2008;

.4 the Administration may exempt ships from the application of the requirements of this paragraph when such ships will be taken permanently out of service within two years after the implementation date specified in subparagraphs .2 and .3;

.5 AIS shall:

.1 provide automatically to appropriately equipped shore stations, other ships and aircraft information, including the ship's identity, type, position, course, speed, navigational status and other safety-related information;

.2 receive automatically such information from similarly fitted ships;

.3 monitor and track ships; and

.4 exchange data with shore-based facilities;

① Refer to *Unified interpretation of the term "first survey" referred to in SOLAS regulations* (MSC.1/Circ.1290).

② Refer to regulation I/8.

③ *The first safety equipment survey* means the first annual survey, the first periodical survey or the first renewal survey for safety equipment, whichever is due first after 1 July 2004, and, in addition, in the case of ships under construction, the initial survey.

.4　航速和航程测量装置,或其他装置,用于指示船舶对水航速和航程;

.5　1台经过适当校正的首向传送装置,或其他装置,用于传送首向信息以输入本条2.3.2、2.3.3和2.4所述的设备中。

2.4　所有300总吨及以上的国际航行船舶、500总吨及以上的非国际航行货船以及不论尺度大小的客船,应按下列要求配备1台自动识别系统(AIS):

.1　在2002年7月1日或以后建造的船舶;

.2　在2002年7月1日以前建造的国际航行船舶:

.1　客船不迟于2003年7月1日;

.2　液货船不迟于2003年7月1日或以后的第一次安全设备①检验②;

.3　除客船和液货船外,50 000总吨及以上的船舶不迟于2004年7月1日;

.4　除客船和液货船外,300总吨及以上但小于50 000总吨的船舶不迟于2004年7月1日以后的第一次安全设备检验③或在2004年12月31日以前,以较早者为准;和

.3　在2002年7月1日以前建造的非国际航行船舶,不迟于2008年7月1日;

.4　若船舶在上述.2和.3所规定的实施日期以后两年内永久退役,则主管机关可对这些船舶免除适用本节的要求;

.5　AIS应:

.1　自动向配有相应设备的岸台、其他船舶和飞机提供信息,包括船舶识别码、船型、船位、航向、航速、航行状况以及其他与安全有关的信息;

.2　自动从其他装有类似设备的船舶接收这种信息;

.3　监视和跟踪其他船舶;和

.4　与岸基设施交换数据;

---

① 参见SOLAS公约中对“第一次检验”的统一解释(第MSC.1/Circ.1290号通函)。

② 参见第I/8条。

③ “第一次安全设备检验”系指安全设备的第一次年度检验、第一次定期检验或者第一次换证检验,以2004年7月1日之后的先到期者为准,此外,对于在建船舶,系指初始检验。

.6 the requirements of paragraph 2.4.5 shall not be applied to cases where international agreements, rules or standards provide for the protection of navigational information; and

.7 AIS shall be operated taking into account the guidelines adopted by the Organization.① Ships fitted with AIS shall maintain AIS in operation at all times except where international agreements, rules or standards provide for the protection of navigational information.

2.5 All ships of 500 gross tonnage and upwards shall, in addition to meeting the requirements of paragraph 2.3, with the exception of paragraphs 2.3.3 and 2.3.5, and the requirements of paragraph 2.4, have:

.1 a gyro-compass, or other means, to determine and display their heading by shipborne non-magnetic means, being clearly readable by the helmsman at the main steering position. These means shall also transmit heading information for input to the equipment referred to in paragraphs 2.3.2, 2.4 and 2.5.5;

.2 a gyro-compass heading repeater, or other means, to supply heading information visually at the emergency steering position if provided;

.3 a gyro-compass bearing repeater, or other means, to take bearings, over an arc of the horizon of 360°, using the gyro-compass or other means referred to in subparagraph .1. However, ships of less than 1,600 gross tonnage shall be fitted with such means as far as possible;

.4 rudder, propeller, thrust, pitch and operational mode indicators, or other means, to determine and display rudder angle, propeller revolutions, the force and direction of thrust and, if applicable, the force and direction of lateral thrust and the pitch and operational mode, all to be readable from the conning position; and

.5 an automatic tracking aid, or other means, to plot automatically the range and bearing of other targets to determine collision risk.

2.6 On all ships of 500 gross tonnage and upwards, failure of one piece of equipment should not reduce the ship's ability to meet the requirements of paragraphs 2.1.1, 2.1.2 and 2.1.4.

2.7 All ships of 3,000 gross tonnage and upwards shall, in addition to meeting the requirements of paragraph 2.5, have:

.1 a 3 GHz radar or, where considered appropriate by the Administration, a second 9 GHz radar, or other means, to determine and display the range and bearing of other surface craft, obstructions, buoys, shorelines and navigational marks to assist in navigation and in collision avoidance, which are functionally independent of those referred to in paragraph 2.3.2; and

① Refer to *Revised guidelines for the onboard operational use of shipborne Automatic Identification Systems (AIS)* (resolution A.1106(29)).

.6 在有国际协议、规则或标准规定要保护航行信息的情况下，本条 2.4.5 的要求应不适用；和

.7 AIS 的操作应考虑到本组织通过的指南①。配备 AIS 的船舶应使 AIS 始终保持运行状态，但国际协定、规则或标准规定要保护航行信息的情况除外。

2.5 所有 500 总吨及以上的船舶，除满足本条 2.3（不包括 2.3.3 和 2.3.5）和 2.4 款的要求外，还应设有：

.1 1 台陀螺罗经，或其他装置，用于通过船载非磁性装置确定和显示船舶首向，操舵人员能在主操舵位置清晰地读取。这些装置也应传送首向信息以输入本条2.3.2、2.4 和 2.5.5 所述的设备中；

.2 1 台陀螺罗经首向复示器，或其他装置，用于将可视首向信息传送到应急操舵位置（如有）；

.3 1 台陀螺罗经首向复示器，或其他装置，通过使用上述.1 所述的陀螺罗经或其他装置，在水平 360°范围内量取方位。但是，小于 1 600 总吨的船舶应尽可能配备该装置；

.4 舵、螺旋桨、推力、螺距和工作模式指示器，或其他装置，用于确定和显示舵角、螺旋桨转速、推力和推力方向以及（如适用）侧推的推力和方向、螺距和工作模式，所有这些指示器都应在指挥驾驶位置清晰可读；和

.5 1 台自动跟踪仪，或其他装置，用于自动标绘其他目标的距离和方位，以确定碰撞危险。

2.6 在所有 500 总吨及以上的船舶上，1 台设备的故障不应降低船舶满足本条 2.1.1、2.1.2 和 2.1.4 要求的能力。

2.7 所有 3 000 总吨及以上的船舶，除满足本条 2.5 款的要求外，还应设有：

.1 1 台 3 GHz 雷达，或（如果主管机关认为合适）第 2 台 9 GHz 雷达，或其他装置，用于确定和显示其他水上船艇、碍航物、浮标、海岸线和航标的距离和方位，借以助航和避碰，并在功能上独立于本条 2.3.2 所述的装置；和

---

① 参见《经修订的船载自动识别系统（AIS）船上操作使用导则》（第 A.1106（29）号决议）。

.2 a second automatic tracking aid, or other means, to plot automatically the range and bearing of other targets to determine collision risk which are functionally independent of those referred to in paragraph 2.5.5.

2.8 All ships of 10,000 gross tonnage and upwards shall, in addition to meeting the requirements of paragraph 2.7 with the exception of paragraph 2.7.2, have:

.1 an automatic radar plotting aid, or other means, to plot automatically the range and bearing of at least 20 other targets, connected to a device to indicate speed and distance through the water, to determine collision risks and simulate a trial manoeuvre; and

.2 a heading or track control system, or other means, to automatically control and keep to a heading and/or straight track.

2.9 All ships of 50,000 gross tonnage and upwards shall, in addition to meeting the requirements of paragraph 2.8, have:

.1 a rate-of-turn indicator, or other means, to determine and display the rate of turn; and

.2 a speed and distance measuring device, or other means, to indicate speed and distance over the ground in the forward and athwartships direction.

2.10 Ships engaged on international voyages shall be fitted with an electronic chart display and information system (ECDIS) as follows:

.1 passenger ships of 500 gross tonnage and upwards constructed on or after 1 July 2012;

.2 tankers of 3,000 gross tonnage and upwards constructed on or after 1 July 2012;

.3 cargo ships, other than tankers, of 10,000 gross tonnage and upwards constructed on or after 1 July 2013;

.4 cargo ships, other than tankers, of 3,000 gross tonnage and upwards but less than 10,000 gross tonnage constructed on or after 1 July 2014;

.5 passenger ships of 500 gross tonnage and upwards constructed before 1 July 2012, not later than the first survey① on or after 1 July 2014;

.6 tankers of 3,000 gross tonnage and upwards constructed before 1 July 2012, not later than the first survey① on or after 1 July 2015;

.7 cargo ships, other than tankers, of 50,000 gross tonnage and upwards constructed before 1 July 2013, not later than the first survey① on or after 1 July 2016;

---

① Refer to *Unified interpretation of the term "first survey" referred to in SOLAS regulations* (MSC.1/Circ.1290).

.2 第2台自动跟踪仪,或其他装置,用于自动标绘其他目标的距离和方位,以确定碰撞危险,并在功能上独立于本条2.5.5所述的装置。

2.8 所有10 000总吨及以上的船舶,除满足本条2.7款(不包括2.7.2)的要求外,还应设有:

.1 1台自动雷达标绘仪,或其他装置,与1台指示船舶相对于水的航速和航程的装置相连,用于自动标绘至少20个其他目标的距离和方位,以确定碰撞危险和模拟试验性操纵;和

.2 1套首向或航迹控制系统,或其他装置,用于自动控制和保持首向和/或直线航迹向。

2.9 所有50 000总吨及以上的船舶,除满足本条2.8的要求外,还应设有:

.1 1台转速仪,或其他装置,用于确定和显示转速;和

.2 1台航速和航程测量装置,或其他装置,用于指示船舶前进方向和横向的相对于地的航速和航程。

2.10 从事国际航行的船舶应按以下要求配备电子海图显示与信息系统(ECDIS):

.1 2012年7月1日或以后建造的500总吨及以上的客船;

.2 2012年7月1日或以后建造的3 000总吨及以上的液货船;

.3 2013年7月1日或以后建造的除液货船以外的10 000总吨及以上的货船;

.4 2014年7月1日或以后建造的除液货船以外的3 000总吨及以上但小于10 000总吨的货船;

.5 2012年7月1日以前建造的500总吨及以上的客船,不迟于2014年7月1日或以后的第一次检验①;

.6 2012年7月1日以前建造的3 000总吨及以上的液货船,不迟于2015年7月1日或以后的第一次检验①;

.7 2013年7月1日以前建造的除液货船以外的50 000总吨及以上的货船,不迟于2016年7月1日或以后的第一次检验①;

① 参见SOLAS公约中对“第一次检验”的统一解释(第MSC.1/Circ.1290号通函)。

.8 cargo ships, other than tankers, of 20,000 gross tonnage and upwards but less than 50,000 gross tonnage constructed before 1 July 2013, not later than the first survey① on or after 1 July 2017; and

.9 cargo ships, other than tankers, of 10,000 gross tonnage and upwards but less than 20,000 gross tonnage constructed before 1 July 2013, not later than the first survey① on or after 1 July 2018.

2.11 Administrations may exempt ships from the application of the requirements of paragraph 2.10 when such ships will be taken permanently out of service within two years after the implementation date specified in subparagraphs .5 to .9 of paragraph 2.10.

3 When "other means" are permitted under this regulation, such means must be approved by the Administration in accordance with regulation 18.

4 The navigational equipment and systems referred to in this regulation shall be so installed, tested and maintained as to minimize malfunction.

5 Navigational equipment and systems offering alternative modes of operation shall indicate the actual mode of use.

6 Integrated bridge systems② shall be so arranged that failure of one sub-system is brought to the immediate attention of the officer in charge of the navigational watch by audible and visual alarms and does not cause failure to any other sub-system. In case of failure in one part of an integrated navigational system③, it shall be possible to operate each other individual item of equipment or part of the system separately.

Regulation 19-1
Long-range identification and tracking of ships④

1 Nothing in this regulation or the provisions of performance standards and functional requirements⑤ adopted by the Organization in relation to the long-range identification and tracking of ships shall prejudice the rights, jurisdiction or obligations of States under international law, in particular, the legal regimes of the high seas, the exclusive economic zone, the contiguous zone, the territorial seas or the straits used for international navigation and archipelagic sea lanes.

2.1 Subject to the provisions of paragraphs 4.1 and 4.2, this regulation shall apply to the following types of ships⑥ engaged on international voyages:

---

① Refer to Unified interpretation of the term "first survey" referred to in SOLAS regulations (MSC.1/Circ.1290).

② Refer to *Guidelines for bridge equipment and systems, their arrangement and integration* (BES) (SN.1/Circ.288).

③ Refer to revised *Recommendation on performance standards for an integrated navigational system* (resolution MSC.252(83), as amended).

④ Refer to *Guidance on the implementation of the LRIT system* (MSC.1/Circ.1298).

⑤ Refer to *Revised performance standards and functional requirements for the long-range identification and tracking of ships* (resolution MSC.263(84), as amended).

⑥ Refer to *Guidance in relation to certain types of ships which are required to transmit LRIT information on exemptions and equivalents and on certain operational matters* (MSC.1/Circ.1295).

.8 2013 年 7 月 1 日以前建造的除液货船以外的 20 000 总吨及以上但小于 50 000 总吨的货船,不迟于 2017 年 7 月 1 日或以后的第一次检验①;以及

.9 2013 年 7 月 1 日以前建造的除液货船以外的 10 000 总吨及以上但小于 20 000 总吨的货船,不迟于 2018 年 7 月 1 日或以后的第一次检验①。

2.11 当这些船舶将在第 2.10 款的第.5 至.9 项中规定的实施日期之后两年内永久退役时,主管机关可免除其适用第 2.10 款的要求。

3 如果根据本条允许使用“其他装置”,则这些装置必须由主管机关按第 18 条进行认可。

4 本条所述的航行设备和系统的安装、试验和维护,应最大限度减少故障。

5 可选择操作模式的航行设备和系统,应指明其实际使用的模式。

6 综合驾驶室系统②的布置,应使一个分系统发生的故障通过听觉和视觉报警立即引起值班驾驶员的注意,并不会导致任何其他分系统的故障。如果一个综合航行系统③的一部分发生故障,该系统的每项其他设备或每一其他部分应可以分别操作。

第 19-1 条
船舶的远程识别和跟踪④

1 本条内容或本组织通过的有关船舶远程识别和跟踪的性能标准和功能要求⑤的规定均不得损害各国根据国际法,特别是公海、专属经济区、毗邻区、领海或用于国际航行海峡和群岛海道的法律制度所具有的权利、管辖权或义务。

2.1 在符合本条 4.1 和 4.2 款规定的条件下,本条应适用于从事国际航行的下列类型船舶⑥:

---

① 参见 SOLAS 公约中对“第一次检验”的统一解释(第 MSC.1/Circ.1290 号通函)。
② 参见《驾驶台设备和系统(BES)的布置和整合》(第 SN.1/Circ.288 号通函)。
③ 参见经修订的《综合航行系统性能标准》(第 MSC.252(83)号决议)。
④ 参见《LRIT 系统实施指南》(第 MSC.1/Circ.1298 号通函)。
⑤ 参见《经修订的船舶远程识别和跟踪系统性能标准和功能要求》(第 MSC.263(84)号决议,经修订的)。
⑥ 参见《关于需要传输 LRIT 信息的某些类型船舶的免除和等效以及某些操作事项的指南》(第 MSC.1/Circ.1295 号通函)。

.1 passenger ships, including high-speed passenger craft;

.2 cargo ships, including high-speed craft, of 300 gross tonnage[1] and upwards; and

.3 mobile offshore drilling units.

2.2 The term ship, when used in paragraphs 3 to 11.2, includes the passenger and cargo ships, the high speed craft and the mobile offshore drilling units which are subject to the provisions of this regulation.

3 This regulation establishes provisions to enable Contracting Governments to undertake the long-range identification and tracking of ships.

4.1 Ships[2] shall be fitted with a system to automatically transmit the information specified in paragraph 5 as follows:

.1 ships constructed on or after 31 December 2008;

.2 ships constructed before 31 December 2008 and certified for operations:

.1 in sea areas A1 and A2, as defined in regulations Ⅳ/2.1.12 and Ⅳ/2.1.13; or

.2 in sea areas A1, A2 and A3, as defined in regulations Ⅳ/2.1.12, Ⅳ/2.1.13 and Ⅳ/2.1.14;

not later than the first survey[3] of the radio installation after 31 December 2008;

.3 ships constructed before 31 December 2008 and certified for operations in sea areas A1, A2, A3 and A4, as defined in regulations Ⅳ/2.1.12, Ⅳ/2.1.13, Ⅳ/2.1.14 and Ⅳ/2.1.15, not later than the first survey[3] of the radio installation after 1 July 2009. However, these ships shall comply with the provisions of subparagraph .2 above whilst they operate within sea areas A1, A2 and A3.

4.2 Ships, irrespective of the date of construction, fitted with an automatic identification system (AIS), as defined in regulation 19.2.4, and operated exclusively within sea area A1, as defined in regulation Ⅳ/2.1.12, shall not be required to comply with the provisions of this regulation.

5 Subject to the provisions of paragraph 4.1, ships shall automatically transmit the following long-range identification and tracking information:

.1 the identity of the ship;

.2 the position of the ship (latitude and longitude); and

.3 the date and time of the position provided.

---

① The *gross tonnage* to be used for determining whether a cargo ship or high-speed craft is required to comply with the provisions of this regulation shall be that determined under the provisions of the International Convention on Tonnage Measurement of Ships, 1969 irrespective of the date on which the ship or high-speed craft has been or is being constructed.

② Refer to *Guidance on the survey and certification of compliance of ships with the requirement to transmit LRIT information* (MSC.1/Circ.1307).

③ Refer to *Unified interpretation of the term "first survey" referred to in SOLAS regulations* (MSC.1/Circ.1290).

.1　客船，包括高速客船；

.2　300 总吨[①]及以上的货船，包括高速船；和

.3　海上移动式钻井平台。

2.2　在本条第 3 至 11.2 款中，"船舶"一词包括受本条规定约束的客船和货船、高速船和海上移动式钻井平台。

3　本条做出使各缔约国政府能进行船舶远程识别和跟踪的规定。

4.1　下列船舶[②]应配备一个自动传送本条第 5 款规定的信息的系统：

.1　2008 年 12 月 31 日或以后建造的船舶；

.2　2008 年 12 月 31 日以前建造并核准在下列海区营运的船舶：

.1　第Ⅳ/2.1.12 和Ⅳ/2.1.13 条定义的 A1 和 A2 海区；或

.2　第Ⅳ/2.1.12、Ⅳ/2.1.13 和Ⅳ/2.1.14 条定义的 A1、A2 和 A3 海区；

不迟于 2008 年 12 月 31 日以后的第一次无线电装置检验[③]；

.3　2008 年 12 月 31 日以前建造并核准在第Ⅳ/2.1.12、Ⅳ/2.1.13、Ⅳ/2.1.14 和Ⅳ/2.1.15 条定义的 A1、A2、A3 和 A4 海区营运的船舶，不迟于 2009 年 7 月 1 日以后的第一次无线电装置检验[③]。但是，这些船舶在 A1、A2 和 A3 海区内营运时应符合上述.2 段的规定。

4.2　无论何时建造，配备第 19.2.4 条定义的自动识别系统（AIS）并专门在第Ⅳ/2.1.12 条定义的 A1 海区内营运的船舶，不要求符合本条的规定。

5　在符合本条 4.1 规定的条件下，船舶应自动传送下列远程识别和跟踪信息：

.1　船舶识别码；

.2　船舶位置（经度和纬度）；和

.3　提供船位的日期和时间。

---

① 为确定货船或高速船是否需要满足本条要求而使用的船舶总吨位，无论该船舶或高速船的建造日期在何时，均应按照《1969 年国际船舶吨位公约》规定的来确定。

② 参见《船舶符合 LRIT 信息传输要求的检验和发证指南》（第 MSC.1/Circ.1307 号通函）。

③ 参见 SOLAS 公约中对"第一次检验"的统一解释（第 MSC.1/Circ.1290 号通函）。

6 Systems and equipment used to meet the requirements of this regulation shall conform to performance standards and functional requirements①,② not inferior to those adopted by the Organization. Any shipboard equipment shall be of a type approved③ by the Administration.

7 Systems and equipment used to meet the requirements of this regulation shall be capable of being switched off on board or be capable of ceasing the distribution of long-range identification and tracking information:

.1 where international agreements, rules or standards provide for the protection of navigational information; or

.2 in exceptional circumstances and for the shortest duration possible where the operation is considered by the master to compromise the safety or security of the ship. In such a case, the master shall inform the Administration without undue delay and make an entry in the record of navigational activities and incidents maintained in accordance with regulation 28 setting out the reasons for the decision and indicating the period during which the system or equipment was switched off.

8.1 Subject to the provisions of paragraphs 8.2 to 11.2, Contracting Governments shall be able to receive long-range identification and tracking information about ships, for security and other purposes④ as agreed by the Organization, as follows:

.1 the Administration shall be entitled to receive such information about ships entitled to fly its flag irrespective of where such ships may be located;

.2 a Contracting Government shall be entitled to receive such information about ships which have indicated their intention to enter a port facility, as defined in regulation XI-2/1.1.9, or a place under the jurisdiction of that Contracting Government, irrespective of where such ships may be located provided they are not located within the waters landward of the baselines, established in accordance with international law, of another Contracting Government; and

.3 a Contracting Government shall be entitled to receive such information about ships entitled to fly the flag of other Contracting Governments, not intending to enter a port facility or a place under the jurisdiction of that Contracting Government, navigating within a distance not exceeding 1,000 nautical miles of its coast provided such ships are not located within the waters landward of the baselines, established in accordance with international law, of another Contracting Government; and

.4 a Contracting Government shall not be entitled to receive, pursuant to subparagraph .3, such information about a ship located within the territorial sea of the Contracting Government whose flag the ship is entitled to fly.

---

① Refer to *Revised performance standards and functional requirements for the long-range identification and tracking of ships* (resolution MSC.263(84), as amended).

② Refer to *LRIT technical documentation* (*part I*) (MSC.1/Circ.1259, as revised).

③ Refer to *Guidance on the survey and certification of compliance of ships with the requirement to transmit LRIT information* (MSC.1/Circ.1307).

④ Refer to *Use of the long-range identification and tracking information for maritime safety and marine environment protection purposes* (resolution MSC.242(83)).

6 用以满足本条要求的系统和设备,其所达到的性能标准和功能要求应不低于本组织通过的性能标准和功能[①,②]要求。任何船载设备应为主管机关认可[③]的类型。

7 用以满足本条要求的系统和设备应能在下列情况下在船上关闭或能停止发送远程识别和跟踪信息:

.1 国际协定、规则或标准规定要保护航行信息的情况;或

.2 在船长认为作业有损船舶安全或保安的特殊情况下并在尽可能短的时间内。在这种情况下,船长应立即通知主管机关,并记入按第 28 条保持的航行活动和事件记录,说明所做决定的理由并指明系统或设备关闭的时间段。

8.1 在符合本条 8.2 至 11.2 规定的条件下,各缔约国政府应能为保安和其他目的[④]按下列要求接收经本组织同意的船舶远程识别和跟踪信息:

.1 主管机关应有权接收悬挂其国旗的船舶的此类信息,而无论此类船舶可能位于何处;

.2 一缔约国政府应有权接收已表示有意进入第Ⅺ-2/1.1.9 条定义的港口设施或该缔约国政府管辖的某地的船舶的此类信息,而无论此类船舶可能位于何处,只要这些船舶不是位于按国际法规定的基线以内(向陆地一侧)另一缔约国政府的水域;

.3 一缔约国政府应有权接收悬挂其他缔约国政府国旗、不准备进入其管辖的港口设施或某地、且在距离其海岸不超过 1 000 n mile 处航行的船舶的此类信息,只要这些船舶不是位于按国际法规定的基线以内(向陆地一侧)另一缔约国政府的水域;和

.4 一缔约国政府无权按.3 接收位于船旗国政府领海内的某一船舶的此类信息。

① 参见《经修订的船舶远程识别和跟踪系统性能标准和功能要求》(第 MSC.263(84)号通函,经修订的)。
② 参见《LRIT 技术文件(第Ⅰ部分)》(第 MSC.1/Circ.1259 号决议,经修订的)。
③ 参见《船舶符合 LRIT 信息传输要求的检验和发证指南》(第 MSC.1/Circ.1307 号通函)。
④ 参见《以海上安全和海洋环境保护目的使用船舶远程识别和跟踪系统》(第 MSC.242(83)号决议)。

8.2 Contracting Governments shall specify and communicate[①] to the Organization relevant details, taking into account the performance standards and functional requirements adopted by the Organization,[②] to enable long-range identification and tracking information to be made available pursuant to the provisions of paragraph 8.1. The Contracting Government concerned may, at any time thereafter, amend or withdraw such communication. The Organization shall inform all Contracting Governments upon receipt of such communication together with the particulars thereof.

9.1 Notwithstanding the provisions of paragraph 8.1.3, the Administration shall be entitled, in order to meet security or other concerns, at any time, to decide that long-range identification and tracking information about ships entitled to fly its flag shall not be provided pursuant to the provisions of paragraph 8.1.3 to Contracting Governments. The Administration concerned may, at any time thereafter, amend, suspend or annul such decisions.

9.2 The Administration concerned shall communicate, pursuant to paragraph 9.1, such decisions to the Organization. The Organization shall inform all Contracting Governments upon receipt of such communication together with the particulars thereof.

9.3 The rights, duties and obligations, under international law, of the ships whose Administration invoked the provisions of paragraph 9.1 shall not be prejudiced as a result of such decisions.

10 Contracting Governments shall, at all times:

.1 recognize the importance of long-range identification and tracking information;

.2 recognize and respect the commercial confidentiality and sensitivity of any long-range identification and tracking information they may receive;

.3 protect the information they may receive from unauthorized access or disclosure; and

.4 use the information they may receive in a manner consistent with international law.

11.1 Contracting Governments shall bear all costs associated with any long-range identification and tracking information they request and receive. Notwithstanding the provisions of paragraph 11.2, Contracting Governments shall not impose any charges on ships in relation to the long-range identification and tracking information they may seek to receive.

11.2 Unless the national legislation of the Administration provides otherwise, ships entitled to fly its flag shall not incur any charges for transmitting long-range identification and tracking information in compliance with the provisions of this regulation.

---

① Refer to *Guidance on the implementation of the LRIT system* (MSC.1/Circ.1298).

② Refer to *Revised performance standards and functional requirements for the long-range identification and tracking of ships* (resolution MSC.263(84), as amended).

8.2　缔约国政府应向本组织详细说明和通报[①]相关细节,并考虑到本组织通过的性能标准和功能要求[②],以便能按 8.1 的规定提供远程识别和跟踪信息。相关的缔约国政府可以在此后的任何时间修正或撤销此类通报。本组织在收到此类通报及其资料后应通知所有缔约国政府。

9.1　尽管有本条 8.1.3 的规定,主管机关有权为应对保安或其他问题,随时决定不按本条 8.1.3 的规定向缔约国政府提供悬挂其国旗的船舶的远程识别和跟踪信息。相关主管机关可在此后任何时候修正、中止或取消此类决定。

9.2　相关主管机关应按本条 9.1 款向本组织通报此类决定。本组织在收到此类通报及其资料后应通知所有缔约国政府。

9.3　主管机关如援用本条 9.1 款的规定,其船舶根据国际法所具有的权利、职责和义务不得因此类决定而受到损害。

10　缔约国政府始终应:

.1　认识到远程识别和跟踪信息的重要性;

.2　认识到并尊重其可能收到的任何远程识别和跟踪信息的商业机密性和敏感性;

.3　防止擅自获取或泄露其可能收到的信息;和

.4　以符合国际法的方式使用其可能收到的信息。

11.1　缔约国政府应承担与其要求和接收的远程识别和跟踪信息相关的所有费用。尽管有本条 11.2 款的规定,缔约国政府不得向船舶征收与其试图接收的远程识别和跟踪信息相关的任何费用。

11.2　除非主管机关的本国法律另有规定,悬挂其国旗的船舶不应为传送符合本条规定的远程识别和跟踪信息而发生任何收费。

---

① 参见《LRIT 系统实施指南》(第 MSC.1/Circ.1298 号通函)。

② 参见《经修订的船舶远程识别和跟踪系统性能标准和功能要求》(第 MSC.263(84)号通函,经修订的)。

12 Notwithstanding the provisions of paragraph 8.1, the search and rescue services① of Contracting Governments shall be entitled to receive, free of any charges, long-range identification and tracking information in relation to the search and rescue of persons in distress at sea.

13 Contracting Governments may report to the Organization any case where they consider that provisions of this regulation or of any other related requirements established by the Organization have not been or are not being observed or adhered to.

14 The Maritime Safety Committee shall determine the criteria, procedures and arrangements for the establishment, review and audit② of the provision of long-range identification and tracking information to Contracting Governments pursuant to the provisions of this regulation.

Regulation 20
Voyage data recorders③

1 To assist in casualty investigations, ships, when engaged on international voyages, subject to the provisions of regulation 1.4, shall be fitted with a voyage data recorder (VDR) as follows:

.1 passenger ships constructed on or after 1 July 2002;

.2 ro-ro passenger ships constructed before 1 July 2002, not later than the first survey④ on or after 1 July 2002;

.3 passenger ships, other than ro-ro passenger ships, constructed before 1 July 2002, not later than 1 January 2004; and

.4 ships, other than passenger ships, of 3,000 gross tonnage and upwards constructed on or after 1 July 2002.

2 To assist in casualty investigations, cargo ships, when engaged on international voyages, shall be fitted with a VDR which may be a simplified voyage data recorder (S-VDR)⑤ as follows:

---

① Refer to *Guidance to search and rescue services in relation to requesting and receiving LRIT information* (MSC.1/Circ.1338, as revised).

② Refer to *Appointment of the LRIT Coordinator* (resolution MSC.275(85)), *Revised performance standards and functional requirements for the long-range identification and tracking of ships* (resolution MSC.263(84), as amended) and *Principles and guidelines relating to the review and audit of the performance of LRIT Data Centres and the International LRIT Data Exchange* (MSC.1/Circ.1412, as revised).

③ Refer to *Performance Standards for Shipborne Voyage Data Recorders (VDRs)* (resolution A.861(20), as amended), *Recommendation on Performance Standards for Shipborne Voyage Data Recorders (VDRs)* (resolution MSC.333(90)) and *Guidelines on voyage data recorder (VDR) ownership and recovery* (MSC/Circ.1024).

④ Refer to *Unified interpretation of the term "first survey" referred to in SOLAS regulations* (MSC.1/Circ.1290).

⑤ Refer to *Performance standards for shipborne simplified voyage data recorders (S-VDRs)* (resolution MSC.163(78), as amended).

12　尽管有本条 8.1 款的规定，缔约国政府的搜救机构[①]应有权免费接收与搜救海上遇险人员有关的远程识别和跟踪信息。

13　缔约国政府可向本组织报告其认为本条规定或本组织制定的任何其他相关要求的规定在过去或现在没有得到遵守或奉行的任何情况。

14　海上安全委员会应为制定、审议和审核[②]按照本条规定向缔约国政府提供远程识别和跟踪信息而确定标准、程序及安排。

第 20 条
航行数据记录仪[③]

1　为有助于事故调查，国际航行船舶应根据第 1.4 款的规定，按下列要求装设航行数据记录仪(VDR)：

.1　在 2002 年 7 月 1 日或以后建造的客船；

.2　在 2002 年 7 月 1 日以前建造的滚装客船，不迟于 2002 年 7 月 1 日或以后的第一次检验[④]；

.3　在 2002 年 7 月 1 日以前建造的客船，除滚装客船外，不迟于 2004 年 1 月 1 日；和

.4　在 2002 年 7 月 1 日或以后建造的 3 000 总吨及以上的船舶，客船除外。

2　为有助于海难调查，从事国际航行的货船应按以下期限装设一台 VDR，该仪器可以是简易型航行数据记录仪(S-VDR)[⑤]：

---

①　参见《搜救机构要求和接收 LRIT 信息指南》(第 MSC.1/Circ.1338 号通函，经修订的)。

②　参见《LRIT 协调人的任命》(第 MSC.275(85)号通函)，《经修订的船舶远程识别和跟踪系统性能标准和功能要求(第 MSC.263(84)号通函，经修订的)》，以及《关于 LRIT 数据中心和国际 LRIT 数据交换效果评估和审核原则和导则》(第 MSC.1/Circ.1412 号通函，经修订的)。

③　参见《船载航行数据记录仪(VDRs)性能标准》(第 A.861(20)号决议，经修订的)，《船载航行数据记录仪(VDRs)性能标准的建议》(第 MSC.333(90)号通函)，以及《航行数据记录仪(VDR)的使用和备份导则》(第 MSC/Circ.1024 号通函)。

④　参见 SOLAS 公约中对“第一次检验”的统一解释(第 MSC.1/Circ.1290 号通函)。

⑤　参见《船载简易型航行数据记录仪(S-VDRs)性能标准》(第 MSC.163(78)号通函，经修订的)。

.1 in the case of cargo ships of 20,000 gross tonnage and upwards constructed before 1 July 2002, at the first scheduled dry-docking after 1 July 2006 but not later than 1 July 2009;

.2 in the case of cargo ships of 3,000 gross tonnage and upwards but less than 20,000 gross tonnage constructed before 1 July 2002, at the first scheduled dry-docking after 1 July 2007 but not later than 1 July 2010; and

.3 Administrations may exempt cargo ships from the application of the requirements of subparagraphs .1 and .2 when such ships will be taken permanently out of service within two years after the implementation date specified in subparagraphs .1 and .2 above.

3 Administrations may exempt ships, other than ro-ro passenger ships, constructed before 1 July 2002 from being fitted with a VDR where it can be demonstrated that interfacing a VDR with the existing equipment on the ship is unreasonable and impracticable.

Regulation 21
International Code of Signals and IAMSAR Manual

1 All ships which, in accordance with the present Convention, are required to carry a radio installation shall carry the International Code of Signals as may be amended by the Organization. The Code shall also be carried by any other ship which, in the opinion of the Administration, has a need to use it.

2 All ships shall carry an up-to-date copy of Volume Ⅲ of the International Aeronautical and Maritime Search and Rescue (IAMSAR) Manual.

Regulation 22
Navigation bridge visibility

1 Ships of not less than 55 m in length, as defined in regulation 2.4, constructed on or after 1 July 1998, shall meet the following requirements:

.1 The view of the sea surface from the conning position shall not be obscured by more than two ship lengths, or 500 m, whichever is less, forward of the bow to 10° on either side under all conditions of draught, trim and deck cargo;

.2 No blind sector, caused by cargo, cargo gear or other obstructions outside of the wheelhouse forward of the beam which obstructs the view of the sea surface as seen from the conning position, shall exceed 10°. The total arc of blind sectors shall not exceed 20°. The clear sectors between blind sectors shall be at least 5°. However, in the view described in .1, each individual blind sector shall not exceed 5°;

.1　对 2002 年 7 月 1 日以前建造的 20 000 总吨及以上货船，在 2006 年 7 月 1 日以后第 1 次计划坞修日，但不迟于 2009 年 7 月 1 日；

.2　对 2002 年 7 月 1 日以前建造的 3 000 总吨及以上，但小于 20 000 总吨的货船，在 2007 年 7 月 1 日以后第 1 次计划坞修日，但不迟于 2010 年 7 月 1 日；和

.3　如果货船在上述.1 和.2 规定的实施日期之后两年以内将永久退役，主管机关可对这类船舶免除.1 和.2 的要求。

3　除滚装客船以外，对于 2002 年 7 月 1 日以前建造的船舶，如果能证明 VDR 与船上的现有设备连接为不合理和不可行，则主管机关可对其免除配备 VDR 的要求。

第 21 条
《国际信号规则》和 IAMSAR 手册

1　按照本公约要求配备无线电装置的所有船舶，应备有可能经本组织修正的《国际信号规则》。主管机关认为有必要使用该规则的任何其他船舶，也应备有此规则。

2　所有船舶均应备有一份最新的《国际航空和海上搜救（IAMSAR ）手册》第Ⅲ卷。

第 22 条
驾驶室可视范围

1　按照第 2.4 条定义的船长不小于 55 m，1998 年 7 月 1 日或以后建造的船舶应满足下列要求：

.1　在吃水、纵倾和甲板货所有状态下，指挥位置上的海面视域，自船首前方至任何一舷 10°范围内的盲视区长度均不应超过两倍船长或 500 m（取其小者）；

.2　从正横向向前，任一由货物、起货装置或操舵室外的其他障碍物造成的遮挡指挥位置上海面视域的盲视区应不超过 10°。盲视区的总角度不应超过 20°。在盲视区之间的可视扇形区域应至少为 5°。但在本条.1 中所述的视域内，每一盲视区均应不超过 5°；

.3 The horizontal field of vision from the conning position shall extend over an arc of not less than 225°, that is from right ahead to not less than 22.5° abaft the beam on either side of the ship;

.4 From each bridge wing, the horizontal field of vision shall extend over an arc of at least 225°, that is from at least 45° on the opposite bow through right ahead and then from right ahead to right astern through 180° on the same side of the ship;

.5 From the main steering position, the horizontal field of vision shall extend over an arc from right ahead to at least 60° on each side of the ship;

.6 The ship's side shall be visible from the bridge wing;

.7 The height of the lower edge of the navigation bridge front windows above the bridge deck shall be kept as low as possible. In no case shall the lower edge present an obstruction to the forward view as described in this regulation;

.8 The upper edge of the navigation bridge front windows shall allow a forward view of the horizon, for a person with a height of eye of 1,800 mm above the bridge deck at the conning position, when the ship is pitching in heavy seas. The Administration, if satisfied that a 1,800 mm height of eye is unreasonable and impractical, may allow reduction of the height of eye but not to less than 1,600 mm;

.9 Windows shall meet the following requirements:

.1 To help avoid reflections, the bridge front windows shall be inclined from the vertical plane top out, at an angle of not less than 10° and not more than 25°;

.2 Framing between navigation bridge windows shall be kept to a minimum and not be installed immediately forward of any work station;

.3 Polarized and tinted windows shall not be fitted;

.4 A clear view through at least two of the navigation bridge front windows and, depending on the bridge configuration, an additional number of clear-view windows shall be provided at all times, regardless of weather conditions.

2 Ships constructed before 1 July 1998 shall, where practicable, meet the requirements of paragraphs 1.1 and 1.2. However, structural alterations or additional equipment need not be required.

3 On ships of unconventional design which, in the opinion of the Administration, cannot comply with this regulation, arrangements shall be provided to achieve a level of visibility that is as near as practical to that prescribed in this regulation.

4 Notwithstanding the requirements of paragraphs 1.1, 1.3, 1.4 and 1.5, ballast water exchange may be undertaken provided that:

.3 指挥位置上的水平视域应为一个不小于225°的扇面,即在船舶任意一侧,从正前方至正横向后不小于22.5°;

.4 每一驾驶室翼桥的水平视域应为一个至少为225°的扇面,即从船首另一侧至少45°的位置,经正前方,然后从正前方延伸180°至本侧正后方;

.5 主操舵位置的水平视域应为一个从正前方至船舶每一舷至少60°的扇面;

.6 船舷应从驾驶室侧翼上可见;

.7 驾驶台甲板上方的驾驶室正前窗下缘高度应尽可能降低。任何情况下,该下部边缘均不得遮挡本条所述的前方视域;

.8 驾驶室正前窗上部边缘的位置,保证驾驶台甲板上视线高度为1 800 mm的人员,当船舶在大浪中纵摇时,在指挥位置具有水平视野。主管机关如认为1 800 mm的视线高度不合理和不切实际,可允许降低视线高度,但不应低于1 600 mm;

.9 窗应满足下列要求:

.1 为避免反射,驾驶室正前窗应自垂直方向顶部向外倾斜,其角度不小于10°且不大于25°;

.2 驾驶室窗之间的窗框应保持最低数量,且不应设置在任何工作台的正前方;

.3 不应设置偏振及着色玻璃窗;

.4 不管天气状况如何,在任何时候应至少两扇驾驶室正前窗和其他一些窗(取决于驾驶台形状)具有清晰的视域。

2 1998年7月1日以前建造的船舶,如实际可行,应满足本条1.1和1.2的要求。但是,不必要求结构变化或另置设备。

3 对非常规设计的船舶,如主管机关认为其不能满足本条规定时,应做出尽可能接近本条规定的可视范围的布置。

4 尽管有1.1、1.3、1.4和1.5款的要求,还是可以进行压载水更换,前提是:

.1 the master has determined that it is safe to do so and takes into consideration any increased blind sectors or reduced horizontal fields of vision resulting from the operation to ensure that a proper lookout is maintained at all times;

.2 the operation is conducted in accordance with the ship's ballast water management plan, taking into account the recommendations on ballast water exchange adopted by the Organization; and

.3 the commencement and termination of the operation are recorded in the ship's record of navigational activities pursuant to regulation 28.

Regulation 23
Pilot transfer arrangements

1 Application

1.1 Ships engaged on voyages in the course of which pilots may be employed shall be provided with pilot transfer arrangements.

1.2 Equipment and arrangements for pilot transfer which are installed① on or after 1 July 2012 shall comply with the requirements of this regulation, and due regard shall be paid to the standards adopted by the Organization.②

1.3 Except as provided otherwise, equipment and arrangements for pilot transfer which are provided on ships before 1 July 2012 shall at least comply with the requirements of regulation 17③ or 23, as applicable, of the International Convention for the Safety of Life at Sea, 1974 in force prior to that date, and due regard shall be paid to the standards adopted by the Organization prior to that date.

1.4 Equipment and arrangements installed on or after 1 July 2012, which are a replacement of equipment and arrangements provided on ships before 1 July 2012, shall, in so far as is reasonable and practicable, comply with the requirements of this regulation.

1.5 With respect to ships constructed before 1 January 1994, paragraph 5 shall apply not later than the first survey④ on or after 1 July 2012.

1.6 Paragraph 6 applies to all ships.

2 General

① Refer to *Unified interpretation of SOLAS regulation V/23* (MSC.1/Circ.1375).

② Refer to *Pilot transfer arrangements* (resolution A.1045(27), as amended).

③ Refer to resolution MSC.99(73), renumbering previous regulation 17 as regulation 23, which entered into force on 1 July 2002.

④ Refer to *Unified interpretation of the term "first survey" referred to in SOLAS regulations* (MSC.1/Circ.1290).

.1 船长已经确定这样做是安全的,而且考虑到了由于该作业导致盲区的增加或水平视野的减少,以确保随时保持适当瞭望;

.2 按照压载水管理计划进行作业,考虑了本组织通过的有关压载水更换的建议案;

.3 按照第28条要求,将作业开始和结束的情况记录在船舶航行活动记录上。

第23条
引航员登离船装置

1 适用范围

1.1 航行中可能雇用引航员的船舶应设有引航员登离船装置。

1.2 在2012年7月1日或以后安装的供引航员登离船使用的设备和装置①,应符合本条要求并须充分考虑本组织通过的标准。②

1.3 除另有规定外,在2012年7月1日以前安装的引航员登离船设备和装置,应至少符合在该日期以前生效的本公约第Ⅴ/17③或Ⅴ/23条(如适用)的要求,并须充分考虑该日期之前本组织通过的标准。

1.4 在2012年7月1日或以后安装的设备和装置(其替换在2012年7月1日以前安装的设备和装置)应在合理和可行的范围内遵守本条的要求。

1.5 对于1994年1月1日以前建造的船舶,应不迟于2012年7月1日或以后的第一次检验④适用本条第5款。

1.6 本条第6款适用于所有船舶。

2 通则

---

① 参见SOLAS公约第Ⅴ/23条的统一解释(第MSC.1/Circ.1375号通函)。
② 参见《引航员登离船安排》(第A.1045(27)号决议,经修订的)。
③ 参见第MSC.99(73)号决议,将此前的第17条重新编号为第23条,于2002年7月1日生效。
④ 参见SOLAS公约中对“第一次检验”的统一解释(第MSC.1/Circ.1290号通函)。

2.1 All arrangements used for pilot transfer shall efficiently fulfil their purpose of enabling pilots to embark and disembark safely. The appliances shall be kept clean, properly maintained and stowed and shall be regularly inspected to ensure that they are safe to use. They shall be used solely for the embarkation and disembarkation of personnel.

2.2 The rigging of the pilot transfer arrangements and the embarkation of a pilot shall be supervised by a responsible officer having means of communication with the navigation bridge and who shall also arrange for the escort of the pilot by a safe route to and from the navigation bridge. Personnel engaged in rigging and operating any mechanical equipment shall be instructed in the safe procedures to be adopted and the equipment shall be tested prior to use.

2.3 A pilot ladder shall be certified by the manufacturer as complying with this regulation or with an international standard acceptable to the Organization.① Ladders shall be inspected in accordance with regulations I/6, 7 and 8.

2.4 All pilot ladders used for pilot transfer shall be clearly identified with tags or other permanent marking so as to enable identification of each appliance for the purposes of survey, inspection and record keeping. A record shall be kept on the ship as to the date the identified ladder is placed into service and any repairs effected.

2.5 Reference in this regulation to an accommodation ladder includes a sloping ladder used as part of the pilot transfer arrangements.

3 Transfer arrangements

3.1 Arrangements shall be provided to enable the pilot to embark and disembark safely on either side of the ship.

3.2 In all ships where the distance from sea level to the point of access to, or egress from, the ship exceeds 9 m, and when it is intended to embark and disembark pilots by means of the accommodation ladder②, or other equally safe and convenient means in conjunction with a pilot ladder, the ship shall carry such equipment on each side, unless the equipment is capable of being transferred for use on either side.

3.3 Safe and convenient access to, and egress from, the ship shall be provided by either:

.1 a pilot ladder requiring a climb of not less than 1.5 m and not more than 9 m above the surface of the water so positioned and secured that:

.1 it is clear of any possible discharges from the ship;

.2 it is within the parallel body length of the ship and, as far as is practicable, within the mid-ship half length of the ship;

---

① Refer to the recommendations by the International Organization for Standardization, in particular publication ISO 799-1:2019, *Ships and marine technology–Pilot ladders*.

② Refer to regulation II-1/3-9 on *Means of embarkation on and disembarkation from ships*.

2.1 供引航员登离船使用的所有装置均应有效地达到使引航员安全登船和离船的目的。装置须保持干净,适当维护保养和存放并须定期检查,以确保其安全使用。这些装置应专门用于人员的登船和离船。

2.2 引航员登离船装置的安装和引航员的登船,应由一名高级船员进行监督,该高级船员应持有与驾驶室联系的通信设备,还应安排护送引航员由安全路线前往和离开驾驶室。安装和操作任何机械设备的人员应遵循安全作业程序,且设备在使用前应进行检测。

2.3 引航员软梯须具有制造商颁发的证书,以证明其符合本条或本组织接受的国际标准①。应按第Ⅰ/6、7和8条检查软梯。

2.4 供引航员登离船使用的所有引航员软梯应使用标签或其他永久性标记清晰地标识,以便在检验、检查和记录时识别每个装置。船上对于所标识的软梯投入使用和进行任何修理时应在当天记录。

2.5 本条所述的舷梯包括作为引航员登离船装置组成部分的斜梯。

3　登离船装置

3.1 船舶应设有能使引航员从船舶的任一舷安全登船和离船的装置。

3.2 在所有船舶上,当海平面至登船处或离船处的距离超过9 m,并欲将舷梯或其他同等安全方便的装置②与引航员软梯一起供引航员登船或离船时,应在每舷均装有这种设备,除非该设备能够移至另一舷使用。

3.3 船舶须配备下列任一装置,以供安全方便地登船或离船:

.1 引航员软梯,所需爬高不小于1.5 m,离水面高度不超过9 m,其位置和系固须做到:

.1 避开任何可能的船舶排放口;

.2 与船长方向平行,并尽可能在船中船长的一半范围内;

① 参见国际标准化组织的建议,尤其是ISO 799-1:2019,船舶和海上技术——引航员梯。

② 参见第Ⅱ-1/3-9条,登船和离船设施。

.3 each step rests firmly against the ship's side; where constructional features, such as rubbing bands, would prevent the implementation of this provision, special arrangements shall, to the satisfaction of the Administration, be made to ensure that persons are able to embark and disembark safely;

.4 the single length of pilot ladder is capable of reaching the water from the point of access to, or egress from, the ship and due allowance is made for all conditions of loading and trim of the ship, and for an adverse list of 15°; the securing strong point, shackles and securing ropes shall be at least as strong as the side ropes; or

.2 an accommodation ladder in conjunction with the pilot ladder (i.e. a combination arrangement), or other equally safe and convenient means, whenever the distance from the surface of the water to the point of access to the ship is more than 9 m. The accommodation ladder shall be sited leading aft. When in use, means shall be provided to secure the lower platform of the accommodation ladder to the ship's side, so as to ensure that the lower end of the accommodation ladder and the lower platform are held firmly against the ship's side within the parallel body length of the ship and, as far as is practicable, within the mid-ship half length and clear of all discharges.

.1 when a combination arrangement is used for pilot access, means shall be provided to secure the pilot ladder and manropes to the ship's side at a point of nominally 1.5 m above the bottom platform of the accommodation ladder. In the case of a combination arrangement using an accommodation ladder with a trapdoor in the bottom platform (i.e. embarkation platform), the pilot ladder and manropes shall be rigged through the trapdoor extending above the platform to the height of the handrail.

4 Access to the ship's deck

Means shall be provided to ensure safe, convenient and unobstructed passage for any person embarking on, or disembarking from, the ship between the head of the pilot ladder, or of any accommodation ladder or other appliance, and the ship's deck. Where such passage is by means of:

.1 a gateway in the rails or bulwark, adequate handholds shall be provided;

.2 a bulwark ladder, two handhold stanchions rigidly secured to the ship's structure at or near their bases and at higher points shall be fitted. The bulwark ladder shall be securely attached to the ship to prevent overturning.

5 Shipside doors

Shipside doors used for pilot transfer shall not open outwards.

6 Mechanical pilot hoists

Mechanical pilot hoists shall not be used.

.3　每级踏板稳固地紧靠在船舷；如果结构特征，如护舷板妨碍本规定的实施，应做出特别布置使主管机关满意，以确保人员能安全登船和离船；

.4　引航员软梯的单一长度能从登船处或离船处抵达水面，并充分考虑所有装载状况和船舶纵倾及横倾至 15°的不利情况；安全加固点、卸扣和系索的强度应至少与扶手索相同；或

.2　当水面至登船处的距离超过 9 m 时，应将舷梯与引航员软梯相连（如组合装置），或采用其他同等安全方便的方法。舷梯设置方向朝向船尾。在使用时，将舷梯的下平台系固在船舷，从而确保舷梯的下端和下平台稳固地紧靠在平行船舷的方向，并尽可能设在船中、船长的一半范围内，且避开所有的排放口。

.1　当使用组合装置用于引航员登船时，须确保软梯和扶手绳系固于船舷上距舷梯底层平台以上 1.5 m 处。当组合装置中底层平台（即登船平台）带有活动门时，应将引航员软梯和扶手索穿过活动门并延伸至平台以上栏杆的高度。

4　到甲板的通道

应配备供任何人员登船和离船的装置，以确保在引航员软梯的上端或任何舷梯或其他设施的上端与船舶甲板之间有安全、方便和无障碍的通道。如果这种通道是：

.1　在栏杆或舷墙中开门，应设有足够的扶手；

.2　舷墙梯，应设有两根扶手支柱，其基部或接近基部处以及较高的几处应以刚性方式系固在船舶结构上。舷墙梯应牢固地固定在船舶上，以防翻转。

5　舷门

引航员登离船的舷门不得向外开启。

6　引航员机械升降器

不得使用引航员机械升降器。

7 Associated equipment

7.1 The following associated equipment shall be kept at hand ready for immediate use when persons are being transferred:

.1 two manropes of not less than 28 mm and not more than 32 mm in diameter properly secured to the ship if required by the pilot; manropes shall be fixed at the rope end to the ring plate fixed on deck and shall be ready for use when the pilot disembarks, or upon request from a pilot approaching to board (the manropes shall reach the height of the stanchions or bulwarks at the point of access to the deck before terminating at the ring plate on deck);

.2 a lifebuoy equipped with a self-igniting light;

.3 a heaving line.

7.2 When required by paragraph 4 above, stanchions and bulwark ladders shall be provided.

8 Lighting

Adequate lighting shall be provided to illuminate the transfer arrangements overside and the position on deck where a person embarks or disembarks.

Regulation 24
Use of heading and/or track control systems

1 In areas of high traffic density, in conditions of restricted visibility and in all other hazardous navigational situations where heading and/or track control systems are in use, it shall be possible to establish manual control of the ship's steering immediately.

2 In circumstances as above, the officer in charge of the navigational watch shall have available without delay the services of a qualified helmsperson who shall be ready at all times to take over steering control.

3 The change-over from automatic to manual steering and vice versa shall be made by, or under the supervision of, a responsible officer.

4 The manual steering shall be tested after prolonged use of heading and/or track control systems and before entering areas where navigation demands special caution.

Regulation 25
Operation of steering gear

In areas where navigation demands special caution, ships shall have more than one steering gear power unit in operation when such units are capable of simultaneous operation.

7　相关设备

7.1　须在易取处配备下列相关设备,以备在人员登离船时随时使用:

.1　两根扶手绳,直径不小于 28 mm 且不大于 32 mm,牢固地系在船上(如引航员有要求);扶手绳的一端须固定在甲板的眼环上,当引航员离船或即将登轮的引航员要求使用时即可使用(在登上甲板处,扶手绳一端系于眼环,自支柱顶端或舷墙的最高处穿过向舷外垂下);

.2　带有自亮灯的救生圈;

.3　撇缆绳。

7.2　为满足在本条第 4 款要求,应配备支柱和舷墙梯。

8　照明

应配备充足照明,以照亮舷外的登离船装置和甲板上人员登离船位置。

第 24 条
首向和/或航迹控制系统的使用

1　如在海上交通密度大的区域,能见度受限制的条件下以及所有其他危及航行的情况下使用首向和/或航迹控制系统,应能实现立即转为人工操舵。

2　在上述情况下,应及时为值班驾驶员配备 1 名适任的舵工,随时准备接过操舵工作。

3　从自动操舵转换为人工操舵,以及从人工操舵换为自动操舵,应由 1 名负责的驾驶员操作或在其监督下进行操作。

4　在长期使用首向和/或航迹控制系统以后,以及在进入需要特别谨慎驾驶的区域以前,均应试验人工操舵。

第 25 条
操舵装置的操作

在需要特别谨慎驾驶的区域,船舶操舵装置应有 1 个以上的电源在工作,且这些电源可以同时工作。

Regulation 26
Steering gear: testing and drills

1 Within 12 hours before departure, the ship's steering gear shall be checked and tested by the ship's crew. The test procedure shall include, where applicable, the operation of the following:

.1 the main steering gear;

.2 the auxiliary steering gear;

.3 the remote steering gear control systems;

.4 the steering positions located on the navigation bridge;

.5 the emergency power supply;

.6 the rudder angle indicators in relation to the actual position of the rudder;

.7 the remote steering gear control system power failure alarms;

.8 the steering gear power unit failure alarms; and

.9 automatic isolating arrangements and other automatic equipment.

2 The checks and tests shall include:

.1 the full movement of the rudder according to the required capabilities of the steering gear;

.2 a visual inspection of the steering gear and its connecting linkage; and

.3 the operation of the means of communication between the navigation bridge and steering gear compartment.

3.1 Simple operating instructions with a block diagram showing the change-over procedures for remote steering gear control systems and steering gear power units shall be permanently displayed on the navigation bridge and in the steering compartment.

3.2 All ships' officers concerned with the operation and/or maintenance of steering gear shall be familiar with the operation of the steering systems fitted on the ship and with the procedures for changing from one system to another.

4 In addition to the routine checks and tests prescribed in paragraphs 1 and 2, emergency steering drills shall take place at least once every three months in order to practise emergency steering procedures. These drills shall include direct control within the steering gear compartment, the communications procedure with the navigation bridge and, where applicable, the operation of alternative power supplies.

第26条
操舵装置:测试和演习

1　船舶开航前12 h内,船员应对操舵装置进行校验和测试。测试程序(如适用)应包括下述操作:

.1　主操舵装置;

.2　辅助操舵装置;

.3　操舵装置遥控系统;

.4　驾驶室内的操舵位置;

.5　应急电源;

.6　指示舵实际位置的舵角指示器;

.7　操舵装置遥控系统电力故障报警器;

.8　操舵装置电源故障报警器;和

.9　自动切断装置及其他自动设备。

2　校验和测试应包括:

.1　根据操舵装置能力进行的满舵操作;

.2　操舵装置及其联动部件的外观检查;和

.3　驾驶室与舵机室之间通信设备的操作。

3.1　在驾驶室及舵机室内,应永久展示操舵装置遥控系统和电源转换程序的操作流程示意图。

3.2　所有与操舵装置的操作和/或维护保养有关的高级船员,应熟悉船上所装的操舵系统的操作以及从一个系统转换到另一系统的程序。

4　除本条1和2款所述的常规校验和测试外,应至少每3个月进行一次应急操舵演习,以演练应急操舵程序。演习应包括在舵机室内的直接控制、与驾驶室的通信程序以及(如适用)转换电源的操作。

5 The Administration may waive the requirements to carry out the checks and tests prescribed in paragraphs 1 and 2 for ships which regularly engage on voyages of short duration. Such ships shall carry out these checks and tests at least once every week.

6 The date upon which the checks and tests prescribed in paragraphs 1 and 2 are carried out and the date and details of emergency steering drills carried out under paragraph 4 shall be recorded.

Regulation 27
Nautical charts and nautical publications

Nautical charts and nautical publications, such as sailing directions, lists of lights, notices to mariners, tide tables and all other nautical publications necessary for the intended voyage, shall be adequate and up to date.

Regulation 28
Records of navigational activities and daily reporting

1 All ships engaged on international voyages shall keep on board a record of navigational activities and incidents which are of importance to safety of navigation and which must contain sufficient detail to restore a complete record of the voyage, taking into account the recommendations adopted by the Organization.① When such information is not maintained in the ship's logbook, it shall be maintained in another form approved by the Administration.

2 Each ship of 500 gross tonnage and above, engaged on international voyages exceeding 48 hours, shall submit a daily report to its company, as defined in regulation IX/1, which shall retain it and all subsequent daily reports for the duration of the voyage. Daily reports may be transmitted by any means, provided that they are transmitted to the company as soon as practicable after determination of the position named in the report. Automated reporting systems may be used, provided that they include a recording function of their transmission and that those functions and interfaces with position-fixing equipment are subjected to regular verification by the ship's master. The report shall contain the following:

.1 ship's position;

.2 ship's course and speed; and

.3 details of any external or internal conditions that are affecting the ship's voyage or the normal safe operation of the ship.

---

① Refer to *Guidelines for the recording of events related to navigation* (resolution A.916(22)).

5　对于定期从事短程航行的船舶，主管机关可免除本条1和2所规定的核查和试验要求，但这些船舶应每周至少进行一次这样的校核和试验。

6　进行本条1和2规定的校验和测试的日期，以及进行本条4所述应急操舵演习的日期和详细内容应做记录。

第27条
海图和航海出版物

海图和航海出版物，如航路指南、灯标表、航海通告、潮汐表，以及预定航程所需的所有其他航海出版物均应充足并保持更新。

第28条
航行活动的记录和每日报告

1　所有从事国际航行的船舶应在船上保持一份有关航行活动和事件的记录，这些活动和事件系对航行安全有重要影响且记录中必须包括足以还原该航次的细节，并考虑到本组织通过的建议案①。如果船舶的航海日志中未记载这些信息，则应以主管机关认可的其他形式做记录。

2　每艘500总吨及以上、航程超过48 h的国际航行船舶应向其公司（第Ⅸ/1条所定义者）提交每日报告，公司应保留该报告和航行期间的所有后续每日报告。每日报告可通过任何方式发送，但应在报告中所述船位确定后尽快发送至公司。可使用自动报告系统，自动报告系统应具备对其发送内容的记录功能，并且这些功能以及与定位设备的接口应由船长定期核验。报告应包含下列内容：

.1　船舶的位置；

.2　船舶的航向和航速；和

.3　影响船舶航行或船舶正常安全营运的任何外部和内部状况的细节。

① 参见《与航行有关的事件记录导则》（第A.916(22)号决议）。

Regulation 29
Life-saving signals to be used by ships, aircraft or persons in distress

An illustrated table describing the life-saving signals① shall be readily available to the officer of the watch of every ship to which this chapter applies. The signals shall be used by ships or persons in distress when communicating with life-saving stations, maritime rescue units and aircraft engaged in search and rescue operations.

Regulation 30
Operational limitations

1 This regulation applies to all passenger ships to which chapter Ⅰ applies.

2 A list of all limitations on the operation of a passenger ship, including exemptions from any of these regulations, restrictions in operating areas, weather restrictions, sea state restrictions, restrictions in permissible loads, trim, speed and any other limitations, whether imposed by the Administration or established during the design or the building stages, shall be compiled before the passenger ship is put in service. The list, together with any necessary explanations, shall be documented in a form acceptable to the Administration, which shall be kept on board readily available to the master. The list shall be kept updated. If the language used is not English or French, the list shall be provided in one of the two languages.

Regulation 31
Danger messages

1 The master of every ship which meets with dangerous ice, a dangerous derelict, or any other direct danger to navigation, or a tropical storm, or encounters sub-freezing air temperatures associated with gale force winds causing severe ice accretion on superstructures, or winds of force 10 or above on the Beaufort scale for which no storm warning has been received, is bound to communicate the information by all means at his disposal to ships in the vicinity, and also to the competent authorities. The form in which the information is sent is not obligatory. It may be transmitted either in plain language (preferably English) or by means of the International Code of Signals.

2 Each Contracting Government will take all steps necessary to ensure that when intelligence of any of the dangers specified in paragraph 1 is received, it will be promptly brought to the knowledge of those concerned and communicated to other interested Governments.

3 The transmission of messages regarding the dangers specified is free of cost to the ships concerned.

---

① Such life-saving signals are described in the International Aeronautical and Maritime Search and Rescue (IAMSAR) Manual, Volume Ⅲ, Mobile Facilities, and illustrated in the International Code of Signals, as amended.

第 29 条
遇险船舶、飞机或人员使用的救生信号

凡适用本章的每艘船舶均应备有一份说明各种救生信号[①]的图表,供值班驾驶员随时取用。遇险船舶或人员在与救生站、海上救助单位和进行搜救作业的飞机通信时,均应使用这种信号。

第 30 条
操作限制

1　本条适用于所有适用第Ⅰ章的客船。

2　无论是由主管机关强制规定还是在设计或建造阶段就已确定的对客船的操作限制,均应在该客船投入使用之前编制一个所有这些操作限制的清单,清单中应包括对任何一条规定的免除、航区限制、天气限制、海况限制、容许负荷限制、纵倾限制、航速限制以及其他任何限制。该清单连同必要的说明应以主管机关可接受的格式,并应保存在船上供船长随时取用。该清单应保持更新。如该清单使用的语言既非英文也非法文,则应配有使用其中一种语言的文本。

第 31 条
危险通报

1　每艘船舶的船长如遇到危险的冰、危险废弃物,或其他任何影响航行的直接危险,或热带风暴,或遇到伴随强风的低于冰点的低温致使上层建筑严重结冰,或未曾收到暴风警报而遇到蒲福风级 10 级或 10 级以上的风力时,一定要通过各种方式将此信息通知附近各船及主管机关。发送这种信息的形式不限,可用明语(最好用英文)或按《国际信号规则》发送。

2　各缔约国政府应采取所有必要的措施,确保其在获悉本条 1 所述的任何危险的情报时,迅速通知有关各方并通报其他相关国家的政府。

3　向有关船舶发送的上述危险通报,不收费用。

---

① 这种救生信号详见《国际航空和海上搜救手册》(IAMSAR),第Ⅲ卷:移动设施,以及经修订的《国际信号规则》。

4 All radio messages issued under paragraph 1 shall be preceded by the safety signal, using the procedure as prescribed by the Radio Regulations as defined in regulation IV/2.

Regulation 32
Information required in danger messages

The following information is required in danger messages:

1 Ice, derelicts and other direct dangers to navigation:

.1 The kind of ice, derelict or danger observed.

.2 The position of the ice, derelict or danger when last observed.

.3 The time and date (Universal Coordinated Time) when the danger was last observed.

2 Tropical cyclones (storms):①

.1 A statement that a tropical cyclone has been encountered. This obligation should be interpreted in a broad spirit, and information transmitted whenever the master has good reason to believe that a tropical cyclone is developing or exists in the neighbourhood.

.2 Time, date (Universal Coordinated Time) and position of ship when the observation was taken.

.3 As much of the following information as is practicable should be included in the message:

- barometric pressure,② preferably corrected (stating millibars, millimetres, or inches, and whether corrected or uncorrected);
- barometric tendency (the change in barometric pressure during the past 3 hours);
- true wind direction;
- wind force (Beaufort scale);
- state of the sea (smooth, moderate, rough, high);
- swell (slight, moderate, heavy) and the true direction from which it comes. Period or length of swell (short, average, long) would also be of value;
- true course and speed of ship.

---

① The term *tropical cyclone* is the generic term used by national meteorological services of the World Meteorological Organization. The term *hurricane*, *typhoon*, *cyclone*, *severe tropical storm*, *etc.*, may also be used, depending on the geographical location.
② The standard international unit for barometric pressure is the hectopascal (hPa), which is numerically equivalent to the millibar (mbar).

4　根据本条第1款所发送的一切无线电通报应冠以安全信号，并按第Ⅳ/2条中定义的《无线电规则》所规定的程序办理。

第32条
危险通报内要求的信息

在危险通报内要求有下列信息：

1　冰、废弃物及其他影响航行的直接危险：

.1　所观测到的冰、废弃物或危险的种类。

.2　最后所观测到的冰、废弃物或危险的位置。

.3　最后所观测到的危险的时间和日期（协调世界时）。

2　热带气旋（风暴）[①]：

.1　遭遇热带气旋的报告。这项义务应从广义理解，每当船长有充分理由确信附近正在形成或存在热带气旋时，即须发送信息。

.2　观测的时间、日期（协调世界时）和船舶的位置。

.3　在通报内应尽可能包括下列信息：

— 气压[②]，最好是修正过的气压（注明其为mbar、mm或in以及是否已经修正）；

— 气压趋势（过去3 h内气压的变化）；

— 真风向；

— 风力（蒲福风级）；

— 海况（小浪，中浪，大浪，巨浪）；

— 涌浪（低，中，巨）及涌浪来自的真方向。涌浪的周期或长度（短，中，长）也会有重要性；

— 船舶真航向及航速。

---

① “热带气旋”一词为世界气象组织所属各国气象服务机构的通用术语。也可使用飓风、台风、气旋、强热带风暴等词语，取决于地理位置。

② 气压的标准国际单位为百帕（hPa），在数值上与毫巴（mbar）相等。

Subsequent observations

3 When a master has reported a tropical cyclone or other dangerous storm, it is desirable, but not obligatory, that further observations be made and transmitted hourly, if practicable, but in any case at intervals of not more than 3 hours, so long as the ship remains under the influence of the storm.

4 Winds of force 10 or above on the Beaufort scale for which no storm warning has been received. This is intended to deal with storms other than the tropical cyclones referred to in paragraph 2; when such a storm is encountered, the message should contain similar information to that listed under the paragraph but excluding the details concerning sea and swell.

5 Sub-freezing air temperatures associated with gale force winds causing severe ice accretion on superstructures:

.1 Time and date (Universal Coordinated Time).

.2 Air temperature.

.3 Sea temperature (if practicable).

.4 Wind force and direction.

Examples

Ice

TTT ICE. LARGE BERG SIGHTED IN 4506 N, 4410 W, AT 0800 UTC. MAY 15.

Derelicts

TTT DERELICT. OBSERVED DERELICT ALMOST SUBMERGED IN 4006 N, 1243 W, AT 1630 UTC. APRIL 21.

Danger to navigation

TTT NAVIGATION. ALPHA LIGHTSHIP NOT ON STATION. 1800 UTC. JANUARY 3.

Tropical cyclone

TTT STORM. 0030 UTC. AUGUST 18. 2004 N, 11354 E. BAROMETER CORRECTED 994 MILLIBARS, TENDENCY DOWN 6 MILLIBARS. WIND NW, FORCE 9, HEAVY SQUALLS. HEAVY EASTERLY SWELL. COURSE 067, 5 KNOTS.

TTT STORM. APPEARANCES INDICATE APPROACH OF HURRICANE. 1300 UTC. SEPTEMBER 14. 2200 N, 7236 W. BAROMETER CORRECTED 29.64 INCHES, TENDENCY DOWN .015 INCHES. WIND NE, FORCE 8, FREQUENT RAIN SQUALLS. COURSE 035, 9 KNOTS.

TTT STORM. CONDITIONS INDICATE INTENSE CYCLONE HAS FORMED. 0200 UTC. MAY 4. 1620 N, 9203 E. BAROMETER UNCORRECTED 753 MILLIMETRES, TENDENCY DOWN 5 MILLIMETRES. WIND S BY W, FORCE 5. COURSE 300, 8 KNOTS.

后续观测

3　在船长已报告热带气旋或其他危险的风暴后，只要该船仍处于受风暴影响的情况下，建议船长（但非强制性）在可行时做进一步观测并每小时发一次通报，但无论如何间隔时间不宜超过 3 h。

4　虽未收到风暴警报而风力已达蒲福风级 10 级或 10 级以上。这里意指除本条 2 所述热带气旋以外的其他风暴；当遇到这种风暴时，通报中应包括本节所列的类似信息，但不包括有关海浪和涌浪的细节。

5　伴随强风的低于冰点的低温致使上层建筑严重结冰：

.1　时间和日期（协调世界时）。

.2　气温。

.3　海水温度（如可行）。

.4　风力和风向。

举例

冰

TTT 冰。5 月 15 日协调世界时 08 点 00 分在北纬 45°06′，西经 44°10′发现大冰山。

废弃物

TTT 废弃物。4 月 21 日协调世界时 16 点 30 分在北纬 40°06′，西经 12°43′观测到几乎淹没的废弃物。

航行危险

TTT 航行。1 月 3 日协调世界时 18 点 00 分。A 灯船不在原位。

热带气旋

TTT 风暴。8 月 18 日协调世界时 00 点 30 分。在北纬 20°04′，西经 113°54′。修正气压 994 mbar，趋势下降 6 mbar。西北风，风力 9 级，烈飑。巨涌偏东向。航向 067°，航速 5 kn。

TTT 风暴。飓风接近的迹象。9 月 14 日协调世界时 13 点 00 分。北纬 22°00′，西经 72°36′。修正气压 29.64 英寸汞柱，趋势下降 0.015 英寸汞柱。东北风，风力 8 级，暴雨频繁。航向 035°，航速 9 kn。

TTT 风暴。情况表明已形成强气旋。5 月 4 日协调世界时 02 点 00 分。北纬 16°20′，东经 92°03′。未修正气压 753 mm，趋势下降 5 mm。风向南偏西，风力 5 级。航向 300°，航速 8 kn。

TTT STORM. TYPHOON TO SOUTHEAST. 0300 UTC. JUNE 12. 1812 N, 12605 E. BAROMETER FALLING RAPIDLY. WIND INCREASING FROM N.

TTT STORM. WIND FORCE 11, NO STORM WARNING RECEIVED. 0300 UTC. MAY 4. 4830 N, 30 W. BAROMETER CORRECTED 983 MILLIBARS, TENDENCY DOWN 4 MILLIBARS. WIND SW, FORCE 11 VEERING. COURSE 260, 6 KNOTS.

Icing

TTT EXPERIENCING SEVERE ICING. 1400 UTC. MARCH 2. 69 N, 10 W. AIR TEMPERATURE 18 ℉ (−7.8 ℃). SEA TEMPERATURE 29 ℉ (−1.7 ℃). WIND NE, FORCE 8.

Regulation 33
Distress situations: obligations and procedures

1 The master of a ship at sea which is in a position to be able to provide assistance, on receiving information from any source that persons are in distress at sea, is bound to proceed with all speed to their assistance, if possible informing them or the search and rescue service that the ship is doing so. This obligation to provide assistance applies regardless of the nationality or status of such persons or the circumstances in which they are found. If the ship receiving the distress alert is unable or, in the special circumstances of the case, considers it unreasonable or unnecessary to proceed to their assistance, the master must enter in the logbook the reason for failing to proceed to the assistance of the persons in distress, taking into account the recommendation of the Organization to inform the appropriate search and rescue service accordingly.

1-1 Contracting Governments shall coordinate and cooperate to ensure that masters of ships providing assistance by embarking persons in distress at sea are released from their obligations with minimum further deviation from the ships' intended voyage, provided that releasing the master of the ship from the obligations under the current regulation does not further endanger the safety of life at sea. The Contracting Government responsible for the search and rescue region in which such assistance is rendered shall exercise primary responsibility for ensuring such coordination and cooperation occurs, so that survivors assisted are disembarked from the assisting ship and delivered to a place of safety, taking into account the particular circumstances of the case and guidelines developed by the Organization.[①] In these cases the relevant Contracting Governments shall arrange for such disembarkation to be effected as soon as reasonably practicable.

2 The master of a ship in distress or the search and rescue service concerned, after consultation, so far as may be possible, with the masters of ships which answer the distress alert, has the right to requisition one or more of those ships as the master of the ship in distress or the search and rescue service considers best able to render assistance, and it shall be the duty of the master or masters of the ship or ships requisitioned to comply with the requisition by continuing to proceed with all speed to the assistance of persons in distress.

---

① Refer to Guidelines on the treatment of persons rescued at sea (resolution MSC.167(78)).

TTT 风暴。台风在东南方向。6 月 12 日协调世界时 03 点 00 分。北纬 18°12′，东经 126°05′。气压急速下降。北风在增强中。

TTT 风暴。风力 11 级,未收到暴风警报。5 月 4 日协调世界时 03 点 00 分。北纬 48°30′,西经 30°。修正气压 983 mbar,趋势下降 4 mbar。西南风,风力 11 级,顺时针转向。航向 260°，航速 6 kn。

冰冻

TTT 经受严重冰冻。3 月 2 日协调世界时 14 点 00 分。北纬 69°,西经 10°。气温 18 ℉(−7.8 ℃)，海水温度 29 ℉(−1.7 ℃)。东北风,风力 8 级。

第 33 条
遇险情况:义务和程序

1　处于能提供援助位置的船舶的船长,在收到来自任何关于海上人员遇险的信息后,有义务立即全速前往提供援助,如有可能通知遇险人员或搜救机构,本船正在全速前往援助中。不论遇险人员的国籍或身份或其被发现时的状况,均适用此提供援助的义务。如果收到遇险报警的船舶不能前往援助,或因情况特殊认为前往援助不合理或不必要,该船长必须将未能前往援助遇险人员的理由载入航海日志,并考虑到本组织的建议,通知相应的搜救机构。

1-1　缔约国政府应协调合作,确保免除救起海上遇险人员的船舶的船长的义务,让其在此后以最低程度偏离船舶原定航线,但对船长免除本条规定的义务不得进一步危及海上人命安全。对该援助活动所在的搜救区域负有责任的缔约国政府应对确保进行这种协调合作履行首要责任,使被救援的幸存者从救援船上岸并送至安全地点,并考虑到特定情况和本组织制定的指南①。为此,有关缔约国政府应在合理可行的范围内尽快安排获救者离船。

2　遇险船舶的船长或有关的搜救机构在尽可能与应答了遇险信号的各船船长协商后,有权召请其中被遇险船舶的船长或搜救机构认为最有能力给予援助的 1 艘或数艘船舶,被召请的 1 艘或数艘船舶的船长有义务履行应召,继续全速前往援助遇险人员。

① 参见《海上获救人员救护导则》(第 MSC.167(78)号决议)。

3 Masters of ships shall be released from the obligation imposed by paragraph 1 on learning that their ships have not been requisitioned and that one or more other ships have been requisitioned and are complying with the requisition. This decision shall, if possible, be communicated to the other requisitioned ships and to the search and rescue service.

4 The master of a ship shall be released from the obligation imposed by paragraph 1 and, if his ship has been requisitioned, from the obligation imposed by paragraph 2 on being informed by the persons in distress or by the search and rescue service or by the master of another ship which has reached such persons that assistance is no longer necessary.

5 The provisions of this regulation do not prejudice the Convention for the Unification of Certain Rules of Law relating to Assistance and Salvage at Sea, signed at Brussels on 23 September 1910, particularly the obligation to render assistance imposed by article 11 of that Convention.[①]

6 Masters of ships who have embarked persons in distress at sea shall treat them with humanity, within the capabilities and limitations of the ship.

Regulation 34
Safe navigation and avoidance of dangerous situations

1 Prior to proceeding to sea, the master shall ensure that the intended voyage has been planned using the appropriate nautical charts and nautical publications for the area concerned, taking into account the guidelines and recommendations developed by the Organization.[②]

2 The voyage plan shall identify a route which:

.1 takes into account any relevant ships' routeing systems;

.2 ensures sufficient sea room for the safe passage of the ship throughout the voyage;

.3 anticipates all known navigational hazards and adverse weather conditions; and

.4 takes into account the marine environmental protection measures that apply, and avoids, as far as possible, actions and activities which could cause damage to the environment.

Regulation 34-1
Master's discretion

The owner, the charterer, the company operating the ship as defined in regulation Ⅸ/1, or any other person shall not prevent or restrict the master of the ship from taking or executing any decision which, in the master's professional judgement, is necessary for safety of life at sea and protection of the marine environment.

---

① Refer to the International Convention on Salvage, 1989, done at London on 28 April 1989, entered into force on 14 July 1996.

② Refer to *Guidelines for voyage planning* (resolution A.893(21)).

3　当船长获知1艘或数艘其他船舶已被召请并正在履行应召,而其船舶未被召请时,应予解除本条1所责成的义务。如有可能,应将这个决定通知其他被召请的船舶和搜救机构。

4　当一艘船舶的船长从遇险人员或搜救机构或已抵达遇险人员处的另一船舶的船长处获知不再需要提供援助时,应予解除本条1所责成的义务,如果其船舶已被召请,则予解除本条2所责成的义务。

5　本条规定与1910年9月23日在布鲁塞尔签订的《关于统一海上救助若干法规的公约》并无抵触,特别是该公约①第11条所责成的援助义务。

6　救起海上遇险人员的船舶的船长应在本船能力和条件范围内,给予他们人道待遇。

第34条
安全航行和避险

1　船长在开航前应考虑到本组织制定的指南和建议案②,确保预定航程已根据有关区域的相应海图和航海出版物制订了计划。

2　航程计划应确定一条航线,该航线:

.1　考虑到任何相关的船舶定线制;

.2　确保船舶在整个航程中有足够的宽阔水域安全通过;

.3　预计所有已知的航行危险和不利的天气条件;和

.4　考虑到适用的海洋环境保护措施,并尽可能避免可能对环境造成破坏的行为和活动。

第34-1条
船长决定权

船东,租船人,第Ⅸ/1条所定义的船舶经营公司,或任何他人均不得阻止或限制船长根据其专业判断做出或执行为海上人命安全和保护海洋环境所必需的任何决定。

① 参见1989年4月28日在伦敦通过,1996年7月14日生效的《1989年国际救助公约》。
② 参见《航次计划指南》(第A.893(21)号决议)。

Regulation 35
Misuse of distress signals

The use of an international distress signal, except for the purpose of indicating that a person or persons are in distress, and the use of any signal which may be confused with an international distress signal are prohibited.

第35条
遇险信号的误用

除用于表示人员遇险外,禁止使用国际遇险信号及任何可能与国际遇险信号相混淆的信号。

Appendix
Rules for the management, operation and financing of the North Atlantic Ice Patrol

1 In these Rules:

.1 Ice season means the annual period between 15 February and 1 July.

.2 Region of icebergs guarded by the Ice Patrol means the south-eastern, southern and south-western limits of the region of icebergs in the vicinity of the Grand Banks of Newfoundland.

.3 Routes passing through regions of icebergs guarded by the Ice Patrol means:

.1 routes between Atlantic coast ports of Canada (including inland ports approached from the North Atlantic through the Gut of Canso and Cabot Straits) and ports of Europe, Asia or Africa approached from the North Atlantic through or north of the Straits of Gibraltar (except routes which pass south of the extreme limits of ice of all types);

.2 routes via Cape Race, Newfoundland, between Atlantic coast ports of Canada (including inland ports approached from the North Atlantic through the Gut of Canso and Cabot Straits) west of Cape Race, Newfoundland, and Atlantic coast ports of Canada north of Cape Race, Newfoundland;

.3 routes between Atlantic and Gulf Coast ports of the United States of America (including inland ports approached from the North Atlantic through the Gut of Canso and Cabot Straits) and ports of Europe, Asia or Africa approached from the North Atlantic through or north of the Straits of Gibraltar (except routes which pass south of the extreme limits of ice of all types);

.4 routes via Cape Race, Newfoundland, between Atlantic and Gulf Coast ports of the United States of America (including inland ports approached from the North Atlantic through the Gut of Canso and Cabot Straits) and Atlantic Coast ports of Canada north of Cape Race, Newfoundland.

.4 Extreme limits of ice of all types in the North Atlantic Ocean is defined by a line connecting the following points:

A—42°23′.00 N, 59°25′.00 W
B—41°23′.00 N, 57°00′.00 W
C—40°47′.00 N, 55°00′.00 W
D—40°07′.00 N, 53°00′.00 W
E—39°18′.00 N, 49°39′.00 W
F—38°00′.00 N, 47°35′.00 W
J—39°49′.00 N, 41°00′.00 W
K—40°39′.00 N, 39°00′.00 W
L—41°19′.00 N, 38°00′.00 W
M—43°00′.00 N, 37°27′.00 W
N—44°00′.00 N, 37°29′.00 W
O—46°00′.00 N, 37°55′.00 W

附录
北大西洋冰区巡逻的管理、运作和费用规则

1　在这些规则中：

.1　冰季系指每年2月15日至7月1日这段时期。

.2　冰区巡逻所警戒冰山区系指纽芬兰大浅滩附近冰山区的东南、南及西南限界。

.3　穿越冰区巡逻所警戒冰山区的航线系指：

.1　在加拿大的北大西洋沿岸各港口（包括从北大西洋经坎索水道和卡伯特海峡抵达的内陆港口）和从北大西洋经直布罗陀海峡或直布罗陀海峡以北抵达的欧洲、亚洲或非洲各港口之间的航线（经过各类冰区最南限界的航线除外）；

.2　在纽芬兰累斯角西部的加拿大北大西洋沿岸各港口（包括从北大西洋经坎索水道和卡伯特海峡抵达的内陆港口）和纽芬兰累斯角北部的加拿大北大西洋沿岸各港口之间经纽芬兰累斯角的航线；

.3　在美国的大西洋和海湾沿岸各港口（包括从北大西洋经坎索水道和卡伯特海峡抵达的内陆港口）和从北大西洋经直布罗陀海峡或直布罗陀海峡以北抵达的欧洲、亚洲或非洲各港口之间的航线（经过各类冰区最南限界的航线除外）；

.4　在美国的大西洋和海湾沿岸各港口（包括从北大西洋经坎索水道和卡伯特海峡抵达的内陆港口）和纽芬兰累斯角北部的加拿大北大西洋沿岸各港口之间经纽芬兰累斯角的航线。

.4　各类冰区的最终限界在北大西洋中系由连接下列各点的一条线限定：

A——北纬42°23′.00，西经59°25′.00　J——北纬39°49′.00，西经41°00′.00

B——北纬41°23′.00，西经57°00′.00　K——北纬40°39′.00，西经39°00′.00

C——北纬40°47′.00，西经55°00′.00　L——北纬41°19′.00，西经38°00′.00

D——北纬40°07′.00，西经53°00′.00　M——北纬43°00′.00，西经37°27′.00

E——北纬39°18′.00，西经49°39′.00　N——北纬44°00′.00，西经37°29′.00

F——北纬38°00′.00，西经47°35′.00　O——北纬46°00′.00，西经37°55′.00

G—37°41′.00 N, 46°40′.00 W	P—48°00′.00 N, 38°28′.00 W
H—38°00′.00 N, 45°33′.00 W	Q—50°00′.00 N, 39°07′.00 W
I—39°05′.00 N, 43°00′.00 W	R—51°25′.00 N, 39°45′.00 W.

.5 Managing and operating means maintaining, administering and operating the Ice Patrol, including the dissemination of information received therefrom.

.6 Contributing Government means a Contracting Government undertaking to contribute to the costs of the Ice Patrol Service pursuant to these Rules.

2 Each Contracting Government specially interested in these services whose ships pass through the region of icebergs during the ice season undertakes to contribute to the Government of the United States of America its proportionate share of the costs for the management and operation of the Ice Patrol Service. The contribution to the Government of the United States of America shall be based on the ratio which the average annual gross tonnage of that contributing Government's ships passing through the region of icebergs guarded by the Ice Patrol during the previous three ice seasons bears to the combined average annual gross tonnage of all ships that passed through the region of icebergs guarded by the Ice Patrol during the previous three ice seasons.

3 All contributions shall be calculated by multiplying the ratio described in paragraph 2 by the average actual annual cost incurred by the Governments of the United States of America and Canada of managing and operating ice patrol services during the previous three years. This ratio shall be computed annually, and shall be expressed in terms of a lump sum per-annum fee.

4 Each of the contributing Governments has the right to alter or discontinue its contribution, and other interested Governments may undertake to contribute to the expense. The contributing Government which avails itself of this right will continue to be responsible for its current contribution up to 1 September following the date of giving notice of intention to alter or discontinue its contribution. To take advantage of the said right it must give notice to the managing Government at least six months before the said 1 September.

5 Each contributing Government shall notify the Secretary-General of its undertaking pursuant to paragraph 2, who shall notify all Contracting Governments.

6 The Government of the United States of America shall furnish annually to each contributing Government a statement of the total cost incurred by the Governments of the United States of America and Canada of managing and operating the Ice Patrol for that year and of the average percentage share for the past three years of each contributing Government.

7 The managing Government shall publish annual accounts including a statement of costs incurred by the Governments providing the services for the past three years and the total gross tonnage using the service for the past three years. The accounts shall be publicly available. Within three months after having received the cost statement, contributing Governments may request more detailed information regarding the costs incurred in managing and operating the Ice Patrol.

8 These Rules shall be operative beginning with the ice season of 2002.

G——北纬 37°41′.00,西经 46°40′.00 P——北纬 48°00′.00,西经 38°28′.00

H——北纬 38°00′.00,西经 45°33′.00 Q——北纬 50°00′.00,西经 39°07′.00

I——北纬 39°05′.00,西经 43°00′.00 R——北纬 51°25′.00,西经 39°45′.00。

.5 管理和运作系指冰区巡逻的保持、行政管理和运作,包括传播由此所收到的信息。

.6 分摊国政府系指遵照本规则承担义务分摊冰区巡逻服务费用的缔约国政府。

2 与这些服务有特殊利害关系且在冰季有船舶穿越冰山区的各缔约国政府,承担义务按比例分摊美利坚合众国政府用于冰区巡逻服务的管理和运作的费用。付给美利坚合众国政府的分摊份额,应根据前三个冰季内各分摊国穿越冰区巡逻所警戒冰山区的船舶的平均年总吨位在前三个冰季内穿越冰区巡逻所警戒冰山区的所有船舶的平均年总吨位中所占比例计取。

3 所有分摊份额的计算,均应为以上 2 所述比例乘以前三年内美利坚合众国政府和加拿大政府为管理和运作冰区巡逻服务所负担的平均实际年度费用。该比例应每年计算一次,并应以年度总付费额表示。

4 每个分摊国政府有权变更或中止其分摊份额,而其他有关政府可以承担义务分摊该项费用。运用这项权利的分摊国政府仍应继续负担其现有分摊份额,直至变更或中止其分摊份额的通知发出之日以后的 9 月 1 日为止。在利用该项权利时,该分摊国必须在上述 9 月 1 日以前至少 6 个月通知管理国政府。

5 各缔约国政府应将其遵照以上 2 所承担的义务通知秘书长,并应由秘书长通知所有缔约国政府。

6 美利坚合众国政府应每年向各分摊国政府提供一份结单,列明美利坚合众国政府和加拿大政府该年为管理和经营冰区巡逻所负担的总费用以及过去 3 年中各分摊国政府所分担的平均百分比份额。

7 管理国政府应公布年度账单,包括一份关于提供该项服务的各国政府在过去 3 年中所负担的费用以及过去 3 年中使用该项服务的船舶总吨位的结单。这些账单应可公开查阅。在收到费用结单后的 3 个月内,分摊国政府可以要求有关为管理和运作冰区巡逻所负担费用的更详细的资料。

8 本规则应于 2002 年冰季起开始施行。

Chapter Ⅵ Carriage of cargoes and oil fuels

第Ⅵ章　货物和燃油运输

Part A
General provisions

Regulation 1
Application

1 Unless expressly provided otherwise, this chapter applies to the carriage of cargoes (except liquids in bulk, gases in bulk and those aspects of carriage covered by other chapters) which, owing to their particular hazards to ships or persons on board, may require special precautions in all ships to which the present regulations apply and in cargo ships of less than 500 gross tonnage. However, for cargo ships of less than 500 gross tonnage, the Administration, if it considers that the sheltered nature and conditions of voyage are such as to render the application of any specific requirements of part A or B of this chapter unreasonable or unnecessary, may take other effective measures to ensure the required safety for these ships.

2 To supplement the provisions of parts A and B of this chapter, each Contracting Government shall ensure that appropriate information on cargo and its stowage and securing is provided, specifying, in particular, precautions necessary for the safe carriage of such cargoes.①

Regulation 1-1
Definition

For the purpose of this chapter, unless expressly provided otherwise, the following definitions shall apply:

1 *IMSBC Code* means the International Maritime Solid Bulk Cargoes (IMSBC) Code adopted by the Maritime Safety Committee of the Organization by resolution MSC.268(85), as may be amended by the Organization, provided that such amendments are adopted, brought into force and take effect in accordance with the provisions of article Ⅷ of the present Convention concerning the amendment procedures applicable to the annex other than chapter Ⅰ.

2 *Solid bulk cargo* means any cargo, other than liquid or gas, consisting of a combination of particles, granules or any larger pieces of material generally uniform in composition, which is loaded directly into the cargo spaces of a ship without any intermediate form of containment.

---

① Refer to:

.1 the *Code of Safe Practice for Cargo Stowage and Securing* (resolution A.714(17), as amended);

.2 the *Code of Safe Practice for Ships Carrying Timber Deck Cargoes, 2011* (2011 TDC Code) (resolution A.1048(27)), *Guidance note on precautions to be taken by the masters of ships of below 100 metres in length engaged in the carriage of logs* (MSC/Circ.525), and *Guidance note on precautions to be taken by masters of ships engaged in the carriage of timber cargoes* (MSC/Circ.548); and

.3 the IMSBC Code (resolution MSC.268(85), as amended).

A 部分
一般规定

第 1 条
适用范围

1 除有另有明文规定外,本章适用于对船舶或船上人员具有特殊危害的货物运输(散装液体、散装气体和其他各章已做出运输规定者除外),并因其运输的危险性而需在本规则适用的所有船舶以及小于 500 总吨的货船上采取特别预防措施。但是,对小于 500 总吨的货船,如果主管机关认为因航行的遮蔽性和条件,应用本章 A 部分或 B 部分的任何具体要求为不合理或不必要时,可采取能够确保这些船舶所需安全的其他有效措施。

2 作为本章 A 部分和 B 部分规定的补充,各缔约国政府应确保提供有关货物及其积载和系固的相应资料,特别应说明安全运输此类货物所必需的预防措施。①

第 1-1 条
定义

除另有明文规定,就本章而言,以下定义适用:

1 **国际固体散货规则**系指本组织海上安全委员会经第 MSC.268(85)号决议通过的《国际海运固体散装货物规则》(国际散货规则)。此规则可由本组织加以修正,但修正案要按照现公约第Ⅷ条有关适用于除第 1 章之外其他附件的修正程序的规定而通过,生效和实施;

2 **固体散装货物**系指除液体或气体之外,任何由通常构成一致的材料的微粒、颗粒或任何较大碎块的组合构成,直接装入船舶货舱,没有任何中间包装的货物。

① 参见:
.1 本组织第 A.714(17)号决议通过并经修正的《货物积载和系固安全操作规则》;
.2 本组织第 A.1048(27)号决议通过并经修正的《船舶载运木材甲板货安全操作规则》(2011 年 TDC 规则);第 MSC/Circ.525 号通函《船长小于 100 m 从事圆木运输的船舶船长应采取的预防措施导则》以及第 MSC/Circ.548 号通函《从事木材货物运输的船舶船长应采取的预防措施导则》;和
.3 本组织第 MSC.268(85)号决议通过的《国际海运固体散货(IMSBC)规则》。

Regulation 1-2
Requirements for the carriage of solid bulk cargoes other than grain

The carriage of solid bulk cargoes other than grain shall be in compliance with the relevant provisions of the IMSBC Code.

Regulation 2
Cargo information

1 The shipper shall provide the master or his representative with appropriate information on the cargo sufficiently in advance of loading to enable the precautions which may be necessary for proper stowage and safe carriage of the cargo to be put into effect. Such information① shall be confirmed in writing② and by appropriate shipping documents prior to loading the cargo on the ship.

2 The cargo information shall include:

.1 in the case of general cargo, and of cargo carried in cargo units, a general description of the cargo, the gross mass of the cargo or of the cargo units, and any relevant special properties of the cargo. For the purpose of this regulation the cargo information required in sub-chapter 1.9 of the Code of Safe Practice for Cargo Stowage and Securing, adopted by the Organization by resolution A.714(17), as may be amended, shall be provided. Any such amendment to sub-chapter 1.9 shall be adopted, brought into force and take effect in accordance with the provisions of article Ⅷ of the present Convention concerning the amendment procedures applicable to the annex other than chapter Ⅰ;

.2 in the case of solid bulk cargo, information as required by section 4 of the IMSBC Code.

3 Prior to loading cargo units on board ships, the shipper shall ensure that the gross mass of such units is in accordance with the gross mass declared on the shipping documents.

4 In the case of cargo carried in a container,③ except for containers carried on a chassis or a trailer when such containers are driven on or off a ro-ro ship engaged in short international voyages as defined in regulation Ⅲ/3, the gross mass according to paragraph 2.1 of this regulation shall be verified by the shipper, either by:

.1 weighing the packed container using calibrated and certified equipment; or

---

① Refer to *Form for cargo information* (MSC/Circ.663).

② Reference to documents in this regulation does not preclude the use of electronic data processing (EDP) and electronic data interchange (EDI) transmission techniques as an aid to paper documentation.

③ The term *container* should be considered as having the same meaning as defined and applied in the International Convention for Safe Containers (CSC), 1972, as amended, taking into account *Guidelines for the approval of offshore containers handled in open seas* (MSC/Circ.860) and *Revised recommendations on harmonized interpretation and implementation of the International Convention for Safe Containers, 1972, as amended* (CSC.1/Circ.138/Rev.1).

第 1-2 条
除谷物外其他固体散货的载运要求

载运谷物食以外的固体散装货物须符合国际固体散货规则的相关规定。

第 2 条
货物资料

1 托运人应在装货前及早向船长或其代表提供关于该货物的相应资料,以便能实施为此种货物的正确积载和安全运输可能是必需的预防措施。此类资料①应在货物装船前以书面形式②和相应的运输单证予以确认。

2 货物资料应包括:

.1 对于杂货和以货物单元运输的货物,应有货物的一般说明、货物或货物单元的毛重和货物的任何有关特性。就本条而言,应提供本组织第 A.714(17)号决议通过并可能经修正的《货物积载和系固安全操作规则》第 1.9 节所要求的货物资料。对第 1.9 节的任何此种修正案应按本公约第Ⅷ条有关适用于除第Ⅰ章外的附则修正程序的规定予以通过、生效和实施;

.2 如果为固体散货,则国际散货规则第 4 节所要求的资料。

3 在货物单元装船前,托运人应确保这类货物单元的毛重与运输单证中表明的毛重一致。

4 对于集装箱装运的货物③,符合本条第 2.1 款的毛重应经托运人以下列方式之一予以验证,但在从事第Ⅲ/3 条界定的短程国际航行的滚装船上装卸的、以底盘车或拖车载运的集装箱除外:

.1 使用经校准和认证的设备对装货集装箱称重;或

---

① 参见第 MSC/Circ.663 号通函《货物资料表》。

② 本条所指的单证并不排除作为书面文件的一种辅助手段而使用电子数据处理(EDP)和电子数据交换(EDI)的传输技术。

③ 术语"集装箱"应视为与经修正的《1972 年国际集装箱安全公约》(CSC)以及《公海上操作的海上集装箱认可指南》(第 MSC/Circ.860 号通函)和经修正的《经修订的 1972 年国际集装箱安全公约协调解释和实施建议案》(第 CSC.1/Circ.138/Rev.1 号通函)中定义和适用的"集装箱"具有相同含义。

.2 weighing all packages and cargo items, including the mass of pallets, dunnage and other securing material to be packed in the container and adding the tare mass of the container to the sum of the single masses, using a certified method approved by the competent authority of the State in which packing of the container was completed.

5 The shipper of a container shall ensure the verified gross mass① is stated in the shipping document. The shipping document shall be:

.1 signed by a person duly authorized by the shipper; and

.2 submitted to the master or his representative and to the terminal representative sufficiently in advance, as required by the master or his representative, to be used in the preparation of the ship stowage plan.②

6 If the shipping document, with regard to a packed container, does not provide the verified gross mass and the master or his representative and the terminal representative have not obtained the verified gross mass of the packed container, it shall not be loaded on to the ship.

Regulation 3
Oxygen analysis and gas detection equipment

1 When transporting a solid bulk cargo which is liable to emit a toxic or flammable gas, or cause oxygen depletion in the cargo space, an appropriate instrument for measuring the concentration of gas or oxygen in the air shall be provided together with detailed instructions for its use. Such an instrument shall be to the satisfaction of the Administration.

2 The Administration shall take steps to ensure that crews of ships are trained in the use of such instruments.

Regulation 4
The use of pesticides in ships③

Appropriate precautions shall be taken in the use of pesticides in ships, in particular for the purposes of fumigation.

---

① Refer to *Guidelines regarding the verified gross mass of a container carrying cargo* (MSC.1/Circ.1475).

② This document may be presented by means of EDP or EDI transmission techniques. The signature may be an electronic signature or may be replaced by the name, in capitals, of the person authorized to sign.

③ Refer to:

.1 *Revised recommendations on the safe use of pesticides in ships* (MSC./Circ.1358);

.2 *Recommendations on the safe use of pesticides in ships applicable to the fumigation of cargo holds* (MSC./Circ.1264, as amended); and

.3 *Revised recommendations on the safe use of pesticides in ships applicable to the fumigation of cargo transport units* (MSC.1/Circ.1361).

.2　对所有包装件和货品进行称重,包括货盘、货垫和其他装入集装箱的系固材料的质量,并使用完成集装箱包装所在国主管当局批准的经认证方法,将集装箱皮质量与前述各项质量之和相加。

5　集装箱托运人须确保运输单证中已载明经验证的毛重①。运输单证须:

.1　由经托运人正式授权的人员签字;和

.2　应船长或其代表的要求,提前足够时间提交给船长或其代表及提交给码头代表,以用于编制船舶积载图②。

6　如果装货集装箱的运输单证上没有提供经验证的毛重,且船长或其代表及码头代表尚未收到该装货集装箱经核实的毛重,该装货集装箱不得装载上船。

第3条
氧气分析和气体探测设备

1　在运输可能释放有毒或易燃气体或可能在货物处所中造成氧气耗尽的固体散装货物时,应备有测量空气中这类气体或氧气浓度的适当仪器,及其详细的使用说明书。这种仪器应使主管机关满意。

2　主管机关应采取措施,确保船员在上述仪器使用方面受到培训。

第4条
船上使用杀虫剂③

在船上使用杀虫剂,特别是为熏舱而使用杀虫剂时,应采取适当预防措施。

---

① 参见《关于装货集装箱验证毛重指南》(第 MSC.1/Circ.1475 号通函)。

② 本文件可通过 EDP 或 EDI 传输技术显示。签名可为电子签名或可由经授权签字人员以大写字母书写的名字替代。

③ 参见:
1.《经修订的关于船上安全使用杀虫剂的建议案》(第 MSC.1/Circ.1358 号通函);
2.《关于船上安全使用杀虫剂进行货舱熏蒸的建议案》(经修正的第 MSC.1/Circ.1264 号通函);和
3.《经修订的关于船上安全使用杀虫剂进行货物运输单元熏蒸的建议案》(第 MSC.1/Circ.1361 号通函)

Regulation 5
Stowage and securing

1 Cargo, cargo units[①] and cargo transport units[②] carried on or under deck shall be so loaded, stowed and secured as to prevent as far as is practicable, throughout the voyage, damage or hazard to the ship and the persons on board, and loss of cargo overboard.

2 Cargo, cargo units and cargo transport units shall be so packed and secured within the unit as to prevent, throughout the voyage, damage or hazard to the ship and the persons on board.

3 Appropriate precautions shall be taken during loading and transport of heavy cargoes or cargoes with abnormal physical dimensions to ensure that no structural damage to the ship occurs and to maintain adequate stability throughout the voyage.

4 Appropriate precautions shall be taken during loading and transport of cargo units and cargo transport units on board ro-ro ships, especially with regard to the securing arrangements on board such ships and on the cargo units and cargo transport units and with regard to the strength of the securing points and lashings.

5 Freight containers shall not be loaded to more than the maximum gross weight indicated on the Safety Approval Plate under the International Convention for Safe Containers (CSC), as amended.

6 All cargoes, other than solid and liquid bulk cargoes, cargo units and cargo transport units, shall be loaded, stowed and secured throughout the voyage in accordance with the Cargo Securing Manual approved by the Administration. In ships with ro-ro spaces, as defined in regulation II-2/3.41, all securing of such cargoes, cargo units, and cargo transport units, in accordance with the Cargo Securing Manual, shall be completed before the ship leaves the berth. The Cargo Securing Manual shall be drawn up to a standard at least equivalent to relevant guidelines developed by the Organization.[③]

Regulation 5-1
Material safety data sheets

Ships carrying oil or oil fuel, as defined in regulation 1 of Annex I of the International Convention for the Prevention of Pollution from Ships, 1973, as modified by the Protocol of 1978 relating thereto, shall be provided with material safety data sheets, based on the recommendations developed by the Organization,[④] prior to the loading of such oil as cargo in bulk or bunkering of oil fuel.

---

① Refer to the *Code of Safe Practice for Cargo Stowage and Securing* (resolution A.714(17), as amended).

② Refer to the *International Maritime Dangerous Goods (IMDG) Code* (resolution MSC.122(75), as amended).

③ Refer to *Revised guidelines for the preparation of the Cargo Securing Manual* (MSC.1/Circ.1353/Rev.1).

④ Refer to *Recommendations for material safety data sheets (MSDS) for MARPOL Annex I oil cargo and oil fuel* (resolution MSC.286(86), as may be amended).

第 5 条
积载和系固

1　在甲板上或甲板下载运的货物、货物单元①和货物运输单元②，其装载、积载和系固应尽可能防止在整个航程中对船舶和船上人员造成损害或危险，以及防止货物落水灭失。

2　货物、货物单元和货物运输单元，其在单元中的包装和系固，应能防止在整个航程中对船舶和船上人员造成损害或危险。

3　在重型货物或异常外形尺寸货物的装载和运输过程中，应采取适当的预防措施，确保不发生船舶结构性损坏，并在整个航程中保持足够的稳性。

4　在滚装船上货物单元和货物运输单元的装载和运输过程中，应采取适当的预防措施，特别是注意这种船上和货物单元和货物运输单元上的系固装置，以及系固点和捆索的强度。

5　货运集装箱的装载应不超过经修正的《国际集装箱安全公约》(CSC)规定的安全核准牌上注明的最大总重量。

6　在整个航程中，除散装固体和液体货物以外的所有货物、货物单元和货物运输单元，应按主管机关认可的《货物系固手册》进行装载、积载和系固。对于具有第Ⅱ-2/3.41 条定义的滚装处所的船舶，应在离开泊位之前按《货物系固手册》完成所有这些货物、货物单元和货物运输单元的系固。《货物系固手册》的编制标准应至少等效于本组织制定的相关指南③。

第 5-1 条
物质安全数据单

对于装运《经 1978 年议定书修订的 1973 年国际防止船舶造成污染公约》附则Ⅰ第 1 条所界定的油类或燃油的船舶，须根据本组织制定的建议，④在这些油类作为散装货物或燃料油装船之前，向船舶提供物质安全数据单。

---

① 参见《货物积载和系固安全操作规则》(经修正的第 A.714(17)号决议)。
② 参见《国际海运危险货物(IMDG)规则》(经修正的第 MSC.122(75)号决议)
③ 参见《经修订的货物系固手册编制指南》(第 MSC.1/Circ.1353/Rev.1 号通函)。
④ 参见《关于 MARPOL 附则Ⅰ货油和燃油所用物质安全数据单(MSDS)的建议案》(可能经修正的第 MSC.286(86)号决议)。

Regulation 5-2
Prohibition of the blending of bulk liquid cargoes and production processes during sea voyages

1 The physical blending of bulk liquid cargoes during sea voyages is prohibited. Physical blending refers to the process whereby the ship's cargo pumps and pipelines are used to internally circulate two or more different cargoes with the intent to achieve a cargo with a new product designation. This prohibition does not preclude the master from undertaking cargo transfers for the safety of the ship or protection of the marine environment.

2 The prohibition in paragraph 1 does not apply to the blending of products for use in the search and exploitation of seabed mineral resources on board ships used to facilitate such operations.

3 Any production process on board a ship during sea voyages is prohibited. Production processes refer to any deliberate operation whereby a chemical reaction between a ship's cargo and any other substance or cargo takes place.

4 The prohibition in paragraph 3 does not apply to the production processes of cargoes for use in the search and exploitation of seabed mineral resources on board ships used to facilitate such operations.[①]

① Refer to *Guidelines for the transport and handling of limited amounts of hazardous and noxious liquid substances in bulk in offshore support vessels* (resolution A.673(16), as amended).

第 5-2 条
禁止在海上航行时进行散装液体货物混合和生产作业

1　禁止在海上航行时将散装液体货物进行物理混合。物理混合系指使用船舶的货泵和管路对两种或以上的不同货物进行内部循环,以形成一种具有新货品名称的货物的过程。该禁止不妨碍船长为保障船舶安全或保护海洋环境而进行的货物过驳。

2　第 1 段中的禁止,对在用于便利勘探和开采海底矿物资源的船舶上,为勘探和开采中的使用而进行的货品混合不适用。

3　海上航行时,禁止在船上进行任何生产作业。生产作业系指使船上某一货物与任何其他物质或货物发生化学反应的任何故意操作。

4　上述第 3 段中的禁止,对在用于便利勘探和开采海底矿物资源的船舶上,为勘探和开采中的使用而进行的货品混合不适用。①

① 参见《近海供应船散装运输和装卸有限数量有毒有害液体物质指南》(经修正的第 A.673(16)号决议)。

Part B
Special provisions for solid bulk cargoes

Regulation 6
Acceptability for shipment

1 Prior to loading a solid bulk cargo, the master shall be in possession of comprehensive information on the ship's stability and on the distribution of cargo for the standard loading conditions. The method of providing such information shall be to the satisfaction of the Administration.①

Regulation 7
Loading, unloading and stowage of solid bulk cargoes②

1 For the purpose of this regulation, terminal representative means a person appointed by the terminal or other facility, where the ship is loading or unloading, who has responsibility for operations conducted by that terminal or facility with regard to the particular ship.

2 To enable the master to prevent excessive stresses in the ship's structure, the ship shall be provided with a booklet, which shall be written in a language with which the ship's officers responsible for cargo operations are familiar. If this language is not English, the ship shall be provided with a booklet written also in the English language. The booklet shall, as a minimum, include:

.1 stability data, as required by regulation Ⅱ-1/5-1;

.2 ballasting and deballasting rates and capacities;

.3 maximum allowable load per unit surface area of the tank top plating;

.4 maximum allowable load per hold;

.5 general loading and unloading instructions with regard to the strength of the ship's structure including any limitations on the most adverse operating conditions during loading, unloading, ballasting operations and the voyage;

.6 any special restrictions such as limitations on the most adverse operating conditions imposed by the Administration or organization recognized by it, if applicable; and

.7 where strength calculations are required, maximum permissible forces and moments on the ship's hull during loading, unloading and the voyage.

① Refer to regulation Ⅱ-1/5-1 on Stability information to be supplied to the master.

② Refer to the *Code of Practice for the Safe Loading and Unloading of Bulk Carriers* (BLU Code) (resolution A.862(20), as amended).

B 部分
固体散装货物的特别规定

第 6 条
装运的可接受性

1　在固体散装货物装船前，船长应获得关于船舶稳性和标准装载工况下货物分布的综合资料。提供此种资料的方法，应使主管机关满意。[①]

第 7 条
固体散装货物的装卸和积载[②]

1　就本条而言，码头代表系指船舶装卸货物的码头或其他设施使用方指定的人员，其负责该码头或设施对特定船舶进行作业。

2　为能使船长防止船体结构中产生过大应力，船舶应配备一份手册，其应使用为负责货物作业的高级船员所熟悉的语言编写。如果该种语言不是英文，则船上还应配备一份用英文写成的手册。该手册应至少包括下列内容：

.1　第Ⅱ-1/5-1 条所要求的稳性资料；

.2　加压载和减压载的速率和能力；

.3　内底板上单位表面积的最大许用载荷；

.4　每舱最大许用载荷；

.5　有关船体结构强度的一般装卸须知，包括在装卸货物、压载作业及航行期间的最不利操作工况的任何限制；

.6　任何特别的限制，例如主管机关或由其认可的组织所施加的最不利操作工况的限制（如适用）；和

.7　如果要求强度计算，在装卸货物及航行期间船体上的最大许用载荷和力矩。

---

① 参见第Ⅱ-1/5-1 条“向船长提供的资料”。

② 参见本组织第 A.862(20)号决议通过并经修正的《散货船安全装卸操作规则(BLU 规则)》。

3 Before a solid bulk cargo is loaded or unloaded, the master and the terminal representative shall agree on a plan① which shall ensure that the permissible forces and moments on the ship are not exceeded during loading or unloading, and shall include the sequence, quantity and rate of loading or unloading, taking into consideration the speed of loading or unloading, the number of pours and the deballasting or ballasting capability of the ship. The plan and any subsequent amendments thereto shall be lodged with the appropriate authority of the port State.

4 The master and terminal representative shall ensure that loading and unloading operations are conducted in accordance with the agreed plan.

5 If during loading or unloading any of the limits of the ship referred to in paragraph 2 are exceeded or are likely to become so if the loading or unloading continues, the master has the right to suspend operation and the obligation to notify accordingly the appropriate authority of the port State with which the plan has been lodged. The master and the terminal representative shall ensure that corrective action is taken. When unloading cargo, the master and terminal representative shall ensure that the unloading method does not damage the ship's structure.

6 The master shall ensure that ship's personnel continuously monitor cargo operations. Where possible, the ship's draught shall be checked regularly during loading or unloading to confirm the tonnage figures supplied. Each draught and tonnage observation shall be recorded in a cargo logbook. If significant deviations from the agreed plan are detected, cargo or ballast operations or both shall be adjusted to ensure that the deviations are corrected.

---

① Refer to the *Code of Practice for the Safe Loading and Unloading of Bulk Carriers* (BLU Code) (resolution A.862(20), as amended).

3 固体散装货物在装货或卸货之前，船长和码头代表应商订一项计划[①]，该计划应确保在装卸货物期间不超过船上的许用应力和力矩，还应包括装卸货物的次序、数量及速率，并考虑到装卸货物的速度、船上添注口的数量及减压载或加压载的能力。该计划及其后的任何修改，应提交给港口国的有关当局。

4 散装货物应在整个货物处所范围内装载并视需要合理平舱，以最大限度减少货物移动的风险，并确保在整个航行期间保持足够的稳性。

5 在甲板间舱载运散装货物时，如果装载资料表明船底结构在舱口开启时的应力会达到不可接受的程度，则这些甲板间的舱口应关闭。货物应合理平舱，并应延伸到两舷，或用具有足够强度的附加纵向隔壁加以固定。应注意甲板间舱的安全承载能力，以确保甲板结构不过载。

6 船长应确保船上人员连续不断地监视货物装卸作业。如有可能，在装卸货物期间应定期校核吃水以确认提供的吨位数。每次测得的吃水和吨位数应记入货物日志。如发现与商定的计划有显著偏差，则应调整货物装卸或压载作业，或两者，以确保偏差被纠正。

① 参见本组织第 A.862(20)号决议通过并经修正的《散货船安全装卸操作规则》(BLU 规则)。

Part C
Carriage of grain

Regulation 8
Definitions

For the purposes of this part, unless expressly provided otherwise:

1 *International Grain Code* means the International Code for the Safe Carriage of Grain in Bulk adopted by the Maritime Safety Committee of the Organization by resolution MSC.23 (59) as may be amended by the Organization, provided that such amendments are adopted, brought into force and take effect in accordance with the provisions of article Ⅷ of the present Convention concerning the amendment procedures applicable to the annex other than chapter Ⅰ.

2 The term *grain* includes wheat, maize (corn), oats, rye, barley, rice, pulses, seeds and processed forms thereof whose behaviour is similar to that of grain in its natural state.

Regulation 9
Requirements for cargo ships carrying grain

1 In addition to any other applicable requirements of the present regulations, a cargo ship carrying grain shall comply with the requirements of the International Grain Code, and hold a document of authorization as required by that Code. For the purpose of this regulation, the requirements of the Code shall be treated as mandatory.

2 A ship without such a document shall not load grain until the master satisfies the Administration, or the Contracting Government of the port of loading on behalf of the Administration, that the ship will comply with the requirements of the International Grain Code in its proposed loaded condition.

C 部分
谷物运输

第 8 条
定义

除另有明文规定外,就本部分而言:

1 **《国际谷物规则》**系指本组织海上安全委员会第 MSC.23(59)号决议通过并可能经本组织修正的《国际散装谷物安全运输规则》,但该修正应按本公约第Ⅷ条有关适用于除第Ⅰ章外的附则修正程序的规定予以通过、生效和实施。

2 **谷物**一词包括小麦、玉蜀黍(玉米)、燕麦、稞麦、大麦、大米、豆类、种子以及由其加工而成并在自然状态下具有类似特征的制品。

第 9 条
货船载运谷物的要求

1 除本规则任何其他适用的要求外,载运谷物的货船还应符合《国际谷物规则》的要求,并持有一份该规则要求的批准文件。就本条而言,该规则要求应视作强制性要求。

2 没有这种批准文件的船舶,在船长使主管机关或代表主管机关的装货港的缔约国政府确信该船所提出的装载工况符合《国际谷物规则》的要求之前,不应装载谷物。

Chapter Ⅶ Carriage of dangerous goods

第Ⅶ章　危险货物运输

Part A
Carriage of dangerous goods in packaged form

Regulation 1
Definitions

For the purpose of this chapter, unless expressly provided otherwise:

1 *IMDG Code* means the International Maritime Dangerous Goods (IMDG) Code adopted by the Maritime Safety Committee of the Organization by resolution MSC.122(75), as may be amended by the Organization, provided that such amendments are adopted, brought into force and take effect in accordance with the provisions of article Ⅷ of the present Convention concerning the amendment procedures applicable to the annex other than chapter Ⅰ.

2 *Dangerous goods* mean the substances, materials and articles covered by the IMDG Code.

3 *Packaged form* means the form of containment specified in the IMDG Code.

Regulation 2
Application①

1 Unless expressly provided otherwise, this part applies to the carriage of dangerous goods in packaged form in all ships to which the present regulations apply and in cargo ships of less than 500 gross tonnage.

2 The provisions of this part do not apply to ships' stores and equipment.

3 The carriage of dangerous goods in packaged form is prohibited except in accordance with the provisions of this chapter.

4 To supplement the provisions of this part, each Contracting Government shall issue, or cause to be issued, detailed instructions on emergency response and medical first aid relevant to incidents involving dangerous goods in packaged form, taking into account the guidelines developed by the Organization.②

---

① Refer to:
.1 part D, which contains special requirements for the carriage of INF cargo; and
.2 regulation Ⅱ-2/19, which contains special requirements for ships carrying dangerous goods.

② Refer to:
.1 the *Revised Emergency Response Procedures for Ships Carrying Dangerous Goods (EmS Guide)* (MSC.1/Circ.1588, as may be amended); and
.2 the *Medical First Aid Guide for Use in Accidents Involving Dangerous Goods (MFAG)*. These Guides are reproduced in the Supplement to the IMDG Code published by the Organization.

A 部分
包装危险货物运输

第1条
定义

除另有明文规定外,就本章而言:

1 **IMDG 规则**系指本组织海上安全委员会第 MSC.122(75)号决议通过并可能经本组织修正的《国际海运危险货物(IMDG)规则》,但这种修正案应按本公约第Ⅷ条有关适用于除第Ⅰ章外的附则修正程序的规定予以通过、生效和实施。

2 **危险货物**系指 IMDG 规则中所述的物质、材料和物品。

3 **包装形式**系指 IMDG 规则中规定的包装形式。

第2条
适用范围①

1 除另有明文规定外,本部分适用于本公约规则所适用的所有船舶和小于 500 总吨的货船包装危险货物的运输。

2 本部分的规定不适用于船用物料和设备。

3 除按本章的规定外,禁止运输包装危险货物。

4 为了补充本部分的规定,各缔约国政府应颁布或促使颁布关于涉及包装危险货物事故的应急响应和医疗急救的详细须知,并考虑到本组织制定的导则②。

---

① 参见:
.1 D 部分,对运输 INF 货物的特殊要求;和
.2 第Ⅱ-2/19 条,对载运危险货物船舶的特殊要求。

② 参见:
.1 《经修订的船舶载运危险货物应急反应措施(EmS 指南)》(第 MSC.1/Circ.1588 号通函,可经修订);和
.2 《危险货物事故医疗急救指南(MFAG)》。这些文件亦见本组织出版的《IMDG 规则》(补充本)。

Regulation 3
Requirements for the carriage of dangerous goods

The carriage of dangerous goods in packaged form shall be in compliance with the relevant provisions of the IMDG Code.

Regulation 4
Documents

1 Transport information relating to the carriage of dangerous goods in packaged form and the container/vehicle packing certificate shall be in accordance with the relevant provisions of the IMDG Code and shall be made available to the person or organization designated by the port State authority.

2 Each ship carrying dangerous goods in packaged form shall have a special list, manifest or stowage plan setting forth, in accordance with the relevant provisions of the IMDG Code, the dangerous goods on board and the location thereof. A copy of one of these documents shall be made available before departure to the person or organization designated by the port State authority.

Regulation 5
Cargo Securing Manual

Cargo, cargo units① and cargo transport units shall be loaded, stowed and secured throughout the voyage in accordance with the Cargo Securing Manual approved by the Administration. The Cargo Securing Manual shall be drawn up to a standard at least equivalent to the guidelines developed by the Organization.②

Regulation 6
Reporting of incidents involving dangerous goods

1 When an incident takes place involving the loss or likely loss overboard of dangerous goods in packaged form into the sea, the master, or other person having charge of the ship, shall report the particulars of such an incident without delay and to the fullest extent possible to the nearest coastal State. The report shall be drawn up based on general principles and guidelines developed by the Organization.③

① As defined in the *Code of Safe Practice for Cargo Stowage and Securing* (resolution A.714(17), as amended).

② Refer to *Revised guidelines for the preparation of the Cargo Securing Manual* (MSC/Circ.1353/Rev.1).

③ Refer to the *General principles for ship reporting systems and ship reporting requirements, including Guidelines for reporting incidents involving dangerous goods, harmful substances and/or marine pollutants* (resolution A.851(20), as amended).

第 3 条
危险货物运输要求

包装危险货物运输应符合 IMDG 规则的有关规定。

第 4 条
单证

1 与包装危险货物运输相关的信息和集装箱/车辆装箱证书须符合《IMDG 规则》的相关规定，并须向港口国主管机关指定的人员或组织提供。

2 每艘载运包装危险货物的船舶须具有一份特别清单、舱单或积载图，按《IMDG 规则》的相关规定，列出船上的危险货物及其位置。这些单证的副本，需在离港前向港口国主管机关指定的人员或组织提供。

第 5 条
货物系固手册

在整个航程中，货物、货物单元①和货物运输单元应按照主管机关认可的《货物系固手册》进行装载、积载和系固。《货物系固手册》的编制标准应至少等效于本组织制定的导则②。

第 6 条
涉及危险货物事故的报告

1 在发生涉及包装危险货物从船上落入海中灭失或可能灭失的事故时，船长或该船的其他负责人应立即将此类事故的详细情况尽可能全面地向最近的沿岸国报告，该报告应根据本组织制定的一般原则和指南③做出。

---

① 与本组织第 A.714(17)号决议通过并经修正的《货物积载和系固安全操作规则》中的定义相同。

② 参见《经修订的货物系固手册编制导则》(第 MSC/Circ.1353/Rev.1 号通函)。

③ 参见《船舶报告系统和船舶报告要求的一般原则，包括涉及危险货物、有害物质和/或海洋污染物事故报告指南》(第 A.851(20)号决议)。

2 In the event of the ship referred to in paragraph 1 being abandoned, or in the event of a report from such a ship being incomplete or unobtainable, the company, as defined in regulation Ⅸ/1.2, shall, to the fullest extent possible, assume the obligations placed upon the master by this regulation.

2　当本条 1 所述的船舶弃船时,或从该船发出的报告不完整或不能获得时,第Ⅸ/1.2 条所定义的公司应在最大可能的范围内承担本条对船长规定的义务。

Part A-1
Carriage of dangerous goods in solid form in bulk

Regulation 7
Definitions

Dangerous goods in solid form in bulk means any material, other than liquid or gas, consisting of a combination of particles, granules or any larger pieces of material, generally uniform in composition, which is covered by the IMDG Code and is loaded directly into the cargo spaces of a ship without any intermediate form of containment, and includes such materials loaded in a barge on a barge-carrying ship.

Regulation 7-1
Application①

1 Unless expressly provided otherwise, this part applies to the carriage of dangerous goods in solid form in bulk in all ships to which the present regulations apply and in cargo ships of less than 500 gross tonnage.

2 The carriage of dangerous goods in solid form in bulk is prohibited except in accordance with the provisions of this part.

3 To supplement the provisions of this part, each Contracting Government shall issue, or cause to be issued, instructions on emergency response and medical first aid relevant to incidents involving dangerous goods in solid form in bulk, taking into account the guidelines developed by the Organization.②

Regulation 7-2
Documents

1 In all documents relating to the carriage of dangerous goods in solid form in bulk by sea, the bulk cargo shipping name of the goods shall be used (trade names alone shall not be used).

2 Each ship carrying dangerous goods in solid form in bulk shall have a special list or manifest setting forth the dangerous goods on board and the location thereof. A detailed stowage plan, which identifies by class and sets out the location of all dangerous goods on board, may be used in place of such a special list or manifest. A copy of one of these documents shall be made available before departure to the person or organization designated by the port State authority.

---

① Refer to regulation Ⅱ-2/19, which contains special requirements for ships carrying dangerous goods.

② Refer to the *Medical First Aid Guide for Use in Accidents involving Dangerous Goods* (MFAG) which is reproduced in the Supplement to the IMDG Code published by the Organization.

A-1 部分
固体散装危险货物运输

第 7 条
定义

固体散装危险货物系指除液体或气体以外,由粒子、颗粒或较大块状物质组成的并在 IMDG 规则中列明的任何物质,成分通常一致,并直接装入船舶的货物处所而无须任何中间围护形式,包括装入载驳船上的驳船内的此类物质。

第 7-1 条
适用范围①

1 除另有明文规定外,本部分适用于本公约规则所适用的所有船舶和小于 500 总吨的货船固体散装危险货物的运输。

2 除按本部分的规定外,禁止运输固体散装危险货物。

3 为了补充本部分的规定,各缔约国政府应颁布或促使颁布关于固体散装危险货物安全运输的详细须知,其应包括涉及固体散装危险货物事故的应急反应和医疗急救的须知,并考虑到本组织制定的导则。②

第 7-2 条
单证

1 在有关海运固体散装危险货物的所有单证中,应使用货物的散货运输名称(不应单独使用商品名称)。

2 每艘载运固体散装危险货物的船舶应具有一份特别清单或舱单,列出船上危险货物及其位置。一份标明所有危险货物的类别并表明其在船上位置的详细积载图,可用于代替上述特别清单或舱单。船舶驶离前应备有一份这些单证的副本,以供港口国当局指定的人员或组织使用。

① 参见第Ⅱ-2/19 条,对载运危险货物船舶的特殊要求。
② 参见《危险货物事故医疗急救指南(MFAG)》,见本组织出版的《IMDG 规则》(补充本)。

Regulation 7-3
Stowage and segregation requirements

1 Dangerous goods in solid form in bulk shall be loaded and stowed safely and appropriately in accordance with the nature of the goods. Incompatible goods shall be segregated from one another.

2 Dangerous goods in solid form in bulk, which are liable to spontaneous heating or combustion, shall not be carried unless adequate precautions have been taken to minimize the likelihood of the outbreak of fire.

3 Dangerous goods in solid form in bulk, which give off dangerous vapours, shall be stowed in a well ventilated cargo space.

Regulation 7-4
Reporting of incidents involving dangerous goods

1 When an incident takes place involving the loss or likely loss overboard of dangerous goods in solid form in bulk into the sea, the master, or other person having charge of the ship, shall report the particulars of such an incident without delay and to the fullest extent possible to the nearest coastal State. The report shall be drawn up based on general principles and guidelines developed by the Organization.①

2 In the event of the ship referred to in paragraph 1 being abandoned, or in the event of a report from such a ship being incomplete or unobtainable, the company, as defined in regulation Ⅸ/1.2, shall, to the fullest extent possible, assume the obligations placed upon the master by this regulation.

Regulation 7-5
Requirements for the carriage of dangerous goods in solid form in bulk

The carriage of dangerous goods in solid form in bulk shall be in compliance with the relevant provisions of the IMSBC Code, as defined in regulation Ⅵ/1-1.1.

① Refer to the General principles for ship reporting systems and ship reporting requirements, including Guidelines for reporting incidents involving dangerous goods, harmful substances and/or marine pollutants (resolution A.851(20), as amended).

第 7-3 条
积载和隔离要求

1 固体散装危险货物应按其性质安全和适当地予以装载和积载。对于互不相容的货物，应将其彼此隔离。

2 不得载运易自热或自燃的固体散装危险货物，除非已采取适当的预防措施以使发生火灾的可能性减至最小。

3 会产生危险蒸气的固体散装危险货物应积载于通风良好的货物处所内。

第 7-4 条
涉及危险货物事故的报告

1 在发生涉及固体散装危险货物从船上落入海中灭失或可能灭失的事故时，船长或该船的其他负责人应立即将此类事故的详细情况尽可能全面地向最近的沿岸国报告，该报告应根据本组织制定的一般原则和指南①做出。

2 当本条 1 所述的船舶弃船时，或从该船发出的报告不完整或不能获得时，第Ⅸ/1.2 条所定义的公司应在最大可能的范围内承担本条对船长规定的义务。

第 7-5 条
固体散装危险货物载运要求

载运固体散装危险货物须符合《国际固体散货规则》的相关规定，如规划Ⅵ/1-1.1 条中定义的国际散货规则的相关要求。

---

① 参见《船舶报告系统和船舶报告要求的一般原则，包括涉及危险货物、有害物质和/或海洋污染物事故报告指南》（第 A.851（20）号决议，经修正的）。

Part B
Construction and equipment of ships carrying dangerous liquid chemicals in bulk

Regulation 8
Definitions

For the purpose of this part, unless expressly provided otherwise:

1 *International Bulk Chemical Code* (*IBC Code*) means the International Code for the Construction and Equipment of Ships Carrying Dangerous Chemicals in Bulk adopted by the Maritime Safety Committee of the Organization by resolution MSC.4(48), as may be amended by the Organization, provided that such amendments are adopted, brought into force and take effect in accordance with the provisions of article Ⅷ of the present Convention concerning the amendment procedures applicable to the annex other than chapter Ⅰ.

2 *Chemical tanker* means a cargo ship constructed or adapted and used for the carriage in bulk of any liquid product listed in chapter 17 of the International Bulk Chemical Code.

3 For the purpose of regulation 9, *ship constructed* means a ship the keel of which is laid or which is at a similar stage of construction.

4 At a *similar stage of construction* means the stage at which:

.1 construction identifiable with a specific ship begins; and

.2 assembly of that ship has commenced comprising at least 50 tonnes or 1% of the estimated mass of all structural material, whichever is less.

Regulation 9
Application to chemical tankers

1 Unless expressly provided otherwise, this part applies to chemical tankers constructed on or after 1 July 1986 including those of less than 500 gross tonnage. Such tankers shall comply with the requirements of this part in addition to any other applicable requirements of the present regulations.

2 Any chemical tanker, irrespective of the date of construction, which undergoes repairs, alterations, modifications and outfitting related thereto shall continue to comply with at least the requirements previously applicable to the ship. Such a ship, if constructed before 1 July 1986, shall, as a rule, comply with the requirements for a ship constructed on or after that date to at least the same extent as before undergoing such repairs, alterations, modifications or outfitting. Repairs, alterations and modifications of a major character, and outfitting related thereto, shall meet the requirements for a ship constructed on or after 1 July 1986 in so far as the Administration deems reasonable and practicable.

B 部分
散装运输危险液体化学品船舶的构造和设备

第 8 条
定义

除另有明文规定外，就本部分而言：

1 **《国际散装化学品规则》(IBC 规则)**系指本组织海上安全委员会第 MSC.4(48)号决议通过并可能经本组织修正的《国际散装运输危险化学品船舶构造和设备规则》，但这种修正案应按本公约第Ⅷ条有关适用于除第Ⅰ章外的附则修正程序的规定予以通过、生效和实施。

2 **化学品液货船**系指经建造或改建用于散装运输《国际散装化学品规则》第 17 章所列的任何液体货品的货船。

3 就第 9 条而言，**建造的船舶**系指安放龙骨或处于类似建造阶段的船舶。

4 **类似建造阶段**系指在此阶段：

.1 可辨认出某一具体船舶建造开始；和

.2 该船业已开始的装配量至少为 50 吨，或为全部结构材料估算重量的 1%，取较小者。

第 9 条
化学品液货船的适用范围

1 除另有明文规定外，本部分适用于 1986 年 7 月 1 日或以后建造的化学品液货船，也包括小于 500 总吨者。此类化学品液货船除符合本规则任何其他适用的要求外，还应符合本部分的要求。

2 任何化学品液货船，无论何时建造，在进行修理、改装以及与之有关的舾装时，应至少继续符合该船原先适用的要求。该船如果系在 1986 年 7 月 1 日以前建造，一般应至少按其修理、改装或舾装之前的同等程度，符合对该日或以后建造的船舶的要求。重大的修理、改装以及与之有关的舾装，在主管机关认为合理和可行的范围内，应满足对 1986 年 7 月 1 日或以后建造的船舶的要求。

3 A ship, irrespective of the date of construction, which is converted to a chemical tanker shall be treated as a chemical tanker constructed on the date on which such conversion commenced.

Regulation 10
Requirements for chemical tankers

1 A chemical tanker shall comply with the requirements of the International Bulk Chemical Code and shall, in addition to the requirements of regulation Ⅰ/8, Ⅰ/9, and Ⅰ/10, as applicable, be surveyed and certified as provided for in that Code.

2 A chemical tanker holding a certificate issued pursuant to the provisions of paragraph 1 shall be subject to the control established in regulation Ⅰ/19. For this purpose such certificate shall be treated as a certificate issued under regulation Ⅰ/12 or Ⅰ/13.

3　无论何时建造的船舶，一经改建成化学品液货船后，应视作在开始改建之日建造的化学品液货船。

第10条
化学品液货船的要求

1　化学品液货船应符合《国际散装化学品规则》的要求，并除第Ⅰ/8条、第Ⅰ/9条和第Ⅰ/10条的适用要求外，还应按该规则中的规定予以检验和发证。

2　持有按本条1的规定签发证书的化学品液货船，均应受到第Ⅰ/19条所规定的控制。为此，该证书应视作按第Ⅰ/12条或第Ⅰ/13条的要求所签发的证书。

Part C
Construction and equipment of ships carrying liquefied gases in bulk

Regulation 11
Definitions

For the purpose of this part, unless expressly provided otherwise:

1 *International Gas Carrier Code (IGC Code)* means the International Code for the Construction and Equipment of Ships Carrying Liquefied Gases in Bulk as adopted by the Maritime Safety Committee of the Organization by resolution MSC.5(48), as may be amended by the Organization, provided that such amendments are adopted, brought into force and take effect in accordance with the provisions of article Ⅷ of the present Convention concerning the amendment procedures applicable to the annex other than chapter I.

2 *Gas carrier* means a cargo ship constructed or adapted and used for the carriage in bulk of any liquefied gas or other product listed in chapter 19 of the International Gas Carrier Code.

3 For the purpose of regulation 12, *ship constructed* means a ship the keel of which is laid or which is at a similar stage of construction.

4 At a *similar stage of construction* means the stage at which:

.1 construction identifiable with a specific ship begins; and

.2 assembly of that ship has commenced comprising at least 50 tonnes or 1% of the estimated mass of all structural material, whichever is less.

Regulation 12
Application to gas carriers

1 Unless expressly provided otherwise, this part applies to gas carriers constructed on or after 1 July 1986 including those of less than 500 gross tonnage. Such gas carriers shall comply with the requirements of this part in addition to any other applicable requirements of the present regulations.

2 Any gas carrier, irrespective of the date of construction, which undergoes repairs, alterations, modifications and outfitting related thereto shall continue to comply with at least the requirements previously applicable to the ship. Such a ship if constructed before 1 July 1986 shall, as a rule, comply with the requirements for a ship constructed on or after that date to at least the same extent as before undergoing such repairs, alterations, modifications or outfitting. Repairs, alterations and modifications of a major character, and outfitting related thereto, shall meet the requirements for a ship constructed on or after 1 July 1986 in so far as the Administration deems reasonable and practicable.

C 部分
散装运输液化气体船舶的构造和设备

第 11 条
定义

除另有明文规定外,就本部分而言:

1 **《国际气体运输船规则》(IGC 规则)**系指本组织海上安全委员会第 MSC.5(48)号决议通过并可能经本组织修正的《国际散装运输液化气体船舶构造和设备规则》,但这种修正案应按本公约第Ⅷ条有关适用于除第Ⅰ章外的附则修正程序的规定予以通过、生效和实施。

2 **气体运输船**系指经建造或改建用于散装运输《国际气体运输船规则》第 19 章所列的任何液化气体或其他货品的货船。

3 就第 12 条而言,**建造的船舶**系指安放龙骨或处于类似建造阶段的船舶。

4 **类似建造阶段**系指在此阶段:

.1 可辨认出某一具体船舶建造开始;和

.2 该船业已开始的装配量至少为 50 t,或为全部结构材料估算重量的 1%,取较小者。

第 12 条
气体运输船的适用范围

1 除另有明文规定外,本部分适用于 1986 年 7 月 1 日或以后建造的气体运输船,也包括小于 500 总吨者。此类气体运输船除符合本规则任何其他适用的要求外,还应符合本部分的要求。

2 任何气体运输船,无论何时建造,在进行修理、改装以及与之有关的舾装时,应至少继续符合该船原先适用的要求。该船如果系在 1986 年 7 月 1 日以前建造,一般应至少按其修理、改装或舾装之前的同等程度,符合对该日或以后建造的船舶的要求。重大的修理、改装以及与之有关的舾装,在主管机关认为合理和可行的范围内,应满足对 1986 年 7 月 1 日或以后建造的船舶的要求。

3 A ship, irrespective of the date of construction, which is converted to a gas carrier shall be treated as a gas carrier constructed on the date on which such conversion commenced.

Regulation 13
Requirements for gas carriers

1 A gas carrier shall comply with the requirements of the International Gas Carrier Code and shall, in addition to the requirements of regulation Ⅰ/8, Ⅰ/9 and Ⅰ/10, as applicable, be surveyed and certified as provided for in that Code. For the purpose of this regulation, the requirements of the Code shall be treated as mandatory.

2 A gas carrier holding a certificate issued pursuant to the provisions of paragraph 1 shall be subject to the control established in regulation Ⅰ/19. For this purpose such certificate shall be treated as a certificate issued under regulation Ⅰ/12 or Ⅰ/13.

3　无论何时建造的船舶，一经改建成气体运输船后，应视作在开始改建之日建造的气体运输船。

第13条
气体运输船的要求

1　气体运输船应符合《国际气体运输船规则》的要求，并除第Ⅰ/8条、第Ⅰ/9条和第Ⅰ/10条的适用要求外，还应按该规则中的规定予以检验和发证。就本条而言，该规则的要求应视作强制性要求。

2　持有按本条1的规定签发证书的气体运输船，均应受到第Ⅰ/19条所规定的控制。为此，该证书应视作按第Ⅰ/12条或第Ⅰ/13条的要求所签发的证书。

Part D
Special requirements for the carriage of packaged irradiated nuclear fuel, plutonium and high-level radioactive wastes on board ships

Regulation 14
Definitions

For the purpose of this part, unless expressly provided otherwise:

1 *INF Code* means the International Code for the Safe Carriage of Packaged Irradiated Nuclear Fuel, Plutonium and High-Level Radioactive Wastes on Board Ships, adopted by the Maritime Safety Committee of the Organization by resolution MSC.88(71), as may be amended by the Organization, provided that such amendments are adopted, brought into force and take effect in accordance with the provisions of article Ⅷ of the present Convention concerning the amendment procedures applicable to the annex other than chapter Ⅰ.

2 *INF cargo* means packaged irradiated nuclear fuel, plutonium and high-level radioactive wastes carried as cargo in accordance with class 7 of the IMDG Code.

3 *Irradiated nuclear fuel* means material containing uranium, thorium and/or plutonium isotopes which has been used to maintain a self-sustaining nuclear chain reaction.

4 *Plutonium* means the resultant mixture of isotopes of that material extracted from irradiated nuclear fuel from reprocessing.

5 *High-level radioactive wastes* means liquid wastes resulting from the operation of the first stage extraction system or the concentrated wastes from subsequent extraction stages, in a facility for reprocessing irradiated nuclear fuel, or solids into which such liquid wastes have been converted.

Regulation 15
Application to ships carrying INF cargo

1 Except as provided for in paragraph 2, this part shall apply to all ships regardless of the date of construction and size, including cargo ships of less than 500 gross tonnage, engaged in the carriage of INF cargo.

2 This part and the INF Code do not apply to warships, naval auxiliary or other vessels owned or operated by a Contracting Government and used, for the time being, only on government non-commercial service; however, each Administration shall ensure, by the adoption of appropriate measures not impairing operations or operational capabilities of such ships owned or operated by it, that such ships carrying INF cargo act in a manner consistent, so far as reasonable and practicable, with this part and the INF Code.

D 部分
船舶运输密封装辐射性核燃料、钚和强放射性废料的特殊要求

第 14 条
定义

除另有明文规定外，就本部分而言：

1 **INF 规则**系指本组织海上安全委员会第 MSC.88(71)号决议通过并可能经本组织修正的《国际船舶安全载运包装的辐射性核燃料、钚和强放射性废料规则》，但这种修正案应按本公约第Ⅷ条有关适用于除第Ⅰ章外的附则修正程序的规定予以通过、生效和实施。

2 **INF 货物**系指按 IMDG 规则中第 7 类货物载运的包装的辐射性核燃料、钚和强放射性废料。

3 **辐射性核燃料**系指含有曾用于维持自续链式核反应的铀、钍和/或钚的同位素的材料。

4 **钚**系指由辐射性核燃料再加工提炼出的材料，其为同位素的合成混合物。

5 **强放射性废料**系指由第一阶段提炼系统作业所产生的废液或由随后提炼阶段在辐射性核燃料再加工装置中浓缩的废物或由液体废料转换成的固体。

第 15 条
载运 INF 货物船舶的适用范围

1 除本条 2 的规定外，本部分应适用于所有船舶，而不论其建造日期和尺度，包括从事于运输 INF 货物的小于 500 总吨的货船。

2 本部分和 INF 规则不适用于军舰、海军辅助船或由缔约国政府拥有或经营，目前仅用于政府非商业性服务的其他船舶；但是，各主管机关均应采取不会影响其所拥有或经营的这类船舶的操作或操作能力的适当措施，确保这类装运 INF 货物的船舶在合理和可行的范围内符合本部分和 INF 规则的要求。

3 Nothing in this part or the INF Code shall prejudice the rights and duties of governments under international law and any action taken to enforce compliance shall be consistent with international law.

Regulation 16
Requirements for ships carrying INF cargo

1 A ship carrying INF cargo shall comply with the requirements of the INF Code in addition to any other applicable requirements of the present regulations and shall be surveyed and certified as provided for in that Code.

2 A ship holding a certificate issued pursuant to the provisions of paragraph 1 shall be subject to the control established in regulations I/19 and XI-1/4. For this purpose, such certificate shall be treated as a certificate issued under regulation I/12 or I/13.

3 本部分或 INF 规则的任何内容均不得损害各国政府根据国际法所具有的权利和义务，且为实施有关要求所采取的任何行动应符合国际法。

第 16 条
载运 INF 货物船舶的要求

1 除本规则任何其他适用要求外，载运 INF 货物的船舶还应符合 INF 规则的要求并应按该规则中的规定予以检验和发证。

2 持有按本条 1 的规定签发证书的船舶，均应受到第Ⅰ/19 条和第Ⅺ/4 条所规定的控制。为此，该证书应视作按第Ⅰ/12 条或第Ⅰ/13 条的要求所签发的证书。

Chapter Ⅷ Nuclear ships

第Ⅷ章　核能船舶

Regulation 1
Application

This chapter applies to all nuclear ships except ships of war.

Regulation 2
Application of other chapters

The regulations contained in the other chapters of the present Convention apply to nuclear ships except as modified by this chapter.①

Regulation 3
Exemptions

A nuclear ship shall not, in any circumstances, be exempted from compliance with any regulations of this Convention.

Regulation 4
Approval of reactor installation

The design, construction and standards of inspection and assembly of the reactor installation shall be subject to the approval and satisfaction of the Administration and shall take account of the limitations which will be imposed on surveys by the presence of radiation.

Regulation 5
Suitability of reactor installation for service on board ship

The reactor installation shall be designed having regard to the special conditions of service on board ship both in normal and exceptional circumstances of navigation.

Regulation 6
Radiation safety

The Administration shall take measures to ensure that there are no unreasonable radiation or other nuclear hazards, at sea or in port, to the crew, passengers or public, or to the waterways or food or water resources.

① Refer to the *Code of Safety for Nuclear Merchant Ships* (resolution A.491(Ⅻ)), which supplements the requirements of this chapter.

第 1 条
适用范围

本章适用于所有核能船舶,但军用舰船除外。

第 2 条
其他各章的适用范围

本公约的其他各章中的规则均适用于核能船舶,但经本章修订者除外。[①]

第 3 条
免除

在任何情况下,核能船舶均不得免于符合本公约的任何规则。

第 4 条
核反应堆装置的认可

核反应堆装置的设计、构造以及检查和装配的标准均应经主管机关认可和使主管机关满意,并应考虑到因有辐射而使检验所受到的限制。

第 5 条
核反应堆装置装船使用的适用性

设计核反应堆装置时,应考虑船舶在正常和特殊两种航行情况下的特殊工作条件。

第 6 条
辐射安全

主管机关应采取措施,确保在海上或港内不使船员、乘客或公众,或水道或食物或水源受到不当的辐射或其他的核能危害。

① 参见《核能商船安全规则》(A.491(Ⅻ)决议),该规则补充本章的要求。

Regulation 7
Safety assessment

(**a**) A safety assessment shall be prepared to permit evaluation of the nuclear power plant and safety of the ship to ensure that there are no unreasonable radiation or other hazards, at sea or in port, to the crew, passengers or public, or to the waterways or food or water resources. The Administration, when satisfied, shall approve such safety assessment which shall always be kept up to date.

(**b**) The safety assessment shall be made available sufficiently in advance to the Contracting Governments of the countries which a nuclear ship intends to visit so that they may evaluate the safety of the ship.

Regulation 8
Operating manual

A fully detailed operating manual shall be prepared for the information and guidance of the operating personnel in their duties on all matters relating to the operation of the nuclear power plant and having an important bearing on safety. The Administration, when satisfied, shall approve such operating manual and a copy shall be kept on board the ship. The operating manual shall always be kept up to date.

Regulation 9
Surveys

Survey of nuclear ships shall include the applicable requirements of regulation 7 of chapter Ⅰ, or of regulations 8, 9 and 10 of chapter Ⅰ, except in so far as surveys are limited by the presence of radiation. In addition, the surveys shall include any special requirements of the safety assessment. They shall in all cases, notwithstanding the provisions of regulations 8 and 10 of chapter Ⅰ, be carried out not less frequently than once a year.

Regulation 10
Certificates

(**a**) The provisions of paragraph (a) of regulation 12 of chapter Ⅰ and of regulation 14 of chapter Ⅰ shall not apply to nuclear ships.

(**b**) A certificate, called a Nuclear Passenger Ship Safety Certificate shall be issued after inspection and survey to a nuclear passenger ship which complies with the requirements of chapters Ⅱ-1, Ⅱ-2, Ⅲ, Ⅳ and Ⅷ, and any other relevant requirements of the present regulations.

第 7 条
安全鉴定书

(a) 应编写安全鉴定书,以评定核动力装置的性能和船舶的安全,从而确保在海上或港内不使船员、乘客或公众,或水道或食物或水源受到不当的辐射或其他的核能危害。主管机关对鉴定书满意时,应予以认可,该鉴定书应始终保持更新。

(b) 应提前足够的时间将安全鉴定书送交核能船舶拟驶往的缔约国政府,以供其评定该核能船舶的安全性。

第 8 条
操作手册

应制定关于核动力装置的所有操作事项且着重于安全的操作手册,作为操作人员在工作时的参考和指导。主管机关对操作手册满意时,应予以认可。应有 1 份操作手册保存在船上,且应始终保持更新。

第 9 条
检验

对核能船舶的检验应包括第Ⅰ章第 7 条或第Ⅰ章第 8、9 和 10 条中的适用要求,但对于因有辐射而受到限制的检验除外。此外,检验还应包括安全鉴定书的任何特殊要求。虽然有第Ⅰ章第 8 条和第 10 条的规定,但在所有情况下,对核能船舶的检验应不少于每年 1 次。

第 10 条
证书

(a) 第Ⅰ/12(a)条和第Ⅰ/14 条的规定不适用于核能船舶。

(b) 对经检查和检验后符合第Ⅱ-1 章、第Ⅱ-2 章、第Ⅲ章、第Ⅳ章和第Ⅷ章的要求及本规则其他有关要求的核能客船,应签发核能客船安全证书。

(c) A certificate, called a Nuclear Cargo Ship Safety Certificate shall be issued after inspection and survey to a nuclear cargo ship which satisfies the requirements for cargo ships on survey set out in regulation 10 of chapter Ⅰ, and complies with the requirements of chapters Ⅱ-1, Ⅱ-2, Ⅲ, Ⅳ and Ⅷ and any other relevant requirements of the present regulations.

(d) Nuclear Passenger Ship Safety Certificates and Nuclear Cargo Ship Safety Certificates shall state: "That the ship, being a nuclear ship, complied with all requirements of chapter Ⅷ of the Convention and conformed to the Safety Assessment approved for the ship."

(e) Nuclear Passenger Ship Safety Certificates and Nuclear Cargo Ship Safety Certificates shall be valid for a period of not more than 12 months.

(f) Nuclear Passenger Ship Safety Certificates and Nuclear Cargo Ship Safety Certificates shall be issued either by the Administration or by any person or organization duly authorized by it. In every case, that Administration assumes full responsibility for the certificate.

Regulation 11
Special control①

In addition to the control established by regulation 19 of chapter Ⅰ, nuclear ships shall be subject to special control before entering the ports and in the ports of Contracting Governments, directed towards verifying that there is on board a valid Nuclear Ship Safety Certificate and that there are no unreasonable radiation or other hazards at sea or in port, to the crew, passengers or public, or to the waterways or food or water resources.

Regulation 12
Casualties

In the event of any accident likely to lead to an environmental hazard the master of a nuclear ship shall immediately inform the Administration. The master shall also immediately inform the competent governmental authority of the country in whose waters the ship may be, or whose waters the ship approaches in a damaged condition.

① Refer to the IMO/IAEA *Safety Recommendations on the Use of Ports by Nuclear Merchant Ships.*

（c）对经检查和检验后满足第Ⅰ章第10条所规定的货船检验要求并符合第Ⅱ-1章、第Ⅱ-2章、第Ⅲ章、第Ⅳ章和第Ⅷ章的要求以及本规则其他有关要求的核能货船，应签发核能货船安全证书。

（d）在核能客船安全证书和核能货船安全证书中应阐明："该船为核能船舶，符合公约第Ⅷ章的所有要求，并与所认可的该船安全鉴定书相一致。"

（e）核能客船安全证书和核能货船安全证书的有效期限均不应超过12个月。

（f）核能客船安全证书和核能货船安全证书均应由主管机关或由其正式授权的任何个人或组织签发。在任何情况下，主管机关应对该证书负有全部责任。

第11条
特殊监督①

除按照第Ⅰ章第19条进行的港口国监督外，核能船舶在进入缔约国港口之前及在港口期间，应对其采取特殊的监督措施，旨在核实船舶持有有效的核能船舶安全证书，并核实其在海上或港口，不使船员、乘客或公众、航道、食物或水源受到不当的辐射或其他损害。

第12条
事故

当核能船舶发生任何可能导致危害周围环境的事故时，该船船长应立即报告主管机关。船长还应立即报告该船在损坏情况下可能处于的水域或驶往的水域所属国家政府的主管当局。

① 参见IMO/IAEA《核能商船使用港口的安全建议》。

Chapter Ⅸ　Management for the safe operation of ships

第Ⅸ章　船舶安全营运管理

Regulation 1
Definitions

For the purpose of this chapter, unless expressly provided otherwise:

1 *International Safety Management (ISM) Code* means the International Management Code for the Safe Operation of Ships and for Pollution Prevention adopted by the Organization by resolution A.741(18), as may be amended by the Organization, provided that such amendments are adopted, brought into force and take effect in accordance with the provisions of article VIII of the present Convention concerning the amendment procedures applicable to the annex other than chapter I.

2 *Company* means the owner of the ship or any other organization or person such as the manager, or the bareboat charterer, who has assumed the responsibility for operation of the ship from the owner of the ship and who on assuming such responsibility has agreed to take over all the duties and responsibilities imposed by the International Safety Management Code.

3 *Oil tanker* means an oil tanker as defined in regulation II-1/2.22.

4 *Chemical tanker* means a chemical tanker as defined in regulation VII/8.2.

5 *Gas carrier* means a gas carrier as defined in regulation VII/11.2.

6 *Bulk carrier* means a ship which is constructed generally with single deck, top-side tanks and hopper side tanks in cargo spaces, and is intended primarily to carry dry cargo in bulk, and includes such types as ore carriers and combination carriers.①

7 *Mobile offshore drilling unit (MODU)* means a vessel capable of engaging in drilling operations for the exploration for or exploitation of resources beneath the sea-bed such as liquid or gaseous hydrocarbons, sulphur or salt.

8 *High-speed craft* means a craft as defined in regulation X/1.

Regulation 2
Application

1 This chapter applies to ships, regardless of the date of construction, as follows:

.1 passenger ships including passenger high-speed craft, not later than 1 July 1998;

.2 oil tankers, chemical tankers, gas carriers, bulk carriers and cargo high-speed craft of 500 gross tonnage and upwards, not later than 1 July 1998; and

---

① Refer to *Interpretation of the provisions of SOLAS chapter XII on additional safety measures for bulk carriers* (resolution MSC.79(70)) and *Clarification of the term "bulk carrier" and guidance for application of regulations in SOLAS to ships which occasionally carry dry cargoes in bulk and are not determined as bulk carriers in accordance with regulation XII/1.1 and chapter II-1* (resolution MSC.277(85)).

第1条
定义

除另有明文规定外，就本章而言：

1 **《国际安全管理(ISM)规则》**系指本组织A.741(18)决议通过并可能经本组织修正的《国际船舶安全营运和防污染管理规则》，但这种修正案应按本公约第Ⅷ条有关适用于除第Ⅰ章外的附则修正程序的规定予以通过、生效和实施。

2 **公司**系指船舶所有人或任何其他组织或个人，诸如管理者或光船租赁人，他们已从船舶所有人处接受船舶营运的责任，同意承担《国际安全管理规则》规定的所有义务和责任。

3 **油船**系指第Ⅱ-1/2.22条定义的油船。

4 **化学品液货船**系指第Ⅶ/8.2条定义的化学品液货船。

5 **气体运输船**系指第Ⅶ/11.2条定义的气体运输船。

6 **散货船**系指在货物处所中通常建有单层甲板、顶边舱和底边舱，且主要用于运输散装干货的船舶，包括诸如矿砂船和兼装船等船型。[①]

7 **海上移动式钻井平台(MODU)**系指能从事勘探或开采诸如液体或气体碳氢化合物、硫或盐等海床下资源的钻井作业的船舶。

8 **高速船**系指第Ⅹ/1条定义的船舶。

第2条
适用范围

1 本章按下述日期适用于各类船舶(不论其建造日期)：

.1 客船(包括高速客船)：不迟于1998年7月1日；

.2 500总吨及以上的油船、化学品液货船、气体运输船、散货船和高速货船：不迟于1998年7月1日；和

① 参见《对SOLAS第Ⅻ章——关于散货船附加安全措施规定的解释》(第MSC.79(70)号决议)，以及对“散货船”一词的澄清和《SOLAS中适用于偶尔运载散装干货且未根据第Ⅻ/1.1条和第Ⅱ-1章被确定为散货船的规定适用指南》(第MSC.277(85)号决议)。

.3 other cargo ships and mobile offshore drilling units of 500 gross tonnage and upwards, not later than 1 July 2002.[①]

2 This chapter does not apply to government-operated ships used for non-commercial purposes.

Regulation 3
Safety management requirements[②]

1 The company and the ship shall comply with the requirements of the International Safety Management Code. For the purpose of this regulation, the requirements of the Code shall be treated as mandatory.

2 The ship shall be operated by a company holding a Document of Compliance referred to in regulation 4.

Regulation 4
Certification[③]

1 A Document of Compliance shall be issued to every company which complies with the requirements of the International Safety Management Code. This document shall be issued by the Administration[④], by an organization recognized by the Administration, or at the request of the Administration by another Contracting Government.

2 A copy of the Document of Compliance shall be kept on board the ship in order that the master can produce it on request for verification.

3 A Certificate, called a Safety Management Certificate, shall be issued to every ship by the Administration or an organization recognized by the Administration. The Administration or organization recognized by it shall, before issuing the Safety Management Certificate, verify that the company and its shipboard management operate in accordance with the approved safety management system.

---

① The Maritime Safety Committee, at its sixty-sixth session, decided that mobile offshore drilling units not propelled by mechanical means need not comply with the requirements of the chapter.

② Refer to *Revised guidelines for the operational implementation of the ISM Code by Companies* (MSC-MEPC.7/Circ.8); *Implementation of the ISM Code – Guidance to companies operating multi-flagged fleets and supplementary guidelines to Administrations* (MSC/Circ.762).

③ Refer to *Unified interpretation of the date of completion of the survey and verification on which the certificates are based* (MSC-MEPC.5/Circ.3) and *Unified interpretation on the expiration date of statutory certificates* (MSC-MEPC.5/Circ.13).

④ Refer to the *Code for Recognized Organizations* (*RO Code*) (MSC.349(92) and MEPC.237(65)); *Communication of information on the authorization of recognized organizations* (*ROs*) (MSC/Circ.1010-MEPC/Circ.382) and the information collected via the Global Integrated Shipping Information System (GISIS).

.3　500 总吨及以上其他货船和海上移动式钻井平台：不迟于 2002 年 7 月 1 日。[①]

2　本章不适用于政府经营的用于非商业目的的船舶。

第 3 条
安全管理要求[②]

1　公司和船舶应符合《国际安全管理规则》的要求。就本条而言，该规则的要求应视作强制性要求。

2　船舶应由持有第 4 条所述的符合证明的公司营运。

第 4 条
发证[③]

1　应为每一符合《国际安全管理规则》要求的公司签发符合证明。该证明文件应由主管机关[④]、主管机关认可的组织或应主管机关的请求由另一缔约国政府签发。

2　船上应存有一份符合证明的副本，以使船长在被要求验证时出示。

3　主管机关或主管机关认可的组织应为每艘船舶签发安全管理证书。在签发安全管理证书前，主管机关或其认可的组织应验证该公司及其船上管理系按经认可的安全管理体系进行营运。

① 海上安全委员会在其第 66 届会议上决定，非机械推进的海上移动式钻井平台不必符合本章要求。

② 参见公司营运实施 ISM 规则的修订指南（MSC-MEPC.7/Circ.8）；ISM 规则的实施——公司营运多国船旗船队的指南及主管机关补充导则（MSC/Circ.762）。

③ 参见《对证书所依据的检验和验证完成日期的统一解释》（MSC-MEPC.5/Circ.3）和对法定证书到期日期的统一解释（MSC-MEPC.5/Circ.13）。

④ 参见《认可组织规则》（RO 规则）（MSC.349（92）和 MEPC.237（65））；《关于认可组织授权的信息交流》（MSC/Circ.1010-MEPC/Circ.382）以及《通过全球综合航运信息系统（GISIS）收集的信息》。

Regulation 5
Maintenance of conditions

The safety management system shall be maintained in accordance with the provisions of the International Safety Management Code.

Regulation 6
Verification and control①

1 The Administration, another Contracting Government at the request of the Administration or an organization recognized by the Administration shall periodically verify the proper functioning of the ship's safety management system.

2 A ship required to hold a certificate issued pursuant to the provisions of regulation 4.3 shall be subject to control in accordance with the provisions of regulation XI-1/4. For this purpose such certificate shall be treated as a certificate issued under regulation I/12 or I/13.

---

① Refer to *Revised guidelines on implementation of the International Safety Management (ISM) Code by Administrations* (resolution A.1118(30)), *Procedures for port State control, 2019* (resolution A.1138(31)); *Procedures concerning observed ISM Code major non-conformities* (MSC/Circ.1059-MEPC/Circ.401) and *IMO requirements on carriage of publications on board ships* (MSC-MEPC.2/Circ.2).

第 5 条
状况的保持

应按《国际安全管理规则》的规定保持安全管理体系。

第 6 条
验证与控制[①]

1 主管机关、应主管机关请求另一缔约国政府或主管机关认可的组织,应定期验证船舶安全管理体系是否正常运行。

2 要求持有按第 4.3 条的规定签发证书的船舶,均应受到第Ⅺ-1/4 条所规定的控制。为此,该证书应视作按第Ⅰ/12 或Ⅰ/13 条的要求所签发的证书。

① 参见《主管机关实施 ISM 的修订指南》(第 A.1118(30)号决议),《2019 年港口国监督程序》(第 A.1138(31)号决议);《ISM 规则严重不合格项的处理程序》(MSC/Circ.1059-MEPC/Circ.401)和《IMO 关于船上携带出版物的规定》(MSC-MEPC.2/Circ.2)。

Chapter X Safety measures for high-speed craft

第X章　高速船安全措施

Regulation 1
Definitions

For the purpose of this chapter:

1 *High-Speed Craft Code, 1994 (1994 HSC Code)* means the International Code of Safety for High-Speed Craft adopted by the Maritime Safety Committee of the Organization by resolution MSC.36(63), as may be amended by the Organization, provided that such amendments are adopted, brought into force and take effect in accordance with the provisions of article VIII of the present Convention concerning the amendment procedures applicable to the annex other than chapter I.

2 *High-Speed Craft Code, 2000 (2000 HSC Code)* means the International Code of Safety for High-Speed Craft, 2000, adopted by the Maritime Safety Committee of the Organization by resolution MSC.97(73), as may be amended by the Organization, provided that such amendments are adopted, brought into force and take effect in accordance with the provisions of article VIII of the present Convention concerning the amendment procedures applicable to the annex other than chapter I.

3 *High-speed craft* is a craft capable of a maximum speed, in metres per second (m/s), equal to or exceeding:

$$3.7\ \nabla^{0.1667}$$

where: ∇ = volume of displacement corresponding to the design waterline (m^3),

excluding craft the hull of which is supported completely clear above the water surface in non-displacement mode by aerodynamic forces generated by ground effect.

4 *Craft constructed* means a craft the keel of which is laid or which is at a similar stage of construction.

5 *Similar stage of construction* means a stage at which:

.1 construction identifiable with a specific craft begins; and

.2 assembly of that craft has commenced comprising at least 50 tonnes or 3% of the estimated mass of all structural material, whichever is the less.

Regulation 2
Application

1 This chapter applies to high-speed craft constructed on or after 1 January 1996, as follows:

.1 passenger craft which do not proceed in the course of their voyage more than 4 h at operational speed from a place of refuge when fully laden; and

.2 cargo craft of 500 gross tonnage and upwards which do not proceed in the course of their voyage more than 8 h at operational speed from a place of refuge when fully laden.

第1条
定义

就本章而言：

1 **《1994年高速船规则》(1994年HSC规则)**系指本组织海上安全委员会MSC.36(63)决议通过并可能经本组织修正的《国际高速船安全规则》,但这种修正案应按本公约第Ⅷ条有关适用于除第Ⅰ章外的附则修正程序的规定予以通过、生效和实施。

2 **《2000年高速船规则》(2000年HSC规则)**系指本组织海上安全委员会MSC.97(73)决议通过并可能经本组织修正的《2000年国际高速船安全规则》,但这种修正案应按本公约第Ⅷ条有关适用于除第Ⅰ章外的附则修正程序的规定予以通过、生效和实施。

3 **高速船**系指最大航速(m/s)等于或大于下列值的船：

$$3.7\ \nabla^{0.1667}$$

式中:∇=相应于设计水线的排水量(m^3),

不包括在非排水状态下船体由地效应产生的气动升力完全支承在水面以上的船舶。

4 **建造的船**系指安放龙骨或处于类似建造阶段的船。

5 **类似建造阶段**系指在此阶段：

.1 可辨认出某一具体高速船建造开始;和

.2 该船业已开始的装配量至少为50 t,或为全部结构材料估算重量的3%,取较小者。

第2条
适用范围

1 本章适用于符合下列条件的1996年1月1日或以后建造的高速船：

.1 在其营运的航线上,满载时以其营运航速航行至避难地不超过4 h的客船;和

.2 在其营运的航线上,满载时以其营运航速航行至避难地不超过8 h的500总吨及以上的货船。

2 Any craft, irrespective of the date of construction, which undergoes repairs, alterations, modifications and outfitting related thereto shall continue to comply with at least the requirements previously applicable to the craft. Such a craft, if constructed before 1 July 2002, shall, as a rule, comply with the requirements for a craft constructed on or after that date to at least the same extent as it did before undergoing such repairs, alterations, modifications or outfitting. Repairs, alterations and modifications of a major character, and outfitting related thereto, shall meet the requirements for a craft constructed on or after 1 July 2002 in so far as the Administration deems reasonable and practicable.

Regulation 3
Requirements for high-speed craft

1 Notwithstanding the provisions of chapters I to IV and regulations V/18, 19 and 20:

.1 a high-speed craft constructed on or after 1 January 1996 but before 1 July 2002 which complies with the requirements of the High-Speed Craft Code, 1994 in its entirety and which has been surveyed and certified as provided in that Code shall be deemed to have complied with the requirements of chapters I to IV and regulations V/18, 19 and 20. For the purpose of this regulation, the requirements of that Code shall be treated as mandatory;

.2 a high-speed craft constructed on or after 1 July 2002 which complies with the requirements of the High-Speed Craft Code, 2000 in its entirety and which has been surveyed and certified as provided in that Code shall be deemed to have complied with the requirements of chapters I to IV and regulations V/18, 19 and 20.

2 The certificates and permits issued under the High-Speed Craft Code shall have the same force and the same recognition as the certificates issued under chapter I.

2 任何高速船,无论其何时建造,在进行修理、改装以及与之有关的舾装时,应至少继续符合该船原先适用的要求。该船如系在2002年7月1日以前建造,一般应至少按其修理、改装或舾装之前的同等程度,符合对该日或以后建造的高速船的要求。重大的修理、改装以及与之有关的舾装,在主管机关认为合理和可行的范围内,应满足对2002年7月1日或以后建造的高速船的要求。

第3条
高速船的要求

1 尽管有第Ⅰ章至第Ⅳ章及第Ⅴ/18、19和20条的规定:

.1 在1996年1月1日或以后,但在2002年7月1日以前建造的高速船,如果完全符合《1994年高速船规则》的要求,并按该规则的规定业已检验和发证,则其应视为符合第Ⅰ章至第Ⅳ章及第Ⅴ/18、19和20条的要求。就本条而言,该规则的要求应视为强制性要求;

.2 在2002年7月1日或以后建造的高速船,如果完全符合《2000年高速船规则》的要求,并按该规则的规定业已检验和发证,则其应视为符合第Ⅰ章至第Ⅳ章及第Ⅴ/18、19和20条的要求。

2 根据《高速船规则》签发的证书和许可证,应与按第Ⅰ章规定签发的证书具有同样的效力和获得同样的承认。

Chapter XI-1 Special measures to enhance maritime safety

第Ⅺ-1章　加强海上安全的特别措施

Regulation 1
Authorization of recognized organizations①

The Administration shall authorize organizations, referred to in regulation I/6, including classification societies, in accordance with the provisions of the present Convention and with the Code for Recognized Organizations (RO Code), consisting of part 1 and part 2 (the provisions of which shall be treated as mandatory) and part 3 (the provisions of which shall be treated as recommendatory), as adopted by the Organization by resolution MSC.349(92), as may be amended by the Organization, provided that:

.1 amendments to part 1 and part 2 of the RO Code are adopted, brought into force and take effect in accordance with the provisions of article VIII of the present Convention;

.2 amendments to part 3 of the RO Code are adopted by the Maritime Safety Committee in accordance with its Rules of Procedure; and

.3 any amendments adopted by the Maritime Safety Committee and the Marine Environment Protection Committee are identical and come into force or take effect at the same time, as appropriate.

Regulation 2
Enhanced surveys②

Bulk carriers as defined in regulation IX/1.6 and oil tankers as defined in regulation II-1/2.22 shall be subject to an enhanced programme of inspections in accordance with the International Code on the Enhanced Programme of Inspections during Surveys of Bulk Carriers and Oil Tankers, 2011 (2011 ESP Code), adopted by the Assembly of the Organization by resolution A.1049(27), as may be amended by the Organization, provided that such amendments are adopted, brought into force and take effect in accordance with the provisions of article VIII of the present Convention concerning the amendment procedures applicable to the annex other than chapter I.

① Refer to *IMO Instruments Implementation Code* (III Code) (resolution A.1070(28)); *Model agreement for the authorization of recognized organizations acting on behalf of the Administration* (MSC/Circ. 710-MEPC/Circ. 307, as may be amended); *Communication of information on the authorization of recognized organizations (ROs)* (MSC/Circ. 1010-MEPC/Circ. 382); *Guidelines for Administrations to ensure the adequacy of transfer of class-related matters between Recognized Organizations* (ROs) (MSC-MEPC.5/Circ.2); and *Notification and circulation through the Global Integrated Shipping Information System (GISIS)* (resolution A.1074(28)).

② Refer to *Guidance for planning the enhanced programme of inspections during surveys of bulk carriers and oil tankers* (MSC/Circ.655) and *Guidelines on the means of access to structures for inspection and maintenance of oil tankers and bulk carriers* (MSC/Circ.686/Rev.1).

第1条
对被认可组织的授权[①]

主管机关须按本公约的规定和本组织以第MSC.349(92)号决议通过的《被认可组织规则》(《RO规则》),对第Ⅰ/6条所述的组织(包括船级社)予以授权,《RO规则》由第1部分和第2部分(须视为强制性规定)和第3部分(须视为建议性规定)组成,并可由本组织修正,条件是:

.1 《RO规则》第1部分和第2部分的修正案应按照本公约第Ⅷ条的规定予以通过、生效和实施;

.2 《RO规则》第3部分的修正案应由海上安全委员会按照其《议事规则》予以通过;和

.3 海上安全委员会和海上环境保护委员会通过的任何相应修正案均应完全一致并且在同一时间生效或实施。

第2条
加强检验[②]

第Ⅸ/1.6条定义的散货船和第Ⅱ-1/2.22条定义的油船,应按本组织大会以第A.1049(27)号决议通过的《2011年国际散货船和油船检验期间加强检验计划规则》(2011年加强检验规则)执行加强检验程序,但这种修正案应按本公约第Ⅷ条有关适用于除第Ⅰ章外的附则修正程序的规定予以通过、生效和实施。

① 参见《国际海事组织文书实施规则》(Ⅲ规则)(第A.1070(28)号决议);《授权代表主管机关的认可组织的示范协议》(经修订的MSC/Circ.710-MEPC/Circ.307);授权认可组织的相关信息交流(MSC/Circ.1010-MEPC/Circ.382);《主管机关确保认可组织(RO)之间充分移交船级事务的指南》(MSC-MEPC.5/Circ.2);和《经全球综合航运信息系统(GISIS)进行的通知和通报》(第A.1074(28)号决议)。

② 参见《散货船和油船检验期间加强检验程序规划导则》(MSC/Circ.655通函)和《油船和散货船进入结构检查和维修指南》(MSC/Circ.686/Rev.1通函)。

Regulation 2-1
Harmonization of survey periods of cargo ships not subject to the ESP Code

For cargo ships not subject to enhanced surveys under regulation XI-1/2, notwithstanding any other provisions, the intermediate and renewal surveys included in regulation I/10 may be carried out and completed over the corresponding periods as specified in the 2011 ESP Code, as may be amended, and the guidelines developed by the Organization,① as appropriate.

Regulation 3
Ship identification number

(Paragraphs 4 and 5 apply to all ships to which this regulation applies. For ships constructed before 1 July 2004, the requirements of paragraphs 4 and 5 shall be complied with not later than the first scheduled dry-docking of the ship after 1 July 2004)

1 This regulation applies to all passenger ships of 100 gross tonnage and upwards and to all cargo ships of 300 gross tonnage and upwards.

2 Every ship shall be provided with an identification number which conforms to the IMO ship identification number scheme adopted by the Organization.②

3 The ship's identification number shall be inserted③ on the certificates and certified copies thereof issued under regulation I/12 or regulation I/13.

4 The ship's identification number shall be permanently marked:

.1 in a visible place either on the stern of the ship or on either side of the hull, amidships port and starboard, above the deepest assigned load line or either side of the superstructure, port and starboard or on the front of the superstructure or, in the case of passenger ships, on a horizontal surface visible from the air; and

.2 in an easily accessible place either on one of the end transverse bulkheads of the machinery spaces, as defined in regulation II-2/3.30, or on one of the hatchways or, in the case of tankers, in the pump-room or, in the case of ships with ro-ro spaces, as defined in regulation II-2/3.41, on one of the end transverse bulkheads of the ro-ro spaces.

5.1 The permanent marking shall be plainly visible, clear of any other markings on the hull and shall be painted in a contrasting colour.

---

① Refer to the *Survey guidelines under the Harmonized System of Survey and Certification (HSSC), 2019* (resolution A.1140(31)), as may be amended.

② Refer to the *IMO ship identification number scheme* (resolution A.1117(30)) and *Implementation of resolution A. 1078(28)—IMO ship identification number scheme* (Circular letter No.1886/Rev.6), as may be amended.

③ Refer to *Marking the ship's plans, manuals and other documents with the IMO ship identification number* (MSC/Circ.1142-MEPC/Circ.425).

第 2-1 条
对不适用《加强检验计划规则》的货船检验期间的协调

对于不适用第 Ⅺ-1/2 条规定的加强检验的货船,尽管有任何其他规定,第 Ⅰ/10 条包括的中间检验和换证检验可按可能经修正的《2011 年加强检验计划规则》中规定的相应周期和本组织制定的合适的导则[①]实施和完成。

第 3 条
船舶识别号

(本条 4 和 5 适用于本条适用的所有船舶。2004 年 7 月 1 日以前建造的船舶,应在不迟于 2004 年 7 月 1 日以后的第一次计划进干坞之日符合本条 4 和 5 的要求。)

1　本条适用于 100 总吨及以上的所有客船和 300 总吨及以上的所有货船。

2　每艘船舶应有一个符合本组织通过的 IMO 船舶编号体系的识别号。[②]

3　该船舶识别号应载入[③]按第Ⅰ/12 条或第Ⅰ/13 条规定签发的证书及其核准无误的副本。

4　船舶识别号应永久性标记在以下位置:

.1　在船尾或船体中部左舷和右舷的最深核定载重线以上,或上层建筑左舷或右舷或上层建筑正面的可见位置,或者就客船而言,在可从空中看见的水平表面;和

.2　在第Ⅱ-2/3.30 条所定义的机器处所的一个端部横舱壁上,或在一个舱口上,或者就油船而言,在泵舱内,或者对于设有第Ⅱ-2/3.41 条所定义的滚装处所的船舶,在滚装处所的一个端部横舱壁上容易接近的位置。

5.1　该永久性标记应清晰可见,与船体上的任何其他标记分开,并应涂成有反差的颜色。

---

① 参见《2019 年检验和发证协调系统下的检验导则》(第 A.1140(31)号决议)。
② 参见《IMO 船舶识别号机制》(第 A.1117(30)号决议)和《第 A.1078(28)号决议的实施情况——IMO 船舶识别号机制》(第 1886/Rev.6 号通函件)。
③ 参见《用 IMO 船舶识别号标记船上图纸、手册和其他文件》(MSC/Circ.1142-MEPC/Circ.425 号通函)。

5.2 The permanent marking referred to in paragraph 4.1 shall be not less than 200 mm in height. The permanent marking referred to in paragraph 4.2 shall not be less than 100 mm in height. The width of the marks shall be proportionate to the height.

5.3 The permanent marking may be made by raised lettering or by cutting it in or by centre-punching it or by any other equivalent method of marking the ship identification number which ensures that the marking is not easily expunged.

5.4 On ships constructed of material other than steel or metal, the Administration shall approve the method of marking the ship identification number.

Regulation 3-1
Company and registered owner identification number

1 This regulation applies to Companies and registered owners of ships to which chapter I applies.

2 For the purpose of this regulation, registered owner shall be as specified by the Administration and Company as defined in regulation IX/1.

3 Every Company and registered owner shall be provided with an identification number which conforms to the IMO Unique Company and Registered Owner Identification Number Scheme adopted by the Organization.[①]

4 The Company identification number shall be inserted on the certificates and certified copies thereof issued under regulation IX/4 and section A/19.2 or A/19.4 of the ISPS Code.

5 This regulation shall take effect when the certificates referred to in paragraph 4 are issued or renewed on or after 1 January 2009.

Regulation 4
Port State control on operational requirements[②]

1 A ship when in a port of another Contracting Government is subject to control by officers duly authorized by such Government concerning operational requirements in respect of the safety of ships, when there are clear grounds for believing that the master or crew are not familiar with essential shipboard procedures relating to the safety of ships.

2 In the circumstances defined in paragraph 1 of this regulation, the Contracting Government carrying out the control shall take such steps as will ensure that the ship shall not sail until the situation has been brought to order in accordance with the requirements of the present Convention.

① Refer to *Adoption of the IMO unique company and registered owner identification number scheme* (resolution MSC.160(78)) and *Implementation of IMO unique company and registered owner identification number scheme* (resolution MSC. 760 (78)) (Circular Letter No.2554/Rev.3), as may be amended.

② Refer to *Procedures for port State control, 2019* (resolution A.1138(31)).

5.2 上述4.1所述的永久性标记的高度应不小于200 mm。上述4.2所述的永久性标记的高度应不小于100 mm。标记的宽度应与其高度成比例。

5.3 该永久性标记可制成凸出的字符，或刻入或用中心冲头冲制，或使用可确保该标记不易被擦除的任何其他标识船舶识别号的等效方法制成。

5.4 对于用钢材或金属以外的材料建造的船舶，船舶标识号的标识方法应经主管机关批准。

第3-1条
公司和注册船东识别号

1 本条适用于第Ⅰ章所适用的船舶公司和注册船东。

2 就本条而言，注册船东应由主管机关和第Ⅸ/1条所定义的公司予以规定。

3 每个公司和船东均应拥有一个与本组织通过的《IMO唯一的公司和注册船东识别号机制》相符的识别号①。

4 公司识别号应载入按第Ⅸ/4条和ISPS规则A/19.2或A/19.4签发的证书及其核准无误的副本。

5 本条4所述的证书在2009年1月1日或以后签发或换新时，本条应予实施。

第4条
关于操作要求的港口国控制②

1 船舶在另一缔约国政府的港口时，若有明显理由确信该船船长或船员不熟悉船上与船舶安全有关的主要操作程序，应接受该国政府正式授权的官员对有关船舶安全方面的操作要求的控制。

2 在本条1定义的情况下，执行控制的缔约国政府应采取措施，确保该船在按本公约的要求调整至正常状态前，不得开航。

① 参见通过的《IMO唯一的公司和注册船东识别号机制》(MSC.160(78)号决议)和《实施IMO唯一公司和注册船东识别号机制(MSC.160(78)号决议)》第2554/Rev.3号通函件。

② 参见《2019年港口国控制程序》(第A.1138(31)号决议)

3 Procedures relating to the port State control prescribed in regulation I/19 shall apply to this regulation.

4 Nothing in the present regulation shall be construed to limit the rights and obligations of a Contracting Government carrying out control over operational requirements specifically provided for in the regulations.

Regulation 5
Continuous Synopsis Record

1 Every ship to which chapter I applies shall be issued with a Continuous Synopsis Record.

2.1 The Continuous Synopsis Record is intended to provide an on-board record of the history of the ship with respect to the information recorded therein.

2.2 For ships constructed before 1 July 2004, the Continuous Synopsis Record shall, at least, provide the history of the ship as from 1 July 2004.

3 The Continuous Synopsis Record shall be issued by the Administration to each ship that is entitled to fly its flag and it shall contain, at least, the following information (the Continuous Synopsis Record shall contain the information in paragraphs 3.7 and 3.10 when it is issued or updated on or after 1 January 2009):

.1 the name of the State whose flag the ship is entitled to fly;

.2 the date on which the ship was registered with that State;

.3 the ship's identification number in accordance with regulation 3;

.4 the name of the ship;

.5 the port at which the ship is registered;

.6 the name of the registered owner(s) and their registered address(es);

.7 the registered owner identification number;

.8 the name of the registered bareboat charterer(s) and their registered address(es), if applicable;

.9 the name of the Company, as defined in regulation IX/1, its registered address and the address (es) from where it carries out the safety management activities;

.10 the Company identification number;

.11 the name of all classification society(ies) with which the ship is classed;

3　第Ⅰ/19 条规定的港口国控制程序应适用于本条。

4　本条的任何内容均不得解释为限制缔约国政府对本规则明确规定的操作要求执行控制的权利和义务。

第 5 条
连续概要记录

1　第Ⅰ章所适用的每艘船舶应予签发连续概要记录。

2.1　连续概要记录旨在就其中所记录的信息在船上提供一份船舶历史记录。

2.2　对于 2004 年 7 月 1 日以前建造的船舶,连续概要记录应至少提供该船自 2004 年 7 月 1 日起的历史。

3　主管机关应为悬挂其国旗的每艘船舶签发连续概要记录,其应至少包括以下信息(连续概要记录在 2009 年 1 月 1 日或以后签发或更新时,应包含本条 3.7 和 3.10 所述的信息):

.1　该船的船旗国国名;

.2　该船在该国注册的日期;

.3　第 3 条所述的船舶识别号;

.4　该船船名;

.5　该船的船籍港;

.6　注册船东姓名及其注册地址;

.7　注册船东识别号;

.8　注册光船租赁人姓名及其注册地址(如适用);

.9　第Ⅸ/1 条所定义的公司的名称,其注册地址及其开展安全管理活动的地址;

.10　公司识别号;

.11　该船所入级的所有船级社的名称;

.12 the name of the Administration or of the Contracting Government or of the recognized organization which has issued the Document of Compliance (or the Interim Document of Compliance), specified in the ISM Code as defined in regulation IX/1, to the Company operating the ship and the name of the body which has carried out the audit on the basis of which the Document was issued, if other than that issuing the Document;

.13 the name of the Administration or of the Contracting Government or of the recognized organization that has issued the Safety Management Certificate (or the Interim Safety Management Certificate), specified in the ISM Code as defined in regulation IX/1, to the ship and the name of the body which has carried out the audit on the basis of which the Certificate was issued, if other than that issuing the Certificate;

.14 the name of the Administration or of the Contracting Government or of the recognized security organization that has issued the International Ship Security Certificate (or the Interim International Ship Security Certificate), specified in part A of the ISPS Code as defined in regulation XI-2/1, to the ship and the name of the body which has carried out the verification on the basis of which the Certificate was issued, if other than that issuing the Certificate; and

.15 the date on which the ship ceased to be registered with that State.

4.1 Any changes relating to the entries referred to in paragraphs 3.4 to 3.12 shall be recorded in the Continuous Synopsis Record so as to provide updated and current information together with the history of the changes.

4.2 In case of any changes relating to the entries referred to in paragraph 4.1, the Administration shall issue, as soon as is practically possible but not later than three months from the date of the change, to the ships entitled to fly its flag either a revised and updated version of the Continuous Synopsis Record or appropriate amendments thereto.

4.3 In case of any changes relating to the entries referred to in paragraph 4.1, the Administration, pending the issue of a revised and updated version of the Continuous Synopsis Record, shall authorize and require either the Company as defined in regulation IX/1 or the master of the ship to amend the Continuous Synopsis Record to reflect the changes. In such cases, after the Continuous Synopsis Record has been amended, the Company shall, without delay, inform the Administration accordingly.

5.1 The Continuous Synopsis Record shall be in English, French or Spanish language. Additionally, a translation of the Continuous Synopsis Record into the official language or languages of the Administration may be provided.

5.2 The Continuous Synopsis Record shall be in the format developed by the Organization and shall be maintained in accordance with guidelines developed by the Organization.① Any previous entries in the Continuous Synopsis Record shall not be modified, deleted or, in any way, erased or defaced.

---

① Refer to *Format and guidelines for the maintenance of the Continuous Synopsis Record (CSR)* (resolution A.959(23), as amended by MSC.198(80)) and *Guidance to port State control officers on the non-security related elements of the 2002 SOLAS amendments* (MSC/Circ.1113).

.12 向经营该船的公司签发第Ⅸ/1条所定义的ISM规则规定的符合证明(或临时符合证明的主管机关或缔约国政府或认可组织名称,如果进行审核并据此发证的机构不是同一机构,还要有审核机构的名称;

.13 向该船签发第Ⅸ/1条所定义的ISM规则规定的安全管理证书(或临时安全管理证书的主管机关或缔约国政府或认可组织名称,如果进行审核并据此发证的机构不是同一机构,还要有审核机构的名称;

.14 向该船签发第Ⅺ-2/1条所定义的ISPS规则A部分规定的国际船舶保安证书(或临时国际船舶保安证书)的主管机关或缔约国政府或认可组织名称,如果进行审核并据此发证的机构不是同一机构,还要有审核机构的名称;和

.15 该船终止在该国注册的日期。

4.1 与3.4至3.12所述记载有关的任何变化均应记录在连续概要记录中,以便提供最新的和当前的信息以及变化的历史。

4.2 如果4.1所述记载发生任何变化,主管机关应按实际可能尽快,但不迟于自发生变化之日起的三个月,向悬挂其国旗的船舶签发一份经修订和更新的连续概要记录或该记录相应的修正文件。

4.3 如果4.1所述记载发生任何变化,主管机关应在签发经修订和更新的连续概要记录之前,授权并要求第Ⅸ/1条所定义的公司或船舶的船长对连续概要记录进行修改,以反映有关变化。此种情况下,公司在修改连续概要记录后,应随即通知主管机关。

5.1 连续概要记录应使用英文、法文或西班牙文。此外,连续概要记录还可提供主管机关的官方语言的译本。

5.2 连续概要记录应使用本组织制定的格式,并应按本组织制定的指南①保持。对连续概要记录的任何已有记载均不得修改、删除或以任何方式擦除或涂改。

---

① 参见《连续概要记录(CSR)的格式和保持指南》(经第MSC.198(80)号决议修正的第A.959(23)号决议)和《2002年SOLAS修正案有关非保安要素的港口国控制官员导则》(第MSC/Circ.1113号通函)。

6 Whenever a ship is transferred to the flag of another State or the ship is sold to another owner (or is taken over by another bareboat charterer) or another Company assumes the responsibility for the operation of the ship, the Continuous Synopsis Record shall be left on board.

7 When a ship is to be transferred to the flag of another State, the Company shall notify the Administration of the name of the State under whose flag the ship is to be transferred so as to enable the Administration to forward to that State a copy of the Continuous Synopsis Record covering the period during which the ship was under its jurisdiction.

8 When a ship is transferred to the flag of another State the Government of which is a Contracting Government, the Contracting Government of the State whose flag the ship was flying hitherto shall transmit to the Administration, as soon as possible after the transfer takes place, a copy of the relevant Continuous Synopsis Record covering the period during which the ship was under their jurisdiction together with any Continuous Synopsis Records previously issued to the ship by other States.

9 When a ship is transferred to the flag of another State, the Administration shall append the previous Continuous Synopsis Records to the Continuous Synopsis Record the Administration will issue to the ship so to provide the continuous history record intended by this regulation.

10 The Continuous Synopsis Record shall be kept on board the ship and shall be available for inspection at all times.

Regulation 6
Additional requirements for the investigation of marine casualties and incidents①

Taking into account regulation I/21, each Administration shall conduct investigations of marine casualties and incidents, in accordance with the provisions of the present Convention, as supplemented by the provisions of the Code of the International Standards and Recommended Practices for a Safety Investigation into a Marine Casualty or Marine Incident (Casualty Investigation Code) adopted by resolution MSC.255(84), and:

---

① Refer to the following resolutions:
IMO Instruments Implementation Code (III Code) (resolution A.1070(28));
Guidelines to assist investigators in the implementation of the Casualty Investigation Code (resolution MSC.255(84)) (resolution A.1075(28));
Recommendation on the conclusion of agreements and arrangements between States on the question of access and employment of foreign seaborne salvage equipment in territorial waters (resolution A.203(VII));
Guidelines on fair treatment of seafarers in the event of a maritime accident (resolution A.987(24));
Promotion as widely as possible of the application of the 2006 *guidelines on fair treatment of seafarers in the event of a maritime accident* (resolution A.1056(27)); and
Notification and circulation through the Global Integrated Shipping Information System (GISIS) (resolution A.1074(28)).
Refer also to:
Revised harmonized reporting procedures—Reports required under SOLAS regulations I/21 and XI-1/6, and MARPOL, articles 8 and 12 (MSC-MEPC.3/Circ.4/Rev.1);
Provision of preliminary information on serious and very serious casualties by rescue coordination centres (MSC/Circ.802-MEPC/Circ.332);
Guidance on near-miss reporting (MSC-MEPC.7/Circ.7); and
Reporting near misses (MSC.Circ.1015).

6 船舶无论何时变更船旗或被售予另一船东(或由另一光船租赁人接管),或由另一公司承担营运责任,连续概要记录均应留在船上。

7 如果船舶将要变更船旗,公司应将新船旗国的国名告知原主管机关,以便原主管机关将该船在受其管辖期间的连续概要记录的副本送交该国。

8 在船舶变更船旗时,如新的船旗国为缔约国政府,该船的原缔约船旗国政府应在换旗后尽快将该船受其管辖期间的有关连续概要记录副本以及先前由其他国家向该船签发的任何连续概要记录送交新的主管机关。

9 在船舶变更船旗时,主管机关应将以前的连续概要记录附在该主管机关将要签发给该船的连续概要记录之后,以提供本条所指的连续历史记录。

10 连续概要记录应保存在船上,并应随时可供检查。

第6条
海难与事故调查附加要求①

考虑到第Ⅰ/21条规定,各主管机关须对海上事故和事件进行调查。进行调查须遵照本公约的规定,和第MSC.255(84)号决议通过的海上事故或海上事件安全调查国际标准和建议做法规则(事故调查规则)中的补充规定,及;

① 参见以下决议:
《IMO文书实施规则》(Ⅲ规则)(第A.1070(28)号决议);
《协助调查员执行海难调查规则(第MSC.255(84)号决议)指南》(第A.1075(28)号决议)。
《关于外国海上救助设备进入本国领海和使用问题在相关国家间缔结协议和协定的建议案》(第A.203(Ⅶ)号决议);
《关于发生海上事故时公平对待海员的导则》(第A.987(24)号决议)
《促进尽可能广泛应用2006年海上事故中公平对待海员指南》(第A.1056(27)号决议);
《经全球综合航运信息系统(GISIS)进行通知和通报》(第A.1074(28)号决议);
又参见:
《经修订的协调报告程序——根据SOLAS公约第Ⅰ/21条和Ⅺ-1/6条及MARPOL公约第8条和第12条要求的报告》(第MSC-MEPC.3/Circ.4/Rev.1号通函);
《由救援协调中心提供严重和非常严重海难的初步信息》(第MSC/Circ.802-MEPC/Circ.332号通函);
《侥幸事故报告指南》(第MSC-MEPC.7/Circ.7号通函)和《报告侥幸事故》(第MSC.Circ.1015号通函)

.1 the provisions of parts Ⅰ and Ⅱ of the Casualty Investigation Code shall be fully complied with;

.2 the related guidance and explanatory material contained in part Ⅲ of the Casualty Investigation Code should be taken into account to the greatest possible extent in order to achieve a more uniform implementation of the Casualty Investigation Code;

.3 amendments to parts Ⅰ and Ⅱ of the Casualty Investigation Code shall be adopted, brought into force and take effect in accordance with the provisions of article Ⅷ of the present Convertion Concerning the amendment procedures applicable to the annex other than chapter Ⅰ; and

.4 part Ⅲ of the Casualty Investigation Code shall be amended by the Maritime Safety Committee in accordance with its rules of procedure.

Regulation 7
Atmosphere testing instrument for enclosed spaces

Every ship to which chapter Ⅰ applies shall carry an appropriate portable atmosphere testing instrument or instruments①. As a minimum, these shall be capable of measuring concentrations of oxygen, flammable gases or vapours, hydrogen sulphide and carbon monoxide prior to entry into enclosed spaces②. Instruments carried under other requirements may satisfy this regulation. Suitable means shall be provided for the calibration of all such instruments.

① Refer to the *Guidelines to facilitate the selection of portable atmosphere testing instruments for enclosed spaces as required by SOLAS regulation XI-1/7* (MSC.1/Circ.1477).

② Refer to the *Revised recommendations for entering enclosed spaces aboard ships* (resolution A.1050(27)).

.1　事故调查规则 第Ⅰ和第Ⅱ部分的规定须完全遵守；

.2　部分须由海上安全委员会按照其程序规则加以部分中的指南和说明内容应尽最大可能地给予事故调查规则第Ⅲ部分考虑以获得对事故调查规则的更加统一的实施；

.3　事故调查规则第Ⅰ和第Ⅱ部分的修正案须按照本公约第Ⅷ条中适用于除第Ⅰ章外的附件修正程序的规定加以通过,生效和实施;及

.4　事故调查规则的第Ⅲ修正。

第7条
围蔽处所的气体测试仪

第Ⅰ章所适用的每艘船舶应配备适当的便携式气体测试仪①。这些测试仪须至少能在进入围蔽处所前测量氧气、可燃气体或蒸气、硫化氢和一氧化碳的浓度②。按其他要求配备的测试仪可满足本条要求。须为所有这些测试仪提供合适的校准设备。

① 参见《便利选择 SOLAS 公约第Ⅺ-1/7 条要求的围蔽处所便携式气体测试仪导则》(第 MSC.1/Circ.1477 号通函)。
② 参见《经修订的进入船上围蔽处所建议案》(第 A.1050(27)号决议)。

Chapter XI-2 Special measures to enhance maritime security

第Ⅺ-2章　加强海上保安的特别措施

Regulation 1
Definitions

1 For the purpose of this chapter, unless expressly provided otherwise:

.1 *Bulk carrie*r means a bulk carrier as defined in regulation IX/1.6.

.2 *Chemical tanker* means a chemical tanker as defined in regulation VII/8.2.

.3 *Gas carrier* means a gas carrier as defined in regulation VII/11.2.

.4 *High-speed craft* means a craft as defined in regulation X/1.2.

.5 *Mobile offshore drilling unit* means a mechanically propelled mobile offshore drilling unit, as defined in regulation IX/1.7, not on location.

.6 *Oil tanker* means an oil tanker as defined in regulation II-1/2.22.

.7 *Company* means a Company as defined in regulation IX/1.2.

.8 *Ship/port interface* means the interactions that occur when a ship is directly and immediately affected by actions involving the movement of persons, goods or the provisions of port services to or from the ship.

.9 *Port facility* is a location, as determined by the Contracting Government or by the Designated Authority, where the ship/port interface takes place. This includes areas such as anchorages, waiting berths and approaches from seaward, as appropriate.

.10 *Ship-to-ship activity* means any activity not related to a port facility that involves the transfer of goods or persons from one ship to another.

.11 *Designated Authority* means the organization(s) or the administration(s) identified, within the Contracting Government, as responsible for ensuring the implementation of the provisions of this chapter pertaining to port facility security and ship/port interface, from the point of view of the port facility.

.12 *International Ship and Port Facility Security (ISPS) Code* means the International Code for the Security of Ships and of Port Facilities consisting of part A (the provisions of which shall be treated as mandatory) and part B (the provisions of which shall be treated as recommendatory), as adopted, on 12 December 2002, by resolution 2 of the Conference of Contracting Governments to the International Convention for the Safety of Life at Sea, 1974 as may be amended by the Organization, provided that:

.1 amendments to part A of the Code are adopted, brought into force and take effect in accordance with article VIII of the present Convention concerning the amendment procedures applicable to the annex other than chapter I; and

.2 amendments to part B of the Code are adopted by the Maritime Safety Committee in accordance with its Rules of Procedure.

第1条
定义

1　除另有明文规定外,就本章而言:

.1　**散货船**系指第Ⅸ/1.6条所定义的散货船。

.2　**化学品液货船**系指第Ⅶ/8.2条所定义的化学品液货船。

.3　**气体运输船**系指第Ⅶ/11.2条所定义的气体运输船。

.4　**高速船**系指第Ⅹ/1.2条所定义的船。

.5　**海上移动式钻井平台**系指第Ⅸ/1.7条所定义的非就位状态的机械推进海上移动式钻井平台。

.6　**油船**系指第Ⅱ-1/2.22条所定义的油船。

.7　**公司**系指第Ⅸ/1.2条所定义的公司。

.8　**船/港界面活动**系指当船舶受到往来于船舶的人员、货物移动或港口服务提供等活动的直接和密切影响时发生的交互活动。

.9　**港口设施**系由缔约国政府或由指定当局确定的发生船/港界面活动的场所,其中包括锚地、候泊区和进港航道等区域。

.10　**船到船活动**系指涉及物品或人员从一船向另一船转移的任何与港口设施无关的活动。

.11　**指定当局**系指在缔约国政府内所确定的负责从港口设施的角度确保实施本章涉及港口设施保安和船/港界面活动规定的机构或行政机关。

.12　**《国际船舶和港口设施保安(ISPS)规则》**系指《1974年国际海上人命安全公约》缔约国政府会议于2002年12月12日以第2号决议通过的《国际船舶保安和港口设施保安规则》,由A部分(其规定应视为具有强制性)和B部分(其规定应视为建议性)组成。该规则可能经本组织修正,但:

.1　该规则A部分的修正案应按本公约第Ⅷ条有关适用于除第Ⅰ章外的附则修正程序的规定予以通过、生效和实施;和

.2　该规则B部分的修正案应由海上安全委员会按照其议事规则通过。

.13 *Security incident* means any suspicious act or circumstance threatening the security of a ship, including a mobile offshore drilling unit and a high-speed craft, or of a port facility or of any ship/port interface or any ship-to-ship activity.

.14 *Security level* means the qualification of the degree of risk that a security incident will be attempted or will occur.

.15 *Declaration of Security* means an agreement reached between a ship and either a port facility or another ship with which it interfaces, specifying the security measures each will implement.

.16 *Recognized security organization* means an organization with appropriate expertise in security matters and with appropriate knowledge of ship and port operations authorized to carry out an assessment, or a verification, or an approval or a certification activity, required by this chapter or by part A of the ISPS Code.

2 The term *ship*, when used in regulations 3 to 13, includes mobile offshore drilling units and high-speed craft.

3 The term *all ships*, when used in this chapter, means any ship to which this chapter applies.

4 The term *Contracting Government*, when used in regulations 3, 4, 7 and 10 to 13, includes a reference to the Designated Authority.

Regulation 2
Application

1 This chapter applies to:

.1 the following types of ships engaged on international voyages:

.1 passenger ships, including high-speed passenger craft;

.2 cargo ships, including high-speed craft, of 500 gross tonnage and upwards; and

.3 mobile offshore drilling units; and

.2 port facilities serving such ships engaged on international voyages.

2 Notwithstanding the provisions of paragraph 1.2, Contracting Governments shall decide the extent of application of this chapter and of the relevant sections of part A of the ISPS Code to those port facilities within their territory which, although used primarily by ships not engaged on international voyages, are required, occasionally, to serve ships arriving or departing on an international voyage.

2.1 Contracting Governments shall base their decisions, under paragraph 2, on a port facility security assessment carried out in accordance with the provisions of part A of the ISPS Code.

.13 **保安事件**系指威胁船舶(包括海上移动式钻井平台和高速船),或港口设施或任何船/港界面活动或任何船到船活动保安的任何可疑行为或情况。

.14 **保安等级**系指企图造成保安事件或发生保安事件的风险级别划分。

.15 **保安声明**系指船舶与作为其界面活动对象的港口设施或其他船舶之间达成的协议,规定各自将实行的保安措施。

.16 **认可的保安组织**系指经授权进行本章或 ISPS 规则 A 部分所要求的评估,或验证,或批准或发证活动,具备相应保安专长并具备相应船舶和港口操作方面知识的组织。

2 在第 3 至 13 条中所使用的"船舶"一词,包括海上移动式钻井平台和高速船。

3 本章所使用的"所有船舶"一词,系指本章所适用的任何船舶。

4 在第 3、4、7 和 10 至 13 条中使用的"缔约国政府"一词,同时也是指"指定当局"。

第 2 条
适用范围

1 本章适用于:

.1 以下各类从事国际航行的船舶:

.1 客船,包括高速客船;

.2 500 总吨及以上的货船,包括高速货船;和

.3 海上移动式钻井平台;和

.2 为此类国际航行船舶服务的港口设施。

2 尽管有 1.2 的规定,但对于其境内主要用于非国际航行船舶,仅偶尔需要为到港或离港的国际航行船舶服务的港口设施,缔约国政府仍应决定本章和 ISPS 规则 A 部分的相关章节在何种程度上适用于这些港口设施。

2.1 缔约国政府应在按照 ISPS 规则 A 部分开展的港口设施保安评估的基础上,根据上述 2 做出决定。

2.2 Any decision which a Contracting Government makes, under paragraph 2, shall not compromise the level of security intended to be achieved by this chapter or by part A of the ISPS Code.

3 This chapter does not apply to warships, naval auxiliaries or other ships owned or operated by a Contracting Government and used only on government non-commercial service.

4 Nothing in this chapter shall prejudice the rights or obligations of States under international law.

Regulation 3
Obligations of Contracting Governments with respect to security

1 Administrations shall set security levels and ensure the provision of security-level information to ships entitled to fly their flag. When changes in security level occur, security-level information shall be updated as the circumstance dictates.

2 Contracting Governments shall set security levels and ensure the provision of security-level information to port facilities within their territory, and to ships prior to entering a port or whilst in a port within their territory. When changes in security level occur, security-level information shall be updated as the circumstance dictates.

Regulation 4
Requirements for Companies and ships

1 Companies shall comply with the relevant requirements of this chapter and of part A of the ISPS Code, taking into account the guidance given in part B of the ISPS Code.

2 Ships shall comply with the relevant requirements of this chapter and of part A of the ISPS Code, taking into account the guidance given in part B of the ISPS Code, and such compliance shall be verified and certified as provided for in part A of the ISPS Code.

3 Prior to entering a port or whilst in a port within the territory of a Contracting Government, a ship shall comply with the requirements for the security level set by that Contracting Government, if such security level is higher than the security level set by the Administration for that ship.

4 Ships shall respond without undue delay to any change to a higher security level.

5 Where a ship is not in compliance with the requirements of this chapter or of part A of the ISPS Code, or cannot comply with the requirements of the security level set by the Administration or by another Contracting Government and applicable to that ship, then the ship shall notify the appropriate competent authority prior to conducting any ship/port interface or prior to entry into port, whichever occurs earlier.

2.2 缔约国政府根据上述2所做的任何决定不应降低本章或ISPS规则A部分所要达到的保安水平。

3 本章不适用于军船、海军辅助船，或由缔约国政府拥有或经营的仅用于政府非商业性服务的其他船舶。

4 本章的任何内容均不得损害各国根据国际法所具有的权利或义务。

第3条
缔约国政府的保安义务

1 主管机关应为悬挂其国旗的船舶规定保安等级并确保向其提供保安等级方面的信息。当保安等级发生变化时，应根据情况对保安等级信息予以更新。

2 缔约国政府应为其境内的港口设施和进入其港口前的船舶或在其港口内的船舶规定保安等级并确保向其提供保安等级方面的信息。当保安等级发生变化时，应根据情况对保安等级信息予以更新。

第4条
对公司和船舶的要求

1 公司应符合本章和ISPS规则A部分的相关要求，并考虑到ISPS规则B部分提供的指导。

2 船舶应符合本章和ISPS规则A部分的相关要求，并考虑到ISPS规则B部分提供的指导，且这种符合应按ISPS规则A部分的规定予以验证和发证。

3 船舶在进入一缔约国境内的港口之前，或在其境内的港口期间，如果缔约国政府规定的保安等级高于该船主管机关为其规定的保安等级，则船舶应符合该缔约国政府规定的保安等级要求。

4 船舶应对改为更高的保安等级做出响应，不得有不当延误。

5 如果船舶不符合本章或ISPS规则A部分的要求，或不能符合主管机关或另一缔约国政府规定的对其适用的保安等级要求，则该船应在进行任何船/港界面活动之前，或在进港之前（以时间在先者为准）通知有关主管当局。

Regulation 5
Specific responsibility of Companies

The Company shall ensure that the master has available on board, at all times, information through which officers duly authorized by a Contracting Government can establish:

.1 who is responsible for appointing the members of the crew or other persons currently employed or engaged on board the ship in any capacity on the business of that ship;

.2 who is responsible for deciding the employment of the ship; and

.3 in cases where the ship is employed under the terms of charter party(ies), who are the parties to such charter party(ies).

Regulation 6
Ship security alert system①

1 All ships shall be provided with a ship security alert system, as follows:

.1 ships constructed on or after 1 July 2004;

.2 passenger ships, including high-speed passenger craft, constructed before 1 July 2004, not later than the first survey of the radio installation after 1 July 2004;

.3 oil tankers, chemical tankers, gas carriers, bulk carriers and cargo high-speed craft, of 500 gross tonnage and upwards constructed before 1 July 2004, not later than the first survey of the radio installation after 1 July 2004; and

.4 other cargo ships of 500 gross tonnage and upward and mobile offshore drilling units constructed before 1 July 2004, not later than the first survey of the radio installation after 1 July 2006.

2 The ship security alert system, when activated, shall:

.1 initiate and transmit a ship-to-shore security alert to a competent authority designated by the Administration, which in these circumstances may include the Company, identifying the ship, its location and indicating that the security of the ship is under threat or it has been compromised;

.2 not send the ship security alert to any other ships;

.3 not raise any alarm on board the ship; and

.4 continue the ship security alert until deactivated and/or reset.

3 The ship security alert system shall:

---

① Refer to the *Performance standards for a ship security alert system* (resolution MSC.136(76)) and *Revised performance standards for ship security alert systems* (resolution MSC.147(77)).

第5条
公司的具体责任

公司应确保船长在任何时候船上有资料可供缔约国政府正式授权的官员使用,使其能确定:

.1 谁负责指派船员或当前以任何职能身份在船上受雇或工作的其他人员;

.2 谁负责决定船舶的使用;和

.3 如果船舶按租船合同的条款使用,则谁是租船合同的各方。

第6条
船舶保安警报系统①

1 所有船舶应按以下规定装设船舶保安警报系统:

.1 在2004年7月1日或以后建造的船舶;

.2 在2004年7月1日以前建造的客船,包括高速客船,不迟于2004年7月1日以后的第一次无线电装置检验;

.3 在2004年7月1日以前建造的500总吨及以上的油船、化学品液货船、气体运输船、散货船和高速货船,不迟于2004年7月1日以后的第一次无线电装置检验;和

.4 在2004年7月1日以前建造的500总吨及以上的其他货船和海上移动式钻井平台,不迟于2006年7月1日以后的第一次无线电装置检验。

2 船舶保安警报系统启动后,应:

.1 开始向主管机关指定的主管当局(在此情况下可包括公司)发送船对岸保安警报,确定船舶身份、船位并指出该船的保安状况受到威胁或已受到危害;

.2 不向任何其他船舶发送船舶保安警报;

.3 不在船上发出任何报警;和

.4 在关闭和/或复位前持续发送船舶保安警报。

3 船舶保安警报系统应:

---

① 参见第MSC.136(76)号决议通过的《船舶保安警报系统性能标准》和第MSC.147(77)号决议通过的《经修订的船舶保安警报系统性能标准》。

.1 be capable of being activated from the navigation bridge and in at least one other location; and

.2 conform to performance standards not inferior to those adopted by the Organization.

4 The ship security alert system activation points shall be designed so as to prevent the inadvertent initiation of the ship security alert.

5 The requirement for a ship security alert system may be complied with by using the radio installation fitted for compliance with the requirements of chapter IV, provided all requirements of this regulation are complied with.

6 When an Administration receives notification of a ship security alert, that Administration shall immediately notify the State(s) in the vicinity of which the ship is presently operating.

7 When a Contracting Government receives notification of a ship security alert from a ship which is not entitled to fly its flag, that Contracting Government shall immediately notify the relevant Administration and, if appropriate, the State(s) in the vicinity of which the ship is presently operating.

Regulation 7
Threats to ships

1 Contracting Governments shall set security levels and ensure the provision of security-level information to ships operating in their territorial sea or having communicated an intention to enter their territorial sea.

2 Contracting Governments shall provide a point of contact through which such ships can request advice or assistance and to which such ships can report any security concerns about other ships, movements or communications.

3 Where a risk of attack has been identified, the Contracting Government concerned shall advise the ships concerned and their Administrations of:

.1 the current security level;

.2 any security measures that should be put in place by the ships concerned to protect themselves from attack, in accordance with the provisions of part A of the ISPS Code; and

.3 security measures that the coastal State has decided to put in place, as appropriate.

.1　能从驾驶台和至少一个其他位置启动；和

.2　其性能标准不低于本组织通过的性能标准。

4　船舶保安警报系统启动点的设计应能防止误发船舶保安警报。

5　在符合本条所有要求的条件下，可通过使用根据第Ⅳ章的要求而安装的无线电装置符合船舶保安警报系统的要求。

6　当主管机关收到船舶保安警报通知时，该主管机关应立即通知船舶当时所在位置附近的国家。

7　当缔约国政府从非悬挂其国旗的船舶收到船舶保安警报通知时，该缔约国政府应立即通知有关主管机关，并在适当时通知船舶当时所在位置附近的国家。

第7条
对船舶的威胁

1　缔约国政府应为在其领海内营运或已向其通报进入其领海意图的船舶规定保安等级并确保向其提供保安等级信息。

2　缔约国政府应提供一个联络点，上述船舶能够通过该联络点请求咨询或协助并报告关于其他船舶、动向或通信的任何保安问题。

3　如果已确定存在受到袭击的风险，有关缔约国政府应将以下情况告知有关船舶及其主管机关：

.1　当前的保安等级；

.2　按照ISPS规则A部分的规定，有关船舶为防备受到袭击而应采取的任何保安措施；和

.3　沿岸国已决定采取的相应保安措施。

Regulation 8
Master's discretion for ship safety and security

1 The master shall not be constrained by the Company, the charterer or any other person from taking or executing any decision which, in the professional judgement of the master, is necessary to maintain the safety and security of the ship. This includes denial of access to persons (except those identified as duly authorized by a Contracting Government) or their effects and refusal to load cargo, including containers or other closed cargo transport units.

2 If, in the professional judgement of the master, a conflict between any safety and security requirements applicable to the ship arises during its operations, the master shall give effect to those requirements necessary to maintain the safety of the ship. In such cases, the master may implement temporary security measures and shall forthwith inform the Administration and, if appropriate, the Contracting Government in whose port the ship is operating or intends to enter. Any such temporary security measures under this regulation shall, to the highest possible degree, be commensurate with the prevailing security level. When such cases are identified, the Administration shall ensure that such conflicts are resolved and that the possibility of recurrence is minimized.

Regulation 9
Control and compliance measures

1 Control of ships in port

1.1 For the purpose of this chapter, every ship to which this chapter applies is subject to control when in a port of another Contracting Government by officers duly authorized by that Government, who may be the same as those carrying out the functions of regulation I/19. Such control shall be limited to verifying that there is on board a valid International Ship Security Certificate or a valid Interim International Ship Security Certificate issued under the provisions of part A of the ISPS Code ("Certificate"), which if valid shall be accepted, unless there are clear grounds for believing that the ship is not in compliance with the requirements of this chapter or part A of the ISPS Code.

1.2 When there are such clear grounds, or when no valid Certificate is produced when required, the officers duly authorized by the Contracting Government shall impose any one or more control measures in relation to that ship as provided in paragraph 1.3. Any such measures imposed must be proportionate, taking into account the guidance given in part B of the ISPS Code.

1.3 Such control measures are as follows: inspection of the ship, delaying the ship, detention of the ship, restriction of operations, including movement within the port, or expulsion of the ship from port. Such control measures may additionally or alternatively include other lesser administrative or corrective measures.

2 Ships intending to enter a port of another Contracting Government

第8条
船长对船舶安全和保安的决定权

1　船长依照其专业判断而做出或执行为维护船舶安全或保安所必需的决定，应不受公司、承租人或任何他人的约束。这包括拒绝人员（经确认的缔约国政府正式授权的人员除外）或其物品上船和拒绝装货，包括集装箱或其他封闭的货运单元。

2　如果依照船长的专业判断，在船舶操作中出现适用于该船的安全和保安要求之间发生冲突的情况，船长应执行为维护船舶安全所必须的要求。在这种情况下，船长可以实施临时性保安措施并应随即通知主管机关，如果情况适宜，还应随即通知该船所在或拟进入的港口所属缔约国政府。根据本条采取的任何此类临时性保安措施应尽最大可能相当于主要的保安等级。在识别这种情况后，主管机关应确保此类冲突得以解决并使其再次发生的可能性减至最低。

第9条
控制和符合措施

1　对在港船舶的控制

1.1　就本章而言，本章所适用的每一艘船在另一缔约国政府的港口内时，均应受到该国政府正式授权官员的控制，该官员可以是行使第Ⅰ/19条所规定职责的同一官员。除非有明显理由确信船舶不符合本章或ISPS规则A部分的要求，此种控制应限于验证船上携有根据ISPS规则A部分规定签发的有效国际船舶保安证书或有效临时国际船舶保安证书（以下简称“证书”）。该证书如系有效，则应予承认。

1.2　如有此类明显理由，或未能按要求出示有效证书时，缔约国政府正式授权的官员应对船舶采取1.3规定的任何一项或几项控制措施。所采取的任何此类措施必须是适度的，并考虑到ISPS规则B部分提供的指导。

1.3　此类控制措施如下：检查船舶，推迟船期，扣留船舶，限制操作（包括限制在港内移动），或将船舶驱逐出港。此类控制措施还可辅以其他较轻的行政或纠正措施，或由其他较轻的行政或纠正措施代替。

2　拟进入另一缔约国港口的船舶

2.1 For the purpose of this chapter, a Contracting Government may require that ships intending to enter its ports provide the following information to officers duly authorized by that Government to ensure compliance with this chapter prior to entry into port with the aim of avoiding the need to impose control measures or steps:

.1 that the ship possesses a valid Certificate and the name of its issuing authority;

.2 the security level at which the ship is currently operating;

.3 the security level at which the ship operated in any previous port where it has conducted a ship/port interface within the timeframe specified in paragraph 2.3;

.4 any special or additional security measures that were taken by the ship in any previous port where it has conducted a ship/port interface within the timeframe specified in paragraph 2.3;

.5 that the appropriate ship security procedures were maintained during any ship-to-ship activity within the timeframe specified in paragraph 2.3; or

.6 other practical security-related information (but not details of the ship security plan), taking into account the guidance given in part B of the ISPS Code.

If requested by the Contracting Government, the ship or the Company shall provide confirmation, acceptable to that Contracting Government, of the information required above.

2.2 Every ship to which this chapter applies intending to enter the port of another Contracting Government shall provide the information described in paragraph 2.1 on the request of the officers duly authorized by that Government. The master may decline to provide such information on the understanding that failure to do so may result in denial of entry into port.

2.3 The ship shall keep records of the information referred to in paragraph 2.1 for the last 10 calls at port facilities.

2.4 If, after receipt of the information described in paragraph 2.1, officers duly authorized by the Contracting Government of the port in which the ship intends to enter have clear grounds for believing that the ship is in non-compliance with the requirements of this chapter or part A of the ISPS Code, such officers shall attempt to establish communication with and between the ship and the Administration in order to rectify the non-compliance. If such communication does not result in rectification, or if such officers have clear grounds otherwise for believing that the ship is in non-compliance with the requirements of this chapter or part A of the ISPS Code, such officers may take steps in relation to that ship as provided in paragraph 2.5. Any such steps taken must be proportionate, taking into account the guidance given in part B of the ISPS Code.

2.5 Such steps are as follows:

.1 a requirement for the rectification of the non-compliance;

.2 a requirement that the ship proceed to a location specified in the territorial sea or internal waters of that Contracting Government;

2.1 就本章而言,为了避免对船舶采取控制措施或步骤的必要性,缔约国政府可要求拟进入其港口的船舶在进港之前向该缔约国政府正式授权的官员提供以下信息,以确保符合本章的要求:

.1 船舶具有有效证书,及证书签发机关名称;

.2 船舶当前营运所处的保安等级;

.3 在2.3规定的时间段内,船舶在其曾进行船/港界面活动的任何港口内时,其营运所处的保安等级;

.4 在2.3规定的时间段内,船舶在其曾进行船/港界面活动的任何港口内时,所采取的任何特别或附加保安措施;

.5 在2.3规定的时间段内,船舶在任何船对船活动中维持了适当的船舶保安程序;或

.6 与保安有关的其他实际信息(但非船舶保安计划的细节),并考虑到ISPS规则B部分提供的指导。

如果缔约国政府提出要求,船舶或公司应就上文所要求的信息向缔约国政府做出其可接受的确认。

2.2 适用本章的每一艘船拟进入另一缔约国政府的港口,在该政府正式授权官员提出要求后,应提供2.1所述信息。船长可以拒绝提供该信息,但须明白不提供该信息可能导致拒绝该船进港。

2.3 该船保存2.1所述信息的范围为其所停靠的前10个港口设施。

2.4 该船所拟进入港口的缔约国政府正式授权的官员在收到2.1所述信息后,如果有明显理由确信该船不符合本章或ISPS规则A部分的要求,应试图与该船及其主管机关或在该船与其主管机关之间建立通信联系,以纠正不符合的情况。如果上述通信未能解决问题,或该官员有其他明显理由确信该船不符合本章或ISPS规则A部分的要求,该官员可对该船采取2.5规定的步骤。所采取的任何此类步骤必须是适度的,并考虑到ISPS规则B部分提供的指导。

2.5 此类步骤如下:

.1 要求纠正不符合的情况;

.2 要求该船驶往该缔约国政府领海或内陆水域中的一个指定位置;

.3 inspection of the ship, if the ship is in the territorial sea of the Contracting Government the port of which the ship intends to enter; or

.4 denial of entry into port.

Prior to initiating any such steps, the ship shall be informed by the Contracting Government of its intentions. Upon this information the master may withdraw the intention to enter that port. In such cases, this regulation shall not apply.

3 Additional provisions

3.1 In the event:

.1 of the imposition of a control measure, other than a lesser administrative or corrective measure, referred to in paragraph 1.3; or

.2 any of the steps referred to in paragraph 2.5 are taken, an officer duly authorized by the Contracting Government shall forthwith inform in writing the Administration specifying which control measures have been imposed or steps taken and the reasons thereof. The Contracting Government imposing the control measures or steps shall also notify the recognized security organization which issued the Certificate relating to the ship concerned and the Organization when any such control measures have been imposed or steps taken.

3.2 When entry into port is denied or the ship is expelled from port, the authorities of the port State should communicate the appropriate facts to the authorities of the State of the next appropriate ports of call, when known, and any other appropriate coastal States, taking into account guidelines to be developed by the Organization. Confidentiality and security of such notification shall be ensured.

3.3 Denial of entry into port, pursuant to paragraphs 2.4 and 2.5, or expulsion from port, pursuant to paragraphs 1.1 to 1.3, shall only be imposed where the officers duly authorized by the Contracting Government have clear grounds to believe that the ship poses an immediate threat to the security or safety of persons, or of ships or other property and there are no other appropriate means for removing that threat.

3.4 The control measures referred to in paragraph 1.3 and the steps referred to in paragraph 2.5 shall only be imposed, pursuant to this regulation, until the non-compliance giving rise to the control measures or steps has been corrected to the satisfaction of the Contracting Government, taking into account actions proposed by the ship or the Administration, if any.

3.5 When Contracting Governments exercise control under paragraph 1 or take steps under paragraph 2:

.1 all possible efforts shall be made to avoid a ship being unduly detained or delayed. If a ship is thereby unduly detained, or delayed, it shall be entitled to compensation for any loss or damage suffered; and

.2 necessary access to the ship shall not be prevented for emergency or humanitarian reasons and for security purposes.

.3　如果该船在所拟进入港口的缔约国政府的领海内，对该船进行检查；或

.4　拒绝该船进港。

缔约国政府在开始采取任何此类步骤之前，应将其意图通知该船。收到此信息后，船长可以撤销其进入该港的意图。在这种情况下，本条不再适用。

3　附加规定

3.1　如果：

.1　采取了 1.3 所述的一项除较轻的行政或纠正措施以外的控制措施；或

.2　采取了 2.5 所述的任何步骤，缔约国政府正式授权的官员应随即通知主管机关，说明已采取的控制措施或步骤及其原因。如果已采取任何此类控制措施或步骤，采取控制措施的缔约国政府还应通知向有关船舶签发证书的认可保安组织和本组织。

3.2　如果拒绝船舶进入港口或船舶被驱逐出港，港口国当局应将有关事实通报该船已知的随后各停靠港口的国家当局以及任何其他有关沿岸国，并应考虑到本组织制定的指南。应确保此类通知的保密性和安全性。

3.3　只有在缔约国政府正式授权的官员有明显理由确信船舶对人员，船舶或其他财产的保安或安全构成紧迫威胁，并且没有其他适当方式来消除该威胁的情况下，才可按照 2.4 和 2.5 拒绝船舶进入港口或依照 1.1 至 1.3 将船舶驱逐出港。

3.4　依照本条所采取的 1.3 所述控制措施和 2.5 所述步骤，应以导致采取控制措施或步骤的不符合情况得到纠正并使缔约国政府满意为限，并应考虑到船舶或主管机关所建议的行动（若有）。

3.5　缔约国政府在根据上述 1 行使控制或根据上述 2 采取步骤时：

.1　应尽一切可能避免船舶被不当扣留或船期被不当延误。如果船舶被不当扣留或船期被不当延误，船舶有权就其所受任何损失或损害取得赔偿；和

.2　不得阻止出于紧急或人道主义原因和出于保安目的而在必要时登船。

Regulation 10
Requirements for port facilities

1 Port facilities shall comply with the relevant requirements of this chapter and part A of the ISPS Code, taking into account the guidance given in part B of the ISPS Code.

2 Contracting Governments with a port facility or port facilities within their territory, to which this regulation applies, shall ensure that:

.1 port facility security assessments are carried out, reviewed and approved in accordance with the provisions of part A of the ISPS Code; and

.2 port facility security plans are developed, reviewed, approved and implemented in accordance with the provisions of part A of the ISPS Code.

3 Contracting Governments shall designate and communicate the measures required to be addressed in a port facility security plan for the various security levels, including when the submission of a Declaration of Security will be required.

Regulation 11
Alternative security agreements

1 Contracting Governments may, when implementing this chapter and part A of the ISPS Code, conclude in writing bilateral or multilateral agreements with other Contracting Governments on alternative security arrangements covering short international voyages on fixed routes between port facilities located within their territories.

2 Any such agreement shall not compromise the level of security of other ships or of port facilities not covered by the agreement.

3 No ship covered by such an agreement shall conduct any ship-to-ship activities with any ship not covered by the agreement.

4 Such agreements shall be reviewed periodically, taking into account the experience gained as well as any changes in the particular circumstances or the assessed threats to the security of the ships, the port facilities or the routes covered by the agreement.

Regulation 12
Equivalent security arrangements

1 An Administration may allow a particular ship or a group of ships entitled to fly its flag to implement other security measures equivalent to those prescribed in this chapter or in part A of the ISPS Code, provided such security measures are at least as effective as those prescribed in this chapter or part A of the ISPS Code. The Administration which allows such security measures shall communicate to the Organization particulars thereof.

第 10 条
对港口设施的要求

1 港口设施应符合本章和 ISPS 规则 A 部分的相关要求，并考虑到 ISPS 规则 B 部分提供的指导。

2 在其境内拥有适用本条的港口设施的缔约国政府应确保：

.1 按照 ISPS 规则 A 部分的规定，开展港口设施保安评估，并对其予以评审和批准；和

.2 按照 ISPS 规则 A 部分的规定制订、评审、批准并实施港口设施保安计划。

3 缔约国政府应指定并通报港口设施保安计划所应涉及的各保安等级的对应措施，包括在何时要求提交保安声明。

第 11 条
替代保安协议

1 缔约国政府在实施本章和 ISPS 规则 A 部分时，可以与其他缔约国政府就其境内港口设施之间的短途固定航线国际航行的替代保安安排达成双边或多边书面协议。

2 任何此类协议均不得降低协议范围以外的其他船舶或港口设施的保安水平。

3 此类协议范围以内的船舶不得与协议范围以外的任何船舶进行船到船活动。

4 对此类协议应予以定期评审，评审时要考虑到所获得的经验以及特定情况发生的变化或对协议范围以内的船舶、港口设施或航线的保安所受威胁的评估。

第 12 条
等效保安安排

1 主管机关可以允许悬挂其国旗的某一特定船舶或一组船舶实施等效于本章或 ISPS 规则 A 部分所述措施的其他保安措施，但此类保安措施至少须与本章或 ISPS 规则 A 部分所述措施同样有效。允许此类保安措施的主管机关应将有关细节通报本组织。

2 When implementing this chapter and part A of the ISPS Code, a Contracting Government may allow a particular port facility or a group of port facilities located within its territory, other than those covered by an agreement concluded under regulation 11, to implement security measures equivalent to those prescribed in this chapter or in part A of the ISPS Code, provided such security measures are at least as effective as those prescribed in this chapter or part A of the ISPS Code. The Contracting Government which allows such security measures shall communicate to the Organization particulars thereof.

Regulation 13
Communication of information

1 Contracting Governments shall, not later than 1 July 2004, communicate to the Organization and shall make available for the information of Companies and ships:

.1 the names and contact details of their national authority or authorities responsible for ship and port facility security;

.2 the locations within their territory covered by approved port facility security plans;

.3 the names and contact details of those who have been designated to be available at all times to receive and act upon the ship-to-shore security alerts referred to in regulation 6.2.1;

.4 the names and contact details of those who have been designated to be available at all times to receive and act upon any communications from Contracting Governments exercising control and compliance measures referred to in regulation 9.3.1; and

.5 the names and contact details of those who have been designated to be available at all times to provide advice or assistance to ships and to whom ships can report any security concerns referred to in regulation 7.2 and thereafter update such information as and when changes relating thereto occur. The Organization shall circulate such particulars to other Contracting Governments for the information of their officers.

2 Contracting Governments shall, not later than 1 July 2004, communicate to the Organization the names and contact details of any recognized security organizations authorized to act on their behalf together with details of the specific responsibility and conditions of authority delegated to such organizations. Such information shall be updated as and when changes relating thereto occur. The Organization shall circulate such particulars to other Contracting Governments for the information of their officers.

3 Contracting Governments shall, not later than 1 July 2004, communicate to the Organization a list showing the approved port facility security plans for the port facilities located within their territory together with the location or locations covered by each approved port facility security plan and the corresponding date of approval and thereafter shall further communicate when any of the following changes take place:

2 缔约国政府在实施本章和 ISPS 规则 A 部分时,可以允许其境内的某一特定港口设施或一组港口设施(根据第 11 条达成的协议范围以内的港口设施除外)实施等效于本章或 ISPS 规则 A 部分所述措施的保安措施,但此类保安措施至少应与本章或 ISPS 规则 A 部分所述的措施同样有效。允许此类保安措施的缔约国政府应将有关细节通报本组织。

第 13 条
资料的送交

1 缔约国政府应不迟于 2004 年 7 月 1 日将以下资料送交本组织并应使公司和船舶能够得到这些资料:

.1 负责船舶和港口设施保安事宜的国家(各)当局的名称和详细联系方式;

.2 经批准的港口设施保安计划在其领土内所覆盖的地点;

.3 被指定全天接收第 6.2.1 条所述的船对岸保安警报和针对警报采取行动的人员的姓名和详细联系方式;

.4 被指定全天接收第 9.3.1 条所述的实施控制和符合措施的缔约国政府任何消息的人员的姓名和详细联系方式;和

.5 被指定全天为船舶提供第 7.2 条所述的咨询或协助以及船舶能够向其报告任何保安问题的人员的姓名和详细联系方式并在此类资料以后发生变化时更新该资料。本组织应将上述各项资料分送其他缔约国政府供其官员知晓。

2 缔约国政府应不迟于 2004 年 7 月 1 日将其所授权代其行事的任何认可保安组织的名称和详细联系方式以及授予此类组织的具体责任和授权条件送交本组织。在此类资料以后发生变化时,应更新该资料。本组织应将上述各项资料分送其他缔约国供其官员知晓。

3 缔约国政府应不迟于 2004 年 7 月 1 日将一份关于其境内港口设施的已批准的港口设施保安计划以及每份已批准的港口设施保安计划所覆盖的地点和相应批准日期的清单送交本组织,并在此后做出以下变动时进一步送交资料:

.1 changes in the location or locations covered by an approved port facility security plan are to be introduced or have been introduced. In such cases the information to be communicated shall indicate the changes in the location or locations covered by the plan and the date as of which such changes are to be introduced or were implemented;

.2 an approved port facility security plan, previously included in the list submitted to the Organization, is to be withdrawn or has been withdrawn. In such cases, the information to be communicated shall indicate the date on which the withdrawal will take effect or was implemented. In these cases, the communication shall be made to the Organization as soon as is practically possible; and

.3 additions are to be made to the list of approved port facility security plans. In such cases, the information to be communicated shall indicate the location or locations covered by the plan and the date of approval.

4 Contracting Governments shall, at five year intervals after 1 July 2004, communicate to the Organization a revised and updated list showing all the approved port facility security plans for the port facilities located within their territory together with the location or locations covered by each approved port facility security plan and the corresponding date of approval (and the date of approval of any amendments thereto) which will supersede and replace all information communicated to the Organization, pursuant to paragraph 3, during the preceding five years.

5 Contracting Governments shall communicate to the Organization information that an agreement under regulation 11 has been concluded. The information communicated shall include:

.1 the names of the Contracting Governments which have concluded the agreement;

.2 the port facilities and the fixed routes covered by the agreement;

.3 the periodicity of review of the agreement;

.4 the date of entry into force of the agreement; and

.5 information on any consultations which have taken place with other Contracting Governments and thereafter shall communicate, as soon as practically possible, to the Organization information when the agreement has been amended or has ended.

6 Any Contracting Government which allows, under the provisions of regulation 12, any equivalent security arrangements with respect to a ship entitled to fly its flag or with respect to a port facility located within its territory shall communicate to the Organization particulars thereof.

7 The Organization shall make available the information communicated under paragraphs 3 to 6 to other Contracting Governments upon request.

.1 已批准的港口设施保安计划所覆盖的地点将有或者已有变动。在这种情况下,送交的资料应指明该计划所覆盖地点的变动以及变动将要开始或已实施的日期;

.2 向本组织提交的清单原来所包括的已批准的港口设施保安计划将被撤销或已被撤销。在这种情况下,送交的资料应指明撤销的生效或已实施的日期。在这些情况下,应按实际可能尽快向本组织送交资料;和

.3 需对已批准的港口设施保安计划清单进行增补。在这种情况下,送交的资料应指明该计划所覆盖的地点和批准日期。

4 缔约国政府应在 2004 年 7 月 1 日以后,每隔 5 年将一份关于其境内港口设施的所有已批准的港口设施保安计划以及每份已批准的港口设施保安计划所覆盖的地点和相应批准日期(以及任何相关修正的批准日期)的经修订和更新的清单送交本组织,该清单将取代并替换前 5 年内依照上述 3 送交本组织的所有资料。

5 缔约国政府应将关于根据第 11 条已达成的协议资料送交本组织。所送交的资料应包括:

.1 缔结协议的缔约国政府的名称;

.2 协议所涉及的港口设施和固定航线;

.3 协议定期评审的间隔期;

.4 协议生效的日期;和

.5 与其他缔约国政府所进行的任何协商的信息并在该协议以后被修正或终止时,应按实际可能尽快将信息通报本组织。

6 任何缔约国政府根据第 12 条的规定允许对悬挂其国旗的船舶或其境内的港口设施采取任何等效保安安排,应将有关详情通报本组织。

7 本组织应在其他缔约国政府有要求时,向其提供根据上述 3 至 6 所送交的资料。

Chapter XII Additional safety measures for bulk carriers

第Ⅻ章　散货船附加安全措施

Regulation 1
Definitions

For the purpose of this chapter:

1 *Bulk carrier* means a ship which is intended primarily to carry dry cargo in bulk, including such types as ore carriers and combination carriers.①

2 *Bulk carrier of single-side skin construction* means a bulk carrier as defined in paragraph 1, in which:

.1 any part of a cargo hold is bounded by the side shell; or

.2 one or more cargo holds are bounded by a double-side skin, the width of which is less than 760 mm in bulk carriers constructed before 1 January 2000 and less than 1,000 mm in bulk carriers constructed on or after 1 January 2000 but before 1 July 2006, the distance being measured perpendicular to the side shell.

Such ships include combination carriers in which any part of a cargo hold is bounded by the side shell.

3 *Bulk carrier of double-side skin construction* means a bulk carrier as defined in paragraph 1, in which all cargo holds are bounded by a double-side skin, other than as defined in paragraph 2.2.

4 *Double-side skin* means a configuration where each ship side is constructed by the side shell and a longitudinal bulkhead connecting the double bottom and the deck. Hopper side tanks and top-side tanks may, where fitted, be integral parts of the double-side skin configuration.

5 *Length* of a bulk carrier means the length as defined in the International Convention on Load Lines in force.

6 *Solid bulk cargo* means any material, other than liquid or gas, consisting of a combination of particles, granules or any larger pieces of material, generally uniform in composition, which is loaded directly into the cargo spaces of a ship without any intermediate form of containment.

---

① Refer to:

.1 For ships constructed before 1 July 2006, resolution 6, Interpretation of the definition of "bulk carrier", as given in chapter IX of SOLAS 1974, as amended in 1994, adopted by the 1997 SOLAS Conference.

.2 *Interpretation of the provisions of SOLAS chapter XII on additional safety measures for bulk carriers* (resolution MSC.79(70)).

.3 The application provisions of annex 1 to the *Interpretation of the provisions of SOLAS chapter XII on additional safety measures for bulk carriers* (resolution MSC.89(71)).

第 1 条
定义

就本章而言：

1 **散货船**系指主要用于运输散装干货的船舶，包括诸如矿砂船和兼装船等船型[①]。

2 **单舷侧结构散货船**系指 1 所定义的散货船，该船：

.1 货舱任何边界均为舷侧壳板；或

.2 一个或多个货舱边界为双舷侧结构；2000 年 1 月 1 日以前建造的散货船，该双舷侧结构宽度小于 760 mm；2000 年 1 月 1 日或以后，但在 2006 年 7 月 1 日以前建造的散货船，该双舷侧结构宽度小于 1 000 mm；该宽距按垂直于舷侧壳板量取。

此类船舶包括货舱任何边界均为舷侧壳板的兼装船。

3 **双舷侧结构散货船**系指 1 所定义的所有货舱边界均为双舷侧结构，与 2.2 所定义者不同的散货船。

4 **双舷侧**系指船舶每侧均由舷侧壳板与纵舱壁组成的构造形式，该纵舱壁连接双层底和甲板。底边舱和顶边舱（若设有）可为双舷侧构造的组成部分。

5 散货船的**船长**系指现行《国际载重线公约》所定义的长度。

6 **固体散货**系指除液体或气体以外，由粒子、颗粒或较大块状物质组成的任何物质，成分通常一致，并直接装入船舶的货物处所而无须任何中间围护形式。

---

① 参见：

.1 对于在 2006 年 7 月 1 日以前建造的船舶，1997 年 SOLAS 公约缔约国大会通过的决议 6《对 1974 年 SOLAS 公约第Ⅸ章经 1994 年修正的“散货船”定义的解释》。

.2 本组织海上安全委员会 MSC.79(70)决议通过的《对 SOLAS 公约第Ⅻ章“散货船附加安全措施”规定的解释》。

.3 本组织海上安全委员会 MSC.89(71)决议通过的《对 SOLAS 公约第Ⅻ章“散货船附加安全措施”规定的解释》附件 1 实施规定。

7 *Bulk carrier bulkhead and double bottom strength standards* means "Standards for the evaluation of scantlings of the transverse watertight vertically corrugated bulkhead between the two foremost cargo holds and for the evaluation of allowable hold loading of the foremost cargo hold" adopted by resolution 4 of the Conference of Contracting Governments to the International Convention for the Safety of Life at Sea, 1974 on 27 November 1997, as may be amended by the Organization, provided that such amendments are adopted, brought into force and take effect in accordance with the provisions of article VIII of the present Convention concerning the amendment procedures applicable to the Annex other than chapter I.

8 *Bulk carriers constructed* means bulk carriers the keels of which are laid or which are at a similar stage of construction.

9 *A similar stage of construction* means the stage at which:

.1 construction identifiable with a specific ship begins; and

.2 assembly of that ship has commenced comprising at least 50 tonnes or 1% of the estimated mass of all structural material, whichever is less.

10 *Breadth* (*B*) of a bulk carrier means the breadth as defined in the International Convention on Load Lines in force.

Regulation 2
Application

Bulk carriers shall comply with the requirements of this chapter in addition to the applicable requirements of other chapters.

Regulation 3
Implementation schedule

Bulk carriers constructed before 1 July 1999 to which regulations 4 or 6 apply shall comply with the provisions of such regulations according to the following schedule, with reference to the enhanced programme of inspections required by regulation XI-1/2:

.1 bulk carriers which are 20 years of age and over on 1 July 1999, by the date of the first intermediate survey or the first periodical survey① after 1 July 1999, whichever comes first;

.2 bulk carriers which are 15 years of age and over but less than 20 years of age on 1 July 1999, by the date of the first periodical survey① after 1 July 1999, but not later than 1 July 2002; and

① Refer to *Application of SOLAS regulations XII/3, XII/7 and XII/11* (MSC.1/Circ.1463).

7　**散货船舱壁和双层底强度标准**系指《1974年国际海上人命安全公约》缔约国政府大会1997年11月27日通过并可能经本组织修正的决议4《最前两个货舱之间垂向槽形水密横舱壁尺寸评估和最前部货舱许可装载评估用标准》,但这种修正案应按本公约第Ⅷ条有关适用于除第Ⅰ章外的附则修正程序的规定予以通过、生效和实施。

8　**建造的散货船**系指安放龙骨或处于类似建造阶段的散货船。

9　**类似建造阶段**系指在此阶段:

.1　可辨认出某一具体船舶建造开始;和

.2　该船业已开始的装配量至少为50 t,或为全部结构材料估算重量的1%,取较小者。

10　**散货船的船宽**(B)系指现行《国际载重线公约》所定义的宽度。

第2条
适用范围

散货船除符合其他各章的适用要求外,还应符合本章的要求。

第3条
实施计划

适用第4条或第6条的1999年7月1日以前建造的散货船,应按下述计划符合其规定,并参照第Ⅺ-1/2条所要求的加强检验程序:

.1　对1999年7月1日船龄满20年及以上的散货船,1999年7月1日以后的第一次中间检验或第一次定期检验日期①,取早者;

.2　对1999年7月1日船龄满15年及以上但不满20年的散货船,在1999年7月1日以后的第一次定期检验日期①,但不迟于2002年7月1日;和

① 参见《〈安全公约〉第Ⅻ/3、Ⅻ/7和Ⅻ/11条的适用》(第MSC.1/Circ.1463号通函)。

.3 bulk carriers which are less than 15 years of age on 1 July 1999, by the date of the first periodical survey① after the date on which the ship reaches 15 years of age, but not later than the date on which the ship reaches 17 years of age.

Regulation 4
Damage stability requirements applicable to bulk carriers

1 Bulk carriers of 150 m in length and upwards of single-side skin construction, designed to carry solid bulk cargoes having a density of 1,000 kg/m^3 and above, constructed on or after 1 July 1999, shall, when loaded to the Summer Load Line, be able to withstand flooding of any one cargo hold in all loading conditions and remain afloat in a satisfactory condition of equilibrium, as specified in paragraph 4.

2 Bulk carriers of 150 m in length and upwards of double-side skin construction in which any part of longitudinal bulkhead is located within *B*/5 or 11.5 m, whichever is less, inboard from the ship's side at right angle to the centreline at the assigned Summer Load Line, designed to carry solid bulk cargoes having a density of 1,000 kg/m^3 and above, constructed on or after 1 July 2006, shall, when loaded to the Summer Load Line, be able to withstand flooding of any one cargo hold in all loading conditions and remain afloat in a satisfactory condition of equilibrium, as specified in paragraph 4.

3 Bulk carriers of 150 m in length and upwards of single-side skin construction, carrying solid bulk cargoes having a density of 1,780 kg/m^3 and above, constructed before 1 July 1999, shall, when loaded to the Summer Load Line, be able to withstand flooding of the foremost cargo hold in all loading conditions and remain afloat in a satisfactory condition of equilibrium, as specified in paragraph 4. This requirement shall be complied with in accordance with the implementation schedule specified in regulation 3.

4 Subject to the provisions of paragraph 7, the condition of equilibrium after flooding shall satisfy the condition of equilibrium laid down in the annex to resolution A.320(IX)—Regulation equivalent to regulation 27 of the International Convention on Load Lines, 1966, as amended by resolution A.514(13). The assumed flooding need only take into account flooding of the cargo hold space to the water level outside the ship in that flooded condition. The permeability of a loaded hold shall be assumed as 0.9 and the permeability of an empty hold shall be assumed as 0.95, unless a permeability relevant to a particular cargo is assumed for the volume of a flooded hold occupied by cargo and a permeability of 0.95 is assumed for the remaining empty volume of the hold.

5 Bulk carriers constructed before 1 July 1999, which have been assigned a reduced freeboard in compliance with regulation 27(7) of the International Convention on Load Lines, 1966, as adopted on 5 April 1966, may be considered as complying with paragraph 3 of this regulation.

① Refer to *Application of SOLAS regulations XII/3, XII/7 and XII/11* (MSC.1/Circ.1463).

.3 对 1999 年 7 月 1 日船龄小于 15 年的散货船，在船龄达到 15 年后的第一次定期检验日期①，但不迟于船龄达到 17 年之日。

第 4 条
适用于散货船的破损稳性要求

1 船长 150 m 及以上，设计用于载运密度为 1 000 kg/m³ 及以上的固体散装货物，于1999 年 7 月 1 日或以后建造的单舷侧结构散货船，当装载至夏季载重线时，应在所有装载工况下均能承受任一货舱进水，并能按本条 4 的规定在令人满意的平衡状态下保持漂浮。

2 船长 150 m 及以上，设计用于载运密度为 1 000 kg/m³ 及以上的固体散装货物，于 2006 年 7 月 1 日或以后建造，纵舱壁任一部分均在舷内 *B*/5 或 11.5 m（取较小者）范围（在核定的夏季载重线处自舷侧向船内垂直于中心线方向量取）内的双舷侧结构散货船，当装载至夏季载重线时，应在所有装载工况下均能承受任一货舱进水，并能按本条 4 的规定在令人满意的平衡状态下保持漂浮。

3 船长 150 m 及以上，载运密度为 1 780 kg/m³ 及以上的固体散装货物，于 1999 年 7 月1 日以前建造的单舷侧结构散货船，当装载至夏季载重线时，应在所有装载工况下均能承受最前部货舱进水，并能按本条 4 的规定在令人满意的平衡状态下保持漂浮。应按第 3 条规定的实施计划符合本要求。

4 按本条 7 的规定，进水后的平衡状态应满足经 A.514（13）决议修正的 A.320（Ⅸ）决议的附件《等效于〈1966 年国际载重线公约〉第 27 条的规则》所规定的平衡状态。假定的进水只需考虑货舱处所进水至该进水状况下船舶的舷外水位。除非进水货舱容积中被货物占据部分的渗透率按该特定货物予以假定，并且该货舱所剩空余容积的渗透率假定为 0.95，否则载货舱的渗透率应假定为 0.9，空货舱的渗透率应假定为 0.95。

5 1999 年 7 月 1 日以前建造并按 1966 年 4 月 5 日通过的《1966 年国际载重线公约》第 27（7）条已核定为减小干舷的散货船，可视为符合本条 3 的要求。

① 参见《〈安全公约〉第Ⅻ/3、Ⅻ/7 和Ⅻ/11 条的适用》（第 MSC.1/Circ.1463 号通函）。

6 Bulk carriers which have been assigned a reduced freeboard in compliance with the provisions of paragraph (8) of the regulation equivalent to regulation 27 of the International Convention on Load Lines, 1966, adopted by resolution A.320 (IX), as amended by resolution A.514 (13), may be considered as complying with paragraphs 1 or 2, as appropriate.

7 On bulk carriers which have been assigned reduced freeboard in compliance with the provisions of regulation 27 (8) of Annex B of the Protocol of 1988 relating to the International Convention on Load Lines, 1966, the condition of equilibrium after flooding shall satisfy the relevant provisions of that Protocol.

Regulation 5
Structural strength of bulk carriers

1 Bulk carriers of 150 m in length and upwards of single-side skin construction, designed to carry solid bulk cargoes having a density of 1,000 kg/m^3 and above, constructed on or after 1 July 1999, shall have sufficient strength to withstand flooding of any one cargo hold to the water level outside the ship in that flooded condition in all loading and ballast conditions, taking also into account dynamic effects resulting from the presence of water in the hold, and taking into account the recommendations adopted by the Organization.①

2 Bulk carriers of 150 m in length and upwards of double-side skin construction, in which any part of longitudinal bulkhead is located within $B/5$ or 11.5 m, whichever is less, inboard from the ship's side at right angle to the centreline at the assigned Summer Load Line, designed to carry bulk cargoes having a density of 1,000 kg/m^3 and above, constructed on or after 1 July 2006, shall comply with the structural strength provisions of paragraph 1.

Regulation 6
Structural and other requirements for bulk carriers

1 Bulk carriers of 150 m in length and upwards of single-side skin construction, carrying solid bulk cargoes having a density of 1,780 kg/m^3 and above, constructed before 1 July 1999, shall comply with the following requirements in accordance with the implementation schedule specified in regulation 3:

.1 The transverse watertight bulkhead between the two foremost cargo holds and the double bottom of the foremost cargo hold shall have sufficient strength to withstand flooding of the foremost cargo hold, taking also into account dynamic effects resulting from the presence of water in the hold, in compliance with the bulk carrier bulkhead and double bottom strength standards. For the purpose of this regulation, the bulk carrier bulkhead and double bottom strength standards shall be treated as mandatory.

---

① Refer to *Recommendation on compliance with SOLAS regulation XII/5* (resolution 3 of the 1997 SOLAS Conference).

6　按经 A.514(13)决议修正的 A.320(Ⅸ)决议通过的《等效于〈1966 年国际载重线公约〉第 27 条的规则》(8)的规定已核定为减小干舷的散货船,可视为符合本条 1 或 2 的要求。

7　按《1966 年国际载重线公约 1988 年议定书》附则 B 第 27(8)条的规定已核定为减小干舷的散货船,进水后的平衡状态应满足该议定书的有关规定。

第 5 条
散货船的结构强度

1　船长 150 m 及以上,设计用于载运密度为 1 000 kg/m^3 及以上的固体散装货物,于 1999 年 7 月 1 日或以后建造的单舷侧结构散货船,应在所有装载和压载工况下均有足够强度承受任一货舱进水至该进水状况下船舶的舷外水位,并计及舱内进水所产生的动力影响,同时考虑到本组织通过的建议案。①

2　船长为 150 m 及以上,设计用于载运密度为 1 000 kg/m^3 及以上的散装货物,于 2006 年 7 月 1 日或以后建造,纵舱壁任一部分均在舷内 *B*/5 或 11.5 m(取较小者)范围(在核定的夏季载重线处自舷侧向船内垂直于中心线方向量取)内的双舷侧结构散货船,应符合本条 1 的结构强度规定。

第 6 条
散货船的结构要求及其他要求

1　船长为 150 m 及以上,载运密度为 1 780 kg/m^3 及以上的固体散装货物,于 1999 年 7 月 1 日以前建造的单舷侧结构散货船,应按第 3 条规定的实施计划符合下述要求:

.1　最前两个货舱间的水密横舱壁及最前部货舱的双层底应符合散货船舱壁和双层底强度标准,有足够强度承受最前部货舱进水,并计及舱内进水所产生的动力影响。就本条而言,散货船舱壁和双层底强度标准应视作强制性标准。

---

①　参见 1997 年 SOLAS 公约缔约国大会通过的决议 3《关于符合 SOLAS 公约第Ⅻ/5 条的建议案》。

.2 In considering the need for, and the extent of, strengthening of the transverse watertight bulkhead or double bottom to meet the requirements of 1.1, the following restrictions may be taken into account:

.1 restrictions on the distribution of the total cargo weight between the cargo holds; and

.2 restrictions on the maximum deadweight.

.3 For bulk carriers using either of, or both, the restrictions given in 1.2.1 and 1.2.2 above for the purpose of fulfilling the requirements of 1.1, these restrictions shall be complied with whenever solid bulk cargoes having a density of 1,780 kg/m^3 and above are carried.

2 Bulk carriers of 150 m in length and upwards constructed on or after 1 July 2006 shall comply in all areas with double-side skin construction with the following requirements:

.1 Primary stiffening structures of the double-side skin shall not be placed inside the cargo hold space.

.2 Subject to the provisions below, the distance between the outer shell and the inner shell at any transverse section shall not be less than 1,000 mm measured perpendicular to the side shell. The double-side skin construction shall be such as to allow access for inspection as provided in regulation II-1/3-6 and the Technical Provisions referring thereto.

.1 The clearances below need not be maintained in way of cross ties, upper and lower end brackets of transverse framing or end brackets of longitudinal framing.

.2 The minimum width of the clear passage through the double-side skin space in way of obstructions such as piping or vertical ladders shall not be less than 600 mm.

.3 Where the inner and/or outer skins are transversely framed, the minimum clearance between the inner surfaces of the frames shall not be less than 600 mm.

.4 Where the inner and outer skins are longitudinally framed, the minimum clearance between the inner surfaces of the frames shall not be less than 800 mm. Outside the parallel part of the cargo hold length this clearance may be reduced where necessitated by the structural configuration, but shall in no case be less than 600 mm.

.5 The minimum clearance referred to above shall be the shortest distance measured between assumed lines connecting the inner surfaces of the frames on the inner and outer skins.

3 The double-side skin spaces, with the exception of top-side wing tanks, if fitted, shall not be used for the carriage of cargo.

4 In bulk carriers of 150 m in length and upwards, carrying solid bulk cargoes having a density of 1,000 kg/m^3 and above, constructed on or after 1 July 2006:

.1 the structure of cargo holds shall be such that all contemplated cargoes can be loaded and discharged by standard loading/discharge equipment and procedures without damage which may compromise the safety of the structure;

.2　在考虑水密横舱壁或双层底为满足本条 1.1 的要求而进行加强的必要性和范围时，以下限制条件可予以考虑：

.1　货舱间总载货量分布的限制；和

.2　最大载重量的限制。

.3　对为满足本条 1.1 的要求而采用以上 1.2.1 和 1.2.2 的一种或两种限制的散货船，载运密度为 1 780 kg/m^3 及以上的固体散货时，均应符合这些限制条件。

2　船长为 150 m 及以上，于 2006 年 7 月 1 日或以后建造的双舷侧结构散货船应符合下述要求：

.1　双舷侧的主要加强结构不应设置在货舱处所内。

.2　根据以下规定，外壳板和内壳板在任何横剖面处的间距不得小于 1 000 mm（按垂直于舷侧壳板量取）。根据第Ⅱ-1/3-6 条及检查通道技术规定，双舷侧结构应留有检查通道。

.1　在横撑材，横骨架的上、下端肘板或纵骨架的端肘板处不必保持下述净空。

.2　在双舷侧处所内的管路或垂直梯子之类障碍物处，净通道的最小宽度不得小于 600 mm。

.3　如果内壳板和/或外壳板系横骨架式，肋骨内表面之间的最小净空不得小于 600 mm。

.4　如果内壳板和外壳板系纵骨架式，肋骨内表面之间的最小净空不得小于 800 mm。在货舱长度的平行部分之外，该净空可按结构形状的需要而减少，但无论如何不得小于 600 mm。

.5　上述最小净空应是按内壳板和外壳板上骨架内表面之间的假想连线量取的最小距离。

3　除顶边翼舱（若设有）外，双舷侧处所不得用于载运货物。

4　船长为 150 m 及以上，载运密度为 1 000 kg/m^3 及以上的固体散装货物，于 2006 年 7 月 1 日或以后建造的散货船：

.1　货舱的结构应使所有拟装货物能以标准装载/卸载设备和程序进行装卸，不会造成有损结构安全的破坏；

.2 effective continuity between the side shell structure and the rest of the hull structure shall be assured; and

.3 the structure of cargo areas shall be such that single failure of one stiffening structural member will not lead to immediate consequential failure of other structural items potentially leading to the collapse of the entire stiffened panels.

Regulation 7
Survey and maintenance of bulk carriers

1 Bulk carriers of 150 m in length and upwards of single-side skin construction, constructed before 1 July 1999, of 10 years of age and over, shall not carry solid bulk cargoes having a density of 1,780 kg/m^3 and above unless they have satisfactorily undergone either:

.1 a periodical survey①, in accordance with the enhanced programme of inspections during surveys required by regulation XI-1/2; or

.2 a survey of all cargo holds to the same extent as required for periodical surveys in the enhanced programme of inspections during surveys required by regulation XI-1/2.

2 Bulk carriers shall comply with the maintenance requirements provided in regulation II-1/3-1 and the Standards for owners' inspection and maintenance of bulk carrier hatch covers, adopted by the Organization by resolution MSC.169(79), as may be amended by the Organization, provided that such amendments are adopted, brought into force and take effect in accordance with the provisions of article VIII of the present Convention concerning the amendment procedures applicable to the Annex other than chapter I.

Regulation 8
Information on compliance with requirements for bulk carriers

1 The booklet required by regulation VI/7.2 shall be endorsed by the Administration, or on its behalf, to indicate that regulations 4, 5, 6 and 7, as appropriate, are complied with.

2 Any restrictions imposed on the carriage of solid bulk cargoes having a density of 1,780 kg/m^3 and above in accordance with the requirements of regulations 6 and 14 shall be identified and recorded in the booklet referred to in paragraph 1.

3 A bulk carrier to which paragraph 2 applies shall be permanently marked on the side shell at midships, port and starboard, with a solid equilateral triangle, having sides of 500 mm and its apex 300 mm below the deck line, and painted a contrasting colour to that of the hull.

① Refer to *Application of SOLAS regulations XII/3, XII/7 and XII/11* (MSC.1/Circ.1463).

.2 应保证舷侧壳板和船体结构其余部分之间的有效连续性；和

.3 货物区域结构应使一个加强构件的单一失效不会导致其他构件立即随之失效，从而可能导致整个加强板格的破坏。

第7条
散货船的检验和维护保养

1 船长为150 m及以上，船龄为10年及以上，于1999年7月1日以前建造的单舷侧结构散货船，除非满足下述条件之一，不得载运密度为1 780 kg/m^3及以上的固体散装货物：

.1 按第Ⅺ-1/2条要求的加强检验程序通过了定期检验①；或

.2 所有货舱按第Ⅺ-1/2条要求的加强检验程序通过了与定期检验同样范围的检验。

2 散货船应符合第Ⅱ-1/3-1条规定的维护保养要求和本组织MSC.169(79)决议通过并可能经本组织修正的《散货船舱口盖船东检查和维护标准》，但这种修正案应按本公约第Ⅷ条有关适用于除第Ⅰ章外的附则修正程序的规定予以通过、生效和实施。

第8条
关于符合散货船要求的资料

1 第Ⅵ/7.2条要求的小册子应由主管机关或其代表签署以表明其符合本章第4、5、6和7条的适用要求。

2 按第6条和第14条的要求对载运密度为1 780 kg/m^3及以上的固体散装货物的任何限制应在本条1所述的小册子上做出标识和记录。

3 适用本条2的散货船应在船中部左、右舷侧外板上勘绘一个实心的永久性等边三角形标志，其边长为500 mm，顶点在甲板线以下300 mm处，并漆成与船体有反差的颜色。

---

① 参见《〈安全公约〉第Ⅻ/3、Ⅻ/7和Ⅻ/11条的适用》(第MSC.1/Circ.1463号通函)。

Regulation 9
Requirements for bulk carriers not being capable of complying with regulation 4.3 due to the design configuration of their cargo holds

For bulk carriers constructed before 1 July 1999 being within the application limits of regulation 4.3, which have been constructed with an insufficient number of transverse watertight bulkheads to satisfy that regulation, the Administration may allow relaxation from the application of regulations 4.3 and 6, on condition that they shall comply with the following requirements:

.1 for the foremost cargo hold, the inspections prescribed for the annual survey in the enhanced programme of inspections during surveys required by regulation XI-1/2 shall be replaced by the inspections prescribed therein for the intermediate survey of cargo holds;

.2 they are provided with bilge well high water level alarms in all cargo holds, or in cargo conveyor tunnels, as appropriate, giving an audible and visual alarm on the navigation bridge, as approved by the Administration or an organization recognized by it in accordance with the provisions of regulation XI-1/1; and

.3 they are provided with detailed information on specific cargo hold flooding scenarios. This information shall be accompanied by detailed instructions on evacuation preparedness under the provisions of section 8 of the International Safety Management (ISM) Code and be used as the basis for crew training and drills.

Regulation 10
Solid bulk cargo density declaration

1 Prior to loading bulk cargo on bulk carriers of 150 m in length and upwards, the shipper shall declare the density of the cargo, in addition to providing the cargo information required by regulation VI/2.

2 For bulk carriers to which regulation 6 applies, unless such bulk carriers comply with all relevant requirements of this chapter applicable to the carriage of solid bulk cargoes having a density of 1,780 kg/m^3 and above, any cargo declared to have a density within the range 1,250 kg/m^3 to 1,780 kg/m^3 shall have its density verified by an accredited testing organization.①

Regulation 11
Loading instrument

(Unless provided otherwise, this regulation applies to bulk carriers regardless of their date of construction)

① In verifying the density of solid bulk cargoes, reference should be made to the *Uniform method of measurement of the density of bulk cargoes* (MSC/Circ.908).

第 9 条
对由于货舱结构设计的原因而不能符合第 4.3 条的散货船的要求

在第 4.3 条应用范围之内,于 1999 年 7 月 1 日以前建造而建造后又不具有足够数量的水密横舱壁以满足该条要求的散货船,如果其能符合下列要求,则主管机关可允许放宽第 4.3 和 6 条的要求:

.1 对最前部货舱按第Ⅺ-1/2 条要求的加强检验程序对年度检验所规定的检查项目,应由对货舱的中间检验所规定的检查项目替代;

.2 在所有的货舱或货物传输装置隧道(如适用)内设置舱底污水井高水位报警装置,使之在驾驶台发出听觉和视觉报警,该报警装置应经主管机关或主管机关按第Ⅺ-1/1条规定所认可的组织认可;和

.3 提供特定货舱进水状况的详细资料。该资料应附有按《国际安全管理(ISM)规则》第 8 节规定制定的有关撤离部署的详细须知,并以此作为船员训练和演习的基础。

第 10 条
固体散货密度的申报

1 船长为 150 m 及以上的散货船装货之前,托运人除按第Ⅵ/2 条要求提交货物资料外,还应申报货物密度。

2 对于适用第 6 条的散货船,除非这些散货船符合本章有关装运密度为 1 780 kg/m^3 及以上的固体散货的所有相关要求,申报密度在 1 250 kg/m^3 至 1 780 kg/m^3 范围内的任何货物应由有资质的试验机构验证其密度①。

第 11 条
装载仪

(除另有规定外,本条适用于无论何时建造的散货船)

① 在验证固体散货密度时,应参见第 MSC/Circ.908 号通函《测量散货密度的统一方法》。

1 Bulk carriers of 150 m in length and upwards shall be fitted with a loading instrument capable of providing information on hull girder shear forces and bending moments, taking into account the recommendation adopted by the Organization.①

2 Bulk carriers of 150 m in length and upwards constructed before 1 July 1999 shall comply with the requirements of paragraph 1 not later than the date of the first intermediate or periodical survey② of the ship to be carried out after 1 July 1999.

3 Bulk carriers of less than 150 m in length constructed on or after 1 July 2006 shall be fitted with a loading instrument capable of providing information on the ship's stability in the intact condition. The computer software shall be approved for stability calculations by the Administration and shall be provided with standard conditions for testing purposes relating to the approved stability information.③

Regulation 12
Hold, ballast and dry space water ingress alarms④

(*This regulation applies to bulk carriers regardless of their date of construction*)

1 Bulk carriers shall be fitted with water level detectors:

.1 in each cargo hold, giving audible and visual alarms, one when the water level above the inner bottom in any hold reaches a height of 0.5 m and another at a height not less than 15% of the depth of the cargo hold but not more than 2 m. On bulk carriers to which regulation 9.2 applies, detectors with only the latter alarm need be installed. The water level detectors shall be fitted in the aft end of the cargo holds. For cargo holds which are used for water ballast, an alarm overriding device may be installed. The visual alarms shall clearly discriminate between the two different water levels detected in each hold;

.2 in any ballast tank forward of the collision bulkhead required by regulation II-1/12, giving an audible and visual alarm when the liquid in the tank reaches a level not exceeding 10% of the tank capacity. An alarm overriding device may be installed to be activated when the tank is in use; and

.3 in any dry or void space other than a chain cable locker, any part of which extends forward of the foremost cargo hold, giving an audible and visual alarm at a water level of 0.1 m above the deck. Such alarms need not be provided in enclosed spaces the volume of which does not exceed 0.1% of the ship's maximum displacement volume.

---

① Refer to the *Recommendation on loading instruments* (resolution 5 of the 1997 SOLAS Conference).

② Refer to *Application of SOLAS regulations XII/3, XII/7 and XII/11* (MSC.1/Circ.1463).

③ Refer to the relevant parts of the appendix to *Guidelines for the on-board use and application of computers* (MSC/Circ.891), *Guidelines on the provision of stability-related information for bulk carriers* (MSC/Circ.1159) and *Uniform method of measurement of the density of bulk cargoes* (MSC/Circ.908).

④ When water level detectors are installed on bulk carriers in compliance with regulation XII/12, the *Performance standards for water level detectors on bulk carriers and single hold cargo ships other than bulk carriers*, annexed to resolution MSC.188(79) adopted on 3 December 2004, should be applied.

1 船长为 150 m 及以上的散货船均应配备装载仪,该装载仪应能提供船体梁的剪力和弯矩资料,并考虑到本组织通过的建议案。①

2 1999 年 7 月 1 日以前建造的船长为 150 m 及以上的散货船,应不迟于 1999 年 7 月 1 日以后的第一次中间检验或定期检验②之日符合本条第 1 款的要求。

3 2006 年 7 月 1 日或以后建造的船长小于 150 m 的散货船应配备能提供船舶完整稳性资料的装载仪。计算机稳性计算的软件应经主管机关认可,该软件还应备有标准工况用于与批准的稳性资料有关的测试。③

第 12 条
货舱、压载舱和干燥处所进水报警装置④

(本条适用于无论何时建造的散货船)

1 散货船应安装水位探测器:

.1 在每一货舱内,当水位达到高出任何货舱内底 0.5 m 时应发出听觉和视觉报警,并在水位高度达到不小于货舱深度 15%但不超过 2 m 时也应发出听觉和视觉报警。对于适用第 9.2 条的散货船,只需要安装后一个报警的探测器。水位探测器应安装在货舱的后端。对于用作水压载的货舱,可安装一个报警越控装置。视觉报警器应能将每一货舱中探测到的两种不同的水位明显区分开;

.2 对第Ⅱ-1/12 条所要求的防撞舱壁前方的任一压载舱,当舱内的液面达到不超过舱容的 10%时应发出听觉和视觉报警。可安装一个报警越控装置,在使用该舱时启动;和

.3 在除锚链舱以外的任何干燥处所或空舱内,延伸至最前部货舱前方的任何部位,在水位高出甲板 0.1 m 时应发出听觉和视觉报警。当围蔽处所内的容量不超过船舶最大排水量的 0.1%时,不必安装此类报警器。

---

① 参见 1997 年 SOLAS 公约缔约国大会通过的决议 5《关于装载仪的建议案》。
② 参见《〈安全公约〉第Ⅻ/3、Ⅻ/7 和Ⅻ/11 条的适用》(第 MSC.1/Circ.1463 号通函)。
③ 参见《船上计算机使用和应用导则》(第 MSC/Circ.891 号通函)附录的相关部分,《散货船稳性相关信息规定的导则》(第 MSC/Circ.1159 号通函)和《散装货物密度测量统一方法》(第 MSC/Circ.908 号通函)。
④ 如散货船按照第Ⅻ/2 条要求安装了水位探测器,则应适用《散货船和单货舱非散货船上的水位探测器性能标准》,见 2004 年 12 月 3 日通过的第 MSC.188(79)号决议的附件。

2 The audible and visual alarms specified in paragraph 1 shall be located on the navigation bridge.

3 Bulk carriers constructed before 1 July 2004 shall comply with the requirements of this regulation not later than the date of the annual, intermediate or renewal survey of the ship to be carried out after 1 July 2004, whichever comes first.

Regulation 13
Availability of pumping systems①

(*This regulation applies to bulk carriers regardless of their date of construction*)

1 On bulk carriers, the means for draining and pumping ballast tanks forward of the collision bulkhead and bilges of dry spaces any part of which extends forward of the foremost cargo hold shall be capable of being brought into operation from a readily accessible enclosed space, the location of which is accessible from the navigation bridge or propulsion machinery control position without traversing exposed freeboard or superstructure decks. Where pipes serving such tanks or bilges pierce the collision bulkhead, valve operation by means of remotely operated actuators may be accepted, as an alternative to the valve control specified in regulation II-1/12, provided that the location of such valve controls complies with this regulation.

2 Bulk carriers constructed before 1 July 2004 shall comply with the requirements of this regulation not later than the date of the first intermediate or renewal survey of the ship to be carried out after 1 July 2004, but in no case later than 1 July 2007.

Regulation 14
Restrictions from sailing with any hold empty

Bulk carriers of 150 m in length and upwards of single-side skin construction, carrying cargoes having a density of 1,780 kg/m^3 and above, if not meeting the requirements for withstanding flooding of any one cargo hold as specified in regulation 5.1 and the Standards and criteria for side structures of bulk carriers of single-side skin construction, adopted by the Organization by resolution MSC.168(79), as may be amended by the Organization, provided that such amendments are adopted, brought into force and take effect in accordance with the provisions of article VIII of the present Convention concerning the amendment procedures applicable to the Annex other than chapter I, shall not sail with any hold loaded to less than 10% of the hold's maximum allowable cargo weight when in the full load condition, after reaching 10 years of age. The applicable full load condition for this regulation is a load equal to or greater than 90% of the ship's deadweight at the relevant assigned freeboard.

① Refer to *Interpretation of SOLAS regulation XII/13* (MSC/Circ.1069).

2　本条1规定的听觉和视觉报警器应设于驾驶台。

3　2004年7月1日以前建造的散货船,应在不迟于2004年7月1日后该船进行的年度检验、中间检验或换证检验时符合本条要求,取早者。

第13条
泵系的有效性①

(本条适用于无论何时建造的散货船)

1　散货船上用于排放和泵吸位于防撞舱壁前方的压载舱的压载水以及延伸至最前部货舱前的干燥处所任何部分的舱底水的设备,应能从一个可进入的围蔽处所内控制其运行。该围蔽处所应能从驾驶台或主机控制站进入而无须穿过露天干舷甲板或上层建筑甲板。如果用于这些舱或舱底水的管路穿过防撞舱壁,也可接受通过遥控启动阀门操作的装置作为第Ⅱ-1/12条规定的阀控制的替代措施,只要此类阀门控制器的位置符合本条的规定。

2　2004年7月1日以前建造的散货船,应在不迟于2004年7月1日以后船舶进行第一次中间检验或换证检验时,但无论如何不得迟于2007年7月1日符合本条要求。

第14条
任何货舱空舱时的航行限制

对船长为150 m及以上,载运货物密度为1 780 kg/m^3及以上的单舷侧结构散货船,如果不满足第5.1条规定的承受任一货舱进水的要求,也不满足本组织第MSC.168(79)号决议通过的《单舷侧结构散货船舷侧结构标准和衡准》(可能经本组织修正,但这种修正案应按本公约第Ⅷ条有关适用于除第Ⅰ章外的附则修正程序的规定予以通过、生效和实施),则在船龄满10年之后,当任何货舱的载货重量低于该货舱在满载工况下最大许可载货重量的10%时,不得开航。本条所适用的满载工况系指其载荷等于或大于在相应的核定干舷时的船舶载重量的90%。

① 参见《对SOLAS公约第Ⅻ/13条的解释》(第MSC/Circ.1069号通函)。

Chapter XIII Verification of compliance

第XIII章　符合性验证

Regulation 1
Definitions

For the purpose of this chapter:

1 Audit means a systematic, independent and documented process for obtaining audit evidence and evaluating it objectively to determine the extent to which audit criteria are fulfilled.

2 Audit Scheme means the IMO Member State Audit Scheme established by the Organization and taking into account the guidelines developed by the Organization.①

3 Code for Implementation means the IMO Instruments Implementation Code (III Code) adopted by the Organization by resolution A.1070(28).

4 Audit Standard means the Code for Implementation.

Regulation 2
Application

Contracting Governments shall use the provisions of the Code for Implementation in the execution of their obligations and responsibilities② contained in the present Convention.

Regulation 3
Verification of compliance

1 Every Contracting Government shall be subject to periodic audits by the Organization in accordance with the audit standard to verify compliance with and implementation of the present Convention.

2 The Secretary-General of the Organization shall have responsibility for administering the Audit Scheme, based on the guidelines developed by the Organization.①

3 Every Contracting Government shall have responsibility for facilitating the conduct of the audit and implementation of a programme of actions to address the findings, based on the guidelines adopted by the Organization.①

4 Audit of all Contracting Governments shall be:

---

① Refer to the *Framework and Procedures for the IMO Member State Audit Scheme* (resolution A.1067(28)).

② Refer to *2019 Non-exhaustive list of obligations under instruments relevant to the IMO Instruments Implementation Code (III Code)* (resolution A.1141(31)), as may be amended, and *Guidance on communication of information by Member States* (resolution A.1139(31)).

第 1 条
定义

1　审核系指为获取和客观地鉴定审核证据以确定审核标准满足程度的系统、独立且有文件记录的一个过程。

2　审核机制系指本组织建立的、考虑到本组织制定的各项导则的《IMO 成员国审核机制》[①]。

3　实施系指本组织以第 A.1070(28)号决议通过的《IMO 文书实施规则》(III 规则)。

4　审核标准系指实施规则。

第 2 条
适用范围

各缔约国政府在履行本附则所含的其义务和责任[②]时,须使用实施规则的规定。

第 3 条
符合性验证

1　每一缔约国政府均须接受本组织按照审核标准进行的定期审核,以对符合和实施本公约进行验证。

2　本组织秘书长基于本组织制定的导则[①],有责任管理该审核机制。

3　每一缔约国政府基于本组织制定的导则[①],均有责任便利开展审核和实施为处理审核结果的行动计划。

4　所有缔约国政府审核均须:

① 参见《IMO 成员国审核机制框架和程序》(第 A.1067(28)号决议)。

② 参见《2019 年 IMO 文书实施规则》(III 规则)下的非详尽义务清单(第 A.1141(31)号决议)和《成员国信息交流指南》(第 A.1139(31)号决议)。

.1 based on an overall schedule developed by the Secretary-General of the Organization, taking into account the guidelines developed by the Organization①; and

.2 conducted at periodic intervals, taking into account the guidelines developed by the Organization.①

① Refer to the *Framework and Procedures for the IMO Member State Audit Scheme* (resolution A.1067(28)).

.1　基于本组织秘书长制订的总体计划，并考虑到本组织制定的导则；和

.2　定期进行，并考虑到本组织制定的导则。[①]

① 参见《IMO 成员国审核机制框架和程序》（第 A.1067（28）号决议）。

Chapter XIV Safety measures for ships operating in polar waters

第XIV章　极地水域营运船舶的安全措施

Regulation 1
Definitions

For the purpose of this chapter:

1 *Polar Code* means the International Code for Ships Operating in Polar Waters, consisting of an introduction and parts I-A and II-A and parts I-B and II-B, as adopted by resolutions MSC.385(94) and of the Marine Environment Protection Committee,① as may be amended, provided that:

.1 amendments to the safety-related provisions of the introduction and part I-A of the Polar Code are adopted, brought into force and take effect in accordance with the provisions of article VIII of the present Convention concerning the amendment procedures applicable to the annex other than chapter I; and

.2 amendments to part I-B of the Polar Code are adopted by the Maritime Safety Committee in accordance with its Rules of Procedure.

2 *Antarctic area* means the sea area south of latitude 60° S.

3 *Arctic waters* means those waters which are located north of a line from the latitude 58°00′.0 Nand longitude 042°00′.0 W to latitude 64°37′.0 N, longitude 035°27′.0 W and thence by a rhumb line to latitude 67°03′.9 N, longitude 026°33′.4 W and thence by a rhumb line to the latitude 70°49′.56 N and longitude 008°59′.61 W (Sørkapp, Jan Mayen) and by the southern shore of Jan Mayen to 73°31′.6 N and 019°01′.0 E by the Island of Bjørnøya, and thence by a great circle line to the latitude 68°38′.29 N and longitude 043°23′.08 E (Cap Kanin Nos) and hence by the northern shore of the Asian Continent eastward to the Bering Strait and thence from the Bering Strait westward to latitude 60° N as far as Il'pyrskiy and following the 60th North parallel eastward as far as and including Etolin Strait and thence by the northern shore of the North American continent as far south as latitude 60° N and thence eastward along parallel of latitude 60°N, to longitude 056°37′.1 W and thence to the latitude 58°00′.0 N, longitude 042°00′.0 W.

4 *Polar waters* means Arctic waters and/or the Antarctic area.

5 *Ship constructed* means a ship the keel of which is laid or which is at a similar stage of construction.

6 *At a similar stage of construction* means the stage at which:

.1 construction identifiable with a specific ship begins; and

.2 assembly of that ship has commenced comprising at least 50 tonnes or 1% of the estimated mass of all structural material, whichever is less.

① Refer to the resolution of adoption of the *International Code for Ships Operating in Polar Waters* (MEPC.264(68)), by the Marine Environment Protection Committee.

第1条
定义

就本章而言：

1　**极地规则**系指第 MSC.385(94)号决议和海上环境保护委员会决议通过的《国际极地水域营运船舶规则》[①]，由引言和Ⅰ-A 和 Ⅱ-A 部分以及Ⅰ-B 和Ⅱ-B 部分组成；它可加以修正，但：

.1　《极地规则》引言和Ⅰ-A 部分中与安全相关的条款的修正案应按照第Ⅷ条关于本公约附则（除第Ⅰ章外）的适用修正程序的规定予以通过、生效和实施；和

.2　《极地规则》Ⅰ-B 部分的修正案由海上安全委员会按其议事规则予以通过。

2　**南极区域**系指南纬 60°以南的海域。

3　**北极水域**系指位于下述连线以北的水域：从北纬 58°00′.0 和西经 042°00′.0 延伸至北纬 64°37′.0 和西经 035°27′.0 的连线，再经一恒向线延伸至北纬 67°03′.9 和西经 026°33′.4，再经一恒向线延伸至北纬 70°49′.56 和西经 008°59′.61（Sørkapp，Jan Mayen），并经由 Jan Mayen 南岸延伸至靠近 Bjørnøya 岛的北纬 73°31′.6 和东经 019°01′.0，再经一大圆线延伸至北纬 68°38′.29 和东经 043°23′.08（Cap Kanin Nos），再经由亚洲大陆北岸向东延伸至白令海峡，再从白令海峡向西延伸至北纬 60° 直到 Il′pyrskiy，并沿北纬 60°平行线向东延伸至并包括 Etolin 海峡，再经由北美大陆北岸向南延伸至北纬 60°，再向东沿北纬 60°平行线延伸至西经 056°37′.1，再延伸至北纬 58°00′.0 和西经 042°00′.0。

4　**极地水域**系指北极水域和（或）南极区域。

5　**建造的船舶**系指安放龙骨或处于类似建造阶段的船舶。

6　**类似建造阶段**系指在此阶段：

.1　可辨认出某一具体船舶的建造开始；和

.2　该船业已开始的装配量至少为 50 吨，或为全部结构材料估算重量的 1%，取较小者。

① 参见海上环境保护委员会通过的《国际极地水域营运船舶规则》决议（MEPC.264(68)）。

Regulation 2
Application

1 Unless expressly provided otherwise, this chapter applies to ships operating in polar waters, certified in accordance with chapter 1.①

2 Ships constructed before 1 January 2017 shall meet the relevant requirements of the Polar Code by the first intermediate or renewal survey, whichever occurs first, after 1 January 2018.

3 In applying part I-A of the Polar Code, consideration should be given to the additional guidance in part I-B of the Polar Code.

4 This chapter shall not apply to ships owned or operated by a Contracting Government and used, for the time being, only in government non-commercial service. However, ships owned or operated by a Contracting Government and used, for the time being, only in government non-commercial service are encouraged to act in a manner consistent, so far as reasonable and practicable, with this chapter.

5 Nothing in this chapter shall prejudice the rights or obligations of States under international law.

Regulation 3
Requirements for ships to which this chapter applies

1 Ships to which this chapter applies shall comply with the requirements of the safety-related provision of the introduction and with part I-A of the Polar Code and shall, in addition to the requirements of regulations I/7, I/8, I/9, and I/10, as applicable, be surveyed and certified, as provided for in that Code.

2 Ships to which this chapter applies holding a certificate issued pursuant to the provisions of paragraph 1 shall be subject to the control established in regulations I/19 and XI-1/4. For this purpose, such certificates shall be treated as a certificate issued under regulation I/12 or I/13.

Regulation 4
Alternative design and arrangement

1 The goal of this regulation is to provide a methodology for alternative design and arrangements for structure, machinery, and electrical installations, fire safety and life saving appliances and arrangements.

---

① Refer to the *Interim safety measures for ships not certified under the SOLAS Convention operating in polar waters* (resolution A.1137(31)).

第 2 条
适用范围

1　除另有明文规定外，本章适用于在极地水域营运并按第Ⅰ章发证的船舶[①]。

2　2017 年 1 月 1 日以前建造的船舶应在 2018 年 1 月 1 日后的第一次中间或换证检验之前（以较早者为准）满足《极地规则》的相关要求。

3　在适用《极地规则》的Ⅰ-A 部分时，应考虑到《极地规则》Ⅰ-B 部分中的补充指南。

4　本章不适用于由缔约国政府拥有或经营的、目前仅用于政府非商业性服务的船舶。但是，仍鼓励缔约国政府拥有或经营的、目前仅用于政府非商业性服务的船舶在合理和可行的范围内符合本章要求。

5　本章的任何内容均不得损害各国根据国际法所具有的权利或义务。

第 3 条
对适用本章的船舶的要求

1　适用本章的船舶应符合《极地规则》的引言和Ⅰ-A 部分中安全相关条款的要求，且除须符合第Ⅰ/7、Ⅰ/8、Ⅰ/9 和Ⅰ/10 条的适用要求外，还应按该规则的规定进行检验和发证。

2　持有按照上述第 1 款规定签发的证书的、适用本章的船舶须接受第Ⅰ/19 和XI-1/4 条规定的监督。为此，此种证书须视为根据第Ⅰ/12 或Ⅰ/13 条签发的证书。

第 4 条
替代设计和布置

1　本条的目的是为结构、机电设备、消防安全以及救生设备和布置的替代设计和布置提供方法。

---

① 参见未在《国际海上人命安全公约》体系下发证的船舶在极地水域作业的临时安全措施（第 A.1137(31)号决议）。

2 Structural arrangements, machinery and electrical installation, fire safety design and arrangement measures and as well as life-saving appliances and arrangements may deviate from the prescriptive requirements set out in chapters 3, 6, 7 and 8 of the Polar Code, provided that the alternative design and arrangements meet the intent of the goal and functional requirements concerned and provide an equivalent level of safety to the requirements in those chapters.

3 When alternative designs or arrangements deviate from the prescriptive requirements of chapters 3, 6, 7 and 8 of the Polar Code, an engineering analysis, evaluation and approval of the design and arrangements shall be carried out based on the guidelines approved by the Organization.①

4 Any alternative designs or arrangement deviating from the prescriptive requirements shall be recorded in the Polar Ship Certificate and the ship's Polar Water Operational Manual, as required by the Polar Code, also defining the technical and operational measures and conditions for the allowed deviation.

① Refer to the *Guidelines for the approval of alternatives and equivalents as provided for in various IMO instruments* (MSC.1/Circ.1455), the *Revised guidelines on alternative design and arrangements for SOLAS chapters II-1 and III* (MSC.1/Circ.1212/Rev.1) and the *Guidelines on alternative design and arrangements for fire safety* (MSC/Circ.1002 and its Corr.1, Corr.2 and Corr.3, as amended by MSC.1/Circ.1552), as applicable.

2　结构布置、机电设备、消防安全的设计和布置措施以及救生设备和布置可偏离《极地规则》第 3、6、7 和 8 章所述的规定性要求，但替代设计和布置应满足相关目的和功能要求的意图并具有与该几章中的要求等效的安全等级。

3　当替代设计或布置偏离《极地规则》第 3、6、7 和 8 章的规定性要求时，应根据本组织批准的导则①进行替代设计和布置的工程分析、评估和认可。

4　任何偏离规定性要求的替代设计或布置均须按照《极地规则》的要求，在极地船舶证书和船舶的极地水域操作手册中予以记录，并对所允许的偏离规定其技术、操作措施和条件。

---

①　参见《IMO 文件规定的替代与等效的认可导则》（第 MSC.1/Circ.1455 号通函）、《经修订的 SOLAS 第Ⅱ-1 和Ⅲ章的替代设计和布置导则》（第 MSC.1/Circ.1212/Rev.1 号通函）和《消防安全替代设计和布置指南》（第 MSC.1/Circ.1002 号通函及其经 MSC.1/Circ.1552 修订的 Corr.1、Corr.2 及 Corr.3），如适用。

Appendix
Certificates①

① The present appendix contains the forms of certificates and records of equipment of the 1974 SOLAS Convention, as modified by the 1988 SOLAS Protocol. States which are Contracting Governments to the 1974 SOLAS Convention but not Parties to the 1988 SOLAS Protocol may issue certificates in the form prescribed by the 1988 SOLAS Protocol in accordance with Assembly resolution A.883(21) relating to the global implementation of the harmonized system of survey and certification.

附录
证书[①]

① 本附录包含经 1988 年 SOLAS 议定书修订的 1974 年 SOLAS 公约的证书和设备记录格式。1974 年 SOLAS 公约缔约国但非 1988 年 SOLAS 议定书缔约国的政府,可根据关于全球执行检验和发证协调系统的 A.883(21) 决议,以 1988 年 SOLAS 议定书规定的格式签发证书。

P88 Form of safety certificate for passenger ships

PASSENGER SHIP SAFETY CERTIFICATE

This Certificate shall be supplemented by a Record of Equipment for Passenger Ship Safety (Form P)

(*official seal*) (*State*)

for an/a short① international voyage

Issued under the provisions of the
INTERNATIONAL CONVENTION FOR THE SAFETY OF LIFE AT SEA, 1974,
as modified by the Protocol of 1988 relating thereto
under the authority of the Government of

____

(*name of the State*)

by ________________________________

(*person or organization authorized*)

Particulars of ship②

Name of ship ________________________________

Distinctive number or letters ________________________________

Port of registry ________________________________

Gross tonnage ________________________________

Sea areas in which ship is certified to operate (regulation Ⅳ/2) ________________

IMO Number③ ________________________________

Date of build

Date of building contract ________________________________

Date on which keel was laid or ship was at similar stage of construction ________________

① Delete as appropriate.
② Alternatively, the particulars of the ship may be placed horizontally in boxes.
③ In accordance with the IMO ship identification number scheme (resolution A.1117(30)).

P88 客船安全证书格式

客船安全证书

本证书须附有客船安全的设备记录（格式 P）

（公章）　　　　　　　　　　　　　　　　　　　　　　　　（国籍）

供国际航行/短程国际航行①用

本证书由________（国名）政府授权____________（被授权的个人或组织）按经 1988 年议定书修订的《1974 年国际海上人命安全公约》的规定签发。

船舶资料②

船名____

船舶编号或呼号____

船籍港____

总吨位____

核准船舶营运的海区（第Ⅳ/2 条）____

IMO 识别号③____

建造日期

建造合同日期____

安放龙骨或处于类似建造阶段的日期____

① 酌情删减。
② 船舶资料也可在表格中横向排列。
③ 按照《IMO 船舶识别号机制》（A.1117(30)决议）。

Date of delivery ______________________________

Date on which work for a conversion or an alteration or modification of

a major character was commenced (where applicable) ____________________

All applicable dates shall be completed.

THIS IS TO CERTIFY:

1 That the ship has been surveyed in accordance with the requirements of regulation Ⅰ/7 of the Convention.

2 That the survey showed that:

2.1 the ship complied with the requirements of the Convention as regards:

.1 the structure, main and auxiliary machinery, boilers and other pressure vessels;

.2 the watertight subdivision arrangements and details;

.3 the following subdivision load lines:

Subdivision load lines assigned and marked on the ship's side amidships (regulation Ⅱ-1/18①)	Freeboard	To apply when the spaces in which passengers are carried include the following alternative spaces
P1		
P2		
P3		

2.2 the ship complied with part G of chapter Ⅱ-1 of the Convention using ________ as fuel/N.A.②;

2.3 the ship complied with the requirements of the Convention as regards structural fire protection, fire safety systems and appliances and fire control plans;

2.4 the life-saving appliances and the equipment of lifeboats, liferafts and rescue boats were provided in accordance with the requirements of the Convention;

2.5 the ship was provided with a line-throwing appliance and radio installations used in life-saving appliances in accordance with the requirements of the Convention;

2.6 the ship complied with the requirements of the Convention as regards radio installations;

2.7 the functioning of the radio installations used in life-saving appliances complied with the requirements of the Convention;

2.8 the ship complied with the requirements of the Convention as regards shipborne navigational equipment, means of embarkation for pilots and nautical publications;

---

① For ships constructed before 1 January 2009, the applicable subdivision notation "C.1", "C.2" and "C.3" should be used.
② Delete as appropriate.

交船日期＿＿＿＿＿＿＿＿＿＿＿＿＿＿＿＿＿＿＿＿

重大改建或改装开始的日期(如适用)＿＿＿＿＿＿＿＿＿＿＿＿

应填写所有适用日期。

兹证明:

1　该船业已按公约第Ⅰ/7 条的要求进行了检验。

2　检验表明:

2.1　该船在以下方面符合公约的要求:

.1　结构、主机和辅机、锅炉及其他压力容器;

.2　水密分舱布置及细节;

.3　下列分舱载重线:

核定并勘绘于船中两舷的分舱载重线(第Ⅱ-1/18 条)[①]	干舷	适用于包括下列其他处所在内的载客处所
P1		
P2		
P3		

2.2　该船符合公约第Ⅱ-1 章 G 部分要求,使用＿＿＿＿作为燃料/不适用[②]。

2.3　该船在结构防火、消防安全系统和设备及防火控制图方面符合公约的要求;

2.4　该船根据公约的要求配备了救生设备和救生艇、救生筏及救助艇用属具;

2.5　该船根据公约的要求在救生设备中配备了抛绳设备和无线电装置;

2.6　该船在无线电装置方面符合公约的要求;

2.7　该船救生设备中使用的无线电装置的功能符合公约的要求;

2.8　该船在船载导航设备、引航员登船设施及航海出版物方面符合公约的要求;

---

① 对于 2009 年 1 月 1 日以前建造的船舶,应使用适用的分舱标志“C.1”、“C.2”和“C.3”。
② 酌情删减。

2.9 the ship was provided with lights, shapes, means of making sound signals and distress signals in accordance with the requirements of the Convention and the International Regulations for Preventing Collisions at Sea in force;

2.10 in all other respects the ship complied with the relevant requirements of the Convention.

2.11 the ship was/was not[①] subjected to an alternative design and arrangements in pursuance of regulation(s) Ⅱ-1/55/Ⅱ-2/17/Ⅲ/38[①] of the Convention;

2.12 a Document of approval of alternative design and arrangements for machinery and electrical installations/fire protection/life-saving appliances and arrangements[①] is/is not[①] appended to this Certificate.

3 That an Exemption Certificate has/has not[①] been issued.

This certificate is valid until____

Completion date of the survey on which this certificate is based:______________(*dd/mm/yyy*)

Issued at ____

(*place of issue of certificate*)

____________________________　　____

(*date of issue*)　　(*signature of authorized official issuing the certificate*)

(*seal or stamp of the issuing authority, as appropriate*)

Endorsement where the renewal survey has been completed and regulation I/14(d) applies

The ship complies with the relevant requirements of the Convention, and this certificate shall, in accordance with regulation Ⅰ/14(d) of the Convention, be accepted as valid until__________

Signed______________________________________

(*signature of authorized official*)

Place_______________________________________

Date____

(*seal or stamp of the authority, as appropriate*)

① Delete as appropriate.

2.9 该船根据公约及现行《国际海上避碰规则》的要求配备了航行灯、号型以及发出声响信号和遇险信号的设备；

2.10 该船所有其他方面均符合公约的有关要求；

2.11 船舶设有/未设[①]符合本公约第Ⅱ-1/55/Ⅱ-2/17/Ⅲ/38[①]条规定的替代设计和布置；

2.12 机电设备/防火/救生设备的替代设计和布置的批准文件附于/未附于[①]本证书之后。

3 已经/尚未[①]签发免除证书。

本证书有效期限至止______________________________

本证书基于的检验完成日期：__________________________（年/月/日）

签发于____

（证书签发地点）

____________________ ____________________

（签发日期） （经授权发证的官员签字）

（发证主管当局盖章或钢印）

在已完成换证检验并适用第Ⅰ/14（d）条情况下的签署该船符合公约的有关要求

该船符合公约的有关要求，本证书根据公约第Ⅰ/14(d)条应视为有效，有效期限至________________止。

签字____________________

（经授权的官员签字）

地点____________________

日期____________________

（主管当局盖章或钢印）

① 酌情删减。

Endorsement to extend the validity of the certificate until reaching the port of survey or for a period of grace where regulation I/14(e) or I/14(f) applies

This certificate shall, in accordance with regulation Ⅰ/14(e)/Ⅰ/14 (f)[①] of the Convention, be accepted as valid until ________________

Signed ________________

(*signature of authorized official*)

Place ________________

Date ________________

(*seal or stamp of the authority, as appropriate*)

① Delete as appropriate.

在适用第Ⅰ/14（e）条或第Ⅰ/14（f）条情况下，将证书有效期展期至驶抵进行检验的港口或给予宽限期的签署

本证书根据公约第Ⅰ/14（e）/Ⅰ/14（f）条[①]应视为有效，有效期限至________________止。

签字______________________________

（经授权的官员签字）

地点______________________________

日期______________________________

（主管当局盖章或钢印）

① 酌情删减。

RECORD OF EQUIPMENT FOR PASSENGER SHIP SAFETY (FORM P)

RECORD OF EQUIPMENT FOR COMPLIANCE WITH THE INTERNATIONAL CONVENTION FOR THE SAFETY OF LIFE AT SEA, 1974, AS AMENDED

1 Particulars of ship

Name of ship ____________________

Distinctive number or letters ____________________

Number of passengers for which certified ____________________

Minimum number of persons with required qualifications to operate the radio installations ______

2 Details of life-saving appliances

1	Total number of persons for which life-saving appliances are provided		
		Port side	Starboard side
2	Total number of lifeboats		
2.1	Total number of persons accommodated by them		
2.2	Number of partially enclosed lifeboats (regulation Ⅲ/21 and LSA Code, section 4.5)		
2.3	Number of self-righting partially enclosed lifeboats (regulation Ⅲ/43)①		
2.4	Number of totally enclosed lifeboats (regulation Ⅲ/21 and LSA Code, section 4.6)		
2.5	Other lifeboats		
2.5.1	Number		
2.5.2	Type		
3	Number of motor lifeboats (included in the total lifeboats shown above)		

① Refer to the 1983 amendments to SOLAS (MSC.6(48)), applicable to ships constructed on or after 1 July 1986, but before 1 July 1998.

客船安全的设备记录（格式P）

证明符合经修正的1974年国际海上人命安全公约有关要求的设备记录

1　船舶资料

船名＿＿＿＿＿＿＿＿＿＿＿＿＿＿＿＿＿＿＿＿

船舶编号或呼号＿＿＿＿＿＿＿＿＿＿＿＿＿＿＿＿＿＿＿＿

核准的乘客数＿＿＿＿＿＿＿＿＿＿＿＿＿＿＿＿＿＿＿＿

持证无线电装置操作人员的最少定员数＿＿＿＿＿＿＿＿＿＿＿＿＿＿＿＿＿＿＿＿

2　救生设备明细表

1	救生设备可供使用的总人数		
		左舷	右舷
2	救生艇的总数		
2.1	救生艇可载总人数		
2.2	半封闭救生艇的数量(第Ⅲ/21条和LSA规则第4.5节)		
2.3	自扶正的部分封闭的救生艇数量(第Ⅲ/43条)①		
2.4	全封闭救生艇的数量(第Ⅲ/21条和LSA规则第4.6节)		
2.5	其他救生艇		
2.5.1	数量		
2.5.2	类型		
3	机动救生艇的数量(包括在上述救生艇总数内)		

① 参见1983年SOLAS修正案(MSC.6(48)决议),其适用于在1986年7月1日或以后,但在1998年7月1日以前建造的船舶。

2 Details of life-saving appliances(*continued*)

3.1	Number of lifeboats fitted with searchlights	
4	Number of rescue boats	
4.1	Number of boats which are included in the total lifeboats shown above	
4.2	Number of boats which are fast rescue boats	
5	Liferafts	
5.1	Those for which approved launching appliances are required	
5.1.1	Number of liferafts	
5.1.2	Number of persons accommodated by them	
5.2	Those for which approved launching appliances are not required	
5.2.1	Number of liferafts	
5.2.2	Number of persons accommodated by them	
6	Number of Marine Evacuation Systems (MES)	
6.1	Number of liferafts served by them	
6.2	Number of persons accommodated by them	
7	Buoyant apparatus	
7.1	Number of apparatus	
7.2	Number of persons capable of being supported	
8	Number of lifebuoys	
9	Number of lifejackets (total)	
9.1	Number of adult lifejackets	
9.2	Number of child lifejackets	
9.3	Number of infant lifejackets	
10	Immersion suits	
10.1	Total number	
10.2	Number of suits complying with the requirements for lifejackets	
11	Number of anti-exposure suits	
12	Number of thermal protective aids①	
13	Radio installations used in life-saving appliances	
13.1	Number of search and rescue locating devices	
13.1.1	Radar search and rescue transponders (SART)	
13.1.2	AIS search and rescue transmitters (AIS-SART)	
13.2	Number of two-way VHF radiotelephone apparatus	

① Excluding those required by the LSA Code, paragraphs 4.1.5.1.24, 4.4.8.31 and 5.1.2.2.13.

2　救生设备明细表(续表)

3.1	装备有探照灯的救生艇的数量	
4	救助艇的数量	
4.1	包括在上述救生艇总数内的艇的数量	
5	救生筏	
5.1	需设置认可降落装置的救生筏	
5.1.1	救生筏的数量	
5.1.2	救生筏可载人数	
5.2	不需设置认可降落装置的救生筏	
5.2.1	救生筏的数量	
5.2.2	救生筏可载人数	
6	海上撤离系统(MES)的数量	
6.1	使用海上撤离系统的救生筏的数量	
6.2	海上撤离系统可载人数	
7	浮具	
7.1	数量	
7.2	可供使用的人数	
8	救生圈的数量	
9	救生衣的数量(总数)	
9.1	成人救生衣的数量	
9.2	儿童救生衣的数量	
10	救生服	
10.1	总数	
10.2	符合救生衣要求的救生服的数量	
11	抗暴露服的数量	
12	保温用具的数量①	
13	救生设备中使用的无线电装置	
13.1	搜救定位装置的数目	
13.1.1	搜救雷达应答器(SART)	
13.1.2	AIS 搜救应答器(AIS-SART)	
13.2	双向 VHF 无线电话设备的数量	

① 不包括 LSA 规则 4.1.5.1.24、4.4.8.31 和 5.1.2.2.13 要求的保温用具。

3 Details of radio facilities

Item		Actual provision
1	Primary systems	
1.1	VHF radio installation	
1.1.1	DSC encoder	
1.1.2	DSC watch receiver	
1.1.3	Radiotelephony	
1.2	MF radio installation	
1.2.1	DSC encoder	
1.2.2	DSC watch receiver	
1.2.3	Radiotelephony	
1.3	MF/HF radio installation	
1.3.1	DSC encoder	
1.3.2	DSC watch receiver	
1.3.3	Radiotelephony	
1.3.4	Direct-printing radiotelegraphy	
1.4	Recognized mobile satellite service ship earth station	
2	Secondary means of alerting	
3	Facilities for reception of maritime safety information	
3.1	NAVTEX receiver	
3.2	EGG receiver	
3.3	HF direct-printing radiotelegraph receiver	
4	Satellite EPIRB	
4.1	COSPAS-SARSAT	
5	VHF EPIRB	
6	Ship's search and rescue locating device	
6.1	Radar search and rescue transponder (SART)	
6.2	AIS search and rescue transmitter (AIS-SART)	

4 Methods used to ensure availability of radio facilities (regulation IV/15.6 and 15.7)

4.1 Duplication of equipment ____________________

4.2 Shore-based maintenance ____________________

4.3 At-sea maintenance capability ____________________

3 无线电设备明细表

	项目	实际配备情况
1	主设备	
1.1	VHF 无线电装置	
1.1.1	DSC 编码器	
1.1.2	DSC 值班接收机	
1.1.3	无线电话	
1.2	MF 无线电装置	
1.2.1	DSC 编码器	
1.2.2	DSC 值班接收机	
1.2.3	无线电话	
1.3	MF/HF 无线电装置	
1.3.1	DSC 编码器	
1.3.2	DSC 值班接收机	
1.3.3	无线电话	
1.3.4	直接印字无线电报	
1.4	经认可的移动卫星业务船舶地面站	
2	辅助警报装置	
3	用于接收海上安全信息的设施	
3.1	NAVTEX 接收机	
3.2	EGC 接收机	
3.3	HF 直接印字无线电报接收机	
4	卫星 EPIRB	
4.1	COSPAS-SARSAT	
5	VHF EPIRB	
6	船舶的搜救定位装置	
6.1	搜救雷达应答器(SART)	
6.2	AIS 搜救应答器(AIS-SART)	

4 用于确保无线电设备有效性的方法(第Ⅳ/15.6 和 15.7 条)

4.1 双套设备 ______________________________

4.2 岸基维护 ______________________________

4.3 海上维护能力 ______________________________

5 Details of navigational systems and equipment

Item		Actual provision
1.1	Standard magnetic compass	
1.2	Spare magnetic compass①	
1.3	Gyro-compass①	
1.4	Gyro-compass heading repeater①	
1.5	Gyro-compass bearing repeater①	
1.6	Heading or track control system①	
1.7	Pelorus or compass bearing device①	
1.8	Means of correcting heading and bearings	
1.9	Transmitting heading device (THD)①	
2.1	Nautical charts/electronic chart display and information system (ECDIS)②	
2.2	Back-up arrangements for ECDIS	
2.3	Nautical publications	
2.4	Back-up arrangements for electronic nautical publications	
3.1	Receiver for a global navigation satellite system/terrestrial radionavigation system/multi-system shipborne radionavigation receiver①,②	
3.2	9 GHz radar①	
3.3	Second radar (3 GHz/9 GHz②)①	
3.4	Automatic radar plotting aid (ARPA)①	
3.5	Automatic tracking aid①	
3.6	Second automatic tracking aid①	
3.7	Electronic plotting aid①	
4.1	Automatic identification system (AIS)	
4.2	Long-range identification and tracking system	
5	Voyage data recorder (VDR)	
6.1	Speed and distance measuring device (through the water)①	

① Alternative means of meeting this requirement are permitted under regulation V/19. In case of other means, they shall be specified.

② Delete as appropriate.

5 航行系统和设备明细表

项目		实际配备情况
1.1	标准磁罗经[①]	
1.2	备用磁罗经[①]	
1.3	陀螺罗经[①]	
1.4	陀螺罗经首向复示器[①]	
1.5	陀螺罗经方位复示器[①]	
1.6	首向或航迹控制系统[①]	
1.7	哑罗经或罗经方位装置[①]	
1.8	首向和方位修正仪	
1.9	首向传送装置(THD)[①]	
2.1	海图/电子海图显示和信息系统(ECDIS)[②]	
2.2	ECDIS 备份装置	
2.3	航海出版物	
2.4	电子海图出版物备份装置	
3.1	全球卫星导航系统/全球无线电导航系统接收装置/多系统船载无线电导航接收装置[①,②]	
3.2	9 GHz 雷达[①]	
3.3	第二台雷达(3 GHz/9 GHz[②])[①]	
3.4	自动雷达标绘仪(ARPA)[①]	
3.5	自动跟踪仪[①]	
3.6	第二台自动跟踪仪[①]	
3.7	电子标绘装置[①]	
4.1	自动识别系统(AIS)	
4.2	远程识别与跟踪系统	
5	航行数据记录仪(VDR)	
6.1	航速和航程测量装置(对水)[①]	

① 根据第Ⅴ/19 条的规定,可允许采用符合本要求的替代装置。如果是其他装置,则应予详细说明。
② 酌情删减。

5 Details of navigational systems and equipment(*continued*)

6.2	Speed and distance measuring device (over the ground in the forward and athwartships direction)①	
7	Echo-sounding device①	
8.1	Rudder, propeller, thrust, pitch and operational mode indicator①	
8.2	Rate-of-turn indicator①	
9	Sound reception system①	
10	Telephone to emergency steering position①	
11	Daylight signalling lamp①	
12	Radar reflector①	
13	International Code of Signals	
14	IAMSAR Manual, Volume Ⅲ	
15	Bridge navigational watch alarm system (BNWAS)	

THIS IS TO CERTIFY that this Record is correct in all respects.

Issued at ____________________

(*place of issue of the Record*)

____________________ ____________________

(*date of issue*) (*signature of duly authorized official issuing the Record*)

(*seal or stamp of the issuing Authority, as appropriate*)

① Alternative means of meeting this requirement are permitted under regulation V/19. In case of other means, they shall be specified.

5　航行系统和设备明细表(续表)

6.2	航速和航程测量装置(对地,正向和横向)①	
7	回声测深仪①	
8.1	舵、螺旋桨、推力、螺距和工作模式指示器①	
8.2	回转速率指示仪①	
9	声响接收系统①	
10	与应急操舵位置联系的电话①	
11	白昼信号灯①	
12	雷达反射器①	
13	国际信号规则	
14	IAMSAR 手册第Ⅲ卷	
15	驾驶台航行值班报警系统(BNWAS)	

签发于________________________________

(记录签发地点)

________________________　　________________________

(签发日期)　　(经正式授权签发记录的官员签字)

(发证主管当局盖章或钢印)

① 根据第Ⅴ/19条的规定,可允许采用符合本要求的替代装置。如果是其他装置,则应予详细说明。

P88 Form of safety construction certificate for cargo ships

CARGO SHIP SAFETY CONSTRUCTION CERTIFICATE

(*official seal*) (*State*)

Issued under the provisions of the
INTERNATIONAL CONVENTION FOR THE SAFETY OF LIFE AT SEA, 1974,
as modified by the Protocol of 1988 relating thereto
under the authority of the Government of

____

(*name of the State*)

by ________________________________

(*person or organization authorized*)

Particulars of ship①

Name of ship ________________________________

Distinctive number or letters ________________________________

Port of registry ________________________________

Gross tonnage ________________________________

Deadweight of ship (metric tons)② ________________________________

IMO Number③ ________________________________

Type of ship④

Bulk carrier

Oil tanker

Chemical tanker

Gas carrier

---

① Alternatively, the particulars of the ship may be placed horizontally in boxes.
② For oil tankers, chemical tankers and gas carriers only.
③ In accordance with the IMO ship identification number scheme (resolution A.1117(30)).
④ Delete as appropriate.

P88 货船构造安全证书格式

货船构造安全证书

(公章)　　　　　　　　　　　　　　　　　　　　　　　　　　　　(国籍)

本证书由________________(国名)政府授权____________________(被授权的个人或组织)按经 1988 年议定书修订的 1974 年国际海上人命安全公约的规定签发。

船舶资料①

船名______________________________

船舶编号或呼号______________________________

船籍港______________________________

总吨位______________________________

载重量(公吨)②______________________________

IMO 识别号③______________________________

船型④

散货船

油船

化学品液

气体运输船

---

① 船舶资料也可在表格中横向排列。
② 仅适用于油船、化学品液货船和气体运输船。
③ 按照《IMO 船舶识别号机制》(A.1117(30)决议)。
④ 酌情删减。

Cargo ship other than any of the above

Date of build

Date of building contract ______

Date on which keel was laid or ship was at similar stage of construction ______

Date of delivery ______

Date on which work for a conversion or an alteration or modification of a major character was commenced (where applicable) ______

All applicable dates shall be completed.

THIS IS TO CERTIFY:

1 That the ship has been surveyed in accordance with the requirements of regulation Ⅰ/10 of the Convention.

2 That the survey showed that:

.1 the condition of the structure, machinery and equipment as defined in the above regulation was satisfactory and the ship complied with the relevant requirements of chapters Ⅱ-1 and Ⅱ-2 of the Convention (other than those relating to fire safety systems and appliances and fire control plans); and

.2 the ship complied with part G of chapter Ⅱ-1 of the Conventionusing ____ as fuel/N.A.①

3 That the last two inspections of the outside of the ship's bottom took place on ______ and ______ (*dd/mm/yyyy*).

4 That an Exemption Certificate has/has not① been issued.

5 That the ship was/was not① subjected to an alternative design and arrangements in pursuance of regulation(s) Ⅱ-1/55/Ⅱ-2/17① of the Convention.

6 A Document of approval of alternative design and arrangements for machinery and electrical installations/fire protection① is/is not① appended to this Certificate.

This certificate is valid until ______ ② subject to the annual and intermediate surveys and inspections of the outside of the ship's bottom in accordance with regulation Ⅰ/10 of the Convention.

① Delete as appropriate.

② Insert the date of expiry as specified by the Administration in accordance with regulation Ⅰ/14(a) of the Convention. The day and the month of this date correspond to the anniversary date, as defined in regulation Ⅰ/2(n) of the Convention, unless amended in accordance with regulation Ⅰ/14(h).

上述船型以外的货船

建造日期

建造合同日期________________________________

安放龙骨或处于类似建造阶段的日期________________________

交船日期________________________________

重大改建或改装开始的日期(如适用)________________________

应填写所有适用日期。

兹证明:

1 该船业已按公约第Ⅰ/10条的要求进行了检验。

2 检验表明:

.1 该船在上述条文所定义的结构、机械和设备等方面的状况令人满意,并符合公约第Ⅱ-1章和第Ⅱ-2章的有关要求(消防安全系统和设备及防火控制图除外);和

.2 该船符合公约第Ⅱ-1章G部分要求,使用________作为燃料/不适用[①]。

3 最近两次的船底外部检查于__________________和__________________(年/月/日)进行。

4 已经/尚未[①]签发免除证书。

5 船舶设有/未设[①]按公约第Ⅱ-1/55/Ⅱ-2/17条[①]规定的替代设计和布置。

6 机电设备/防火[①]的替代设计和布置的批准文件附于/未附于[①]本证书之后。

本证书有效期限至____________止[②],但应视公约第Ⅰ/10条规定的年度检验和中间检验以及船底外部检查情况而定。

---

① 酌情删减。

② 填入主管机关根据公约第Ⅰ/14(a)条规定的失效日期。该日期如未根据公约第Ⅰ/14(h)条予以修正,其日、月相当于第Ⅰ/2(n)条定义的周年日。

Completion date of the survey on which this certificate is based____________(*dd/mm/yyyy*)

Issued at ____

(*place of issue of certificate*)

________________ ________________________________

(*date of issue*) (*signature of authorized official issuing the certificate*)

(*seal or stamp of the issuing authority, as appropriate*)

本证书基于的检验完成日期：________________________________（年/月/日）

签发于____

（证书签发地点）

______________________　　　　______________________

（签发日期）　　　　　　　　（经授权发证的官员签字）

（发证主管当局盖章或钢印）

Endorsement for annual and intermediate surveys

THIS IS TO CERTIFY that, at a survey required by regulation Ⅰ/10 of the Convention, the ship was found to comply with the relevant requirements of the Convention.

Annual survey

Signed ______________________________

(*signature of authorized official*)

Place ______________________________

Date ______________________________

(*seal or stamp of the authority, as appropriate*)

Annual/Intermediate[①] Survey

Signed ______________________________

(*signature of authorized official*)

Place ______________________________

Date ______________________________

(*seal or stamp of the authority, as appropriate*)

Annual/Intermediate[①] survey

Signed ______________________________

(*signature of authorized official*)

Place ______________________________

Date ______________________________

(*seal or stamp of the authority, as appropriate*)

Annual survey

Signed ______________________________

(*signature of authorized official*)

Place ______________________________

Date ______________________________

(*seal or stamp of the authority, as appropriate*)

---

① Delete as appropriate.

年度检验和中间检验的签署

兹证明业已按公约第Ⅰ/10条的要求对该船进行了检验,查明该船符合公约的有关要求。

年度检验　　签字________________________

(经授权的官员签字)

地点________________________

日期________________________

(主管当局盖章或钢印)

年度/中间[①]检验　　签字________________________

(经授权的官员签字)

地点________________________

日期________________________

(主管当局盖章或钢印)

年度/中间[①]检验　　签字________________________

(经授权的官员签字)

地点________________________

日期________________________

(主管当局盖章或钢印)

年度检验　　签字________________________

(经授权的官员签字)

地点________________________

日期________________________

(主管当局盖章或钢印)

① 酌情删减。

Annual/intermediate survey in accordance with regulation　I/14(h)(iii)

THIS IS TO CERTIFY that, at an annual/intermediate survey[①] in accordance with regulation I/14(h)(iii) of the Convention, the ship was found to comply with the relevant requirements of the Convention.

Signed ______________________________

(*signature of authorized official*)

Place ______________________________

Date ______________________________

(*seal or stamp of the authority, as appropriate*)

Endorsement for inspections of the outside of the ship's bottom[①]

THIS IS TO CERTIFY that, at an inspection required by regulation Ⅰ/10 of the Convention, the ship was found to comply with the relevant requirements of the Convention.

First inspection

Signed ______________________________

(*signature of authorized official*)

Place ______________________________

Date ______________________________

(*seal or stamp of the authority, as appropriate*)

Second inspection

Signed ______________________________

(*signature of authorized official*)

Place ______________________________

Date ______________________________

(*seal or stamp of the authority, as appropriate*)

Endorsement to extend the certificate if valid for less than five years where regulation　I/14(c) applies

The ship complies with the relevant requirements of the Convention, and this certificate shall, in accordance with regulation Ⅰ/14(c) of the Convention, be accepted as valid until ________

Signed ______________________________

(*signature of authorized official*)

① Provision may be made for additional inspections.

按第Ⅰ/14(h)(iii)条进行的年度/中间检验

兹证明业已按公约第Ⅰ/14(h)(iii)条的要求对该船进行了年度/中间[①]检验，查明该船符合公约的有关要求。

签字＿＿＿＿＿＿＿＿＿＿＿＿＿＿

（经授权的人员签名）

地点＿＿＿＿＿＿＿＿＿＿＿＿＿＿

日期＿＿＿＿＿＿＿＿＿＿＿＿＿＿

（主管当局盖章或钢印）

船底外部检查的签署[①]

兹证明业已按公约第Ⅰ/10条的要求对该船进行了检查，查明该船符合公约的有关要求。

第1次检查

签字＿＿＿＿＿＿＿＿＿＿＿＿＿＿

（经授权的官员签字）

地点＿＿＿＿＿＿＿＿＿＿＿＿＿＿

日期＿＿＿＿＿＿＿＿＿＿＿＿＿＿

（主管当局盖章或钢印）

第2次检查

签字＿＿＿＿＿＿＿＿＿＿＿＿＿＿

（经授权的官员签字）

地点＿＿＿＿＿＿＿＿＿＿＿＿＿＿

日期＿＿＿＿＿＿＿＿＿＿＿＿＿＿

（主管当局盖章或钢印）

在适用第Ⅰ/14(c)条情况下，有效期少于5年的证书展期签署

该船符合公约的有关要求，本证书根据公约第Ⅰ/14(c)条应视为有效，有效期限至＿＿＿＿＿止。

签字＿＿＿＿＿＿＿＿＿＿＿＿＿＿

（经授权的官员签字）

① 可规定进行附加检查。

Place ________________________________

Date ________________________________

(*seal or stamp of the authority, as appropriate*)

Endorsement where the renewal survey has been completed and regulation I/14(d) applies

The ship complies with the relevant requirements of the Convention, and this certificate shall, in accordance with regulation Ⅰ/14(d) of the Convention, be accepted as valid until ________

Signed ________________________________

(*signature of authorized official*)

Place ________________________________

Date ________________________________

(*seal or stamp of the authority, as appropriate*)

Endorsement to extend the validity of the certificate until reaching the port of survey or a period of grace where regulation I/14(e) or I/14(f) applies

This certificate shall, in accordance with regulation Ⅰ/14(e)/ Ⅰ/14 or (f)[①] of the Convention be accepted as valid until ________________________________

Signed ________________________________

(*signature of authorized official*)

Place ________________________________

Date ________________________________

(*seal or stamp of the authority, as appropriate*)

Endorsement for advancement of anniversary date where regulation I/14(h) applies

In accordance with regulation Ⅰ/14(h) of the Convention, the new anniversary date is

____

Signed ________________________________

(*signature of authorized official*)

Place ________________________________

Date ________________________________

① Delete as appropriate.

地点＿＿＿＿＿＿＿＿＿＿＿＿＿＿＿＿＿

日期＿＿＿＿＿＿＿＿＿＿＿＿＿＿＿＿＿

（主管当局盖章或钢印）

在已完成换证检验并适用第Ⅰ/14(d)条情况下的签署

该船符合公约的有关要求，本证书根据公约第Ⅰ/14(d)条应视为有效，有效期限至＿＿＿＿止。

签字＿＿＿＿＿＿＿＿＿＿＿＿＿＿＿＿＿

（经授权的官员签字）

地点＿＿＿＿＿＿＿＿＿＿＿＿＿＿＿＿＿

日期＿＿＿＿＿＿＿＿＿＿＿＿＿＿＿＿＿

（主管当局盖章或钢印）

在适用第Ⅰ/14(e)条或第Ⅰ/14(f)条情况下，将证书有效期展期至驶抵进行检验的港口或给予宽限期的签署

本证书根据公约第Ⅰ/14(e)/Ⅰ/14(f)条①应视为有效，有效期限至＿＿＿＿＿＿止。

签字＿＿＿＿＿＿＿＿＿＿＿＿＿＿＿＿＿

（经授权的官员签字）

地点＿＿＿＿＿＿＿＿＿＿＿＿＿＿＿＿＿

日期＿＿＿＿＿＿＿＿＿＿＿＿＿＿＿＿＿

（主管当局盖章或钢印）

在适用第Ⅰ/14(h)条情况下，周年日提前的签署

根据公约第Ⅰ/14(h)条，新的周年日为＿＿＿＿＿＿＿＿＿＿。

签字＿＿＿＿＿＿＿＿＿＿＿＿＿＿＿＿＿

（经授权的官员签字）

地点＿＿＿＿＿＿＿＿＿＿＿＿＿＿＿＿＿

日期＿＿＿＿＿＿＿＿＿＿＿＿＿＿＿＿＿

① 酌情删减。

(*seal or stamp of the authority, as appropriate*)

In accordance with regulation Ⅰ/14(h) of the Convention, the new anniversary date is

____

Signed ______________________________

(*signature of authorized official*)

Place ______________________________

Date ______________________________

(*seal or stamp of the authority, as appropriate*)

（主管当局盖章或钢印）

根据公约第Ⅰ/14(h)条,新的周年日为________________。

签字________________________________

（经授权的官员签字）

地点________________________________

日期________________________________

（主管当局盖章或钢印）

P88 Form of safety equipment certificate for cargo ships

CARGO SHIP SAFETY EQUIPMENT CERTIFICATE

This Certificate shall be supplemented by a Record of Equipment for Cargo Ship Safety (Form E)

(*official seal*) (*State*)

Issued under the provisions of the
INTERNATIONAL CONVENTION FOR THE SAFETY OF LIFE AT SEA, 1974,
as modified by the Protocol of 1988 relating thereto
under the authority of the Government of

____

(*name of the State*)

by ______________________________________

(*person or organization authorized*)

Particulars of ship①

Name of ship ______________________________________

Distinctive number or letters ______________________________

Port of registry ____________________________________

Gross tonnage ____________________________________

Deadweight of ship (metric tons)② __________________________

Length of ship (regulation Ⅲ/3.12) _________________________

IMO Number③ ____________________________________

Type of ship④

① Alternatively, the particulars of the ship may be placed horizontally in boxes.
② For oil tankers, chemical tankers and gas carriers only.
③ In accordance with the IMO ship identification number scheme (resolution A.1117(30)).
④ Delete as appropriate.

P88 货船设备安全证书格式

货船设备安全证书

本证书应附有货船安全的设备记录(格式 E)

(公章)　　　　　　　　　　　　　　　　　　　　　　　　　　　　(国籍)

本证书由________(国名)政府授权________(被授权的个人或组织)按经 1988 年议定书修订的 1974 年国际海上人命安全公约的规定签发。

船舶资料①

船名____

船舶编号或呼号____

船籍港____

总吨位____

载重量(公吨)②____

船舶长度(第Ⅲ/3.12 条)____

IMO 识别号③____

船型④

---

① 船舶资料也可在表格中横向排列。
② 仅适用于油船、化学品液货船和气体运输船。
③ 按照《IMO 船舶编号体系》(第 A.1078(28)号决议)。
④ 酌情删减。

Bulk carrier

Oil tanker

Chemical tanker

Gas carrier

Cargo ship other than any of the above

Date on which keel was laid or ship was at a similar stage of construction or, where applicable, date on which work for a conversion or an alteration or modification of a major character was commenced ______________________________

THIS IS TO CERTIFY:

1 That the ship has been surveyed in accordance with the requirements of regulation Ⅰ/8 of the Convention.

2 That the survey showed that:

2.1 the ship complied with the requirements of the Convention as regards fire safety systems and appliances and fire control plans;

2.2 the life-saving appliances and the equipment of lifeboats, liferafts and rescue boats were provided in accordance with the requirements of the Convention;

2.3 the ship was provided with a line-throwing appliance and radio installations used in life-saving appliances in accordance with the requirements of the Convention;

2.4 the ship complied with the requirements of the Convention as regards shipborne navigational equipment, means of embarkation for pilots and nautical publications;

2.5 the ship was provided with lights, shapes and means of making sound signals and distress signals in accordance with the requirements of the Convention and the International Regulations for Preventing Collisions at Sea in force;

2.6 in all other respects the ship complied with the relevant requirements of the Convention;

2.7 the ship was/was not① subjected to an alternative design and arrangements in pursuance of regulation(s) Ⅱ-2/17/Ⅲ/38① of the Convention;

2.8 a Document of approval of alternative design and arrangements for fire protection/life-saving appliances and arrangements① is/is not① appended to this Certificate.

3 That the ship operates in accordance with regulation Ⅲ/26.1.1.1② within the limits of the trade area

4 That an Exemption Certificate has/has not① been issued.

---

① Delete as appropriate.

② Refer to the 1983 amendments to SOLAS (MSC.6(48)), applicable to ships constructed on or after 1 July 1986, but before 1 July 1998 in the case of self-righting partially enclosed lifeboats on board.

散货船

油船

化学品液货船

气体运输船

上述船型以外的货船

安放龙骨或处于类似建造阶段的日期,或(如适用)重大改建或改装开始的日期。

兹证明:

1　该船业已按公约第Ⅰ/8条的要求进行了检验。

2　检验表明:

2.1　该船符合公约有关消防安全系统和设备及防火控制图的要求;

2.2　该船根据公约的要求配备了救生设备及救生艇、救生筏和救助艇用属具;

2.3　该船根据公约的要求在救生设备中配备了抛绳设备和无线电装置;

2.4　该船在船载导航设备、引航员登船设施及航海出版物方面符合公约的要求;

2.5　该船根据公约及现行《国际海上避碰规则》的要求配备了航行灯、号型以及发出声响信号和遇险信号的设备;

2.6　该船所有其他方面均符合公约的有关要求;

2.7　船舶设有/未设①按公约第Ⅱ-2/17/Ⅲ/38条①规定的替代设计和布置;

2.8　防火/救生设备和装置①的替代设计和布置的批准文件附于/未附于①本证书之后。

3　船舶按照第Ⅲ/26.1.1.1条②的要求在贸易区域限制范围内营运。

4　已经/尚未①签发免除证书。

---

①　酌情删减。

②　参见SOLAS 1983年修正案(MSC.6(48)决议),适用于在1986年7月1日或以后,但在1998年7月1日以前建造的配有自扶正的部分封闭救生艇的船舶。

This certificate is valid until ________________________ [1] subject to the annual and periodical surveys in accordance with regulation Ⅰ/8 of the Convention.

Completion date of the survey on which this certificate is based ____________ *(dd/mm/yyyy)*

Issued at ____

(place of issue of certificate)

____________ ____

(date of issue) *(signature of authorized official issuing the certificate)*

(seal or stamp of the issuing authority, as appropriate)

Endorsement for annual and periodical surveys

THIS IS TO CERTIFY that, at a survey required by regulation Ⅰ/8 of the Convention, the ship was found to comply with the relevant requirements of the Convention.

Annual survey Signed ________________________________

(signature of authorized official)

Place ________________________________

Date ________________________________

(seal or stamp of the authority, as appropriate)

Annual/periodical[2] survey Signed ________________________________

(signature of authorized official)

Place ________________________________

Date ________________________________

(seal or stamp of the authority, as appropriate)

Annual/periodical/[2] survey Signed ________________________________

(signature of authorized official)

Place ________________________________

---

① Insert the date of expiry as specified by the Administration in accordance with regulation Ⅰ/14(a) of the Convention. The day and the month of this date correspond to the anniversary date, as defined in regulation Ⅰ/2(n) of the Convention, unless amended in accordance with regulation Ⅰ/14(h).

② Delete as appropriate.

本证书有效期限至________止[①]，但应视公约第Ⅰ/8 条规定的年度检验和定期检验情况而定。本证书基于的检验完成日期：________________（年/月/日）

签发于____

（证书签发地点）

________________　　________________________

（签发日期）　　（经授权发证的官员签字）

（发证主管当局盖章或钢印）

年度检验和定期检验的签署

兹证明业已按公约第Ⅰ/8 条的要求对该船进行了检验，查明该船符合公约的有关要求。

年度检验　　签字________________

（经授权的官员签字）

地点________________

日期________________

（主管当局盖章或钢印）

年度/定期[②]检验　　签字________________

（经授权的官员签字）

地点________________

日期________________

（主管当局盖章或钢印）

年度/定期[②]检验　　签字________________

（经授权的官员签字）

地点________________

① 填入主管机关根据第Ⅰ/14(a)条规定的失效日期。该日期如未根据公约第Ⅰ/14(h)条予以修正，其日、月相当于第Ⅰ/2(n)条定义的周年日。

② 酌情删减。

Date ______________________

(*seal or stamp of the authority, as appropriate*)

Annual survey

Signed ______________________

(*signature of authorized official*)

Place ______________________

Date ______________________

(*seal or stamp of the authority, as appropriate*)

Annual/periodical survey in accordance with regulation I/14(h)(iii)

THIS IS TO CERTIFY that, at an annual/periodical[①] survey in accordance with regulation Ⅰ/14(h)(iii) of the Convention, the ship was found to comply with the relevant requirements of the Convention.

Signed ______________________

(*signature of authorized official*)

Place ______________________

Date ______________________

(*seal or stamp of the authority, as appropriate*)

Endorsement to extend the certificate if valid for less than five years where regulation I/14(c) applies

The ship complies with the relevant requirements of the Convention, and this certificate shall, in accordance with regulation Ⅰ/14(c) of the Convention, be accepted as valid until __________

Signed ______________________

(*signature of authorized official*)

Place ______________________

Date ______________________

(*seal or stamp of the authority, as appropriate*)

① Delete as appropriate.

日期＿＿＿＿＿＿＿＿＿＿＿＿＿＿＿＿

（主管当局盖章或钢印）

年度检验

签字＿＿＿＿＿＿＿＿＿＿＿＿＿＿＿＿

（经授权的官员签字）

地点＿＿＿＿＿＿＿＿＿＿＿＿＿＿＿＿

日期＿＿＿＿＿＿＿＿＿＿＿＿＿＿＿＿

（主管当局盖章或钢印）

按第Ⅰ/14(h)(iii)条进行的年度/定期检验

兹证明业已按公约第Ⅰ/14(h)(iii)条的要求对该船进行了年度/定期[①]检验，查明该船符合公约的有关要求。

签字＿＿＿＿＿＿＿＿＿＿＿＿＿＿＿＿

（经授权的官员签字）

地点＿＿＿＿＿＿＿＿＿＿＿＿＿＿＿＿

日期＿＿＿＿＿＿＿＿＿＿＿＿＿＿＿＿

（主管当局盖章或钢印）

在适用第Ⅰ/14(c)条情况下，有效期少于5年的证书展期签署

该船符合公约的有关要求，本证书根据公约第Ⅰ/14(c)条应视为有效，有效期限至＿＿＿＿＿止。

签字＿＿＿＿＿＿＿＿＿＿＿＿＿＿＿＿

（经授权的官员签字）

地点＿＿＿＿＿＿＿＿＿＿＿＿＿＿＿＿

日期＿＿＿＿＿＿＿＿＿＿＿＿＿＿＿＿

（主管当局盖章或钢印）

① 酌情删减。

Endorsement where the renewal survey has been completed and regulation I/14(d) applies

The ship complies with the relevant requirements of the Convention, and this certificate shall, in accordance with regulation Ⅰ/14(d) of the Convention, be accepted as valid until ________

Signed ________________________

(*signature of authorized official*)

Place ________________________

Date ________________________

(*seal or stamp of the authority, as appropriate*)

Endorsement to extend the validity of the certificate until reaching the port of survey or for a period of grace where regulation I/14(e) or I/14(f) applies

This certificate shall, in accordance with regulation Ⅰ/14(e)/ Ⅰ/14(f)① of the Convention, be accepted as valid until ________________________

Signed ________________________

(*signature of authorized official*)

Place ________________________

Date ________________________

(*seal or stamp of the authority, as appropriate*)

Endorsement for advancement of anniversary date where regulation I/14(h) applies

In accordance with regulation Ⅰ/14(h) of the Convention, the new anniversary date is

____

Signed ________________________

(*signature of authorized official*)

Place ________________________

Date ________________________

(*seal or stamp of the authority, as appropriate*)

① Delete as appropriate.

在已完成换证检验并适用第Ⅰ/14(d)条情况下的签署

该船符合公约的有关要求,本证书根据公约第Ⅰ/14(d)条应视为有效,有效期限至________止。

签字________________________________

(经授权的官员签字)

地点________________________________

日期________________________________

(主管当局盖章或钢印)

在适用第Ⅰ/14(e)条或第Ⅰ/14(f)条情况下,将证书有效期展期至驶抵进行检验的港口或给予宽限期的签署

本证书根据公约第Ⅰ/14(e)/Ⅰ/14(f)[①]条应视为有效,有效期限至________________止。

签字________________________________

(经授权的官员签字)

地点________________________________

日期________________________________

(主管当局盖章或钢印)

在适用第Ⅰ/14(h)条情况下,周年日提前的签署

根据公约第Ⅰ/14(h)条,新的周年日为____。

签字________________________________

(经授权的官员签字)

地点________________________________

日期________________________________

(主管当局盖章或钢印)

① 酌情删减。

In accordance with regulation Ⅰ/14(h) of the Convention, the new anniversary date is

____

Signed ______________________________

(*signature of authorized official*)

Place ______________________________

Date ______________________________

(*seal or stamp of the authority, as appropriate*)

根据公约第Ⅰ/14(h)条,新的周年日为＿＿＿＿＿＿＿＿＿＿＿＿＿＿＿＿＿＿＿＿＿＿＿＿。

签字＿＿＿＿＿＿＿＿＿＿＿＿＿＿＿＿＿＿＿＿

(经授权的官员签字)

地点＿＿＿＿＿＿＿＿＿＿＿＿＿＿＿＿＿＿＿＿

日期＿＿＿＿＿＿＿＿＿＿＿＿＿＿＿＿＿＿＿＿

(主管当局盖章或钢印)

RECORD OF EQUIPMENT FOR CARGO SHIP SAFETY (Form E)

RECORD OF EQUIPMENT FOR COMPLIANCE WITH THE INTERNATIONAL CONVENTION FOR THE SAFETY OF LIFE AT SEA, 1974, AS MODIFIED

1 Particulars of ship

Name of ship ____________________________

Distinctive number or letters ____________________________

2 Details of life-saving appliances

1	Total number of persons for which life-saving appliances are provided		
		Port side	Starboard side
2	Total number of davit-launched lifeboats		
2.1	Total number of persons accommodated by them		
2.2	Number of self-righting partially enclosed lifeboats (regulation Ⅲ/43)①		
2.3	Number of totally enclosed lifeboats (regulation Ⅲ/31 and LSA Code, section 4.6)		
2.4	Number of lifeboats with a selfcontained air support system (regulation Ⅲ/31 and LSA Code, section 4.8)		
2.5	Number of fire-protected lifeboats (regulation Ⅲ/31 and LSA Code, section 4.9)		
2.6	Other lifeboats		
2.6.1	Number		
2.6.2	Type		
3	Total number of free-fall lifeboats		
3.1	Total number of persons accommodated by them		

① Refer to the 1983 amendments to SOLAS (MSC.6(48)), applicable to ships constructed on or after 1 July 1986, but before 1 July 1998.

货船安全的设备记录（格式 E）

证明符合经修正的 1974 年国际海上人命安全公约有关要求的设备记录

1 船舶资料

船名______________________________

船舶编号或呼号______________________________

2 救生设备明细表

1	救生设备可供使用的总人数		
		左舷	右舷
2	吊架降落式救生艇的总数		
2.1	吊架降落式救生艇可载总人数		
2.2	自行扶正部分封闭救生艇的数量(第Ⅲ/43 条①)		
2.3	全封闭救生艇的数量(第Ⅲ/31 条和 LSA 规则第 4.6 节)		
2.4	自备空气补给系统的救生艇的数量(第Ⅲ/31 条和 LSA 规则第 4.8 节)		
2.5	耐火救生艇的数量(第 Ⅲ/31 条和 LSA 规则第 4.9 节)		
2.6	其他救生艇		
2.6.1	数量		
2.6.2	型式		
3	自由降落救生艇的数量		
3.1	自由降落救生艇可载总人数		

① 参见 1983 年 SOLAS 修正案(第 MSC.6(48)号决议)，适用于在 1986 年 7 月 1 日或以后但在 1998 年 7 月 1 日以前建造的船舶。

2 Details of life-saving appliances(*continued*)

3.2	Number of totally enclosed lifeboats (regulation Ⅲ/31 and LSA Code, section 4.7)	
3.3	Number of lifeboats with a self-contained air support system (regulation Ⅲ/31 and LSA Code, section 4.8)	
3.4	Number of fire-protected lifeboats (regulation Ⅲ/31 and LSA Code, section 4.9)	
4	Number of motor lifeboats (included in the total lifeboats shown in 2 and 3 above	
4.1	Number of lifeboats fitted with searchlights	
5	Number of rescue boats	
5.1	Number of boats which are included in the total lifeboats shown in 2 and 3 above	
6	Liferafts	
6.1	Those for which approved launching appliances are required	
6.1.1	Number of liferafts	
6.1.2	Number of persons accommodated by them	
6.2	Those for which approved launching appliances are not required	
6.2.1	Number of liferafts	
6.2.2	Number of persons accommodated by them	
6.3	Number of liferafts required by regulation Ⅲ/31.1.4	
7	Number of lifebuoys	
8	Number of lifejackets	
9	Immersion suits	
9.1	Total number	
9.2	Number of suits complying with the requirements for lifejackets	
10	Number of anti-exposure suits	
11	Radio installations used in life-saving appliances	
11.1	Number of search and rescue locating devices	
11.1.1	Radar search and rescue transponders (SART)	
11.1.2	AIS search and rescue transmitters (AIS-SART)	
11.2	Number of two-way VHF radiotelephone apparatus	

3 Details of navigational systems and equipment

Item		Actual provision
1.1	Standard magnetic compass①	
1.2	Spare magnetic compass①	
1.3	Gyro-compass①	

① Alternative means of meeting this requirement are permitted under regulation V/19. In case of other means they shall be specified.

2　救生设备明细表(续表)

3.2	全封闭救生艇的数量(第Ⅲ/31 条和 LSA 规则第 4.7 节)	
3.3	自备空气补给系统的救生艇的数量(第Ⅲ/31 条和 LSA 规则第 4.8 节)	
3.4	耐火救生艇的数量(第Ⅲ/31 条和 LSA 规则第 4.9 节)	
4	机动救生艇的数量(包括在上述 2 和 3 救生艇总数内)	
4.1	装备有探照灯的救生艇的数量	
5	救助艇的数量	
5.1	包括在上述 2 和 3 救生艇总数内的艇的数量	
6	救生筏	
6.1	需设置认可降落装置的救生筏	
6.1.1	救生筏的数量	
6.1.2	救生筏可载人数	
6.2	不需设置认可降落装置的救生筏	
6.2.1	救生筏的数量	
6.2.2	救生筏可载人数	
6.3	第 Ⅲ/31.1.4 条要求的救生筏数量	
7	救生圈的数量	
8	救生衣的数量	
9	救生服	
9.1	总数	
9.2	符合救生衣要求的救生服的数量	
10	防暴露服的数量	
11	救生设备中使用的无线电装置	
11.1	搜救定位装置的数量	
11.1.1	搜救雷达应答器(SART)	
11.1.2	AIS 搜救应答器(AIS-SART)	
11.2	双向 VHF 无线电话设备的数量	

3　航行系统和设备明细表

项目		实际配备情况
1.1	标准磁罗经①	
1.2	备用磁罗经①	
1.3	陀螺罗经①	

① 根据第Ⅴ/19 条的规定,可允许采用符合本要求的替代装置。如果是其他装置,则应予详细说明。

3 Details of navigational systems and equipment(*continued*)

1.4	Gyro-compass heading repeater①	
1.5	Gyro-compass bearing repeater①	
1.6	Heading or track control system①	
1.7	Pelorus or compass bearing device①	
1.8	Means of correcting heading and bearings	
1.9	Transmitting heading device (THD)①	
2.1	Nautical charts/Electronic chart display and information system (ECDIS)②	
2.2	Back-up arrangements for ECDIS	
2.3	Nautical publications	
2.4	Back-up arrangements for electronic nautical publications	
3.1	Receiver for a global navigation satellite system/terrestrial radionavigation system/multi-system shipborne radionarvigation receive①,②	
3.2	9 GHz radar①	
3.3	Second radar (3 GHz/ 9 GHz②)①	
3.4	Automatic radar plotting aid (ARPA)①	
3.5	Automatic tracking aid①	
3.6	Second automatic tracking aid①	
3.7	Electronic plotting aid①	
4.1	Automatic identification system (AIS)	
4.2	Long-range identification and tracking system	
5.1	Voyage data recorder (VDR)②	
5.2	Simplified voyage data recorder (S-VDR)②	
6.1	Speed and distance measuring device (through the water)①	
6.2	Speed and distance measuring device (over the ground in the forward and athwartship direction)①	
7	Echo-sounding device①	
8.1	Rudder, propeller, thrust, pitch and operational mode indicator①	
8.2	Rate-of-turn indicator①	
9	Sound reception system①	
10	Telephone to emergency steering position①	
11	Daylight signalling lamp①	
12	Radar reflector①	
13	International Code of Signals	
14	IAMSAR Manual, Volume Ⅲ	
15	Bridge navigational watch alarm system (BNWAS)	

① Alternative means of meeting this requirement are permitted under regulation V/19. In case of other means, they shall be specified.

② Delete as appropriate.

3 航行系统和设备明细表(续表)

1.4	陀螺罗经首向复示器[①]	
1.5	陀螺罗经方位复示器[①]	
1.6	首向或航迹控制系统[①]	
1.7	哑罗经或罗经方位装置[①]	
1.8	首向和方位修正仪	
1.9	首向传送输装置(THD)[①]	
2.1	海图/电子海图显示和信息系统(ECDIS)[②]	
2.2	ECDIS 备份装置	
2.3	航海出版物	
2.4	电子海图出版物备份装置	
3.1	全球卫星导航系统/全球无线电导航系统接收装置/多系统船载无线电导航接收装置[①,②]	
3.2	9 GHz 雷达[①]	
3.3	第二台雷达(3 GHz/9 GHz[②])[①]	
3.4	自动雷达标绘仪(ARPA)[①]	
3.5	自动跟踪仪[①]	
3.6	第二台自动跟踪仪[①]	
3.7	电子标绘装置[①]	
4.1	自动识别系统(AIS)	
4.2	远程识别与跟踪系统	
5.1	航行数据记录仪(VDR)[②]	
5.2	简化航行数据记录仪(S-VDR)[②]	
6.1	航速和航程测量装置(对水)[①]	
6.2	航速和航程测量装置(对地,正向和横向)[①]	
7	回声测深仪[①]	
8.1	舵、螺旋桨、推力、螺距和工作模式指示器[①]	
8.2	回转速率指示仪[①]	
9	声响接收系统[①]	
10	与应急操舵位置联系的电话[①]	
11	白昼信号灯[①]	
12	雷达反射器[①]	
13	国际信号规则	
14	IAMSAR 手册第Ⅲ卷	
15	驾驶台航行值班报警系统(BNWAS)	

① 根据第Ⅴ/19 条的规定,可允许采用符合本要求的替代装置。如果是其他装置,则应予详细说明。

② 酌情删减。

THIS IS TO CERTIFY that this Record is correct in all respects.

Issued at ____

(place of issue of the Record)

______________ ____

(date of issue) *(signature of duly authorized official issuing the Record)*

(seal or stamp of the issuing Authority, as appropriate)

兹证明该记录在各方面均正确无误。

签发于＿＿＿＿＿＿＿＿＿＿＿＿＿＿＿＿＿＿＿＿＿＿＿＿＿＿＿＿＿＿＿＿＿＿

（记录签发地点）

＿＿＿＿＿＿＿＿＿＿＿＿＿＿＿＿　＿＿＿＿＿＿＿＿＿＿＿＿＿＿＿＿

（签发日期）　（经正式授权签发记录的官员签字）

（发证主管当局盖章或钢印）

P88 Form of safety radio certificate for cargo ships

CARGO SHIP SAFETY RADIO CERTIFICATE

This Certificate shall be supplemented by a Record of Equipment for Cargo Ship Safety Radio (Form R)

(*official seal*) (*State*)

Issued under the provisions of the
INTERNATIONAL CONVENTION FOR THE SAFETY OF LIFE AT SEA, 1974,
as modified by the Protocol of 1988 relating thereto
under the authority of the Government of

____

(*name of the State*)

by ____

(*person or organization authorized*)

Particulars of ship①

Name of ship____

Distinctive number or letters ____

Port of registry____

Gross tonnage____

Sea areas in which ship is certified to operate (regulation Ⅳ/2)____________________

IMO Number②____

Date on which keel was laid or ship was at a similar stage of construction or, where applicable, date on which work for a conversion or an alteration or modification of a major character was commenced____

---

① Alternatively, the particulars of the ship may be placed horizontally in boxes.
② In accordance with the IMO ship identification number scheme (resolution A.1117(30)).

P88 货船无线电安全证书格式

货船无线电安全证书

本证书应附有无线电设备的记录(格式 R)

(公章) (国籍)

本证书由________________(国名)政府授权____________________(被授权的个人或组织)按经 1988 年议定书修订的 1974 年国际海上人命安全公约的规定签发。

船舶资料①

船名____

船舶编号或呼号____________________________________

船籍港____

总吨位____

核准船舶营运的海区(第Ⅳ/2 条)____________________

IMO 编号②_______________________________________

安放龙骨或处于类似建造阶段的日期,或(如适用)重大改建或改装开始的日期

____

① 船舶资料也可在表格中横向排列。
② 按照《IMO 船舶识别号机制》(第 A.1117(30)号决议)。

THIS IS TO CERTIFY:

1 That the ship has been surveyed in accordance with the requirements of regulation Ⅰ/9 of the Convention.

2 That the survey showed that:

2.1 the ship complied with the requirements of the Convention as regards radio installations;

2.2 the functioning of the radio installations used in life-saving appliances complied with the requirements of the Convention.

3 That an Exemption Certificate has/has not① been issued.

This certificate is valid until ______________________________ ②
subject to the periodical surveys in accordance with regulation Ⅰ/9 of the Convention.

Completion date of the survey on which this certificate is based____________ (*dd/mm/yyyy*)

Issued at ______________________________

(*place of issue of certificate*)

____________ ______________________________

(*date of issue*) (*signature of authorized official issuing the certificate*)

(*seal or stamp of the issuing authority, as appropriate*)

Endorsement for periodical surveys

THIS IS TO CERTIFY that, at a survey required by regulation Ⅰ/9 of the Convention, the ship was found to comply with the relevant requirements of the Convention.

Periodical survey Signed ______________________________

(*signature of authorized official*)

Place ______________________________

Date ______________________________

(*seal or stamp of the authority, as appropriate*)

Periodical survey Signed ______________________________

(*signature of authorized official*)

Place ______________________________

① Delete as appropriate.

② Insert the date of expiry as specified by the Administration in accordance with regulation Ⅰ/14(a) of the Convention. The day and the month of this date correspond to the anniversary date, as defined in regulation Ⅰ/2(n) of the Convention, unless amended in accordance with regulation Ⅰ/14(h).

兹证明：

1　该船业已按公约第Ⅰ/9条的要求进行了检验。

2　检验表明：

2.1　该船符合公约有关无线电装置的要求；

2.2　救生设备中使用的无线电装置的功能符合公约的要求。

3　已经/尚未①签发免除证书。

本证书有效期限至＿＿＿＿＿＿＿＿＿＿止②，但应视公约第Ⅰ/9条规定的定期检验情况而定。

本证书基于的检验完成日期：＿＿＿＿＿＿＿＿＿＿＿＿＿＿＿（年/月/日）

签发于＿＿＿＿＿＿＿＿＿＿＿＿＿＿＿＿＿＿＿＿＿＿＿＿＿＿＿＿＿＿＿

（证书签发地点）

＿＿＿＿＿＿＿＿＿＿＿＿＿＿＿　　＿＿＿＿＿＿＿＿＿＿＿＿＿＿＿＿＿＿＿＿

（签发日期）　　（经授权发证的官员签字）

（发证主管当局盖章或钢印）

定期检验的签署

兹证明业已按公约第Ⅰ/9条的要求对该船进行了检验，查明该船符合公约的有关要求。

定期检验　　签字＿＿＿＿＿＿＿＿＿＿＿＿＿＿

（经授权的官员签字）

地点＿＿＿＿＿＿＿＿＿＿＿＿＿＿

日期＿＿＿＿＿＿＿＿＿＿＿＿＿＿

（主管当局盖章或钢印）

定期检验　　签字＿＿＿＿＿＿＿＿＿＿＿＿＿＿

（经授权的官员签字）

地点＿＿＿＿＿＿＿＿＿＿＿＿＿＿

① 酌情删减。

② 填入主管机关根据公约第Ⅰ/14(a)条规定的失效日期。该日期如未根据公约第Ⅰ/14(h)条予以修正，其日、月相当于第Ⅰ/2(n)条定义的周年日。

Date ____________________

(*seal or stamp of the authority, as appropriate*)

Periodical survey Signed ____________________

(*signature of authorized official*)

Place ____________________

Date ____________________

(*seal or stamp of the authority, as appropriate*)

Periodical survey Signed ____________________

(*signature of authorized official*)

Place ____________________

Date ____________________

(*seal or stamp of the authority, as appropriate*)

Periodical survey in accordance with regulation I/14(h)(iii)

THIS IS TO CERTIFY that, at a periodical survey in accordance with regulation Ⅰ/14(h)(iii) of the Convention, the ship was found to comply with the relevant requirements of the Convention.

Signed ____________________

(*signature of authorized official*)

Place ____________________

Date ____________________

(*seal or stamp of the authority, as appropriate*)

Endorsement to extend the certificate if valid for less than 5 years where regulation I/14(c) applies

The ship complies with the relevant requirements of the Convention, and this certificate shall, in accordance with regulation Ⅰ/14(c) of the Convention, be accepted as valid until ________

Signed ____________________

(*signature of authorized official*)

Place ____________________

Date ____________________

(*seal or stamp of the authority, as appropriate*)

日期________________________

（主管当局盖章或钢印）

定期检验　　　　　　　　　　签字________________________

（经授权的官员签字）

地点________________________

日期________________________

（主管当局盖章或钢印）

定期检验　　　　　　　　　　签字________________________

（经授权的官员签字）

地点________________________

日期________________________

（主管当局盖章或钢印）

按第Ⅰ/14(h)(iii)条进行的定期检验

兹证明业已按公约第Ⅰ/14(h)(iii)条的要求对该船进行了定期检验，查明该船符合公约的有关要求。

签字________________________

（经授权的官员签字）

地点________________________

日期________________________

（主管当局盖章或钢印）

在适用第Ⅰ/14(c)条情况下，有效期少于5年的证书展期签署

该船符合公约的有关要求，本证书根据公约第Ⅰ/14(c)条应视为有效，有效期限至________止。

签字________________________

（经授权的官员签字）

地点________________________

日期________________________

（主管当局盖章或钢印）

Endorsement where the renewal survey has been completed and regulation I/14(d) applies.

The ship complies with the relevant requirements of the Convention, and this certificate shall, in accordance with regulation Ⅰ/14(d) of the Convention, be accepted as valid until ________

Signed ______________________________

(*signature of authorized official*)

Place ______________________________

Date ______________________________

(*seal or stamp of the authority, as appropriate*)

Endorsement to extend the validity of the certificate until reaching the port of survey or for a period of grace where regulation I/14(e) or I/14(f) applies

This certificate shall, in accordance with regulation Ⅰ/14(e) or Ⅰ/14(f)① of the Convention, be accepted as valid until ______________________________

Signed ______________________________

(*signature of authorized official*)

Place ______________________________

Date ______________________________

(*seal or stamp of the authority, as appropriate*)

Endorsement for advancement of anniversary date where regulation I/14(h) applies

In accordance with regulation Ⅰ/14(h) of the Convention, the new anniversary date is

____

Signed ______________________________

(*signature of authorized official*)

Place ______________________________

Date ______________________________

(*seal or stamp of the authority, as appropriate*)

① Delete as appropriate.

在已完成换证检验并适用第Ⅰ/14(d)条情况下的签署

该船符合公约的有关要求,本证书根据公约第Ⅰ/14(d)条应视为有效,有效期限至________止。

签字________________________

(经授权的官员签字)

地点________________________

日期________________________

(主管当局盖章或钢印)

在适用第Ⅰ/14(e)条或第Ⅰ/14(f)条情况下,将证书有效期展期至驶抵进行检验的港口或给予宽限期的签署

本证书根据公约第Ⅰ/14(e)/Ⅰ/14(f)①条应视为有效,有效期限至________止。

签字________________________

(经授权的官员签字)

地点________________________

日期________________________

(主管当局盖章或钢印)

在适用第Ⅰ/14(h)条情况下,周年日提前的签署

根据公约第Ⅰ/14(h)条,新的周年日为________________。

签字________________________

(经授权的官员签字)

地点________________________

日期________________________

(主管当局盖章或钢印)

① 酌情删减。

In accordance with regulation Ⅰ/14(h) of the Convention, the new anniversary date is

____

Signed ______________________________

(*signature of authorized official*)

Place ______________________________

Date ______________________________

(*seal or stamp of the authority, as appropriate*)

根据公约第Ⅰ/14(h)条,新的周年日为________________。

签字________________________________

(经授权的官员签字)

地点________________________________

日期________________________________

(主管当局盖章或钢印)

RECORD OF EQUIPMENT FOR CARGO SHIP SAFETY RADIO (FORM R)

RECORD OF EQUIPMENT FOR COMPLIANCE WITH THE INTERNATIONAL CONVENTION FOR THE SAFETY OF LIFE AT SEA, 1974, AS AMENDED

1　Particulars of ship

Name of ship ____________________

Distinctive number or letters ____________________

Minimum number of persons with required

qualifications to operate the radio installations ____________________

2　Details of radio facilities

Item		Actual provision
1	Primary systems	
1.1	VHF radio installation	
1.1.1	DSC encoder	
1.1.2	DSC watch receiver	
1.1.3	Radiotelephony	
1.2	MF radio installation	
1.2.1	DSC encoder	
1.2.2	DSC watch receiver	
1.2.3	Radiotelephony	
1.3	MF/HF radio installation	
1.3.1	DSC encoder	
1.3.2	DSC watch receiver	
1.3.3	Radiotelephony	
1.3.4	Direct-printing telegraphy	
1.4	Recognized mobile satellite service ship earth station	
2	Secondary means of alerting	
3	Facilities for reception of maritime safety information	

货船无线电安全的设备记录（格式 R）

证明符合经修正的 1974 年国际海上人命安全公约有关要求的设备记录

1　船舶资料

船名＿＿＿＿＿＿＿＿＿＿＿＿＿＿＿＿＿＿＿＿

船舶编号或呼号＿＿＿＿＿＿＿＿＿＿＿＿＿＿＿＿＿＿＿＿

持证无线电装置操作人员的最少定员数＿＿＿＿＿＿＿＿＿＿＿＿＿＿＿＿＿＿＿＿

2　无线电设备明细表

项目		实际配备情况
1	主设备	
1.1	VHF 无线电装置	
1.1.1	DSC 编码器	
1.1.2	DSC 值班接收机	
1.1.3	无线电话	
1.2	MF 无线电装置	
1.2.1	DSC 编码器	
1.2.2	DSC 值班接收机	
1.2.3	无线电话	
1.3	MF/HF 无线电装置	
1.3.1	DSC 编码器	
1.3.2	DSC 值班接收机	
1.3.3	无线电话	
1.3.4	直接印字无线电报	
1.4	经认可的移动卫星业务船舶地面站	
2	辅助警报装置	
3	用于接收海上安全信息的设施	

2 Details of radio facilities(*continued*)

Item		Actual provision
3.1	NAVTEX receiver	
3.2	EGC receiver	
3.3	HF direct-printing radiotelegraph receiver	
4	Satellite EPIRB	
4.1	COSPAS-SARSAT	
5	VHF EPIRB	
6	Ship's search and rescue locating device	
6.1	Radar search and rescue transponder (SART)	
6.2	AIS search and rescue transmitter (AIS-SART)	

3 Methods used to ensure availability of radio facilities (regulations Ⅳ/15.6 and 15.7)

3.1 Duplication of equipment ______________________

3.2 Shore-based maintenance ______________________

3.3 At-sea maintenance capability ______________________

THIS IS TO CERTIFY that this Record is correct in all respects.

Issued at ______________________

(*place of issue of the Record*)

______________ ______________________

(*date of issue*) (*signature of duly authorized official issuing the Record*)

(*seal or stamp of the issuing authority, as appropriate*)

2　无线电设备明细表(续表)

项目		实际配备情况
3.1	NAVTEX 接收机	
3.2	EGC 接收机	
3.3	HF 直接印字无线电报接收机	
4	卫星 EPIRB	
4.1	COSPAS-SARSAT	
5	VHF EPIRB	
6	船舶搜救定位装置	
6.1	搜救雷达应答器(SART)	
6.2	AIS 搜救应答器(AIS-SART)	

3　用于确保无线电设备有效性的方法(第Ⅳ/15.6 和 15.7 条)

3.1　双套设备____________________

3.2　岸基维护____________________

3.3　海上维护能力____________________

兹证明该记录在各方面均正确无误。

签发于____

(证书签发地点)

____________________　　　　____________________

(签发日期)　　　　(经授权发证的官员签字)

(发证主管当局盖章或钢印)

P88 Form of safety certificate for cargo ships

CARGO SHIP SAFETY CERTIFICATE

This Certificate shall be supplemented by a Record of Equipment for Cargo Ship Safety (Form C)

(*official seal*)　　　　　　　　　　　　　　　　　　　　　　　　　　　　　　　　(*State*)

Issued under the provisions of the
INTERNATIONAL CONVENTION FOR THE SAFETY OF LIFE AT SEA, 1974,
as modified by the Protocol of 1988 relating thereto
under the authority of the Government of

____

(*name of the State*)

by _______________________________________

(*person or organization authorized*)

Particulars of ship[①]

Name of ship _______________________________________

Distinctive number or letters _______________________________________

Port of registry _______________________________________

Gross tonnage _______________________________________

Deadweight of ship (metric tons)[②] _______________________________________

Length of ship (regulation Ⅲ/3.12) _______________________________________

Sea areas in which ship is certified to operate (regulation Ⅳ/2) ____________________

IMO Number[③] _______________________________________

① Alternatively, the particulars of the ship may be placed horizontally in boxes.
② For oil tankers, chemical tankers and gas carriers only.
③ In accordance with the IMO ship identification number scheme (resolution A.1117(30)).

P88 货船安全证书格式

货船安全证书

本证书应附有货船安全的设备记录(格式 C)

(公章)　　　　　　　　　　　　　　　　　　　　　　　　(国籍)

本证书由________________(国名)政府授权____________________(被授权的个人或组织)按经 1988 年议定书修订的 1974 年国际海上人命安全公约的规定签发。

船舶资料①

船名____

船舶编号或呼号____

船籍港____

总吨位____

载重量(公吨)②____

船舶长度(第Ⅲ/3.12 条)____

核准营运的海区(第Ⅳ/2 条)____

IMO 编号③____

---

① 船舶资料也可在表格中横向排列。
② 仅适用于油船、化学品液货船和气体运输船。
③ 按照《IMO 船舶识别号机制》(第 A.1117(30)号决议)。

Type of ship[①]

Bulk carrier

Oil tanker

Chemical tanker

Gas carrier

Cargo ship other than any of the above

Date of build

Date of building contract ______________________________

Date on which keel was laid or ship was at similar stage of construction ______________

Date of delivery ______________________________

Date on which work for a conversion or an alteration or modification of a major character was commenced (where applicable) ______________

All applicable dates shall be completed.

THIS IS TO CERTIFY:

1 That the ship has been surveyed in accordance with the requirements of regulations Ⅰ/8, Ⅰ/9 and Ⅰ/10 of the Convention.

2 That the survey showed that:

2.1 the condition of the structure, machinery and equipment as defined in regulation Ⅰ/10 was satisfactory and the ship complied with the relevant requirements of chapter Ⅱ-1 and chapter Ⅱ-2 of the Convention (other than those relating to fire safety systems and appliances and fire control plans);

2.2 the ship complied with part G of chapter Ⅱ-1 of the Convention using ________ as fuel/N.A.[①];

2.3 the last two inspections of the outside of the ship's bottom took place on __________ and __________ (dates);

2.4 the ship complied with the requirements of the Convention as regards fire safety systems and appliances and fire control plans;

2.5 the life-saving appliances and the equipment of the lifeboats, liferafts and rescue boats were provided in accordance with the requirements of the Convention;

2.6 the ship was provided with a line-throwing appliance and radio installations used in life-saving appliances in accordance with the requirements of the Convention;

---

① Delete as appropriate.

船型①

散货船

油船

化学品液货船

气体运输船

上述船型以外的货船

建造日期

建造合同日期________________________________

安放龙骨或处于类似建造阶段的日期________________________________

交船日期________________________________

重大改建或改装开始的日期(如适用)________________________________

应填写所有适用日期。

兹证明:

1 该船业已按公约第Ⅰ/8条、第Ⅰ/9条和第Ⅰ/10条的要求进行了检验。

2 检验表明:

2.1 该船在第Ⅰ/10条所定义的结构、机器和设备均处于合格状态,并符合公约第Ⅱ-1章和第Ⅱ-2章的有关要求(消防安全系统和设备及防火控制图除外);

2.2 该船符合公约第Ⅱ-1章G部分要求,使用________作为燃料/不适用①。

2.3 最近两次的船底外部检查于________________和________________(日期)进行;

2.4 该船在消防安全系统和设施及防火控制图方面符合公约的要求;

2.5 该船根据公约的要求配备了救生设备及救生艇、救生筏和救助艇用属具;

2.6 该船根据公约的要求在救生设备中配备了抛绳设备和无线电装置;

① 酌情删减。

2.7 the ship complied with the requirements of the Convention as regards radio installations;

2.8 the functioning of the radio installation used in life-saving appliances complied with the requirements of the Convention;

2.9 the ship complied with the requirements of the Convention as regards shipborne navigational equipment, means of embarkation for pilots and nautical publications;

2.10 the ship was provided with lights, shapes, means of making sound signals and distress signals in accordance with the requirements of the Convention and the International Regulations for Preventing Collisions at Sea in force;

2.11 in all other respects, the ship complied with the relevant requirements of the Convention;

2.12 the ship was/was not① subjected to an alternative design and arrangements in pursuance of regulation(s) Ⅱ-1/55/Ⅱ-2/17/Ⅲ/38① of the Convention;

2.13 a Document of approval of alternative design and arrangements for machinery and electrical installations/fire protection/life-saving appliances and arrangements① is/is not① appended to this Certificate.

3 That the ship operates in accordance with regulation Ⅲ/26.1.1.1② within the limits of the trade area ________________

4 That an Exemption Certificate has/has not① been issued.

This certificate is valid until ________________③ subject to the annual, intermediate and periodical surveys and inspections of the outside of the ship's bottom in accordance with regulations Ⅰ/8, Ⅰ/9 and Ⅰ/10 of the Convention.

Completion date of the survey on which this certificate is based ____________ (*dd/mm/yyyy*)

Issued at ____

(*place of issue of certificate*)

____________ ____

(*date of issue*) (*signature of authorized official issuing the certificate*)

(*seal or stamp of the issuing authority, as appropriate*)

① Delete as appropriate.

② Refer to the 1983 amendments to SOLAS (MSC.6(48)), applicable to ships constructed on or after 1 July 1986, but before 1 July 1998 in the case of self-righting partially enclosed lifeboat(s) on board.

③ Insert the date of expiry as specified by the Administration in accordance with regulation Ⅰ/14(a) of the Convention. The day and the month of this date correspond to the anniversary date as defined in regulation Ⅰ/2(n) of the Convention, unless amended in accordance with regulation Ⅰ/14(h).

2.7　该船在无线电装置方面符合公约的要求；

2.8　该船救生设备中使用的无线电装置的功能符合公约的要求；

2.9　该船在船载导航设备、引航员登船设施及航海出版物方面符合公约的要求；

2.10　该船根据公约及现行《国际海上避碰规则》的要求配备了航行灯、号型以及发出声响信号和遇险信号的设备；

2.11　该船所有其他方面均符合公约的有关要求；

2.12　船舶设有/未设①符合本公约第Ⅱ-1/55/Ⅱ-2/17/Ⅲ/38①条规定的替代设计和布置；

2.13　机电设备/防火/救生设备①的替代设计和布置的批准文件附于/未附于①本证书之后。

3　船舶按照第Ⅲ/26.1.1.1条②的要求在贸易区域限制范围________内营运。

4　已经/尚未①签发免除证书。

本证书有效期限至________止③，但应视公约第Ⅰ/8条、第Ⅰ/9条和第Ⅰ/10条规定的年度检验、中间检验和定期检验及船底外部检查情况而定。

本证书基于的检验完成日期：________________（年/月/日）

签发于____

（证书签发地点）

________________________　　　　________________________

（签发日期）　　　　（经授权发证的官员签字）

（发证主管当局盖章或钢印）

① 酌情删减。
② 参见1983年SOLAS修正案（MSC.6(48)决议），适用于在1986年7月1日或以后，但在1998年7月1日以前建造的配有自扶正的部分封闭救生艇的船舶。
③ 填入主管机关根据公约第Ⅰ/14(a)条规定的失效日期。该日期如未根据公约第Ⅰ/14(h)条予以修正，其日、月相当于第Ⅰ/2(n)条定义的周年日。

Endorsement for annual and intermediate surveys relating to structure, machinery and equipment referred to in paragraph 2.1 of this certificate

THIS IS TO CERTIFY that, at a survey required by regulation Ⅰ/10 of the Convention, the ship was found to comply with the relevant requirements of the Convention.

Annual survey Signed ______________________

(*signature of authorized official*)

Place ______________________

Date ______________________

(*seal or stamp of the authority, as appropriate*)

Annual/Intermediate[①] survey Signed ______________________

(*signature of authorized official*)

Place ______________________

Date ______________________

(*seal or stamp of the authority, as appropriate*)

Annual/Intermediate[①] survey Signed ______________________

(*signature of authorized official*)

Place ______________________

Date ______________________

(*seal or stamp of the authority, as appropriate*)

Annual survey Signed ______________________

(*signature of authorized official*)

Place ______________________

Date ______________________

(*seal or stamp of the authority, as appropriate*)

本证书2.1要求的结构、机器和设备的年度检验和中间检验的签署

兹证明业已按公约第Ⅰ/10条的要求对该船进行了检验，查明该船符合公约的有关要求。

年度检验

签字＿＿＿＿＿＿＿＿＿＿＿＿＿＿

（经授权的官员签字）

地点＿＿＿＿＿＿＿＿＿＿＿＿＿＿

日期＿＿＿＿＿＿＿＿＿＿＿＿＿＿

（主管当局盖章或钢印）

年度/中间[①]检验

签字＿＿＿＿＿＿＿＿＿＿＿＿＿＿

（经授权的官员签字）

地点＿＿＿＿＿＿＿＿＿＿＿＿＿＿

日期＿＿＿＿＿＿＿＿＿＿＿＿＿＿

（主管当局盖章或钢印）

年度/中间[①]检验

签字＿＿＿＿＿＿＿＿＿＿＿＿＿＿

（经授权的官员签字）

地点＿＿＿＿＿＿＿＿＿＿＿＿＿＿

日期＿＿＿＿＿＿＿＿＿＿＿＿＿＿

（主管当局盖章或钢印）

年度检验

签字＿＿＿＿＿＿＿＿＿＿＿＿＿＿

（经授权的官员签字）

地点＿＿＿＿＿＿＿＿＿＿＿＿＿＿

日期＿＿＿＿＿＿＿＿＿＿＿＿＿＿

（主管当局盖章或钢印）

Annual/intermediate survey in accordance with regulation I/14(h)(iii)

THIS IS TO CERTIFY that, at an annual/intermediate[①] survey in accordance with regulations Ⅰ/10 and Ⅰ/14(h)(iii) of the Convention, the ship was found to comply with the relevant requirements of the Convention.

Signed ______________________________

(*signature of authorized official*)

Place ______________________________

Date ______________________________

(*seal or stamp of the authority, as appropriate*)

Endorsement for inspections of the outside of the ship's bottom[②]

THIS IS TO CERTIFY that, at an inspection required by regulation Ⅰ/10 of the Convention, the ship was found to comply with the relevant requirements of the Convention.

First inspection

Signed ______________________________

(*signature of authorized official*)

Place ______________________________

Date ______________________________

(*seal or stamp of the authority, as appropriate*)

Second inspection

Signed ______________________________

(*signature of authorized official*)

Place ______________________________

Date ______________________________

(*seal or stamp of the authority, as appropriate*)

Endorsement for annual and periodical surveys relating to life-saving appliances and other equipment referred to in paragraph 2.3, 2.4, 2.5, 2.8 and 2.9 of this certificate

THIS IS TO CERTIFY that, at a survey required by regulation Ⅰ/8 of the Convention, the ship was found to comply with the relevant requirements of the Convention.

Annual survey

Signed ______________________________

① Delete as appropriate.

② Provision may be made for additional inspections.

按第Ⅰ/14(h)(iii)条进行的年度/中间检验

兹证明业已按公约第Ⅰ/10条和第Ⅰ/14(h)(iii)条的要求对该船进行了年度/中间[①]检验,查明该船符合公约的有关要求。

签字____________________

(经授权的官员签字)

地点____________________

日期____________________

(主管当局盖章或钢印)

船底外部检查的签署[②]

兹证明业已按公约第Ⅰ/10条的要求对该船进行了检查,查明该船符合公约的有关要求。

第1次检查

签字____________________

(经授权的官员签字)

地点____________________

日期____________________

(主管当局盖章或钢印)

第2次检查

签字____________________

(经授权的官员签字)

地点____________________

日期____________________

(主管当局盖章或钢印)

本证书2.3、2.4、2.5、2.8和2.9要求的救生设备和其他设备的年度检验和定期检验的签署

兹证明业已按公约第Ⅰ/8条的要求对该船进行了检验,查明该船符合公约的有关要求。

年度检验

签字____________________

① 酌情删减。
② 可规定进行附加检查。

(*signature of authorized official*)

Place ______________________________

Date ______________________________

(*seal or stamp of the authority, as appropriate*)

Annual/Periodical[①] survey Signed ______________________________

(*signature of authorized official*)

Place ______________________________

Date ______________________________

(*seal or stamp of the authority, as appropriate*)

Annual/periodical[①] survey Signed ______________________________

(*signature of authorized official*)

Place ______________________________

Date ______________________________

(*seal or stamp of the authority, as appropriate*)

Annual survey Signed ______________________________

(*signature of authorized official*)

Place ______________________________

Date ______________________________

(*seal or stamp of the authority, as appropriate*)

Annual/Periodical survey in accordance with regulation I/14(h)(iii)

THIS IS TO CERTIFY that, at an annual/periodical[②] survey in accordance with regulations Ⅰ/8 and Ⅰ/14(h)(iii) of the Convention, the ship was found to comply with the relevant requirements of the Convention.

Signed ______________________________

(*signature of authorized official*)

① Delete as appropriate.
② Delete as appropriate.

（经授权的官员签字）

地点＿＿＿＿＿＿＿＿＿＿＿＿＿＿＿

日期＿＿＿＿＿＿＿＿＿＿＿＿＿＿＿

（主管当局盖章或钢印）

年度/中间[1]检验　　签字＿＿＿＿＿＿＿＿＿＿＿＿＿＿＿

（经授权的官员签字）

地点＿＿＿＿＿＿＿＿＿＿＿＿＿＿＿

日期＿＿＿＿＿＿＿＿＿＿＿＿＿＿＿

（主管当局盖章或钢印）

年度/中间[1]检验　　签字＿＿＿＿＿＿＿＿＿＿＿＿＿＿＿

（经授权的官员签字）

地点＿＿＿＿＿＿＿＿＿＿＿＿＿＿＿

日期＿＿＿＿＿＿＿＿＿＿＿＿＿＿＿

（主管当局盖章或钢印）

年度检验　　签字＿＿＿＿＿＿＿＿＿＿＿＿＿＿＿

（经授权的官员签字）

地点＿＿＿＿＿＿＿＿＿＿＿＿＿＿＿

日期＿＿＿＿＿＿＿＿＿＿＿＿＿＿＿

（主管当局盖章或钢印）

按第Ⅰ/14(h)(iii)条进行的年度/定期检验

兹证明业已按公约第Ⅰ/8条和第Ⅰ/14(h)(iii)条的要求对该船进行了年度/定期检验[2]，查明该船符合公约的有关要求。

签字＿＿＿＿＿＿＿＿＿＿＿＿＿＿＿

（经授权的官员签字）

① 酌情删减。
② 酌情删减。

Place ______________________________

Date ______________________________

(seal or stamp of the authority, as appropriate)

Endorsement for periodical surveys relating to radio installations referred to in paragraphs 2.6 and 2.7 of this certificate

THIS IS TO CERTIFY that, at a survey required by regulation I/9 of the Convention, the ship was found to comply with the relevant requirements of the Convention.

Periodical survey

Signed ______________________________

(signature of authorized official)

Place ______________________________

Date ______________________________

(seal or stamp of the authority, as appropriate)

Periodical survey Signed ______________________________

(signature of authorized official)

Place ______________________________

Date ______________________________

(seal or stamp of the authority, as appropriate)

Periodical survey Signed ______________________________

(signature of authorized official)

Place ______________________________

Date ______________________________

(seal or stamp of the authority, as appropriate)

Periodical survey Signed ______________________________

(signature of authorized official)

Place ______________________________

Date ______________________________

(seal or stamp of the authority, as appropriate)

地点＿＿＿＿＿＿＿＿＿＿＿＿＿＿＿＿

日期＿＿＿＿＿＿＿＿＿＿＿＿＿＿＿＿

（主管当局盖章或钢印）

本证书 2.6 和 2.7 要求的无线电装置定期检验的签署

兹证明业已按公约第Ⅰ/9 条的要求对该船进行了检验，查明该船符合公约的有关要求。

定期检验

签字＿＿＿＿＿＿＿＿＿＿＿＿＿＿＿＿

（经授权的官员签字）

地点＿＿＿＿＿＿＿＿＿＿＿＿＿＿＿＿

日期＿＿＿＿＿＿＿＿＿＿＿＿＿＿＿＿

（主管当局盖章或钢印）

定期检验

签字＿＿＿＿＿＿＿＿＿＿＿＿＿＿＿＿

（经授权的官员签字）

地点＿＿＿＿＿＿＿＿＿＿＿＿＿＿＿＿

日期＿＿＿＿＿＿＿＿＿＿＿＿＿＿＿＿

（主管当局盖章或钢印）

定期检验

签字＿＿＿＿＿＿＿＿＿＿＿＿＿＿＿＿

（经授权的官员签字）

地点＿＿＿＿＿＿＿＿＿＿＿＿＿＿＿＿

日期＿＿＿＿＿＿＿＿＿＿＿＿＿＿＿＿

（主管当局盖章或钢印）

定期检验

签字＿＿＿＿＿＿＿＿＿＿＿＿＿＿＿＿

（经授权的官员签字）

地点＿＿＿＿＿＿＿＿＿＿＿＿＿＿＿＿

日期＿＿＿＿＿＿＿＿＿＿＿＿＿＿＿＿

（主管当局盖章或钢印）

Periodical survey in accordance with regulation I/14(h)(iii)

THIS IS TO CERTIFY that, at a periodical-survey in accordance with regulations I/9 and I/14(h)(iii) of the Convention, the ship was found to comply with the relevant requirements of the Convention.

Signed ______________________________

(*signature of authorized official*)

Place ______________________________

Date ______________________________

(*seal or stamp of the authority, as appropriate*)

Endorsement to extend the Certificate if valid for less than five years where regulation I/14(c) applies

The ship complies with the relevant requirements of the Convention, and this certificate shall, in accordance with regulation I/14(c) of the Convention, be accepted as valid until ________

Signed ______________________________

(*signature of authorized official*)

Place ______________________________

Date ______________________________

(*seal or stamp of the authority, as appropriate*)

Endorsement where the renewal survey has been completed and regulation I/14(d) applies

The ship complies with the relevant requirements of the Convention, and this certificate shall, in accordance with regulation I/14(d) of the Convention, be accepted as valid until ________

Signed ______________________________

(*signature of authorized official*)

Place ______________________________

Date ______________________________

(*seal or stamp of the authority, as appropriate*)

按第Ⅰ/14(h)(iii)条进行的定期检验

兹证明业已按公约第Ⅰ/9条和第Ⅰ/14(h)(iii)条的要求对该船进行了定期检验，查明该船符合公约的有关要求。

签字＿＿＿＿＿＿＿＿＿＿＿＿＿＿＿＿

（经授权的官员签字）

地点＿＿＿＿＿＿＿＿＿＿＿＿＿＿＿＿

日期＿＿＿＿＿＿＿＿＿＿＿＿＿＿＿＿

（主管当局盖章或钢印）

在适用第Ⅰ/14(c)条情况下，有效期少于5年的证书展期签署

该船符合公约的有关要求，本证书根据公约第Ⅰ/14(c)条应视为有效，有效期限至＿＿＿＿止。

签字＿＿＿＿＿＿＿＿＿＿＿＿＿＿＿＿

（经授权的官员签字）

地点＿＿＿＿＿＿＿＿＿＿＿＿＿＿＿＿

日期＿＿＿＿＿＿＿＿＿＿＿＿＿＿＿＿

（主管当局盖章或钢印）

在已完成换证检验并适用第Ⅰ/14(d)条情况下的签署

该船符合公约的有关要求，本证书根据公约第Ⅰ/14(d)条应视为有效，有效期限至＿＿＿＿止。

签字＿＿＿＿＿＿＿＿＿＿＿＿＿＿＿＿

（经授权的官员签字）

地点＿＿＿＿＿＿＿＿＿＿＿＿＿＿＿＿

日期＿＿＿＿＿＿＿＿＿＿＿＿＿＿＿＿

（主管当局盖章或钢印）

Endorsement to extend the validity of the certificate until reaching the port of survey or for a period of grace where regulation I/14(e) or I/14(f) applies

This certificate shall, in accordance with regulation Ⅰ/14(e)/Ⅰ/14(f)[①] of the Convention, be accepted as valid until ____________________

Signed ____________________

(signature of authorized official)

Place ____________________

Date ____________________

(seal or stamp of the authority, as appropriate)

Endorsement for advancement of anniversary date where regulation I/14(h) applies

In accordance with regulation Ⅰ/14(h) of the Convention, the new anniversary date is

____

Signed ____________________

(signature of authorized official)

Place ____________________

Date ____________________

(seal or stamp of the authority, as appropriate)

In accordance with regulation Ⅰ/14(h) of the Convention, the new anniversary date is ______

Signed ____________________

(signature of authorized official)

Place ____________________

Date ____________________

(seal or stamp of the authority, as appropriate)

① Delete as appropriate.

在适用第Ⅰ/14(e)条或第Ⅰ/14(f)条情况下,将证书有效期展期至驶抵进行检验的港口或给予宽限期的签署

本证书根据公约第Ⅰ/14(e)/Ⅰ/14(f)[①]条应视为有效,有效期限至________止。

签字________________________________

(经授权的官员签字)

地点________________________________

日期________________________________

(主管当局盖章或钢印)

在适用第Ⅰ/14(h)条情况下,周年日提前的签署

根据公约第Ⅰ/14(h)条,新的周年日为________________。

签字________________________________

(经授权的官员签字)

地点________________________________

日期________________________________

(主管当局盖章或钢印)

根据公约第Ⅰ/14(h)条,新的周年日为________________。

签字________________________________

(经授权的官员签字)

地点________________________________

日期________________________________

(主管当局盖章或钢印)

① 酌情删减。

P88 Form of exemption certificate

EXEMPTION CERTIFICATE

(*official seal*) (*State*)

Issued under the provisions of the
INTERNATIONAL CONVENTION FOR THE SAFETY OF LIFE AT SEA, 1974,
as modified by the Protocol of 1988 relating thereto
under the authority of the Government of

____

(*name of the State*)

by ________________________________

(*person or organization authorized*)

Particulars of ship①

Name of ship ________________________________

Distinctive number or letters ________________________________

Port of registry ________________________________

Gross tonnage ________________________________

IMO Number② ________________________________

THIS IS TO CERTIFY:

That the ship is, under the authority conferred by regulation _______ of the Convention, exempted from the requirements ________________________________ of the Convention.

Conditions, if any, on which the Exemption Certificate is granted __________________________

____

Voyages, if any, for which the Exemption Certificate is granted __________________________

____

① Alternatively, the particulars of the ship may be placed horizontally in boxes.
② In accordance with IMO ship identification number scheme (resolution A.1117(30)).

P88 免除证书格式

免除证书

(公章) (国籍)

本证书由________(国名)政府授权__________(被授权的个人或组织)按经 1988 年议定书修订的 1974 年国际海上人命安全公约的规定签发。

船舶资料①

船名____________________

船舶编号或呼号____________________

船籍港____________________

总吨位____________________

IMO 编号②____________________

兹证明:

根据公约第________条授予的权限,准予该船免除公约中____条的要求。

准予本免除证书的条件(如有)____________________

准予本免除证书的航线(如有)____________________

① 船舶资料也可在表格中横向排列。

② 按照《IMO 船舶识别号机制》(第 A.1117(30)号决议)。

This certificate is valid until ________________________________ subject to the ________________________________ Certificate, to which this certificate is attached, remaining valid.

Issued at ________________________________

(*Place of issue of certificate*)

______________ ________________________________

(*Date of issue*) (*signature of authorized official issuing the certificate*)

(*seal or stamp of the issuing authority, as appropriate*)

Endorsement to extend the certificate if valid for less than five years where regulation I/14 (c) applies

This certificate shall, in accordance with regulation I/14(c) of the Convention, be accepted as valid until ______________ subject to the ________________________ Certificate, to which this certificate is attached remaining valid.

Signed ________________________________

(*signature of authorized official*)

Place ________________________________

Date ________________________________

(*seal or stamp of the authority, as appropriate*)

Endorsement where the renewal survey has been completed and regulation I/14(d) applies

This certificate shall, in accordance with regulation I/14(d) of the Convention, be accepted as valid until ____________ subject to the ________________________________ Certificate, to which this certificate remaining valid.

Signed ________________________________

(*signature of authorized official*)

Place ________________________________

Date ________________________________

(*seal or stamp of the authority, as appropriate*)

本证书为＿＿＿＿＿＿＿＿证书的附件,在该证书有效的情况下,本免除证书的有效期限至＿＿＿＿＿＿＿＿止。

签发于＿＿＿＿＿＿＿＿＿＿＿＿＿＿＿＿

（证书签发地点）

＿＿＿＿＿＿＿＿＿＿＿＿　　＿＿＿＿＿＿＿＿＿＿＿＿

（签发日期）　　（经授权发证的官员签字）

（发证主管当局盖章或钢印）

在适用第Ⅰ/14(c)条情况下,有效期少于5年的证书展期签署

本证书为＿＿＿＿证书的附件,在该证书有效的情况下,本免除证书根据公约第Ⅰ/14(c)条应视为有效,有效期限至＿＿＿＿＿＿＿＿止。

签字＿＿＿＿＿＿＿＿＿＿＿＿

（经授权的官员签字）

地点＿＿＿＿＿＿＿＿＿＿＿＿

日期＿＿＿＿＿＿＿＿＿＿＿＿

（主管当局盖章或钢印）

在已完成换证检验并适用第Ⅰ/14(d)条情况下的签署

本证书为＿＿＿＿证书的附件,在该证书有效的情况下,本免除证书根据公约第Ⅰ/14(d)条应视为有效,有效期限至＿＿＿＿＿＿＿＿止。

签字＿＿＿＿＿＿＿＿＿＿＿＿

（经授权的官员签字）

地点＿＿＿＿＿＿＿＿＿＿＿＿

日期＿＿＿＿＿＿＿＿＿＿＿＿

（主管当局盖章或钢印）

Endorsement to extend the validity of the certificate until reaching the port of survey or for a period of grace where regulation I/14(e) or I/14(f) applies

This certificate shall, in accordance with regulation Ⅰ/14(e) Ⅰ/14(f)①/ of the Convention, be accepted as valid until____________subject to the______________________Certificate, to which this certificate is attached, remaining valid.

Signed______________________________________

(*signature of authorized official*)

Place ______________________________________

Date_______________________________________

(*seal or stamp of the authority, as appropriate*)

① Delete as appropriate.

在适用第Ⅰ/14(e)条或第Ⅰ/14(f)条情况下,将证书有效期展期至驶抵进行检验的港口或给予宽限期的签署

本证书为________________证书的附件,在该证书有效的情况下,本免除证书根据公约第Ⅰ/14(e)/Ⅰ/14(f)条[①]应视为有效,有效期限至____________________止。

签字________________________________

(经授权的官员签字)

地点________________________________

日期________________________________

(主管当局盖章或钢印)

① 酌情删减。

Form of safety certificate for nuclear passenger ships

NUCLEAR PASSENGER SHIP SAFETY CERTIFICATE

This Certificate shall be supplemented by a Record of Equipment for Passenger Ship Safety (Form P)

(*official seal*) (*State*)

for an/a short[1] international voyage

Issued under the provisions of the
INTERNATIONAL CONVENTION FOR THE SAFETY OF LIFE AT SEA, 1974,
as amended under the authority of the Government of

____

(*name of the State*)

by ______________________________

(*person or organization authorized*)

Particulars of ship[2]

Name of ship ____________________

Distinctive number or letters ____________________

Port of registry ____________________

Gross tonnage ____________________

Sea areas in which ship is certified to operate (regulation Ⅳ/2) __________

IMO Number [3] ____________________

Date of build

Date of building contract ____________________

Date on which keel was laid or ship was at similar stage of construction __________

① Delete as appropriate.

② Alternatively, the particulars of the ship may be placed horizontally in boxes.

③ In accordance with the *IMO ship identification number scheme* (resolution A.1117(30)).

核能客船安全证书格式

核能客船安全证书

本证书应附有客船安全的设备记录 （格式 P）

（公章） （国籍）

供国际航行/短程国际航行[①]使用

本证书由＿＿＿＿＿＿＿＿（国名）政府授权＿＿＿＿＿＿＿＿（被授权的个人或组织）按经修正的1974年国际海上人命安全公约的规定签发。

船舶资料[②]

船名＿＿＿＿＿＿＿＿＿＿＿＿＿＿＿＿

船舶编号或呼号＿＿＿＿＿＿＿＿＿＿＿＿＿＿＿＿

船籍港＿＿＿＿＿＿＿＿＿＿＿＿＿＿＿＿

总吨位＿＿＿＿＿＿＿＿＿＿＿＿＿＿＿＿

核准船舶营运的海区（第Ⅳ条）＿＿＿＿＿＿＿＿＿＿＿＿＿＿＿＿

IMO 编号[③]＿＿＿＿＿＿＿＿＿＿＿＿＿＿＿＿

建造日期

建造合同日期＿＿＿＿＿＿＿＿＿＿＿＿＿＿＿＿

安放龙骨或处于类似建造阶段的日期＿＿＿＿＿＿＿＿＿＿＿＿＿＿＿＿

① 酌情删减。
② 船舶资料也可在表格中横向排列。
③ 按照《IMO 船舶识别号机制》（第 A.1117(30)号决议）。

Date of delivery ________________________________

Date on which work for a conversion or an alteration or modification

of a major character was commenced (where applicable) ____________________

All applicable dates shall be completed.

THIS IS TO CERTIFY:

1 That the ship has been surveyed in accordance with the requirements of regulation Ⅷ/9 of the Convention.

2 That the ship, being a nuclear ship, complied with all the requirements of chapter Ⅷ of the Convention and conformed to the Safety Assessment approved for the ship; and that:

2.1 the ship complied with the requirements of the Convention as regards:

.1 the structure, main and auxiliary machinery, boilers and other pressure vessels, including the nuclear propulsion plant and the collision protective structure;

.2 the watertight subdivision arrangements and details;

.3 the following subdivision load lines:

Subdivision load lines assigned and marked on the ship's side amidships (regulation Ⅱ-1/18)①	Freeboard	To apply when the spaces in which passengers are carried include the following alternative spaces
P1		
P2		
P3		

2.2 the ship complied with the requirements of the Convention as regards structural fire protection, fire safety systems and appliances and fire control plans;

2.3 the ship complied with the requirements of the Convention as regards radiation protection systems and equipment;

2.4 the life-saving appliances and the equipment of the lifeboats, liferafts and rescue boats were provided in accordance with the requirements of the Convention;

2.5 the ship was provided with a line-throwing appliance and radio installations used in life-saving appliances in accordance with the requirements of the Convention;

2.6 the ship complied with the requirements of the Convention as regards radio installations;

2.7 the functioning of the radio installations used in life-saving appliances complied with the requirements of the Convention;

① For ships constructed before 1 January 2009, the applicable subdivision notation "C.1", "C.2" and "C.3" should be used.

交船日期____

重大改建或改装开始的日期(如适用)____________________________

应填写所有适用日期。

兹证明:

1 该船业已按公约第Ⅷ/9 条的要求进行了检验。

2 该船为核能船舶,符合公约第Ⅷ章的所有要求,并与经认可的该船安全鉴定书相一致;和:

2.1 该船在以下方面符合公约的要求:

.1 结构、主机和辅机、锅炉及其他压力容器,包括核能推进装置和防撞结构;

.2 水密分舱布置及细节;

.3 下列分舱载重线:

核定并戡划于船中两舷的分舱载重线(第Ⅱ-1/18 条①)	干舷	适用于包括下列其他处所在内的载客处所
P1		
P2		
P3		

2.2 该船在结构防火、消防安全系统和设备及防火控制图方面符合公约的要求;

2.3 该船在辐射防护系统和设备方面符合公约的要求;

2.4 该船根据公约的要求配备了救生设备和救生艇、救生筏及救助艇用属具;

2.5 该船根据公约的要求在救生设备中配备了抛绳设备和无线电装置;

2.6 该船在无线电装置方面符合公约的要求;

2.7 该船救生设备中使用的无线电装置的功能符合公约的要求;

① 对 2009 年 1 月 1 日以前建造的船舶,应使用适用的分舱标志“C.1”、“C.2”和“C.3”。

2.8 the ship complied with the requirements of the Convention as regards shipborne navigational equipment, means of embarkation for pilots and nautical publications;

2.9 the ship was provided with lights, shapes, means of making sound signals and distress signals, in accordance with the requirements of the Convention and the International Regulations for Preventing Collisions at Sea in force;

2.10 in all other respects the ship complied with the relevant requirements of the Convention;

2.11 the ship was/was not① subjected to an alternative design and arrangements in pursuance of regulation(s) Ⅱ-1/55/Ⅱ-2/17/Ⅲ/38① of the Convention;

2.12 a Document of approval of alternative design and arrangements for machinery and electrical installations/fire protection/life-saving appliances and arrangements① is/is not① appended to this Certificate.

This certificate is valid until ____________________

Completion date of the survey on which this certificate is based ____________ (*dd/mm/yyyy*)

Issued at ____________________

(*place of issue of certificate*)

____________ ____________________

(*date of issue*) (*signature of authorized official issuing the certificate*)

(*seal or stamp of the issuing authority, as appropriate*)

① Delete as appropriate.

2.8　该船在船载导航设备、引航员登船设施及航海出版物方面符合公约的要求；

2.9　该船根据公约及现行《国际海上避碰规则》的要求配备了航行灯、号型以及发出声响信号和遇险信号的设备；

2.10　该船在所有其他方面均符合公约的有关要求；

2.11　船舶设有/未设[①]符合公约第Ⅱ-1/55/Ⅱ-2/17/Ⅲ/38[①]条规定的替代设计和布置；

2.12　机电设备/防火/救生设备和装置[①]的替代设计和布置的批准文件附于/未附于[①]本证书之后。

本证书有效期限至________________止。

本证书基于的检验完成日期：______________________________（年/月/日）

签发于____

（证书签发地点）

____________________________　　　　____________________________

（签发日期）　　　　（经授权发证的官员）

（发证主管当局盖章或钢印）

① 酌情删减。

Form of safety certificate for nuclear cargo ships

NUCLEAR CARGO SHIP SAFETY CERTIFICATE

This Certificate shall be supplemented by a Record of Equipment for Cargo Ship Safety (Form C)

(*official seal*) (*State*)

Issued under the provisions of the
INTERNATIONAL CONVENTION FOR THE SAFETY OF LIFE
AT SEA, 1974, as amended
under the authority of the Government of

____

(*name of the State*)

by ________________________________

(*person or organization authorized*)

Particulars of ship①

Name of ship ________________________________

Distinctive number or letters ________________________________

Port of registry ________________________________

Gross tonnage ________________________________

Deadweight of ship (metric tons)② ________________________________

Length of ship (regulation Ⅲ/3.12) ________________________________

Sea areas in which ship is certified to operate (regulation Ⅳ/2) ________________

IMO Number③ ________________________________

Type of ship④

① Alternatively, the particulars of the ship may be placed horizontally in boxes.
② For oil tankers, chemical tankers and gas carriers only.
③ In accordance with the *IMO ship identification number scheme* (resolution A.1117(30)).
④ Delete as appropriate.

核能货船安全证书格式

核能货船安全证书

本证书应附有货船安全的设备记录(格式 C)

(公章)　　　　　　　　　　　　　　　　　　　　　　　　　　　　(国家)

本证书由________________(国名)政府授权________________(被授权的个人或组织)按经修正的 1974 年国际海上人命安全公约的规定签发。

船舶资料①

船名____

船舶编号或呼号____

船籍港____

总吨位____

船舶载重量(吨)②____

船长(第Ⅲ/3.12 条)____

核准船舶营运的海区(第Ⅳ/2 条)____

IMO 识别号③____

船型④

---

① 船舶资料也可在表格中横向排列。
② 仅适用于油船、化学品液货船和气体运输船。
③ 按照《IMO 船舶识别号机制》(第 A.1117(30)号决议)。
④ 酌情删减。

Bulk carrier

Oil tanker

Chemical tanker

Gas carrier

Cargo ship other than any of the above

Date of build

Date of building contract ____________________

Date on which keel was laid or ship was at similar stage of construction ____________

Date of delivery ____________________

Date on which work for a conversion or an alteration or modification

of a major character was commenced (where applicable) ____________

All applicable dates shall be completed.

THIS IS TO CERTIFY:

1 That the ship has been surveyed in accordance with the requirements of regulation Ⅷ/9 of the Convention.

2 That the ship, being a nuclear ship, complied with all the requirements of chapter Ⅷ of the Convention and conformed to the Safety Assessment approved for the ship; and that:

2.1 the condition of the structure, machinery and equipment as defined in regulation Ⅰ/10 (as applicable to comply with regulation Ⅷ/9), including the nuclear propulsion plant and the collision protective structure, was satisfactory and the ship complied with the relevant requirements of chapter Ⅱ-1 and chapter Ⅱ-2 of the Convention (other than those relating to fire safety systems and appliances and fire control plans);

2.2 the ship complied with the requirements of the Convention as regards fire safety systems and appliances and fire control plans;

2.3 the life-saving appliances and the equipment of the lifeboats, liferafts and rescue boats were provided in accordance with the requirements of the Convention;

2.4 the ship was provided with a line-throwing appliance and radio installations used in life-saving appliances in accordance with the requirements of the Convention;

2.5 the ship complied with the requirements of the Convention as regards radio installations;

2.6 the functioning of the radio installations used in life-saving appliances complied with the requirements of the Convention;

2.7 the ship complied with the requirements of the Convention as regards shipborne navigational equipment, means of embarkation for pilots and nautical publications;

散货船

油船

化学品液货船

气体运输船

上述船型以外的货船

建造日期

建造合同日期________________________________

安放龙骨或处于类似建造阶段的日期________________________________

交船日期________________________________

重大改建或改装开始的日期(如适用)________________________________

应填写所有适用日期。

兹证明:

1 该船业已按公约第Ⅷ/9条的要求进行了检验。

2 该船为核能船舶,符合公约第Ⅷ章的所有要求,并与经认可的该船安全鉴定书相一致;和:

2.1 该船在第Ⅰ/10条(在按第Ⅷ/9条办理时适用)所定义的结构、机器及设备,包括核能推进装置和防撞结构处于合格状态,并符合公约第Ⅱ-1章和第Ⅱ-2章的有关要求(消防安全系统和设备及防火控制图除外);

2.2 该船在消防安全系统和设备及防火控制图方面符合公约的要求;

2.3 该船根据公约的要求配备了救生设备和救生艇、救生筏及救助艇用属具;

2.4 该船根据公约的要求在救生设备中配备了抛绳设备和无线电装置;

2.5 该船在无线电装置方面符合公约的要求;

2.6 该船救生设备中使用的无线电装置的功能符合公约的要求;

2.7 该船在船载航行设备、引航员登船设施及航海出版物方面符合公约的要求;

2.8 the ship was provided with lights, shapes, means of making sound signals and distress signals in accordance with the requirements of the Convention and the International Regulations for Preventing Collisions at Sea in force;

2.9 in all other respects the ship complied with the relevant requirements of the regulations, so far as these requirements apply thereto;

2.10 the ship was/was not① subjected to an alternative design and arrangements in pursuance of regulation(s) Ⅱ-1/55/Ⅱ-2/17/Ⅲ/38① of the Convention;

2.11 a Document of approval of alternative design and arrangements for machinery and electrical installations/fire protection/life-saving appliances and arrangements① is/is not① appended to this Certificate.

This certificate is valid until ______________________

Completion date of the survey on which this certificate is based ____________ (*dd/mm/yyyy*)

Issued at ______________________

(*place of issue of certificate*)

______________ ______________________

(*date of issue*) (*signature of authorized official issuing the certificate*)

(*seal or stamp of the issuing authority, as appropriate*)

① Delete as appropriate.

2.8 该船根据公约及现行《国际海上避碰规则》的要求配备了航行灯、号型以及发出声响信号和遇险信号的设备；

2.9 该船在所有其他方面均符合公约适用的有关要求；

2.10 船舶设有/未设 按公约第Ⅱ-1/55/Ⅱ-2/17/Ⅲ/38①条规定的替代设计和布置；

2.11 机电设备/防火/救生设备和装置的替代设计和布置的批准文件附于/未附于本证书之后。

本证书有效期限至____________止。本证书基于的检验完成日期：_______（年/月/日）

签发于____

（证书签发地点）

____________________ ____________________

（签发日期） （经授权发证的官员）

（发证主管当局盖章或钢印）

① 酌情删减。

RECORD OF EQUIPMENT FOR CARGO SHIP SAFETY (FORM C)

RECORD OF EQUIPMENT FOR COMPLIANCE WITH THE INTERNATIONAL CONVENTION FOR THE SAFETY OF LIFE AT SEA, 1974, AS AMENDED

1 Particulars of ship

Name of ship ______________________________

Distinctive number or letters ______________________________

Minimum number of persons with required qualifications to operate the radio installations ______

2 Details of life-saving appliances

1	Total number of persons for which life-saving appliances are provided		
		Port side	Starboard Side
2	Total number of davit-launched lifeboats		
2.1	Total number of persons accommodated by them		
2.2	Number of self-righting partially enclosed lifeboats (regulation Ⅲ/43)[1]		
2.3	Number of totally enclosed lifeboats (regulation Ⅲ/31 and LSA Code, section 4.6)		
2.4	Number of lifeboats with a self-contained air support system (regulation Ⅲ/31 and LSA Code, section 4.8)		
2.5	Number of fire-protected lifeboats (regulation Ⅲ/31 and LSA Code, section 4.9)		
2.6	Other lifeboats		
2.6.1	Number		
2.6.2	Type		
3	Total number of free-fall lifeboats		
3.1	Total number of persons accommodated by them		
3.2	Number of totally enclosed lifeboats (regulation Ⅲ/31 and LSA Code, section 4.7)		
3.3	Number of lifeboats with a self-contained air support system (regulation Ⅲ/31 and LSA Code, section 4.8)		

[1] Refer to the 1983 amendments to SOLAS (MSC.6(48)), applicable to ships constructed on or after 1 July 1986, but before 1 July 1998.

货船安全的设备记录（格式C）

证明符合经修正的1974年国际海上人命安全公约有关要求的设备记录

1　船舶资料

船名______________________

船舶编号或呼号______________________

持证无线电装置操作人员的最少定员数______________________

2　救生设备明细表

1	救生设备可供使用的总人数		
		左舷	右舷
2	救生艇的总数		
2.1	救生艇可载总人数		
2.2	自扶正的部分封闭的救生艇数量（第Ⅲ/43条）①		
2.3	全封闭救生艇的数量（第Ⅲ/31条和LSA规则第4.6节）		
2.4	自备空气补给系统的救生艇的数量（第Ⅲ/31条和LSA规则第4.8节）		
2.5	耐火救生艇的数量（第Ⅲ/31条和LSA规则第4.9节）		
2.6	其他救生艇		
2.6.1	数量		
2.6.2	型式		
3	自由降落救生艇的数量		
3.1	自由降落救生艇可载总人数		
3.2	全封闭救生艇（第Ⅲ/31条和LSA规则第4.7节）		
3.3	自备空气补给系统的救生艇（第Ⅲ/31条和LSA规则第4.8节）		

① 参见1983年SOLAS修正案（第MSC.6（48）号决议），其适用于在1986年7月1日或以后，但在1998年7月1日以前建造的船舶。

2 Details of life saving appliances (*continued*)

3.4	Number of fire-protected lifeboats (regulation Ⅲ/31 and LSA Code, section 4.9)	
4	Number of motor lifeboats (included in the total lifeboats shown in 2 and 3 above)	
4.1	Number of lifeboats fitted with searchlights	
5	Number of rescue boats	
5.1	Number of boats which are included in the total lifeboats shown in 2 and 3 above	
6	Liferafts	
6.1	Those for which approved launching appliances are required	
6.1.1	Number of liferafts	
6.1.2	Number of persons accommodated by them	
6.2	Those for which approved launching appliances are not required	
6.2.1	Number of liferafts	
6.2.2	Number of persons accommodated by them	
6.3	Number of liferafts required by regulation Ⅲ/31.1.4	
7	Number of lifebuoys	
8	Number of lifejackets	
9	Immersion suits	
9.1	Total number	
9.2	Number of suits complying with the requirements for lifejackets	
10	Number of anti-exposure suits	
11	Radio installations used in life-saving appliances	
11.1	Number of search and rescue locating devices	
11.1.1	Radar search and rescue transponders (SART)	
11.1.2	AIS search and rescue transmitters (AIS-SART)	
11.2	Number of two-way VHF radiotelephone apparatus	

3 Details of radio facilities

Item		Actual provision
1	Primary systems	
1.1	VHF radio installation	
1.1.1	DSC encoder	
1.1.2	DSC watch receiver	
1.1.3	Radiotelephony	
1.2	MF radio installation	
1.2.1	DSC encoder	
1.2.2	DSC watch receiver	
1.2.3	Radiotelephony	
1.3	MF/HF radio installation	
1.3.1	DSC encoder	
1.3.2	DSC watch receiver	

2　救生设备明细表(续表)

3.4	耐火救生艇(第Ⅲ/31 条和 LSA 规则第 4.9 节)	
4	机动救生艇的数量(包括在上述救生艇总数内)	
4.1	装备有探照灯的救生艇的数量	
5	救助艇的数量	
5.1	包括在上述救生艇总数内的艇的数量	
6	救生筏	
6.1	需设置认可降落装置的救生筏	
6.1.1	救生筏的数量	
6.1.2	救生筏可载人数	
6.2	不需设置认可降落装置的救生筏	
6.2.1	救生筏的数量	
6.2.2	救生筏可载人数	
6.3	第Ⅲ/31.1.4 条要求的救生筏数量	
7	救生圈的数量	
8	救生衣的数量	
9	救生服	
9.1	总数	
9.2	符合救生衣要求的救生服的数量	
10	抗暴露服的数量	
11	救生设备中使用的无线电装置	
11.1	搜救定位装置的数量	
11.1.1	搜救雷达应答器(SART)	
11.1.2	AIS 搜救应答器(AIS-SART)	
11.2	双向 VHF 无线电话设备的数量	

3　无线电设备明细表

项目		实际配备情况
1	主设备	
1.1	VHF 无线电装置	
1.1.1	DSC 编码器	
1.1.2	DSC 值班接收机	
1.1.3	无线电话	
1.2	MF 无线电装置	
1.2.1	DSC 编码器	
1.2.2	DSC 值班接收机	
1.2.3	无线电话	
1.3	MF/VHF 无线电装置	
1.3.1	DSC 编码器	
1.3.2	DSC 值班接收机	

3 **Details of radio facilities**(*continued*)

1.3.3	Radiotelephony	
1.3.4	Direct-printing telegraphy	
1.4	Recognized mobile satellite service ship earth station	
2	Secondary means of alerting	
3	Facilities for reception of maritime safety information	
3.1	NAVTEX receiver	
3.2	EGC receiver	
3.3	HF direct-printing radiotelegraph receiver	
4	Satellite EPIRB	
4.1	COSPAS-SARSAT	
5	VHF EPIRB	
6	Ship's search and rescue locating device	
6.1	Radar search and rescue transponder (SART)	
6.2	AIS search and rescue transmitter (AIS-SART)	

4 Methods used to ensure availability of radio facilities (regulations Ⅳ/15.6 and 15.7)

4.1 Duplication of equipment ____________________

4.2 Shore-based maintenance ____________________

4.3 At-sea maintenance capability ____________________

5 Details of navigation systems and equipment

Item		Actual provision
1.1	Standard magnetic compass①	
1.2	Spare magnetic compass①	
1.3	Gyro-compass①	
1.4	Gyro-compass heading repeater①	
1.5	Gyro-compass bearing repeater①	
1.6	Heading or track control system①	
1.7	Pelorus or compass bearing device①	
1.8	Means of correcting heading and bearings	
1.9	Transmitting heading device (THD)①	
2.1	Nautical charts/Electronic chart display and information system (ECDIS)②	
2.2	Back-up arrangements for ECDIS②	
2.3	Nautical publications	
2.4	Back-up arrangements for electronic nautical publications	
3.1	Receiver for a global navigation satellite system/terrestrial radionavigation system/multi-system shipborne radionavigation receiver①,②	

① Alternative means of meeting this requirement are permitted under regulation V/19. In case of other means they shall be specified.

② Delete as appropriate.

3　无线电设备明细表(续表)

1.3.3	无线电话	
1.3.4	直接印字无线电报	
1.4	经认可的移动卫星业务船舶地面站	
2	辅助警报装置	
3	用于接收海上安全信息的设施	
3.1	NAVTEX 接收机	
3.2	EGC 接收机	
3.3	HF 直接印字无线电报接收机	
4	卫星 EPIRB	
4.1	COSPAS-SARSAT	
5	VHF EPIRB	
6	船舶的搜救定位装置	
6.1	搜救雷达应答器(SART)	
6.2	AIS 搜救应答器(AIS-SART)	

4　用于确保无线电设备有效性的方法(第Ⅳ/15.6 和 15.7 条)

4.1　双套设备______________________________

4.2　岸基维护______________________________

4.3　海上维护能力______________________________

5　航行系统和设备明细表

项目		实际配备情况
1.1	标准磁罗经①	
1.2	备用磁罗经①	
1.3	陀螺罗经①	
1.4	陀螺罗经首向复示器①	
1.5	陀螺罗经方位复示器①	
1.6	首向或航迹控制系统①	
1.7	哑罗经或罗经方位装置①	
1.8	首向和方位修正仪	
1.9	首向传送装置(THD)①	
2.1	海图/电子海图显示和信息系统(ECDIS)②	
2.2	ECDIS 备份装置②	
2.3	航海出版物	
2.4	电子海图出版物备份装置	
3.1	全球卫星导航系统/全球无线电导航系统接收装置/多系统船载无线电导航接收装置①,②	

① 根据第Ⅴ/19 条的规定,可允许采用符合本要求的替代装置。如果是其他装置,则应予详细说明。
② 酌情删减。

5 Details of navigation systems and equipment(*continued*)

3.2	9 GHz radar①	
3.3	Second radar (3 Ghz/ 9 GHz②)①	
3.4	Automatic radar plotting aid (ARPA)①	
3.5	Automatic tracking aid①	
3.6	Second automatic tracking aid①	
3.7	Electronic plotting aid①	
4.1	Automatic identification system (AIS)	
4.2	Long-range identification and tracking system	
5.1	Voyage data recorder (VDR)②	
5.2	Simplified voyage data recorder (S-VDR)②	
6.1	Speed and distance measuring device (through the water)①	
6.2	Speed and distance measuring device (over the ground in the forward and athwartship direction)①	
7	Echo-sounding device①	
8.1	Rudder, propeller, thrust, pitch and operational mode indicator①	
8.2	Rate-of-turn indicator①	
9	Sound reception system①	
10	Telephone to emergency steering position①	
11	Daylight signalling lamp①	
12	Radar reflector①	
13	International Code of Signals	
14	IAMSAR Manual, Volume Ⅲ	
15	Bridge navigational watch alarm system (BNWAS)	

THIS IS TO CERTIFY that this record is correct in all respects.

Issued at ______________________________

(*place of issue of certificate*)

______________ ______________________________

(*date of issue*) (*signature of authorized official issuing the certificate*)

(*seal or stamp of the issuing authority, as appropriate*)

① Alternative means of meeting this requirement are permitted under regulation V/19. In case of other means, they shall be specified.

② Delete as appropriate

5　航行系统和设备明细表(续表)

3.2	9 GHz 雷达①	
3.3	第二台雷达(3 GHz/9 GHz②)①	
3.4	自动雷达标绘仪(ARPA)①	
3.5	自动跟踪仪①	
3.6	第二台自动跟踪仪①	
3.7	电子标绘装置①	
4.1	自动识别系统(AIS)	
4.2	远程识别与跟踪系统	
5.1	航行数据记录仪(VDR)②	
5.2	简化航行数据记录仪(S-VDR)②	
6.1	航速和航程测量装置(对水)①	
6.2	航速和航程测量装置(对地,正向和横向)①	
7	回声测深仪①	
8.1	舵、螺旋桨、推力、螺距和工作模式指示器①	
8.2	回转速率指示仪①	
9	声响接收系统①	
10	与应急操舵位置联系的电话①	
11	白昼信号灯①	
12	雷达反射器①	
13	国际信号规则	
14	IAMSAR 手册第Ⅲ卷	
15	驾驶台航行值班报警系统(BNWAS)	

兹证明该记录在各方面均正确无误。

签发于______________________________

(证书签发地点)

______________________　　　______________________

(签发日期)　　　(经授权发证的官员签字)

(发证主管当局盖章或钢印)

① 根据第Ⅴ/19 条的规定,可允许采用符合本要求的替代装置。如果是其他装置,则应予详细说明。
② 酌情删减。